D1482775

Social Stratification

SOCIAL INEQUALITY SERIES
Marta Tienda and David B. Grusky, *Series Editors*

Social Stratification

Class, Race, and Gender in Sociological Perspective

edited by
David B. Grusky
Stanford University

Westview Press

Boulder • San Francisco • Oxford

For my parents and
in memory of my grandparents

Social Inequality Series

Copyright © 1994 by Westview Press, Inc.

Additional copyright information appears on p. 745 and is an extension of the information on this page.

Published in 1994 in the United States of America by Westview Press, Inc., 5500 Central Avenue, Boulder, Colorado 80301-2877, and in the United Kingdom by Westview Press, 36 Lonsdale Road, Summertown, Oxford OX2 7EW

Library of Congress Cataloging-in-Publication Data
Grusky, David B.
Social stratification : class, race, and gender in sociological
    perspective / David B. Grusky.
      p.   cm. — (Social inequality series)
    ISBN 0-8133-1064-4. — ISBN 0-8133-1065-2 (pbk.)
    1. Equality.   2. Social status.   3. Social classes.   I. Title.
II. Series.
HM146.G78   1994
305—dc20   93-34904
                                                                                                        CIP

Printed and bound in the United States of America

The paper used in this publication meets the requirements of the American National Standard for Permanence of Paper for Printed Library Materials Z39.48-1984.

10   9   8   7

Contents

Part I Introduction

Part II Forms and Sources of Stratification

Part III The Structure of Modern Stratification

Part IV   Generating Stratification

Part V   The Consequences of Stratification

Part VI   Ascriptive Processes

Part VII   The Evolution of Modern Stratification

Study Guide

This book is designed to be used either as a stand-alone text or as a source of supplementary readings that might be assigned in conjunction with other texts. Although most of the chapters are reprints of past and present classics in the field, some are newly commissioned pieces that provide students with the conceptual background and introductory commentary that a stand-alone text requires. The lead chapter was formulated with this didactic objective explicitly in mind, and the concluding chapter for each of the other six parts of the book provides further commentary on the main subfields of stratification research and the analytic orientations underlying them. In all cases, the contributing authors were permitted to write with their own "voice," and the present book thus departs from conventional texts that seek to represent fields of research in (putatively) objective or balanced fashion.

In assembling this text, every effort was made to select articles that were both path-breaking *and* readable, yet on occasion it proved necessary to compromise on either of these two objectives. The following chapters, in particular, rest on concepts or methods that might be challenging to some undergraduate students:

Karl Marx, "Alienation and Social Classes" (p. 65)
Edward Shils, "Deference" (p. 197)
David L. Featherman and Robert M. Hauser, "A Refined Model of Occupational Mobility" (p. 265)
David B. Grusky and Robert M. Hauser, "Comparative Social Mobility Revisited: Models of Convergence and Divergence in 16 Countries" (p. 275)
James A. Davis, "Achievement Variables and Class Cultures: Family, Schooling, Job, and Forty-Nine Dependent Variables in the Cumulative GSS" (p. 439)
Michael T. Hannan, "Dynamics of Ethnic Boundaries" (p. 500)
Michael Hout, "Occupational Mobility of Black Men: 1962 to 1973" (p. 531)
Paula England, "Wage Appreciation and Depreciation: A Test of Neoclassical Economic Explanations of Occupational Sex Segregation" (p. 590)
William T. Bielby and James N. Baron, "Men and Women at Work: Sex Segregation and Statistical Discrimination" (p. 606)
William H. Sewell, Robert M. Hauser, and Wendy C. Wolf, "Sex, Schooling, and Occupational Status" (p. 633)
Talcott Parsons, "Equality and Inequality in Modern Society, or Social Stratification Revisited" (p. 670)

Although the foregoing chapters present materials that should be mastered by all advanced students (both graduates and undergraduates), they can be safely excised for the purposes of a purely introductory course. The remaining readings were selected so as to ensure that introductory students will still be acquainted with the most important concepts, findings, and debates in the field.

David B. Grusky

Preface and Acknowledgments

The standard rationale for publishing an anthology is that new concepts, theories, and findings have been accumulating so rapidly that some sort of organizing or synthesizing effort is needed. Indeed, given the frequency with which rhetoric of this kind appears in the prefaces of anthologies, the skeptical consumer of sociology might reasonably ask whether such a wide array of subfields and specialties can possibly be flourishing at once. In this context, there is something to be said for passing over the usual partisan rhetoric and providing, as much as possible, a more dispassionate reading of the current standing of stratification research. If, for example, one uses publication rates as an arbiter of disciplinary standing, the available evidence suggests that the position of stratification research has remained quite stable over the last thirty-five years (almost eerily so), with issues of inequality and mobility playing a featured role in roughly 25 percent of all articles published in major sociology journals (see Figure 1 in Mary Diane Burton and David B. Grusky, 1992, "A Quantitative History of Comparative Stratification Research," *Contemporary Sociology* 21, pp. 623–631). In characterizing the field, the appropriate conclusion is not that some sort of "take-off period" is still underway but rather that stratification research is firmly institutionalized and has successfully consolidated its standing as one of the dominant approaches within sociology.

The research literature has therefore become so large and complex that the task of culling it into a necessarily limited anthology poses difficulties of all kinds. In carrying out this task, it was clearly useful to start off with some "priors" about the types of contributions that should be featured, yet much of the organizational structure of the present volume emerged rather more gradually as the project unfolded. As a result, one might view the prefatory comments that follow as a dissonance reduction exercise in which the goal is to infer, after the fact, the larger logic that presumably guided the project. The six organizing principles listed below should be interpreted accordingly:

1. In assembling this collection, the first and foremost objective was to represent the diversity of research traditions on offer while at the same time giving precedence to those traditions that have so far borne the greatest fruit. As is often the case, the pool of disciplinary knowledge has developed in uneven and ramshackle fashion, so much so that any attempt to cover all subjects equally would grossly misrepresent the current strengths and weaknesses of contemporary stratification research.

2. This sensitivity to disciplinary fashion reveals itself, for example, in the relatively large number of selections addressing and discussing issues of race, ethnicity, and gender. Among contemporary scholars, the prevailing view seems to be that race and gender are no longer secondary forms of status affiliation but rather are increasingly dominant forces in the evolution and functioning of modern stratification systems. If the concepts of class, status, and power formed the holy trinity of postwar stratification theorizing, then the (partly overlapping) concepts of class, race, and gender are playing analogous roles now.

3. The second disciplinary development of interest is the growing popularity of quantitative models of stratification and the consequent emergence of stratification analysis as the preferred forum for introducing, testing, and marketing new methods. Although the study of stratification has become increasingly technical in method, most of the articles selected for this anthology are nonetheless accessible to introductory sociology stu-

dents and other novices (see the Study Guide for details).

4. The readers of this volume will thus be disproportionately exposed to *contemporary* approaches to analyzing stratification systems. However, given that most stratification research has a strongly cumulative character to it, there is didactic value in incorporating earlier sociological classics as well as some of the "near-classics" that were written well after the foundational contributions of Karl Marx or Max Weber. The latter body of intervening work is often ignored by editors of anthologies, thereby perpetuating (in some small way) the view that all sociological research can or should be stamped with an exclusively Marxian or Weberian imprimatur.

5. In most anthologies, the classics so chosen make the research literature appear more coherent and cumulative than it truly is, since the natural tendency is to emphasize those aspects of the sociological past that seem to best anticipate or motivate current disciplinary interests. The novice reader may be left, then, with the impression that all past sociological work leads directly and inevitably to current disciplinary interests. This form of academic teleology will likely always be popular, yet in the present case I am hopeful that some innoculation against it was secured by commissioning a series of concluding essays that locate the selections within a broader historical and substantive context.

6. The final, and most difficult, task faced by editors of anthologies is to chart an optimal course between the Scylla of overly aggressive excerpting and the Charybdis of excessive editorial timidity. By the usual standards of anthologies, the course charted here was very much an average one; the (obvious) objective was to eliminate all inessential material while still preserving the analytic integrity of the contributions. To be sure, some of our readers and contributors would no doubt oppose *all* forms of excerpting, yet the practical cost of implementing such a radical stance would be a substantial reduction in the number of articles that could be reproduced.

The editing rules adopted throughout this anthology were in most cases conventional. For example, brackets were used to mark off a passage that was inserted for the purpose of clarifying meaning, whereas ellipses were used whenever a passage appearing in the original contribution was excised altogether. The latter convention was violated, however, if the excised text was merely a footnote or a minor reference to a table or passage (e.g., "see table 1") that was itself excerpted out. When necessary, tables and footnotes were renumbered without so indicating in the text, and all articles that were cited in excised passages were likewise omitted, without indication, from the list of references appearing at the end of each chapter. The spelling, grammar, and stylistic conventions of the original contributions were otherwise preserved. In this respect, the reader should be forewarned that some of the terms appearing in the original contributions would now be regarded as pejorative (e.g., *Negro*), whereas others have passed out of common usage and will possibly be unfamiliar. Although a strong argument could clearly be made for eliminating all language that is no longer acceptable, this type of sanitizing would not only exceed usual editorial license but would also generate a final text that contained inconsistent, and possibly confusing, temporal cues.

The truism that scholarly research is a collective enterprise probably holds for this book more so than others. Among the various functions that an anthology fills, one of the more obvious ones is to define and celebrate what a field has achieved and in so doing to pay tribute to those who made such achievement possible. I am duly grateful, therefore, to the dozens of scholars who allowed their work to be reproduced for this anthology or who agreed to write one of the commissioned essays that glue the various sections of it together. This book provides a well-deserved occasion to recognize the many successes of a field that is perhaps better known for its contentiousness and controversy.

The task of fashioning a book out of such a large and diverse field rested, in large part, on the careful labor of dedicated graduate research assistants. I relied extensively on Karen Aschaffenburg and Ivan K. Fukumoto to locate and review hundreds of possible selections, and Mariko Lin Chang provided invaluable help in constructing the subject index and proofing the galleys. At the early planning stages of this project, I also profited from the advice and suggestions of the following scholars: James N. Baron, Mary Diane Burton, Phillip A. Butcher, Maria Charles, Paul J. DiMaggio, Thomas A. DiPrete, Oscar Grusky, Robert M. Hauser, Jerald R. Herting, Gerhard E. Lenski, Leonard J. Hochberg, Harold R. Kerbo, Robert D. Mare, John W. Meyer, Manuela Romero, Rachel A. Rosenfeld, Aage B. Sørensen, Jesper B. Sørensen, Eve B. Spangler, Ivan Szelényi, Marta Tienda, Nancy B. Tuma, Raymond S. Wong, and Morris Zelditch, Jr. If this book proves to be at all useful, it is in large part because my friends and colleagues guided me in fruitful directions.

The selections reproduced here have all been pretested in graduate and undergraduate stratification classes at the University of Chicago and Stanford University. I am indebted to the many students in these classes who shared their reactions to the selections and thereby shaped the final product more than they may appreciate or realize. The students attending my most recent stratification class require special mention in this regard, since they all read the galleys in their entirety and thus caught many errors both minor and major.

The funding for this project came from the usual assortment of public and private sources. The final draft of my introductory essay was completed while I was on fellowship leave funded by the National Science Foundation through the Center for Advanced Study in the Behavioral Sciences (NSF BNS-8700864). The honoraria for some of the commissioned essays were paid by the Stanford University Dean's Research Fund, and the monies for research assistance were provided by the Presidential Young Investigator Program of the National Science Foundation (NSF SES-8858467) and the Stanford Center for the Study of Families, Children, and Youth. Although I am most grateful for the funding that these organizations so generously provided, they are of course in no way responsible for the views and opinions expressed herein.

It is fitting to conclude by singling out those contributions that make the concept of altruism seem all the more necessary. I would like to give special thanks to Kenneth I. Spenner for reading the entire manuscript and providing comments of a most helpful sort, to Ida May B. Norton for superb copy editing that made many of us seem more intelligent than we truly are, and to Dean Birkenkamp and Libby Barstow of Westview Press for their advice and support throughout the ordeal that publishing a book inevitably becomes. I am most appreciative, finally, of the grace with which Szonja Szelényi shouldered the triple burden of being a wife, an academic, and an in-house scholarly adviser to her husband. This book bears her imprint in innumerable ways.

D.B.G.

Part I
Introduction

DAVID B. GRUSKY

The Contours of Social Stratification

In advanced industrial societies, much rhetoric and social policy have been directed against economic and social inequality, yet despite such efforts the brute facts of poverty and massive inequality are still everywhere with us. The human condition has so far been a fundamentally unequal one; indeed, *all* known societies have been characterized by inequalities of some kind, with the most privileged individuals or families enjoying a disproportionate share of the total wealth, power, or prestige. The task of contemporary stratification research is to describe the contours and distribution of inequality and to explain its persistence despite modern egalitarian or antistratification values.

The term "stratification system" refers to the complex of social institutions that generate inequalities of this sort. The key components of such systems are (1) the institutional processes that define certain types of goods as valuable and desirable, (2) the rules of allocation that distribute these goods across various positions or occupations in the division of labor (e.g., doctor, farmer, or "housewife"), and (3) the mobility mechanisms that link individuals to occupations and thereby generate unequal control over valued resources. It follows that inequality is produced by two types of matching processes: The jobs, occupations, and social roles in society are first matched to "reward packages" of unequal value, and individual members of society are then allo-

cated to the positions so defined and rewarded.[1] In all societies, there is a constant flux of occupational incumbents as new individuals enter the system (and replace dying, retiring, or out-migrating individuals), yet the positions themselves and the reward packages attached to them typically remain much the same. As Schumpeter (1953) puts it, the occupational structure can be seen as "a hotel ... which is always occupied, but always by different persons" (p. 171).

The contents of these reward packages may well differ across modern societies, but the range of variability appears not to be great (e.g., Treiman 1976). We have listed in Table 1 the various goods and assets that have been socially valued in past or present societies (for related listings, see Svalastoga 1965, p. 70; Duncan 1968, pp. 686–690; Runciman 1968).[2] In constructing this table, we have followed the usual objective of including all those goods that are valuable in their own right (i.e., consumption goods) but excluding any "second-order goods" (i.e., investments) that are deemed valuable only insofar as they provide access to other intrinsically desirable goods. The resulting list nonetheless includes resources and assets that serve some investment functions. For example, most economists regard schooling as an investment that generates future streams of income (see Becker 1975), and some sociologists likewise regard cultural resources (e.g., Bourdieu 1977) or social networks (e.g., Coleman 1990) as forms of capital that can be parlayed into educational credentials and other goods.[3] Although most of the assets listed in Table 1 are clearly convertible in this fashion, they are not necessarily re-

_____
This is an original article prepared for this book.

TABLE 1

Types of Assets, Resources, and Valued Goods Underlying Stratification Systems

Asset Group	Selected Examples	Relevant Scholars
1. Economic	Ownership of land, farms, factories, professional practices, businesses, liquid assets, humans (i.e., slaves), labor power (e.g., serfs)	Karl Marx; Erik Wright
2. Political	Household authority (e.g., head of household); workplace authority (e.g., manager); party and societal authority (e.g., legislator); charismatic leader	Max Weber; Ralf Dahrendorf
3. Cultural	High-status consumption practices; "good manners"; privileged life-style	Pierre Bourdieu; Paul DiMaggio
4. Social	Access to high-status social networks, social ties, associations and clubs, union memberships	W. Lloyd Warner; James Coleman
5. Honorific	Prestige; "good reputation"; fame; deference and derogation; ethnic and religious purity	Edward Shils; Donald Treiman
6. Civil	Rights of property, contract, franchise, and membership in elective assemblies; freedom of association and speech	T. H. Marshall; Rogers Brubaker
7. Human	Skills; expertise; on-the-job training; experience; formal education; knowledge	Kaare Svalastoga; Gary Becker

garded as investments by the individuals involved. In fact, many of these assets are secured at birth or through childhood socialization (e.g., the "good manners" of the aristocracy), and they are therefore acquired without the beneficiaries explicitly weighing the costs of acquisition against the benefits of future returns (see DiMaggio 1979).[4]

The implicit claim underlying Table 1 is that these assets exhaust all possible consumption goods and, as such, constitute the raw materials of stratification systems. Given this formulation, one might expect modern stratification scholars to adopt an analytic approach that is multidimensional in orientation, with their objective being to specify the distribution of individuals on each asset in Table 1. Although some scholars have indeed proceeded in multidimensional fashion (e.g., Landecker 1981), most have instead opted to characterize stratification systems in terms of discrete classes or strata whose members are (allegedly) endowed with similar levels or amounts of assets. In the most extreme versions of this approach, the resulting classes are assumed to be real entities that exist prior to the distribution of assets, and many scholars therefore refer to the "effects" of class location on the assets that their

incumbents control (see the following section for details).

The goal of stratification research has thus devolved to describing the structure of these social classes and specifying the processes by which they are generated and maintained. The following types of questions are central to the field:

1. What are the major forms of stratification in human history? Is inequality an inevitable feature of human life?

2. How many social classes are there? What are the principal "fault lines" or social cleavages that define the class structure? Are these cleavages strengthening or weakening with the transition to advanced industrialism?

3. How frequently do individuals cross occupational or class boundaries? Are educational degrees, social contacts, and "individual luck" important forces in matching individuals to jobs and class positions? What other types of social or institutional forces underlie occupational attainment and allocation?

4. How are the life-styles, attitudes, and personalities of individuals shaped by their class locations? Are there identifiable "class cultures" in past and present societies?

5. What types of social processes and state policies serve to maintain or alter racial, ethnic, and sex discrimination in labor markets? Have these forms of discrimination weakened or strengthened with the transition to advanced industrialism?

6. Will stratification systems take on completely new and distinctive forms in the future? Is a "new class" of professionals and intellectuals emerging? Are the stratification systems of modern societies gradually shedding their distinctive features and converging toward some common (i.e., post-industrial) regime?

The foregoing questions reflect a critical orientation to human stratification systems that is distinctively modern in its underpinnings. For the greater part of human history, the existing stratification order was regarded as an immutable feature of society, and the implicit objective of commentators was to explain or justify this order in terms of religious or quasi-religious doctrines (see Tawney 1931; Bottomore 1965). It was only with the Enlightenment that a critical "rhetoric of equality" emerged in opposition to the civil and legal advantages of the aristocracy and other privileged status groupings. After these advantages were largely eliminated in the eighteenth and nineteenth centuries, the same egalitarian ideal was extended and recast to encompass not merely civil assets (e.g., voting rights) but also economic assets in the form of land, property, and the means of production. In its most radical form, this economic egalitarianism led to Marxist interpretations of human history, and it ultimately provided the intellectual underpinnings for socialist stratification systems. Although much of stratification theory has been formulated in reaction to these early forms of Marxist scholarship,[5] the field nonetheless shares with Marxism a distinctively modern (i.e., Enlightenment) orientation based on the premise that individuals are

"ultimately morally equal" (see Meyer 1994, p. 733; also see Tawney 1931). This premise implies that issues of inequality are critical in evaluating the justice and efficiency of stratification systems.

The purpose of this book is to acquaint readers with some of these modern theories and analyses. As has frequently been noted (e.g., Grusky and Takata 1992), the field of stratification covers an exceedingly diverse terrain. It is therefore useful to delimit our review by first defining some core stratification concepts and then focusing on the six empirical questions previously identified. The readings presented after this introductory essay are likewise organized around the same set of empirical questions.

Basic Concepts and Simplifying Strategies

The stratification literature has developed its own vocabulary to describe the distribution of assets, goods, and resources listed in Table 1. The key concepts of this literature can be defined as follows:

1. The degree of *inequality* in a given asset (e.g., income) depends, of course, on its dispersion or concentration across the individuals in the population. Although many scholars seek to characterize the overall level of societal inequality with a single parameter, such attempts will obviously be compromised insofar as some types of assets are distributed more equally than others. This complexity clearly arises in the case of modern stratification systems; for instance, the recent emergence of "citizenship rights" suggests that civil goods are now widely dispersed across all citizens, whereas economic and political goods continue to be disproportionately controlled by a relatively small elite (see, e.g., Parsons 1970; Marshall 1981).

2. The *rigidity* of a stratification system refers to the continuity (over time) in the social standing of its members. The stratification

system is said to be highly rigid, for example, if the current wealth, power, or prestige of individuals can be accurately predicted on the basis of their prior statuses or those of their parents. The amount of rigidity (or "social closure") in any given society will typically vary across the different types of resources and assets listed in Table 1.

3. The stratification system rests on *ascriptive* processes to the extent that traits present at birth (e.g., sex, race, ethnicity, parental wealth, nationality) influence the subsequent social standing of individuals. If ascriptive processes of this sort are in operation, it is possible (but by no means guaranteed) that the underlying traits themselves will become bases for group formation and collective action (e.g., race riots and feminist movements). In modern societies, ascription of all kinds is usually seen as undesirable or discriminatory, and much governmental policy is therefore directed toward fashioning a stratification system in which individuals acquire resources solely by virtue of their achievements.[6]

4. The degree of status *crystallization* is indexed by the correlations among the resources in Table 1. If these correlations are strong, then the same individuals (the "upper class") will consistently appear at the top of all status hierarchies, and other individuals (the "lower class") will consistently appear at the bottom of the stratification system. By contrast, various types of status inconsistencies (e.g., a poorly educated millionaire) will emerge in stratification systems with weakly correlated hierarchies, and it is correspondingly difficult in such systems to define a unitary set of classes that have predictive power with respect to all resources.

The foregoing discussion suggests that stratification systems are complex and multidimensional. However, many scholars are quick to argue that this complexity is mere surface appearance and that stratification systems can in fact be adequately understood with a smaller and simpler set of principles. We shall proceed by reviewing the three simplifying assumptions that have proved to be especially popular.

Reductionism

The prevailing approach is to claim that only one of the asset groups in Table 1 is truly fundamental in understanding the structure, sources, or evolution of societal stratification.[7] There are nearly as many claims of this sort as there are dimensions in Table 1. To be sure, Marx is most commonly criticized (with some justification) for placing "almost exclusive emphasis on economic factors as determinants of social class" (Lipset 1968, p. 300), but in fact much of what passes for stratification theorizing amounts to reductionism of one form or another. Among non-Marxist scholars, inequalities in honor or power are frequently regarded as the most fundamental sources of class formation, whereas the distribution of economic assets is seen as purely secondary. For example, Dahrendorf (1959) argues that "differential authority in associations is the ultimate 'cause' of the formation of conflict groups" (p. 172; also see Lenski 1966), and Shils (1968) suggests that "without the intervention of considerations of deference position the … inequalities in the distribution of any particular facility or reward would not be grouped into a relatively small number of vaguely bounded strata" (p. 130). The contributions in Part III of this volume were selected, in part, to acquaint readers with these various claims and the arguments on which they are based.[8]

Synthesizing Approaches

There is an equally long tradition of research based on synthetic measures that simultaneously tap a wide range of assets and resources. As was noted earlier, many of the rewards in Table 1 (e.g., income) are directly allocated through the jobs that individuals hold, and one can therefore measure the standing of individuals by classifying them in terms of their positions. In this context, Parkin (1971) refers to the occupational structure as the "backbone of the entire reward system of modern Western society" (p. 18), and Hauser and Featherman (1977) argue that studies "framed in terms of occupational mobility ... yield information simultaneously (albeit, indirectly) on status power, economic power, and political power" (p. 4; also see Parsons 1954, pp. 326–329; Duncan 1968, pp. 689–690). Although occupational measures are currently the preferred form of classification within this tradition, the same synthesizing objective can be achieved by simply asking community members to locate their peers in a hierarchy of social classes (e.g., Warner 1949). Under the latter approach, a synthetic classification is no longer secured by ranking and sorting occupations in terms of the bundles of rewards attached to them but rather by passing the raw data of inequality through the fulcrum of individual judgment.[9]

Classification Exercises

Regardless of whether a reductionist or synthesizing approach is taken, most scholars adopt the final simplifying step of defining a relatively small number of discrete "classes."[10] For example, Parkin (1971) argues for six occupational classes with the principal "cleavage falling between the manual and non-manual categories" (p. 25), whereas Dahrendorf (1959) argues for a two-class solution with a "clear line drawn between those who participate in the exercise [of authority] ... and those who are subject to the authoritative commands of others" (p. 170).[11] These types of classificatory exercises may seem relatively benign, but the question that necessarily arises is whether the categories so constructed are purely nominal entities or are truly meaningful to the individuals involved. If the categories are intended to be meaningful, one would expect class members not only to be aware of their membership ("class awareness") but also to identify with their class ("class identification") and occasionally act in its behalf ("class action").[12] There is no shortage of debates about the conditions under which classes of this (real) sort are generated.

The simplifying devices listed here are discussed in greater detail in our review of contemporary models of class and status groupings (see

"The Structure of Modern Stratification"). However, rather than turning directly to the analysis of contemporary systems, we first set the stage by outlining a highly stylized and compressed history of the stratification forms that appear in modern and premodern periods.

Forms of Stratification

The starting point for any comparative analysis of social inequality is the purely descriptive task of classifying the various types of stratification systems. The staple of modern classification efforts has been the tripartite distinction among class, caste, and estate (e.g., Svalastoga 1965; Mayer and Buckley 1970; Tumin 1985), but there is also a long and illustrious tradition of Marxian typological work that introduces the additional categories of primitive communism, slave society, and socialism (see Marx [1939] 1971; Wright 1985). As shown in Table 2, these conventional approaches are largely (but not entirely) complementary, and it is therefore possible to fashion a hybrid classification that incorporates most of the standard distinctions (see Runciman 1974; Rossides 1990; Kerbo 1991 for related work).

The typology presented here relies heavily on some of the simplifying devices discussed earlier. For each of the stratification forms listed in Table 2, we have assumed not only that certain types of assets tend to emerge as the dominant stratifying forces (see column 2) but also that the asset groups so identified constitute the major axis around which social classes or status groupings are organized (see column 3). If the latter assumptions hold, the rigidity of stratification systems can be indexed by the amount of *class* persistence (see column 5), and the degree of crystallization can be indexed by the correlation between *class* membership and each of the assets listed in Table 1 (see column 6).[13] The final column in Table 2 rests on the further assumption that stratification systems have (reasonably) coherent ideologies that legitimate the rules and criteria by which individuals are allocated to positions in the class structure (see column 7). In most cases, ideologies of this kind are largely conservative in their effects, but they can sometimes

TABLE 2
Basic Parameters of Stratification for Eight Ideal-Typical Systems

System (1)	Principal Assets (2)	Major Strata or Classes (3)	Inequality (4)	Rigidity (5)	Crystallization (6)	Justifying Ideology (7)
A. Hunting and gathering society						
1. Tribalism	Human (hunting and magic skills)	Chiefs, shamans, and other tribe members	Low	Low	High	Meritocratic selection
B. Horticultural and agrarian society						
2. Asiatic mode	Political (i.e., incumbency of state office)	Office-holders and peasants	High	Medium	High	Tradition and religious doctrine
3. Feudalism	Economic (land and labor power)	Nobility, clergy, and commoners	High	Medium-High	High	Tradition and Roman Catholic doctrine
4. Slavery	Economic (human property)	Slave owners, slaves, "free men"	High	Medium-High	High	Doctrine of natural and social inferiority (of slaves)
5. Caste society	Honorific and cultural (ethnic purity and "pure" lifestyles)	Castes and subcastes	High	High	High	Tradition and Hindu religious doctrine
C. Industrial society						
6. Class system	Economic (means of production)	Capitalists and workers	Medium-High	Medium	High	Classical liberalism
7. State socialism	Political (party and workplace authority)	Managers and managed	Low-Medium	Low-Medium	High	Marxism and Leninism
8. "Advanced" industrialism	Human (i.e., education, expertise)	Skill-based occupational groupings	Medium	Low-Medium	Medium	Classical liberalism

serve as forces for change as well as stability. For example, if the facts of labor market processes are inconsistent with the prevailing ideology (e.g., racial discrimination in advanced industrial societies), then various sorts of ameliorative action might be anticipated (e.g., affirmative action programs).

The stratification forms represented in Table 2 should thus be seen as ideal types rather than as viable descriptions of existing systems. In constructing these categories, our intention was not to make empirical claims about how existing systems operate in practice but rather to capture (and distill) the accumulated wisdom about how these systems might operate in their purest form. These ideal-typical models can nonetheless assist us in understanding empirical systems. Indeed, insofar as societies evolve through the gradual overlaying of new stratification forms on older (and partly superseded) ones, it becomes possible to interpret contemporary systems as a complex mixture of several of the ideal types presented in Table 2 (see Schumpeter 1951).

The first panel in this table pertains to the "primitive" tribal systems that dominated human society from the very beginning of human evolution until the Neolithic revolution of 10,000 years ago. As might be expected, our summary assessments in columns 2–7 conceal much variability; it should be kept in mind that "merely in the night of our ignorance [do] all alien shapes take on the same hue" (Anderson 1974, p. 549). The variable features of tribal societies are clearly of interest, yet what is crucial for our purposes is that (1) the total size of the distributable surplus was quite limited in all such societies, and (2) this cap on the surplus placed corresponding limits on the overall level of economic inequality (but not necessarily on other forms of inequality). It should also be noted that customs such as gift exchange, food sharing, and the like were commonly practiced in tribal societies and had obvious redistributive effects. In fact, some observers (e.g., Marx [1939] 1971) treated these societies as examples of "primitive communism" because the means of production (e.g., tools, land) were owned collectively, and other types of property typically were distributed evenly among tribal members. This is not to suggest that a perfect equality prevailed; after all, the more powerful medicine men (shamans) often secured a disproportionate share of resources, and the tribal chief could exert considerable influence on the political decisions of the day. However, these residual forms of power and privilege were never directly inherited, nor were they typically allocated in accord with well-defined ascriptive traits (e.g., racial traits).[14] It was only by demonstrating superior skills in hunting, magic, or leadership that tribal members could secure political office or acquire status and prestige (see Lenski 1966 for further details). Although meritocratic forms of allocation are often seen as prototypically modern, in fact they were present in incipient form at the very earliest stages of human evolution.

With the emergence of agrarian forms of production, the economic surplus became large enough to support more complex systems of stratification. Among contemporary Marxist theorists (e.g., Godelier 1978; Chesneaux 1964), the "Asiatic mode" is often treated as an intermediate formation in the transition to advanced agrarian society (e.g., feudalism); we have therefore led off our typology with the Asiatic case (see line B2).[15] In this regard we should emphasize that the explicit evolutionary theories of Godelier (1978) and others have not been well received, yet many scholars still take the fallback position that Asiaticism is an important "analytical, though not chronological, stage" in the development of class society (Hobsbawm 1965, p. 37; also see Mandel 1971, pp. 116–139; Anderson 1974, p. 486). The main features of this formation are (1) a large peasant class residing in agricultural villages that are "almost autarkic" (O'Leary 1989, p. 17), (2) the absence of strong legal institutions recognizing private property rights (with village life taking on a correspondingly communal character), (3) a state elite that extracts the surplus agricultural production through rents or taxes and expends it on "defense, opulent living, and the construction of public works" (Shaw 1978, p. 127),[16] and (4) a constant flux in elite personnel due to "wars of dynastic succession and wars of conquest by nomadic warrior tribes" (O'Leary 1989, p. 18; for more extensive reviews, also see Brook 1989; Krader 1975).

Beyond this skeletal outline, all else is open to dispute. There are long-standing debates, for example, about how widespread the Asiatic mode was (see Mandel 1971, pp. 124–128) and about the appropriateness of reducing all forms of Asian development to a "uniform residual category" (Anderson 1974, pp. 548–549). These issues are clearly of significance, but more important for our purposes is that the Asiatic mode provides the conventional example of how a "dictatorship of officialdom" can flourish in the absence of private property and a well-developed proprietary class (Gouldner 1980, pp. 327–328). Under this reading of Asiaticism, the parallel with modern socialism looms large (at least in some quarters), so much so that various scholars have suggested that Marx downplayed the Asian case for fear of exposing it as a "parable for socialism" (see Gouldner 1980, pp. 324–352; also see Wittfogel

1981). It is hardly surprising that O'Leary (1989) nominates Asiaticism as the "most controversial mode" (p. 7) within the Marxist typology.

Whereas the institution of private property was underdeveloped in the East, the ruling class under Western feudalism was very much a propertied one.[17] The distinctive feature of feudalism was that the nobility not only owned large estates or manors but also held legal title to the labor power of its serfs (see line B3).[18] If a serf fled to the city, this was considered a form of theft: The serf was stealing that portion of his or her labor power owned by the lord (Wright 1985, p. 78). With this interpretation, the statuses of serf and slave differ only in degree, and slavery thereby constitutes the "limiting case" in which workers lose all control over their labor power (see line B4).[19] At the same time, it would obviously be a mistake to reify this distinction, given that the history of agrarian Europe reveals "almost infinite gradations of subordination" (Bloch 1961, p. 256) that confuse and blur the conventional dividing lines between slavery, serfdom, and freedom (see Finley 1960 on the complex gradations of Greek slavery; also see Patterson 1982, pp. 21–27). The slavery of Roman society provides the best example of complete subordination (see Sio 1965), whereas some of the slaves of the early feudal period were bestowed with rights of real consequence (e.g., the right to sell surplus product), and some of the (nominally) free men were in fact obliged to provide rents or services to the manorial lord (Bloch 1961, pp. 255–274).[20] The social classes that emerged under European agrarianism were thus structured in quite diverse ways. In all cases, we nonetheless find that rights of property ownership were firmly established, and that the life chances of individuals were defined, in large part, by their control over property in its differing forms. Unlike the ideal-typical Asiatic system, the feudal stratification system was not state centered because the means of production (i.e., land, labor) were controlled by a proprietary class that emerged independently of the state.[21]

The historical record makes it clear that agrarian stratification systems were not always based on strictly hereditary forms of social closure (see panel B, column 5). The case of European feudalism is especially instructive in this regard because

it suggests that stratification systems often become more rigid as the underlying institutional forms mature and take shape (see Mosca 1939; Kelley 1981). Although it is well known that the era of classical feudalism (i.e., post-twelfth century) was characterized by a "rigid stratification of social classes" (Bloch 1961, p. 325),[22] the feudal structure appears to have been more permeable during the period prior to the institutionalization of the manorial system and the associated transformation of the nobility into a legal class. In this transitional period, access to the nobility was not yet legally restricted to the offspring of nobility, nor was marriage across classes or estates formally prohibited (see Bloch 1961, pp. 320–331, for further details). The case of ancient Greece provides a complementary example of a (relatively) open agrarian society. As Finley (1960) and others have noted, the condition of slavery was indeed heritable under Greek law, yet manumission (the freeing of slaves) was so common that the slave class had to be constantly replenished with new captives secured through war or piracy. The possibility of servitude was thus something which "no man, woman, or child, regardless of status or wealth, could be sure to escape" (Finley 1960, p. 161). At the same time, some slave systems rested more fully on hereditary forms of closure; the familiar case of American slavery provides the conventional example of a closed system. As Sio (1965) notes, slavery in the antebellum South was "hereditary, endogamous, and permanent" (p. 303), with the annual manumission rate apparently falling as low as 0.04 percent by 1850 (see Patterson 1982, p. 273). The slave societies of Jamaica, South Africa, and rural Iraq were likewise based on largely permanent slave populations (Patterson 1982).

The most extreme examples of hereditary closure are of course found in caste societies (see line B5). In some respects, American slavery might be seen as having "caste-like features" (see Berreman 1981), but Hindu India clearly provides the defining case of caste organization.[23] The Indian caste system is based on (1) a hierarchy of status groupings (castes) that are ranked by ethnic purity, wealth, and access to goods or services, (2) a corresponding set of "closure rules" that restrict all forms of intercaste marriage or mobility and thereby make caste membership both hereditary and permanent, (3) a high degree of physical and occupational segregation enforced by elaborate rules and rituals governing intercaste contact, and (4) a justifying ideology (Hinduism) that successfully induces the population to regard such extreme forms of inequality as legitimate and appropriate (Jalali 1992; Brass 1985, 1983; Berreman 1981; Dumont 1970; Srinivas 1962; Leach 1960). What makes this system so distinctive, then, is not merely its well-developed closure rules but also the fundamentally honorific (and noneconomic) character of the underlying social hierarchy. As indicated in Table 2, the castes of India are ranked on a continuum of ethnic and ritual purity, with the highest positions in the system reserved for castes that prohibit behaviors deemed dishonorable or "polluting." Under some circumstances, castes that acquired political and economic power eventually advanced in the status hierarchy, yet they typically did so only after mimicking the behaviors and life-styles of higher castes (Srinivas 1962).

The defining feature of the industrial era (see panel C) has been the emergence of egalitarian ideologies and the consequent delegitimation of the extreme forms of stratification found in caste, feudal, and slave systems. This can be seen, for example, in the European revolutions (of the eighteenth and nineteenth centuries) that pitted the egalitarian ideals of the Enlightenment against the privileges of rank and the political power of the nobility. In the end, these struggles eliminated the last residue of feudal privilege, but they also made new types of inequality and stratification possible. Under the class system that ultimately emerged (see line C6), the estates of the feudal era were replaced by purely economic groups ("classes"), and the old closure rules based on heredity were likewise supplanted by (formally) meritocratic processes. The resulting classes were neither legal entities nor closed status groupings, and the associated class-based inequalities could therefore be represented and justified as the natural outcome of competition among individuals with differing abilities, motivation, or moral character ("classical liberalism"). As indicated in line C6 of Table 2, the class structure of early industrialism had a clear "economic base" (Kerbo 1991, p. 23), so

much so that Marx ([1894] 1972) defined classes in terms of their relationship to the means of economic production. The precise contours of the industrial class structure are nonetheless a matter of continuing debate; for example, a simplistic Marxian model focuses on the cleavage between capitalists and workers, whereas more refined Marxian and neo-Marxian models identify additional intervening or "contradictory" classes (e.g., Wright 1985), and yet other (non-Marxian) approaches represent the class structure as a continuous gradation of socioeconomic status or "monetary wealth and income" (Mayer and Buckley 1970, p. 15).[24]

Whatever the relative merits of these models might be, the ideology underlying the socialist revolutions of the nineteenth and twentieth centuries was of course explicitly Marxist. The intellectual heritage of these revolutions and their legitimating ideologies can ultimately be traced to the Enlightenment, but the new rhetoric of equality that emerged was now directed against the economic power of the capitalist class rather than the status and honorific privileges of the nobility. The evidence from Eastern Europe and elsewhere suggests that these egalitarian ideals were only partially realized (e.g., Lenski 1994). In the immediate post-revolutionary period, factories and farms were indeed collectivized or socialized, and various fiscal and economic reforms were instituted for the express purpose of reducing income inequality and wage differentials among manual and nonmanual workers (Parkin 1971, pp. 137–159; Giddens 1973, pp. 226–230). Although these egalitarian policies were subsequently weakened or reversed through the reform efforts of Stalin and others, this is not to say that inequality on the scale of pre-revolutionary society was ever reestablished among rank-and-file workers (cf. Lenski 1994). It has long been argued, however, that the socialization of productive forces did not have the intended effect of empowering workers because the capitalist class was simply replaced by a "new class" of party officials and managers who continued to control the means of production and to allocate the resulting social surplus (see I. Szelényi 1994). This class has been variously identified with intellectuals or intelligentsia (e.g., Gouldner 1979), bureaucrats or managers (e.g.,

Rizzi 1985), and party officials or appointees (e.g., Djilas 1965). Regardless of the formulation adopted, the presumption is that the working class ultimately lost out in contemporary socialist revolutions, just as it did in the so-called bourgeois revolutions of the eighteenth and nineteenth centuries.[25]

Whereas the means of production were socialized in the revolutions of Eastern Europe and the former Soviet Union, the capitalist class remained largely intact throughout the process of industrialization in the West. However, the propertied class may ultimately be weakened by ongoing structural changes, with the most important of these being (1) the rise of a service economy and the associated growth of a professional-managerial class (Ehrenreich and Ehrenreich 1979), (2) the transition to an "information society" (Masuda 1980) and the increasing "centrality of theoretical knowledge as the source of innovation" (Bell 1973, p. 14), and (3) the consequent emergence of technical expertise, educational degrees, and training certificates as "new forms of property" (Berg 1973, p. 183). The foregoing developments all suggest that human and cultural capital are replacing economic capital as the principal stratifying forces in advanced industrial society (see line C8). According to Gouldner (1979) and others (e.g., Galbraith 1967), a dominant class of cultural elites is therefore emerging in the West, much as the transition to state socialism (allegedly) generated a new class of intellectuals in the East.[26]

This is not to suggest that all theorists of advanced industrialism posit a grand divide between the cultural elite and a working mass. In fact, some commentators (e.g., Dahrendorf 1959, pp. 48–57) have argued that skill-based cleavages are crystallizing throughout the occupational structure and that a continuous gradation or hierarchy of socioeconomic classes is therefore emerging. In nearly all models of advanced industrial society, it is further assumed that education is the principal mechanism by which individuals are sorted into such classes; the shared premise is that educational institutions serve to "license" human capital and thereby convert it to cultural currency.[27] The rise of mass education is sometimes seen as a rigidifying force (e.g.,

Bourdieu and Passeron 1977), but the prevailing view seems to be that the transition to advanced industrialism has equalized life chances and produced a more open society (see line C8, column 5).[28]

Sources of Stratification

The preceding sketch makes it clear that a wide range of stratification systems emerged over the course of human history. The question that arises, then, is whether some form of stratification or inequality is an inevitable feature of human society. In discussing this question, one turns naturally to the functionalist theory of Davis and Moore (1945) because it addresses explicitly "the universal necessity which calls forth stratification in any system" (p. 242; also see Davis 1953; Moore 1963a, 1963b). The starting point for any functionalist approach is the premise that all societies must devise some means to motivate the best workers to fill the most important and difficult occupations. This "motivational problem" might be addressed in a variety of ways, but perhaps the simplest solution is to construct a hierarchy of rewards (e.g., prestige, property, power) that privileges the incumbents of functionally significant positions. As noted by Davis and Moore (1945, p. 243), this amounts to setting up a system of institutionalized inequality (a "stratification system"), with the occupational structure then serving as a conduit through which unequal rewards and perquisites are allocated. The stratification system thus may be seen as an "unconsciously evolved device by which societies insure that the important positions are conscientiously filled by the most qualified persons" (Davis and Moore 1945, p. 243). Under the Davis-Moore formulation, the only empirical claim is that *some form* of inequality is needed to allocate labor efficiently; the authors are silent, however, when it comes to specifying *how much* inequality is sufficient for this purpose. It is well to bear in mind that the extreme forms of stratification found in existing societies may exceed the "minimum … necessary to maintain a complex division of labor" (Wrong 1959, p. 774).

The Davis-Moore hypothesis has come under considerable criticism from several quarters (see

Huaco 1966 for an early review). The prevailing view, at least among postwar commentators, is that the original hypothesis cannot adequately account for inequalities in "stabilized societies where statuses are ascribed" (Wesolowski 1962, p. 31; Tumin 1953). Indeed, whenever the vacancies in the occupational structure are allocated on purely hereditary grounds, one cannot reasonably argue that the reward system is serving its putative function of matching qualified workers to important positions. What must be recognized, however, is that a purely hereditary system is rarely achieved in practice; in fact, even in caste societies of the most rigid sort, one typically finds that talented and qualified individuals have some opportunities for upward mobility. With the Davis-Moore formulation (1945), this slow trickle of mobility is regarded as essential to the functioning of the social system, so much so that elaborate systems of inequality have evidently been devised to ensure that the trickle continues (see Davis 1948, pp. 369–370, for additional and related comments). Although the Davis-Moore hypothesis can therefore be used to explain stratification in societies with *some* mobility, the original hypothesis is of course untenable insofar as there is complete closure.

The functionalist approach has been further criticized for neglecting the "power element" in stratification systems (Wrong 1959, p. 774). It has long been argued that Davis and Moore failed "to observe that incumbents [of functionally important positions] have the power not only to insist on payment of expected rewards but to demand even larger ones" (Wrong 1959, p. 774; also see Dahrendorf 1968). In this regard, the stratification system might be seen as self-reproducing: The incumbents of important positions can use their power to influence the distribution of resources and to preserve or extend their own privileges. It would be difficult, for instance, to account fully for the advantages of feudal lords without referring to their ability to enforce their claims through moral, legal, or economic sanctions. By this line of reasoning, the distribution of rewards reflects not only the "latent needs" of the larger society but also the balance of power among competing groups and their members (see Collins 1975).

Whereas the early debates addressed conceptual issues of this kind, subsequent researchers shifted their emphasis to constructing "critical tests" of the Davis-Moore hypothesis. This research effort continued apace throughout the 1970s, with some commentators reporting evidence consistent with functionalist theorizing (e.g., Cullen and Novick 1979) and others providing less sympathetic assessments (e.g., Broom and Cushing 1977). The following decade was a period of relative quiescence, but Lenski (1994) has now reopened the debate with his suggestion that "many of the internal, systemic problems of Marxist societies were the result of inadequate motivational arrangements" (p. 57). According to Lenski, the socialist commitment to wage leveling made it difficult to recruit and motivate highly skilled workers, and the "visible hand" of the socialist economy could never be calibrated to mimic adequately the natural incentive of capitalist profit-taking. These results led Lenski to conclude that "successful incentive systems involve ... motivating the best qualified people to seek the most important positions" (p. 59). It remains to be seen whether this reading of the socialist "experiments in destratification" (Lenski 1978) will generate a new round of functionalist theorizing and debate.

The Structure of Modern Stratification

The recent history of stratification theory is in large part a history of debates about the contours of class, status, and prestige hierarchies in advanced industrial societies. These debates might appear to be nothing more than academic infighting, but the participants treat them with high seriousness as a "necessary prelude to the conduct of political strategy" (Parkin 1979, p. 16). For instance, considerable energy has been devoted to drawing the correct dividing line between the working class and the bourgeoisie, if only because the task of identifying the oppressed class is seen as a prerequisite to devising a political strategy that might appeal to it. It goes without saying that political and intellectual goals are often conflated in such mapmaking efforts, and the assorted debates in this subfield are thus infused with more than the usual amount of scholarly contention. These debates are complex and wide-ranging, but it suffices for our purposes to distinguish among four schools of thought (see Wright 1979, pp. 3–18, for a more comprehensive review).

Marxists and Post-Marxists

The debates within the Marxist and neo-Marxist camps have been especially contentious, not only because of the foregoing political motivations but also because the discussion of class within *Capital* (Marx [1894] 1972) is too fragmentary and unsystematic to adjudicate between various competing interpretations. At the end of the third volume of *Capital,* one finds the now-famous fragment on "the classes" (Marx [1894] 1972, pp. 862–863), but this discussion breaks off just when Marx appeared ready to advance a formal definition of the term. It is clear, nonetheless, that his abstract model of capitalism was resolutely dichotomous, with the conflict between capitalists and workers constituting the driving force behind further social development. This simple two-class model should be viewed as an ideal type designed to capture the developmental tendencies of capitalism; indeed, whenever Marx carried out concrete analyses of existing capitalist systems, he acknowledged that the class structure was complicated by the persistence of transitional classes (e.g., landowners), quasi-class groupings (e.g., peasants), and class fragments (e.g., the lumpen proletariat). It was only with the progressive maturation of capitalism that Marx expected these complications to disappear as the "centrifugal forces of class struggle and crisis flung all *dritte Personen* [third persons] to one camp or the other" (Parkin 1979, p. 16).

The recent history of modern capitalism suggests that the class structure has not evolved in such a precise and tidy fashion. As Dahrendorf (1959) points out, the old middle class of artisans and shopkeepers has indeed declined in relative size, yet a new middle class of managers, professionals, and nonmanual workers has expanded to occupy the newly vacated space (cf. Steinmetz and Wright 1989). The last fifty years of neo-Marxist theorizing can be seen as the intellectual fallout from this development. Whereas some commentators have sought to minimize its implications, others have put forward a revised mapping of the class structure that accommodates the new middle class in explicit terms. Within the former camp, the principal tendency is to claim that the lower sectors of the new middle class are in the process of being proletarianized because "capital subjects [nonmanual labor] ... to the forms of rationalization characteristic of the capitalist mode of production" (Braverman 1974, p. 408). This line of reasoning suggests that the working class may gradually expand in relative size and therefore regain its earlier power.

At the other end of the continuum, Poulantzas (1974) has argued that most members of the new intermediate stratum fall outside the working class proper because they are not exploited in the classical Marxian sense (i.e., surplus value is not extracted). The latter approach may have the merit of keeping the working class conceptually pure, but it also reduces the size of this class to "pygmy proportions" (see Parkin 1979, p. 19), thereby dashing the hopes of those who would see workers as a viable political force within advanced industrial society. This result has motivated contemporary scholars to develop class models that fall somewhere between the extremes advocated by Braverman (1974) and Poulantzas (1974). For example, the neo-Marxist model proposed by Wright (1978) generates an American working class that is acceptably large (approximately 46 percent of the labor force), yet the class mappings in this model still pay tribute to the various cleavages and divisions among workers who sell their labor power. That is, professionals are placed in a distinct "semiautonomous class" by virtue of their control over the work process, and upper-level supervisors are located in a "managerial class" by virtue of their authority over workers (Wright 1978; also see Wright 1985). It should be noted that the dividing lines proposed in this model rest on concepts (e.g., autonomy, authority relations) that were once purely the province of Weberian or neo-Weberian sociology. This type of synthetic approach has become quite popular (e.g., see Westergaard and Resler 1975), so much so that Parkin (1979) suggested that "inside every neo-Marxist there seems to be a Weberian struggling to get out" (p. 25).[29]

Weberians and Post-Weberians

The rise of the "new middle class" is less problematic for scholars working within a Weberian framework. The class model advanced by Weber suggests, in fact, a multiplicity of class cleavages because it equates the economic class of workers with their "market situation" in the competition for jobs and valued goods (Weber [1922] 1968, pp. 926–940). Under this formulation, the class of skilled workers is privileged because its incumbents are in high demand on the labor market and because its economic power can be parlayed into high wages and an advantaged position in commodity markets (Weber [1922] 1968, pp. 927–928). At the same time, the stratification system is further complicated by the existence of "status groupings," which Weber saw as forms of social affiliation that can compete, coexist, or overlap with class-based groupings. Although an economic class is merely an aggregate of individuals in a similar market situation, a status grouping is defined as a community of individuals who share a style of life and interact as status equals (e.g., the nobility or an ethnic caste). In some circumstances, the boundaries of a status grouping are determined by purely economic criteria, yet Weber noted that "status honor normally stands in sharp opposition to the pretensions of sheer property" (Weber [1922] 1968, p. 932).

The Weberian approach has been elaborated and extended by sociologists seeking to understand the "American form" of stratification. During the postwar decades, American sociologists typically dismissed the Marxist model of class as overly simplistic and one-dimensional, whereas they celebrated the Weberian model as properly distinguishing between the numerous variables that Marx had conflated in his definition of class (see, e.g., Barber 1968). In the most extreme versions of this approach, the dimensions identified by Weber were disaggregated into a multiplicity of stratification variables (e.g., income, education, ethnicity), and the correlations between these variables were then shown to be weak enough to generate various forms of "status inconsistency" (e.g., a poorly educated millionaire). The resulting picture suggested a "pluralistic model" of stratification; that is, the class system was represented as intrinsically multidimen-

sional, with a host of cross-cutting affiliations producing a complex patchwork of internal class cleavages. The multidimensionalists were often accused of providing a "sociological portrait of America as drawn by Norman Rockwell" (Parkin 1979, p. 604), but it should be kept in mind that some of these theorists also emphasized the seamy side of pluralism. In fact, Lenski (1954) and others (e.g., Lipset 1959) have argued that modern stratification systems might be seen as breeding grounds for personal stress and political radicalism, given that individuals with contradictory statuses may feel relatively deprived and thus support "movements designed to alter the political *status quo*" (Lenski 1966, p. 88). This line of research ultimately died out in the early 1970s under the force of negative and inconclusive findings (e.g., Jackson and Curtis 1972). There has been a recent resurgence of theorizing about issues of status disparity and relative deprivation (e.g., Beck 1987; Wegener 1991; Baron 1994), yet much of this work focuses on the generic properties of all postmodern stratification systems rather than the (allegedly) exceptional features of the American case.

It would be a mistake to regard multidimensionalists of this kind as the only intellectual descendants of Weber. In recent years, the standard multidimensionalist interpretation of "Class, Status, and Party" (Weber 1946, pp. 180–195) has fallen into disfavor, and an alternative version of neo-Weberian stratification theory has gradually taken shape. This revised reading of Weber draws on the concept of social closure as defined and discussed in the essay "Open and Closed Relationships" (Weber [1922] 1968, pp. 43–46, 341–348; also see Weber 1947, pp. 424–429). By social closure, Weber was referring to the processes by which groups devise and enforce rules of membership; the purpose of such rules typically is to "improve the position [of the group] by monopolistic tactics" (Weber [1922] 1968, p. 43). Although Weber did not directly link this discussion with his other contributions to stratification theory, subsequent commentators have pointed out that social classes and status groupings are generated by simple exclusionary processes operating at the macrostructural level (e.g., Goldthorpe 1987; Breiger 1981; Parkin 1979; Westergaard and

Resler 1975; Giddens 1973; Sørensen and Kalleberg 1981).[30] Under modern industrialism, there are obviously no formal sanctions preventing labor from crossing class boundaries, yet various institutional forces (e.g., private property, union shops) are nonetheless quite effective in limiting the amount of class mobility over the life course and between generations. These exclusionary mechanisms not only "maximize claims to rewards and opportunities" among the incumbents of closed classes (Parkin 1979, p. 44), but they also provide the demographic continuity needed to generate distinctive class cultures and to "reproduce common life experience over the generations" (Giddens 1973, p. 107). As noted by Giddens (1973, pp. 107–112), barriers of this sort are not the only source of "class structuration," yet they clearly play a contributing role in the formation of identifiable classes under modern industrialism.[31] This revisionist interpretation of Weber has reoriented the discipline toward examining the causes and sources of class formation rather than the (potentially) fragmenting effects of cross-cutting affiliations and cleavages.

The Ruling Class and Elites

The classical elite theorists (Pareto 1935; Mosca 1939; Mills 1956) sought to replace the Marxian (and Weberian) model of economic classes with a purely political analysis resting on the distinction between the rulers and the ruled. Whereas Marx formulated the "short-cut theory that the economic class rules politically" (Mills 1956, p. 277), elite theorists typically contend that the composition of the ruling class reflects the outcome of political struggles that may not necessarily favor the owners of productive resources. As a corollary to this thesis, Pareto and Mosca further claim that the movement of history can be understood as a cyclical succession of elites, with the relative size of the governing minority tending to diminish as the political community grows (Mosca 1939, p. 53). The common end point of all revolutions is, therefore, the "dominion of an organized minority" (Mosca 1939, p. 53); indeed, Mosca points out that all historical class struggles have culminated with a new elite taking power, whereas the lowliest class invariably remains as such (also see

Gouldner 1979, p. 93). Although Marx would perhaps have agreed with this oligarchical interpretation of presocialist revolutions, he nonetheless insisted that the socialist revolution would break the pattern and culminate in a dictatorship of the proletariat (and ultimately a classless state).[32] The elite theorists were, by contrast, unconvinced that the "iron law of oligarchy" (Michels 1949) could be so conveniently suspended for this final revolution.

As elite theory evolved, this original interest in the dynamics of class systems was largely abandoned, and the emphasis shifted to describing the structure and composition of the modern ruling class (cf. Lachmann 1990; Szelényi and Szelényi 1993). The research agenda of contemporary elite theorists is dominated by the following types of questions:

- What are the principal lines of cleavage and structuration at the top of the stratification system? Is there an "inner circle" of powerful corporate leaders (Useem 1984), a "governing class" of hereditary political elites (Mosca 1939; also see Shils 1982), or a more encompassing "power elite" that cuts across political, economic, and military domains (Mills 1956)?

- How solidaristic and cohesive are the elite groupings so defined? Do their members form a unified "social class" (Mills 1956, p. 11), or are they divided by conflicting interests and "unable to weld themselves into a solidified group" (Berg and Zald 1978, p. 137)?

- How are the members of elite groupings recruited and retained? Is there a continuous and rapid "circulation of elites" (see Shils 1982; also see Pareto 1935), or have hereditary forms of closure remained largely intact even today (see Baltzell 1958, 1964, 1991)?

There are nearly as many elite theories as there are possible permutations of responses to questions of this sort. If there is any unifying theme to contemporary theorizing, it is merely that the subordinate classes are seen as "effectively dispossessed" (Mills 1956) of any meaningful control over the major economic and political decisions of the day. It was once fashionable to argue that "ordinary citizens can acquire as much power ... as their free time, ability, and inclination permit" (Rose 1967, p. 247), but such extreme versions of pluralism have now fallen into disrepute (see Dahl 1967 for a classic statement of the pluralist perspective).

Gradational Status Groupings

The foregoing theorists have all proceeded by mapping individuals or families into mutually exclusive and exhaustive categories (i.e., classes). As our review indicates, there continues to be much debate about the location of the boundaries separating these categories, yet the shared assumption is that fundamental class boundaries of some kind are present, if only in latent or incipient form. By contrast, the implicit claim underlying gradational approaches is that such dividing lines are largely the construction of overzealous sociologists, and that the underlying structure of modern stratification can, in fact, be more closely approximated with gradational measures of income, status, or prestige (Nisbet 1959; also see Clark and Lipset 1991; cf. Hout, Brooks, and Manza 1993). The standard concepts of class action and consciousness are likewise typically discarded; indeed, whereas most categorical models are based on the (realist) assumption that the constituent categories are "structures of interest that provide the basis for collective action" (Wright 1979, p. 7), gradational models are usually represented as taxonomic or statistical classifications of purely heuristic interest.[33]

There is no shortage of gradational measures that might be used to characterize the social welfare or reputational ranking of individuals. Although there is some sociological precedent for treating income as an indicator of class (e.g., Mayer and Buckley 1970, p. 15), most sociologists seem content with a disciplinary division of labor that leaves matters of income to economists. It does not follow that distinctions of income are sociologically uninteresting; after all, if one is truly intent on assessing the "market situation" of workers (Weber [1922] 1968), there is much to rec-ommend a direct measurement of their income and wealth. The preferred approach has nonetheless been to define classes as "groups of persons who are members of effective kinship units which, as units, are approximately equally valued" (Parsons 1954, p. 77). This formulation was first operationalized in the postwar community studies (e.g., Warner 1949) by constructing broadly defined categories of reputational equals ("upper-upper class," "upper-middle class," and so on).[34] However, when the disciplinary focus shifted to the national stratification system, the measure of choice soon became occupational scales of prestige (e.g., Treiman 1976, 1977), socio-economic status (e.g., Blau and Duncan 1967), or global "success in the labor market" (Jencks, Perman, and Rainwater 1988). The latter scales now serve as standard measures of class background in sociological research of all kinds (see Grusky and Van Rompaey 1992 for a recent review).

Generating Stratification

The language of stratification theory makes a sharp distinction between the distribution of social rewards (e.g., the income distribution) and the distribution of opportunities for securing these rewards. As sociologists have frequently noted (e.g., Kluegel and Smith 1986), it is the latter distribution that governs popular judgments about the legitimacy of stratification: The typical American, for example, is quite willing to tolerate substantial inequalities in power, wealth, or prestige provided that the opportunities for securing these social goods are distributed equally across all individuals (Hochschild 1981). Whatever the wisdom of this popular logic might be, stratification researchers have long sought to explore its factual underpinnings by monitoring and describing the structure of mobility chances.

In most of these analyses, the liberal ideal of an open and class-neutral system is treated as an explicit benchmark, and the usual objective is to expose any inconsistencies between this ideal and the empirical distribution of life chances (see, especially, Tawney 1931; Glass 1954). This is not to suggest, however, that all mobility scholars necessarily take a positive interest in mobility or regard liberal democracy as "the good society itself in operation" (Lipset 1959, p. 439). In fact, Lipset and Bendix (1959) themselves argue that open stratification systems can lead to high levels of "social and psychic distress" (p. 286), and not merely because the heightened aspirations that such systems engender are so frequently frustrated (Young 1958). The further difficulty that arises is that open stratification systems will typically generate various types of status inconsistency, given that mobility trajectories in plural societies are often "partial and incomplete" (Lipset and Bendix 1959, p. 286) and therefore trap individuals between collectivities that have conflicting expectations. The nouveaux riches, for example, are typically unable to parlay their economic mobility into social esteem and acceptance from their new peers; the alleged result is personal resentment and consequent "combativeness, frustration, and rootlessness" (Lipset and Bendix 1959, p. 285). Although the empirical evidence for such inconsistency effects is at best weak (e.g., Davis 1982), the continuing effort to uncover them makes it clear that mobility researchers are motivated by a wider range of social interests than commentators and critics have often allowed (see Osipov 1969 for a representative critique; also see Goldthorpe 1987, pp. 1–36, for a relevant review).

The study of social mobility continues to be a major sociological industry, with new findings and developments coming "faster and more furiously in this field than in any other" (Hout 1984, p. 1379). It is convenient to distinguish among the following three traditions of mobility research:

1. The conventional starting point has been to analyze bivariate "mobility tables" formed by cross-classifying the occupational origins and destinations of individuals. The tables so constructed can be used to estimate the densities of occupational inheritance, to describe patterns of mobility and exchange between occupations, and to map the social distances between classes and their constituent occupations (see, e.g., Featherman and Hauser 1978; Stier and Grusky 1990). Moreover, when comparable mobility tables are assembled from several countries, it becomes possible to address long-standing debates about

the underlying contours of cross-national variation in stratification systems (e.g., Lipset and Bendix 1959; Grusky and Hauser 1984; Hauser and Grusky 1988; Erikson and Goldthorpe 1994).

2. It is by now a sociological truism that Blau and Duncan (1967) and their colleagues (e.g., Sewell, Haller, and Portes 1969) revolutionized the field with their formal "path models" of stratification. These models were intended to represent, if only partially, the process by which background advantages could be converted into socioeconomic status through the mediating variables of schooling, aspirations, and parental encouragement (e.g., Sewell, Haller, and Portes 1969; Hauser and Featherman 1977; Hauser, Tsai, and Sewell 1983; Grusky and DiPrete 1990). Under formulations of this kind, the main sociological objective was to show that socioeconomic outcomes were structured not only by family origins but also by various intervening variables (e.g., schooling) that were themselves only partly determined by origins and other ascriptive forces (see, especially, Blau and Duncan 1967, pp. 199–205). The picture of modern stratification that emerged suggested that market outcomes depended in large part on unmeasured career contingencies (i.e., individual luck) rather than influences of a more structural sort (Blau and Duncan 1967, p. 174; Jencks et al. 1972; cf. Jencks et al. 1979; Hauser, Tsai, and Sewell 1983).

3. The latter tradition has been frequently criticized for failing to attend to the social structural constraints that operate on the stratification process independently of individual-level traits (e.g., Horan 1978; Beck, Horan, and Tolbert 1978; Sørensen and Kalleberg 1981; Granovetter 1981). The structuralist accounts that ultimately emerged from these critiques amounted, in most cases, to refurbished versions of dual economy and market segmentation models that were introduced and popularized several decades ago by institutional economists (e.g., Averitt 1968; Doeringer and Piore 1971; Piore 1975; also see Smith 1990). When these models were redeployed by sociologists in the early 1980s, the usual objective was to demonstrate that women and minorities were disadvantaged not merely by virtue of deficient human capital investments (e.g., inadequate schooling and experience) but also by their

consignment to secondary labor markets that, on average, paid out lower wages and offered fewer opportunities for promotion or advancement.

The history of these research traditions is marked more by statistical and methodological signposts than substantive ones. Although such methodological innovations obviously cannot be reviewed here, it should at least be noted that most scholars regard the development of structural equation, log-linear, and event-history models as watershed events in the history of mobility research (see Featherman 1981; Ganzeboom, Treiman, and Ultee 1991). At the same time, it is typically conceded that "theory formulation in the field [of social mobility] has become excessively narrow" (Ganzeboom, Treiman, and Ultee 1991, p. 278), and that "little, if any, refinement of major theoretical positions has recently occurred" (Featherman 1981, p. 364; also see Blau and Duncan 1967, pp. 2–10; Burton and Grusky 1992, p. 628). In a now-classic critique of contemporary stratification analysis, Coser (1975) further argued that mobility researchers are so entranced by quantitative models and methods that "the methodological tail [may soon be] wagging the substantive dog" (p. 652). The latter argument can no longer be taken exclusively in the (intended) pejorative sense because these new models and methods have often provided revealing insights into mobility processes and thus opened up questions of some substantive importance (Burton and Grusky 1992).

The Consequences of Stratification

We have so far taken it for granted that the sociological study of classes and status groupings is more than a purely academic exercise. For Marxist scholars, there is of course a strong *macrostructural* rationale for class analysis: The defining assumption of Marxism is that human history unfolds through the conflict between classes and the "revolutionary reconstruction of society" (Marx 1948, p. 9) that such conflict ultimately brings about. By contrast, macrostructural claims of this sort have typically been deemphasized by subsequent (non-Marxist) scholars, and there has been a consequent ratcheting down of analytic in-

terest to the *individual* level. The rationale for class analysis that now tends to be offered rests, in most cases, on the simple empirical observation that class background affects a wide range of individual outcomes (e.g., consumption practices, life-styles, religious affiliation, voting behavior, mental health and deviance, fertility and mortality, values and attitudes). As DiMaggio (1994) puts it, measures of social class serve as modern-day "crack troops in the war on unexplained variance" (p. 458); one would be hard-pressed to identify any aspect of human experience that sociologists have not linked to class-based variables in some way. The resulting analyses of the "consequences of class" continue to account for a substantial proportion of contemporary stratification research (see Burton and Grusky 1992).

The relationship between class, status, and life-styles has been framed and conceptualized in various ways (for reviews, see Gartman 1991; Brubaker 1985; Sobel 1981; Zablocki and Kanter 1976). We shall review in turn three of the most popular approaches to studying the consequences of social stratification.

Models of Status Groupings

There is a long and honorable tradition of market research (e.g., Mitchell 1983; Weiss 1988) that operationalizes the Weberian concept of status by constructing detailed typologies of modern life-styles and consumption practices. It should be kept in mind that Weber joined two analytically separable elements in his definition of status; that is, members of a given status grouping were not only assumed to be honorific equals in the symbolic (or subjective) sphere but were also seen as sharing a certain style of life and having similar tastes or preferences in the sphere of consumption (see Giddens 1973, pp. 80, 109). The former feature of status groupings can be partly captured by conventional prestige scales, but the latter can only be indexed by classifying the actual consumption practices of individuals as revealed by their "cultural possessions, material possessions, and participation in the group activities of the community" (Chapin 1935, p. 374; also see Sewell 1940). The status groups so defined are usually regarded as analytically distinct from classes; indeed, the standard Weberian approach is to define classes within the domain of *production,* whereas status groups are determined by the "*consumption* of goods as represented by special styles of life" (Weber [1922] 1968, p. 937; italics in original).

Reproduction Theory

The recent work of Bourdieu (e.g., 1977; 1984) can be read as an explicit effort to rethink this conventional distinction between class and status groupings. If one assumes, as does Bourdieu, that classes are highly efficient agents of selection and socialization, then their members will necessarily evince the shared dispositions, tastes, and styles of life that demarcate and define status groupings (see Gartman 1991; Brubaker 1985). Although it is hardly controversial to treat classes as socializing forces (see, e.g., Hyman 1966), Bourdieu takes the more extreme stance that class-based conditioning "structures the whole experience of subjects" (1979, p. 2) and thus creates a near-perfect correspondence between the objective conditions of existence and internalized dispositions or tastes. This is not to suggest that the "subjects" themselves always fully appreciate the class-based sources of their tastes and preferences. As argued by Bourdieu (1977), the conditioning process is typically so seamless and unobtrusive that the sources of individual dispositions are concealed from view, and the "superior" tastes and privileged outcomes of socioeconomic elites are therefore misperceived (and legitimated) as the product of individual merit or worthiness.

Structuration Theory

The foregoing approach is increasingly popular, but there is also continuing support for a middle-ground position that neither treats status groupings in isolation from class (e.g., Mitchell 1983) nor simply conflates them with class (e.g., Bourdieu 1984). The starting point for this position is the proposition that status and class are related in historically specific and contingent ways. For instance, Giddens (1973, p. 109) adopts the

usual assumption that classes are founded in the sphere of production, yet he further maintains that the "structuration" of such classes depends on the degree to which incumbents are unified by shared patterns of consumption and behavior (also see Weber [1922] 1968, pp. 932–938). The twofold conclusion reached by Giddens is that (1) classes become distinguishable formations only insofar as they *overlap* with status groupings, and (2) the degree of overlap should be regarded as an empirical matter rather than something resolvable by conceptual fiat (cf. Bourdieu 1984). This type of formula appears to inform much of the current research on the consequences of class (e.g., Clark and Lipset 1991; Hout, Brooks, and Manza 1993; also see Goldthorpe and Marshall 1992). If contemporary commentators are so often exercised about the strength of "class effects" (see, e.g., Wright 1985), this is largely because these effects (purportedly) speak to the degree of class structuration and the consequent viability of class analysis in modern society.

The empirical results coming out of these research programs have been interpreted in conflicting ways. Although some researchers have emphasized the strength and pervasiveness of class effects (e.g., Kohn 1980; Fussell 1983; Bourdieu 1984), others have argued that consumption practices are becoming uncoupled from class and that new theories that are "more cultural than structural" (Davis 1982 p. 585) are now required to account for the attitudes and life-styles that individuals adopt. The evidence adduced for the latter view has often been impressionistic in nature: For example, Nisbet (1959) concluded from his analysis of popular literature that early industrial workers could be readily distinguished by class-specific markers (e.g., distinctive dress, speech), whereas their postwar counterparts were increasingly participating in a "mass culture" that offered the same commodities to all classes and produced correspondingly standardized tastes, attitudes, and behaviors (also see Hall 1992; Clark and Lipset 1991, p. 405; Parkin 1979, p. 69; Goldthorpe et al. 1969, pp. 1–29). The critical issue, of course, is not merely whether a mass culture of this sort is indeed emerging but also whether the resulting standardization of life-styles constitutes convincing evidence of a decline in class-based forms of social organization. As we have noted earlier, some commentators would regard the rise of mass culture as an important force for class destructuration (e.g., Giddens 1973), yet others have suggested that the "thin veneer of mass culture" (Adorno 1976) only serves to legitimate the class system by obscuring and concealing the more fundamental inequalities upon which classes are based (also see Horkheimer and Adorno 1972).

Ascriptive Processes

The forces of race, ethnicity, and gender have long been relegated to the sociological sidelines by class theorists of both Marxist and non-Marxist persuasion.[35] In most versions of class-analytic theory, status groups are treated as secondary forms of affiliation, whereas class-based ties are seen as more fundamental and decisive determinants of social and political action (see, e.g., Althusser 1969). This is not to suggest that race and gender have been ignored altogether in such treatments; however, when competing forms of communal solidarity are incorporated into conventional class-analytic models, they are typically represented as vestiges of traditional loyalties that will wither away under the rationalizing influence of socialism (e.g., Kautsky 1903), industrialism (e.g., Levy 1966), or modernization (e.g., Parsons 1975).

The first step in the intellectual breakdown of this model was the fashioning of a multidimensional approach to stratification. Whereas many class theorists gave theoretical or conceptual priority to the economic dimension of stratification, the early multidimensionalists emphasized that social behavior could only be understood by taking into account all status group memberships (e.g., racial, gender) and the complex ways in which these interacted with one another and with class outcomes. The class-analytic approach was further undermined by the apparent reemergence of racial, ethnic, and nationalis[...] late postwar period. Far from wi[...] der the force of industrialism, the bo[...] and ethnicity seemed to be alive and we[...] modern world was witnessing a "sudden increas[...] in tendencies by people in many countries and many circumstances to insist on the significance of their group distinctiveness" (Glazer and Moynihan 1975, p. 3). This resurgence of status politics continues apace today. Indeed, not only have ethnic and regional solidarities intensified with the decline of conventional class politics in Eastern Europe and elsewhere (see Jowitt 1992), but gender-based affiliations and loyalties have likewise strengthened as feminist movements diffuse throughout much of the modern world.

The latter turn of events has led some commentators to proclaim that the factors of race, ethnicity, or gender are now the driving force behind the evolution of stratification systems. In one such formulation, Glazer and Moynihan (1975) conclude that "property relations [formerly] obscured ethnic ones" (p. 16), but now it is "property that begins to seem derivative, and ethnicity that becomes a more fundamental source of stratification" (p. 17). The analogue position favored by at least some feminists is that "men's dominance over women is the cornerstone on which all other oppression (class, age, race) rests" (see Hartmann 1981, p. 12; Firestone 1972). It should be noted that formulations of this kind beg the question of timing; after all, if the forces of gender or ethnicity are truly primordial, it is natural to ask why they only began to be expressed with relative vigor in recent decades. In addressing this issue, Bell (1975) suggests that a trade-off exists between class-based and ethnic forms of solidarity, with the latter strengthening whenever the former weaken (see Hannan 1994, p. 506, for a related interpretation; also see Weber 1946, pp. 193–194). As the conflict between labor and capital is institutionalized (via trade unionism), Bell argues that class-based affiliations typically lose their affective content, and that workers must therefore turn to racial or ethnic ties to provide them with a renewed sense of identification and commitment (see Horowitz 1985; Nielsen 1985; Olzak 1983 for alternative interpretations). It could well be argued that gender politics often fills the same "moral vacuum" that this decline in class politics has allegedly generated (Parkin 1979, p. 34).

It may be misleading, of course, to treat the competition between ascriptive and class-based forces as a sociological horse race in which one, and only one, of these two principles can ultimately win out. In a pluralist society of the American kind, workers can choose an identity appropriate to the situational context; a modern-day worker might behave as "an industrial laborer in the morning, a black in the afternoon, and an American in the evening" (Parkin 1979, p. 34). Although this situational model of status has not been widely adopted in contemporary research, there is nonetheless some evidence of renewed interest in conceptualizing the diverse affiliations of individuals and the "multiple oppressions" (see Wright 1989, pp. 5–6) that these affiliations engender. It is now fashionable, for example, to assume that the major status groupings in contemporary stratification systems are defined by the *intersection* of ethnic, gender, or class affiliations (e.g., black working-class women, white middle-class men). The theoretical framework motivating this approach is not always well-articulated, but the implicit claim seems to be that these subgroupings shape the "life chances and experiences" of individuals (Ransford and Miller 1983, p. 46) and thus define the social settings in which subcultures typically emerge (also see Gordon 1978; Baltzell 1964). The obvious effect of this approach is to invert the traditional post-Weberian perspective on status groupings; that is, whereas orthodox multidimensionalists described the stress experienced by individuals in inconsistent statuses (e.g., poorly educated doctors), these new multidimensionalists emphasize the shared interests and cultures generated within commonly encountered status sets (e.g., black working-class women).

The sociological study of gender, race, and ethnicity has thus burgeoned of late. As noted by Lieberson (1994, p. 649), there has been a certain faddishness in the types of research topics that scholars of gender and race have chosen for study, and the resulting body of literature has a correspondingly haphazard and scattered feel to it. The following research questions have nonetheless emerged as (relatively) central ones in the field:

1. How are class relations affected by ascriptive forms of stratification? Can capitalists exploit ethnic antagonisms and patriarchy to their advantage (e.g., Reich 1977)? Do male majority workers also benefit from stratification by race and gender (Bonacich 1972; also see Hartmann 1981)?

2. What accounts for variability across time and space in ethnic conflict and solidarity? Will ethnic loyalties weaken as modernization diffuses across ethnically diverse populations (e.g., Lipset and Rokkan 1967)? Or does modernization produce a "cultural division of labor" (Hechter 1975) that strengthens communal ties by making ethnicity the principal arbiter of life chances? Is ethnic conflict further intensified when ethnic groups compete for the same niche in the occupational structure (see Bonacich 1972; Hannan 1994)?

3. What are the generative forces underlying ethnic, racial, and gender differentials in income and other socioeconomic outcomes? Do such differentials proceed from supply-side variability in the occupational aspirations or human capital that workers bring to the market (e.g., Marini and Brinton 1984; Polachek and Siebert 1993)? Or are they produced by demand-side forces such as market segmentation, statistical or institutional discrimination, and the (seemingly) irrational tastes and preferences of employers (e.g., Piore 1975; Arrow 1973; Becker 1957)?

4. Is the underlying structure of ascriptive stratification changing with the transition to advanced industrialism? Does the "logic" of industrialism require universalistic personnel practices and consequent declines in overt discrimination? Can this logic be reconciled with the rise of a modern ghetto underclass (Wilson 1987), the persistence of massive segregation by sex and race (e.g., Bielby and Baron 1986), and the emergence of new forms of poverty and hardship among women and recent immigrants (e.g., Benería and Stimpson 1987)?

The preceding questions make it clear that ethnic, racial, and gender inequalities are often classed together and treated as analytically equivalent forms of ascription. Although Parsons (1951) and others (e.g., Mayhew 1970) have indeed emphasized the shared features of "communal ties," one should bear in mind that such ties can be maintained (or subverted) in very different ways. It has long been argued, for example, that some forms of inequality can be rendered more palatable by the practice of pooling resources (e.g., income) across all family members. As Lieberson (1994) points out, the family operates to bind males and females together in a single unit of consumption, whereas extrafamilial institutions (e.g., schools, labor markets) must be relied upon to provide the same integrative functions for ethnic groups. If these functions are left wholly unfilled, one might expect ethnic separatist and nationalist movements to emerge (e.g., Hechter 1975). The same "nationalist" option is obviously less viable for single-sex groups; indeed, barring any revolutionary changes in family structure or kinship relations, it seems unlikely that separatist solutions will ever garner much support among men or women. The latter considerations may account for the absence of a well-developed literature on *overt* conflict between single-sex groups (cf. Firestone 1972; Hartmann 1981).[36]

The Evolution of Modern Stratification

We will conclude our introductory commentary by briefly reviewing current approaches to understanding the changing structure of modern stratification. As indicated in Figure 1, some commentators have suggested that future forms of stratification will be defined by structural changes in the productive system (i.e., structural approaches), whereas others have argued that modernity and postmodernity can only be understood by looking beyond the economic system and its putative consequences (i.e., cultural approaches). It will suffice to review these various approaches in cursory fashion because they are based on theories and models that have been covered extensively elsewhere in this introduction.

The natural starting point for our discussion is the now-familiar claim that human and political capital are replacing economic capital as the principal stratifying forces in advanced industrial society. In the most extreme versions of this claim, the old class of moneyed capital is represented as a dying force, and a new class of intellectuals (e.g., Gouldner 1979), managers (e.g., Bunrham 1962), or party bureaucrats (e.g., Djilas 1965) is assumed to be on the road to power. The latter formulations have of course been widely criticized, and not by the academic Left alone. Whereas the (orthodox) Marxist stance is that "news of the demise of the capitalist class is … somewhat premature" (Zeitlin 1982, p. 216),[37] the contrary position taken by Bell (1973) is that neither the old capitalist class nor the so-called new class will have unfettered power in the postindustrial future. To be sure, there is widespread agreement among postindustrial theorists that human capital is becoming a dominant form of property, yet this need not imply that "the amorphous bloc designated as the knowledge stratum has sufficient community of interest to form a class" (Bell 1987, p. 464). The members of the knowledge stratum have diverse interests because they are drawn from structurally distinct situses (e.g., military, business, university) and because their attitudes are further influenced (and thus rendered heterogeneous) by noneconomic forces of various sorts.[38]

The foregoing variants of structuralism are nonetheless unified by the simple functionalist premise that new classes or strata rise to prominence because they take on increasingly central (i.e., "functionally important") roles in the productive system. The just-so histories that new class theorists tend to advance have a correspondingly zero-sum character to them; that is, the presumption is that all class systems are defined by a single dominant asset and that the history of stratification is therefore the history of old forms of capital (e.g., economic capital) being superseded and supplanted by new forms (e.g., human capital).[39] This framework might be contrasted, then, to stratification theories that treat the emergence of multiple bases of solidarity and affiliation as one of the distinctive features of modernity. For example, Parsons (1970) argues that the oft-cited "separation of ownership from control" (e.g., Berle and Means 1932) is not a unique historical event but instead is merely one example of

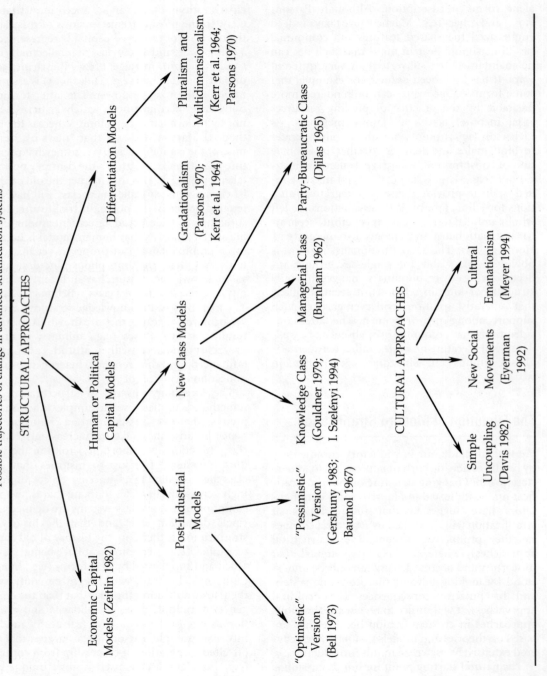

FIGURE 1
Possible trajectories of change in advanced stratification systems

STRUCTURAL APPROACHES

Economic Capital Models (Zeitlin 1982)

Human or Political Capital Models

Differentiation Models

Gradationalism (Parsons 1970; Kerr et al. 1964)

Pluralism and Multidimensionalism (Kerr et al. 1964; Parsons 1970)

New Class Models

Party-Bureaucratic Class (Djilas 1965)

Managerial Class (Burnham 1962)

Knowledge Class (Gouldner 1979; I. Szelényi 1994)

Post-Industrial Models

"Pessimistic" Version (Gershuny 1983; Baumol 1967)

"Optimistic" Version (Bell 1973)

CULTURAL APPROACHES

Cultural Emanationism (Meyer 1994)

New Social Movements (Eyerman 1992)

Simple Uncoupling (Davis 1982)

the broader tendency for ascriptively fused structures to break down into separate substructures and create a "complex composite of differentiated and articulating ... units of community" (Parsons 1970, p. 25). This process of differentiation is further revealed in (1) the emergence of a finely graded hierarchy of specialized occupations (Parsons 1970; Kerr et al. 1964), (2) the spread of professional and voluntary associations that provide additional and competing bases of affiliation and solidarity (e.g., Parsons 1970; Kerr et al. 1964), and (3) the breakdown of the "kinship complex" as evidenced by the declining salience of family ties for careers, marriages, and other stratification outcomes (e.g., Parsons 1970; also see Treiman 1970; Blau and Duncan 1967, pp. 429–431; Featherman and Hauser 1978, pp. 222–232). The latter tendencies imply that the class standing of modern individuals is becoming "divorced from its historic relation to both kinship and property" (Parsons 1970, p. 24). As Parsons (1970) argues, the family may have once been the underlying unit of stratification, yet increasingly the class standing of individuals is determined by all the collectivities to which they belong, both familial and otherwise. This multidimensionalist approach thus provides the analytic basis for rejecting the conventional family-based model of stratification that Parsons himself earlier espoused (e.g., Parsons 1954).[40]

The driving force behind these accounts is, of course, structural change of the sort conventionally described by such terms as *industrialism* (Kerr et al. 1964), *postindustrialism* (Bell 1973), and *social differentiation* or *integration* (Parsons 1970). By contrast, cultural accounts of change tend to deemphasize these forces or to cast them as epiphenomenal, with the focus thus shifting to the independent role of ideologies, social movements, and cultural practices in generating modern forms of stratification. The culturalist tradition encompasses a host of accounts that have not, as yet, been fashioned into a unitary or cohesive whole. The following positions within this tradition might therefore be distinguished:

1. The weakest form of culturalism rests on the straightforward claim that economic interests are no longer decisive determinants of attitudes or lifestyles (e.g., Davis 1982; see Goldthorpe et al. 1969 on the embourgeoisement hypothesis). This "uncoupling" of class and culture is not necessarily inconsistent with structuralist models of change; for example, Adorno (1976) has long argued that mass culture only serves to obscure the more fundamental class divisions that underlie all historical change, and other neo-Marxians (e.g., Althusser 1969) have suggested that some forms of ideological convergence are merely transitory and will ultimately wither away as economic interests reassert themselves in the "last instance." The uncoupling thesis can therefore be rendered consistent with assorted versions of structuralism, yet it nonetheless lays the groundwork for theories that are fundamentally antistructuralist in tone or character.

2. The "strong form" of the uncoupling thesis suggests that the cultural sphere is not merely increasingly autonomous but also is the locus of permanent and fundamental change in patterns of stratification. This line of argumentation underlies, for example, all forms of postmodernism that seek to represent "new social movements" (e.g., feminism, ethnic and peace movements, environmentalism) as the vanguard force behind future stratificatory change. As argued by Eyerman (1992) and others (e.g., Touraine 1981), the labor movement can be seen as a fading enterprise rooted in the old conflicts of the workplace and industrial capitalism, whereas the new social movements provide a more appealing call for collective action by virtue of their emphasis on issues of lifestyle, personal identity, and normative change. With this formulation, the proletariat is stripped of its privileged status as a universal class, and the new social movements emerge as an alternative force "shaping the future of modern societies" (Haferkamp and Smelser 1992, p. 17).

3. The popularity of modern social movements might be attributed to ongoing structural transformations (e.g., the rise of the new class) rather than to any intrinsic appeal of the egalitarian ideals or values that these movements typically represent. Although structural arguments of this kind continue to be pressed (see, e.g., Eyerman 1992; Brint 1984), the alternative position staked out by Meyer (1994) and others (e.g., Eisenstadt 1992) is that cultural premises such as egalitarianism and functionalism are true generative forces

underlying the rise and spread of modern stratification systems (also see Parsons 1970). As Meyer (1994) points out, egalitarian values not only produce a real reduction in some forms of inequality (e.g., civil inequalities) but also underlie various societal subterfuges (e.g., differentiation) by which inequality is merely concealed from view rather than eliminated. The recent work of Meyer (1994) provides, then, an extreme example of how classical idealist principles can be deployed to account for modern stratificational change.

The final, and more pragmatic, question that might be posed is whether changes of the preceding sort presage a general decline in the field of stratification itself. It could well be argued that Marxian and neo-Marxian models of class will decline in popularity with the rise of postmodern stratification systems and the associated uncoupling of class from lifestyles, consumption patterns, and political behavior (see Clark and Lipset 1991). This line of reasoning is not without merit, but it is worth noting that (1) past predictions of this sort have generated protracted debates that, if anything, have reenergized the field (see, e.g., Nisbet 1959); (2) the massive facts of economic, political, and honorific inequality will still be with us even if narrowly conceived models of class ultimately lose out in such debates; and (3) the continuing diffusion of egalitarian values suggests that all departures from equality, no matter how small, will be the object of considerable interest among sociologists and the lay public alike (see Meyer 1994). In making the latter point, our intent is not merely to note that sociologists may become "ever more ingenious" (Nisbet 1959, p. 12) in teasing out increasingly small departures from perfect equality but also to suggest that entirely new forms and sources of inequality will likely be discovered and marketed by sociologists. This orientation is already very much in evidence; for example, when the now-famous *Scientific American* studies (e.g., Taylor, Sheatsley, and Greeley 1978) revealed that overt forms of racial and ethnic prejudice were withering away, the dominant reaction within the discipline was to ask whether such apparent change concealed the emergence of more subtle and insidious forms of symbolic racism (see, e.g., Sears, Hensler, and Speer 1979). In

similar fashion, when Beller (1982) reported a modest decline in occupational sex segregation, other sociologists were quick to ask whether the models and methods being deployed misrepresented the structure of change (e.g., Charles and Grusky 1995) or whether the classification system being used disguised counteracting trends at the intraoccupational level (e.g., Bielby and Baron 1986). The point here is not to suggest that revisionist stories of this kind are either deficient or misleading but only to emphasize that modern sociologists are highly sensitized to inequalities and have a special interest in uncovering those "deep structures" of social differentiation (e.g., Baron 1994, p. 390) that are presumably concealed from ordinary view. This sensitivity to all things unequal bodes well for the future of the field even in the (unlikely) event of a long-term secular movement toward diminishing inequality.

Notes

1. In some stratification systems, individuals receive rewards directly rather than by virtue of the social positions that they occupy, and it therefore becomes possible to describe the regime in terms of a single matching algorithm. The limiting case here would be the tribal economies of Melanesia in which "Big Men" (Oliver 1955) secured prestige and power through personal influence rather than through incumbency of any well-defined roles (also see Granovetter 1981, pp. 12–14).

2. It goes without saying that the assets listed in Table 1 are institutionalized in quite diverse ways. Whereas some types of assets are legally recognized by the state or by professional associations (e.g., civil rights, property ownership, educational credentials), other types are reserved for incumbents of specified work roles (e.g., workplace authority), and yet others have no formal legal or institutional standing and are revealed probabilistically through patterns of behavior and action (e.g., high-status consumption practices, deference, and derogation).

3. It is sometimes claimed that educational credentials are *entirely* investment goods and should therefore be excluded from any listing of the primitive dimensions underlying stratification systems (e.g., Runciman 1968, p. 33). In evaluating this claim, it is worth noting that an investment rhetoric for schooling became fashionable only quite recently (e.g., Becker 1975), whereas

intellectuals and humanists have long viewed education as a simple consumption good.

4. This is not to gainsay the equally important point that parents often encourage their children to acquire such goods because of their putative benefits.

5. The term "stratification" has itself been seen as anti-Marxist by some commentators (e.g., Duncan 1968) because it places emphasis on the vertical ranking of classes rather than the exploitative relations between them. The geological metaphor implied by this term does indeed call attention to issues of hierarchy; nonetheless, whenever it is used in this essay, our intention is to refer generically to inequality of all forms (including those involving exploitation).

6. Although "native ability" is by definition established at birth, it is often seen as a legitimate basis for allocating rewards (because it is presumed to be relevant to judgments of merit). The inherent ambiguity of such judgments is discussed in more detail by Bell (1973).

7. The scholars listed in the right-hand column of Table 1 are not necessarily reductionists of this sort.

8. This section also includes contributions by scholars who recognize two or three "primitive" stratification dimensions (e.g., Wright 1985; also see Bourdieu 1984; Runciman 1968).

9. The viability of a synthesizing approach clearly depends on the extent to which the stratification system is crystallized. If the degree of crystallization is low, then one cannot construct a unidimensional scale that is strongly correlated with its constituent parts.

10. There is, of course, an ongoing tradition of research in which the class structure is represented in gradational terms (see, e.g., Blau and Duncan 1967). However, no attempt has been made to construct an exhaustive rank-ordering of individuals based on their control over the resources listed in Table 1, nor is there any available rank-ordering of the thousands of detailed occupational titles that can be found in modern industrial societies (but see Cain and Treiman 1981; Jencks, Perman, and Rainwater 1988). The approach taken by most gradationalists has been (1) to map individuals into a relatively small number (approximately 500) of broad occupational categories and (2) to subsequently map these categories into an even smaller number of prestige or socioeconomic scores.

11. According to Dahrendorf (1959), the classes so formed are always specific to particular organizational settings (see Dahrendorf 1959, pp. 171–173), and thus the social standing of any given individual will typically differ across the various associations in which he or she participates (e.g., workplace, church, polity). This line of reasoning leads Dahrendorf to conclude that "if individuals in a given society are ranked according to the sum of their authority positions in all associations, the resulting pattern will not be a dichotomy but rather like scales of stratification according to income or prestige" (p. 171).

12. The class structure can also operate in less obtrusive ways; for example, one might imagine a social system in which classes have demonstrable macrolevel consequences (and are therefore "real"), yet their members are not aware of these consequences nor of their membership in any particular class.

13. The assumptions embedded in columns 4–6 of Table 2 are clearly far-reaching. Unless a stratification system is perfectly crystallized, its parameters for inequality and rigidity cannot be represented as scalar quantities, nor can the intercorrelations between the multiple stratification dimensions be easily summarized (in a single "crystallization" parameter). Moreover, even in stratification systems that are perfectly crystallized, there is no reason to believe that persistence over the life course (intragenerational persistence) will always vary in tandem with persistence between generations (intergenerational inheritance). We have nonetheless assumed that each of our ideal-typical stratification systems can be characterized in terms of a single "rigidity parameter" (see column 5).

14. In all hunting and gathering societies, men and women were assigned to different roles or occupations (e.g., see Pfeiffer 1977; Leakey and Lewin 1977), and this led to consequent differences (across genders) in the distribution of rewards. We address this form of ascription in more detail subsequently.

15. It should again be stressed that our typology by no means exhausts the variability of agrarian stratification forms (see Kerbo 1991, pp. 63–79, for an extended review).

16. The state elite was charged with constructing and maintaining the massive irrigation systems that made agriculture possible in regions such as China, India, and the Middle East (cf. Anderson 1974, pp. 490–492).

17. This is not to suggest that feudalism can only be found in the West or that the so-called Asiatic mode is limited to the East. Indeed, the social structure of Japan was essentially feudalistic until the mid-nineteenth century (with the rise of the Meiji state), and the Asiatic mode has been recently discovered in areas as diverse as Africa, pre-Columbian America, and even Mediterranean Europe (see Godelier 1978). The latter "discoveries" were of course predicated on a broad and ahistorical definition of the underlying ideal type. As always, there is a tension between scholars who seek to construct ideal types that are closely tied to historical social systems, and those who seek to construct ones that are more encompassing in their coverage.

18. This economic interpretation of feudalism is clearly not favored by all scholars. For example, Bloch (1961, pp. 288–289) argues that the defining feature of feudalism is the monopolization of *authority* by a small group of nobles, with the implication of this being that the economic concomitants of authority (e.g., land ownership) are reduced to a position of secondary importance. The "authority classes" that emerge under his specification might be seen as feudal analogues to the social classes that Dahrendorf (1959) posits for the capitalist case.

19. We have adopted the conventional definition of a slave as "a man [who] is in the eyes of the law and of public opinion and with respect to all other parties a possession of another man" (Finley 1960, p. 53).

20. In the so-called secondary stage of feudalism (Bloch 1961), the obligations of serfs and free men became somewhat more formalized and standardized, yet regional variations of various sorts often persisted.

21. It was not until the early fourteenth century that states of the modern sort appeared in Europe (see Hechter and Brustein 1980).

22. In describing this period of classical feudalism, Bloch (1961) noted that "access to the circle of knights … was not absolutely closed, [yet] the door was nevertheless only very slightly ajar" (p. 325).

23. The Indian caste system flourished during the agrarian period, yet it persists in attenuated form within modern industrialized India (see Jalali 1992).

24. This is by no means an exhaustive listing of the various approaches that have been taken (see pp. 13–17 for a more detailed review).

25. There is an emerging consensus that the power of intellectuals and the intelligentsia has been further strengthened with the recent antisocialist revolutions in Eastern Europe (I. Szelényi 1994). The irony in this development is that the intellectual elite may ultimately be sowing the seeds of its own demise by reconstituting the old capitalist class.

26. The long-standing claim of convergence theorists (e.g., Kerr et al. 1964) has been that socialist and capitalist societies are simultaneously moving toward some common structural pattern. This was assumed to be occurring despite the surface differences between socialism and capitalism; however, with the subsequent fall of socialism in Eastern Europe and elsewhere, we are now seeing convergence of a more overt sort.

27. Although educational institutions clearly play a certifying role, it does not follow that they emerge merely to fill a "functional need" for highly trained workers (see Collins 1979).

28. This issue is addressed in greater detail in Part IV (see, e.g., "A Refined Model of Occupational Mobility," "Comparative Social Mobility Revisited: Models of Convergence and Divergence in 16 Countries," and "Trends in Class Mobility: The Post-war European Experience").

29. The rise of synthetic approaches makes it increasingly difficult to label scholars in meaningful ways. Although we have avoided standard "litmus test" definitions of what constitutes a true Marxist or Weberian, we have nonetheless found it possible (and useful) to classify scholars in terms of the types of intellectual problems, debates, and literatures that they address.

30. This position contrasts directly with the conventional wisdom that "social mobility as such is irrelevant to the problem of the existence of classes" (Dahrendorf 1959, p. 109; also see Poulantzas 1974, p. 37; Schumpeter 1951).

31. It should be stressed that Giddens departs from the usual neo-Weberian formulations on issues such as "the social and political significance of the new middle class, the importance of bureaucracy as a form of domination, and the character of the state as a focus of political and military power" (Giddens 1980, p. 297). As indicated in the Contents (p. viii), we have nonetheless reluctantly imposed the neo-Weberian label on Giddens, if only because he follows the lead of Weber in treating the foregoing issues as central to understanding modern industrialism and capitalism (see Note 29).

32. However, insofar as "every new class achieves its hegemony on a broader basis than that of the class ruling previously" (Marx and Engels [1947] 1970, p. 66), the presocialist revolutions can be interpreted as partial steps toward a classless society.

33. It is frequently argued that Americans have an elective affinity for gradational models of class. In accounting for this affinity, Ossowski (1963) and others (e.g., Lipset and Bendix 1959) have cited the absence of a feudal or aristocratic past in American history and the consequent reluctance of Americans to recognize differences in status or power with overt forms of deference or derogation.

34. Although some of the research completed by Warner was gradational in character (e.g., Warner 1949, ch. 2), it should be emphasized that his preferred mapping of the American class structure is based on purely discrete categories.

35. The defining feature of ethnic groups is that their members "entertain a subjective belief in their common descent because of similarities of physical type or of customs or both, or because of memories of colonization and migration" (Weber [1922] 1968, p. 389). This definition implies that "races" are particular types of ethnic groups in which putative physical similarities provide the basis for a subjective belief in common de-

scent (see Alba 1992, pp. 575–576, for competing definitions).

36. There is, of course, a large popular literature that represents gender conflict in wholly individualistic terms. This tendency to personalize gender conflicts reflects the simple fact that men and women interact frequently and intimately in family settings.

37. The position that Zeitlin (1982) takes here is directed against the conventional argument that corporate ownership in Western industrialized societies is so diffused across multiple stockholders that effective corporate power has now defaulted to managers. This argument does not, of course, apply directly to the case of socialist societies. Although such societies were once seen as a future bastion of new class rule (e.g., Konrad and Szelényi 1979), it is now possible that a neobourgeoisie will regain power in Russia and Eastern Europe as the postsocialist transition unfolds.

38. We have indicated in Figure 1 that two distinct postindustrial trajectories have been envisaged. The prevailing view has long been that advanced industrialism generates some form of skill upgrading (e.g., Piore and Sabel 1984), yet one continues to find "pessimistic" scenarios that project growing joblessness, underemployment, and deindustrialization (e.g., Gershuny 1983; Baumol 1967).

39. The work by Wright (1985) is similarly zero-sum in character. Although Wright emphasizes that multiple forms of capital tend to coexist in any given historical system, he nonetheless defines the march of history in terms of transitions from one dominant form of capital to another.

40. The importance of distinguishing between the early and mature Parsons on matters of stratification should therefore be stressed. This distinction has not been sufficiently appreciated in recent debates about the appropriateness of treating families as the primitive units of modern stratification analysis (see S. Szelényi 1994).

References

Adorno, Theodore. 1976. *Introduction to the Sociology of Music.* New York: Continuum.

Alba, Richard D. 1992. "Ethnicity." Pp. 575–584 in *Encyclopedia of Sociology,* edited by Edgar F. Borgatta and Marie L. Borgatta. New York: Macmillan.

Althusser, Louis. 1969. *For Marx.* London: Verso.

Anderson, Perry. 1974. *Lineages of the Absolutist State.* London: Verso.

Arrow, Kenneth J. 1973. "The Theory of Discrimination." Pp. 3–33 in *Discrimination in Labor Markets,* edited by Orley Ashenfelter and Albert Rees. Princeton: Princeton University Press.

Averitt, Robert T. 1968. *The Dual Economy: The Dynamics of American Industry Structure.* New York: Norton.

Baltzell, Edward D. 1958. *Philadelphia Gentlemen.* Glencoe, Ill.: Free Press.

———. 1964. *The Protestant Establishment.* New York: Random House.

———. 1991. *The Protestant Establishment Revisited.* New Brunswick, N.J.: Transaction Publishers.

Barber, Bernard. 1968. "Social Stratification." Pp. 288–295 in *International Encyclopedia of the Social Sciences,* edited by D. L. Sills. New York: Macmillan.

Baron, James N. 1994. "Reflections on Recent Generations of Mobility Research." Pp. 384–393 in *Social Stratification: Class, Race, and Gender in Sociological Perspective,* edited by David B. Grusky. Boulder: Westview.

Baumol, William J. 1967. "The Macro-Economics of Unbalanced Growth." *American Economic Review* 57:415–426.

Beck, E. M., Patrick Horan, and Charles Tolbert. 1978. "Stratification in a Dual Economy: A Structural Model of Earnings Determination." *American Sociological Review* 43:704–720.

Beck, Ulrich. 1987. "Beyond Status and Class: Will There Be an Individualized Class Society?" in *Modern German Sociology,* edited by Volker Meja, Dieter Misgeld, and Nico Stehr. New York: Columbia University Press.

Becker, Gary S. 1957. *The Economics of Discrimination.* Chicago: University of Chicago Press.

———. 1975. *Human Capital.* Chicago: University of Chicago Press.

Bell, Daniel. 1973. *The Coming of Post-Industrial Society.* New York: Basic Books.

———. 1975. "Ethnicity and Social Change." Pp. 141–174 in *Ethnicity: Theory and Experience,* edited by Nathan Glazer and Daniel P. Moynihan. Cambridge: Harvard University Press.

———. 1987. "The New Class: A Muddled Concept." Pp. 455–468 in *Structured Social Inequality,* edited by Celia S. Heller. 2d ed. New York: Macmillan.

Beller, Andrea H. 1982. "Occupational Segregation by Sex and Race, 1960–81." Pp. 11–26 in *Sex Segregation in the Workplace,* edited by Barbara F. Reskin. Washington, D.C.: National Academy.

Benería, Lourdes, and Catharine R. Stimpson (eds.). 1987. *Women, Households, and the Economy.* New Brunswick, N.J.: Rutgers University Press.

Berg, Ivar. 1973. *Education and Jobs: The Great Training Robbery.* Harmondsworth: Penguin Books.

Berg, Ivar, and Mayer N. Zald. 1978. "Business and Society." *Annual Review of Sociology* 4:115–143.

Berle, Adolf, and Gardiner Means. 1932. *The Modern Corporation and Private Property.* New York: Macmillan.

Berreman, Gerald. 1981. *Caste and Other Inequities.* Delhi: Manohar.

Bielby, William T., and James N. Baron. 1986. "Men and Women at Work: Sex Segregation and Statistical Discrimination." *American Journal of Sociology* 91: 759–799.

Blau, Peter M., and Otis Dudley Duncan. 1967. *The American Occupational Structure.* New York: Wiley.

Bloch, Marc. 1961. *Feudal Society.* London: Routledge and Kegan Paul.

Bonacich, Edna. 1972. "A Theory of Ethnic Antagonism: The Split Labor Market" *American Sociological Review* 37:547–559.

Bottomore, Thomas B. 1965. *Classes in Modern Society.* London: Allen and Unwin.

Bourdieu, Pierre. 1977. *Outline of a Theory of Practice,* translated by Richard Nice. New York: Cambridge University Press.

_____. 1979. *Algeria 1960,* translated by Richard Nice. Cambridge: Cambridge University Press.

_____. 1984. *Distinction: A Social Critique of the Judgement of Taste,* translated by Richard Nice. Cambridge: Harvard University Press.

Bourdieu, Pierre, and Jean-Claude Passeron. 1977. *Reproduction in Education, Society, and Culture.* Beverly Hills: Sage.

Brass, Paul R. 1983. *Caste, Faction, and Party in Indian Politics: Faction and Party,* vol. 1. Delhi: Chanakya Publications.

_____. 1985. *Caste, Faction, and Party in Indian Politics: Elections Studies,* vol. 2. Delhi: Chanakya Publications.

Braverman, Harry. 1974. *Labor and Monopoly Capital.* New York and London: Monthly Review Press.

Breiger, Ronald L. 1981. "The Social Class Structure of Occupational Mobility." *American Journal of Sociology* 87:578–611.

Brint, Steven. 1984. "'New Class' and Cumulative Trend Explanations of Liberal Political Attitudes of Professionals." *American Journal of Sociology* 90:30–71

Brook, Timothy. 1989. *The Asiatic Mode of Production in China.* Armonk, N.Y.: M. E. Sharpe.

Broom, Leonard, and Robert G. Cushing. 1977. "A Modest Test of an Immodest Theory: The Functional Theory of Stratification." *American Sociological Review* 42(1):157–169.

Brubaker, Rogers. 1985. "Rethinking Classical Theory: The Sociological Vision of Pierre Bourdieu." *Theory and Society* 14:745–775.

Burnham, James. 1962. *The Managerial Revolution.* Bloomington: Indiana University Press.

Burton, Mary D., and David B. Grusky. 1992. "A Quantitative History of Comparative Stratification Research." *Contemporary Sociology* 21:623–631.

Cain, Pamela S., and Donald J. Treiman. 1981. "The Dictionary of Occupational Titles as a Source of Occupational Data." *American Sociological Review* 46:253–278.

Chapin, Francis S. 1935. *Contemporary American Institutions: A Sociological Analysis.* New York: Harper and Row.

Charles, Maria, and David B. Grusky. 1995. "Models for Describing the Underlying Structure of Sex Segregation." *American Journal of Sociology.* Forthcoming.

Chesneaux, Jean. 1964. "Le mode de production asiatique: Une nouvelle étape de la discussion." *Eirenc* 3:131–146.

Clark, Terry N., and Seymour M. Lipset. 1991. "Are Social Classes Dying?" *International Sociology* 6:397–410.

Coleman, James S. 1990. *Foundations of Social Theory.* Cambridge: Harvard University Press.

Collins, Randall. 1975. *Conflict Sociology.* New York: Academic Press.

_____. 1979. *The Credential Society.* New York: Academic Press.

Coser, Lewis A. 1975. "Presidential Address: Two Methods in Search of a Substance." *American Sociological Review* 40:691–700.

Cullen, John B., and Shelley M. Novick. 1979. "The Davis-Moore Theory of Stratification: A Further Examination and Extension." *American Journal of Sociology* 84(6):1424–1437.

Dahl, Robert. 1967. *Pluralist Democracy in the United States.* Chicago: Rand McNally.

Dahrendorf, Ralf. 1959. *Class and Class Conflict in Industrial Society.* Stanford: Stanford University Press.

_____. 1968. *Essays in the Theory of Society.* Stanford: Stanford University Press.

Davis, James. 1982. "Achievement Variables and Class Cultures: Family, Schooling, Job, and Forty-Nine Dependent Variables in the Cumulative GSS." *American Sociological Review* 47:569–586.

Davis, Kingsley. 1948. *Human Society.* New York: Macmillan.

_____. 1953. "Reply." *American Sociological Review* 18:394–397.

Davis, Kingsley, and Wilbert E. Moore. 1945. "Some Principles of Stratification." *American Sociological Review* 10:242–249.

DiMaggio, Paul. 1979. "Review Essay on Pierre Bourdieu." *American Journal of Sociology* 84:1460–1474.

————. 1994. "Social Stratification, Life-Style, and Social Cognition." Pp. 458–465 in *Social Stratification: Class, Race, and Gender in Sociological Perspective,* edited by David B. Grusky. Boulder: Westview.

Djilas, Milovan. 1965. *The New Class.* New York: Praeger.

Doeringer, Peter, and Michael Piore. 1971. *Internal Labor Markets and Manpower Analysis.* Lexington, Mass.: D. C. Heath.

Dumont, Louis. 1970. *Homo Hierarchicus.* Chicago: University of Chicago Press.

Duncan, Otis Dudley. 1968. "Social Stratification and Mobility: Problems in the Measurement of Trend." Pp. 675–719 in *Indicators of Social Change,* edited by Eleanor B. Sheldon and Wilbert E. Moore. New York: Russell Sage Foundation.

Ehrenreich, Barbara, and John Ehrenreich. 1979. "The Professional-Managerial Class." Pp. 5–45 in *Between Labor and Capital,* edited by Pat Walker. Boston: South End Press.

Eisenstadt, S. N. 1992. "A Reappraisal of Theories of Social Change and Modernization." Pp. 412–429 in *Social Change and Modernity,* edited by Hans Haferkamp and Neil J. Smelser. Berkeley: University of California Press.

Erikson, Robert, and John H. Goldthorpe. 1994. "Trends in Class Mobility: The Post-War European Experience." Pp. 289–316 in *Social Stratification: Class, Race, and Gender in Sociological Perspective,* edited by David B. Grusky. Boulder: Westview.

Eyerman, Ron. 1992. "Modernity and Social Movements." Pp. 37–54 in *Social Change and Modernity,* edited by Hans Haferkamp and Neil J. Smelser. Berkeley: University of California Press.

Featherman, David L. 1981. "Social Stratification and Mobility." *American Behavioral Scientist* 24:364–385.

Featherman, David L., and Robert M. Hauser. 1978. *Opportunity and Change.* New York: Academic Press.

Finley, Moses J. 1960. *Slavery in Classical Antiquity.* Cambridge: W. Heffer and Sons.

Firestone, Shulamith. 1972. *The Dialectic of Sex.* New York: Bantam.

Fussell, Paul. 1983. *Class.* New York: Ballantine Books.

Galbraith, John K. 1967. *The New Industrial State.* Boston: Houghton Mifflin.

Ganzeboom, Harry B.G., Donald J. Treiman, and Wout C. Ultee. 1991. "Comparative Intergenerational Stratification Research: Three Generations and Beyond." *Annual Review of Sociology* 17:277–302.

Gartman, David. 1991. "Culture as Class Symbolization or Mass Reification? A Critique of Bourdieu's *Distinction.*" *American Journal of Sociology* 97:421–447.

Gershuny, Jonathan. 1983. *Social Innovation and the Division of Labor.* Oxford: Oxford University Press.

Giddens, Anthony. 1973. *The Class Structure of the Advanced Societies.* London: Hutchinson.

————. 1980. "Postscript." *The Class Structure of the Advanced Societies.* 2d ed. London: Hutchinson.

Glass, David V. 1954. *Social Mobility in Britain.* London: Routledge and Kegan Paul.

Glazer, Nathan, and Daniel P. Moynihan. 1975. "Introduction." Pp. 3–26 in *Ethnicity: Theory and Experience,* edited by Nathan Glazer and Daniel P. Moynihan. Cambridge: Harvard University Press.

Godelier, Maurice. 1978. "The Concept of the 'Asiatic Mode of Production' and Marxist Models of Social Evolution." Pp. 209–257 in *Relations of Production, Marxist Approaches to Economic Anthropology,* edited by D. Seddon. London: Cass.

Goldthorpe, John H. 1987. *Social Mobility and Class Structure in Modern Britain.* Oxford: Clarendon Press.

Goldthorpe, John H., David Lockwood, Frank Bechhofer, and Jennifer Platt. 1969. *The Affluent Worker in the Class Structure.* London: Cambridge University Press.

Goldthorpe, John H., and Gordon Marshall. 1992. "The Promising Future of Class Analysis: A Response to Recent Critiques." *Sociology* 26:381–400.

Gordon, Milton M. 1978. *Human Nature, Class, and Ethnicity.* New York: Oxford University Press.

Gouldner, Alvin. 1979. *The Future of Intellectuals and the Rise of the New Class.* New York: Seabury.

————. 1980. *The Two Marxisms: Contradictions and Anomalies in the Development of Theory.* New York: Seabury.

Granovetter, Mark. 1981. "Toward a Sociological Theory of Income Differences." Pp. 11–47 in *Sociological Perspectives on Labor Markets,* edited by Ivar Berg. New York: Academic Press.

Grusky, David B., and Thomas A. DiPrete. 1990. "Recent Trends in the Process of Stratification." *Demography* 27:617–637.

Grusky, David B., and Robert M. Hauser. 1984. "Comparative Social Mobility Revisited: Models of Convergence and Divergence in Sixteen Countries." *American Sociological Review* 49:19–38.

Grusky, David B., and Ann Azumi Takata. 1992. "Social Stratification." Pp. 1955–1970 in *Encyclopedia of Sociology,* edited by Edgar F. Borgatta and Marie L. Borgatta. New York: Macmillan.

Grusky, David B., and Stephen E. Van Rompaey. 1992. "The Vertical Scaling of Occupations: Some Cautionary Comments and Reflections." *American Journal of Sociology* 97:1712–1728.

Haferkamp, Hans, and Neil J. Smelser. 1992. "Introduction." Pp. 1–33 in *Social Change and Modernity,* edited by Hans Haferkamp and Neil J. Smelser. Berkeley: University of California Press.

Hall, John R. 1992. "The Capital(s) of Cultures: A Nonholistic Approach to Status Situations, Class, Gender, and Ethnicity." Pp. 257–285 in *Cultivating Differences: Symbolic Boundaries and the Making of Inequality,* edited by Michèle Lamont and Marcel Fournier. Chicago: University of Chicago Press.

Hannan, Michael. 1994. "Dynamics of Ethnic Boundaries." Pp. 500–508 in *Social Stratification: Class, Race, and Gender in Sociological Perspective,* edited by David B. Grusky. Boulder: Westview Press.

Hartmann, Heidi. 1981. "The Unhappy Marriage of Marxism and Feminism: Towards a More Progressive Union." Pp. 1–41 in *Women and Revolution,* edited by Lydia Sargent. Boston: South End Press.

Hauser, Robert M., and David L. Featherman. 1977. *The Process of Stratification: Trends and Analyses.* New York: Academic Press.

Hauser, Robert M., and David B. Grusky. 1988. "Cross-National Variation in Occupational Distributions, Relative Mobility Chances, and Intergenerational Shifts in Occupational Distributions." *American Sociological Review* 53:723–741.

Hauser, Robert M., Shu-Ling Tsai, and William H. Sewell. 1983. "A Model of Stratification with Response Error in Social and Psychological Variables." *Sociology of Education* 56:20–46.

Hechter, Michael. 1975. *Internal Colonialism: The Celtic Fringe in British National Development, 1536–1966.* Berkeley: University of California Press.

Hechter, Michael, and William Brustein. 1980. "Regional Modes of Production and Patterns of State Formation in Western Europe." *American Journal of Sociology* 85:1061–1094.

Hobsbawm, Eric J. 1965. "Introduction." Pp. 9–65 in *Pre-Capitalist Economic Formations,* translated by Jack Cohen, edited by Eric J. Hobsbawm. New York: International Publishers.

Hochschild, Jennifer L. 1981. *What's Fair? American Beliefs About Distributive Justice.* Cambridge: Harvard University Press.

Horan, Patrick. 1978. "Is Status Attainment Research Atheoretical?" *American Sociological Review* 43:534–541.

Horkheimer, Max, and Theodore Adorno. 1972. *Dialectic of Enlightenment.* New York: Herder and Herder.

Horowitz, Donald. 1985. *Ethnic Groups in Conflict.* Berkeley: University of California Press.

Hout, Michael. 1984. "Status, Autonomy, and Training in Occupational Mobility." *American Journal of Sociology* 89:1379–1409.

Hout, Michael, Clem Brooks, and Jeff Manza. 1993. "The Persistence of Classes in Post-Industrial Societies." *International Sociology* 8:259–277.

Huaco, George A. 1966. "The Functionalist Theory of Stratification: Two Decades of Controversy." *Inquiry* 9:215–240.

Hyman, Herbert H. 1966. "The Value Systems of Different Classes: A Social Psychological Contribution to the Analysis of Stratification." Pp. 488–499 in *Class, Status, and Power,* edited by Reinhard Bendix and Seymour M. Lipset. New York: Free Press.

Jackson, Elton F., and Richard F. Curtis. 1972. "Effects of Vertical Mobility and Status Inconsistency: A Body of Negative Evidence." *American Sociological Review* 37:701–713.

Jalali, Rita. 1992. "Caste and Class." Pp. 172–176 in *Encyclopedia of Sociology,* edited by Edgar F. Borgatta and Marie L. Borgatta. New York: Macmillan.

Jencks, Christopher, Susan Bartlett, Mary Corcoran, James Crouse, David Eaglesfield, Gregory Jackson, Kent McClelland, Peter Mueser, Michael Olneck, Joseph Schwartz, Sherry Ward, and Jill Williams. 1979. *Who Gets Ahead? The Determinants of Economic Success in America.* New York: Basic Books.

Jencks, Christopher, Lauri Perman, and Lee Rainwater. 1988. "What Is a Good Job? A New Measure of Labor-Market Success." *American Journal of Sociology* 93:1322–1357.

Jencks, Christopher, Marshall Smith, Henry Acland, Mary Jo Bane, David Cohen, Herbert Gintis, Barbara Heyns, and Stephen Michelson. 1972. *Inequality: A Reassessment of the Effect of Family and Schooling in America.* New York: Basic Books.

Jowitt, Ken. 1992. *New World Disorder: The Leninist Extinction.* Berkeley: University of California Press.

Kautsky, Karl. 1903. *The Social Revolution.* Chicago: C. H. Kerr and Company.

Kelley, Jonathan. 1981. *Revolution and the Rebirth of Inequality.* Berkeley: University of California Press.

Kerbo, Harold R. 1991. *Social Stratification and Inequality: Class Conflict in Historical and Comparative Perspective.* New York: McGraw-Hill.

Kerr, Clark, John T. Dunlop, Frederick H. Harbison, and Charles A. Myers. 1964. *Industrialism and Industrial Man.* New York: Oxford University Press.

Kluegel, James R., and Eliot R. Smith. 1986. *Beliefs About Inequality: Americans' Views of What Is and What Ought to Be.* New York: Aldine de Gruyter.

Kohn, Melvin L. 1980. "Job Complexity and Adult Personality." Pp. 193–210 in *Themes of Work and Love in Adulthood,* edited by Neil J. Smelser and Erik H. Erikson. Cambridge: Harvard University Press.

Konrád, George, and Iván Szelényi. 1979. *The Intellectuals on the Road to Class Power.* New York: Harcourt Brace Jovanovich.

Krader, Lawrence. 1975. *The Asiatic Mode of Production: Sources, Development, and Critique in the Writings of Karl Marx.* Assen: Van Gorcum.

Lachmann, Richard. 1990. "Class Formation Without Class Struggle: An Elite Conflict Theory of the Transition to Capitalism." *American Sociological Review* 55:398–414.

Landecker, Werner S. 1981. *Class Crystallization.* New Brunswick, N.J.: Rutgers University Press.

Leach, Edmund R. 1960. *Aspects of Caste in South India, Ceylon, and North-West Pakistan.* Cambridge: Cambridge University Press.

Leakey, Richard, and Roger Lewin. 1977. *Origins.* New York: Dutton.

Lenski, Gerhard E. 1954. "Status Crystallization: A Non-Vertical Dimension of Social Status." *American Sociological Review* 19:405–413.

———. 1966. *Power and Privilege.* New York: McGraw-Hill.

———. 1978. "Marxist Experiments in Destratification: An Appraisal." *Social Forces* 57:364–383.

———. 1994. "New Light on Old Issues: The Relevance of 'Really Existing Socialist Societies' for Stratification Theory." Pp. 55–61 in *Social Stratification: Class, Race, and Gender in Sociological Perspective,* edited by David B. Grusky. Boulder: Westview.

Levy, Marion, Jr. 1966. *Modernization and the Structure of Societies.* Princeton: Princeton University Press.

Lieberson, Stanley. 1994. "Understanding Ascriptive Stratification: Some Issues and Principles." Pp. 649–656 in *Social Stratification: Class, Race, and Gender in Sociological Perspective,* edited by David B. Grusky. Boulder: Westview Press.

Lipset, Seymour M. 1959. *Political Man: The Social Bases of Politics.* Baltimore: The Johns Hopkins University Press.

———. 1968. "Social Class." Pp. 296–316 in *International Encyclopedia of the Social Sciences,* edited by D. L. Sills. New York: Macmillan.

Lipset, Seymour M., and Reinhard Bendix. 1959. *Social Mobility in Industrial Society.* Berkeley: University of California Press.

Lipset, Seymour H., and Stein Rokkan. 1967. *Party Systems and Voter Alignments.* New York: Free Press.

Mandel, Ernest. 1971. *The Formation of the Economic Thought of Karl Marx.* New York: Monthly Review Press.

Marini, Margaret M., and Mary C. Brinton. 1984. "Sex Typing in Occupational Socialization." Pp. 192–232 in *Sex Segregation in the Workplace,* edited by Barbara Reskin. Washington, D.C.: National Academy Press.

Marshall, Thomas H. 1981. *The Right to Welfare and Other Essays.* New York: Free Press.

Marx, Karl. 1948. *Manifesto of the Communist Party.* New York: International Publishers.

———. [1939] 1971. *The Grundrisse.* New York: Harper and Row.

———. [1894] 1972. *Capital.* 3 vols. London: Lawrence and Wishart.

Marx, Karl, and Frederich Engels. [1947] 1970. *The German Ideology,* edited by C. J. Arthur. New York: International Publishers.

Masuda, Yoneji. 1980. *The Information Society as Post-Industrial Society.* Tokyo: Institute for the Information Society.

Mayer, Kurt B., and Walter Buckley. 1970. *Class and Society.* New York: Random House.

Mayhew, Leon. 1970. "Ascription in Modern Societies." Pp. 308–323 in *The Logic of Social Hierarchies,* edited by Edward O. Laumann, Paul M. Siegel, and Robert W. Hodge. Chicago: Markham Publishing.

Meyer, John W. 1994. "The Evolution of Modern Stratification Systems," Pp. 730–737 in *Social Stratification: Class, Race, and Gender in Sociological Perspective,* edited by David B. Grusky. Boulder: Westview Press.

Michels, Robert. 1949. *Political Parties,* translated by Eden Paul and Cedar Paul. Glencoe, Ill.: Free Press.

Mills, C. Wright. 1956. *The Power Elite.* New York: Oxford University Press.

Mitchell, Arnold. 1983. *The Nine American Lifestyles.* New York: Macmillan.

Moore, Wilbert E. 1963a. "But Some Are More Equal Than Others." *American Sociological Review* 28:13–28.

———. 1963b. "Rejoinder." *American Sociological Review* 28:27.

Mosca, Gaetano. 1939. *The Ruling Class.* New York: McGraw-Hill.

Nielsen, François. 1985. "Toward a Theory of Ethnic Solidarity in Modern Societies." *American Sociological Review* 50:133–149.

Nisbet, Robert A. 1959. "The Decline and Fall of Social Class." *Pacific Sociological Review* 2:11–17.

O'Leary, Brendan. 1989. *The Asiatic Mode of Production.* Oxford: Basil Blackwell.

Oliver, Douglas L. 1955. *A Solomon Island Society.* Cambridge: Harvard University Press.

Olzak, Susan. 1983. "Contemporary Ethnic Mobilization." *Annual Review of Sociology* 9:355–374.

Osipov, G. B. 1969. "The Class Character of the Theory of Social Mobility." Pp. 135–137 in *American and So-*

viet Society, edited by Paul Hollander. Englewood Cliffs, N.J.: Prentice-Hall.

Ossowski, Stanislaw. 1963. *Class Structure in the Social Consciousness.* New York: Free Press.

Pareto, Vilfredo. 1935. *The Mind and Society,* translated by A. Bongiorno and A. Livingston, edited by A. Livingston. New York: Harcourt, Brace, and Company.

Parkin, Frank. 1971. *Class Inequality and Political Order: Social Stratification in Capitalist and Communist Societies.* New York: Praeger.

_____. 1979. *Marxism and Class Theory: A Bourgeois Critique.* New York: Columbia University Press.

Parsons, Talcott. 1951. *The Social System.* Glencoe, Ill.: The Free Press.

_____. 1954. *Essays in Sociological Theory.* Glencoe, Ill.: Free Press.

_____. 1970. "Equality and Inequality in Modern Society, or Social Stratification Revisited." Pp. 13–72 in *Social Stratification: Research and Theory for the 1970s,* edited by Edward O. Laumann. Indianapolis, Ind.: Bobbs-Merrill Company.

_____. 1975. "Some Theoretical Considerations on the Nature and Trends of Change of Ethnicity." Pp. 53–83 in *Ethnicity: Theory and Experience,* edited by Nathan Glazer and Daniel P. Moynihan. Cambridge: Harvard University Press.

Patterson, Orlando. 1982. *Slavery and Social Death.* Cambridge: Harvard University Press.

Pfeiffer, John. 1977. *The Emergence of Society: A Prehistory of the Establishment.* New York: McGraw-Hill.

Piore, Michael J. 1975. "Notes for a Theory of Labor Market Segmentation." Pp. 125–171 in *Labor Market Segmentation,* edited by Richard C. Edwards, Michael Reich, and David M. Gordon. Lexington, Mass.: D.C. Heath.

Piore, Michael J., and Charles F. Sabel. 1984. *The Second Industrial Divide.* New York: Basic.

Polachek, Solomon W., and W. Stanley Siebert. 1993. *The Economics of Earnings.* Cambridge: Cambridge University Press.

Poulantzas, Nicos. 1974. *Classes in Contemporary Capitalism.* London: Verso.

Ransford, H. Edward, and Jon Miller. 1983. "Race, Sex, and Feminist Outlooks." *American Sociological Review* 48:46–59.

Reich, Michael. 1977. "The Economics of Racism." Pp. 184–188 in *Problems in Political Economy: An Urban Perspective,* edited by David M. Gordon. Lexington, Mass.: D.C. Heath.

Rizzi, Bruno. 1985. *The Bureaucratization of the World.* London: Tavistock Publications.

Rose, Arnold. 1967. *The Power Structure.* New York: Oxford University Press.

Rossides, Daniel W. 1990. *Social Stratification: The American Class System in Comparative Perspective.* Englewood Cliffs, N.J.: Prentice-Hall.

Runciman, Walter G. 1968. "Class, Status, and Power?" Pp. 25–61 in *Social Stratification,* edited by J. A. Jackson. New York: Cambridge University Press.

_____. 1974. "Towards a Theory of Social Stratification." Pp. 55–81 in *The Social Analysis of Class Structure,* edited by Frank Parkin. London: Tavistock Publications.

Schumpeter, Joseph. 1951. *Imperialism and Social Classes.* New York: Augustus M. Kelley, Inc.

_____. 1953. *Aufsätze zur Soziologie.* Tübingen: Mohr/Siebeck.

Sears, David O., Carl P. Hensler, and Leslie K. Speer. 1979. "Whites' Opposition to 'Busing': Self-Interest or Symbolic Politics?" *American Political Science Review* 73:369–384.

Sewell, William H. 1940. *The Construction and Standardization of a Scale for the Measurement of Oklahoma Farm Families Socioeconomic Status.* Agricultural Experiment Station, Technical Bulletin no 9. Stillwater: Oklahoma Agricultural and Mechanical College.

Sewell, William H., Archibald O. Haller, and Alejandro Portes. 1969. "The Educational and Early Occupational Attainment Process." *American Sociological Review* 34:82–92.

Shaw, William H. 1978. *Marx's Theory of History.* Stanford: Stanford University Press.

Shils, Edward. 1968. Pp. 104–132 in *Social Stratification,* edited by J. A. Jackson. New York: Cambridge University Press.

_____. 1982. "The Political Class in the Age of Mass Society: Collectivistic Liberalism and Social Democracy." Pp. 13–32 in *Does Who Governs Matter? Elite Circulation in Contemporary Societies,* edited by Moshe M. Czudnowski. DeKalb: Northern Illinois University Press.

Sio, Arnold A. 1965. "Interpretations of Slavery: The Slave Status in the Americas." *Comparative Studies in Society and History* 7:289–308.

Smith, Michael R. 1990. "What Is New in 'New Structuralist' Analyses of Earnings?" *American Sociological Review* 55:827–841.

Sobel, Michael E. 1981. *Lifestyle and Social Structure: Concepts, Definitions, Analyses.* New York: Academic Press.

Sørensen, Aage B., and Arne L. Kalleberg. 1981. "An Outline of a Theory of the Matching of Persons to Jobs." Pp. 49–74 in *Sociological Perspectives on Labor Markets,* edited by Ivar Berg. New York: Academic Press.

Srinivas, Mysore N. 1962. *Caste in Modern India*. London: Asia Publishing House.

Steinmetz, George, and Erik O. Wright. 1989. "The Fall and Rise of the Petty Bourgeoisie: Changing Patterns of Self-Employment in the Postwar United States." *American Journal of Sociology* 94:973–1018.

Stier, Haya, and David B. Grusky. 1990. "An Overlapping Persistence Model of Career Mobility." *American Sociological Review* 55:736–756.

Svalastoga, Kaare. 1965. *Social Differentiation*. New York: D. McKay Co.

Szelényi, Iván. 1994. "Post-Industrialism, Post-Communism, and the New Class." Pp. 723–729 in *Social Stratification: Class, Race, and Gender in Sociological Perspective*, edited by David B. Grusky. Boulder: Westview.

Szelényi, Szonja. 1994. "Women and the Class Structure." Pp. 577–582 in *Social Stratification: Class, Race, and Gender in Sociological Perspective*, edited by David B. Grusky. Boulder: Westview.

Szelényi, Szonja, and Iván Szelényi. 1993. "The Making of a New Elite in Post-Communist Central Europe: An Outline of a Dynamic Model of Social Spaces." Paper presented at the Annual Meeting of the Hungarian Sociological Association, Miskolc, Hungary, July 1993.

Tawney, R. H. 1931. *Equality*. London: George Allen and Unwin.

Taylor, D. Garth, Paul B. Sheatsley, and Andrew M. Greeley. 1978. "Attitudes Toward Racial Integration." *Scientific American* 238:42–51.

Touraine, Alain. 1981 *The Voice and the Eye: An Analysis of Social Movements*. Cambridge: Cambridge University Press.

Treiman, Donald J. 1970. "Industrialization and Social Stratification." Pp. 207–234 in *Social Stratification: Research and Theory for the 1970s*, edited by Edward O. Laumann. Indianapolis: Bobbs-Merrill.

———. 1976. "A Standard Occupational Prestige Scale for Use with Historical Data." *Journal of Interdisciplinary History* 7:283–304.

———. 1977. *Occupational Prestige in Comparative Perspective*. New York: Academic Press.

Tumin, Melvin M. 1953. "Some Principles of Stratification: A Critical Analysis." *American Sociological Review* 18:378–394.

———. 1985. *Social Stratification: The Forms and Functions of Inequality*. Englewood Cliffs, N.J.: Prentice-Hall.

Useem, Michael. 1984. *The Inner Circle*. New York: Oxford University Press.

Warner, W. Lloyd. 1949. *Social Class in America*. Chicago: Science Research Associates.

Weber, Max. 1946. *From Max Weber: Essays in Sociology*, edited and translated by Hans Gerth and C. Wright Mills. New York: Oxford University Press.

———. 1947. *The Theory of Social and Economic Organization*, edited by Talcott Parsons. New York: Free Press.

———. [1922] 1968. *Economy and Society*. Berkeley: University of California Press.

Wegener, Bernd. 1991. "Relative Deprivation and Social Mobility: Structural Constraints on Distributive Justice Judgments." *European Sociological Review* 7:3–18.

Weiss, Michael J. 1988. *The Clustering of America*. New York: Harper and Row.

Wesolowski, Wlodzimierz. 1962. "Some Notes on the Functional Theory of Stratification." *Polish Sociological Bulletin* 3-4:28–38.

Westergaard, John, and Henrietta Resler. 1975. *Class in a Capitalist Society: A Study of Contemporary Britain*. London: Heinemann.

Wilson, William J. 1987. *The Truly Disadvantaged: The Inner City, the Underclass, and Public Policy*. Chicago: University of Chicago Press.

Wittfogel, Karl A. 1981. *Oriental Despotism: A Comparative Study of Total Power*. New York: Vintage Books.

Wright, Erik O. 1978. *Class, Crisis, and the State*. London: New Left Books.

———. 1979. *Class Structure and Income Determination*. New York: Academic Press.

———. 1985. *Classes*. London: Verso.

———. 1989. *The Debate on Classes*. London: Verso.

Wrong, Dennis H. 1959. "The Functional Theory of Stratification: Some Neglected Considerations." *American Sociological Review* 24:772–782.

Young, Michael. 1958. *The Rise of the Meritocracy*. Harmondsworth: Penguin Books.

Zablocki, Benjamin D., and Rosabeth M. Kanter. 1976. "The Differentiation of Life-Styles." *Annual Review of Sociology* 2:269–298.

Zeitlin, Maurice. 1982. "Corporate Ownership and Control: The Large Corporation and the Capitalist Class." Pp. 196–223 in *Classes, Power, and Conflict*, edited by Anthony Giddens and David Held. Berkeley: University of California Press.

Part II
Forms and Sources of Stratification

The Functions of Stratification

The Dysfunctions of Stratification

The Functions of Stratification

KINGSLEY DAVIS AND WILBERT E. MOORE

Some Principles of Stratification

In a previous paper some concepts for handling the phenomena of social inequality were presented.[1] In the present paper a further step in stratification theory is undertaken—an attempt to show the relationship between stratification and the rest of the social order.[2] Starting from the proposition that no society is "classless," or unstratified, an effort is made to explain, in functional terms, the universal necessity which calls forth stratification in any social system. Next, an attempt is made to explain the roughly uniform distribution of prestige as between the major types of positions in every society. Since, however, there occur between one society and another great differences in the degree and kind of stratification, some attention is also given to the varieties of social inequality and the variable factors that give rise to them.

Clearly, the present task requires two different lines of analysis—one to understand the universal, the other to understand the variable features of stratification. Naturally each line of inquiry aids the other and is indispensable, and in the treatment that follows the two will be interwoven, although, because of space limitations, the emphasis will be on the universals.

Throughout, it will be necessary to keep in mind one thing—namely, that the discussion relates to the system of positions, not to the individuals occupying those positions. It is one thing to ask why different positions carry different degrees of prestige, and quite another to ask how certain individuals get into those positions. Although, as the argument will try to show, both questions are related, it is essential to keep them separate in our thinking. Most of the literature on stratification has tried to answer the second question (particularly with regard to the ease or difficulty of mobility between strata) without tackling the first. The first question, however, is logically prior and, in the case of any particular individual or group, factually prior.

The Functional Necessity of Stratification

Curiously the main functional necessity explaining the universal presence of stratification is precisely the requirement faced by any society of placing and motivating individuals in the social structure. As a functioning mechanism a society must somehow distribute its members in social positions and induce them to perform the duties of these positions. It must thus concern itself with motivation at two different levels: to instill in the proper individuals the desire to fill certain positions, and, once in these positions, the desire to perform the duties attached to them. Even though the social order may be relatively static in form, there is a continuous process of metabolism as new individuals are born into it, shift with age, and die off. Their absorption into the positional system must somehow be arranged and motivated. This is true whether the system is competitive or non-competitive. A competitive system gives greater importance to the motivation to achieve positions, whereas a non-competitive sys-

39

tem gives perhaps greater importance to the motivation to perform the duties of the positions; but in any system both types of motivation are required.

If the duties associated with the various positions were all equally pleasant to the human organism, all equally important to societal survival, and all equally in need of the same ability or talent, it would make no difference who got into which positions, and the problem of social placement would be greatly reduced. But actually it does make a great deal of difference who gets into which positions, not only because some positions are inherently more agreeable than others, but also because some require special talents or training and some are functionally more important than others. Also, it is essential that the duties of the positions be performed with the diligence that their importance requires. Inevitably, then, a society must have, first, some kind of rewards that it can use as inducements, and, second, some way of distributing these rewards differentially according to positions. The rewards and their distribution become a part of the social order, and thus give rise to stratification.

One may ask what kind of rewards a society has at its disposal in distributing its personnel and securing essential services. It has, first of all, the things that contribute to sustenance and comfort. It has, second, the things that contribute to humor and diversion. And it has, finally, the things that contribute to self respect and ego expansion. The last, because of the peculiarly social character of the self, is largely a function of the opinion of others, but it nonetheless ranks in importance with the first two. In any social system all three kinds of rewards must be dispensed differentially according to positions.

In a sense the rewards are "built into" the position. They consist in the "rights" associated with the position, plus what may be called its accompaniments or perquisites. Often the rights, and sometimes the accompaniments, are functionally related to the duties of the position. (Rights as viewed by the incumbent are usually duties as viewed by other members of the community.) However, there may be a host of subsidiary rights and perquisites that are not essential to the function of the position and have only an indirect and symbolic connection with its duties, but which still may be of considerable importance in inducing people to seek the positions and fulfil the essential duties.

If the rights and perquisites of different positions in a society must be unequal, then the society must be stratified, because that is precisely what stratification means. Social inequality is thus an unconsciously evolved device by which societies insure that the most important positions are conscientiously filled by the most qualified persons. Hence every society, no matter how simple or complex, must differentiate persons in terms of both prestige and esteem, and must therefore possess a certain amount of institutionalized inequality.

It does not follow that the amount or type of inequality need be the same in all societies. This is largely a function of factors that will be discussed presently.

The Two Determinants of Positional Rank

Granting the general function that inequality subserves, one can specify the two factors that determine the relative rank of different positions. In general those positions convey the best reward, and hence have the highest rank, which (a) have the greatest importance for the society and (b) require the greatest training or talent. The first factor concerns function and is a matter of relative significance; the second concerns means and is a matter of scarcity.

Differential Functional Importance. Actually a society does not need to reward positions in proportion to their functional importance. It merely needs to give sufficient reward to them to insure that they will be filled competently. In other words, it must see that less essential positions do not compete successfully with more essential ones. If a position is easily filled, it need not be heavily rewarded, even though important. On the other hand, if it is important but hard to fill, the reward must be high enough to get it filled anyway. Functional importance is therefore a necessary but not a sufficient cause of high rank being assigned to a position.[3]

Differential Scarcity of Personnel. Practically all positions, no matter how acquired, require some form of skill or capacity for performance. This is implicit in the very notion of position, which implies that the incumbent must, by virtue of his incumbency, accomplish certain things.

There are, ultimately, only two ways in which a person's qualifications come about: through inherent capacity or through training. Obviously, in concrete activities both are always necessary, but from a practical standpoint the scarcity may lie primarily in one or the other, as well as in both. Some positions require innate talents of such high degree that the persons who fill them are bound to be rare. In many cases, however, talent is fairly abundant in the population but the training process is so long, costly, and elaborate that relatively few can qualify. Modern medicine, for example, is within the mental capacity of most individuals, but a medical education is so burdensome and expensive that virtually none would undertake it if the position of the M.D. did not carry a reward commensurate with the sacrifice.

If the talents required for a position are abundant and the training easy, the method of acquiring the position may have little to do with its duties. There may be, in fact, a virtually accidental relationship. But if the skills required are scarce by reason of the rarity of talent or the costliness of training, the position, if functionally important, must have an attractive power that will draw the necessary skills in competition with other positions. This means, in effect, that the position must be high in the social scale—must command great prestige, high salary, ample leisure, and the like.

How Variations Are to Be Understood. In so far as there is a difference between one system of stratification and another, it is attributable to whatever factors affect the two determinants of differential reward—namely, functional importance and scarcity of personnel. Positions important in one society may not be important in another, because the conditions faced by the societies, or their degree of internal development, may be different. The same conditions, in turn, may affect the question of scarcity; for in some societies the stage of development, or the external situation, may wholly obviate the necessity of certain kinds of skill or talent. Any particular system of stratification, then, can be understood as a product of the special conditions affecting the two aforementioned grounds of differential reward.

Major Societal Functions and Stratification

Religion

The reason why religion is necessary is apparently to be found in the fact that human society achieves its unity primarily through the possession by its members of certain ultimate values and ends in common. Although these values and ends are subjective, they influence behavior, and their integration enables the society to operate as a system. Derived neither from inherited nor from external nature, they have evolved as a part of culture by communication and moral pressure. They must, however, appear to the members of the society to have some reality, and it is the role of religious belief and ritual to supply and reinforce this appearance of reality. Through belief and ritual the common ends and values are connected with an imaginary world symbolized by concrete sacred objects, which world in turn is related in a meaningful way to the facts and trials of the individual's life. Through the worship of the sacred objects and the beings they symbolize, and the acceptance of supernatural prescriptions that are at the same time codes of behavior, a powerful control over human conduct is exercised, guiding it along lines sustaining the institutional structure and conforming to the ultimate ends and values.

If this conception of the role of religion is true, one can understand why in every known society the religious activities tend to be under the charge of particular persons, who tend thereby to enjoy greater rewards than the ordinary societal member. Certain of the rewards and special privileges may attach to only the highest religious functionaries, but others usually apply, if such exists, to the entire sacerdotal class.

Moreover, there is a peculiar relation between the duties of the religious official and the special privileges he enjoys. If the supernatural world governs the destinies of men more ultimately than does the real world, its earthly representative, the person through whom one may communicate with the supernatural, must be a powerful individual. He is a keeper of sacred tradition, a skilled performer of the ritual, and an interpreter of lore and myth. He is in such close contact with the gods that he is viewed as possessing some of their characteristics. He is, in short, a bit sacred, and hence free from some of the more vulgar necessities and controls.

It is no accident, therefore, that religious functionaries have been associated with the very highest positions of power, as in theocratic regimes. Indeed, looking at it from this point of view, one may wonder why it is that they do not get *entire* control over their societies. The factors that prevent this are worthy of note.

In the first place, the amount of technical competence necessary for the performance of religious duties is small. Scientific or artistic capacity is not required. Anyone can set himself up as enjoying an intimate relation with deities, and nobody can successfully dispute him. Therefore, the factor of scarcity of personnel does not operate in the technical sense.

One may assert, on the other hand, that religious ritual is often elaborate and religious lore abstruse, and that priestly ministrations require tact, if not intelligence. This is true, but the technical requirements of the profession are for the most part adventitious, not related to the end in the same way that science is related to air travel. The priest can never be free from competition, since the criteria of whether or not one has genuine contact with the supernatural are never strictly clear. It is this competition that debases the priestly position below what might be expected at first glance. That is why priestly prestige is highest in those societies where membership in the profession is rigidly controlled by the priestly guild itself. That is why, in part at least, elaborate devices are utilized to stress the identification of the person with his office—spectacular costume,

abnormal conduct, special diet, segregated residence, celibacy, conspicuous leisure, and the like. In fact, the priest is always in danger of becoming somewhat discredited—as happens in a secularized society—because in a world of stubborn fact, ritual and sacred knowledge alone will not grow crops or build houses. Furthermore, unless he is protected by a professional guild, the priest's identification with the supernatural tends to preclude his acquisition of abundant worldly goods.

As between one society and another it seems that the highest general position awarded the priest occurs in the medieval type of social order. Here there is enough economic production to afford a surplus, which can be used to support a numerous and highly organized priesthood; and yet the populace is unlettered and therefore credulous to a high degree. Perhaps the most extreme example is to be found in the Buddhism of Tibet, but others are encountered in the Catholicism of feudal Europe, the Inca regime of Peru, the Brahminism of India, and the Mayan priesthood of Yucatan. On the other hand, if the society is so crude as to have no surplus and little differentiation, so that every priest must be also a cultivator or hunter, the separation of the priestly status from the others has hardly gone far enough for priestly prestige to mean much. When the priest actually has high prestige under these circumstances, it is because he also performs other important functions (usually political and medical).

In an extremely advanced society built on scientific technology, the priesthood tends to lose status, because sacred tradition and supernaturalism drop into the background. The ultimate values and common ends of the society tend to be expressed in less anthropomorphic ways, by officials who occupy fundamentally political, economic, or educational rather than religious positions. Nevertheless, it is easily possible for intellectuals to exaggerate the degree to which the priesthood in a presumably secular milieu has lost prestige. When the matter is closely examined the urban proletariat, as well as the rural citizenry, proves to be surprisingly god-fearing and priest-ridden. No society has become so completely secularized as to liquidate entirely the belief in transcendental ends and supernatural entities. Even in a secularized society some system must exist for the integration of ultimate values, for their ritualistic expression, and for the emotional adjustments required by disappointment, death, and disaster.

Government

Like religion, government plays a unique and indispensable part in society. But in contrast to religion, which provides integration in terms of sentiments, beliefs, and rituals, it organizes the society in terms of law and authority. Furthermore, it orients the society to the actual rather than the unseen world.

The main functions of government are, internally, the ultimate enforcement of norms, the final arbitration of conflicting interests, and the overall planning and direction of society; and externally, the handling of war and diplomacy. To carry out these functions it acts as the agent of the entire people, enjoys a monopoly of force, and controls all individuals within its territory.

Political action, by definition, implies authority. An official can command because he has authority, and the citizen must obey because he is subject to that authority. For this reason stratification is inherent in the nature of political relationships.

So clear is the power embodied in political position that political inequality is sometimes thought to comprise all inequality. But it can be shown that there are other bases of stratification, that the following controls operate in practice to keep political power from becoming complete: (a) The fact that the actual holders of political office, and especially those determining top policy must necessarily be few in number compared to the total population. (b) The fact that the rulers represent the interest of the group rather than of themselves, and are therefore restricted in their behavior by rules and mores designed to enforce this limitation of interest. (c) The fact that the holder of political office has his authority by virtue of his office and nothing else, and therefore any special knowledge, talent, or capacity he may claim is purely incidental, so that he often has to depend upon others for technical assistance.

In view of these limiting factors, it is not strange that the rulers often have less power and prestige than a literal enumeration of their formal rights would lead one to expect.

Wealth, Property, and Labor

Every position that secures for its incumbent a livelihood is, by definition, economically rewarded. For this reason there is an economic aspect to those positions (e.g. political and religious) the main function of which is not economic. It therefore becomes convenient for the society to use unequal economic returns as a principal means of controlling the entrance of persons into positions and stimulating the performance of their duties. The amount of the economic return therefore becomes one of the main indices of social status.

It should be stressed, however, that a position does not bring power and prestige *because* it draws a high income. Rather, it draws a high income because it is functionally important and the available personnel is for one reason or another scarce. It is therefore superficial and erroneous to regard high income as the cause of a man's power and prestige, just as it is erroneous to think that a man's fever is the cause of his disease.[4]

The economic source of power and prestige is not income primarily, but the ownership of capital goods (including patents, good will, and professional reputation). Such ownership should be distinguished from the possession of consumers' goods, which is an index rather than a cause of social standing. In other words, the ownership of producers' goods is properly speaking, a source of income like other positions, the income itself remaining an index. Even in situations where social values are widely commercialized and earnings are the readiest method of judging social position, income does not confer prestige on a position so much as it induces people to compete for the position. It is true that a man who has a high income as a result of one position may find this money helpful in climbing into another position as well, but this again reflects the effect of his initial, economically advantageous status, which exercises its influence through the medium of money.

In a system of private property in productive enterprise, an income above what an individual spends can give rise to possession of capital wealth. Presumably such possession is a reward for the proper management of one's finances originally and of the productive enterprise later. But as social differentiation becomes highly advanced and yet the institution of inheritance persists, the phenomenon of pure ownership, and reward for pure ownership, emerges. In such a case it is difficult to prove that the position is functionally important or that the scarcity involved is anything other than extrinsic and accidental. It is for this reason, doubtless, that the institution of private property in productive goods becomes more subject to criticism as social development proceeds toward industrialization. It is only this pure, that is, strictly legal and functionless ownership, however, that is open to attack; for some form of active ownership, whether private or public, is indispensable.

One kind of ownership of production goods consists in rights over the labor of others. The most extremely concentrated and exclusive of such rights are found in slavery, but the essential principle remains in serfdom, peonage, encomienda, and indenture. Naturally this kind of ownership has the greatest significance for stratification, because it necessarily entails an unequal relationship.

But property in capital goods inevitably introduces a compulsive element even into the nominally free contractual relationship. Indeed, in some respects the authority of the contractual employer is greater than that of the feudal landlord, inasmuch as the latter is more limited by traditional reciprocities. Even the classical economics recognized that competitors would fare unequally, but it did not pursue this fact to its necessary conclusion that, however it might be acquired, unequal control of goods and services must give unequal advantage to the parties to a contract.

Technical Knowledge

The function of finding means to single goals, without any concern with the choice between goals, is the exclusively technical sphere. The explanation of why positions requiring great technical skill receive fairly high rewards is easy to see,

for it is the simplest case of the rewards being so distributed as to draw talent and motivate training. Why they seldom if ever receive the highest rewards is also clear: the importance of technical knowledge from a societal point of view is never so great as the integration of goals, which takes place on the religious, political, and economic levels. Since the technological level is concerned solely with means, a purely technical position must ultimately be subordinate to other positions that are religious, political, or economic in character.

Nevertheless, the distinction between expert and layman in any social order is fundamental, and cannot be entirely reduced to other terms. Methods of recruitment, as well as of reward, sometimes lead to the erroneous interpretation that technical positions are economically determined. Actually, however, the acquisition of knowledge and skill cannot be accomplished by purchase, although the opportunity to learn may be. The control of the avenues of training may inhere as a sort of property right in certain families or classes, giving them power and prestige in consequence. Such a situation adds an artificial scarcity to the natural scarcity of skills and talents. On the other hand, it is possible for an opposite situation to arise. The rewards of technical position may be so great that a condition of excess supply is created, leading to at least temporary devaluation of the rewards. Thus "unemployment in the learned professions" may result in a debasement of the prestige of those positions. Such adjustments and readjustments are constantly occurring in changing societies; and it is always well to bear in mind that the efficiency of a stratified structure may be affected by the modes of recruitment for positions. The social order itself, however, sets limits to the inflation or deflation of the prestige of experts: an over-supply tends to debase the rewards and discourage recruitment or produce revolution, whereas an under-supply tends to increase the rewards or weaken the society in competition with other societies.

Particular systems of stratification show a wide range with respect to the exact position of technically competent persons. This range is perhaps most evident in the degree of specialization. Extreme division of labor tends to create many specialists without high prestige since the training is short and the required native capacity relatively small. On the other hand it also tends to accentuate the high position of the true experts—scientists, engineers, and administrators—by increasing their authority relative to other functionally important positions. But the idea of a technocratic social order or a government or priesthood of engineers or social scientists neglects the limitations of knowledge and skills as a basis for performing social functions. To the extent that the social structure is truly specialized the prestige of the technical person must also be circumscribed.

Variation in Stratified Systems

The generalized principles of stratification here suggested form a necessary preliminary to a consideration of types of stratified systems, because it is in terms of these principles that the types must be described. This can be seen by trying to delineate types according to certain modes of variation. For instance, some of the most important modes (together with the polar types in terms of them) seem to be as follows:

(a) The Degree of Specialization. The degree of specialization affects the fineness and multiplicity of the gradations in power and prestige. It also influences the extent to which particular functions may be emphasized in the invidious system, since a given function cannot receive much emphasis in the hierarchy until it has achieved structural separation from the other functions. Finally, the amount of specialization influences the bases of selection. Polar types: *Specialized, Unspecialized.*

(b) The Nature of the Functional Emphasis. In general when emphasis is put on sacred matters, a rigidity is introduced that tends to limit specialization and hence the development of technology. In addition, a brake is placed on social mobility, and on the development of bureaucracy. When the preoccupation with the sacred is withdrawn, leaving greater scope for purely secular preoccupations, a great development, and rise in status, of economic and technological positions seemingly takes place. Curiously, a concomitant rise in

political position is not likely, because it has usually been allied with the religious and stands to gain little by the decline of the latter. It is also possible for a society to emphasize family functions—as in relatively undifferentiated societies where high mortality requires high fertility and kinship forms the main basis of social organization. Main types: *Familistic, Authoritarian (Theocratic* or sacred, and *Totalitarian* or secular), *Capitalistic.*

(c) The Magnitude of Invidious Differences. What may be called the amount of social distance between positions, taking into account the entire scale, is something that should lend itself to quantitative measurement. Considerable differences apparently exist between different societies in this regard, and also between parts of the same society. Polar types: *Equalitarian, Inequalitarian.*

(d) The Degree of Opportunity. The familiar question of the amount of mobility is different from the question of the comparative equality or inequality of rewards posed above, because the two criteria may vary independently up to a point. For instance, the tremendous divergences in monetary income in the United States are far greater than those found in primitive societies, yet the equality of opportunity to move from one rung to the other in the social scale may also be greater in the United States than in a hereditary tribal kingdom. Polar types: *Mobile* (open), *Immobile* (closed).

(e) The Degree of Stratum Solidarity. Again, the degree of "class solidarity" (or the presence of specific organizations to promote class interests) may vary to some extent independently of the other criteria, and hence is an important principle in classifying systems of stratification. Polar types: *Class organized, Class unorganized.*

External Conditions

What state any particular system of stratification is in with reference to each of these modes of variation depends on two things: (1) its state with reference to the other ranges of variation, and (2) the conditions outside the system of stratification which nevertheless influence that system. Among the latter are the following:

(a) The Stage of Cultural Development. As the cultural heritage grows, increased specialization becomes necessary, which in turn contributes to the enhancement of mobility, a decline of stratum solidarity, and a change of functional emphasis.

(b) Situation with Respect to Other Societies. The presence or absence of open conflict with other societies, of free trade relations or cultural diffusion, all influence the class structure to some extent. A chronic state of warfare tends to place emphasis upon the military functions, especially when the opponents are more or less equal. Free trade, on the other hand, strengthens the hand of the trader at the expense of the warrior and priest. Free movement of ideas generally has an equalitarian effect. Migration and conquest create special circumstances.

(c) Size of the Society. A small society limits the degree to which functional specialization can go, the degree of segregation of different strata, and the magnitude of inequality.

Composite Types

Much of the literature on stratification has attempted to classify concrete systems into a certain number of types. This task is deceptively simple, however, and should come at the end of an analysis of elements and principles, rather than at the beginning. If the preceding discussion has any validity, it indicates that there are a number of modes of variation between different systems, and that any one system is a composite of the society's status with reference to all these modes of variation. The danger of trying to classify whole societies under such rubrics as *caste, feudal,* or *open class* is that one or two criteria are selected and others ignored, the result being an unsatisfactory solution to the problem posed. The present discussion has been offered as a possible approach to the more systematic classification of composite types.

Notes

1. Kingsley Davis, "A Conceptual Analysis of Stratification," *American Sociological Review.* 7:309–321, June, 1942.

2. The writers regret (and beg indulgence) that the present essay, a condensation of a longer study, covers so much in such short space that adequate evidence and qualification cannot be given and that as a result what is actually very tentative is presented in an unfortunately dogmatic manner.

3. Unfortunately, functional importance is difficult to establish. To use the position's prestige to establish it, as is often unconsciously done, constitutes circular reasoning from our point of view. There are, however, two independent clues: (a) the degree to which a position is functionally unique, there being no other positions that can perform the same function satisfactorily; (b) the degree to which other positions are dependent on the one in question. Both clues are best exemplified in organized systems of positions built around one major function. Thus, in most complex societies the religious, political, economic, and educational functions are handled by distinct structures not easily interchangeable. In addition, each structure possesses many different positions, some clearly dependent on, if not subordinate to, others. In sum, when an institutional nucleus becomes differentiated around one main function, and at the same time organizes a large portion of the population into its relationships, the *key* positions in it are of the highest functional importance. The absence of such specialization does not prove functional unimportance, for the whole society may be relatively unspecialized; but it is safe to assume that the more important functions receive the first and clearest structural differentiation.

4. The symbolic rather than intrinsic role of income in social stratification has been succinctly summarized by Talcott Parsons, "An Analytical Approach to the Theory of Social Stratification," *American Journal of Sociology.* 45:841–862, May, 1940.

The Dysfunctions of Stratification

MELVIN M. TUMIN

Some Principles of Stratification: A Critical Analysis

The fact of social inequality in human society is marked by its ubiquity and its antiquity. Every known society, past and present, distributes its scarce and demanded goods and services unequally. And there are attached to the positions which command unequal amounts of such goods and services certain highly morally-toned evaluations of their importance for the society.

The ubiquity and the antiquity of such inequality has given rise to the assumption that there must be something both inevitable and positively functional about such social arrangements.

Clearly, the truth or falsity of such an assumption is a strategic question for any general theory of social organization. It is therefore most curious that the basic premises and implications of the assumption have only been most casually explored by American sociologists.

The most systematic treatment is to be found in the well-known article by Kingsley Davis and Wilbert Moore, entitled "Some Principles of Stratification."[1] More than twelve years have passed since its publication, and though it is one of the very few treatments of stratification on a high level of generalization, it is difficult to locate a single systematic analysis of its reasoning. It will be the principal concern of this paper to present the beginnings of such an analysis.

The central argument advanced by Davis and Moore can be stated in a number of sequential propositions, as follows:

(1) Certain positions in any society are functionally more important than others, and require special skills for their performance.

(2) Only a limited number of individuals in any society have the talents which can be trained into the skills appropriate to these positions.

(3) The conversion of talents into skills involves a training period during which sacrifices of one kind or another are made by those undergoing the training.

(4) In order to induce the talented persons to undergo these sacrifices and acquire the training, their future positions must carry an inducement value in the form of differential, i.e., privileged and disproportionate access to the scarce and desired rewards which the society has to offer.[2]

(5) These scarce and desired goods consist of the rights and perquisites attached to, or built into, the positions, and can be classified into those things which contribute to (a) sustenance and comfort, (b) humor and diversion, (c) self-respect and ego expansion.

(6) This differential access to the basic rewards of the society has as a consequence the differentiation of the prestige and esteem which various strata acquire. This may be said, along with the rights and perquisites, to constitute institutionalized social inequality, i.e., stratification.

(7) Therefore, social inequality among different strata in the amounts of scarce and desired goods, and the amounts of prestige and esteem which they receive, is both

positively functional and inevitable in any society.

Let us take these propositions and examine them *seriatim.*[3]

(1) Certain positions in any society are more functionally important than others and require special skills for their performance.

The key term here is "functionally important." The functionalist theory of social organization is by no means clear and explicit about this term. The minimum common referent is to something known as the "survival value" of a social structure.[4] This concept immediately involves a number of perplexing questions. Among these are: (a) the issue of minimum vs. maximum survival, and the possible empirical referents which can be given to those terms; (b) whether such a proposition is a useless tautology since any *status quo* at any given moment is nothing more and nothing less than everything present in the *status quo.* In these terms, all acts and structures must be judged positively functional in that they constitute essential portions of the *status quo;* (c) what kind of calculus of functionality exists which will enable us, at this point in our development, to add and subtract long and short range consequences, with their mixed qualities, and arrive at some summative judgment regarding the rating an act or structure should receive on a scale of greater or lesser functionality? At best, we tend to make primarily intuitive judgments. Often enough, these judgments involve the use of value-laden criteria, or, at least, criteria which are chosen in preference to others not for any sociologically systematic reasons but by reason of certain implicit value preferences.

Thus, to judge that the engineers in a factory are functionally more important to the factory than the unskilled workmen involves a notion regarding the dispensability of the unskilled workmen, or their replaceability, relative to that of the engineers. But this is not a process of choice with infinite time dimensions. For at some point along the line one must face the problem of adequate motivation for *all* workers at all levels of skill in the factory. In the long run, *some* labor force of unskilled workmen is as important and as indispensable to the factory as *some* labor force of engineers. Often enough, the labor force situation is such that this fact is brought home sharply to the entrepreneur in the short run rather than in the long run.

Moreover, the judgment as to the relative indispensability and replaceability of a particular segment of skills in the population involves a prior judgment about the bargaining-power of that segment. But this power is itself a culturally shaped *consequence* of the existing system of rating, rather than something inevitable in the nature of social organization. At least the contrary of this has never been demonstrated, but only assumed.

A generalized theory of social stratification must recognize that the prevailing system of inducements and rewards is only one of many variants in the whole range of possible systems of motivation which, at least theoretically, are capable of working in human society. It is quite conceivable, of course, that a system of norms could be institutionalized in which the idea of threatened withdrawal of services, except under the most extreme circumstances, would be considered as absolute moral anathema. In such a case, the whole notion of relative functionality, as advanced by Davis and Moore, would have to be radically revised.

(2) Only a limited number of individuals in any society have the talents which can be trained into the skills appropriate to these positions (i.e., the more functionally important positions).

The truth of this proposition depends at least in part on the truth of proposition 1 above. It is, therefore, subject to all the limitations indicated above. But for the moment, let us assume the validity of the first proposition and concentrate on the question of the rarity of appropriate talent.

If all that is meant is that in every society there is a *range* of talent, and that some members of any society are by nature more talented than others, no sensible contradiction can be offered, but a question must be raised here regarding the amount of sound knowledge present in any society concerning the presence of talent in the population.

For, in every society there is some demonstrable ignorance regarding the amount of talent present in the population. *And the more rigidly strati-*

fied a society is, the less chance does that society have of discovering any new facts about the talents of its members. Smoothly working and stable systems of stratification, wherever found, tend to build-in obstacles to the further exploration of the range of available talent. This is especially true in those societies where the opportunity to discover talent in any one generation varies with the differential resources of the parent generation. Where, for instance, access to education depends upon the wealth of one's parents, and where wealth is differentially distributed, large segments of the population are likely to be deprived of the chance even to *discover* what are their talents.

Whether or not differential rewards and opportunities are functional in any one generation, it is clear that if those differentials are allowed to be socially inherited by the next generation, then, the stratification system is specifically dysfunctional for the discovery of talents in the next generation. In this fashion, systems of social stratification tend to limit the chances available to maximize the efficiency of discovery, recruitment and training of "functionally important talent."[5]

Additionally, the unequal distribution of rewards in one generation tends to result in the unequal distribution of motivation in the succeeding generation. Since motivation to succeed is clearly an important element in the entire process of education, the unequal distribution of motivation tends to set limits on the possible extensions of the educational system, and hence, upon the efficient recruitment and training of the widest body of skills available in the population.[6]

Lastly, in this context, it may be asserted that there is some noticeable tendency for elites to restrict further access to their privileged positions, once they have sufficient power to enforce such restrictions. This is especially true in a culture where it is possible for an elite to contrive a high demand and a proportionately higher reward for its work by restricting the numbers of the elite available to do the work. The recruitment and training of doctors in modern United States is at least partly a case in point.

Here, then, are three ways, among others which could be cited, in which stratification systems, once operative, tend to reduce the survival value of a society by limiting the search, recruitment and training of functionally important personnel far more sharply than the facts of available talent would appear to justify. It is only when there is genuinely equal access to recruitment and training for all potentially talented persons that differential rewards can conceivably be justified as functional. And stratification systems are apparently *inherently antagonistic* to the development of such full equality of opportunity.

(3) *The conversion of talents into skills involves a training period during which sacrifices of one kind or another are made by those undergoing the training.*

Davis and Moore introduce here a concept, "sacrifice" which comes closer than any of the rest of their vocabulary of analysis to being a direct reflection of the rationalizations, offered by the more fortunate members of a society, of the rightness of their occupancy of privileged positions. It is the least critically thought-out concept in the repertoire, and can also be shown to be least supported by the actual facts.

In our present society, for example, what are the sacrifices which talented persons undergo in the training period? The possibly serious losses involve the surrender of earning power and the cost of the training. The latter is generally borne by the parents of the talented youth undergoing training, and not by the trainees themselves. But this cost tends to be paid out of income which the parents were able to earn generally by virtue of *their* privileged positions in the hierarchy of stratification. That is to say, the parents' ability to pay for the training of their children is part of the differential *reward* they, the parents, received for their privileged positions in the society. And to charge this sum up against sacrifices made by the youth is falsely to perpetrate a bill or a debt already paid by the society to the parents.

So far as the sacrifice of earning power by the trainees themselves is concerned, the loss may be measured relative to what they might have earned had they gone into the labor market instead of into advanced training for the "important" skills. There are several ways to judge this. One way is to take all the average earnings of age peers who did go into the labor market for a period equal to the average length of the training period. The total income, so calculated, roughly equals an amount which the elite can, on the average, earn back in the first decade of professional work, over and above the earnings of his age peers who are not trained. Ten years is probably the maximum amount needed to equalize the differential.[7] There remains, on the average, twenty years of work during each of which the skilled person then goes on to earn far more than his unskilled age peers. And, what is often forgotten, there is then still another ten or fifteen year period during which the skilled person continues to work and earn when his unskilled age peer is either totally or partially out of the labor market by virtue of the attrition of his strength and capabilities.

One might say that the first ten years of differential pay is perhaps justified, in order to regain for the trained person what he lost during his training period. But it is difficult to imagine what would justify continuing such differential rewards beyond that period.

Another and probably sounder way to measure how much is lost during the training period is to compare the per capita income available to the trainee with the per capita income of the age peer on the untrained labor market during the so-called sacrificial period. If one takes into account the earlier marriage of untrained persons, and the earlier acquisition of family dependents, it is highly dubious that the per capita income of the wage worker is significantly larger than that of the trainee. Even assuming, for the moment, that there is a difference, the amount is by no means sufficient to justify a lifetime of continuing differentials.

What tends to be completely overlooked, in addition, are the psychic and spiritual rewards which are available to the elite trainees by comparison with their age peers in the labor force. There is, first, the much higher prestige enjoyed by the college student and the professional-school student as compared with persons in shops and offices. There is, second, the extremely highly valued privilege of having greater opportunity for self-development. There is, third, all the psychic gain involved in being allowed to delay the assumption of adult responsibilities such as earning a living and supporting a family. There is, fourth, the access to leisure and freedom of a kind not likely to be experienced by the persons already at work.

If these are never taken into account as rewards of the training period it is not because they are not concretely present, but because the emphasis in American concepts of reward is almost exclusively placed on the material returns of positions. The emphases on enjoyment, entertainment, ego enhancement, prestige and esteem are introduced only when the differentials in these which accrue to the skilled positions need to be justified. If these other rewards were taken into account, it would be much more difficult to demonstrate that the training period, as presently operative, is really sacrificial. Indeed, it might turn out to be the case that even at this point in their careers, the elite trainees were being differentially rewarded relative to their age peers in the labor force.

All of the foregoing concerns the quality of the training period under our present system of motivation and rewards. Whatever may turn out to be the factual case about the present system—and the factual case is moot—the more important theoretical question concerns the assumption that the training period under *any* system must be sacrificial.

There seem to be no good theoretical grounds for insisting on this assumption. For, while under any system certain costs will be involved in training persons for skilled positions, these costs could easily be assumed by the society-at-large. Under these circumstances, there would be no need to compensate anyone in terms of differential rewards once the skilled positions were staffed. In short, there would be no need or justification for stratifying social positions on *these* grounds.

(4) In order to induce the talented persons to undergo these sacrifices and acquire the training, their future positions must carry an inducement value in the form of differential, i.e., privileged and disproportionate access to the scarce and desired rewards which the society has to offer.

Let us assume, for the purposes of the discussion, that the training period is sacrificial and the talent is rare in every conceivable human society. There is still the basic problem as to whether the allocation of differential rewards in scarce and desired goods and services is the only or the most efficient way of recruiting the appropriate talent to these positions.

For there are a number of alternative motivational schemes whose efficiency and adequacy ought at least to be considered in this context. What can be said, for instance, on behalf of the motivation which De Man called "joy in work," Veblen termed "instinct for workmanship" and which we latterly have come to identify as "intrinsic work satisfaction?" Or, to what extent could the motivation of "social duty" be institutionalized in such a fashion that self interest and social interest come closely to coincide? Or, how much prospective confidence can be placed in the possibilities of institutionalizing "social service" as a widespread motivation for seeking one's appropriate position and fulfilling it conscientiously?

Are not these types of motivations, we may ask, likely to prove most appropriate for precisely the "most functionally important positions?" Especially in a mass industrial society, where the vast majority of positions become standardized and routinized, it is the skilled jobs which are likely to retain most of the quality of "intrinsic job satisfaction" and be most readily identifiable as socially serviceable. Is it indeed impossible then to build these motivations into the socialization pattern to which we expose our talented youth?

To deny that such motivations could be institutionalized would be to overclaim our present knowledge. In part, also, such a claim would seem to derive from an assumption that what has not been institutionalized yet in human affairs is incapable of institutionalization. Admittedly, historical experience affords us evidence we cannot afford to ignore. But such evidence cannot legitimately be used to deny absolutely the possibility of heretofore untried alternatives. Social innovation is as important a feature of human societies as social stability.

On the basis of these observations, it seems that Davis and Moore have stated the case much too strongly when they insist that a "functionally important position" which requires skills that are scarce, "must command great prestige, high salary, ample leisure, and the like," if the appropriate talents are to be attracted to the position. Here, clearly, the authors are postulating the unavoidability of very specific types of rewards and, by implication, denying the possibility of others.

(5) These scarce and desired goods consist of rights and perquisites attached to, or built into, the positions and can be classified into those things which contribute to (a) sustenance and comfort; (b) humor and diversion; (c) self respect and ego expansion.

(6) This differential access to the basic rewards of the society has as a consequence the differentiation of the prestige and esteem which various strata acquire. This may be said, along with the rights and perquisites, to constitute institutionalized social inequality, i.e., stratification.

With the classification of the rewards offered by Davis and Moore there need be little argument. Some question must be raised, however, as to whether any reward system, built into a general stratification system, must allocate equal amounts of all three types of reward in order to function effectively, or whether one type of reward may be emphasized to the virtual neglect of others. This raises the further question regarding which type of emphasis is likely to prove most effective as a differential inducer. Nothing in the known facts about human motivation impels us to favor one type of reward over the other, or to insist that all three types of reward must be built into the positions in comparable amounts if the position is to have an inducement value.

It is well known, of course, that societies differ considerably in the kinds of rewards they emphasize in their efforts to maintain a reasonable balance between responsibility and reward. There are, for instance, numerous societies in which the conspicuous display of differential economic advantage is considered extremely bad taste. In short, our present knowledge commends to us the possibility of considerable plasticity in the way in which different types of rewards can be structured into a functioning society. This is to say, it cannot yet be demonstrated that it is *unavoidable* that differential prestige and esteem shall accrue to positions which command differential rewards in power and property.

What does seem to be unavoidable is that differential prestige shall be given to those in any society who conform to the normative order as against those who deviate from that order in a way judged immoral and detrimental. On the assumption that the continuity of a society depends on the continuity and stability of its normative order, some such distinction between conformists and deviants seems inescapable.

It also seems to be unavoidable that in any society, no matter how literate its tradition, the older, wiser and more experienced individuals who are charged with the enculturation and socialization of the young must have more power than the young, on the assumption that the task of effective socialization demands such differential power.

But this differentiation in prestige between the conformist and the deviant is by no means the same distinction as that between strata of individuals each of which operates *within* the normative order, and is composed of adults. The *latter* distinction, in the form of differentiated rewards and prestige between social strata is what Davis and Moore, and most sociologists, consider the structure of a stratification system. The *former* distinctions have nothing necessarily to do with the workings of such a system nor with the efficiency of motivation and recruitment of functionally important personnel.

Nor does the differentiation of power between young and old necessarily create differentially valued strata. For no society rates its young as less morally worthy than its older persons, no matter how much differential power the older ones may temporarily enjoy.

(7) *Therefore, social inequality among different strata in the amounts of scarce and desired goods, and the amounts of prestige and esteem which they receive, is both positively functional and inevitable in any society.*

If the objections which have heretofore been raised are taken as reasonable, then it may be stated that the only items which any society *must* distribute unequally are the power and property necessary for the performance of different tasks. If such differential power and property are viewed by all as commensurate with the differential responsibilities, and if they are culturally defined as

resources and not as rewards, then, no differentials in prestige and esteem need follow.

Historically, the evidence seems to be that every time power and property are distributed unequally, no matter what the cultural definition, prestige and esteem differentiations have tended to result as well. Historically, however, no systematic effort has ever been made, under propitious circumstances, to develop the tradition that each man is as socially worthy as all other men so long as he performs his appropriate tasks conscientiously. While such a tradition seems utterly utopian, no known facts in psychological or social science have yet demonstrated its impossibility or its dysfunctionality for the continuity of a society. The achievement of a full institutionalization of such a tradition seems far too remote to contemplate. Some successive approximations at such a tradition, however, are not out of the range of prospective social innovation.

What, then, of the "positive functionality" of social stratification? Are there other, negative, functions of institutionalized social inequality which can be identified, if only tentatively? Some such dysfunctions of stratification have already been suggested in the body of this paper. Along with others they may now be stated, in the form of provisional assertions, as follows:

(1) Social stratification systems function to limit the possibility of discovery of the full range of talent available in a society. This results from the fact of unequal access to appropriate motivation, channels of recruitment and centers of training.

(2) In foreshortening the range of available talent, social stratification systems function to set limits upon the possibility of expanding the productive resources of the society, at least relative to what might be the case under conditions of greater equality of opportunity.

(3) Social stratification systems function to provide the elite with the political power necessary to procure acceptance and dominance of an ideology which rationalizes the *status quo*, whatever it may be, as "logical,"

"natural" and "morally right." In this manner, social stratification systems function as essentially conservative influences in the societies in which they are found.

(4) Social stratification systems function to distribute favorable self-images unequally throughout a population. To the extent that such favorable self-images are requisite to the development of the creative potential inherent in men, to that extent stratification systems function to limit the development of this creative potential.

(5) To the extent that inequalities in social rewards cannot be made fully acceptable to the less privileged in a society, social stratification systems function to encourage hostility, suspicion and distrust among the various segments of a society and thus to limit the possibilities of extensive social integration.

(6) To the extent that the sense of significant membership in a society depends on one's place on the prestige ladder of the society, social stratification systems function to distribute unequally the sense of significant membership in the population.

(7) To the extent that loyalty to a society depends on a sense of significant membership in the society, social stratification systems function to distribute loyalty unequally in the population.

(8) To the extent that participation and apathy depend upon the sense of significant membership in the society, social stratification systems function to distribute the motivation to participate unequally in a population.

Each of the eight foregoing propositions contains implicit hypotheses regarding the consequences of unequal distribution of rewards in a society in accordance with some notion of the functional importance of various positions. These are empirical hypotheses, subject to test. They are offered here only as exemplary of the kinds of consequences of social stratification which are not often taken into account in dealing with the problem. They should also serve to reinforce the doubt that social inequality is a device which is uniformly functional for the role of guaranteeing that the most important tasks in a society will be performed conscientiously by the most competent persons.

The obviously mixed character of the functions of social inequality should come as no surprise to anyone. If sociology is sophisticated in any sense, it is certainly with regard to its awareness of the mixed nature of any social arrangement, when the observer takes into account long as well as short range consequences and latent as well as manifest dimensions.

Summary

In this paper, an effort has been made to raise questions regarding the inevitability and positive functionality of stratification, or institutionalized social inequality in rewards, allocated in accordance with some notion of the greater and lesser functional importance of various positions. The possible alternative meanings of the concept "functional importance" has been shown to be one difficulty. The question of the scarcity or abundance of available talent has been indicated as a principal source of possible variation. The extent to which the period of training for skilled positions may reasonably be viewed as sacrificial has been called into question. The possibility has been suggested that very different types of motivational schemes might conceivably be made to function. The separability of differentials in power and property considered as resources appropriate to a task from such differentials considered as rewards for the performance of a task has also been suggested. It has also been maintained that differentials in prestige and esteem do not necessarily follow upon differentials in power and property when the latter are considered as appropriate resources rather than rewards. Finally, some negative functions, or dysfunctions, of institutionalized social inequality have been tentatively identified, revealing the mixed character of the outcome of social stratification, and casting doubt on the contention that

Social inequality is thus an unconsciously evolved device by which societies insure that the most important positions are conscientiously filled by the most qualified persons.[8]

Notes

The writer has had the benefit of a most helpful criticism of the main portions of this paper by Professor W. J. Goode of Columbia University. In addition, he has had the opportunity to expose this paper to criticism by the Staff Seminar of the Sociology Section at Princeton. In deference to a possible rejoinder by Professors Moore and Davis, the writer has not revised the paper to meet the criticisms which Moore has already offered personally.

1. *American Sociological Review,* X (April, 1945), pp. 242–249. An earlier article by Kingsley Davis, entitled, "A Conceptual Analysis of Stratification," *American Sociological Review,* VII (June, 1942), pp. 309–321, is devoted primarily to setting forth a vocabulary for stratification analysis. A still earlier article by Talcott Parsons, "An Analytical Approach to the Theory of Social Stratification," *American Journal of Sociology,* XLV (November, 1940), pp. 849–862, approaches the problem in terms of why "differential ranking is considered a really fundamental phenomenon of social systems and what are the respects in which such ranking is important." The principal line of integration asserted by Parsons is with the fact of the normative orientation of any society. Certain crucial lines of connection are left unexplained, however, in this article, and in the Davis

and Moore article of 1945 only some of these lines are made explicit.

2. The "scarcity and demand" qualities of goods and services are never explicitly mentioned by Davis and Moore. But it seems to the writer that the argument makes no sense unless the goods and services are so characterized. For if rewards are to function as differential inducements they must not only be differentially distributed but they must be both scarce and demanded as well. Neither the scarcity of an item by itself nor the fact of its being in demand is sufficient to allow it to function as a differential inducement in a system of unequal rewards. Leprosy is scarce and oxygen is highly demanded.

3. The arguments to be advanced here are condensed versions of a much longer analysis entitled, *An Essay on Social Stratification.* Perforce, all the reasoning necessary to support some of the contentions cannot be offered within the space limits of this article.

4. Davis and Moore are explicitly aware of the difficulties involved here and suggest two "independent clues" other than survival value. See footnote 3 on p. 244 of their article.

5. Davis and Moore state this point briefly on p. 248 but do not elaborate it.

6. In the United States, for instance, we are only now becoming aware of the amount of productivity we, as a society, lose by allocating inferior opportunities and rewards, and hence, inferior motivation, to our Negro population. The actual amount of loss is difficult to specify precisely. Some rough estimate can be made, however, on the assumption that there is present in the Negro population about the same range of talent that is found in the White population.

7. These are only very rough estimates, of course, and it is certain that there is considerable income variation within the so-called elite group, so that the proposition holds only relatively more or less.

8. Davis and Moore, *op. cit.,* p. 243.

GERHARD LENSKI

New Light on Old Issues: The Relevance of "Really Existing Socialist Societies" for Stratification Theory

Scholars have long debated the causes, consequences, and legitimacy of systems of social inequality, with some defending them as natural, inevitable, or even divinely ordained, and others challenging them as unnatural, unnecessary, and immoral (Lenski 1966, ch. 1). In the twentieth century, the most important challenges have come from groups and individuals inspired, directly or indirectly, by the work of Marx and his followers.

One does not need to look far in sociology to see the impact of Marx's vision and the controversies it has created. As many have observed, the long-running debate between functionalists and their critics is, in many ways, a debate over the merits of Marxism: Functionalists maintain that economic inequality is both necessary for societies and beneficial for the vast majority of their members, whereas their critics argue that it is neither.

Unfortunately, from the standpoint of our understanding of the causes and consequences of systems of stratification and the merits of Marx's ideas, the debate among sociologists has focused almost entirely on the experience of Western "capitalist" societies.[1] Surprisingly little attention has been devoted to the experience of the former Soviet republics, Poland, East Germany before unification, the once-united Czechoslovakia,

Hungary, the former Yugoslavia, Romania, Bulgaria, Albania, China, Cuba, North Korea, Vietnam, and other societies that were or have been governed for extended periods by dedicated Marxists. Yet, as East European sociologists have often pointed out in recent years, these societies have provided a unique set of laboratories for observing the effects of "really existing socialism."[2] They allow us to observe socialist societies functioning in the real world under real-life conditions. In these societies, we can see what actually happens when private ownership is abolished and the emphasis in a society's system of rewards is shifted from material incentives to moral incentives. Imperfect though these tests have been, they shed valuable new light on the causes and consequences of inequalities in power and privilege.[3] The results have been much too consistent to be ignored or written off as simply a matter of chance, and the consistency is especially impressive when one considers the great cultural diversity of the societies involved.

For many years, Western sociologists could justify their inattention to "really existing socialist societies" because of the difficulties of obtaining reliable data. By the early 1970s, however, a sufficient body of evidence had accumulated, and political conditions in a number of Marxist societies had improved to the point that one could, with some confidence, begin to form a fairly accurate view of a number of important aspects of the new Marxist systems of stratification. On the basis of materials available at the time, I concluded in an

---

This is an original article prepared for this book.

earlier article (Lenski 1978) that these "experiments in destratification" had enjoyed their greatest successes in reducing *economic* inequality: Differentials in wealth and income appeared to be substantially less in societies governed by Marxist elites than in other societies. These successes were offset, however, by two major failures: (1) *Political* inequalities in these societies were enormous, far greater than in any of the Western industrial democracies, and (2) none of these societies had achieved anything remotely resembling the critical transformation in human nature that Marx had predicted would follow the abolition of private property and would lay the foundation for the subsequent evolution of societies from socialism to communism. These failures, I concluded, were due in large measure to a critical flaw in Marxian theory—its unrealistic assumptions about human nature.

Looking back, I believe these conclusions have stood the test of time fairly well. Of course, information that has since emerged and the wisdom of hindsight would lead me to modify and extend them. For example, recent revelations following the overthrow of the Marxist regimes in Eastern Europe indicate that the level of economic inequality in those societies was greater than I was then aware. To cite but three examples: (1) After the overthrow of Todor Zhikov, the Bulgarian public and the rest of the world learned that during his years in power he had acquired no fewer than thirty separate homes for his personal use and that he and other top leaders had accumulated millions of dollars in secret foreign bank accounts (Laber 1990); (2) the longtime leader of Romania, Nicolae Ceaușescu, amassed forty villas and twenty palaces for himself and his family and accumulated millions in Swiss bank accounts at a time when the bulk of the population was often living without heat or light (*Washington Post* 1990); and (3) in East Germany, Erich Honecker accumulated millions of dollars in Swiss bank accounts by skimming profits from arms sales to Third World nations, while sharing with other top Communist Party leaders exclusive private hunting preserves and other luxuries that were denied to and hidden from the rest of the population. Although it has long been clear that Communist Party elites enjoyed many privileges that

were denied to others (Matthews 1978), the extent of these privileges has proved to be much greater than most had supposed. That these were not merely aberrations of East European Marxism is indicated by non-European examples: In Nicaragua, the villas and much of the other property once owned by Anastasio Somoza and his associates became the personal property of top Sandinista leaders and their families, while in China and Vietnam, Communist Party elites continue to live in closed compounds (similar to those in the former East Germany) where living conditions are carefully hidden from public scrutiny (Salisbury 1992).

At the other extreme, poverty in these societies was more widespread and more serious than Western observers generally realized. Reports by Soviet authorities in the late 1980s indicated that at least 20 percent of the population was living at or below the official poverty level (Fein 1989). Homelessness was also reported to be a problem in Moscow and other Soviet cities, while studies in Hungary at the end of the Communist era found that a quarter of the population was living in poverty (Kamm 1989).

Despite these revelations, it still appears that the level of economic inequality in Marxist societies never equaled the level found in Japan and most of the Western democracies. Wealthy and privileged though the Zhikovs, Ceaușescus, and Honeckers were by comparison with their fellow citizens, the magnitude of their wealth never compared with the great fortunes amassed by leading Western and Japanese businessmen and by oil-rich Middle Eastern leaders. Furthermore, passing wealth on to the next generation has always been much more difficult in Marxist societies than elsewhere, as the unhappy experiences of the Leonid Brezhnev family and others indicate.[4]

A more serious flaw in my earlier assessment was its failure to anticipate the speed and magnitude of the changes that lay ahead. Although I anticipated that the gradual process of political liberalization that began after Stalin's death would continue, and that other changes would occur in response to problems encountered and to the changing needs and growing demands of a better educated population, I cannot pretend to have foreseen the sudden collapse of Communist Party hegemony, the rapid emergence of multiparty systems, or the radical economic changes that have occurred in most of Eastern Europe.

The benefit of hindsight makes clear that the internal, systemic problems of the command economies and one-party polities of Marxist societies were far more serious than most Western observers suspected. In fact, it now appears that the greatest success of Marxist regimes was their ability to dissimulate—a success that was too often achieved because of the readiness of large numbers of Western journalists, scholars, and others to accept glowing reports of socialist successes uncritically (Hollander 1981; Fang 1990). With the revelations that have followed in the wake of the democratic revolutions in Eastern Europe, we now know that the economies of these societies had been stagnating for years and that much of the population had become disaffected and hostile. Worse, Marxism and Marxist elites had lost whatever legitimacy they once enjoyed in the minds of many people, especially intellectuals and other opinion leaders and even Party members. (Ironically, this was at a time when Marxism was becoming increasingly fashionable among Western intellectuals.)

These developments have great relevance for our understanding of the causes and consequences of inequality, since it seems that many of the internal, systemic problems of Marxist societies were the result of inadequate motivational arrangements of the sort debated by stratification theorists such as Davis and Moore (1945), Davis (1953), and Tumin (1953). These problems were of two basic types: (1) undermotivation of ordinary workers and (2) misdirected motivation of managers, bureaucrats, and other decision-makers.

The first of these problems was summarized succinctly years ago by East European workers themselves who said, "They pretend to pay us, and we pretend to work" (Dobbs 1981). The rewards for most kinds of work simply did not justify anything more than minimal, perfunctory effort (Shlapentokh 1989, ch. 2). Shoddy workmanship, sullen workers, absenteeism, corruption, and bureaucratic pathologies of various kinds came to typify worker performance in

Marxist societies (*The Economist* 1988). These problems are present in every society to some degree, but they became far more prevalent and far more serious in the socialist economies of Marxist societies than in most others. They became so serious, in fact, that they had demoralizing consequences for the vast majority of citizens: endless hours spent in lines queuing for merchandise that was either of poor quality or in short supply, frequent confrontations with surly state employees, unsatisfactory housing, an inadequate health-care system, and more. To add insult to injury, most citizens became aware that a small minority of their fellows was exempted from most of these problems: For them, there were well-stocked stores with better quality merchandise in ample supply and more responsive employees, better housing, better health-care facilities, better schools for their children, second homes, and countless other perks. Worse, this elite preached socialism and the need for sacrifice while enjoying all these special privileges.

To describe the conditions that developed in these societies is to raise the question of why the system failed so badly. What went wrong, and why was the promise of freedom and affluence for the masses never achieved?

For many years, Marxist elites in Eastern Europe and their Western sympathizers explained away these problems on the grounds of *external factors:* the historic backwardness of Eastern Europe, the damage to the Soviet economy caused by the civil war that followed the 1917 revolution, and the hostility of the Western democracies. Although there was much truth to these claims, it has become increasingly clear that *internal, systemic factors* were also a major source of problems for many years. By the late 1980s, this had become obvious even to the leaders of these societies, with many of them becoming advocates of change, and some abandoning Marxism altogether.

Over the years, Marxist societies experimented with a variety of incentive systems, but the egalitarian nature of Marxist ideology always led to substantial limitations on wage differentials for the masses of workers.[5] Over time, however, the severity of these limitations varied as Party elites attempted either to improve the economic performance of their societies or, alternatively, to conform more closely to socialist principles. In a few instances, in an excess of socialist zeal, wage differentials were virtually eliminated: In Czechoslovakia in the early 1960s, for example, wage differences were reduced to the point that engineers and highly skilled workers earned only 5 percent more than unskilled workers. Because of this, large numbers of talented young people dropped out of school, feeling that it was not worth the effort required and the income that would be sacrificed to continue their education. Morale problems also developed among skilled workers, engineers, and other professionals. Within several years, problems had become so acute that authorities were forced to reverse themselves and increase rewards for better educated and more highly skilled workers. A similar crisis developed in the Soviet Union in the early 1930s, forcing Stalin to increase material incentives and wage differentials substantially (Inkeles 1950), and there is growing evidence that the economic crisis in the Soviet Union of the 1980s developed initially in response to a process of wage leveling begun under Brezhnev.

The chief reason for these problems appears to be a basic flaw in Marxist theory. Writing in the nineteenth century, Marx was heir to the eighteenth-century Enlightenment view of human nature—an optimistic view that saw the unattractive aspects of human life as products of corrupting social institutions that could be eliminated by rational social engineering. Whereas the French philosophes blamed the defects in human nature on the influence of church and state, Marx saw private property as the ultimate source of society's ills: If it were abolished, human nature would be transformed. Once socialism was established and the means of production were owned by all, moral incentives could replace material incentives and workers would find work intrinsically rewarding (see also Tumin [1953] on this point). They would work for the sheer joy of working and for the satisfaction of contributing to society's needs, not simply to earn a livelihood.

Unfortunately, the abolition of private property failed to produce the happy transformation in human nature that Marx anticipated. On the contrary, freed from the fear of unemployment and lacking adequate material incentives, workers

did not live up to the ideal—worker performance deteriorated and production stagnated or declined in Marxist societies everywhere (Shlapentokh 1989; *The Economist* 1988; Silk 1990; Kamm 1989; Jones 1981; Scammel 1990; Huberman and Sweezy 1967; Zeitlin 1970). The most compelling evidence of this has come from the two Germanys, which shared a common cultural heritage that involved a long tradition of worker pride. Yet by the closing days of the German Democratic Republic, reports of slack work patterns were widespread, and many East German workers were quoted as expressing concern that they would be unable to adapt to the more demanding standards of West German industry. In 1990, at the twenty-eighth Communist Party congress in the Soviet Union, President Mikhail Gorbachev's close associate, Aleksandr Yakovlev, asserted that labor productivity in capitalist South Korea was substantially greater than in socialist North Korea (New York Times News Service 1990). Tatiana Zaslavskaia, a leading Soviet sociologist, found that as many as a third of Soviet workers hated work and were unresponsive to incentives of any kind (Shlapentokh 1987).

But the motivational problems of workers in Marxist societies stemmed from more than faulty assumptions about human nature. They were also due to defective organizational arrangements spawned by the command economies of those societies. Lacking the system of automatic controls inherent in a market economy, economic planners were forced to devise elaborate plans and assign production quotas for the managers of every enterprise. To ensure fulfillment of these quotas, managers were awarded bonuses for meeting or exceeding them and were penalized severely for any shortfall. One unanticipated consequence of this seemingly rational procedure was that managers acquired a strong incentive to stockpile essential resources of every kind—*including labor* (Kostakov 1989; Smith 1976; Greenhouse 1989). Thus, labor resources in these societies came to be used very inefficiently; the result was that workers became cynical about the value of what they were called on to do.

Managers also developed a variety of other unfortunate adaptations to central planning. They learned, for example, that quantity, not quality, was what their bosses, the central planners, cared about (Parkhomovsky 1982).[6] They also learned that production figures could be inflated without much risk because their bosses were also rewarded for good statistics and no one had any interest in seeing if actual performance matched reported performance (G. Medvedev 1989; Z. Medvedev 1990).

Finally, managers learned that there were only minimal rewards for reinvestment and for technological innovation. Lacking pressures from direct economic competition, Party leaders and planners failed to appreciate the importance of continuous modernization of their industrial plant. According to one account, Soviet managers received bonuses of 33 percent for fulfilling production quotas but only 8 percent for fulfilling the plan for new technology (*The Economist* 1988, 11). Thus, because capital investment and technological advance were badly neglected, the command economies of Marxist societies became less and less competitive in world markets.[7]

All of this evidence seems to confirm Davis's (1953) assertion that successful incentive systems involve (1) motivating the best qualified people to seek the most important positions and (2) motivating them to perform to the best of their ability once they are in them. Marxist societies seem to have failed on both counts, using political criteria primarily both to allocate positions and to reward incumbents (Voslensky 1984; Kennedy and Bialecki 1989; Voinovich 1989).

The many malfunctions in the command economies of Marxist societies raise the question of whether they were more or less inevitable consequences of the system itself. This is a question of considerable importance, since command economies are not confined to Marxist societies. The public sector in every society functions as a command economy, and the public sector has been expanding in most societies in recent decades.

Although it is not possible to explore this question in depth here, several observations are in order. First, a substantial majority of the citizens in most of the once socialist societies of Eastern Europe have rejected the system when given the chance. Even many Party leaders now have little faith in central planning and the command economy. As one member of the Soviet Congress of

People's Deputies said on the floor of that body, his nation taught the world a valuable lesson by testing, at great cost to itself, what proved to be "an impossible system of economic development" (Zakharov 1990).

Second, there have been remarkable similarities in the performance of command economies in otherwise widely divergent Marxist societies. Most of the pathologies found in Eastern Europe—absenteeism, poor work discipline, low levels of productivity, failure to reinvest in plants and to encourage innovation—have also been reported in China, Cuba, and elsewhere.

Finally, many of these same problems are also evident in the public sector of non-Marxist societies. Government workers and workers in state-owned Western enterprises are widely perceived as less diligent, innovative, enterprising, and responsive than workers in private industry: Negative associations with the term "bureaucrat" are almost as strong in non-Marxist societies as in Marxist ones. In addition, government agencies in these societies are noted for their inefficient use of human and other resources. Managers in these bureaucracies quickly learn that they are much more likely to maximize their own rewards by expanding the size of the work force and other resources under their supervision (regardless of need) than by using these resources efficiently.

Some observers have argued that the massive failures of the socialist economies of Marxist societies in Eastern Europe and elsewhere demonstrate the obvious superiority of capitalism and indicate that the future lies with capitalism. That conclusion, however, seems unwarranted. As noted earlier, even those societies that are usually referred to as "capitalist" have, in reality, very *mixed economies*. To paraphrase Marx, they are societies in which rewards are allocated partly on the basis of *need*, partly on the basis of *work*, and partly on the basis of *property*. In short, they combine elements of communism, socialism, and capitalism and are the product of trial-and-error experimentation guided, in large measure, by a spirit of pragmatism. It is a system that recognizes the need for material incentives and acknowledges the benefits of economic inequality. But it is also a system that recognizes the necessity of allocating a part of the economic product on the basis of need and most on the basis of work.[8] In short, the old view of societies as being either capitalist or socialist seems increasingly irrelevant.

Over time, an ever-increasing number of societies and their leaders have accomplished what scholarly theorists have so notably failed to achieve: They have created a workable synthesis out of seemingly contradictory principles of allocation. One of the urgent tasks for students of inequality in the years ahead will be to catch up with this new social reality and create the kind of theoretical synthesis that does justice to the economic synthesis that has been created in most Western democracies in recent decades. Too much of stratification theory still resembles the work of the proverbial blind men struggling to describe an elephant.

No real synthesis is likely to emerge, however, so long as students of stratification ignore the crucial body of evidence that has accumulated concerning the effects on motivation and productivity of the massive experiments in destratification conducted in the twentieth century by Marxist elites. In effect, these experiments have provided us with far better evidence than any we have had before of the limits of what is possible in terms of the reduction of differentials in wealth and income. And although these tests cannot be considered definitive, neither can they be written off and ignored as most analysts have done so far.

societies were able to implement the basic socialist principle of abolishing private property far more successfully than socialists in Western Europe ever were.

3. Unfortunately, imperfect tests are a fact of life in the social sciences. If the tests of Marxist theory that are possible in Marxist societies fall short of the scientific ideal, the same is true of almost every test in the social sciences. To deny the relevance of evidence from imperfect tests would be to deny the relevance of most of what has been learned over the years in the social sciences.

4. Shortly after Brezhnev's death, his son-in-law was arrested and sentenced to prison on charges of corruption.

5. The salaries of Party leaders were also kept quite low, but they were compensated generously in a variety of other ways.

6. Quality controls are far more likely when consumers can choose among competing products. When people must use their own money to purchase goods and services, they are not nearly so willing to accept inferior products as when they are using public funds.

7. For example, only 23 percent of Soviet inventions were put to use within two years of their date of patenting, compared to 66 percent of American inventions and 64 percent of West German (*The Economist* 1988).

8. Internal Revenue Service data indicate that approximately 10 percent of U.S. GNP is allocated on the basis of need (public health, welfare, and education expenditures), 70 percent on work (wages and salaries), and 20 percent on property (interest, rents, dividends, capital gains) (Lenski 1984, 202).

Notes

I wish to thank Peter Bearman, David Grusky, Michael Kennedy, and Anthony Oberschall for valuable suggestions concerning a prior draft of this paper. They are, of course, in no way responsible for flaws and errors in this final version.

1. I have qualified the label *capitalist* because all Western industrial societies now have mixed economies with substantial state controls over and limitations on the rights of ownership.

2. The terms *really existing socialism* and *really existing socialist societies* were coined by East European sociologists. Although the Marxist-Leninist societies, to which the terms have been applied, represent but one version of socialism, they are especially important for stratification theory because the former leaders of these

References

Davis, Kingsley. 1953. "Reply [to Tumin, 1945]." *American Sociological Review* 18:394–397.

Davis, Kingsley, and Wilbert Moore. 1945. "Some Principles of Stratification." *American Sociological Review* 10:242–249.

Dobbs, Michael. 1981. "'They Pretend to Pay Us, We Pretend to Work,' East Europeans Say." *Washington Post*, April 22.

The Economist. 1988. "The Soviet Economy." April 9, pp. 3–18.

Fang, Lizhi. 1990. "The Chinese Amnesia." *New York Review of Books*, September 27, pp. 30–31.

Fein, Esther. 1989. "Glasnost Is Opening the Door on Poverty." *New York Times*, January 29.

Greenhouse, Steven. 1989. "Can Poland's Dinosaur Evolve?" *New York Times*, November 27.

Hollander, Paul. 1981. *Political Pilgrims: Travels of Western Intellectuals to the Soviet Union, China, and Cuba, 1928–1978.* New York: Oxford University Press.

Huberman, Leo, and Paul Sweezy. 1967. *Socialism in Cuba.* New York: Modern Reader Paperbacks.

Inkeles, Alex. 1950. "Social Stratification and Mobility in the Soviet Union: 1940–1950." *American Sociological Review* 15:465–479.

Jones, T. Anthony. 1981. "Work, Workers, and Modernization in the USSR." *Sociology of Work* 1:249–283.

Kamm, Henry. 1989. "Hungarians Shocked by News of Vast Poverty in Their Midst." *New York Times,* February 6.

Kennedy, Michael, and Ireneusz Bialecki. 1989. "Power and the Logic of Distribution in Poland." *Eastern European Politics and Societies* 3:300–328.

Kostakov, Vladimir. 1989. "Employment: Scarcity or Surplus?" Pp. 159–175 in Anthony Jones and William Moskoff, eds., *Perestroika and the Economy.* Armonk, N.Y.: Sharpe.

Laber, Jeri. 1990. "The Bulgarian Difference." *New York Review of Books,* May 17, pp. 34–36.

Lenski, Gerhard. 1966. *Power and Privilege: A Theory of Social Stratification.* New York: McGraw-Hill.

———. 1978. "Marxist Experiments in Destratification: An Appraisal." *Social Forces* 57:364–383.

———. 1984. "Income Stratification in the United States: Toward a Revised Model of the System." *Research in Social Stratification and Mobility* 3:173–205.

Matthews, Mervyn. 1978. *Privilege in the Soviet Union.* London: Allen & Unwin.

Medvedev, Grigorii. 1989. *Chernobyl'skaia Kronika.* Moscow: Sovremennik. Cited by David Holloway.

1990. "The Catastrophe and After." *New York Review of Books,* July 19, p. 5.

Medvedev, Zhores. 1990. *The Legacy of Chernobyl.* New York: Norton.

New York Times News Service. 1990. "Gorbachev Checks Headstrong Congress." July 8.

Parkhovmosky, Elrad. 1982. "Can't Anybody Here Make Shoes?" *Izvestia.* Reprinted in *World Press Review,* July, p. 36.

Salisbury, Harrison. 1992. *The New Emperors: China in the Era of Mao and Deng.* Boston: Little, Brown.

Scammel, Michael. 1990. "Yugoslavia: The Awakening." *New York Review of Books,* June 28, pp. 42–47.

Shlapentokh, Vladimir. 1987. "Soviet People: Too Rich for Reform." *New York Times,* November 23.

———. 1989. *Public and Private Life of the Soviet People.* New York: Oxford University Press.

Silk, Leonard. 1990. "Soviet Crisis Worse, Economists Declare." *New York Times,* March 15.

Smith, Hedrick. 1976. *The Russians.* New York: Quadrangle.

Tumin, Melvin. 1953. "Some Principles of Stratification: A Critical Analysis." *American Sociological Review* 18:387–394.

Voinovich, Vladimir. 1989. *The Fur Hat.* New York: Harcourt Brace Jovanovich.

Voslensky, Michael. 1984. *Nomenklatura: The Soviet Ruling Class.* Garden City, N.Y.: Doubleday.

Washington Post. 1990. May 6.

Zakharov, Mark. 1990. "A Glimpse in 1990: Politics and Democracy." *Literaturnaya Gazetta* (international ed.), March, p. 5.

Zeitlin, Maurice. 1970. *Revolutionary Politics and the Cuban Working Class.* New York: Harper & Row.

Part III
The Structure of Modern Stratification

Theories of Class
  Marx and Post-Marxists
  Weber and Post-Weberians
  The Ruling Class and Elites

Gradational Status Groupings
  Reputation, Deference, and Prestige
  Occupational Hierarchies

Part III
The Structure of
Modern Stratification

Theories of Class

 ## MARX AND POST-MARXISTS

KARL MARX

Alienation and Social Classes

We shall begin from a *contemporary* economic fact. The worker becomes poorer the more wealth he produces and the more his production increases in power and extent. The worker becomes an ever cheaper commodity the more goods he creates. The *devaluation* of the human world increases in direct relation with the *increase in value* of the world of things. Labour does not only create goods; it also produces itself and the worker as a *commodity,* and indeed in the same proportion as it produces goods.

This fact simply implies that the object produced by labour, its product, now stands opposed to it as an *alien being,* as a *power independent* of the producer. The product of labour is labour which has been embodied in an object and turned into a physical thing; this product is an *objectification* of labour. The performance of work is at the same time its objectification. The performance of work appears in the sphere of political economy as a *vitiation* of the worker, objectification as a *loss* and as *servitude to the object,* and appropriation as *alienation.*

So much does the performance of work appear as vitiation that the worker is vitiated to the point of starvation. So much does objectification appear as loss of the object that the worker is deprived of the most essential things not only of life but also of work. Labour itself becomes an object which he can acquire only by the greatest effort and with unpredictable interruptions. So much

does the appropriation of the object appear as alienation that the more objects the worker produces the fewer he can possess and the more he falls under the domination of his product, of capital.

All these consequences follow from the fact that the worker is related to the *product of his labour* as to an *alien* object. For it is clear on this presupposition that the more the worker expends himself in work the more powerful becomes the world of objects which he creates in face of himself, the poorer he becomes in his inner life, and the less he belongs to himself. It is just the same as in religion. The more of himself man attributes to God the less he has left in himself. The worker puts his life into the object, and his life then belongs no longer to himself but to the object. The greater his activity, therefore, the less he possesses. What is embodied in the product of his labour is no longer his own. The greater this product is, therefore, the more he is diminished. The *alienation* of the worker in his product means not only that his labour becomes an object, assumes an *external* existence, but that it exists independently, *outside himself,* and alien to him, and that it stands opposed to him as an autonomous power. The life which he has given to the object sets itself against him as an alien and hostile force.
...

So far we have considered the alienation of the worker only from one aspect; namely, *his relation-*

ship with the products of his labour. However, alienation appears not merely in the result but also in the *process* of *production,* within *productive activity* itself. How could the worker stand in an alien relationship to the product of his activity if he did not alienate himself in the act of production itself? The product is indeed only the *résumé* of activity, of production. Consequently, if the product of labour is alienation, production itself must be active alienation—the alienation of activity and the activity of alienation. The alienation of the object of labour merely summarizes the alienation in the work activity itself.

What constitutes the alienation of labour? First, that the work is *external* to the worker, that it is not part of his nature; and that, consequently, he does not fulfil himself in his work but denies himself, has a feeling of misery rather than well-being, does not develop freely his mental and physical energies but is physically exhausted and mentally debased. The worker, therefore, feels himself at home only during his leisure time, whereas at work he feels homeless. His work is not voluntary but imposed, *forced labour.* It is not the satisfaction of a need, but only a *means* for satisfying other needs. Its alien character is clearly shown by the fact that as soon as there is no physical or other compulsion it is avoided like the plague. External labour, labour in which man alienates himself, is a labour of self-sacrifice, of mortification. Finally, the external character of work for the worker is shown by the fact that it is not his own work but work for someone else, that in work he does not belong to himself but to another person.

Just as in religion the spontaneous activity of human fantasy, of the human brain and heart, reacts independently as an alien activity of gods or devils upon the individual, so the activity of the worker is not his own spontaneous activity. It is another's activity and a loss of his own spontaneity.

We arrive at the result that man (the worker) feels himself to be freely active only in his animal functions—eating, drinking and procreating, or at most also in his dwelling and in personal adornment—while in his human functions he is reduced to an animal. The animal becomes human and the human becomes animal.

Eating, drinking and procreating are of course also genuine human functions. But abstractly considered, apart from the environment of human activities, and turned into final and sole ends, they are animal functions.

We have now considered the act of alienation of practical human activity, labour, from two aspects: (1) the relationship of the worker to the *product of labour* as an alien object which dominates him. This relationship is at the same time the relationship to the sensuous external world, to natural objects, as an alien and hostile world; (2) the relationship of labour to the *act of production* within *labour.* This is the relationship of the worker to his own activity as something alien and not belonging to him, activity as suffering (passivity), strength as powerlessness, creation as emasculation, the *personal* physical and mental energy of the worker, his personal life (for what is life but activity?), as an activity which is directed against himself, independent of him and not belonging to him. This is *self-alienation* as against the above-mentioned alienation of the *thing.*

We have now to infer a third characteristic of *alienated labour* from the two we have considered.

Man is a species-being not only in the sense that he makes the community (his own as well as those of other things) his object both practically and theoretically, but also (and this is simply another expression for the same thing) in the sense that he treats himself as the present, living species, as a *universal* and consequently free being.

Species-life, for man as for animals, has its physical basis in the fact that man (like animals) lives from inorganic nature, and since man is more universal than an animal so the range of inorganic nature from which he lives is more universal. Plants, animals, minerals, air, light, etc. constitute, from the theoretical aspect, a part of human consciousness as objects of natural science and art; they are man's spiritual inorganic nature, his intellectual means of life, which he must first prepare for enjoyment and perpetuation. So also, from the practical aspect, they form a part of human life and activity. In practice man lives only from these natural products, whether in the form of food, heating, clothing, housing, etc. The universality of man appears in practice in the universality which makes the whole of nature into his inorganic body: (1) as a direct means of life; and equally (2) as the material object and instrument of his life activity. Nature is the inorganic body of man; that is to say nature, excluding the human body itself. To say that man *lives* from nature means that nature is his *body* with which he must remain in a continuous interchange in order not to die. The statement that the physical and mental life of man, and nature, are interdependent means simply that nature is interdependent with itself, for man is a part of nature.

Since alienated labour: (1) alienates nature from man; and (2) alienates man from himself, from his own active function, his life activity; so it alienates him from the species. It makes *species-life* into a means of individual life. In the first place it alienates species-life and individual life, and secondly, it turns the latter, as an abstraction, into the purpose of the former, also in its abstract and alienated form.

For labour, *life activity, productive life,* now appear to man only as *means* for the satisfaction of a need, the need to maintain his physical existence. Productive life is, however, species-life. It is life creating life. In the type of life activity resides the whole character of a species, its species-character; and free, conscious activity is the species-character of human beings. Life itself appears only as a *means of life.*

The animal is one with its life activity. It does not distinguish the activity from itself. It is *its activity.* But man makes his life activity itself an object of his will and consciousness. He has a conscious life activity. It is not a determination with which he is completely identified. Conscious life activity distinguishes man from the life activity of animals. Only for this reason is he a species-being. Or rather, he is only a self-conscious being, i.e. his own life is an object for him, because he is a species-being. Only for this reason is his activity free activity. Alienated labour reverses the relationship, in that man because he is a self-conscious being makes his life activity, his *being,* only a means for his *existence.*

The practical construction of an *objective world,* the *manipulation* of inorganic nature, is the confirmation of man as a conscious species-being, i.e. a being who treats the species as his own being or himself as a species-being. Of

course, animals also produce. They construct nests, dwellings, as in the case of bees, beavers, ants, etc. But they only produce what is strictly necessary for themselves or their young. They produce only in a single direction, while man produces universally. They produce only under the compulsion of direct physical needs, while man produces when he is free from physical need and only truly produces in freedom from such need. Animals produce only themselves, while man reproduces the whole of nature. The products of animal production belong directly to their physical bodies, while man is free in face of his product. Animals construct only in accordance with the standards and needs of the species to which they belong, while man knows how to produce in accordance with the standards of every species and knows how to apply the appropriate standard to the object. Thus man constructs also in accordance with the laws of beauty.

It is just in his work upon the objective world that man really proves himself as a *species-being.* This production is his active species-life. By means of it nature appears as *his* work and his reality. The object of labour is, therefore, the *objectification of man's species-life;* for he no longer reproduces himself merely intellectually, as in consciousness, but actively and in a real sense, and he sees his own reflection in a world which he has constructed. While, therefore, alienated labour takes away the object of production from man, it also takes away his *species-life,* his real objectivity as a species-being, and changes his advantage over animals into a disadvantage in so far as his inorganic body, nature, is taken from him.

Just as alienated labour transforms free and self-directed activity into a means, so it transforms the species-life of man into a means of physical existence.

Consciousness, which man has from his species, is transformed through alienation so that species-life becomes only a means for him. (3) Thus alienated labour turns the *species-life of man,* and also nature as his mental species-property, into an *alien* being and into a *means* for his *individual existence.* It alienates from man his own body, external nature, his mental life and his *human* life. (4) A direct consequence of the alienation of man from the product of his labour, from his life activity and from his species-life, is that *man* is *alienated* from other *men*. When man confronts himself he also confronts *other* men. What is true of man's relationship to his work, to the product of his work and to himself, is also true of his relationship to other men, to their labour and to the objects of their labour.

In general, the statement that man is alienated from his species-life means that each man is alienated from others, and that each of the others is likewise alienated from human life.

Human alienation, and above all the relation of man to himself, is first realized and expressed in the relationship between each man and other men. Thus in the relationship of alienated labour every man regards other men according to the standards and relationships in which he finds himself placed as a worker.

We began with an economic fact, the alienation of the worker and his production. We have expressed this fact in conceptual terms as *alienated labour,* and in analysing the concept we have merely analysed an economic fact.

Let us now examine further how this concept of alienated labour must express and reveal itself in reality. If the product of labour is alien to me and confronts me as an alien power, to whom does it belong? If my own activity does not belong to me but is an alien, forced activity, to whom does it belong? To a being *other* than myself. And who is this being? The *gods?* It is apparent in the earliest stages of advanced production, e.g. temple building, etc. in Egypt, India, Mexico, and in the service rendered to gods, that the product belonged to the gods. But the gods alone were never the lords of labour. And no more was *nature.* What a contradiction it would be if the more man subjugates nature by his labour, and the more the marvels of the gods are rendered superfluous by the marvels of industry, the more he should abstain from his joy in producing and his enjoyment of the product for love of these powers.

The *alien* being to whom labour and the product of labour belong, to whose service labour is devoted, and to whose enjoyment the product of labour goes, can only be *man* himself. If the product of labour does not belong to the worker, but confronts him as an alien power, this can only be because it belongs to *a man other than the worker.*

If his activity is a torment to him it must be a source of *enjoyment* and pleasure to another. Not the gods, nor nature, but only man himself can be this alien power over men.

Consider the earlier statement that the relation of man to himself is first *realized, objectified,* through his relation to other men. If he is related to the product of his labour, his objectified labour, as to an *alien,* hostile, powerful and independent object, he is related in such a way that another alien, hostile, powerful and independent man is the lord of this object. If he is related to his own activity as to unfree activity, then he is related to it as activity in the service, and under the domination, coercion and yoke, of another man. ...

Thus, through alienated labour the worker creates the relation of another man, who does not work and is outside the work process, to this labour. The relation of the worker to work also produces the relation of the capitalist (or whatever one likes to call the lord of labour) to work. *Private property* is, therefore, the product, the necessary result, of *alienated labour,* of the external relation of the worker to nature and to himself.

Private property is thus derived from the analysis of the concept of *alienated labour;* that is, alienated man, alienated labour, alienated life, and estranged man.

We have, of course, derived the concept of *alienated labour* (*alienated life*) from political economy, from an analysis of the *movement of private property*. But the analysis of this concept shows that although private property appears to be the basis and cause of alienated labour, it is rather a consequence of the latter, just as the gods are *fundamentally* not the cause but the product of confusions of human reason. At a later stage, however, there is a reciprocal influence.

Only in the final stage of the development of private property is its secret revealed, namely, that it is on one hand the *product* of alienated labour, and on the other hand the *means* by which labour is alienated, *the realization of this alienation.*

The Economic and Philosophical Manuscripts, pp. 121–131

The possessing class and the proletarian class represent one and the same human self-alienation.

But the former feels satisfied and affirmed in this self-alienation, experiences the alienation as a sign *of its own power,* and possesses in it the *appearance* of a human existence. The latter, however, feels destroyed in this alienation, seeing in it its own impotence and the reality of an inhuman existence. To use Hegel's expression, this class is, within depravity, an *indignation* against this depravity, an indignation necessarily aroused in this class by the contradiction between its human *nature* and its life-situation, which is a blatant, out-right and all-embracing denial of that very nature.

Within the antagonism as a whole, therefore, private property represents the *conservative* side and the proletariat the *destructive* side. From the former comes action aimed at preserving the antagonism; from the latter, action aimed at its destruction.

The Holy Family: A Critique of Critical Criticism, pp. 133–134

KARL MARX

Classes in Capitalism and Pre-Capitalism

The history of all hitherto existing society[1] is the history of class struggles.

Freeman and slave, patrician and plebeian, lord and serf, guild-master[2] and journeyman, in a word, oppressor and oppressed, stood in constant opposition to one another, carried on an uninterrupted, now hidden, now open fight, a fight that each time ended, either in a revolutionary re-constitution of society at large, or in the common ruin of the contending classes.

In the earlier epochs of history, we find almost everywhere a complicated arrangement of society into various orders, a manifold gradation of social rank. In ancient Rome we have patricians, knights, plebeians, slaves; in the Middle Ages, feudal lords, vassals, guild-masters, journeymen, apprentices, serfs; in almost all of these classes, again, subordinate gradations.

The modern bourgeois society that has sprouted from the ruins of feudal society has not done away with class antagonisms. It has but established new classes, new conditions of oppression, new forms of struggle in place of the old ones.

Our epoch, the epoch of the bourgeoisie, possesses, however, this distinctive feature: it has simplified the class antagonisms. Society as a whole is more and more splitting up into two great hostile camps, into two great classes directly facing each other: Bourgeoisie and Proletariat.

From the serfs of the Middle Ages sprang the chartered burghers of the earliest towns. From these burgesses the first elements of the bourgeoisie were developed.

The discovery of America, the rounding of the Cape, opened up fresh ground for the rising bourgeoisie. The East-Indian and Chinese markets, the colonisation of America, trade with the colonies, the increase in the means of exchange and in commodities generally, gave to commerce, to navigation, to industry, an impulse never before known, and thereby, to the revolutionary element in the tottering feudal society, a rapid development.

The feudal system of industry, under which industrial production was monopolised by closed guilds, now no longer sufficed for the growing wants of the new markets. The manufacturing system took its place. The guild-masters were pushed on one side by the manufacturing middle class; division of labour between the different corporate guilds vanished in the face of division of labour in each single workshop.

Meantime the markets kept ever growing, the demand ever rising. Even manufacture no longer sufficed. Thereupon, steam and machinery revolutionised industrial production. The place of manufacture was taken by the giant, Modern Industry, the place of the industrial middle class, by industrial millionaires, the leaders of whole industrial armies, the modern bourgeois.

Modern industry has established the world-market, for which the discovery of America paved the way. This market has given an immense development to commerce, to navigation, to communication by land. This development has, in its turn, reacted on the extension of industry; and in proportion as industry, commerce, navigation, railways extended, in the same proportion the bourgeoisie developed, increased its capital, and pushed into the background every class handed down from the Middle Ages.

We see, therefore, how the modern bourgeoisie is itself the product of a long course of development, of a series of revolutions in the modes of production and of exchange.

Each step in the development of the bourgeoisie was accompanied by a corresponding political advance of that class. An oppressed class under the sway of the feudal nobility, an armed and self-governing association in the mediaeval commune[3]; here independent urban republic (as in Italy and Germany), there taxable "third estate" of the monarchy (as in France), afterwards, in the period of manufacture proper, serving either the semi-feudal or the absolute monarchy as a counterpoise against the nobility, and, in fact, cornerstone of the great monarchies in general, the bourgeoisie has at last, since the establishment of Modern Industry and of the world-market, conquered for itself, in the modern representative State, exclusive political sway. The executive of the modern State is but a committee for managing the common affairs of the whole bourgeoisie.

The bourgeoisie, historically, has played a most revolutionary part.

The bourgeoisie, wherever it has got the upper hand, has put an end to all feudal, patriarchal, idyllic relations. It has pitilessly torn asunder the motley feudal ties that bound man to his "natural superiors," and has left remaining no other nexus between man and man than naked self-interest, than callous "cash payment." It has drowned the most heavenly ecstasies of religious fervour, of chivalrous enthusiasm, of philistine sentimentalism, in the icy water of egotistical calculation. It has resolved personal worth into exchange value, and in place of the numberless indefeasible chartered freedoms, has set up that single, unconscionable freedom—Free Trade. In one word, for exploitation, veiled by religious and political illusions, it has substituted naked, shameless, direct, brutal exploitation.

The bourgeoisie has stripped of its halo every occupation hitherto honoured and looked up to with reverent awe. It has converted the physician, the lawyer, the priest, the poet, the man of science, into its paid wage-labourers.

The bourgeoisie has torn away from the family its sentimental veil, and has reduced the family relation to a mere money relation.

The bourgeoisie has disclosed how it came to pass that the brutal display of vigour in the Middle Ages, which Reactionists so much admire, found its fitting complement in the most slothful indolence. It has been the first to show what man's activity can bring about. It has accomplished wonders far surpassing Egyptian pyramids, Roman aqueducts, and Gothic cathedrals; it has conducted expeditions that put in the shade all former Exoduses of nations and crusades.

The bourgeoisie cannot exist without constantly revolutionising the instruments of production, and thereby the relations of production, and with them the whole relations of society. Conservation of the old modes of production in unaltered form, was, on the contrary, the first condition of existence for all earlier industrial classes. Constant revolutionising of production, uninterrupted disturbance of all social conditions, everlasting uncertainty and agitation distinguish the bourgeois epoch from all earlier ones. All fixed, fast-frozen relations, with their train of ancient and venerable prejudices and opinions, are swept away, all new-formed ones become antiquated before they can ossify. All that is solid melts into air, all that is holy is profaned, and man is at last compelled to face with sober senses, his real conditions of life, and his relations with his kind.

The need of a constantly expanding market for its products chases the bourgeoisie over the whole surface of the globe. It must nestle everywhere, settle everywhere, establish connexions everywhere.

The bourgeoisie has through its exploitation of the world-market given a cosmopolitan character to production and consumption in every country. To the great chagrin of Reactionists, it has drawn from under the feet of industry the national ground on which it stood. All old-established national industries have been destroyed or are daily being destroyed. They are dislodged by new industries, whose introduction becomes a life and death question for all civilised nations, by industries that no longer work up indigenous raw material, but raw material drawn from the remotest zones; industries whose products are consumed, not only at home, but in every quarter of the globe. In place of the old wants, satisfied by the productions of the country, we find new wants, requiring for their satisfaction the products of distant lands and climes. In place of the old local and national seclusion and self-sufficiency, we have intercourse in every direction, universal inter-dependence of nations. And as in material, so also in intellectual production. The intellectual creations of individual nations become common property. National one-sidedness and narrow-mindedness become more and more impossible, and from the numerous national and local literatures, there arises a world literature.

The bourgeoisie, by the rapid improvement of all instruments of production, by the immensely facilitated means of communication, draws all, even the most barbarian, nations into civilisation. The cheap prices of its commodities are the heavy artillery with which it batters down all Chinese walls, with which it forces the barbarians' intensely obstinate hatred of foreigners to capitulate. It compels all nations, on pain of extinction, to adopt the bourgeois mode of production; it compels them to introduce what it calls civilisation into their midst, *i.e.,* to become bourgeois

themselves. In one word, it creates a world after its own image.

The bourgeoisie has subjected the country to the rule of the towns. It has created enormous cities, has greatly increased the urban population as compared with the rural, and has thus rescued a considerable part of the population from the idiocy of rural life. Just as it has made the country dependent on the towns, so it has made barbarian and semi-barbarian countries dependent on the civilised ones, nations of peasants on nations of bourgeois, the East on the West.

The bourgeoisie keeps more and more doing away with the scattered state of the population, of the means of production, and of property. It has agglomerated population, centralised means of production, and has concentrated property in a few hands. The necessary consequence of this was political centralisation. Independent, or but loosely connected provinces, with separate interests, laws, governments and systems of taxation, became lumped together into one nation, with one government, one code of laws, one national class-interest, one frontier and one customs-tariff.

The bourgeoisie, during its rule of scarce one hundred years, has created more massive and more colossal productive forces than have all preceding generations together. Subjection of Nature's forces to man, machinery, application of chemistry to industry and agriculture, steam-navigation, railways, electric telegraphs, clearing of whole continents for cultivation, canalisation of rivers, whole populations conjured out of the ground—what earlier century had even a presentiment that such productive forces slumbered in the lap of social labour?

We see then: the means of production and of exchange, on whose foundation the bourgeoisie built itself up, were generated in feudal society. At a certain stage in the development of these means of production and of exchange, the conditions under which feudal society produced and exchanged, the feudal organisation of agriculture and manufacturing industry, in one word, the feudal relations of property became no longer compatible with the already developed productive forces; they became so many fetters. They had to be burst asunder; they were burst asunder.

Into their place stepped free competition, accompanied by a social and political constitution adapted to it, and by the economical and political sway of the bourgeois class.

A similar movement is going on before our own eyes. Modern bourgeois society with its relations of production, of exchange and of property, a society that has conjured up such gigantic means of production and of exchange, is like the sorcerer, who is no longer able to control the powers of the nether world whom he has called up by his spells. For many a decade past the history of industry and commerce is but the history of the revolt of modern productive forces against modern conditions of production, against the property relations that are the conditions for the existence of the bourgeoisie and of its rule. It is enough to mention the commercial crises that by their periodical return put on its trial, each time more threateningly, the existence of the entire bourgeois society. In these crises a great part not only of the existing products, but also of the previously created productive forces, are periodically destroyed. In these crises there breaks out an epidemic that, in all earlier epochs, would have seemed an absurdity—the epidemic of over-production. Society suddenly finds itself put back into a state of momentary barbarism; it appears as if a famine, a universal war of devastation had cut off the supply of every means of subsistence; industry and commerce seem to be destroyed; and why? Because there is too much civilisation, too much means of subsistence, too much industry, too much commerce. The productive forces at the disposal of society no longer tend to further the development of the conditions of bourgeois property; on the contrary, they have become too powerful for these conditions, by which they are fettered, and so soon as they overcome these fetters, they bring disorder into the whole of bourgeois society, endanger the existence of bourgeois property. The conditions of bourgeois society are too narrow to comprise the wealth created by them. And how does the bourgeoisie get over these crises? On the one hand by enforced destruction of a mass of productive forces; on the other, by the conquest of new markets, and by the more thorough exploitation of the old ones. That is to say, by paving the way for more extensive and more destructive crises, and by diminishing the means whereby crises are prevented.

The weapons with which the bourgeoisie felled feudalism to the ground are now turned against the bourgeoisie itself.

But not only has the bourgeoisie forged the weapons that bring death to itself; it has also called into existence the men who are to wield those weapons—the modern working class—the proletarians.

In proportion as the bourgeoisie, i.e., capital, is developed, in the same proportion is the proletariat, the modern working class, developed—a class of labourers, who live only so long as they find work, and who find work only so long as their labour increases capital. These labourers, who must sell themselves piecemeal, are a commodity, like every other article of commerce, and are consequently exposed to all the vicissitudes of competition, to all the fluctuations of the market.

Owing to the extensive use of machinery and to division of labour, the work of the proletarians has lost all individual character, and, consequently, all charm for the workman. He becomes an appendage of the machine, and it is only the most simple, most monotonous, and most easily acquired knack, that is required of him. Hence, the cost of production of a workman is restricted, almost entirely, to the means of subsistence that he requires for his maintenance, and for the propagation of his race. But the price of a commodity, and therefore also of labour, is equal to its cost of production. In proportion, therefore, as the repulsiveness of the work increases, the wage decreases. Nay more, in proportion as the use of machinery and division of labour increases, in the same proportion the burden of toil also increases, whether by prolongation of the working hours, by increase of the work exacted in a given time or by increased speed of the machinery, etc.

Modern industry has converted the little workshop of the patriarchal master into the great factory of the industrial capitalist. Masses of labourers, crowded into the factory, are organised like soldiers. As privates of the industrial army they are placed under the command of a perfect hierarchy of officers and sergeants. Not only are they slaves of the bourgeois class, and of the bourgeois State; they are daily and hourly enslaved by the machine, by the overlooker, and, above all, by the individual bourgeois manufacturer himself. The more openly this despotism proclaims gain to be its end and aim, the more petty, the more hateful and the more embittering it is.

The less the skill and exertion of strength implied in manual labour, in other words, the more modern industry becomes developed, the more is the labour of men superseded by that of women. Differences of age and sex have no longer any distinctive social validity for the working class. All are instruments of labour, more or less expensive to use, according to their age and sex.

No sooner is the exploitation of the labourer by the manufacturer, so far, at an end, and he receives his wages in cash, than he is set upon by the other portions of the bourgeoisie, the landlord, the shopkeeper, the pawnbroker, etc.

The lower strata of the middle class—the small tradespeople, shopkeepers, and retired tradesmen generally, the handicraftsmen and peasants—all these sink gradually into the proletariat, partly because their diminutive capital does not suffice for the scale on which Modern Industry is carried on, and is swamped in the competition with the large capitalists, partly because their specialised skill is rendered worthless by new methods of production. Thus the proletariat is recruited from all classes of the population.

The proletariat goes through various stages of development. With its birth begins its struggle with the bourgeoisie. At first the contest is carried on by individual labourers, then by the workpeople of a factory, then by the operatives of one trade, in one locality, against the individual bourgeois who directly exploits them. They direct their attacks not against the bourgeois conditions of production, but against the instruments of production themselves: they destroy imported wares that compete with their labour, they smash to pieces machinery, they set factories ablaze, they seek to restore by force the vanished status of the workman of the Middle Ages.

At this stage the labourers still form an incoherent mass scattered over the whole country, and broken up by their mutual competition. If anywhere they unite to form more compact bodies, this is not yet the consequence of their own active union, but of the union of the bourgeoisie, which

class, in order to attain its own political ends, is compelled to set the whole proletariat in motion, and is moreover yet, for a time, able to do so. At this stage, therefore, the proletarians do not fight their enemies, but the enemies of their enemies, the remnants of absolute monarchy, the landowners, the non-industrial bourgeois, the petty bourgeoisie. Thus the whole historical movement is concentrated in the hands of the bourgeoisie; every victory so obtained is a victory for the bourgeoisie.

But with the development of industry the proletariat not only increases in number; it becomes concentrated in greater masses, its strength grows, and it feels that strength more. The various interests and conditions of life within the ranks of the proletariat are more and more equalised, in proportion as machinery obliterates all distinctions of labour, and nearly everywhere reduces wages to the same low level. The growing competition among the bourgeois, and the resulting commercial crises, make the wages of the workers ever more fluctuating. The unceasing improvement of machinery, ever more rapidly developing, makes their livelihood more and more precarious; the collisions between individual workmen and individual bourgeois take more and more the character of collisions between two classes. Thereupon the workers begin to form combinations (Trades' Unions) against the bourgeois; they club together in order to keep up the rate of wages; they found permanent associations in order to make provision beforehand for these occasional revolts. Here and there the contest breaks out into riots.

Now and then the workers are victorious, but only for a time. The real fruit of their battles lies, not in the immediate result, but in the ever-expanding union of the workers. This union is helped on by the improved means of communication that are created by modern industry and that place the workers of different localities in contact with one another. It was just this contact that was needed to centralise the numerous local struggles, all of the same character, into one national struggle between classes. But every class struggle is a political struggle. And that union, to attain which the burghers of the Middle Ages, with their miserable highways, required centuries, the modern proletarians, thanks to railways, achieve in a few years.

This organisation of the proletarians into a class, and consequently into a political party, is continually being upset again by the competition between the workers themselves. But it ever rises up again, stronger, firmer, mightier. It compels legislative recognition of particular interests of the workers, by taking advantage of the divisions among the bourgeoisie itself. Thus the ten-hours' bill in England was carried.

Altogether collisions between the classes of the old society further, in many ways, the course of development of the proletariat. The bourgeoisie finds itself involved in a constant battle. At first with the aristocracy; later on, with those portions of the bourgeoisie itself, whose interests have become antagonistic to the progress of industry; at all times, with the bourgeoisie of foreign countries. In all these battles it sees itself compelled to appeal to the proletariat, to ask for its help, and thus, to drag it into the political arena. The bourgeoisie itself, therefore, supplies the proletariat with its own elements of political and general education, in other words, it furnishes the proletariat with weapons for fighting the bourgeoisie.

Further, as we have already seen, entire sections of the ruling classes are, by the advance of industry, precipitated into the proletariat, or are at least threatened in their conditions of existence. These also supply the proletariat with fresh elements of enlightenment and progress.

Finally, in times when the class struggle nears the decisive hour, the process of dissolution going on within the ruling class, in fact within the whole range of old society, assumes such a violent, glaring character, that a small section of the ruling class cuts itself adrift, and joins the revolutionary class, the class that holds the future in its hands. Just as, therefore, at an earlier period, a section of the nobility went over to the bourgeoisie, so now a portion of the bourgeoisie goes over to the proletariat, and in particular, a portion of the bourgeois ideologists, who have raised themselves to the level of comprehending theoretically the historical movement as a whole.

Of all the classes that stand face to face with the bourgeoisie today, the proletariat alone is a really revolutionary class. The other classes decay and finally disappear in the face of Modern Industry; the proletariat is its special and essential product.

The lower middle class, the small manufacturer, the shopkeeper, the artisan, the peasant, all these fight against the bourgeoisie, to save from extinction their existence as fractions of the middle class. They are therefore not revolutionary, but conservative. Nay more, they are reactionary, for they try to roll back the wheel of history. If by chance they are revolutionary, they are so only in view of their impending transfer into the proletariat, they thus defend not their present, but their future interests, they desert their own standpoint to place themselves at that of the proletariat.

The "dangerous class," the social scum, that passively rotting mass thrown off by the lowest layers of old society, may, here and there, be swept into the movement by a proletarian revolution, its conditions of life, however, prepare it far more for the part of a bribed tool of reactionary intrigue.

In the conditions of the proletariat, those of old society at large are already virtually swamped. The proletarian is without property; his relation to his wife and children has no longer anything in common with the bourgeois family-relations; modern, industrial labour, modern subjection to capital, the same in England as in France, in America as in Germany, has stripped him of every trace of national character. Law, morality, religion, are to him so many bourgeois prejudices, behind which lurk in ambush just as many bourgeois interests.

All the preceding classes that got the upper hand, sought to fortify their already acquired status by subjecting society at large to their conditions of appropriation. The proletarians cannot become masters of the productive forces of society, except by abolishing their own previous mode of appropriation, and thereby also every other previous mode of appropriation. They have nothing of their own to secure and to fortify; their mission is to destroy all previous securities for, and insurances of, individual property.

All previous historical movements were movements of minorities, or in the interests of minorities. The proletarian movement is the self-conscious, independent movement of the immense majority, in the interests of the immense majority. The proletariat, the lowest stratum of our present society, cannot stir, cannot raise itself up, without the whole superincumbent strata of official society being sprung into the air.

Though not in substance, yet in form, the struggle of the proletariat with the bourgeoisie is at first a national struggle. The proletariat of each country must, of course, first of all settle matters with its own bourgeoisie.

In depicting the most general phases of the development of the proletariat, we traced the more or less veiled civil war, raging within existing society, up to the point where that war breaks out into open revolution, and where the violent overthrow of the bourgeoisie lays the foundation for the sway of the proletariat.

Hitherto, every form of society has been based, as we have already seen, on the antagonism of oppressing and oppressed classes. But in order to oppress a class, certain conditions must be assured to it under which it can, at least, continue its slavish existence. The serf, in the period of serfdom, raised himself to membership in the commune, just as the petty bourgeois, under the yoke of feudal absolutism, managed to develop into a bourgeois. The modern labourer, on the contrary, instead of rising with the progress of industry, sinks deeper and deeper below the conditions of existence of his own class. He becomes a pauper, and pauperism develops more rapidly than population and wealth. And here it becomes evident, that the bourgeoisie is unfit any longer to be the ruling class in society, and to impose its conditions of existence upon society as an overriding law. It is unfit to rule because it is incompetent to assure an existence to its slave within his slavery, because it cannot help letting him sink into such a state, that it has to feed him, instead of being fed by him. Society can no longer live under this bourgeoisie, in other words, its existence is no longer compatible with society.

The essential condition for the existence, and for the sway of the bourgeois class, is the formation and augmentation of capital; the condition for capital is wage-labour. Wage-labour rests exclusively on competition between the labourers. The advance of industry, whose involuntary promoter is the bourgeoisie, replaces the isolation of the labourers, due to competition, by their revolutionary combination, due to association. The

development of Modern Industry, therefore, cuts from under its feet the very foundation on which the bourgeoisie produces and appropriates products. What the bourgeoisie, therefore, produces, above all, is its own grave-diggers. Its fall and the victory of the proletariat are equally inevitable.

Notes

1. That is, all *written* history. In 1847, the pre-history of society, the social organisation existing previous to recorded history, was all but unknown. [*Note by Engels to the English edition of 1888.*]

2. Guild-master, that is, a full member of a guild, a master within, not a head of a guild. [*Note by Engels to the English edition of 1888.*]

3. "Commune" was the name taken, in France, by the nascent towns even before they had conquered from their feudal lords and masters local self-government and political rights as the "Third Estate". Generally speaking, for the economical development of the bourgeoisie, England is here taken as the typical country; for its political development, France. [*Note by Engels to the English edition of 1888.*]

This was the name given their urban communities by the townsmen of Italy and France, after they had purchased or wrested their initial rights of self-government from their feudal lords. [*Note by Engels to the German edition of 1890.*]

The Communist Manifesto, pp. 108–119

The first attempts of workers to *associate* among themselves always take place in the form of combinations.

Large-scale industry concentrates in one place a crowd of people unknown to one another. Competition divides their interests. But the maintenance of wages, this common interest which they have against their boss, unites them in a common thought of resistance—*combination*. Thus combination always has a double aim, that of stopping competition among the workers, so that they can carry on general competition with the capitalist. If the first aim of resistance was merely the maintenance of wages, combinations, at first isolated, constitute themselves into groups as the capitalists in their turn unite for the purpose of repression, and in face of always united capital, the maintenance of the association becomes more necessary to them than that of wages. This is so true that English economists are amazed to see the workers sacrifice a good part of their wages in favour of associations, which, in the eyes of these economists, are established solely in favour of wages. In this struggle—a veritable civil war—all the elements necessary for a coming battle unite and develop. Once it has reached this point, association takes on a political character.

Economic conditions had first transformed the mass of the people of the country into workers. The combination of capital has created for this mass a common situation, common interests. This mass is thus already a class as against capital, but not yet for itself. In the struggle, of which we have noted only a few phases, this mass becomes united, and constitutes itself as a class for itself. The interests it defends become class interests. But the struggle of class against class is a political struggle.

In the bourgeoisie we have two phases to distinguish: that in which it constituted itself as a class under the regime of feudalism and absolute monarchy, and that in which, already constituted as a class, it overthrew feudalism and monarchy to make society into a bourgeois society. The first of these phases was the longer and necessitated the greater efforts. This too began by partial combinations against the feudal lords.

Much research has been carried out to trace the different historical phases that the bourgeoisie has passed through, from the commune up to its constitution as a class.

But when it is a question of making a precise study of strikes, combinations and other forms in which the proletarians carry out before our eyes their organization as a class, some are seized with real fear and others display a *transcendental* disdain.

An oppressed class is the vital condition for every society founded on the antagonism of classes. The emancipation of the oppressed class thus implies necessarily the creation of a new society. For the oppressed class to be able to emancipate itself it is necessary that the productive powers already acquired and the existing social relations should no longer be capable of existing side by side. Of all the instruments of production, the greatest productive power is the revolutionary class itself. The organization of revolutionary elements as a class supposes the existence of all the productive forces which could be engendered in the bosom of the old society.

Does this mean that after the fall of the old society there will be a new class domination culminating in a new political power? No.

The condition for the emancipation of the working class is the abolition of every class, just as the condition for the liberation of the third estate, of the bourgeois order, was the abolition of all estates[1] and all orders.

The working class, in the course of its development, will substitute for the old civil society an association which will exclude classes and their antagonism, and there will be no more political power properly so-called, since political power is precisely the official expression of antagonism in civil society.

Meanwhile the antagonism between the proletariat and the bourgeoisie is a struggle of class against class, a struggle which carried to its highest expression is a total revolution. Indeed, is it at all surprising that a society founded on the opposition of classes should culminate in brutal *contradiction,* the shock of body against body, as its final *dénouement?*

Do not say that social movement excludes political movement. There is never a political movement which is not at the same time social.

It is only in an order of things in which there are no more classes and class antagonisms that *social evolutions* will cease to be *political revolutions.* Till then, on the eve of every general reshuffling of society, the last word of social science will always be:

"*Le combat ou la mort; la lutte sanguinaire ou le néant. C'est ainsi que la question est invinciblement posée.*"[2]

Notes

1. Estates here in the historical sense of the estates of feudalism, estates with definite and limited privileges. The revolution of the bourgeoisie abolished the estates and their privileges. Bourgeois society knows only

classes. It was, therefore, absolutely in contradiction with history to describe the proletariat as the "fourth estate." [*Note by F. Engels to the German edition,* 1885.]

2. "Combat or death; bloody struggle or extinction. It is thus that the question is inexorably put." George Sand, *Jean Ziska*.

The Poverty of Philosophy, pp. 172–175

The small-holding peasants form a vast mass, the members of which live in similar conditions but without entering into manifold relations with one another. Their mode of production isolates them from one another instead of bringing them into mutual intercourse. The isolation is increased by France's bad means of communication and by the poverty of the peasants. Their field of production, the small holding, admits of no division of labour in its cultivation, no application of science and, therefore, no diversity of development, no variety of talent, no wealth of social relationships. Each individual peasant family is almost self-sufficient; it itself directly produces the major part of its consumption and thus acquires its means of life more through exchange with nature than in intercourse with society. A small holding, a peasant and his family; alongside them another small holding, another peasant and another family. A few score of these make up a village, and a few score of villages make up a Department. In this way, the great mass of the French nation is formed by simple addition of homologous magnitudes, much as potatoes in a sack form a sack of potatoes. In so far as millions of families live under economic conditions of existence that separate their mode of life, their interests and their culture from those of the other classes, and put them in hostile opposition to the latter, they form a class. In so far as there is merely a local interconnection among these small-holding peasants, and the identity of their interests begets no community, no national bond and no political organisation among them, they do not form a class. They are consequently incapable of enforcing their class interests in their own name, whether through a parliament or through a convention. They cannot represent themselves, they must be represented. Their representative must at

the same time appear as their master, as an authority over them, as an unlimited governmental power that protects them against the other classes and sends them rain and sunshine from above. The political influence of the small-holding peasants, therefore, finds its final expression in the executive power subordinating society to itself.

The Eighteenth Brumaire of Louis Bonaparte, pp. 478–479

The owners merely of labour-power, owners of capital, and landowners, whose respective sources of income are wages, profit and ground-rent, in other words, wage-labourers, capitalists and landowners, constitute then three big classes of modern society based upon the capitalist mode of production.

In England, modern society is indisputably most highly and classically developed in economic structure. Nevertheless, even here the stratification of classes does not appear in its pure form. Middle and intermediate strata even here obliterate lines of demarcation everywhere (although incomparably less in rural districts than in the cities). However, this is immaterial for our analysis. We have seen that the continual tendency and law of development of the capitalist mode of production is more and more to divorce the means of production from labour, and more and more to concentrate the scattered means of production into large groups, thereby transforming labour into wage-labour and the means of production into capital. And to this tendency, on the other hand, corresponds the independent separation of landed property from capital and labour, or the transformation of all landed property into the form of landed property corresponding to the capitalist mode of production.

The first question to be answered is this: What constitutes a class?—and the reply to this follows naturally from the reply to another question, namely: What makes wage-labourers, capitalists and landlords constitute the three great social classes?

At first glance—the identity of revenues and sources of revenue. There are three great social groups whose members, the individuals forming them, live on wages, profit and ground-rent respectively, on the realisation of their labour-power, their capital, and their landed property.

However, from this standpoint, physicians and officials, e.g., would also constitute two classes, for they belong to two distinct social groups, the members of each of these groups receiving their revenue from one and the same source. The same would also be true of the infinite fragmentation of interest and rank into which the division of social labour splits labourers as well as capitalists and landlords—the latter, e.g., into owners of vineyards, farm owners, owners of forests, mine owners and owners of fisheries.

[Here the manuscript breaks off.]

Capital, Vol. III, pp. 885–886

KARL MARX

Ideology and Class

The ideas of the ruling class are in every epoch the ruling ideas, i.e. the class which is the ruling *material* force of society, is at the same time its ruling *intellectual* force. The class which has the means of material production at its disposal, has control at the same time over the means of mental production, so that thereby, generally speaking, the ideas of those who lack the means of mental production are subject to it. The ruling ideas are nothing more than the ideal expression of the dominant material relationships, the dominant material relationships grasped as ideas; hence of the relationships which make the one class the ruling one, therefore, the ideas of its dominance. The individuals composing the ruling class possess among other things consciousness, and therefore think. Insofar, therefore, as they rule as a class and determine the extent and compass of an epoch, it is self-evident that they do this in its whole range, hence among other things rule also as thinkers, as producers of ideas, and regulate the production and distribution of the ideas of their age: thus their ideas are the ruling ideas of the epoch. For instance, in an age and in a country where royal power, aristocracy, and bourgeoisie are contending for mastery and where, therefore, mastery is shared, the doctrine of the separation of powers proves to be the dominant idea and is expressed as an "eternal law".

The division of labour manifests itself in the ruling class as the division of mental and material labour, so that inside this class one part appears as the thinkers of the class (its active, conceptive ideologists, who make the perfecting of the illusion of the class about itself their chief source of livelihood), while the others' attitude to these ideas and illusions is more passive and receptive, because they are in reality the active members of this class and have less time to make up illusions and ideas about themselves. Within this class this cleavage can even develop into a certain opposition and hostility between the two parts, which, however, in the case of a practical collision, in which the class itself is endangered, automatically comes to nothing, in which case there also vanishes the semblance that the ruling ideas were not the ideas of the ruling class and had a power distinct from the power of this class. The existence of revolutionary ideas in a particular period presupposes the existence of a revolutionary class.

If now in considering the course of history we detach the ideas of the ruling class from the ruling class itself and attribute to them an independent existence, if we confine ourselves to saying that these or those ideas were dominant at a given time, without bothering ourselves about the conditions of production and the producers of these ideas, if we thus ignore the individuals and world conditions which are the source of the ideas, we can say, for instance, that during the time that the aristocracy was dominant, the concepts honour, loyalty, etc. were dominant, during the dominance of the bourgeoisie the concepts freedom, equality, etc. The ruling class itself on the whole imagines this to be so. This conception of history, which is common to all historians, particularly since the eighteenth century, will necessarily come up against the phenomenon that increasingly abstract ideas hold sway, i.e. ideas which increasingly take on the form of universality. For each new class which puts itself in the place of one ruling before it, is compelled, merely in order to carry through its aim, to represent its interest as the common interest of all the members of society, that is, expressed in ideal form: it has to give its ideas the form of universality, and represent them as the only rational, universally valid ones. The class making a revolution appears from the very start, if only because it is opposed to a *class,* not as a class but as the representative of the whole of society; it appears as the whole mass of society confronting the one ruling class.[1] It can do this because, to start with, its interest really is more connected with the common interest of all other non-ruling classes, because under the pressure of hitherto existing conditions its interest has not yet been able to develop as the particular interest of a particular class. Its victory, therefore, benefits also many individuals of the other classes which are not winning a dominant position, but

only insofar as it now puts these individuals in a position to raise themselves into the ruling class. When the French bourgeoisie overthrew the power of the aristocracy, it thereby made it possible for many proletarians to raise themselves above the proletariat, but only insofar as they become bourgeois. Every new class, therefore, achieves its hegemony only on a broader basis than that of the class ruling previously, whereas the opposition of the non-ruling class against the new ruling class later develops all the more sharply and profoundly. Both these things determine the fact that the struggle to be waged against this new ruling class, in its turn, aims at a more decided and radical negation of the previous conditions of society than could all previous classes which sought to rule.

This whole semblance, that the rule of a certain class is only the rule of certain ideas, comes to a natural end, of course, as soon as class rule in general ceases to be the form in which society is organised, that is to say, as soon as it is no longer necessary to represent a particular interest as general or the "general interest" as ruling.

Notes

1. Universality corresponds to (1) the class versus the estate, (2) the competition, world-wide intercourse, etc., (3) the great numerical strength of the ruling class, (4) the illusion of the *common* interests (in the beginning this illusion is true), (5) the delusion of the ideologists and the division of labour. [*Marginal note by Marx.*]

KARL MARX

Value and Surplus Value

What is the common *social substance* of all commodities? It is *Labour.* To produce a commodity a certain amount of labour must be bestowed upon it, or worked up in it. And I say not only *Labour,* but *social Labour.* A man who produces an article for his own immediate use, to consume it himself, creates a *product,* but not a *commodity.* As a self-sustaining producer he has nothing to do with society. But to produce a *commodity,* a man must not only produce an article satisfying some *social* want, but his labour itself must form part and parcel of the total sum of labour expended by society. It must be subordinate to the *Division of Labour within Society.* It is nothing without the other divisions of labour, and on its part is required to *integrate* them.

If we consider *commodities as values,* we consider them exclusively under the single aspect of *realised, fixed,* or, if you like, *crystallised social labour.* In this respect they can *differ* only by representing greater or smaller quantities of labour, as, for example, a greater amount of labour may be worked up in a silken handkerchief than in a brick. But how does one measure *quantities of labour?* By the *time the labour lasts,* in measuring the labour by the hour, the day, etc. Of course, to apply this measure, all sorts of labour are reduced to average or simple labour as their unit.

We arrive, therefore, at this conclusion. A commodity has a *value,* because it is a *crystallisation of social labour.* The *greatness* of its value, of its *relative* value, depends upon the greater or less amount of that social substance contained in it; that is to say, on the relative mass of labour necessary for its production. The *relative values of commodities* are, therefore, determined by the *respective quantities or amounts of labour, worked up,*

realised, fixed in them. The *correlative* quantities of commodities which can be produced in the *same time of labour* are *equal.* Or the value of one commodity is to the value of another commodity as the quantity of labour fixed in the one is to the quantity of labour fixed in the other. ...

What, then, is the *Value of Labouring Power?*

Like that of every other commodity, its value is determined by the quantity of labour necessary to produce it. The labouring power of a man exists only in his living individuality. A certain mass of necessaries must be consumed by a man to grow up and maintain his life. But the man, like the machine, will wear out, and must be replaced by another man. Beside the mass of necessaries required for *his own* maintenance, he wants another amount of necessaries to bring up a certain quota of children that are to replace him on the labour market and to perpetuate the race of labourers. Moreover, to develop his labouring power, and acquire a given skill, another amount of values must be spent. For our purpose it suffices to consider only *average* labour, the costs of whose education and development are vanishing magnitudes. Still I must seize upon this occasion to state that, as the costs of producing labouring powers of different quality differ, so must differ the values of the labouring powers employed in different trades. The cry for an *equality of wages* rests, therefore, upon a mistake, is an *insane* wish never to be fulfilled. It is an offspring of that false and superficial radicalism that accepts premises and tries to evade conclusions. Upon the basis of the wages system the value of labouring power is settled like that of every other commodity; and as different kinds of labouring power have different values, or require different quantities of labour for their production, they *must* fetch different prices in the labour market. To clamour for *equal or even equitable retribution* on the basis of the wages system is the same as to clamour for *freedom* on the basis of the slavery system. What you think just or equitable is out of the question. The question is: What is necessary and unavoidable with a given system of production?

After what has been said, it will be seen that the *value of labouring power* is determined by the *value of the necessaries* required to produce, develop, maintain, and perpetuate the labouring power.

Now suppose that the average amount of the daily necessaries of a labouring man require *six hours of average labour* for their production. Suppose, moreover, six hours of average labour to be also realised in a quantity of gold equal to 3s. Then 3s. would be the *Price,* or the monetary expression of the *Daily Value* of that man's *Labouring Power.* If he worked daily six hours he would daily produce a value sufficient to buy the average amount of his daily necessaries, or to maintain himself as a labouring man.

But our man is a wages labourer. He must, therefore, sell his labouring power to a capitalist. If he sells it at 3s. daily, or 18s. weekly, he sells it at its value. Suppose him to be a spinner. If he works six hours daily he will add to the cotton a value of 3s. daily. This value, daily added by him, would be an exact equivalent for the wages, or the price of his labouring power, received daily. But in that case *no surplus value* or *surplus produce* whatever would go to the capitalist. Here, then, we come to the rub.

In buying the labouring power of the workman, and paying its value, the capitalist, like every other purchaser, has acquired the right to consume or use the commodity bought. You consume or use the labouring power of a man by making him work as you consume or use a machine by making it run. By paying the daily or weekly value of the labouring power of the workman, the capitalist has, therefore, acquired the right to use or make that labouring power work during the *whole day or week.* ...

For the present I want to turn your attention to one decisive point.

The *value* of the labouring power is determined by the quantity of labour necessary to maintain or reproduce it, but the *use* of that labouring power is only limited by the active energies and physical strength of the labourer. The daily or weekly *value* of the labouring power is quite distinct from the daily or weekly exercise of that power, the same as the food a horse wants and the time it can carry the horseman are quite distinct. The quantity of labour by which the *value* of the workman's labouring power is limited forms by no means a limit to the quantity of labour which his labouring power is apt to perform. Take the example of our spinner. We have seen that, to daily reproduce his labouring power, he must daily reproduce a value of three shillings, which he will do by working six hours daily. But this does not disable him from working ten or twelve or more hours a day. But by paying the daily or weekly *value* of the spinner's labouring power, the capitalist has acquired the right of using that labouring power during *the whole day or week.* He will, therefore, make him work say, daily, *twelve* hours. *Over and above* the six hours required to replace his wages, or the value of his labouring power, he will, therefore, have to work *six other hours,* which I shall call hours of *surplus labour,* which surplus labour will realise itself in a *surplus value* and a *surplus produce.* If our spinner, for example, by his daily labour of six hours, added three shillings' value to the cotton, a value forming an exact equivalent to his wages, he will, in twelve hours, add six shillings' worth to the cotton, and produce *a proportional surplus of yarn.* As he has sold his labouring power to the capitalist, the whole value or produce created by him belongs to the capitalist, the owner *pro tem.* of his labouring power. By advancing three shillings, the capitalist will, therefore, realise a value of six shillings, because, advancing a value in which six hours of labour are crystallised, he will receive in return a value in which twelve hours of labour are crystallised. By repeating this same process daily, the capitalist will daily advance three shillings and daily pocket six shillings, one-half of which will go to pay wages anew, and the other half of which will form *surplus value,* for which the capitalist pays no equivalent. It is this *sort of exchange between capital and labour* upon which capitalistic production, or the wages system, is founded, and which must constantly result in reproducing the working man as a working man, and the capitalist as a capitalist.

The rate of surplus value, all other circumstances remaining the same, will depend on the proportion between that part of the working day necessary to reproduce the value of the labouring power and the *surplus time* or *surplus labour* performed for the capitalist. It will, therefore, depend on the *ratio in which the working day is prolonged over and above that extent*, by working which the working man would only reproduce the value of his labouring power, or replace his wages.

RALF DAHRENDORF

Class and Class Conflict in Industrial Society

One of the main questions which the present investigation is supposed to answer is: Do classes and class conflicts belong to that group of phenomena by which only the capitalist type of industrial society is characterized, or is their existence a consequence of industrial production itself, and are they therefore a lasting feature of industrial societies? This question will accompany us throughout the following analysis of changes in the structure of industrial societies since Marx.

Ownership and Control, or the Decomposition of Capital

Marx was right in seeking the root of social change in capitalist society in the sphere of industrial production, but the direction these changes took turned out to be directly contrary to Marx's expectations. With respect to capital, he had, in his later years, at least a vision of what was going to happen, as his brief and somewhat puzzled analysis of joint-stock companies shows. Joint-stock companies were legally recognized in Germany, England, France, and the United States in the second half of the nineteenth century. Laws often indicate the conclusion of social developments, and indeed early forms of joint-stock companies can be traced back at least to the commercial companies and trade societies of the seventeenth century. But it was in the nineteenth and early twentieth centuries that this type of enterprise first gained wide recognition and expanded into all branches of economic activity. Today, more than two-thirds of all companies in advanced industrial societies are joint-stock companies, and their property exceeds four-fifths of the total property in economic enterprises. The enterprise owned and run by an individual, or even a family, has long ceased to be the dominant pattern of economic organization. ...

According to the radical view, joint-stock companies involve a complete break with earlier capitalist traditions. By separating what has come to be called ownership and control, they give rise to a new group of managers who are utterly different from their capitalist predecessors. Thus for Marx, the joint-stock company involves a complete alienation of capital "from the real producers, and its opposition as alien property to all individuals really participating in production, from the manager down to the last day-laborer" (1953, Vol. III, p. 478). In other words, by separating ownership and control, the joint-stock company reduces the distance between manager and worker while at the same time removing the owners altogether from the sphere of production and thereby isolating their function as exploiters of others. It is merely a step from this kind of analysis to the thesis that, as Renner has it, the "capitalists without function" yield to the "functionaries without capital," and that this new ruling group of industry bears little resemblance to the old "full capitalists" (1953, pp. 182, 198). Burnham, Geiger, Sering, and others followed Marx (and Renner) in this radical interpretation of the social effects of joint-stock companies.

The conservative view, on the other hand, holds that the consequences of the apparent separation of ownership and control have been vastly overrated. It is argued that in fact owners and controllers, i.e., stockholders and managers, are a fairly homogeneous group. There are often direct connections between them, and where this is not the case, their outlook is sufficiently similar to justify insisting on the old assumption of a homogeneous class of capitalists opposed to an equally homogeneous class of laborers. This view is not often heard in the West nowadays, although traces of it are evident in the work of C. Wright Mills (1954, 1956). It may be added that this conservative view is clearly contrary to Marx's own analysis.

We cannot here exhaust the complex subject of ownership and control, but it seems desirable not to leave the subject without considering which of these two views seems more plausible and appropriate. There can be little doubt that the social structure of joint-stock companies as well as co-operative and state-owned enterprises differs from that of the classical capitalist enterprise, and that therefore a transition from the latter to the former is a process of social change. However, what type of change are we dealing with in this problem? Is it a change involving the transference of certain rights and duties attached to social positions from an old to a new group? Or is it a change that involves some rearrangement of the positions endowed with rights and duties themselves? These questions are not quite as rhetorical as they may sound. In fact, I would claim that the separation of ownership and control involved both a change in the structure of social positions and a change in the recruitment of personnel to

these positions. But it is evident that, in the first place, joint-stock companies differ from capitalist enterprises in the structure of their leading positions. In the sphere with which we are here concerned, the process of transition from capitalist enterprises to joint-stock companies can be described as a process of role differentiation. The roles of owner and manager, originally combined in the position of the capitalist, have been separated and distributed over two positions, those of stockholder and executive.

At the very least, this process of differentiation means that two physical entities occupy the positions formerly occupied by one. But this is not all. Apart from its manifest effects, the separation of ownership and control has a number of latent effects of even greater importance; i.e., it seems clear that the resulting positions, those of stockholder and executive, differ not only with respect to the obvious rights and duties of their incumbents, but also in other respects. Generally, the "capitalist without function" is indeed, as Marx emphasized, alienated from production, i.e., largely removed from the enterprise whose stock he owns. He does not participate in the day-to-day life of the enterprise, and above all he does not have a defined place in the formal hierarchy of authority in the enterprise. The "functionary without capital," on the other hand, has this place, although he typically has no property in the enterprise which he runs.

From the point of view of the social structure of industrial enterprises, this means a significant change in the basis of legitimacy of entrepreneurial authority. The old-style capitalist exercised authority because he owned the instruments of production. The exercise of authority was part and parcel of his property rights, as indeed property may always be regarded from one point of view as simply an institutionalized form of authority over others. By contrast to this legitimation by property, the authority of the manager resembles in many ways that of the heads of political institutions. It is true that even for the manager property has not ceased to function as a basis of authority. The right of the manager to command and expect obedience accrues in part from the property rights delegated to him by the shareholders, acting either as a group or through an elected board of directors. But besides these delegated property rights, the manager, by virtue of his more immediate contact with the participants of production, has to seek a second, and often more important, basis of legitimacy for his authority, namely, some kind of consensus among those who are bound to obey his commands. Typically, this consensus merely takes the form of an absence of dissensus. However, the manager, unlike the "full capitalist," can ill afford to exercise his authority in direct and deliberate contravention to the wishes and interests of his subordinates. The mechanisms by which manual and clerical workers who object to a member of top management can make their interests felt are complex and largely unregulated.[1] But there are such mechanisms, and managers have ways and means to forestall their being brought to bear. In this sense, the "human relations" movement is nothing but a symptom of the changing basis of legitimacy of entrepreneurial authority once ownership and control are separated.

With the differentiation of capitalist roles, the composition of the entrepreneurial class—if it is a class—changes too. This is probably a gradual development, but one that is far advanced in most of the highly industrialized societies today. If we follow Bendix (1956, p. 228) in distinguishing capitalists, heirs, and bureaucrats as three types of entrepreneurs, it is evident that three significantly different patterns of recruitment correspond to these types. The capitalist in this sense is a man who owns and manages an enterprise which he has founded himself. From having been perhaps a skilled craftsman or a shopkeeper at the beginning of his career, he has built up, "from scratch," a sizable firm or factory and one that continues to grow in scope, size, and production. The heir, by contrast, is born into the ownership of an enterprise, and apart from perhaps a few years' experience in some of its departments he has known nothing but the property he has inherited. Both the capitalist and the heir are owner-managers.

For mere managers, however, there are two typical patterns of recruitment, and both of them differ radically from those of capitalists and heirs. One of these patterns is the bureaucratic career. In the early joint-stock companies in particular, executives were often chosen from among the firm's leading employees, both technical and clerical. They had worked their way up from the ranks. More recently, a different pattern has gained increasing importance. Today, a majority of top management officials in industrial enterprises have acquired their positions on the strength of some specialized education, and of university degrees. Lawyers, economists, and engineers often enter management almost immediately after they have completed their education, and gradually rise to the top positions. There can be little doubt that both these patterns of recruitment—but in particular the latter—distinguish managerial groups significantly from those of old-style owner-managers as well as new-style mere owners. Their social background and experience place these groups into different fields of reference, and it seems at least likely that the group of professionally trained managers "increasingly develops its own functionally determined character traits and modes of thought" (Sering, 1947, p. 205). For this is, in our context, the crucial effect of the separation of ownership and control in industry: that it produces two sets of roles the incumbents of which increasingly move apart in their outlook on and attitudes toward society in general and toward the enterprise in particular. Their reference groups differ, and different reference groups make for different values. Among classical capitalists, the "organization man" is an unthinkable absurdity. Yet the manager is "not the individualist but the man who works through others for others" (Whyte, 1957, p. 21). Never has the imputation of a profit motive been further from the real motives of men than it is for modern bureaucratic managers. Economically, managers are interested in such things as rentability, efficiency, and productivity. But all these are indissolubly linked with the imponderables of what has been called the social "climate of the enterprise" (Betriebsklima). The manager shares with the capitalist two important social reference groups: his peers and his subordinates. But his attitude toward these differs considerably from that of the capitalist (as does consequently, the attitude expected from him by his peers). For him, to be successful means to be liked, and to be liked means, in many ways, to be alike. The manager is an involuntary ruler, and his attitudes betray his feelings.

Before concluding this analysis it would perhaps be well to point out briefly what it does not mean or imply. Despite many differences, there are without doubt considerable similarities in the positions, roles, and attitudes of both the capitalist and the manager. Both are entrepreneurial roles, and both are therefore subject to certain expectations which no social context can remove. Moreover, there are numerous personal and social ties between owners and managers in all industrial societies. If anything, the unpropertied managers are more active in political affairs, both as individuals and through their associations and lobbies. Also, while the joint-stock company has conquered the sphere of industrial production (i.e., of secondary industries), it is still of only minor importance in the tertiary industries of trade and commerce and in the services. Thus, the separation of ownership and control is not as fundamental a change as, say, the industrial revolution. But it is a change, and one with very definite, if restricted, implications for class structure and conflict.

There is little reason to follow Marx and describe the condition of separation of ownership and control as a transitional form of historical development. It is no more transitional than any other stage of history, and it has already proven quite a vital pattern of social and economic structure. But I think that we can follow Marx in his radical interpretation of this phenomenon. The separation of ownership and control has replaced one group by two whose positions, roles, and outlooks are far from identical. In taking this view, one does of course agree with Marx against himself. For it follows from this that the homogeneous capitalist class predicted by Marx has in fact not developed. Capital—and thereby capitalism—has dissolved and given way in the economic sphere, to a plurality of partly agreed, partly competing, and partly simply different groups. The effect of this development on class conflict is threefold: first, the replacement of capitalists by managers involves a change in the composition of the groups participating in conflict; second, and as a consequence of this change in recruitment and composition, there is a change in

the nature of the issues that cause conflicts, for the interests of the functionaries without capital differ from those of full-blown capitalists, and so therefore do the interests of labor vis-à-vis their new opponents; and third, the decomposition of capital involves a change in the patterns of conflict. One might question whether this new conflict, in which labor is no longer opposed to a homogeneous capitalist class, can still be described as a class conflict at all. In any case, it is different from the division of the whole society into two great and homogeneous hostile camps with which Marx was concerned. While I would follow the radical view of the separation of ownership and control in industry to this point, there is one thing to be said in favor of the conservative view. Changes in the composition of conflict groups, of the issues, and of patterns of conflict do not imply the abolition of conflict or even of the specific conflict between management and labor in industry. Despite the effects of the decomposition of capital on class structure, we have no reason to believe that antagonisms and clashes of interest have now been banned from industrial enterprises.

Skill and Stratification, or the Decomposition of Labor

While Marx had at least a premonition of things to come with respect to capital, he remained unaware of developments affecting the unity and homogeneity of labor. Yet in this respect, too, the sphere of production which loomed so large in Marx's analyses became the starting point of changes that clearly refute his predictions. The working class of today, far from being a homogeneous group of equally unskilled and impoverished people, is in fact a stratum differentiated by numerous subtle and not-so-subtle distinctions. Here, too, history has dissolved one position, or role, and has substituted for it a plurality of roles that are endowed with diverging and often conflicting expectations.

In trying to derive his prediction of the growing homogeneity of labor from the assumption that the technical development of industry would tend to abolish all differences of skill and qualification, Marx was a genuine child of his century. Only the earliest political economists had believed that the division of labor in manufacturing would make for an "increase of dexterity in every particular workman" (Adam Smith, 1937, p. 7) by allowing him to refine the "skill acquired by frequent repetition of the same process" (Babbage, 1832, p. 134). Already in the following generation, social scientists were quite unanimous in believing that the processes of industrial production "effect a substitution of labor comparatively unskilled, for that which is more skilled" (Ure, 1835, p. 30), and that the division of labor had reached a phase "in which we have seen the skill of the worker decrease at the rate at which industry becomes more perfect" (Proudhon, 1867, p. 153). Marx was only too glad to adopt this view which tallied so well with his general theories of class structure: "The interests and life situations of the proletariat are more and more equalized, since the machinery increasingly obliterates the differences of labor and depresses the wage almost everywhere to an equally low level" (1953, p. 17). "The hierarchy of specialized workmen that characterizes manufacture is replaced, in the automatic factory, by a tendency to equalize and reduce to one and the same level every kind of work that has to be done" (1953, Vol. I, p. 490).

Indeed, so far as we can tell from available evidence, there was, up to the end of the nineteenth century, a tendency for most industrial workers to become unskilled, i.e., to be reduced to the same low level of skill. But since then, two new patterns have emerged which are closely related on the one hand to technical innovations in production, on the other hand to a new philosophy of industrial organization as symbolized by the works of F. W. Taylor (1947) and H. Fayol (1916). First, there emerged, around the turn of the century, a new category of workers which today is usually described as semiskilled. As early as 1905, Max Weber referred to the growing importance of "the semiskilled workers trained directly on the job" (1924, p. 502). By the 1930's, the theory had become almost commonplace that "there is a tendency for all manual laborers to become semiskilled machine minders, and for highly skilled as well as unskilled workers to become relatively less

important" (Carr-Saunders and Jones, 1937, p. 61). The semiskilled differ from the unskilled not so much in the technical qualifications required from them for their work, as in certain less easily defined extrafunctional skills which relate to their capacity to accept responsibility, to adapt to difficult conditions, and to perform a job intelligently. These extrafunctional skills are acquired not by formal training (although many semiskilled workers receive this also), but by experience on the job; yet these "skills of responsibility" constitute a clear line of demarcation between those who have them and the unskilled who lack both training and experience. Apart from the semiskilled, there appeared, more recently, a new and ever-growing demand for highly skilled workers of the engineer type in industry. Carr-Saunders and Jones, in their statement above, still expected the simultaneous reduction of unskilled as well as skilled labor. Today we know—as Friedmann (1953), Geiger (1949), Moore (1947), and others have pointed out—that the second half of this expectation has not come true. Increasingly complex machines require increasingly qualified designers, builders, maintenance and repair men, and even minders, so that Drucker extrapolates only slightly when he says: "Within the working class a new shift from unskilled to skilled labor has begun—reversing the trend of the last fifty years. The unskilled worker is actually an engineering imperfection, as unskilled work, at least in theory, can always be done better, faster and cheaper by machines" (1950, pp. 42–43).

Because of changing classifications, it is a little difficult to document this development statistically. As for the unskilled, a slight decrease in their proportion can be shown for England where, in 1951, they amounted to 12.5 per cent of the occupied male population, as against 16.5 per cent in 1931. In the United States, an even sharper decrease has been noted, from 36 per cent of the labor force in 1910 to just over 28 per cent in 1930 and, further, to less than 20 per cent in 1950 (see Caplow, 1954, p. 299). But statistics are here neither very reliable nor even indispensable evidence. Analysis of industrial conditions suggests quite clearly that within the labor force of advanced industry we have to distinguish at least three skill groups: a growing stratum of highly skilled workmen who increasingly merge with both engineers and white-collar employees, a relatively stable stratum of semiskilled workers with a high degree of diffuse as well as specific industrial experience, and a dwindling stratum of totally unskilled laborers who are characteristically either newcomers to industry (beginners, former agricultural laborers, immigrants) or semi-unemployables. It appears, furthermore, that these three groups differ not only in their level of skill, but also in other attributes and determinants of social status. The semiskilled almost invariably earn a higher wage than the unskilled, whereas the skilled are often salaried and thereby participate in white-collar status. The hierarchy of skill corresponds exactly to the hierarchy of responsibility and delegated authority within the working class. From numerous studies it would seem beyond doubt that it also correlates with the hierarchy of prestige, at the top of which we find the skilled man whose prolonged training, salary, and security convey special status, and at the bottom of which stands the unskilled man who is, according to a recent German investigation into workers' opinions, merely "working" without having an "occupation" proper (see Kluth, 1955, p. 67). Here as elsewhere Marx was evidently mistaken. "Everywhere, the working class differentiates itself more and more, on the one hand into occupational groups, on the other hand into three large categories with different, if not contradictory, interests: the skilled craftsmen, the unskilled laborers, and the semiskilled specialist workers" (Philip, 1955, p. 2).

In trying to assess the consequences of this development, it is well to remember that, for Marx, the increasing uniformity of the working class was an indispensable condition of that intensification of the class struggle which was to lead, eventually, to its climax in a revolution. The underlying argument of what for Marx became a prediction appears quite plausible. For there to be a revolution, the conflicts within a society have to become extremely intense. For conflicts to be intense, one would indeed expect its participants to be highly unified and homogeneous groups. But neither capital nor labor have developed along these lines. Capital has dissolved into at least two, in many ways distinct, elements, and so has labor.

The proletarian, the impoverished slave of industry who is indistinguishable from his peers in terms of his work, his skill, his wage, and his prestige, has left the scene. What is more, it appears that by now he has been followed by his less depraved, but equally alienated successor, the worker. In modern industry, "the worker" has become precisely the kind of abstraction which Marx quite justly resented so much. In his place, we find a plurality of status and skill groups whose interests often diverge. Demands of the skilled for security may injure the semiskilled; wage claims of the semiskilled may raise objections by the skilled; and any interest on the part of the unskilled is bound to set their more highly skilled fellow workmen worrying about differentials.

Again, as in the case of capital, it does not follow from the decomposition of labor that there is no bond left that unites most workers—at least for specific goals; nor does it follow that industrial conflict has lost its edge. But here, too, a change of the issues and, above all, of the patterns of conflict is indicated. As with the capitalist class, it has become doubtful whether speaking of the working class still makes much sense. Probably Marx would have agreed that class "is a force that unites into groups people who differ from one another, by overriding the differences between them" (Marshall, 1950, p. 114), but he certainly did not expect the differences to be so great, and the uniting force so precarious as it has turned out to be in the case both of capital and of labor.

The "New Middle Class"

Along with the decomposition of both capital and labor a new stratum emerged within, as well as outside, the industry of modern societies, which was, so to speak, born decomposed. Since Lederer and Marschak first published their essay on this group, and coined for it the name "new middle class" (*neuer Mittelstand*), so much has been written by sociologists about the origin, development, position, and function of white-collar or black-coated employees that whatever one says is bound to be repetitive. However, only one conclusion is borne out quite clearly by all these studies of salaried employees in industry, trade, commerce, and public administration: that there is no word in any modern language to describe this group that is no group, class that is no class, and stratum that is no stratum. To be sure, there have been attempts to describe it. In fact, we are here in the comparatively fortunate position of having to decide between two or, perhaps, three conflicting theories. But none of these attempts has been free of innumerable qualifications to the effect that it is impossible to generalize. Although the following brief discussion will not distinguish itself in this respect, it could not be avoided in an account of social changes of the past century that have a bearing on the problem of class. ...

According to the first [theory], the "new middle class" constitutes in fact an extension of the old, capitalist or bourgeois, ruling class, and is in this sense part of the ruling class. Croner—who, apart from Renner (1953), Bendix (1956, chap. iv), and others, recently espoused this theory—argues that "the explanation of the special social position of salaried employees can be found in the fact that their work tasks have once been entrepreneurial tasks" (1954, p. 36). This statement is meant by Croner both in a historical and in a structural sense. Historically, most clerical occupations were differentiated out of the leading positions in industry, commerce, and the state. Structurally they are, according to this view, characterized by the exercise of delegated authority—delegated, that is, from the real seat of authority in social organizations, from, in other words, their leading positions. In contrast to this view, Geiger, C. Wright Mills, and others claim that the "new middle class" is, if not exactly an extension of the proletariat, at any rate closer to the working class than to the ruling class, whether capitalist or managerial. "Objectively, ... the structural position of the white-collar mass is becoming more and more similar to that of the wage-workers. Both are, of course, propertyless, and their incomes draw closer and closer together. All the factors of their status position, which have enabled white-collar workers to set themselves apart from wage-workers, are now subject to definite decline" (Mills, 1951, p. 297). Mills does not say so, but he would probably have no quarrel with Geiger's conclusion that "from the point of view of class structure in Marx's sense the salaried employee is un-

doubtedly closer to the worker than to any other figure of modern society" (1949, p. 167).

The two views are clearly in conflict, and it seems desirable to come to a decision as to their relative merits. Fortunate as it is, from a methodological point of view, to have to decide between two conflicting theories, our situation here does not, upon closer inspection, turn out to be quite so simple. In fact, Mills may well be right when he suspects that because of the vastly different "definitions" of the "new middle class" the two theories not only may peacefully co-exist but even both be correct (1951, pp. 291 ff.). Clearly the theory that salaried employees have delegated authority and are therefore part of the ruling class cannot have meant the office boy, the salesgirl, or even the skilled worker who has been granted the status symbol of a salary; equally clearly, the theory that salaried employees resemble the working class does not apply to senior executives, higher civil servants, and professional people. However, there is more than a question of definition involved in this difficulty.

Instead of asking which of two apparently conflicting theories applies to the "new middle class," we can, so to speak, reverse our question and ask whether there is any criterion that would allow us to distinguish between those sectors of the "new middle class" to which one theory applies and those to which the other theory applies. I think that there is such a criterion, and that its application provides at least a preliminary solution to our wider problem of the effects of the growth of a "new middle class" on class structure and class conflict. It seems to me that a fairly clear as well as significant line can be drawn between salaried employees who occupy positions that are part of a bureaucratic hierarchy and salaried employees in positions that are not. The occupations of the post-office clerk, the accountant, and, of course, the senior executive are rungs on a ladder of bureaucratic positions; those of the salesgirl and the craftsman are not. There may be barriers in bureaucratic hierarchies which are insurmountable for people who started in low positions; salaried employees outside such hierarchies may earn more than those within, and they may also change occupations and enter upon a bureaucratic career; but these and similar facts are irrelevant to the distinction between bureaucrats and white-collar workers proposed here. Despite these facts I suggest that the ruling-class theory applies without exception to the social position of bureaucrats, and the working-class theory equally generally to the social position of white-collar workers.

There is, in other words, one section of the "new middle class" the condition of which, from the point of view of class conflict, closely resembles that of industrial workers. This section includes many of the salaried employees in the tertiary industries, in shops and restaurants, in cinemas, and in commercial firms, as well as those highly skilled workers and foremen who have acquired salaried status. It is hard to estimate, from available evidence, the numerical size of this group, but it probably does not at present exceed one-third of the whole "new middle class"—although it may do so in the future, since the introduction of office machinery tends to reduce the number of bureaucrats while increasing the demand for salaried office technicians. Although some white-collar workers earn rather more than industrial workers, and most of them enjoy a somewhat higher prestige, their class situation appears sufficiently similar to that of workers to expect them to act alike. In general, it is among white-collar workers that one would expect trade unions as well as radical political parties to be successful.

The bureaucrats, on the other hand, share, if often in a minor way, the requisites of a ruling class. Although many of them earn less than white-collar and even industrial workers, they participate in the exercise of authority and thereby occupy a position vis-à-vis rather than inside the working class. The otherwise surprising fact that many salaried employees identify themselves with the interests, attitudes, and styles of life of the higher-ups can be accounted for in these terms. For the bureaucrats, the supreme social reality is their career that provides, at least in theory, a direct link between every one of them and the top positions which may be described as the ultimate seat of authority. It would be false to say that the bureaucrats are a ruling class, but in any case they are part of it, and one would there-

fore expect them to act accordingly in industrial, social, and political conflicts.

The decomposition of labor and capital has been the result of social developments that have occurred since Marx, but the "new middle class" was born decomposed. It neither has been nor is it ever likely to be a class in any sense of this term. But while there is no "new middle class," there are, of course, white-collar workers and bureaucrats, and the growth of these groups is one of the striking features of historical development in the past century. What is their effect on class structure and class conflict, if it is not that of adding a new class to the older ones Marx described? It follows from our analysis that the emergence of salaried employees means in the first place an extension of the older classes of bourgeoisie and proletariat. The bureaucrats add to the bourgeoisie, as the white-collar workers add to the proletariat. Both classes have become, by these extensions, even more complex and heterogeneous than their decomposition has made them in any case. By gaining new elements, their unity has become a highly doubtful and precarious feature. White-collar workers, like industrial workers, have neither property nor authority, yet they display many social characteristics that are quite unlike those of the old working class. Similarly, bureaucrats differ from the older ruling class despite their share in the exercise of authority. Even more than the decomposition of capital and labor, these facts make it highly doubtful whether the concept of class is still applicable to the conflict groups of post-capitalist societies. In any case, the participants, issues, and patterns of conflict have changed, and the pleasing simplicity of Marx's view of society has become a nonsensical construction. If ever there have been two large, homogeneous, polarized, and identically situated social classes, these have certainly ceased to exist today, so that an unmodified Marxian theory is bound to fail in explaining the structure and conflicts of advanced industrial societies. ...

The Institutionalization of Class Conflict

A historian might argue that all the tendencies of change here described as changes in the structure of industrial societies since Marx had in fact begun before and in some cases long before Marx died in 1883. ... There is, however, one line of social development in industrial societies which has both originated and spread since about the time of Marx's death, and which is directly relevant to our problem. Geiger, who has described this change as the "institutionalization of class conflict," says: "The tension between capital and labor is recognized as a principle of the structure of the labor market and has become a legal institution of society. ... The methods, weapons, and techniques of the class struggle are recognized—and are thereby brought under control. The struggle evolves according to certain rules of the game. Thereby the class struggle has lost its worst sting, it is converted into a legitimate tension between power factors which balance each other. Capital and labor struggle with each other, conclude compromises, negotiate solutions, and thereby determine wage levels, hours of work, and other conditions of work" (1949, p. 184).

Marx displayed a certain sociological naïveté when he expressed his belief that capitalist society would be entirely unable to cope with the class conflict generated by its structure. In fact, every society is capable of coping with whatever new phenomena arise in it, if only by the simple yet effective inertia which can be described, a little pretentiously, as the process of institutionalization. In the case of class conflict, institutionalization assumed a number of successive and complementary forms. It began with the painful process of recognition of the contending parties as legitimate interest groups. Within industry, a "secondary system of industrial citizenship" (Marshall, 1950, p. 68) enabled both workers and entrepreneurs to associate and defend their interests collectively. Outside industry, the primary system of political citizenship had the same effect. And while, in the stage of organization, conflict may develop a greater visible intensity, organization has at least two side effects which operate in the opposite direction. Organization presupposes the legitimacy of conflict groups, and it thereby removes the permanent and incalculable threat of guerrilla warfare. At the same time, it makes systematic regulations of conflicts possible. Organization is institutionalization, and whereas its manifest function is usually an increasingly articulate and outspoken defense of interests, it invariably has the latent function also of inaugurating routines of conflict which contribute to reducing the violence of clashes of interest. ...

Nobody can, of course, ever be sure that a given pattern of conflict regulation will always prove successful. There are still strikes, and for all we know they will continue to occur. But it has proved possible for industrial society to get along with the clashes of interest arising from its industrial and political structure—and it has proved possible for interest groups to get along with industrial society. Instead of a battlefield, the scene of group conflict has become a kind of market in which relatively autonomous forces contend according to certain rules of the game, by virtue of which nobody is a permanent winner or loser. This course of development must naturally be bitter for the orthodox and the dogmatic, but theirs is the kind of bitterness which makes liberal minds rejoice. ...

Power and Authority

From the point of view of the integration theory of social structure, units of social analysis ("social systems") are essentially voluntary associations of people who share certain values and set up institutions in order to ensure the smooth functioning of cooperation. From the point of view of coercion theory, however, the units of social analysis present an altogether different picture. Here, it is not voluntary cooperation or general consensus but enforced constraint that makes social organizations cohere. In institutional terms, this means that in every social organization some positions are entrusted with a right to exercise control over other positions in order to ensure effective coercion; it means, in other words, that there is a differential distribution of power and authority. One of the central theses of this study consists in the assumption that this differential distribution of authority invariably becomes the determining factor of systematic social conflicts of a type that is germane to class conflicts in the traditional (Marxian) sense of this term. The structural origin of such group conflicts must be sought in the arrangement of social roles endowed with expectations of domination or subjection. Wherever there are such roles, group conflicts of the type in question are to be expected. Differentiation of groups engaged in such conflicts follows the lines of differentiation of roles that are relevant from the point of view of the exercise of authority. Identification of variously equipped authority roles is the first task of conflict analysis;[2] conceptually and empirically all further steps of analysis follow from the investigation of distributions of power and authority.

"Unfortunately, the concept of power is not a settled one in the social sciences, either in political science or in sociology" (Parsons, 1957, p. 139). Max Weber (1947), Pareto (1955), Mosca (1950), later Russell (1938), Bendix (1952), Lasswell (1936), and others have explored some of the dimensions of this category; they have not, however, reached such a degree of consensus as would enable us to employ the categories of power and authority without at least brief conceptual preliminaries. So far as the terms "power" and "authority" and their distinction are concerned, I shall follow in this study the useful and well-considered definitions of Max Weber. For Weber, power is the "probability that one actor within a social relationship will be in a position to carry out his own will despite resistance, regardless of the basis on which this probability rests"; whereas authority (*Herrschaft*) is the "probability that a command with a given specific content will be obeyed by a given group of persons" (1947, p. 28). The important difference between power and authority consists in the fact that whereas power is essentially tied to the personality of individuals, authority is always associated with social positions or roles. The demagogue has power over the masses to whom he speaks or whose actions he controls; but the control of the officer over his men, the manager over his workers, the civil servant over his clientele is authority, because it exists as an expectation independent of the specific person occupying the position of officer, manager, civil servant. It is only another way of putting this difference if we say—as does Max Weber—that while power is merely a factual relation, authority is a legitimate relation of domination and subjection. In this

sense, authority can be described as legitimate power.

In the present study we are concerned exclusively with relations of authority, for these alone are part of social structure and therefore permit the systematic derivation of group conflicts from the organization of total societies and associations within them. The significance of such group conflicts rests with the fact that they are not the product of structurally fortuitous relations of power but come forth wherever authority is exercised— and that means in all societies under all historical conditions. (1) Authority relations are always relations of super- and subordination. (2) Where there are authority relations, the superordinate element is socially expected to control, by orders and commands, warnings and prohibitions, the behavior of the subordinate element. (3) Such expectations attach to relatively permanent social positions rather than to the character of individuals; they are in this sense legitimate. (4) By virtue of this fact, they always involve specification of the persons subject to control and of the spheres within which control is permissible. Authority, as distinct from power, is never a relation of generalized control over others. (5) Authority being a legitimate relation, noncompliance with authoritative commands can be sanctioned; it is indeed one of the functions of the legal system (and of course of quasi-legal customs and norms) to support the effective exercise of legitimate authority.

Alongside the term "authority," we shall employ in this study the terms "domination" and "subjection." These will be used synonymously with the rather clumsy expressions "endowed with authority" or "participating in the exercise of authority" (domination), and "deprived of authority" or "excluded from the exercise of authority" (subjection).

It seems desirable for purposes of conflict analysis to specify the relevant unit of social organization in analogy to the concept of social system in the analysis of integration. To speak of specification here is perhaps misleading. "Social system" is a very general concept applicable to all types of organization; and we shall want to employ an equally general concept which differs from that of social system by emphasizing a different aspect of the same organizations. It seems to me that Max

Weber's category "imperatively coordinated association" (*Herrschaftsverband*) serves this purpose despite its clumsiness. …

Empirically it is not always easy to identify the border line between domination and subjection. Authority has not remained unaffected by the modern process of division of labor. But even here, groups or aggregates can be identified which do not participate in the exercise of authority other than by complying with given commands or prohibitions. Contrary to all criteria of social stratification, authority does not permit the construction of a scale. So-called hierarchies of authority (as displayed, for example, in organization charts) are in fact hierarchies of the "plus-side" of authority, i.e., of the differentiation of domination; but there is, in every association, also a "minus-side" consisting of those who are subjected to authority rather than participate in its exercise.

In two respects this analysis has to be specified, if not supplemented. First, for the individual incumbent of roles, domination in one association does not necessarily involve domination in all others to which he belongs, and subjection, conversely, in one association does not mean subjection in all. The dichotomy of positions of authority holds for specific associations only. In a democratic state, there are both mere voters and incumbents of positions of authority such as cabinet ministers, representatives, and higher civil servants. But this does not mean that the "mere voter" cannot be incumbent of a position of authority in a different context, say, in an industrial enterprise; conversely, a cabinet minister may be, in his church, a mere member, i.e., subject to the authority of others. Although empirically a certain correlation of the authority positions of individuals in different associations seems likely, it is by no means general and is in any case a matter of specific empirical conditions. It is at least possible, if not probable, that if individuals in a given society are ranked according to the sum total of their authority positions in all associations, the resulting pattern will not be a dichotomy but rather like scales of stratification according to income or prestige. For this reason it is necessary to emphasize that in the sociological analysis of group conflict the unit of analysis is always a specific association and the dichotomy of positions within it.

As with respect to the set of roles associated with an individual, total societies, also, do not usually present an unambiguously dichotomic authority structure. There are a large number of imperatively coordinated associations in any given society. Within every one of them we can distinguish the aggregates of those who dominate and those who are subjected. But since domination in industry does not necessarily involve domination in the state, or a church, or other associations, total societies can present the picture of a plurality of competing dominant (and, conversely, subjected) aggregates. This, again, is a problem for the analysis of specific historical societies and must not be confounded with the clearer lines of differentiation within any one association. Within the latter, the distribution of authority always sums up to zero, i.e., there always is a division involving domination and subjection.

I need hardly emphasize that from the point of view of "settling" the concepts of power and authority, the preceding discussion has raised more problems than it has solved. I believe, however, that for the purposes of this study, and of a sociological theory of conflict, little needs to be added to what has been stated here. In order somewhat to substantiate this perhaps rather bold assertion, it seems useful to recapitulate briefly the heuristic purpose and logical status of the considerations of this section.

I have introduced, as a structural determinant of conflict groups, the category of authority as exercised in imperatively coordinated associations. While agreeing with Marx that source and level of income—even socioeconomic status—cannot usefully be conceived as determinants of conflict groups, I have added to this list of erroneous approaches Marx's own in terms of property in the means of production. Authority is both a more general and a more significant social relation. The former has been shown in our critique of Marx; the latter will have to be demonstrated [elsewhere (see Dahrendorf 1959)]. The concept of authority is used, in this context, in a specific sense. It is differentiated from power by what may roughly be referred to as the element of legitimacy; and it has to be understood throughout in the restricted sense of authority as distributed and exercised in imperatively coordinated associations. While its "disruptive" or conflict-generating consequences are not the only aspect of authority, they are the one relevant in terms of the coercion model of society. Within the frame of reference of this model, (1) the distribution of authority in associations is the ultimate "cause" of the formation of conflict groups, and (2) being dichotomous, it is, in any given association, the cause of the formation of two, and only two, conflict groups.

Notes

1. They extend from direct pressure aimed at forcing the manager to resign or change his attitudes to indirect means of disturbing the operation of the enterprise which may result in the manager's being reprimanded or deposed by the directors, who, in this case, act in a sense on behalf of the employees.

2. To facilitate communication, I shall employ in this study a number of abbreviations. These must not however be misunderstood. Thus, "conflict analysis" in this context stands for "analysis of group conflicts of the class type, class being understood in the traditional sense." At no point do I want to imply a claim for a generalized theory of social conflict.

Bibliography

Charles Babbage. 1832. *On the Economy of Machinery and Manufactures*. London.

Reinhard Bendix. 1952. "Bureaucracy and the Problem of Power." *Reader in Bureaucracy*. Edited by R.K. Merton, A.P. Gray, B. Hockey, and H.C. Selvin. Glencoe.

Reinhard Bendix. 1956. *Work and Authority in Industry: Ideologies of Management in the Course of Industrialization*. New York and London.

Theodore Caplow. 1954. *The Sociology of Work*. Minneapolis.

A.M. Carr-Saunders and D.C. Jones. 1937. *A Survey of the Social Structure of England and Wales*. 2d ed. Oxford.

Fritz Croner. 1954. *Die Angestellten in der modernen Gesellschaft*. Frankfurt.

Ralf Dahrendorf. 1959. *Class and Class Conflict in Industrial Society*. Stanford.

P.F. Drucker. 1950. *The New Society: The Anatomy of the Industrial Order*. New York.

Henri Fayol. 1916. *Administration industrielle et générale*. Paris.

Georges Friedmann. 1953. *Zukunft der Arbeit*. Cologne.

Theodor Geiger. 1949. *Die Klassengesellschaft im Schmelztiegel*. Cologne and Hagen.

Heinz B. Kluth. 1955. "Arbeiterjugend—Begriff und Wirklichkeit," in Helmut Schelsky, ed., *Arbeiterjugend—gestern und heute*. Heidelberg.

Harold Lasswell. 1936. *Politics—Who Gets What, When, and How?* New York.

T.H. Marshall. 1950. *Citizenship and Social Class*. Cambridge.

Karl Marx. 1953. *Das Kapital*. Vols. I, III. New ed. Berlin.

Karl Marx. 1953. *Manifest der kommunistischen Partei*. New ed. Berlin.

C.W. Mills. 1951. *White Collar: The American Middle Classes*. New York.

C.W. Mills. 1954. *The New Men of Power*. New York.

C.W. Mills. 1956. *The Power Elite*. New York.

W.E. Moore. 1947. *Industrial Relations and the Social Order*. New York.

Gaetano Mosca. 1950. *Die herrschende Klasse*. Bern.

Vilfredo Pareto. 1955. *Allgemeine Soziologie*. Translated and edited by C. Brinkmann. Tübingen.

Talcott Parsons. 1957. "The Distribution of Power in American Society," *World Politics* X, No. 1, October.

André Philip. 1955. *La démocratie industrielle*. Paris.

P.J. Proudhon. 1867. *Système des contradictions économiques, ou Philosopie de la misère*. 3d ed. Paris.

Karl Renner. 1953. *Wandlungen der modernen Gesellschaft: zwei Abhandlungen über die Probleme der Nachkriegszeit*. Vienna.

Bertrand Russell. 1938. *Power: A New Social Analysis*. London.

Paul Sering. 1947. *Jenseits des Kapitalismus*. Nürnberg.

Adam Smith. 1937. *An Inquiry into the Nature and Causes of the Wealth of Nations*. New ed. New York.

F.W. Taylor. 1947. "The Principles of Scientific Management," in *Scientific Management*. New York and London.

Andrew Ure. 1835. *The Philosophy of Manufacturers*.

Max Weber. 1924. "Der Sozialismus," in *Gesammelte Aufsätze zur Soziologie und Sozialpolitik*. Tübingen.

Max Weber. 1947. *Wirtschaft und Gesellschaft* (Grundriss der Sozialökonomik, section III). 4th ed. Tübingen.

W.H. Whyte. 1957. *The Organization Man*. New York.

ERIK OLIN WRIGHT

Varieties of Marxist Conceptions of Class Structure

The general outlines of the theory of contradictory locations within class relations were first presented in an essay in the *New Left Review* in 1976 and later elaborated in a series of other publications.[1] The basic argument revolves around an analysis of three interconnected dimensions of domination and subordination within production. Each of these dimensions involves a social relation of domination and subordination with respect to some particular resource within production: *money capital,* that is, the flow of investments into production and the direction of the over-all accumulation process (accumulation of surplus value); *physical capital,* that is, the actual means of production within the production process; and *labor,* that is, the laboring activity of the direct producers within production. These relations can be characterized as relations of domination and subordination because each relation simultaneously defines those positions that have the capacity to control the particular resource and those that are excluded from such control. The first of these dimensions is often referred to as "real economic ownership"; the second and third together are often referred to as "possession."

In no sense should these three *dimensions* be thought of as three independent *types* of relations. Within capitalist production they are each necessary conditions for the existence of the others; there is no sense in which they can exist autonomously. Nevertheless, while these three dimensions of social relations are intrinsically interdependent, there is still a clear hierarchy of determination among them. The social relations

of control over money capital structure, or set limits upon, the relations of control over physical capital, which in turn limit the direct control over labor within production. A rentier capitalist, therefore, who is not directly involved in control over physical capital or labor, nevertheless falls within the capitalist class because of the social relations of control over money capital ("real economic ownership" of the means of production).

The fundamental class relation between labor and capital can be thought of as a polarized, antagonistic relation along all three of these dimensions: The capitalist class occupies the dominant position with respect to the social relations of control over money capital, physical capital, and labor; the working class occupies the subordinate position within each of these dimensions of social relations.

When the class structure is analyzed at the highest level of abstraction—the level of the "pure" capitalist mode of production—these are the only two classes defined by these three dimensions of relations of production. When we move to a lower level of abstraction—the level of what Marxists call the "social formation"—other classes enter the analysis. This occurs for two basic reasons. First, concrete capitalist social formations are never characterized simply by the capitalist mode of production. Various kinds of precapitalist relations of production exist side by side with capitalist relations, although typically these are of marginal importance and are socially subordinated in various ways to the capitalist mode of production. Of particular importance in these terms is simple commodity production: the production and sale of goods by self-employed individuals who employ no workers. In terms of the three dimensions of social relations of production discussed above, such "petty bourgeois" class locations involve control over money capital and physical capital but not over labor (since no labor power is employed within production).

The second way in which additional class locations appear when we study class structures within concrete capitalist societies is that the three dimensions of social relations of production need not necessarily coincide perfectly—indeed, there are systemic forces in capitalist development working against their doing so. Such noncorrespondence generates what I have termed "contradictory locations within class relations." Three such contradictory locations are particularly important.

Managers and supervisors occupy a contradictory location between the working class and the capitalist class. Like the working class they are excluded from control over money capital (that is, from basic decisions about allocation of investments and the direction of accumulation), but unlike workers they have a certain degree of control of the physical means of production and over the labor of workers within production. Within the manager-supervisor contradictory location, top managers occupy the position closest to the capitalist class, whereas foremen occupy the location closest to the working class.

Small employers occupy a contradictory location between the petty bourgeoisie and the capitalist class proper. Unlike the petty bourgeoisie, they do employ some labor power and thus are in a relation of exploitation with workers. But unlike the capitalist class, they are themselves directly engaged in production alongside their workers, and they do not employ sufficient quantities of labor power to accumulate large masses of capital.

Semiautonomous employees occupy a contradictory location between the petty bourgeoisie and the working class. Like the working class, they are excluded from any control over money capital and the labor of others, but like the petty bourgeoisie they do have some real control over their immediate physical means of production, over their direct activity within the labor process.

These three contradictory locations are schematically represented in the accompanying figure and in a more formal way in table 1.

It should be noted that in table 1 there is more than one position (or "level") within each of the three dimensions of social relations of production. Take, for example, the social relations of control over physical capital, one of the two aspects of "possession" of the means of production. "Full" control in this instance implies that the position is involved in decisions concerning the operation and planning of the entire production process; "partial" control implies participation in decisions concerning specific segments of the production process; "minimal" control implies control over one's immediate means of production within the labor process; "no" control implies complete exclusion from decisions concerning the operation of the means of production. Each of these "levels" of control must be understood in terms of the social relations with other levels; they are not simply points on a scale. Taken together, they make it possible to identify more precisely specific positions within each contradictory location.

It is important to understand the precise sense in which these class locations are "contradictory" locations within class relations. They are not contradictory simply because they cannot be neatly pigeonholed in any of the basic classes. The issue is not one of typological aesthetics. Rather they are contradictory locations because they simultaneously share the relational characteristics of two distinct classes. As a result, they share class interests with two different classes but have interests identical to neither. It is in this sense that they can be viewed as being objectively torn between class locations.

The schema represented in the figure and table 1 is not without its difficulties. While it does provide a fairly comprehensive way of locating positions within the social relations of production, there is a degree of arbitrariness involved in trying to define precisely the boundaries of each of these contradictory locations. On the one hand, at a certain point, supervisors become mere conduits for information from above and lose any capacity for actually controlling the labor of subor-

The basic class relations of capitalist society

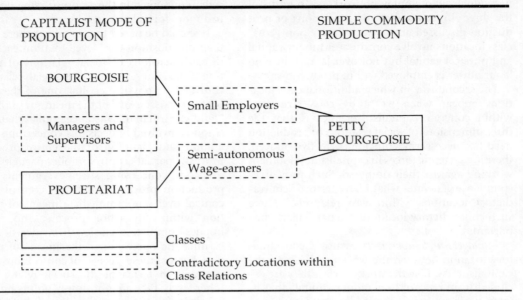

dinates. Such nominal supervisors should be considered part of the working class. As top managers shade into top executives, on the other hand, and begin to participate in the control of basic investment decisions, then they should be placed within the bourgeoisie proper. Similar problems are encountered in defining the "boundaries" of the semiautonomous-employee location and the small-employer category.

Furthermore, in the case of semiautonomous employees there is a real ambiguity in the very content of the "autonomy" that defines the contradictory class location. Does the possession of specialized skills or knowledge constitute control over the immediate labor process? Does one have to have some control over *what* is produced as well as *how* it is produced? Is the issue autonomy vis-à-vis supervisors per se, or is it autonomy with respect to concrete tasks?

Finally, the schema as represented above only includes positions directly engaged in production. Positions located outside immediate capitalist production—state employees, housewives, pensioners, students, and so forth—are not directly defined by the criteria. Are these positions in some sense "outside" the class structure, or are

they situated within class relations through social relations other than production relations? Elsewhere I have offered a provisional solution to this problem.[2]

These and other issues are still in the process of resolution. It may well be that in the course of adequately solving these problems, the basic schema itself will undergo substantial modification. It is precisely through such a process of "theoretical practice," to use the Althusserian expression, that concepts are transformed.

Notes

1. The initial formulation was in Erik Olin Wright, "Class Boundaries in Advanced Capitalist Societies," *New Left Review,* no. 98 (1976), pp. 3–41. This essay was then revised as chap. 2 in *Class, Crisis and the State* (London: New Left Books, 1978). Other discussions of contradictory locations include: idem, "Intellectuals and the Working Class," *The Insurgent Sociologist,* Summer 1978; idem, *Class Structure and Income Determination* (New York: Academic Press, 1979); and idem, "Class, Occupation and Organization," *International Yearbook of Organizational Theory,* vol. 1, ed. David Dunkerley and Graham Saleman (London: Routledge

TABLE 1
Formal Criteria for Contradictory Locations Within Class Relations

| | | Dimensions of Social Relations of Production[a] | | |
| | | Relations of Economic Ownership | Relations of Possession | |
Class Positions		Control over Money Capital	Control over Physical Capital	Control over Labor
Bourgeoisie	Traditional capitalist	+	+	+
	Top corporate executive	+	+	+
Contradictory class location between the bourgeoisie and the proletariat	Top managers	Partial/minimal	+	+
	Middle managers	Minimal/−	Partial	Partial
	Technocrats	−	Minimal	Minimal
	Foremen/supervisors	−	−	Minimal
Proletariat		−	−	−
Contradictory class location between the proletariat and the petty bourgeoisie	Semiautonomous employees	−	Minimal	−
Petty Bourgeoisie		+	+	−
Contradictory class location between the petty bourgeoisie and the bourgeoisie	Small employers	+	+	Minimal

NOTE: + = Full control; − = no control

[a]Levels of control within each dimension of production relations may be defined, schematically, as follows:

| | Relations of Economic Ownership | Relations of Possession | |
		Control of Means of Production	Control of Labor
Full control	Control over the overall investment and accumulation process	Control over the entire apparatus of production	Control over the entire supervisory hierarchy
Partial control	Participation in decisions concerning either subunits of the total production process or partial aspects of the entire investment process	Control over one segment of the total production process	Control over one segment of the supervisory hierarchy
Minimal control	Participation in decisions concerning narrow aspects of subunits of production	Control over one's immediate instruments of production; some autonomy in the immediate labor process	Control over the direct producers, over immediate subordinates, but not part of the hierarchy as such
No control	Complete exclusion from participation in investment and accumulation decisions	Negligible control over any aspect of the means of production	No ability to invoke sanctions on other workers

and Kegan Paul, 1979). For some critical remarks on the analysis of contradictory locations, see Edward S. Greenberg and Thomas F. Mayer, "Review of *Class, Crisis and the State*," *Kapitalistate*, no. 7 (1979), pp. 167–86; and Barbara Ehrenreich and John Ehrenreich, "Rejoin-

der," in *Between Capital and Labor*, ed. Pat Walker (Boston: South End Press, 1979), esp. pp. 325, 331–32.

2. See *Class, Crisis and the State*, chap. 2; and idem, "Intellectuals and the Working Class," *The Insurgent Sociologist*, Summer 1978.

ERIK OLIN WRIGHT

A General Framework for the Analysis of Class Structure

The Point of Departure: Neo-Marxist Analyses of Class Structure

At the heart of the recent resurgence of Marxist theorizing on the problem of class has been what might be termed the "embarrassment" of the middle class. For all of their disagreements, all Marxists share a basic commitment to a polarized abstract concept of class relations. Yet, at least at first glance, the concrete class structures of contemporary advanced capitalist societies look anything but polarized. This empirical evidence of a large middle class has provided critics of Marxism with one of their principal arguments against Marxist class theory. In response, a variety of solutions to the problem of the middle class have been proposed in the recent Marxist debates.

Without going into any detail, it is possible to identify four broadly different strategies that Marxists have adopted to deal with the conceptual problem of nonpolarized class positions within a logic of polarized class relations.[1] First, the class structure of advanced capitalist societies really *is* polarized; the "middle class" is strictly an ideological illusion. This position deals with the problem of the middle class by denying the problem itself. Second, the middle class should be viewed as a *segment* of some other class, typically a "new petty bourgeoisie" or "new working

class."[2] In this strategy the basic class map of capitalism remains intact, but significant internal differentiations within classes are added to the analysis of class structure. Third, the middle class is really a new class in its own right, completely distinct from either the bourgeoisie, the proletariat, or the petty bourgeoisie. Sometimes this class is given a specific name, such as the Professional Managerial Class,[3] sometimes it is simply called "the New Class."[4] By adding entirely new classes to the class structure, this approach more radically alters the class map of capitalism than the class-segment strategy. Fourth, the positions aggregated under the popular rubric "middle class" are not really in *a* class at all. Rather they should be viewed as locations that are simultaneously in more than one class, positions that I have characterized as "contradictory locations within class relations."[5] Managers, for example, should be viewed as simultaneously in the working class (in so far as they are wage laborers dominated by capitalists) and in the capitalist class (in so far as they control the operation of production and the labor of workers). This strategy departs most from the traditional Marxist vision of class structure since the very meaning of a "location" is altered: there is no longer a one-to-one correspondence between structural locations filled by individuals and classes.

I no longer feel that this fourth solution is satisfactory. Specifically, it suffers from two important problems that it shares with most other neo-Marxist conceptualizations of class structure: it tends to shift the analysis of class relations from exploitation to domination; and it implicitly regards socialism—a society within which the working class is the "ruling class"—as the only possible alternative to capitalism.

Domination Versus Exploitation

Throughout the development of the concept of contradictory class locations I have insisted that this was a reformulation of a distinctively Marxist class concept. As part of the rhetoric of such an enterprise, I affirmed the relationship between class and exploitation. Nevertheless, in practice the concept of contradictory locations within class relations rested almost exclusively on relations of *domination* rather than exploitation. Reference to exploitation functioned more as a background concept to the discussion of classes than as a constitutive element of the analysis of class structures. Managers, for example, were basically defined as a contradictory location because they were simultaneously dominators and dominated. Domination relations were also decisive in defining the class character of "semiautonomous employees"—locations that, I argued, were simultaneously petty bourgeois and proletarian by virtue of their self-direction within the labor process—since "autonomy" defines a condition with respect to domination. This same tendency of substituting domination for exploitation at the core of the concept of class is found in most other neo-Marxist conceptualizations of class structure.

For some people, of course, marginalizing the concept of exploitation is a virtue, not a sin. My own view, however, is that this is a serious weakness. The marginalization of exploitation both undermines claims that classes have "objective" interests and erodes the centrality Marxists have accorded class in social theory.

The concept of domination does not in and of itself imply any specific interest of actors. Parents dominate small children, but this does not imply that they have intrinsically opposed interests to their children. What would make those interests

antagonistic is if the relation of parents to children were exploitative as well. Exploitation, unlike domination, intrinsically implies a set of opposing material interests. If we wish to retain some sense in which the interests of individuals as members of classes are not simply whatever interests those individuals subjectively hold, then the shift to a domination-centered concept renders this more difficult.

Domination-centered concepts of class also tend to slide into what can be termed "the multiple oppressions" approach to understanding society. Societies, in this view, are characterized by a plurality of oppressions each rooted in a different form of domination—sexual, racial, national, economic—none of which has any explanatory priority over any other. Class, then, becomes just one of many oppressions, with no particular centrality for social and historical analysis. How important class is in a given society becomes an historically contingent question.

Again, this displacement of class from the center stage may be viewed as an achievement rather than a problem. It may be that class should not occupy a privileged place in social theory. But if one believes, as Marxists traditionally have believed, that only by giving class this central place is it possible to develop a scientific theory of the trajectory of historical development, and in particular, a theory of the real historical alternatives to capitalism, then the domination-centered concept of class risks eroding the theoretical justification for Marxian class analysis itself.

Classes in Postcapitalist Societies

Classical Marxism was absolutely unequivocal about the historical prognosis for capitalism: socialism—and ultimately communism—was the future of capitalist societies. The bearer of that necessary future was the working class. The polarized class structure *within* capitalism between the bourgeoisie and the proletariat thus paralleled the polarized historical alternatives *between* capitalism and socialism.

The actual historical experience of the twentieth century has called into question, although not unambiguously refuted, this historical vision. As I have argued elsewhere, it is necessary to at least entertain the possibility of postcapitalist class structures.[6] The difficulty is that with very few exceptions, the conceptual frameworks adopted by Marxists for analyzing capitalist class relations do not contain adequate criteria for understanding postcapitalist classes.[7] In particular, all of the class categories in my analysis of contradictory locations within class relations were either situated firmly within capitalist relations (bourgeoisie, managers, workers) or in contradictory locations involving basically precapitalist relations (semi-autonomous employees, the petty bourgeoisie, small employers). There were no elements within this analysis of class relations in capitalist society that could point the direction for the analysis of postcapitalist classes. The result is a tendency for discussions of postcapitalist class structures—the class structures of "actually existing socialism"—to have a very ad hoc character to them.

Given these conceptual problems—the shift from exploitation to domination and the lack of a conceptual basis for analyzing postcapitalist classes—there are really two theoretical alternatives that could be pursued. One possibility is to celebrate the shift to a domination-centered concept and use this new class concept as the basis for analyzing both capitalist and postcapitalist society. This would lead class analysis firmly in the direction of Dahrendorf's analysis of classes as positions within authority relations.[8] A second alternative is to attempt to restore exploitation as the center of class analysis in such a way that it can both accommodate the empirical complexities of the middle class within capitalism and the historical reality of postcapitalist class structures. It is this second course of action that I will pursue in the rest of this paper.

The basis for this reconstruction of an exploitation-centered concept of class comes from the recent work of John Roemer.[9] While Roemer himself has not been particularly concerned with problems of empirical investigation or the elaboration of concrete maps of class structures, nevertheless his work does provide a rich foundation for such endeavors. As I will attempt to show, with suitable modification and extension, his strategy of analysis can provide a rigorous basis

for resolving the problems in the concept of contradictory class locations.

Roemer's Account of Class and Exploitation

The Concept of Exploitation

We observe inequalities in the distribution of incomes, the real consumption packages available to individuals, families, groups. The concept of exploitation is a particular way of analyzing such inequalities. To describe an inequality as reflecting exploitation is to make the claim that there exists a particular kind of causal relationship between the incomes of different actors. More concretely, we will say that the rich exploit the poor when two things can be established: that the welfare of the rich causally depends on the deprivations of the poor—the rich are rich *because* the poor are poor; and that the welfare of the rich depends upon the *effort* of the poor—the rich, through one mechanism or another, appropriate part of the fruits of labor of the poor. The first of these criteria by itself defines *economic oppression*, but not exploitation. Unemployed workers, in these terms, are economically oppressed but not exploited. Exploitation implies both economic oppression and appropriation of at least part of the social surplus by the oppressor.

The traditional Marxist concept of exploitation is clearly a special case of this general concept. In Marxian exploitation one class appropriates the surplus labor performed by another class through various mechanisms. The income of the exploiting class comes from the labor performed by the exploited class. There is thus a straightforward causal linkage between the poverty and effort of the exploited and the affluence of the exploiter. The latter benefits at the expense of the former.

Roemer has attempted to elaborate this view of exploitation using two strategies. The first of these involves studying through a series of formal mathematical models the flows of "surplus labor" from one category of actors to another in the course of various exchange relations; the second involves adopting a kind of game-theory approach to specifying different forms of exploitation. Let us briefly examine each of these in turn.

The Labor-Transfer Approach

The analysis of labor transfers is an extension of the traditional Marxist view of exploitation, although Roemer self-consciously does not rely on the labor theory of value in order to explore such labor transfers. The main target of his analysis is the view, commonly held by Marxists, that a necessary condition for the exploitation of labor in a market economy is the institution of wage labor. Roemer demonstrates two basic propositions. First, Roemer demonstrates that exploitation can occur in an economy in which all producers own their own means of production and in which there is no market in labor power and no credit market (that is, no borrowing). The only things that are traded are products. In such an economy if different producers own different amounts of productive assets such that different producers have to work different numbers of hours to produce the exchange-equivalent of their own subsistence, then free trade among these producers will lead to exploitation of the asset poor by the asset rich. What Roemer shows in this simple economy is not simply that some producers work less than others for the same subsistence, but that the workers who work less are able to do so *because* the less-endowed producers have to work more. The critical proof in this example is that if the asset-poor person simply stopped producing—died—and the asset-rich person took over the asset-poor's assets, then the asset-rich producer would have to work longer hours than before to maintain the same subsistence. There is thus not merely an inequality among the producers in this economy, but exploitation as well.

Second, Roemer demonstrates that there is complete symmetry in the structure of exploitation in a system in which capital hires wage laborers and in a system in which workers rent capital (that is, systems with credit and labor markets). For this analysis, he compares the class structures and patterns of exploitation on the two imaginary islands, "labor-market island" and "credit-market island." On both islands some people own no means of production and other people own vary-

ing amounts of the means of production. The distribution of these assets is identical on the two islands. And on both islands people have the same motivations: they all seek to minimize the amount of labor-time they must expend to achieve a common level of subsistence. The two islands differ in only one respect: on the labor-market island people are allowed to sell their labor power, whereas on the credit-market island people are prohibited from selling their labor power but are allowed to borrow, at some interest rate, the means of production. Roemer shows that on each island there is a strict correspondence between class location (derived from ownership of differing amounts of means of production, including no means of production) and exploitation status (having one's surplus labor appropriated by someone else). This is what he terms the "Class-Exploitation Correspondence Principle." He also shows that the two class structures are completely isomorphic: every individual on one island would be in exactly the same exploitation status on the other island.

The upshot of these two propositions (and others that Roemer explores) is the claim that market-based exploitation is strictly a consequence of inequalities in the distribution of the means of production. However, while this may typically play itself out through a labor market, this is only one concrete institutional form for such exploitation: it is not the necessary condition for the exploitation to occur.

The Game-Theory Approach

While the labor-transfer analyses of exploitation were primarily designed to reveal the underlying logic of exploitation in market exchanges, the game-theory approach is used by Roemer to compare different systems of exploitation. The idea is to compare different systems of exploitation by treating the organization of production as a "game" and asking if a coalition of players would be better off if they withdrew from the game under certain specified procedures. Different types of exploitation are defined by the withdrawal rules that would make certain agents better off.

More formally, Roemer argues that a coalition of actors S can be said to be exploited, and another coalition S' (the complement of S) can be said to be exploiting, if "there is no alternative, which we may conceive of as hypothetically feasible, in which S would be better off than in its present situation, [and if,] under this alternative, the complement to S ... would be worse off than at present."[10] The counterfactual in these two conditions is meant to convey the sense in which the welfare of S' is causally dependent upon the deprivation of S.

Roemer uses this strategy to define three kinds of exploitation: feudal exploitation, capitalist exploitation, and what he refers to as socialist exploitation. Let's begin with capitalist exploitation. Workers own no physical assets (means of production) and sell their labor power to capitalists for a wage. Are workers exploited under capitalism? The answer to this question, in the game theoretic formulation, requires posing an alternative game to the game of capitalism within which the two conditions specified above hold. What is the alternative? It is a game within which each worker receives his/her *per capita share of society's total productive assets*. What Roemer demonstrates is that if the coalition of all wage-earners were to leave the game of capitalism with their per capita share of society's assets, then they would be better off than staying in capitalism, and capitalists would be worse off. The "withdrawal rule" in this case—leaving the game with per capita shares of physical assets—then becomes the formal "test" of whether or not a particular social system involves capitalistic exploitation.

In contrast, the withdrawal rule to specify feudal exploitation is leaving the game with one's *personal assets* (rather than one's per capita share of total social assets). This is equivalent to the feudal serf being freed from all obligations based on personal bondage. Peasants would be better off under such circumstances; feudal lords would be worse off.[11]

The concept of the socialist exploitation is the least systematically worked out in Roemer's analysis. The withdrawal rule in this case is leaving the game with one's *per capita share of inalienable assets* (skills). A coalition will be said to be socialistically exploited if it would improve its position by leaving with its per capita skills while its complement would be worse off under such circum-

stances. This implies that people with high levels of skills in the game receive high income not simply because they have high skills, but because of the differentials in skill levels across actors. The highly skilled would become worse off if the unskilled obtained skills; they thus have an interest in maintaining skill differentials, and this is what underpins the claim that their income reflects exploitation.[12] If a skilled person's income reflected no more than the amount of time and resources it takes to obtain the skill, then there would be no skill-based exploitation. The higher incomes would simply be reimbursement for real costs incurred. The argument behind skill exploitation is that people with scarce skills receive incomes above the costs of producing those skills, a "rent" component to their income; it is this element that constitutes exploitation.

Class and Exploitation

The central message of both of Roemer's strategies for analyzing exploitation is that the material basis of exploitation is inequalities in distributions of productive assets, or what is usually referred to as property relations. On the one hand, inequalities of assets are sufficient to account for transfers of labor surplus; on the other hand, different forms of asset inequality specify different systems of exploitation. Classes are then defined as positions within the social relations of production derived from these relations of exploitation.[13]

These conclusions have led Roemer to challenge directly the tendency of Marxists (like myself) to define class relations primarily in terms of domination relations within production. Of course, exploiting classes dominate exploited classes in the sense of preventing the exploited classes from taking the exploiting class's productive assets. But domination *within* production, Roemer insists, is not a central part of defining class relations as such.

In previous work I have criticized Roemer's position on this issue.[14] I argued that class relations intrinsically involved domination *at the point of production*, not simply in the repressive protection of the property relations as such. I now think that Roemer is correct on this point. That capitalists boss workers around within production is unquestionably an important feature of most historic forms of capitalist production and may play an important role in explaining the forms of class organization and class conflict within production. However, the basis of the capital-labor relation should be identified with relations of effective control (that is, real economic ownership) over productive assets as such.

One of the reasons why I resisted Roemer's conceptualization of classes in terms of property relations is that it seemed to blur the difference between Marxist definitions of class and Weberian definitions. Weberian definitions, as I construed them, were "market based" definitions of class, whereas Marxist definitions were "production based." The reputed advantage of the latter was that production was more "fundamental" than exchange, and therefore production-based class concepts had more explanatory power than market-based concepts.

What now seems clear to me is that definitions of classes in terms of property relations should not be identified with strictly market-based definitions. Property-relations accounts of classes do not define classes by income shares, by the results of market transactions, but by the productive assets that classes control, which lead them to adopt certain strategies within exchange relations and which thereby determine the outcomes of those market transactions.

Toward a General Framework of Class Analysis

Extending Roemer's Analysis

The heart of Roemer's analysis is the linkage between the distribution of productive assets of various sorts and exploitation. Different mechanisms of exploitation are defined by different kinds of assets, and different class systems are defined by which of these assets is most important for shaping the patterns of exploitation in the society.

In Roemer's own explicit formulation, only two kinds of assets are formally considered: physical assets (alienable assets in his terminology) and skill assets (inalienable assets). The distinction between exploitation in feudalism and exploitation in capitalism revolves around the nature of the withdrawal rules with respect to physical assets (withdrawing with one's personal assets to define feudal exploitation versus withdrawing with one's per capita share of assets to define capitalist exploitation). The feudal case, however, can be characterized in a somewhat different way. Labor power is a productive asset.[15] In capitalist societies everyone owns one unit of this asset, namely themselves. In feudalism, on the other hand, ownership rights over labor power are unequally distributed: feudal lords have more than one unit, serfs have less than one unit. To be sure, it is not typical of feudalism for serfs to own no labor power—they are generally not slaves divested of all ownership rights in their own labor power—but they do not have complete effective control over their own persons as productive actors, and this is what it means to "own" one's own labor power assets. The withdrawal rule that defines feudal exploitation can then be specified as leaving the feudal game with one's per capita share of society's assets in labor power, namely one unit. Feudal exploitation is thus exploitation (transfers of labor) that results from inequalities in the distribution of assets in labor power.

Reformulating feudal exploitation in this manner makes the game-theory specification of different exploitations in Roemer's analysis symmetrical: feudal exploitation is based on inequalities generated by ownership of labor-power assets; capitalist exploitation on inequalities generated by ownership of alienable assets; socialist exploitation on inequalities generated by ownership of inalienable assets. And corresponding to each of these exploitation-generating inequalities of assets, there is a specific class relation: lords and serfs in feudalism, bourgeoisie and proletariat in capitalism, experts and workers in socialism.

But how, it might be asked, should "actually existing socialist societies" be theorized within these categories? The anticapitalist revolution in Russia resulted in the virtual elimination of private property in the means of production: individuals cannot own means of production, they cannot inherit them or dispose of them on a market, and so on. And yet it seems unsatisfactory to characterize such societies simply in terms of skill-based exploitation. Experts do not appear to be the "ruling class" in those societies, and the dynamic of the societies does not seem to revolve around skill inequalities as such.

Roemer recognized this problem and introduced what he termed "status exploitation" to deal with it. The exploitation exercised by bureaucrats is the prototypical example. "If these positions," Roemer writes, "required special skills, then one might be justified in calling the differential remuneration to these positions an aspect of socialist [skill-based] exploitation. ... [However] there is some extra remuneration to holders of those positions which accrues solely by virtue of the position and not by virtue of the skill necessary to carry out the tasks associated with it. These special payments to positions give rise to *status exploitation*."[16]

Roemer's concept of status exploitation is unsatisfactory for two principal reasons. First, it is outside of the logic of the rest of his analysis of exploitation. In each of the other cases, exploitation is rooted in relations to the forces of production. Each of the other forms of exploitation is "materialist" not only because the concept is meant to explain material distribution, but also because it is based on the relation to the material conditions of production. "Status" exploitation has no necessary relationship to production at all. Second, it is hard to rigorously distinguish status exploitation from feudal exploitation. The "lord" receives remuneration strictly because of an incumbency in a position, not because of skills or ownership of capital. Yet, it hardly seems reasonable to consider the logic of exploitation and class in the contemporary Soviet Union and in fourteenth-century feudal Europe as being essentially the same.

The problems with the concept of status exploitation can be solved by analyzing exploitation based on a fourth element in the inventory of productive assets, an asset that can be referred to as "organization." As both Adam Smith and Marx noted, the technical division of labor among producers is itself a source of productivity. The way the production process is organized is a produc-

tive resource independent of the expenditure of labor power, the use of means of production, or the skills of the producer. Of course there is an interrelationship between organization and these other assets, just as there is an interdependence between means of production and skills. But organization—the conditions of coordinated cooperation among producers in a complex division of labor—is a productive resource in its own right.

How is this asset distributed in different kinds of societies? In contemporary capitalism, organization assets are generally controlled by managers and capitalists: managers control the organization assets within specific firms under constraints imposed by the ownership of the capital assets by capitalists. Entrepreneurial capitalists directly control both kinds of assets (and probably skill assets as well); pure rentier capitalists ("coupon clippers") only own capital assets. Because of the anarchy of the capitalist market, no set of actors controls the technical division of labor across firms.

In state bureaucratic socialism, organization assets assume a much greater importance. Controlling the technical division of labor—the coordination of productive activities within and across labor processes—becomes a societal task organized at the center. The control over organization assets is no longer simply the task of firm-level managers but extends into the central organs of planning within the state. Exploitation in such societies is thus based on bureaucratic power: the control over organization assets defines the material basis for class relations and exploitation.

This notion of organization assets bears a close relation to the problem of authority and hierarchy. The asset is organization. The activity of using that asset is coordinated decision making over a complex technical division of labor. When that asset is distributed unequally, so some positions have effective control over much more of the asset than others, then the social relation with respect to that asset takes the form of hierarchical authority. Authority, however, is not the asset as such; organization is the asset and is controlled through a hierarchy of authority.

The claim that effective control over organization assets is a basis of exploitation is equivalent to saying that nonmanagers would be better off

TABLE 1
Assets, Exploitation, and Classes

Type of class structure	*Principal asset that is unequally distributed*	*Mechanism of exploitation*	*Classes*	*Central task of revolutionary transformation*
Feudalism	Labor power	Coercive extraction of surplus labor	Lords and serfs	Individual liberty
Capitalism	Means of production	Market exchanges of labor power and commodities	Capitalists and workers	Socializing means of production
State bureaucratic socialism	Organization	Planned appropriation and distribution of surplus based on hierarchy	Managers/ bureaucrats and nonmanagement	Democratization of organizational control
Socialism	Skills	Negotiated redistribution of surplus from workers to experts	Experts and workers	Substantive equality

and managers/bureaucrats worse off if nonmanagers were to withdraw with their per capita share of organization assets (or equivalently, if organizational control were democratized); and that by virtue of effectively controlling organization assets managers/bureaucrats control part or all of the socially produced surplus.[17]

A Typology of Class Structures, Assets, and Exploitation

If we add organization assets to the list in Roemer's analysis, we generate the more complex typology presented in Table 1. Let us briefly look at each row of this table and examine its logic. Feudalism is a class system based on unequal distribution of ownership rights in labor power. What "personal bondage" means is that feudal lords have partial effective economic control over vassals. The empirical manifestation of this unequal distribution of ownership rights over labor power in classical feudalism is the coercive extraction of labor dues from serfs. When corvée labor is commuted to rents in kind and eventually money rents, the feudal character of the exploitation relation is reflected in legal prohibitions on the movement of peasants off the land. The "flight" of a peasant to the city is, in effect, a form of theft: the peasant is stealing part of the labor power owned by the lord. Feudal lords may also have more

means of production than serfs, more organizational assets, and more productive skills (although this is unlikely), and thus they may be exploiters with respect to these assets as well. What defines the society as "feudal", however, is the primacy of the distinctively feudal mechanisms of exploitation. Accordingly, feudal class relations will be the primary structural basis of class struggle.

The bourgeois revolutions radically redistributed productive assets in people: everyone, at least in principle, owns one unit. This is what is meant by "bourgeois freedoms," and in this sense capitalism can be regarded as an historically progressive force. But capitalism raises the second type of exploitation, exploitation based on property relations in means of production, to an unprecedented level.

The typical institutional form of capitalist class relations is capitalists having full ownership rights in the means of production and workers none. Other possibilities, however, have existed historically. Cottage industries in early capitalism involved workers owning some of their means of production, but not having sufficient assets to actually produce commodities without the assistance of merchant capitalists. Such workers were still being capitalistically exploited even though there was no formal labor market with wages. In all capitalist exploitation, the mediating mechanism is market exchanges. Unlike in feudalism, surplus is not directly appropriated from workers in the form of coerced labor. Rather, it is appropriated through market exchanges: workers are paid a wage that covers the costs of production of their labor power; capitalists receive an income from the sale of the commodities produced by workers. The difference in these quantities constitutes the exploitative surplus appropriated by capitalists.

Anticapitalist revolutions attempt to eliminate the distinctively capitalist form of exploitation, exploitation based on private ownership of the means of production. The nationalization of the principal means of production is, in effect, a radical equalization of ownership of capital: everyone owns one citizen-share. Such revolutions, however, do not eliminate, and indeed may considerably strengthen and deepen, inequalities of effective control over organization assets. Whereas in capitalism the control over organization assets does not extend beyond the firm, in state bureaucratic socialism the coordinated integration of the division of labor extends to the whole society through institutions of central state planning. The mechanism by which this generates exploitative transfers of surplus involves the centrally planned bureaucratic appropriation and distribution of the surplus along hierarchical principles. The corresponding class relation is therefore between managers/bureaucrats—people who control organization assets—and nonmanagers.

The historical task of revolutionary transformation of state bureaucratic socialism revolves around the equalization of effective economic control over organization assets, or, equivalently, the democratization of bureaucratic apparatuses of production. This does not imply total direct democracy, where all decisions of any consequence are directly made in democratic assemblies. There will still inevitably be delegated responsibilities, and there certainly can be representative forms of democratic control. But it does mean that the basic parameters of planning and coordinating social production are made through democratic mechanisms and that incumbency within delegated positions of responsibility does not give incumbents any personal claims on the social surplus. Such equalization, however, would not necessarily affect exploitation based on skills/credentials. Such exploitation would remain a central feature of socialism.

"Skill" in this context is not a trivial concept. The mere possession of enhanced laboring capabilities acquired through training is not sufficient to generate relations of exploitation, since the income of such trained labor may simply reflect the costs of acquiring the training. In such cases there is neither a transfer of surplus, nor would the untrained be better off under the game-theory specification of exploitation. For a skill to be the basis of exploitation, therefore, it has to be in some sense scarce relative to its demand, and there must be a mechanism through which individual owners of scarce skills are able to translate that scarcity into higher incomes.

There are basically three ways that skills can become scarce: first, they may require special *talents* that are naturally scarce in a population; second, access to the training needed to develop the skill may be restricted through various mechanisms, creating an artificial scarcity of trained people; third, a certification system may be established that prohibits uncertified people from being employed to use the skill even if they have it. In all of these cases, the exploitation comes from the skilled/certified individual receiving an income that is above the costs of production of the skills by virtue of the scarcity of the availability of the skill.

In this conceptualization of socialism, a socialist society is essentially a kind of democratic technocracy. Experts control their own skills and knowledge within production, and by virtue of such control are able to appropriate some of the surplus out of production. However, because of the democratization of organization assets, actual planning decisions will not be made under the direct control of experts but will be made through some kind of democratic procedure (this is in effect what democratization of organization assets means: equalizing control over the planning and coordinating of social production). This means that the actual class power of a socialist technocratic exploiting class will be much weaker than the class power of exploiting classes in other class systems. Their ownership rights extend to only a limited part of the social surplus.

This much more limited basis of *domination* implied by skill-based exploitation is consistent with the spirit, if not the letter, of Marx's claim that socialism is the "lower stage" of "communism," since classes are already in a partial state of dissolution in a society with only skill-based exploitation. Communism itself, then, would be understood as a society within which skill-based exploitation itself had "withered away," that is, in which ownership rights in skills had been equalized. This does not mean, it must be stressed, that all individuals would actually *possess* the same skills in communism, any more than eliminating property rights in means of production implies that all individuals would actively use the same amount of physical capital. What is equalized is effective control over skills as a productive resource and claims to differential incomes resulting from differential use of skills.[18] ...

The Middle Classes and Contradictory Locations

The framework in Table 1 enables us to pose the problem of middle classes in a new way. Two different kinds of nonpolarized class locations can be defined in the logic of this framework:

1. There are class locations that are neither exploiters nor exploited, that is, people who have precisely the per capita level of the relevant asset. A petty bourgeois, self-employed producer with average capital stock, for example, would be neither exploiter nor exploited within capitalist relations. These kinds of positions are what can be called the "traditional" or "old" middle class of a particular kind of class system.

2. Since concrete societies are rarely, if ever, characterized by a single mode of production, the actual class structures of given societies will be characterized by complex patterns of intersecting exploitation relations. There will therefore tend to be some positions that are exploiting along one dimension of exploitation relations and are exploited along another. Highly skilled wage-earners (for example, professionals) in capitalism are a good example: they are capitalistically exploited because they lack

assets in capital, and yet they are skill exploiters. Such positions are what are typically referred to as the "new middle class" of a given system.

Table 2 presents a schematic typology of such complex class locations for capitalism. The typology is divided into two segments: one for owners of the means of production and one for non-owners. Within the wage-earner section of the typology, locations are distinguished by the two subordinate relations of exploitation characteristic of capitalist society—organization assets and skill/credential assets. It is thus possible within this framework to distinguish a whole terrain of class locations in capitalist *society* that are distinct from the polarized classes of the capitalist *mode of production*: expert managers, nonmanagerial experts, nonexpert managers, and so on.[19]

What is the relationship between this heterogeneous exploitation definition of the middle class and my previous conceptualization of such positions as contradictory locations within class relations? There is still a sense in which such positions could be characterized as "contradictory locations," for they will typically hold contradictory interests with respect to the primary forms of class struggle in capitalist society, the struggle between labor and capital. On the one hand, they are like workers, in being excluded from ownership of the means of production. On the other hand, they have interests opposed to workers because of their effective control of organization and skill assets. Within the struggles of capitalism, therefore, these new middle classes do constitute contradictory locations, or more precisely, contradictory locations within exploitation relations.

This conceptualization of the middle classes also suggests that historically the principal forms of contradictory locations will vary depending upon the particular combinations of exploitation relations in a given society. These principal contradictory locations are presented in Table 3. In feudalism, the critical contradictory location is constituted by the bourgeoisie, the rising class of the successor mode of production. Within capitalism, the central contradictory location within exploitation relations is constituted by managers and state bureaucrats. They embody a principle

TABLE 2
Basic Typology of Exploitation and Class

Assets in the means of production

Owners (%)	Nonowners (wage laborers) (%)			
1 Bourgeoisie US 1.8 Sweden 0.7	**4 Expert manager** US 3.9 Sweden 4.4	**7 Semicredentialed manager** US 6.2 Sweden 4.0	**10 Uncredentialed manager** US 2.3 Sweden 2.5	+
2 Small employer US 6.0 Sweden 4.8	**5 Expert supervisor** US 3.7 Sweden 3.8	**8 Semicredentialed supervisor** US 6.8 Sweden 3.2	**11 Uncredentialed supervisor** US 6.9 Sweden 3.1	>0 Organization assets
3 Petty bourgeoisie US 6.9 Sweden 5.4	**6 Expert nonmanager** US 3.4 Sweden 6.8	**9 Semicredentialed worker** US 12.2 Sweden 17.8	**12 Proletarian** US 39.9 Sweden 43.5	−
	+	>0 Skill assets	−	

United States: N = 1487
Sweden: N = 1179

Note: Distributions are of people working in the labor force, thus excluding unemployed, housewives, pensioners, etc.
Source: Comparative Project on Class Structure and Class Consciousness.

TABLE 3
Basic Classes and Contradictory Locations
in Successive Modes of Production

Mode of production	Basic classes	Principal contradictory location
Feudalism	Lords and serfs	Bourgeoisie
Capitalism	Bourgeoisie and proletariat	Managers/bureaucrats
State bureaucratic socialism	Bureaucrats and workers	Intelligentsia/experts

of class organization that is quite distinct from capitalism and that potentially poses an alternative to capitalist relations. This is particularly true for state managers who, unlike corporate managers, are less likely to have their careers tightly integrated with the interests of the capitalist class. Finally, in state bureaucratic socialism, the "intelligentsia" broadly defined constitutes the pivotal contradictory location.

One of the upshots of this reconceptualization of the middle class is that it is no longer axiomatic that the proletariat is the unique, or perhaps even the central, rival to the capitalist class for class power in capitalist society. That classical Marxist assumption depended upon the thesis that there were no other classes within capitalism that could be viewed as the "bearers" of an historical alternative to capitalism. Socialism (as the transition to communism) was the only possible future for capitalism. What Table 3 suggests is that there are other class forces within capitalism that potentially pose an alternative to capitalism. This does not imply that there is any inevitability to the sequence feudalism–capitalism–state bureaucratic socialism–socialism–communism; state bureaucrats are not inevitably destined to be the future ruling class of present-day capitalisms. But it does suggest that the process of class formation and class struggle is considerably more complex and indeterminate than the traditional Marxist story has allowed.

Notes

1. For a more detailed review of these alternatives, see E.O. Wright, "Varieties of Marxist Concepts of Class Structure," *Politics and Society*, vol. 9, no. 3 (1980).

2. The leading proponent of the concept of the "new petty bourgeoisie" is N. Poulantzas, *Classes in Contem-*

porary Capitalism (London: Verso, 1975). For the new-working-class concept, see S. Mallet, *La Nouvelle Classe Ouvrière* (Paris: Seuil, 1963).

3. B. Ehrenreich and J. Ehrenreich, "The Professional and Managerial Class," *Radical America,* vol. 11, no. 2 (1977).

4. A. Gouldner, *The Future of Intellectuals and the Rise of the New Class* (New York: Seabury Press, 1979); and G. Konrad and I. Szelényi, *Intellectuals on the Road to Class Power* (New York: Harcourt, Brace, Jovanovich, 1979).

5. E.O. Wright, "Class Boundaries in Advanced Capitalist Societies," *New Left Review,* no. 98 (1976); and *Class, Crisis and the State* (London: New Left Books, 1978). See also G. Carchedi, *The Economic Identification of Social Classes* (London: Routledge and Kegan Paul, 1977).

6. E.O. Wright, "Capitalism's Futures," *Socialist Review,* no. 68 (1983).

7. A partial exception to this can be found in arguments for the existence of a "new class" of intellectuals and/or bureaucrats in capitalist and postcapitalist society. See: A. Gouldner, *The Future of Intellectuals;* and I. Szelényi and W. Martin, *New Class Theory and Beyond* (unpublished book manuscript, Department of Sociology, University of Wisconsin, 1985).

8. R. Dahrendorf, *Class and Class Conflict in Industrial Society* (Palo Alto: Stanford University Press, 1959).

9. Roemer is a Marxist economist engaged in a long-term project of elaborating what he calls the "micro-foundations" of Marxist theory. His most important work is entitled *A General Theory of Exploitation and Class* (Cambridge: Harvard University Press, 1982).

10. Roemer, *A General Theory,* pp. 194–95.

11. But note: workers in capitalism are *not* feudalistically exploited; they would be worse off, not better off, if they withdrew from the game of capitalism with only their personal assets. As Roemer argues, the claim by neoclassical theorists that wage earners in capitalism are not exploited is generally equivalent to the claim that they are not feudalistically exploited, that is, that they are not subjected to surplus extraction based on relations of personal bondage. See Roemer, *A General Theory,* p. 206.

12. The asset-exploitation nexus thus depends upon the capacity of asset-holders to deprive others of that asset. The social basis of exploitation, understood in this way, is quite similar to Frank Parkin's characterization of Weber's concept of social closure as "the process by which social collectivities seek to maximize rewards by restricting access to resources and opportunities to a limited circle of eligibles." F. Parkin, *Marxism and Class Theory: A Bourgeois Critique* (New York: Columbia University Press, 1979). While Parkin's central concern is with the kinds of attributes that serve as the basis for closure—race, religion, language—Roemer's is with the nature of the resources (productive assets) over which closure is organized.

13. Roemer's conceptualization of the relationship between class and exploitation is similar in certain aspects to Alvin Gouldner's, although Roemer is unaware of Gouldner's work. Gouldner defines the "New Class" as a *cultural* bourgeoisie defined by its control over "cultural capital," where "capital" is defined as "any produced object used to make saleable utilities, thus providing its possessor with *incomes,* or claims to incomes defined as legitimate because of their imputed contribution to economic productivity." (*Future of Intellectuals,* p. 21). While Gouldner does not characterize this income allocation process in terms of exploitation, Roemer's exploitation concept would fit comfortably within Gouldner's general approach.

14. E.O. Wright, "The Status of the Political in the Concept of Class Structure," *Politics and Society,* vol. 11, no. 3 (1982).

15. See G.A. Cohen, *Karl Marx's Theory of History: A Defense* (Princeton: Princeton University Press, 1978), pp. 40–41, for a discussion of why labor power should be considered part of the forces of production (that is, a productive asset).

16. Roemer, *A General Theory,* p. 243.

17. This "control of the surplus," it must be noted, is *not* the equivalent of the *actual* personal consumption income of managers and bureaucrats, any more than capitalist profits or feudal rents are the equivalent of the personally consumed income of capitalists and feudal lords. It is historically variable both within and between types of societies what fraction of the surplus effectively controlled by exploiting classes is used for personal consumption and what portion is used for other purposes (feudal military expenditures, capitalist accumulation, organization growth). The claim that managers-bureaucrats would be "worse off" under conditions of a redistribution of organization assets refers to the amount of income they effectively control, which is therefore potentially available for personal appropriation, not simply the amount they personally consume.

18. It may be utopian to imagine a society without skill-based exploitation, or even a society without organization-asset exploitation, particularly if we reject the claim that a future society will ever exist in a state of absolute abundance. In the absence of absolute abundance, all societies will face dilemmas and trade-offs around the problem of distribution of consumption, and such dilemmas may pose intractable incentive problems in the absence of exploitation. For a careful exposition of the problem of utopian fantasies in Marxist theory, see A. Nove, *The Economics of Feasible Social-*

ism (Hemel Hempstead: George Allen and Unwin, 1983).

19. The labor-force data in this table come from the comparative project on class structure and class con-

sciousness, University of Wisconsin. Details of the coding of categories and the operationalization of variables can be found in E.O. Wright, *Classes* (London: Verso, 1985), appendix 2.

IMMANUEL WALLERSTEIN

Class Conflict in the Capitalist World Economy

What is capitalism as a mode of production? This is not an easy question, and for that reason is not in fact a widely discussed one. It seems to me that there are several elements that combine to constitute the 'model'. Capitalism is the *only* mode of production in which the *maximization* of surplus creation is rewarded *per se*. In every historical system, there has been *some* production for *use,* and *some* production for *exchange,* but only in capitalism are all producers rewarded primarily in terms of the exchange value they produce and penalized to the extent they neglect it. The 'rewards' and 'penalties' are mediated through a structure called the 'market'. It is a structure but not an institution. It is a structure molded by *many* institutions (political, economic, social, even cultural), and it is the principal arena of economic struggle.

Not only is surplus maximized for its own sake, but those who use the surplus to accumulate more capital to produce still more surplus are further rewarded. Thus the pressure is for constant expansion, although the individualistic premise of the system simultaneously renders *constant* expansion impossible.

How does the search for profit operate? It operates by creating legal protections for individual firms (which can range in size from individuals to quite large organizations, including parastatal agencies) to appropriate the surplus value created by the labor of the primary producers. Were all or most of this surplus value however consumed by the few who owned or controlled the 'firms', we would not have capitalism. This is in fact approximately what had happened in various pre-capitalist systems.

Capitalism involves in addition structures and institutions which reward primarily that subsegment of the owners and controllers who use the surplus value only *in part* for their own consumption, and in another (usually larger) part for further investment. The structure of the market ensures that those who do not accumulate capital (but merely consume surplus value) lose out economically over time to those who do accumulate capital.

We may thereupon designate as the bourgeoisie those who receive a part of the surplus value they do not themselves create and use some of it to accumulate capital. What defines the bourgeois is not a particular profession and not even the legal status of proprietor (although this was historically important) but the fact that the bourgeois obtains, either as an individual or a member of some collectivity, a part of the surplus that he did not create and is in the position to invest (again either individually or as part of a collectivity) some of this surplus in capital goods.

There is a very large gamut of organizational arrangements which can permit this, of which the classic model of the 'free entrepreneur' is only one. Which organizational arrangements prevail at particular moments of time in particular states (for these arrangements are dependent on the legal framework) is a function of the state of development of the world-economy as a whole (and the role of a particular state in that world-economy) on the one hand, and the consequent forms of class struggle in the world-economy (and within the particular state) on the other. Hence, like all other social constructs, the 'bourgeoisie' is not a static phenomenon. It is the designation of a class in the process of perpetual re-creation and hence of constant change of form and composition. …

The fundamental role of the state as an institution in the capitalist world-economy is to augment the advantage of some against others in the market—that is, to *reduce* the 'freedom' of the market. Everyone is in favor of this, as long as one is the beneficiary of the 'distortion', and everyone opposed to the extent that one loses. It is all a matter of whose ox is being gored.

The modes of augmenting advantage are many. The state can transfer income by taking it from some and giving it to others. The state can restrict access to the market (of commodities or of labor) which favor those who thereby share in the oligopoly or oligopsony. The state can restrain persons from organizing to change the actions of the state. And, of course, the state can act not only within its jurisdiction but beyond it. This may be licit (the rules concerning transit over boundaries) or illicit (interference in the internal affairs of another state). Warfare is of course one of the mechanisms used.

What is crucial to perceive is that the state is a special kind of organization. Its 'sovereignty', a notion of the modern world, is the claim to the monopolization (regulation) of the legitimate use of force within its boundaries, and it is in a relatively strong position to interfere effectively with the flow of factors of production. Obviously also it is possible for particular social groups to alter advantage by altering state boundaries; hence both movements for secession (or autonomy) and movements for annexation (or federation).

It is this realistic ability of states to interfere with the flow of factors of production that provides the political underpinnings of the structural division of labor in the capitalist world-economy as a whole. Normal market considerations may account for recurring initial thrusts to specialization (natural or socio-historical advantages in the production of one or another commodity), but it is the state system which encrusts, enforces, and exaggerates the patterns, and it has regularly required the use of state machinery to revise the pattern of the world-wide division of labor.

Furthermore, the ability of states to interfere with flows becomes differentiated. That is, core states become *stronger* than peripheral states, and use this differential power to maintain a differential degree of interstate freedom of flow. Specifically, core states have historically arranged that world-wide and over time, money and goods have flowed more 'freely' than labor. The reason for doing this is that core states have thereby received the advantages of 'unequal exchange'.

In effect, unequal exchange is simply a part of the world-wide process of the appropriation of surplus. We analyze falsely if we try to take literally the model of *one* proletarian relating to *one* bourgeois. In fact, the surplus value that the producer creates passes through a series of persons and firms. It is therefore the case that *many* bourgeois *share* the surplus value of *one* proletarian. The exact share of different groups in the chain (property owner, merchants, intermediate consumers) is subject to much historical change and is itself a principal analytical variable in the functioning of the capitalist world-economy.

This chain of the transfer of surplus value frequently (often? almost always?) traverses national boundaries and, when it does, state operations intervene to tilt the sharing among bourgeois towards those bourgeois located in core states. This is unequal exchange, a mechanism in the overall process of the appropriation of surplus value.

One of the socio-geographic consequences of this system is the uneven distribution of the bourgeoisie and proletariat in different states, core states containing a higher percentage nationally of bourgeois than peripheral states. In addition, there are systematic differences in *kinds* of bourgeois and proletarians located in the two zones. For example, the percentage of wage-earning proletarians is systematically higher in core states.

Since states are the primary arena of political conflict in a capitalist world-economy, and since the functioning of the world-economy is such that national class composition varies widely, it is easy to perceive why the politics of states differentially located in relation to the world-economy should be so dissimilar. It is also then easy to perceive that using the political machinery of a given state to change the social composition and world-economic function of national production does not *per se* change the capitalist world-system as such.

Obviously, however, these various national thrusts to a change in structural position (which we misleadingly often call 'development') do in fact affect, indeed over the long run do in fact transform, the world-system. But they do so via the intervening variable of their impact on world-wide class consciousness of the proletariat.

Core and periphery then are simply phrases to locate one crucial part of the system of surplus appropriation by the bourgeoisie. To oversimplify, capitalism is a system in which the surplus value of the proletarian is appropriated by the bourgeois. When this proletarian is located in a different country from this bourgeois, one of the mechanisms that has affected the process of appropriation is the manipulation of controlling flows over state boundaries. This results in patterns of 'uneven development' which are *summarized* in the concepts of core, semiperiphery, and periphery. This is an intellectual tool to help analyze the multiple forms of class conflict in the capitalist world-economy.

MAX WEBER

Class, Status, Party

Economically Determined Power and the Social Order

Law exists when there is a probability that an order will be upheld by a specific staff of men who will use physical or psychical compulsion with the intention of obtaining conformity with the order, or of inflicting sanctions for infringement of it.[1] The structure of every legal order directly influences the distribution of power, economic or otherwise, within its respective community. This is true of all legal orders and not only that of the state. In general, we understand by 'power' the chance of a man or of a number of men to realize their own will in a communal action even against the resistance of others who are participating in the action.

'Economically conditioned' power is not, of course, identical with 'power' as such. On the contrary, the emergence of economic power may be the consequence of power existing on other grounds. Man does not strive for power only in order to enrich himself economically. Power, including economic power, may be valued 'for its own sake.' Very frequently the striving for power is also conditioned by the social 'honor' it entails. Not all power, however, entails social honor: The typical American Boss, as well as the typical big speculator, deliberately relinquishes social honor. Quite generally, 'mere economic' power, and especially 'naked' money power, is by no means a recognized basis of social honor. Nor is power the only basis of social honor. Indeed, social honor, or prestige, may even be the basis of political or economic power, and very frequently has been.

Power, as well as honor, may be guaranteed by the legal order, but, at least normally, it is not their primary source. The legal order is rather an additional factor that enhances the chance to hold power or honor; but it cannot always secure them.

The way in which social honor is distributed in a community between typical groups participating in this distribution we may call the 'social order.' The social order and the economic order are, of course, similarly related to the 'legal order.' However, the social and the economic order are not identical. The economic order is for us merely the way in which economic goods and services are distributed and used. The social order is of course conditioned by the economic order to a high degree, and in its turn reacts upon it.

Now: 'classes,' 'status groups,' and 'parties' are phenomena of the distribution of power within a community.

Determination of Class-Situation by Market-Situation

In our terminology, 'classes' are not communities; they merely represent possible, and frequent, bases for communal action. We may speak of a 'class' when (1) a number of people have in common a specific causal component of their life chances, in so far as (2) this component is represented exclusively by economic interests in the possession of goods and opportunities for income, and (3) is represented under the conditions of the commodity or labor markets. [These points refer to 'class situation,' which we may express more briefly as the typical chance for a supply of goods, external living conditions, and personal life experiences, in so far as this chance is determined by the amount and kind of power, or lack of such, to dispose of goods or skills for the sake of income in a given economic order. The term 'class' refers to any group of people that is found in the same class situation.]

It is the most elemental economic fact that the way in which the disposition over material property is distributed among a plurality of people, meeting competitively in the market for the purpose of exchange, in itself creates specific life chances. According to the law of marginal utility this mode of distribution excludes the non-owners from competing for highly valued goods; it favors the owners and, in fact, gives to them a monopoly to acquire such goods. Other things being equal, this mode of distribution monopolizes the opportunities for profitable deals for all those who, provided with goods, do not necessarily have to exchange them. It increases, at least generally, their power in price wars with those who, being propertyless, have nothing to offer but their services in native form or goods in a form constituted through their own labor, and who above all are compelled to get rid of these products in order barely to subsist. This mode of distribution gives to the propertied a monopoly on the possibility of transferring property from the sphere of use as a 'fortune,' to the sphere of 'capital goods'; that is, it gives them the entrepreneurial function and all chances to share directly or indirectly in returns on capital. All this holds true within the area in which pure market conditions prevail. 'Property' and 'lack of property' are, therefore, the basic categories of all class situations. It does not matter whether these two categories become effective in price wars or in competitive struggles.

Within these categories, however, class situations are further differentiated: on the one hand, according to the kind of property that is usable for returns; and, on the other hand, according to the kind of services that can be offered in the market. Ownership of domestic buildings; productive establishments; warehouses; stores; agriculturally usable land, large and small holdings—quantitative differences with possibly qualitative consequences—; ownership of mines; cattle; men (slaves); disposition over mobile instruments of production, or capital goods of all sorts, especially money or objects that can be exchanged for money easily and at any time; disposition over products of one's own labor or of others' labor differing according to their various distances from consumability; disposition over transferable monopolies of any kind—all these distinctions differentiate the class situations of the propertied just as does the 'meaning' which they can and do give to the utilization of property, especially to property which has money equivalence. Accordingly, the propertied, for instance, may belong to the class of rentiers or to the class of entrepreneurs.

Those who have no property but who offer services are differentiated just as much according to their kinds of services as according to the way in which they make use of these services, in a continuous or discontinuous relation to a recipient. But always this is the generic connotation of the concept of class: that the kind of chance in the *market* is the decisive moment which presents a common condition for the individual's fate. 'Class situation' is, in this sense, ultimately 'market situation.' The effect of naked possession *per se*, which among cattle breeders gives the nonowning slave or serf into the power of the cattle owner, is only a forerunner of real 'class' formation. However, in the cattle loan and in the naked severity of the law of debts in such communities, for the first time mere 'possession' as such emerges as decisive for the fate of the individual. This is very much in contrast to the agricultural communities based on labor. The creditor-debtor relation becomes the basis of 'class situations' only in those cities where a 'credit market,' however primitive, with rates of interest increasing according to the extent of dearth and a factual monopolization of credits, is developed by a plutocracy. Therewith 'class struggles' begin.

Those men whose fate is not determined by the chance of using goods or services for themselves on the market, e.g. slaves, are not, however, a 'class' in the technical sense of the term. They are, rather, a 'status group.'

Communal Action Flowing from Class Interest

According to our terminology, the factor that creates 'class' is unambiguously economic interest, and indeed, only those interests involved in the existence of the 'market.' Nevertheless, the concept of 'class-interest' is an ambiguous one: even as an empirical concept it is ambiguous as soon as one understands by it something other than the factual direction of interests following with a certain probability from the class situation for a certain 'average' of those people subjected to the class situation. The class situation and other circumstances remaining the same, the direction in which the individual worker, for instance, is likely to pursue his interests may vary widely, according to whether he is constitutionally qualified for the task at hand to a high, to an average, or to a low degree. In the same way, the direction of interests may vary according to whether or not a *communal* action of a larger or smaller portion of those commonly affected by the 'class situation,' or even an association among them, e.g. a 'trade union,' has grown out of the class situation from which the individual may or may not expect promising results. [Communal action refers to that action which is oriented to the feeling of the actors that they belong together. Societal action, on the other hand, is oriented to a rationally motivated adjustment of interests.] The rise of societal or even of communal action from a common class situation is by no means a universal phenomenon.

The class situation may be restricted in its effects to the generation of essentially *similar* reactions, that is to say, within our terminology, of 'mass actions.' However, it may not have even this result. Furthermore, often merely an amorphous communal action emerges. For example, the 'murmuring' of the workers known in ancient oriental ethics: the moral disapproval of the work-master's conduct, which in its practical significance was probably equivalent to an increasingly typical phenomenon of precisely the latest industrial development, namely, the 'slow down' (the deliberate limiting of work effort) of laborers by virtue of tacit agreement. The degree in which 'communal action' and possibly 'societal action,'

emerges from the 'mass actions' of the members of a class is linked to general cultural conditions, especially to those of an intellectual sort. It is also linked to the extent of the contrasts that have already evolved, and is especially linked to the *transparency* of the connections between the causes and the consequences of the 'class situation.' For however different life chances may be, this fact in itself, according to all experience, by no means gives birth to 'class action' (communal action by the members of a class). The fact of being conditioned and the results of the class situation must be distinctly recognizable. For only then the contrast of life chances can be felt not as an absolutely given fact to be accepted, but as a resultant from either (1) the given distribution of property, or (2) the structure of the concrete economic order. It is only then that people may react against the class structure not only through acts of an intermittent and irrational protest, but in the form of rational association. There have been 'class situations' of the first category (1), of a specifically naked and transparent sort, in the urban centers of Antiquity and during the Middle Ages; especially then, when great fortunes were accumulated by factually monopolized trading in industrial products of these localities or in foodstuffs. Furthermore, under certain circumstances, in the rural economy of the most diverse periods, when agriculture was increasingly exploited in a profit-making manner. The most important historical example of the second category (2) is the class situation of the modern 'proletariat.'

Types of 'Class Struggle'

Thus every class may be the carrier of any one of the possibly innumerable forms of 'class action,' but this is not necessarily so: In any case, a class does not in itself constitute a community. To treat 'class' conceptually as having the same value as 'community' leads to distortion. That men in the same class situation regularly react in mass actions to such tangible situations as economic ones in the direction of those interests that are most adequate to their average number is an important and after all simple fact for the understanding of historical events. Above all, this fact must not lead to that kind of pseudo-scientific operation with the concepts of 'class' and 'class interests' so frequently found these days, and which has found its most classic expression in the statement of a talented author, that the individual may be in error concerning his interests but that the 'class' is 'infallible' about its interests. Yet, if classes as such are not communities, nevertheless class situations emerge only on the basis of communalization. The communal action that brings forth class situations, however, is not basically action between members of the identical class; it is an action between members of different classes. Communal actions that directly determine the class situation of the worker and the entrepreneur are: the labor market, the commodities market, and the capitalistic enterprise. But, in its turn, the existence of a capitalistic enterprise presupposes that a very specific communal action exists and that it is specifically structured to protect the possession of goods *per se,* and especially the power of individuals to dispose, in principle freely, over the means of production. The existence of a capitalistic enterprise is preconditioned by a specific kind of 'legal order.' Each kind of class situation, and above all when it rests upon the power of property *per se,* will become most clearly efficacious when all other determinants of reciprocal relations are, as far as possible, eliminated in their significance. It is in this way that the utilization of the power of property in the market obtains its most sovereign importance.

Now 'status groups' hinder the strict carrying through of the sheer market principle. In the present context they are of interest to us only from this one point of view. Before we briefly consider them, note that not much of a general nature can be said about the more specific kinds of antagonism between 'classes' (in our meaning of the term). The great shift, which has been going on continuously in the past, and up to our times, may be summarized, although at the cost of some precision: the struggle in which class situations are effective has progressively shifted from consumption credit toward, first, competitive struggles in the commodity market and, then, toward price wars on the labor market. The 'class struggles' of antiquity—to the extent that they were genuine class struggles and not struggles between

status groups—were initially carried on by indebted peasants, and perhaps also by artisans threatened by debt bondage and struggling against urban creditors. For debt bondage is the normal result of the differentiation of wealth in commercial cities, especially in seaport cities. A similar situation has existed among cattle breeders. Debt relationships as such produced class action up to the time of Cataline. Along with this, and with an increase in provision of grain for the city by transporting it from the outside, the struggle over the means of sustenance emerged. It centered in the first place around the provision of bread and the determination of the price of bread. It lasted throughout antiquity and the entire Middle Ages. The propertyless as such flocked together against those who actually and supposedly were interested in the dearth of bread. This fight spread until it involved all those commodities essential to the way of life and to handicraft production. There were only incipient discussions of wage disputes in antiquity and in the Middle Ages. But they have been slowly increasing up into modern times. In the earlier periods they were completely secondary to slave rebellions as well as to fights in the commodity market.

The propertyless of antiquity and of the Middle Ages protested against monopolies, pre-emption, forestalling, and the withholding of goods from the market in order to raise prices. Today the central issue is the determination of the price of labor.

This transition is represented by the fight for access to the market and for the determination of the price of products. Such fights went on between merchants and workers in the putting-out system of domestic handicraft during the transition to modern times. Since it is quite a general phenomenon we must mention here that the class antagonisms that are conditioned through the market situation are usually most bitter between those who actually and directly participate as opponents in price wars. It is not the rentier, the share-holder, and the banker who suffer the ill will of the worker, but almost exclusively the manufacturer and the business executives who are the direct opponents of workers in price wars. This is so in spite of the fact that it is precisely the cash boxes of the rentier, the share-holder, and the banker into which the more or less 'unearned' gains flow, rather than into the pockets of the manufacturers or of the business executives. This simple state of affairs has very frequently been decisive for the role the class situation has played in the formation of political parties. For example, it has made possible the varieties of patriarchal socialism and the frequent attempts—formerly, at least—of threatened status groups to form alliances with the proletariat against the 'bourgeoisie.'

Status Honor

In contrast to classes, *status groups* are normally communities. They are, however, often of an amorphous kind. In contrast to the purely economically determined 'class situation' we wish to designate as 'status situation' every typical component of the life fate of men that is determined by a specific, positive or negative, social estimation of *honor*. This honor may be connected with any quality shared by a plurality, and, of course, it can be knit to a class situation: class distinctions are linked in the most varied ways with status distinctions. Property as such is not always recognized as a status qualification, but in the long run it is, and with extraordinary regularity. In the subsistence economy of the organized neighborhood, very often the richest man is simply the chieftain. However, this often means only an honorific preference. For example, in the so-called pure modern 'democracy,' that is, one devoid of any expressly ordered status privileges for individuals, it may be that only the families coming under approximately the same tax class dance with one another. This example is reported of certain smaller Swiss cities. But status honor need not necessarily be linked with a 'class situation.' On the contrary, it normally stands in sharp opposition to the pretensions of sheer property.

Both propertied and propertyless people can belong to the same status group, and frequently they do with very tangible consequences. This 'equality' of social esteem may, however, in the long run become quite precarious. The 'equality' of status among the American 'gentlemen,' for instance, is expressed by the fact that outside the

subordination determined by the different functions of 'business,' it would be considered strictly repugnant—wherever the old tradition still prevails—if even the richest 'chief,' while playing billiards or cards in his club in the evening, would not treat his 'clerk' as in every sense fully his equal in birthright. It would be repugnant if the American 'chief' would bestow upon his 'clerk' the condescending 'benevolence' marking a distinction of 'position,' which the German chief can never dissever from his attitude. This is one of the most important reasons why in America the German 'clubby-ness' has never been able to attain the attraction that the American clubs have.

Guarantees of Status Stratification

In content, status honor is normally expressed by the fact that above all else a specific *style of life* can be expected from all those who wish to belong to the circle. Linked with this expectation are restrictions on 'social' intercourse (that is, intercourse which is not subservient to economic or any other of business's 'functional' purposes). These restrictions may confine normal marriages to within the status circle and may lead to complete endogamous closure. As soon as there is not a mere individual and socially irrelevant imitation of another style of life, but an agreed-upon communal action of this closing character, the 'status' development is under way.

In its characteristic form, stratification by 'status groups' on the basis of conventional styles of life evolves at the present time in the United States out of the traditional democracy. For example, only the resident of a certain street ('the street') is considered as belonging to 'society,' is qualified for social intercourse, and is visited and invited. Above all, this differentiation evolves in such a way as to make for strict submission to the fashion that is dominant at a given time in society. This submission to fashion also exists among men in America to a degree unknown in Germany. Such submission is considered to be an indication of the fact that a given man *pretends* to qualify as a gentleman. This submission decides, at least *prima facie,* that he will be treated as such. And this recognition becomes just as important for his employment chances in 'swank' establishments, and above all, for social intercourse and marriage with 'esteemed' families, as the qualification for dueling among Germans in the Kaiser's day. As for the rest: certain families resident for a long time, and, of course, correspondingly wealthy, e.g. 'F. F. V., i.e. First Families of Virginia,' or the actual or alleged descendants of the 'Indian Princess' Pocahontas, of the Pilgrim fathers, or of the Knickerbockers, the members of almost inaccessible sects and all sorts of circles setting themselves apart by means of any other characteristics and badges … all these elements usurp 'status' honor. The development of status is essentially a question of stratification resting upon usurpation. Such usurpation is the normal origin of almost all status honor. But the road from this purely conventional situation to legal privilege, positive or negative, is easily traveled as soon as a certain stratification of the social order has in fact been 'lived in' and has achieved stability by virtue of a stable distribution of economic power.

'Ethnic' Segregation and 'Caste'

Where the consequences have been realized to their full extent, the status group evolves into a closed 'caste.' Status distinctions are then guaranteed not merely by conventions and laws, but also by *rituals*. This occurs in such a way that every physical contact with a member of any caste that is considered to be 'lower' by the members of a 'higher' caste is considered as making for a ritualistic impurity and to be a stigma which must be expiated by a religious act. Individual castes develop quite distinct cults and gods.

In general, however, the status structure reaches such extreme consequences only where there are underlying differences which are held to be 'ethnic.' The 'caste' is, indeed, the normal form in which ethnic communities usually live side by side in a 'societalized' manner. These ethnic communities believe in blood relationship and exclude exogamous marriage and social intercourse. Such a caste situation is part of the phenomenon of 'pariah' peoples and is found all over the world. These people form communities, acquire specific occupational traditions of handicrafts or of other arts, and cultivate a belief in their ethnic community. They live in a 'diaspora' strictly segregated from all personal intercourse, except that of an unavoidable sort, and their situation is legally precarious. Yet, by virtue of their economic indispensability, they are tolerated, indeed, frequently privileged, and they live in interspersed political communities. The Jews are the most impressive historical example.

A 'status' segregation grown into a 'caste' differs in its structure from a mere 'ethnic' segregation: the caste structure transforms the horizontal and unconnected coexistences of ethnically segregated groups into a vertical social system of super- and subordination. Correctly formulated: a comprehensive societalization integrates the ethnically divided communities into specific political and communal action. In their consequences they differ precisely in this way: ethnic coexistences condition a mutual repulsion and disdain but allow each ethnic community to consider its own honor as the highest one; the caste structure brings about a social subordination and an acknowledgment of 'more honor' in favor of the privileged caste and status groups. This is due to the fact that in the caste structure ethnic distinctions as such have become 'functional' distinctions within the political societalization (warriors, priests, artisans that are politically important for war and for building, and so on). But even pariah people who are most despised are usually apt to continue cultivating in some manner that which is equally peculiar to ethnic and to status communities: the belief in their own specific 'honor.' This is the case with the Jews.

Only with the negatively privileged status groups does the 'sense of dignity' take a specific deviation. A sense of dignity is the precipitation in individuals of social honor and of conventional demands which a positively privileged status group raises for the deportment of its members. The sense of dignity that characterizes positively privileged status groups is naturally related to their 'being' which does not transcend itself, that is, it is to their 'beauty and excellence.' Their kingdom is 'of this world.' They live for the present and by exploiting their great past. The sense of dignity of the negatively privileged strata naturally refers to a future lying beyond the present, whether it is of this life or of another. In other words, it must be nurtured by the belief in a providential 'mission' and by a belief in a specific honor before God. The 'chosen people's' dignity is nurtured by a belief either that in the beyond 'the last will be the first,' or that in this life a Messiah will appear to bring forth into the light of the world which has cast them out the hidden honor of the pariah people. This simple state of affairs, and not the 'resentment' which is so strongly emphasized in Nietzsche's much admired construction in the *Genealogy of Morals,* is the source of the religiosity cultivated by pariah status groups. In passing, we may note that resentment may be accurately applied only to a limited extent; for one of Nietzsche's main examples, Buddhism, it is not at all applicable.

Incidentally, the development of status groups from ethnic segregations is by no means the normal phenomenon. On the contrary, since objective 'racial differences' are by no means basic to every subjective sentiment of an ethnic community, the ultimately racial foundation of status structure is rightly and absolutely a question of the concrete individual case. Very frequently a status group is instrumental in the production of a thoroughbred anthropological type. Certainly a status group is to a high degree effective in producing extreme types, for they select personally qualified individuals (e.g. the Knighthood selects those who are fit for warfare, physically and psychically). But selection is far from being the only, or the predominant, way in which status groups are formed: Political membership or class situation has at all times been at least as frequently decisive. And today the class situation is by far the predominant factor, for of course the possibility of a style of life expected for members of a status group is usually conditioned economically.

Status Privileges

For all practical purposes, stratification by status goes hand in hand with a monopolization of ideal and material goods or opportunities, in a manner we have come to know as typical. Besides the specific status honor, which always rests upon distance and exclusiveness, we find all sorts of material monopolies. Such honorific preferences may consist of the privilege of wearing special costumes, of eating special dishes taboo to others, of carrying arms—which is most obvious in its consequences—the right to pursue certain non-professional dilettante artistic practices, e.g. to play certain musical instruments. Of course, material monopolies provide the most effective motives for the exclusiveness of a status group; although, in themselves, they are rarely sufficient, almost always they come into play to some extent. Within a status circle there is the question of intermarriage: the interest of the families in the monopolization of potential bridegrooms is at least of equal importance and is parallel to the interest in the monopolization of daughters. The daughters of the circle must be provided for. With an increased inclosure of the status group, the conventional preferential opportunities for special employment grow into a legal monopoly of special offices for the members. Certain goods become objects for monopolization by status groups. In the typical fashion these include 'entailed estates' and frequently also the possessions of serfs or bondsmen and, finally, special trades. This monopolization occurs positively when the status group is exclusively entitled to own and to manage them; and negatively when, in order to maintain its specific way of life, the status group must *not* own and manage them.

The decisive role of a 'style of life' in status 'honor' means that status groups are the specific bearers of all 'conventions.' In whatever way it may be manifest, all 'stylization' of life either originates in status groups or is at least conserved by them. Even if the principles of status conventions differ greatly, they reveal certain typical traits, especially among those strata which are most privileged. Quite generally, among privileged status groups there is a status disqualification that operates against the performance of common physical labor. This disqualification is now 'setting in' in America against the old tradition of esteem for labor. Very frequently every rational economic pursuit, and especially 'entrepreneurial activity,' is looked upon as a disqualification of status. Artistic and literary activity is also considered as degrading work as soon as it is exploited for income, or at least when it is connected with hard physical exertion. An example is the sculptor working like a mason in his dusty smock as over against the painter in his salon-like 'studio' and those forms of musical practice that are acceptable to the status group.

Economic Conditions and Effects of Status Stratification

The frequent disqualification of the gainfully employed as such is a direct result of the principle of status stratification peculiar to the social order, and of course, of this principle's opposition to a distribution of power which is regulated exclusively through the market. These two factors operate along with various individual ones, which will be touched upon below.

We have seen above that the market and its processes 'knows no personal distinctions': 'functional' interests dominate it. It knows nothing of 'honor.' The status order means precisely the reverse, viz.: stratification in terms of 'honor' and of styles of life peculiar to status groups as such. If mere economic acquisition and naked economic power still bearing the stigma of its extra-status origin could bestow upon anyone who has won it the same honor as those who are interested in status by virtue of style of life claim for themselves, the status order would be threatened at its very root. This is the more so as, given equality of status honor, property *per se* represents an addition even if it is not overtly acknowledged to be such. Yet if such economic acquisition and power gave the agent any honor at all, his wealth would result in his attaining more honor than those who successfully claim honor by virtue of style of life. Therefore all groups having interests in the status order react with special sharpness precisely against the pretensions of purely economic acquisition. In most cases they react the more vigorously the more they feel themselves threatened. Calderon's respectful treatment of the peasant, for instance, as opposed to Shakespeare's simultaneous and ostensible disdain of the *canaille* illustrates the different way in which a firmly structured status order reacts as compared with a status order that has become economically pre-

carious. This is an example of a state of affairs that recurs everywhere. Precisely because of the rigorous reactions against the claims of property *per se,* the 'parvenu' is never accepted, personally and without reservation, by the privileged status groups, no matter how completely his style of life has been adjusted to theirs. They will only accept his descendants who have been educated in the conventions of their status group and who have never besmirched its honor by their own economic labor.

As to the general *effect* of the status order, only one consequence can be stated, but it is a very important one: the hindrance of the free development of the market occurs first for those goods which status groups directly withheld from free exchange by monopolization. This monopolization may be effected either legally or conventionally. For example, in many Hellenic cities during the epoch of status groups, and also originally in Rome, the inherited estate (as is shown by the old formula for indication against spendthrifts) was monopolized just as were the estates of knights, peasants, priests, and especially the clientele of the craft and merchant guilds. The market is restricted, and the power of naked property *per se,* which gives its stamp to 'class formation,' is pushed into the background. The results of this process can be most varied. Of course, they do not necessarily weaken the contrasts in the economic situation. Frequently they strengthen these contrasts, and in any case, where stratification by status permeates a community as strongly as was the case in all political communities of antiquity and of the Middle Ages, one can never speak of a genuinely free market competition as we understand it today. There are wider effects than this direct exclusion of special goods from the market. From the contrariety between the status order and the purely economic order mentioned above, it follows that in most instances the notion of honor peculiar to status absolutely abhors that which is essential to the market: higgling. Honor abhors higgling among peers and occasionally it taboos higgling for the members of a status group in general. Therefore, everywhere some status groups, and usually the most influential, consider almost any kind of overt participation in economic acquisition as absolutely stigmatizing.

With some over-simplification, one might thus say that 'classes' are stratified according to their relations to the production and acquisition of goods; whereas 'status groups' are stratified according to the principles of their *consumption* of goods as represented by special 'styles of life.'

An 'occupational group' is also a status group. For normally, it successfully claims social honor only by virtue of the special style of life which may be determined by it. The differences between classes and status groups frequently overlap. It is precisely those status communities most strictly segregated in terms of honor (viz. the Indian castes) who today show, although within very rigid limits, a relatively high degree of indifference to pecuniary income. However, the Brahmins seek such income in many different ways.

As to the general economic conditions making for the predominance of stratification by 'status,' only very little can be said. When the bases of the acquisition and distribution of goods are relatively stable, stratification by status is favored. Every technological repercussion and economic transformation threatens stratification by status and pushes the class situation into the foreground. Epochs and countries in which the naked class situation is of predominant significance are regularly the periods of technical and economic transformations. And every slowing down of the shifting of economic stratifications leads, in due course, to the growth of status structures and makes for a resuscitation of the important role of social honor.

Parties

Whereas the genuine place of 'classes' is within the economic order, the place of 'status groups' is within the social order, that is, within the sphere of the distribution of 'honor.' From within these spheres, classes and status groups influence one another and they influence the legal order and are in turn influenced by it. But 'parties' live in a house of 'power.'

Their action is oriented toward the acquisition of social 'power,' that is to say, toward influencing a communal action no matter what its content may be. In principle, parties may exist in a social 'club' as well as in a 'state.' As over against the actions of classes and status groups, for which this is not necessarily the case, the communal actions of 'parties' always mean a societalization. For party actions are always directed toward a goal which is striven for in planned manner. This goal may be a 'cause' (the party may aim at realizing a program for ideal or material purposes), or the goal may be 'personal' (sinecures, power, and from these, honor for the leader and the followers of the party). Usually the party action aims at all these simultaneously. Parties are, therefore, only possible within communities that are societalized, that is, which have some rational order and a staff of persons available who are ready to enforce it. For parties aim precisely at influencing this staff, and if possible, to recruit it from party followers.

In any individual case, parties may represent interests determined through 'class situation' or 'status situation,' and they may recruit their following respectively from one or the other. But they need be neither purely 'class' nor purely 'status' parties. In most cases they are partly class parties and partly status parties, but sometimes they are neither. They may represent ephemeral or enduring structures. Their means of attaining power may be quite varied, ranging from naked violence of any sort to canvassing for votes with coarse or subtle means: money, social influence, the force of speech, suggestion, clumsy hoax, and so on to the rougher or more artful tactics of obstruction in parliamentary bodies.

The sociological structure of parties differs in a basic way according to the kind of communal action which they struggle to influence. Parties also differ according to whether or not the community is stratified by status or by classes. Above all else, they vary according to the structure of domination within the community. For their leaders normally deal with the conquest of a community. They are, in the general concept which is maintained here, not only products of specially modern forms of domination. We shall also designate as parties the ancient and medieval 'parties,' despite the fact that their structure differs basically from the structure of modern parties. By virtue of these structural differences of domination it is impossible to say anything about the structure of parties without discussing the structural forms of social domination *per se.* Parties, which are always structures struggling for domination, are very frequently organized in a very strict 'authoritarian' fashion. ...

Concerning 'classes,' 'status groups,' and 'parties,' it must be said in general that they necessarily presuppose a comprehensive societalization, and especially a political framework of communal action, within which they operate. This does not mean that parties would be confined by the frontiers of any individual political community. On the contrary, at all times it has been the order of the day that the societalization (even when it aims at the use of military force in common) reaches beyond the frontiers of politics. This has been the case in the solidarity of interests among the Oligarchs and among the democrats in Hellas, among the Guelfs and among Ghibellines in the Middle Ages, and within the Calvinist party during the period of religious struggles. It has been the case up to the solidarity of the landlords (in-

ternational congress of agrarian landlords), and has continued among princes (holy alliance, Karlsbad decrees), socialist workers, conservatives (the longing of Prussian conservatives for Russian intervention in 1850). But their aim is not necessarily the establishment of new international political, i.e. *territorial,* dominion. In the main they aim to influence the existing dominion.[2]

Notes

1. *Wirtschaft und Gesellschaft*, part III, chap. 4, pp. 631–40. The first sentence in paragraph one and the several definitions in this chapter which are in brackets do not appear in the original text. They have been taken from other contexts of *Wirtschaft und Gesellschaft*.

2. The posthumously published text breaks off here. We omit an incomplete sketch of types of 'warrior estates.'

MAX WEBER

Status Groups and Classes

The Concepts of Class and Class Situation

The term 'class situation'[1] will be applied to the typical probability that a given state of (a) provision with goods, (b) external conditions of life, and (c) subjective satisfaction or frustration will be possessed by an individual or a group. These probabilities define class situation in so far as they are dependent on the kind and extent of control or lack of it which the individual has over goods or services and existing possibilities of their ex-

ploitation for the attainment of income or receipts within a given economic order.

A 'class' is any group of persons occupying the same class situation. The following types of classes may be distinguished: (a) A class is a 'property class' when class situation for its members is primarily determined by the differentiation of property holdings; (b) a class is an 'acquisition class' when the class situation of its members is primarily determined by their opportunity for the exploitation of services on the market; (c) the 'social class' structure is composed of the plurality of class situations between which an interchange of individuals on a personal basis or in the course of generations is readily possible and typically observable. On the basis of any of the three types of class situation, associative relationships between those sharing the same class interests, namely, corporate class organizations may develop. This need not, however, necessarily happen. The concepts of class and class situation as such designate only the fact of identity or similarity in the typical situation in which a given individual and many others find their interests defined. In principle control over different combinations of consumer goods, means of production, investments, capital funds or marketable abilities constitute class situations which are different with each variation and combination. Only persons who are completely unskilled, without property and dependent on employment without regular occupation, are in a strictly identical class situation. Transitions from one class situation to another vary greatly in fluidity and in the ease with which an individual can enter the class. Hence the unity of 'social' classes is highly relative and variable.

The Significance of Property Classes

The primary significance of a positively privileged property class lies in the following facts: (i) Its members may be able to monopolize the purchase of high-priced consumer goods. (ii) They may control the opportunities of pursuing a systematic monopoly policy in the sale of economic goods. (iii) They may monopolize opportunities for the accumulation of property through unconsumed surpluses. (iv) They may monopolize opportunities to accumulate capital by saving, hence, the possibility of investing property in loans and the related possibility of control over executive positions in business. (v) They may monopolize the privileges of socially advantageous kinds of education so far as these involve expenditures.

Positively privileged property classes typically live from property income. This may be derived from property rights in human beings, as with slaveowners, in land, in mining property, in fixed equipment such as plant and apparatus, in ships, and as creditors in loan relationships. Loans may consist of domestic animals, grain, or money. Finally they may live on income from securities.

Class interests which are negatively privileged with respect to property belong typically to one of the following types: (a) They are themselves objects of ownership, that is they are unfree. (b) They are 'outcasts,' that is 'proletarians' in the sense meant in Antiquity. (c) They are debtor classes and, (d) the 'poor.'

In between stand the 'middle' classes. This term includes groups who have all sorts of property, or of marketable abilities through training, who are in a position to draw their support from these sources. Some of them may be 'acquisition' classes. Entrepreneurs are in this category by virtue of essentially positive privileges; proletarians, by virtue of negative privileges. But many types such as peasants, craftsmen, and officials do not fall in this category.

The differentiation of classes on the basis of property alone is not 'dynamic,' that is, it does not necessarily result in class struggles or class revolutions. It is not uncommon for very strongly privileged property classes, such as slaveowners, to exist side by side with such far less privileged groups as peasants or even outcasts without any class struggle. There may even be ties of solidarity between privileged property classes and unfree elements. However, such conflicts as that between land owners and outcast elements or between creditors and debtors, the latter often being a question of urban patricians as opposed to either rural peasants or urban craftsmen, may lead to revolutionary conflict. Even this, however, need not necessarily aim at radical changes in economic organization. It may, on the contrary, be concerned in the first instance only with a redistribution of wealth. These may be called 'property revolutions.'

A classic example of the lack of class antagonism has been the relation of the 'poor white trash,' originally those not owning slaves, to the planters in the Southern States of the United States. The 'poor whites' have often been much more hostile to the Negro than the planters who have frequently had a large element of patriarchal sentiment. The conflict of outcast against the property classes, of creditors and debtors, and of landowners and outcasts are best illustrated in the history of Antiquity.

The Significance of Acquisition and Social Classes

The primary significance of a positively privileged acquisition class is to be found in two directions. On the one hand it is generally possible to go far toward attaining a monopoly of the management of productive enterprises in favour of the members of the class and their business interests. On the other hand, such a class tends to insure the security of its economic position by exercising influence on the economic policy of political bodies and other groups.

The members of positively privileged acquisition classes are typically entrepreneurs. The following are the most important types: merchants, shipowners, industrial and agricultural entrepreneurs, bankers and financiers. Under certain circumstances two other types are also members of such classes, namely, members of the 'liberal' professions with a privileged position by virtue of their abilities or training, and workers with special skills commanding a monopolistic position, regardless of how far they are hereditary or the result of training.

Acquisition classes in a negatively privileged situation are workers of the various principal types. They may be roughly classified as skilled, semi-skilled and unskilled.

In this connexion as well as the above, independent peasants and craftsmen are to be treated as belonging to the 'middle classes.' This category often includes in addition officials, whether they are in public or private employment, the liberal professions, and workers with exceptional monopolistic assets or positions.

Examples of 'social classes' are: (a) The 'working' class as a whole. It approaches this type the more completely mechanized the productive process becomes. (b) The petty bourgeoisie.[2] (c) The 'intelligentsia' without independent property and the persons whose social position is primarily dependent on technical training such as engineers, commercial and other officials, and civil servants. These groups may differ greatly among themselves, in particular according to costs of training. (d) The classes occupying a privileged position through property and education.

The unfinished concluding section of Karl Marx's *Kapital* was evidently intended to deal with the problem of the class unity of the proletariat, which he held existed in spite of the high degree of qualitative differentiation. A decisive factor is the increase in the importance of semi-skilled workers who have been trained in a relatively short time directly on the machines themselves, at the expense of the older type of 'skilled' labour and also of unskilled. However, even this type of skill may often have a monopolistic aspect. Weavers are said to attain the highest level of productivity only after five years' experience.

At an earlier period every worker could be said to have been primarily interested in becoming an independent small bourgeois, but the possibility of realizing this goal is becoming progressively smaller. From one generation to another the most readily available path to advancement both for skilled and semi-skilled workers is into the class of technically trained individuals. In the most highly privileged classes, at least over the period of more than one generation, it is coming more and more to be true that money is overwhelmingly decisive. Through the banks and corporate enterprises members of the lower middle class and the salaried groups have certain opportunities to rise into the privileged class.

Organized activity of class groups is favoured by the following circumstances: (a) The possibility of concentrating on opponents where the immediate conflict of interests is vital. Thus workers organize against management and not against security holders who are the ones who really draw income without working. Similarly peasants are not apt to organize against landlords. (b) The existence of a class situation which is typically similar for large masses of people. (c) The technical possibility of being easily brought together. This is particularly true where large numbers work together in a small area, as in the modern factory. (d) Leadership directed to readily understandable goals. Such goals are very generally imposed or at least are interpreted by persons, such as intelligentsia, who do not belong to the class in question.

Status and Status Group

The term of 'status'[3] will be applied to a typically effective claim to positive or negative privilege with respect to social prestige so far as it rests on one or more of the following bases: (a) mode of living, (b) a formal process of education which may consist in empirical or rational training and the acquisition of the corresponding modes of life, or (c) on the prestige of birth, or of an occupation.

The primary practical manifestations of status with respect to social stratification are conubium, commensality, and often monopolistic appropriation of privileged economic opportunities and also prohibition of certain modes of acquisition. Finally, there are conventions or traditions of other types attached to a status.

Status may be based on class situation directly or related to it in complex ways. It is not, however, determined by this alone. Property and managerial positions are not as such sufficient to lend their holder a certain status, though they may well lead to its acquisition. Similarly, poverty is not as such a disqualification for high status though again it may influence it.

Conversely, status may partly or even wholly determine class situation, without, however, being identical with it. The class situation of an officer, a civil servant, and a student as determined by their income may be widely different while their status remains the same, because they adhere to the same mode of life in all relevant respects as a result of their common education.

A 'status group' is a plurality of individuals who, within a larger group, enjoy a particular kind and level of prestige by virtue of their position and possibly also claim certain special monopolies.

The following are the most important sources of the development of distinct status groups: (a) The most important is by the development of a peculiar style of life including, particularly, the type of occupation pursued. (b) The second basis is hereditary charisma arising from the successful claim to a position of prestige by virtue of birth. (c) The third is the appropriation of political or hierocratic authority as a monopoly by socially distinct groups.

The development of hereditary status groups is usually a form of the hereditary appropriation of privileges by an organized group or by individual qualified persons. Every well-established case of appropriation of opportunities and abilities, especially of exercising imperative powers, has a tendency to lead to the development of distinct status groups. Conversely, the development of status groups has a tendency in turn to lead to the monopolistic appropriation of governing powers and of the corresponding economic advantages.

Acquisition classes are favoured by an economic system oriented to market situations, whereas status groups develop and subsist most readily where economic organization is of a monopolistic and liturgical character and where the economic needs of corporate groups are met on a feudal or patrimonial basis. The type of class which is most closely related to a status group is the 'social' class, while the 'acquisition' class is the farthest removed. Property classes often constitute the nucleus of a status group.

Every society where status groups play a prominent part is controlled to a large extent by conventional rules of conduct. It thus creates economically irrational conditions of consumption and hinders the development of free markets by monopolistic appropriation and by restricting free disposal of the individual's own economic ability. This will have to be discussed further elsewhere.

Notes

[1]. Although Parsons chooses to translate *Klasse* as "class status" in this context, to do so is potentially confusing because Weber so carefully distinguishes between the concepts of class and status. I have therefore followed the lead of Roth and Wittich (*Economy and Society*, 1968) and opted for the term "class situation" throughout this essay.—ED.

[2]. I have again followed Roth and Wittich (*Economy and Society*, 1968) in translating the German term *Kleinbürgertum* as "petty bourgeoisie," whereas Parsons opted for the more ambiguous term "lower middle" class.—ED.

[3]. For the purposes of consistency with the other selections, I have translated the term *ständische Lage* as "status" (see Roth and Wittich, *Economy and Society*, 1968), whereas Parsons opted for the terms "social status," "stratifactory status," and the like.—ED.

MAX WEBER

Open and Closed Relationships

Social Relationships

A social relationship, regardless of whether it is communal or associative in character, will be spoken of as "open" to outsiders if and insofar as its system of order does not deny participation to anyone who wishes to join and is actually in a position to do so. A relationship will, on the other hand, be called "closed" against outsiders so far as, according to its subjective meaning and its binding rules, participation of certain persons is excluded, limited, or subjected to conditions. Whether a relationship is open or closed may be determined traditionally, affectually, or rationally in terms of values or of expediency. It is especially likely to be closed, for rational reasons, in the following type of situation: a social relationship may provide the parties to it with opportunities for the satisfaction of spiritual or material interests, whether absolutely or instrumentally, or whether it is achieved through co-operative action or by a compromise of interests. If the participants expect that the admission of others will lead to an improvement of their situation, an improvement in degree, in kind, in the security or the value of the satisfaction, their interest will be in keeping the relationship open. If, on the other hand, their expectations are of improving their position by monopolistic tactics, their interest is in a closed relationship.

There are various ways in which it is possible for a closed social relationship to guarantee its monopolized advantages to the parties. (a) Such advantages may be left free to competitive struggle within the group; (b) they may be regulated or rationed in amount and kind, or (c) they may be appropriated by individuals or sub-groups on a permanent basis and become more or less inalienable. The last is a case of closure within, as well as against outsiders. Appropriated advantages will be called "rights." As determined by the relevant order, appropriation may be (1) for the benefit of the members of particular communal or associative groups (for instance, household groups), or (2) for the benefit of individuals. In the latter case, the individual may enjoy his rights on a purely personal basis or in such a way that in case of his death one or more other persons related to the holder of the right by birth (kinship), or by some other social relationship, may inherit the rights in question. Or the rights may pass to one or more individuals specifically designated by the holder. These are cases of hereditary appropriation. Finally, (3) it may be that the holder is more or less fully empowered to alienate his rights by voluntary agreement, either to other specific persons or to anyone he chooses. This is alienable appropriation. A party to a closed social relationship will be called a "member"; in case his participation is regulated in such a way as to guarantee him appropriated advantages, a privileged member (*Rechtsgenosse*). Appropriated rights which are enjoyed by individuals through inheritance or by hereditary groups, whether communal or associative, will be called the "property" of the individual or of groups in question; and, insofar as they are alienable, "free" property.

The apparently gratuitous tediousness involved in the elaborate definition of the above concepts is an example of the fact that we often neglect to think out clearly what seems to be obvious, because it is intuitively familiar.

1. (a) Examples of communal relationships, which tend to be closed on a traditional basis, are those in which membership is determined by family relationship.

(b) Personal emotional relationships are usually affectually closed. Examples are erotic relationships and, very commonly, relations of personal loyalty.

(c) Closure on the basis of value-rational commitment to values is usual in groups sharing a common system of explicit religious belief.

(d) Typical cases of rational closure on grounds of expediency are economic associations of a monopolistic or a plutocratic character.

A few examples may be taken at random. Whether a group of people engaged in conversation is open or closed depends on its content. General conversation is apt to be open, as contrasted with intimate conversation or the imparting of official information. Market relationships are in most, or at least in many, cases essentially open. In the case of many relationships, both communal and associative, there is a tendency to shift from a phase of expansion to one of exclusiveness. Examples are the guilds and the democratic city-states of Antiquity and the Middle Ages. At times these groups sought to increase their membership in the interest of improving the security of their position of power by adequate numbers. At other times they restricted their membership to protect the value of their monopolistic position. The same phenomenon is not uncommon in monastic orders and religious sects which have passed from a stage of religious proselytizing to one of restriction in the interest of the maintenance of an ethical standard or for the protection of material interests. There is a similar close relationship between the extension of market relationships in the interest of increased turnover on the one hand, their monopolistic restriction on the other. The promotion of linguistic uniformity is today a natural result of the interests of publishers and writers, as opposed to the earlier, not uncommon, tendency for status groups to maintain linguistic peculiarities or even for secret languages to emerge.

2. Both the extent and the methods of regulation and exclusion in relation to outsiders may vary widely, so that the transition from a state of openness to one of regulation and closure is gradual. Various conditions of participation may be laid down; qualifying tests, a period of probation, requirement of possession of a share which can be purchased under certain conditions, election of new members by ballot, membership or eligibility by birth or by virtue of achievements open to anyone. Finally, in case of closure and the appropriation of rights within the group, participation may be dependent on the acquisition of an appropriated right. There is a wide variety of different degrees of closure and of conditions of participation. Thus regulation and closure are relative concepts. There are all manner of gradual shadings as between an exclusive club, a theatrical audience the members of which have purchased tickets, and a party rally to which the largest possible number has been urged to come; similarly, from a church service open to the general public through the rituals of a limited sect to the mysteries of a secret cult.

3. Similarly, closure within the group may also assume the most varied forms. Thus a caste, a guild, or a group of stock exchange brokers, which is closed to outsiders, may allow to its members a perfectly free competition for all the advantages which the group as a whole monopolizes for itself. Or it may assign every member strictly to the enjoyment of certain advantages, such as claims over customers or particular business opportunities, for life or even on a hereditary

basis. This is particularly characteristic of India. Similarly, a closed group of settlers (*Markgenossenschaft*) may allow its members free use of the resources of its area or may restrict them rigidly to a plot assigned to each individual household. A closed group of colonists may allow free use of the land or sanction and guarantee permanent appropriation of separate holdings. In such cases all conceivable transitional and intermediate forms can be found. Historically, the closure of eligibility to fiefs, benefices, and offices within the group, and the appropriation on the part of those enjoying them, have occurred in the most varied forms. Similarly, the establishment of rights to and possession of particular jobs on the part of workers may develop all the way from the "closed shop" to a right to a particular job. The first step in this development may be to prohibit the dismissal of a worker without the consent of the workers' representatives. The development of the "works councils" [in Germany after 1918] might be a first step in this direction, though it need not be. ...

4. The principal motives for closure of a relationship are: (a) The maintenance of quality, which is often combined with the interest in prestige and the consequent opportunities to enjoy honor, and even profit; examples are communities of ascetics, monastic orders, especially, for instance, the Indian mendicant orders, religious sects like the Puritans, organized groups of warriors, of *ministeriales* and other functionaries, organized citizen bodies as in the Greek states, craft guilds; (b) the contraction of advantages in relation to consumption needs (*Nahrungsspielraum*); examples are monopolies of consumption, the most developed form of which is a self-subsistent village community; (c) the growing scarcity of opportunities for acquisition (*Erwerbsspielraum*). This is found in trade monopolies such as guilds, the ancient monopolies of fishing rights, and so on. Usually motive (a) is combined with (b) or (c). ...

Economic Relationships

One frequent economic determinant [of closure] is the competition for a livelihood—offices, cli-

ents and other remunerative opportunities. When the number of competitors increases in relation to the profit span, the participants become interested in curbing competition. Usually one group of competitors takes some externally identifiable characteristic of another group of (actual or potential) competitors—race, language, religion, local or social origin, descent, residence, etc.—as a pretext for attempting their exclusion. It does not matter which characteristic is chosen in the individual case: whatever suggests itself most easily is seized upon. Such group action may provoke a corresponding reaction on the part of those against whom it is directed.

In spite of their continued competition against one another, the jointly acting competitors now form an "interest group" toward outsiders; there is a growing tendency to set up some kind of association with rational regulations; if the monopolistic interests persist, the time comes when the competitors, or another group whom they can influence (for example, a political community), establish a legal order that limits competition through formal monopolies; from then on, certain persons are available as "organs" to protect the monopolistic practices, if need be, with force. In such a case, the interest group has developed into a *"legally privileged group"* (*Rechtsgemeinschaft*) and the participants have become *"privileged members"* (*Rechtsgenossen*). Such closure, as we want to call it, is an ever-recurring process; it is the source of property in land as well as of all guild and other group monopolies.

The tendency toward the monopolization of specific, usually economic opportunities is always the driving force in such cases as: "cooperative organization," which always means closed monopolistic groups, for example, of fishermen taking their name from a certain fishing area; the establishment of an association of engineering graduates, which seeks to secure a legal, or at least factual, monopoly over certain positions; the exclusion of outsiders from sharing in the fields and commons of a village; "patriotic" associations of shop clerks; the *ministeriales,* knights, university graduates and craftsmen of a given region or locality; ex-soldiers entitled to civil service positions—all these groups first engage in some joint action (*Gemeinschaftshandeln*) and later perhaps an explicit association. This monopolization is directed against competitors who share some positive or negative characteristics; its purpose is always the closure of social and economic opportunities to *outsiders*. Its extent may vary widely, especially so far as the group member shares in the apportionment of monopolistic advantages. ...

This monopolistic tendency takes on specific forms when groups are formed by persons with shared qualities *acquired* through upbringing, apprenticeship and training. These characteristics may be economic qualifications of some kind, the holding of the same or of similar offices, a knightly or ascetic way of life, etc. If in such a case an association results from social action, it tends toward the *guild*. Full members make a vocation out of monopolizing the disposition of spiritual, intellectual, social and economic goods, duties and positions. Only those are admitted to the unrestricted practice of the vocation who (1) have completed a novitiate in order to acquire the proper training, (2) have proven their qualification, and (3) sometimes have passed through further waiting periods and met additional requirements. This development follows a typical pattern in groups ranging from the juvenile student fraternities, through knightly associations and craft-guilds, to the qualifications required of the modern officials and employees. It is true that the interest in guaranteeing an efficient performance may everywhere have some importance; the participants may desire it for idealistic or materialistic reasons in spite of their possibly continuing competition with one another: local craftsmen may desire it for the sake of their business reputation, *ministeriales* and knights of a given association for the sake of their professional reputation and also their own military security, and ascetic groups for fear that the gods and demons may turn their wrath against all members because of faulty manipulations. (For example, in almost all primitive tribes, persons who sang falsely during a ritual dance were originally slain in expiation of such an offense.) But normally this concern for efficient performance recedes behind the interest in limiting the supply of candidates for the benefices and honors of a given occupation. The novitiates, waiting periods, masterpieces and other demands, particularly the expensive entertainment of group members, are more often economic than professional tests of qualification.

MAX WEBER

The Rationalization of Education and Training

We cannot here analyze the far-reaching and general cultural effects that the advance of the rational bureaucratic structure of domination, as such, develops quite independently of the areas in which it takes hold. Naturally, bureaucracy promotes a 'rationalist' way of life, but the concept of rationalism allows for widely differing contents. Quite generally, one can only say that the bureaucratization of all domination very strongly furthers the development of 'rational matter-of-factness' and the personality type of the professional expert. This has far-reaching ramifications, but only one important element of the process can be briefly indicated here: its effect upon the nature of training and education.

Educational institutions on the European continent, especially the institutions of higher learning—the universities, as well as technical academies, business colleges, gymnasiums, and other middle schools—are dominated and influenced by the need for the kind of 'education' that produces a system of special examinations and the trained expertness that is increasingly indispensable for modern bureaucracy.

The 'special examination,' in the present sense, was and is found also outside of bureaucratic structures proper; thus, today it is found in the 'free' professions of medicine and law and in the guild-organized trades. Expert examinations are neither indispensable to nor concomitant phenomena of bureaucratization. The French, English, and American bureaucracies have for a long time foregone such examinations entirely or to a large extent, for training and service in party organizations have made up for them.

'Democracy' also takes an ambivalent stand in the face of specialized examinations, as it does in the face of all the phenomena of bureaucracy—although democracy itself promotes these developments. Special examinations, on the one hand, mean or appear to mean a 'selection' of those who qualify from all social strata rather than a rule by notables. On the other hand, democracy fears that a merit system and educational certificates will result in a privileged 'caste.' Hence, democracy fights against the special-examination system.

The special examination is found even in prebureaucratic or semi-bureaucratic epochs. Indeed, the regular and earliest locus of special examinations is among prebendally organized dominions. Expectancies of prebends, first of church prebends—as in the Islamite Orient and in the Occidental Middle Ages—then, as was especially the case in China, secular prebends, are the typical prizes for which people study and are examined. These examinations, however, have in truth only a partially specialized and expert character.

The modern development of full bureaucratization brings the system of rational, specialized, and expert examinations irresistibly to the fore. The civil-service reform gradually imports expert training and specialized examinations into the United States. In all other countries this system also advances, stemming from its main breeding place, Germany. The increasing bureaucratization of administration enhances the importance of the specialized examination in England. In China, the attempt to replace the semi-patrimonial and ancient bureaucracy by a modern bureaucracy brought the expert examination; it took the place of a former and quite differently structured system of examinations. The bureaucratization of capitalism, with its demand for expertly trained technicians, clerks, et cetera, carries such examinations all over the world. Above all, the development is greatly furthered by the social prestige of the educational certificates acquired through such specialized examinations. This is all the more the case as the educational patent is turned to economic advantage. Today, the certificate of education becomes what the test for ancestors has been in the past, at least where the nobility has remained powerful: a prerequisite for equality of birth, a qualification for a canonship, and for state office.

The development of the diploma from universities, and business and engineering colleges, and the universal clamor for the creation of educational certificates in all fields make for the formation of a privileged stratum in bureaus and in offices. Such certificates support their holders' claims for intermarriages with notable families (in business offices people naturally hope for preferment with regard to the chief's daughter), claims to be admitted into the circles that adhere to 'codes of honor,' claims for a 'respectable' remuneration rather than remuneration for work done, claims for assured advancement and old-age insurance, and, above all, claims to monopolize socially and economically advantageous positions. When we hear from all sides the demand for an introduction of regular curricula and special examinations, the reason behind it is, of course, not a suddenly awakened 'thirst for education' but the desire for restricting the supply for these positions and their monopolization by the owners of educational certificates. Today, the 'examination' is the universal means of this monopolization, and therefore examinations irresistibly advance. As the education prerequisite to the acquisition of the educational certificate requires considerable expense and a period of waiting for full remuneration, this striving means a setback for talent (charisma) in favor of property. For the 'intellectual' costs of educational certificates are always low, and with the increasing volume of such certificates, their intellectual costs do not increase, but rather decrease. …

Social prestige based upon the advantage of special education and training as such is by no means specific to bureaucracy. On the contrary! But educational prestige in other structures of domination rests upon substantially different foundations.

Expressed in slogan-like fashion, the 'cultivated man,' rather than the 'specialist,' has been the end sought by education and has formed the basis of social esteem in such various systems as the feudal, theocratic, and patrimonial structures of dominion: in the English notable administration, in the old Chinese patrimonial bureaucracy, as well as under the rule of demagogues in the so-called Hellenic democracy.

The term 'cultivated man' is used here in a completely value-neutral sense; it is understood to mean solely that the goal of education consists in the quality of a man's bearing in life which was *considered* 'cultivated,' rather than in a specialized training for expertness. The 'cultivated' personality formed the educational ideal, which was stamped by the structure of domination and by the social condition for membership in the ruling stratum. Such education aimed at a chivalrous or an ascetic type; or, at a literary type, as in China; a gymnastic-humanist type, as in Hellas; or it aimed at a conventional type, as in the case of the Anglo-Saxon gentleman. The qualification of the ruling stratum as such rested upon the possession of 'more' cultural quality (in the absolutely changeable, value-neutral sense in which we use the term here), rather than upon 'more' expert knowledge. Special military, theological, and juridical ability was of course intensely practiced; but the point of gravity in Hellenic, in medieval, as well as in Chinese education, has rested upon educational elements that were entirely different from what was 'useful' in one's specialty.

Behind all the present discussions of the foundations of the educational system, the struggle of the 'specialist type of man' against the older type of 'cultivated man' is hidden at some decisive point. This fight is determined by the irresistibly expanding bureaucratization of all public and private relations of authority and by the ever-increasing importance of expert and specialized knowledge. This fight intrudes into all intimate cultural questions.

ANTHONY GIDDENS

The Class Structure of the Advanced Societies

The Weberian Critique

For the most significant developments in the theory of classes since Marx, we have to look to those forms of social thought whose authors, while being directly influenced by Marx's ideas, have attempted at the same time to criticise or to reformulate them. This tendency has been strongest, for a combination of historical and intellectual reasons, in German sociology, where a series of attempts have been made to provide a fruitful critique of Marx—beginning with Max Weber, and continuing through such authors as Geiger, Renner and Dahrendorf.[1] Weber's critique of Marx here has been of particular importance. But, especially in the English-speaking world, the real import of Weber's analysis has frequently been misrepresented. The customary procedure has been to contrast Weber's discussion of 'Class, status and party', a fragment of *Economy and Society*, with the conception of class supposedly taken by Marx, to the detriment of the latter. Marx, so it is argued, treated 'class' as a purely economic phenomenon and, moreover, regarded class conflicts as in some way the 'inevitable' outcome of clashes of material interest. He failed to realise, according to this argument, that the divisions of economic interest which create classes do not necessarily correspond to sentiments of communal identity which constitute differential 'status'. Thus, status, which depends upon subjective evaluation, is a separate 'dimension of stratification' from class, and the two may vary independently. There is yet a third dimension, so the argument continues, which Weber recognised as an independently variable factor in 'stratification', but which Marx treated as directly contingent upon class interests. This is the factor of 'power'.[2]

Evaluation of the validity of this interpretation is difficult because there is no doubt that Weber himself accepted it—or certain elements of it. What is often portrayed in the secondary literature as a critique of 'Marx's conception of class' actually takes a stilted and impoverished form of crude Marxism as its main target of attack. But this sort of determinist Marxism was already current in Germany in Weber's lifetime, and since Weber himself set out to question this determinism, the true lines of similarity and difference between his and Marx's analysis of classes are difficult to disentangle.[3] ...

In the two versions of 'Class, status and party' which have been embodied in *Economy and Society*,[4] Weber provides what is missing in Marx: an explicit discussion of the concept of class. There are two principal respects in which this analysis differs from Marx's 'abstract model' of classes. One is that which is familiar from most secondary accounts—the differentiation of 'class' from 'status' and 'party'. The second, however, as will be argued below, is equally important: this is that, although Weber employs for some purposes a dichotomous model which in certain general respects resembles that of Marx, his viewpoint strongly emphasises a *pluralistic conception of*

classes. Thus Weber's distinction between 'ownership classes' (*Besitzklassen*) and 'acquisition classes' (*Erwerbsklassen*) is based upon a fusion of two criteria: 'on the one hand ... the kind of property that is usable for returns; and, on the other hand ... the kind of services that can be offered on the market', thus producing a complex typology. The sorts of property which may be used to obtain market returns, although dividing generally into two types—creating ownership (*rentier*) and acquisition (entrepreneurial) classes—are highly variable, and may produce many differential interests within dominant classes:

Ownership of dwellings; workshops; warehouses; stores; agriculturally usable land in large or small-holdings—a quantitative difference with possibly qualitative consequences; ownership of mines; cattle; men (slaves); disposition over mobile instruments of production, or capital goods of all sorts, especially money or objects that can easily be exchanged for money; disposition over products of one's own labour or of others' labour differing according to their various distances from consumability; disposition over transferable monopolies of any kind—all these distinctions differentiate the class situations of the propertied ...[5]

But the class situations of the propertyless are also differentiated, in relation both to the types and the degree of 'monopolisation' of 'marketable skills' which they possess. Consequently, there are various types of 'middle class' which stand between the 'positively privileged' classes (the propertied) and the 'negatively privileged' classes (those who possess neither property nor marketable skills). While these groupings are all nominally propertyless, those who possess skills which have a definite 'market value' are certainly in a different class situation from those who have nothing to offer but their (unskilled) labour. In acquisition classes—i.e., those associated particularly with the rise of modern capitalism—educational qualifications take on a particular significance in this respect; but the monopolisation of trade skills by manual workers is also important.

Weber insists that a clear-cut distinction must be made between class 'in itself' and class 'for itself': 'class', in his terminology, always refers to market interests, which exist independently of whether men are aware of them. Class is thus an 'objective' characteristic influencing the life-chances of men. But only under certain conditions do those sharing a common class situation become conscious of, and act upon, their mutual economic interests. In making this emphasis, Weber undoubtedly intends to separate his position from that adopted by many Marxists, involving what he calls a 'pseudo-scientific operation' whereby the link between class and class consciousness is treated as direct and immediate.[6] Such a consideration evidently also underlies the emphasis which Weber places upon 'status groups' (*Stände*) as contrasted to classes. The contrast between class and status group, however, is not, as often seems to be assumed, merely, nor perhaps even primarily, a distinction between subjective and objective aspects of differentiation. While class is founded upon differentials of economic interest in market relationships, Weber nowhere denies that, under certain given circumstances, a class may be a subjectively aware 'community'. The importance of status groups—which are normally 'communities' in this sense—derives from the fact that they are built upon criteria of grouping other than those stemming from market situation. The contrast between classes and status groups is sometimes portrayed by Weber as one between the objective and the subjective; but it is also one between production and consumption. Whereas class expresses relationships involved in production, status groups express those involved in consumption, in the form of specific 'styles of life'.

Status affiliations may cut across the relationships generated in the market, since membership of a status group usually carries with it various sorts of monopolistic privileges. Nonetheless, classes and status groups tend in many cases to be closely linked, through property: possession of property is both a major determinant of class situation and also provides the basis for following a definite 'style of life'. The point of Weber's analysis is not that class and status constitute two 'dimensions of stratification', but that classes and status communities represent two possible, and competing, modes of group formation in relation to the distribution of power in society. Power is *not*, for Weber, a 'third dimension' in some sense comparable to the first two. He is quite explicit

about saying that classes, status groups and parties are all 'phenomena of the distribution of power'.[7] The theorem informing Weber's position here is his insistence that power is not to be assimilated to economic domination—again, of course, a standpoint taken in deliberate contrast to that of Marx. The party, oriented towards the acquisition or maintenance of political leadership, represents, like the class and the status group, a major focus of social organisation relevant to the distribution of power in a society. It is, however, only characteristic of the modern rational state. ...

In his conceptual discussion of class, besides distinguishing the purely economic *Besitzklassen* and *Erwerbsklassen*, Weber also refers to what he calls 'social classes'. A social class, in Weber's sense, is formed of a cluster of class situations which are linked together by virtue of the fact that they involve common mobility chances, either within the career of individuals or across the generations. Thus while a worker may fairly readily move from an unskilled to a semi-skilled manual occupation, and the son of an unskilled worker may become a semi-skilled or perhaps a skilled worker, the chances of either intra- or inter-generational mobility into non-manual occupations are much less. While the conception of the 'social class' remains relatively undeveloped in Weber's writings, it is of particular interest in relation to his model of capitalist development. As Weber himself points out, the notion of 'social class' comes much closer to that of 'status group' than does the conception of purely economic class (although, as with economic class situation, individuals who are in the same social class are not necessarily conscious of the fact). The notion of social class is important because it introduces a unifying theme into the diversity of cross-cutting class relationships which may stem from Weber's identification of 'class situation' with 'market position'. If the latter is applied strictly, it is possible to distinguish an almost endless multiplicity of class situations. But a 'social class' exists only when these class situations cluster together in such a way as to create a common nexus of social interchange between individuals. In capitalism, Weber distinguishes four main social class groupings: the manual working class; the petty bourgeoisie; propertyless white-collar workers: 'technicians, various kinds of white-collar employees, civil servants—possibly with considerable social differences depending on the cost of their training'; and those 'privileged through property and education'.[8] Of these social class groupings, the most significant are the working class, the propertyless 'middle class' and the propertied 'upper class'. Weber agrees with Marx that the category of small property-owners (*Kleinbürgertum*) tends to become progressively more restricted with the increasing maturity of capitalism. The result of this process, however, is not normally that they 'sink into the proletariat', but that they become absorbed into the expanding category of skilled manual or non-manual salaried workers.

To emphasise, therefore, that Weber's 'abstract model' of classes is a pluralistic one is not to hold that he failed to recognise unifying ties between the numerous combinations of class interests made possible by his conception of 'class situation'. But there is no doubt that his viewpoint drastically amends important elements of Marx's picture of the typical trend of development of the capitalist class structure. Even Weber's simplified ('social class') model of capitalism diverges significantly from the Marxian conception, in treating the propertyless 'middle class' as the category which tends to expand most with the advance of capitalism. Moreover, the social classes do not necessarily constitute 'communities', and they may be fragmented by interest divisions deriving from differentials in market position; and finally, as Weber shows in his historical writings, the relationship between class structure and the political sphere is a contingent one. ...

Rethinking the Theory of Class

The deficiency in Weber's reinterpretation of Marx's view is that it is not sufficiently radical. While Weber recognises the unsatisfactory character of the Marxian standpoint, particularly as regards the undifferentiated category of the 'propertyless', he does not pursue the implications of his own conception far enough. Dahrendorf has suggested that we may stand the Marxian concept of property on its head in terms of its relation to authority;[9] the implications of the Weberian analysis, however, are that the conception of property may be 'inverted' or generalised in a different way, which does not sacrifice the economic foundation of the concept of class. 'Property' refers, not to any characteristics of physical objects as such, but to rights which are associated with them, which in turn confer certain capacities upon the 'owner'. ... In the market, of course, the significance of capital as private property is that it confers certain very definite capacities upon its possessor as compared to those who are 'propertyless'—those who do not own their means of production. But we can readily perceive that, even in the Marxian view, the notion of 'propertylessness' is something of a misnomer. For if 'property' is conceived of as a set of capacities of action with reference to the operations of the market, it is evident that the wage-labourer does possess such capacities. The 'property' of the wage-labourer is the labour-power which he brings for sale in entering into the contractual relation. While this fundamentally disadvantages him in the competitive bargaining situation in relation to the owner of capital, this is not simply a one-way power relationship: the 'property' which the wage-labourer possesses is needed by the employer, and he must pay at least some minimal attention to the demands of the worker—providing a basis for the collective withdrawal of labour as a possible sanction. It would be departing too much from usual terminology to refer to capital and to the labour-power of the worker both as 'property'; and, anyway, the point is rather that 'property' (capital) is a particular case of capacity to determine the bargaining outcome, rather than vice versa. So I shall continue to speak below of 'property' (in the means of production) in a conventional sense, and shall use the term 'market capacity' in an inclusive manner *to refer to all forms of relevant attributes which individuals may bring to the bargaining encounter.*

It is an elementary fact that where ownership of property is concentrated in the hands of a minority and in a society in which the mass of the population is employed in industrial production, the vast majority consequently offer their labour for sale on the market. Because of his general emphasis upon 'productive labour', and because of his expectation that it is in the nature of modern technology to reduce productive operations to a homogeneous skill-level, Marx failed to recognise the potential significance of differentiations of market capacity which do not derive directly from the factor of property ownership. Such differentiations, it seems clear, are contingent upon the scarcity value of what the individual 'owns' and is able to offer on the market. As Weber indicates, possession of recognised 'skills'—including educational qualifications—is the major factor influencing market capacity. Differentiations in market capacity may be used, as various recent authors have indicated, to secure economic returns other than income as such. These include, principally, security of employment, prospects of career advancement, and a range of 'fringe benefits', such as pension rights, etc.[10] In the same way as the capacities which individuals bring to the bargaining process may be regarded as a form of 'property' which they exchange on the market, so these material returns may be regarded as forms of 'good' which are obtained through the sale of labour-power.

In the market structure of competitive capitalism, *all* those who participate in the exchange process are in a certain sense in (interest) conflict with one another for access to scarce returns. Conflict of interest may be created by the existence of many sorts of differential market capacities. Moreover, the possible relationships between property and 'propertyless' forms of market capacity are various. Speculative investment in property may, for example, be one of the specific market advantages used by those in certain occupations (thus directors are often able to use 'inside knowledge' to profit from property deals). Marx himself, of course, recognised the existence of persistent conflicts of interest within property-owning groupings: notably, between financial and industrial sectors of the large bourgeoisie, and between large and petty bourgeoisie.

The difficulty of identifying 'class' with common market capacity has already been alluded to with reference to Weber. While Weber's concept of 'market situation' successfully moves away from some of the rigidities of the Marxian scheme, it tends to imply the recognition of a cumbersome plurality of classes. There would appear to be as many 'classes', and as many 'class conflicts', as there are differing market positions. The problem here, however, is not the recognition of the diversity of the relationships and conflicts created by the capitalist market as such, but that of making the *theoretical transition from such relationships and conflicts to the identification of classes as structured forms.* The unsatisfactory and ill-defined character of the connections between 'class position', the typology of *Besitzklassen* and *Erwerbsklassen,* and 'social classes' in Weber's work has already been mentioned. But the problem is by no means confined to Weber's theoretical scheme. Marx was certainly conscious of the problematic character of the links between class as a latent set of characteristics generated by the capitalist system and class as an historical, dynamic entity, an 'historical actor'. But his contrast between class 'in itself' and class 'for itself' is primarily one distinguishing between class relationships as a cluster of economic connections on the one hand and class consciousness on the other. This emphasis was very much dictated by the nature of Marx's interests, lying as they did above all in understanding and promoting the rise of a revolutionary class consciousness within capitalism. While it would by no means be true to hold that Marx ignored this completely, it can be said that he gave only little attention to the modes in which classes, founded in a set of economic relationships, take on or 'express' themselves in definite social forms.

Nor has the matter been adequately dealt with in the writings of later authors. In fact, one of the leading dilemmas in the theory of class—which figures prominently, for example, in Aron's discussion—is that of identifying the 'reality' of class.[11] Not only has there been some considerable controversy over whether class is a 'real' or 'nominal' category, but many have argued that, since it is difficult or impossible to draw the 'boundaries' between classes with any degree of clarity, we should abandon the notion of class as a useful sociological concept altogether.[12] Only Dahrendorf seems to have attempted to give attention to the problem within the framework of an overall theory of class, and since his identification of class with authority divisions is unacceptable [for reasons outlined elsewhere],[13] his analysis does not help greatly.

The major problems in the theory of class, I shall suggest, do not so much concern the nature and application of the class concept itself, as what, for want of a better word, I shall call the *structuration* of class relationships.[14] Most attempts to revise class theory since Marx have sought to accomplish such a revision primarily by refining, modifying, or substituting an altogether different notion for the Marxian concept of class. While it is useful to follow and develop certain of Weber's insights in this respect, the most important blank spots in the theory of class concern the processes whereby 'economic classes' become 'social classes', and whereby in turn the latter are related to other social forms. As Marx was anxious to stress in criticising the premises of political economy, all economic relationships, and any sort of 'economy', presuppose a set of social ties between producers. In arguing for the necessity of conceptualising the structuration of class relationships, I do not in any way wish to question the legitimacy of this insight, but rather to focus upon *the modes in which* 'economic' relationships become translated into 'non-economic' social structures.

One source of terminological ambiguity and conceptual confusion in the usage of the term 'class' is that it has often been employed to refer both to an economic *category* and to a specifiable cluster of social groupings. Thus Weber uses the term in both of these ways, although he seeks terminologically to indicate the difference between 'class' (as a series of 'class positions') and 'social class'. But in order to insist that the study of class and class conflict must concern itself with the interdependence of economy and society, it is not necessary to identify the term 'class' with the divisions and interests generated by the market as such. Consequently, in the remainder of this [essay], I shall use the term in the sense of Weber's 'social class'—appropriately explicated. While there may be an indefinite multiplicity of cross-cutting interests created by differential market capacities, there are only, in any given society, a limited number of classes.

It will be useful at this juncture to state what class is *not*. First, a class is not a specific 'entity'— that is to say, a bounded social form in the way in which a business firm or a university is—and a class has no publicly sanctioned identity. It is extremely important to stress this, since established linguistic usage often encourages us to apply active verbs to the term 'class'; but the sense in which a class 'acts' in a certain way, or 'perceives' elements in its environment on a par with an individual actor, is highly elliptical, and this sort of verbal usage is to be avoided wherever possible. Similarly, it is perhaps misleading to speak of 'membership' of a class, since this might be held to imply participation in a definite 'group'. This form of expression, however, is difficult to avoid altogether, and I shall not attempt to do so in what follows. Secondly, class has to be distinguished from 'stratum', and class theory from the study of 'stratification' as such. The latter, comprising what Ossowski terms a gradation scheme, involves a criterion or set of criteria in terms of which individuals may be ranked descriptively along a scale.[15] The distinction between class and stratum is again a matter of some significance, and bears directly upon the problem of class 'boundaries'. For the divisions between strata, for analytical purposes, may be drawn very precisely, since they may be set upon a measurement scale—as, for example, with 'income strata'. The divisions between classes are *never* of this sort; nor, moreover, do they lend themselves to easy visualisation, in terms of any ordinal scale of 'higher' and 'lower', as strata do—although this sort of imagery cannot be escaped altogether. Finally we must distinguish clearly between class and elite. Elite theory, as formulated by Pareto and Mosca, developed in part as a conscious and deliberate repudiation of class analysis.[16] In place of the concept of class relationships, the elite theorists substituted the opposition of 'elite' and 'mass'; and in place of the Marxian juxtaposition of class society and classlessness they substituted the idea of the cyclical replacement of elites *in perpetuo*. ...

The Structuration of Class Relationships

It is useful, initially, to distinguish the *mediate* from the *proximate* structuration of class relationships. By the former term, I refer to the factors which intervene between the existence of certain given market capacities and the formation of classes as identifiable social groupings, that is to say which operate as 'overall' connecting links between the market on the one hand and structured systems of class relationships on the other. In using the latter phrase, I refer to 'localised' factors which condition or shape class formation. The mediate structuration of class relationships is governed above all by the distribution of mobility chances which pertain within a given society. Mobility has sometimes been treated as if it were in large part separable from the determination of class structure. According to Schumpeter's famous example, classes may be conceived of as like conveyances, which may be constantly carrying different 'passengers' without in any way changing their shape. But, compelling though the analogy is at first sight, it does not stand up to closer examination, especially within the framework I am suggesting here.[17] In general, the greater the degree of 'closure' of mobility chances—both intergenerationally and within the career of the individual—the more this facilitates the formation of identifiable classes. For the effect of closure in terms of intergenerational movement is to provide for the *reproduction* of common life experience over the generations; and this homogenisation of experience is reinforced to the degree to which the individual's movement within the labour market is confined to occupations which generate a similar range of material outcomes. In general we may state that the structuration of classes is facilitated *to the degree to which mobility closure exists in relation to any specified form of market capacity*. There are three sorts of market capacity which can be said to be normally of importance in this respect: ownership of property in the means of production; possession of educational or technical qualifications; and possession of manual labour-power. In so far as it is the case that these tend to be tied to closed patterns of inter- and intragenerational mobility, this yields the foundation of *a basic three-class system* in capitalist society: an 'upper', 'middle', and 'lower' or 'working' class. But as has been indicated previously, it is an intrinsic characteristic of the development of the capitalist market that there exist no legally sanctioned or formally prescribed limitations upon mobility, and hence it must be

emphasised that there is certainly never anything even approaching complete closure. In order to account for the emergence of structured classes, we must look in addition at the proximate sources of structuration.

There are three, related, sources of proximate structuration of class relationships: the division of labour within the productive enterprise; the authority relationships within the enterprise; and the influence of what I shall call 'distributive groupings'. I have already suggested that Marx tended to use the notion of 'division of labour' very broadly, to refer both to market relationships and to the allocation of occupational tasks within the productive organisation. Here I shall use the term only in this second, more specific, sense. In capitalism, the division of labour in the enterprise is in principle governed by the promotion of productive efficiency in relation to the maximisation of profit; but while responding to the same exigencies as the capitalist market in general, the influence of the division of labour must be analytically separated as a distinctive source of structuration (and, as will be discussed later, as a significant influence upon class consciousness). The division of labour, it is clear, may be a basis of the fragmentation as well as the consolidation of class relationships. It furthers the formation of classes to the degree to which it creates homogeneous groupings which cluster along the same lines as those which are fostered by mediate structuration. Within the modern industrial order, the most significant influence upon proximate structuration in the division of labour is undoubtedly that of technique. The effect of industrial technique (more recently, however, modified by the introduction of cybernetic systems of control) is to create a decisive separation between the conditions of labour of manual and non-manual workers. 'Machine-minding', in one form or another, regardless of whether it involves a high level of manual skill, tends to create a working environment quite distinct from that of the administrative employee, and one which normally enforces a high degree of physical separation between the two groupings.[18]

This effect of the division of labour thus overlaps closely with the influence of the mediate structuration of class relationships through the differential apportionment of mobility chances; but it is, in turn, potentially heavily reinforced by the typical authority system in the enterprise. In so far as administrative workers participate in the framing, or merely in the enforcement, of author- itative commands, they tend to be separated from manual workers, who are subject to those com- mands. But the influence of differential authority is also basic as a reinforcing agent of the struc- turation of class relationships at the 'upper' levels. Ownership of property, in other words, confers certain fundamental capacities of command, maximised within the 'entrepreneurial' enterprise in its classical form. To the extent to which this serves to underlie a division at 'the top', in the control of the organisation (something which is manifestly influenced, but not at all destroyed, if certain of the suppositions advanced by the advo- cates of the theory of the separation of 'ownership and control' are correct) it supports the differen- tiation of the 'upper' from the 'middle' class.

The third source of the proximate structura- tion of class relationships is that originating in the sphere of consumption rather than produc- tion. Now according to the traditional interpreta- tions of class structure, including those of Marx and Weber, 'class' is a phenomenon of produc- tion: relationships established in consumption are therefore quite distinct from, and secondary to, those formed in the context of productive ac- tivity. There is no reason to deviate from this gen- eral emphasis. But without dropping the concep- tion that classes are founded ultimately in the economic structure of the capitalist market, it is still possible to regard consumption patterns as a major influence upon class structuration. Weber's notions of 'status' and 'status group', as I previ- ously pointed out, confuse two separable ele- ments: the formation of groupings in consump- tion, on the one hand, and the formation of types of social differentiation based upon some sort of non-economic value providing a scale of 'honour' or 'prestige' on the other. While the two may often coincide, they do not necessarily do so, and it seems worthwhile to distinguish them termino- logically. Thus I shall call 'distributive groupings' those relationships involving common patterns of the consumption of economic goods, regardless of whether the individuals involved make any type of conscious evaluation of their honour or prestige relative to others; 'status' refers to the existence of such evaluations, and a 'status group' is, then, any set of social relationships which de- rives its coherence from their application.[19]

In terms of class structuration, distributive groupings are important in so far as they interre- late with the other sets of factors distinguished above in such a way as to reinforce the typical sep- arations between forms of market capacity. The most significant distributive groupings in this re- spect are those formed through the tendency to- wards community or neighbourhood segrega- tion. Such a tendency is not normally based only upon differentials in income, but also upon such factors as access to housing mortgages, etc. The creation of distinctive 'working-class neighbour- hoods' and 'middle-class neighbourhoods', for example, is naturally promoted if those in manual labour are by and large denied mortgages for house buying, while those in non-manual occu- pations experience little difficulty in obtaining such loans. Where industry is located outside of the major urban areas, homogeneous 'working- class communities' frequently develop through the dependence of workers upon housing pro- vided by the company.

In summary, to the extent to which the various bases of mediate and proximate class structura- tion overlap, classes will exist as distinguishable formations. I wish to say that *the combination of the sources of mediate and proximate structuration distinguished here, creating a threefold class struc- ture, is generic to capitalist society.* But the mode in which these elements are merged to form *a spe- cific class system,* in any given society, differs signi- ficantly according to variations in economic and political development. It should be evident that structuration is never an all-or-nothing matter. The problem of the existence of distinct class 'boundaries', therefore, is not one which can be settled *in abstracto:* one of the specific aims of class analysis in relation to empirical societies must necessarily be that of determining how strongly, in any given case, the 'class principle' has become established as a mode of structuration. Moreover, the operation of the 'class principle' may also involve the creation of forms of structuration within the major class divisions.

One case in point is that which Marx called the 'petty bourgeoisie'. In terms of the preceding analysis, it is quite easy to see why ownership of small property in the means of production might come to be differentiated both from the upper class and from the ('new') middle class. If it is the case that the chances of mobility, either inter- or intragenerationally, from small to large property ownership are slight, this is likely to isolate the small property-owner from membership of the upper class as such. But the fact that he enjoys directive control of an enterprise, however minute, acts to distinguish him from those who are part of a hierarchy of authority in a larger organisation. On the other hand, the income and other economic returns of the petty bourgeois are likely to be similar to the white-collar worker, and hence they may belong to similar distributive groupings. A second potentially important influence upon class formation is to be traced to the factor of skill differential within the general category of manual labour. The manual worker who has undergone apprenticeship, or a comparable period of training, possesses a market capacity which sets him apart from the unskilled or semi-skilled worker. This case will be discussed in more detail [elsewhere];[20] it is enough merely to indicate at this point that there are certain factors promoting structuration on the basis of this differentiation in market capacity (e.g., that the chances of intergenerational mobility from skilled manual to white-collar occupations are considerably higher than they are from unskilled and semi-skilled manual occupations).

So far I have spoken of structuration in a purely formal way, as though class could be defined in terms of relationships which have no 'content'. But this obviously will not do: if classes become social realities, this must be manifest in the formation of common patterns of behaviour and attitude. Since Weber's discussion of classes and status groups, the notion of 'style of life' has normally come to be identified as solely pertaining to the mode whereby a status group expresses its claim to distinctiveness. However, in so far as there is marked convergence of the sources of structuration mentioned above, classes will also tend to manifest common styles of life.

An initial distinction can be drawn here between 'class awareness' and 'class consciousness'.[21] We may say that, in so far as class is a structurated phenomenon, there will tend to exist a common awareness and acceptance of similar attitudes and beliefs, linked to a common style of life, among the members of the class. 'Class awareness', as I use the term here, does *not* involve a recognition that these attitudes and beliefs signify a particular class affiliation, or the recognition that there exist other classes, characterised by different attitudes, beliefs, and styles of life; 'class consciousness', by contrast, as I shall use the notion, does *imply* both of these. The difference between class awareness and class consciousness is a fundamental one, because class awareness may take the form of *a denial of the existence or reality of classes.*[22] Thus the class awareness of the middle class, in so far as it involves beliefs which place a premium upon individual responsibility and achievement, is of this order.

Within ethnically and culturally homogeneous societies, the degree of class structuration will be determined by the interrelationship between the sources of structuration identified previously. But many, if not the majority, of capitalist societies are not homogeneous in these respects. Traditionally, in class theory, racial or religious divisions have been regarded as just so many 'obstacles' to the formation of classes as coherent unities. This may often be so, where these foster types of structuration which deviate from that established by the 'class principle' (as typically was the case in the battles fought by the rearguard of feudalism against the forces promoting the emergence of capitalism). The idea that ethnic or cultural divisions serve to dilute or hinder the formation of classes is also very explicitly built into Weber's separation of (economic) 'class' and 'status group'. But this, in part at least, gains its cogency from the contrast between estate, as a legally constituted category, and class, as an economic category. While it may be agreed, however, that the *bases* of the formation of classes and status groups (in the sense in which I have employed these concepts) are different, nonetheless the tendency to class structuration may receive a considerable impetus *where class coincides with the criteria of status group membership*—in other words, where structuration deriving from economic organisation 'overlaps' with, or, in Dahrendorf's terms, is 'superimposed' upon, that deriving from evaluative categorisations based upon ethnic or cultural differences.[23] Where this is so, status group membership itself becomes a form of market capacity. Such a situation frequently offers the strongest possible source of class structuration, whereby there develop clearcut differences in attitudes, beliefs and style of life between the classes. Where ethnic differences serve as a 'disqualifying' market capacity, such that those in the category in question are heavily concentrated among the lowest-paid occupations, or are chronically unemployed or semi-employed, we may speak of the existence of an *underclass*.[24]

Notes

1. Theodor Geiger, *Die Klassengesellschaft im Schmeltztiegel* (Cologne 1949); Karl Renner, *Wandlungen der modernen Gesellschaft* (Vienna 1953); Ralf Dahrendorf, *Class and Class Conflict in Industrial Society* (Stanford 1959).

2. For a cogent representation of this view, see W. G. Runciman, 'Class, status and power', in J. A. Jackson, *Social Stratification* (Cambridge 1968).

3. See my *Capitalism and Modern Social Theory* (Cambridge 1971), pp. 185ff. and *passim*.

4. *Economy and Society,* vol. 2 (New York 1968), pp. 926–40, and vol. 1, pp. 302–7.

5. ibid., vol. 2, p. 928.

6. ibid., p. 930.

7. ibid., p. 927.

8. ibid., p. 305.

9. Dahrendorf, *Class and Class Conflict.*

10. See, for example, David Lockwood, *The Blackcoated Worker* (London 1958), pp. 202–4; Frank Parkin, *Class Inequality and Political Order* (London 1971).

11. Raymond Aron, *La lutte des classes* (Paris 1964).

12. See Robert A. Nisbet, 'The decline and fall of social class', *Pacific Sociological Review* 2, 1959.

13. Anthony Giddens, *The Class Structure of the Advanced Societies* (New York 1973), ch. 4.

14. What I call class structuration, Gurvitch calls negatively 'résistance à la pénétration par la société globale'. Georges Gurvitch, *Le concept de classes sociales de Marx à nos jours* (Paris 1954), p. 116 and *passim*.

15. Stanislaw Ossowski, *Class Structure in the Social Consciousness* (London 1963).

16. Vilfredo Pareto, *The Mind and Society* (New York 1935); Gaetano Mosca, *The Ruling Class* (New York 1939).

17. We may, however, agree with Schumpeter that 'The family, not the physical person, is the true unit of class and class theory' (Joseph Schumpeter, *Imperialism, Social Classes,* Cleveland 1961). This is actually completely consistent with the idea that mobility is fundamental to class formation.

18. Lockwood, *The Blackcoated Worker,* op. cit.

19. It might be pointed out that it would easily be possible to break down the notion of status group further: according, for example, to whether the status evaluations in question are made primarily by others outside the group, and rejected by those inside it, etc.

20. Giddens, *The Class Structure of the Advanced Societies.*

21. This is not, of course, the same as Lukács' 'class-conditioned unconsciousness'; but I believe that Lukács is correct in distinguishing qualitatively different 'levels' of class consciousness. Georg Lukács, *History and Class Consciousness* (London 1971), pp. 52ff.

22. cf. Nicos Poulantzas, *Pouvoir politique et classes sociales de l'état capitaliste* (Paris 1970). It is misleading, however, to speak of *classes sans conscience,* as Crozier does. See Michel Crozier, 'Classes sans conscience ou préfiguration de la société sans classes', *Archives européenes de sociologie* 1, 1960; also 'L'ambiguité de la conscience de classe chez les employés et les petits fonctionnaires', *Cahiers internationaux de sociologie* 28, 1955.

23. Or, to use another terminology, where there is 'overdetermination' (Louis Althusser, *For Marx,* London 1969, pp. 89–128).

24. Marx's *Lumpenproletariat,* according to this usage, is only an underclass when the individuals in question tend to derive from distinctive ethnic backgrounds. Leggett has referred to the underclass as the 'marginal working class', defining this as 'a sub-community of workers who belong to a subordinate ethnic or racial group which is usually proletarianised and highly segregated' (John C. Leggett, *Class, Race, and Labor,* New York 1968, p. 14).

FRANK PARKIN

Marxism and Class Theory: A Bourgeois Critique

The 'Boundary Problem' in Sociology

The persistent attractions of Marxist class theory have almost certainly been boosted by the less than inspiring alternative offered by academic sociology. In so far as there is any sort of tacitly agreed upon model of class among western social theorists it takes the form of the familiar distinction between manual and non-manual labour. No other criterion for identifying the class boundary seems to enjoy such widespread acceptance among those who conduct investigations into family structure, political attitudes, social imagery, life-styles, educational attainment, and similar enquiries that keep the wheels of empirical sociology endlessly turning. Paradoxically, however, although the manual/non-manual model is felt to be highly serviceable for research purposes, it is not commonly represented as a model of class cleavage and conflict. That is to say, the two main social categories distinguished by sociology for purposes of class analysis are not invested with antagonistic properties comparable to those accorded to proletariat and bourgeoisie in Marxist theory. This would be less cause for comment if proponents of the manual/non-manual model normally construed the social order as a harmonious and integrated whole; but to construe it instead in terms of conflict, dichotomy, and cleavage, as most of these writers now appear to do, seems to reveal an awkward contrast between the empirical model of class and the general conception of capitalist society.

The strongest case that could be made out for identifying the line between manual and non-manual labour as the focal point of class conflict

would be one that treated capitalist society as the industrial firm writ large. It is only within the framework of 'factory despotism' that the blue-collar/white-collar divide closely corresponds to the line of social confrontation over the distribution of spoils and the prerogatives of command. And this is particularly the case in those industrial settings where even the lowest grades of white-collar staff are cast in the role of managerial subalterns physically and emotionally removed from the shop-floor workers. Within the microcosm of capitalism represented by the typical industrial firm, the sociological model of class has something to recommend it as an alternative to one constructed around the rights of property.

The drawback is, however, that social relations within the capitalist *firm* are a less accurate guide to class relations within capitalist *society* than they might once have been. The reason for this is that the post-war expansion of the public sector has given rise to an ever-increasing assortment of non-manual groups in local government and welfare services that cannot in any real sense be thought of as the tail-end of a broad managerial stratum aligned against a manual workforce. Frequently, in fact there is no manual workforce to confront in the occupational settings within which these white-collar groups are employed.[1] And even where teachers, social workers, nurses, local government clerks, lower civil servants, and the like do form part of an organization that includes janitors, orderlies, cleaners, and other workers by hand, they do not usually stand in the same quasi-managerial relationship to them as does the staff employee to the industrial worker in the capitalist firm.

The usual rationale for treating intermediate

and lower white-collar groups as a constituent element of a dominant class is that these groups traditionally have identified themselves with the interests of capital and management rather than with the interests of organized labour. But for various reasons this identification is easier to accomplish in the sphere of private industry and commerce than in the public sector. In the latter, as already pointed out, not only is there usually no subordinate manual group physically present to inspire a sense of white-collar status elevation, but also the charms of management are likely to seem less alluring when the chain of command stretches ever upwards and out of sight into the amorphous and unlovely body of the state. Moreover, public sector employees do not have the same opportunities as those in the commercial sector for transferring their special skills and services to different and competing employers; all improvements in pay and conditions must be negotiated with a monopoly employer, and one who is under close budgetary scrutiny. All this makes for a relationship of some tension between white-collar employees and the state *qua* employer, a condition more akin to that found between manual labour and management than between white-collar employees and management in the private sector. Thus, the validity of the manual/non-manual model as a representation of class conflict relies more heavily upon a view of the commercial employee as the prototypical case of the white-collar worker than really is justified, given the enormous growth of public-sector employment.

What this suggests is that manual and non-manual groups can usefully be thought of as entities socially differentiated from each other in terms of life-chances and opportunities, but not as groups standing in a relationship of exploiter and exploited, of dominance and subordination, in the manner presumably required of a genuine conflict model. Expressed differently, the current sociological model does not fulfil even the minimal Weberian claim that the relations between classes are to be understood as 'aspects of the distribution of power'. Instead of a theoretical framework organized around the central ideas of mutual antagonism and the incompatibility of interests we find one organized around the recorded facts of mere social differentiation. ...

The 'Boundary Problem' in Marxism

The variety of [Marxist] interpretations on offer make it more than usually difficult to speak of 'the' Marxist theory of class. In some respects the range of differences within this camp has tended to blur the simple contrast between Marxist and bourgeois theories; and this is particularly so given the tendency for Marxists to adopt familiar sociological categories under substitute names. The most striking example of this is the tacit acknowledgment of the role of *authority* in the determination of bourgeois status. This arises from the need to find some theoretical principle by which the managerial stratum, in particular, can be assigned to the same class as the owners of capital. Although allusions may occasionally be made to the fact that managers are sometimes shareholders in the companies that employ them, it is clear that this is a contingent feature of managerial status and could not be regarded as theoretically decisive. Managers with and without private company shares do not appear to be different political and ideological animals.

The exercise of discipline over the workforce, on the other hand, is a necessary feature of the managerial role, not a contingent one; and as such it recommends itself as a major criterion of bourgeois class membership. Indeed, for some Marxists managerial authority has in certain respects superseded property ownership as *the* defining attribute of a capitalist class. According to Carchedi, 'the manager, rather than the capitalist rentier, is the central figure, he, rather than the capitalist rentier, is the non-labourer, the non-producer, the exploiter. He, rather than the capitalist rentier, is capital personified.'[2]

Interestingly, by proclaiming that the supervision and control of subordinates is the new hallmark of bourgeois status, Marxist theorists have come surprisingly close to endorsing Dahrendorf's view of the determinate role of authority in establishing the class boundary.[3] Their strict avoidance of this term in favour of some synonym or circumlocution ('mental labour', 'global function of capital', 'labour of superintendence') is perhaps a tacit admission of this embarrassing affinity with Dahrendorf's position. Although none of these writers would accept Dahrendorf's proposition that authority is a general phenomenon that encompasses property, it is nevertheless the case that their treatment of authority relations, however phrased, takes up far more of their analysis than the discussion of property relations.

To make property the centrepiece of class analysis would bring with it the duty of explaining precisely why the apparatus of managerial authority and control was thought to grow out of the institution of private ownership. Presumably it has come to the attention of western Marxists that societies that have done away with property in its private forms nevertheless have their own interesting little ways of seeing to the 'superintendence of labour'. The view that class and authority relations under capitalism are a unique product of private ownership must rest on a belief that these things are ordered in a very different way under the socialist mode of production. The fact that this mode of production figures not at all in any of the class analyses referred to suggests that Marxists are none too happy about drawing the very comparisons that are so essential to their case. After all, supposing it was discovered that factory despotism, the coercive uses of knowledge, and the privileges of mental labour were present not only in societies where the manager was 'capital personified', but also in societies where he was the party personified? Marxists would then be faced with the unwelcome choice of either having to expand the definition of capitalism to embrace socialist society, or of disowning the cherished concepts of private property and surplus extraction upon which their class theory is grounded. The obvious reluctance to engage in the comparative analysis of class under the two ostensibly different modes of production is therefore understandable enough. As for the credibility of Marxist class theory, it would seem that the advent of socialist society is about the worst thing that could have happened to it.

A further difficulty encountered by this theory is the attempt to arrive at some general principles by which to demarcate the established professions from routine white-collar employees, a distinction required by the evident self-identification of the former with the general interests of the bourgeoisie. In place of any general principles, however, resort is had to an eclectic assortment of de-scriptive indices demonstrating that 'higher' white-collar groups are in various ways simply better off than 'lower' white-collar groups. Braverman, for example, lists advantages such as higher pay, security of employment, and the privileged market position of the professions.[4] In similar vein, Westergaard and Resler suggest drawing a line of class demarcation beneath professional and managerial groups on the grounds that 'they are not dependent on the markets in which they sell their labour in anything like the way that other earners are'.[5] Their incomes 'are determined by market rules and mechanisms over which, in effect, they themselves have considerable influence in their own corners of the market'.[6]

The one notable thing about this kind of analysis is that despite its avowedly Marxist provenance it is indistinguishable from the approach of modern bourgeois social theory. It is, after all, Weber rather than Marx who provides the intellectual framework for understanding class in terms of market opportunities, life-chances, and symbolic rewards. The focus upon income differences and other market factors is difficult to reconcile with the standard Marxist objection to bourgeois sociology that it mistakenly operates on the level of distribution instead of on the level of productive relations. It might also be said that it is from Weber rather than Marx that the postulated link between class position and bureaucratic authority most clearly derives. The fact that these normally alien concepts of authority relations, life-chances, and market rewards have now been comfortably absorbed by contemporary Marxist theory is a handsome, if unacknowledged, tribute to the virtues of bourgeois sociology. Inside every neo-Marxist there seems to be a Weberian struggling to get out. ...

Social Closure

By social closure Weber means the process by which social collectivities seek to maximize rewards by restricting access to resources and opportunities to a limited circle of eligibles. This entails the singling out of certain social or physical attributes as the justificatory basis of exclusion. Weber suggests that virtually any group attribute—race, language, social origin, religion—may be seized upon provided it can be used for 'the monopolization of specific, usually economic opportunities'.[7] This monopolization is directed against competitors who share some positive or negative characteristic; its purpose is always the closure of social and economic opportunities to *outsiders*.[8] The nature of these exclusionary practices, and the completeness of social closure, determine the general character of the distributive system.

Surprisingly, Weber's elaboration of the closure theme is not linked in any immediate way with his other main contributions to stratification theory, despite the fact that processes of exclusion can properly be conceived of as an aspect of the distribution of power, which for Weber is practically synonymous with stratification. As a result, the usefulness of the concept for the study of class and similar forms of structured inequality becomes conditional on the acceptance of certain refinements and enlargements upon the original usage.

An initial step in this direction is to extend the notion of closure to encompass other forms of collective social action designed to maximize claims to rewards and opportunities. Closure strategies would thus include not only those of an exclusionary kind, but also those adopted by the excluded themselves as a direct response to their status as outsiders. It is in any case hardly possible to consider the effectiveness of exclusion practices without due reference to the countervailing actions of socially defined ineligibles. As Weber acknowledges: 'Such group action may provoke a corresponding reaction on the part of those against whom it is directed.'[9] In other words, collective efforts to resist a pattern of dominance governed by exclusion principles can properly be regarded as the other half of the social closure equation. This usage is in fact employed by Weber in his discussion of 'community closure' which, as Neuwirth has shown, bears directly upon those forms of collective action mounted by the excluded—that is, 'negatively privileged status groups'.[10]

The distinguishing feature of exclusionary closure is the attempt by one group to secure for itself a privileged position at the expense of some other group through a process of subordination. That is to say, it is a form of collective social action which, intentionally or otherwise, gives rise to a social category of ineligibles or outsiders. Expressed metaphorically, exclusionary closure represents the use of power in a 'downward' direction because it necessarily entails the creation of a group, class, or stratum of legally defined inferiors. Countervailing action by the 'negatively privileged', on the other hand, represents the use of power in an upward direction in the sense that collective attempts by the excluded to win a greater share of resources always threaten to bite into the privileges of legally defined superiors. It is in other words a form of action having usurpation as its goal. *Exclusion* and *usurpation* may therefore be regarded as the two main generic types of social closure, the latter always being a consequence of, and collective response to, the former.[11]

Strategies of exclusion are the predominant mode of closure in all stratified systems. Where the excluded in their turn also succeed in closing off access to remaining rewards and opportunities, so multiplying the number of substrata, the stratification order approaches the furthest point of contrast to the Marxist model of class polarization. The traditional caste system and the stratification of ethnic communities in the United States provide the clearest illustrations of this closure pattern, though similar processes are easily detectable in societies in which class formation is paramount. Strategies of usurpation vary in scale from those designed to bring about marginal redistribution to those aimed at total expropriation. But whatever their intended scale they nearly always contain a potential challenge to the prevailing system of allocation and to the authorized version of distributive justice.

All this indicates the ease with which the language of closure can be translated into the language of power. Modes of closure can be thought of as different means of mobilizing power for the purpose of engaging in distributive struggle. To conceive of power as a built-in attribute of closure is at the very least to dispense with those fruitless searches for its 'location' inspired by Weber's more familiar but completely unhelpful definition in terms of the ubiquitous struggle between contending wills. Moreover, to speak of power in the light of closure principles is quite consistent with the analysis of class relations. Thus, to anticipate the discussion, the familiar distinction between bourgeoisie and proletariat, in its classic as well as in its modern guise, may be conceived of as an expression of conflict between classes defined not specifically in relation to their place in the productive process but in relation to their prevalent modes of closure, exclusion and usurpation, respectively. ...

In modern capitalist society the two main exclusionary devices by which the bourgeoisie constructs and maintains itself as a class are, first, those surrounding the institutions of property; and, second, academic or professional qualifications and credentials. Each represents a set of legal arrangements for restricting access to rewards and privileges: property ownership is a form of closure designed to prevent general access to the means of production and its fruits; credentialism is a form of closure designed to control and monitor entry to key positions in the division of labour. The two sets of beneficiaries of these state-enforced exclusionary practices may thus be thought of as the core components of the dominant class under modern capitalism. Before taking up the discussion of common class interests fostered by private property and credentials it may be useful to consider each of the two principal closure strategies separately.

It has already been remarked upon how the concept of property has been devalued in the modern sociology of class as a result of the heavy weighting accorded to the division of labour. This has not always been true of bourgeois sociology. Weber was in full accord with Marx in asserting that '"Property" and "lack of property" are ... the basic characteristics of all class situations'.[12] The post-Weberian tendency to analyse social relations as if the propertyless condition had painlessly arrived is perhaps a natural extension of the use of 'western' or 'industrial' to denote societies formerly referred to as capitalist. The post-war impact of functionalist theory certainly contributed to this tendency, since the proclamation of belief in the ultimate victory of achievement values and the merit system of reward naturally cast doubt on the importance of property as an institution. The inheritance of wealth after all requires notably little expenditure of those talents and efforts that are said to be the only keys to the gates of fortune.

The extent to which property has come to be regarded as something of an embarrassing theoretical anomaly is hinted at in the fact that it receives only the most cursory acknowledgment in Davis and Moore's functionalist manifesto, and even then in the shape of an assertion that 'strictly legal and functionless ownership ... is open to attack' as capitalism develops.[13] To propose that the imposition of death duties and estate taxes constitutes evidence for an assault upon property rights is somewhat like suggesting that the introduction of divorce laws is evidence of state support for the dissolution of the family. Property in this scheme of things can only be understood as a case of cultural lag—one of those quaint institutional remnants from an earlier epoch which survives by the grace of social inertia.

Several generations earlier Durkheim had reasoned along similar lines in declaring that property inheritance was 'bound up with archaic concepts and practices that have no part in our present day ethics'.[14] And although he felt it was not bound to disappear on this account he was willing to predict that inherited wealth would 'lose its importance more and more', and if it survived at all it would only be 'in a weakened form'.[15] Durkheim was not of course opposed to private property as such, only its transmission through the family. 'It is obvious that inheritance, by creating inequalities amongst men from birth, that are unrelated to merit or services, invalidates the whole contractual system at its very roots.'[16] Durkheim wanted society made safe for property by removing those legal practices that could not be squared with conceptions of liberal individualism and which therefore threatened to cause as much moral and social disturbance as the 'forced' division of labour.

There was not much likelihood of property itself declining as an institution because it was part of the order of things invested with a sacred character, understood in that special Durkheimian sense of an awesome relationship rooted deeply in the *conscience collective*. Although the sacred character of property arose originally from its communal status, the source of all things holy, the marked evolutionary trend towards the individualization of property would not be accompanied by any decline in its divinity. Personal rights to property were therefore seen by Durkheim as part of that general line of social development by which the individual emerges as a distinct and separate entity from the shadow of the group. The individual affirms himself as such by claiming exclusive rights to things over and above the rights of the collectivity. There is more than an echo here of Hegel's dictum that 'In his property a person exists for the first time as reason'.[17] As Plamenatz comments:

'It makes sense to argue, as Hegel does, that it is partly in the process of coming to own things, and to be recognised as their owners, that human beings learn to behave rationally and responsibly, to lead an ordered life. It is partly in the process of learning to distinguish mine from thine that a child comes to recognise itself as a person, as a bearer of rights and duties, as a member of a community with a place of its own inside it.'[18]

As Plamenatz goes on to say, however plausible as a defence of personal property this may be, as a defence of capitalist property relations it is 'lamentably inadequate'.[19]

The reason for this is that Hegel, like Durkheim, and many contemporary sociologists, never clearly distinguishes between property as rights to personal *possessions* and property as capital. Parsons is only one of many who reduces all forms of property to the status of a possession; this is understood as 'a right or a bundle of rights. In other words it is a set of expectations relative to social behaviour and attitudes.'[20] If property is simply a specific form of possession, or a certain bundle of rights, then everyone in society is a proprietor to some degree. On this reckoning there can be no clear social division between owners and non-owners, only a gradual, descending scale from those with very much to those with very little. This is well in line with Parsons' usual theoretical strategy of asserting the benign quality of any resource by reference to its widespread distribution. The possession of a toothbrush or an oilfield confers similar rights and obligations upon their owners, so that property laws cannot be inter-

preted as class laws. As Rose and his colleagues have suggested:

'the ideological significance of such a universalistic and disinterested legal interpretation of property in modern capitalist society is two-fold. First, as the law protects and recognises *all* private property, and as virtually all members of the society can claim title to *some* such property, it may be claimed that all members of society have some vested interest in the *status quo*. From such a perspective, therefore, it can be argued that, far from representing an irreconcilable conflict of interests, the distribution of property in modern capitalist society gives rise to a commensurability of interests, any differences being variations of degree rather than kind. The office developer, the shareholder, the factory-owner, the householder and even the second-hand car owner may thus be represented as sharing fundamentally common interests, if not identities.'[21]

What the sociological definition of property as possessions interestingly fails to ask is why only certain limited forms of possession are legally admissible. It is patently not the case, for example, that workers are permitted to claim legal possession of their jobs; nor can tenants claim rights of possession to their homes, nor welfare claimants enforceable rights to benefits. Possession in all these cases is pre-empted by the conflicting claims of employers, landlords, and the state respectively, which are accorded legal priority. Although the law may treat the rights of ownership in true universalistic fashion it is silent on the manner by which only some 'expectations' are successfully converted to the status of property rights and others not. ...

The case for restoring the notion of property into the centre of class analysis is that it is the most important single form of social closure common to industrial societies. That is to say, rights of ownership can be understood not as a special case of authority so much as a specific form of exclusion. As Durkheim expresses it, 'the right of property is the right of a given individual to exclude other individual and collective entities from the usage of a given thing'.[22] Property is defined negatively by 'the exclusion it involves rather than the prerogatives it confers'.[23] Durkheim's reference to *individual* rights of exclusion clearly indicates that once again he has possessions in mind, and that, characteristically, he sees no important distinction between objects of personal ownership, and the control of resources resulting in the exercise of power.

It is clearly necessary to distinguish property as possessions from property as capital, since only the latter is germane to the analysis of class systems. Property as capital is, to paraphrase Macpherson, that which 'confers the right to deny men access to the means of life and labour'.[24] This exclusionary right can obviously be vested in a variety of institutional forms, including the capitalist firm, a nationalized industry, or a Soviet enterprise. All these are examples of property that confers legal powers upon a limited few to grant or deny general access to the means of production and the distribution of its fruits. Although personal possessions and capital both entail rights of exclusion, it is only the exclusionary rights embedded in the latter that have important consequences for the life-chances and social condition of the excluded. To speak of property in the context of class analysis is, then, to speak of capital only, and not possessions.

Once property is conceptualized as a form of exclusionary social closure there is no need to become entangled in semantic debates over whether or not workers in socialist states are 'really' exploited. The relevant question is not whether surplus extraction occurs, but whether the state confers rights upon a limited circle of eligibles to deny access to the 'means of life and labour' to the rest of the community. If such exclusionary powers are legally guaranteed and enforced, an exploitative relationship prevails as a matter of definition. It is not of overriding importance to know whether these exclusionary powers are exercised by the formal owners of property or by their appointed agents, since the social consequences of exclusion are not demonstrably different in the two cases. Carchedi and other neo-Marxists may therefore be quite correct in suggesting that 'the manager is capital personified'; but all that needs to be added is first, that this dictum holds good not only for monopoly capitalism, but for *all*, including socialism, systems in which access to property and its benefices is in the legal gift of a select few; and, second, that it squares far more comfortably with the assump-

tions of bourgeois, or at least Weberian, sociology than with classical Marxist theory.

Of equal importance to the exclusionary rights of property is that set of closure practices sometimes referred to as 'credentialism'—that is, the inflated use of educational certificates as a means of monitoring entry to key positions in the division of labour. Well before the onset of mass higher education, Weber had pointed to the growing use of credentials as a means of effecting exclusionary closure.

'The development of the diploma from universities, and business and engineering colleges, and the universal clamour for the creation of educational certificates in all fields make for the formation of a privileged stratum in bureaus and offices. Such certificates support their holders' claims for intermarriages with notable families … , claims to be admitted into the circles that adhere to "codes of honour", claims for a "respectable" remuneration rather than remuneration for work well done, claims for assured advancement and old-age insurance, and, above all, claims to monopolize social and economically advantageous positions. When we hear from all sides the demand for an introduction of regular curricula and special examinations, the reason behind it is, of course, not a suddenly awakened "thirst for education" but the desire for restricting the supply of these positions and their monopolization by the owners of educational certificates. Today the "examination" is the universal means of this monopolization, and therefore examinations irresistibly advance.'[25]

The use of credentials for closure purposes, in the manner elaborated by Weber, has accompanied the attempt by an ever-increasing number of white collar occupations to attain the status of professions. Professionalization itself may be understood as a strategy designed, amongst other things, to limit and control the supply of entrants to an occupation in order to safeguard or enhance its market value. Much of the literature on the professions has tended to stress their differences from workaday occupations, usually accepting the professions' own evaluation of their singularity in creating rigorous codes of technical competence and ethical standards. It is perfectly possible to accept that the monopolization of skills and services does enable the professions to exercise close control over the moral and technical standards of their members, whilst also endorsing

Weber's judgment that 'normally this concern for efficient performance recedes behind the interest in limiting the supply of candidates for the benefices and honours of a given occupation.'[26]

It would seem to be the professions' anxiety to control the supply side of labour that accounts, in part at least, for the qualifications epidemic referred to by Dore as the 'diploma disease'.[27] This is the universal tendency among professions to raise the minimum standards of entry as increasing numbers of potential candidates attain the formerly scarce qualifications. The growing reliance upon credentials as a precondition of professional candidature is commonly justified by reference to the greater complexity of the tasks to be performed and the consequent need for more stringent tests of individual capacity. Yet Berg's careful analysis of these claims was able to turn up no evidence to show that variations in the level of formal education were matched by variations in the quality of work performance.[28] Nor was there anything to suggest that professional tasks were in fact becoming more complex such as to justify a more rigorous intellectual screening of potential entrants. Berg's conclusion, in line with Weber's, is that credentials are accorded their present importance largely because they simplify and legitimate the exclusionary process. It is on these grounds, among others, that Jencks suggests that 'the use of credentials or tests scores to exclude "have not" groups from desirable jobs can be viewed in the same light as any other arbitrary form of discrimination'.[29]

Formal qualifications and certificates would appear to be a handy device for ensuring that those who possess 'cultural capital' are given the best opportunity to transmit the benefits of professional status to their own children. Credentials are usually supplied on the basis of tests designed to measure certain class-related qualities and attributes rather than those practical skills and aptitudes that may not so easily be passed on through the family line. It is illuminating in this respect to contrast the white-collar professions with the sporting and entertaining professions. What is especially remarkable about the latter is how relatively few of the children of successful footballers, boxers, baseball and tennis stars, or the celebrities of stage and screen have succeeded in reproducing their parents' elevated status. One reason for this would seem to be that the skills called for in these pursuits are of a kind that must be acquired and cultivated by the individual in the actual course of performance, and which are thus not easily transferred from parent to child. That is, there seems to be no equivalent to cultural capital that can be socially transmitted to the children of those gifted in the performing arts that could give them a head start in the fiercely competitive world of professional sport and show business. Presumably, if the rewards of professional sport could be more or less guaranteed along conventional career or bureaucratic lines serious proposals would eventually be put forward to limit entry to those candidates able to pass qualifying examinations in the theory of sporting science. This would have the desired effect of giving a competitive edge to those endowed with examination abilities over those merely excelling in the activity itself.[30]

The reason why professional sports, and the entertainment professions in general, are likely to be resistant to the 'diploma disease' offers a further instructive comment upon the nature of the white-collar professions. The supreme advantage of occupational closure based upon credentials is that all those in possession of a given qualification are deemed competent to provide the relevant skills and services for the rest of their professional lives. There is no question of retesting abilities at a later stage in the professional career. The professional bodies' careful insistence that members of the lay public are not competent to sit in judgement on professional standards effectively means that a final certificate is a meal ticket for life. In the sporting and entertainment professions, by contrast, the skills and abilities of the performers are kept under continuous open review by the public; those who consume the services are themselves the ultimate arbiters of an individual's competence and hence his market value, as expressed via their aggregate purchasing power. There can be no resort to the umbrella protection of a professional licence when sporting prowess and the ability to entertain are felt to be in decline in the eyes of those who pass collective judgement.

Against this exacting yardstick, then, credentialism stands out as a doubly effective device for protecting the learned professions from the hazards of the marketplace. Not merely does it serve the convenient purpose of monitoring and restricting the supply of labour, but also effectively masks all but the most extreme variations in the level of ability of professional members, thereby shielding the least competent from ruinous economic punishment. The small irony is that credentialist strategies aimed at neutralizing the competitive effects of the market confer most benefit upon that class that is most prone to trumpet the virtues of a free market economy and the sins of collectivism.

The use of systematic restrictions upon occupational entry has not of course been wholly confined to the white-collar professions. Certain skilled manual trades have adopted similar techniques designed to regulate supply, as in the case of the apprenticeship system or certain forms of the closed shop. Some unskilled occupations such as dock work and market-portering have also sought to restrict entry to the kinsmen of those already employed, though this does not normally guarantee control over the actual volume of labour supply. The crucial difference between these attempts at occupational exclusion by manual trades and those adopted by the professions is that the latter generally seek to establish a *legal monopoly* over the provision of services through licensure by the state. Whereas the learned professions have been remarkably successful in winning for themselves the status of what Weber calls 'legally privileged groups', it has been far less common for the manual trades to secure the blessing of the state for their exclusionary tactics. Indeed, the resort to 'restrictive practices' on the part of organized labour is commonly condemned as a breach of industrial morality that should be curbed rather than sanctified by law. Presumably the fact that governments have usually been reluctant to legislate formally against such practices is not unrelated to the awkwardness that might arise in drawing legal distinctions between these practices and the exclusionary devices of the professions, including the profession of law itself.

A further point of difference between professional closure and restrictive practices by trade unions is that the main purpose behind the latter activity has been the attempt to redress in some small part the disadvantages accruing to labour in its uneven contest with capital. Closure by skilled workers has been a strategy embarked upon in the course of struggle against a superior and highly organized opponent, and not primarily with the conscious intent of reducing the material opportunities of other members of the labour force. Credentialism, on the other hand, cannot be seen as a response to exploitation by powerful employers; the learned or free professions were never directly subordinate to an employing class during the period when they were effecting social closure. Their conflict, concealed beneath the rhetoric of professional ethics was, if anything, with the lay public. It was the struggle to establish a monopoly of certain forms of knowledge and practice and to win legal protection from lay interference. The aim was to ensure that the professional-client relationship was one in which the organized few confronted the disorganized many. Under modern conditions, where many professionals are indirectly in the service of the state and occasionally in conflict with the government of the day over pay and conditions, a somewhat better case could perhaps be made for likening the position of professions to that of craft unions, in so far as both could be said to employ closure for purposes of bargaining with a more powerful agency. But however acrimonious relations may become between professional bodies and the state, it is worth noting that the state rarely if ever threatens to take sanctions against professions in the way that would most seriously damage their interests—namely, by rescinding their legal monopoly.

On all these grounds it is necessary to regard credentialism as a form of exclusionary social closure comparable in its importance for class formation to the institution of property. Both entail the use of exclusionary rules that confer benefits and privileges on the few through denying access to the many, rules that are enshrined in law and upheld by the coercive authority of the state. It follows from this that the dominant class under modern capitalism can be thought of as comprising those who possess or control productive capital and those who possess a legal monopoly of professional services. These groups represent the core body of the dominant or exploiting class by virtue of their exclusionary powers which necessarily have the effect of creating a reciprocal class of social inferiors and subordinates. ...

Class Reproduction

There is a definite tension between the commitment to closure by way of property and credentials on the part of one generation and the desire to pass on benefits to subsequent generations of kith and kin. It is not in the least necessary to deny that most members of the exclusionary class will strive to put their own advantages to the service of their children, while asserting at the same time that bourgeois forms of closure are not exactly tailor-made for self-recruiting purposes. In fact exclusionary institutions formed under capitalism do not seem to be designed first and foremost to solve the problem of class reproduction through the family line. The kinship link can only be preserved as a result of *adaptation* by the bourgeois family to the demands of institutions designed to serve a different purpose; it does not come about as a natural consequence of the closure rules themselves. In systems based on aristocratic, caste, or racial exclusion, families of the dominant group can expect to pass on their privileged status to their own descendants as a direct result of the closure rules in operation, however socially lethargic those families might be. The bourgeois family, by contrast, cannot rest comfortably on the assumption of automatic class succession; it must make definite social exertions of its own or face the very real prospect of generational decline. In other words, although the typical bourgeois family will certainly be better equipped than most to cope with the closure system on its children's behalf, it must still approach the task more in the manner of a challenge with serious risks attached than as a foregone conclusion. Even when it is successful it must face the prospect of sharing bourgeois status with uncomfortably large numbers of parvenus. What kind of system is this to provoke such anxieties in the breasts of those supposedly in command?

The answer must be that it is a system designed to promote a class formation biased more in the direction of sponsorship and careful selection of successors than of hereditary transmission. Although *both* aims might be held desirable, the first takes ideological precedence over the second, so that succession along kinship lines must be accomplished in conformity with the application of criteria that are ostensibly indifferent to the claims of blood. There is nothing especially bizarre about an arrangement whereby a dominant class relinquishes its children's patrimony in order to ensure that the calibre of its replacements is of the highest possible order. It would only appear strange to those unable to conceive that the attachment to doctrine could ever take precedence over the claims of kinship. As Orwell noted in his discussion of communist party oligarchies:

'The essence of oligarchical rule is not father-to-son inheritance, but the persistence of a certain world-view and a certain way of life, imposed by the dead upon the living. A ruling group is a ruling group so long as it can nominate its successors. The Party is not concerned with perpetuating its blood but with perpetuating itself.'[31]

There are also powerful forces in capitalist society that are more dedicated to the perpetuation of bourgeois values than bourgeois blood. Ideological commitment to the rights of property and the value of credentials may be just as fierce as any faith in Leninist party principles. Each represents a set of ideals that can be held quite irrespective of the consequences upon the family fortunes of their advocates. The party militant's belief in a system of political selection and exclusion that could tell against his own ideologically wayward children has its counterpart in the liberal's belief in the validity of meritocratic criteria that would find against his not too clever offspring. It was perhaps examples of this kind that Weber had in mind when referring to patterns of closure distinguished by a 'rational commitment to values'. The same idea is also more than hinted at in Marx's well-known assertion that the bourgeoisie always puts the interests of the whole class above the interests of any of its individual members. These priorities are not, presumably, reversed whenever the individual members in question happen to be someone's children.

To suggest that predominant forms of closure under modern capitalism are in some tension with the common desire to transmit privileges to one's own is to point up politically significant differences of interpretation of bourgeois ideology. The classical liberal doctrine of individualism contains a powerful rejection of those principles and practices that evaluate men on the basis of group or collectivist criteria. The political driving force of individualist doctrines arose in part from the opposition of the emergent middle classes to aristocratic pretensions and exclusiveness centred around the notion of descent. The emphasis upon lineage was an obvious hindrance to those who had raised themselves into the ranks of property by way of industry and commerce, but who lacked the pedigree necessary to enter the charmed circles inhabited by those of political power and social honour. Although non-landed wealth could occasionally be cleansed through marriage into the nobility, the new rising class sought to make property respectable in its own right by divorcing it from its associations with particular status groups. Property in all its forms was to become the hallmark of moral worth without reference back, as it were, to the quality of proprietorial blood. In the individualist credo, property thus assumed the same characteristic as money in the marketplace, where the ability to pay overrides all questions as to the actual source of the buyer's cash. ...

One reason for pressing the distinction between collectivist and individualist criteria underlying all forms of exclusion is to suggest that subordinate classes or strata are likely to differ in their political character according to which of the two sets of criteria is predominant. Looked at in ideal-typical terms, purely collectivist types of exclusion, such as those based on race, religion, ethnicity, and so on, would produce a subordinate group of a communal character—that is, one defined in terms of a total all-encompassing negative status. Blacks under *apartheid* or minority groups herded into religious and racial ghettoes are the familiar modern examples. The polar archetypal case would be that of exclusion based solely on individualist criteria, giving rise to a subordinate group marked by intense social fragmentation and inchoateness. The example here is

furnished by the model of a pure meritocracy in which class is virtually replaced by a condition of discrete segmental statuses never quite reaching the point of coalescence. In non-fictional societies, of course, individualist and collectivist criteria are usually applied in some combination or other, so producing stratified systems located at various points between these two extremes. This can be depicted in simplified form as follows:

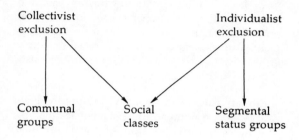

Thus, of the three major types of subordination, classes are presented as a combination of both types of exclusionary criteria. Schematically, a subordinate class could be located towards either of the opposite poles according to the relative weighting of the two sets of criteria. The proletariat of early and mid-nineteenth century Europe, for example, would approximate to the communal pole by virtue of its wholesale exclusion from civil society arising from the treatment of its members as a *de facto* collectivity. The badge of proletarian status carried with it the kinds of stigmata commonly associated with subordinate racial and ethnic groups. It was a total condition which permitted little leeway for the cultivation of those small part-time identities that bring temporary release from the humilities of servile status. Correspondingly, of course, the proletarian condition under communal exclusion offered fertile ground for movements and ideologies which raised large questions about the nature of the political order and its legitimacy, and not merely about the fact of unequal shares.

It is the very hallmark of the communal condition that subordination is experienced through a myriad of direct personal degradations and affronts to human dignity, encouraged by the submersion of the individual into the stereotype of his 'membership' group. It is largely as a result of this that the politics of communal exclusion so frequently stresses the need for subordinate groups to create an alternative moral identity to that fashioned for them by their oppressors. Although the condition of the early proletariat was never completely of a communal kind, it was not so different from that of a despised ethnic group, if only because the visible signs and trappings of status were as unmistakably clear as racial features. Certainly the mixture of horror, fear, and revulsion felt by the upper classes for the great unwashed was not a far remove from the sentiments usually held by dominant racial or ethnic groups towards those whom they simultaneously exploit and despise.

To speak of a gradual shift in the nature of exclusionary rules, from collectivism to individualism, is thus to point to those tendencies making for the progressive erosion of the communal components of proletarian status, otherwise referred to as working-class incorporation into civil society. Although under advanced capitalism labour remains an exploited commodity, the status of the worker does not derive to anything like the same extent from his immersion in a total collective identity and its accompanying rituals of personal degradation. Mills' portrayal of the pattern of 'status cycles' by which the modern urban worker is able to find escape in class anonymity during leisure periods and vacations may be somewhat overdrawn;[32] but there is a real sense in which the absence of clearly visible and unambiguous marks of inferior status has made the enforcement of an all-pervasive deference system almost impossible to sustain outside the immediate work situation. It would now take an unusually sharp eye to detect the social class of Saturday morning shoppers in the High Street, whereas to any earlier generation it would have been the most elementary task. More to the point, even assuming that a lynx-eyed bourgeois could accurately spot a worker in mufti, what real hope could he now entertain of having any claim to deference actually honoured? A system of deference can only operate effectively when the status of strangers can accurately be judged, and the information required for this is difficult to come by without the aid of a collectivist stereotype. In this respect the personal dignity of the modern worker has been enhanced by the evolution towards individualist exclusion, even though his subordination to capital remains a central fact of life.

As class subordination becomes increasingly less communal in character, the political ideals and programmes that flourish among its members tend to become less inspired by visions of a new moral order and the promise of emancipation, and rather more preoccupied with the issues of distributive justice. Those who deplore the apparent flickering of those energies and passions that produced nineteenth-century socialism might care to reflect on the possibility that this has less to do with the iniquities of working-class leadership than with the system of modern exploitation, in which the engines of political resentment are not so lavishly fuelled by the personal degradations arising from wholesale collectivist exclusion. ...

Conclusion

By way of concluding this part of the discussion, it might be appropriate to offer some general remarks on the explanatory status of the closure model. This model, like any other, recommends the use of a particular sociological vocabulary and an attendant battery of concepts that contain barely disguised moral assumptions about the nature of class society. It is not strictly speaking a 'theory' of class but a way of conceptualizing it that differs from that proposed by other variants of bourgeois sociology or by Marxism. Most of what we conventionally call theories of class are in fact conceptual methods of this kind. They are, for the most part, take-it-or-leave-it moral classifications, not sets of propositions that stand or fall under the impact of evidence. What conceivable social facts could destroy either the Marxist conception of class as an exploitative relationship, or the liberal conception of class as an exchange relationship? Since conceptual models are ways of presenting social reality, it follows that the preference for one presentation over another entails a personal judgement of some kind about the moral standing of class society.

On this score, the closure model is almost bound to appear defective by liberal and Marxist theorists alike. Liberal theory endorses a contractual view of class, in which the notion of mutual interest and harmony is the essential ingredient. Marxism, on the other hand, assumes not merely the absence of harmony and common class interests, but, more importantly, the presence of irresolvable antagonisms that drive the system to ultimate breakdown. The neo-Weberian position advanced here is that the relation between classes is neither one of harmony and mutual benefit, nor of irresolvable and fatal contradiction. Rather, the relationship is understood as one of mutual antagonism and permanent *tension*; that is, a condition of unrelieved distributive struggle that is not necessarily impossible to 'contain'. Class conflict may be without cease, but it is not inevitably fought to a conclusion. The competing notions of harmony, contradiction, and tension could thus be thought of as the three broad possible ways of conceptualizing the relation between classes, and on which all class models are grounded.

Since class models are not subject to direct empirical assault, the case for advancing the cause of one in preference to another rests partly on the claim that it draws attention to a set of problems and issues that are otherwise obscured. Thus, one of the attractions of the closure model is that it highlights the fact of communal cleavage and its relationship to class, and seeks to analyse both within the same conceptual framework. More generally, it proposes that intra-class relations be treated as conflict phenomena of the same general order as inter-class relations, and not as mere disturbances or complications within a 'pure' class model. Hence the extension of the concept of exploitation to cover both sets of phenomena. There is, in addition, a recommendation that social classes be defined by reference to their mode of collective action rather than to their place in the productive process or the division of labour. The reason for this is that incumbency of position in a formally defined structure does not normally correspond to class alignment where it really counts—at the level of organized political sentiment and conduct. This serious lack of fit between all positional or systemic definitions of class and the actual behaviour of classes in the course of distributive struggle, is not due to any lack othe categories employed. It arises from the initial theoretical decision to discount the significance and effect of variations in the cultural and social make-up of the groups assigned to the categories in question. Models constructed upon such formal, systemic definitions require of their advocates much ingenuity in accounting for the continuous and wholesale discrepancies between class position and class behaviour. A good deal of the intellectual energy of western Marxism has been dissipated in wrestling with this very problem which is of its own conceptual making.

Notes

1. The hospital setting provides, perhaps, the most important exception. Industrial conflicts between medical staff and the manual workers' unions over issues such as 'pay beds' are unusual in having clear-cut ideological, rather than bread-and-butter, causes.

2. Carchedi 1975:48. For Braverman, too, managers and executives are 'part of the class that personifies capital ...' (1974:405).

3. Dahrendorf 1959.

4. Braverman 1974: Chapter 18.

5. Westergaard and Resler 1975:92.

6. Westergaard and Resler 1975:346.

7. Weber (eds Roth and Wittich) 1968:342.

8. Weber (eds Roth and Wittich) 1968:342.

9. Weber (eds Roth and Wittich) 1968:342.

10. Neuwirth 1969.

11. These arguments were first tentatively sketched out in my 'Strategies of Social Closure in Class Formation' (Parkin 1974). In that publication the two types of closure were referred to as *exclusion* and *solidarism*. This latter term does not, however, satisfactorily describe a mode of collective action standing in direct opposition to exclusion, since solidaristic behaviour can itself be used for blatantly exclusionary ends. That is to say, solidarism does not properly refer to the purposes for which power is employed. The term *usurpation* more adequately captures the notion of collective action designed to improve the lot of a subordinate group at the expense of a dominant group. Solidarism is simply one means among others to this end.

12. Weber (eds Gerth and Mills) 1948:182.

13. Davis and Moore 1945:247.

14. Durkheim 1957:174.

15. Durkheim 1957:175 and 217.
16. Durkheim 1957:213.
17. Plamenatz 1975:120.
18. Plamenatz 1975:121.
19. Plamenatz 1975:121.
20. Parsons 1951:119. The entry in the index under 'Property' invites the reader to 'see Possessions'.
21. Rose *et al.* 1976:703.
22. Durkheim 1957:142.
23. Durkheim 1957:142.
24. Macpherson 1973.
25. Weber (eds Gerth and Mills) 1948:241–42.
26. Weber (eds Roth and Wittich) 1968:344.
27. Dore 1976.
28. Berg 1973.
29. Jencks 1972:192.
30. It transpires that the idea is not so far-fetched after all. The Council for National Academic Awards has recently approved the syllabus for a BA Degree in Sports Studies. Undergraduates will be instructed in 'the variables influencing performance in sport; a science and its sports application; scientific methods, statistics and computing; and wide practical experience in a number of sports.' *Daily Telegraph,* Monday, 28 August 1978, p. 3.
31. Orwell 1949:215.
32. Mills 1956:257–58.

Bibliography

Berg, I. (1973) *Education and Jobs: The Great Training Robbery.* Harmondsworth: Penguin Books.
Braverman, H. (1974) *Labor and Monopoly Capital.* New York: Monthly Review Press.
Carchedi, G. (1975) On the Economic Identification of the New Middle Class. *Economy and Society* 4 (1).
Dahrendorf, R. (1959) *Class and Class Conflict in Industrial Society.* London: Routledge.
Davis, K. and Moore, W. E. (1945) Some Principles of Stratification. *American Sociological Review* X (2).
Dore, R. (1976) *The Diploma Disease.* London: Allen and Unwin.
Durkheim, E. (1957) *Professional Ethics and Civic Morals.* London: Routledge.
Jencks, C. (1972) *Inequality.* New York: Basic Books.
Macpherson, C. B. (1973) A Political Theory of Property. In, *Democratic Theory: Essays in Retrieval.* Oxford University Press.
Mills, C. W. (1956) *White Collar.* New York: Oxford University Press.
Neuwirth, G. (1969) A Weberian Outline of a Theory of Community: Its Application to the 'Dark Ghetto'. *British Journal of Sociology* 20 (2).
Orwell, G. (1949) *Nineteen Eighty-Four.* London: Secker and Warburg.
Parkin, F. (ed.) (1974) *The Social Analysis of Class Structure.* London: Tavistock.
Parsons, T. (1951) *The Social System.* London: Routledge.
Plamenatz, J. (1975) *Karl Marx's Philosophy of Man.* Oxford: Clarendon Press.
Rose, D., Saunders, P., Newby, H., and Bell, C. (1976) Ideologies of Property: A Case Study. *Sociological Review* 24 (4).
Weber, M. (1945) *From Max Weber.* Gerth, H. H. and Mills, C. W. (eds) London: Routledge.
———. (1968) *Economy and Society.* Roth, G. and Wittich, C. (eds) New York: Bedminster Press.
Westergaard, J. and Resler, H. (1975) *Class in a Capitalist Society.* London: Heinemann.

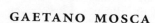

GAETANO MOSCA

The Ruling Class

1. Among the constant facts and tendencies that are to be found in all political organisms, one is so obvious that it is apparent to the most casual eye. In all societies—from societies that are very meagerly developed and have barely attained the dawnings of civilization, down to the most advanced and powerful societies—two classes of people appear—a class that rules and a class that is ruled. The first class, always the less numerous, performs all political functions, monopolizes power and enjoys the advantages that power brings, whereas the second, the more numerous class, is directed and controlled by the first, in a manner that is now more or less legal, now more or less arbitrary and violent, and supplies the first, in appearance at least, with material means of subsistence and with the instrumentalities that are essential to the vitality of the political organism.

In practical life we all recognize the existence of this ruling class (or political class, as we have elsewhere chosen to define it).[1] We all know that, in our own country, whichever it may be, the management of public affairs is in the hands of a minority of influential persons, to which management, willingly or unwillingly, the majority defer. We know that the same thing goes on in neighboring countries, and in fact we should be put to it to conceive of a real world otherwise organized—a world in which all men would be directly subject to a single person without relationships of superiority or subordination, or in which all men would share equally in the direction of political affairs. If we reason otherwise in theory, that is due partly to inveterate habits that we follow in our thinking and partly to the exaggerated importance that we attach to two political facts that loom far larger in appearance than they are in reality.

The first of these facts—and one has only to open one's eyes to see it—is that in every political organism there is one individual who is chief among the leaders of the ruling class as a whole and stands, as we say, at the helm of the state. That person is not always the person who holds supreme power according to law. At times, alongside of the hereditary king or emperor there is a prime minister or a major-domo who wields an actual power that is greater than the sovereign's. At other times, in place of the elected president the influential politician who has procured the president's election will govern. Under special circumstances there may be, instead of a single person, two or three who discharge the functions of supreme control.

The second fact, too, is readily discernible. Whatever the type of political organization, pressures arising from the discontent of the masses who are governed, from the passions by which they are swayed, exert a certain amount of influence on the policies of the ruling, the political, class.

But the man who is at the head of the state would certainly not be able to govern without the support of a numerous class to enforce respect for his orders and to have them carried out; and granting that he can make one individual, or indeed many individuals, in the ruling class feel the weight of his power, he certainly cannot be at odds with the class as a whole or do away with it. Even if that were possible, he would at once be forced to create another class, without the support of which action on his part would be completely paralyzed. On the other hand, granting that the discontent of the masses might succeed in deposing a ruling class, inevitably, as we shall later show, there would have to be another organized minority within the masses themselves to discharge the functions of a ruling class. Otherwise all organization, and the whole social structure, would be destroyed.

2. From the point of view of scientific research the real superiority of the concept of the ruling, or political, class lies in the fact that the varying structure of ruling classes has a preponderant importance in determining the political type, and also the level of civilization, of the different peoples. According to a manner of classifying forms of government that is still in vogue, Turkey and Russia were both, up to a few years ago, absolute monarchies, England and Italy were constitutional, or limited, monarchies, and France and the United States were classed as republics. The classification was based on the fact that, in the first two countries mentioned, headship in the state was hereditary and the chief was nominally omnipotent; in the second two, his office is hereditary but his powers and prerogatives are limited; in the last two, he is elected.

That classification is obviously superficial. Absolutisms though they were, there was little in common between the manners in which Russia and Turkey were managed politically, the levels of civilization in the two countries and the organization of their ruling classes being vastly different. On the same basis, the regime in Italy, a monarchy, is much more similar to the regime in France, a republic, than it is to the regime in England, also a monarchy; and there are important differences between the political organizations of the United States and France, though both countries are republics.

As we have already suggested, ingrained habits of thinking have long stood, as they still stand, in the way of scientific progress in this matter. The classification mentioned above, which divides governments into absolute monarchies, limited monarchies and republics, was devised by Montesquieu and was intended to replace the classical categories of Aristotle, who divided governments into monarchies, aristocracies and de-

mocracies. What Aristotle called a democracy was simply an aristocracy of fairly broad membership. Aristotle himself was in a position to observe that in every Greek state, whether aristocratic or democratic, there was always one person or more who had a preponderant influence. Between the day of Polybius and the day of Montesquieu, many writers perfected Aristotle's classification by introducing into it the concept of "mixed" governments. Later on the modern democratic theory, which had its source in Rousseau, took its stand upon the concept that the majority of the citizens in any state can participate, and in fact *ought* to participate, in its political life, and the doctrine of popular sovereignty still holds sway over many minds in spite of the fact that modern scholarship is making it increasingly clear that democratic, monarchical and aristocratic principles function side by side in every political organism. We shall not stop to refute this democratic theory here, since that is the task of this work as a whole. Besides, it would be hard to destroy in a few pages a whole system of ideas that has become firmly rooted in the human mind. As Las Casas aptly wrote in his life of Christopher Columbus, it is often much harder to unlearn than to learn.

3. We think it may be desirable, nevertheless, to reply at this point to an objection which might very readily be made to our point of view. If it is easy to understand that a single individual cannot command a group without finding within the group a minority to support him, it is rather difficult to grant, as a constant and natural fact, that minorities rule majorities, rather than majorities minorities. But that is one of the points—so numerous in all the other sciences—where the first impression one has of things is contrary to what they are in reality. In reality the dominion of an organized minority, obeying a single impulse, over the unorganized majority is inevitable. The power of any minority is irresistible as against each single individual in the majority, who stands alone before the totality of the organized minority. At the same time, the minority is organized for the very reason that it is a minority. A hundred men acting uniformly in concert, with a common understanding, will triumph over a thousand men who are not in accord and can

therefore be dealt with one by one. Meanwhile it will be easier for the former to act in concert and have a mutual understanding simply because they are a hundred and not a thousand. It follows that the larger the political community, the smaller will the proportion of the governing minority to the governed majority be, and the more difficult will it be for the majority to organize for reaction against the minority.

However, in addition to the great advantage accruing to them from the fact of being organized, ruling minorities are usually so constituted that the individuals who make them up are distinguished from the mass of the governed by qualities that give them a certain material, intellectual or even moral superiority; or else they are the heirs of individuals who possessed such qualities. In other words, members of a ruling minority regularly have some attribute, real or apparent, which is highly esteemed and very influential in the society in which they live.

4. In primitive societies that are still in the early stages of organization, military valor is the quality that most readily opens access to the ruling, or political, class. In societies of advanced civilization, war is the exceptional condition. It may be regarded as virtually normal in societies that are in the initial stages of their development; and the individuals who show the greatest ability in war easily gain supremacy over their fellows—the bravest become chiefs. The fact is constant, but the forms it may assume, in one set of circumstances or another, vary considerably.

As a rule the dominance of a warrior class over a peaceful multitude is attributed to a superposition of races, to the conquest of a relatively unwarlike group by an aggressive one. Sometimes that is actually the case—we have examples in India after the Aryan invasions, in the Roman Empire after the Germanic invasions and in Mexico after the Aztec conquest. But more often, under certain social conditions, we note the rise of a warlike ruling class in places where there is absolutely no trace of a foreign conquest. As long as a horde lives exclusively by the chase, all individuals can easily become warriors. There will of course be leaders who will rule over the tribe, but we will not find a warrior class rising to exploit, and at the same time to protect, another class that is de-

voted to peaceful pursuits. As the tribe emerges from the hunting stage and enters the agricultural and pastoral stage, then, along with an enormous increase in population and a greater stability in the means of exerting social influence, a more or less clean-cut division into two classes will take place, one class being devoted exclusively to agriculture, the other class to war. In this event, it is inevitable that the warrior class should little by little acquire such ascendancy over the other as to be able to oppress it with impunity. ...

5. Everywhere—in Russia and Poland, in India and medieval Europe—the ruling warrior classes acquire almost exclusive ownership of the land. Land, as we have seen, is the chief source of production and wealth in countries that are not very far advanced in civilization. But as civilization progresses, revenue from land increases proportionately. With the growth of population there is, at least in certain periods, an increase in rent, in the Ricardian sense of the term, largely because great centers of consumption arise—such at all times have been the great capitals and other large cities, ancient and modern. Eventually, if other circumstances permit, a very important social transformation occurs. Wealth rather than military valor comes to be the characteristic feature of the dominant class: the people who rule are the rich rather than the brave.

The condition that in the main is required for this transformation is that social organization shall have concentrated and become perfected to such an extent that the protection offered by public authority is considerably more effective than the protection offered by private force. In other words, private property must be so well protected by the practical and real efficacy of the laws as to render the power of the proprietor himself superfluous. This comes about through a series of gradual alterations in the social structure whereby a type of political organization, which we shall call the "feudal state," is transformed into an essentially different type, which we shall term the "bureaucratic state." We are to discuss these types at some length hereafter, but we may say at once that the evolution here referred to is as a rule greatly facilitated by progress in pacific manners and customs and by certain moral habits which societies contract as civilization advances.

Once this transformation has taken place, wealth produces political power just as political power has been producing wealth. In a society already somewhat mature—where, therefore, individual power is curbed by the collective power—if the powerful are as a rule the rich, to be rich is to become powerful. And, in truth, when fighting with the mailed fist is prohibited whereas fighting with pounds and pence is sanctioned, the better posts are inevitably won by those who are better supplied with pounds and pence.

There are, to be sure, states of a very high level of civilization which in theory are organized on the basis of moral principles of such a character that they seem to preclude this overbearing assertiveness on the part of wealth. But this is a case—and there are many such—where theoretical principles can have no more than a limited application in real life. In the United States all powers flow directly or indirectly from popular elections, and suffrage is equal for all men and women in all the states of the Union. What is more, democracy prevails not only in institutions but to a certain extent also in morals. The rich ordinarily feel a certain aversion to entering public life, and the poor a certain aversion to choosing the rich for elective office. But that does not prevent a rich man from being more influential than a poor man, since he can use pressure upon the politicians who control public administration. It does not prevent elections from being carried on to the music of clinking dollars. It does not prevent whole legislatures and considerable numbers of national congressmen from feeling the influence of powerful corporations and great financiers.[2] ...

6. In societies in which religious beliefs are strong and ministers of the faith form a special class a priestly aristocracy almost always arises and gains possession of a more or less important share of the wealth and the political power. Conspicuous examples of that situation would be ancient Egypt (during certain periods), Brahman India and medieval Europe. Oftentimes the priests not only perform religious functions. They possess legal and scientific knowledge and constitute the class of highest intellectual culture. Consciously or unconsciously, priestly hierarchies often show a tendency to monopolize learning and hamper the dissemination of the methods and procedures that make the acquisition of knowledge possible and easy. To that tendency may have been due, in part at least, the painfully slow diffusion of the demotic alphabet in ancient Egypt, though that alphabet was infinitely more simple than the hieroglyphic script. The Druids in Gaul were acquainted with the Greek alphabet but would not permit their rich store of sacred literature to be written down, requiring their pupils to commit it to memory at the cost of untold effort. To the same outlook may be attributed the stubborn and frequent use of dead languages that we find in ancient Chaldea, in India, and in medieval Europe. Sometimes, as was the case in India, lower classes have been explicitly forbidden to acquire knowledge of sacred books.

Specialized knowledge and really scientific culture, purged of any sacred or religious aura, become important political forces only in a highly advanced stage of civilization, and only then do they give access to membership in the ruling class to those who possess them. But in this case too, it is not so much learning in itself that has political value as the practical applications that may be made of learning to the profit of the public or the state. Sometimes all that is required is mere possession of the mechanical processes that are indispensable to the acquisition of a higher culture. This may be due to the fact that on such a basis it is easier to ascertain and measure the skill which a candidate has been able to acquire—it is easier to "mark" or grade him. So in certain periods in ancient Egypt the profession of scribe was a road to public office and power, perhaps because to have learned the hieroglyphic script was proof of long and patient study. In modern China, again, learning the numberless characters in Chinese script has formed the basis of the mandarin's education.[3] In present-day Europe and America the class that applies the findings of modern science to war, public administration, public works and public sanitation holds a fairly important position, both socially and politically, and in our western world, as in ancient Rome, an altogether privileged position is held by lawyers. They know the complicated legislation that arises in all peoples of long-standing civilization, and they become especially powerful if their knowledge of law is coupled with the type of eloquence that chances to have a strong appeal to the taste of their contemporaries.

There are examples in abundance where we see that longstanding practice in directing the military and civil organization of a community creates and develops in the higher reaches of the ruling class a real art of governing which is something better than crude empiricism and better than anything that mere individual experience could suggest. In such circumstances aristocracies of functionaries arise, such as the Roman senate, the Venetian nobility and to a certain extent the English aristocracy. Those bodies all stirred John Stuart Mill to admiration and certainly they all three developed governments that were distinguished for carefully considered policies and for great steadfastness and sagacity in carrying them out. This art of governing is not political science, though it has, at one time or another, anticipated applications of a number of the postulates of political science. However, even if the art of governing has now and again enjoyed prestige with certain classes of persons who have long held possession of political functions, knowledge of it has never served as an ordinary criterion for admitting to public offices persons who were barred from them by social station. The degree of mastery of the art of governing that a person possesses is, moreover, apart from exceptional cases, a very difficult thing to determine if the person has given no practical demonstration that he possesses it.

7. In some countries we find hereditary castes. In such cases the governing class is explicitly restricted to a given number of families, and birth is the one criterion that determines entry into the class or exclusion from it. Examples are exceedingly common. There is practically no country of long-standing civilization that has not had a hereditary aristocracy at one period or another in its history. We find hereditary nobilities during certain periods in China and ancient Egypt, in India, in Greece before the wars with the Medes, in ancient Rome, among the Slavs, among the Latins and Germans of the Middle Ages, in Mexico at the time of the Discovery and in Japan down to a few years ago.

In this connection two preliminary observations are in point. In the first place, all ruling clas-ses tend to become hereditary in fact if not in law. All political forces seem to possess a quality that in physics used to be called the force of inertia. They have a tendency, that is, to remain at the point and in the state in which they find themselves. Wealth and military valor are easily maintained in certain families by moral tradition and by heredity. Qualification for important office—the habit of, and to an extent the capacity for, dealing with affairs of consequence—is much more readily acquired when one has had a certain familiarity with them from childhood. Even when academic degrees, scientific training, special aptitudes as tested by examinations and competitions, open the way to public office, there is no eliminating that special advantage in favor of certain individuals which the French call the advantage of *positions déjà prises*. In actual fact, though examinations and competitions may theoretically be open to all, the majority never have the resources for meeting the expense of long preparation, and many others are without the connections and kinships that set an individual promptly on the right road, enabling him to avoid the gropings and blunders that are inevitable when one enters an unfamiliar environment without any guidance or support.

The democratic principle of election by broad-based suffrage would seem at first glance to be in conflict with the tendency toward stability which, according to our theory, ruling classes show. But it must be noted that candidates who are successful in democratic elections are almost always the ones who possess the political forces above enumerated, which are very often hereditary. In the English, French and Italian parliaments we frequently see the sons, grandsons, brothers, nephews and sons-in-law of members and deputies, ex-members and ex-deputies.

In the second place, when we see a hereditary caste established in a country and monopolizing political power, we may be sure that such a status de jure was preceded by a similar status de facto. Before proclaiming their exclusive and hereditary right to power the families or castes in question must have held the scepter of command in a firm grasp, completely monopolizing all the political forces of that country at that period. Otherwise such a claim on their part would only have aroused the bitterest protests and provoked the bitterest struggles.

Hereditary aristocracies often come to vaunt supernatural origins, or at least origins different from, and superior to, those of the governed classes. Such claims are explained by a highly significant social fact, namely that every governing class tends to justify its actual exercise of power by resting it on some universal moral principle. This same sort of claim has come forward in our time in scientific trappings. A number of writers, developing and amplifying Darwin's theories, contend that upper classes represent a higher level in social evolution and are therefore superior to lower classes by organic structure. Gumplowicz goes to the point of maintaining that the divisions of populations into trade groups and professional classes in modern civilized countries are based on ethnological heterogeneousness.[4]

Now history very definitely shows the special abilities as well as the special defects—both very marked—which have been displayed by aristocracies that have either remained absolutely closed or have made entry into their circles difficult. The ancient Roman patriciate and the English and German nobilities of modern times give a ready idea of the type we refer to. Yet in dealing with this fact, and with the theories that tend to exaggerate its significance, we can always raise the same objection—that the individuals who belong to the aristocracies in question owe their special qualities not so much to the blood that flows in their veins as to their very particular upbringing, which has brought out certain intellectual and moral tendencies in them in preference to others.
...

8. Finally, if we were to keep to the idea of those who maintain the exclusive influence of the hereditary principle in the formation of ruling classes, we should be carried to a conclusion somewhat like the one to which we were carried by the evolutionary principle: The political history of mankind ought to be much simpler than it is. If the ruling class really belonged to a different race, or if the qualities that fit it for dominion were transmitted primarily by organic heredity, it is difficult to see how, once the class was formed, it could decline and lose its power. The peculiar qualities of a race are exceedingly tenacious.

Keeping to the evolutionary theory, acquired capacities in the parents are inborn in their children and, as generation succeeds generation, are progressively accentuated. The descendants of rulers, therefore, ought to become better and better fitted to rule, and the other classes ought to see their chances of challenging or supplanting them become more and more remote. Now the most commonplace experience suffices to assure one that things do not go in that way at all.

What we see is that as soon as there is a shift in the balance of political forces—when, that is, a need is felt that capacities different from the old should assert themselves in the management of the state, when the old capacities, therefore, lose some of their importance or changes in their distribution occur—then the manner in which the ruling class is constituted changes also. If a new source of wealth develops in a society, if the practical importance of knowledge grows, if an old religion declines or a new one is born, if a new current of ideas spreads, then, simultaneously, far-reaching dislocations occur in the ruling class. One might say, indeed, that the whole history of civilized mankind comes down to a conflict between the tendency of dominant elements to monopolize political power and transmit possession of it by inheritance, and the tendency toward a dislocation of old forces and an insurgence of new forces; and this conflict produces an unending ferment of endosmosis and exosmosis between the upper classes and certain portions of the lower. Ruling classes decline inevitably when they cease to find scope for the capacities through which they rose to power, when they can no longer render the social services which they once rendered, or when their talents and the services they render lose in importance in the social environment in which they live. So the Roman aristocracy declined when it was no longer the exclusive source of higher officers for the army, of administrators for the commonwealth, of governors for the provinces. So the Venetian aristocracy declined when its nobles ceased to command the galleys and no longer passed the greater part of their lives in sailing the seas and in trading and fighting.

In inorganic nature we have the example of our air, in which a tendency to immobility produced by the force of inertia is continuously in conflict with a tendency to shift about as the result of inequalities in the distribution of heat. The two tendencies, prevailing by turn in various regions on our planet, produce now calm, now wind and storm. In much the same way in human societies there prevails now the tendency that produces closed, stationary, crystallized ruling classes, now the tendency that results in a more or less rapid renovation of ruling classes.

Notes

1. Mosca, *Teorica dei governi e governo parlamentare,* chap. I.
2. Jannet, *Le istituzioni politiche e sociali degli Stati Uniti d'America,* part II, chap. X f.
3. This was true up to a few years ago, the examination of a mandarin covering only literary and historical studies—as the Chinese understood such studies, of course.
4. *Der Rassenkampf.* This notion transpires from Gumplowicz's whole volume. It is explicitly formulated in book II, chap. XXXIII.

C. WRIGHT MILLS

The Power Elite

The powers of ordinary men are circumscribed by the everyday worlds in which they live, yet even in these rounds of job, family, and neighborhood they often seem driven by forces they can neither understand nor govern. 'Great changes' are beyond their control, but affect their conduct and outlook none the less. The very framework of modern society confines them to projects not their own, but from every side, such changes now press upon the men and women of the mass society, who accordingly feel that they are without purpose in an epoch in which they are without power.

But not all men are in this sense ordinary. As the means of information and of power are centralized, some men come to occupy positions in American society from which they can look down upon, so to speak, and by their decisions mightily affect, the everyday worlds of ordinary men and women. They are not made by their jobs; they set up and break down jobs for thousands of others; they are not confined by simple family responsibilities; they can escape. They may live in many hotels and houses, but they are bound by no one community. They need not merely 'meet the demands of the day and hour'; in some part, they create these demands, and cause others to meet them. Whether or not they profess their power, their technical and political experience of it far transcends that of the underlying population. What Jacob Burckhardt said of 'great men,' most Americans might well say of their elite: 'They are all that we are not.'[1]

The power elite is composed of men whose positions enable them to transcend the ordinary environments of ordinary men and women; they are in positions to make decisions having major consequences. Whether they do or do not make such decisions is less important than the fact that they do occupy such pivotal positions: their failure to act, their failure to make decisions, is itself an act that is often of greater consequence than the decisions they do make. For they are in command of the major hierarchies and organizations of modern society. They rule the big corporations. They run the machinery of the state and claim its prerogatives. They direct the military establishment. They occupy the strategic command posts of the social structure, in which are now centered the effective means of the power and the wealth and the celebrity which they enjoy.

The power elite are not solitary rulers. Advisers and consultants, spokesmen and opinion-makers are often the captains of their higher thought and decision. Immediately below the elite are the professional politicians of the middle levels of power, in the Congress and in the pressure groups, as well as among the new and old upper classes of town and city and region. Mingling with them in curious ways are those professional celebrities who live by being continually displayed but are never, so long as they remain celebrities, displayed enough. If such celebrities are not at the head of any dominating hierarchy, they do often have the power to distract the attention of the public or afford sensations to the masses, or, more directly, to gain the ear of those who do occupy positions of direct power. More or less unattached, as critics of morality and technicians of power, as spokesmen of God and creators of mass sensibility, such celebrities and consultants are part of the immediate scene in which the drama of the elite is enacted. But that drama itself is centered in the command posts of the major institutional hierarchies.

1

The truth about the nature and the power of the elite is not some secret which men of affairs know but will not tell. Such men hold quite various theories about their own roles in the sequence of event and decision. Often they are uncertain about their roles, and even more often they allow their fears and their hopes to affect their assessment of their own power. No matter how great their actual power, they tend to be less acutely aware of it than of the resistances of others to its use. Moreover, most American men of affairs have learned well the rhetoric of public relations, in some cases even to the point of using it when they are alone, and thus coming to believe it. The personal awareness of the actors is only one of the several sources one must examine in order to understand the higher circles. Yet many who believe that there is no elite, or at any rate none of any

consequence, rest their argument upon what men of affairs believe about themselves, or at least assert in public.

There is, however, another view: those who feel, even if vaguely, that a compact and powerful elite of great importance does now prevail in America often base that feeling upon the historical trend of our time. They have felt, for example, the domination of the military event, and from this they infer that generals and admirals, as well as other men of decision influenced by them, must be enormously powerful. They hear that the Congress has again abdicated to a handful of men decisions clearly related to the issue of war or peace. They know that the bomb was dropped over Japan in the name of the United States of America, although they were at no time consulted about the matter. They feel that they live in a time of big decisions; they know that they are not making any. Accordingly, as they consider the present as history, they infer that at its center, making decisions or failing to make them, there must be an elite of power.

On the one hand, those who share this feeling about big historical events assume that there is an elite and that its power is great. On the other hand, those who listen carefully to the reports of men apparently involved in the great decisions often do not believe that there is an elite whose powers are of decisive consequence.

Both views must be taken into account, but neither is adequate. The way to understand the power of the American elite lies neither solely in recognizing the historic scale of events nor in accepting the personal awareness reported by men of apparent decision. Behind such men and behind the events of history, linking the two, are the major institutions of modern society. These hierarchies of state and corporation and army constitute the means of power; as such they are now of a consequence not before equaled in human history—and at their summits, there are now those command posts of modern society which offer us the sociological key to an understanding of the role of the higher circles in America.

Within American society, major national power now resides in the economic, the political, and the military domains. Other institutions seem off to the side of modern history, and, on occasion, duly subordinated to these. No family is as directly powerful in national affairs as any major corporation; no church is as directly powerful in the external biographies of young men in America today as the military establishment; no college is as powerful in the shaping of momentous events as the National Security Council. Religious, educational, and family institutions are not autonomous centers of national power; on the contrary, these decentralized areas are increasingly shaped by the big three, in which developments of decisive and immediate consequence now occur. ...

Within each of the big three, the typical institutional unit has become enlarged, has become administrative, and, in the power of its decisions, has become centralized. Behind these developments there is a fabulous technology, for as institutions, they have incorporated this technology and guide it, even as it shapes and paces their developments.

The economy—once a great scatter of small productive units in autonomous balance—has become dominated by two or three hundred giant corporations, administratively and politically interrelated, which together hold the keys to economic decisions.

The political order, once a decentralized set of several dozen states with a weak spinal cord, has become a centralized, executive establishment which has taken up into itself many powers previously scattered, and now enters into each and every cranny of the social structure.

The military order, once a slim establishment in a context of distrust fed by state militia, has become the largest and most expensive feature of government, and, although well versed in smiling public relations, now has all the grim and clumsy efficiency of a sprawling bureaucratic domain.

In each of these institutional areas, the means of power at the disposal of decision makers have increased enormously; their central executive powers have been enhanced; within each of them modern administrative routines have been elaborated and tightened up.

As each of these domains becomes enlarged and centralized, the consequences of its activities become greater, and its traffic with the others increases. The decisions of a handful of corpora-

tions bear upon military and political as well as upon economic developments around the world. The decisions of the military establishment rest upon and grievously affect political life as well as the very level of economic activity. The decisions made within the political domain determine economic activities and military programs. There is no longer, on the one hand, an economy, and, on the other hand, a political order containing a military establishment unimportant to politics and to money-making. There is a political economy linked, in a thousand ways, with military institutions and decisions. On each side of the world-split running through central Europe and around the Asiatic rimlands, there is an ever-increasing interlocking of economic, military, and political structures.[2] If there is government intervention in the corporate economy, so is there corporate intervention in the governmental process. In the structural sense, this triangle of power is the source of the interlocking directorate that is most important for the historical structure of the present.

The fact of the interlocking is clearly revealed at each of the points of crisis of modern capitalist society—slump, war, and boom. In each, men of decision are led to an awareness of the interdependence of the major institutional orders. In the nineteenth century, when the scale of all institutions was smaller, their liberal integration was achieved in the automatic economy, by an autonomous play of market forces, and in the automatic political domain, by the bargain and the vote. It was then assumed that out of the imbalance and friction that followed the limited decisions then possible a new equilibrium would in due course emerge. That can no longer be assumed, and it is not assumed by the men at the top of each of the three dominant hierarchies.

For given the scope of their consequences, decisions—and indecisions—in any one of these ramify into the others, and hence top decisions tend either to become co-ordinated or to lead to a commanding indecision. It has not always been like this. When numerous small entrepreneurs made up the economy, for example, many of them could fail and the consequences still remain local; political and military authorities did not intervene. But now, given political expectations and military commitments, can they afford to allow key units of the private corporate economy to break down in slump? Increasingly, they do intervene in economic affairs, and as they do so, the controlling decisions in each order are inspected by agents of the other two, and economic, military, and political structures are interlocked.

At the pinnacle of each of the three enlarged and centralized domains, there have arisen those higher circles which make up the economic, the political, and the military elites. At the top of the economy, among the corporate rich, there are the chief executives; at the top of the political order, the members of the political directorate; at the top of the military establishment, the elite of soldier-statesmen clustered in and around the Joint Chiefs of Staff and the upper echelon. As each of these domains has coincided with the others, as decisions tend to become total in their consequence, the leading men in each of the three domains of power—the warlords, the corporation chieftains, the political directorate—tend to come together, to form the power elite of America.

2

The higher circles in and around these command posts are often thought of in terms of what their members possess: they have a greater share than other people of the things and experiences that are most highly valued. From this point of view, the elite are simply those who have the most of what there is to have, which is generally held to include money, power, and prestige—as well as all the ways of life to which these lead.[3] But the elite are not simply those who have the most, for they could not 'have the most' were it not for their positions in the great institutions. For such institutions are the necessary bases of power, of wealth, and of prestige, and at the same time, the chief means of exercising power, of acquiring and retaining wealth, and of cashing in the higher claims for prestige.

By the powerful we mean, of course, those who are able to realize their will, even if others resist it. No one, accordingly, can be truly powerful unless he has access to the command of major institutions, for it is over these institutional means of

power that the truly powerful are, in the first instance, powerful. Higher politicians and key officials of government command such institutional power; so do admirals and generals, and so do the major owners and executives of the larger corporations. Not all power, it is true, is anchored in and exercised by means of such institutions, but only within and through them can power be more or less continuous and important. ...

If we took the one hundred most powerful men in America, the one hundred wealthiest, and the one hundred most celebrated away from the institutional positions they now occupy, away from their resources of men and women and money, away from the media of mass communication that are now focused upon them—then they would be powerless and poor and uncelebrated. For power is not of a man. Wealth does not center in the person of the wealthy. Celebrity is not inherent in any personality. To be celebrated, to be wealthy, to have power requires access to major institutions, for the institutional positions men occupy determine in large part their chances to have and to hold these valued experiences.

3

The people of the higher circles may also be conceived as members of a top social stratum, as a set of groups whose members know one another, see one another socially and at business, and so, in making decisions, take one another into account. The elite, according to this conception, feel themselves to be, and are felt by others to be, the inner circle of 'the upper social classes.'[4] They form a more or less compact social and psychological entity; they have become self-conscious members of a social class. People are either accepted into this class or they are not, and there is a qualitative split, rather than merely a numerical scale, separating them from those who are not elite. They are more or less aware of themselves as a social class and they behave toward one another differently from the way they do toward members of other classes. They accept one another, understand one another, marry one another, tend to work and to think if not together at least alike.

Now, we do not want by our definition to pre-judge whether the elite of the command posts are conscious members of such a socially recognized class, or whether considerable proportions of the elite derive from such a clear and distinct class. These are matters to be investigated. Yet in order to be able to recognize what we intend to investigate, we must note something that all biographies and memoirs of the wealthy and the powerful and the eminent make clear: no matter what else they may be, the people of these higher circles are involved in a set of overlapping 'crowds' and intricately connected 'cliques.' There is a kind of mutual attraction among those who 'sit on the same terrace'—although this often becomes clear to them, as well as to others, only at the point at which they feel the need to draw the line; only when, in their common defense, they come to understand what they have in common, and so close their ranks against outsiders.

The idea of such ruling stratum implies that most of its members have similar social origins, that throughout their lives they maintain a network of informal connections, and that to some degree there is an interchangeability of position between the various hierarchies of money and power and celebrity. We must, of course, note at once that if such an elite stratum does exist, its social visibility and its form, for very solid historical reasons, are quite different from those of the noble cousinhoods that once ruled various European nations.

That American society has never passed through a feudal epoch is of decisive importance to the nature of the American elite, as well as to American society as a historic whole. For it means that no nobility or aristocracy, established before the capitalist era, has stood in tense opposition to the higher bourgeoisie. It means that this bourgeoisie has monopolized not only wealth but prestige and power as well. It means that no set of noble families has commanded the top positions and monopolized the values that are generally held in high esteem; and certainly that no set has done so explicitly by inherited right. It means that no high church dignitaries or court nobilities, no entrenched landlords with honorific accouterments, no monopolists of high army posts have opposed the enriched bourgeoisie and in the name of birth and prerogative successfully resisted its self-making.

But this does *not* mean that there are no upper strata in the United States. That they emerged from a 'middle class' that had no recognized aristocratic superiors does not mean they remained middle class when enormous increases in wealth made their own superiority possible. Their origins and their newness may have made the upper strata less visible in America than elsewhere. But in America today there are in fact tiers and ranges of wealth and power of which people in the middle and lower ranks know very little and may not even dream. There are families who, in their well-being, are quite insulated from the economic jolts and lurches felt by the merely prosperous and those farther down the scale. There are also men of power who in quite small groups make decisions of enormous consequence for the underlying population.

The American elite entered modern history as a virtually unopposed bourgeoisie. No national bourgeoisie, before or since, has had such opportunities and advantages. Having no military neighbors, they easily occupied an isolated continent stocked with natural resources and immensely inviting to a willing labor force. A framework of power and an ideology for its justification were already at hand. Against mercantilist restriction, they inherited the principle of *laissez-faire;* against Southern planters, they imposed the principle of industrialism. The Revolutionary War put an end to colonial pretensions to nobility, as loyalists fled the country and many estates were broken up. The Jacksonian upheaval with its status revolution put an end to pretensions to monopoly of descent by the old New England families. The Civil War broke the power, and so in due course the prestige, of the antebellum South's claimants for the higher esteem. The tempo of the whole capitalist development made it impossible for an inherited nobility to develop and endure in America.

No fixed ruling class, anchored in agrarian life and coming to flower in military glory, could contain in America the historic thrust of commerce and industry, or subordinate to itself the capitalist elite—as capitalists were subordinated, for example, in Germany and Japan. Nor could such a ruling class anywhere in the world contain that of the United States when industrialized violence came to decide history. Witness the fate of Germany and Japan in the two world wars of the twentieth century; and indeed the fate of Britain herself and her model ruling class, as New York became the inevitable economic, and Washington the inevitable political capital of the western capitalist world.

4

The elite who occupy the command posts may be seen as the possessors of power and wealth and celebrity; they may be seen as members of the upper stratum of a capitalistic society. They may also be defined in terms of psychological and moral criteria, as certain kinds of selected individuals. So defined, the elite, quite simply, are people of superior character and energy.

The humanist, for example, may conceive of the 'elite' not as a social level or category, but as a scatter of those individuals who attempt to transcend themselves, and accordingly, are more noble, more efficient, made out of better stuff. It does not matter whether they are poor or rich, whether they hold high position or low, whether they are acclaimed or despised; they are elite because of the kind of individuals they are. The rest of the population is mass, which, according to this conception, sluggishly relaxes into uncomfortable mediocrity.[5]

This is the sort of socially unlocated conception which some American writers with conservative yearnings have recently sought to develop. But most moral and psychological conceptions of the elite are much less sophisticated, concerning themselves not with individuals but with the stratum as a whole. Such ideas, in fact, always arise in a society in which some people possess more than do others of what there is to possess. People with advantages are loath to believe that they just happen to be people with advantages. They come readily to define themselves as inherently worthy of what they possess; they come to believe themselves 'naturally' elite; and, in fact, to imagine their possessions and their privileges as natural extensions of their own elite selves. In this sense,

the idea of the elite as composed of men and women having a finer moral character is an ideology of the elite as a privileged ruling stratum, and this is true whether the ideology is elite-made or made up for it by others.

In eras of equalitarian rhetoric, the more intelligent or the more articulate among the lower and middle classes, as well as guilty members of the upper, may come to entertain ideas of a counter-elite. In western society, as a matter of fact, there is a long tradition and varied images of the poor, the exploited, and the oppressed as the truly virtuous, the wise, and the blessed. Stemming from Christian tradition, this moral idea of a counter-elite composed of essentially higher types condemned to a lowly station, may be and has been used by the underlying population to justify harsh criticism of ruling elites and to celebrate utopian images of a new elite to come.

The moral conception of the elite, however, is not always merely an ideology of the overprivileged or a counter-ideology of the underprivileged. It is often a fact: having controlled experiences and select privileges, many individuals of the upper stratum do come in due course to approximate the types of character they claim to embody. Even when we give up—as we must—the idea that the elite man or woman is born with an elite character, we need not dismiss the idea that their experiences and trainings develop in them characters of a specific type. ...

5

These several notions of the elite, when appropriately understood, are intricately bound up with one another, and we shall use them all in this examination of American success. We shall study each of several higher circles as offering candidates for the elite, and we shall do so in terms of the major institutions making up the total society of America; within and between each of these institutions, we shall trace the interrelations of wealth and power and prestige. But our main concern is with the power of those who now occupy the command posts, and with the role which they are enacting in the history of our epoch.

Such an elite may be conceived as omnipotent, and its powers thought of as a great hidden design. Thus, in vulgar Marxism, events and trends are explained by reference to 'the will of the bourgeoisie'; in Nazism, by reference to 'the conspiracy of the Jews'; by the petty right in America today, by reference to 'the hidden force' of Communist spies. According to such notions of the omnipotent elite as historical cause, the elite is never an entirely visible agency. It is, in fact, a secular substitute for the will of God, being realized in a sort of providential design, except that usually non-elite men are thought capable of opposing it and eventually overcoming it.

The opposite view—of the elite as impotent—is now quite popular among liberal-minded observers. Far from being omnipotent, the elites are thought to be so scattered as to lack any coherence as a historical force. Their invisibility is not the invisibility of secrecy but the invisibility of the multitude. Those who occupy the formal places of authority are so check-mated—by other elites exerting pressure, or by the public as an electorate, or by constitutional codes—that, although there may be upper classes, there is no ruling class; although there may be men of power, there is no power elite; although there may be a system of stratification, it has no effective top. In the extreme, this view of the elite, as weakened by compromise and disunited to the point of nullity, is a substitute for impersonal collective fate; for, in this view, the decisions of the visible men of the higher circles do not count in history.

Internationally, the image of the omnipotent elite tends to prevail. All good events and pleasing happenings are quickly imputed by the opinion-makers to the leaders of their own nation; all bad events and unpleasant experiences are imputed to the enemy abroad. In both cases, the omnipotence of evil rulers or of virtuous leaders is assumed. Within the nation, the use of such rhetoric is rather more complicated: when men speak of the power of their own party or circle, they and their leaders are, of course, impotent; only 'the people' are omnipotent. But, when they speak of the power of their opponent's party or circle, they impute to them omnipotence; 'the people' are now powerlessly taken in.

More generally, American men of power tend, by convention, to deny that they are powerful. No American runs for office in order to rule or even govern, but only to serve; he does not become a bureaucrat or even an official, but a public servant. And nowadays, as I have already pointed out, such postures have become standard features of the public-relations programs of all men of power. So firm a part of the style of power-wielding have they become that conservative writers readily misinterpret them as indicating a trend toward an 'amorphous power situation.'

But the 'power situation' of America today is less amorphous than is the perspective of those who see it as a romantic confusion. It is less a flat, momentary 'situation' than a graded, durable structure. And if those who occupy its top grades are not omnipotent, neither are they impotent. It is the form and the height of the gradation of power that we must examine if we would understand the degree of power held and exercised by the elite.

If the power to decide such national issues as are decided were shared in an absolutely equal way, there would be no power elite; in fact, there would be no *gradation* of power, but only a radical homogeneity. At the opposite extreme as well, if the power to decide issues were absolutely monopolized by one small group, there would be no gradation of power; there would simply be this small group in command, and below it, the undifferentiated, dominated masses. American society today represents neither the one nor the other of these extremes, but a conception of them is none the less useful: it makes us realize more clearly the question of the structure of power in the United States and the position of the power elite within it.

Within each of the most powerful institutional orders of modern society there is a gradation of power. The owner of a roadside fruit stand does not have as much power in any area of social or economic or political decision as the head of a multi-million-dollar fruit corporation; no lieutenant on the line is as powerful as the Chief of Staff in the Pentagon; no deputy sheriff carries as much authority as the President of the United States. Accordingly, the problem of defining the power elite concerns the level at which we wish to draw the line. By lowering the line, we could define the elite out of existence; by raising it, we could make the elite a very small circle indeed. In a preliminary and minimum way, we draw the line crudely, in charcoal as it were: By the power elite, we refer to those political, economic, and military circles which as an intricate set of overlapping cliques share decisions having at least national consequences. In so far as national events are decided, the power elite are those who decide them. ...

6

It is not my thesis that for all epochs of human history and in all nations, a creative minority, a ruling class, an omnipotent elite, shape all historical events. Such statements, upon careful examination, usually turn out to be mere tautologies,[6] and even when they are not, they are so entirely general as to be useless in the attempt to understand the history of the present. The minimum definition of the power elite as those who decide whatever is decided of major consequence, does not imply that the members of this elite are always and necessarily the history-makers; neither does it imply that they never are. We must not confuse the conception of the elite, which we wish to define, with one theory about their role: that they are the history-makers of our time. To define the elite, for example, as 'those who rule America' is less to define a conception than to state one hypothesis about the role and power of that elite. No matter how we might define the elite, the extent of its members' power is subject to historical variation. If, in a dogmatic way, we try to include that variation in our generic definition, we foolishly limit the use of a needed conception. If we insist that the elite be defined as a strictly coordinated class that continually and absolutely rules, we are closing off from our view much to which the term more modestly defined might open to our observation. In short, our definition of the power elite cannot properly contain dogma concerning the degree and kind of power that ruling groups everywhere have. Much less should it permit us to smuggle into our discussion a theory of history.

During most of human history, historical change has not been visible to the people who were involved in it, or even to those enacting it. Ancient Egypt and Mesopotamia, for example, endured for some four hundred generations with but slight changes in their basic structure. That is six and a half times as long as the entire Christian era, which has only prevailed some sixty generations; it is about eighty times as long as the five generations of the United States' existence. But now the tempo of change is so rapid, and the means of observation so accessible, that the interplay of event and decision seems often to be quite historically visible, if we will only look carefully and from an adequate vantage point.

When knowledgeable journalists tell us that 'events, not men, shape the big decisions,' they are echoing the theory of history as Fortune, Chance, Fate, or the work of The Unseen Hand. For 'events' is merely a modern word for these older ideas, all of which separate men from history-making, because all of them lead us to believe that history goes on behind men's backs. History is drift with no mastery; within it there is action but no deed; history is mere happening and the event intended by no one.[7]

The course of events in our time depends more on a series of human decisions than on any inevitable fate. The sociological meaning of 'fate' is simply this: that, when the decisions are innumerable and each one is of small consequence, all of them add up in a way no man intended—to history as fate. But not all epochs are equally fateful. As the circle of those who decide is narrowed, as the means of decision are centralized and the consequences of decisions become enormous, then the course of great events often rests upon the decisions of determinable circles. This does not necessarily mean that the same circle of men follow through from one event to another in such a way that all of history is merely their plot. The power of the elite does not necessarily mean that history is not also shaped by a series of small decisions, none of which are thought out. It does not mean that a hundred small arrangements and compromises and adaptations may not be built into the going policy and the living event. The idea of the power elite implies nothing about the process of decision-making as such: it is an attempt to delimit the social areas within which that process, whatever its character, goes on. It is a conception of who is involved in the process.

The degree of foresight and control of those who are involved in decisions that count may also vary. The idea of the power elite does not mean that the estimations and calculated risks upon which decisions are made are not often wrong and that the consequences are sometimes, indeed often, not those intended. Often those who make decisions are trapped by their own inadequacies and blinded by their own errors.

Yet in our time the pivotal moment does arise, and at that moment, small circles do decide or fail to decide. In either case, they are an elite of power. The dropping of the A-bombs over Japan was such a moment; the decision on Korea was such a moment; the confusion about Quemoy and Matsu, as well as before Dienbienphu were such moments; the sequence of maneuvers which involved the United States in World War II was such a 'moment.' Is it not true that much of the history of our times is composed of such moments? And is not that what is meant when it is said that we live in a time of big decisions, of decisively centralized power?

Most of us do not try to make sense of our age by believing in a Greek-like, eternal recurrence, nor by a Christian belief in a salvation to come, nor by any steady march of human progress. Even though we do not reflect upon such matters, the chances are we believe with Burckhardt that we live in a mere succession of events; that sheer continuity is the only principle of history. History is merely one thing after another; history is meaningless in that it is not the realization of any determinate plot. It is true, of course, that our sense of continuity, our feeling for the history of our time, is affected by crisis. But we seldom look beyond the immediate crisis or the crisis felt to be just ahead. We believe neither in fate nor providence; and we assume, without talking about it, that 'we'—as a nation—can decisively shape the future but that 'we' as individuals somehow cannot do so.

Any meaning history has, 'we' shall have to give to it by our actions. Yet the fact is that although we are all of us within history we do not all possess equal powers to make history. To pretend that

we do is sociological nonsense and political irresponsibility. It is nonsense because any group or any individual is limited, first of all, by the technical and institutional means of power at its command; we do not all have equal access to the means of power that now exist, nor equal influence over their use. To pretend that 'we' are all history-makers is politically irresponsible because it obfuscates any attempt to locate responsibility for the consequential decisions of men who do have access to the means of power.

From even the most superficial examination of the history of the western society we learn that the power of decision-makers is first of all limited by the level of technique, by the *means* of power and violence and organization that prevail in a given society. In this connection we also learn that there is a fairly straight line running upward through the history of the West; that the means of oppression and exploitation, of violence and destruction, as well as the means of production and reconstruction, have been progressively enlarged and increasingly centralized.

As the institutional means of power and the means of communications that tie them together have become steadily more efficient, those now in command of them have come into command of instruments of rule quite unsurpassed in the history of mankind. And we are not yet at the climax of their development. We can no longer lean upon or take soft comfort from the historical ups and downs of ruling groups of previous epochs. In that sense, Hegel is correct: we learn from history that we cannot learn from it.

Notes

1. Jacob Burckhardt, *Force and Freedom* (New York: Pantheon Books, 1943), pp. 303 ff.
2. Cf. Hans Gerth and C. Wright Mills, *Character and Social Structure* (New York: Harcourt, Brace, 1953), pp. 457 ff.
3. The statistical idea of choosing some value and calling those who have the most of it an elite derives, in modern times, from the Italian economist, Pareto, who puts the central point in this way: 'Let us assume that in every branch of human activity each individual is given an index which stands as a sign of his capacity, very

much the way grades are given in the various subjects in examinations in school. The highest type of lawyer, for instance, will be given 10. The man who does not get a client will be given 1—reserving zero for the man who is an out-and-out idiot. To the man who has made his millions—honestly or dishonestly as the case may be—we will give 10. To the man who has earned his thousands we will give 6; to such as just manage to keep out of the poor-house, 1, keeping zero for those who get in … So let us make a class of people who have the highest indices in their branch of activity, and to that class give the name of *elite.*' Vilfredo Pareto, *The Mind and Society* (New York: Harcourt, Brace, 1935), par. 2027 and 2031. Those who follow this approach end up not with one elite, but with a number corresponding to the number of values they select. Like many rather abstract ways of reasoning, this one is useful because it forces us to think in a clear-cut way. For a skillful use of this approach, see the work of Harold D. Lasswell, in particular, *Politics: Who Gets What, When, How* (New York: McGraw-Hill, 1936); and for a more systematic use, H. D. Lasswell and Abraham Kaplan, *Power and Society* (New Haven: Yale University Press, 1950).

4. The conception of the elite as members of a top social stratum, is, of course, in line with the prevailing common-sense view of stratification. Technically, it is closer to 'status group' than to 'class,' and has been very well stated by Joseph A. Schumpeter, 'Social Classes in an Ethically Homogeneous Environment,' *Imperialism and Social Classes* (New York: Augustus M. Kelley, Inc., 1951), pp. 133 ff., especially pp. 137–47. Cf. also his *Capitalism, Socialism and Democracy,* 3rd ed. (New York: Harper, 1950), Part II. For the distinction between class and status groups, see *From Max Weber: Essays in Sociology* (trans. and ed. by Gerth and Mills; New York: Oxford University Press, 1946). For an analysis of Pareto's conception of the elite compared with Marx's conception of classes, as well as data on France, see Raymond Aron, 'Social Structure and Ruling Class,' *British Journal of Sociology,* vol. I, nos. 1 and 2 (1950).

5. The most popular essay in recent years which defines the elite and the mass in terms of a morally evaluated character-type is probably José Ortega y Gasset's, *The Revolt of the Masses,* 1932 (New York: New American Library, Mentor Edition, 1950), esp. pp. 91 ff.

6. As in the case, quite notably, of Gaetano Mosca, *The Ruling Class* (New York: McGraw-Hill, 1939). For a sharp analysis of Mosca, see Fritz Morstein Marx, 'The Bureaucratic State,' *Review of Politics,* vol. I, 1939, pp. 457 ff. Cf. also Mills, 'On Intellectual Craftsmanship,' April 1952, mimeographed, Columbia College, February 1955.

7. Cf. Karl Löwith, *Meaning in History* (Chicago: University of Chicago Press, 1949), pp. 125 ff. for concise and penetrating statements of several leading philosophies of history.

ANTHONY GIDDENS

Elites and Power

It is certainly one of the most characteristic emphases of the Marxian perspective that, in capitalism especially (but also, in a general sense, in the prior types of class system), the realm of the 'political' is subordinate to that of the 'economic'. What remains relatively obscure in Marx is the specific form of this dependence, and how it is expressed concretely in the domination of the ruling class.[1] The importance of this is not confined to the analysis of the social structure of capitalism, but bears directly upon the question of the classless character of socialism. It relates, in addition, to issues brought to the forefront by the critique of the Marxian standpoint advanced by the 'elite theorists' of the turn of the century. The substance of this critique, in the writings of such as Pareto and Mosca, may be expressed as an attempt to transmute the Marxian concept of class, as founded in the relations of production, into an essentially *political* differentiation between those 'who rule' and those who 'are ruled'—a transmutation which was, indeed, in part made possible by Marx's failure to specify in a systematic fashion the modes whereby the economic hegemony of the capitalist class becomes 'translated' into the political domination of the *ruling* class. For if it is simply the case that economic control directly yields political power, the way is open for the assertion that, in socialism, as in capitalism (indeed as in any other conceivable type of complex society), whoever controls the means of production thereby achieves political domination as a ruling class. The movement of history from capitalism to socialism then becomes conceived of as a mere succession of 'ruling classes' ('elites'), as in classical 'elite theory', or more specifically as the emergence of the sort of 'managerial' or 'technocratic' ruling class described in Burnham's writings, and more recently in some of the variants of the theory of the 'technocratic society'.[2]

The points at issue between the Marxian standpoint and 'elite theory' have become further complicated in recent years by the use of concepts drawn from the latter, such as that of 'power elite', as if they were synonymous with that of 'ruling class'. It will be useful to clarify the usage of the terms 'ruling class', 'elite', 'power elite', 'governing class', etc., which involves, in part, looking more closely at the structuration of the upper class.

In the analysis which follows, I shall be interested primarily in developing a set of formulations which illuminate significant conceptual distinctions, rather than adhering to conventional terminological usage—if it can be said, in any case, that there is any conventional practice in a field in which there has been so much confusion.[3] I shall suggest that, given the distinctions set out below, there can exist a 'governing class' without it necessarily being a 'ruling class'; that there can exist a 'power elite' without there necessarily being either a 'ruling' or a 'governing class'; that there can be what I shall call a system of 'leadership groups' which constitutes neither a 'ruling class', 'governing class', nor 'power elite'; and that *all* of these social formations are, in principle, compatible with the existence of a society which is 'capitalist' in its organisation. To begin with, a few elementary remarks are necessary about the notion of 'elite'. As it is sometimes employed,

'elite' may refer to those who 'lead' in any given category of activity: to actors and sportsmen as well as to political or economic 'leaders'. There is evidently a difference, however, between the first and the second, in that the former 'lead' in terms of some sort of scale of 'fame' or 'achievement', whereas the second usage may be taken to refer to persons who are at the head of a specific social organisation which has an internal authority structure (the state, an economic enterprise, etc.). I shall use the term 'elite group' in this latter sense, to designate those individuals who occupy positions of formal authority at the head of a social organisation or institution; and 'elite' very generally, to refer either to an elite group or cluster of elite groups.

In these terms, it can be said that a major aspect of the structuration of the upper class concerns, first, the process of mobility into or recruitment to, elite positions and, second, the degree of social 'solidarity' within and between elite groups. Mediate structuration thus concerns how 'closed' the process of recruitment to elite positions is, in favour of those drawn from propertied backgrounds. Proximate structuration depends primarily upon the frequency and nature of the social contacts between the members of elite groups. These may take various forms, including the formation of marriage connections or the existence of other kin ties, the prevalence of personal ties of acquaintance or friendship, etc. If the extent of social 'integration' of elite groups is high, there is also likely to be a high degree of moral solidarity characterising the elite as a whole and, probably, a low incidence of either latent or manifest conflicts between them. There has never been any elite, however solidary, which has been free of conflicts and struggles; but the degree and intensity of overt conflict has varied widely, and thus it is reasonable to speak broadly of differentials in the solidarity of elite groups.

Combining these two aspects of structuration, we can establish a typology of elite formations [see diagram on p. 172].

A 'uniform' elite is one which shares the attributes of having a restricted pattern of recruitment and of forming a relatively tightly knit unity. It hardly needs emphasising that the classifications involved are not of an all-or-nothing character.

Recruitment

	Open	Closed
High	solidary elite	uniform elite
Low	abstract elite	established elite

Integration

The point has been made that even among traditional aristocracies there was never a completely 'closed' pattern of recruitment, something which has only been approached by the Indian caste system—all elites open their ranks, in some degree, to individuals from the lower orders, and may enhance their stability thereby. A relatively closed type of recruitment, however, is likely to supply the sort of coherent socialisation process producing a high level of solidarity between (and within) elite groups. But it is quite feasible to envisage the existence of instances which approximate more closely to the case of an 'established' elite, where there is a relatively closed pattern of recruitment, but only a low level of integration between elite groups. A 'solidary' elite, as defined in the classification, might also appear to involve an unlikely combination of elements, since it might seem difficult to attain a high degree of integration among elite groups whose members are drawn from diverse class backgrounds. But, while this type of social formation is probably rare in capitalist societies, at least some of the state socialist countries fit quite neatly into this category: the Communist Party is the main channel of access to elite positions, and while it provides an avenue of mobility for individuals drawn in substantial proportions from quite lowly backgrounds, at the same time it ensures a high degree of solidarity among elite groups. An 'abstract' elite, involving both relatively open recruitment and a low level of elite solidarity, whatever its empirical reality, approximates closely to the picture of certain contemporary capitalist societies as these are portrayed in the writings of the theorists of so-called 'pluralist democracy'.

The distinguishing of different types of elite formation does not, in itself, enable us to conceptualise the phenomenon of power. As in the case of class structuration itself, we may distinguish two forms of the mediation of power relationships in society. The first I shall call the *institutional* mediation of power; the other, the mediation of power in terms of *control*. By the institutional mediation of power, I mean the general form of state and economy within which elite groups are recruited and structured. This concerns, among other things, the role of property in the overall organisation of economic life, the nature of the legal framework defining economic and political rights and obligations, and the institutional structure of the state itself. The mediation of control refers to the actual (effective) power of policy-formation and decision-making held by the members of particular elite groups: how far, for example, economic leaders are able to influence decisions taken by politicians, etc. To express it another way, we can say that power has two aspects: a 'collective' aspect, in the sense that the 'parameters' of any concrete set of power relationships are contingent upon the overall system of organisation of a society; and a 'distributive' aspect, in the sense that certain groups are able to exert their will at the expense of others.[4] The mediation of control is thus expressed in terms of 'effective' power, manifest in terms of the capacity either to take or to influence the taking of decisions which affect the interests of two or more parties differentially.

We may conceptually separate two variable factors in analysing effective power (that is to say, power as differentiated from 'formal authority') in relation to types of elite formation. The first

| | Issue-strength | |
	Broad	Restricted
Consolidated power	autocratic	oligarchic
Diffused power	hegemonic	democratic

concerns how far such power is 'consolidated' in the hands of elite groups; the second refers to the 'issue-strength' of the power wielded by those in elite positions. While the former designates limitations upon effective power, deriving from constraints imposed from 'below', the latter concerns how far that power is limited *because it can only be exercised in relation to a range of restricted issues*. Thus it is often held to be characteristic of modern capitalist societies that there are quite narrowly defined limitations upon the issues over which elite groups are able to exercise control.[5] By combining these two aspects of effective power as exercised by elite groups, we can establish a classification of forms of power-structure [see diagram on this page]. Like the previous typology, this sets out an abstract combination of possibilities; it goes almost without saying that this is no more than an elementary categorisation of a very complex set of phenomena, and the labels applied here in no way exhaust the variety of characteristics which are frequently subsumed under these terms.

According to these definitions, the consolidation of effective power is greatest where it is not restricted to clearly defined limits in terms of its 'lateral range' (broad 'issue-strength'), and where it is concentrated in the hands of the elite, or an elite group. Power-holding is 'oligarchic' rather than 'autocratic' where the degree of centralisation of power in the hands of elite groups is high, but where the issue-strength of that power is limited. In the case of 'hegemonic' control, those in elite positions wield power which, while it is not clearly defined in scope and limited to a restricted range of issues, is 'shallow'. A 'democratic' order,

in these terms, is one in which the effective power of elite groups is limited in both respects.

Finally, bringing together both classifications formulated above, we can set up an overall typology of elite formations and power within the class structure [see diagram on p. 174]. This makes possible a clarification of the four concepts already mentioned—'ruling class', 'governing class', 'power elite' and 'leadership groups'. It must be emphasised that these partially cross-cut some of the existing usages in the literature on class and elite theory. The Paretian term 'governing class' is here not, as in Pareto's own writing, a replacement for the Marxian 'ruling class'; in this scheme, a governing class is 'one step down', both in terms of elite formation and power-holding, from a 'ruling class'.

In this scheme, the 'strongest' case of a ruling class is defined as that where a uniform elite wields 'autocratic' power; the weakest is where an established elite holds 'oligarchic' power. Where a relatively closed recruitment pattern is linked with the prevalence of defined restrictions upon the effective power of elite groups, a governing class exists, but not a ruling class. A governing class borders upon being a ruling class where a uniform elite possesses 'hegemonic' power; and comes closest to being a system of leadership groups where an established elite holds 'democratic' power. Where a governing class involves a combination of an established elite and 'hegemonic' power, it stands close to being a power elite. A power elite is distinguished from a ruling class in terms of pattern of recruitment, as is a governing class from a system of leadership groups. The latter exists where elite groups only

	Elite formation	Power-holding
Ruling class	uniform/established elite	autocratic/oligarchic
Governing class	uniform/established elite	hegemonic/democratic
Power elite	solidary elite	autocratic/oligarchic
Leadership groups	abstract elite	hegemonic/democratic

hold limited power, and where, in addition, elite recruitment is relatively open in character.

In terms of the mediation of control, this classification leaves undefined the relative primacy of the power of any one elite group over others. This can be conceptually expressed as referring to the nature of the *hierarchy* which exists among elite groups. A hierarchy exists among elite groups in so far as one such group holds power of broader issue-strength than others, and is thereby able to exert a degree of control over decisions taken by those within them. Thus it may be that the economic elite, or certain sectors of the economic elite, are able to significantly condition political decisions through the use of 'influence', 'inducement', or the 'direct' control of political positions—i.e., through the fact that members of the economic elite are also incumbents of political positions. We may refer to all of these modes of obtaining, or striving for, control as the *media of interchange* between elite groups. It is precisely one of the major tasks of the analysis of elite formations to examine the media of interchange which operate between elite groups in any given

society in order to determine what kinds of elite hierarchy exist.

Notes

1. Most subsequent Marxist authors have either been content with the most generalised assertions about this issue, or have wanted to have their cake and eat it by insisting that capitalism is dominated by a ruling class who do not actually 'rule'; cf. Nicos Poulantzas, *Pouvoir politique et classes sociales de l'état capitaliste* (Paris 1970), pp. 361ff.

2. James Burnham, *The Managerial Revolution* (New York 1941).

3. In this section of this chapter I have drawn upon part of my article 'Elites in the British class structure', *Sociological Review* 20, 1972.

4. cf. Talcott Parsons, 'On the concept of political power', *Proceedings of the American Philosophical Society* 107, 1963. The error in Parsons' analysis, however, is to take insufficient account of the fact that the 'collective' aspect of power is asymmetrical in its consequences for the different groupings in society.

5. As in Keller's 'strategic elites'. See Suzanne Keller, *Beyond the Ruling Class* (New York 1963).

MICHAEL USEEM

The Inner Circle

Recent studies of the politics of big business could hardly be more divided on the extent to which the corporate community is socially unified, cognizant of its classwide interests, and prepared for concerted action in the political arena. In a number of original investigations, for instance, G. William Domhoff finds "persuasive evidence for the existence of a socially cohesive national upper class."[1] These "higher circles," composed chiefly of corporate executives, primary owners, and their descendents, constitute, in his view, "the governing class in America," for these businesspeople and their families dominate the top positions of government agencies, the political parties, and the governing boards of nonprofit organizations. Drawing on studies of the U.S., Great Britain, and elsewhere, Ralph Miliband reaches a similar conclusion, finding that " 'elite pluralism' does not ... prevent the separate elites in capitalist society from constituting a dominant economic class, possessed of a high degree of cohesion and solidarity, with common interests and common purposes which far transcend their specific differences and disagreements."[2]

Yet other analysts have arrived at nearly opposite conclusions. In an extensive review of studies of business, Ivar Berg and Mayer Zald argue that "businessmen are decreasingly a coherent and self-sufficient autonomous elite; increasingly business leaders are differentiated by their heterogeneous interests and find it difficult to weld themselves into a solidified group."[3] Similarly, Daniel Bell contends that the disintegration of family capitalism in America has thwarted the emergence of a national "ruling class," and, as a result, "there are relatively few political issues on which the managerial elite is united."[4] Leonard

Silk and David Vogel, drawing on their observations of private discussions among industrial managers, find that the "enormous size and diversity of corporate enterprise today makes it virtually impossible for an individual group to speak to the public or government with authority on behalf of the entire business community."[5]

Observers of the British corporate community express equally disparate opinion, though the center of gravity is closer to that of discerning cohesion than disorganization. Drawing on their own study of British business leaders during the past century, Philip Stanworth and Anthony Giddens conclude that "we may correctly speak of the emergence, towards the turn of the century, of a consolidated and unitary 'upper class' in industrial Britain."[6] More recently, according to John Westergaard and Henrietta Resler, "the core" of the privileged and powerful is "those who own and those who control capital on a large scale: whether top business executives or rentiers makes no difference in this context. Whatever divergences of interests there may be among them on this score and others, latent as well as manifest, they have a common stake in one overriding cause: to keep the working rule of the society capitalist."[7] The solidity is underpinned by a unique latticework of old school ties, exclusive urban haunts, and aristocratic traditions that are without real counterpart in American life. Thus, "a common background and pattern of socialization, reinforced through intermarriage, club memberships, etc. generated a community feeling among the members of the propertied class," writes another analyst, and "this feeling could be articulated into a class awareness by the most active members of the class."[8]

Yet even if the concept of "the establishment" originated in British attempts to characterize the seamless web at the top that seemed so obvious to many, some observers still discern little in British business on which to pin such a label. Scanning the corporate landscape in the early 1960s, for instance, J. P. Nettl finds that the "business community" is in "a state of remarkable weakness and diffuseness—compared, say, to organized labour or the professions," for British businessmen lack "a firm sense of their distinct identity, and belief in their distinct purpose."[9] The years since have brought little consolidation, according to Wyn Grant: business "is neither homogeneous in its economic composition nor united on the appropriate strategy and tactics to advance its interests." Thus, "businessmen in Britain are not bound by a strong sense of common political purpose."[10]

Scholarly disagreement on this question, not surprisingly, is reflected in the textbooks used in university social-science courses. Every year American undergraduate students enter courses whose main textbook declares that business leaders have "a strong sense of identity as a class and a rather sophisticated understanding of their collective interest on which they tend to act in a collective way."[11] But students on other campuses find themselves studying textbooks with entirely different conclusions. They will be taught that the capitalist class has ceased to exist altogether or, at the minimum, that the received wisdom is, at best, agnostic on its degree of cohesion. The required reading in some courses asserts that "the question of whether [the] upper class forms a unified, cohesive, dominant group is still the subject of unresolved debate."[12] The correct view according to the assigned textbook in still other courses is that "until more data are gathered the question of whether national power is in the control of a power elite or veto group remains moot."[13] Still other students, especially those enrolled in management courses, are informed that fragmentation rather than cohesion now prevails. "A great deal of evidence," asserts a text for business school instruction, "suggests that our society is leaning toward the pluralistic model" rather than the "power-elite" model. "Few, if any, books are written about an 'establishment' anymore,

suggesting that if one did exist it either has disappeared or is not influential enough to worry about."[14] The theory of the "power elite" is, according to another widely used textbook on business and society, "a gross distortion of reality and the conclusions derived from it are largely erroneous."[15]

Social theory itself divides along this very line. Both traditional pluralist thought and a neo-Marxist strand sometimes labeled "structuralism" have generally argued that the parochial concerns of individual firms receive far greater expression in the political process than do the general collective concerns of business. Competition among firms, sectoral cleavages, and executives' and directors' primary identification with their own enterprise all inhibit even the formation of classwide awareness, let alone an organizational vehicle for promoting their shared concerns. Business disorganization, it is argued, prevails. Arguments based on pluralism and those on structural Marxism radically diverge in the implications they draw from the presumed disunity. To the pluralists, the corporate elite is far too divided to be any more effective than any other interest group in imposing its views on the government, thus enabling the state to avoid having its prerogatives co-opted by business. But for structural Marxism, it is precisely because of this disorganization of big business that the state can and does (for other reasons) assume the role of protecting the common interests of its major corporations.

Counterposed to both of these theoretical perspectives is an equally familiar thesis, advanced by what are now known as "instrumental" neo-Marxists and by many non-Marxists as well: that the government is more responsive to the outlook of big business than to that of any other sector or class, certainly of labor. According to these theories, this responsiveness is the result, in part, of the social unity and political cohesion of the corporate elite. With such cohesion and coordination, business is able to identify and promote successfully those public policies that advance the general priorities shared by most large companies.[16]

Resolution of these opposing visions of the internal organization of the business community is essential if we are to understand how, and with what effect, business enters the political process, or, in Anthony Giddens's more abstract framing, how we are to comprehend "the modes in which … economic hegemony is translated into political domination."[17] But the resolution offered here is not one of establishing which of these competing views is more "correct," for either answer would be, as we shall see, incorrect; in their own limited and specific fashions, both descriptions are also partly true. …

The Inner Circle

I will argue that a politicized leading edge of the leadership of a number of major corporations has come to play a major role in defining and promoting the shared needs of large corporations in two of the industrial democracies, the United States and the United Kingdom. Rooted in intercorporate networks through shared ownership and directorship of large companies in both countries, this politically active group of directors and top managers gives coherence and direction to the politics of business. Most business leaders are not part of what I shall term here the *inner circle*. Their concerns extend little beyond the immediate welfare of their own firms. But those few whose positions make them sensitive to the welfare of a wide range of firms have come to exercise a voice on behalf of the entire business community.

Central members of the inner circle are both top officers of large firms and directors of several other large corporations operating in diverse environments. Though defined by their corporate positions, the members of the inner circle constitute a distinct, semi-autonomous network, one that transcends company, regional, sectoral, and other politically divisive fault lines within the corporate community.

The inner circle is at the forefront of business outreach to government, nonprofit organizations, and the public. Whether it be support for political candidates, consultation with the highest levels of the national administration, public defense of the "free enterprise system," or the governance of foundations and universities, this politically dominant segment of the corporate community assumes a leading role, and corporations whose leadership involves itself in this pan-corporate network assume their own distinct political role as well. Large companies closely allied to the highest circle are more active than other firms in promoting legislation favorable to all big business and in assuming a more visible presence in public affairs, ranging from philanthropy to local community service.

The inner circle has assumed a particularly critical role during the past decade. The 1970s and early 1980s were a period of unprecedented expansion of corporate political activities, whether through direct subvention of candidates, informal lobbying at the highest levels of government, or formal access to governmental decision-making processes through numerous business-dominated panels created to advise government agencies and ministries. This political mobilization of business can be traced to the decline of company profits in both the United States and the United Kingdom and to heightened government regulation in America and labor's challenge of management prerogatives in Britain. As large companies have increasingly sought to influence the political process, the inner circle has helped direct their activities toward political ends that will yield benefits for all large firms, not just those that are most active. This select group of directors and senior managers has thus added a coherence and effectiveness to the political voice of business, one never before so evident. The rise to power of governments attentive to the voice of business, if not always responsive to its specific proposals, is, in part, a consequence of the mobilization of corporate politics during the past decade and the inner circle's channeling of this new energy into a range of organizational vehicles.

Both the emergence of the inner circle and the degree to which it has come to define the political interests of the entire business community are unforeseen consequences of a far-reaching transformation of the ways in which large corporations and the business communities are organized. In the early years of the rise of the modern corporation, self-made entrepreneurs were at the organizational helm, ownership was shared with, but limited to, kin and descendents, and the owning families merged into a distinct, intermarrying upper class. It was the era of family capitalism, and upper-class concerns critically informed business political activity. In time, however, family capitalism was slowly but inexorably pushed aside by the emergence of a new pattern of corporate organization and control—managerial capitalism. Business political activity increasingly came to address corporate, rather upper-class, agendas, as the corporation itself became the central organizing force. If family capitalism was at its height at the end of the nineteenth century and managerial capitalism was ascendent during the first half of the twentieth, both are now yielding in this era to institutional capitalism, a development dating to the postwar period and rapidly gaining momentum in recent decades. In the era of institutional capitalism, it is not only family or individual corporate interests that serve to define how business political activity is organized and expressed but rather concerns much more classwide—the shared interests and needs of all large corporations taken together. Increasingly a consciousness of a generalized corporate outlook shapes the content of corporate political action.

The large business communities in Britain and America have thus evolved, for the most part without conscious design, the means for aggregating and promoting their common interests. While government agencies add further coherence to the policies sought, the inner circle now serves to fashion, albeit in still highly imperfect ways, the main elements of public policies suited to serve the broader requirements of the entire corporate community. This conclusion is not in accord with predominant thinking, nor with those theories about business-government relations more fully described below. Of these, most fall into one of two opposing schools. According to the first, corporate leadership is presumed to be either too-little organized to act politically at all, or, as the second goes, so fully organized that it acts as a single, politically unified bloc. This [essay] rejects both schools of thought and argues for a new perception, a new theory of the nature of the politics of big business in contemporary British and American society.

A new conception of the business firm is also needed. Most corporate business decisions are viewed, correctly, as a product of the internal logic of the firm. Yet when decisions are made on the allocation of company monies to political candidates, the direction of its philanthropic activities, and other forms of political outreach, an external logic is important as well. This is the logic of classwide benefits, involving considerations that lead to company decisions beneficial to all large companies, even when there is no discernible, direct gain for the individual firm. The inner circle is the carrier of this extracorporate logic; the strategic presence of its members in the executive suites of major companies allows it to shape corporate actions to serve the entire corporate community.

The power of the transcorporate network even extends into the selection of company senior managers. In considering an executive for promotion to the uppermost positions in a firm, the manager's reputation within the firm remains of paramount importance, but it is not the only reputation that has come to count. The executive's standing within the broader corporate community—as cultivated through successful service on the boards of several other large companies, leadership in major business associations, and the assumption of civic and public responsibilities—is increasingly a factor. Acceptance by the inner circle has thus become almost a prerequisite for accession to the stewardship of many of the nation's largest corporations. Our traditional conception of the firm must accordingly be modified. No longer is the large company an entirely independent actor, striving for its own profitable success without regard for how its actions are affecting the profitability of others. While it retains its independence in many areas of decision-making, its autonomy is compromised. And this is especially true for company actions targeted at improving the political environment. Through the agency of the inner circle, large corporations are now subject to a new form of collective political discipline by their corporate brethren. ...

Principles of Social Organization

The organization is simultaneously structured by a number of distinct principles, of which three are of overriding importance.[18] Each contains a fundamentally different implication for the ways in which business enters the political arena.

The *upper-class principle* asserts that the first and foremost defining element is a social network of established wealthy families, sharing a distinct culture, occupying a common social status, and unified through intermarriage and common experience in exclusive settings, ranging from boarding schools to private clubs. This principle is the point of departure for virtually all analyses of the British "establishment," or the group that has sometimes been more termed "the great and the good."[19] Yet the lesser visibility and heterogeneity of an American "establishment" has not discouraged scholars from treating the U.S. circles in terms analogous to those applied to the British upper class. This is evident, for instance, in E. Digby Baltzell's studies of the national and metropolitan "business aristocracies"; in G. William Domhoff's inquiries into America's "upper-social class"; in Randall Collins's treatment of the preeminence of upper-class cultural dominance in America; and in Leonard and Mark Silk's study of what they have simply called "the American establishment."[20]

Many, if not most members of the upper class also occupy positions in or around large companies. But from the standpoint of this principle, these corporate locations are useful but not defining elements. Individuals are primarily situated instead according to a mixture of such factors as family reputation, kinship connections, academic pedigree, social prominence, and patrician bearing. As the upper class enters politics, this principle supports the conclusions that its main objectives would be to preserve the social boundaries of the upper class, its intergenerational transmission of its position, and the privately held wealth on which its privileged station resides. Control of the large corporation is only one means to this end, though in the U.S. it has emerged as the single most important means. Thus, one "of the functions of upper class solidarity," writes Baltzell, "is the retention, within a primary group of families, of the final decision-making positions within the social structure. As of the first half of the twentieth century in America, the final decisions affecting the goals of the social structure

have been made primarily by members of the financial and business community."[21]

A parallel movement into British industry is suggested by other analysts. "Without stigma," writes one observer, "peers, baronets, knights and country squires [accepted] directorships in the City, in banks, large companies and even in the nationalized industries." But the entry into commerce, necessitated by political and financial reality, was not at the price of assimilation, it is argued, for the upper class moved to rule business with the same self-confident sense of special mission with which it had long overseen land, politics, and the empire. Aristocratic identity ran far too deep to permit even capitalist subversion of traditional values: "Heredity, family connections, going to the same schools, belonging to the same clubs, the same social circle, going to the same parties, such were the conditions that enabled 'the charmed circle' to survive all change, unscathed, whether economic, political, religious or cultural."[22] Business enterprise is simply the newest means for preserving upper-class station, and, as such, is largely subordinated to that project.

The *corporate principle* of organization suggests by contrast that the primary defining element is the corporation itself. Location is determined not by patrician lineage, but by the individual's responsibilities in the firm and the firm's position in the economy. Coordinates for the latter include such standard dimensions as company size, market power, sector, organizational complexity, source of control, financial performance, and the like. Upper-class allegiances are largely incidental to this definition of location, for the manager is locked into corporate-determined priorities no matter what family loyalties may still be maintained. This is the point of departure, of course, for most journalists covering business, corporate self-imagery, and analysts working within the traditional organizational behavior paradigm.[23] Not only are upper-class commitments viewed as largely incidental, but loyalties to the corporate elite as a whole are taken to be faint by comparison with the manager's single-minded drive to advance the interests of his own firm ahead of those of his competitors. By implication, corporate leaders enter politics primarily to promote conditions favorable to the profitability of their own corporations. Policies designed to preserve upper-class station or the long-term collective interests of all large companies receive weak articulation at best. Capitalist competition and its political spillover might be described as one of the few remaining illustrations of Hobbes's infamous state of a war of all against all.

The *classwide principle* resides on still different premises about the main elements defining the social organization of the corporate community. In this framework, location is primarily determined by position in a set of interrelated, quasi-autonomous networks encompassing virtually all large corporations. Acquaintanceship circles, interlocking directorates, webs of interfirm ownership, and major business associations are among the central strands of these networks. Entry into the transcorporate networks is contingent on successfully reaching the executive suite of some large company, and it is further facilitated by old school ties and kindred signs of a proper breeding. But corporate credentials and upper-class origins are here subordinated to a distinct logic of classwide organization. ...

Upper-class, corporate, and classwide principles of social organization distinctively shape the basic thrust of business political activity. Thus, their relative importance is of fundamental interest for comprehending contemporary corporate activity—from the orchestration of public opinion on behalf of "reindustrialization" to renewed assaults on organized labor and government regulation. The underlying theme of the present analysis is that the relative balance long ago shifted in the U.S. from upper-class to corporate principle, and that American business is currently undergoing still another transformation, this time from corporate to classwide principles of organization. By the middle of this century, family capitalism had largely given way to managerial capitalism, and in recent decades managerial capitalism itself has been giving way to institutional capitalism, bringing us into an era in which classwide principles are increasingly dominant. In the U.K., the corporate principle never quite so fully eclipsed the upper-class principle, but both logics are now yielding there as well to the rise of classwide organization within the business community. This transformation has profound implications for the power and ideology of big business in both countries. ...

The Power Elite

Business, military, and the government—these were the three pillars of C. Wright Mills's famous American "power elite."[24] Since publication of this classic study in 1956, several generations of university students have been required to master its elements, even as, or perhaps because, they were soon themselves to become part of one of the three pillars. As contested as it was, Mills's thesis was assimilated into the shared perception of most educated circles, a touchstone for informed conversation about how our society governs itself, if not proven fact. In opening an article profiling the chief executives of the largest U.S. corporations some two decades after *The Power Elite* first appeared, *Fortune* magazine could still frame a question whose reference most readers were certain to comprehend: "Is [the chief executive], as often supposed outside the business world, an aristocrat of what C. Wright Mills called the Power Elite?"[25]

Less remembered than the general thesis, but more useful for understanding corporate politics, is Mills's prescient insight regarding why business had become a pillar of the establishment. American capitalism, he observed, has been marked by continuously increasing centralization and concentration. This process, in Mills's view, had led to the emergence of a new breed of corporate executives committed to industry-wide concerns reaching far beyond the interests of their own firms. Moreover, a fraction of these executives took an even broader view of business problems: "They move from the industrial point of interest and outlook to the interests and outlook of the class of all big corporate property as a whole."[26]

Mills identified two features of business organization as primarily responsible for the change in outlook. First, the personal and family investments of top managers and owners had become dispersed among a number of firms. As a result, he wrote, "the executives and owners who are in and of and for this propertied class cannot merely push the narrow interests of each property; their interests become engaged by the whole corporate class."[27]

Second, the emergence of an extensive network of interlocking directorships among the major corporations also meant that a number of managers had assumed responsibility for the prosperity of several corporations, and thus those holding multiple directorships constituted "a more sophisticated executive elite which now possesses a certain autonomy from any specific property interests. Its power is the power ... of classwide property."[28] It is this power that had so well positioned the business elite to serve as a dominant pillar of the American power elite.

Surveying much the same landscape, other analysts have offered kindred hypotheses. Maurice Zeitlin has suggested that centralizing tendencies akin to those discussed by Mills are creating an overarching unity within the business community. Prominent among such tendencies is "the establishment of an effective organizational apparatus of interlocking directorates" cutting across both financial and industrial sectors. Such interlocking directorates may be very important in any effort to maintain the "cohesiveness of the capitalist class and its capacity for common action and unified policies."[29] The number of owners and managers holding diversified corporate investments and positions is viewed by both Zeitlin and Mills as a potentially dominant political segment of the business community, one that is increasingly in a position to impose its outlook as it recognizes itself as the national network that it is.

The growing concentration of economic power in this network has been recognized in official circles as well, with equanimity in some, alarm in others. A U.S. congressional study of shared directorships warns, for instance, that "the interlocking management device" could lead to a situation in which "inordinate control over the major part of the U.S. commerce would be concentrated in the hands of [a] few individuals," creating the possibility that "an 'inner group' would control the destiny of American commerce."[30]

Central to these analyses is the potentially critical political role played by top managers holding multi-firm connections. Executives with ties to several, often disparate, companies necessarily become concerned with the joint welfare of the several companies. Their indirect ties to other firms through the interlocking directorate further enlarges the scope of their concern. "Even more than other large corporation executives," writes one group of analysts, "those who sit at the center of the web of interlocking directorates must have an outlook and executive policies that, while yet serving particular and more narrow interests, conform to the general interests of the corporate community and of the principal owners of capital within it."[31] The inner circle, in short, constitutes a distinct, politicized business segment, if a segment is defined as a subset of class members sharing a specific social location with partially distinct interests.[32] Though members of the inner circle share with other corporate managers a common commitment to enhancing company profits, their heightened sensitivity to business interests more general than those that look solely to support individual company profits also sets them apart. ...

The business pillar of the establishment is indeed a pillar, but as powerful as those who occupy the pillar's base may be within their own large corporation, they lack the means and incentives for shaping classwide policy. The top of the pillar does not. It has the power to act through its umbrella of intercorporate connections. It has the unity to act by virtue of its shared social cohesion. Its upper-class connections opens doors when it chooses to act. And at its disposal are the business associations when formal representation is needed.

The inner circle is not all powerful, however. Nor is it seamless. The upper-class credentials are partial, the ability to control the associations imperfect. Yet in all these respects it is more prepared to act than are other individuals or groups of corporate managers and directors. The pluralist and structuralist claims of elite disorganization capture a relative truth when applied to the bulk of the corporate community. The claim of disunity is far less applicable, however, to the inner circle.

Even then the inner circle does not act as a committee of the whole. Political action is taken not by the inner circle, but by organized entities within it. Resources are actually mobilized through (1) the intercorporate and informal networks linking members of the inner circle, and

(2) the formal associations over which the inner circle exercises substantial influence. The real unit of classwide corporate politics, then, is not the business elite as a whole, nor even this select stratum of the elite. As blocs, neither business nor the inner circle act on behalf of anything. But within the inner circle are a set of horizontally organized networks and vertically structured organizations that do act. These are the real motors of business political motion. The inner circle, then, refers not just to the company executive directors who constitute its membership, but also to the networks that constitute its internal structure. It is the power of these internal networks that propel members of the inner circle into leadership roles on behalf of the entire corporate community.

Notes

1. Domhoff 1974, p. 109; 1967; 1970; 1972; 1979.
2. Miliband 1969, p. 47.
3. Berg and Zald 1978, p. 137.
4. Bell 1962, pp. 62–63.
5. Silk and Vogel 1976, p. 181.
6. Stanworth and Giddens 1974, p. 100.
7. Westergaard and Resler 1975, p. 346.
8. Scott 1979, pp. 125–26.
9. Nettl 1965, p. 23.
10. Grant 1980, p. 146.
11. Szymanski 1978, p. 39.
12. Rothman 1978, p. 89.
13. Duberman 1976, p. 74.
14. Buchholz 1982, pp. 58–59.
15. Steiner and Steiner 1980, p. 9.
16. Many elements of the several perspectives are summarized in Alford (1975). The less well-known intra-Marxist debate is described within or exemplified by the works of Miliband (1969), Offe (1973), O'Connor (1973), Poulantzas (1973), Gold et al. (1975), Jessop (1977), Domhoff (1979), Whitt (1980, 1982), and Skocpol (1980).
17. Giddens 1974, p. xi.
18. Other principles are described in Useem (1980).
19. See, for instance, Cole (1955), pp. 101–23; Guttsman (1963); Perrott (1968); Sampson (1971); Johnson (1973); Giddens (1976).
20. Baltzell 1958, 1964, 1966, 1979; Domhoff 1967, 1970, 1974, 1979; Collins 1971, 1979; Silk and Silk 1980.
21. Baltzell 1966, p. 273.
22. Bedardia 1979, pp. 202–4.
23. Westhues (1976) provides a description of this approach.

24. Mills 1956.
25. Burck 1976, p. 173.
26. Mills 1956, p. 121.
27. Mills 1956, p. 121.
28. Mills 1956, p. 122.
29. Zeitlin 1974, p. 1, 112.
30. U.S. House Committee on the Judiciary, 1965, Antitrust Subcommittee, pp. 225–26.
31. Zeitlin et al. 1974, p. 4.
32. A helpful conceptualization of class segments within the business community can be found in Zeitlin et al. (1976).

References

Alford, Robert. 1975. "Paradigms of relations between state and society." In *Stress and Contradiction in Modern Capitalism,* Leon Lindberg et al., eds. Lexington, Ma.: Heath.

Baltzell, E. Digby. 1958. *Philadelphia Gentlemen: The Making of a National Upper Class.* New York: Free Press.

Baltzell, E. Digby. 1964. *The Protestant Establishment: Aristocracy and Caste in America.* New York: Random House.

Baltzell, E. Digby. 1966. "'Who's Who in America' and 'The Social Register': elite and upper class indexes in metropolitan America." Pp. 266-275 in *Class, Status, and Power,* Reinhard Bendix and Seymour Martin Lipset, eds. New York: Free Press, 2nd edition.

Baltzell, E. Digby. 1979. *Puritan Boston and Quaker Philadelphia.* New York: Free Press.

Bedardia, Francois. 1979. *A Social History of England, 1851–1975.* A. S. Foster, trans. London: Methuen.

Bell, Daniel. 1962. *The End of Ideology.* New York: Free Press.

Berg, Ivar, and Mayer N. Zald. 1978. "Business and society." *Annual Review of Sociology* 4: 115–143.

Buchholz, Rogene A. 1982. *Business Environment and Public Policy: Implications for Management.* Englewood Cliffs, N.J.: Prentice-Hall.

Burck, Charles G. 1976. "A group profile of the Fortune 500 chief executive." *Fortune,* May, pp. 173ff.

Cole, G. D. K. 1955. *Studies in Class Structure.* London: Routledge and Kegan Paul.

Collins, Randall. 1971. "Functional and conflict theories of educational stratification." *American Sociological Review* 36: 1002–1019.

Collins, Randall. 1979. *The Credential Society: An Historical Sociology of Education and Stratification.* New York: Academic Press.

Domhoff, G. William. 1967. *Who Rules America?* Englewood Cliffs, N.J.: Prentice-Hall.

Domhoff, G. William. 1970. *The Higher Circles: The Governing Class in America.* New York: Random House.

Domhoff, G. William. 1972. *Fat Cats and Democrats: The Role of the Big Rich in the Party of the Common Man.* Englewood Cliffs, N.J.: Prentice-Hall.

Domhoff, G. William. 1974. *The Bohemian Grove and Other Retreats: A Study of Ruling-Class Consciousness.* New York: Harper and Row.

Domhoff, G. William. 1979. *The Powers That Be: Processes of Ruling-Class Domination in America.* New York: Random House.

Duberman, Lucile. 1976. *Social Inequality: Class and Caste in America.* New York: Lippincott.

Giddens, Anthony. 1974. "Preface." In *Elites and Power in British Society,* Philip Stanworth and Anthony Giddens, eds. London: Cambridge University Press.

Giddens, Anthony. 1976. "The Rich." *New Society* 38 (October): 63–66.

Gold, David A., Clarence P. H. Lo, and Erik Olin Wright. 1975. "Recent developments in Marxist theories of the capitalist state." *Monthly Review* 27 (October): 29–43.

Grant, Wyn. 1980. "Business interests and the British Conservative Party." *Government and Opposition* 15: 143–161.

Guttsman, W. L. 1963. *The British Political Elite.* London: MacGibbon and Kee.

Jessop, Bob. 1977. "Recent theories about the capitalist state." *Cambridge Journal of Economics* 1: 353–373.

Johnson, R. W. 1973. "The British political elite, 1955–1972." *European Journal of Sociology* 14: 35–77.

Miliband, Ralph. 1969. *The State in Capitalist Society.* New York: Basic Books.

Mills, C. Wright. 1956. *The Power Elite.* New York: Oxford University Press.

O'Connor, James. 1973. *The Fiscal Crisis of the State.* New York: St. Martin's Press.

Offe, Claus. 1973. "The abolition of market control and the problem of legitimacy (I)." *Kapitalistate* 1: 109–116.

Nettl, J. P. 1965. "Consensus or elite domination: the case of business." *Political Studies* 8: 22–44.

Perrott, Roy. 1968. *The Aristocrats.* London: Weidenfeld and Nicolson.

Poulantzas, Nicos. 1973. *Political Power and Social Classes.* Timothy O'Hagen, trans. London: New Left Books, and Sheed Ward.

Rothman, Robert A. 1978. *Inequality and Stratification in the United States.* Englewood Cliffs, N.J.: Prentice-Hall.

Sampson, Anthony. 1971. *The New Anatomy of Britain.* London: Hodder and Stoughton.

Scott, John. 1979. *Corporations, Classes and Capitalism.* London: Hutchinson.

Silk, Leonard, and David Vogel. 1976. *Ethics and Profits: The Crisis of Confidence in American Business.* New York: Simon and Schuster.

Silk, Leonard, and Mark Silk. 1980. *The American Establishment.* New York: Basic Books.

Skocpol, Theda. 1980. "Political response to capitalist crisis: Neo-Marxist theories of the state and the case of the New Deal." *Politics and Society* 10: 155–201.

Stanworth, Philip, and Anthony Giddens. 1974. "An economic elite: a demographic profile of company chairmen." In *Elites and Power in British Society,* Philip Stanworth and Anthony Giddens, eds. London: Cambridge University Press.

Steiner, George A., and John F. Steiner. 1980. *Business, Government, and Society: A Managerial Perspective.* New York: Random House.

Szymanski, Albert. 1978. *The Capitalist State and the Politics of Class.* Cambridge, Ma.: Winthrop Publishing Company.

U.S. House Committee on the Judiciary. 1965. Antitrust Subcommittee. *Interlocks in Corporate Management.* Washington, D.C.: U.S. Government Printing Office.

Useem, Michael. 1980. "Corporations and the corporate elite." In *Annual Review of Sociology,* Alex Inkeles, Neil J. Smelser, and Ralph Turner, eds. Palo Alto, Ca.: Annual Reviews.

Westergaard, John, and Henrietta Resler. 1975. *Class in Capitalist Society: A Study of Contemporary Britain.* London: Heinemann.

Westhues, Kenneth. 1976. "Class and organization as paradigms in social science." *The American Sociologist* 11: 38–49.

Whitt, J. Allen. 1980. "Can capitalists organize themselves?" In *Power Structure Research,* G. William Domhoff, ed. Beverly Hills, Ca.: Sage.

Zeitlin, Maurice, Richard Earl Ratcliff, and Lynda Ann Ewen. 1974. "The 'Inner Group': interlocking directorates and the internal differentiation of the capitalist class in Chile." Presented at the annual meeting of the American Sociological Association.

Zeitlin, Maurice, W. Lawrence Newman, and Richard Earl Ratcliff. 1976. "Class segments: agrarian property and political leadership in the capitalist class in Chile." *American Sociological Review* 41: 1006–1029.

EDWARD A. SHILS

The Political Class in the Age of Mass Society: Collectivistic Liberalism and Social Democracy

The very subject of the study of elites is anathema to the anti-elitists. Mosca and Pareto have always been suspect among progressivistic, collectivistic liberals and radicals, partly because they were suspected of having been Fascists, partly because some Fascists invoked them as witnesses to their oligarchical ideals and their admiration—and practice—of brutality. But, in fact, the study of elites is an evaluatively neutral subject. Insofar as it confines itself to the description of what happens between two or more generations, it is silent at the question as to whether inequality in the distribution of opportunities and rewards is inherent in the nature of societies. Indeed, the descriptive accounts contained in elite studies are quite compatible with the beliefs that inequalities are inevitable and with beliefs that they are necessary and useful or at least have advantages which more than compensate for their disadvantages. They are quite compatible with beliefs that the distributions which they disclose are good or evil.

Mosca certainly regarded the kinds of inequalities that he discovered in his studies as inevitable. He thought there could be no society without elites and that elites perform functions which are absolutely fundamental for the working of society. He thought moreover that they could not be dispensed with and that some of their vices were an inevitable concomitant of that existence. These did not seem to be controvertible issues to Mosca, nor indeed did they take a central position in his thought. He was more concerned with the conditions under which political elites were effective. This seems to me to set the proper problem in the study of elites. The demographic or "elite-recruit-

ment" studies find their justification when the information that they bring is put to the task of explaining the success or failure of elites in maintaining their domination over their societies and avoiding violent disruptions in their tenure. Mosca did not conceive of the tenure of a particular set of individuals; he thought of tenure as running beyond the lifetime or the political careers of single individuals, conceived simply as individuals. He thought of the success of elites as political lineages or political classes. The ruling or political class was not the aggregate of all individuals participating in political life; it was not the aggregate of all those sections of the population whose members participated in politics. The ruling or political class was narrower than the latter; it was more a collective than the former. The political class was, according to Mosca, marked by a sense of political vocation, which was shared by its individual members who, at the same time, perceived that sense of vocation in the other members of the class. There was, on this basis, a sense of solidarity of individuals with each other, even though the political class as a whole was divided by rivalries.

The concept of a political class referred to a cluster of families or, to a lesser extent, professions and institutions from which the individuals who held important elective and appointive positions in the government came. Membership in these lineages or membership in these professions or the fact of having been a student at certain schools or colleges or universities offered to their members a sense of identity as parts of a loose collectivity whose "business" was ruling the society. The concept of a political class refers not only to the families, professions, and schools from which politicians and political organizers come; it refers to more than these and to the sense of identity focused on the shared right and obligation to rule. It is also a reference to an accumulating tradition of outlook and skill. The tradition provides each new generational group in the lineages, the professions, or the schools and the protégés of these groups, with the knowledge and skill that it needs to remain in power, to contend for power if it is not in power, and to do its job of exercising power with sufficient effectiveness to enable its collectivity to survive, to leave the peripheries of the ruled, in their significant parts, sufficiently satisfied and, if not satisfied, then sufficiently impotent so as to leave the political class at the center of society.

Mosca—and Schumpeter—seemed to think that these traditions of ruling provided the dispositions and attitudes needed to rule effectively, the self-confidence in confronting the decisions inherent in ruling, the ability to weigh and calculate the chances of success, and the knowledge of human beings with whom one must collaborate and against whom one must act. They thought that political experience is the best teacher of the art of politics and that the accumulated experiences of generations, concentrated into streams of traditions which flow into and through institutions, such as lineages, professions and schools, colleges and universities, are the sources of the knowledge which enables political classes to be successful. The idea of a political class is relevant to the understanding of politics because it implies that certain kinds of attitudes and knowledge are necessary for effective rule and that the sources of recruitment are connected with the qualities that make for effectiveness or ineffectiveness of rule.

Mosca wrote his great book a century ago, and he looked back over all of human history in the way in which an educated man in the Italy of his time, well read in the classics and in history, could do. He wrote in a period that was on the verge of political and social developments which made the existence of the kind of political class which he had in mind more difficult. Political classes in Mosca's sense are greatly attenuated in the West, to the extent that they exist at all. And the tasks which they would have faced, and which their successors do face in the second half of the 20th century, render the efficacy of rulers more difficult. ...

Whatever the complex of conditions that brought forth the present situation of "popular democracy," collectivistic liberalism, and social democracy and whatever the differences among these, the present situation is one that requires a tremendous concentration of power in the government to assemble and dispose of resources and to cope with a very high level of demands in various parts of the population.

Contemporary Western governments have taken the responsibility for full employment and economic growth, as well as for the provision of goods and services beyond those provided by the market, for the fostering of individual happiness and personal development, for the care of health and the conservation of nature, for the progress of scientific knowledge and the promotion of technological innovation, for the well-being of the arts and the quality of culture and for social justice—not just the rule of law—and for the remedying of past wrongs. This is a tremendous distance from the welfare state as it was conceived in Germany in the 19th century and by humanitarian reformers in the United States and Great Britain at the beginning of the 20th century. There is scarcely any sphere of life into which modern governments have not entered as a result of their own conception of their obligations and their sensitivity to the imperfections of man's life on earth and in response to the demands of various parts of the electorate and the prevailing intellectual opinion as to what governments should do and how they can do it.

No "political class," when political classes were still the reservoirs from which governing political elites came, ever had to cope with such a situation. The situation is a novel one; the tasks placed on and accepted by or actually sought by government are to some extent novel in substance and certainly unprecedented in scope. Moreover, the tasks change rapidly. Tasks are redefined. Failures must be remedied by renewed and more extensive measures. The undertakings of governments are so numerous and so comprehensive are the responsibilities that have been demanded of or proclaimed by governments as their "programs" that tasks of coordination of unexampled complexity arise. Governments have long ceased to regard governing as their first, perhaps even their only task; every government on its accession to office has a program of positive actions intended to carry further its past achievements, to broaden them and to improve on them. (Mistakes of one's own commission are seldom admitted.) On the rare occasions when an ostensibly less expansive government accedes to office, its program of undoing some of the arrangements instituted by its more expansive predecessors is as complicated as the positive program it would cancel. Furthermore, programs of cancellation of the arrangements of previous governments are never as comprehensive as the programs of preceding more positive administrations.

How different this is from the budget of tasks that political classes, when they still existed, accepted and were expected to accept! Even in the "absolute" monarchies of the *ancien régime,* government aspired to nothing comparable in scale and intensity to what contemporary Western governments accept as their objectives.

The great merit of the political class was its inheritance of a tradition of the arts of politics and ruling. The knowledge borne by that tradition was wisdom; it was not technical knowledge. Governments formed by political classes did not use much technical knowledge, and they used practically nothing of what would now be called scientific knowledge and scientific technology. Details of road building, the maintenance of waterways, the registration of titles to property, the construction of tax rolls, and the keeping of accounts of revenues and expenditures could be left to officials; decisions at the higher levels of government, insofar as they drew on this kind of knowledge, could be made by delegation of authority or by placing oneself in the hands of "expert advisors." Turgot and Colbert knew as much of the "science of economics" as anyone in France at that time. The fact is that there was little "science" which was thought to have bearing on the affairs of state; the challenge to know it and to incorporate it into decisions was not a burden which the "political class" had to bear. That bur-

den is, however, one which contemporary politicians must bear.

The kinds of problems with which government dealt were not beyond the cognitive possessions of the political class. The failures of a political class could not be attributed to its failure to master and use an available stock of scientific knowledge. The problems political classes faced, to the extent that they faced them, did not lie outside the powers gained from the assimilation of the traditional political and governmental wisdom available to members of the political class and their own experience.

To do all the things which are demanded of them and to which they have committed themselves, legislators of the present century have called into being an immense bureaucracy. The bureaucracy, competent or incompetent though it might be in taking these tasks in hand, is certainly able to hold its own with the legislators who are constitutionally the rulers of Western societies, whether they be systems of parliamentary government dominated by a cabinet made up of the leaders of the dominant party or the presidential system which provides for an independent legislature and an independent executive. It was long ago pointed out by Max Weber that the bureaucracy would become the dominant power in government, unless it could be held in check by a system of competitive parties which, through elections and the competition in parliament, brought charismatic leaders to the fore. The American Congress, not knowing how to generate charismatic politicians, has sought a makeweight against the bureaucracy through the expansion of congressional staffs. They have now become dependent on a bureaucracy of their own making which is nearly as dominating over its superiors as the bureaucracy of the civil service. The President, to cope in his turn with the civil service on the one hand and with the legislature, which is increasingly wagged by the bureaucratic tail of its own creation, has created a large bureaucracy of his own in the Executive Office of the President. …

The Soviet Union is the only country that can be said to have a political class—a very limited circle of long duration from which the highest political elite is chosen by co-optation and calculation. It is not a political class in Mosca's sense because it lacks the element of recruitment from lineage, but this is a secondary matter. The present Soviet elite comes from a political class, the higher ranks of the Communist party of the Soviet Union; it comes primarily from Russia. Its members were not born into the Soviet political class, but they must enter it very early in their careers and make those careers within it and through the patronage of its then reigning leaders. It is a closed circle; intrusions from the outside are not compatible with its continued existence. Progress within the political class is dependent almost entirely on decisions within the political class which, having the formal organization of the Communist party of the Soviet Union as its frame, maintains—at least thus far—a strict control over succession.

Has the Communist political class been successful? In certain important respects, it has been successful. It has remained in power for about two thirds of a century; it has avoided subversion or replacement from outside itself. It has succeeded in achieving this success by ruthlessness, in brutal suppression of even mild-mannered internal criticism. In this sense, it goes beyond one of the features of political classes. Whereas political classes could assimilate some of their potential rivals or antagonists and could bring them into the system—this is how constitutional liberalism came to live together with monarchically centered conservatism in the 19th century in Western and Central Europe—the Soviet political elite suppresses potential rivals.

Since remaining in power is one of the tests of success of a political elite or of a political class (which is the variant of concern to us here), the Soviet elite has been successful. But one of the features of modern political elites is that they possess programs which they claim to be able to realize. The Soviet elite has certainly been quite successful in its external policies, in its intrusions into other countries. It has possessed the readiness to use force, corruption, manipulation, and conspiracy in the pursuit of its ends abroad, and it has done so with self-confidence. In this respect it has had all the qualities of relatively successful political classes of early modern times up to almost the end of the 19th century; these were the features of political classes which Mosca, and especially Pareto, admired.

Communism is, however, an ideal arrangement of the internal affairs of a society, and it is through the establishment everywhere of such a system that the Soviet elite justifies its extrusions beyond its own boundaries. There it has not been successful, neither within its own boundaries nor in the regimes which it has established and maintained in power outside those boundaries. There, all the qualities which are sustained by the culture of a political class have not helped it—with the exception of its readiness to suppress by the harshest methods those who appear to endanger it. In those fields of activity, like the economic sphere, in which force is not sufficient, the Soviet political class and those lesser political classes which it supports have not been at all successful. Being a political class is thus not anything like a guarantee of success, although it does have certain advantages.

When we turn away from Communist regimes and consider the political elites of modern Western countries, we contemplate a scene which is fairly devoid of the qualities of organization and culture characteristic of political classes. Modern liberalism, with its emphasis on individual achievement, modern taxation, and the changes in the technology and organization of agriculture have doomed one of the pillars of the system of political classes, namely the great landowning families which in many large societies supplied cultural centers of interaction and much of the personnel of the political classes.

The church, the religious orders, and lay, para-ecclesiastical organizations once constituted a set of adjuncts of the political class, particularly in Roman Catholic countries in the *anciens régimes* and to a smaller, but still some, extent in Protestant countries. This has changed greatly in Roman Catholic countries as a consequence of anticlericalism and more recently as a consequence of radicalism in the priesthood; priests in some Latin countries have become the enemies of what remains of the political class. In Protestant countries too there has been a clerical withdrawal from the political elite.

The political elites have become less self-enclosed, and their different and rival sectors have become less conciliatory toward each other than when they formed a political class. The fate of the system of *versuiling* which prevailed for more than a century in the Netherlands illustrates this process. As long as the political elites of the various "vertical" sectors of Dutch society maintained their ascendancy in consequence of the compliance of their following, they could collaborate more easily with their rivals or competitors of the other "vertical" sectors. When the rank and file of the various parties became more demanding, more consciously "self-esteeming," and more insistent on their being heeded by their leaders, the political class of the Netherlands lost some of its self-enclosedness, its control over recruitment, and its self-assurance. Similar developments, *mutatis mutandis,* have occurred in other Western countries. The churches have become uneasy about their links with the center of their respective societies. They have sought to disavow their participation in the earthly center in order to espouse the causes and to seek the approval of the peripheries of society, while claiming thereby to affirm their link with the transcendent center of all existence.

Lineages ceased to be as significant in the self-consciousness of individuals and in their influence on the conduct and loyalties of their members. Churches became somewhat dissociated from the centers of society—either by the constitutional separation of church and state or through voluntary withdrawal and disavowal by the churches.

Great Britain and France were the only countries in which educational institutions served to form and rally the political class. In the former, the great public schools—above all Eton, Harrow, Rugby, and a few others—and Oxford University (also Cambridge to a lesser degree) provided places for inculcation of the outlook of the political class, a sense of solidarity—the "old school tie"—and places of recruitment into the political class. In France, in different ways, a few of the great *lycées* in Paris, e.g., the Lycée Louis le Grand and the Ecole libre des sciences politiques and, around the time of the First World War, the Ecole normale supérieure, played a similar role.[1] More

recently, the Ecole d'administration has been added to the set of formative institutions of the French political elite. (The Ecole polytechnique, important though it has been in the administration of the country, does not seem to have been quite as important in the formation and maintenance of the political elite in contemporary France, although it is conceivable that the technological, scientific training which it offers might lead to its displacement of the more humanistic Ecole normale supérieure. The same applies to the forward movement of the Ecole nationale d'administration.)

Neither the United States nor Germany have had any higher educational institutions which have performed approximately similar functions. No German university, despite the intellectual achievements and the nationalistic devotion (sometimes excessive) of German professors, ever played a role like that of Oxford in Great Britain. The role of the universities in the United States is somewhat similar. In some of the states, the state university played a part of some importance in the formation of a state-wide political elite. (I think particularly of the University of Wisconsin and, with less certainty, of the University of Minnesota.) Harvard University has never been in a position in national political life in the United States comparable to that of Oxford or the French *grandes écoles.* It has, from time to time, appeared to be on the verge of that situation, for example, during the administrations of Theodore Roosevelt, Franklin Roosevelt, and John Kennedy. Many of its members would have liked it to be such, and, recently, the Kennedy School of Public Affairs tries to perform a partial function of an institution which contributes to the formation of a political class through its courses for newly elected members of Congress. Nevertheless, despite aspirations and occasional flickerings, Harvard has not attained that position, and no other American educational institution has come even that near.

The United States is too large and, despite the recent aggrandizement of the national center, it is still too decentralized in its interests, functions, and loyalties for a political class to emerge. Populism would have resisted it. But even without populism and the diversity of American society, local and regional interests and the local and federal structure of the American governmental system would have prevented it. The local and state political machines did create some of the constitutive elements of a political class, but the weakness, between presidential elections, of the national institutions of the two major parties has also stood in the way of the fusion of these constituents into a national political class.

Insofar as the United States has a political class—and it has one only in a most rudimentary and partial form—it does so through its national legislative bodies. Of these, the Senate is by far the most important in many respects. The United States Senate and the British House of Commons have each claimed or, had claimed for them, the standing of "the best club in the world." A club has its atmosphere and its rules; it has its own distinctive culture which new members must acquire and through which they acquire "the art of politics." It is, however, another matter as to whether the "best club in the world" can generate and sustain the skill, knowledge, solidarity, and self-confidence necessary for keeping on top of the problems which the demands of the electorate and of the particular interests within it, and their own ideas about the rightful sphere of government, have presented to modern politicians for solution.

The strain on the political culture of the main centers of Western societies is aggravated by the unceasingly critical and demanding scrutiny which the contemporary apparatus of knowledge, on the one side, and demanding and increasingly aggrieved assertiveness of the mass of population on the other, directs toward the political elite.

When Mosca discussed a closed or a partially closed political class he had in mind primarily the reservoir of recruitment and the extent to which that reservoir was open to persons who came from outside the main political families, institutions, and circles. Modern political life under conditions of popular democracy is too open for the generation and maintenance of a political class. Mosca's emphasis on the partial closedness of recruitment as a condition of the existence and continuity of a political class might also have been

extended, and it should now be extended to include closedness from external scrutiny.

Bentham conceived of the "eye of the public" as "the virtue of the statesman," but he never conceived of that eye as having such a depth of penetration, such brightness, and such constancy as the present eye of the public represented in the professional staffs of the mass media of communication. Like many of the critics of the closure of the political classes of the 18th and 19th centuries who wanted a pattern of government more open to the public gaze, he did not imagine how imaginative, how powerful, how detailed, and omnipresent that eye would become.

It would be very difficult for a political elite, nurtured by a combination of open and closed recruitment, to withstand that insistent eye, especially under conditions in which the minds and voices behind that eye demand so much and demand it so insistently and censoriously. The invention of sample surveys of the political attitudes of Western societies, the frequency of those surveys, and the specificity of the objects on which they seek to discover the distribution of attitudes mean that political elites have to think unceasingly about whether their measures are popular. Popularity of measures becomes a criterion of the success of a measure, long before it has had a chance to become effective. Effectiveness and popularity are not the same thing, and their divergence renders the formation of a political class in Mosca's sense impossible. A political class in Mosca's sense did not have to be continuously on the alert to its popularity, and since it did not try to do as much as contemporary political elites in societies dominated by collectivistic liberal and social democratic beliefs and demands, it was easier for it to be effective. Neither of these conditions is present today.

Notes

1. Albert Thibaudet puts this thesis forward explicitly in *La Republique des professeurs* (Paris: Grasset, 1927).

Gradational Status Groupings

▶ **REPUTATION, DEFERENCE, AND PRESTIGE**

W. LLOYD WARNER, WITH MARCHIA MEEKER
AND KENNETH EELLS

Social Class in America

Our great state papers, the orations of great men, and the principles and pronouncements of politicians and statesmen tell us of the equality of all men. Each school boy learns and relearns it; but most of us are dependent upon experience and indirect statement to learn about "the wrong side of the tracks," "the Gold Coast and the slums," and "the top and bottom of the social heap." We are proud of those facts of American life that fit the pattern we are taught, but somehow we are often ashamed of those equally important social facts which demonstrate the presence of social class. Consequently, we tend to deny them or, worse, denounce them and by so doing deny their existence and magically make them disappear from consciousness. We use such expressions as "the Century of the Common Man" to insist on our democratic faith; but we know that, ordinarily, for Common Men to exist as a class, un-Common superior and inferior men must also exist. We know that every town or city in the country has its "Country Club set" and that this group usually lives on its Gold Coast, its Main Line, North Shore, or Nob Hill, and is the top of the community's social heap. ...

Class Among the New England Yankees

Studies of communities in New England clearly demonstrate the presence of a well-defined social-class system.[1] At the top is an aristocracy of birth and wealth. This is the so-called "old family" class. The people of Yankee City say the families who belong to it have been in the community for a long time—for at least three generations and preferably many generations more than three. "Old family" means not only old to the community but old to the class. Present members of the class were born into it; the families into which they were born can trace their lineage through many generations participating in a way of life characteristic of the upper class back to a generation marking the lowly beginnings out of which their family came. Although the men of this level are occupied gainfully, usually as large merchants, financiers, or in the higher professions, the wealth of the family, inherited from the husband's or the wife's side, and often from both, has been in the family for a long time. Ideally, it should stem from the sea trade when Yankee City's merchants and sea captains made large fortunes, built great Georgian houses on elm-lined Hill Street, and filled their houses and gardens with the proper symbols of their high position. They became the 400, the Brahmins, the Hill Streeters to whom others looked up; and they, well-mannered or not, looked down on the rest. They counted themselves, and were so counted, equals of similar levels in Salem, Boston, Providence, and other New England cities. Their sons and daughters married into the old families from these towns and at times, when family fortune was low or love was great, they married wealthy sons and daughters from the newly rich who occupied the class level below them. This was a happy event for the fathers and mothers of such fortunate young people in the lower half of the upper class, an event well publicized and sometimes not too discreetly bragged about by the parents of the lower-upper-class children, an occasion to be explained by the mothers from the old families in terms of the spiritual demands of romantic love and by their friends as "a good deal and a fair exchange all the way around for everyone concerned."

The new families, the lower level of the upper class, came up through the new industries—shoes, textiles, silverware—and finance. Their fathers were some of the men who established New England's trading and financial dominance throughout America. When New York's Wall Street rose to power, many of them transferred their activities to this new center of dominance. Except that they aspire to old-family status, if not for themselves then for their children, these men and their families have a design for living similar to the old-family group. But they are consciously aware that their money is too new and too recently earned to have the sacrosanct quality of wealth inherited from a long line of ancestors. They know, as do those about them, that, while a certain amount of wealth is necessary, birth and old family are what really matter. Each of them can cite critical cases to prove that particular individuals have no money at all, yet belong to the top class because they have the right lineage and right name. While they recognize the worth and importance of birth, they feel that somehow their family's achievements should be better rewarded than by a mere second place in relation to those who need do little more than be born and stay alive.

The presence of an old-family class in a community forces the newly rich to wait their turn if they aspire to "higher things." Meanwhile, they must learn how to act, fill their lives with good deeds, spend their money on approved philanthropy, and reduce their arrogance to manageable proportions.

The families of the upper and lower strata of the upper classes are organized into social cliques and exclusive clubs. The men gather fortnightly in dining clubs where they discuss matters that concern them. The women belong to small clubs or to the Garden Club and give their interest to subjects which symbolize their high status and evoke those sentiments necessary in each individual if the class is to maintain itself. Both sexes join philanthropic organizations whose good deeds are an asset to the community and an expression of the dominance and importance of the top class to those socially beneath them. They are the members of the Episcopalian and Unitarian and, occasionally, the Congregational and Presbyterian churches.

Below them are the members of the solid, highly respectable upper-middle class, the people who get things done and provide the active front in civic affairs for the classes above them. They aspire to the classes above and hope their good deeds, civic activities, and high moral principles will somehow be recognized far beyond the usual pat on the back and that they will be invited by those above them into the intimacies of upper-class cliques and exclusive clubs. Such recognition might increase their status and would be likely to make them members of the lower-upper group. The fact that this rarely happens seldom stops members of this level, once activated, from continuing to try. The men tend to be owners of stores and belong to the large proprietor and professional levels. Their incomes average less than those of the lower-upper class, this latter group having a larger income than any other group, including the old-family level.

These three strata, the two upper classes and the upper-middle, constitute the levels above the Common Man. There is a considerable distance socially between them and the mass of the people immediately below them. They comprise three of the six classes present in the community. Although in number of levels they constitute half the community, in population they have no more than a sixth, and sometimes less, of the Common Man's population. The three levels combined include approximately 13 per cent of the total population.

The lower-middle class, the top of the Common Man level, is composed of clerks and other white-collar workers, small tradesmen, and a fraction of skilled workers. Their small houses fill "the side streets" down from Hill Street, where the upper classes and some of the upper-middle live, and are noticeably absent from the better suburbs where the upper-middle concentrate. "Side Streeter" is a term often used by those above them to imply an inferior way of life and an inconsequential status. They have accumulated little property but are frequently home owners. Some of the more successful members of ethnic groups, such as the Italians, Irish, French-Canadians, have reached this level. Only a few members of these cultural minorities have gone beyond it; none of them has reached the old-family level.

The old-family class (upper-upper) is smaller in size than the new-family class (lower-upper) below them. It has 1.4 per cent, while the lower-upper class has 1.6 per cent, of the total population. Ten per cent of the population belongs to the upper-middle class, and 28 per cent to the lower-middle level. The upper-lower is the most populous class, with 34 per cent, and the lower-lower has 25 per cent of all the people in the town.

The prospects of the upper-middle-class children for higher education are not as good as those of the classes above. One hundred per cent of the children of the two upper classes take courses in the local high school that prepare them for college, and 88 per cent of the upper-middle do; but only 44 percent of the lower-middle take these courses, 28 per cent of the upper-lower, and 26 per cent of the lower-lower. These percentages provide a good index of the position of the lower-middle class, ranking it well below the three upper classes, but placing it well above the upper-lower and the lower-lower.[2]

The upper-lower class, least differentiated from the adjacent levels and hardest to distinguish in the hierarchy, but clearly present, is composed of the "poor but honest workers" who more often

than not are only semi-skilled or unskilled. Their relative place in the hierarchy of class is well portrayed by comparing them with the classes superior to them and with the lower-lower class beneath them in the category of how they spend their money.

A glance at the ranking of the proportion of the incomes of each class spent on ten items (including such things as rent and shelter, food, clothing, and education, among others) shows, for example, that this class ranks second for the percentage of the money spent on food, the lower-lower class being first and the rank order of the other classes following lower-middle according to their place in the social hierarchy. The money spent on rent and shelter by upper-lower class is also second to the lower-lower's first, the other classes' rank order and position in the hierarchy being in exact correspondence. To give a bird's-eye view of the way this class spends its money, the rank of the upper-lower, for the percentage of its budget spent on a number of common and important items, has been placed in parentheses after every item in the list which follows: food (2), rent (2), clothing (4), automobiles (5), taxes (5), medical aid (5), education (4), and amusements (4–5). For the major items of expenditure the amount of money spent by this class out of its budget corresponds fairly closely with its place in the class hierarchy, second to the first of the lower-lower class for the major necessities of food and shelter, and ordinarily, but not always, fourth or fifth to the classes above for the items that give an opportunity for cutting down the amounts spent on them. Their feelings about doing the right thing, of being respectable and rearing their children to do better than they have, coupled with the limitations of their income, are well reflected in how they select and reject what can be purchased on the American market.[3]

The lower-lower class, referred to as "Riverbrookers" or the "low-down Yankees who live in the clam flats," have a "bad reputation" among those who are socially above them. This evaluation includes beliefs that they are lazy, shiftless, and won't work, all opposites of the good middle-class virtues belonging to the essence of the Protestant ethic. They are thought to be improvident and unwilling or unable to save their money for a rainy day and, therefore, often dependent on the philanthropy of the private or public agency and on poor relief. They are sometimes said to "live like animals" because it is believed that their sexual mores are not too exacting and that pre-marital intercourse, post-marital infidelity, and high rates of illegitimacy, sometimes too publicly mixed with incest, characterize their personal and family lives. It is certain that they deserve only part of this reputation. Research shows many of them guilty of no more than being poor and lacking in the desire to get ahead, this latter trait being common among those above them. For these reasons and others, this class is ranked in Yankee City below the level of the Common Man (lower-middle and upper-lower). For most of the indexes of status it ranks sixth and last.

Class in the Democratic Middle West and Far West

Cities large and small in the states west of the Alleghenies sometimes have class systems which do not possess an old-family (upper-upper) class. The period of settlement has not always been sufficient for an old-family level, based on the security of birth and inherited wealth, to entrench itself. Ordinarily, it takes several generations for an old-family class to gain and hold the prestige and power necessary to impress the rest of the community sufficiently with the marks of its "breeding" to be able to confer top status on those born into it. The family, its name, and its lineage must have had time to become identified in the public mind as being above ordinary mortals.

While such identification is necessary for the emergence of an old-family (upper-upper) class and for its establishment, it is also necessary for the community to be large enough for the principles of exclusion to operate. For example, those in the old-family group must be sufficiently numerous for all the varieties of social participation to be possible without the use of new-family members; the family names must be old enough to be easily identified; and above all there should always be present young people of marriageable age to become mates of others of their own class and a

sufficient number of children to allow mothers to select playmates and companions of their own class for their children.

When a community in the more recently settled regions of the United States is sufficiently large, when it has grown slowly and at an average rate, the chances are higher that it has an old-family class. If it lacks any one of these factors, including size, social and economic complexity, and steady and normal growth, the old-family class is not likely to develop.

One of the best tests of the presence of an old-family level is to determine whether members of the new-family category admit, perhaps grudgingly and enviously and with hostile derogatory remarks, that the old-family level looks down on them and that it is considered a mark of advancement and prestige by those in the new-family group to move into it and be invited to the homes and social affairs of the old families. When a member of the new-family class says, "We've only been here two generations, but we still aren't old-family," and when he or she goes on to say that "they (old family) consider themselves better than people like us and the poor dopes around here let them get away with it," such evidence indicates that an old-family group is present and able to enforce recognition of its superior position upon its most aggressive and hostile competitors, the members of the lower-upper, or new-family, class.

When the old-family group is present and its position is not recognized as superordinate to the new families, the two tend to be co-ordinate and view each other as equals. The old-family people adroitly let it be known that their riches are not material possessions alone but are old-family lineage; the new families display their wealth, accent their power, and prepare their children for the development of a future lineage by giving them the proper training at home and later sending them to the "right" schools and marrying them into the "right" families.

Such communities usually have a five-class pyramid, including an upper class, two middle, and two lower classes.[4] ...

The communities of the mountain states and Pacific Coast are new, and many of them have changed their economic form from mining to other enterprises; consequently, their class orders are similar to those found in the Middle West. The older and larger far western communities which have had a continuing, solid growth of population which has not destroyed the original group are likely to have the old-family level at the top with the other classes present; the newer and smaller communities and those disturbed by the destruction of their original status structure by large population gains are less likely to have an old-family class reigning above all others. San Francisco is a clear example of the old-family type; Los Angeles, of the more amorphous, less well-organized class structure.

Class in the Deep South

Studies in the Deep South demonstrate that, in the older regions where social changes until recently have been less rapid and less disturbing to the status order, most of the towns above a few thousand population have a six-class system in which an old-family elite is socially dominant.

For example, in a study of a Mississippi community, a market town for a cotton-growing region around it, Davis and the Gardners found a six-class system.[5] Perhaps the southern status order is best described by Chart I on page 195 which gives the names used by the people of the community for each class and succinctly tells how the members of each class regard themselves and the rest of the class order.

The people of the two upper classes make a clear distinction between an old aristocracy and an aristocracy which is not old. There is no doubt that the first is above the other; the upper-middle class views the two upper ones much as the upper classes do themselves but groups them in one level with two divisions, the older level above the other; the lower-middle class separates them but considers them co-ordinate; the bottom two classes, at a greater social distance than the others, group all the levels above the Common Man as "society" and one class. An examination of the terms used by the several classes for the other classes shows that similar principles are operating.

The status system of most communities in the South is further complicated by a color-caste system which orders and systematically controls the relations of those categorized as Negroes and whites.

Although color-caste in America is a separate problem and the present [essay] does not deal with this American status system, it is necessary that we describe it briefly to be sure a clear distinction is made between it and social class. Color-caste is a system of values and behavior which places all people who are thought to be white in a superior position and those who are thought of as black in an inferior status. ...

The members of the two groups are severely punished by the formal and informal rules of our society if they intermarry, and when they break this rule of "caste endogamy," their children suffer the penalties of our caste-like system by being placed in the lower color caste. Furthermore, unlike class, the rules of this system forbid the members of the lower caste from climbing out of it. Their status and that of their children are fixed forever. This is true no matter how much money they have, how great the prestige and power they may accumulate, or how well they have acquired correct manners and proper behavior. There can be no social mobility out of the lower caste into the higher one. (There may, of course, be class mobility within the Negro or white caste.) The rigor of caste rules varies from region to region in the United States.[6]

The Mexicans, Spanish Americans, and Orientals occupy a somewhat different status from that of the Negro, but many of the characteristics of their social place in America are similar.[7]

The social-class and color-caste hypotheses, inductively established as working principles for understanding American society, were developed in the researches which were reported in the "Yankee City" volumes, *Deep South,* and *Caste and Class in a Southern Town.* Gunnar Myrdal borrowed them, particularly color-caste, and made then known to a large, non-professional American audience.[8]

The Generalities of American Class

It is now time to ask what are the basic characteristics of social status common to the communities

CHART I

The social perspectives of the social classes*

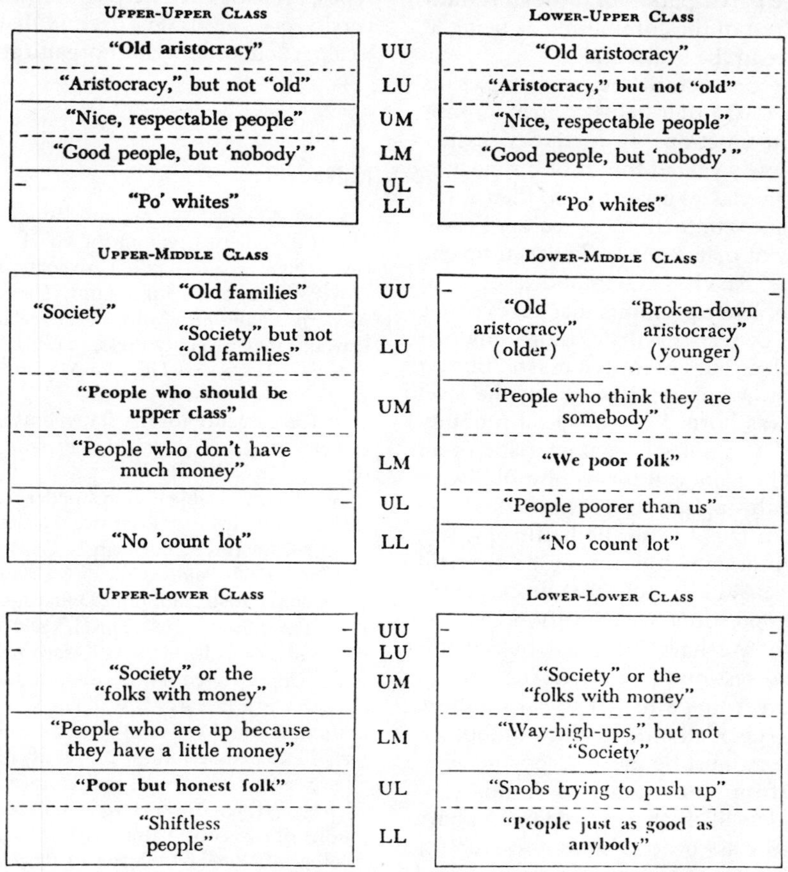

UPPER-UPPER CLASS		LOWER-UPPER CLASS
"Old aristocracy"	UU	"Old aristocracy"
"Aristocracy," but not "old"	LU	"Aristocracy," but not "old"
"Nice, respectable people"	UM	"Nice, respectable people"
"Good people, but 'nobody' "	LM	"Good people, but 'nobody' "
"Po' whites"	UL / LL	"Po' whites"

UPPER-MIDDLE CLASS		LOWER-MIDDLE CLASS
"Society" — "Old families"	UU	"Old aristocracy" (older) — "Broken-down aristocracy" (younger)
"Society" but not "old families"	LU	
"People who should be upper class"	UM	"People who think they are somebody"
"People who don't have much money"	LM	"We poor folk"
	UL	"People poorer than us"
"No 'count lot"	LL	"No 'count lot"

UPPER-LOWER CLASS		LOWER-LOWER CLASS
	UU	
	LU	
"Society" or the "folks with money"	UM	"Society" or the "folks with money"
"People who are up because they have a little money"	LM	"Way-high-ups," but not "Society"
"Poor but honest folk"	UL	"Snobs trying to push up"
"Shiftless people"	LL	"People just as good as anybody"

* Allison Davis, Burleigh B. Gardner, and Mary R. Gardner, *Deep South* (Chicago: University of Chicago Press, 1941), p. 65.

of all regions in the United States and, once we have answered this question, to inquire what the variations are among the several systems. Economic factors are significant and important in determining the class position of any family or person, influencing the kind of behavior we find in any class, and contributing their share to the present form of our status system. But, while significant and necessary, the economic factors are not sufficient to predict where a particular family or individual will be or to explain completely the phenomena of social class. Something more than a large income is necessary for high social position. Money must be translated into socially approved behavior and possessions, and they in turn must be translated into intimate participation with, and acceptance by, members of a superior class. ...

The "right" kind of house, the "right" neighborhood, the "right" furniture, the proper behavior—all are symbols that can ultimately be translated into social acceptance by those who have sufficient money to aspire to higher levels than they presently enjoy.

To belong to a particular level in the social-class system of America means that a family or individual has gained acceptance as an equal by those who belong in the class. The behavior in this class and the participation of those in it must be rated by the rest of the community as being at a particular place in the social scale.

Although our democratic heritage makes us disapprove, our class order helps control a number of important functions. It unequally divides the highly and lowly valued things of our society among the several classes according to their rank. Our marriage rules conform to the rules of class, for the majority of marriages are between people of the same class. No class system, however, is so rigid that it completely prohibits marriages above and below one's own class. Furthermore, an open class system such as ours permits a person during his lifetime to move up or down from the level into which he was born. Vertical social mobility for individuals or families is characteristic of all class systems. The principal forms of mobility in this country are through the use of money, education, occupation, talent, skill, philanthropy, sex, and marriage. Although economic mobility is still important, it seems likely now that more people move to higher positions by education than by any other route. We have indicated before this that the mere possession of money is insufficient for gaining and keeping a higher social position. This is equally true of all other forms of mobility. In every case there must be social acceptance.

Class varies from community to community. The new city is less likely than an old one to have a well-organized class order; this is also true for cities whose growth has been rapid as compared with those which have not been disturbed by huge increases in population from other regions or countries or by the rapid displacement of old industries by new ones. The mill town's status hierarchy is more likely to follow the occupational hierarchy of the mill than the levels of evaluated participation found in market towns or those with diversified industries. Suburbs of large metropolises tend to respond to selective factors which reduce the number of classes to one or a very few. They do not represent or express all the cultural factors which make up the social pattern of an ordinary city.

Yet systematic studies from coast to coast, in cities large and small and of many economic types, indicate that, despite the variations and diversity, class levels do exist and that they conform to a particular pattern of organization.

Notes

1. See W. Lloyd Warner and Paul S. Lunt, *The Social Life of a Modern Community*, Vol. I, "Yankee City Series" (New Haven: Yale University Press, 1941); W. Lloyd Warner and Paul S. Lunt, *The Status System of a Modern Community*, Vol. II, "Yankee City Series" (New Haven: Yale University Press, 1942).

2. See *The Social Life of a Modern Community*, pp. 58–72.

3. The evidence for the statements in this paragraph can be found in *The Social Life of a Modern Community*, pp. 287–300.

4. It is conceivable that in smaller communities there may be only three, or even two, classes present.

5. Allison Davis, Burleigh B. Gardner, and Mary R. Gardner, *Deep South* (Chicago: University of Chicago Press, 1941). Also read: John Dollard, *Caste and Class in a Southern Town* (New Haven: Yale University Press, 1937); Mozell Hill, "The All-Negro Society in Oklahoma" (Unpublished Ph.D. dissertation, University of Chicago, 1936); Harry J. Walker, "Changes in Race Accommodation in a Southern Community" (Unpublished Ph.D. dissertation, University of Chicago, 1945).

6. See St. Clair Drake and Horace R. Cayton, *Black Metropolis* (New York: Harcourt, Brace & Co., 1945), for studies of two contrasting caste orders; read the "Methodological Note" by Warner in *Black Metropolis* for an analysis of the difference between the two systems.

7. See W. Lloyd Warner and Leo Srole, *The Social Systems of American Ethnic Groups*, Vol. III, "Yankee City Series" (New Haven: Yale University Press, 1945). Chapter X discusses the similarities and differences and presents a table of predictability on their probable assimilation and gives the principles governing these phenomena.

8. Gunnar Myrdal, *An American Dilemma* (New York: Harper & Bros., 1944). For an early publication on color-caste, see W. Lloyd Warner, "American Caste and Class," *American Journal of Sociology*, XLII, No. 2 (September, 1936), 234–37, and "Formal Education and the Social Structure," *Journal of Educational Sociology*, IX (May, 1936), 524–31.

EDWARD SHILS

Deference

Into every action of one human being towards another there enters an element of appreciation or derogation of the 'partner' towards whom the action is directed. It enters in varying degrees; some actions contain very little of it, some consist almost entirely of appreciation or derogation, in most actions the appreciative or derogatory elements are mingled with others, such as commanding, coercing, cooperating, purchasing, loving, etc.

Appreciation and derogation are responses to properties of the 'partner', of the role which he is performing, of the categories into which he is classified or the relationships in which he stands to third persons or categories of persons—against the background of the actor's own image of himself with respect to these properties. This element of appreciation or derogation is different from those responses to the past or anticipated actions of the 'partner' which are commands, acts of obedience, the provision of goods or services, the imposition of injuries such as the withholding or withdrawal of goods and services, and acts of love or hatred.

These acts of appreciation or derogation I shall designate as *deference*. The term *deference* shall refer both to positive or high deference and to negative or low deference or derogation. Ordinarily, when I say that one person defers to another, I shall mean that he is acknowledging that person's worth or dignity but when I speak of a person's 'deference-position', that might refer either to a high or low deference-position. What I call deference here is sometimes called 'status' by other writers. There is nothing wrong with that designation, except that it has become associated with a conception of the phenomenon which I wish to modify. The term 'deference' with its clear

intimation of a person who defers, brings out the aspect which has in my view not been made sufficiently explicit in work on this subject in recent years. ...

The Bases of Deference

The disposition to defer and the performance of acts of deference are evoked by the perception, in the person or classes of persons perceived, of certain characteristics or properties of their roles or actions. These characteristics or properties I shall call deference-entitling properties or entitlements. While they do not by themselves and automatically arouse judgments of deference, they must be seen or believed to exist for deference to be granted. Deference-entitlements include: occupational role and accomplishment, wealth (including type of wealth), income and the mode of its acquisition, style of life, level of educational attainment, political or corporate power, proximity to persons or roles exercising political or corporate power, kinship connections, ethnicity, performance on behalf of the community or society in relation to external communities or societies, and the possession of 'objective acknowledgments' of deference such as titles or ranks.

It is on the basis of the perception of these entitlements that individuals and classes or more or less anonymous individuals who are believed to possess some constellation of these entitlements are granted deference; it is on the basis of the possession of these properties that they grant deference to themselves and claim it from others. It is on the basis of simultaneous assessments of their own and of others' deference-entitlements that they regulate their conduct towards others and anticipate the deferential (or derogatory) responses of others.

Why should these properties be singled out as pertinent to deference? What is it about them which renders them deference-relevant? Why are they and not kindness, amiability, humour, manliness, femininity, and other temperamental qualities which are so much appreciated in life, regarded as deference-relevant?

The cognitive maps which human beings form of their world include a map of their society. This map locates the primary or corporate groups of which they are active members and the larger society which includes these groups, but with which they have little active contact. The map which delineates this society entails a sense of membership in that society and a sense of the vital character of that membership. Even though the individual revolts against that society, he cannot completely free himself from his sense of membership in it. The society is not just an ecological fact or an environment; it is thought to possess a vitality which is inherent in it and membership in it confers a certain vitality on those who belong to it. It is a significant cosmos from which members derive some of their significance to themselves and to others. This significance is a charismatic significance; i.e. it signifies the presence and operation of what is thought to be of ultimate and determinative significance.

If we examine each of the deference-relevant properties with reference to this charismatic content, i.e. with reference to the extent to which it tends to have charisma attributed to it, we will see that each of these properties obtains its significance as an entitlement to deference primarily on these grounds.

Occupational role is ordinarily thought of as one of the most significant entitlements to deference. The most esteemed occupations in societies, for which there are survey or impressionistic data, are those which are in their internal structure and in their functions closest to the *centres*. The centres of society are those positions which exercise earthly power and which mediate man's relationship to the order of existence—spiritual forces, cosmic powers, values and norms—which legitimates or withholds legitimacy from the earthly powers or which dominates earthly existence. The highest 'authorities' in society—governors, judges, prime ministers and presidents and fundamental scientists—are those whose roles enable them to control society or to penetrate into the ultimate laws and forces which are thought to control the world and human life. Occupational roles are ranked in a sequence which appears approximately to correspond with the extent to which each role possesses these properties. The charismatic content of a given occupational role will vary with the centrality of the corporate body or sector in which it is carried on. The most authoritative role in a peripheral corporate body will carry less charisma than the same type of role in a more centrally located corporate body. The roles which exercise no authority and which are thought to have a minimum of contact with transcendent powers call forth least deference.

Of course, occupational roles and their incumbents are also deferred to on account of certain highly correlated deference-entitling properties such as the income which the practice of the occupation provides, the educational level of its practitioners, the ethnic qualities of its incumbents, etc. Conversely, occupational roles which are ill-remunerated and the incumbents of which have little education and are of derogatory ethnic stocks receive little deference on the grounds of these traits as well as on the grounds of the nature and functions of the occupational role itself. Nonetheless, occupational role is an independent entitlement to deference. ...

Deference Behaviour

The term *status*, when it is used to refer to deference-position, ordinarily carries with it overtones of the stability, continuity and pervasiveness which are possessed by sex and age. A person who has a given status tends to be thought of as having that status at every moment of his existence as long as that particular status is not replaced by another status. One of the reasons why I have chosen to use the term 'deference-position' in place of 'status' is that it makes a little more prominent the fact that status is not a substantial property of the person arising automatically from the possession of certain entitlements but is in fact an element in a relationship between the person deferred to and the deferent person. Deference towards another person is an attitude which is manifested in behaviour.

Acts of deference judgments are evaluative classifications of self and other. As classifications they transcend in their reference the things classified. A person who is evaluatively classified by an act of deference on the basis of his occupation is in that classification even when he is not performing his occupational role. The classificatory deference judgment, because it is a generalization, attains some measure of independence from the intermittence of entitlements. It has an intermittence of its own which is not necessarily synchronized with that of the entitlements.

Overt concentrated acts of deference such as greetings and presentations are usually shortlived, i.e. they are performed for relatively short periods and then 'disappear' until the next appropriate occasion. The appropriate occasions for the performance of concentrated acts of deference might be regular in their recurrence, e.g. annually or weekly or even daily, but except for a few 'deference-occupations' they are not performed with the high frequency and density over extended periods in the way in which occupational roles are performed. But does deference consist exclusively of the performance of concentrated deferential actions? Is there a 'deference vacuum' when concentrated deferential actions are not being performed? Where does deference go when it is not being expressed in a grossly tangible action?

To answer this question, it is desirable to examine somewhat more closely the character of attenuated deference actions. There are concentrated, exclusively deferential actions which are nothing but deferential actions just as there are exclusively power or style of life or occupational actions but in a way different from these others. Occupational actions are substantial; all effort within a given space and time is devoted to their performance. They can be seen clearly by actor and observer as occupational actions; the exercise of authority has many of these features, especially when it is exercised in an authoritative occupational role. Expenditures of money are of shorter duration but they too are clearly definable. The acts of consumption and conviviality which are comprised in a style of life are of longer duration but they too are also clearly defined. On the other hand,

level of educational attainment and kinship connection and ethnicity are not actual actions at all, they are classifications in which 'objectively' the classified person is continuously present although once present in the class he does nothing to manifest or affirm.

But deference actions—deferring to self and other, receiving deference from self and other—are actions. They result in and are performed with reference to classifications but they are actions nonetheless. They are not however always massive actions of much duration. They occur moreover mainly at the margin of other types of action. Deference actions performed alone are usually very shortlived; they open a sequence of interaction and they close it. Between beginning and end, deference actions are performed in fusion with non-deferential actions. Throughout the process of interaction they are attenuated in the substance of the relationship in which the performance of tasks appropriate to roles in corporate bodies, to civil roles, to personal relationships, etc., occurs. Deference actions have always been largely components of other actions; they are parts of the pattern of speaking to a colleague, a superior or an inferior about the business at hand in an authoritatively hierarchical corporate body, of speaking about or to a fellow citizen, of acting towards him over a distance (as in an election). In other words, deference actions seldom appear solely as deference actions and those which do are not regarded, especially in the United States, as a particularly important part of interaction in most situations. Nonetheless, deference is demanded and it is accepted in an attenuated form.

This then is the answer to the question as to where deference goes when it ceases to be concentrated: it survives in attenuation, in a pervasive, intangible form which enters into all sorts of relationships through tone of speech, demeanour, precedence in speaking, frequency and mode of contradiction, etc. ...

The Distribution of Deference

It has long been characteristic of the study of deference and of the deference-positions (status) which it helps to produce to ascribe to them a distribution similar in important respects to the distribution of entitlements such as occupational roles and power, income, wealth, styles of life, levels of educational attainment, etc. The entitlements are all relatively 'substantial' things which are not matters of opinion but rather 'objective', more or less quantifiable, conditions or attributes and as such capable of being ranged in a univalent and continuous distribution. Every individual has one occupation or another at any given period in time or for a specifiable duration; every individual has—if it could be measured—such and such an average amount of power over a specifiable time period. Every individual has some style of life, certain components of which at least are enduring and observable—and he either possesses them or does not possess them. There are of course cases of persons having two widely different kinds of occupational roles within the same limited time period ('moonlighting'), of persons having widely divergent incomes within a given period, but these and other anomalies can quite easily be resolved by specifiable procedures for the collection of data and for their statistical treatment and presentation.

Present-day sociological notions of deference (status, esteem, prestige, honour, etc.) grew up in association with the 'objective'[1] conception of social stratification. For reasons of convenience in research and also because common usage practised a system of classification into 'middle', 'upper', 'lower',[2] etc., classes, research workers and theorists attempted to construct a composite index which would amalgamate the positions of each individual in a number of distributions (in particular, the distributions of occupational role and education) into some variant of the three-class distribution. The resultant was called 'social-economic status' (sometimes, 'socio-economic status').

The 'subjective' conception of social stratification appreciated the 'opinion'-like character of deference but for reasons of convenience in research procedure and because of the traditional mode of discourse concerning social stratification, the 'subjective factor' itself tended to be 'substantialized' and it too was regarded as capable of being ranged in a univalent distribution.[3] Sometimes as in the Edwards classification in the

United States or in the Registrar-General's classification in the United Kingdom, this 'subjective factor' impressionistically assessed by the research worker was amalgamated with the 'objective factors' in arriving at a single indicator of 'status'. Status was taken to mean a total status, which included both deference-position and entitlements, constructed by an external observer (not a participant in the system). But this conception has not found sufferance because it is patently unsatisfactory. Deference-position—or esteem, prestige or status—does belong to a different order of events in comparison with events like occupational distribution, income and wealth distribution, etc. It belongs to the realm of values; it is the outcome of evaluative judgments regarding positions in the distributions of 'objective' characteristics.

The improvement of techniques of field work in community studies and sample surveys has rendered it possible to collect data, relatively systematically, about these evaluations and to assign to each person in a small community or to each occupation on a list a single position in a distribution. Research technique has served to obscure a fundamental conceptual error. As a result, since each person possessed a status (or deference-position), they could be ranged in a single distribution. Such a distribution could occur, however, only under certain conditions. The conditions include (a) an evaluative consensus throughout the society regarding the criteria in accordance with which deference is allocated; (b) cognitive consensus throughout the society regarding the characteristics of each position in each distribution and regarding the shape of the distributions of entitlements; (c) consensus throughout the society regarding the weights to be assigned to the various categories of deference-entitling properties;[4] (d) equal attention to and equal differentiation by each member of the society of strata which are adjacent to his own and those which are remote from it;[5] (e) equal salience of deference judgments throughout the society; (f) univalence of all deference judgments.

Were these conditions to obtain, then the distribution of deference-positions in such a society might well have the form which the distributions of 'objective' entitlements possess. There are, however, numerous reasons why the distribution of deference-positions or status does not have this form. Some of these reasons are as follows: (*a*) Some consensus concerning the criteria for the assessment of entitlements might well exist but like any consensus it is bound to be incomplete. Furthermore criteria are so ambiguously apprehended that any existent consensus actually covers a wide variety of beliefs about the content of the criteria. (*b*) Cognitive consensus throughout the society regarding the properties of entitlements and the shape of their distributions is rather unlikely because of the widespread and unequal ignorance about such matters as the occupational roles, incomes, educational attainments of individuals and strata. (*c*) The weighting of the various criteria is not only ambiguous, it is likely to vary from stratum to stratum depending on the deference position of the various strata and their positions on the various distributions; it is likely that each stratum will give a heavier weight to that distribution on which it stands more highly or on which it has a greater chance of improving its position or protecting it from 'invaders'. (*d*) The perceptions of one's own stratum or of adjacent strata are usually much more differentiated and refined and involve more subsidiary criteria than is the case in their perceptions of remote strata. Thus even if they are compatible with each other there is no identity of the differentiations made by the various strata. (*e*) Some persons are more sensitive to deference than are others and this difference in the salience of deference occurs among strata as well. Some persons think frequently in terms of deference position, others think less frequently in those terms. Accordingly assessments of other human beings and the self may differ markedly within a given society, among individuals, strata, regions and generations with respect to their tendency to respond deferentially rather than affectionately or matter-of-factly or instrumentally. The arrangement of the members of a society into a stratified distribution as if each of them had a determinate quantity of a homogeneous thing called deference (or status or prestige) does violence to the nature of deference and deference-positions; it further obscures in any case sufficiently opaque reality. The possibility of dissensus in each of the component judgments—cognitive and evaluative—which go to make up a deference-judgment can, of course,

be covered by the construction of measures which hide the dispersion of opinions. If all inter-individual disagreements are confined to differences in ranking within a given stratum, the procedure would perhaps be acceptable. But, if 80 per cent of a population place certain persons in stratum I and if 20 per cent place them in stratum II, is it meaningful to say that the persons so judged are in stratum I?

The dissensus which results in inter-individually discordant rankings seriously challenges the validity of procedures which construct univalent deference distributions and then disjoin them into strata. This difficulty would exist even if there were agreement about the location of the boundary lines which allegedly separate one deference stratum from the other. But there is no certainty that there will be consensus on this matter, and the purpose of realistic understanding is not served by assuming that there is such consensus or by constructing measures which impose the appearance of such a consensus on the data. ...

Deference Systems

Deference systems tend to become territorially dispersed into local systems which are more differentiated to those who participate in them than is the national system. I do not mean to say that the several systems ranging from local to national are in conflict with each other. Indeed they can be quite consensual and the local usually could not be constituted without reference to persons, roles and symbols of the centre. In the various zones and sectors of the periphery where the centre is more remote, the imagery of the centre still enters markedly into the deference system and local differentiations are often simply refined applications of perceptions and evaluations which have the centre as their point of reference. Thus, for example, local deference judgments will make more subtle internal distinctions about occupational role and authority, income and style of life than would judgments made from a distant point either peripheral or central. Still the distinctions will refer to distances from some standard which enjoys its highest fulfilment at the centre. It seems unlikely that centre-blindness can ever be complete in any society.

Nevertheless, the various systems do to some extent have lives of their own. The local deference system is probably more continuously or more frequently in operation than the national system—although as national societies become more integrated and increasingly incorporate with local and regional societies, the national deference system becomes more frequently and more intensely active.

In all societies, the deference system is at its most intense and most continuous at the centre. The high concentrations of power and wealth, the elaborateness of the style of life, all testify to this and call it forth. It is at the centre that deference institutions function and this gives an added focus and stimulus to deference behaviour. The centre adds the vividness of a local deference system to the massive deference-evoking powers of centrality. Within each local or regional deference system, there are some persons who are more sensitive than others to the centre and they infuse into the local system some awareness of and sensitivity to the centre.

At some times and at others, individuals whose preoccupations are mainly with the local deference systems—insofar as they are at all concerned with deference—place themselves on the macro-social deference map. This self-location and the perception that others are also locating themselves is the precondition of a sense of affinity among those who place themselves macro-socially on approximately the same position in the distribution of deference. The placement of others is made of course on the basis of fragmentary evidence about occupational role, style of life, or elements of these and the sense of affinity is loose, the self-location very vague, very inarticulated and very approximate. In this way deference (or status) strata are constituted. They have no clear boundaries and membership cannot be certified or specified. It is largely a matter of sensing one's membership and being regarded by others as a member. Those one 'knows' are usually members, and beyond them the domain spreads out indefinitely and anonymously in accordance with vague cognitive stratification maps and an inchoate image of the 'average man'; within each stratum, an 'average man' possesses the proper combination of positions on the distribution of significant deference-entitlements.

Thus the formation of deference-strata is a process of the mutual assimilation of local deference systems into a national deference system. It is through class consciousness that deference-strata are formed.

In the course of its self-constitution a deference stratum also defines in a much vaguer way the other deference strata of its society. It draws boundary lines but, except for those it draws about itself, the boundaries are matters of minor significance. Boundary lines are of importance only or mainly to those who are affected by the location of the boundary, i.e. those who live close to it on one side or the other. The location of a line of division in the distribution of deference is regarded as important primarily by those who fear that they themselves are in danger of expulsion or who are refused admission to the company of members of a stratum to whom they regard themselves as equal or to whom they wish to be equal and whose company they regard as more desirable than the one to which they would otherwise be confined. The members of any deference stratum are likely to be ignorant about the location of deference stratum boundaries which are remote from them and if they are not ignorant, they are indifferent.

The various deference strata of local deference systems are in contact with each other through occasional face-to-face contacts. They are present in each others' imaginations and this deferential presence enters into all sorts of non-deferential actions of exchange, conflict and authority.

In national deference systems too the different strata are in contact with each other, not very much through face-to-face contact but through their presence in each other's imagination. This presence carries with it the awareness of one's distance from the centre and it entails some acceptance of the centrality of the centre and some acceptance of the greater dignity of the centre. It is an implicit belief that the centre embodies and enacts standards which are important in the assessment of oneself and one's own stratum.

In some sense, the centre 'is' the standard which is derived from the perception, correct or incorrect, of its conduct and bearing. These remote persons and strata which form the centre might be deferred to, or condemned in speech, and the pattern of their conduct, bearing, outlook, etc., might be emulated or avoided. An 'objective existence' is attributed to the rank ordering from centrality to peripherality of the other strata and within this rank ordering one's own stratum is located. The ontological, non-empirical reality which is attributed to position in the distribution of deference makes it different from 'mere' evaluation and sometimes even antithetical to it.

On a much more earthly level, contacts between deference strata occur and in many forms—particularly through the division of labour and its coordination through the market and within corporate bodies and in the struggle for political power. This does not mean that the strata encounter each other in corporately organized forms[6] or that, when there is interstratum contact in the encounter of corporate bodies, these bodies include all or most members of their respective strata. Much of this inter-stratum contact takes place through intermediaries who act as agents and who receive a deference which is a response both to their own deference-entitling properties and those of their principals. Those who act on behalf of these corporate bodies do so in a state of belief that they are 'representing' the deference-stratum to which they belong or feel akin.

A society can then have a deference system of relatively self-distinguishing and self-constituting deference strata, with the strata being in various kinds of relationship with each other. Such a situation is entirely compatible with the absence of the type of objective deference distribution which we rejected in the foregoing section. Each of the deference strata possesses in a vague form an image of a society-wide deference distribution but these images cannot be correct in the sense of corresponding to an objective deference distribution, which might or might not actually exist.

Notes

This paper is a further exploration of the theme of my earlier papers 'Charisma, order and status', *American Sociological Review*, vol. 30 (April 1965), pp. 199–213; 'Centre and periphery', in *The Logic of Personal Knowledge: Essays in Honour of Michael Polanyi* (London: Routledge, Kegan Paul, 1961), pp. 117–30; 'The concentration and dispersion of charisma', *World Politics*, vol. XI, 1, pp. 1–19; and 'Metropolis and province in the intellectual community' in N. V. Sovani and V. M. Dandekar (eds.), *Changing India: Essays in Honour of Professor D. R. Cadgil* (Bombay: Asia Publishing House, 1961), pp. 275–94.

1. The 'objective' conception concerned itself with the relatively substantial entitlements, the 'subjective' with the 'opinion'-like elements.

2. The prevalence of the trichotomous classification and variations on it is probably of Aristotelian origin. There is no obvious reason why reflection on experience and observation alone should have resulted in three classes. This might well be a case where nature has copied art.

3. It is quite possible that this pattern of thought which emerged in the nineteenth century was deeply influenced by the conception of social class of the nineteenth-century critics of the *ancien régime* and of the bourgeois social order which succeeded it. In the *ancien régime* the most powerful ranks were designated by legally guaranteed titles which entered into the consciousness of their bearers and those who associated with or considered them. These designations were not 'material' or 'objective'. They did not belong to the 'substructure' of society. They were therefore 'subjective' but they were also unambiguous. They could be treated in the same way as 'objective' characteristics. By extension, the same procedure could be applied to the other strata.

4. Where these three conditions exist, there would also exist a consensus between the judgment which a person makes of his own deference-position and the judgments which others render about his position.

5. It also presupposes equal knowledge by all members of the society about all other members.

6. Corporate organizations, membership in which is determined by a sense of affinity of deference positions and of positions in other distributions, seldom enlist the active membership of all the members of the stratum or even of all the adult male members of the stratum. Those who are not members of the corporate body are not, however, to be regarded as completely devoid of the sense of affinity with other members of their stratum. 'Class consciousness' in this sense is very widespread but it is a long step from this type of 'class consciousness' to the aggressively alienated class consciousness which Marxist doctrine predicted would spread throughout the class of manual workers in industry and Marxist agitation has sought to cultivate.

► OCCUPATIONAL HIERARCHIES

PETER M. BLAU AND OTIS DUDLEY DUNCAN,
WITH THE COLLABORATION OF ANDREA TYREE

Measuring the Status of Occupations

Two approaches have dominated the investigations of occupational hierarchy carried out by students of social stratification. One is the effort to develop a socioeconomic classification scheme for occupations. Perhaps the most influential work here was that of the census statistician Alba M. Edwards.[1] His "social-economic grouping" of occupations has been widely used in studies of occupational stratification and mobility. With certain modifications it led to the "major occupation groups" used by the Bureau of the Census since 1940. ... To suggest that his grouping supplied a "scale," Edwards contented himself with showing differences in average or typical levels of education and income of the workers included in the several categories: "Education is a very large factor in the social status of workers, and wage or salary income is a very large factor in their economic status."[2]

A more recent development is the derivation of scores for *detailed* census occupation titles representing a composite index of education and income levels of workers in each such occupation. Priority for this specific technique probably belongs to social scientists in Canada,[3] with a similar approach being taken in this country by both a private researcher worker[4] and, lately, in official

publications of the U. S. Bureau of the Census.[5]

The second approach to occupational stratification is to secure, from samples more or less representative of the general public, ratings of the "general standing" or "prestige" of selected occupations. Such ratings have been shown to be remarkably close to invariant with respect to (a) the composition and size of the sample of raters; (b) the specific instructions or form of the rating scale; (c) the interpretation given by respondents to the notion of "general standing"; and (d) the passage of time.[6] The high order of reliability and stability evidenced by prestige ratings would commend their use in problems requiring social distance scaling of the occupations pursued by a general sample of the working force, but for one fact: ratings have hitherto been available only for relatively small numbers of occupation titles. Many research workers have resorted to ingenious schemes for splicing *ad hoc* judgments into the series of rated occupations, but no general solution to the problem has been widely accepted.

Work currently in progress at the National Opinion Research Center promises to overcome this difficulty by supplying prestige ratings for a comprehensive list of occupations. In the absence of such ratings at the time of the Occupational

TABLE 1

Occupations Illustrating Various Scores on the Index of Occupational Status*

Score Interval	Title of Occupation (Frequency per 10,000 Males in 1960 Experienced Civilian Labor Force in Parentheses)
90 to 96	Architects (7); dentists (18); chemical engineers (9); lawyers and judges (45); physicians and surgeons (47)
85 to 89	Aeronautical engineers (11); industrial engineers (21); salaried managers, banking and finance (30); self-employed proprietors, banking and finance (5)
80 to 84	College presidents, professors and instructors (31); editors and reporters (14); electrical engineers (40); pharmacists (19); officials, federal public administration and postal service (13); salaried managers, business services (11)
75 to 79	Accountants and auditors (87); chemists (17); veterinarians (3); salaried managers, manufacturing (133); self-employed proprietors, insurance and real estate (9)
70 to 74	Designers (12); teachers (105); store buyers and department heads (40); credit men (8); salaried managers, wholesale trade (41); self-employed proprietors, motor vehicles and accessories retailing (12); stock and bond salesmen (6)
65 to 69	Artists and art teachers (15); draftsmen (45); salaried managers, motor vehicles and accessories retailing (18); self-employed proprietors, apparel and accessories retail stores (8); agents, n.e.c. (29); advertising agents and salesmen (7); salesmen, manufacturing (93); foremen, transportation equipment manufacturing (18)
60 to 64	Librarians (3); sports instructors and officials (12); postmasters (5); salaried managers, construction (31); self-employed proprietors, manufacturing (35); stenographers, typists, and secretaries (18); ticket, station, and express agents (12); real estate agents and brokers (33); salesmen, wholesale trade (106); foremen, machinery manufacturing (28); photoengravers and lithographers (5)
55 to 59	Funeral directors and embalmers (8); railroad conductors (10); self-employed proprietors, wholesale trade (28); electrotypers and stereotypers (2); foremen, communications, utilities, and sanitary services (12); locomotive engineers (13)
50 to 54	Clergymen (43); musicians and music teachers (19); officials and administrators, local public administration (15); salaried managers, food and dairy products stores (21); self-employed proprietors, construction (50); bookkeepers (33); mail carriers (43); foremen, metal industries (28); toolmakers, and die-makers and setters (41)
45 to 49	Surveyors (10); salaried managers, automobile repair services and garages (4); office machine operators (18); linemen and servicemen, telephone, telegraph and power (60); locomotive firemen (9); airplane mechanics and repairmen (26); stationary engineers (60)
40 to 44	Self-employed proprietors, transportation (8); self-employed proprietors, personal services (19); cashiers (23); clerical and kindred workers, n.e.c. (269); electricians (77); construction foremen (22); motion picture projectionists (4); photographic process workers (5); railroad switchmen (13); policemen and detectives, government (51)

Changes in a Generation (OCG) survey we fell back on the idea of a socioeconomic index of occupational status. The particular index we used, however, was one designed to give near-optimal reproduction of a set of prestige ratings. A full account of the construction of this index is given elsewhere,[7] and only a few general points need to be made before presenting some illustrations of the scale values assigned to occupations.

In the derivation of the socioeconomic index of occupational status, prestige ratings obtained from a sizable sample of the U.S. population in

TABLE 1

(continued)

Score Interval	Title of Occupation (Frequency per 10,000 Males in 1960 Experienced Civilian Labor Force in Parentheses)
35 to 39	Salaried and self-employed managers and proprietors, eating and drinking places (43); salesmen and sales clerks, retail trade (274); bookbinders (3); radio and television repairmen (23); firemen, fire protection (30); policemen and detectives, private (3)
30 to 34	Building managers and superintendents (7); self-employed proprietors, gasoline service stations (32); boilermakers (6); machinists (111); millwrights (15); plumbers and pipe fitters (72); structural metal workers (14); tinsmiths, coppersmiths, and sheet metal workers (31); deliverymen and routemen (93); operatives, printing, publishing and allied industries (13); sheriffs and bailiffs (5)
25 to 29	Messengers and office boys (11); newsboys (41); brickmasons, stonemasons, and tile setters (45); mechanics and repairmen, n.e.c. (266); plasterers (12); operatives, drugs and medicine manufacturing (2); ushers, recreation and amusement (2); laborers, petroleum refining (3)
20 to 24	Telegraph messengers (1); shipping and receiving clerks (59); bakers (21); cabinetmakers (15); excavating, grading, and road machine operators (49); railroad and car shop mechanics and repairmen (9); tailors (7); upholsterers (12); bus drivers (36); filers, grinders, and polishers, metal (33); welders and flame-cutters (81)
15 to 19	Blacksmiths (5); carpenters (202); automobile mechanics and repairmen (153); painters (118) attendants, auto service and parking (81); laundry and dry cleaning operatives (25); truck and tractor drivers (362); stationary firemen (20); operatives, metal industries (103); operatives, wholesale and retail trade (35); barbers (38); bartenders (36); cooks, except private household (47)
10 to 14	Farmers (owners and tenants)(521); shoemakers and repairers, except factory (8); dyers (4); taxicab drivers and chauffeurs (36); attendants, hospital and other institution (24); elevator operators (11); fishermen and oystermen (9); gardeners, except farm, and groundskeepers (46); longshoremen and stevedores (13); laborers, machinery manufacturing (10)
5 to 9	Hucksters and peddlers (5); sawyers (20); weavers, textile (8); operatives, footwear, except rubber, manufacturing (16); janitors and sextons (118); farm laborers, wage workers (241); laborers, blast furnaces, steel works, and rolling mills (26); construction laborers (163)
0 to 4	Coal mine operatives and laborers (31); operatives, yarn, thread and fabric mills (30); porters (33); laborers, saw mills, planing mills, and millwork (21)

*n.e.c. means "not elsewhere classified"

SOURCES: Reiss, op. cit., Table B-1; and U.S. Bureau of the Census, 1960 Census of Population, Final Report, PC(1)-1D, Table 201.

1947 were taken as the criterion. These were available for 45 occupations whose titles closely matched those in the census detailed list. Data in the 1950 Census of Population were converted to two summary measures: per cent of male workers with four years of high school or a higher level of educational attainment, and per cent with incomes of $3,500 or more in 1949 (both variables being age-standardized). The multiple regression of per cent "excellent" or "good" prestige ratings on the education and income measures was calculated. The multiple correlation, with the 45 occupations as units of observation, came out as .91, implying that five-sixths of the variation in aggregate prestige ratings was taken into account by the combination of the two socioeconomic variables. Using the regression weights obtained in this calculation, all census occupations were assigned scores on the basis of their education and income distributions. Such scores may be interpreted either as estimates of (unknown) prestige ratings or simply as values on a scale of occupational socioeconomic status ("occupational status" for short). The scale is represented by two-digit numbers ranging from 0 to 96. It closely resembles the scales of Blishen, Bogue, and the U.S. Bureau of the Census mentioned earlier, although there are various differences in detail among the four sets of scores.

One of the most serious issues in using any index of occupational status in the study of mobility has to do with the problem of temporal stability. ... Fortunately, we now have a detailed study of temporal stability in occupational prestige ratings. The results are astonishing to most sociologists who have given the matter only casual thought. A set of ratings obtained as long ago as 1925 is correlated to the extent of .93 with the latest set available, obtained in 1963. The analysts conclude, "There have been no substantial changes in occupational prestige in the United States since 1925."[8] Less complete evidence is available for the socioeconomic components of our index, but information available in the Censuses of 1940, 1950, and 1960 points to a comparably high order of temporal stability,[9] despite major changes in the value of the dollar and the generally rising levels of educational attainment. ...

Two-digit status scores are available for 446 detailed occupation titles. Of these, 270 are specific occupation categories; the remainder are subgroupings, based on industry or class of worker, of 13 general occupation categories. The reader may consult the source publication for the scores of particular occupations of interest.[10] Here we shall only illustrate the variation of the scores by citing illustrative occupations, not always those of the greatest numerical importance (see Table 1). ...

Table 1 makes it clear that occupations of very different character may have similar status scores. In particular, there is considerable overlap of scores of occupations in distinct major occupa-

tion groups. Indeed, only five points separate the lowest occupation in the "professional, technical, and kindred workers" group from the highest among "laborers, except farm and mine." Nevertheless, the major occupation group classification accounts for three-fourths of the variation in scores among detailed occupations. The status scores offer a useful refinement of the coarser classification but not a radically different pattern of grading.

Table 1 probably does not illustrate adequately the variation by industry subclass of such occupation categories as "operatives, not elsewhere classified" and "laborers, not elsewhere classified." Such variation is fairly substantial. It must be understood, however, that particularly at these levels of the census classification scheme the occupation-industry categories represent groups of jobs with quite heterogeneous specifications, although the groups are thought to be somewhat homogeneous as to the degree of skill and experience required for their performance. No one has yet faced the question of what a study of occupational mobility would look like if all the 20,000 or more detailed titles in the *Dictionary of Occupational Titles* were coded without prior grouping.

The use of occupational status scores carries a theoretical implication. We are assuming, in effect, that the occupation structure is more or less continuously graded in regard to status rather than being a set of discrete status classes. The justification of such an assumption is not difficult. One needs only to look at any tabulation of social and economic characteristics of persons engaged in each specific occupation (whatever the level of refinement in the system of occupational nomenclature). We discover that the occupations overlap—to a greater or lesser degree, to be sure—in their distributions of income, educational attainment, consumer expenditures, measured intelligence, political orientations, and residential locations (to mention but a few items). One may sometimes find evidence supporting the interpretation that there are "natural breaks" in such distributions. Interpretations of this kind were advanced [elsewhere][11] in respect to the dividing line between farm and nonfarm and between white-collar and manual occupations. The evidence did not permit the conclusion that such occupation categories are entirely disjunct. The analysis ... suggests that boundaries may be discerned between the three broad groups, [but] also shows that these are by no means sharp lines without any overlap.

If we choose to think of occupational status as exhibiting continuous variation, the appropriate analytical model is one that treats status as a quantitative variable. This point of view has far-reaching implications for the conceptualization of the process of mobility as well as for the analysis and manipulation of data purporting to describe the process.

Notes

1. Alba M. Edwards, *Comparative Occupation Statistics for the United States,* 1870 to 1940, Washington: Government Printing Office, 1943.

2. *Ibid.,* p. 180.

3. Enid Charles, *The Changing Size of the Family in Canada,* Census Monograph No. One, Eighth Census of Canada, 1941, Ottawa: The Kings Printer and Con-

troller of Stationery, 1948; Bernard R. Blishen, "The Construction and Use of an Occupational Class Scale," *Canadian Journal of Economics and Political Science,* 24 (1958), 519–531.

4. Donald J. Bogue, *Skid Row in American Cities,* Chicago: Community and Family Study Center, University of Chicago, 1963, Chapter 14 and Appendix B.

5. U. S. Bureau of the Census, *Methodology and Scores of Socioeconomic Status,* Working Paper, No. 15 (1963); U. S. Bureau of the Census, "Socioeconomic Characteristics of the Population: 1960," *Current Population Reports,* Series P-23, No. 12 (July 31, 1964).

6. Albert J. Reiss, Jr., *et al., Occupations and Social Status,* New York: Free Press of Glencoe, 1961; Robert W. Hodge, Paul M. Siegel, and Peter H. Rossi, "Occupational Prestige in the United States, 1925–63," *American Journal of Sociology,* 70 (1964), 286–302.

7. Otis Dudley Duncan, "A Socioeconomic Index for All Occupations," in Reiss, *op. cit.,* pp. 109–138.

8. Hodge, Siegel, and Rossi, *op. cit.,* p. 296.

9. Reiss, *op. cit.,* p. 152. (Work in progress by Hodge and Treiman further supports this point.)

10. Duncan, *op. cit.,* Table B-1, pp. 263–275.

11. Peter M. Blau and Otis Dudley Duncan, *The American Occupational Structure,* New York: The Free Press, 1967, Chapter 2.

DONALD J. TREIMAN

Occupational Prestige in Comparative Perspective

In the three decades since World War II there have been some eighty-five studies of occupational prestige conducted in more than sixty countries throughout the world, ranging from highly industrialized places such as the U.S. to traditional societies such as India, Thailand, Nigeria, and New Guinea. Although these studies vary somewhat in their specific details, they all utilize the same basic procedure: a sample of the population is asked to rate or rank a set of occupational titles with respect to their prestige or social standing. These ratings are then aggregated into mean scores (or other measures of central tendency) and the scores are treated as indicators of the relative prestige of the evaluated occupations.

A remarkable feature of these studies is that they yield the same results regardless of the exact wording of the questionnaire. It does not matter whether respondents are asked about the "prestige" or "social standing" or "respect" accorded certain occupations, or whether they are asked to rate occupations on a scale or to rank them in any other way. The results are the same. A second striking feature is that the educated and uneducated, the rich and poor, the urban and rural, the old and young, all on the average have the same perceptions of the prestige hierarchy. There is no systematic subgroup variation in the relative ratings of jobs. This is of considerable importance since it allows us to make use of data drawn from rather poor samples of the population—for example, students, members of voluntary organizations, representatives of special subcultures—without fear that if we had a different sample we would get different answers. The third noteworthy feature is that although the distribution of the labor force in various occupations varies substantially from place to place, the same sorts of occupations tend to exist everywhere. Even if there are not many airplane pilots or professors in a given country, there tend to be at least a few of them and the population at large knows what these jobs are. In general, the organization of work into specific jobs is amazingly uniform across societies. Pretty much everywhere there are distinctions between weavers and tailors, and between carpenters, painters, and plumbers. And the uniformity in occupations across societies is reflected in the uniformity of occupational titles appearing in prestige studies. As a result, matching occupational titles across countries is a less onerous task than might be expected.

These three features, uniform results regardless of measurement procedures, minimal subgroup variations, and similarity of occupational titles, make possible a systematic comparison of occupational prestige hierarchies among countries. The basic procedure is to match titles across countries, e.g., "physician" in the U.S. with "doctor" in Australia, "medecin" in Mauritania, "medico" in Argentina, "laege" in Denmark, and then to compute a product moment correlation between the prestige scores for all matching titles for each pair of countries. The correlation coefficients thus generated can be taken as measures of the similarity of prestige evaluations between each pair of countries. The fundamental conclusion from such computations is that there is substantial uniformity in occupational evaluations throughout the world: the average intercorrelation between pairs of countries is .81.[1] As such numbers go, it is extremely high and fully justifies treatment of the prestige hierarchy in any given country as reflecting, in large part, a single worldwide occupational prestige hierarchy. On the basis of this result, and in view of the need for a standard occupational scaling procedure, it seemed desirable to attempt to construct a standard occupational prestige scale which could be applied to any country.

In order to match occupational titles across countries, it was necessary to devise a comprehensive occupational classification scheme. To do this, I took advantage of an already existing scheme: the *International Standard Classification of Occupations,* Revised Edition (ISCO).[2] This classification is a "nested" scheme which clusters occupations into nine major groups, eighty-three minor groups, 284 unit groups, and 1,506 specific occupations. It was developed by the International Labour Office as a guide for national census offices to encourage the comparability of occupational statistics. Many foreign census bureaus do, in fact, utilize the ISCO scheme and do publish occupational statistics according to its guidelines.

However, since the 1,506 ISCO occupational categories did not correspond very well to the occupational titles for which I had prestige ratings, I followed the ISCO scheme (with minor variations) down to the unit group level and then, within this level, made distinctions among specific occupations when they appeared warranted by my prestige data. The resulting classification contains 509 distinct occupational titles.

To derive generic prestige scores for each of these occupations, I converted all the data to a standard metric and then simply averaged scores across all countries in which a given title appeared. Scores for higher levels of aggregation (unit groups, minor groups, and major groups) were derived by various averaging procedures.[3]

How good is the prestige scale created by this procedure? The answer is—very good. Evidence for contemporary societies is extremely convincing. The average correlation of the new Standard Scale with the reported prestige hierarchies of fifty-five countries is .91 and only seven of the correlations are less than .87. Thus the Standard Scale is, on the average, the best available predictor of the prestige of occupations in any contemporary society.[4] ...

A Theory of the Determinants of Prestige

Analysis of the universally shared occupational prestige hierarchy suggests that high prestige is allocated to those occupations which require a high degree of skill or which entail authority over other individuals or control over capital. Moreover, the nature of occupational specialization is such that specific occupations are relatively invariant in these characteristics across time and space. As a result, the prestige of specific occupations is relatively invariant as well. In fact, it is so uniform that a single occupational prestige scale will capture the basic features of the occupational hierarchy of any society.

Specialization of functions into distinct occupational roles necessarily results in inequalities among occupations with respect to skill, authority, and control over capital. Some occupations, by their very definitions, require specific skills. For example, literacy is required of clerks because one cannot be a clerk if one is illiterate. Similarly, some occupations require control over capital or authority over other individuals as inherent definitions of their functions. For instance, a managerial job is one which involves "planning, direction, control, and co-ordination";[5] otherwise, it is not a managerial job but something else. Examples of these inherent inequalities can be located throughout the prestige hierarchy.

Skill, authority, and economic control are singled out as the basic resources which differentiate occupations because these are the fundamental aspects of power—they provide the crucial means to the achievement of desired goals. But the more powerful an occupation, the more important it is that it be performed well, since the consequences of competent or incompetent performances are more telling for such occupations. For example, if a garbage collector does his job poorly, little is lost; but if a surgeon is incompetent, a life can be lost. Or, similarly, if a chain store manager makes a poor business decision it may cost a firm a few hundred or at the most a few thousand dollars; but a poor decision on the part of a major executive can run into millions. Consequently, the more powerful an occupation, the greater the incentive to attract competent personnel to it. And since the basic mechanism for inducing people to perform tasks is to reward them, it follows that the most powerful positions will also be the most highly rewarded.

Other factors do enter into the determination of rewards, so that the relationship between power and privilege is not perfect. Some functions are in greater demand than others, depending upon the needs of society at any particular time. For example, in a hunting and gathering society, hunting is in greater demand than farming and thus hunting is more highly rewarded. And in a commercial economy, law is of great importance and therefore highly rewarded. But these differences are relatively minor compared to the differences in occupational requisites and perquisites which are inherent in the definitions of jobs and therefore stable across time and space.

Not only is the relative power and privilege of occupations essentially similar across societies, but so is the prestige accorded them, for prestige is granted in recognition of power and privilege. Prestige is the metric of "moral worth," and the moral worth of positions reflects their control over socially valued resources and rewards, that is, their power and privilege.[6] Since occupations are differentiated with respect to power, they will in turn be differentiated with respect to privilege and prestige. Thus, if this theory of prestige determinants is correct, these attributes of occupations will be highly correlated across societies.[7] In particular, skill level, authority, economic power, wealth, income, and prestige will be highly intercorrelated with one another and will be highly correlated across countries.

In my work on occupational prestige in contemporary societies, I amassed data on the education levels of occupations for fifteen nations (as a surrogate measure for "skill") and on income levels of occupations for eleven countries; no comparable measures of authority or control of capital were available. These data indicate a striking uniformity in occupational hierarchies. Like occupational prestige evaluations, occupational variations in education and in income proved to be highly similar from society to society. When measures of the average level of schooling of incumbents of each occupation were computed for the U.S., Argentina, Canada, West Germany, Ghana, Great Britain, India, Israel, Japan, the

Netherlands, Norway, Taiwan, the U.S.S.R., Yugoslavia, and Zambia and these measures were intercorrelated, the average intercorrelation was .76, which is almost as high as the average prestige intercorrelation reported above (.81). And when measures of the average income of incumbents of each occupation were computed for the U.S., Canada, Ceylon, Costa Rica, India, New Zealand, Pakistan, Surinam, Sweden, Taiwan, and Yugoslavia and these measures were intercorrelated, the average intercorrelation was .65, which is still a substantial correlation. Moreover, education, income, and prestige levels of occupations were highly correlated within each country: the average correlations were, respectively, .77 between education and income, .72 between education and prestige, and .69 between income and prestige. The average correlations with the Standard Scale were .79 for education and .70 for income.[8]

In short, the available data indicate that in the contemporary world occupational hierarchies are substantially invariant from place to place, even among countries varying widely in level of industrialization. This finding lends considerable empirical support to the theoretical argument outlined above.

Notes

This is a revised version of a paper presented at the Conference on International Comparisons of Social Mobility in Past Societies held in 1972. Preparation of the paper was supported by a grant from the National Science Foundation to Columbia University (NSF #28050). I am grateful to the following for making unpublished material available or for giving leads to the work of others: Peter Decker, Sigmund Diamond, Clyde Griffen, James Henretta, David Herlihy, Theodore Hershberg, Richard Hopkins, Michael Katz, William Sewell, Jr., James Smith, and Stephan Thernstrom. Thanks are also extended to Vincent Covello, Theodore Riccardi, Jr., Rose M. Cascio, Michael Freeman, John Hammond, Jr., Herbert Klein, and Jane Ferrar. The comments of the participants at the MSSB Conference, and especially those of Griffen, were extremely helpful in preparing the revision.

1. This average correlation was computed over all pairs of countries with at least 10 occupational titles rated in common.

2. International Labour Office (Geneva, 1969).

3. These are described more fully in Donald J. Treiman, *Occupational Prestige in Comparative Perspective* (New York, 1976), ch. 8.

4. I have shown that the Standard Scale does a uniformly better job of predicting occupational prestige hierarchies in individual countries than do occupational status scales developed specifically for use in occupational mobility studies in those countries. See Donald J. Treiman, "Problems of Concept and Measurement in the Comparative Study of Occupational Mobility," *Social Science Research*, IV (1975), 183–230.

5. I.L.O., *International Standard Classification*, 95.

6. Cf. Edward Shils, "Deference," in John A. Jackson (ed.), *Social Stratification* (Cambridge, 1968), 104–132.

7. Some readers will recognize the similarity between this theory and that of Kingsley Davis and Wilbert E. Moore, "Some Principles of Stratification," *American Sociological Review*, X (1945), 242–249. The principal difference between the two lies in the claim by Davis and Moore that prestige is granted by society as an inducement to competent people to fill important jobs. My claim is that occupational income may be seen as such an inducement but that prestige must be viewed as a measure of moral worth, that is, of the extent to which an occupation embodies that which is valued by members of society. Since power and privilege are universally valued and since hierarchies of power and privilege are relatively invariant, prestige will also be relatively invariant.

8. The education data typically derive from the population censuses of each of the countries in question. The income data also typically derive from population censuses, but in some cases they are from enterprise censuses. Ordinarily annual income was utilized but in some instances weekly or monthly wage rates were available rather than annual income. In practice, alternative measures of the relative income of occupational groups tend to be highly correlated, despite differences among occupations in part-time or seasonal employment rates. See Treiman, *Occupational Prestige*, ch. 5, Tables 5.1 and 5.2. Data on both income and education levels were available for only five countries: the U.S., Canada, India, Taiwan, and Yugoslavia.

JOHN H. GOLDTHORPE AND KEITH HOPE

Occupational Grading and Occupational Prestige

Introduction

Over the last forty years or so, there has accumulated in the literature of sociology and social psychology a relatively large number (probably several score) of studies in which respondents have been required to grade a selection of occupations in some hierarchical fashion. It has become customary to refer to such studies as being ones of 'occupational prestige.' Indeed, when the matter of occupational prestige is now considered, it is almost invariably in terms of studies of the kind in question. Furthermore, the data provided by these enquiries have come to play an important part both in theoretical discussion and in the conduct of empirical investigation in the general problem-area of social stratification and mobility. Yet, oddly enough, 'occupational prestige' studies have rarely been subjected to critical examination other than from a technical point of view. …

The Meaning of Prestige

An appropriate starting point for a more radical appraisal of 'occupational prestige' studies than seems hitherto to have been made is with the concept of 'prestige' itself. In a sociological context, we would suggest, prestige can be most usefully understood as referring to a particular form of social advantage and power, associated with the incumbency of a role or membership of a collectivity: specifically, to advantage and power which are of a *symbolic,* rather than of an economic or political nature. That is to say, such advantage and power imply the ability of an actor to exploit—in the pursuit of his goals—*meanings* and *values,* rather than superior material resources or positions of authority or of *force majeure.*

From this conception it follows that a hierarchy of prestige is constituted by intersubjective communication among actors, and must therefore be characterized in attitudinal and relational terms. It cannot be characterized—other than misleadingly—as a distribution in which units have differing amounts of some particular substance or quality. As a provisional statement, a prestige hierarchy might be one in which actors

(i)   *defer* to their superiors—that is, acknowledge by speech or other action their own social inferiority—and seek, or at least appreciate, association with superiors;

(ii)   *accept* their equals as partners, associates etc. in intimate social interaction—entertainment, friendship, courtship, marriage, etc.;

(iii)   *derogate*[1] their inferiors, if only by accepting their deference and avoiding association with them other than where their own superiority is confirmed.

The attributes of roles or collectivities which differentiate actors in respect of their prestige are various. What they have in common is some symbolic significance—some generally recognised meaning—which, in conjunction with prevailing values, constitutes a claim to social superiority or, conversely, some stigma of inferiority. For example, having the role of doctor and working in a hospital or clinic implies having knowledge of, control over and close involvement with matters which are generally regarded as ones of ultimate concern—matters of life and death. Belonging to an aristocratic family and owning a landed estate signifies descent from illustrious forebears and participation in an historically-rooted, distinctive and exclusive way of life. Working as a clerk in a bank evokes such generally valued characteristics as honesty, trustworthiness, discretion and dependability, and again in relation to 'important'—in this case, financial—matters. In all of these cases, then, 'deference-entitlements' (Shils, 1968) exist, and are likely to be honoured at least by some actors in some contexts. In contrast, being, say, a gypsy scrap-metal dealer or a West Indian refuse-collector is likely to mean relatively frequent exposure to derogation, on account both of the symbolic significance of the ethnic memberships in question and of the implied occupational contact with what is spoiled, discarded and dirty.[2] In other words, prestige positions do not derive directly from the attributes of a role or collectivity 'objectively' considered, but rather from the way in which certain of these attributes are perceived and evaluated in some culturally determined fashion. ...

Occupational Prestige

Assuming that a conception of prestige consistent with classical analyses is adopted, then the reference of 'occupational prestige' follows from it directly: it is to the chances of deference, acceptance and derogation associated with the incumbency of occupational roles and membership in occupational collectivities. Such prestige will be related to the 'objective' attributes of occupations—their rewards, requisite qualifications, work-tasks, work environments etc.—but only indirectly: only, that is, in so far as these attributes carry symbolic significance of a kind that is likely to be interpreted as indicative of social superiority or inferiority, with corresponding interactional consequences.

We may, therefore, now go on to ask such questions as: (i) whether such a conception of occupational prestige has been that generally held by the authors of conventional occupational prestige studies; (ii) whether the results of such studies provide valid indicators of prestige in the sense in

question; (iii) whether the uses to which results have been put have been appropriate ones. ...

The Interpretation of Occupational Prestige Ratings

It has been regularly remarked that in occupational prestige ratings, as conventionally carried out, both cognitive and evaluative processes are involved. However, precisely what are supposed to be the objects of these processes has rarely been made clear. For example, if it really were occupational prestige in the sense we would favour which was being assessed, then what would have to be cognized (or, rather, *re*cognized) and evaluated would be the symbolic significance of certain features of an occupation with regard to the chances of those engaged in the occupation meeting with deference, acceptance or derogation in their relations with others. If, for instance, the occupational 'stimulus' given were that of 'coal miner', a possible response might be on the lines of

'dirty, degrading work' →
'rough, uncultivated men' →
'likely to be looked down on by most groups'

or, alternatively perhaps

'difficult, dangerous work' →
'able, courageous men' →
'likely to be respected by many groups'

But is this in fact the kind of thing that usually happens? There is little reason to believe so, at least if we are guided by respondents' own accounts of what chiefly influenced their ratings.[3] Rather, we would suggest, the operation that most respondents have tended to perform (perhaps in accordance with the principle of least effort) is a far more obvious and simple one: namely, that of rating the occupations on the basis of what they know, or think they know, about a number of objective characteristics, evaluated in terms of what they contribute to the general 'goodness' of a job. In other words—and consistently with their own accounts—respondents in occupational prestige studies have not typically been acting within a distinctively 'prestige' frame of reference at all. The sensitivity to symbolic indications of social superiority and inferiority which this would imply has not usually been evoked by the task of grading set them. Rather, this task has led them to assess occupations only in some far less specific fashion, according to a composite judgment on an assortment of their attributes which might be thought of as more or less desirable.[4]

Such an interpretation of what 'occupational prestige' ratings are actually about would seem, moreover, to fit far better with what is known of the pattern of variation in such ratings than would the idea that they relate to prestige *stricto sensu.* The basic feature of this pattern is that while some considerable amount of disagreement in rating occurs as between *individuals,* differences between the mean ratings of age, sex, regional, occupational and other collectivities are never very great. If one assumes that in making their judgments, respondents more or less consciously (i) consider a number of different occupational attributes which they take as determining how 'good' a job is; (ii) attach some subjective 'weight' to each of these; (iii) for each occupation presented apply their rating 'formula' to what they know about the occupation, and thus (iv) come to some overall assessment of it—then one might well anticipate some appreciable degree of variation in ratings at the individual level. Individuals are likely to differ in their familiarity with particular jobs and in their priorities as regards what makes a job 'good'. However, one would not expect—other than in somewhat special and limited cases[5]—that such differences would be socially structured in any very striking way. Knowledge about the more general characteristics of other than rather esoteric occupations is relatively 'open'; and, again in general terms, the kinds of thing thought of as 'good' in a job are unlikely to give rise to systematic differences in ratings, especially since there is, in any case, a clear tendency for such advantages to go together. To take a particular example—from the NORC data—it is not surprising, given an interpretation of the kind we have proposed, that individuals should quite often disagree about the ratings of 'building contractor' *vis-à-vis* 'welfare-worker'—*nor* that, at the same time, in the case of age, sex, regional, occupational or other categories, the former job should invariably have the higher *mean* rating. (See Reiss 1961, pp. 55–6, 225–8).[6]

On the other hand, if we were to suppose that 'occupational prestige' scores did give a valid indication of a structure of prestige relations, then the degree of consensus that is shown among different social groups would indeed be remarkable, at least in those societies where other research has indicated some notable diversity in value systems and in particular between members of different social strata. For in this case it would not be a matter of evaluative consensus simply on what attributes make a job 'good', but rather on certain symbolic criteria of generalized superiority and inferiority, with all their attitudinal and behavioural implications. As Shils has observed, the conditions necessary for an entirely, or even a largely, 'integrated' prestige order to exist are in fact demanding ones. It would seem, therefore, the safest assumption to make that, within modern industrial societies, such conditions will prevail only locally, transiently or imperfectly, and thus that social relations expressive of a prestige order will occur only in an intermittent or discontinuous fashion. On the basis of available empirical data, one might suggest that while derogation is still quite widely manifest—as, for example, in the form of differential association or statusgroup exclusivity—the claim to superiority thus made by one group is not necessarily, or even usually, acknowledged by those regarded as inferior; that is to say, the latter are often not inclined to display deference.[7] This refusal may be revealed passively—by disregard for the claim to superiority, in that no particular 'respect' is shown, and little concern to reduce social distance from the 'superior' group; or, perhaps, some direct challenge to the claim may be made where real interests are felt to be threatened by it—as, say, by 'exclusivity' in housing areas, use of amenities, etc. ...

The Uses of 'Occupational Prestige' Ratings

One notable use of the data in question results from the fact that over the last two decades occupational prestige studies have been carried out in a steadily increasing number of countries at different levels of economic development. The opportunity has therefore arisen of making cross-national comparisons which, it has been supposed, can throw light on the relationship between value systems and social structural characteristics and are thus relevant to the thesis of the 'convergent' development of societies as industrialism advances. For example, Inkeles and Rossi (1956), comparing occupational prestige ratings in studies from six industrial societies, showed that a high degree of similarity prevailed. On this basis, they concluded that common structural features of these societies were of greater influence on the evaluation of occupations than were differences in cultural traditions. Subsequently, however, occupational prestige ratings from several countries as yet little industrialized have *also* been shown to be broadly in line with the hierarchy found in economically advanced societies— in so far, that is, as comparisons can be made. This result has then led to the modified argument (Hodge, Treiman and Rossi, 1966) that what is chiefly reflected in prestige ratings is the set of structural features shared by national societies of *any* degree of complexity—'specialized institutions to carry out political, religious, and economic functions, and to provide for the health, education and welfare of the population …'. Occupations at the top of these institutional structures, it is suggested, are highly regarded because of their functional importance and also because they are those which require the most training and ability and those to which the highest rewards accrue. Thus, 'any major prestige inversion would produce a great deal of inconsistency in the stratification system.' (p. 310).

In this way, therefore, it is clearly indicated how occupational prestige data may further be employed in support of a general theory of social stratification of a structural-functional type. Such an application has in fact been made quite explicitly in the work of Barber (1957). Following a Parsonian approach, Barber takes the results of the Inkeles-Rossi study as the main empirical foundation for the view that the factual order of stratification in modern societies tends in the main to be consistent with the dominant normative order. Inequality in social rewards and relationships, it is held, is structured in accordance

with functional 'needs', and this arrangement is then seen as receiving general moral support: 'functionally important roles are congruent with or partly determine a system of values'. (p. 6).

Clearly, for occupational prestige data to be used in the ways in question, it is necessary to assume that such data reflect prevailing values and norms *of a particular kind:* ones pertaining to the 'goodness'—in the sense of the 'fairness' or 'justice'—of the existing distribution of social power and advantage. However, in view of our previous discussion, it is difficult to regard such an assumption as a valid one or indeed to understand why it ever should have been made. Even if it were to be supposed that data on publicly recognized occupational hierarchies do indicate a prestige order in something approximating the classical conception, it still then would not follow that they can provide evidence that the objective reality of stratification is morally legitimated. For while prestige relations do depend upon a certain range of shared understandings, consensus on principles of distributive justice is not necessarily involved.[8] Moreover, as we have argued, by far the most plausible interpretation is that occupational prestige ratings reflect prevailing ideas at a much lower level of abstraction: that is, ideas of what is 'good' in the sense simply of what is generally found desirable in an occupation. And if *this* is the case, then the consensus that exists is obviously of no very great moral or legitimatory significance at all. Apart from quite unsurprising agreement on such matters as, for example, that high pay is preferable to low pay, more security to less, qualifications to lack of qualifications, etc., the consensus that is implied is of a cognitive and perceptual kind, not an evaluative one. The fact that, on average, all groups and strata agree that certain occupations should be rated higher than others tells one nothing at all about whether the occupational hierarchy that is thus represented is regarded as that which *ought* to exist. And in so far as the publicly recognized hierarchy corresponds to that proposed by structural-functional theorists, this would seem to indicate no more than that broadly similar sets of rating criteria are being applied: i.e. occupational rewards and occupational requirements.[9]

Thus, as regards the utilization of occupational prestige data in the advancement of stratification theory, our view must be that this has been fundamentally misguided. What, now, of their application in research? Primarily, of course, occupational prestige ratings have been used in studies of social mobility, in which they have constituted the hierarchy—scalar or categorical—in the context of which mobility has been assessed. Assumptions about what prestige ratings rate are thus necessarily involved in the interpretation of mobility patterns, and the crucial issues that arise are once more ones of 'validity'.

Concerning the question: What, in mobility studies, may occupational prestige ratings be taken to indicate?—three main positions can be distinguished. These can be usefully considered in turn, together with their implications and problems.

(i) Ratings may be taken—as, for example, by Svalastoga (1959)—as indicative of the position of an occupation within a prestige order; that is, as indicative of the chances of those holding that occupation encountering deference, acceptance or derogation in their social lives. In this case, therefore, mobility between different occupational levels, other than of a marginal kind, may be interpreted as involving the probability of subcultural and relational discontinuity. While such a perspective does not necessarily mean that society is seen as divided up into more or less discrete strata, it does imply that social mobility, as measured, is not just a matter of individuals gaining more qualifications, more income, more interesting work etc., but further of their experiencing changes in their life-styles and patterns of association. The difficulty is, however, as already remarked, that the validity of occupational prestige ratings construed in this way has never been established, and that there are indeed strong grounds for doubting their validity. In other words, we are simply not in a position to infer, with any acceptable degree of precision and certitude, what are the typical consequences of mobility, as measured via occupational prestige ratings, for the actual social experience of those deemed to be mobile.

(ii) Prestige ratings may be taken as indicative of the status of occupations in the generic sense—that is, as being in effect comparable with composite measures of 'socio-economic' status, de-

rived from data on income, education, housing, possessions etc. Justification for this position is twofold: first, to [quote] the observation of Reiss (1961), respondents in prestige-rating studies appear 'to emphasize the relevance of indicators sociologists use to measure socio-economic status ...'; secondly, as shown by Duncan (1961), it is possible, at least in the American case, to predict prestige ratings fairly accurately from census data on occupational income and education. If then, 'occupational prestige' is understood in the way in question, some reasonable basis may be claimed for interpreting occupationally-measured mobility in terms of movement between grades of occupation differentiated chiefly by their levels of rewards and requirements. At the same time, though, it must be emphasized that in this case no good grounds exist for any interpretation in terms of prestige *stricto sensu*, and, of course, no basis at all for any consideration of how far mobility may be incongruent from one form of stratification to another. Precisely because of the inevitably 'synthetic' nature (Ossowski, 1963) of socio-economic status, as indicated by prestige scores, the analysis of mobility must be strictly unidimensional. These limitations would lead one to suggest, therefore, that if it is accepted that occupational prestige ratings are not valid indicators of a prestige order but are being used simply to stand proxy for socio-economic status, then it would be preferable, where possible, to seek to measure the latter more directly—and without any concern to combine components so that a good 'fit' with prestige scores may be obtained. To discard the notion of prestige altogether would, in this case, mean losing nothing but the possibility of terminological confusion; and developing separate indices of occupational income, education etc., as well as some composite measure, would permit the analysis of mobility in a multi-dimensional manner. In short, there seems no good argument for basing mobility research on occupational prestige ratings, interpreted as socio-economic status scores, other than where a lack of data on the socio-economic attributes of occupations makes this procedure an unavoidable *pis aller*.

(iii) Prestige ratings may be taken as indicating popular evaluations of the relative 'goodness' of occupations in terms of the entire range of pre-vailing criteria. In this case, related mobility data are open to interpretation as showing, basically, the chances of individuals entering more or less desirable grades of occupation, given certain grades of origin. While an interpretation of the data on these lines has rarely, if ever, been pursued consistently throughout a mobility study, it is that which, on grounds of validity, could best be defended. First, as we have already argued, grading occupations according to notions of their general 'goodness' is what respondents in occupational prestige studies appear, in the main, to be doing. Secondly, it is in regard to *this* understanding of prestige scores that it would seem most relevant to claim, following Duncan and Artis (1951) and Reiss (1961), that their validity lies in the degree of consensus which emerges, despite the use of quite various criteria of evaluation. The argument that this consensus points to 'the existence of an underlying and agreed upon structure of occupational prestige' is difficult to sustain once it is recognized just what consensus on a prestige order entails. But the idea of a broadly agreed upon ordering of occupations in terms of 'goodness' does, on the evidence in question, receive some clear—and not very surprising—support. Furthermore, if prestige ratings are taken as indicative of an occupational hierarchy of this kind, then the fact that they represent synthetic judgments and cannot be 'disaggregated' is no longer a problem in the analysis of mobility patterns. For if mobility is being interpreted as being simply between grades of occupation of differing desirability in some overall sense, a unidimensional approach would appear the appropriate one. However, it must be added that what would then be a dubious and potentially dangerous step would be to shift from such an interpretation of specifically occupational mobility to one in which conclusions were drawn regarding the stability of status groups, income classes, or social strata in any sense whatsoever; that is, conclusions regarding *social* mobility as generally understood. In effect, of course, a shift of this nature has been made in most large-scale mobility studies carried out in the recent past. But while it might reasonably be held that such a manoeuvre is unlikely to be very misleading so far as the 'gross' patterns of

social mobility are concerned, the difficulty is (apart from the limitation of unidimensionality) that we have no way of knowing at just *what* point and in *what* ways it might turn out to be quite deceptive. Yet again, the problem of validity recurs.

The general—and rather pessimistic—conclusion to which one is led is, therefore, the following: that to the extent that the meaning of occupational prestige ratings is correctly construed, the less useful they appear to be as a basis for mobility studies which pursue the 'classical' sociological interests of mobility research.

Notes

1. We use 'derogate' in this context following Shils (1968). Were it not that its usual connotations go beyond its strict meaning, 'disparage'—literally 'to make unequal'—might be a preferable term.

2. On 'stigma symbols' as the obverse of 'prestige symbols', see Goffman (1963).

3. See Reiss (1961).

4. As regards the NORC [National Opinion Research Center] study, it is worth recalling what is usually forgotten: that this enquiry, at least in the view of those who devised it, was in fact specifically aimed at finding out what people thought were the best jobs, in the sense of the most desirable. Where 'prestige' and 'standing' are referred to in the initial report on the study, they are obviously equated with desirability. See NORC (1947).

5. E.g. where respondents are rating occupations within their own status or situs areas, c.f. Gerstl and Cohen (1964).

6. Our interpretation of the meaning of 'occupational prestige' ratings is also consistent with the fact that certain variations in the task set to respondents appear to make little difference to the results achieved: e.g. whether respondents are asked to rate occupations according to their 'social prestige', 'social standing', 'social status', 'general desirability' etc: or whether they are asked for their own opinions or what they believe are generally prevailing opinions. It seems reasonable to suppose that if respondents are required to grade occupations according to any one criterion which, while rather imprecise, implies a 'better-worse' dimension, they will produce results of the kind in question; and further, that the level of consensus in this respect is such that the distinction between personal and general opinion is of little consequence—provided that there is

no suggestion of a normative judgment being required; that is, one in terms of which jobs *ought* to be the best.

7. Cf. for example, Goldthorpe, Lockwood, Bechhofer and Platt (1969) chapters 4 and 5.

8. In fact, one might suggest the hypothesis that societies of the kind in which an integrated and stable prestige order is to be found will tend to be ones in which the factual order of stratification is not commonly appraised in terms of distributive justice, or indeed envisaged as capable of being in any way substantially different from what it is.

The distinction between the recognition of prestige and the attribution of justice is foreshadowed—as are several other points in the above paragraph—by Gusfield and Schwartz (1963) in a paper that has been curiously neglected by subsequent American writers on occupational grading.

9. It is a well-known problem of the structural-functional theory of stratification that other usable criteria of the functional importance of occupational roles are hard to find: employing the two criteria in question does, of course, introduce a serious degree of circularity into the argument.

References

Barber, B. (1957). *Social stratification.* Harcourt, Brace & Co., New York.

Duncan, O.D. (1961). A socioeconomic index for all occupations. In A.J. Reiss, *Occupations and social status.* Free Press of Glencoe. New York.

Duncan, O.D. and Artis, J.W. (1951). *Social stratification in a Pennsylvania rural community.* Pennsylvania State College: Agricultural Experiment Station Bulletin 543.

Gerstl, J. and Cohen, L.K. (1964). Dissensus, situs and egocentrism in occupational ranking. *Brit. J. Sociol.,* 15, 254–61.

Goffman, E. (1963). *Stigma.* Prentice Hall, Englewood Cliffs.

Goldthorpe, J.H., Lockwood, D., Bechhofer, F. and Platt, J. (1969). *The affluent worker in the class structure.* Cambridge University Press.

Gusfield, J.R. and Schwartz, M. (1963). The meaning of occupational prestige: reconsideration of the NORC scale. *Amer. Sociol. Rev.,* 28, 265–71.

Hodge, R.W., Treiman, D.J. and Rossi, P. (1966). A comparative study of occupational prestige. In *Class, status and power* (2nd edn.). (ed. R. Bendix and S.M. Lipset). Free Press of Glencoe, New York.

Inkeles, A. and Rossi, P. (1956). National comparisons of occupational prestige. *Amer. J. Sociol.,* 61, 329–39.

N.O.R.C. (1947). Jobs and occupations: a popular evaluation. *Opinion News,* 9th September. Reprinted in *Class, status and power* (1st edn.). (ed. R. Bendix and S.M. Lipset). Free Press of Glencoe, New York.

Ossowski, S. (1963). *Class structure in the social consciousness.* Routledge, London.

Reiss, A.J. (1961). *Occupations and social status.* Free Press of Glencoe, New York.

Shils, E.A. (1968). Deference. In *Social stratification* (ed. J.A. Jackson). Cambridge University Press.

Svalastoga, K. (1959). *Prestige, class and mobility.* Gyldendal, Copenhagen.

DAVID L. FEATHERMAN AND ROBERT M. HAUSER

Prestige or Socioeconomic Scales in the Study of Occupational Achievement?

At least in the United States and Australia, the processes of allocation to educational and occupational statuses from social origins (i.e., the process of stratification or of status attainment) seem largely socioeconomic in character (Featherman, Jones, and Hauser, 1975). Put another way, inter- and intragenerational movements of men among categories of their own and their parents' educations and occupations more closely follow the dimensions of social space defined by the "socioeconomic" distances among occupation groups than by the "prestige" distances among occupations. Evidence for this interpretation is drawn from parallel results for the United States and Australia in which estimates for the structural equations of "status attainment" models with occupations scaled in units of Duncan's (1961) socioeconomic index (SEI) yield higher coefficients of multiple determination (R^2) than do estimates based on occupations scaled in units of NORC prestige (Siegel, 1971) or of Treiman's (1977) international prestige index. In addition, the canonical structure of generational and career occupational mobility in both societies more nearly approximates a socioeconomic "space," as the canonical weights for occupation categories correlated higher with mean SEI scores for these occupations than with mean Siegel or Treiman scores.

In interpreting these data we suggest that prestige scores for occupations are less valid indicators of the dimensions of occupations pertinent to occupational mobility in industrial societies and of the status attainment processes operating therein than are socioeconomic scores. We reason from evidence for the United States (Reiss, 1961;

Siegel, 1971) and Great Britain (Goldthorpe and Hope, 1974) that occupational prestige scores represent a congeries of salient dimensions or occupational characteristics. For example, the British ratings of the "social standing" of occupations are a linear combination (to the extent of 97% of their variance) of four oblique dimensions: standard of living, power and influence over other people, level of qualifications, and value to society (Goldthorpe and Hope, 1974: 14). Any two pairs of raters produce rankings which are modestly correlated at best ($r = .4$), consistent with the notion that unique variance in prestige gradings is quite high. Conversely, the mean ranks for the same occupations over socially and demographically defined groups correlate in the range of 0.8 and 0.9. This common variance appears to be socioeconomic; that is, over three-quarters of the linear variance in prestige scores is a reflection of the educational and economic properties of the ranked occupations. Thus, while raters in the United States and Britain used many and idiosyncratic features of occupations in assessing their relative social standing, apparently they all were aware of and utilized the socioeconomic "desirability" of titles, to some extent, in reaching their decisions.

The salience of the socioeconomic properties of occupations across persons, groups, and perhaps societies may follow from the rather similar social organization of occupations in functionally similar economic systems (e.g., industrial capitalism). But more to the point of the relative centrality of "prestige" or socioeconomic dimensions to the process of status attainment, we speculate that commonalities in prestige grades and in the responsiveness of these rankings to socioeconomic attributes of occupations may reflect popular awareness of (what further comparative research may show to be) similar processes of status allocation across societies. In at least the cases of Australia and the United States, the socioeconomic model, patterned after the work of Blau and Duncan (1967), yields estimates of effect parameters which are substantially the same. Moreover, loglinear adjustments of mobility matrices for the effects of differential occupation structures (to wit, as provided in the table margins) uncovers largely similar interactions within the tables (to wit, constant patterns of inflow and outflow both between and within generations for both societies).

Our provisional conclusion is that prestige scores are "error-prone" estimates of the socioeconomic attributes of occupations. Whatever it is that prestige scores scale—and this does not appear to be prestige in the classical sense of deference/derogation (see Goldthorpe and Hope, 1972)—it is substantively different from socioeconomic status. Yet one is best advised to use a scale for occupations which most accurately captures the features of occupations having force for the social process one is studying. In instances of occupational mobility and related processes of status allocation, socioeconomic dimensions and socioeconomic scores for occupations are the more central, and therefore are preferable over prestige scores.

Notes

This research was supported by NSF Grant #44336, NICHHD Grant #HD-05876 and institutional support from the College of Agricultural and Life Sciences, University of Wisconsin–Madison. Any opinions, findings, conclusions, or recommendations are those of the authors and do not necessarily reflect the views of the National Science Foundation.

References

Blau, P. M. and O. D. Duncan (1967) The American Occupational Structure. New York: Wiley.

Duncan, O.D. (1961) "A socioeconomic index for all occupations," pp. 139–161 in A. Reiss, Occupations and Social Status. New York: Free Press.

Featherman, D. L., F. L. Jones, and R. M. Hauser (1975) "Assumptions of social mobility research in the U.S.: the case of occupational status." Social Science Research 4 (December): 329–360.

Goldthorpe, J. and K. Hope (1974) The Social Grading of Occupations: A New Approach and Scale. Oxford: Oxford Univ. Press.

———.(1972) "Occupational grading and occupational prestige," pp. 19–79 in K. Hope (ed.) The Analysis of Social Mobility: Methods and Approaches. Oxford: Clarendon.

Reiss, A. J. (1961) Occupations and Social Status. New York: Free Press.

Siegel, P. M. (1971) "Prestige in the American occupational structure." Unpublished doctoral dissertation, University of Chicago.

Treiman, D. J. (1977) Occupational Prestige in Comparative Perspective. New York: Academic Press.

ROBERT W. HODGE

The Measurement of Occupational Status

Since the appearance of Blau and Duncan's monumental inquiry into "The American Occupational Structure" (1967), we have learned a great deal about processes of inter- and intrageneration occupational mobility. Indeed, there has been a virtual explosion of research on processes of status attainment. Much of this research rests upon the reduction of information about a person's detailed occupational pursuit to a single continuous variable, a transformation typically accomplished by utilizing Duncan's Socioeconomic Index for All Occupations (Duncan, 1961a) to assign status scores to the occupations held by fathers and sons at various points in their careers (see, for example, Blau and Duncan, 1967; Hauser and Featherman, 1977). Despite the reliance of most inquiries into processes of status attainment on Duncan's SEI scale, there has been little discussion of the properties and characteristics of this index by its users (see, however, Duncan, 1961b, and Featherman and Hauser, 1976). The purpose of this essay is to discuss the characteristics of Duncan's SEI scale, as well as several difficulties encountered in its use in studies of occupational mobility. ...

On the Interpretation of Duncan's Index

The conceptual meaning of Duncan's SEI scale is by no means clear; at least three alternative interpretations are available and none of these is entirely satisfactory. All of these interpretations rest upon features of the construction of Duncan's index and/or characteristics of the estimated weights of its components.

The most obvious interpretation of Duncan's SEI scale follows from the technique by which the weights of its components were derived. The reader will recall that they were established by regressing the percentage of excellent plus good ratings received by a few titles in the North–Hatt study which matched census lines on census-derived indicators of the age-standardized educational and income levels of these occupations. Scale values for all occupations were then obtained by substituting the education and income measures, available for all occupations from census data, into the resulting equation. Consequently, Duncan's SEI scale may be interpreted as *the expected percentage of excellent plus good ratings an occupation would receive in a prestige inquiry of the North–Hatt type.*

There are two defects with this interpretation of Duncan's SEI scale. First, the prediction equation for the prestige indicator is less than satisfactory. It accounts for a bit more than four-fifths of the variance in prestige ratings. One could, of course, regard the error variance as random, on the view that prestige ratings are just "error-prone" proxies for the education and income levels of occupations. However, such a view cannot be sustained in the light of the substantial consensus which exists between subgroups of raters. The education and income levels of occupations fail to account for the consensus observed between subgroups of raters differing in their own occupations, their sex, race, and so forth. Not only is there consensus between subgroups of raters about overall prestige ratings, there is also consensus about that part of the prestige of an occupation which is not accounted for by the income and educational levels of its incumbents.

This fact enables one to discount the view that prestige scores are just "error-prone" indicators of the "socioeconomic" level of an occupation, a point which appears to have escaped Featherman and Hauser who state (1976, p. 405), "Our provisional conclusion is that prestige scores are 'error-prone' estimates of the socioeconomic attributes of occupations." This claim is quite possibly true *with respect to the intergenerational transmission of occupational status.* However, in view of the consensus over them from one subgroup of raters to the next, the "errors" themselves appear to be social facts in Durkheim's sense, rather than random disturbances which have no life of their own. For this reason, the interpretation of Duncan's SEI scale as a predicted prestige score flies in the face of what is known about occupational prestige.

Since the publication of Duncan's SEI scale, pure prestige scales have become available for all occupations (Siegel, 1971; Treiman, 1977). Comparisons of the performance of these scales with Duncan's index in studies of status attainment leave no doubt that the association between the detailed occupations of fathers and their sons is captured more completely by their values on Duncan's index than on either Siegel's or Treiman's prestige scale (see, for example, Duncan *et al.,* 1972; Featherman and Hauser, 1976; Stevens and Featherman, 1981). This is yet another reason why the interpretation of Duncan's scale as expected prestige scores is dubious.

A second interpretation of Duncan's SEI scale pays no attention to the method of its construction and makes reference only to its components. Without specifying the precise meaning of either, sociologists commonly make a distinction between "social status" and "economic status." (These concepts, whatever they are, should not be confused with Weber's concepts of "status honor" and "class," which have quite specific meanings that are analytically, if not statistically, independent of the usual measures of "social status" and "economic status.") Education is frequently utilized as an indicator of "social status," while current income is a common measure of "economic status." Since aggregate measures of the educational and income levels of an occupation's incumbents enter into the computation of Duncan's index, it is natural to refer to the combination of them as a *socioeconomic index of occupational status.*

This interpretation of Duncan's SEI scale is, obviously, the one most frequently made in the literature. Duncan indicated his own preference for it by his decision to name his index as he did. The socioeconomic interpretation of Duncan's SEI scale is clearly embedded in its use in Blau and Duncan's study of occupational mobility (1967), Hauser and Featherman's replication of it (1977), and Featherman and Hauser's important discussion (1976) of the properties of socioeconomic and prestige indicators of occupational standing. Most users of the Duncan index have accepted this interpretation without serious consideration of alternatives. Despite the overwhelming consensus in the published literature about the proper interpretation of Duncan's scale, it is interesting to note that Duncan himself, in his original presentation of the scale, is more than slightly ambiguous about its proper interpretation. At one point, he remarks (1961a, p.115),

Our problem, then, is defined as that of obtaining a socioeconomic index for each of the occupations in the detailed classification of the 1950 Census of Population. This index is to have both face validity, in terms of its constituent variables, and *sufficient predictive efficiency with respect to the NORC occupational prestige ratings that it can serve as an acceptable substitute for them* [emphasis is added] in any research where it is necessary to grade or rank occupations in the way that the NORC score does but where some of the occupations are not on the NORC list.

This quotation seems to make clear that Duncan wanted to cut the cake both ways: the index was a socioeconomic one, but it was also a substitute for prestige ratings. Subsequently, Duncan made clear that he did not regard his index as the equivalent of a pure prestige scale, noting (1961a, p. 129) that, "It should be made perfectly clear that the socioeconomic index does *not* [Duncan's italics] purport to be a prediction of the prestige ratings that occupations excluded from the NORC list would receive in a similarly conducted study of prestige ratings." Subsequent research has clearly demonstrated that Duncan was absolutely correct in this judgment: his scale and prestige scales are very definitely not the same thing. But that still leaves open how his scale should be interpreted.

The interpretation of Duncan's SEI scale as a socioeconomic index is seemingly agreeable and consistent with what its constituent indicators are thought to measure at the individual level. Nonetheless, this interpretation of Duncan's and similar scales is not without its problems. In our view, there are two primary difficulties with socioeconomic indicators of an occupation's location in the social structure of work. First, the combination of indicators of social and economic status such as education and income into a composite index of socioeconomic level begs the question of whether or not the effects of these factors are proportional to their weights in the index—a crucial and necessary assumption whenever the index is subsequently employed in empirical research. There is ample evidence *at the individual level* that education and income can even have *effects of opposite sign* on some dependent variables such as fertility; combining them together with a person's occupational level into an overall index of an individual's socioeconomic level presumes unidimensionality where there is none and should be avoided. (For a further discussion of this point and additional examples, see Hodge, 1970.) But if it is sound practice to keep such variables as income and education separated at the individual level, one can at least question the wisdom of combining them *at the aggregate level* of occupations. It may well be that alternative, aggregate characteristics of occupations are not just alternative indicators of an occupation's location in a single hierarchy, but reflect somewhat different forces at work on an occupation's incumbents and their behavior.

What we regard, however, as an even greater difficulty with the socioeconomic interpretation of Duncan's SEI scale stems from the analytical status of the concept of "socioeconomic" level. As far as we can see, it has none: its relationship to such *well-defined*, though *poorly measured*, concepts of stratification theory as "class," "status," and "power" is at best vague and imprecise. The concept of socioeconomic status has no independent analytical status in stratification theory: at the individual level it is no more or no less than whatever is measured by a person's education, oc-

cupational pursuit, and income and, at the aggregate level of occupations, it is just some combination of whatever skills it takes to enter the occupation and whatever rewards are obtained from pursuing it at a given point in time within a given market structure. Socioeconomic status is what socioeconomic status scales measure; there is no underlying analytical concept to which we can refer a proposed indicator of socioeconomic status to decide whether it is well or ill conceived or to assess how it might be improved. For example, referring to "the choice of summary statistics to represent the education and income distributions of the occupations, and the adjustment of these statistics for age differences among occupations," Duncan observed (1961a, p. 119), "Reasonable procedures for accomplishing these two steps, different from the ones followed [in the construction of Duncan's index]´ are easily proposed." In a world like this, of course, there is no theoretical justification for the choice of one, as opposed to another plausible means of summarizing the constituent indicators and the choice of any one of the competing alternatives rests on the assumption that they all measure the same thing in approximately the same way. As Duncan put it (1961a, p. 119), "... it seems doubtful that the final result would be greatly altered by switching to one of the alternatives." Whether this is literally the case, we cannot say, for while students of status attainment have been especially diligent at exposing the weaknesses of pure prestige scales in the study of occupational mobility, they have devoted but limited energy to examining the properties of alternative socioeconomic scales, to exposing the behavior of the component variables in these scales, and to making these scales temporally relevant to their research, a fault remedied in considerable measure by the work of Stevens and Featherman (1981).

We offer now a third and final interpretation of Duncan's SEI scale. In Duncan's SEI index, the weights of the education and income variables are nearly equal and the intercept is close to zero. We can find the constant k which will center the coefficients of the income and education variables in Duncan's SEI scale around .5 by solving $.50 - .55k = .59k - .50$ for $K = (1)/(1.14) = .8772$.[1] Multiplying the values of Duncan's SEI scale ($= D$) by this value and adding $6(k) = 6(.8772) = 5.26$ to eliminate the constant term leaves us with

$$D' = k(D) + 6(k) = .8772(D) + 5.26$$
$$= .4825(E) + .5175(I),$$

a transformed index $(= D')$ in which the education $(= E)$ and income $(= I)$ indicators are for all practical purposes simply averaged together. This transformation of Duncan's SEI scale is, of course, made possible only because the summary measures of the education and income distributions of the occupations receive nearly equal weights when prestige is regressed on them. Our ability to effect this transformation suggests another interpretation of the Duncan SEI scale scores, viz., *a linear transformation of the best guess we could make of the age-standardized percentage of an occupation's male incumbents either with at least a high school diploma or with 1949 incomes of $3500 or more if neither percentage was known.* In fact, one would not go far awry in interpreting the untransformed values of Duncan's SEI scale in this fashion, since the transformation required to effect this interpretation is roughly equal to the identity operator.

This interpretation of Duncan's SEI scale is, we believe, novel, though Cain (1974, p. 1501) comes close to making it. And while it sounds ridiculous, that is not necessarily a disadvantage. It keeps one's attention focused upon the essential feature of Duncan's SEI scale, to wit, the particular way it glues education and income together to construct "socioeconomic" status. Beyond that, it makes clear the inherent uncertainty which necessarily surrounds any results obtained by the use of Duncan's SEI scale: having used it, there is absolutely no way of knowing whether the observed effects are brought about by the economic rewards attached to occupations or by the skills required to pursue them. Instead, one must resort to casting the results in terms of an occupation's "socioeconomic" status—a concept which seems more nearly contrived for convenience than a social fact in Durkheim's sense. In keeping with the bulk of the literature on status attainment, we will continue throughout this paper to accept the *socioeconomic* interpretation of Duncan's SEI scale, but it should be obvious that the serious questions which can be raised about this or any other interpretation of Duncan's scale also make the interpretation of any findings based upon it problematical.

Occupation as a Contextual Variable

In recent years, a considerable amount of sociological inquiry has been directed toward detecting contextual effects on individual behavior. In this research tradition, individual behavior is seen in part as a function of the characteristics of the other individuals with whom the subject shares group memberships (see, e.g., Blau, 1957, 1960; Davis, Spaeth, and Huson, 1961; Tannenbaum and Bachman, 1964; Farkas, 1974). Research of this kind has not been without its critics, of which Hauser (1970a, 1970b, 1974) is by far the most outspoken.

There are several strategies of research for examining so-called group, contextual, and structural effects upon individual behavior. We need not detail these here, although we should note that the most general of all these models is the one embedded in the analysis of covariance. The particular strategy of interest in the present context is the one where the consequences for an individual's behavior of his membership in a social group or population aggregate are summarized by an indicator which reflects the average or some other measure of the central tendency on a particular trait of the individual members comprising the social groups or population aggregates to which he belongs. An example of this research strategy would be characterizing schoolchildren by the proportion of minority group members in the school they attend. Such a characterization of an individual has nothing to do with the structural features of the school he attends, such as library books per capita. Instead, it rests solely upon the individual characteristics of his fellow classmates.

The fundamental difficulty with this strategy for analyzing contextual or compositional effects is put quite simply: there is *no logically conceivable way in which one could run an experiment to test for any observed effects.* This is the fundamental defect with the analysis of all compositional effects; Hauser (1970a) comes close to stating this principle, but does not make it as explicit as he might have. To illustrate this principle, we may pursue the foregoing example. Suppose we wanted to run an experiment to examine the effects of minority composition on school achievement among white students. Now obviously, our first step would be to make random assignments of white students to schools; in this way the white students in each school would be expected to have equivalent means and variances on all characteristics save those we experimentally manipulate; this is the advantage we realize from experimentation. So far, so good. Now we must construct our experimental variable. To do this, we can again make random assignments, this time of minority students, of subjects to schools. However, while we can make random assignments of minority students to schools so that their expected means and variances on all variables are equal from school to school, *we must assign them in differential numbers.* If we failed to do this, the schools would not differ in their minority composition and there would be no between-school variance in our experimental variable. The situation is now this: by making random assignments we have secured an expected equality from school to school in the means and variances of both white and minority students on all variables. However, the ratio of white to minority students varies from school to school and that, necessary to conduct the experiment at all, proves fatal.

Minority and white students *do not differ on their minority status alone.* They differ in their socioeconomic backgrounds, in the numbers of their siblings, in the quality of their experiences, and almost surely in their attitudes and values as well. Because the schools vary in their minority composition, *they will necessarily vary in every individual level correlate of minority status as well.* Consequently, any observed effect of minority composition is confounded by every individual correlate of minority status and *there is no logically possible way of experimentally separating these confounding factors.* Having found an effect of minority composition, we can generate additional compositional effects by the carload lot. All we need to do is to refer to the individual level correlates of minority status. Furthermore, although it is not essential to the argument advanced herein, any attempt to separate these confounding factors via nonexperimental methods will certainly flounder on the barricade of multicollinearity, since the relevant associations are the typically high, ecological correlations across the units of the experiment—in this case schools.

The foregoing argument requires comment. First, there is nothing about it which denies the existence of contextual or compositional effects. Indeed, they may be large and substantial, but the argument clearly implies that *there is no logically possible way of isolating them.* Second, while *practically* speaking, most social-science findings are not subject to verification via experimentation, one can at least *logically* conceive of an experiment to test them. Contextual effects, however, are in a different ball park from most other social-science findings. There is no conceivable way of contriving an experiment to test them. That should give one pause, for it is far from clear that the limited resources for social-science research should be expended on discovering effects *whose causes can never be experimentally isolated.* Finally, while it is technically possible to detect a generalized contextual effect—indeed, the experiment outlined above could do that—the impossibility of specifying the precise causal force which generates the effect means that contextual analysis is profoundly and fundamentally irrelevant to policy decisions. Any effort to formulate policy on the basis of presumed, *specific* contextual effects is foolhardy, for there is no way of knowing whether the effects are generated by the specific causes one has identified or by one of their confounding correlates.

Occupation is not inherently a contextual variable. Although other considerations enter the picture, one can at least think of detailed occupational groupings as clusters of jobs whose incumbents are mutually substitutable. Thus, it is the similarity in the work required by the jobs forming an occupational group, rather than the similarity in the personal characteristics of their incumbents, which delineates one occupation from another. However, once occupational information is scored with a socioeconomic index like Duncan's, occupation *is turned into a contextual variable.* All of the reservations that one might have about contextual analysis similarly apply to the analysis of occupational information coded in this particular way. One can, of course, *logically* conceive of an experiment to test for the effects of occupation as such; though practically such an experiment might be unfeasible, at least logically one can imagine randomly assigning subjects to occupational groups. But there is no logical way to conduct an experiment about *occupational status*. Duncan's SEI scale includes the education and income levels of *incumbents* as its factors; if one tried to run an experiment on occupations by randomly assigning subjects to occupations, the expected means and variances in their educational and income levels would be identical from one occupation to the next and the occupations would no longer be differentiated according to their socioeconomic status as it is measured by Duncan's scale. In order to keep the Duncan scale scores of the occupations differentiated, one would have to assign relatively more high school graduates and high-income earners to some occupations than to others. Once one has done this, the entire advantage of experimentation is lost and one's experiment would be confounded by every individual level correlate of educational attainment and income. There is just no logically conceivable way to reproduce experimentally any results derived by scoring occupational data with Duncan's scale scores; this fact alone ought to give one pause before using such a scale, particularly in analyses which purport to be causal, rather than merely descriptive in character.

The educational component of Duncan's index strikes us as the most problematical in this regard. Although the income component refers to individuals and to total income, rather than earnings from one's main occupation, one can at least think of this component of Duncan's scale as a characteristic of *jobs* rather than of *people*. To the extent this is so, one could go ahead and make random assignments of persons to posts in an experimental situation without destroying the income differentiation of occupations. But education is another matter: it is attached to people not posts. There is no way around this fact and this component of Duncan's SEI scale indubitably means that its use, both conceptually and practically, serves to reduce "occupation" to a contextual variable. There is more than a little intellectual irony in the fact that perhaps the leading critic of contextual analysis (Hauser, 1970a, 1970b, 1974) is also one of the principal proponents of Duncan's SEI scale (Featherman, Jones, and Hauser, 1975; Featherman and Hauser, 1976). ...

Prestige and Socioeconomic Status as Occupational Indicators

Prestige scores have two distinct advantages and one very definite disadvantage relative to socioeconomic indices in the study of status attainment and related phenomena. The most obvious advantage of prestige scores is that, unlike socioeconomic indices derived from the characteristics of an occupation's incumbents, they do not reduce occupation to a contextual variable. Because prestige scores are *operationally* independent of the characteristics of an occupation's incumbents, one can logically conceive of an experiment in which subjects are randomly allocated to occupations differing in the prestige they are accorded by the general public. Of course, it may well be that the individual characteristics of an occupation's incumbents are a source of its prestige, in which case one consequence of the experiment might be to reduce the between-occupational variance in prestige scores, since occupations would no longer differ in the characteristics of their incumbents. If, however, the socioeconomic characteristics of an occupation's incumbents are merely *correlates* rather than *causes* of an occupation's prestige rating, then no change would be observed in their prestige ratings, a situation which would be obtained if prestige ratings are derived from, say, the desirability of the work performed in an occupation, the authority built into occupational positions regardless of their incumbents, and features of the typical work setting.

Another advantage of using prestige scores in the study of occupational stratification flows from its status as a well-defined analytical concept in stratification theory. Although Featherman and Hauser (1976, p. 404) conclude "that occupational prestige scores represent a congeries of salient dimensions or occupational characteristics," such a definition of occupational prestige has little to do with the concept as it is typically used in stratification theory. We would venture that the appropriate definition of occupational prestige is analytically parallel to Weber's definition of power. In this view, the relative prestige of two occupations may be defined as the expectation that a member of one will give (or receive) deference from a member of the other. The concept of expectation or probability is crucial to this definition, as it also is to Weber's definition of power, for it admits the possibility that some members of an occupation may receive deference from members of another occupation while others will give deference to members of the same occupation. In keeping with this view of the relative prestige of two occupations, we can think of the overall prestige of an occupation as the expectation that one of its members will receive (or give) deference to a randomly selected member of any other occupation.

The foregoing definition of occupational prestige implies that it has both a formal and informal component—a part that is built into an occupation by virtue of its formal authority relations with other occupations and a part that devolves upon an occupation by virtue of the performance of its members in situations which are not organized by authority relations. Prestige, in this view, is not identical with power, but it does represent a significant resource—viz., command over the respect of others—which can be mobilized in the effort to secure desired outcomes in the face of competing alternatives. Whether or not occupational prestige conceived in this way is, in fact, what prestige scales measure is, of course, another question. One advantage of using occupational prestige scales, however, rests precisely on one's ability to raise this question intelligibly. Because one analytically knows what prestige is, one can query whether one has measured it satisfactorily. A parallel question cannot be posed of socioeconomic scales, since as best we can tell the socioeconomic status of an occupation is whatever is measured by a socioeconomic scale of occupations.

But whatever analytical advantage prestige scales of occupational status may have is in large measure undercut by their performance, relative to socioeconomic scales, in empirical research. As we have already noted, whatever it is that socioeconomic scales of occupational status measure more nearly governs the process of intergenerational occupational mobility and the entire process of status attainment than do the occupational differences reflected in prestige scales. This is one very sound reason for preferring the former to the latter, even if one can be less than analytically clear about what it is that socioeconomic scales measure. It is, of course, possible that prestige scales perform poorly because they are inferior measures of the underlying analytical concept. We think a case to that effect could be sketched out, but space does not permit us to do so here.

Notes

[1]. This is because Duncan's SEI scale is constructed from the regression equation

$$\hat{P} = 0.55(E) + 0.59(I) - 6.0,$$

where E is the age-standardized percentage of the male experienced civilian labor force with 4 years of high school or more, and I is the age-standardized percentage of males who had incomes in 1949 of $3500 or more.—ED.

References

Blau, P. M. (1957), "Formal organization: Dimensions of analysis," *American Journal of Sociology* **63**, 58–69.

Blau, P. M. (1960), "Structural effects," *American Sociological Review* **25**, 178–193.

Blau, P. M., and Duncan, O. D. (1967), *The American Occupational Structure*, Wiley, New York.

Cain, G. G. (1974), "Review of *Socioeconomic Background and Achievement* by O. D. Duncan, D. L. Featherman, and B. Duncan," *American Journal of Sociology* **79**, 1497–1509.

Davis, J. A., Spaeth, J. L., and Huson, C. (1961), "A technique for analyzing the effects of group composition," *American Sociological Review* **26**, 215–226.

Duncan, O. D. (1961a), "A socioeconomic index for all occupations," *in* Occupations and Social Status (A. J.

Reiss, Jr. *et al.*, Eds.), pp. 109–138, The Free Press of Glencoe, New York.

Duncan, O. D. (1961b), "Properties and characteristics of the socioeconomic index," *in* Occupations and Social Status (A. J. Reiss, Jr. *et al.*, Eds.), pp. 139–161, The Free Press of Glencoe, New York.

Duncan, O. D., Featherman, D. L., and Duncan, B. (1972), Socioeconomic Background and Achievement, Seminar, New York.

Farkas, G. (1974), "Specification, residuals, and contextual effects," Sociological Methods and Research 2, 333–363.

Featherman, D. L., and Hauser, R. M. (1976), "Prestige or socioeconomic scales in the study of occupational achievement?" Sociological Methods and Research 4, 403–422.

Featherman, D. L., Jones, F. L., and Hauser, R. M. (1975), "Assumptions of social mobility research in the U.S.: The case of occupational status," Social Science Research 4, 329–360.

Hauser, R. M. (1970a), "Context and consex: A cautionary tale," American Journal of Sociology 75, 645–664.

Hauser, R. M. (1970b), "Hauser replies," American Journal of Sociology 76, 517–520.

Hauser, R. M. (1974), "Contextual analysis revisited," Sociological Methods and Research 2, 365–375.

Hauser, R. M., and Featherman, D. L. (1977), The Process of Stratification: Trends and Analyses, Academic Press, New York.

Hodge, R. W. (1970), "Social integration, psychological well-being and their socioeconomic correlates," Sociological Inquiry 40, 182–206.

Siegel, P. M. (1971), Prestige in the American Occupational Structure, unpublished Ph.D. dissertation, University of Chicago Library, Chicago.

Stevens, G., and Featherman, D. L. (1981), "A revised socioeconomic index of occupational status," Social Science Research 10, 364–395.

Tannenbaum, A. S., and Bachman, J. G. (1964), "Structural versus individual effects," American Journal of Sociology 69, 585–595.

Treiman, D. J. (1977), Occupational Prestige in Comparative Perspective, Academic Press, New York.

AAGE B. SØRENSEN

The Basic Concepts of Stratification Research: Class, Status, and Power

Many good things come in three parts—God, Montesquieu's concept of the modern democratic state, and the major dimensions of social structure. All sociology students are told that class, status, and power are the main variables in stratification research. Weber's brief essay, in the English translation entitled "Class, Status, Party" (1946), is probably the closest thing to a universally required text for all sociologists. Most agree that these three variables are what sociologists use when they analyze processes and structures of stratification. Little else is agreed upon. There is wide disagreement about the relative importance of the three variables. There is equally wide disagreement over the concepts behind the variables. This essay attempts to sort out some of these disagreements and, it is hoped, provide some order.

In addition to the disagreements, there is unequal attention to the three variables. Power never has been a frequently used variable in empirical stratification research. It is a slippery concept and a difficult variable to measure. The study of elites is the main research tradition using power in stratification research; other empirical uses of the concept tend to be located in political science or political sociology. The elite studies make assumptions about the distribution of power and then examine only one part of the distribution, the elite. We have no agreed-upon measures that

allow a test of these assumptions about the distribution, and there is surprisingly little attention given in stratification research to characterizing empirically the structure of power in society. Debates about the usefulness of elite studies tend to be debates about untestable assumptions concerning the distribution of power.

To Weber, studies of class and of status are studies of bases of power, in the sense that class or status positions may be seen as resources for affecting the action of others. However, matters are rarely conceived of that way in stratification research. Sociologists study class and status because they are interested in class and status. Marxists especially tend to think of the class structure as the most important thing about social structure from which everything else, including the power structure, derives. The discussions about the validity of this claim occur in debates about the relation between class and the state. These discussions usually take place in political sociology. The main application of the concept of power in stratification research is the frequent use of authority as an element in the concept of class.

I focus in this essay on class and status and survey some of the main distinctions and conceptual properties that dominate the literature and are well represented in the readings. Few concepts in sociology carry as much conceptual baggage as these two. For many sociologists, the choice between concepts of status and class is a fundamental choice between basic assumptions about the nature of society. Indeed, for some, it is a choice

---

This is an original article prepared for this book.

reflecting basic ideological positions. My main conclusion is that the choices are simpler to make and the conceptual baggage less burdensome than many claim. The essay devotes most attention to the concept of class, which is the most complicated and most ambitious concept in the field of stratification, if not in sociology.

Basic Ideas

It is useful to think of distinct levels of status and class concepts. These levels are differentiated by how close the concepts are connected to theories of inequality. Most measures of status seem to capture overall welfare along several dimensions of inequality and have no theory of inequality implied. Not all status concepts are like this. Weber's original idea of status groups captures a one-dimensional concept of prestige or honor with more theoretical implications. In addition to the socioeconomic or welfare concept and the prestige concept of status, I distinguish among three concepts of class. The first one, a "stratum concept" of class, is not unlike socioeconomic status. It is meant to convey the idea of homogeneous groupings along several dimensions of inequality. Like socioeconomic status, the concept provides no theory of how inequality is obtained. The other two, which I call the market or Weberian concept of class and the Marxist concept of class, have theories of inequality attached to them. The Marxist concept also attaches antagonistic interests to class categories, while the Weberian concept is more ambiguous about this.

Theoretical power is related to the empirical requirements of the concept. The Marxist concept makes the most stringent requirements: A Marxist class category may or may not exist depending on whether or not positions in social structure have certain properties; in particular, positions should be associated with interests that are in conflict with the interests associated with other positions. The prestige concept of status also suggests empirical requirements in the form of strategies of exclusion. The socioeconomic status concept and the stratum concept of class make no such requirements; they are purely nominal classifications of people or positions and therefore especially simple to apply in empirical research. A main task for this essay is a critical review of some of the attempts to meet empirical requirements of such concepts, especially the classic Marxist class concept.

For purposes of this review, it is important to distinguish between positions in social structure and persons occupying these positions. This distinction is the main theoretical contribution of sociological theory about inequality—the distinction is, for example, completely absent from economic theory. A structural theory of inequality is one in which inequality is created by relationships between positions. The structural explanation may be complete, as in the Marxist theory of exploitation; or it may be partial with the theory positing an interaction between characteristics of position and characteristics of person. The most obvious examples of a partial explanation are functionalist theories of the Davis and Moore (1945) variety and organizational theories of inequality that emphasize motivational consequences of organizations, such as internal labor markets (e.g., Stinchcombe 1974; Sørensen 1983; Lazear and Rosen 1981).

In the discussion that follows, I detail the most important status and class concepts. I try to show that the basic choices are not between class and status but between concepts that are useful for different types of research tasks. There is more to say about class than about status. The claims about the theoretical power of the class concepts have been greater.

Social Status: Welfare or Honor?

Sociology students are often told that Weber's discussion of status groups is the original source for the concept of status. This is a bit bizarre. Weber did not use the word *status* or *status group*. He used the words *stand* and *ehre,* which most would translate as estate and honor, in describing what these groups were about. We are meant to be brought back to, or reminded of, the world of feudalism and knights. This world was not so far from Wilhelmian Germany as it is from the contemporary United States. In any event, Weber's ideas about this had little to do with the concept of socioeconomic status that produces the standard variable in all of status-attainment research and the standard independent variable in much other sociological research, especially of the survey variety.

Sorokin's discussion of the basic concepts of stratification is a much more accurate point of departure for the concept and variable that dominate modern stratification research under the name "social status." Sorokin (1927) explicitly adopts a spatial metaphor for society with vertical and horizontal dimensions. The vertical or status dimension has three components: economic status, political status, and occupational status. There are distances and movements (in the form of social mobility) along these dimensions. The vertical dimension is a measuring rod put through society to capture what inequality is about; it tells us what is up and what is down and how far up and down people and positions are.

Sorokin's status concept makes it possible to talk meaningfully about directions and distances. Weber's concept of honor does not. The differentiation of honor depends on who differentiates. Peasants are equally dishonorable to lords but unequally honorable to each other. This imbalance is not useful if one wants to measure distances and movements. Sorokin receives less honor than Weber from modern sociologists, so Weber remains the original source of wisdom about status despite the confusion it creates to compare his comments on the topic with the properties of the concept that is most often used in empirical research. This is the concept of socioeconomic status with the properties described by Sorokin.

It would have made more sense to translate *ehre* as prestige. The concepts of prestige employed by, for example, Goode (1978) and Shils (1970) are similar to the relational concept of *ehre*. Prestige as *ehre* is an extremely interesting variable and in certain institutions—academia, the arts, and the military—an extremely important variable. It is a concept with more theoretical implications than the concept of socioeconomic status. High prestige causes deference, and low prestige causes contempt. Prestige groups practice exclusion or closure, for example with respect to marriage. If prestige groups are to be equated

with Weber's status groups, they must be seen as discrete groupings.

Prestige groups should be identified empirically by demonstrating practices of exclusion or closure. Not all occupational groups or categories of people with similar levels of socioeconomic status necessarily practice such explicit exclusion. Therefore, the identification of prestige groups poses the same type of empirical problems as the empirical identification of the higher-level class concepts, as discussed later. There is some theoretical work on the issue of closure and exclusion (Parkin 1979). Unfortunately, the measurement of prestige and the empirical identification of prestige groups are neglected because of the conceptual confusion created by a misleading translation of Weber and the neglect of Sorokin. The best work on the topic is qualitative (e.g., Goode 1978; Shils 1970).

Empirical research on prestige was derailed also because the concept was contaminated by loose usage in empirical practices. With the arrival of modern survey techniques, it became possible to have national samples rank occupations from one to five according to labels ranging from "excellent" to "poor." This was said to measure the prestige of occupations. However, the occupational ratings do not measure prestige in the sense of honor or deference. There is empirical evidence for this claim. Goldthorpe and Hope (1974) directly asked respondents about what they had in mind when rating occupations. They responded that they thought about things such as income, education, job security, and the like that enter into people's ideas of a good job. Thus, respondents seem to rate occupations according to the general level of welfare that they provide incumbents. The second piece of evidence is that it does not matter much who does the ratings. This is one of the most well established findings in all of sociology. Occupations are rated about the same by all, at all times, and wherever these occupations are found.[1] What is measured by occupational prestige is not a relational concept.

Duncan (1961) used the occupational prestige ratings to generate an index of socioeconomic status. The procedure is simple: For the subset of occupations for which ratings exist, regress the ratings of occupations on aggregate characteristics of those who occupy these occupations. (Duncan used income and education of incumbents.) Then use the regression equation to derive scores for all occupations. The result is called the Socioeconomic Index (SEI). Since SEI is based on occupational prestige scores, it can be seen as an approximation to such scores, with the degree of approximation reflecting the quality of the prediction. Although the approximation is generally quite good, for some occupations the SEI and occupational prestige scores differ, most notably for farmers. Farmers have low income and low formal education but are rated higher than other occupations with the same level of income and education. This may be the result of Americans' nostalgia for a rural past, or it may simply mean that Americans carry around images of farmers that overstate their true income and schooling. Featherman and Hauser (1976) find that SEI explains more variance in status-attainment models than occupational prestige measures, and they conclude from this that SEI is the better measure. This is really a conclusion about how best to measure the socioeconomic status of farmers; it has nothing to do with the difference between the concept of prestige as *ehre* and the concept of socioeconomic status.

Socioeconomic status and occupational prestige are characteristics of occupations. Older American sociology (Warner et al. 1949; Hollingshead and Redlick 1958) constructed measures of the socioeconomic status of persons using indexes based on education, occupation, type of residence, source of income, and other individual attributes. These synthetic measures of the socioeconomic status of persons should perform even better than the occupational-level socioeconomic status measure when the issue is to predict individual behavior, such as voting, deviance, school performance of children, and so forth.

Socioeconomic status measured at the level of occupation nevertheless remains the favorite independent variable in research on all kinds of individual behaviors and attitudes, probably because of the ease with which the measure is obtained. Much has been made of the difference between status, measured at the level of occupation, and class. It is claimed that the use of status assumes that the occupational structure is more fundamental than the class structure (Wright 1979). However, the relative merit of seeing occupations as the basic dimension of social structure has nothing to do with the usefulness of socioeconomic status in empirical research. It is research practice, not theory, that conflates socioeconomic status and occupation. One might equally well have a socioeconomic status measure based on the ranking of class categories.

Class

Most sociologists recognize that the concept of class is among our most important concepts. It is perhaps the most influential formulation of the central idea of sociology—that is, the idea of a social structure. Some claim the concept has a status as gravity does in physics. The analogy is imperfect: Physics without a concept of gravity is impossible, but some pursue sociology without ever employing the term *class* and claim the concept is not needed. Further, those who employ the term use it to denote quite different concepts. This is an expression of the well-known disagreements about what are the central ideas of sociology.

In much of modern sociology, class has come to mean nothing more than a homogeneous categorical grouping of social positions in contrast to the gradation provided by socioeconomic status. An explicit formulation of this emphasis on social homogeneity can be found in Geiger (1951) and Carlsson (1958). It appears to have been decisive for the formulation of the class scheme proposed by Goldthorpe (see Goldthorpe [1984] for an elaboration of the rationale). The difference, if any, between such a *stratum concept of class* and the welfare or socioeconomic concept of social status is the emphasis on the resources that are responsible for a person's welfare rather than the welfare dimensions themselves. This approach usually results in a class scheme that is not completely ordered as socioeconomic status is. A good example is Goldthorpe's class scheme (1987). Such stratum class schemes may be very useful in empirical research. They are nominal categories that do not imply theories of inequality. I concentrate on Marxist or market concepts of class that do imply positional theories of inequality, in particular theories of exploitation.

Marxist Concept of Class

The core of the Marxist concept is a theory of exploitation that explains inequality between classes and the resulting antagonistic interests that generate conflict. Unfortunately, this theory has certain defects, and the concept cannot account for an important part of the inequality we observe—the inequality generated in the labor market. In this section, I first elaborate these points and then show that the defects perhaps can be overcome by identifying the circumstances when market mechanisms produce a form of inequality in which the advantages of some are obtained at the disadvantage of others.

In Marx's own analysis, the ability of one party to become better off at the expense of another is conferred by ownership of the means of production. The two components of ownership—authority and legal ownership—are the means to establish the exploitative relationship. It is the exploitative relationship that defines classes. If there are ways other than ownership of property to maintain a relationship of exploitation, classes presumably would be created.

Exploitation takes place in a social relationship without regard to who occupies this relationship. Capitalists exploit workers because the logic of capitalist production forces them to do so, not because they are evil or conservative or white males. Smart capitalists are no better at exploiting than dumb capitalists. Smart capitalists may get higher profits, but the relation between profits and the rate of exploitation is very complicated. Marx demonstrates this at great length in volume three of *Capital*. Class relations that are relations of exploitation create inequality independently of the personal characteristics of those who occupy class positions. Class positions are "empty places" (Simmel 1908). This is of fundamental importance for the relation between the class structure and the structure of inequality. Only by changing the class structure can the structure of inequality be changed. Therefore, class conflict will produce social change.

This does not mean that Marx did not recognize sources of inequality other than class. He describes but does not analyze inequality in the labor market by education, skills, and ability. These are all inequalities associated with personal characteristics and not with class positions. According to Marx, many inequalities will disappear with the advance of capitalism as the working class becomes more homogeneous. The inequalities caused by effort and ability will continue into socialism. These inequalities are less important for Marx. No tinkering with the structure of society will remove them.

Since exploitation is rooted in positions, class positions become associated with antagonistic interests. Those in positions to exploit wish to preserve their ability to obtain advantage; those being exploited want to destroy the relationship that creates their disadvantage. The model includes a scenario, called the formation of revolutionary class consciousness, describing how the "structural" interests are translated into collective action. The stages are class awareness, class conflict, class struggle, and eventually the destruction of the relationships that define classes.

To Marx, exploitation in capitalist society is created in the employment relationship, but he pays no systematic attention to variation in employment relationships that would form classes within the employed labor force. In fact, I argue later that Marx probably conceived of only one type of employment relationship, at least in advanced capitalism. This is the employment relationship conceived of in classical and neoclassical economics. Regardless of whether the original exploitation theory is valid, it is of little assistance in providing a structural theory of inequality among positions that are jobs. The Marxist concept is useless for analyzing inequality and conflict within the labor market as opposed to the inequality and conflict between capitalists and workers.

There is an even more important theoretical problem. It was Marx's great discovery that voluntary employment relationships create involuntary exploitation of one party by the other. The exploitation comes about by the appropriation by the capitalist of surplus value created by the worker. This assumes the validity of the labor theory of value. Unfortunately, this theory has been abandoned by everyone.[2] The labor theory of value generates a set of relationships among unobservables. It has great appeal as a claim of injustice but no appeal as an economic theory.

Abandoning the labor theory of value removes the basis for the whole theory of inequality and social change, unless some other concept of exploitation can be developed to explain inequality associated with class positions. This other concept should also make empirical requirements that can be met in analysis of labor market structures. The next section considers if the market power concept can provide such an alternative.

Class and Market Power

The Weberian concept of class as market power appears to provide a straightforward rationale for why classes create inequality. In light of the difficulties with the Marxist concept, it is understandable why the market power concept is appealing.

In the Weberian conception, classes are people with similar command over economic resources. The market creates inequality, and class is a proxy for variables that cause inequality in the market, such as occupation, skill, and property. Weberian classes group people according to their resources and their access to resources for obtaining welfare and well-being in the market, but class relations are usually not seen as the direct cause of inequality. Market mechanisms are responsible.

It is presumably to be expected that the market concept will identify positions in social structure associated with interests in preserving advantages and removing disadvantages caused by occupancy of these positions. However, since advantages and disadvantages are created in the market, the realizations of interests by different groups are not necessarily interdependent. In the market the advantage of some does not necessarily reduce the advantage of others. This will only happen when advantage is based on a mechanism of exploitation in the market. Identifying such a mechanism of exploitation is needed for the market concept to be useful in specifying class categories that are conflict groups rather than simply strata.

Roemer's (1982) reformulation of the Marxist exploitation idea is a useful starting point for such an effort. The basic idea is quite simple: Inequality in productive assets will produce exploitation in a market economy with private property and trade. Those with superior assets will need to work less to obtain the same level of welfare as those with inferior assets. If the superior assets were divided among the disadvantaged, they would be better off. Defining classes by absence and presence of property and by amount of property produces a class scheme correlating perfectly with the amount of exploitation.

Roemer's concept of exploitation creates a class concept in which inequalities among classes are created in the market. They are produced by returns to productive assets traded in the market. This market concept of class makes the theory consistent with modern economics. However, the development of the theory relies mainly on the consequences of returns to alienable productive assets—that is, physical property. Here the problem is to define a type of exploitation based on properties of positions in the labor market. This is not a matter dealt with extensively by Roemer (1982). Indeed, he does not emphasize the distinction between people and positions.

It is possible to derive some insights into the exploitation-creating properties of jobs by conceiving of exploitation as generated by economic rent. This seems consistent with Roemer's formulation. Returns on productive assets are payments for use of factors of production. It is important to note that there are two types of productive assets: assets in inherently fixed supply and "normal" assets in variable supply. In the case of normal assets, an increase in return or pay for their use will generate a corresponding increase in the supply of such assets. The increase in supply will then reduce returns to the level obtained for other factors of production. In the long run, therefore, such assets do not create the type of inequality in which the welfare of those possessing the asset is obtained at the expense of those not possessing the asset. All assets will tend to provide the same return, and these returns in turn compensate for the consumption forgone when making the investment. The advantage of some caused by the return on their investments will not reduce the advantage of others.

However, some assets, such as fertile land and superior ability, may be in fixed supply. These assets create a "rent"—a payment that is in addition to the one needed to employ the assets. They produce advantages that are not Pareto-optimal. Those individuals not obtaining the rent are worse off than they would have been without the rent payments to those owning the assets in fixed supply. Roemer's idea of exploitation is consistent with inequalities created by rent-generating assets. These assets will satisfy his test for exploitation. The test is that dividing the assets among owners and nonowners will make the nonowners better off.[3]

To create a positional theory of inequality in the labor market, it is therefore necessary to search for rent-generating assets attached to employment positions. These assets will provide an advantage to the incumbent of the position not available to those not in the position. I show later that many employment positions, including some treated by recent scholars as class categories in the labor market, do not form class positions. In fact, not even all forms of rents generated in employment relationships will create class positions.

Class Formation

While the market power concept of class does identify a source of antagonistic interests in certain labor market structures, exploitation does not unavoidably create the conditions in which latent antagonistic interests result in manifest collective action. Indeed, Roemer (1988) shows that exploitation in the abstract may produce a number of paradoxical consequences. The class formation analyses of Giddens (1973), Parkin (1979), and Goldthorpe (1987) are useful for the identification of the conditions that make exploitation produce class action.

Class formation analysis relies on a simple theory of the formation of collective action. The theory is that persons with the same location in the class structure might realize over time their common interests and form class movements. This is a Durkheimian theory of mechanical solidarity emphasizing similarity and time together. If the boundaries between classes are relatively rigid, class incumbents may come to identify with their

class and act in its behalf. Therefore, the study of mobility patterns becomes a major vehicle for the identification of social classes that might become actors in changing social structure. This is an approach already suggested by Weber's remarks on the matter (Weber 1968). Although there are other sources of "class structuration" (Giddens 1973), such as residential segregation, the analysis of mobility processes represents the best-known empirical example of the class formation perspective.

The class formation approach assumes that some theory explains why classes are unequal and why they have antagonistic interests. While silent on the nature of this theory, it adds an important requirement to the definition of positions that create class categories. Incumbency in these positions must have some permanency over time. Thus, to identify class categories within the employed part of the labor force, we need to know the stability of the employment relationships that create the corresponding job categories. This dimension of employment relationships is the major focus in the remainder of this essay.

In conclusion, exploitation among groups within the labor market has been argued to derive from rent-generating properties of jobs. The mere existence of exploitation is not sufficient for the formation of classes. The class formation perspective suggests identifying properties of jobs generating stable interests and stable membership.

Employment Relationships and Class Properties of Jobs

In this section, I briefly survey the properties of jobs that generate economic rents and stable membership and then ask if some of the proposals for defining class categories in the labor market satisfy these necessary conditions.

Jobs are defined by employment relationships. They form (often implicit) contracts between employer and employee about the execution of certain tasks in return for payment over a period of time. It is useful to characterize employment relations according to who typically has the initiative in terminating the contract. The result is a continuum ranging from employment relationships that are completely *open* (the employer will dismiss the worker whenever a better worker is available for the job) to those that are *closed* (the worker typically has the initiative and therefore high job security). For an elaboration of the distinction and the arguments for when open and closed jobs are likely to emerge, see Sørensen (1983) and Sørensen and Kalleberg (1981).

Open and Closed Relationships

Open employment relationships, of course, assume the employer knows that a different worker can do the job better and that there are no significant costs in dismissing the incumbent. They are assumed in the basic price theory applied to competitive labor markets that constitutes neoclassical economic theory of wage rates. In this scenario, wage rates are a function of individual productivity; equally productive persons should, except for short-term disequilibria, obtain the same wage.

Open employment relationships define jobs that do not satisfy the requirement of permanency needed to create class categories within the labor market. They are of considerable interest anyway. First, they establish a baseline for determining positional sources of inequality. This baseline is the market or competitive wage. Second, in the present context, it is of interest to note that Marx saw open employment relations as being typical of advanced capitalism.

Marx saw the essence of capitalist society in the treatment of labor as a commodity, purchased and sold on the market in the manner of other commodities. This is the very scenario assumed in neoclassical economic theory of the labor market. Such a theory was not available to Marx. Marginalism had not yet been invented. Further, the question of how different prices of labor are created in the labor market apparently was of little interest to him. Thus, we find nowhere in Marx an analysis of wage inequalities similar to the analysis presented by John Stuart Mill. There is, however, nothing to suggest that Marx would not have accepted the now-standard theory about this wage structure. In particular, Marx's analysis

of the dynamics of capitalist society predicts the development of a labor market satisfying the assumptions made in neoclassical labor economics. As Roemer puts it: "The neoclassical model of the competitive economy is not a bad place for Marxists to start their study of idealized capitalism" (Roemer 1988, 196).

This view of Marx's "theory" of the labor market of course implies that Marxist theory will be the same as neoclassical theory in conceptualizing income differences among the employed. There will be no subclasses created in the labor market, consistent with the basic homogenization thesis of Karl Marx. The dynamics of capitalism will destroy those deviating employment relationships that survive from earlier modes of production, such as artisans. With this perspective, the emiseration thesis is not a prediction of wage equality. It is a prediction of a uniform labor market with no positional advantages but with inequality due to skill and ability that will remain also into socialism and only disappear with the ultimate compensating differentials introduced by communism.

It should be noted that open employment relationships may generate economic rents. Scarce and unusual abilities may command a rent so that the person with the rare ability has an advantage obtained at the expense of the welfare of others. Others might be better off if the scarce ability was equally distributed. This does not create classes. Abilities are attributes of people and not of positions, and no reorganization of labor market structures will change the distribution of innate and unique talents.

Skills acquired through training and experience create inequality, but they do not necessarily command rents. The main economic theory about the acquisition of skills—human capital theory—argues that training is undertaken at a cost and results in skills that increase the pay for the individual. Training will only be undertaken if the returns equal the costs. If returns exceed costs, more workers will seek training, thereby lowering the returns on skills. Therefore, in equilibrium, differentials caused by skills exactly compensate for training costs. The cumulated lifetime earnings of people with unequal skills will be equal, except for the variation due to compensating differentials, to effort, and to ability and other resources that affect training costs (such as family background). Skills of general usefulness in the labor market will produce cross-sectional inequality. However, when returns on training equal costs of training, skills do not generate rents and therefore cannot be a basis for exploitation.

Skills may generate rents if training opportunities are in fixed, limited supply because of restrictions of admissions to schools and apprenticeships. This will create an advantage that is a rent. It will be a higher return on the skill than would be necessary to bring about training for the skill. There are numerous examples of situations in which this seems to occur: the training for medical doctors; for most crafts and other skilled occupations; and for artisans and other self-employed occupations typical of the petit bourgeoisie. However, in open employment relations, these rents do not create class categories within the labor market. Open jobs do not provide the needed permanency. Furthermore—regardless of whether skills are rent-generating—they are not properties of positions.[4] The advantages produced outside the labor market seem difficult to maintain unless the advantaged group also can restrict access to the employment of these skills or their substitutes.

Closed employment relationships satisfy the requirement of permanency. Furthermore, closed employment creates the positions that have the potential of providing advantages that may be obtained independently of the productivity of persons. However, only when the resulting job rewards systematically differ from the competitive wage over some period of time will these properties be class properties.

There is a considerable literature on the causes of closed employment relationships. Specific on-the-job training, financed by the employer (Becker 1964), and transaction costs (Williamson 1975) are among the most important causes. These explanations suggest that closed employment may be more efficient than open employment in certain production technologies. If this is so, closed employment does not create rents and therefore does not create the bases for separate classes within the labor market.

If training opportunities are rationed and employment relationships closed, economic rents

should emerge. It is indeed in such job structures that collective action to preserve positional advantage has been more successful. The resulting social organizations, such as craft unions, are particularly important when the use of credentials is underwritten by the state in the form of licensing. This is also the case for professions, such as medicine and law, in which the restriction on employment opportunities is not at the level of a job but at the level of the occupation. It is important to note that a measure of skill level, such as educational attainment, is not in itself informative as to whether skills are rent-generating or not. We need information on the actual rationing of training opportunities.[5] This makes many proposals to define "new" classes by skills and education of quite dubious validity.

Classes in Internal Labor Markets

The use of authority and the use of incentives are properties of closed employment relationships that are solutions to the main problem for the employer involved: the problem of how to match wage rates and productivity, especially effort, in the absence of open competition. Both solutions have been used to justify the emergence of class categories within the labor market. What follows is a brief evaluation of a recent proposal to use authority and incentive structures to define class categories within the labor market.

Authority relations are an inherent part of the employment relationship. Marx emphasizes the importance of authority for employment contracts: That is, when workers sell their labor power, they also sell control over their own activities.[6] Indeed, authority is often identified as the basis for the formation of class categories (Dahrendorf 1959; Wright 1979), and among many sociologists of the labor market, authority has become the defining characteristic of "class" (Kalleberg and Berg 1987).

The class schemes using authority relations to define classes often do not provide a rationale in terms of exploitation mechanisms. It is possible, for example, that Dahrendorf's scheme (1959) may be justified by a justice theory of exploitation, but the theory is not presented. It is difficult to provide a rationale in terms of an economic theory of exploitation. Wright (1985) suggests that there is an advantage accruing to authority that derives from having control over the organization of production. The organization itself is seen as a productive asset, and authority becomes a measure of the asset. This approach is not convincing. The asset of organization is not in fixed supply and therefore does not necessarily generate rents. Further, those in authority in an organization do not "own" the organization of production; they execute it. Finally, authority is not a measure of the value of the asset—of the productive effectiveness of an organizational arrangement. It is difficult, without an incentive argument, to formulate a convincing theory for why those with authority should have higher wages than those who produce. Wright does not try.

Incentive systems provide a way of reducing the costs of exercising authority, in particular, the cost of wages to supervisors. Two such incentive systems have been suggested to create class categories. In "efficiency wage theory" (see, e.g., Akerlof and Yellen 1986), the argument is that paying above-market wages creates an incentive for high performance. Wright (1979) suggests the existence of such a "loyalty" wage for his class category of "semiautonomous employees." However, the efficiency wage increases the productivity of the worker. It therefore need not deviate from the competitive wage, that is, the wage obtained in the open labor market by the worker exercising the same level of effort. The efficiency wage is a solution to the possible inefficiency caused by closed employment relationships. If the solution works, there are no positional advantages caused by efficiency wages.

Promotion systems in internal labor markets are another important solution to the incentive problems created by closed employment relations. It is a common and old idea among sociologists (Weber 1968; Stinchcombe 1974) that promotion schemes can be important for generating effort. In promotion schemes, inequality in the cross section clearly is associated with occupancy of positions. The question is whether the advantages and disadvantages associated with positions constitute rents and therefore represent exploitation.

It is important to consider the career implications of the promotion scheme. The job ladders create an upward-sloping career trajectory. To the extent that the age slope in productivity is lower than the slope in wages, older workers will be paid more than their productivity would justify in a different job structure. If firms maximize profits, they should attempt to equalize total wages paid over the career to the overall productivity of the worker. Younger workers, therefore, will be paid less than their productivity would justify elsewhere.

The implications of this scenario for positional advantages and interests are straightforward but perhaps surprising. For the duration of the employment contract, the overall outcome may well be that there is no advantage in lifetime income of entering an internal labor market. In other words, access to an internal labor market does not necessarily provide a positional advantage that is a rent.[7] The situation is much the same as the one predicted by human capital theory for the returns to training, where the inequality observed in the cross section also misinforms about the overall advantage.

This leaves the use of rationed skills and credentials in matching persons to closed jobs as the main source of positional advantages that can form class categories within the labor market. There is nothing surprising in the proposition that closed skilled jobs for which training opportunities are rationed will form the main example of such categories. These are the positions that form the traditional basis of craft unions and professional organizations. Nevertheless, in recent work on the labor market, scholars employing class analysis strangely ignore these categories.

Conclusion

The general argument has been that the choice of basic concepts in stratification research is a question of balancing theoretical power and specificity with empirical requirements of concepts. The Marxist class concept is the most powerful, but it is also the most unsatisfactory concept for analyzing inequality and conflict within the large majority of the population of modern industrialized societies. The stratum concept of class and the concept of socioeconomic status pose the fewest empirical requirements. They are also least informative about the causes and consequences of inequality.

Some analysts see the choice between class and status concepts as a fundamental one. Certain class concepts indeed make stronger theoretical claims than the socioeconomic status concepts (which basically make none). Unless one believes that Marxist theory explains everything, this does not mean class concepts are more useful. It depends on what is being studied. The Marxist class concept and the market concept may be useful for studies of political processes and social movements, since they make claims about the sources of conflict and social change. However, in studies of attainment and in analyses that predict behavior or attitudes from the level of welfare obtained by individuals, the Marxist or market concepts of class are less useful than socioeconomic status. These class categories often are more heterogeneous than socioeconomic status categories. Further, since SEI and related measures form continuous variables, socioeconomic status is very convenient for use in the estimation of individual linear regression models. The stratum concept of class also emphasizes homogeneity, yet the discrete form may make it an awkward variable to use in attainment studies. Nevertheless, this discrete form may make it especially useful when the emphasis is on certain outcomes, as in mobility research, or when it is desired to study the consequences that changes in industrial structure have for the distribution of welfare.

I have tried to show that an economic theory of rent can be used to identify class categories that have the potential to form class actors. The Weberian idea of prestige or status groups also makes the claim that such groups practice exclusion. This suggests that status groups establish strategies to protect an advantage that is threatened because it is obtained at the expense of others. The market concept of class, therefore, may be seen as a latent basis for status groups consistent with Weber's discussion. There is one difficulty. It has been argued that market-generated class categories form around rents and property, whereas status groups presumably are about

honor or prestige. The transition from rents to honor needs analysis.

The controversies in sociology over the last twenty years have surrounded the choice of basic concepts with a minefield of ideological and epistemological connotations. This confusion has not been useful for research and theoretical development. The main message of this essay is to treat the basic concepts as tools useful for some purposes but not for every purpose.

Notes

I am indebted to Patricia Chang, Liah Greenfeld, Annemette Sørensen, and Jesper B. Sørensen for valuable comments and suggestions.

1. There are, of course, some variations, but they are relatively minor. A comprehensive treatment is provided by Treiman (1977).

2. The start of the demise of the Marxist labor theory of value is usually attributed to the German economist Eugene von Böhm-Bahwerk a hundred years ago. The history of the debate has been reviewed by many: See, for example, Gordon (1990) for a review that includes the attempt by so-called analytical Marxists (e.g., G. A. Cohen, Jon Elster, and John Roemer) to revise the basis for Marxist theory.

3. It is important to note that cross-sectional inequality, in my opinion, does not necessarily provide evidence for exploitation. When some individuals have higher income because of the returns they receive on earlier investments, they are being compensated for consumption forgone when making the investment. Those who do not receive the return, because they did not make the investment, would obviously gladly share in the returns. However, they should then also "pay back" the added gratification they received when choosing consumption over investment. This hypothetical exchange would only be advantageous to those owning assets when these assets are in fixed supply and rents are extracted. The need to consider lifetime incomes when identifying exploitation becomes important for my criticism later of recent formulations of class concepts within the labor market.

4. Roemer (1982) does not provide a discussion of this implication of human capital theory in his formulation of "skill assets" as a basis for exploitation. In fact, he does not present a precise definition of skills. In one place he seems to refer to any type of endowment that leads to unequal productivity (1982, 111); in another he

explicitly states, "Let us treat skills as embodied and innate" (1982, 24). Only the latter should generate rents. Wright (1985) uses the former interpretation and therefore confuses returns with rents. Wright does attempt to make skills a property of positions by defining "skill requirements" of jobs.

5. Wright (1985) violates this principle by operationalizing skill assets as levels of educational attainment. He identifies what he calls skill requirements of positions in an attempt to implement Roemer's notion of exploitation based on skill assets. However, the concept of skill requirements does not distinguish between skills that generate true rents and those for which the income payoff is merely compensation for training costs.

6. The importance attached to authority in Marxist theory seems to contradict the argument presented previously that Marx would have accepted the neoclassical scenario for the labor market in which authority has no role. There is no doubt that Marx thought that the authority exercised by capitalists was important for the creation of classes. However, the importance of authority derives from Marx's belief in the labor theory of value. This theory implies that the wage paid to the worker is independent of his productivity—it represents the cost of reproducing the worker. Therefore, the amount of surplus generated will depend on how much work the employer extracts from the labor purchased. However, if the labor theory of value is abandoned, the need for authority disappears. In the open employment relationships assumed in modern marginal productivity theory, workers are paid according to their productivity, including their effort. As a result, effort is of no concern to the firm. Workers who do not work hard are simply paid less than workers who work hard.

7. Internal labor markets also create other problems for class analysis; see Sørensen (1991) for a discussion.

References

Akerlof, George A., and Janet L. Yellen. 1986. "Introduction." Pp. 1–21 in George A. Akerlof and Janet L. Yellen, eds., *Efficiency Wage Models of the Labor Market*. New York: Cambridge University Press.

Becker, Gary S. 1964. *Human Capital*. New York: National Bureau of Economic Research.

Carlsson, Gösta. 1958. *Social Mobility and Class Structure*. Lund: C.W.K. Gleerup.

Dahrendorf, Ralf. 1959. *Class and Class Conflict in Industrialized Society*. Stanford: Stanford University Press.

Davis, Kingsley, and Wilbert E. Moore. 1945. "Some Principles of Stratification." *American Sociological Review* 10:242–249.

Duncan, Otis D. 1961. "A Socioeconomic Index for All Occupations." Pp. 109–138 in A. J. Reiss, Jr., ed., *Occupations and Social Status*. New York: Free Press.

Featherman, David L., and Robert M. Hauser. 1976. "Prestige or Socioeconomic Scales in the Study of Occupational Achievement." *Sociological Methods and Research* 4:402–422.

Geiger, Theodor. 1951. *Soziale Umschichtungen in einer dänischer Mittelstadt*. Vol. 23 of *Acta Jutlandica*. Aarhus, Denmark: University of Aarhus.

Giddens, Anthony. 1973. *The Class Structure of Advanced Societies*. New York: Harper & Row.

Goldthorpe, John H. 1984. "Social Mobility and Class Formation: On the Renewal of a Tradition in Sociological Inquiry." CASMIN-Projekt. Institut für Sozialwissenschaften. Universität Mannheim.

———. 1987. *Social Class and Mobility in Modern Britain*. 2d ed. Oxford: Clarendon Press.

Goldthorpe, John H., and Keith Hope. 1974. *The Social Grading of Occupations: A New Approach and Scale*. Oxford: Clarendon Press.

Goode, William J. 1978. *The Celebration of Heroes: Prestige as a Control System*. Berkeley: University of California Press.

Gordon, David. 1990. *Resurrecting Marx: The Analytical Marxists on Freedom, Exploitation, and Justice*. New Brunswick, N.J.: Transaction Books.

Hollingshead, August B., and Frederick C. Redlick. 1958. *Social Class and Mental Illness: A Community Study*. New York: Wiley.

Kalleberg, Arne L., and Ivar Berg. 1987. *Work and Industry: Structures, Markets, and Processes*. New York: Plenum.

Lazear, Edward P., and Sherwin Rosen. 1981. "Rank-Order Tournaments as Optimum Labor Contracts." *Journal of Political Economy* 89 (2):841–864.

Parkin, Frank. 1979. *Marxism and Class Theory: A Bourgeois Critique*. New York: Columbia University Press.

Roemer, John E. 1982. *A General Theory of Exploitation and Class*. Cambridge, Mass.: Harvard University Press.

———. 1988. "Should Marxists Be Interested in Exploitation?" Pp. 260–282 in John E. Roemer, ed., *Analytical Marxism*. New York: Cambridge University Press.

Shils, Edward A. 1970. "Deference." Pp. 420–448 in Edward O. Laumann, Paul M. Siegel, and Robert W. Hodge, eds., *The Logic of Social Hierarchies*. Chicago: Markham.

Simmel, Georg. 1908. *Soziologie*. Leipzig: Duncker and C. Humblot.

Sørensen, Aage B. 1983. "Processes of Allocation to Open and Closed Positions in Social Structure." *Zeitschrift für Soziologie* 12 (July): 203–224.

———. 1991. "On the Usefulness of Class Analysis in Research on Social Mobility and Socioeconomic Inequality." *Acta Sociologica* 34:71–87.

Sørensen, Aage B., and Arne L. Kalleberg. 1981. "An Outline of a Theory of the Matching of Persons to Jobs." Pp. 49–74 in Ivar Berg, ed., *Sociological Perspectives on Labor Markets*. New York: Academic Press.

Sorokin, Pitirim. 1927. *Social Mobility*. New York: Harper & Bros.

Stinchcombe, Arthur L. 1974. *Creating Efficient Industrial Administrations*. New York: Academic Press.

Treiman, Donald J. 1977. *Occupational Prestige in Comparative Perspective*. New York: Academic Press.

Warner, W. Lloyd, Marchia Meeker, and Kenneth Eells. 1949. *Social Class in America*. New York: Science Research Associates.

Weber, Max. 1946. "Class, Status, and Party." Pp. 180–195 in Hans H. Gerth and C. Wright Mills, eds., *From Max Weber*. London: Routledge.

———. 1968. *Economy and Society*. New York: Bedminster Press.

Williamson, Oliver E. 1975. *Markets and Hierarchies: Analysis and Antitrust Implications*. New York: Free Press.

Wright, Erik O. 1979. *Class Structure and Income Determination*. New York: Academic Press.

———. 1985. *Classes*. London: Verso.

Part IV
Generating Stratification

Social Mobility
Classical Viewpoints
Modern Analyses

Status and Income Attainment
Basic Models
Social Psychological Models

The "New Structuralism"

Social Mobility

▶ CLASSICAL VIEWPOINTS

PITIRIM A. SOROKIN

Social and Cultural Mobility

Conception of Social Mobility and Its Forms

By social mobility is understood any transition of an individual or social object or value—anything that has been created or modified by human activity—from one social position to another. There are two principal types of social mobility, *horizontal* and *vertical*. By horizontal social mobility or shifting, is meant the transition of an individual or social object from one social group to another situated on the same level. Transitions of individuals, as from the Baptist to the Methodist religious group, from one citizenship to another, from one family (as a husband or wife) to another by divorce and remarriage, from one factory to another in the same occupational status, are all instances of social mobility. So too are transitions of social objects, the radio, automobile, fashion, Communism, Darwin's theory, within the same social stratum, as from Iowa to California, or from any one place to another. In all these cases, "shifting" may take place without any noticeable change of the social position of an individual or social object in the vertical direction. By *vertical* social mobility is meant the relations involved in a transition of an individual (or a social object)

from one social stratum to another. According to the direction of the transition there are two types of vertical social mobility: *ascending* and *descending,* or *social climbing* and *social sinking.* According to the nature of the stratification, there are ascending and descending currents of economic, political, and occupational mobility, not to mention other less important types. The ascending currents exist in two principal forms: as an *infiltration* of the individuals of a lower stratum into an existing higher one; and as a *creation of a new group by such individuals, and the insertion of such a group into a higher stratum instead of, or side by side with, the existing groups of this stratum.* Correspondingly, the descending current has also two principal forms: the first consists in a dropping of individuals from a higher social position into an existing lower one, without a degradation or disintegration of the higher group to which they belonged; the second is manifested in *a degradation of a social group as a whole, in an abasement of its rank among other groups, or in its disintegration as a social unit.* The first case of "sinking" reminds one of an individual falling from a ship; the second of the sinking of the ship itself with all on board, or of the ship as a wreck breaking itself to pieces. ...

Immobile and Mobile Types of Stratified Societies

Theoretically, there may be a stratified society in which the vertical social mobility is nil. This means that within it there is no ascending or descending, no circulation of its members; that every individual is forever attached to the social stratum in which he was born; that the membranes or hymens which separate one stratum from another are absolutely impenetrable, and do not have any "holes" through which, nor any stairs and elevators with which, the dwellers of the different strata may pass from one floor to another. *Such a type of stratification may be styled as absolutely closed, rigid, impenetrable, or immobile.* The opposite theoretical type of the inner structure of the stratification of the same height and profile is that in which the vertical mobility is very intensive and general; here the membranes between the strata are very thin and have the largest holes to pass from one floor to another. Therefore, though the social building is as stratified as the immobile one, nevertheless, the dwellers of its different strata are continually changing; they do not stay a very long time in the same "social story," and with the help of the largest staircases and elevators are *en masse* moving "up and down." *Such a type of social stratification may be styled open, plastic, penetrable, or mobile.* Between these two extreme types there may be many middle or intermediary types of stratification. ...

General Principles of Vertical Mobility

As far as the corresponding historical and other materials permit seeing, in the field of vertical mobility there seems to be no definite perpetual trend toward either an increase or a decrease of the intensiveness and generality of mobility. This is proposed as valid for the history of a country, for that of a large social body, and, finally, for the history of mankind.

In these dynamic times, with the triumph of the electoral system, with the industrial revolution, and especially a revolution in transportation, this proposition may appear strange and improbable. The dynamism of our epoch stimulates

the belief that history has tended and will tend in the future toward a perpetual and "eternal" increase of vertical mobility. There is no need to say that many social thinkers have such an opinion.[1] And yet, if its bases and reasons are investigated it may be seen that they are far from convincing.

In the first place, the partisans of the acceleration and increase of mobility used to point out that in modern societies there are no juridical and religious obstacles to circulation, which existed in a caste—or in a feudal society. Granting for a moment that this statement is true, the answer is: first of all, it is impossible to infer an "eternal historical tendency" on the basis of an experience only of some 130 years; this is too short a period, beside the course of thousands of years of human history, to be a solid basis for the assertion of the existence of a perpetual trend. In the second place, even within this period of 130 years, the trend has not been manifested clearly throughout the greater part of mankind. Within the large social aggregates of Asia and Africa, the situation is still indefinite; the caste-system is still alive in India; in Tibet and Mongolia, in Manchuria and China, among the natives of many other countries, there has been either no alteration of the situation or only such as had happened many times before. In the light of these considerations reference to feudalism compared with the "free" modern times loses a great deal of its significance.

Grant that the removal of the juridical and religious obstacles tended to increase mobility. Even this may be questioned. It would have been valid if, in place of the removed obstacles, there were not introduced some other ones. In fact, such new obstacles were introduced. If in a caste-society it is rarely possible to be noble unless born from a noble family, it is possible nevertheless to be noble and privileged without being wealthy; in the present society it is possible to be noble without being born in a prominent family; but, as a general rule, it is necessary to be wealthy.[2] One obstacle gone, another has taken its place. In theory, in the United States of America, every citizen may become the President of the United States. In fact, 99.9 per cent of the citizens have as little chance of doing it as 99.9 per cent of the subjects of a monarchy have of becoming a monarch. One kind of obstacle removed, others have been estab-

lished. By this is meant that the abolition of obstacles to an intensive vertical circulation, common in caste-society and feudal society, did not
mean an absolute decrease of the obstacles, but
only a substitution of one sort of impediment for
another. And it is not yet known what kind of obstacles—the old or the new—is more efficient in
restraining social circulation. ...

Occupational Dispersion and Recruitment

*In present Western societies different occupational
groups are strongly interwoven, and the cleavages
between them are considerably obliterated, or, more
accurately, are somewhat indefinite and not clearly
cut.* Indeed, since one son of a family is an unskilled laborer, another a business man, and the
third a physician, it is not easy to decide to what
group such a family belongs. On the other hand,
since the offspring of the same family or of many
families of the same occupational status enter the
most different occupations, the cleavages between
occupations are thereby considerably obliterated,
their "strangeness" toward each other is weakened; their social heterogeneity and repulsion diminished. As a result, the precipice between occupational groups becomes less than it is in a society
where such dispersion of the children of fathers
who belong to the same occupation does not take
place, or is a very rare phenomenon. This means
that there is a fallacy in the statement of many
theorizers of class struggle who continue to talk
about the present social classes as though they
were still a kind of caste. They forget completely
about the fluid composition of present occupational groups. However, a part of the truth is in
their statement. What is it? The answer is given in
the next propositions.

*In spite of the above-shown dispersion among
different occupations, the "hereditary" transmission of occupation still exists, and, on the average, it
is still high enough. It is likely also that the fathers'
occupation is still entered by the children in a
greater proportion than any other.* This means that
a part of the population, during one or two or
more generations, still remains in a régime like a
caste-system. Shall we wonder, therefore, that this
part has habits, traditions, standards, mores, psychology, and behavior similar to that of a caste-
society? Shall we wonder that the cleavages between such "rigid" parts of each occupation are
quite clearly cut—economically, socially, mentally, morally, and even biologically? Under specific conditions, such a part of the population
may give a real basis for the existence of a class
psychology and class antagonisms. To this extent
the partisans of the class struggle may have a reason for their theory and aspirations. As an illustration of this, the following fact may be mentioned. Among the German proletariat, the
narrow-proletarian psychology and ideology—in
the form of social-democratic and communist affiliations—have existed principally among those
who have been "hereditary proletarians" or used
to remain within this class throughout their life.[3]
The same may be said of any "hereditary and
non-shifting part" of any occupation.

The next basis for the aspirations of partisans
of class theories is given by the fact which may be
generalized as follows: *The closer the affinity between occupations, the more intensive among them
is mutual interchange of their members; and,* vice
versa, *the greater the difference between occupations the less is the number of individuals who shift
from one group to another.* Since such is the case, it
is natural that there are cleavages not so much between occupational groups in the narrow sense of
the word, as between bigger social subdivisions
going on along the lines of the "affine" and "non-
affine" occupational subdivisions. In a class composed totally of the affine occupational groups,
e.g., of different groups of unskilled and semi-
skilled labor, there appears and exists a community of interests, habits, morals, traditions, and
ideologies considerably different from those of
another class composed totally of other affine occupational groups, *e.g.,* of different professional
and business groups. These differences, being reinforced by differences in the economic status of
such classes, create a basis for what is styled as the
present class-differentiation, with its satellites in
the form of the class antagonisms and class friction. Thus far the partisans of the class struggle
may have a basis for their activity and propa-
ganda. ...

Mobility Facilitates Atomization and Diffusion of Solidarity and Antagonisms

In an immobile society the social solidarity of its members is concentrated within the social box to which they belong. It rarely surpasses its limits because the social contact of an individual with the members of other different "boxes" is very weak and rare. Under such conditions the members of different boxes are likely to be strangers or to be in quite neutral relations. But within each box the ties of solidarity of its members are most intensive; for the same reason that the solidarity of the members of an old-fashioned family is strong. They have a complete understanding and a complete community of interests, or a complete like-mindedness, elaborated in the closest face-to-face contacts throughout a life span. The same may be said of hatred and antagonisms. All these socio-psychical phenomena are "localized" within and "centered" around a definite social box. In a mobile social body a "delocalization," and "atomization," and diffusion tend to take place. Since an individual belongs to different social groups and shifts from one box to another, his "area" of solidarity is not limited within one box. It becomes larger. It involves many individuals of different boxes. It ceases to "concentrate" within one box. It becomes "individualized" and selects not "boxes" but persons, or social atoms. The same may be said of the attitudes of hatred and antagonism. At the same time the phenomena of solidarity and antagonism are likely to lose their intensiveness. They become colder and more moderate. The reason for this is at hand: an individual now is not secluded for life in his box. He stays for a shorter time within each box; his face-to-face contacts with the members of each social group become shorter, the number of persons with whom he "lives together," more numerous: he becomes like a polygamist who is not obliged and does not invest all his love in one wife, but divides it among many women. Under such conditions, the attachment becomes less hot; the intensiveness of feeling, less concentrated.

In the social field this calls forth two important changes. In the first place, the map of solidarity and antagonisms within any mobile society becomes more complex and curved than in an immobile one. It is relatively clear in an immobile society. It goes along the lines separating one caste, order, or clear-cut stratum from another. The vertical and horizontal trenches are in general simple and conspicuous. In periods of social struggle, slaves fight with slaves against masters; serfs against their lords; plebeians, against patricians; peasants, against landlords. Much more complex is the map of solidarity and antagonism in a mobile society. Since the boxes are less clearly cut off from each other, and since each of them is filled by a fluid population from different strata, the lines of solidarity and antagonism become more whimsical, and assume the most fanciful character. During the World War the citizens of the United States showed a considerable difference in their attitudes toward the belligerent countries. Anglo-Saxon, French, and Slavic citizens sympathized with the Allies; the German-Americans, with the Central Powers. The unity of the citizenship did not prevent this splitting. If, further, is taken into consideration the difference in religion, political aspiration, economic and occupational status, the lines of solidarity and antagonism for and against the War appear to be most fanciful. People of the same nationality, or of the same religion, or occupational status, or economic status, or children of the same family, very often happen to be in opposite factions.

In the second place, the lines of solidarity and antagonism in a mobile society become more flexible and more changeable. A man, who yesterday was an antagonist of a definite measure, to-day becomes its partisan because his social position has been changed. Shifting from one social position to another calls forth a similar shifting of interests and solidarity. Fluidity of social groups facilitates the same result. Therefore, it is not strange when we see that yesterday's foes are to-day's friends. The group, which last year was an enemy to be exterminated, to-day turns out an ally. In the contemporary interrelations of groups and whole countries this flexibility of the map of solidarity and antagonism is conspicuous. ...

Mobility Favors an Increase of Individualism Followed by a Vague Cosmopolitanism and Collectivism

Mobility facilitates an increase of individualism because it destroys this "seclusion for life in one social box" typical of an immobile society. When a man is for life attached to his "box," a knowledge of the box is enough to know the characteristics of the man. On the other hand, the man feels himself not so much as a particular personality, but only as a cell or a component of the group to which he belongs.[4] Under such conditions, the "boxes" but not the individuals are the social atoms or units. When the "boxes" are less definite and rigid, when their population is fluid, when an individual passes from position to position and often belongs to several overlapping groups, his attachment to the box becomes less intensive; his characteristics cannot be decided through his temporary position; in order to know him one must take him as an individual and study his personality. This participation in many groups, shifting from one group to another, and impossibility of identification with any one group makes an individual something separate from a social box; awakens his personality, transforms him from the component of a group to an individual person. As he is shifting from group to group, he now must secure rights and privileges for himself, not for a specific group, because he himself does not know in what group he will be to-morrow. Hence the "Declaration of the Rights of Men" but not that of a group. Hence the demands of liberty of speech, religion, freedom, self-realization for a *man*, but not for a group. Hence the equality of all individuals before law; and individual responsibility instead of that of a group, as is the case in an immobile society. A mobile society inevitably must "invest" all rights and responsibilities in an individual but not in a group. .,.

Complete social isolation or loneliness is unbearable for the majority of people. It has been mentioned that mobility facilitates such an isolation. Detached from an intimate oneness with any group, losing even family shelter against loneliness, modern individuals try by every means to attach themselves to some social body to avoid their isolation. And the more the family is disintegrated, the stronger is this need. Some enter labor and occupational unions; some try to fight their isolation through an affiliation with political parties; some, through a participation in different societies, clubs, churches; some through a mad rush from one dancing hall to another. Some try to belong at once to many and often opposite groups. All these "collectivist tendencies" are nothing but the other side of individualism and isolation, created by mobility. They are attempts to substitute for the previous lost "boxes" something similar to them. To some extent all these unions, clubs, societies, and so forth, serve this purpose. But only to some extent. Shifting does not permit one to attach himself to such groups strongly. Hence arise the trends to go further in this direction. This trend is conspicuously manifested in the social schemes of Communists, revolutionary syndicalists, and guild socialists. They contemplate a complete engulfment of an individual within the commune, or syndicate, or a restored guild. They unintentionally try to reëstablish "the lost paradise" of an immobile society, and to make an individual again only a "finger of the hand" of a social body. The greater is the loneliness, the more urgent the need. I fear, however, that until social mobility is diminished, such attempts, even being realized, cannot give what is expected of them. In the best case they may create a kind of a compulsory "social box" which will be felt to be a prison by its members. In conditions of social mobility such a cell will be destroyed by its prisoners. In order to realize the program it is necessary to diminish the mobility. If we are entering such a period, then in some form these schemes may be realized. Are we entering one? I cannot confidently say. Some symptoms are in favor of such an hypothesis. But they are not quite clear as yet; the topic is too big to be discussed briefly, and the writer too much likes the mobile type of society to prophesy its funeral; therefore, he prefers to finish the discussion right here. Whatever may happen in the future, our mobile period is far from ended. And if our aristocracy would try to be a real aristocracy, strong in its rights and duties, creative in its achievements, less sensual in its proclivities and free from parasitism; if it would raise its fecundity; if the channels of climbing are open to every talent among the lower strata; if the machinery of social testing and selection is properly reorganized; if the lower strata are raised to levels as high as possible; and if we are not permeated by the ideologies of false sentimentality and "humanitarian impotency," then the chances for a long and *brilliant* existence of present mobile societies are great and high. Let history do what it has to do; and let us do what we ought to do without wavering and hesitation.

Notes

1. See, *e.g.*, Fahlbeck, "Les classes sociales"; "La noblesse de Suede"; "La décadence et la chute des peuples," in *Bull. de l'Inst. Int. de Stat.*, Vols. XII, XV, and XVIII; D'Aeth, F. G., "Present Tendencies of Class Differentiation," *The Sociological Review*, pp. 269–272 et seq., 1910.

2. Such is the condition necessary for a man to be included in the American "Social Register."

3. See Lurie, *Sostav Proletariata*, p. 9; see also the series "Auslese und Anpassung der Arbeiterschaft," *Schriften des Vereins für Sozialpolitik.*

4. Durkheim, E., *La division du travail social,* and Bouglé, Charles, "Revue générale des théories récentes sur la division du travail," *L'Année sociologique*, Vol. VI; Palant, *Les antinomies entre l'individu et société, passim.*

SEYMOUR MARTIN LIPSET, REINHARD BENDIX, AND HANS L. ZETTERBERG

Social Mobility in Industrial Society

Widespread social mobility has been a concomitant of industrialization and a basic characteristic of modern industrial society. In every industrial country, a large proportion of the population has had to find occupations considerably different from those of their parents. During the nineteenth century, the proportion of the labor force in urban occupations increased rapidly, while the proportion in agriculture decreased.

In the twentieth century the West has been characterized by a rapid growth of trade and of service industries, as well as of bureaucracy in industry and government; more people have become employed in white-collar work, and the comparative size of the rural population has declined even more rapidly than before.[1] These changes in the distribution of occupations from generation to generation mean that no industrial society can be viewed as closed or static.

This apparently simple statement runs counter to widely held impressions concerning the different social structures of American and Western European societies. According to these impressions, America has an "open society" with considerable social mobility, but the countries of Western Europe (specifically England, France, Italy, Germany, the Low Countries, and the Scandinavian nations) have societies that are "closed," in the sense that the children of workers are forced to remain in the social position of their parents. This judgment reflects earlier European beliefs. In the age of the French Revolution, America appeared to be a land free from traditional institutions and historical legacies: the country of the future, Hegel called it, where each man was master of his fate just as American democracy itself was the product of human reason. This notion has been reiterated in many analyses, all contrasting American and European societies.

For the most part these discussions deal with the differences between democratic and autocratic institutions; but they also express assumptions about contrasting patterns of social mobility. Sometimes the political and social aspects of the contrast between America and Europe have been linked as cause and effect: differences in political institutions and values have been cited as evidence for the assertion that the society of America is "open," those of Europe "closed"; and the supposedly greater rate of social mobility in American society has been viewed as a major reason for the success of American democracy. For example, some fifty years ago Werner Sombart referred to the opportunities abundant in America as the major reason why American workers rejected the Marxist view that there is little opportunity under capitalism, while European workers accepted it because their opportunities were more restricted.[2] Such judgments as Sombart's were, however, no more than inferences based on the general contrast between the American tradition which proclaimed the goal of opportunity for all and the European emphasis upon social stability and class differences.[3] For as a matter of fact, it is not really clear whether the different political orientation of the American and European worker reflects different opportunities for social mobility or only a difference in their ethos!

The questions implicit in these alternative interpretations can be answered today with somewhat more assurance than was possible even two decades ago because of recent research in social mobility. In this chapter we attempt to summarize the findings available for a number of countries. Since our object is to assemble a large amount of empirical evidence, it will be useful to state at the outset that *the overall pattern of social mobility appears to be much the same in the industrial societies of various Western countries.* This is startling—even if we discount the mistaken efforts to explain differences in political institutions by reference to different degrees of social mobility in the United States and in Western Europe. Further, although it is clear that social mobility is related in many ways to the economic expansion of industrial societies, it is at least doubtful that the rates of mobility and of expansion are correlated. Since a number of the countries for which we have data have had different rates of economic expansion but show comparable rates of social mobility, our tentative interpretation is that the social mobility of societies becomes relatively high once their industrialization, and hence their economic expansion, reaches a certain level.

Occupational Mobility

Before World War II, studies of social mobility were usually limited to investigations of the social origins of different occupational groups, employees of single factories, or inhabitants of single communities. Since World War II there have been at least fifteen different national surveys in eleven countries which have secured from representative samples of the population information that relates the occupations of the respondents to the occupations of their fathers. In addition, there have been a number of studies conducted in different cities of various countries. Taken together, these investigations permit the comparison of current variations in occupational mobility, as well as some estimate of differences during the past half century.

To make such comparisons and estimates is difficult. Few of the studies were made with the intention of facilitating the comparison of findings in different countries. Many of them employ systems of classifying occupations which cannot be compared with each other and the questions concerning the occupations of respondents and fathers are seldom similar. In order to use the results for a comparative analysis, we have reduced the occupational categories for most countries to the closest approximation of manual, nonmanual, and farm occupations. In presenting these materials, we make the assumption that a move from manual to nonmanual employment constitutes upward mobility among *males*. ...

The lack of comparable classifications in nationwide surveys of social mobility makes it difficult to [reach] more than general impressions. Moreover, we must bear in mind that we deal here exclusively with a single index to complex and quite diverse societies, so that inferences can carry us only part of the way and should be made with caution. Yet, the value of a comparative approach to social mobility becomes apparent when we set side by side for each country the figures which are most clearly indicative of upward, downward, and total mobility across the line between the middle and the working class (table 1). Because of the varying systems of occupational classification the Italian figures cannot be compared with any of the others, and the British and Danish figures can be compared only with each other. The remainder, however, are reasonably comparable.

The figures in the first column give the proportion of all sons of manual workers who now occupy middle-class positions. In the second column the figures indicate the proportion of all sons of middle-class fathers who are now in manual occupations. In order to get some index of the total mobility in society, the figures in the third column were computed: out of all the sons of fathers in urban occupations who are themselves in urban occupations, those who were mobile in either direction were added together, and this figure was expressed as a percentage of the total. For example, of those persons in the nonfarm population of the United States who were sons of fathers in nonfarm occupations, 30 per cent had either fallen into a manual position from their fathers' nonmanual position, or had risen from their fathers' working-class occupation into a middle-class one. Though this is, to be sure, a very crude index, it should give a rough indication of the fluidity of the urban occupational structure. It expresses the proportion of the native urban population which has, in one way or another, "changed class."

The first impression one gains from table 1 is that all the countries studied are characterized by a high degree of mobility. From one generation to another, a quarter to a third of the nonfarm population moves from working class to middle class or vice versa. Second, there is among the first six countries a high degree of similarity in this total mobility rate. The total range is between 23 and 31 per cent, and five of the six countries (United States, Germany, Sweden, Japan, France) range between 27 and 31 per cent. Such narrow differences lead quickly to one interpretation: total mo-

bility rates in these countries are practically the same.

This similarity does not hold, of course, if the relationship between parental occupations and sons' occupations are compared in terms either of upward or of downward mobility, rather than the total amount of mobility. Then it appears that there is considerable variation among countries in the degree to which a father's occupation is an asset or a handicap. Thus, we see that the sons of middle-class fathers are more likely to fall in status in the United States and Germany than they are in Japan, France, or Switzerland. There is less variation in the degree to which a working-class family background handicaps a man in securing a nonmanual position; only Switzerland stands out as permitting higher rates of upward movement than the other countries. Given the variations in the methods of collecting data, it would be premature to place much reliance on these differences. ...

Mobility Trends and Social Structure

Several different processes inherent in all modern social structures have a direct effect on the rate of social mobility, and help account for the similarities in rates in different countries: (1) changes in the number of available vacancies; (2) different rates of fertility; (3) changes in the rank accorded to occupations; (4) changes in the number of inheritable status-positions; and (5) changes in the legal restrictions pertaining to potential opportunities.

By examining the relationship between these features of the social structure and the trends of mobility in different countries, we may be able to account for the similarities and differences among these trends.

1. The number of vacancies in a given stratum is not always, or even usually, constant. For example, in every industrialized or industrializing country, the increase in the proportion of professional, official, managerial, and white-collar positions and the decline in the proportion of unskilled-labor jobs creates a surge of mobility, which is upward—provided these positions retain their relative standing and income. More and

TABLE 1

Comparative Indices of Upward and Downward Mobility (percentages)

NONFARM POPULATIONS

Country	Upward mobility (Nonmanual sons of manual fathers)	Downward mobility (Manual sons of nonmanual fathers)	Total vertical mobility (Nonfarm population mobile across the line between working and middle class)
United States[a]	33	26	30
Germany[b]	29	32	31
Sweden	31	24	29
Japan	36	22	27
France	39	20	27
Switzerland	45	13	23

POPULATIONS WITH RURAL AND URBAN OCCUPATIONS CLASSIFIED TOGETHER[a]

Country	High prestige occupation sons of fathers in low prestige occupations	Low prestige occupation sons of fathers in high prestige occupations	Proportion mobile across high and low occupation prestige lines
Denmark	22	44	31
Great Britain	20	49	29
Italy	8	34	16

SOURCES—UNITED STATES: Average of three studies [Natalie Rogoff, "Jobs and Occupations," *Opinion News*, September 1 (1947): 3–33; Survey Research Center, University of Michigan, 1952 Presidential Election Survey; R. Centers, "Occupational Mobility of Urban Occupational Strata," *American Sociological Review*, 13 (1948): 203]. GERMANY: Average of three studies [Erich Reigratski, *Soziale Verflechtungen in der Bundesrepublik* (Tubingen: Mohr-Siebeck, 1956); Institut für Demoskopie, Allensbach, Germany; DIVO, Frankfurt A.M.]. SWEDEN: Data collected by H.L. Zetterberg, partly reported in "Sveriges fem rangrullor," *Vecko-Journalen*, 48 (1957): 40. JAPAN: Research Committee on Stratification and Social Mobility of The Japanese Sociological Association, *Social Stratification and Mobility* (Tokyo: 1956, mimeographed), p. 13. FRANCE: M. Bresard, "Mobilité sociale et dimension de la famille," *Population*, 5 (1950): 553–566. SWITZERLAND: Recalculated from information supplied by Professor Roger Girod. DENMARK: Computed from data furnished by Professor K. Svalastoga, Copenhagen, Denmark. GREAT BRITAIN: Calculated from David V. Glass, *Social Mobility in Britain* (London: Routledge and Kegan Paul, 1954). ITALY: L. Livi, "Sur la mesure de la mobilité sociale," *Population*, 5 (1950): 65–76.

[a]Occupations of high prestige are high levels of nonmanual occupations and farm owners, except in the high-prestige data for Italy, which include all nonmanual occupations and well-to-do peasants. Occupations of low prestige include routine nonmanual occupations, manual occupations, and farm occupations, except the low-prestige data for Italy, which include only manual occupations (including farm workers) and poor peasants.

more people are needed to manage industry, to distribute goods, to provide personal services, and to run the ever-growing state bureaucracy. A comparison of the ratio of administrative (white-collar) to production (manual) workers in manufacturing industries over the last half-century in the United States, the United Kingdom, and Sweden shows that the correspondence in trends is very great. Thus, in the United States in 1899 there were 8 administrative employees per 100 production workers, in 1947 there were 22 administrative employees per 100 production workers, and in 1957 there were 30 administrative employees per 100 production workers.[4] The corresponding rise in Britain between 1907 and 1948 is from 9 to 20 administrative employees per 100 production workers, and in Sweden the number rose from 7 to 21 between 1915 and 1950. In none of these countries did the proportion of those self-employed in urban occupations decline.

2. An important determinant of upward mobility is the difference in rates of fertility. In all industrialized countries for which we have data, fertility tends to vary inversely with income.[5] Although changes in the economic structure are increasing the proportion of persons engaged in high-level occupations, the families of men who are now in such occupations are not contributing their proportionate share of the population. Consequently, even if every son of a high-status father were to retain that status, there would still be room for others to rise.

A similar consideration also applies to the process of urbanization. In all industrialized countries the urban centers continue to grow, requiring migrants to fill new positions or to replace urbanites, who characteristically fail to reproduce themselves. Although the urban birth rate is below reproduction level, the proportion of the population living in large cities (100,000 and over) grew in England from 26 per cent in 1871 to 38 per cent in 1951; in Germany from 5 per cent in 1870 to 27 per cent in 1950; in France, from 9 per cent in 1870 to 17 per cent in 1946; and in the United States from 11 per cent in 1870 to 30 per cent in 1950. And, as [shown elsewhere],[6] the process of migration into urban areas permits a large proportion of the sons of workers who grow up in metropolitan centers to fill the newly created or demographically vacated middle-class positions, while the manual jobs left open are filled by migrants from small towns or rural areas.

3. In our rapidly changing world some positions lose, some gain, prestige. Thus, a person can be mobile in the eyes of society without changing his job. Admittedly, most of these losses or gains are barely noticeable within one generation. For example, a rating of twenty-five occupations made in 1925 was compared with a rating made in 1947, and a correlation of .97 was obtained, indicating practically no change.[7] However, another study of the same period has indicated that government positions in the United States have enhanced their prestige since the 'twenties.[8] Moreover, the addition of new occupations may sometimes inadvertently alter the prestige of certain ranks; for example, the emergence of the occupation of airplane pilot during the last generation served to deglamorize such occupations as ship captain and locomotive engineer. And significant changes in a given profession such as were effected in those of physicist, mathematician, and others by the atomic research programs during World War II, are also likely to better—or to lower—its prestige. However, we do not have studies with which to test such guesses.

4. In modern social structures there is a relative decline in the number of inheritable positions.[9] Many middle-class fathers in salaried positions have little to give their children except a good education and motivation to obtain a high-status position. If for any reason, such as the early death of the father or family instability, a middle-class child does not complete his higher education, he is obviously in a poorer position, in terms of prospective employment, than the son of a manual worker who completes college. Clearly, some of the children of the middle class are so handicapped, others simply do not have the ability to complete college or to get along in a bureaucratic hierarchy, and many of these fall into a status below that of their fathers. Whatever the reason, persons of middle-class origin who fall in status leave room for others of lower-class background to rise.

The importance of this factor is emphasized by the sharp increase in the educational level among the working classes. No nation approaches the

United States in terms of the number of university students who come from the working class. Even sons of working-class Negroes in the United States are more likely to go to college than sons of European workers.[10] The effect of the difference in university attendance among workers on the two continents, of course, is reduced by the fact that higher education is a more certain way of achieving a privileged position in Europe than in the United States.

5. Many earlier legal restrictions upon the right of a person to create a new and higher occupational status for himself have been removed. The abolition of the guild system is the classic example of this. All the countries we have discussed in this chapter have legal guarantees of the freedom of occupational choice. A peculiar consequence of such guarantees is the phenomenon of "increased upward mobility" during depressions. In these periods many manual workers are fired and cannot find jobs in their normal occupations. To survive, many of them become small entrepreneurs and, thus, according to the conventional classification, move upward on the social ladder. ...

The Consequences of Social Mobility

Although it appears, then, that the *amount* of social mobility is largely determined by the more or less uniform structural changes of industrialized societies and is therefore much the same in all such societies, it should be emphasized that the *consequences* of that mobility have been most diverse. To take an extreme example: if a Negro in South Africa obtains a nonmanual position, he is a ready candidate for leadership in a movement of radical protest. But if a white American from a working-class family makes the same move, he usually becomes politically and socially conservative. Perhaps the most important key to an explanation of such varying consequences of mobility across the line between manual and nonmanual occupations, is the concept of *status discrepancies.* Every society may be thought of as comprising a number of separate hierarchies—e.g., social, economic, educational, ethnic, etc.—each of which has its own status structure, its own conditions for the attainment of a position of prestige within

that structure. There are likely to be a number of discrepancies among the positions in the different hierarchies that every person occupies simultaneously, for, as Georg Simmel pointed out, every person maintains a unique pattern of group affiliations. Mobility merely adds to these discrepancies by creating or accentuating combinations of a high position in one rank and a low one in another; for example, a high position in an occupation combined with a low ethnic status, or a high position in the social-class hierarchy (based on the status of people with whom one associates) combined with a low income.

The few analyses of the psychological dimension of this problem that have been made indicate that status discrepancies may cause difficulties in personal adjustment because high self-evaluations in one sphere of life conflict with low ones in another. Durkheim, for example, suggested that both upward and downward mobility result in increased suicide rates by increasing the number of persons who find themselves in an *anomic* situation, one in which they do not know how to react to the norms involved.[11] Studies of mental illness have suggested that people moving up in America are more likely to have mental breakdowns than the nonmobile.[12]

Since it is primary-group relations which give individuals the psychic support which "protects" them against suicide and mental illness, the hypotheses developed by Janowitz and Curtis on the social consequences of occupational mobility may help explain the above findings. They suggest that social mobility is likely to have disruptive consequences on primary group structures, such as family, clique, and friendships, but that the integration of secondary group structures is less likely to be influenced. They further suggest that primary group strains will be greatest for extreme upward-mobile and downward-mobile families and least for stable and moderately upward-mobile families; greater for intra-generational than for inter-generational mobility.[13]

Of greater interest in the present context are studies which focus attention upon structural sources of status discrepancies, rather than upon the psychological adjustment to the experiences which typically result from these discrepancies. For example, in a society in which there is a

TABLE 2

Party Choice of German, Finnish, Swedish, and American Middle-Class Men Related to Their Social Origin

Country and party choice	Father's occupation					
	Manual		Nonmanual		Farm	
	Per cent	Number in sample	Per cent	Number in sample	Per cent	Number in sample
Germany: 1953						
Social Democratic.........	32	200	20	142	22	58
Finland: 1949						
Social Democratic and						
Communist.............	23	357	6	356	10	183
Sweden: 1950						
Social Democratic.........	47	135	20	315	..	..
Norway: 1957						
Labor and Communist.....	49	61	29	73	24	46
United States: 1952						
Democratic..............	22	67	30	79	34	59

SOURCES: The German data are from a study made by UNESCO Institute at Cologne, Germany; the Finnish data were supplied by Dr. Erik Allerdt and were collected by the Finnish Gallup Poll; the Swedish data are from H. L. Zetterberg, "Overages Erlander?" *Vecko-Journalen,* 48 (1957): 18 and 36; the Norwegian figures are recomputed from data provided by the Oslo Institute for Social Research; the American data are from material supplied by the Survey Research Center of the University of Michigan.

marked difference between the consumption patterns of the working class and the middle class, status discrepancies are more likely to arise from occupational mobility than in societies in which the consumption patterns of workers and middle-class persons are similar.[14] Unfortunately, only in the field of political values do we have comparative data on the differential consequences of social mobility. The data derived from a number of European and American studies (table 2) indicate that in America the successfully mobile members of the middle class are more conservative (that is, more often Republican) than those class members who are in a social position comparable to that of their parents. In Germany, Finland, Norway, and Sweden, on the other hand, the former group is more radical (that is, more often Social Democratic or Communist).

The data from these five countries suggest that individuals moving up occupationally in Northern Europe where shifts from one class to another require major adjustments in living style are more likely than comparably successful Americans to retain links to their class of origin. In the United States there is also presumably less concern with

personal background in much of the middle class, and more likelihood that the successful individual need only change his residential neighborhood to bring his economic and his social status into line. These findings seem related to variations in the working-class vote. In Germany and Sweden, the skilled workers are more radical than the semi- and unskilled; in America, Britain, and Australia, the skilled workers are more conservative.[15] This leads us to the hypothesis that skilled workers experience more status rejection in these North European countries, so that their higher economic status results in frustrations, while the other countries mentioned may give the highly paid skilled worker more real opportunities to aspire to middle-class status. The differences between the working- and middle-class styles of life may also be an important factor, since in America it is presumably easier to take on middle-class consumption patterns. A suggestive indication that the retention of working-class political values by upward-mobile persons is related to other working-class elements in their style of life, is indicated by the following data (see table 3) from Sweden: white-collar workers who have risen from work-

TABLE 3

Relationship Between Social Origin, Consumption Patterns, and Voting Behavior Among Men in Sweden
(percentages)

Voting	Manual from manual homes		Nonmanual from manual homes		Nonmanual from nonmanual homes	
	Without car	With car	Without car	With car	Without car	With car
Non-Socialist.........	15	14	38	74	79	83
Socialist..............	85	86	63	26	21	17
Number in sample.....	221	72	78	55	170	145

SOURCE: From H. L. Zetterberg, "Overages Erlander?"

ing-class backgrounds will generally continue to vote for the working-class party unless they change their style of consumption (symbolized here by the automobile); on assuming a middle-class consumption pattern, they also adopt the voting pattern of the middle class.

This attempt to interpret what little data we have on the consequences of upward mobility in different cultures rests on the unproven assumption that in Europe men who move up in the economic hierarchy find it difficult to adjust to the life style of higher levels, while in the United States men can more easily fulfill the requirements of the social position that corresponds to their economic success. ...

Ideological Equalitarianism

The data presented in the preceding [section] raise questions about the validity of the widely-accepted belief that the United States is *the* land of opportunity. Yet how can we account for the persistence of the assumption that in this country the position of an individual's family is less likely to determine his social and economic destiny than in Europe? And how is this image related to patterns of social mobility? ...

We can only speculate when we attempt to assess the effects of the absence of a feudal past in America. Clearly it has not meant the absence of status distinctions—which have frequently been every bit as invidious, though more surrepti-

tiously introduced, on this side of the Atlantic as on the other. But it has led to, among other things, an ideological equalitarianism, which is not any the less important because it has been contradicted on every side by the existence of status differences. No act is perhaps as symbolic of this ideology as Thomas Jefferson's order to have a round table replace the rectangular one at the White House because this would relieve him of the necessity of stipulating the order of precedence at official receptions. This act was not a denial of the existing differences in rank and authority; it was rather a testimony to the belief that these were the accidental, not the essential, attributes of man. Among men of equal worth it is not in good taste to insist on the accidental distinctions which divide them.

Such ideological equalitarianism has played, and continues to play, an important role in facilitating social mobility in the United States. It enables the person of humble birth to regard upward mobility as attainable for himself, or for his children. It facilitates his acceptance as a social equal if he succeeds in rising economically. It mitigates the emotional distance between persons of different social rank. And it fosters in any existing elite the persuasion (however mistaken this may be) that its eminence is the result of individual effort, and hence temporary. The point to emphasize is, not that these beliefs are often contradicted by the experience of those who hold them, but that this equalitarian ideology has persisted in the face of facts which contradict it. We would suggest that the absence of hereditary aristocracy has done much to foster this persistence. Americans have rarely been exposed to persons whose conduct displays a belief in an inherited and God-given superiority and also demands that others demonstrate (by deferential behavior) their recognition of this superiority.

The existence of ideological equalitarianism in the United States is generally acknowledged, but interpretations of its significance vary widely. One of these interpretations holds that this ideology is a delusion which must be dispelled by presenting the people with the hard facts of status differences. Accordingly, W. Lloyd Warner has called for systematic, explicit training to combat half-knowledge and confused emotions, in order that the adult student will learn "what he needs to know about our status order, how it operates, how he fits into the system, and what he should do to improve his position or make his present one more tolerable."[16] Whatever may be said of the usefulness of such studies, we find it difficult to believe that significant numbers of Americans are not aware of the existence of status differences. We doubt that instruction of the kind envisaged by Warner will have any notable effect upon the belief in equal opportunity. All the available evidence points, rather, to the fact that people continue to believe in the "equalitarianism" of American society despite their daily familiarity with economic inequality and status distinctions.

Another interpretation of ideological equalitarianism takes a much more optimistic view. In his great work on the American Negro, Gunnar Myrdal has pictured the dilemma which arises for every white American out of the profound contradiction between the theory of equal rights and the practice of racial segregation.[17] In the actions prompted by this deep moral conflict Myrdal sees the lever that can be used to bring about progressive social change. This too we find difficult to accept. It is our belief that *this* approach overemphasizes the urgency of a moral conflict. We would not deny that the conflict is present and that it has often led the way from equalitarian theory to equalitarian practice. Indeed, this conflict and its resultant social agitation is a mainspring of the American liberal tradition. Yet the available evidence indicates that the development of both the theory and the practice of "equalitarianism" among the white majority has been aided by the continued presence of large, ethnically segregated castes. That is, one of the reasons why the belief in this system has been sustained is because opportunities to rise socially and economically have been available to "majority-Americans," and a disproportionate share of poverty, unemployment, sickness and all forms of deprivation have fallen to the lot of minority groups, especially fifteen million Negro Americans.

Our own interpretation of "ideological equalitarianism" differs from these overpessimistic or overoptimistic views. We think that the equalitarianism of manners is not merely a matter of belief, but a reality: differences in status and power have no great effect upon the casual social contacts which set the tone of everyday human relations. This is linked to the fact that these differences have not been elaborated ideologically as they have in Europe. Surely this has not diminished these differences of status and power, but it has helped to prevent the ideological hardening of interest- and status-groups, so that the representation of collective interests is a thing apart from the intellectual life of the country. As a result, Americans frequently think of the differences of status and power, not as being what they really are, but rather as differences in the distribution of material goods. This well-known materialism of American society can also be thought of as an ideology—an ideology which purports to measure men by the single yardstick of material success. As such it is unlike the class and status ideologies of Europe; it involves instead quite an idealistic belief in equality, for all the differences in material status which it accentuates.

Such ideological equalitarianism implies an ideal which is best expressed by the familiar phrase, "equality of opportunity." It is conceivable that a people might adhere to such an ideal for some time even in the face of declining opportunities for occupational advancement. Some of the evidence concerning the response to the experience of the Great Depression suggests that the traditional belief in America as the land of opportunity imparted to people a spirit of resilience which helped to sustain them through great adversity.[18] However, it is our guess that *a sharp and lasting decline* in the opportunities for occupational advancement would jeopardize these beliefs and lead to a change in the system of values. Such a decline has not yet occurred.

Notes

1. See Colin Clark, *The Conditions of Economic Progress*, 3d ed. (London: Macmillan, 1957), pp. 490–520.

2. Werner Sombart, *Warum gibt es in den Vereinigten Staaten keinen Sozialismus?* (Tuebingen: J. C. B. Mohr, 1906), p. 135.

3. It may be noted, however, that Sombart also emphasized the subjective factor: "Consideration should also be given to the mere awareness of the worker that he could become an independent farmer at any time. This consciousness was bound to give the American worker a feeling of security and peace of mind which the European worker did not know. One can tolerate any coercive situation much more easily if one has at least the illusion that one could escape that situation if worse came to worst." *Ibid.*, p. 140. Such an awareness was, in Sombart's opinion, relatively independent of the actual number of workers who availed themselves of opportunities for upward mobility, though he did not develop this point further.

4. Reinhard Bendix, *Work and Authority in Industry* (New York: Wiley, 1956), pp. 211–226.

5. An exception is the big cities of Sweden in the earlier part of this century. However, data in the 1935 census indicate that differential fertility was at that time a characteristic of the nation as a whole.

6. Seymour M. Lipset and Reinhard Bendix, *Social Mobility in Industrial Society* (Berkeley and Los Angeles: University of California Press, 1964), chapter viii.

7. Martha E. Deeg and Donald G. Paterson, "Changes in the Social Status of Occupations," *Occupations*, 25 (1947): 205–208.

8. M. Janowitz and Deil Wright, "The Prestige of Public Employment: 1929 and 1954," *Public Administration Review*, 16 (1956): 15–21.

9. See S. M. Lipset and R. Bendix, *Social Mobility in Industrial Society*, chapters iii and iv.

10. C. Arnold Anderson, "The Social Status of University Students in Relation to Type of Economy: An International Comparison," in *Transactions of the Third World Congress of Sociology*, Vol. V (London: International Sociological Association, 1956), p. 57.

11. E. Durkheim, *Suicide* (Glencoe: The Free Press, 1951), pp. 246–254.

12. A. B. Hollingshead, R. Ellis, and E. Kirby, "Social Mobility and Mental Illness," *American Sociological Review*, 19 (1954): 577–584. A. B. Hollingshead and F. C. Redlich, "Schizophrenia and Social Structure," *American Journal of Psychiatry*, 110 (1954): 695–701. The possibility that the same factors cause social mobility that cause mental illness is suggested by Evelyn Ellis, "Social Psychological Correlates of Upward Social Mobility among Unmarried Career Women," *American Sociological Review*, 17 (1952): 558–563.

13. Morris Janowitz and Richard Curtis, "Sociological Consequences of Occupational Mobility in a U. S. Metropolitan Community," (Working Paper One submitted to the Fourth Working Conference on Social Stratification and Social Mobility, International Sociological Association, December, 1957).

14. See S. M. Lipset and R. Bendix, *Social Mobility in Industrial Society*, chapter iii.

15. See S. M. Lipset and J. Linz, *The Social Basis of Political Diversity* (Stanford: Center for Advanced Study in the Behavioral Sciences, 1956; mimeographed.) Data from the Swedish Gallup Poll for different Swedish elections, and from a 1953 study of German elections conducted by the UNESCO Institute at Cologne, and the 1957 study conducted by DIVO indicate that the better paid and higher skilled Swedish and German workers are much more likely to vote for the left parties than the lower paid and less skilled.

16. W. Lloyd Warner, *et al., Social Class in America* (Chicago: Science Research Associates, Inc., 1949), p. v. It is perhaps paradoxical that a theory of class which emphasizes reciprocal status evaluations, should, nevertheless, justify itself on these grounds. The very ambiguity of these evaluations is an important part of the evidence, and an approach that deliberately eliminates this ambiguity in the name of scientific accuracy may obscure this part of the evidence.

17. See G. Myrdal, *The American Dilemma* (New York: Harper, 1942).

18. See E. Wight Bakke, *The Unemployed Worker* (New Haven: Yale University Press, 1940), pp. 83–89, and by the same author, *Citizens Without Work* (New Haven: Yale University Press, 1940), pp. 66–68.

RALPH H. TURNER

Sponsored and Contest Mobility and the School System

This paper suggests a framework for relating certain differences between American and English systems of education to the prevailing norms of upward mobility in each country. Others have noted the tendency of educational systems to support prevailing schemes of stratification, but this discussion concerns specifically the manner in which the *accepted mode of upward mobility* shapes the school system directly and indirectly through its effects on the values which implement social control.

Two ideal-typical normative patterns of upward mobility are described and their ramifications in the general patterns of stratification and social control are suggested. In addition to showing relationships among a number of differences between American and English schooling, the ideal-types have broader implications than those developed in this paper: they suggest a major dimension of stratification which might be profitably incorporated into a variety of studies in social class; and they readily can be applied in further comparisons between other countries.

The Nature of Organizing Norms

Many investigators have concerned themselves with rates of upward mobility in specific countries or internationally,[1] and with the manner in which school systems facilitate or impede such mobility.[2] But preoccupation with the *extent* of mobility has precluded equal attention to the predominant *modes* of mobility. The central assumption underlying this paper is that within a formally open class system that provides for mass education the organizing folk norm which defines the accepted mode of upward mobility is a crucial factor in shaping the school system, and may be even more crucial than the extent of upward mobility. In England and the United States there appear to be different organizing folk norms, here termed *sponsored mobility* and *contest mobility*, respectively. *Contest* mobility is a system in which elite[3] status is the prize in an open contest and is taken by the aspirants' own efforts. While the "contest" is governed by some rules of fair play, the contestants have wide latitude in the strategies they may employ. Since the "prize" of successful upward mobility is not in the hands of an established elite to give out, the latter can not determine who shall attain it and who shall not. Under *sponsored* mobility elite recruits are chosen by the established elite or their agents, and elite status is *given* on the basis of some criterion of supposed merit and cannot be *taken* by any amount of effort or strategy. Upward mobility is like entry into a private club where each candidate must be "sponsored" by one or more of the members. Ultimately the members grant or deny upward mobility on the basis of whether they judge the candidate to have those qualities they wish to see in fellow members. ...

Social Control and the Two Norms

Every society must cope with the problem of maintaining loyalty to its social system and does so in part through norms and values, only some of which vary by class position. Norms and values especially prevalent within a given class must direct behavior into channels that support the total system, while those that transcend strata must support the general class differential. The way in which upward mobility takes place determines in part the kinds of norms and values that serve the indicated purposes of social control in each class and throughout the society.

The most conspicuous control problem is that of ensuring loyalty in the disadvantaged classes toward a system in which their members receive less than a proportional share of society's goods. In a system of contest mobility this is accomplished by a combination of futuristic orientation, the norm of ambition, and a general sense of fellowship with the elite. Each individual is encouraged to think of himself as competing for an elite position so that loyalty to the system and conventional attitudes are cultivated in the process of preparation for this possibility. It is essential that this futuristic orientation be kept alive by delaying a sense of final irreparable failure to reach elite status until attitudes are well established. By thinking of himself in the successful future the elite aspirant forms considerable identification with elitists, and evidence that they are merely ordinary human beings like himself helps to reinforce this identification as well as to keep alive the conviction that he himself may someday succeed in like manner. To forestall rebellion among the disadvantaged majority, then, a contest system must avoid absolute points of selection for mobility and immobility and must delay clear recognition of the realities of the situation until the individual is too committed to the system to change radically. A futuristic orientation cannot, of course, be inculcated successfully in all members of lower strata, but sufficient internalization of a norm of ambition tends to leave the unambitious as individual deviants and to forestall the latters' formation of a genuine subcultural group able to offer collective threat to the established system. Where this kind of control system operates rather effectively it is notable that organized or gang deviancy is more likely to take the form of an attack upon the conventional or moral order rather than upon the class system itself. Thus the United States has its "beatniks"[4] who repudiate ambition and most worldly values and its delinquent and criminal gangs who try to evade the limitations imposed by conventional means,[5] but very few active revolutionaries.

These social controls are inappropriate in a system of sponsorship since the elite recruits are chosen from above. The principal threat to the system would lie in the existence of a strong group the members of whom sought to *take* elite positions themselves. Control under this system is maintained by training the "masses" to regard themselves as relatively incompetent to manage society, by restricting access to the skills and manners of the elite, and by cultivating belief in the superior competence of the elite. The earlier that selection of the elite recruits is made the sooner others can be taught to accept their inferiority and to make "realistic" rather than fantasy plans. Early selection prevents raising the hopes of large numbers of people who might otherwise become the discontented leaders of a class challenging the sovereignty of the established elite. If it is assumed that the difference in competence between masses and elite is seldom so great as to support the usual differences in the advantages accruing to each,[6] then the differences must be artificially augmented by discouraging acquisition of elite skills by the masses. Thus a sense of mystery about the elite is a common device for supporting in the masses the illusion of a much greater hiatus of competence than in fact exists.

While elitists are unlikely to reject a system that benefits them, they must still be restrained from taking such advantage of their favorable situation as to jeopardize the entire elite. Under the sponsorship system the elite recruits—who are selected early, freed from the strain of competitive struggle, and kept under close supervision—may be thoroughly indoctrinated in elite culture. A norm of paternalism toward inferiors may be inculcated, a heightened sensitivity to the good opinion of fellow elitists and elite recruits may be cultivated, and the appreciation of the more complex forms of aesthetic, literary, intellectual, and sporting activities may be taught. Norms of courtesy and altruism easily can be maintained under sponsorship since elite recruits are not required to compete for their standing and since the elite may deny high standing to those who strive for position by "unseemly" methods. The system of sponsorship provides an almost perfect setting for the development of an elite culture characterized by a sense of responsibility for "inferiors" and for preservation of the "finer things" of life.

Elite control in the contest system is more difficult since there is no controlled induction and apprenticeship. The principal regulation seems to lie in the insecurity of elite position. In a sense there is no "final arrival" because each person may be displaced by newcomers throughout his life. The limited control of high standing from above prevents the clear delimitation of levels in the class system, so that success itself becomes relative: each success, rather than an accomplishment, serves to qualify the participant for competition at the next higher level.[7] The restraints upon the behavior of a person of high standing, therefore, are principally those applicable to a contestant who must not risk the "ganging up" of other contestants, and who must pay some attention to the masses who are frequently in a position to impose penalties upon him. But any special norm of paternalism is hard to establish since there is no dependable procedure for examining the means by which one achieves elite credentials. While mass esteem is an effective brake upon over-exploitation of position, it rewards scrupulously ethical and altruistic behavior much less than evidence of fellow-feeling with the masses themselves.

Under both systems, unscrupulous or disreputable persons may become or remain members of the elite, but for different reasons. In contest mobility, popular tolerance of a little craftiness in the successful newcomer, together with the fact that he does not have to undergo the close scrutiny of the old elite, leaves considerable leeway for unscrupulous success. In sponsored mobility, the unpromising recruit reflects unfavorably on the judgments of his sponsors and threatens the myth of elite omniscience; consequently he may be tolerated and others may "cover up" for his deficiencies in order to protect the unified front of the elite to the outer world.

Certain of the general values and norms of any society reflect emulation of elite values by the masses. Under sponsored mobility, a good deal of the protective attitudes toward and interest in classical subjects percolates to the masses. Under contest mobility, however, there is not the same degree of homogeneity of moral, aesthetic, and

intellectual values to be emulated, so that the conspicuous attribute of the elite is its high level of material consumption—emulation itself follows this course. There is neither effective incentive nor punishment for the elitist who fails to interest himself in promoting the arts or literary excellence, or who continues to maintain the vulgar manners and mode of speech of his class origin. The elite has relatively less power and the masses relatively more power to punish or reward a man for his adoption or disregard of any special elite culture. The great importance of accent and of grammatical excellence in the attainment of high status in England as contrasted with the twangs and drawls and grammatical ineptitude among American elites is the most striking example of this difference. In a contest system, the class order does not function to support the *quality* of aesthetic, literary, and intellectual activities; only those well versed in such matters are qualified to distinguish authentic products from cheap imitations. Unless those who claim superiority in these areas are forced to submit their credentials to the elite for evaluation, poor quality is often honored equally with high quality and class prestige does not serve to maintain an effective norm of high quality.

This is not to imply that there are no groups in a "contest" society devoted to the protection and fostering of high standards in art, music, literature, and intellectual pursuits, but that such standards lack the support of the class system which is frequently found when sponsored mobility prevails. In California, the selection by official welcoming committees of a torch singer to entertain a visiting king and queen and "can-can" dancers to entertain Mr. Khrushchev illustrates how American elites can assume that high prestige and popular taste go together.

Formal Education

Returning to the conception of an organizing ideal norm, we assume that to the extent to which one such norm of upward mobility is prevalent in a society there are constant strains to shape the educational system into conformity with that norm. These strains operate in two fashions: directly, by blinding people to alternatives and coloring their judgments of successful and unsuccessful solutions to recurring educational problems; indirectly, through the functional interrelationships between school systems and the class structure, systems of social control, and other features of the social structure which are neglected in this paper.

The most obvious application of the distinction between sponsored and contest mobility norms affords a partial explanation for the different policies of student selection in the English and American secondary schools. Although American high school students follow different courses of study and a few attend specialized schools, a major educational preoccupation has been to avoid any sharp social separation between the superior and inferior students and to keep the channels of movement between courses of study as open as possible. Recent criticisms of the way in which superior students may be thereby held back in their development usually are nevertheless qualified by the insistence that these students must not be withdrawn from the mainstream of student life.[8] Such segregation offends the sense of fairness implicit in the contest norm and also arouses the fear that the elite and future elite will lose their sense of fellowship with the masses. Perhaps the most important point, however, is that schooling is presented as an opportunity, and making use of it depends primarily on the student's own initiative and enterprise.

The English system has undergone a succession of liberalizing changes during this century, but all of them have retained the attempt to sort out early in the educational program the promising from the unpromising so that the former may be segregated and given a special form of training to fit them for higher standing in their adult years. Under the Education Act of 1944, a minority of students has been selected each year by means of a battery of examinations popularly known as "eleven plus," supplemented in varying degrees by grade school records and personal interviews, for admission to grammar schools.[9] The remaining students attend secondary modern or technical schools in which the opportunities to prepare for college or to train for the more prestigeful occupations are minimal. The grammar schools supply what by comparative standards is a high quality of college preparatory education. Of course, such a scheme embodies the logic of sponsorship, with early selection of those destined for middle-class and higher-status occupations, and specialized training to prepare each group for its destined class position. This plan facilitates considerable mobility, and recent research reveals surprisingly little bias against children from manual laboring-class families in the selection for grammar school, when related to measured intelligence.[10] It is altogether possible that adequate comparative study would show a closer correlation of school success with measured intelligence and a lesser correlation between school success and family background in England than in the United States. While selection of superior students for mobility opportunity is probably more efficient under such a system, the obstacles for persons not so selected of "making the grade" on the basis of their own initiative or enterprise are probably correspondingly greater. ...

Effects of Mobility on Personality

Brief note may be made of the importance of the distinction between sponsored and contest mobility with relation to the supposed effects of upward mobility on personality development. Not a great deal is yet known about the "mobile personality" nor about the specific features of importance to the personality in the mobility experience.[11] However, today three aspects of this experience are most frequently stressed: first, the stress or tension involved in striving for status higher than that of others under more difficult conditions than they; second, the complication of interpersonal relations introduced by the necessity to abandon lower-level friends in favor of uncertain acceptance into higher-level circles; third, the problem of working out an adequate personal scheme of values in the face of movement between classes marked by somewhat variant or even contradictory value systems.[12] The impact of each of these three mobility problems, it is suggested, differ depending upon whether the pattern is that of the contest or of sponsorship.

Under the sponsorship system, recruits are selected early, segregated from their class peers, grouped with other recruits and with youth from the class to which they are moving, and trained specifically for membership in this class. Since the selection is made early, the mobility experience should be relatively free from the strain that comes with a series of elimination tests and long-extended uncertainty of success. The segregation and the integrated group life of the "public" school or grammar school should help to clarify the mobile person's social ties. (One investigator failed to discover clique formation along lines of social class in a sociometric study of a number of grammar schools.[13]) The problem of a system of values may be largely met when the elite recruit is taken from his parents and peers to be placed in a boarding school, though it may be less well clarified for the grammar school boy who returns each evening to his working-class family. Undoubtedly this latter limitation has something to do with the observed failure of working-class boys to continue through the last years of grammar school and into the universities.[14] In general, then, the factors stressed as affecting personality formation among the upwardly mobile probably are rather specific to the contest system, or to incompletely functioning sponsorship system.

Notes

This is an expanded version of a paper presented at the Fourth World Congress of Sociology, 1959, and abstracted in the *Transactions* of the Congress. Special indebtedness should be expressed to Jean Floud and Hilde Himmelweit for helping to acquaint the author with the English school system.

1. A comprehensive summary of such studies appears in Seymour M. Lipset and Reinhard Bendix, *Social Mobility in Industrial Society,* Berkeley and Los Angeles: University of California Press, 1959.

2. *Cf.* C. A. Anderson, "The Social Status of University Students in Relation to Type of Economy: An International Comparison," *Transactions of the Third World Congress of Sociology,* London, 1956, Vol. V, pp. 51–63; J. E. Floud, *Social Class and Educational Opportunity,* London: Heinemann, 1956; W. L. Warner, R. J. Havighurst, and M. B. Loeb, *Who Shall Be Educated?* New York: Harper, 1944.

3. Reference is made throughout the paper to "elite" and "masses." The generalizations, however, are intended to apply throughout the stratification continuum to relations between members of a given class and the class or classes above it. Statements about mobility are intended in general to apply to mobility from manual to middle-class levels, lower-middle to upper-middle class, and so on, as well as into the strictly elite groups. The simplified expressions avoid the repeated use of cumbersome and involved statements which might otherwise be required.

4. See, e.g., Lawrence Lipton, *The Holy Barbarians,* New York: Messner, 1959.

5. *Cf.* Albert K. Cohen, *Delinquent Boys: The Culture of the Gang,* Glencoe, Ill.: Free Press, 1955.

6. D. V. Glass, editor, *Social Mobility in Britain,* Glencoe, Ill.: Free Press, 1954, pp. 144–145, reports studies showing only small variations in intelligence between occupational levels.

7. Geoffrey Gorer, *The American People,* New York: Norton, 1948, pp. 172–187.

8. See, e.g., *Los Angeles Times,* May 4, 1959, Part I, p. 24.

9. The nature and operation of the "eleven plus" system are fully reviewed in a report by a committee of the British Psychological Society and in a report of extensive research into the adequacy of selection methods. See P. E. Vernon, editor, *Secondary School Selection: A British Psychological Inquiry,* London: Methuen, 1957; and Alfred Yates and D. A. Pidgeon, *Admission to Grammar Schools,* London: Newnes Educational Publishing Co., 1957.

10. J. E. Floud, A. H. Halsey, and F. M. Martin, *Social Class and Educational Opportunity,* London: Heinemann, 1956.

11. *Cf.* Lipset and Bendix, *op. cit.,* pp. 250 ff.

12. See, e.g., August B. Hollingshead and Frederick C. Redlich, *Social Class and Mental Illness,* New York: Wiley, 1958; W. Lloyd Warner and James C. Abegglen, *Big Business Leaders in America,* New York: Harper, 1955; Warner *et al., Who Shall Be Educated?, op. cit.;* Peter M. Blau, "Social Mobility and Interpersonal Relations," *American Sociological Review,* 21 (June, 1956), pp. 290–300.

13. A. N. Oppenheim, "Social Status and Clique Formation among Grammar School Boys," *British Journal of Sociology,* 6 (September, 1955), pp. 228–245. Oppenheim's findings may be compared with A. B. Hollingshead, *Elmtown's Youth,* New York: Wiley, 1949, pp. 204–242. See also Joseph A. Kahl, *The American Class Structure,* New York: Rinehart, 1957, pp. 129–138.

14. Floud *et al., op. cit.,* pp. 115 ff.

DAVID L. FEATHERMAN AND ROBERT M. HAUSER

A Refined Model of Occupational Mobility

In this [article] we describe and apply a loglinear model of the mobility table. ... The model permits us to locate groups or clusters of cells in the classification that share similar chances of mobility or immobility, freed of the confounding influences of the relative numbers of men in each origin or destination category and of changes in those relative numbers between origin and destination distributions.

By modeling the mobility table in this way we obtain new insights into the process of mobility, changes in that process, and the interactions of the mobility process with changes in the occupational structure within one mobility classification or between two or more mobility classifications. For example, we take a fresh look at the differing tendencies toward immobility in the several occupational strata, at the existence of "class" boundaries limiting certain types of mobility, at differences in upward and downward exchanges between occupational strata, and at differences among strata in the dispersion of recruitment and supply. In these purposes our analysis parallels Blau and Duncan's treatment of manpower flows (1967:Chap. 2; also, see Blau, 1965).

Several sociologists have recently drawn attention to relationships between occupational mobility and class formation, for example, Giddens (1973), Parkin (1971), and Westergaard and Resler (1975). Goldthorpe and Llewellyn (1977) have critically reviewed these and related works in light of British mobility data collected in 1972. It would be easy to identify our present analytic interests with those of the class theorists, but we think such an inference unwarranted.

Although we are attempting a description of the mobility regime that is free of the distributions of occupational origins and destinations, we believe with Goldthorpe and Llewellyn that the class theorists are attempting to interpret what [might be] termed the gross flows of manpower. For the American case we have already described those flows [see Featherman and Hauser (1978:Chapter 3)], and our interest now centers on the net or underlying patterns of association in the mobility table.

We have approached the mobility table without strong theoretical presuppositions about affinities among occupational strata. Like Blau and Duncan, we have worked inductively, but our more refined analytic tools have led to substantively different conclusions than theirs about the major features of the mobility process in the United States.

Some readers may find the following discussion excessively technical, but we have tried to minimize the presentation of methodological detail. We have tried to avoid describing the methods by which empirical specifications of the mobility table may be explored, although we believe these are interesting in their own right. We have focused on the rationale and interpretation of our model, including comparisons with other ways of looking at the mobility table that seem likely to elucidate the properties of the model.

Mobility Models

The record of sociological mobility studies is paralleled by a history of statistical analysis in which occupational mobility has often served as stimulus, object, or illustration of statistical ideas (for example, see Pearson, 1904; Chessa, 1911; Rogoff, 1953; Glass, 1954; Goodman, 1961, 1968, 1969a, 1972c; Tyree, 1973; White, 1963, 1970a; Singer and Spilerman, 1976). Indeed, it is consistent with the historical pattern that sociologists were introduced to the method of path analysis primarily by way of its successful application in studies of occupational mobility (Duncan and Hodge, 1963; Blau and Duncan, 1967). Devices for the statistical analysis of mobility data range from simple descriptive measures to complex analytic schemes. We make no systematic effort to review these measures and models, for there are several recent and comprehensive reviews (Boudon, 1973; Pullum, 1975; Bibby, 1975). We focus almost exclusively on multiplicative (loglinear) representations of the occupational mobility table. In so doing we do not intend to suggest that other methods and approaches are inferior, but to exploit features of the loglinear model that seem interesting and fruitful. ...

In a series of papers, Goodman (1963, 1965, 1968, 1969a, 1969b, 1972c) developed and exposited methods for the analysis of contingency tables (including mobility tables) in which the significant interactions were localized in specified cells or sets of cells in the table (also, see Pullum, 1975). For example, in the case of highly aggregated (3 × 3 or 5 × 5) mobility tables Goodman showed that most of the interaction pertained to cells on or near the main diagonal (when the occupation categories of origin and destination were listed in order of increasing status). White (1963, 1970b) has made essentially the same suggestion, but some aspects of his models and methods are less appealing. Goodman (1965, 1969a) proposed that the analyst ignore or "blank out" those cells where interaction was greatest (where frequencies were thought to be especially dense or especially sparse) and attempt to fit a modified model of statistical independence, termed "quasi-independence," to the remaining frequencies in the table. In the case where only diagonal cells were blanked out in a mobility table, Goodman called the model one of "quasi-perfect mobility," after the term "perfect mobility," which

had earlier been applied to the model of statistical independence in a mobility table. For an early application of this model to a large (17 × 17) table see Blau and Duncan (1967:64–67). Goodman (1965, 1968, 1969a) noted that quasi-independence might hold over all cells in a table whose entries were not ignored, or it might hold within, but not between certain subsets of cells whose entries were not ignored. ...

Models of quasi-independence have provided important insights into the structure of mobility tables. Aside from Goodman's expository papers, they have been applied in cross-national, interurban, and cross-temporal analyses (Iutaka et al., 1975; Featherman et al., 1975; Pullum, 1975; Hauser et al., 1975; Ramsøy, 1977; Goldthorpe et al., 1978). Goodman (1969a) also has shown how related ideas may be supplied to test any specific hypothesis about the pattern of association in a mobility table.

At the same time the application of quasi-independence models in mobility analysis has been less than satisfying in some ways. Even where large numbers of cells are blocked, quasi-independence models do not fit large tables very well (Pullum, 1975; Hauser et al., 1975). That is, when mobility data are not highly aggregated, it appears that association is not limited to the small number of cells on or near the main diagonal. The larger the number of entries blocked (or fitted exactly) before a good fit is obtained, the less substantively appealing is the model of quasi-independence. Moreover, by treating departures from quasi-independence in the blocked or ignored cells as parameters or indices of mobility and departures in the unblocked cells as error, the quasi-independence model attaches too much theoretical importance to occupational inheritance (Hope, 1976). Of course, occupational inheritance is always defined by reference to a given classification of occupations, and the problem is exacerbated by the fact that the model of quasi-independence fits best when the mobility table is based on broad occupation groups. The model is of greatest validity in the measurement of immobility in classifications where the concept of occupational inheritance becomes vague.

The focus on fit on or near the main diagonal

follows a traditional sociological interest in occupational inheritance, but it also draws our attention away from other aspects of association in the table. For example, one might hypothesize that certain types of mobility are as prevalent as other types of mobility or immobility. More generally, one might wish to construct a parametric model of mobility and immobility for the full table that would recognize the somewhat arbitrary character of occupational inheritance and the possible gradations of association throughout the table.

Goodman's (1972c) general multiplicative model of mobility tables and other cross-classifications substantially advanced the sophistication and precision of mobility analysis. For example, Goodman proposed and applied to the classic British and Danish mobility data a number of alternative specifications, all but two of which—the simple independence model and that of quasi-perfect mobility—assumed ordinality in the occupational categories. The models incorporated combinations of parameters for upward and downward mobility, for the number of boundaries crossed, and for barriers to crossing particular categoric boundaries. Many of these models—as well as problems in comparing their goodness of fit—are reviewed by Bishop *et al.* (1975:Chaps. 5, 8, 9), and some of the same models are discussed by Haberman (1974:Chap. 6). Applying Goodman's (1972c) general model we take a slightly different approach in developing models of the mobility table. Elsewhere, Hauser (1978) has applied this approach in an analysis of the classic British mobility table, and Baron (1977) has used it in a reanalysis of Rogoff's (1953) Indianapolis data.

A Refined Multiplicative Model of the Mobility Table[1]

Let x_{ij} be the observed frequency in the ijth cell of the classification of men by their own occupations ($j = 1,...,J$) and their own occupations or fathers' occupations at an earlier time ($i = 1,...,I$). In the context of mobility analysis the same categories will appear in rows and columns, and the table will be square with $I = J$. For $k = 1,...,K$, let H_k be a mutually exclusive and exhaustive partition of the pairs (i, j) in which

$$E[x_{ij}] = m_{ij} = \alpha\beta_i\gamma_j\delta_{ij}, \qquad (1)$$

where $\delta_{ij} = \delta_k$ for $(i, j) \in H_k$, subject to the normalization $\Pi_i\beta_i = \Pi_j\gamma_j = \Pi_i\Pi_j\delta_{ij} = 1$. The normalization of parameters is a matter of convenience, and we choose the value of α so that it will hold. Note that, unlike the usual set-up, the interaction effects are not constrained within rows or columns although the marginal frequencies are fixed. The model says the expected frequencies are a product of an overall effect (α), a row effect (β_i), a column effect (γ_j), and an interaction effect (δ_{ij}). The row and column parameters represent conditions of occupational supply and demand; they reflect demographic replacement processes and past and present technologies and economic conditions. The cells (i, j) are assigned to K mutually exclusive and exhaustive levels, and each of those levels shares a common interaction parameter δ_k. Thus, aside from total, row, and column effects, each expected frequency is determined by only one parameter, which reflects the level of mobility or immobility in that cell relative to that in other cells in the table.

The interaction parameters of the model correspond directly to our notions of variations in the density of observations (White, 1963:26). Unlike several models fitted by Goodman (1972c), this model does not assume ordinal measurement of occupations. Of course, the assumption of ordinality may help us interpret results, or our findings may be used to explore the metric properties of our occupational classification. For the model to be informative, the distribution of levels across the cells of the table must form a meaningful pattern, and one in which the parameters are identified (Mason *et al.*, 1973; Haberman, 1974: 217). Furthermore, the number of levels (K) should be substantially less than the number of cells in the table. These latter properties are partly matters of substantive and statistical interpretation and judgment, rather than characteristics of the model or of the data. We have found it diffi-

TABLE 1

Frequencies in a Classification of Mobility from Father's (or Other Family Head's) Occupation to Son's First
Full-Time Civilian Occupation: U.S. Men Aged 20–64 in March 1973

| Father's occupation | Son's occupation | | | | | |
	Upper nonmanual	Lower nonmanual	Upper manual	Lower manual	Farm	Total
Upper nonmanual	1414	521	302	643	40	2920
Lower nonmanual	724	524	254	703	48	2253
Upper manual	798	648	856	1676	108	4086
Lower manual	756	914	771	3325	237	6003
Farm	409	357	441	1611	1832	4650
Total	4101	2964	2624	7958	2265	19,912

NOTE: Frequencies are based on observations weighted to estimate population counts and compensate for departures of the sampling design from simple random sampling (see Featherman and Hauser [1978: Appendix B]). Broad occupation groups are upper nonmanual: professional and kindred workers, managers and officials, and non-retail sales workers; lower nonmanual: proprietors, clerical and kindred workers, and retail salesworkers; upper manual: craftsmen, foremen and kindred workers; lower manual: service workers, operatives and kindred workers, and laborers, except farm; farm: farmers and farm managers, farm laborers and foremen.

cult to interpret models where the number of levels is much greater than the number of categories recognized in the occupational classification.
...

Mobility to First Jobs: An Illustration

Table 1 gives frequencies in a classification of son's first, full-time civilian occupation by father's (or other family head's) occupation at the son's sixteenth birthday among American men who were ages 20–64 in 1973 and were not currently enrolled in school.[2] Table 2 gives the design matrix of a model for the data of Table 1. Each numerical entry in the body of the table gives the level of H_k to which the corresponding entry in the frequency table was assigned. Formally, the entries are merely labels, but, for convenience in interpretation, the numerical values are inverse to the estimated density of mobility or immobility in the cells to which they refer.

On this understanding the design says that, aside from conditions of supply and demand, immobility is highest in farm occupations (Level 1) and next highest in the upper nonmanual category (Level 2). If we take the occupation groups as ranked from high to low in the order listed, we may say that there are zones of high and almost

TABLE 2

Asymmetric 5-Level Model of Mobility from Father's Occupation to First Full-Time Civilian Occupation

| Father's occupation | Son's occupation | | | | |
	(1)	(2)	(3)	(4)	(5)
1. Upper nonmanual	2	4	5	5	5
2. Lower nonmanual	3	4	5	5	5
3. Upper manual	5	5	5	5	5
4. Lower manual	5	5	5	4	4
5. Farm	5	5	5	4	1

NOTE: Broad occupation groups are upper nonmanual: professional and kindred workers, managers and officials, and non-retail sales workers; lower nonmanual: proprietors, clerical and kindred workers, and retail sales-workers; upper manual: craftsmen, foremen and kindred workers; lower manual: service workers, operatives and kindred workers, and laborers, except farm; farm: farmers and farm managers, farm laborers and foremen.

uniform density bordering the peaks at either end of the status distribution. There is one zone of high density that includes upward or downward movements between the two nonmanual groups and immobility in the lower nonmanual group. Mobility from lower to upper nonmanual occupations (Level 3) is more likely than the opposite movement, and the latter is as likely as stability in the lower nonmanual category (Level 4). Moreover, the densities of immobility in the lower nonmanual category and of downward mobility to it are identical to those in the second zone of relatively high density, which occurs at the lower end of the occupational hierarchy. The second zone includes movements from the farm to the lower manual group and back as well as immobility in the lower manual group. Last, there is a broad zone of relatively low density (Level 5) that includes immobility in the upper manual category, upward and downward mobility within the manual stratum, mobility between upper manual and farm groups, and all movements between nonmanual and either manual or farm groups. The design says that an upper manual worker's son is equally likely to be immobile or to move to the bottom or top of the occupational distribution; obversely, it says that an upper manual worker is equally likely to have been recruited from any location in the occupational hierarchy, including his own. Also, it is worth noting that four of the five density levels recognized in the model occur along the main diagonal, and two of these (Levels 4 and 5) are assigned both to diagonal and off-diagonal cells.

With a single exception the design is symmetric. That is, the upward and downward flows between occupations are assigned to the same density levels, except mobility from lower to upper nonmanual strata (Level 3) exceeds that from upper to lower nonmanual strata (Level 4). This asymmetry in the design is striking because it suggests the power of upper white-collar families to block at least one type of status loss and because it is the *only* asymmetry in the design. For example, Blau and Duncan (1967:58–67) suggest that there are semipermeable class boundaries separating white-collar, blue-collar, and farm occupations, which permit upward mobility but inhibit downward mobility. The only asymmetry in the present design occurs *within* one of the broad classes delineated by Blau and Duncan.

Overall, the design resembles a river valley in which two broad plains are joined by a narrow strip of land between two great peaks. The contours of the peaks differ in that the one forming one side of the valley is both taller and more nearly symmetric than that forming the other side. This representation appears in Figure 1.

In some respects, this design matrix parallels Levine's (1967:Chap. 4) description of the surface of the British mobility table as a saddle (also see Levine, 1972). However, our interpretation is more extreme, since the density reaches an absolute minimum in the center of the table, not merely a minimum among the diagonal cells. In this way our model for the American 5 × 5 table is closer to Goodman's (1969a:38, 1969b:846) conclusion that a British 5 × 5 table shows "status disinheritance" in the middle category. We show elsewhere (Featherman and Hauser, 1978) that Levine's interpretation of the British data is based on a confounding of marginal effects and interactions which parallels that entailed in the use of mobility ratios, even though Levine did not use mobility ratios.

The model of Table 2 provides less than a complete description of the mobility data in Table 1. Under the model of statistical independence we obtain a likelihood-ratio statistic, $G^2 = 6167.7$, which is asymptotically distributed as χ^2 with 16 *df*. With the model of Table 2 as null hypothesis we obtain $G^2 = 66.5$ with 12 *df*, since we lose 4 *df* in creating the five categories of *H*. Clearly the model does not fit, if we take the probability associated with the test statistic as our only guide. On the other hand the model does account for 98.9% of the association in the data, that is, of the value of G^2 under independence. Given the extraordinarily large sample size we might expect small departures from frequencies predicted by the model to be statistically significant. ...

The measures of fit we have examined have told us nothing about the several parameters of the model. That is, we have not shown that our suggested interpretation of the design matrix (Table 2) is substantively appealing, or even that the design correctly sorts the cells of the mobility table into zones of high and low density. Certainly, we want to look at the way in which the model fits and interprets the data as well as at deviations from fitted values.

The upper panel of Table 3 shows the row, column, and level parameters estimated under the model of Table 2 for mobility in the 1973 data from father's (or head's) occupation at son's sixteenth birthday to son's first full-time civilian occupation. The parameters are expressed in addi-

FIGURE 1

Volume of mobility from father's occupation to first full-time civilian occupation: U.S. men aged 20–64 in March 1973. The base is a unit square, and the total volume under the surface is one. Length and breadth can be read as probabilities, and height is proportionate to probability. The vertical scale has been compressed by a factor of 10.

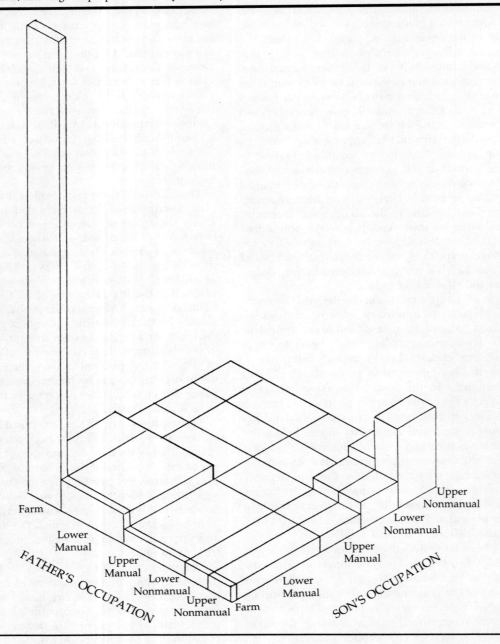

TABLE 3

Parameters and Residuals (in Additive Form) from Main, Row, and Column Effects in the Model of Table 2: Mobility from Father's (or Other Family Head's) Occupation to Son's First Full-Time Civilian Occupation, U.S. Men Aged 20–64 in March 1973

A.   Additive parameters

Design factor	Category of row, column, or level				
	(1)	*(2)*	*(3)*	*(4)*	*(5)*
Rows (father's occupation)	−.466	−.451	.495	.570	−.148
Columns (son's occupation)	.209	.190	.240	1.020	−1.660
Levels (density)	3.044	1.234	.549	.243	−.356

Grand mean = 6.277

B.   Level parameter plus residual (log R_{ij}^*)

Father's occupation	Son's occupation				
	(1)	*(2)*	*(3)*	*(4)*	*(5)*
1. Upper nonmanual	1.23	.25	−.34	−.36	−.45
2. Lower nonmanual	.55	.25	−.53	−.29	−.29
3. Upper manual	−.30	−.49	−.26	−.37	−.43
4. Lower manual	−.43	−.22	−.44	.24	.28
5. Farm	−.32	−.44	−.28	.24	3.04

NOTE: See text for explanation.

tive form, that is, they are effects on logs of frequencies under the model of Eq. (1). The row and column parameters clearly show an intergenerational shift out of farming and into white-collar or lower blue-collar occupations. Of course these parameters reflect a number of factors, including temporal shifts in the distribution of the labor force across occupations, differential fertility, and life cycle differences in occupational positions. The level parameters show very large differences in mobility and immobility across the several cells of the classification, and these differences closely follow our interpretation of the design matrix. Differences between level parameters may readily be interpreted as differences in logs of frequencies, net of row and column effects. For example, the estimates say that immobility in farm occupations is 3.40 = 3.044 − (−.356) greater (in the metric of logged frequencies) than the estimated mobility or immobility in cells assigned to Level 5 in the design matrix. In multiplicative terms, immobility in farm occupations is $e^{3.40}$ = 29.96 times greater than mobility or immobility at Level 5. It would be incorrect to attach too much importance to the signs of the level parameters as reported in Table 3, for they simply reflect our normalization rule that level parameters sum to zero (in the log-frequency metric) across the cells of the table. For example, while the parameters for Levels 4 and 5 each reflect relatively low densities, it is not clear that either parameter indicates "status disinheritance" in the diagonal cells to which it pertains (compare Goodman, 1969a, 1969b).

In any event the parameters do show a sharp density gradient across the levels of the design. The smallest difference, between Levels 3 and 4, indicates a relative density $e^{.549 - .243} = e^{.306} = 1.36$ times as great at Level 3 than at Level 4. The heterogeneity of Level 5 is indicated by the fact that the difference in density between Levels 3 and 4 is about as large as the range of residuals within Level 5. Immobility in farm occupations and in upper nonmanual occupations is quite distinct from densities at other levels, but also immobility in the farm occupations is $e^{3.044 - 1.234}$ 5 $e^{1.810}$ = 6.11 times as great as in the upper nonmanual occupations.

We can write the sample counterpart of Eq. (1) as

$$\hat{m}_{ij} = \hat{\alpha}\hat{\beta}_i\hat{\gamma}_j\hat{\delta}_{ij}. \tag{2}$$

Recalling that

$$e_{ij} = x_{ij}/\hat{m}_{ij}, \tag{3}$$

we substitute Eq. (2) into (3) and rearrange terms to obtain

$$x_{ij} = \hat{\alpha}\hat{\beta}_i\hat{\gamma}_j\hat{\delta}_{ij}e_{ij}. \tag{4}$$

We divide both sides of Eq. (4) by the first three terms on the right-hand side to obtain

$$R_{ij}^{*} = \frac{x_{ij}}{\hat{\alpha}\hat{\beta}_i\hat{\gamma}_j} = \hat{\delta}_{ij}e_{ij}. \tag{5}$$

We shall call R_{ij}^{*} the new mobility ratio, or, simply, the mobility ratio. In the case of diagonal cells R_{ij}^{*} is equivalent to the new immobility ratio proposed by Goodman (1969a,b, 1972c; also, see Pullum, 1975:7–8), but we suggest the ratio be computed for all cells of the table as an aid both to substantive interpretation and to the evaluation of model design.

The lower panel of Table 3 gives logs of the new mobility ratios for the model of Table 2 fitted to the classification of mobility to first jobs. While the entries in this panel depend on our specification of the model, neither need that specification rigidly govern our interpretation of the relative densities. Obviously, the pattern of relative densities does conform substantially to our earlier description of the design. The fit is good enough so there is no overlap in densities across levels recognized in the design, and all of the negative entries are neatly segregated in Level 5 of the design. If immobility among skilled workers—in cell (3, 3)—is high relative to mobility in other cells at Level 5, it is still clear that the immobility in that category is substantially less than the immobility in any other occupation group. ...

Mobility Chances: A New Perspective

As an alternative to the Blau-Duncan interpretation, we think our multiplicative models yield a cogent and parsimonious description of occupational mobility among American men. Unlike its

precursor, our description does not reflect the shape of occupational distributions of origin or destination, but only the underlying patterns of immobility and exchange between occupational strata. It may be useful here to review the major features of this description that appear in mobility between generations and within the occupational career. In doing so, of course, we do some injustice to details reported in the preceding analysis.

First, there is great immobility at the top and at the bottom of the occupational hierarchy, here represented by upper nonmanual and by farm occupations, respectively. This immobility is far more extreme than has heretofore been supposed by most students of the mobility process; it may even be consistent with the beliefs of the more extreme critics of rigidity in the American class structure.

Second, surrounding the extremes of the occupational hierarchy at both top and bottom are transitional zones, within which there are relatively homogeneous chances of immobility and of exchange with adjacent extreme strata.

Third, taken as aggregates the extreme and transitional zones of the occupational hierarchy are relatively closed both to upward and to downward movements. That is, there are sharp breaks between the density of observations within the extreme and transitional zones and the density of mobility beyond those zones. In this sense (but not in others) we may say that the data suggest the existence of barriers to movement across class boundaries.

Fourth, once the boundaries of the transitional zones have been crossed, no social distance gradient seems to underly variations in long-distance mobility chances. These are surprisingly uniform, and observed variations in them show no consistent pattern.

Fifth, if immobility is very great at the extremes of the occupational hierarchy, it is almost nonexistent in the middle of the hierarchy. Contrary to widespread belief, men of upper blue-collar origin are about as likely to end up anywhere higher or lower in the occupational hierarchy as in their stratum of origin. Obversely, upper blue-collar workers are about as likely to have originated anywhere higher or lower in the occupational hierarchy as in their stratum of destination. Those who would find their beliefs about "class" rigidity confirmed by our estimates of immobility at the extremes of the occupational hierarchy must reconcile these with our finding that between generations immobility in upper manual occupations is no more prevalent than most types of extreme, long-distance mobility. There is no evidence of "class" boundaries limiting the chances of movement to or from the skilled manual occupations.

Sixth, there is a rough equality in the propensities to move in one direction or the other between occupational strata. There are several exceptions to this symmetric mobility pattern, some of which may be quite important, but none suggests a dominant tendency toward upward relative to downward mobility across or within class boundaries.

Last, from a methodological perspective, our description of the mobility regime is extremely simple. In broad outline it might be fitted to a 5×5 table with the expenditure of as few as 2 *df*. None of our analyses of American mobility tables required the expenditure of more than 6 of the 16 *df* left unused by the model of simple statistical independence.

We reemphasize that the present description of relative mobility chances does not conflict in any way with our earlier description (Featherman and Hauser 1978:Chapter 3) of occupational inflow and outflow patterns. Rather, relative mobility chances are components of inflows and outflows, but the latter are also affected by distributions of occupational origins and destinations. Major features of the inflow and outflow tables, like the pervasiveness of upward mobility between generations and within the occupational career, are absent from the present account because they are functions of changing distributions of occupational origins and destinations.

Notes

1. We assume the familiarity of the reader with loglinear models for frequency data. Fienberg (1970a, 1977) and Goodman (1972a,b) give useful introductions, as does the comprehensive treatise by Bishop *et al.* (1975). We rely heavily on methods for the analysis of incomplete tables, which have been developed by Goodman (1963, 1965, 1968, 1969a,b, 1971, 1972c), Bishop and Fienberg (1969), Fienberg (1970b, 1972), and Mantel (1970); again, Bishop *et al.* (1975, especially pp. 206–211, 225–228, 282–309, 320–324) is valuable. Our model is a special case of Goodman's (1972c) general model.

2. The reported frequencies are based on a complex sampling design and have been weighted to estimate population counts while compensating for certain types of survey nonresponse. The estimated population counts have been scaled down to reflect underlying sample frequencies, and an additional downward adjustment was made to compensate for departures of the sampling design from simple random sampling (see Featherman and Hauser [1978:Appendix B]). The frequency estimates in Table 1 have been rounded to the nearest integer, but our computations have been based on unrounded figures. We treat the adjusted frequencies as if they had been obtained under simple random sampling.

Bibliography

Baron, James N. 1977. "The structure of intergenerational occupational mobility: Another look at the Indianapolis mobility data." Unpublished masters thesis, University of Wisconsin–Madison.

Bibby, John. 1975. "Methods of measuring mobility." *Quality and Quantity* 9 (March):107–136.

Bishop, Yvonne M. M., and Stephen E. Fienberg. 1969. "Incomplete two-dimensional contingency tables." *Biometrics* 25:119–128.

Bishop, Yvonne M. M., Stephen E. Fienberg, and Paul W. Holland. 1975. *Discrete Multivariate Analysis: Theory and Practice.* Cambridge: M.I.T. Press.

Blau, Peter M. 1965. "The flow of occupational supply and recruitment." *American Sociological Review* 30 (August):475–490.

Blau, Peter M., and Otis Dudley Duncan. 1967. *The American Occupational Structure.* New York: Wiley.

Boudon, Raymond. 1973. *Mathematical Structure of Social Mobility.* San Francisco: Jossey-Bass.

Chessa, Frederico. 1911. *La Trasmissione Erediteria delle Professioni.* Torino: Fratelli Bocca.

Duncan, Otis Dudley, and Robert W. Hodge. 1963. "Education and occupational mobility." *American Journal of Sociology* 68 (May):629–644.

Featherman, David L., and Robert M. Hauser. 1978. *Opportunity and Change.* New York: Academic Press.

Featherman, David L., F. Lancaster Jones, and Robert M. Hauser. 1975. "Assumptions of social mobility research in the United States: the case of occupational status." *Social Science Research* 4:329–360.

Fienberg, Stephen E. 1970a. "The analysis of multidimensional contingency tables." *Ecology* 51:419–433.

———. 1970b. "Quasi-independence and maximum likelihood estimation in incomplete contingency tables." *Journal of the American Statistical Association* 65:1610–1616.

———. 1972. "The analysis of incomplete multiway contingency tables." *Biometrics* 23 (March):177–202.

———. 1977. *The Analysis of Cross-Classified Categorical Data*. Cambridge: M.I.T. Press.

Giddens, Anthony. 1973. *The Class Structure of the Advanced Societies*. New York: Harper and Row.

Glass, D. B. 1954. *Social Mobility in Britain*. London: Routledge and Kegan Paul.

Goldthorpe, John W., and Catriona Llewellyn. 1977. "Class mobility in modern Britain: three theses examined." *Sociology* 11 (May):257–287.

Goldthorpe, John W., Clive Payne, and Catriona Llewellyn. 1978. "Trends in class mobility." *Sociology* 12 (September):441–468.

Goodman, Leo A. 1961. "Statistical methods for the mover-stayer model." *Journal of the American Statistical Association* 56 (December):841–868.

———. 1963. "Statistical methods for the preliminary analysis of transaction flows." *Econometrica* 31 (January):197–208.

———. 1965. "On the statistical analysis of mobility tables." *American Journal of Sociology* 70 (March):564–585.

———. 1968. "The analysis of cross-classified data: independence, quasi-independence, and interaction in contingency tables with or without missing entries." *Journal of the American Statistical Association* 63 (December):1091–1131.

———. 1969a. "How to ransack social mobility tables and other kinds of cross-classification tables." *American Journal of Sociology* 75 (July):1–39.

———. 1969b. "On the measurement of social mobility: an index of status persistence." *American Sociological Review* 34 (December):831–850.

———. 1971. "A simple simultaneous test procedure for quasi-independence in contingency tables." *Applied Statistics* 20:165–177.

———. 1972a. "A general model for the analysis of surveys." *American Journal of Sociology* 77 (May):1035–1086.

———. 1972b. "A modified multiple regression approach to the analysis of dichotomous variables." *American Sociological Review* 37 (February):28–46.

———. 1972c. "Some multiplicative models for the analysis of cross-classified data." Pp. 649–696 in *Proceedings of the Sixth Berkeley Symposium on Mathematical Statistics and Probability*. Berkeley: University of California Press.

Haberman, Shelby J. 1974. *The Analysis of Frequency Data*. Chicago: University of Chicago Press.

Hauser, Robert M. 1978. "A structural model of the mobility table." *Social Forces* 56 (March):919–953.

Hauser, Robert M., Peter J. Dickinson, Harry P. Travis, and John M. Koffel. 1975. "Temporal change in occupational mobility: evidence for men in the United States." *American Sociological Review* 40 (June):279–297.

Hope, Keith. 1976. Review of Thomas W. Pullum's *Measuring Occupational Inheritance*. *American Journal of Sociology* 82 (November):726–730.

Iutaka, S., B. F. Bloomer, R. E. Burke, and O. Wolowyna. 1975. "Testing the quasi-perfect mobility model for intergenerational data: international comparisons." *Economic and Social Review* 6:215–236.

Levine, Joel Harvey. 1967. Measurement in the study of intergenerational status mobility. Unpublished doctoral dissertation. Department of Social Relations. Harvard University.

———. 1972. "A two-parameter model of interaction in father-son status mobility." *Behavioral Science* 17 (September):455–465.

Mantel, Nathan. 1970. "Incomplete contingency tables." *Biometrics* 26:291–304.

Mason, Karen Oppenheim, William M. Mason, Halliman H. Winsborough, and Kenneth W. Poole. 1973. "Some methodological issues in cohort analysis of archival data." *American Sociological Review* 38 (April):242–258.

Parkin, Frank. 1971. *Class Inequality and Political Order: Social Stratification in Capitalist and Communist Societies*. New York: Praeger.

Pearson, Karl. 1904. "On the theory of contingency and its relation to association and normal correlation." Reprinted, 1948, in *Karl Pearson's Early Papers*. Cambridge: Cambridge University Press.

Pullum, Thomas. 1975. *Measuring Occupational Inheritance*. New York: Elsevier.

Ramsøy, Natalie. 1977. *Social Mobilitet i Norge (Social Mobility in Norway)*. Oslo: Tiden Forlag.

Rogoff, Natalie. 1953. *Recent Trends in Occupational Mobility*. Glencoe, Illinois: Free Press.

Singer, Burton, and Seymour Spilerman. 1976. "The representation of social processes by Markov models." *American Journal of Sociology* 82 (July):1–54.

Tyree, Andrea. 1973. "Mobility ratios and association in mobility tables." *Population Studies* 27 (July):577–588.

Westergaard, John, and Henrietta Resler. 1975. *Class in a Capitalist Society: A Study of Contemporary Britain.* New York: Basic Books.

White, Harrison C. 1963. "Cause and effect in social mobility tables." *Behavioral Science* 8:14–27.

———. 1970a. *Chains of Opportunity: System Models of Occupational Mobility in Organizations.* Cambridge: Harvard University Press.

———. 1970b. "Stayers and movers." *American Journal of Sociology* 76 (September):307–324.

DAVID B. GRUSKY AND ROBERT M. HAUSER

Comparative Social Mobility Revisited: Models of Convergence and Divergence in 16 Countries

The starting point for most mobility research is the thesis advanced by Lipset and Zetterberg (1959) that observed mobility rates are much the same in all Western industrialized societies. However, more recent and detailed data lend little support for this position (Hauser and Featherman, 1977; Erikson et al., 1979; Hope, 1982), and Featherman et al. (1975) thus suggested that variation in observed mobility rates might derive from historical and cultural differences in occupational structures, but not from differences in exchanges between occupations. This hypothesis, labelled the FJH revision by Erikson et al., leads to the prediction that mobility chances are invariant once variations in origin and destination distributions have been controlled. Although the FJH revision has been supported by pairwise or three-way comparisons (Erikson et al., 1982; McRoberts and Selbee, 1981; Hope, 1982; Portocarero, 1983; Hauser, 1983), research with a larger sample of countries has tended to emphasize cross-national variability (Tyree et al., 1979; Hazelrigg and Garnier, 1976; McClendon, 1980a).[1] There is also some disagreement about the degree to which "structural influences," reflected in the margins of the mobility table, can account for national differences in observed mobility rates. The FJH revision implies that variation in observed mobility must be attributed to marginal differences, yet McClendon (1980b) has recently reported a contrary finding for industrialized nations.

Among "second generation" mobility scholars (e.g., Treiman, 1970), the long-standing contention has been that mobility increases with industrialization, even after controls are introduced for changes in class or occupation distributions. This contention, typically labelled the "thesis of industrialism," is to be contrasted with the FJH revision; the latter allows an initial developmental effect on mobility, but it implies there is no further effect once a certain level of industrialization is reached. Unfortunately, evidence on the industrialism thesis is no more conclusive than that addressing the FJH revision. Some studies report a positive relationship between industrialization and mobility (Tyree et al., 1979; Hazelrigg, 1974; Cutright, 1968), but others report no significant association (Hazelrigg and Garnier, 1976; Hardy and Hazelrigg, 1978). In an effort to reconcile these findings, McClendon (1980a) claims that the positive relationship holds only when the sample is restricted to men of nonfarm origins. By virtue of his distinction among immobility parameters of different occupational strata, McClendon's research leads in a fruitful direction. ...

The goals of this paper are to address both the convergence and industrialism theses and to explore the role of noneconomic variables in mobility processes. The preceding review shows these issues are not new, nor are the data we shall employ. These data are 3 × 3 classifications of son's by father's occupation for sixteen countries; each table categorizes occupations as white-collar, blue-collar, or farm. The tables were originally assembled by Hazelrigg and Garnier (1976) from mobility surveys of the 1960s and early 1970s, but they have been reanalyzed extensively (Hardy and Hazelrigg, 1978; McClendon, 1980a, 1980b; Tyree et al., 1979; Heath, 1981; Urton, 1981; Raftery, 1983).[2] We will not discuss problems of validity and comparability associated with these data because they have been outlined by Hazelrigg and Garnier (1976:500). Suffice it to say that this three-stratum classification captures important barriers to occupational mobility and other significant differences in life chances (e.g., see Blau and Duncan, 1967:59). …

In the course of the analysis, we reject several models of the 3 × 3 mobility classifications; however, a satisfactory fit can be obtained with several equivalent models that are theoretically appealing. One such model is quasi-perfect mobility, which specifies the association between origins and destinations in terms of parameters for inheritance in each of the three strata. A second family of models specifies barriers between strata, and a third family of models specifies a vertical hierarchy with unequal distances between strata. A rationale for each of these models may be drawn from well-developed research traditions, but their formal equivalence in the 3 × 3 table means that each model produces exactly the same fitted counts. Our analysis shows the algebraic relationships among these models and suggests that two of them are preferable to the others.

Using the quasi-perfect mobility model, we investigate differences between occupational strata in opportunities for mobility or inheritance. We believe that these differences in relative mobility chances arise primarily from variation in the resources and desirability accorded occupations. However, we emphasize variation in economic resources since their transmission is perhaps the most decisive and reliable mechanism of intergenerational inheritance (Goldthorpe, 1980:100). It follows that white-collar immobility should be strong since fathers within this stratum can trans-

mit resources in the form of a business enterprise, professional practice, or privileged education. The desirability of white-collar positions strengthens inheritance further, as white-collar sons wish to retain their fathers' positions. In contrast, sons from the blue-collar stratum do not receive economic resources that bind them to their fathers' stratum, nor do they typically find inheritance as desirable as mobility to the white-collar stratum; the absence of these processes implies considerable mobility for sons of blue-collar origins. The structure of farm inheritance contrasts quite sharply with this blue-collar fluidity. Not only is land a tangible economic good, but there are strong cultural practices and traditions favoring its transfer from generation to generation.[3] Farm inheritance is further strengthened by spatial isolation from urban labor markets (Featherman and Hauser, 1978:188). Given the distinctive skills of farmers, traditions of land tenure, and spatial isolation, one might expect farm inheritance to be even stronger than that of the white-collar stratum.

Two implications follow from these observations about inheritance. First, the relative strengths of stratum-specific inheritance may be uniform across nations simply because there is substantial uniformity in the economic resources and desirability of occupations (Treiman, 1977).[4] It is commonly argued that the latter uniformities also account for the cross-national regularity in occupational prestige hierarchies (Treiman, 1977; Goldthorpe and Hope, 1974). Thus, invariance in mobility processes may be closely related to other constancies in stratification. Second, rather than deriving from the standardizing logic of industrialism, the common structure of mobility may apply to all societies regardless of their economic development. The FJH hypothesis may be broadened in this manner because occupational resources and desirability are similar in all complex societies, industrialized or not (Treiman, 1977). …

The Cross-National Structure of Mobility

There has been no direct test of the Lipset-Zetterberg hypothesis in earlier studies. To carry

TABLE 1
Selected Models of Mobility with and Without Cross-National Equality Constraints:
Sixteen-Country Sample and Industrialized Subsample[a]

Model	Full Sample			Industrialized Countries		
	L^2	df	L^2_H/L^2_T	L^2	df	L^2_H/L^2_T
A. Unconstrained Models						
1. Independence	42970	64	100.0	12020	36	100.0
2. Quasi-perfect mobility	150	16	0.3	77	9	0.6
3. Uniform inheritance	6222	48	14.5	2233	27	18.6
4. Perfect blue-collar mobility	841	32	2.0	206	18	1.7
5. Symmetry	24636	48	—	6748	27	—
B. Models with Cross-National Constraints						
6. Quasi-perfect mobility	1500	61	3.5	513	33	4.3
7. Uniform inheritance	7069	63	16.5	2429	35	20.2
8. Perfect blue-collar mobility	1640	62	3.8	538	34	4.5
9. All two-way interactions	1329	60	3.1	438	32	3.6
C. Contrasts Between Constrained and Unconstrained Models						
10. 2 vs. 6	1350	45	3.1	436	24	3.6
11. 3 vs. 7	847	15	2.0	196	8	1.6
12. 4 vs. 8	799	30	1.9	332	16	2.8

[a] The full sample includes Australia, Belgium, France, Hungary, Italy, Japan, Philippines, Spain, United States, West Germany, West Malaysia, Yugoslavia, Denmark, Finland, Norway and Sweden. The industrialized subsample includes Australia, Belgium, France, United States, West Germany, Denmark, Finland, Norway and Sweden.

out this test, we set up a model of global equality between the mobility classifications in the full set of 16 nations and in the 9 most industrialized, nonsocialist nations. Within the more industrialized subsample, this model yields a highly significant likelihood-ratio chi-square test statistic, L^2 = 3,201 with 64 degrees of freedom (df), and the ratio of the test statistic to its degrees of freedom is L^2/df = 50.0. In the full sample, L^2 = 18,390 with 120 df and L^2/df = 153.3. There is no less evidence of heterogeneity among mobility classifications within the industrialized subsample than within the full set of 16 countries, for there are 3 times as many observations in the full sample as in the industrialized subsample. Thus, we reject the Lipset-Zetterberg hypothesis. Not only is there highly significant variation in observed mobility rates among industrialized nations, but there is no less variation among these nations than among nations that vary widely in level of industrialization.

The remainder of our analysis focuses on the

FJH revision of the Lipset-Zetterberg hypothesis, that is, on the measurement and explanation of intersocietal variation in social fluidity.[5] Table 1 shows the fit of selected models of mobility and immobility. The left-hand side of the table pertains to the full set of countries, while the right-hand side of the table pertains to nine highly industrialized nations. In Panel A, the models do not place any cross-country equality constraints on parameters, so the fit statistic for each model is simply the sum of the fit statistics for that model applied to each country separately.[6] Panel B reports the fit of several of the models of Panel A, each subject to the additional restriction that all of the interaction parameters of that model (but not the marginal effects) are the same in each country. Panel C displays contrasts between corresponding models in Panel A and in Panel B.

Models 1 through 4 in Table 1 are of the form

$$E[X_{ijk}] = \alpha_k \beta_{ik} \gamma_{jk} \delta_{ijk} \qquad (1)$$

where $\delta_{ijk} = \delta_{mk}$ for $(i,j) \in H_m$. In this context, X_{ijk} is the observed frequency in the ijk^{th} cell of the classification of father's stratum (i) by son's stratum (j) by country (k), and H_m is a partition of the pairs (i,j), which is mutually exclusive, exhaustive, and cross-nationally invariant. Subject to the usual normalizations, this model implies that expected frequencies in the kth country are the product of a grand mean (α_k), a row effect (β_{ik}), a column effect (γ_{jk}), and an interaction effect (δ_{ijk}). Models 1 through 4 differ only by partitioning the pairs (i,j) according to various theories of the structure of interaction. These partitions are displayed in Figure 1; cells sharing a numeric value within a matrix are assigned the same interaction parameter in the corresponding model. Note that we have specialized the model to impose the same partition of cells in each country, but not necessarily to specify the same interaction parameters in each country. Since this general model has been discussed in detail elsewhere (e.g., Hauser, 1978, 1979), we will not elaborate it further.

Model 1 specifies conditional independence of father's and son's stratum, so $\delta_{ijk} = 1$ for all pairs (i,j) in all countries (k); this says there is no intergenerational association in any of the 16 countries. Although the global chi-square statistic, $L^2 = 42,970$, reveals that independence is patently inconsistent with these data, this model provides a baseline statistic representing the association to be explained by subsequent models. Model 2, quasi-perfect mobility, fits a distinct inheritance parameter to each diagonal cell and posits independence among the remaining cells off the diagonal. This model fits extremely well, accounting for 99.7 percent of the association under the baseline model of independence. Indeed, the model cannot be rejected at the .05 level in ten of the sixteen countries, and in all countries it explains at least 97.3 percent of the association. Since this is one of our preferred models, we shall consider its implications in some detail.[7]

First, quasi-perfect mobility implies quasi-symmetry in a 3 × 3 table. In a mobility classification, quasi-symmetry means that upward and downward moves are equally likely, net of differences in the prevalence of occupations. Thus, our results do not support the interpretation of semipermeable class boundaries advanced by Blau

FIGURE 1

Parameter displays describing the structure of association for selected models of mobility

Independence

Quasi-Perfect Mobility

Uniform Inheritance

Perfect Blue-Collar Mobility

and Duncan (1967) for the United States. Featherman and Hauser (1978:184–87) and Hauser (1981) report a similar finding in disaggregated American mobility tables; we extend that finding to a larger set of countries.[8]

Symmetry in exchange mobility is entirely consistent with intergenerational occupational change and consequent differences between observed inflow and outflow distributions. We can see this by contrasting the model of quasi-perfect mobility (quasi-symmetry) with that of complete symmetry (Model 5), which posits equal frequencies in corresponding cells above and below the main diagonal of each mobility classification, $E[X_{ijk}] = E[X_{jik}]$. The fit of Model 5, $L^2 = 24,636$, shows that observed frequencies are highly asymmetric. However, from the excellent fit of quasi-perfect mobility (quasi-symmetry), we know this observed asymmetry derives from heterogeneity between origin and destination distributions rather than an intrinsic asymmetry of exchange between occupational strata.

Second, the quasi-perfect mobility model says that mobility does not follow a social distance gradient. Those who move off the diagonal are equally likely to reach either of the two remaining strata regardless of distance or direction. The implication is that long-range mobility is no less frequent than short-range mobility after controlling for marginal effects. Featherman and Hauser (1978: Ch. 4) offer a similar interpretation of disaggregated American mobility tables.[9]

Third, the parameters of the quasi-perfect mobility model reveal wide differences among strata in the strength of inheritance.[10] For purposes of summary, it is instructive to consider Model 6, which constrains parameter estimates to be the same in all sixteen countries. Net of row and column effects, farm inheritance is 12.3 times more likely than mobility off the diagonal, white-collar inheritance is 5.2 times more likely than mobility, and blue-collar inheritance is only 1.2 times more likely than mobility. The picture that emerges is one of severe immobility at the two extremes of the occupational hierarchy and considerable fluidity in the middle (compare Featherman and Hauser, 1978: Ch. 4). Indeed, the United States and Hungary show significant blue-collar disinheritance.[11] A net propensity for mobility out of the blue-collar stratum was first noted by Goodman (1965:575, 1969a) in the classic British and Danish mobility tables of the early postwar period; the results presented here extend his finding to additional countries.[12] Friendly critics have suggested to us that blue-collar disinheritance is implausible and, for that reason, should lead us to reject quasi-perfect mobility in favor of other equivalent models (Goodman, 1979b; Hauser, 1979:453–54, 1981; MacDonald, 1981). On the basis of our earlier discussion of mechanisms of stratum inheritance, we do not think it is possible to rule out blue-collar status disinheritance (see Featherman and Hauser 1978:179–89). Moreover, we will show that quasi-perfect mobility is more plausible than some other equivalent models of the 3 × 3 table.

The remaining models in Panel A of Table 1 help us to test, elaborate, and qualify these interpretations. The uniform inheritance model (Line 3) posits a single inflation factor for the main diagonal; the model says that occupational strata share a uniform propensity for inheritance. This model fits poorly, confirming our observation of substantial variability among inheritance parameters.[13] The model of perfect blue-collar mobility

(Line 4) equates densities of mobility and immobility for men of blue-collar origin or destination (Goodman, 1965:569–71). Net of marginal effects, this model says that blue-collar workers are recruited equally from all three occupational strata and that men of blue-collar origins are selected equally into all three strata. Further, the model says that blue-collar mobility and immobility are as likely as exchange between the white-collar and farm strata. This model does not fit satisfactorily ($L^2 = 841$ with 32 df), yet it does account for 98 percent of the test statistic under conditional independence (compare Lines 1 and 4). Moreover, Model 4 does fit well in 6 countries: Italy, West Malaysia, Yugoslavia, Denmark, Norway, and Sweden. The contrast between Models 2 and 4 tests whether there is significant blue-collar stratum inheritance or disinheritance. Although the global contrast between these models is clearly significant ($L^2 = 691$ with 16 df), the contrast is nonsignificant in Australia and in the other 6 countries where Model 4 fits the data. This provides further evidence for attenuated blue-collar inheritance; it is so weak that densities of mobility and blue-collar immobility can be equated in several of the countries in our data.[14]

These findings about interstratum mobility would not change if we were to analyze disaggregations of the present data. Although it is commonly found that models with 1 parameter for each diagonal cell do not fit detailed mobility classifications (Pullum, 1975; Goodman, 1972), those models are not the logical extension of quasi-perfect mobility in the 3-stratum table. The proper extension of the model assigns interaction parameters to cells in the disaggregated table according to their origin and destination strata in the aggregated table. This is quite different from fitting the diagonal cells in the disaggregated table because the extension of our model equates densities on and off the main diagonal for all cells pertaining to stratum immobility (Hauser, 1979:444–50; Goodman, 1981a; Breiger, 1981). Extended in this manner, the quasi-perfect mobility model explains the same component of association (likelihood-ratio test statistic) in any disaggregation of the 3 × 3 table, and the difference in the test statistics of that model in aggregated and disaggregated classifications measures association within strata of the collapsed table (Goodman, 1968; Bishop et al., 1975:126–30; Featherman and Hauser, 1978:180–84; Allison, 1980). Furthermore, residuals from the extension of quasi-perfect mobility may be useful in elaborating that model in the disaggregated table (Hauser, 1979:444–50). Similar observations hold for other models of the present 3 × 3 classifications and disaggregations of them.

Convergence in Social Fluidity

The cross-national consistency in the fit of quasi-perfect mobility provides some evidence of similarity in processes of mobility, but we have not yet tested the cross-national variation in the parameters estimated under this model. If the same model fits, but its coefficients vary from country to country, then convergence obtains only in a limited sense. The remainder of Table 1 addresses this issue. Whereas each model in Panel A allows interactions between strata to vary across countries, each model in Panel B equates those interactions.[15] The statistics in Panel B reflect lack of fit in the models of Panel A as well as cross-national differences in coefficients, whereas the contrasts between fit statistics in Panels A and B reflect the latter component alone. As shown in Panel C, each of these contrasts is highly significant statistically. At the same time, there is also a great deal of cross-national similarity in parameter estimates; no more than 3.6 percent of the chi-square statistic under conditional independence is attributable to variation in parameters. A similar conclusion may be drawn from the fit of the model of all two-way interactions, which allows 4 df for interaction between origin and outcome strata (Line 9 of Panel B).

These results make it quite clear that the "cross-nationally common element heavily predominates over the cross-nationally variable one" (Erikson et al., 1982:12). Not only does one simple model, quasi-perfect mobility, fit all of these data satisfactorily, but its coefficients do not vary greatly between countries. These findings of cross-national invariance support the FJH revision of the Lipset-Zetterberg hypothesis.

The results of Table 1 imply convergence among industrialized countries in our sample, but they also suggest that conclusions of invariance apply equally to the full sample. Under each of the models of Table 1, the share of association due to cross-national interaction effects (L_H^2/L_T^2) is virtually the same in the full sample as in the industrialized subsample. This suggests an extension of the scope of the FJH hypothesis to state that mobility regimes are much the same in all complex societies, regardless of economic development.[16] This uniformity is perhaps the analogue in comparative mobility analysis to the finding of invariant prestige hierarchies in complex societies (Treiman, 1977). ...

Explained and Unexplained Variation in Social Fluidity

Although the hypothesis of constant social fluidity is rejected at conventional levels of statistical significance, small departures from the model are sufficient to generate a significant chi-square value with a sample of more than 110,000 cases. Assertions of nonconvergence would be more convincing if cross-national variations in social fluidity were linked explicitly to exogenous variables. For this reason we have estimated log-linear or log-multiplicative models in which measures of industrialization, educational enrollment, social democracy, and income inequality are used to explain cross-national variation. These are the major explanatory variables identified in previous research, and for the most part we have used standard measurements of these variables.[17]

Our models also include a dummy variable with the value "1" for Hungary and "0" for all other countries. We have found that Hungary is an outlier in every one of our models, and its presence tends to dominate and distort relationships that appear for other countries. We experimented with numerous treatments of the data, including shifts in functional form and the creation of a dummy variable for socialism in both Hungary and Yugoslavia, but we are unable to explain the Hungarian case. Simkus (1981) has documented the marked shifts in occupational inher-

TABLE 2
Explained and Unexplained Variation in Parameters of Social Fluidity[a]

Model	L^2	df	L^2/df	L^2_H/L^2_T	L^2_H/L^2_T
1. {FC}{SC}	42970	64	671.4	100.0	—
2. {FC}{SC}{QC}	150	16	9.4	0.3	—
3. {FC}{SC}{Q}	1500	61	24.6	3.5	—
4. {FC}{SC}{QI}{QE}{QH}{QD}{QN}	490	46	10.7	1.1	—
5. 4 vs. 3 (Explained variation)	1010	15	67.3	2.4	74.8
6. 4 vs. 2 (Unexplained variation)	340	30	11.3	0.8	25.2
7. 3 vs. 2 (Total variation)	1350	45	30.0	3.1	100.0

[a] F = Father's stratum, S = Son's stratum, C = Country, Q = Quasi-perfect mobility or Model UII*, I = Industrialization, E = Educational enrollment, H = Hungary, D = Social democracy, N = Inequality. The denominator in the first L^2_H/L^2_T ratio is the association under the model of independence (Line 1). The denominator in the second such ratio is the total variation in quasi-perfect mobility or Model UII* (Line 7).

itance that followed the Hungarian transition to socialism.

Table 2 reports fit statistics for the baseline models of conditional independence (Model 1) and variable social fluidity (Model 2). Model 3 specifies constant social fluidity, and Model 4 permits each of the 5 explanatory variables to interact with each of the parameters of the mobility model.[18] The contrast between Model 3 and Model 4 shows the amount of cross-national variability that is explained by the 5 exogenous variables (Line 5), and the contrast between Model 4 and Model 2 shows the amount of cross-national variability that is not explained by the exogenous variables (Line 6). The contrast between Lines 2 and 3 gives the total cross-national variation in social fluidity (Line 7). The exogenous variables account for most of the cross-national variation in stratum inheritance; 74.8 percent of the test statistic is explained by the five variables (1010/1350 = .748). This evidence of systematic, cross-national variation in mobility parameters lends greater credence to assertions of nonconvergence.[19]

Equivalent Models of Vertical Mobility

Several researchers have noted that seemingly different models of cross-classifications may be algebraically equivalent and thus yield the same fitted counts (Goodman, 1979b; Hauser, 1979, 1981; MacDonald, 1981; Pontinen, 1982; Hout, 1983).

The choice between equivalent models cannot be made on the basis of fit. This problem is highly visible in the analysis of 3 × 3 classifications; for example, a great many models imply quasi-symmetry in the 3 × 3 table, and this is the overidentifying restriction in the quasi-perfect mobility model. Some models that are equivalent in the 3 × 3 table are not equivalent in larger tables, but the same problem arises in classifications with many categories and in all other nonexperimental research. If there are some areas of study where the problem seems not to appear, it is because there is substantial consensus in the field. Nonetheless, there are many criteria of model selection other than fit, and these may be helpful in choosing among equivalent models. These criteria include the theoretical rationale of competing models, the plausibility of estimated parameters, and the invariance and autonomy of parameters across populations. We have used these criteria in assessing several equivalent models of the present data.

We focus on equivalent models that assume the three strata can be ranked or scaled. Some models are equivalent to quasi-perfect mobility but do not assume at least a rank order of strata; we have rejected these a priori. As we have stated, we think there is ample theoretical rationale to posit differences among strata in inheritance, and thus we have given priority to the model of quasi-perfect mobility (and possible restrictions of it that equate diagonal parameters) relative to models that distinguish among levels of mobility off the main diagonal. Similarly, we have rejected models that imply quasi-symmetry but appear to posit asymmetric interactions between strata.

Among models that assume the strata can be rank ordered or scaled, we have estimated crossings models (Goodman, 1972; Pontinen, 1982), uniform association (Duncan, 1979; Hope, 1981), and homogeneous row and column effects (Goodman, 1979a, 1981b). Table 3 shows a display of the multiplicative parameters of several equivalent models that elucidates the relationships among them (Goodman, 1979b). In Panel A, δ_1, δ_2, and δ_3 are the immobility parameters for white-collar, blue-collar, and farm strata, respectively, in the model of quasi-perfect mobility. In Panel B, we specify a crossings model in which the density of observations depends on the stratum boundaries that have been crossed; γ_1 is the parameter for the boundary between white- and blue-collar strata, and γ_2 is the parameter for the boundary between blue-collar and farm strata. This model also specifies a parameter, δ, for blue-collar immobility. By equating expressions for the distinct odds ratios in Model A and Model B, we obtain $\gamma_1 = \delta_1^{-1/2}$, $\gamma_2 = \delta_3^{-1/2}$, and $\delta = \delta_2$. There are one-to-one correspondences between the parameter for white-collar immobility and the crossing from white- to blue-collar strata, between the respective parameters for blue-collar immobility, and between the parameter for farm immobility and the crossing from blue-collar to farm strata. Thus, not only are these two models equivalent algebraically and statistically, but their parameters are the same up to a power transformation. Immobility in the extreme categories is simply an inverse measure of the barriers to movement in or out of them. Nothing in the parameter estimates of one model could lead one to prefer it to the other on grounds of plausibility.

Panel C shows another equivalent crossings model, in which the immobility parameter pertains not merely to the blue-collar stratum, but to all three strata. Here, γ_1 is the parameter for the boundary between white- and blue-collar strata, γ_2 is the parameter for the boundary between blue-collar and farm strata, and δ is the parameter for uniform immobility. By equating expressions for the distinct odds ratios in Model A and Model C, we obtain $\gamma_1 = (\delta_2/\delta_1)^{1/2}$, $\gamma_2 = (\delta_2/\delta_3)^{1/2}$, and $\delta = \delta_2$. The blue-collar inheritance

TABLE 3

Some Equivalent Multiplicative Models of the 3 × 3 Mobility Classification[a]

Origin	Destination		
	White-Collar	Blue-Collar	Farm
A. Quasi-Perfect Mobility			
White-Collar	δ_1	1	1
Blue-Collar	1	δ_2	1
Farm	1	1	δ_3
B. Crossings with Blue-Collar Immobility			
White-Collar	1	γ_1	$\gamma_1\gamma_2$
Blue-Collar	γ_1	δ	γ_2
Farm	$\gamma_1\gamma_2$	γ_2	1
C. Crossings with Uniform Immobility			
White-Collar	δ	γ_1	$\gamma_1\gamma_2$
Blue-Collar	γ_1	δ	γ_2
Farm	$\gamma_1\gamma_2$	γ_2	δ
D. Model I* (homogeneous row and column effects) Plus Uniform Immobility			
White-Collar	$\delta\gamma_1^2$	$\gamma_1^2\gamma_2$	$\gamma_1^3\gamma_3$
Blue-Collar	$\gamma_1^2\gamma_2$	$\delta\gamma_2^4$	$\gamma_3^2\gamma_2^3$
Farm	$\gamma_1^3\gamma_3$	$\gamma_3^3\gamma_2^3$	$\delta\gamma_3^6$
E. Model UII* (homogeneous row and column effects with uniform immobility)			
White-Collar	$\delta e^{\mu_1^2}$	$e^{\mu_1\mu_2}$	$e^{\mu_1\mu_3}$
Blue-Collar	$e^{\mu_1\mu_2}$	$\delta e^{\mu_2^2}$	$e^{\mu_2\mu_3}$
Farm	$e^{\mu_1\mu_3}$	$e^{\mu_2\mu_3}$	$\delta e^{\mu_3^2}$

[a] Marginal effects are suppressed in this display. See text for explanation.

parameter of Models A and B is unchanged, while the crossings parameters of Model B are multiplied by the square root of the inheritance parameter. By applying the inheritance parameter of the middle stratum to the two extreme strata, Model C reduces the barriers (crossing parameters) between the extremes and the middle category. Although Model C does not estimate any negative barriers between strata, it still yields negative estimates of status inheritance in Hungary, the United States and Sweden, just as does the model of quasi-perfect mobility. Model C is less appealing to us than quasi-perfect mobility (Model A) because we expect low levels of inheritance only in the blue-collar stratum, but Model C generalizes status disinheritance to all three strata in these countries.

Before discussing the remaining panels of Table 3, it is necessary to introduce some of Goodman's (1979a) association models. Uniform association assigns numeric values to the strata at equal intervals, while homogeneous row and column effect Models I* and II* permit distances between strata to differ. "Homogeneity" refers to the assumption that the distances between the same origin and destination strata are equal. In Model I* and uniform association, we assume that the blue-collar stratum lies between the white-collar and farm strata; homogeneous row and column effect Model II* does not require prior assumptions about the rank order of strata.[20] None of these models satisfactorily accounts for stratum inheritance, and they do not fit the 16-nation data.[21]

In less-aggregated tables, it is possible to fit uniform association or row and column effects while also fitting distinct parameters for immobility in each category (Goodman, 1979a). Those parameters are not identified in the 3 × 3 classifications, but it is possible to identify a single parameter that pertains to inheritance in all strata. Adding a single immobility parameter for each country to the model of uniform association improves fit substantially, but still does not yield a satisfactory fit.[22] The addition of a single immobility parameter makes Model I* or Model II* equivalent to quasi-perfect mobility. The former model is shown in Panel D of Table 3, where γ_1, γ_2, and γ_3 are scale values for the white-collar, blue-collar, and farm strata, respectively. Without loss of generality, we normalize these three parameters by fixing $\gamma_2 = 1$. Consequently, γ_1 pertains (inversely) to the distance between blue-collar and farm strata. As in Model C, δ pertains to immobility in all strata. By equating expressions for the distinct odds ratios in Model A and Model D, we obtain

$$\gamma_1 = (\delta_2 \delta_3 / \delta_1^2)^{1/6},$$
$$\gamma_3 = (\delta_3^2 / \delta_1 \delta_2)^{1/6}, \qquad (2)$$

and
$$\delta = (\delta_1 \delta_2^4 \delta_3)^{1/6}.$$

Clearly, the parameters of Model D are a far more complex mixture of the parameters of Model A

than are those of Models B or C. The distance between white-collar and blue-collar strata varies directly with white-collar inheritance, but inversely with blue-collar and farm inheritance; similarly, the distance between blue-collar and farm strata varies directly with farm inheritance, but inversely with blue-collar and white-collar inheritance.[23]

Given our findings about Model A, these relationships imply that the parameters of Model D should show a moderate level of stratum inheritance, a large distance between the farm stratum and either the blue- or white-collar stratum, and a smaller distance between the blue-collar and white-collar strata. While the parameters for most nations fall within this description, there is a serious anomaly in the estimates for 7 nations: Australia, Belgium, France, the Philippines, Denmark, Finland, and Sweden. In each of these nations, the estimated distance between white-collar and blue-collar strata is negative. We find these results less plausible than the estimates of blue-collar status disinheritance under quasi-perfect mobility. It is difficult to believe that the white-collar stratum is closer to the farm stratum than is the blue-collar stratum. Also, these anomalous distances are contrary to the ranking of strata that was assumed in Model I*, and this renders the model internally inconsistent.[24]

Panel E of Table 3 displays the parameters of Model II* with a uniform immobility parameter (hereafter, Model UII*). The μ_i are scale values for the occupational strata and appear as exponents; in these terms the model is log-multiplicative, not log-linear. Without loss of generality, we normalize the parameters of the model by the restriction $\mu_2 = 0$, so μ_1 is the distance between white- and blue-collar strata and μ_3 is the distance between blue-collar and farm strata. As in Models C and D, δ is a multiplicative (log-linear) effect pertaining to immobility in all strata. By equating expressions for the distinct odds ratios in Model A and Model E, we obtain

$$\delta_1 = \delta e^{\mu_1(\mu_1 - \mu_3)},$$
$$\delta_2 = \delta e^{\mu_1 \mu_3}, \qquad (3)$$

and
$$\delta_3 = \delta e^{\mu_3(\mu_3 - \mu_1)}.$$

In this model, the μ_i and δ are quadratic functions of the logarithms of the δ_i. Our expectations about the parameters of Model E are similar to those for Model D, and in this case the estimates are more plausible. That is, in every country the blue-collar stratum is estimated to lie between the white-collar and farm strata; the distance between the white- and blue-collar strata is less than that between the blue-collar and farm strata; and there is positive status inheritance.[25]

We also estimated the variability of parameters across nations under quasi-perfect mobility and Model UII*. On grounds of parsimony, we would prefer the model that captured cross-national variability in the least number of its parameters. However, we found substantial cross-national variation in each of the parameters of these two and other equivalent models.

There is a trade-off between the specification of heterogeneous interstratum distances in Model UII* and heterogeneous immobility parameters under quasi-perfect mobility. Model UII* specifies unequal distances between strata by equating densities of immobility across strata. For example, if $\mu_1 = \mu_3$, then $\delta_1 = \delta_3 = \delta$. Obversely, the quasi-perfect mobility model specifies stratum differences in inheritance by ignoring interstratum distances. For example, if $\delta_1 = \delta_3$, then $\mu_1 = \pm \mu_3$. While the two models use different imagery to describe the mobility process, the differences between them cannot be resolved on the basis of fit or, in our opinion, the parameter estimates in the 16-nation sample. By virtue of their equivalence many, but not all, cross-national comparisons are indifferent to the choice between the two models. ...

Conclusions

We have gained new insights into the leading issues of comparative social mobility by reanalyzing a standard set of data. Although we know the limitations of these data, we think that our results set a provisional baseline for future comparative research with "second generation" studies. We expect and hope that many of our findings will be elaborated, challenged, and falsified in future work.

The preceding analysis provides considerable support for the FJH revision of the Lipset-Zetterberg hypothesis, which implies that historical and cultural variations affect the shape of the occupational structure but not the interactions between occupational strata; this invariance is perhaps stronger than heretofore supposed. We have also proposed that the FJH revision might be elaborated in two respects. First, we suggested that uniformity in mobility regimes is not limited to highly industrialized societies but may extend across levels of economic development. Industrialized countries share a common pattern of mobility, but the pattern can not derive from the "logic of industrialism" if it applies equally to less-developed societies. This uniformity in mobility patterns may be the analogue to invariance in prestige hierarchies, in the sense that both may result from cross-national regularities in the resources and desirability accorded occupations.

Second, we provided greater substance to the FJH revision by specifying the structure of the shared mobility regime. Since the revision remains agnostic with regard to this structure, we proceeded inductively by fitting a series of mobility models. It is most striking that quasi-symmetry (and equivalent models) provided superior fit in nearly all the countries. This finding implies that Blau and Duncan's (1967) hypothesis of semipermeable class boundaries is not confirmed in the United States, nor in the other countries in our sample. Rather, there is a symmetry of exchanges between occupational strata, once intergenerational shifts in the marginal distributions are controlled.

We have examined several models of mobility that are equivalent to quasi-symmetry, and among these there are reasons to prefer quasi-perfect mobility and Model UII*. The former model yields distinct parameters for stratum-specific inheritance, while the latter specifies unequal distances between strata, plus an inheritance parameter that pertains to all strata. Both of these models are theoretically appealing; both yield plausible parameter estimates; and both display cross-national variation in their parameters. Consequently, a choice between these models must rest upon criteria outside the mobility process per se, and we have used both models in our analysis.

Under the quasi-perfect mobility model, we find strong white-collar inheritance and even stronger farm inheritance, perhaps consonant with the beliefs of the more extreme critics of rigidity in the class structure. Although the strength of inheritance within these strata might lend the impression of distinct class boundaries, this must be reconciled with extreme fluidity in the blue-collar stratum. Indeed, in several countries there is actually a net propensity for blue-collar disinheritance; this finding extends Goodman's (1965, 1969a, 1969b) results on the classic British and Danish mobility tables. Within all sixteen countries, the picture that emerges is one of severe immobility at the two extremes of the occupational hierarchy and considerable fluidity in the middle. Under this model, the cross-national structure of mobility closely resembles the pattern described by Featherman and Hauser (1978) in the United States. Correspondingly, under Model UII*, we find a large distance between the white-collar and blue-collar strata, an even larger distance between the blue-collar and farm strata, and a moderately strong residue of stratum inheritance.

Although we have found substantial similarities in mobility regimes across countries, we have also analyzed deviations from the common pattern. In this respect we departed from earlier international comparisons by directly incorporating several explanatory variables within a mobility model and by estimating and comparing the effects of these variables on the parameters of social fluidity. …

The need to extend and elaborate our analysis is accentuated by our finding that intersocietal differences in observed mobility are induced principally by variations in the marginal distributions of the mobility tables. This suggests that future research should explore the effects of economic and political variables on the shape of the social hierarchy. Much the same conclusion was advanced by Hauser et al. (1975) in their longitudinal analysis of American mobility classifications. They argued that further research cannot treat marginal differences as a nuisance factor if they are the driving force behind temporal change in observed mobility rates. We might add that economic and political variables may well have a greater effect on the structure of occupational supply and demand than on social fluidity. Although issues of this nature may be addressed within the general analytic framework presented here, we leave this task for future research.

Notes

An earlier draft of this paper was presented at the 47th Annual Meeting of the Midwest Sociological Society, Kansas City, 1983. Computations were supported by a grant to the Center for Demography and Ecology of the University of Wisconsin–Madison from the National Institute for Child Health and Human Development (HD-5876). During the preparation of this paper Grusky was supported by a predoctoral fellowship from the National Science Foundation, and Hauser was supported by the Graduate School of the University of Wisconsin–Madison. We thank Lawrence Hazelrigg for furnishing the mobility data, and Peter Smith for providing sample counts for the Philippines table. We have benefited greatly from the comments of Michael Hout, O. D. Duncan, Clifford C. Clogg, Walter Mueller, Michael Sobel, Robert D. Mare, McKee J. McClendon, and from unpublished memoranda and correspondence with Leo A. Goodman that O. D. Duncan shared with us. The opinions expressed herein are those of the authors.

1. Of course, there is an element of subjectivity in any evaluation of the FJH revision; it is unclear how much similarity in mobility regimes is necessary to confirm the hypothesis.

2. Following McClendon (1980a, 1980b), Bulgaria was omitted from the data because the sample included both males and females. Some of the cited studies have supplemented these data with mobility classifications from other countries. We have revised the counts for the U.S., France, Hungary, and the Philippines to reflect the sizes and designs of those samples. These data are available from the authors by request.

3. Although there is intergenerational transfer of skills in the blue-collar stratum, we think it is far stronger in the farm sector, where the family is more often the unit of production.

4. This argument for uniformity may need qualification in the case of socialist societies to the degree that they accord greater desirability to blue-collar occupations and prohibit formal ownership of economic resources (Parkin, 1971; Giddens, 1973).

5. Goldthorpe (1980) uses the term social fluidity for mobility and immobility net of marginal effects. We

use it to refer globally to interaction effects, rather than using "mobility" as an inclusive term.

6. On request the authors will supply a table showing the fit of the models in Panel A in each of the 16 countries.

7. Iutaka et al. (1975) also found that the quasi-perfect mobility model adequately fitted a number of national mobility tables, primarily drawn from Miller (1960). Our preference for this model is specific to the 3 × 3 classification used here. In other mobility tables, including disaggregations of this one, other models may well be preferable.

8. For an explanation of quasi-symmetry, see Bishop et al. (1975: Ch. 8). Featherman and Hauser (1978:184–87) and Hauser (1981) discuss the relevance of quasi-symmetry to the interpretation of social mobility. Featherman and Hauser did find some asymmetries in their analysis of intergenerational mobility to current occupations, but the majority of these pertained to mobility within the broad strata of the present analysis.

9. This property of the model is also consistent with certain social distance models, for example, crossings models (Goodman, 1972; Pontinen, 1982).

10. As Goodman (1969b:15) has demonstrated, the quasi-perfect mobility model is especially useful in comparisons of occupational or stratum persistence because the inheritance parameters are not confounded with one another. The stratum inheritance parameters analyzed by McClendon (1980b:499–500) do not have this desirable property.

11. On request the authors will provide estimates of stratum inheritance under quasi-perfect mobility in each of the sixteen countries. References to statistical significance in the text are based on the $\alpha = .05$ level, two-tailed.

12. Note that Great Britain is not included in the present analysis, and our Danish classification, obtained from a 1972 survey, does not show blue-collar status disinheritance. However, in 1972 the parameter for blue-collar immobility in Denmark is still among the lowest in our sample.

13. The contrast between Model 2 and Model 3 yields $L^2 = 6,072$ with 32 df. We also reject all three hypotheses of pairwise equality between stratum inheritance parameters. The test statistics are $L^2 = 2,734$ for equality of white-collar and blue-collar inheritance, $L^2 = 1,087$ for equality of white-collar and farm inheritance, and $L^2 = 5,577$ for equality of blue-collar and farm inheritance, each with 16 df.

14. The model of perfect blue-collar mobility is equivalent in the 3 × 3 table to a crossings model without a parameter for blue-collar immobility. It would be interesting to recast some of our comparative findings in the terms of either of these models: we have not done

so here because of the more satisfactory fit of quasi-perfect mobility.

15. The models in Panel B substitute terms δ_{ij} for the corresponding terms δ_{ijk} in equation 1.

16. Since the data are primarily from Western industrialized nations, this finding is most tentative.

17. Industrialization is per capita energy consumption in kilograms of coal, matched to the date of the corresponding mobility study (McClendon, 1980a). Educational enrollment is the proportion of the population between the ages of five and nineteen enrolled in primary or secondary education, computed for 1964 or 1965 (Taylor and Hudson, 1972). Inequality is the percentage of the national income going to the top five percent of households, matched as closely as possible to the date of the mobility study (Jain, 1975). When this statistic was not available, comparable figures were estimated from data on inequality among income recipients or workers (Jain, 1975), or from sectoral income distributions (Taylor and Hudson, 1972). These estimates were calculated with the regression procedure outlined by Tyree et al. (1979:416). Social democracy is the proportion of seats in the national legislature held by socialist or "social democratic" parties averaged over the elections immediately preceding and following 1960 (Jackman, 1975). The authors will supply the values of these variables for each country on request.

18. On request the authors will supply a brief appendix that shows how to estimate log-linear models with exogenous variables that affect interaction parameters.

19. The Hungarian case accounts for about 25 percent of the test statistic for cross-national variation in social fluidity. Thus, when we exclude Hungary from the analysis, the other 4 explanatory variables account for proportionately less of the cross-national variation; our results are otherwise unaffected by the choice between excluding Hungary and the specification of a dummy variable for that nation.

20. See Goodman (1979a:547–48) for a statement of the invariance properties of these models.

21. Goodman (1979a:550–51, 1981c:228–35) and Clogg (1982) extend association models to multi-way classifications. Without cross-national constraints on parameters, uniform association yields $L^2 = 9,058$ with 48 df, homogeneous row and column effect Model I* yields $L^2 = 8,091$ with 32 df, and homogeneous row and column effect Model II* yields $L^2 = 7,399$ with 32 df. On request the authors will report the fit of these models in each country.

22. The fit statistic is $L^2 = 1,237$ with 32 df; this model is equivalent to equal crossings with a single diagonal parameter in the 3 × 3 table. It is not possible to add a parameter for immobility in each stratum to the uniform association model, for the model would then

be underidentified in the 3 × 3 classification. That model meets the order condition, but not the rank condition for identification because quasi-perfect mobility and uniform association both imply quasi-symmetry.

23. We thank Michael Hout and O. D. Duncan for suggesting this and related models to us.

24. The estimated parameters of Model I* with uniform inheritance are available from the authors upon request.

25. The algebraic results and parameter estimates are available from the authors upon request. Model UII* cannot be estimated with the ANOASC program (Shockey and Clogg, 1983) because we fit a single parameter for the main diagonal. We have estimated the model within GLIM (Baker and Nelder, 1978) by successively fitting models of row effects and models of column effects to the mobility classifications and their transposes, and updating the estimated scale values at each step. This parallels procedures described by Goodman (1979a:551) and Breen (1984).

References

Allison, Paul D. 1980. "Analyzing collapsed contingency tables without actually collapsing." *American Sociological Review* 45:123–30.

Baker, R. J. and J. A. Nelder. 1978. The GLIM System, Release 3: Generalized Linear Interactive Modelling. Oxford: Numerical Algorithms Group.

Bishop, Yvonne M., Stephen E. Fienberg and Paul W. Holland. 1975. Discrete Multivariate Analysis: Theory and Practice. Cambridge: MIT Press.

Blau, Peter M. and Otis D. Duncan. 1967. The American Occupational Structure. New York: Wiley.

Breen, Richard. 1984. "Fitting non-hierarchical and association log linear models using GLIM." *Sociological Methods and Research* 13:77–107.

Breiger, Ronald L. 1981. "The social class structure of occupational mobility." *American Journal of Sociology* 87:578–611.

Clogg, Clifford C. 1982. "Some models for the analysis of association in multiway cross-classifications having ordered categories." *Journal of the American Statistical Association* 77:803–15.

Cutright, Phillips. 1968. "Occupational inheritance: a cross-national analysis." *American Journal of Sociology* 73:400–16.

Duncan, Otis D. 1979. "How destination depends on origin in the occupational mobility table." *American Journal of Sociology* 84:793–803.

Erikson, Robert, John H. Goldthorpe and Lucienne Portocarero. 1979. "Intergenerational class mobility in three Western European societies: England, France, and Sweden." *British Journal of Sociology* 30:415–41.

———. 1982. "Social fluidity in industrial nations: England, France, and Sweden." *British Journal of Sociology* 33:1–34.

Featherman, David L. and Robert M. Hauser. 1978. Opportunity and Change. New York: Academic Press.

Featherman, David L., F. Lancaster Jones and Robert M. Hauser. 1975. "Assumptions of mobility research in the United States: the case of occupational status." *Social Science Research* 4:329–60.

Giddens, Anthony. 1973. The Class Structure of the Advanced Societies. New York: Harper & Row.

Goldthorpe, John H. 1980. Social Mobility and Class Structure in Modern Britain. Oxford: Clarendon Press.

Goldthorpe, John H. and Keith Hope. 1974. The Social Grading of Occupations: A New Approach and Scale. Oxford: Clarendon Press.

Goodman, Leo A. 1965. "On the statistical analysis of mobility tables." *American Journal of Sociology* 70:564–85.

———. 1968. "The analysis of cross-classified data: independence, quasi-independence, and interaction in contingency tables with or without missing entries." *Journal of the American Statistical Association* 63:1091–1131.

———. 1969a. "On the measurement of social mobility: an index of status persistence." *American Sociological Review* 34:831–50.

———. 1969b. "How to ransack social mobility tables and other kinds of cross-classification tables." *American Journal of Sociology* 75:1–39.

———. 1972. "Some multiplicative models for the analysis of cross-classified data." Pp. 649–96 in Proceedings of the Sixth Berkeley Symposium on Mathematical Statistics and Probability. Berkeley: University of California Press.

———. 1979a. "Simple models for the analysis of association in cross-classifications having ordered categories." *Journal of the American Statistical Association* 70:755–68.

———. 1979b. "Multiplicative models for the analysis of occupational mobility tables and other kinds of cross-classification tables." *American Journal of Sociology* 84:804–19.

———. 1981a. "Criteria for determining whether certain categories in a cross-classification table should be combined, with special reference to occupational categories in an occupational mobility table." *American Journal of Sociology* 87:612–50.

———. 1981b. "Association models and canonical correlation in the analysis of cross-classifications having ordered categories." Journal of the American Statistical Association 76:320–34.

_____. 1981c. "Three elementary views of log linear models for the analysis of cross-classifications having ordered categories." Pp. 193–239 in Samuel Leinhardt (ed.), Sociological Methodology, 1981. San Francisco: Jossey-Bass.

Hardy, Melissa A. and Lawrence E. Hazelrigg. 1978. "Industrialization and the circulatory rate of mobility: further tests of some cross-sectional hypotheses." Sociological Focus 11:1–10.

Hauser, Robert M. 1978. "A structural model of the mobility table." Social Forces 56:919–53.

_____. 1979. "Some exploratory methods for modeling mobility tables and other cross-classified data." Pp. 413–58 in Karl F. Schuessler (ed.), Sociological Methodology, 1980. San Francisco: Jossey-Bass.

_____. 1981. "Hope for the mobility ratio." Social Forces 60:572–84.

_____. 1983. "Vertical class mobility in Great Britain, France, and Sweden." Center for Demography and Ecology, University of Wisconsin–Madison: Working Paper 82-36.

Hauser, Robert M. and David L. Featherman. 1977. "Commonalities in social stratification and assumptions about status mobility in the United States." Pp. 3–50 in Robert M. Hauser and David L. Featherman (eds.), The Process of Stratification. New York: Academic Press.

Hauser, Robert M., John N. Koffel, Harry P. Travis and Peter J. Dickinson. 1975. "Temporal change in occupational mobility: evidence for men in the United States." American Sociological Review 40:279–97.

Hazelrigg, Lawrence E. 1974. "Cross-national comparisons of father-to-son occupational mobility." Pp. 469–93 in Joseph Lopreato and Lionel S. Lewis (eds.), Social Stratification. New York: Harper & Row.

Hazelrigg, Lawrence E. and Maurice A. Garnier. 1976. "Occupational mobility in industrial societies: a comparative analysis of differential access to occupational ranks in seventeen countries." American Sociological Review 41:498–511.

Heath, Anthony. 1981. Social Mobility. London: Fontana.

Hope, Keith. 1981. "Vertical mobility in Britain: a structured analysis." Sociology 15:19–55.

_____. 1982. "Vertical and nonvertical class mobility in three countries." American Sociological Review 47:100–113.

Hout, Michael. 1983. Mobility Tables. Beverly Hills: Sage.

Iutaka, S., B. F. Bloomer, R. E. Burke and O. Wolowyna. 1975. "Testing the quasi-perfect mobility model for intergenerational data: international comparisons." Economic and Social Review 6:215–36.

Jackman, Robert W. 1975. Politics and Social Equality: A Comparative Analysis. New York: Wiley.

Jain, Shail. 1975. Size Distribution of Income: A Compilation of Data. Washington, D.C.: World Bank.

Lipset, Seymour M. and Hans L. Zetterberg. 1959. "Social mobility in industrial societies." Pp. 11–75 in Seymour M. Lipset and Reinhard Bendix (eds.), Social Mobility in Industrial Society. Berkeley: University of California Press.

MacDonald, K. I. 1981. "On the formulation of a structural model of the mobility table." Social Forces 60:557–71.

McClendon, McKee J. 1980a. "Occupational mobility and economic development: a cross-national analysis." Sociological Focus 13:331–42.

_____. 1980b. "Structural and exchange components of occupational mobility: a cross-national analysis." The Sociological Quarterly 21:493–509.

McRoberts, Hugh A. and Kevin Selbee. 1981. "Trends in occupational mobility in Canada and the United States: a comparison." American Sociological Review 46:406–21.

Miller, S. M. 1960. "Comparative social mobility." Current Sociology 9:1–89.

Parkin, Frank. 1971. Class Inequality and Political Order. New York: Praeger.

Pontinen, Seppo. 1982. "Models and social mobility research: a comparison of some log-linear models of a social mobility matrix." Quality and Quantity 16:91–107.

Pullum, Thomas. 1975. Measuring Occupational Inheritance. New York: Elsevier.

Portocarero, Lucienne. 1983. "Social fluidity in France and Sweden." Acta Sociologica 26:127–39.

Raftery, Adrian E. 1983. "Comment on 'Gaps and Glissandos…'" American Sociological Review 48:581–83.

Shockey, James W. and Clifford C. Clogg. 1983. ANOASC: A Computer Program for the Analysis of Association in a Set of K I-by-J Conditional Tables. Population Issues Research Center, Pennsylvania State University.

Simkus, Albert A. 1981. "Historical change in occupational inheritance under socialism: Hungary, 1930–1973." Pp. 171–203 in Donald J. Treiman and Robert V. Robinson (eds.), Research in Social Stratification and Mobility. Greenwich, CT: JAI Press.

Taylor, Charles L. and Michael C. Hudson. 1972. World Handbook of Political and Social Indicators. New Haven: Yale University Press.

Treiman, Donald J. 1970. "Industrialization and social stratification." Pp. 207–34 in Edward O. Laumann (ed.), Social Stratification: Research and Theory for the 1970s. New York: Bobbs-Merrill.

———. 1977. *Occupational Prestige in Comparative Perspective.* New York: Academic Press.

Tyree, Andrea, Moshe Semyonov and Robert Hodge. 1979. "Gaps and glissandos: inequality, economic de-

velopment, and social mobility in 24 countries." *American Sociological Review* 44:410–24.

Urton, William L. 1981. "Mobility and economic development revisited." *American Sociological Review* 46:128–37.

ROBERT ERIKSON AND JOHN H. GOLDTHORPE

Trends in Class Mobility: The Post-War European Experience

Introduction

The issue of trends in class mobility in industrial societies is one characterised by a wide-ranging dissensus which, unfortunately, extends to matters of fact as well as of interpretation. We do not suppose that in this paper we will be able to resolve all the disagreements that are apparent. We do, however, believe that we can address the issue on the basis of comparative mobility data of a distinctively higher quality than those previously utilised, and that the results we report have significant consequences—positive or negative—for most of the rival positions that have been taken up.[1]

From the 1960s onwards, perhaps the dominant view on mobility trends has been that derived from what we will refer to as the 'liberal theory' of industrialism, as developed by various American authors (Kerr *et al.*, 1960, 1973; Kerr, 1969, 1983; Dunlop *et al.*, 1975; cf. also Parsons, 1960: chs. 3 and 4; 1967: chs. 4 and 15; 1971). This theory is a functionalist one which aims at establishing the distinctive properties of industrial societies in terms of the essential prerequisites for, or necessary consequences of, the technical and economic rationality that is seen as their defining

characteristic. What is implied so far as social mobility is concerned may be put in the form of the following three-part proposition.

In industrial societies, in comparison with pre-industrial ones

(i) absolute rates of social mobility are generally high, and moreover upward mobility—i.e. from less to more advantaged positions—predominates over downward mobility;

(ii) relative rates of mobility—or, that is, mobility opportunities—are more equal, in the sense that individuals of differing social origins compete on more equal terms to attain (or to avoid) particular destinations; and

(iii) both the level of absolute rates of mobility and the degree of equality in relative rates tend to increase over time.

To explain *why* these contrasts between mobility in pre-industrial and industrial society should arise, a number of arguments are deployed which have, moreover, been elaborated and extended in the specialist literature by authors generally sympathetic to the liberal position (see esp. Blau and

Duncan, 1967: ch. 12; Treiman, 1970). While all the arguments in question take on a functionalist form, one may usefully distinguish between those relating to three different kinds of effect—*structural, processual* and *compositional.*

First, it is held that within industrial society the dynamism of a rationally developed technology calls for continuous, and often rapid, change in the structure of the social division of labour, which also tends to become increasingly differentiated. High rates of mobility thus follow as from generation to generation, and in the course of individual lifetimes, the redistribution of the active population is required: that is, among economic sectors—first, from agriculture to manufacturing and then from manufacturing to services—and, in turn, among industries and among a growing diversity of occupations. Furthermore, the overall tendency is for advancing technology to *upgrade* levels of employment. Although some skills are rendered obsolete, new ones are created and the *net* effect is a reduction in the number of merely labouring and routine occupations and a rising demand for technically and professionally qualified personnel. At the same time, both the increasing scale of production, dictated by economic rationality, and the expansion of the services sector of the economy promote the growth of large bureaucratic organisations in which managerial and administrative positions also multiply. Industrial societies become increasingly 'middle-class' or at least 'middle-mass' societies. Consequently, upward mobility is more likely than downward in both intergenerational and worklife perspective. Under industrialism, the chances of 'success' are steadily improved for all.

Secondly, it is further claimed that as well as thus reshaping the objective structure of opportunity, industrialism transforms the processes through which particular individuals are allocated to different positions within the division of labour. Most fundamentally, rational procedures of social selection require a shift away from *acription* and towards *achievement* as the leading criterion: what counts is increasingly what individuals can do, and not who they are. Moreover, the growing demand for highly qualified personnel promotes the expansion of education and

training, and also the reform of educational institutions so as to increase their accessibility to individuals of all social backgrounds. Human resources cannot be wasted; talent must be fully exploited wherever it is to be found. Thus, as within a society of widening educational provision 'meritocratic' selection comes to predominate, the association between individuals' social origins and their eventual destinations tends steadily to weaken and the society takes on a more 'open' character. And at the same time various other features of industrialism also serve to reduce the influence of social origins on individuals' future lives. For example, urbanisation and greater geographical mobility loosen ties of kinship and community; mass communications spread information, enlarge horizons and raise aspirations; and a greater equality of condition—that is, in incomes and living standards—means that the resources necessary for the realisation of ambition are more widely available.

Thirdly, it is argued that the foregoing effects interact with each other, in that the emphasis on achievement as the basis for social selection will be strongest within the expanding sectors of the economy—that is, the more technologically advanced manufacturing industries and services—and within the increasingly dominant form of large-scale bureaucratic organisation. Conversely, ascriptive tendencies will persist chiefly within declining sectors and organisational forms—for example, within agriculture or small-scale, family-based business enterprise. In other words, compositional effects on mobility occur in that, once a society begins to industrialise, the proportion of its population that is subject to the new 'mobility regime' characteristic of industrialism not only increases as that regime imposes itself, but further as those areas and modes of economic activity that are most resistant to it become in any event ever more marginal.

One reason that may then be suggested for the degree of dominance exerted by the liberal position is the coherent way in which the underlying theory has been developed. Another is the manifest failure of the main attempt made directly to controvert it. That is, the revision and extension of the Marxist theory of proletarianisation (cf. Braverman, 1974; Carchedi, 1977; Wright and

Singelmann, 1982; Crompton and Jones, 1984) which sought to show the necessity for the systematic 'degrading', rather than upgrading, of labour under the exigencies of late capitalism—with the consequence of large-scale *downward* mobility of a collective kind. This undertaking lacked from start any secure empirical foundation, and the accumulation of results incompatible with the new theory resulted in its eventual abandonment even by those who had been among its most resourceful supporters (see e.g. Singelmann and Tienda, 1985; Wright and Martin, 1987). However, various other positions can still be identified that to a greater or lesser extent come into conflict with the liberal view and that continue to merit serious attention.

First of all, it should be noted that the theory of mobility in industrial society advanced by Lipset and Zetterberg (1956, 1959) and sometimes simply assimilated to the liberal theory (see e.g. Kerr, 1983: 53) does in fact differ from it in crucial respects. For example, Lipset and Zetterberg do not seek to argue that mobility steadily *increases* with industrial development: indeed, they remark that *among* industrial societies no association is apparent between mobility rates and rates of economic growth. What they propose (1959: 13) is, rather, some kind of 'threshold' effect: 'our tentative interpretation is that the social mobility of societies becomes relatively high once their industrialization, and hence their economic expansion, reaches a certain level.' And although Lipset and Zetterberg's claim that (absolute) mobility rates in industrial societies become *uniformly* high would now be generally regarded as empirically untenable, their suggestion that a historic upward shift in such rates tends to occur at some—perhaps quite early—stage in the industrialisation process has not been similarly disconfirmed. Again, it is not part of Lipset and Zetterberg's case that the high mobility that they see as characteristic of industrial societies is the result of a tendency towards greater openness. Rather, they place the emphasis firmly on the effects of structural change, and in turn they are at pains to point out (1959: 27) that 'the fact that one country contains a greater percentage of mobile individuals than another does *not* mean that that

country approximates a model of equal opportunity more closely'.

Secondly, a yet more radical challenge to the liberal view may be derived from the pioneering work of Sorokin (1927/1959). Taking a synoptic view, as much dependent on historical and ethnographic evidence as on contemporary social research, Sorokin was led to the conclusion that in modern western societies mobility was at a relatively high level, and he was further ready to acknowledge the possibility that, from the eighteenth century onwards, mobility rates had in general shown a tendency to rise. However, he was at the same time much concerned to reject the idea that what was here manifested was in effect 'the end of history' and the start of a 'perpetual and "eternal" increase of vertical mobility'. Rather, Sorokin argued, the present situation represented no more than a specific historical phase; in some societies in some periods mobility increased, while in other periods it declined. Overall, no 'definite perpetual trend' was to be seen towards either greater or less mobility, but only 'trendless fluctuation'. Those who were impressed by the distinctiveness of the modern era knew too little about historical societies and their diversity: 'What has been happening is only an alternation—the waves of greater mobility superseded by the cycles of greater immobility—and that is all' (1959: 152–4).

It might from the foregoing appear that Sorokin's position was merely negative. But, in fact, underlying his denial of developmental trends in mobility and his preference for a cyclical view, at least the elements of a theory can be discerned. In arguing against the supposition that rates of mobility in the modern period are quite unprecedented, one of the points Sorokin most stresses is that while certain barriers to mobility have been largely removed—for example, juridical and religious ones—it is important to recognise that other barriers have become more severe or have been newly introduced: for example, those represented by systems of educational selection and occupational qualification (1959: 153–4, 169–79). This, moreover, is what must always be expected: the forms of social stratification which provide the context for mobility are themselves structures expressing differential power and advantage, and thus possess important self-maintaining properties. Those who hold privileged positions will not readily cede them and, in the nature of the case, can draw on superior resources in their defence. Indeed, Sorokin remarks that if he *had* to believe in the existence of a permanent trend in mobility, it would be in a declining one, since social strata are often observed to become more 'closed' over time as the cumulative result of those in superior positions using their power and advantage to restrict entry from below (1959: 158–60). However, this propensity for closure—which we may understand as being *endogenous* to all forms of stratification—is not the only influence on mobility rates. A further point that Sorokin several times makes (see e.g. 1959: 141–152, 466–72) is that in periods of both political and economic upheaval—associated, say, with revolution or war or with rapid commercial, industrial and technological change—marked surges in mobility are typically produced as the social structure as a whole, including the previously existing distribution of power and advantage, is disrupted. In other words, increased mobility here results from the impact of factors that are *exogenous* to the stratification order.

Thirdly and finally, one may note a more recently developed position which, however, has evident affinities with that of Sorokin. Featherman, Jones and Hauser (1975) aim at presenting a reformulation of Lipset and Zetterberg's hypothesis that across industrial societies rates of social mobility display a basic similarity. This hypothesis cannot stand if expressed in terms of absolute rates but, they argue, becomes far more plausible if applied, rather, to relative rates. When mobility is considered at the 'phenotypical' level of absolute rates cross-national similarity can scarcely be expected. This is because these rates are greatly influenced by the structural context of mobility and, in turn, by effects deriving from a range of economic, technological and demographic circumstances which are known to vary widely and which, so far as particular individuals and families are concerned, must be regarded as 'exogenously determined'. When, however, mobility is considered *net of* all such effects, or that is, at the 'genotypical' level of relative rates, the likelihood

of cross-national similarity being found is much greater. For at this level only those factors are involved that bear on the relative chances of individuals of differing social origin achieving or avoiding, in competition with each other, particular destination positions among those that are structurally given. And there is reason to suppose that in modern societies the conditions under which such 'endogenous mobility regimes' operate—for example, the degree of differentiation in occupational hierarchies and in job rewards and requirements—may not be subject to substantial variation.

For present purposes, then, the chief significance of the FJH hypothesis lies in the rather comprehensive challenge that it poses to the claims of liberal theorists. On the one hand, so far as absolute mobility rates are concerned, it implies a basic scepticism, essentially akin to that of Sorokin, about the possibility of *any* long-term, developmentally-driven trend; while, on the other hand, it stands directly opposed to the proposition that under industrialism a steady increase occurs in the equality of mobility chances. Although some initial developmental effect in this direction early in the industrialisation process might be compatible with the hypothesis, any continuing change in relative mobility rates is clearly precluded (cf. Grusky and Hauser, 1984: 20). Once societies can be deemed to have become industrial, their mobility regimes should stabilise in some approximation to the common pattern that the FJH hypothesis proposes, and should not thereafter reveal any specific or persistent tendencies, whether towards convergence on greater openness or otherwise. No forces are recognised inherent in the functional dynamics of industrialism that work systematically to expand mobility opportunities.

The divergent arguments concerning mobility trends that we have reviewed in this section will then provide the context within which we present our empirical analyses of data for European nations. First, though, we must say something about what we take to be the particular relevance to evaluating these arguments of the European experience over the post-war years.

The Relevance of the European Experience

It is not difficult to detect within the liberal theory of industrialism a degree of American or, more accurately perhaps, of Anglo-American, ethnocentricity. Historically, the origins of modern industrial society are traced back to late eighteenth- and early nineteenth-century England; and other western nations, including the USA, are then seen as having successively followed England's lead in breaking free of the constraints of a traditional social order and entering the industrial world.[2] Contemporaneously, it is the USA rather than England that is recognised as the vanguard nation; and with industrialisation now on the global agenda, the major differences between industrial and pre-industrial, or modern and traditional, society are seen as best revealed through explicit or implicit USA–Third World comparisons. Within these perspectives, therefore, the experience of industrialisation of the mainland European nations is viewed in only a rather restrictive way. It tends either to be taken for granted, as fitting unproblematically into the trajectories defined by the two paradigm cases, or alternatively as providing interesting instances of 'deviations', over which, however, the logic of industrialism has eventually to prevail.[3]

This schematic background to the liberal theory must be regarded as excessively simplified, and possibly misleading, in at least two respects. On the one hand, while England did indeed industrialise early, the supposition that other western nations then followed along the same path, being differentiated only by the degree of their 'retardation', is one that has no sound historiographic basis. What is chiefly significant about the process of industrialisation in England is that—in part *because* of England's priority, but for other reasons too—it took on a quite distinctive character which subsequent cases could scarcely reflect (cf. Kemp, 1978: ch. 1 esp.). Rather than having simply followed in England's wake, other European nations do in fact display in their recent economic histories a great diversity of developmental paths; and it is, furthermore, impor-

tant to recognise that later industrialisation and economic retardation should not always be equated—as, for example, the French case can well illustrate (cf. O'Brien and Keyder, 1978).

On the other hand, it would also be mistaken to suppose that by the end of the nineteenth century the industrialisation of Europe was essentially completed. This would be to neglect the great economic and social importance that agriculture and also artisanal and other 'pre-industrial' forms of production continued to have throughout the nineteenth, and for well into the twentieth, century—and in many of the more advanced European nations as well as in those on the 'periphery'. It was in fact, as Bell has remarked (1980: 233), only in the period *after the second world war* that Europe as a whole became an industrial society. Indeed, various interpretations of the 'long boom' of this period have seen it as reflecting aspects of this culmination—for example, as being driven by the final phase of the supply of surplus rural labour (Kindleberger, 1967) or as marking the ultimate overcoming of the dualism of traditional and modern sectors within European economies (Lutz, 1984).[4]

The fact, then, that we here concentrate on the experience of European nations by no means implies that we will be treating questions of mobility trends within an unduly limited context. To the contrary, we have the advantage that while these nations can supply us with high quality data (far better, for example, than those usually available from Third World nations), they do also display a remarkably wide range of variation in their levels and patterns of industrial development—and even if we consider only that time-span to which our mobility data have some reference: that is, from the 1970s back to the first two decades of the century, in which the oldest respondents within our national samples were born. (For details of the surveys utilised, see Appendix Table 1).
…

It will from the foregoing have become evident that, in seeking to exploit the historical richness of our European data, we are prepared to make a large assumption: namely, that valid inferences about the presence or absence of mobility trends can be drawn from the data of single inquiries.

What we are in effect proposing is that age-groups distinguished within our samples from the 1970s can be treated as successive birth-cohorts, and that the mobility experience of their members can then be taken as indicative of whether or not change over time has occurred in mobility rates and patterns. In such an approach certain well-known difficulties arise, above all in treating intergenerational mobility, and in conclusion of this section we should therefore give these some attention.

To begin with, we must recognise that we are not in fact dealing with true birth cohorts within the nations we consider but only with what might better be called 'quasi-cohorts': that is, with the survivors of true cohorts, following on losses due to mortality and emigration, to whom immigrants will then be added. In such cases as those of the FRG, Ireland and Poland, the numbers here involved will obviously be substantial. This, however, is a situation that we can do little to remedy; we can only trust that no serious distortions will be introduced into our data of a kind that might affect our conclusions regarding trends.[5]

Further, there is the so-called 'identification problem'. If for the members of a national sample one compares their present class position (i.e. at time of inquiry) with their class of origin (i.e. father's class), the mobility experience of the individuals within successive 'quasi-cohorts' will be likely to reflect several different effects: not only those of the historical period through which they have lived but also those of their age and of their cohort membership *per se*. Thus, the problem is that of how we can assess 'period' effects—which are those relevant to questions of mobility trends—separately from effects of the other kinds. No clear-cut solution is, or can be, available (cf. Glenn, 1977), since birth-cohorts and age-groups are inescapably 'embedded' in historical time. However, several considerations would lead us to believe that in pursuing our present purposes we need not in fact be at so great a disadvantage in this respect as might initially appear.

First, it would seem empirically defensible to regard men of around 30–35 years of age as having reached a stage of 'occupational maturity', beyond which further major changes in their class positions become relatively unlikely (Goldthorpe, 1980, 1987: ch. 3; cf. also Blossfeld, 1986). Thus, we may take results for cohorts of this age or older as giving a reasonably reliable indication of the 'completed' pattern of the collective class mobility of their members.

Secondly, for all of our European nations except one, the Federal Republic of Germany, we have information on individuals' experience of mobility from their class of origin to their class of *first* employment. For this transition, therefore, age effects at least will obviously be much reduced, since attention is focused on a fairly well defined life-cycle stage. We would not wish to regard data on this transition as a very satisfactory basis for cross-national comparisons of intergenerational mobility, on grounds that we discuss elsewhere (Erikson and Goldthorpe, 1992: ch. 8). None the less, we are thus provided with the possibility of checking whether or not the conclusions that we reach on trends, or their absence, in mobility from class of origin to present class are consistent with ones that pertain to mobility rates of a more age-specific kind.[6]

Thirdly, it is important for us to emphasise that in the analyses that follow our concern will be not so much with the actual empirical description of mobility trends as with the evaluation of particular claims about such trends. What, therefore, we can always consider is whether, if we were to suppose some confounding of effects in our results, these would be of a kind that would tend unduly to favour or disfavour a given position. Thus, for example, in the case of the liberal claim that within industrial nations mobility and openness tend steadily to increase, it is difficult to see why any confounding of period effects by age effects should produce unfairly *negative* results: that is to say, it would appear unlikely that an actual increase in openness and mobility among the more recent cohorts within our national samples would be concealed by the fact that these cohorts are made up of young persons. If anything, one might expect the contrary, since younger persons will have benefited more widely from the expansion of educational provision which, according to the liberal theory, is one of the major sources of greater mobility and equality of opportunity. Likewise, there would seem no reason why age effects should obscure any trends within our data for the mobility rates of different nations to converge—as would be expected under the liberal theory as differences between nations' levels of industrial development are reduced. For if, as the theory maintains, the determinants and processes of mobility become increasingly standardised through the logic of industrialism, then convergence in mobility rates should, presumably, be *more* apparent among the younger than the older age groups in our samples (for an elaboration of this point, see Erikson, Goldthorpe and Portocarero, 1983: 307–10 and Figure 1).

As Glenn has observed (1977: 17), cohort analysis should never be a mechanical exercise, uninformed by theory and by additional 'external' evidence; and this point obviously applies *a fortiori* in the case of analyses, such as those we shall present, which rest only on 'quasi-cohorts'. But since we do have some knowledge about both the historical setting of the mobility that we consider and its life-course phasing, and since we are addressing a number of more or less specific and theoretically grounded hypotheses rather than proceeding quite empirically, our strategy is, we believe, one capable of producing results that can be interpreted in a reasonably reliable and consequential way. It is to these results that we now turn.

Absolute Rates

In seeking to assess the arguments that we have earlier reviewed, we start with evidence on intergenerational class mobility in the form of absolute rates: that is, rates based on differing versions of our class schema (see Appendix Table 2) and expressed in simple percentage terms. So as to avoid marked age effects in considering the transition from class of origin to present class, we restrict our attention to men in our national samples who were over age 30 at the time of inquiry (i.e. at some point in the early or mid-1970s; cf. Appendix Table 1). These men, we suppose, would be approaching, or would have attained, a stage of relative occupational maturity. The maximum age-limit that we apply here—and in all subsequent analyses—is 64.[7]

First of all, we consider *total* mobility rates. That is, the percentage of all men in our national samples found in cells off the main diagonal of the intergenerational mobility table based on the sevenfold version of the class schema; or, in other words, the percentage of all men whose 'present', or destination, class was different to their class of origin—the latter being indexed by the respondent's *father's* class at the time of the respondent's early adolescence.[8] In Figure 1 we seek to plot the course followed by the total mobility rate in each of our nine European nations on the basis of moving weighted averages of this rate for men *in successive birth years*, using a method of graduation that has been developed by Hoem and Linneman (1987).[9]

From inspection of Figure 1, the general impression gained must be one of support for the contention that absolute mobility rates display merely trendless change. It would, at all events, be difficult to ally the data here presented with the idea of mobility increasing steadily as industrialism advances. No regular tendency is apparent for the mobility of older respondents—of men born, say, in the first two decades of the century—to be exceeded by that of respondents who were born some twenty years later, and who would have reached occupational maturity during the long boom of the post-war years. And we may add that no essentially different picture emerges if, using the same technique, we plot total mobility rates from class of origin to class of *first* employment.[10] It would thus seem improbable that the failure of the graphs of Figure 1 to move upwards to the right, as would be expected from the liberal theory, can be explained simply in terms of the confounding of period by age effects.

The one possible pattern that might be discerned in Figure 1 is some tendency for total mobility rates to converge—even if not while steadily rising. That is to say, some narrowing down could be claimed in the cross-national range of mobility levels as between those displayed by the oldest and the youngest cohorts in our samples. For the former, as can be seen, the range of total mobility rates is from around 40 to over 70 percent, while for the latter it is from 50 to under 70 per cent—and, one might add, would be some ten percent-

FIGURE 1
Total mobility rates for men in nine nations by birth year

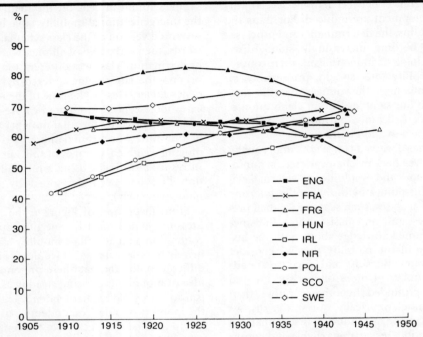

age points narrower still if the one case of Scotland were to be discounted.

However, it is important to note how this convergence comes about. It is in fact to a large extent the result of an increase in total mobility in two nations, Ireland and Poland, in which the rate among older cohorts, at around the 40 per cent mark, was substantially lower than in other nations. Ireland and Poland are—together with Hungary—those nations in our sample in which, as we have earlier indicated, industrialisation was most delayed. An alternative interpretation of Figure 1 would therefore be that instead of revealing a general tendency towards convergence in mobility rates, it rather supports a hypothesis of the kind suggested by Lipset and Zetterberg: that is, of a specific upturn in mobility occurring at a stage relatively early in the industrialisation process when the first major impact of structural change is felt.

That Hungary would then appear as deviant, in showing a high total mobility rate even among the oldest men considered, need not be found surprising. This could be seen as the result of the quite exceptional amount of mobility imposed upon the Hungarian agricultural workforce through direct political intervention, and which is thus reflected across the experience of all age-groups alike. In the period immediately following the second world war, the land reforms of the provisional government created over half-a-million new peasant proprietors; but then, under the subsequent state socialist regime, agriculture was within a decade almost entirely collectivised through the establishment of co-operatives or state farms (Kulcsár, 1984: 78–84, 96–100; Brus, 1986a, 1986b). Thus, respondents to our 1973 survey who were the sons of agricultural proprietors—over a quarter of the total—held different class positions to their fathers more or less of necessity, and even in fact where they continued to work the same land.[11]

These findings on total mobility do, we believe, carry significant implications, to which we shall wish to return. It is, however, of further interest here to try to obtain a somewhat more detailed picture of tendencies in absolute rates by considering also intergenerational *outflow* rates. Unfortunately, the relative smallness of the sizes of certain of our national samples means that we cannot reliably base our examination of such rates on the seven-class version of our schema but must, for the most part, resort to the three-class version (cf. Appendix Table 2) which distinguishes simply between nonmanual, manual and farm classes.[12]

Figures 2 to 6, which are produced via the same procedures as Figure 1, show the course followed in each of our nations by five different outflow rates calculated from 3 × 3 intergenerational mobility tables (again for men aged 30–64). As is indicated, the rates in question are those for intergenerational immobility within the farm class, for mobility from farm origins to manual and to nonmanual destinations, and for mobility from manual origins to nonmanual destinations and *vice versa*. Of the other transitions possible within the 3 × 3 tables, those from manual and nonmanual origins to farm positions were generally followed by too few individuals to allow any reliable rates to be established; and the fact that the numbers involved here are more or less negligible means in turn that trends in the remaining rates—that is, rates of immobility within the manual and nonmanual classes—need scarcely be plotted separately, since they will be essentially the complements of those already examined of mobility between these two classes.

Figure 2 displays the changing proportions of men across birth-cohorts in our nine nations who were of farm origins and who were themselves found in farm work. A broad tendency is apparent for such intergenerational immobility to decline, which might be expected in consequence of the general contraction of agricultural employment. The decline in the cases of Ireland and Poland from farm immobility rates of upwards of 70 per cent in the oldest cohorts is of particular interest in view of the interpretation we have suggested of the increases in total mobility in these nations revealed in Figure 1. By resorting to the raw data, we can in fact show that changes within the farm sector here played a crucial part. Thus, the contribution of this sector to the total *immobility* rate (i.e. the proportion of all cases in the mobility table found in cells on the main diagonal) fell in the Irish case from 69 per cent for men born before 1925 to only 27 per cent for those born after 1940, while in the Polish case the corresponding decline was from 77 to 35 per cent.

In two other nations, France and Hungary, the decline in farm immobility is also more or less continuous over the period to which our data refer. However, the cases of England, Scotland and Northern Ireland and likewise that of the FRG would suggest that, once the decline of agriculture has reached a certain point, rates of farm immobility tend to level out or to become rather variable. And Sweden appears quite distinctive in that farm immobility is shown at a low level— never more than 25 per cent—throughout the decades in which agricultural employment was falling. Here, though, we do have evidence to suggest some distortion in our results. Our corresponding plot for the transition to class of first employment indicates a strong decline in farm immobility; but, on account perhaps of the very rapidity of agricultural contraction in the post-war years, it would seem that many men also left the farm workforce at a quite late age, thus obscuring the downward trend when the transition to present class is considered.

Finally, it may be observed that in Figure 2, as in Figure 1, any impression of converging rates is created essentially by the rather dramatic Irish and Polish graphs. If these are disregarded, the cross-national range in rates of farm immobility merely fluctuates, being, for example, no narrower—at around 15 to 50 per cent—for men born from the mid-1930s onwards than it was for men born around 1920.

Figures 3 and 4 then display the course of outflow rates from farm origins to manual and nonmanual destinations respectively. Figure 3 would suggest that in those cases where declining trends in intergenerational immobility in farming were revealed in Figure 2, their counterpart has been increased outflows from farm origins into manual wage-earning positions in industry. France, Hungary, Ireland and Poland all show

FIGURE 2
Outflow rates from farm origins to farm destinations for men in nine nations by birth year

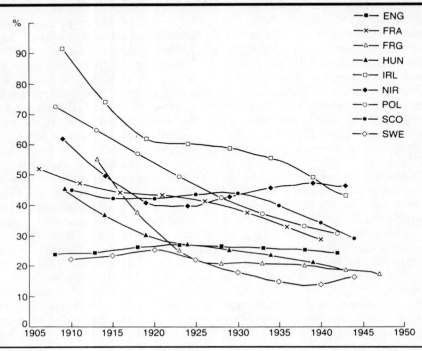

such increases of a continuous kind. In the remaining nations, however, trends are less readily discerned. In the cases of the FRG and Sweden, increasing proportions of men in the cohorts born up to about 1930 moved from farm origins into manual work—following what might perhaps be taken as a characteristic tendency of the drive to 'mature' industrialism. But in later cohorts this tendency is clearly not sustained, although for Sweden there is probably some underestimation of the rate in question as the converse of the distortion noted in regard to farm immobility. For England, Northern Ireland and Scotland, the graphs undulate in no readily interpretable way. Turning to the outflow rates from farm origins to nonmanual destinations presented in Figure 4, we find that trendless change is here still more manifest. The most remarkable feature of the graphs displayed is indeed their flatness, apart from the early rise from a near-zero level in the Irish case.[13]

The remaining point to be observed from Figures 3 and 4 together is that we find little indication at all of national mobility rates converging. Over the period covered, the cross-national range for farm-to-manual outflows shifts upwards, but with little narrowing, from around 10 to 55 per cent to 30 to 70 per cent; while the rates for farm-to-nonmanual outflows are notable for being almost entirely confined within a range of 10 to 25 per cent.

The last two Figures in the series, 5 and 6, show changes in rates of intergenerational mobility between the broad manual and nonmanual classes that we distinguish. From inspection of the graphs, it would once again seem difficult to avoid the conclusion that no clear trends emerge. Although some impression may perhaps be given that, overall, mobility from manual origins to nonmanual destinations has decreased while that in the reverse direction has increased, it is in fact only in the Polish case that monotonic trends in

FIGURE 3

Outflow rates from farm origins to manual destinations for men in nine nations by birth year

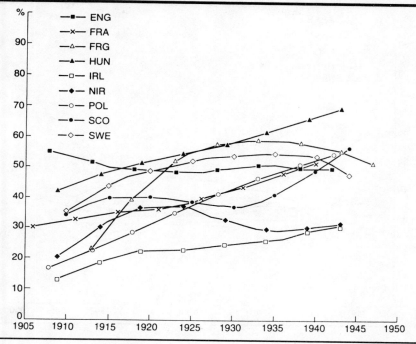

FIGURE 4

Outflow rates from farm origins to non-manual destinations for men in nine nations by birth year

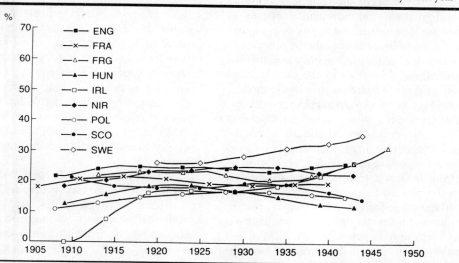

FIGURE 5
Outflow rates from manual origins to non-manual destinations for men in nine nations by birth year

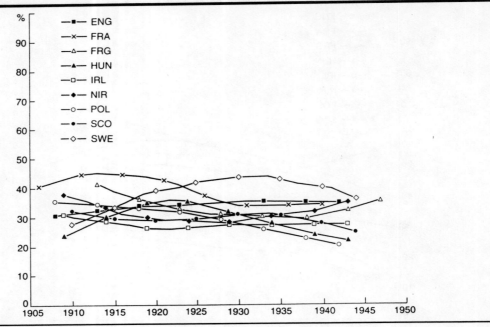

these directions can be found. In general, fluctuating rates are displayed, and the graphs for different nations frequently cross. Moreover, as earlier remarked, the negligible volume of outflows from both manual and nonmanual origins to farm destinations means that the plots of Figures 5 and 6 can be taken as essentially the obverses of those relating to *im*mobility within our manual and nonmanual classes; so in the case of these rates too an absence of trends may be claimed.

Finally, Figures 5 and 6 again fail to provide evidence of cross-national convergence in mobility rates. Over the period covered, the cross-national range for rates of mobility from manual origins to nonmanual destinations narrows only slightly as it falls from around 30 to 55 per cent for the oldest cohorts down to 20 to 40 per cent for the youngest; and the range for mobility in the reverse direction shows no narrowing at all in moving from 20 to 45 up to 30 to 55 per cent.[14]

It is the results contained in these last two Figures—and also in Figure 4—that may occasion

most surprise among those presented so far. It would be generally accepted that nonmanual work tends to grow and manual work to contract as industrial societies reach the more advanced stages of their development—regardless of whether this is seen as contributing to a net degrading or upgrading of the employment structure overall. And thus, within the context of the three-class version of our schema, increasing mobility into nonmanual destinations from farm and manual origins alike should be 'structurally' favoured. Yet, in our data, no consistent indication of such tendencies is to be found, even within the more advanced nations or among the younger cohorts.

However, it must in this connection be noted that our nonmanual class is very widely defined. It includes some groupings, such as routine nonmanual employees in administration, commerce and services, which have grown primarily through the greater workforce participation of women; and others, such as small proprietors and

FIGURE 6

Outflow rates from non-manual origins to manual destinations for men in nine nations by birth year

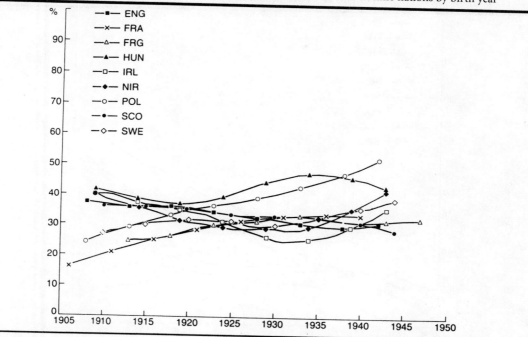

other self-employed workers, which, over the period that our data cover, were typically in decline. If, then, we wish to consider mobility flows into the nonmanual groupings that have most clearly expanded among the male workforce, which are in fact mostly at the higher levels of the white-collar range, we need to draw on data from mobility tables of a more elaborated kind. Although, as we have explained, we cannot go over entirely to the seven-class version of our schema, we can, for present purposes, make a useful compromise: we can construct mobility tables that apply the seven-class version to destinations while retaining the three-class version for origins.

In Figures 7 and 8 we show the course followed by two outflow rates derived from such 3 × 7 tables: that is, outflow rates from farm and from manual origins respectively into Class I+II of the seven-class version—the service class of primarily professional, higher technical, administrative and managerial employees. In other words, we here focus on subsets of the rates presented in Figures

4 and 5 where the mobility in question is into types of employment that *have* been in general expansion. Furthermore, we can also in this way examine changes in mobility flows which, in the light of the hierarchical divisions that we make within our class schema (cf. Appendix Table 3), could be regarded as representing mobility *upwards* from less to more advantaged class positions.[15]

A preliminary point to be noted about Figures 7 and 8 is that, because the rates we are here concerned with are generally lower and less differentiated than those presented in previous figures, we have doubled the vertical scale, thus of course 'enlarging' the changes that are depicted. Even so, they do not appear as highly dramatic.

In Figure 7, some increase in mobility from farm origins into the service class is shown up among younger cohorts in several nations—that is, in England, the FRG and Sweden and, more weakly, in Ireland. But in the remainder any increase that can be detected occurs among older

FIGURE 7

Outflow rates from farm origins to service class destinations for men in nine nations by birth year

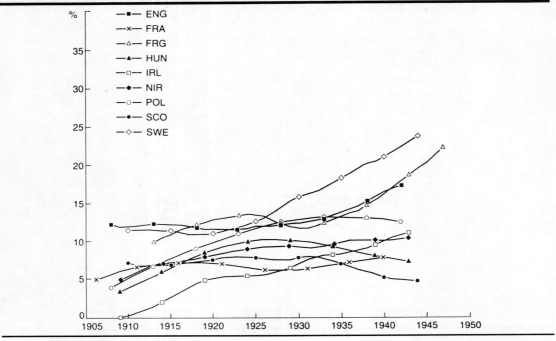

cohorts, and the trend then fades out—so that cross-national differences in rates in fact *widen*. In Figure 8, rates of mobility from manual origins into the service class likewise display an increase in England and Sweden which is at least held, and in the FRG they turn sharply upwards among the youngest cohorts. But again, too, the other nations differ, with the most common tendency being for rates first to rise but then at some later point to decline. It is of interest to note that this tendency is most marked in Figure 8, and also appears in Figure 7, in the graphs for our two eastern European nations. Upward mobility into the service class among Hungarian and Polish men born in the early 1920s—who would reach occupational maturity in the period of post-war 'socialist reconstruction'—rose to a level that later cohorts quite fail to match.

Where, among younger cohorts, the graphs of Figures 7 and 8 level out or turn down, we cannot preclude the possibility that this is in some part the result of age effects—so that in fact, as the men

in these cohorts become older, a larger proportion will enter into service-class positions. However, what we would doubt is that such effects are likely to an extent that would make the graphs seriously misleading. There are good empirical grounds for supposing—and the liberal theory would certainly predict—that the younger the men in our samples, the more probable it is that they will achieve upward mobility through education, so that this mobility will be apparent at a relatively early stage in their working lives. And in this connection, it is then further relevant to emphasise that the graphs corresponding to those of Figures 7 and 8 which depict mobility to class of first employment similarly fail to reveal consistently rising trends. It emerges rather that even if one considers only men born from the 1920s onwards, a steady increase in mobility into the service class from farm and manual origins alike is found in just one nation—namely, Sweden.

What, we believe, should be emphasised here is that although the service class does show a gen-

FIGURE 8
Outflow rates from manual origins to service class destinations for men in nine nations by birth year

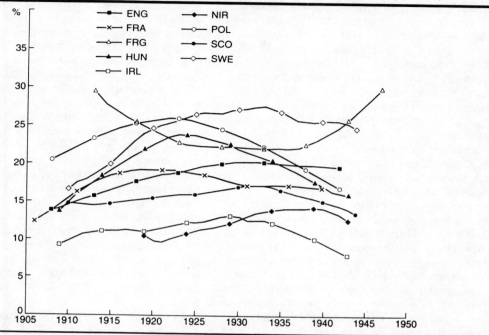

eral tendency to expand within modern societies, it does not do so at a steady pace simply in response to the exigencies of industrial development. Periods of relatively rapid growth and of stasis will alternate under the influence of other factors, not least political ones, thus producing rises and falls in rates of upward mobility into this class of a kind which the Hungarian and Polish cases do no more perhaps than exemplify at their most striking.[16]

How, then, can we best sum up the foregoing findings in regard to trends in absolute rates? To begin with, we can say that our investigation of outflow rates points to certain trends which seem likely to have occurred in most, if not all, of the nations we consider at *some* stage of their industrial development:

(i) a decline in intergenerational immobility within the farm sector;

(ii) an increase in mobility from farm origins

into manual employment in industry; and

(iii) some upturn in mobility from farm and manual origins into service-class positions.

To this extent, therefore, we might stop short of an extreme antinomianism of the kind that Sorokin could be taken to represent, and recognise that industrialism does carry typical implications for the direction of several broad mobility flows—as indeed Carlsson (1963) argued some time ago in a critique of Sorokin's position.

However, we must then also say that the trends that we are able to identify have rarely appeared as continuous over the period to which our data refer; that from nation to nation their phasing within the developmental process evidently differs; and moreover that changes in all other rates that we have examined would appear to be essentially directionless. In turn, therefore, we can produce little evidence that within our European nations mobility rates overall are moving steadily towards some relatively well defined 'industrial' pattern in the way that the liberal theory would suggest—and certainly not towards one that is characterised by steadily rising mobility. The outflow rates that we have considered show no clear tendency to converge; and, whatever course they may follow, they are not associated with any consistent upward trend in total mobility rates. In the light of the evidence presented, and in particular of that of Figure 1, it could not be claimed that men in our national samples whose working lives began, say, after the second world war have generally lived in more mobile societies than those who first entered employment in the 1920s.

The one possible qualification that might here be made is suggested by our findings for Ireland and Poland. These could be taken as meeting the expectation that an upward shift in the level of total mobility will occur in the course of industrialisation where a rapid decline in agricultural employment or, more specifically perhaps, the break-up of a predominantly peasant economy, goes together with a rising demand for industrial labour. But even if, as Lipset and Zetterberg would hold, a shift of this kind can be regarded as a general characteristic of the emergence of industrial societies, at least two further points would still, on our evidence, need to be made. First, the upturn in mobility has to be seen as being of a delimited, once-and-for-all kind; and secondly, it still leaves ample room for subsequent variation in absolute mobility rates and patterns as nations proceed to the further stages of their development.[17]

Relative Rates

We move on now to consider trends in intergenerational class mobility from the standpoint of relative rates, which we shall treat in terms of odds ratios. That is, ratios which show the relative odds of individuals in two different classes of origin being found in one rather than another of two different classes of destination; or, alternatively, one could say, which show the degree of *net* association that exists between the classes of origin

and of destination involved. Two further points concerning such ratios may here be noted.

First, the total set of odds ratios that can be calculated within a mobility table may be taken as representing the 'endogenous mobility regime' or 'pattern of social fluidity' that the table embodies. And since odds ratios are 'margin insensitive' measures, it is then possible for this underlying regime or pattern to remain unaltered as between two or more mobility tables even though their marginal distributions differ and, thus, all absolute rates that can be derived from them. Further, we might add, it would be possible for relative rates as expressed by odds ratios to differ from table to table in some systematic way without this being readily apparent from an inspection of absolute rates.

Secondly, odds ratios are the elements of loglinear models; and, thus, where these ratios are taken as the measure of relative mobility rates, hypotheses about the latter can be presented and formally tested through the application of such models. This is the approach that we shall here follow.

In examining relative rates, we shall attempt, in the same way as we did with absolute rates, to make inferences about the extent of changes over time from the mobility experience of successive birth-cohorts within our national samples. However, instead of here working with yearly cohorts, we distinguish four ten-year birth-cohorts, which can then be regarded, given the closeness of the dates of the inquiries from which the samples derive, as having more or less comparable locations within the broad sweep of recent European economic history.

The first—that is, the earliest—of these cohorts comprises men aged 55 to 64, who were thus mostly born in the first two decades of the century, and who entered employment before or during the inter-war depression years. The second is of men aged 45 to 54, the majority of whom were born in the 1920s and entered employment in the later 1930s or the war years. The third is that of men aged 35 to 44, who were born between the late 1920s and the early 1940s, and whose working lives have fallen very largely within the post-war period. And finally the fourth cohort is that of men aged 25 to 34, who were born from the end of the 1930s onwards and who mostly entered employment while the long boom was in train. This last cohort is clearly made up of respondents who could not be generally assumed to have reached a stage of occupational maturity, and this we must recall where it might be relevant to the interpretation of our results.

When we thus divide our national samples into cohorts, we again have a potential problem of unduly low cell counts in the mobility tables for each cohort. To obviate this, we base our analyses throughout on the five-class version of our schema (cf. Appendix Table 2).

As regards relative rates, there is, as we have noted, an obvious opposition between the expectations that follow from the liberal theory and those that may be derived from the FJH hypothesis. According to the former, a tendency should be found in the course of the development of industrial societies for relative rates to become more equal—or, one could say, for all odds ratios to move closer to the value of 1, which signifies the complete independence of class origins and destinations or 'perfect mobility'. According to the latter, relative rates will be basically the same across all societies that have market economies and (at least) nuclear family systems, whatever stage their level of industrial development may have reached; and thus, when examined over time within particular industrial societies, relative rates should reveal little change at all.

We may then start off from an attempt at evaluating these rival positions, and, to this end, we introduce a rather simple loglinear model which is, however, able to provide a direct representation of expectations under the FJH hypothesis, at least if this is taken *stricto sensu*. This model, which we have earlier labelled the 'constant social fluidity' (CnSF) model (Goldthorpe, 1980, 1987: ch.3; Erikson, Goldthorpe and Portocarero, 1983) may, for present purposes, be written as

$$\log F_{ijk} = \mu + \lambda_i^O + \lambda_j^D + \lambda_k^C + \lambda_{ik}^{OC} + \lambda_{jk}^{DC} + \lambda_{ij}^{OD} \quad (1)$$

where F_{ijk} is the expected frequency in cell ijk of a three-way table comprising class of origin (O), class of destination (D) and cohort (C) and, on the right-hand side of the equation, μ is a scale factor, λ_i^O, λ_j^D and λ_k^C represent the 'main' effects of the distribution of individuals over origins, destinations and cohorts respectively, and the remaining terms represent the effects for the three possible two-way associations in the table.

Thus, the model entails a number of substantive propositions, most of which are unproblematic: for example, that an association exists between class of origin and class of destination; and that further associations exist between class of origin and cohort and between class of destination and cohort—in other words, men in different cohorts have different origin and destination distributions. It is, however, a further proposition that is critical. Since no *three-way* association is provided for in the model (the λ_{ijk}^{ODC} term does not appear), it is also entailed that the level of association between class of origin and of destination is *constant across cohorts* or, one could alternatively say, that over the mobility tables for successive cohorts all corresponding relative rates, as measured by odds ratios, are identical.

We can then consider our nine nations separately, and in each case fit the above CnSF model to a three-way table which comprises the five classes of origin, five classes of destination and four cohorts that we propose to distinguish. The results of so doing are presented in Table 1.

In this table we also report the results of applying a model that represents the hypothesis of the (conditional) independence of class origins and destinations; that is, the CnSF model minus the λ_{ij}^{OD} term. We do not expect this independence model to fit the data—and, as can be seen, in no case does it; but it serves as a useful baseline, by reference to which we can assess, through the rG^2 statistic in the fourth column of the table, how much of the total association between class of origin and class of destination the CnSF model is able to account for.[18]

Also in addition to the more usual 'goodness of fit' statistics, we give in the last column of Table 1 values for the statistic $G^2(S)$. This we introduce here to attempt to deal with a difficulty arising from the large variation in the sizes of our national samples. In consequence of this variation, our national mobility tables differ quite widely in their capacity to show up as statistically significant relatively small deviations from models that

TABLE 1
Results of Fitting the CnSF Model to Intergenerational Class Mobility for Four Birth-Cohorts

Model*	G^2	df	p	$rG^{2\dagger}$	$\Delta^{\ddagger}$	$G^2(S)$ (1,746)
ENG						
(N = 8,343)						
OC DC (con. ind.)	1,695.0	64	0.00	—	16.1	405
OC DC OD (CnSF)	53.1	48	0.28	96.9	2.6	49
FRA						
(N = 16,431)						
OC DC	6,370.6	64	0.00	—	24.7	734
OC DC OD	96.7	48	0.00	98.5	·2.0	53
FRG						
(N = 3,570)						
OC DC	1,092.0	64	0.00	—	21.2	567
OC DC OD	81.9	48	0.00	92.5	4.4	65
HUN						
(N = 10,319)						
OC DC	2,386.0	64	0.00	—	19.2	457
OC DC OD	69.9	48	0.02	97.1	2.4	52
IRL						
(N = 1,746)						
OC DC	902.3	64	0.00	—	29.2	902
OC DC OD	60.2	48	0.11	93.3	5.2	60
NIR						
(N = 1,808)						
OC DC	780.6	64	0.00	—	25.5	756
OC DC OD	44.5	48	>0.50	94.3	5.0	45
POL						
(N = 27,993)						
OC DC	7,357.7	64	0.00	—	19.6	519
OC DC OD	66.7	48	0.04	99.1	1.4	49
SCO						
(N = 3,985)						
OC DC	1,146.6	64	0.00	—	18.1	538
OC DC OD	66.3	48	0.04	94.2	4.4	56
SWE						
(N = 1,882)						
OC DC	403.9	64	0.00	—	17.3	379
OC DC OD	45.2	48	>0.50	88.8	5.1	45

Notes:
  * O = origin class; D = destination class; C = cohort.
  † rG^2 shows the percentage reduction in the G^2 for a model taken as baseline (here the conditional independence model) that is achieved by a more complex model (here the CnSF model). For further discussion of this statistic, see n. 18.
  ‡ Δ is the dissimilarity index, showing the percentage of all cases in the table analysed that are misclassified—that is, allocated to the wrong cell—by a particular model.

we fit to them. It is as if we were looking at slides through microscopes of greatly differing power: we have the possibility of seeing far more detail in some cases than in others. Thus, there is the evident danger that we do not evaluate a model in an evenhanded way from nation to nation. We could, for example, be led to reject a model in the Polish case on account of deviations which, were they present also in the case of, say, Ireland, we would simply not observe. Thus, we evidently need some measure of goodness of fit that is standardised by sample size. One possibility would be to take G^2/N. However, we prefer, as a more refined measure, Schwartz's suggestion of $G^2(S)$ which is given by $((G^2 - df) / N) \times K + df$, where K is the sample size which is to be taken as standard.[19] We will follow the conservative practice of setting K equal to the size of the *smallest* of the national samples with which we are concerned—and thus, in Table 1, at 1746. To help remind the reader of the hypothetical nature of $G^2(S)$—that it is the G^2 value that we would expect from a sample of size K, all other things being equal—we report it only to the nearest integer.

What, then, can we learn from the content of Table 1? It would in fact appear that the CnSF model performs fairly well. It is true that the p values reported indicate that in only four of the nine nations—England, Ireland, Northern Ireland and Sweden—would one retain this model, taken as the null hypothesis, according to the conventional 0.05 criterion. However, it is also evident that much of the variation in the G^2 and p values returned is attributable to differences in sample size. When one examines the $G^2(S)$ values in the final column of the table, one finds that these are in fact contained within a rather narrow range, and moreover that in no case do they exceed the 65 mark, thus implying, with df = 48, p values of above 0.05. In other words, if we were restricted throughout to sample sizes of 1746, such as that we have for Ireland, we would find it difficult to reject the CnSF model for any nation—although the FRG would have to be regarded as a borderline case.

What could therefore be claimed on the basis of the foregoing is that while significant deviations from the CnSF model do have to be recognised in

some at least of our nations, such deviations would not appear to be at all substantial. In this connection, it is of further relevance to note that in all cases but one the CnSF model accounts for more than 90 per cent of the total association existing between class of origin and of destination—the exception being Sweden, where the independence model fits least badly; and again, that within the different national mobility tables the CnSF model leads to the misclassification of, at most, only a little over 5 per cent of all cases.[20] ...

Conclusions

We have sought in this paper to use data from European nations in order to evaluate various arguments concerning mobility trends within industrial societies. The major outcome, it might be said, has been a negative one: that is, considerable doubt has been thrown on claims associated with what we have called the liberal theory of industrialism. We have found no evidence of general and abiding trends towards either higher levels of total mobility or of social fluidity within the nations we have considered; nor evidence that mobility rates, whether absolute or relative, are changing in any other consistent direction; nor again evidence that such rates show a tendency over time to become cross-nationally more similar. The most that could be said on the side of arguments proposing some linkage between industrial development and increased and more standardised mobility rates would be that structural changes—most importantly, the decline in agriculture—appear likely to generate upturns in total, and also perhaps in certain outflow rates over periods of limited duration and of very variable phasing.

Such results are all the more damaging to the liberal theory since, as we earlier emphasised, Europe over the middle decades of the twentieth century, and above all in the post-war era, provides a context in which the theory should have every chance of showing its force. Furthermore, we may reiterate the point that any distortions in our findings that derive from our reliance on (quasi-) cohort analysis, and in particular from the confounding of age and period effects, are unlikely to be ones that tell unfairly against liberal claims: if anything, the contrary should be supposed.

We would therefore believe that the attempt to represent changes in mobility rates in modern societies as displaying regular developmental patterns, driven by a functional logic of industrialism, is one that faces serious empirical difficulties; and, in turn, we would argue that the need must be recognised to search for ways in which these changes might be more satisfactorily understood. In this connection, there is then one further outcome of the analyses of the present chapter which should, in our judgment, be seen as having major significance: namely, that while it appears that liberal expectations of directional tendencies in absolute and relative mobility rates are in both respects largely unfounded, *the nature of the contrary evidence is quite different from one case to the other: with absolute rates it is evidence of trendless, though often quite wide, fluctuation, but with relative rates it is evidence of considerable stability.* What is thus suggested is that in attempts to go beyond the liberal theory, the treatment of absolute and of relative rates is likely to set quite different kinds of problem and of analytical task.

As regards absolute rates, liberal expectations most obviously fail, we would suggest, because changes in structural influences on mobility do not themselves have the regularity that liberal theorists have been wont to suppose. Analyses of economic growth advanced in the 1950s and 1960s by authors such as Clark (1957), Rostow (1960) and Kuznets (1966) were taken as demonstrating clear sequences of change in the sectoral and occupational, and hence in the class, composition of labour forces. However, it would by now be widely accepted that, whatever theoretical insights the work of these authors may provide, it does *not* allow one to think, at a historical level, in terms of a well-defined series of developmental stages through which the structure of the labour forces of different nations will pass in turn as industrialisation proceeds. While certain very general tendencies of change may in this respect be identified, considerable variation still prevails from case to case in relation to the speed with which change occurs and the extent to which dif-

ferent aspects of change are separated in time or overlap (Singelmann, 1978; Gagliani, 1985).

The European experience of industrialisation, which has provided the setting for our analyses in this paper, itself well illustrates the variety of paths that the development of labour forces may follow; and it does, moreover, bring out the diversity of the causal factors at work here—by no means all of which can be plausibly seen as part of some englobing developmental process. Thus, the historical formation of national class structures has to be seen as reflecting not only early or late industrialisation but, in addition, important influences stemming, on the one hand, from the international political economy and, on the other, from the various strategies pursued by national governments in response to both external and internal pressures. To take but one example here, the contraction of agriculture—which we have found to play a major part in the pattern of change in absolute class mobility rates—cannot be understood, as it has occurred in particular cases, simply in terms of the shifting marginal productivity of sectors and differences in the elasticities of demand for their products that the theory of economic growth would emphasise. As the agrarian histories of our nations can amply show (see, e.g., Priebe, 1976), the pace and timing of agricultural contraction also—and often far more decisively—reflects whether nations were at the centre or on the periphery of international trading relations, in a position of economic dominance or dependence; and, further, the policies that their governments adopted towards agriculture both in regard to its social organisation and its protection against or exposure to market forces.[21]

Once, therefore, the variability and complexity of the determination of the structural contexts of mobility is appreciated, the extent to which the movement of absolute rates over time appears as merely trendless can no longer be found especially surprising. If changes in such rates do largely express the shifting conjunctures of a diversity of exogenous effects, then 'trendlessness', as suggested by Sorokin, is indeed what must be expected. It is noteworthy that it is essentially an argument on these lines that has been pursued by the several European economic and social historians who have sought to join in the sociological debate. In rejecting 'the idea of a sustained growth in social mobility during industrialization', these authors have emphasised the 'multitude of factors' which affect mobility levels; and, in place of developmental stages, they have sought rather to establish empirically a number of different 'eras' or 'phases' of both rising *and falling* mobility within the period in which European industrialisation has occurred (see esp. Kaelble, 1984: 490; also Kaelble, 1981; Mendels, 1976; Kocka, 1980).

Thus, we would maintain, the crucial issue that arises so far as absolute rates of mobility are concerned is that of whether, or how far, the course of change they follow is in fact a phenomenon open to explanation in macrosociological terms. Investigators who have been impressed by the degree of temporal variation in absolute, as compared with relative, rates have gone on to conclude that the dynamism of the former must lie primarily in structural effects, and in turn they have urged that these should not be treated as merely a 'nuisance factor' but should become themselves the focus of inquiry (e.g. Hauser *et al.,* 1975; Grusky and Hauser, 1984; Goldthorpe, 1985). However, while this argument has an evident logic, it does leave quite undecided the question of just what *kind* of understanding of structural effects—and thence of change in absolute rates—it might be possible to achieve. In so far as generalisations about such effects can be made, will they prove to be of any great explanatory value when applied to particular instances? Or may one be in this respect forced back willy-nilly to a reliance largely on specific historical descriptions—as a position such as that of Sorokin would in effect imply? Or again are there perhaps intermediate possibilities?

Turning now to relative rates, we meet with a very different situation. In this case, the liberal theory is undermined because, instead of the anticipated trend of change, in the direction of greater equality, we find evidence of an essential stability. Although shifts in relative rates can in some cases be detected [see Erikson and Goldthorpe 1992: 90–101], these are not only ones which go in various directions but, more importantly, ones which, as against those observed in absolute rates, are of very limited magnitude—so

that one might wish to speak more of 'oscillation' than of fluctuation. In other words, the liberal theory would here appear to fail because the logic of industrialism has not in fact automatically generated the changes within processes of social selection which were expected of it, and through which a steady increase in fluidity and openness would be promoted.

It is in this connection of interest to note that of late exponents of the liberal theory appear to have modified their position in regard to relative rates quite significantly. Thus, for example, Treiman initially sought to provide the hypothesis of a trend towards greater openness with a rationale largely in terms of the functional exigencies of industrialism (1970: 218). However, in a recent paper (with Yip), he puts much stronger emphasis on the part that is played in creating greater openness and equality of opportunity by the more proximate factor of greater *equality of condition*—that is, by a greater equality in the economic, cultural and social resources that families possess. And while it is still maintained that this increase in equality of condition itself ultimately derives from the development of industrialism, it is at the same time accepted that 'industrialization and inequality do not move in perfect concert' and, further, that *other* factors, especially political ones—for example, whether a nation has a socialist regime—may also affect the degree of inequality that exists (Treiman and Yip, 1989: 376–7). That is to say, it would here seem to be recognised that even in cases where a trend towards greater fluidity may be empirically established, this cannot be regarded as simply a matter of developmental necessity but must rather be explained as the contingent outcome of quite complex patterns of social action (cf. also Ganzeboom, Luijkx and Treiman, 1989; Simkus *et al.,* 1990). And conversely, this revised, and evidently much weaker, position is then of course able to accommodate the alternative possibility that, in particular instances, no trend of this kind is observed—because countervailing forces have in fact proved too strong.

The stability in relative rates that we have shown gains in significance, we may add, not only because the period that our data cover comprised decades of unprecedented economic growth but also because it was, of course, one of major political upheavals, in which, in the train of war and revolution, national frontiers were redrawn and massive shifts of population occurred.[22] The fact that the relative rates underlying the mobility experience of cohorts within our national samples should then reveal so little change—whether directional or otherwise—becomes all the more remarkable. While we have not been able to support the claim of a sustained developmental trend, we have, it appears, found indications of something of no less sociological interest: that is, of a constancy in social process prevailing within our several nations over decades that would in general have to be characterised in terms of the transformation and turbulence that they witnessed.

Furthermore, this finding is, as we have indicated, one which may be related to a larger sociological argument, namely, that represented by the FJH hypothesis. We have presented analyses which indicate that *some* variation in fluidity patterns does in fact occur among nations—indeed, more than within nations over time—and also that this variation shows no tendency to diminish [see Erikson and Goldthorpe 1992: 90–101]. Thus, expectations of convergence are not met. However, neither would cross-national variation appear to be increasing; and, more importantly, as we have elsewhere sought to show (Erikson and Goldthorpe 1987, 1992: ch. 5), it could not be reckoned as sufficiently wide to rule out the possibility that the 'basic' similarity in relative rates that the FJH hypothesis claims is the major source of the temporal stability that we have observed; or, that is, the possibility that *constancy* above all reflects *commonality*.

In other words, in so far as the degree of similarity proposed by the FJH hypothesis is established, we may think of temporal shifts in fluidity within nations as being no more than oscillations occurring around the standard pattern that the hypothesis implies or, at all events, as being restricted in their frequency and extent by whatever set of effects it is that generates this pattern. And in this regard, then, the ultimate task becomes that of understanding these effects; or, that is, of seeking to explain not variance, to which, as Lieberson (1987) has observed, analytical strategies within macrosociology have thus far been chiefly oriented, but rather a *lack* of variance—for which, unfortunately, appropriate strategies remain largely to be devised.

APPENDIX TABLE 1
National Inquiries Used as Data Sources

	Inquiry	Date	References for survey details
England & Wales (ENG)	Oxford National Occupational Mobility Inquiry	1972	Goldthorpe (1980)
France (FRA)	INSEE Enquête Formation-Qualification Professionelle	1970	Pohl, Thélot and Jousset (1974)
Federal Republic of Germany (FRG)	ZUMA Superfile	1976–1978	Erikson *et al.* (1988)
Hungary (HUN)	Social Mobility and Occupational Change in Hungary	1973	Andorka and Zagórski (1980)
Irish Republic (IRL)	Determinants of Occupational Mobility	1973–1974	O'Muircheartaigh and Wiggins (1977)
Northern Ireland (NIR)	Determinants of Occupational Mobility	1973–1974	O'Muircheartaigh and Wiggins (1977)
Poland (POL)	Change in the Socio-Occupational Structure	1972	Zagórski (1977–8)
Scotland (SCO)	Scottish Mobility Study	1974–1975	Payne (1987)
Sweden (SWE)	Level of Living Survey	1974	Andersson (1987)

APPENDIX TABLE 2
The Class Schema

Full version	Collapsed versions		
	Seven-class*	Five-class	Three-class
I Higher-grade professionals, administrators, and officials; managers in large industrial establishments; large proprietors	I+II Service class: professionals, administrators and managers; higher-grade technicians; supervisors of non-manual workers		
II Lower-grade professionals, administrators, and officials; higher-grade technicians; managers in small industrial establishments; supervisors of non-manual employees		I–III White-collar workers	
IIIa Routine non-manual employees, higher grade (administration and commerce)	III Routine non-manual workers: routine non-manual employees in administration and commerce; sales personnel; other rank-and-file service workers		Non-manual workers
IIIb Routine non-manual employees, lower grade (sales and services)			
IVa Small proprietors, artisans, etc., with employees	IVa+b Petty bourgeoisie: small proprietors and artisans, etc., with and without employees	IVa+b Petty bourgeoisie	
IVb Small proprietors, artisans, etc., without employees			
IVc Farmers and smallholders; other self-employed workers in primary production	IVc Farmers: farmers and smallholders and other self-employed workers in primary production	IVc+VIIb Farm workers	Farm workers
V Lower-grade technicians; supervisors of manual workers	V+VI Skilled workers: lower-grade technicians; supervisors of manual workers; skilled manual workers	V+VI Skilled workers	Manual workers
VI Skilled manual workers			
VIIa Semi- and unskilled manual workers (not in agriculture, etc.)	VIIa Non-skilled workers: semi- and unskilled manual workers (not in agriculture, etc.)	VIIa Non-skilled workers	
VIIb Agricultural and other workers in primary production	VIIb Agricultural labourers: agricultural and other workers in primary production		

APPENDIX TABLE 3

Scores for Classes of the Schema on Different Occupational Scales as a Basis for a Threefold Hierarchical Division

Scale*	Class						
	I+II	III	IVa+b	IVc	V+VI	VIIa	VIIb
Treiman	56	35	42	44	35	29	24
Hope–Goldthorpe (England)	63	36	39	47	40	29	31
Wegener (FRG)	92	50	49	50	49	39	30
Irish Occupational Index (all Ireland)	58	30	42	42	37	24	26
de Lillo–Schizzerotto (Italy)	71	41	51	48	34	20	11
Naoi (Japan)	62	41	37	37	41	33	30
Duncan (USA)	66	27	46	25	33	17	14
Division	1		2			3	

Note:
 * The international Treiman scale and those for the FRG, Ireland, and Japan are intended as scales of occupational prestige, although constructed in different ways; the English scale and also, it would seem, the Italian, are intended as ones of the general desirability of occupations in popular estimation; and the US scale, while originally constructed as a proxy for a prestige scale, is now generally interpreted as one of the socio-economic status of occupations. For further details, see Treiman (1977), Goldthorpe and Hope (1974), Wegener (1988), Boyle (1976), de Lillo and Schizzerotto (1985), Naoi (1979), and Duncan (1961).

Notes

1. This paper is based on chapter 3 of Robert Erikson and John H. Goldthorpe, *The Constant Flux: A Study of Class Mobility in Industrial Societies,* The Clarendon Press, Oxford, 1992. The research on which this book reports was carried out under the auspices of the CASMIN-Projekt, based at the Institüt für Sozialwissenschaften of the University of Mannheim and funded by grants from the Stiftung Volkswagenwerk, Hanover. Readers are referred to the above work (chapter 2 esp.) for full details of the comparative methodology followed in research.

2. The influence here of the 'stages-of-growth' model of Rostow (1960: see esp. Chart 1) would seem to be of particular importance and also, perhaps—though the evidence is indirect—the interpretation of European industrial development provided by Landes (1957, 1965, 1972), which places major emphasis upon the rate and pattern of diffusion of techniques of production from Britain to the more 'backward' economies of the European mainland.

3. Thus, for example, in Kerr *et al.* (1960) discussion of France and Italy is largely concerned with the impediments to industrial development that result from the persisting importance of 'family-dominated enterprises' with 'patrimonial management' (see e.g. pp. 80, 141–2; and cf. Landes, 1957); and discussion of Germany, with difficulties of social rigidity and authoritarianism, following from the promotion of industrialisation by a dynastic elite (e.g. pp. 54–5, 150–1).

4. It is of interest that Bell should refer to the situation on which he comments as one 'that has gone relatively unexamined'. This statement may well be true for American theorists of industrialism, but it can scarcely hold in the case of European economic and social historians. See, for example, the discussion of issues central to the 'reperiodisation' of the development of industrial society in Europe that are found in Wrigley (1972) and Mayer (1981).

5. So far as emigration is concerned, a detailed review of the possible and likely effects on mobility rates and propensities is provided in Hout (1989), with special reference to the Irish case.

6. For our present purposes, it is the confounding of period by age effects that is most likely to create problems. To the extent that cohort effects are present in the data, this may be regarded as valid evidence against the occurrence of secular trends.

7. This is in fact the highest maximum age that we could apply across all nine of our national samples.

8. The wording of the questions from which this information was derived varied somewhat from one national inquiry to another but not, we believe, in ways likely to have any significant effects on the comparability of data. In this and all similar instances full details of question wording, construction of variables, etc. are to be found in the documentation to the CASMIN International Social Mobility Superfile (Erikson *et al.*, 1988).

9. We are greatly endebted to Jan Hoem for his most generous help in this aspect of our work.

10. These plots are not shown but in what follows it may be assumed that where no reference is made to rates of mobility from class origins to class of first employment, our findings in this respect would not lead us seriously to qualify those we have obtained for rates from class origins to present class.

11. The results that we report here for Hungary do of course depend on our treating workers on agricultural co-operatives or state farms as having a different class position (VIIb) from that of peasant proprietors (IVc). Some analysts of mobility in Hungary have not made this distinction; but we would argue the desirability of so doing, wherever it is practically feasible. It was, after all, precisely the aim both of the immediate post-war land reform and of the subsequent collectivisation programme to *change* agrarian class relations. In the Polish case, it should be noted, the attempt to collectivise agriculture that the regime launched at the end of the 1940s met with fierce peasant opposition and was finally abandoned in 1956 (cf. Lewis, 1973).

12. Although, then, we are here forced back to the obviously rather crude three-class basis of much earlier comparative research, we must stress that we still do achieve a much higher standard of data comparability. As a result of our systematic recoding of the original unit-record data (see Erikson and Goldthorpe, 1992: ch. 2), we have a reasonable assurance that the categories of 'nonmanual', 'manual' and 'farm' are being applied in a consistent manner from nation to nation, rather than providing comparability of a merely nominal kind.

13. It may be noted that in Figure 4 the left tail of the curve for Sweden has been deleted. This is on account of its unreliability, as determined by a test developed by Hoem (see Erikson and Goldthorpe, 1992: ch. 3, Annex). For the same reason, we have also deleted the left tail of the curve for Northern Ireland in Figure 8.

14. These results are of direct relevance to the Lipset-Zetterberg hypothesis of cross-national similarity in absolute rates, since this was in fact formulated in terms of outflow rates from nonmanual to manual positions and *vice versa*. We do not take up this issue here (but see further Erikson and Goldthorpe, 1992: ch. 6).

15. Following the hierarchical levels that we propose, a further upward flow—that our 3×7 tables do not enable us to distinguish—would be represented by men entering Class I+II positions from Class III origins.

16. Thus, for example, in the English case the more or less continuous rise in upward mobility into the service class across the cohorts we distinguish can be related to a corresponding steady expansion of this class from a time somewhere between 1931 and 1951 (there was no 1941 Census)—following, however, on several decades in which it grew scarcely at all (see Goldthorpe, 1980, 1987: ch. 2 esp.). As regards socialist societies, it may further be noted that evidence of a 'parabolic' curve for upward mobility, similar to that we record in Hungary and Poland, is also found for post-war Czechoslovakia in data from a survey conducted in 1984 (personal communication from Marek Boguszak and cf. Boguszak, 1990).

17. It would, moreover, be mistaken simply to equate a peasant economy—or society—with a 'traditional' one. Thus, while one may with justification speak of a peasant economy existing in substantial areas of Ireland at least up to the 1940s, many of its key institutional features—most importantly, perhaps, non-partible inheritance—were relatively new (cf. Hannan, 1979). The Irish peasant community, as classically depicted by Arensberg and Kimball (1940, 1968), has in fact to be seen as the historical product of economic and social conditions in Ireland following the Great Famine of 1846–9 and then of the land reform legislation introduced between 1870 and the First World War.

18. It is important that rG^2, referred to by Goodman (1972) as the 'coefficient of multiple determination', should be interpreted within the particular context of loglinear modelling, rather than being taken as the equivalent of the perhaps more familiar R^2 of regression analysis. As Schwartz has pointed out (1985), the fact that R^2s are typically much lower than rG^2s reflects the fact that in regression the units of analysis are usually individuals while in loglinear modelling they are the cells of cross-tabulations and the scores are the numbers of individuals in a cell. Such aggregate data must then be expected to reveal stronger regularities than individual-level data. Schwartz's summary (1985: 2–3) is apt: rG^2 'measures how adequately a model accounts for the observed *associations* among a pre-specified set of variables while R^2 and Eta^2 measure the amount of *variation* in one variable that can be ac-

counted for by its (linear) association with specified independent variables.' The point may be added that the substantive meaning of rG^2 will of course depend on the model that is chosen as baseline.

19. This suggestion was made to us by Joseph E. Schwartz in a personal communication, for which we are duly grateful.

20. We may add that results from equivalent analyses of data referring to mobility from class of origin to class of first employment are essentially similar. In only one case, that of Ireland, would the CnSF model be rejected on the basis of the $G^2(S)$ statistic; and again only in the Swedish case does the model not account for at least 90 per cent of the total origin-destination association, while at most only a little over 5 per cent of all cases are misclassified. It should, however, be recalled that we cannot undertake an analysis of the kind in question for the FRG, owing to lack of information on first employment.

21. Moreover, while we would believe that 'demand side' factors are generally of major importance in promoting structural change, 'supply side' ones may also have to be taken into account—for example, the effects of demographic change, including in- and out-migration, and of changes in the workforce participation rates of women and of different age-groups. And in these respects too political intervention may obviously play a crucial role.

22. Most importantly, in the aftermath of World War II the FRG was created out of the division of the Third Reich, and Poland's frontiers were moved some 150–200 miles to the west—both changes being accompanied by large population movements. In addition, one may note the truncation of Hungary in 1920 (with the loss of almost 70 per cent of its area and 60 per cent of its population); and the partition of Ireland in 1920–2, following the War of Independence and the Civil War, so as to create the Irish Free State (which became the Irish Republic in 1949) and the six counties of Northern Ireland, a constituent element of the United Kingdom with, up to 1973, its own parliament and executive.

Bibliography

Andersson, L. (1987): 'Appendix A: Sampling and Data Collection' in R. Erikson and R. Åberg eds., *Welfare in Transition: A Survey of Living Conditions in Sweden 1968–1981*. Oxford: Clarendon Press.

Andorka, R. and K. Zagórski (1980): *Socio-Occupational Mobility in Hungary and Poland*. Warsaw: Polish Academy of Sciences.

Arensberg, C.M. and S.T. Kimball (1940, 2nd ed. 1968): *Family and Community in Ireland*. Cambridge, Mass.: Harvard University Press.

Bell, D. (1980): 'Liberalism in the Post-Industrial Society' in *Sociological Journeys*. London: Heinemann.

Blau, P.M. and O.D. Duncan (1967): *The American Occupational Structure*. New York: Wiley.

Blossfeld, H.-P. (1986): 'Career Opportunities in the Federal Republic of Germany'. *European Sociological Review* 2.

Boguszak, M. (1990): 'Transition to Socialism and Intergenerational Class Mobility: The Model of Core Social Fluidity Applied to Czechoslovakia' in M. Haller ed., *Class Structure in Europe*. Armonk, N.Y.: Sharpe.

Boyle, J.F. (1976): 'Analysis of the Irish Occupational Index'. Department of Social Studies, The Queen's University, Belfast.

Braverman, H. (1974): *Labor and Monopoly Capitalism*. New York: Monthly Review Press.

Brus, W. (1986a): 'Postwar Reconstruction and Socio-Economic Transformation' in M.C. Kaser and E.A. Radice eds., *The Economic History of Eastern Europe, 1919–1975*, vol. 2. Oxford: Clarendon Press.

Brus, W. (1986b): '1950 to 1953: The Peak of Stalinism' in M.C. Kaser ed., *The Economic History of Eastern Europe, 1919–1975*, vol. 3. Oxford: Clarendon Press.

Carchedi, G. (1977): *On the Economic Identification of Classes*. London: Routledge.

Carlsson, G. (1963): 'Sorokin's Theory of Social Mobility' in P.J. Allen ed., *Pitirim A. Sorokin in Review*. Durham, N.C.: Duke University Press.

Clark, C. (3rd ed., 1957): *The Conditions of Economic Progress*. London: Macmillan.

Crompton, R. and G. Jones (1984): *White-Collar Proletariat: Deskilling and Gender in Clerical Work*. London: Macmillan.

Duncan, O.D. (1961): 'A Socioeconomic Index for All Occupations' in A.J. Reiss ed., *Occupations and Social Status*. New York: Free Press.

Dunlop, J.T., F.H. Harbison, C. Kerr and C.A. Myers (1975): *Industrialism and Industrial Man Reconsidered*. Princeton: Inter-University Study of Human Resources in National Development.

Erikson, R. and J.H. Goldthorpe (1987): 'Commonality and Variation in Social Fluidity in Industrial Nations. Part I: A Model for Evaluating the "FJH Hypothesis"; Part II: The Model of Core Social Fluidity Applied'. *European Sociological Review* 3.

Erikson, R. and J.H. Goldthorpe (1992): *The Constant Flux: A Study of Class Mobility in Industrial Societies*. Oxford: Clarendon Press.

Erikson, R., J.H. Goldthorpe and L. Portocarero (1983): 'Intergenerational Class Mobility and the Convergence Thesis'. *British Journal of Sociology* 34.

Erikson, R., J.H. Goldthorpe, W. König, P. Lüttinger and W. Müller (1988): 'CASMIN International Mobility Superfile: Documentation'. Mannheim: Institut für Sozialwissenschaften, University of Mannheim.

Featherman, D.L., F.L. Jones and R.M. Hauser (1975): 'Assumptions of Social Mobility Research in the US: The Case of Occupational Status'. *Social Science Research* 4.

Gagliani, G. (1985): 'Long-Term Changes in the Occupational Structure'. *European Sociological Review* 1.

Ganzeboom, H., R. Luijkx and D.J. Treiman (1989): 'Intergenerational Class Mobility in Comparative Perspective'. *Research in Social Stratification and Mobility* 8.

Glenn, N.D. (1977): *Cohort Analysis.* Beverly Hills: Sage.

Goldthorpe, J.H. (with Catriona Llewellyn and Clive Payne) (1980, 2nd ed. 1987): *Social Mobility and Class Structure in Modern Britain.* Oxford: Clarendon Press.

Goldthorpe, J.H. (1985): 'On Economic Development and Social Mobility'. *British Journal of Sociology* 36.

Goldthorpe, J.H. and K. Hope (1974): *The Social Grading of Occupations: A New Approach and Scale.* Oxford: Clarendon Press.

Goodman, L.A. (1972): 'A General Model for the Analysis of Surveys'. *American Journal of Sociology* 77.

Grusky, D.B. and R.M. Hauser (1984): 'Comparative Social Mobility Revisited: Models of Convergence and Divergence in 16 Countries'. *American Sociological Review* 49.

Hannan, D.F. (1979): *Displacement and Development: Class, Kinship and Social Change in Irish Rural Communities.* Dublin: The Economic and Social Research Institute.

Hauser, R.M., P.J. Dickinson, H.P. Travis and J.M. Koffel (1975): 'Temporal Change in Occupational Mobility: Evidence for Men in the United States'. *American Sociological Review* 40.

Hoem, J.M. and P. Linneman (1987): 'The Tails in Moving Average Graduation'. Stockholm: Research Reports in Demography 37, University of Stockholm.

Hout, M. (1989): *Following in Father's Footsteps: Social Mobility in Ireland.* Cambridge, Mass.: Harvard University Press.

Kaelble, H. (1981): *Historical Research on Social Mobility.* London: Croom Helm.

Kaelble, H. (1984): 'Eras of Social Mobility in 19th and 20th Century Europe'. *Journal of Social History* 17.

Kemp, T. (1978): *Historical Patterns of Industrialization.* London: Longman.

Kerr, C. (1969): *Marshall, Marx and Modern Times.* Cambridge: Cambridge University Press.

Kerr, C. (1983): *The Future of Industrial Societies.* Cambridge, Mass.: Harvard University Press.

Kerr, C., J.T. Dunlop, F.H. Harbison and C.A. Myers (1960, 2nd ed. 1973): *Industrialism and Industrial Man.* Cambridge, Mass.: Harvard University Press.

Kindleberger, C.P. (1967): *Europe's Postwar Growth: The Role of Labor Supply.* Cambridge, Mass.: Harvard University Press.

Kocka, J. (1980): 'The Study of Social Mobility and the Formation of the Working Class in the 19th Century'. *Le mouvement social* 111.

Kulcsár, K. (1984): *Contemporary Hungarian Society.* Budapest: Corvina.

Kuznets, S. (1966): *Modern Economic Growth.* New Haven: Yale University Press.

Landes, D.S. (1957): 'Observations on France: Economy, Society and Politics'. *World Politics,* April.

Landes, D.S. (1965, 2nd ed. 1972): *The Unbound Prometheus: Technological Change and Industrial Development in Western Europe from 1750 to the Present.* Cambridge: Cambridge University Press.

Lewis, P. (1973): 'The Peasantry' in D. Lane and G. Kolankiewicz eds., *Social Groups in Polish Society.* London: Macmillan.

Lieberson, S. (1985, 2nd ed. 1987): *Making It Count.* Berkeley, University of California Press.

de Lillo, A. and A. Schizzerotto (1985): *La valutazione sociale delle occupazioni.* Bologna: Il Mulino.

Lipset, S.M. and H.L. Zetterberg (1956): 'A Theory of Social Mobility'. *Transactions of the Third World Congress of Sociology,* vol. 3. London: International Sociological Association.

Lipset, S.M. and H.L. Zetterberg (1959): 'Social Mobility in Industrial Societies' in S.M. Lipset and R. Bendix, *Social Mobility in Industrial Society.* Berkeley: University of California Press.

Lutz, B. (1984): *Der kurze Traum immerwährender Prosperität.* Frankfurt: Campus.

Mayer, A.J. (1981): *The Persistence of the Old Regime: Europe to the Great War.* New York: Pantheon.

Mendels, F.F. (1976): 'Social Mobility and Phases of Industrialisation'. *Journal of Interdisciplinary History* 7.

Naoi, A. (1979): 'Shokugyoteki Chiishakudo no Kosei' (The Construction of the Occupational Status Scale) in K. Tominaga ed., *Nihon no Kaiso Kozo* (The Stratification Structure in Japan). Tokyo: Todai Shuppan Kai.

O'Brien, P. and C. Keyder (1978): *Economic Growth in Britain and France, 1780–1914.* London: Allen and Unwin.

O'Muircheartaigh, C.A. and R.D. Wiggins (1977): 'Sample Design and Evaluation for an Occupational Mobility Study'. *Economic and Social Review* 8.

Parsons, T. (1960): *Structure and Process in Modern Societies*. Glencoe: Free Press.

Parsons, T. (1967): *Sociological Theory and Modern Society*. New York: Free Press.

Parsons, T. (1971): *The System of Modern Societies*. Englewood Cliffs: Prentice-Hall.

Payne, G. (1987): *Employment and Opportunity*. London: Macmillan.

Pohl, R., C. Thélot and M-F. Jousset (1974): *L'Enquête Formation-Qualification Professionelle de 1970*. Paris: INSEE.

Priebe, H. (1976): 'The Changing Role of Agriculture, 1920–1970' in C.M. Cipolla ed., *Fontana Economic History of Europe*, vol. 5 (ii). London: Fontana.

Rostow, W.W. (1960): *The Stages of Economic Growth: A Non-Communist Manifesto*. Cambridge: Cambridge University Press.

Schwartz, J.E. (1985): 'Goodman's Coefficient of Multiple Determination: Why it is *Not* Analogous to R²'. Stockholm: Swedish Institute for Social Research.

Simkus, A.A., R. Andorka, J. Jackson, K-B. Yip and D.J. Treiman (1990): 'Changes in Social Mobility in Two Societies in the Crux of Transition: A Hungarian-Irish Comparison, 1943–1973'. *Research in Social Stratification and Mobility* 9.

Singelmann, J. (1978): *From Agriculture to Services: The Transformation of Industrial Employment*. Beverly Hills: Sage.

Singelmann, J. and M. Tienda (1985): 'The Process of Occupational Change in a Service Society: The Case of the United States, 1960–1980' in B. Roberts, R. Finnegan and D. Gallie, eds., *New Approaches to Economic Life*. Manchester: Manchester University Press.

Sorokin, P.A. (1927, 2nd ed. 1959): *Social and Cultural Mobility*. Glencoe: Free Press.

Treiman, D.J. (1970): 'Industrialisation and Social Stratification' in E.O. Laumann ed., *Social Stratification: Research and Theory for the 1970s*. Indianapolis: Bobbs Merrill.

Treiman, D.J. (1977): *Occupational Prestige in Comparative Perspective*. New York: Academic Press.

Treiman, D.J. and K-B. Yip (1989): 'Educational and Occupational Attainment in 21 Countries' in M.L. Kohn ed., *Cross-National Research in Sociology*. Newbury Park: Sage.

Wegener, B. (1988): *Kritik des Prestiges*. Opladen: Westdeutscher Verlag.

Wright, E.O. and J. Singelmann (1982): 'Proletarianization in the Changing American Class Structure'. *American Journal of Sociology* 88.

Wright, E.O. and B. Martin (1987): 'The Transformation of the American Class Structure, 1960–1980'. *American Journal of Sociology* 93.

Wrigley, E.A. (1972): 'The Process of Modernization and the Industrial Revolution in England'. *Journal of Interdisciplinary History* 3.

Zagórski, K. (1977–8): 'Transformations of Social Structure and Social Mobility in Poland'. *International Journal of Sociology* 7.

Status and Income Attainment

▶ **BASIC MODELS**

**PETER M. BLAU AND OTIS DUDLEY DUNCAN,
WITH THE COLLABORATION OF ANDREA TYREE**

The Process of Stratification

Stratification systems may be characterized in various ways. Surely one of the most important has to do with the processes by which individuals become located, or locate themselves, in positions in the hierarchy comprising the system. At one extreme we can imagine that the circumstances of a person's birth—including the person's sex and the perfectly predictable sequence of age levels through which he is destined to pass—suffice to assign him unequivocally to a ranked status in a hierarchical system. At the opposite extreme his prospective adult status would be wholly problematic and contingent at the time of birth. Such status would become entirely determinate only as adulthood was reached, and solely as a consequence of his own actions taken freely—that is, in the absence of any constraint deriving from the circumstances of his birth or rearing. Such a pure achievement system is, of course, hypothetical, in much the same way that motion without friction is a purely hypothetical possibility in the physical world. Whenever the stratification system of any moderately large and complex society is described, it is seen to involve both ascriptive and achievement principles.

In a liberal democratic society we think of the more basic principle as being that of achieve-ment. Some ascriptive features of the system may be regarded as vestiges of an earlier epoch, to be extirpated as rapidly as possible. Public policy may emphasize measures designed to enhance or to equalize opportunity—hopefully, to overcome ascriptive obstacles to the full exercise of the achievement principle.

The question of how far a society may realisti-cally aspire to go in this direction is hotly debated, not only in the ideological arena but in the aca-demic forum as well. Our contribution, if any, to the debate will consist largely in submitting mea-surements and estimates of the strength of ascrip-tive forces and of the scope of opportunities in a large contemporary society. The problem of the relative importance of the two principles in a given system is ultimately a quantitative one. We have pushed our ingenuity to its limit in seeking to contrive relevant quantifications.

The governing conceptual scheme in the analy-sis is quite a commonplace one. We think of the individual's life cycle as a sequence in time that can be described, however partially and crudely, by a set of classificatory or quantitative measure-ments taken at successive stages. Ideally we should like to have under observation a cohort of births, following the individuals who make up the cohort as they pass through life. As a practical matter we resorted to retrospective questions put to a representative sample of several adjacent cohorts so as to ascertain those facts about their life histories that we assumed were both relevant to our problem and accessible by this means of observation.

Given this scheme, the questions we are continually raising in one form or another are: how and to what degree do the circumstances of birth condition subsequent status? and, how does status attained (whether by ascription or achievement) at one stage of the life cycle affect the prospects for a subsequent stage? The questions are neither idle nor idiosyncratic ones. Current policy discussion and action come to a focus in a vaguely explicated notion of the "inheritance of poverty." Thus a spokesman for the Social Security Administration writes:

It would be one thing if poverty hit at random and no one group were singled out. It is another thing to realize that some seem destined to poverty almost from birth—by their color or by the economic status or occupation of their parents.[1]

Another officially sanctioned concept is that of the "dropout," the person who fails to graduate from high school. Here the emphasis is not so much on circumstances operative at birth but on the presumed effect of early achievement on subsequent opportunities. Thus the "dropout" is seen as facing "a lifetime of uncertain employment,"[2] probable assignment to jobs of inferior status, reduced earning power, and vulnerability to various forms of social pathology.

In this study we do not have measurements on all the factors implicit in a full-blown conception of the "cycle of poverty" nor all those variables conceivably responding unfavorably to the achievement of "dropout" status. … This limitation, however, is not merely an analytical convenience. We think of the selected quantitative variables as being sufficient to describe the major outlines of status changes in the life cycle of a cohort. Thus a study of the relationships among these variables leads to a formulation of a basic model of the process of stratification.

A Basic Model

To begin with, we examine only five variables. For expository convenience, when it is necessary to resort to symbols, we shall designate them by arbitrary letters but try to remind the reader from time to time of what the letters stand for. These variables are:

V: Father's educational attainment

X: Father's occupational status

U: Respondent's educational attainment

W: Status of respondent's first job

Y: Status of respondent's occupation in 1962

Each of the three occupational statuses is scaled by the [socioeconomic] index described [elsewhere],[3] ranging from 0 to 96. The two education variables are scored on the following arbitrary scale of values ("rungs" on the "educational ladder") corresponding to specified numbers of years of formal schooling completed:

0: No school

1: Elementary, one to four years

2: Elementary, five to seven years

3: Elementary, eight years

4: High school, one to three years

5: High school, four years

6: College, one to three years

7: College, four years

8: College, five years or more (i.e., one or more years of postgraduate study)

Actually, this scoring system hardly differs from a simple linear transformation, or "coding," of the exact number of years of school completed. In retrospect, for reasons given [elsewhere],[4] we feel that the score implies too great a distance between intervals at the lower end of the scale; but the resultant distortion is minor in view of the very small proportions scored 0 or 1.

A basic assumption in our interpretation of regression statistics—though not in their calculation as such—has to do with the causal or temporal ordering of these variables. In terms of the father's career we should naturally assume precedence of V (education) with respect to X (occupation when his son was 16 years old). We are not concerned with the father's career, however, but only with his statuses that comprised a configuration of background circumstances or origin conditions for the cohorts of sons who were respondents in the Occupational Changes in a Generation (OCG) study. Hence we generally make no assumption as to the priority of V with respect to X; in effect, we assume the measurements on these variables to be contemporaneous from the son's viewpoint. The respondent's education, U, is supposed to follow in time—and thus to be susceptible to causal influence from—the two measures of father's status. Because we ascertained X as of respondent's age 16, it is true that some respondents may have completed school before the age to which X pertains. Such cases were doubtlessly a small minority and in only a minor proportion of them could the father (or other family head) have changed status radically in the two or three years before the respondent reached 16.

The next step in the sequence is more problematic. We assume that W (first job status) follows U (education). The assumption conforms to the wording of the questionnaire, which stipulated "the first full-time job you had after you left school." In the years since the OCG study was designed we have been made aware of a fact that should have been considered more carefully in the design. Many students leave school more or less definitively, only to return, perhaps to a different school, some years later, whereupon they often finish a degree program.[5] The OCG questionnaire contained information relevant to this problem, namely the item on age at first job. Through an oversight no tabulations of this item were made for the present study. Tables prepared for another study[6] using the OCG data, however, suggest that approximately one-eighth of the respondents report a combination of age at first job and education that would be very improbable unless (a) they violated instructions by reporting a part-time or school-vacation job as the first job, or (b) they did, in fact, interrupt their schooling to enter

regular employment. (These "inconsistent" responses include men giving 19 as their age at first job and college graduation or more as their education; 17 or 18 with some college or more; 14, 15, or 16 with high-school graduation or more; and under 14 with some high school or more.) When the two variables are studied in combination with occupation of first job, a very clear effect is evident. Men with a given amount of education beginning their first jobs early held lower occupational statuses than those beginning at a normal or advanced age for the specified amount of education.

Despite the strong probability that the U-W sequence is reversed for an appreciable minority of respondents, we have hardly any alternative to the assumption made here. If the bulk of the men who interrupted schooling to take their first jobs were among those ultimately securing relatively advanced education, then our variable W is downwardly biased, no doubt, as a measure of their occupational status immediately after they finally left school for good. In this sense, the correlations between U and W and between W and Y are probably attenuated. Thus, if we had really measured "job after completing education" instead of "first job," the former would in all likelihood have loomed somewhat larger as a variable intervening between education and 1962 occupational status. We do not wish to argue that our respondents erred in their reports on first job. We are inclined to conclude that their reports were realistic enough, and that it was our assumption about the meaning of the responses that proved to be fallible.

The fundamental difficulty here is conceptual. If we insist on *any* uniform sequence of the events involved in accomplishing the transition to independent adult status, we do violence to reality. Completion of schooling, departure from the parental home, entry into the labor market, and contracting of a first marriage are crucial steps in this transition, which all normally occur within a few short years. Yet they occur at no fixed ages nor in any fixed order. As soon as we aggregate individual data for analytical purposes we are forced into the use of simplifying assumptions. Our assumption here is, in effect, that "first job" has a uniform significance for all men in terms of its temporal relationship to educational preparation and subsequent work experience. If this assumption is not strictly correct, we doubt that it could be improved by substituting any other *single* measure of initial occupational status. (In designing the OCG questionnaire, the alternative of "job at the time of first marriage" was entertained briefly but dropped for the reason, among others, that unmarried men would be excluded thereby.)

One other problem with the *U-W* transition should be mentioned. Among the younger men in the study, 20 to 24 years old, are many who have yet to finish their schooling or to take up their first jobs or both—not to mention the men in this age group missed by the survey on account of their military service.[7] Unfortunately, an early decision on tabulation plans resulted in the inclusion of the 20 to 24 group with the older men in aggregate tables for men 20 to 64 years old. We have ascertained that this results in only minor distortions by comparing a variety of data for men 20 to 64 and for those 25 to 64 years of age. Once over the *U-W* hurdle, we see no serious objection to our assumption that both *U* and *W* precede *Y*, except in regard to some fraction of the very young men just mentioned.

In summary, then, we take the somewhat idealized assumption of temporal order to represent an order of priority in a causal or processual sequence, which may be stated diagrammatically as follows:

$$(V, X) - (U) - (W) - (Y).$$

In proposing this sequence we do not overlook the possibility of what Carlsson calls "delayed effects,"[8] meaning that an early variable may affect a later one not only via intervening variables but also directly (or perhaps through variables not measured in the study).

In translating this conceptual framework into quantitative estimates the first task is to establish the pattern of associations between the variables in the sequence. This is accomplished with the correlation coefficient. Table 1 supplies the correlation matrix on which much of the subsequent analysis is based. In discussing causal interpretations of these correlations, we shall have to be clear about the distinction between two points of view. On the one hand, the simple correlation—

TABLE 1

Simple Correlations for Five Status Variables

Variable	Variable				
	Y	W	U	X	V
Y: 1962 occ. status		.541	.596	.405	.322
W: First-job status		...	.538	.417	.332
U: Education			...	.438	.453
X: Father's occ. status				...	.516
V: Father's education					...

given our assumption as to direction of causation—measures the gross magnitude of the effect of the antecedent upon the consequent variable. Thus, if $r_{YW} = .541$, we can say that an increment of one standard deviation in first job status produces (whether directly or indirectly) an increment of just over half of one standard deviation in 1962 occupational status. From another point of view we are more concerned with net effects. If both first job and 1962 status have a common antecedent cause—say, father's occupation—we may want to state what part of the effect of *W* on *Y* consists in a transmission of the prior influence of *X*. Or, thinking of *X* as the initial cause, we may focus on the extent to which its influence on *Y* is transmitted by way of its prior influence on *W*.

We may, then, devote a few remarks to the pattern of gross effects before presenting the apparatus that yields estimates of net direct and indirect effects. Since we do not require a causal ordering of father's education with respect to his occupation, we may be content simply to note that $r_{XV} = .516$ is somewhat lower than the corresponding correlation, $r_{YU} = .596$, observed for the respondents themselves. The difference suggests a heightening of the effect of education on occupational status between the fathers' and the sons' generations. Before stressing this interpretation, however, we must remember that the measurements of *V* and *X* do not pertain to some actual cohort of men, here designated "fathers." Each "father" is represented in the data in proportion to the number of his sons who were 20 to 64 years old in March 1962.

The first recorded status of the son himself is education (*U*). We note that r_{UV} is just slightly greater than r_{UX}. Apparently both measures on the father represent factors that may influence the son's education.

In terms of gross effects there is a clear ordering of influences on first job. Thus $r_{WU} > r_{WX} > r_{WV}$. Education is most strongly correlated with first job, followed by father's occupation, and then by father's education.

Occupational status in 1962 (Y) apparently is influenced more strongly by education than by first job; but our earlier discussion of the first-job measure suggests we should not overemphasize the difference between r_{YW} and r_{YU}. Each, however, is substantially greater than r_{YX}, which in turn is rather more impressive than r_{YV}.

Figure 1 is a graphic representation of the system of relationships among the five variables that we propose as our basic model. The numbers entered on the diagram, with the exception of r_{XV}, are path coefficients, the estimation of which will be explained shortly. First we must become familiar with the conventions followed in constructing this kind of diagram. The link between V and X is shown as a curved line with an arrowhead at both ends. This is to distinguish it from the other lines, which are taken to be paths of influence. In the case of V and X we may suspect an influence running from the former to the latter. But if the diagram is logical for the respondent's generation, we should have to assume that for the fathers, likewise, education and occupation are correlated not only because one affects the other but also because common causes lie behind both, which we have not measured. The bidirectional arrow merely serves to sum up all sources of correlation between V and X and to indicate that the explanation thereof is not part of the problem at hand.

The straight lines running from one measured variable to another represent *direct* (or net) influences. The symbol for the path coefficient, such as p_{YW}, carries a double subscript. The first subscript is the variable at the head of the path, or the effect; the second is the causal variable. (This resembles the convention for regression coefficients, where the first subscript refers to the "dependent" variable, the second to the "independent" variable.)

Finally, we see lines with no source indicated carrying arrows to each of the effect variables. These represent the residual paths, standing for all other influences on the variable in question, including causes not recognized or measured, errors of measurement, and departures of the true

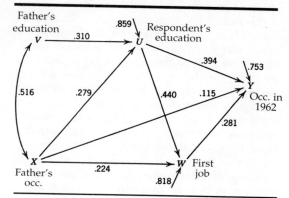

FIGURE 1

Path coefficients in basic model of the process of stratification

relationships from additivity and linearity, properties that are assumed throughout the analysis.

An important feature of this kind of causal scheme is that variables recognized as effects of certain antecedent factors may, in turn, serve as causes for subsequent variables. For example, U is caused by V and X, but it in turn influences W and Y. The algebraic representation of the scheme is a system of equations, rather than the single equation more often employed in multiple regression analysis. This feature permits a flexible conceptualization of the *modus operandi* of the causal network. Note that Y is shown here as being influenced directly by W, U, and X, but not by V (an assumption that will be justified shortly). But this does not imply that V has no influence on Y. V affects U, which does affect Y both directly and indirectly (via W). Moreover, V is correlated with X, and thus shares in the gross effect of X on Y, which is partly direct and partly indirect. Hence the gross effect of V on Y, previously described in terms of the correlation r_{YV}, is here interpreted as being entirely indirect, in consequence of V's effect on intervening variables and its correlation with another cause of Y.

Path Coefficients

Whether a path diagram, or the causal scheme it represents, is adequate depends on both theoretical and empirical considerations. At a minimum, before constructing the diagram we must know, or be willing to assume, a causal ordering of the observed variables (hence the lengthy discussion of this matter earlier in this chapter). This information is external or *a priori* with respect to the data, which merely describe associations or correlations. Moreover, the causal scheme must be complete, in the sense that all causes are accounted for. Here, as in most problems involving analysis of observational data, we achieve a formal completeness of the scheme by representing unmeasured causes as a residual factor, presumed to be uncorrelated with the remaining factors lying behind the variable in question. If any factor is known or presumed to operate in some other way it must be represented in the diagram in accordance with its causal role, even though it is not measured. Sometimes it is possible to deduce interesting implications from the inclusion of such a variable and to secure useful estimates of certain paths in the absence of measurements on it, but this is not always so. A partial exception to the rule that all causes must be explicitly represented in the diagram is the unmeasured variable that can be assumed to operate strictly as an intervening variable. Its inclusion would enrich our understanding of a causal system without invalidating the causal scheme that omits it. Sociologists have only recently begun to appreciate how stringent are the logical requirements that must be met if discussion of causal processes is to go beyond mere impressionism and vague verbal formulations.[9] We are a long way from being able to make causal inferences with confidence, and schemes of the kind presented here had best be regarded as crude first approximations to adequate causal models.

On the empirical side, a minimum test of the adequacy of a causal diagram is whether it satisfactorily accounts for the observed correlations among the measured variables. In making such a test we employ the fundamental theorem in path analysis, which shows how to obtain the correlation between any two variables in the system, given the path coefficients and correlations entered on the diagram.[10] Without stating this theorem in general form we may illustrate its application here. For example,

$$r_{YX} = p_{YX} + p_{YU}r_{UX} + p_{YW}r_{WX};$$

and

$$r_{WX} = p_{WX} + p_{WU}r_{UX}.$$

We make use of each path leading to a given variable (such as Y in the first example) and the correlations of each of its causes with all other variables in the system. The latter correlations, in turn, may be analyzed; for example, r_{WX}, which appeared as such in the first equation, is broken down into two parts in the second. A complete expansion along these lines is required to trace out all the indirect connections between variables; thus,

$$r_{YX} = p_{YX} + p_{YU}p_{UX} + p_{YU}p_{UV}r_{VX} + p_{YW}p_{WX} \\ + p_{YW}p_{WU}p_{UX} + p_{YW}p_{WU}p_{UV}r_{VX}.$$

Now, if the path coefficients are properly estimated, and if there is no inconsistency in the diagram, the correlations calculated by a formula like the foregoing must equal the observed correlations. Let us compare the values computed from such a formula with the corresponding observed correlations:

$$\begin{aligned} r_{WV} &= p_{WX}r_{XV} + p_{WU}r_{UV} \\ &= (.224)(.516) + (.440)(.453) \\ &= .116 + .199 = .315 \end{aligned}$$

which compares with the observed value of .332; and

$$\begin{aligned} r_{YV} &= p_{YU}r_{UV} + p_{YX}r_{XV} + p_{YW}r_{WV} \\ &= (.394)(.453) + (.115)(.516) + (.281)(.315) \\ &= .326 \end{aligned}$$

(using here the calculated rather than the observed value of r_{WV}), which resembles the actual value, .322. Other such comparisons—for r_{YX}, for example—reveal, at most, trivial discrepancies (no larger than .001).

We arrive, by this roundabout journey, at the problem of getting numerical values for the path coefficients in the first place. This involves using equations of the foregoing type inversely. We have illustrated how to obtain correlations if the path coefficients are known, but in the typical empirical problem we know the correlations (or at least some of them) and have to estimate the paths. For a diagram of the type of Figure 1 the solution involves equations of the same form as those of linear multiple regression, except that we work with a recursive system of regression equations[11] rather than a single regression equation.

Table 2 records the results of the regression calculations. It can be seen that some alternative combinations of independent variables were studied. It turned out that the net regressions of both *W* and *Y* on *V* were so small as to be negligible. Hence *V* could be disregarded as a direct influence on these variables without loss of information. The net regression of *Y* on *X* was likewise small but, as it appears, not entirely negligible. Curiously, this net regression is of the same order of magnitude as the proportion of occupational inheritance in this population—about 10 per cent, as discussed [elsewhere].[12] We might speculate that the direct effect of father's occupation on the occupational status of a mature man consists of this modest amount of strict occupational inheritance. The remainder of the effect of *X* on *Y* is indirect, inasmuch as *X* has previously influenced *U* and *W,* the son's education and the occupational level at which he got his start. For reasons noted [elsewhere][13] we do not assume that the full impact of the tendency to take up the father's occupation is registered in the choice of first job.

With the formal properties of the model in mind we may turn to some general problems confronting this kind of interpretation of our results. One of the first impressions gained from Figure 1 is that the largest path coefficients in the diagram are those for residual factors, that is, variables not measured. The residual path is merely a convenient representation of the extent to which measured causes in the system fail to account for the variation in the effect variables. (The residual is obtained from the coefficient of determination; if $R^2_{Y(WUX)}$ is the squared multiple correlation of *Y* on the three independent variables, then the residual for *Y* is $\sqrt{1 - R^2_{Y(WUX)}}$.) Sociologists are often disappointed in the size of the residual, assuming that this is a measure of their success in "explaining" the phenomenon under study. They seldom reflect on what it would mean to live in a society where nearly perfect explanation of the depend-

TABLE 2

Partial Regression Coefficients in Standard Form (Beta Coefficients) and Coefficients of Determination, for Specified Combinations of Variables

Dependent Variable[a]	Independent Variables[a]				Coefficient of Determination (R^2)
	W	U	X	V	
U[b]	...	...	.279	.310	.26
W	...	.433	.214	.026	.33
W[b]	...	.440	.224	...	.33
Y	.282	.397	.120	-.014	.43
Y[b]	.281	.394	.115	...	.43
Y	.311	.428	...	...	.42

[a] V: Father's education.
X: Father's occ. status.
U: Respondent's education.
W: First-job status.
Y: 1962 occ. status.
[b] Beta coefficients in these sets taken as estimates of path coefficients for Figure 1.

ent variable could be secured by studying causal variables like father's occupation or respondent's education. In such a society it would indeed be true that some are "destined to poverty almost from birth ... by the economic status or occupation of their parents" (in the words of the reference cited in footnote 1). Others, of course, would be "destined" to affluence or to modest circumstances. By no effort of their own could they materially alter the course of destiny, nor could any stroke of fortune, good or ill, lead to an outcome not already in the cards.

Thinking of the residual as an index of the adequacy of an explanation gives rise to a serious misconception. It is thought that a high multiple correlation is presumptive evidence that an explanation is correct or nearly so, whereas a low percentage of determination means that a causal interpretation is almost certainly wrong. The fact is that the size of the residual (or, if one prefers, the proportion of variation "explained") is *no* guide whatever to the validity of a causal interpretation. The best-known cases of "spurious correlation"—a correlation leading to an egregiously wrong interpretation—are those in which the coefficient of determination is quite high.

The relevant question about the residual is not really its size at all, but whether the unobserved factors it stands for are properly represented as being uncorrelated with the measured antecedent variables. We shall entertain [elsewhere][14] some conjectures about unmeasured variables that clearly are not uncorrelated with the causes depicted in Figure 1. It turns out that these require us to acknowledge certain possible modifications of the diagram, whereas other features of it remain more or less intact. A delicate question in this regard is that of the burden of proof. It is all too easy to make a formidable list of unmeasured variables that someone has alleged to be crucial to the process under study. But the mere existence of such variables is already acknowledged by the very presence of the residual. It would seem to be part of the task of the critic to *show,* if only hypothetically, but *specifically,* how the modification of the causal scheme to include a new variable would disrupt or alter the relationships in the original diagram. His argument to this effect could then be examined for plausibility and his evidence, if any, studied in terms of the empirical possibilities it suggests.

Our supposition is that the scheme in Figure 1 is most easily subject to modification by introducing additional measures of the same kind as those used here. If indexes relating to socioeconomic background other than V and X are inserted we will almost certainly estimate differently the direct effects of these particular variables. If occupational statuses of the respondent intervening between W and Y were known we should have to modify more or less radically the right-hand portion of the diagram. Yet we should argue that such modifications may amount to an enrichment or extension of the basic model rather than an invalidation of it. The same may be said of other variables that function as intervening causes. In theory, it should be possible to specify these in some detail, and a major part of the research worker's task is properly defined as an attempt at such specification. In the course of such work, to be sure, there is always the possibility of a discovery that would require a fundamental reformulation, making the present model obsolete. Discarding the model would be a cost gladly paid for the prize of such a discovery.

Postponing the confrontation with an altered model, the one at hand is not lacking in interest. An instructive exercise is to compare the magnitudes of gross and net relationships. Here we make use of the fact that the correlation coefficient and the path coefficient have the same dimensionality. The correlation $r_{YX} = .405$ (Table 1) means that a unit change (one standard deviation) in X produces a change of 0.4 unit in Y, in gross terms. The path coefficient, $p_{YX} = .115$ (Figure 1), tells us that about one-fourth of this gross effect is a result of the direct influence of X on Y. (We speculated above on the role of occupational inheritance in this connection.) The remainder $(.405 - .115 = .29)$ is indirect, via U and W. The sum of all indirect effects, therefore, is given by the difference between the simple correlation and the path coefficient connecting two variables. We note that the indirect effects on Y are generally substantial, relative to the direct. Even the variable temporally closest (we assume) to Y has "indirect effects"—actually, common antecedent causes—nearly as large as the direct. Thus $r_{YW} = .541$ and $p_{YW} = .281$, so that the aggregate of "indirect effects" is .26, which in this case are common determinants of Y and W that spuriously inflate the correlation between them.

To ascertain the indirect effects along a given chain of causation we must multiply the path coefficients along the chain. The procedure is to locate on the diagram the dependent variable of interest, and then trace back along the paths linking it to its immediate and remote causes. In such a tracing we may reverse direction once but only once, following the rule "first back, then forward." Any bidirectional correlation may be traced in either direction. If the diagram contains more than one such correlation, however, only one may be used in a given compound path. In tracing the indirect connections no variable may be intersected more than once in one compound path. Having traced all such possible compound paths, we obtain the entirety of indirect effects as their sum.

Let us consider the example of effects of education on first job, U on W. The gross or total effect is $r_{WU} = .538$. The direct path is $p_{WU} = .440$. There are two indirect connections or compound paths: from W back to X then forward to U; and from W back to X, then back to V, and then forward to U. Hence we have:

$$r_{WU} = p_{WU} + \underbrace{p_{WX}p_{UX} + p_{WX}r_{XV}p_{UV}}_{\text{(indirect)}}$$
$$\text{(gross)} \quad \text{(direct)}$$

or, numerically,

$$.538 = .440 + (.224)(.279) + (.224)(.516)(.310)$$
$$= .440 + .062 + .036$$
$$= .440 + .098.$$

In this case all the indirect effect of *U* on *W* derives from the fact that both *U* and *W* have *X* (plus *V*) as a common cause. In other instances, when more than one common cause is involved and these causes are themselves interrelated, the complexity is too great to permit a succinct verbal summary.

A final stipulation about the scheme had best be stated, though it is implicit in all the previous discussion. The form of the model itself, but most particularly the numerical estimates accompanying it, are submitted as valid only for the population under study. No claim is made that an equally cogent account of the process of stratification in another society could be rendered in terms of this scheme. For other populations, or even for subpopulations within the United States, the magnitudes would almost certainly be different, although we have some basis for supposing them to have been fairly constant over the last few decades in this country. The technique of path analysis is not a method for discovering causal laws but a procedure for giving a quantitative interpretation to the manifestations of a known or assumed causal system as it operates in a particular population. When the same interpretive structure is appropriate for two or more populations there is something to be learned by comparing their respective path coefficients and correlation patterns. We have not yet reached the stage at which such comparative study of stratification systems is feasible. ...

The Concept of a Vicious Circle

Although the concept of a "cycle of poverty" has a quasi-official sanction in U. S. public policy discussion, it is difficult to locate a systematic explication of the concept. As clear a formulation as any that may be found in academic writing is perhaps the following:[15]

Occupational and social status are to an important extent self-perpetuating. They are associated with many factors which make it difficult for individuals to modify their status. Position in the social structure is usually associated with a certain level of income, education, family structure, community reputation, and so forth. These become part of a vicious circle in which each factor acts on the other in such a way as to preserve the social structure in its present form, as well as the individual family's position in that structure. ... The cumulation of disadvantages (or of advantages) affects the individual's entry into the labor market as well as his later opportunities for social mobility.

The suspicion arises that the authors in preparing this summary statement were partly captured by their own rhetoric. Only a few pages earlier they had observed that the "widespread variation of educational attainment within classes suggests that one's family background plays an enabling and motivating rather than a determining role."[16] But is an "enabling and motivating role" logically adequate to the function of maintaining a "vicious circle"? In focusing closely on the precise wording of the earlier quotation we are not interested in splitting hairs or in generating a polemic. It merely serves as a convenient point of departure for raising the questions of what is specifically meant by "vicious circle," what are the operational criteria for this concept, and what are the limits of its usefulness.

To begin with, there is the question of fact—or, rather, of how the quantitative facts are to be evaluated. How "difficult" is it, in actuality, "for individuals to modify their status" (presumably reference is to the status of the family of orientation)? We have found that the father-son correlation for occupational status is of the order of .4. (Assuming attenuation by errors of measurement, this should perhaps be revised slightly upward.) Approaching the measurement problem in an entirely different way, we find that the amount of intergenerational mobility between census major occupation groups is no less than seven-eighths as much as would occur if there were no statistical association between the two statuses whatsoever, or five-sixths as much as the difference between the "minimum" mobility involved in the intergenerational shift in occupation distributions and the amount required for "perfect" mobility.[17] Evidently a very considerable amount of "status modification" or occupational mobility does occur. (There is nothing in the data exhibited by Lipset and Bendix to indicate the contrary.) If the existing amount of modification of status is insufficient in terms of some functional or normative criterion implicitly employed, the precise criterion should be made explicit: *How much mobility must occur to contradict the diagnosis of a "vicious circle"?*

Next, take the postulate that occupational status (of origin) is "associated with many factors" and that "each factor acts on the other" so as "to preserve … the individual family's position." Here the exposition virtually cries out for an explicit *quantitative* causal model; if not one of the type set forth in the first section of this chapter, then some other model that also takes into account the way in which several variables combine their effects. Taking our own earlier model, for want of a better alternative, as representative of the situation, what do we learn about the "associated factors"? Family "position" is, indeed, "associated with … education," and education in turn makes a sizable difference in early and subsequent occupational achievement. Yet of the total or gross effect of education (U) on Y, occupational status in 1962 ($r_{YU} = .596$), only a minor part consists in a transmission of the prior influence of "family position," at least as this is indicated by measured variables V (father's education) and X (father's occupation). … A relevant calculation concerns the compound paths through V and X linking Y to U. Using data for men 20 to 64 years old with nonfarm background, we find:

$$p_{YX}p_{UX} = .025$$
$$p_{YX}r_{XV}p_{UV} = .014$$
$$p_{YX}p_{WX}p_{UX} = .014$$
$$p_{YW}p_{WX}r_{XV}p_{UV} = \underline{.008}$$
$$\text{Sum} = .061$$

This is the *entire* part of the effect of education that has to do with "perpetuating" the "family's position." By contrast, the direct effect is $p_{YU} = .407$ and the effect via W (exclusive of prior influ-

ence of father's education and occupation on respondent's first job) is $p_{YW}p_{WU} = .128$, for a total of .535. Far from serving in the main as a factor perpetuating initial status, education operates *primarily* to induce variation in occupational status that is independent of initial status. The simple reason is that the large residual factor for U is an indirect cause of Y. But by definition it is quite uncorrelated with X and V. This is not to gainsay the equally cogent point that the degree of "perpetuation" (as measured by r_{YX}) that does occur is mediated in large part by education.

This conclusion is so important that we should not allow it to rest on a single calculation. The reader accustomed to a calculus of "explained variation" may prefer the following. For men 35 to 44 years of age with nonfarm background (a convenient and not unrepresentative illustration), we have these pertinent results: $r_{YX} = .400$; $R_{Y(XV)} = .425$; $R_{Y(UXV)} = .651$. Note that adding the "associated factor" of father's education to father's occupation increases very slightly our estimate of the influence of "family position" on occupational achievement. Including respondent's education, however, makes quite a striking difference. Squaring these coefficients to yield an accounting of the total variation in respondent's 1962 occupational status (Y), we obtain these percentages:

(*i*) Gross (or total) effect of father's education and occupation	18.06
(*ii*) Education of respondent, independent of (*i*)	24.32
(*iii*) All other factors, independent of (*i*) and (*ii*)	57.62
TOTAL	100.00

An analogous calculation, derived from multiple-classification rather than linear-regression statistics, was offered [elsewhere].[18] The results are rather similar. Here we have imputed to the measures of "family position," X and V, their *total* influence, including such part of this as works through education; the 24 per cent contribution of respondent's education refers only to the part of the effect of education that is net of the background factors. Still, education has a greater influence, *independent of these factors*, than they have themselves, operating both directly and indirectly. Overshadowing both these components, of course, is the unexplained variation of nearly 58 per cent, which can have nothing to do with "perpetuating status."

Whatever the merit of these observations, they should at least make clear that statistical results do not speak for themselves. Rather, the findings of a statistical analysis must be controlled by an interpretation—one that specifies the form the analysis will take—and be supplemented by further interpretations that (ideally) make explicit the assumptions on which the analyst is proceeding. The form in which our results are presented is dictated by a conception of status achievement as a temporal process in which later statuses depend, in part, on earlier statuses, intervening achievements, and other contingent factors. In such a framework it may not be a meaningful task to evaluate the relative importance of different causal factors. Instead, attention is focused on how the causes combine to produce the end result. From this point of view we can indicate, first, the gross effect of the measured background factors or origin statuses of a cohort of men on their adult achievement. We can then show how and to what extent this effect is transmitted via measured intervening variables and, finally, to what extent such intervening variables contribute to the outcome, independently of their role in transmission of prior statuses. In a balanced interpretation all these questions should be dealt with explicitly.

Our treatment seems to indicate the advisability of keeping in perspective the magnitude of the gross relationship of background factors and status of origin to subsequent achievement. The relationship is not trivial, nor is it, on the other hand, great enough in itself to justify the conception of a system that insures the "inheritance of poverty" or otherwise renders wholly ineffectual the operation of institutions supposedly based on universalistic principles.

Our model also indicates where the "vicious circle" interpretation is vulnerable. In the passage on the vicious circle quoted there seems to be an assumption that because of the substantial intercorrelations between a number of background factors, each of which has a significant relationship to subsequent achievement, the total effect of

origin on achievement is materially enhanced. Here, in other words, the concept of "cumulation" appears to refer to the intercorrelations of a collection of independent variables. But the effect of such intercorrelations is quite opposite to what the writers appear to suppose. They are not alone in arguing from a fallacious assumption that was caustically analyzed by Karl Pearson half a century ago.[19] The crucial point is that if the several determinants are indeed substantially intercorrelated with each other, then their combined effect will consist largely in redundancy, not in "cumulation." This circumstance does not relieve us from the necessity of trying to understand better *how* the effects come about (a point also illustrated in a less fortunate way in Pearson's work). It does imply that a refined estimate of how much effect results from a combination of "associated factors" will not differ greatly from a fairly crude estimate based on the two or three most important ones. Sociologists have too long followed the mirage of "increasing the explained variance." ...

We do not wish to imply that the idea of cumulation of influences, or even the particular form of cumulation describable as a "vicious circle," is without merit. Our aim is to call attention to the necessity of specifying the actual mechanism that is only vaguely suggested by such terms. One legitimate meaning of cumulation is illustrated by the model of a synthetic cohort presented [elsewhere].[20] In this case what is cumulative is the experience of an individual or a cohort of individuals over the life cycle, so that in the latter part of the life cycle achieved status depends heavily on prior achievements, whatever the factors determining those achievements may have been. The cumulation here consists in large measure of the effects of contingent factors not related to social origins or measured background factors.

The situation of the Negro American, which is analyzed [elsewhere],[21] exemplifies mechanisms inviting the label of a vicious circle. What is crucial in this case is not merely that Negroes begin life at a disadvantage and that this initial disadvantage, transmitted by intervening conditions, has adverse effects on later careers. Rather, what happens is that, in addition to the initial handicap, the Negro experiences further handicaps at each stage of the life cycle. When Negroes and whites are equated with respect to socioeconomic circumstances of origin and rearing, Negroes secure inferior education. But if we allow for this educational disadvantage as well as the disadvantage of low social origins, Negroes find their way into first jobs of lower status than whites. Again, allowing for the handicap of inferior career beginnings, the handicap of lower education, and the residual effect of low socioeconomic origins—even with all these allowances—Negroes do not enjoy comparable occupational success in adulthood. Indeed, even though we have not carried our own analysis this far, there is good evidence that Negroes and whites do not have equal incomes even after making allowance for the occupational status difference and the educational handicap of Negroes.[22] Thus there surely are disadvantaged minorities in the United States who suffer from a "vicious circle" that is produced by discrimination. But not all background factors that create occupational handicaps are necessarily indicative of such a vicious circle of *cumulative* disadvantages; the handicaps of the Southern whites, for example, are not cumulative in the same sense.[23] A vicious circle of cumulative impediments is a distinctive phenomenon that should not be confused with any and all forms of differential occupational achievement.

As noted earlier, the issue of equalitarianism is one that has generally been more productive of debate than of cogent reasoning from systematized experience. Without becoming fully involved in such a debate here, we must at least attempt to avoid having our position misunderstood. We have *not* vouchsafed a "functional interpretation" that asserts that somehow American society has just the right amount of stratification and just the appropriate degree of intergenerational status transmission. We *have* indicated that it is easy to exaggerate the latter and, in particular, that it is possible seriously to misconstrue the nature of the causal relationships in the process that characterizes status transmission between generations.

In conclusion, one question of policy may be briefly mentioned, which pertains to the distinction between the plight of the minorities who do suffer disadvantages due to their ascribed status and the influence of ascribed factors on occupational life in general. To help such minorities to break out of the vicious circle resulting from discrimination and poverty is a challenge a democratic society must face, in our opinion. To advocate this policy, however, is not the same as claiming that *all* ascriptive constraints on opportunities and achievements could or should be eliminated. To eliminate all *dis*advantages that flow from membership in a family of orientation—with its particular structure of interpersonal relationships, socioeconomic level, community and regional location, and so on—would by the same token entail eliminating any *advantages* the family can confer or provide. If parents, having achieved a desirable status, can *ipso facto* do nothing to make comparable achievement easier for their offspring, we may have "equal opportunity." But we will no longer have a family system—at least not in the present understanding of the term. (This point has not been misunderstood in radical, particularly Marxist, ideologies.)

We do not contemplate an effortless equilibrium at some optimum condition where the claims of egalitarian values and the forces of family attachment are neatly balanced to the satisfaction of all. A continuing tension between these ultimately incompatible tendencies may, indeed, be a requisite for social progress. We do contend that both equity and effectiveness in the policy realm call for a deeper understanding of the process of stratification than social science and politics yet can claim.

Notes

1. Mollie Orshansky, "Children of the Poor," *Social Security Bulletin,* 26(July 1963).

2. Forrest A. Bogan, "Employment of High School Graduates and Dropouts in 1964," *Special Labor Force Report,* No. 54 (U. S. Bureau of Labor Statistics, June 1965), p. 643.

3. Peter M. Blau and Otis Dudley Duncan, *The American Occupational Structure,* New York: The Free Press, 1967, ch. 4.

4. *Ibid.*

5. Bruce K. Eckland, "College Dropouts Who Came Back," *Harvard Educational Review,* 34(1964), 402–420.

6. Beverly Duncan, *Family Factors and School Drop-out: 1920–1960*, U. S. Office of Education, Cooperative Research Project No. 2258, Ann Arbor: Univ. of Michigan, 1965.

7. Blau and Duncan, *op. cit.*, Appendix C.

8. Gösta Carlsson, *Social Mobility and Class Structure*, Lund: CWK Gleerup, 1958, p. 124.

9. H. M. Blalock, Jr., *Causal Inferences in Nonexperimental Research*, Chapel Hill: Univ. of North Carolina Press, 1964.

10. Sewall Wright, "Path Coefficients and Path Regressions," *Biometrics*, 16(1960), 189–202; Otis Dudley Duncan, "Path Analysis," *American Journal of Sociology*, 72(1966), 1–16.

11. Blalock, *op. cit.*, pp. 54ff.

12. Blau and Duncan, *op. cit.*, ch. 4.

13. *Ibid.*, ch. 3.

14. *Ibid.*, ch. 5.

15. Seymour M. Lipset and Reinhard Bendix, *Social Mobility in Industrial Society*, Berkeley: Univ. of California Press, 1959, pp. 198–199.

16. *Ibid.*, p. 190.

17. U. S. Bureau of the Census, "Lifetime Occupational Mobility of Adult Males: March 1962," *Current Population Reports*, Series P-23, No. 11 (May 12, 1964), Table B.

18. Blau and Duncan, *op. cit.*, ch. 4.

19. Karl Pearson, "On Certain Errors with Regard to Multiple Correlation Occasionally Made by Those Who Have Not Adequately Studied This Subject," *Biometrika*, 10(1914), 181–187.

20. Blau and Duncan, *op. cit.*, ch. 5.

21. *Ibid.*, ch. 6.

22. See Herman P. Miller, *Rich Man, Poor Man*, New York: Crowell, 1964, pp. 90–96.

23. Blau and Duncan, *op. cit.*, ch. 6.

CHRISTOPHER JENCKS, MARSHALL SMITH, HENRY ACLAND, MARY JO BANE, DAVID COHEN, HERBERT GINTIS, BARBARA HEYNS, AND STEPHAN MICHELSON

Inequality: A Reassessment of the Effect of Family and Schooling in America

Most Americans say they believe in equality. But when pressed to explain what they mean by this, their definitions are usually full of contradictions. Many will say, like the Founding Fathers, that "all men are created equal." Many will also say that all men are equal "before God," and that they are, or at least ought to be, equal in the eyes of the law. But most Americans also believe that some people are more competent than others, and that this will always be so, no matter how much we reform society. Many also believe that competence should be rewarded by success, while incompetence should be punished by failure. They have no commitment to ensuring that everyone's job is equally desirable, that everyone exercises the same amount of political power, or that everyone receives the same income.

But while most Americans accept inequality in virtually every sphere of day-to-day life, they still believe in what they often call "equal opportunity." By this they mean that the rules determining who succeeds and who fails should be fair. People are, of course, likely to disagree about precisely what is "fair" and what is "unfair." Still, the general principle of fair competition is almost universally endorsed.

During the 1960s, many reformers devoted enormous effort to equalizing opportunity. More specifically, they tried to eliminate inequalities based on skin color, and to a lesser extent on economic background. They also wanted to eliminate absolute deprivation: "poverty," "ignorance," "powerlessness," and so forth. But only a handful of radicals talked about eliminating inequality per se. Almost none of the national legislation passed during the 1960s tried to reduce disparities in adult status, power, or income in any direct way. There was no significant effort, for example, to make taxation more progressive, and very little effort to reduce wage disparities between highly paid and poorly paid workers. Instead, attention focused on helping workers in poorly paid jobs to move into better paid jobs. Nor was there much effort to reduce the social or psychological distance between high- and low-status occupations. Instead, the idea was to help people in low-status occupations leave these occupations for more prestigious ones. Even in the political arena, "maximum feasible participation" implied mainly that more "leaders" should be black and poor, not that power should be equally distributed between leaders and followers.

Because the reforms of the 1960s did not tackle the problem of adult inequality directly, they accomplished only a few of their goals. Equalizing opportunity is almost impossible without greatly reducing the absolute level of inequality, and the same is true of eliminating deprivation.

Consider the case of equal opportunity. One can equalize the opportunities available to blacks and whites without equalizing anything else, and considerable progress was made in this direction during the late 1960s. But equalizing the opportunities available to different children of the same race is far more difficult. If a society is competitive and rewards adults unequally, some parents are bound to succeed while others fail. Successful parents will then try to pass along their advantages to their children. Unsuccessful parents will inevitably pass along some of their disadvantages. Unless a society completely eliminates ties between parents and children, inequality among parents guarantees some degree of inequality in the opportunities available to children. The only real question is how serious these inequalities must be.

Or consider the problem of deprivation. When the war on poverty began in late 1963, it was conceived as an effort to raise the living standards of the poor. The rhetoric of the time described the persistence of poverty in the midst of affluence as a "paradox," largely attributable to "neglect." Official publications all assumed that poverty was an absolute rather than a relative condition. Having assumed this, they all showed steady progress toward the elimination of poverty, since fewer and fewer people had incomes below the official "poverty line."

Yet despite all the official announcements of progress, the feeling that lots of Americans were poor persisted. The reason was that most Americans define poverty in relative rather than absolute terms. Public opinion surveys show, for example, that when people are asked how much money an American family needs to "get by," they typically name a figure about half what the average American family actually receives.[1] This has been true for the last three decades, despite the fact that real incomes (i.e. incomes adjusted for inflation) have doubled in the interval.

Political definitions of poverty have reflected these popular attitudes. During the Depression, the average American family was living on about $30 a week. A third of all families were living on less than half this amount, i.e. less than $15 a week. This made it natural for Franklin Roosevelt to speak of "one third of a nation" as ill-housed, ill-clothed, and ill-fed. One third of the nation was below what most people then regarded as the poverty line.

By 1964, when Lyndon Johnson declared war on poverty, incomes had risen more than fivefold. Even allowing for inflation, living standards had doubled. Only about 10 percent of all families had real incomes as low as the bottom third had had during the Depression. But popular conceptions of what it took to "get by" had also risen since the Depression. Mean family income was about $160 a week, and popular opinion now held that it took $80 a week for a family of four to make ends meet. About a quarter of all families were still poor by this definition. As a matter of political convenience, the Administration set the official poverty line at $60 a week for a family of four rather than $80, ensuring that even conservatives would admit that those below the line were poor. But by 1970 inflation had raised mean family income to about $200 a week, and the National Welfare Rights Organization was rallying liberal support for a guaranteed income of $100 a week for a family of four.

These political changes in the definition of poverty were not just a matter of "rising expectations" or of people's needing to "keep up with the Joneses." The goods and services that made it possible to live on $15 a week during the Depression were no longer available to a family with the same "real" income (i.e. $40 a week) in 1964. Eating habits had changed, and many cheap foods had disappeared from the stores. Most people had enough money to buy an automobile, so public transportation had atrophied, and families without automobiles were much worse off than during the Depression. The labor market had also changed, and a person without a telephone could not get or keep many jobs. A home without a telephone was more cut off socially than when few people had telephones and more people "dropped by." Housing arrangements had changed, too. During the Depression, many people could not afford indoor plumbing and "got by" with a privy. By the 1960s, privies were illegal in most places. Those who could not afford an indoor toilet ended up in buildings which had broken toilets. For this they paid more than their parents had paid for privies.

Examples of this kind suggest that the "cost of living" is not the cost of buying some fixed set of goods and services. It is the cost of participating in a social system. The cost of participation depends in large part on how much other people habitually spend to participate. Those who fall far below the norm, whatever it may be, are excluded. It follows that raising the incomes of the poor will not eliminate poverty if the incomes of other Americans rise even faster. If people with incomes less than half the national average cannot afford what "everyone" regards as "necessities," the only way to eliminate poverty is to make sure everyone has an income at least half the average.

This line of reasoning applies to wealth as well as poverty. The rich are not rich because they eat filet mignon or own yachts. Millions of people can now afford these luxuries, but they are still not "rich" in the colloquial sense. The rich are rich because they can afford to buy other people's time. They can hire other people to make their beds, tend their gardens, and drive their cars. These are not privileges that become more widely available as people become more affluent. If all workers' wages rise at the same rate, the highly paid professional will have to spend a constant percentage of his income to get a maid, a gardener, or a taxi. The number of people who are "rich," in the sense of controlling more than their share of other people's time and effort, will therefore remain the same, even though consumption of yachts and filet mignon is rising.

If the distribution of income becomes more equal, as it did in the 1930s and 1940s, the number of people who are "rich" in this sense of the term will decline, even though absolute incomes are rising. If, for example, the wages of domestic servants rise faster than the incomes of their prospective employers, fewer families will feel they can afford full-time servants. This will lower the living standards of the elite to some extent, regardless of what happens to consumption of yachts and filet mignon.

This same logic applies not only to income but to the cognitive skills taught in school. Young people's performance on standardized tests rose dramatically between World War I and World War II, for example. But the level of competence required for many adult roles rose too. When America was a polyglot nation of immigrants, all sorts of jobs were open to those who could not read English. Such people could, for example, join the army, drive a truck, or get a job in the construction industry. Today, when almost everyone can read English, the range of choices open to nonreaders has narrowed. The military no longer takes an appreciable number of illiterates, a driver's license requires a written examination, and apprenticeships in the construction trades are restricted to those who can pass tests. Those who cannot read English are at a disadvantage, simply because they are atypical. America is not organized with their problems in mind. The same thing applies to politics. If the average citizen's vocabulary expands, the vocabulary used by politicians and newspapers will expand too. Those with very limited vocabularies relative to their neighbors will still have trouble following events, even though their vocabulary is larger than, say, their parents' vocabulary was.

Arguments of this kind suggest that it makes more sense to think of poverty and ignorance as relative than as absolute conditions. They also suggest that eliminating poverty and ignorance, at least as these are usually defined in America, depends on eliminating, or at least greatly reducing, inequality. This is no simple matter. Since a competitive system means that some people "succeed" while others "fail," it also means that people will end up unequal. If we want to reduce inequality, we therefore have two options. The first possibility is to make the system less competitive by reducing the benefits that derive from success and the costs paid for failure. The second possibility is to make sure that everyone enters the competition with equal advantages and disadvantages.

The basic strategy of the war on poverty during the 1960s was to try to give everyone entering the job market or any other competitive arena comparable skills. This meant placing great emphasis on education. Many people imagined that if schools could equalize people's cognitive skills this would equalize their bargaining power as adults. In such a system nobody would end up very poor—or, presumably, very rich.

This strategy rested on a series of assumptions which went roughly as follows:

1. Eliminating poverty is largely a matter of helping children born into poverty to rise out of it. Once families escape from poverty, they do not fall back into it. Middle-class children rarely end up poor.

2. The primary reason poor children do not escape from poverty is that they do not acquire basic cognitive skills. They cannot read, write, calculate, or articulate. Lacking these skills, they cannot get or keep a well-paid job.

3. The best mechanism for breaking this vicious circle is educational reform. Since children born into poor homes do not acquire the skills they need from their parents, they must be taught these skills in school. This can be done by making sure that they attend the same schools as mid-

dle-class children, by giving them extra compensatory programs in school, by giving their parents a voice in running their schools, or by some combination of all three approaches.

So far as we can discover, each of these assumptions is erroneous.

1. Poverty is not primarily hereditary. While children born into poverty have a higher-than-average chance of ending up poor, there is still an enormous amount of economic mobility from one generation to the next. Indeed, there is nearly as much economic inequality among brothers raised in the same homes as in the general population. This means that inequality is recreated anew in each generation, even among people who start life in essentially identical circumstances.

2. The primary reason some people end up richer than others is not that they have more adequate cognitive skills. While children who read well, get the right answers to arithmetic problems, and articulate their thoughts clearly are somewhat more likely than others to get ahead, there are many other equally important factors involved. Thus there is almost as much economic inequality among those who score high on standardized tests as in the general population. Equalizing everyone's reading scores would not appreciably reduce the number of economic "failures."

3. There is no evidence that school reform can substantially reduce the extent of cognitive inequality, as measured by tests of verbal fluency, reading comprehension, or mathematical skill. Neither school resources nor segregation has an appreciable effect on either test scores or educational attainment.

Our work suggests, then, that many popular explanations of economic inequality are largely wrong. We cannot blame economic inequality primarily on genetic differences in men's capacity for abstract reasoning, since there is nearly as much economic inequality among men with equal test scores as among men in general. We cannot blame economic inequality primarily on the fact that parents pass along their disadvantages to their children, since there is nearly as much inequality among men whose parents had the same economic status as among men in general. We cannot blame economic inequality on differences between schools, since differences between schools seem to have very little effect on any measurable attribute of those who attend them.

Economic success seems to depend on varieties of luck and on-the-job competence that are only moderately related to family background, schooling, or scores on standardized tests. The definition of competence varies greatly from one job to another, but it seems in most cases to depend more on personality than on technical skills. This makes it hard to imagine a strategy for equalizing competence. A strategy for equalizing luck is even harder to conceive.

The fact that we cannot equalize luck or competence does *not* mean that economic inequality is inevitable. Still less does it imply that we cannot eliminate what has traditionally been defined as poverty. It only implies that we must tackle these problems in a different way. Instead of trying to reduce people's capacity to gain a competitive advantage on one another, we would have to change the rules of the game so as to reduce the rewards of competitive success and the costs of failure. Instead of trying to make everyone equally lucky or equally good at his job, we would have to devise "insurance" systems which neutralize the effects of luck, and income-sharing systems which break the link between vocational success and living standards.

This could be done in a variety of ways. Employers could be constrained to reduce wage disparities between their best- and worst-paid workers.[2] The state could make taxes more progressive, and could provide income supplements to those who cannot earn an adequate living from wages alone. The state could also provide free public services for those who cannot afford to buy adequate services in the private sector. Pursued with vigor, such a strategy would make "poverty" (i.e. having a living standard less than half the national average) virtually impossible. It would also make economic "success," in the sense of having, say, a living standard more than twice the national average, far less common than it now is. The net effect would be to make those with the most competence and luck subsidize those with the least competence and luck to a far greater extent than they do today.

This strategy was rejected during the 1960s for the simple reason that it commanded relatively little popular support. The required legislation could not have passed Congress. Nor could it pass today. But that does not mean it was the wrong strategy. It simply means that until we change the political and moral premises on which most Americans now operate, poverty and inequality of opportunity will persist at pretty much their present level.

At this point the reader may wonder whether trying to change these premises is worthwhile. Why, after all, should we be so concerned about economic equality? Is it not enough to ensure equal opportunity? And does not the evidence we have described suggest that opportunities are already quite equal in America? If economic opportunities are relatively equal, and if the lucky and the competent then do better for themselves than the unlucky and incompetent, why should we feel guilty about this? Such questions cannot be answered in any definitive way, but a brief explanation of our position may help avoid misunderstanding.

We begin with the premise that every individual's happiness is of equal value. From this it is a short step to Bentham's dictum that society should be organized so as to provide the greatest good for the greatest number. In addition, we assume that the law of diminishing returns applies to most of the good things in life. In economic terms this means that people with low incomes value extra income more than people with high incomes.[3] It follows that if we want to maximize the satisfaction of the population, the best way to divide any given amount of money is to make everyone's income the same. Income disparities (except those based on variations in "need") will always reduce overall satisfaction, because individuals with low incomes will lose more than individuals with high incomes gain.

The principal argument against equalizing incomes is that some people contribute more to the general welfare than others, and that they are therefore entitled to greater rewards. The most common version of this argument is that unless those who contribute more than their share are rewarded (and those who contribute less than their share punished) productivity will fall and everyone will be worse off. A more sophisticated version is that people will only share their incomes on an equal basis if all decisions that affect these incomes are made collectively. If people are left free to make decisions on an individual basis, their neighbors cannot be expected to pay the entire cost of their mistakes.

We accept the validity of both these arguments. We believe that men need incentives to contribute to the common good, and we prefer monetary incentives to social or moral incentives, which tend to be inflexible and very coercive. We believe, in other words, that virtue should be rewarded, and we assume that there will be considerable variation in virtue from one individual to another. This does not, however, mean that incomes must remain as unequal as they are now. Even if we assume, for example, that the most productive fifth of all workers accounts for half the Gross National Product, it does not follow that they need receive half the income. A third or a quarter might well suffice to keep both them and others productive.

Most people accept this logic to some extent. They believe that the rich should pay more taxes than the poor, although they often disagree about how much more. Conversely, they believe that the poor should not starve, even if they contribute nothing to the general welfare. They believe, in other words, that people should not be rewarded solely for their contribution to the general welfare, but that other considerations, such as need, should also be taken into account. Our egalitarianism is simply another way of saying that we think need should play a larger role than it now does in determining what people get back from society. We do not think it can or should be the sole consideration.

When we turn from the distribution of income to the distribution of other things, our commitment to equality is even more equivocal. We assume, for example, that occupational prestige resembles income in that those who have low-prestige occupations usually value additional prestige more than those who have high-prestige occupations. Insofar as prestige is an end in itself, then, the optimal distribution is again egalitarian. But occupational prestige derives from a variety of factors, most of which are more difficult to redistribute than income. We cannot imagine a social system in which all occupations have equal prestige, except in a society where all workers are equally competent. Since we do not see any likelihood of equalizing competence, we regard the equalization of occupational prestige as a desirable but probably elusive goal.

When we turn from occupational prestige to educational attainment and cognitive skills, the arguments for and against equality are reversed. If schooling and knowledge are thought of strictly as ends in themselves, it is impossible to make a case for distributing them equally. We can see no reason to suppose, for example, that people with relatively little schooling value additional schooling more than people who have already had a lot of schooling. Experience suggests that the reverse is the case. Insofar as schooling is an end in itself, then, Benthamite principles imply that those who want a lot should get a lot, and those who want very little should get very little. The same is true of knowledge and cognitive skills. People who know a lot generally value additional knowledge and skills more than those who know very little. This means that insofar as knowledge or skill is valued for its own sake, an unequal distribution is likely to give more satisfaction to more people than an equal distribution.

The case for equalizing the distribution of schooling and cognitive skill derives not from the idea that we should maximize consumer satisfaction, but from the assumption that equalizing schooling and cognitive skill is necessary to equalize status and income. This puts egalitarians in the awkward position of trying to impose equality on people, even though the natural demand for both cognitive skill and schooling is very unequal. Since we have found rather modest relationships between cognitive skill and schooling on the one hand and status and income on the other, we are much less concerned than most egalitarians with making sure that people end up alike in these areas.

Our commitment to equality is, then, neither all-embracing nor absolute. We do not believe that everyone can or should be made equal to everyone else in every respect. We assume that some differences in cognitive skill and vocational competence are inevitable, and that efforts to eliminate such differences can never be 100 percent successful. But we also believe that the distribution of income can be made far more equal than it is, even if the distribution of cognitive skill and vocational competence remains as unequal as it is now. We also think society should get on with the task of equalizing income rather than waiting for the day when everyone's earning power is equal.

Notes

1. This material has been collected and analyzed by Lee Rainwater at Harvard University, as part of a forthcoming study of the social meaning of low income.

2. Lester C. Thurow and Robert E.B. Lucas, in "The American Distribution of Income" [Washington, D.C.: U.S. Government Printing Office, March 17, 1972], discuss the possibility of such constraints in some detail. The principal virtue of this approach is that it reduces the incomes of the rich *before* they are defined as "income" rather than afterwards. This means that the recipient is less conscious of what he is giving up and less likely to feel he is being cheated of his due.

3. If everyone had equal earning power we could assume that people "chose" their incomes voluntarily and that those with low incomes were those who were maximizing something else (e.g. leisure, autonomy, etc.). But as we note [elsewhere], people's concern with income as against other objectives has no apparent effect on their actual income, at least while they are young [see Christopher Jencks, Marshall Smith, Henry Acland, Mary Jo Bane, David Cohen, Herbert Gintis, Barbara Heyns, and Stephan Michelson, *Inequality: A Reassessment of the Effect of Family and Schooling in America*, New York: Harper and Row, 1972, ch. 7, note 64]. Thus we infer that income differences derive largely from differences in earning power and luck.

WILLIAM H. SEWELL, ARCHIBALD O. HALLER,
AND ALEJANDRO PORTES

The Educational and Early Occupational
Attainment Process

Blau and Duncan (1967:165–172) have recently presented a path model of the occupational attainment process of the American adult male population. This basic model begins with two variables describing the early stratification position of each person; these are his father's educational and occupational attainment statuses. It then moves to two behavioral variables; these are the educational level the individual has completed and the prestige level of his first job. The dependent variable is the person's occupational prestige position in 1962. That the model is not without power is attested by the fact that it accounts for about 26 percent of the variance in educational attainment, 33 percent of the variance in first job, and 42 percent of the variance in 1962 level of occupational attainment. Various additions to the basic model are presented in the volume, but none is clearly shown to make much of an improvement in it. These include nativity, migration, farm origin, subgroup position, marriage, and assortative mating. Without detracting from the excellence of the Blau and Duncan analysis, we may make several observations.

1) Because the dependent behaviors are occupational prestige attainments—attainment levels in a stratification system, it is appropriate to single out variables indicating father's stratification position as the most relevant social structural inputs. It is unfortunate that practical considerations prevented the inclusion of psychological inputs in their model, especially considering the repeated references to one such—mental abil-

ity—in the literature on differential occupational attainment (Lipset and Bendix, 1959:203–226; Sewell and Armer, 1966). More recently, this gap has been partially filled (Duncan, 1968a).

2) Also omitted are social psychological factors which mediate the influence of the input variables on attainment. This, too, is unfortunate in view not only of the speculative theory but also the concrete research in social psychology, which suggests the importance of such intervening variables as reference groups (Merton, 1957:281–386), significant others (Gerth and Mills, 1953:84–91), self-concept (Super, 1957:80–100), behavior expectations (Gross et al., 1958), levels of educational and occupational aspiration (Haller and Miller, 1963; Kuvlesky and Ohlendorf, 1967; Ohlendorf et al., 1967), and experiences of success or failure in school (Parsons, 1959; Brookover et al., 1965).

It remains to be seen whether the addition of such psychological and social psychological variables is worthwhile, although there are reasons for believing that at least some of them may be. First, an explanation of a behavior system requires a plausible causal argument, not just a set of path coefficients among temporally ordered variables. As indicated in Duncan's (1969) recent work, the introduction of social psychological mediating variables offers this possibility, but it does not guarantee it. As it stands, the Blau-Duncan model fails to indicate why any connection at all would be expected between the input variables, father's education and occupation, and the three subsequent factors: respondent's education, respondent's first job, and respondent's 1962 occupation. Granting differences among social psychological positions, they all agree that one's cognitions and motivations (including, among others, knowledge, self-concept and aspirations) are developed in structured situations (including the expectations of others), and that one's actions (attainments in this case) are a result of the cognitive and motivational orientations one brings to the action situation, as well as the factors in the new situation itself. Second, if valid, a social psychological model will suggest new points at which the causal system may be entered in order to change the attainment behaviors of persons, an issue not addressed by the Blau and Duncan volume. Variables such as the expectations of significant others offer other possibilities for manipulating the outcomes, including educational attainments. Third, in addition to the above advantages, a social psychological model of educational and occupational attainment might add to the explanation of variance in the dependent variables.

The Problem

The present report extends the attempts of the writers (Sewell and Armer, 1966; Sewell and Orenstein, 1965; Sewell and Shah, 1967; Sewell, 1964; Haller and Sewell, 1967; Portes *et al.*, 1968; Haller, 1966; Haller and Miller, 1963; Miller and Haller, 1964; Sewell *et al.*, 1957) to apply social psychological concepts to the explanation of variation in levels of educational and occupational attainment. We assume (1) that certain social structural and psychological factors—initial stratification position and mental ability, specifically—affect both the sets of significant others' influences bearing on the youth, and the youth's own observations of his ability; (2) that the influence of significant others, and possibly his estimates of his ability, affect the youth's levels of educational and occupational aspiration; (3) that the levels of aspiration affect subsequent levels of educational attainment; (4) that education in turn affects levels of occupational attainment. In the present analysis we assume that all effects are

linear; also, that the social psychological variables perform only mediating functions.

More specifically, we present theory and data regarding what we believe to be a logically consistent social psychological model. This provides a plausible causal argument to link stratification and mental ability inputs through a set of social psychological and behavioral mechanisms to educational and occupational attainments. One compelling feature of the model is that some of the inputs may be manipulated through experimental or other purposive interventions. This means that parts of it can be experimentally tested in future research and that practical policy agents can reasonably hope to use it in order to change educational and occupational attainments.

A Social Psychological Model

The model treats causal relationships among eight variables. X_1 is the occupational prestige level attained by the adult person, or *occupational attainment* (OccAtt); X_2 is the educational level he had previously attained, or *educational attainment* (EdAtt); X_3 is the occupational prestige level to which he aspired as a youth, or *level of occupational aspiration* (LOA); X_4 is his *level of educational aspiration* as a youth (LEA); X_5 is the influence for educational achievement exerted upon him by significant others while still in high school, or *significant others' influence* (SOI); X_6 is the quality of his *academic performance* in high school (AP); X_7 is the level of his family in the stratification system, or *socioeconomic status* (SES); and X_8 is his *mental ability* as measured while he was in high school (MA). Path models (Blau and Duncan, 1967:165–172; Wright, 1934; Wright, 1960; Heise, 1969) require a knowledge of the causal order among the variables. Beyond the causal arguments presented below, additional credibility is suggested by the existence of a plausible temporal order among variables. X_7 (SES) and X_8 (MA) precede everything else. X_5 (SOI) and X_6 (AP) precede both aspirations and attainments, and it can be assumed that for the most part X_6 precedes X_5. Youthful aspirations obviously precede later educational and occupational

DIAGRAM 1
Path coefficients of antecedents of educational and occupational attainment levels

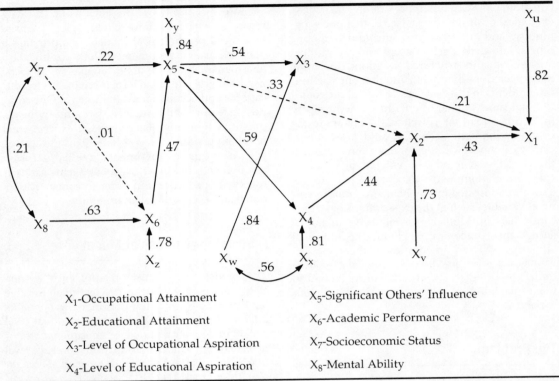

X_1-Occupational Attainment

X_2-Educational Attainment

X_3-Level of Occupational Aspiration

X_4-Level of Educational Aspiration

X_5-Significant Others' Influence

X_6-Academic Performance

X_7-Socioeconomic Status

X_8-Mental Ability

attainments. Pre-adult educational attainments precede adult occupational attainments.

By no means do all of the possible causal linkages seem defensible. The most likely ones are indicated in Diagram 1. In it straight solid lines stand for causal lines that are to be theoretically expected, dotted lines stand for possible but theoretically debatable causal lines, and curved lines represent unanalyzed correlations among variables which cannot be assigned causal priority in present data.

Commencing from the left of the diagram, we assume, as has often been found before (Sewell and Shah, 1967; Sewell *et al.*, 1957), that a low positive correlation, r_{78}, exists between the youth's measured mental ability (MA) and his parents' socioeconomic status (SES). This is the case: r_{78}=.21. We anticipate the existence of stheorize

that significant others' influence (SOI) is controlled by AP, and by socioeconomic status, as well as by exogenous factors, that they exert profound effects on aspiration, and that the latter in turn influences later attainments. A more detailed examination of the theory follows.

Working with partial conceptions of SOI (and using different terminology), Bordua (1960) and Sewell and Shah (1968) have shown that parents' expectations for the youths' attainments are important influences on later aspirations and attainment. Similarly, Cramer (1967), Alexander and Campbell (1964), Campbell and Alexander (1965), Haller and Butterworth (1960), and Duncan *et al.* (1968) have investigated peer influences on aspirations and attainments. Each of these sets of actors, plus some others, may be seen as a special case of reference group influence. Building on such thinking, we have concluded that the key variable here is significant others' influence. Significant others are the specific persons from whom the individual obtains his level of aspiration, either because they serve as models or because they communicate to him their expectations for his behavior (Woelfel, 1967). The term "significant others" is more appropriate than that of "reference group" because it eliminates the implication that collectivities such as one's friends, or work groups, or parents are necessarily the influential agents for all individuals. Experimental research, beginning with Sherif's work (1935), has shown the importance of other persons in defining one's own situation. One obtains his social behavior tendencies largely through the influence of others. Herriott (1963) has carried this line of thinking into the present area of research. He has shown that one's conception of the educational behavior others think appropriate to him is highly correlated with his level of educational aspiration. Thus, significant others' influence is a central variable in a social psychological explanation of educational and occupational attainment. It is obviously important to discover the causal paths determining SOI, as well as those by which it exerts its effects on attainment. We hypothesize a substantial direct path (p_{57}) from socioeconomic status (SES) to SOI. We also hypothesize a substantial effect of mental ability on SOI. This is because we expect that the significant others with whom the youth interacts base their expectations for his educational and occupational attainments in part on his demonstrated abilities. In turn, this implies that the path from mental ability (MA) to SOI is indirect by way of academic performance (AP). Thus, we hypothesize the existence of a pronounced path from MA to AP (p_{68}) and another from AP to SOI (p_{56}). So far we assume that one's grades in school are based on the quality of his performance. A strong undercurrent in the literature seems to have held, however, that the youth's family's SES has a direct influence on his grades (Havighurst and Neugarten, 1957:236–237). To our knowledge, this has not been adequately demonstrated, and in large high schools, often far removed from the youth's home and neighborhood, this may well be debatable. Nevertheless, since it is at least possible that school grades (the

evidences of performance) are partly determined by teachers' desires to please prestigious parents or to reward "middle-class" behavior, we have drawn a dotted path (p_{67}) from SES to AP, allowing for the possibility of such an influence.

We hypothesize that the major effects of significant others' influence (SOI) on attainment are mediated by its effects on levels of aspiration. Thus, we have indicated a path (p_{35}) from SOI to level of occupational aspiration (LOA) and another (p_{45}) from SOI to level of educational aspiration (LEA). It is not inconsistent with this to suspect the possibility that SOI might have a direct influence on later educational attainment (EdAtt); we have thus included a dotted or debatable path (p_{25}) from SOI to EdAtt. Because we are here referring to SOI during late high school, it must necessarily refer largely to college education. There is, therefore, no reason to include such a path from SOI to occupational attainment.

Levels of educational aspiration (LEA) and occupational aspirations (LOA) are known to be highly correlated, since education is widely, and to some extent validly, considered to be a necessary condition for high occupational attainment (Haller and Miller, 1963:30, 39–42, 96). But LOA and LEA are not identical. (In these data, $r_{34.5} = r_{WX} = .56$.) We expect that LEA will have a pronounced effect on EdAtt (p_{24}), and that its entire effect on level of occupational attainment will be expressed through EdAtt. On the other hand, we do not hypothesize any effect of LOA on EdAtt which is not already contained in its correlation with LEA. Hence, there is no hypothetical path for LOA to EdAtt. A direct effect of LOA on OccAtt (p_{13}) is hypothesized, however.

There are 26 possible paths, given the sequence laid out above. As one can see by counting the paths (straight lines) in Diagram 1, we hypothesize noteworthy effects for only eight of these—ten if the dotted lines are counted. If this were a rigorous theoretical model, path coefficients would be calculated only for these eight (or ten) supposed causal connections. We believe that because of the fact that it is not rigorous, and at this stage of our knowledge probably cannot be, it would be well to calculate all of the possible 26 path coefficients, using the calculated values as rough indicators of the influences operating in the system. If the theoretic reasoning is a fair description of the reality to which it is addressed, the path coefficients for the eight (or ten) predicted causal lines should be considerably greater than those for the remainder where no causal prediction was made. Also, it is entirely possible that some unhypothesized causal lines might turn out to be of importance. This, too, argues for calculating the whole set of 26. These data are presented in tabular form (Table 3) below.

Method

In 1957 all high school seniors in Wisconsin responded to an extensive questionnaire concerning their educational and occupational aspirations and a number of potentially related topics. In 1964 one of the authors (Sewell) directed a follow-up in which data on later educational and occupational attainments were collected from an approximately one-third random sample of the respondents in the original survey.

This study is concerned with those 929 subjects for whom data are available at both times, in 1957 and 1964, and who (a) are males and (b) whose fathers were farmers in 1957. Zero-order correlations are computed on all 929 cases, using a computer program which accepts missing data. All higher order coefficients are based on 739 cases for whom data on each variable were complete. (The matrices of zero-order correlations between all eight variables for those two sets of cases are practically identical.)

Variables

Level of occupational attainment (X_1—OccAtt) was measured by Duncan's (1961) socioeconomic index of occupational status.

Level of educational attainment (X_2—EdAtt) was operationalized with data obtained in 1964 by dividing the sample into those who have had at least some college education and those who have not had any at all.[1]

Level of occupational aspiration (X_3—LOA) was determined by assigning Duncan's (1961) socioeconomic index scores to the occupation indi-

TABLE 1

Zero-Order Correlations Between Indicators of Significant Others' Influence Regarding College

	Teachers' Influence	Friends' Influence	Index of Significant Others' Influence
Parental Influence	.37	.26	.74
Teachers' Influence	...	.32	.72
Friends' Influence	...	...	.68
Significant Others' Influence	...	...	...

cated by the respondent as the one he desired to fill in the future.

Level of educational aspiration (X_4—LEA) is a dichotomous variable corresponding to the respondent's statement in 1957 of whether or not he planned to attend college after graduating from high school.

Index of significant others' influence (X_5—SOI) is a simple summated score (range: zero to three) of three variables: (a) The youth's report of his parents' encouragement for college, dichotomized according to whether or not the respondent perceived direct parental encouragement for going to college. (b) The youth's report of his teachers' encouragement for college, dichotomized in a similar manner, according to whether or not direct teacher encouragement for college was perceived by the respondent. (c) Friends' college plans, dichotomized according to the respondent's statement that most of his close friends planned or did not plan to go to college. These variables, all emphasizing education, were combined because they reflect the same conceptual dimension, and that dimension is theoretically more relevant than any of its component parts. That the three components do in fact measure the same dimension is attested by the positive correlations among them and a subsequent factor analysis. These correlations and the correlation of each with the summated variable, significant others' influence, are shown in Table 1. It may be relevant to point out the composition of this significant others' index in the light of Kelley's distinction (1952). Clearly, the perceptions of direct parental and teacher pressures toward college conform to the classic case of normative reference groups. The educational plans of close friends, on the other hand, may be thought of as having mixed functions. First, close peer groups may exercise pressure toward conformity, and second, friends' plans also serve for the individual's cognitive comparison of himself with "people like himself." Therefore, though the main character of the dimension indicated by this index is clearly normative, it can be thought of as containing some elements of an evaluative function as well.

Quality of academic performance (X_6—AP) is measured by a reflected arc sine transformation of each student's rank in his high school class.

Socioeconomic status (X_7—SES) is measured by a factor-weighted combination of the education of the respondent's father and mother, his perception of the economic status of the family, his perception of possible parental support should he choose to go to college and the approximate amount of such support, and the occupation of his father.[2]

Measured mental ability (X_8—MA) is indexed by Henmon-Nelson test scores (1942). The data were taken when the youths were in the junior year of high school. The scores, originally recorded as percentile-ranks, were treated with an arc sine transformation to approximate a normal distribution.[3]

Results

The zero-order correlation coefficients among eight variables are presented in Table 2. A complete path diagram would involve too many lines to be intelligible, because path coefficients presented in Diagram 1 were calculated for all 26 possible lines implied in the causal order specified above. With the exception of the theoretically dubious direct path from SES to AP, which turned out to be $p_{67} = .01$, each of the path coefficients for causal lines hypothesized in Diagram 1 is larger than those not hypothesized. Both sets of standardized beta (or path) coefficients are presented in Table 3.

This table shows that the reasoning presented in the above section, offering a social psychological explanation for educational and occupational attainment, cannot be too far off the mark. We had hypothesized that SOI (significant others' influence) was of central importance. In fact, it has notable direct effects on three subsequent variables, each of which bears ultimately on prestige level of occupational attainment. Both theory and data agree that SOI has direct effects on levels of educational and occupational aspiration, as well as educational (*i.e.,* college) attainment. In turn, each aspiration variable appears to have the predicted substantial effects on its respective attainment variable. Looking at its antecedents, we note theory and data again agree that SOI is affected directly by SES and indirectly by measured mental ability through the latter's effect on the youth's academic performance. The latter variable is crucial because it provides (or is correlated with) palpable evidence that significant others can observe and, thus to a degree, align their expectations for the youth with his demonstrated ability.

None of the unpredicted paths is very strong, but we must recognize that there may be more operating in such a system than we were able to anticipate from previous thinking. There is a pair of perhaps consequential direct paths from academic performance to educational aspiration ($p_{46} = .18$) and to educational attainment ($p_{26} = .17$). There are several possibilities. The data might imply the existence of a mediating factor, such as one's self conception of his ability, a factor which could influence both educational aspirations and attainment. They also suggest that not all of the effect of ability on educational aspiration and attainments is mediated by SOI. Finally, one's ability may exert a continuing effect on his educational attainments quite apart from the mediation of either significant others or aspirations—and therefore apart from one's conception of his ability. Arguments such as these, however, should not be pressed too far because the figures are small. Another unexpected but noteworthy path links mental ability directly to level of occupational aspiration. We offer no speculation regarding it.

So far we have seen that a consistent and plausible social psychological position is at least moderately well borne out by the analysis of lines of apparent influence of its variables when they are

TABLE 2
Zero-Order Correlations

	X_1 Occupational Attainment (Prestige Scores— Duncan)	X_2 Educational Attainment (Years College)	X_3 Level of Occupational Aspiration	X_4 Level of Educational Aspiration	X_5 Significant Others' Influence	X_6 Academic Performance (Grade Point)	X_7 Socioeconomic Status	X_8 Measured Mental Ability
X_1-Occ. Att.	...	.52	.43	.38	.41	.37	.14	.33
X_2-Ed. Att.	...	...	.53	.61	.57	.48	.23	.40
X_3-LOA	...	...	...	.70	.53	.43	.15	.41
X_4-LEA	...	...	...	...	.59	.46	.26	.40
X_5-SOI	...	...	...	...	...	.49	.29	.41
X_6-AP	...	...	...	...	...	...	.16	.62
X_7-SES	...	...	...	...	...	...	...	.21
X_8-MA	...	...	...	...	...	...	...	...

TABLE 3
Standardized Beta Coefficients for Hypothesized and Non-Hypothesized Causal Paths*

Dependent Variables	Independent Variables						
	X_2 EdAtt	X_3 LOA	X_4 LEA	X_5 SOI	X_6 AP	X_7 SES	X_8 MA
X_6 AP	...	...	...	...	...	(.01)	.62
X_5 SOI	...	...	...	...	.39	.21	.13
X_4 LEA	...	...	...	.45	.18	.07	.08
X_3 LOA	...	...	...	.42	.12	—.02	.16
X_2 EdAtt	...	.07	.34	(.23)	.17	.05	.03
X_1 OccAtt	.38	.19	—.10	.11	.06	.00	.04

* Figures in italics are coefficients for paths hypothesized in Diagram 1.
Figures in parentheses refer to theoretically debatable causal lines.

arranged in causal order. How well does the total set of independent variables work in accounting for variance in the attainment variables? In brief, $R^2_{1.2345678} = .34$ and $R^2_{2.345678} = .50$. Thus, the variables account for 34 percent of the variance in level of occupational attainment and 50 percent of the variance in level of educational attainment. Obviously, variables X_3 through X_8 are much more effective in accounting for educational attainment than in accounting for occupational attainment. Indeed, educational attainment alone accounts for 27 percent of the variance in occupational attainment (from Table 3, $r^2_{12} = .52^2 = .27$). What we have here, then, is a plausible causal system functioning primarily to explain variation in

educational attainment. This, in turn, has considerable effect on occupational attainment. The same set of variables adds a small but useful amount to the explanation of occupational attainment variance beyond that contributed by its explanation of educational attainment.[4]

Discussion and Conclusions

Using father's occupational prestige, the person's educational attainment, and his first job level, Blau and Duncan (1967:165–172) were able to account for 33 percent of the variance in occupational attainment of a nationwide sample of

American men. Neither our sample nor our variables are identical with theirs; so it is impossible to assess the total contribution of this study to the state of knowledge as reflected in their work. Educational attainment is strategic in both studies and in this regard the studies are fairly comparable. The present model adds a great deal to the explanation of the social psychological factors affecting that variable. The prospects seem good, too, that if the present model were to be applied to a sample coming from a wider range of the American stratification system with greater age variation, it might prove to be more powerful than it appears with our sample of young farm-reared men. In general, the present take-off on the Blau-Duncan approach to occupational attainment levels seems worthy of further testing and elaboration.

Several comments are appropriate regarding the social psychological position and data presented here. (1) Clearly, the variable we have called significant others' influence is an important factor. The present evidence appears to show that once formed its effects are far-reaching. Also, besides being a powerful explanatory factor, significant others' influence should be amenable to manipulation. It thus suggests itself as a point at which external agents might intervene to change educational and occupational attainment levels. This means that at least part of the system is theoretically amenable to experimental testing. The parts of the present model which are hypothetically dependent upon this variable might be more securely tested if such experiments can be worked out. Also, practical change agents might be able to change levels of attainment, either by inserting themselves or others as new significant others or by changing the expectations existing significant others have for the individual. There may well be a substantial pay-off from more refined work with this variable.

(2) The results seem to indicate, too, that aspirations (a special class of attitudes) are in fact performing mediational functions in transmitting anterior factors into subsequent behaviors. This has been a subject of recent debate, much of which has in effect held that attitudinal variables are useless epiphenomena. This was recently discussed by Fendrich (1967).

Such encouraging results do not, however, mitigate the need for (a) general experimental determination of the supposed effects of attitudes on behaviors, and (b) specific experimental determination of the effects of aspirations on attainments.

(3) The question may be raised as to the extent to which this system is inherently culture-bound. One might wonder whether attainment behavior within an institutionalized pattern of "sponsored" rather than "contest" achievement (Turner, 1960) would change the path model. Besides this (and perhaps other institutionalized types of achievement patterns), there is also the question of the relevance of the model for ascribed occupational attainment systems. Obviously we do not have data bearing on these questions but we may at least discuss them. Let us suppose that the same eight variables are measured on youth in a "sponsored" achievement context. We speculate that if measured mental ability is the basis of selection of those who are to be advanced, then the direct path from mental ability to significant others' influence would increase because sponsors are significant others. (This would require a more general measure of significant others' influence than was used here.) If a variable other than mental ability or socioeconomic status is important to the sponsors, then the residual effect of unmeasured variables on significant others' influence would increase. Since one's sponsors presumably influence one's aspirations and aspirations in turn mediate attainment, the rest of the model probably would not change much.

Consider the case of ascribed attainment. Here one's parents' position determines what one's significant others will expect of one; mental ability is either irrelevant or controlled by family position; and one's aspirations are controlled by the family. The importance of higher education may vary among basically ascribed systems: in one it may be unimportant, in another it may merely validate one's status, or in still another it may train ascribed elites to fulfill the key social roles in the society. If educational attainment is important within the social system, aspirations will mediate the influence of significant others upon it, and it in turn will mediate occupational attainment. If not, occupational aspirations will mediate occupational attainment and educational attainment will drop out of the path model. In short, by allowing for variations in the path coefficients, the same basic social psychological model might work well to describe attainment in stratification and mobility systems quite different from that of the present sample.

(4) The linear model used here seems to be an appropriate way to operationalize social psychological positions holding that the function of "intervening" attitudinal variables is to mediate the influence of more fundamental social structural and psychological variables on behavior. By assuming linear relations among variables and applying a path system to the analysis, we have cast the attainment problem in such a framework. It seems to have worked quite well. We are sufficiently encouraged by this attempt to recommend that a parallel tack might be made on problems in which the overt behavior variables are quite different from educational and occupational attainment.

(5) Nonetheless, satisfactory as such a linear model and its accompanying theory seems to be, there is still the possibility that other techniques flowing from somewhat different social psychological assumptions might be better. It is possible that, in the action situation, enduring attitudes (such as educational and occupational aspirations) may function as independent forces which express themselves in relevant overt behaviors to the degree that other personality and situational variables permit. Linear models would thus be effective to the degree that the persons modify their aspirations to bring them in line with potentials for action offered by the latter variables. More importantly, the combined effects of aspirational and facilitational variables would produce nonlinear accelerating curves of influence on behavior variables. For the present types of data, this would imply that parental stratification position, mental ability, and significant others' influence not only produce aspirations, but also, to the extent to which these influences continue more or less unchanged on into early adulthood, they function as differential facilitators for the expression of aspirations in attainments. If this is true, a nonlinear system of statistical analysis handling

interaction effects would be even more powerful than the one used in this paper.

(6) It should be remembered that the most highly educated of these young men had just begun their careers when the final data were collected. If the distance between them and the less educated widens, the occupational attainment variance accounted for by the model may well increase. The direct relations of some of the antecedents to occupational attainment may also change. In particular, mental ability may show a higher path to occupational attainment.

(7) Finally, although the results reported in this paper indicate that the proposed model has considerable promise for explaining educational and early occupational attainment of farm boys, its adequacy should now be tested on populations with a more differentiated socioeconomic background. It is quite possible that in such populations the effects of socioeconomic status on subsequent variables may be significantly increased. The effects of other variables in the system may also be altered when the model is applied to less homogeneous populations.

The present research appears to have extended knowledge of the causal mechanism influencing occupational attainment. Most of this was accomplished by providing a consistent social psychological model which adds to our ability to explain what is surely one of its key proximal antecedents, educational attainment.

Notes

Revision of paper originally prepared for delivery at the joint sessions of the Rural Sociological Society and the American Sociological Association, San Francisco, August, 1967. The research reported here was supported by the University of Wisconsin Graduate School, by the Cooperative State Research Service and the University's College of Agriculture for North Central Regional Research Committee NC-86, by funds to the Institute for Research on Poverty at the University of Wisconsin provided by the Office of Economic Opportunity pursuant to the provisions of the Economic Opportunity Act of 1964, and by a grant from the National Institute of Health, U. S. Public Health Service (M-6275). The writers wish to thank Otis Dudley Duncan for his careful reading and incisive criticisms and Vimal P.

Shah for help in the statistical analysis. The conclusions are the full responsibility of the authors.

1. It is important to note that the timing of the follow-up was such as to allow most individuals to complete their education up to the bachelor's degree and beyond. It is unlikely that the educational attainment of the sample as a whole will change much in the years to come. On the other hand, while the span of seven years allowed those individuals who did not continue their education to find a stable position in the occupational structure and even improve upon it, there was not enough time for those who continued their education to do the same. A few of the latter were still in school; most had just begun their occupational careers. It is therefore possible that a follow-up taken five or ten years from now would show greater differentiation in attainments as the educated group gathers momentum and moves up in the occupational world.

2. Naturally, father's occupation is a constant in this subsample of farm-reared males. It is important to note that the SES mean and standard deviations for this subsample are considerably lower than for the total sample. The low and homogeneous SES levels of this subsample may yield atypical relations among the variables.

3. Our previous research (Sewell and Armer, 1966; Haller and Sewell, 1967) has led us to be skeptical of claims that local ecological and school class compositional factors influence aspirations and attainments. Nevertheless the zero-order intercorrelations of five such variables and their correlations with $X_1 - X_8$ are available (although they are not presented here). Two of these pertain to the county in which the youth attended high school: county level of living and degree of urbanization. Three pertain to his high school senior class: average SES of the class, percentage of the class members whose fathers attended college, and percentage of the class members whose fathers had professional-level occupations. Though substantially correlated with each other, the variables are uncorrelated with the variables in the above model.

4. Some readers will be interested in the path coefficients as calculated only for the lines hypothesized in the diagram. For this reason and because of the diagram's parsimony, we have calculated the values for each of its eight paths (or ten, including dubious ones). The restricted model explains 47 and 33 percent of the variance in X_2 and X_1, respectively. Data not presented here show that the model reproduces the zero-order correlation matrix quite well. For this reason and because the model is an effective predictor of X_2 and X_1, it may be considered to be fairly valid. Nonetheless, it seems more prudent to rest our case on the less presumptuous data already presented in Table 3. This is

why the coefficients presented in the diagram are not discussed here.

References

Alexander, C. Norman, Jr., and Ernest Q. Campbell. 1964. "Peer influences on adolescent educational aspirations and attainments." American Sociological Review 29 (August):568–575.

Blau, Peter M., and Otis Dudley Duncan. 1967. The American Occupational Structure. New York: Wiley.

Bordua, David J. 1960. "Educational aspirations and parental stress on college." Social Forces 38 (March):262–269.

Brookover, Wilbur B., Jean M. LePere, Don E. Hamachek, Shailer Thomas, and Edsel L. Erickson. 1965. Self-concept of ability and school achievement. East Lansing: Michigan State University, Bureau of Educational Research Services.

Campbell, Ernest Q., and C. Norman Alexander. 1965. "Structural effects and interpersonal relationships." American Journal of Sociology 71 (November):284–289.

Cramer, M. R. 1967. "The relationship between educational and occupational plans of high school students." Paper presented at the meeting of the Southern Sociological Society, Atlanta (unpublished).

Duncan, Otis Dudley. 1961. "A socioeconomic index for all occupations." Pp. 109–138 in Albert J. Reiss, Jr. (ed.), Occupations and Social Status. New York: Free Press.

———. 1968a. "Ability and achievement." Eugenics Quarterly 15 (March):1–11.

———. 1969. "Contingencies in the construction of causal models," Edgar F. Borgatta, (ed.), Sociological Methodology.

Duncan, Otis Dudley, Archibald O. Haller, and Alejandro Portes. 1968. "Peer influences on aspirations: a reinterpretation." American Journal of Sociology 74 (September):119–137.

Fendrich, James M. 1967. "Perceived reference group support: racial attitudes and overt behavior." American Sociological Review 32 (December):960–970.

Gerth, Hans, and C. Wright Mills. 1953. Character and Social Structure. New York: Harcourt, Brace and World.

Gross, Neal, Ward S. Mason, and Alexander W. McEachern. 1958. Explorations in Role Analysis. New York: Wiley.

Haller, Archibald O. 1966. "Occupational choices of rural youth." Journal of Cooperative Extension 4 (Summer):93–102.

Haller, Archibald O., and Charles E. Butterworth. 1960. "Peer influences on levels of occupational and educational aspiration." Social Forces 38 (May):289–295.

Haller, Archibald O., and Irwin W. Miller. 1963. The Occupational Aspiration Scale: Theory, Structure and Correlates. East Lansing: Michigan Agricultural Experiment Station Bulletin 288.

Haller, Archibald O., and William H. Sewell. 1967. "Occupational choices of Wisconsin farm boys." Rural Sociology 32 (March):37–55.

Havighurst, Robert J., and Bernice L. Neugarten. 1957. Society and Education. Boston: Allyn and Bacon.

Heise, David R. 1969. "Problems in path analysis and causal inference," Edgar F. Borgatta, (ed.), Sociological Methodology.

Henmon, V. A. C., and M. J. Nelson. 1942. The Henmon-Nelson Test of Mental Ability. Boston: Houghton Mifflin Company.

Herriott, Robert E. 1963. "Some social determinants of educational aspiration." Harvard Educational Review 33 (Spring):157–177.

Kelley, Harold H. 1952. "Two functions of reference groups." Pp. 410–414 in Guy E. Swanson, et al. (eds.), Readings in Social Psychology. New York: Henry Holt and Company.

Kuvlesky, William P., and George W. Ohlendorf. 1967. A Bibliography of Literature on Status Projections of Youth: I. Occupational Aspirations and Expectations. College Station: Texas A&M University, Department of Agricultural Economics and Sociology.

Lipset, Seymour M., and Reinhard Bendix. 1959. Social Mobility in Industrial Society. Berkeley: University of California Press.

Merton, Robert K. 1957. Social Theory and Social Structure. New York: Free Press.

Miller, I. W., and Archibald O. Haller. 1964. "The measurement of level of occupational aspiration." Personnel and Guidance Journal 42 (January):448–455.

Ohlendorf, George W., Sherry Wages, and William P. Kuvlesky. 1967. A Bibliography of Literature on Status Projections of Youth: II. Educational Aspirations and Expectations. College Station: Texas A and M University, Department of Agricultural Economics and Sociology.

Parsons, Talcott. 1959. "The school class as a social system." Harvard Educational Review 29 (Summer):297–318.

Portes, Alejandro, Archibald O. Haller, and William H. Sewell. 1968. "Professional-executive vs. farming as unique occupational choices." Rural Sociology 33 (June):153–159.

Sewell, William H. 1964. "Community of residence and college plans." American Sociological Review 29 (February):24–38.

Sewell, William H., and J. Michael Armer. 1966. "Neighborhood context and college plans." American Sociological Review 31 (April): 159–168.

Sewell, William H., Archibald O. Haller, and Murray A. Straus. 1957. "Social status and educational and occupational aspiration." American Sociological Review 22 (February):67–73.

Sewell, William H., and Alan M. Orenstein. 1965. "Community of residence and occupational choice." American Journal of Sociology 70 (March):551–563.

Sewell, William H., and Vimal P. Shah. 1967. "Socioeconomic status, intelligence, and the attainment of higher education." Sociology of Education 40 (Winter):1–23.

_____. 1968. "Social class, parental encouragement, and educational aspirations." American Journal of Sociology 73 (March):559–572.

Sherif, Muzafer. 1935. "A study of some social factors in perception." Archives of Psychology Number 187.

Super, Donald E. 1957. The Psychology of Careers. New York: Harper.

Turner, Ralph H. 1960. "Sponsored and contest mobility and the school system." American Sociological Review 25 (December):855–867.

Woelfel, Joseph. 1967. "A paradigm for research on significant others." Paper presented at the Joint Session of the Society for the Study of Social Problems and the American Sociological Association, San Francisco (unpublished).

Wright, Sewall. 1934. "The method of path coefficients." Annals of Mathematical Statistics 5 (September):161–215.

_____. 1960. "Path coefficients and regression coefficients: alternative or complementary concept?" Biometrics 16 (June):189–202.

JAY MACLEOD

Ain't No Makin' It: Leveled Aspirations in a Low-income Neighborhood

"Any child can grow up to be president." So maintains the dominant ideology in the United States. This perspective characterizes American society as an open one in which barriers to success are mainly personal rather than social. In this meritocratic view, education ensures equality of opportunity for all individuals, and economic inequalities result from differences in natural qualities and in one's motivation and will to work. Success is based on achievement rather than ascription. Individuals do not inherit their social status— they attain it on their own. Because schooling mitigates gender, class, and racial barriers to success, the ladder of social mobility is there for all to climb. A favorite Hollywood theme, the rags-to-riches story resonates in the psyche of the American people. We never tire of hearing about Andrew Carnegie, for his experience validates much that we hold dear about America, the land of opportunity. Horatio Alger's accounts of the spectacular mobility achieved by men of humble origins through their own unremitting efforts occupy a treasured place in our national folklore. The American Dream is held out as a genuine prospect for anyone with the drive to achieve it.

"I ain't goin' to college. Who wants to go to college? I'd just end up gettin' a shitty job anyway." So says Freddie Piniella,[1] an intelligent eleven-year-old boy from Clarendon Heights, a low-income housing development in a northeastern city. This statement, pronounced with certitude and feeling, completely contradicts our achievement ideology. Freddie is pessimistic about his prospects for social mobility and disputes schooling's capacity to "deliver the goods." Such a view offends our sensibilities and seems a rationalization. But Freddie has a point. What of Carnegie's grammar school classmates, the great bulk of whom no doubt were left behind to occupy positions in the class structure not much different from those held by their parents? What about the static, nearly permanent element in the working class, whose members consider the chances for mobility remote and thus despair of all hope? These people are shunned, hidden, forgotten— and for good reason—because just as the self-made man is a testament to certain American ideals, so the very existence of an "underclass" in American society is a living contradiction to those ideals.

Utter hopelessness is the most striking aspect of Freddie's outlook. Erik H. Erikson writes that hope is the basic ingredient of all vitality;[2] stripped of hope, there is little left to lose. How is it that in contemporary America a boy of eleven can feel bereft of a future worth embracing? This is not what the United States is supposed to be. The United States is the nation of hopes and dreams and opportunity. As Ronald Reagan remarked in his 1985 State of the Union Address, citing the accomplishments of a young Vietnamese immigrant, "Anything is possible in America if we have the faith, the will, and the heart."[3] But to Freddie Piniella and many other Clarendon Heights young people who grow up in households where their parents and older siblings are unemployed, undereducated, or imprisoned, Reagan's words ring hollow. For them the American Dream, far from being a genuine prospect, is not even a dream. It is a hallucination.

I first met Freddie Piniella in the summer of 1981 when as a student at a nearby university I worked as a counselor in a youth enrichment program in Clarendon Heights. For ten weeks I lived a few blocks from the housing project and worked intensively with nine boys, aged eleven to thirteen. While engaging them in recreational and educational activities, I was surprised by the modesty of their aspirations. The world of middle-class work was entirely alien to them; they spoke about employment in construction, factories, the armed forces, or, predictably, professional athletics. In an ostensibly open society, they were a group of boys whose occupational aspirations did not even cut across class lines. ...

The male teenage world of Clarendon Heights is populated by two divergent peer groups. The first group, dubbed the Hallway Hangers because of the group's propensity for "hanging" in a particular hallway in the project [i.e., outside doorway #13], consists predominantly of white boys. Their characteristics and attitudes stand in marked contrast to the second group, which is composed almost exclusively of black youths who call themselves the Brothers. Surprisingly, the Brothers speak with relative optimism about their futures, while the Hallway Hangers are despondent about their prospects for social mobility. ...

Before describing the boys' orientation toward work [in more detail], I would like to make an analytical distinction between aspirations and expectations. Both involve assessments of one's desires, abilities, and the character of the opportunity structure. In articulating one's aspirations, an individual weighs his or her preferences more heavily; expectations are tempered by perceived capabilities and available opportunities. Aspirations are one's preferences relatively unsullied by anticipated constraints; expectations take these constraints squarely into account.[4]

The Hallway Hangers: Keeping a Lid on Hope

Conventional, middle-class orientations toward employment are inadequate to describe the Hallway Hangers' approach to work. The notion of a career, a set of jobs that are connected to one another in a logical progression, has little relevance to these boys. They are hesitant when asked about their aspirations and expectations. This hesitancy is not the result of indecision; rather it stems from the fact that these boys see little choice involved in getting a job. No matter how hard I pressed him, for instance, Jinks refused to articulate his aspirations: "I think you're kiddin' yourself to have any. We're just gonna take whatever we can get." Jinks is a perceptive boy, and his answer seems to be an accurate depiction of the situation. Beggars cannot be choosers, and these boys have nothing other than unskilled labor to offer on a credential-based job market.

It is difficult to gauge the aspirations of most of the Hallway Hangers. Perhaps at a younger age they had dreams for their futures. At ages sixteen, seventeen, and eighteen, however, their own job experiences as well as those of family members have contributed to a deeply entrenched cynicism about their futures. What is perceived as the cold, hard reality of the job market weighs very heavily on the Hallway Hangers; they believe their preferences will have almost no bearing on the work they actually will do. Their expectations are not merely tempered by perceptions of the opportunity structure; even their aspirations are crushed by their estimation of the job market. These generalizations may seem bold and rather extreme, but they do not lack ethnographic support.

The pessimism and uncertainty with which the Hallway Hangers view their futures emerge clearly when the boys are asked to speculate on what their lives will be like in twenty years.

(*all in separate interviews*)
STONEY: Hard to say. I could be dead tomorrow. Around here, you gotta take life day by day.
BOO-BOO: I dunno. I don't want to think about it. I'll think about it when it comes.
FRANKIE: I don't fucking know. Twenty years. I may be fucking dead. I live a day at a time. I'll probably be in the fucking pen.
SHORTY: Twenty years? I'm gonna be in jail.

These responses are striking not only for the insecurity and despondency they reveal, but also because they do not include any mention of work. It is not that work is unimportant—for people as strapped for money as the Hallway Hangers are, work is crucial. Rather, these boys are indifferent to the issue of future employment. Work is a given; they all hope to hold jobs of one kind or another in order to support themselves and their families. But the Hallway Hangers believe the character of work, at least all work in which they are likely to be involved, is essentially the same: boring, undifferentiated, and unrewarding. Thinking about their future jobs is a useless activity for the Hallway Hangers. What is there to think about?

For Steve and Jinks, although they do see themselves employed in twenty years, work is still of tangential importance.

JM: If you had to guess, what do you think you'll be doing twenty years from now?

(*in separate interviews*)

STEVE: I don't fucking know. Working probably. Have my own pad, my own house. Bitches, kids. Fucking fridge full of brewskies. Fine wife, likes to get laid.

JINKS: Twenty years from now? Probably kicked back in my own apartment doing the same shit I'm doing now—getting high. I'll have a job, if I'm not in the service, if war don't break out, if I'm not dead. I just take one day at a time.

Although the Hallway Hangers expect to spend a good portion of their waking hours on the job, work is important to them not as an end in itself, but solely as a means to an end—money.

In probing the occupational aspirations and expectations of the Hallway Hangers, I finally was able to elicit from them some specific hopes. Although Shorty never mentions his expectations, the rest of the Hallway Hangers have responded to my prodding with some definite answers. The range of answers as well as how they change over time are as significant as the particular hopes each boy expresses.

Boo-Boo's orientation toward work is typical of the Hallway Hangers. He has held a number of jobs in the past, most of them in the summer.

During his freshman year in high school Boo-Boo worked as a security guard at school for $2.50 an hour in order to make restitution for a stolen car he damaged. Boo-Boo also has worked on small-scale construction projects through a summer youth employment program called Just-A-Start, at a pipe manufacturing site, and as a clerk in a gift shop. Boo-Boo wants to be an automobile mechanic. Upon graduating from high school, he studied auto mechanics at a technical school on a scholarship. The only black student in his class, Boo-Boo was expelled early in his first term after racial antagonism erupted into a fight. Boo-Boo was not altogether disappointed, for he already was unhappy with what he considered the program's overly theoretical orientation. (Howard London found this kind of impatience typical of working-class students in the community college he studied.[5]) Boo-Boo wanted hands-on training, but "all's they were doing was telling me about how it's made, stuff like that." Boo-Boo currently is unemployed, but he recently had a chance for a job as a cook's helper. Although he was not hired, the event is significant nevertheless because prior to the job interview, Boo-Boo claimed that his ambition now was to work in a restaurant. Here we have an example of the primacy of the opportunity structure in determining the aspirations of the Hallway Hangers. One job opening in another field was so significant that the opening prompted Boo-Boo to redefine totally his aspirations.

In contrast to the rest of the Hallway Hangers who are already on the job market, Steve wants to stay in school for the two years required to get his diploma. Yet he has a similar attitude toward his future work as do the other youths. He quit his summer job with the Just-A-Start program and has no concrete occupational aspirations. As for expectations, he believes he might enlist in the air force after graduation but adds, "I dunno. I might just go up and see my uncle, do some fuckin' construction or something."

Many of these boys expect to enter military service. Jinks and Frankie mention it as an option; Stoney has tried to enlist, but without success. Although Jinks refuses to think in terms of aspirations, he will say what he expects to do after he finishes school.

JM: What are you gonna do when you get out?

JINKS: Go into the service, like everybody else. The navy.

JM: What about after that?

JINKS: After that, just get a job, live around here.

JM: Do you have any idea what job you wanna get?

JINKS: No. No particular job. Whatever I can get.

Jinks subsequently quit school. He had been working twenty hours a week making clothes-racks in a factory with his brother. He left school with the understanding that he would be employed full-time, and he was mildly content with his situation: "I got a job. It ain't a good job, but other things will come along." Two weeks later, he was laid off. For the past three months he has been unemployed, hanging full-time in doorway #13.

Shorty has worked construction in the past and has held odd jobs such as shoveling snow. Shorty, an alcoholic, has trouble holding down a steady job, as he freely admits. He was enrolled in school until recently. Ordered by the court to a detoxification center, Shorty apparently managed to convince the judge that he had attended enough Alcoholics Anonymous meetings in the meantime to satisfy the court. He has not returned to school since, nor has he landed a job. Given that Shorty is often on the run from the police, he is too preoccupied with pressing everyday problems to give serious thought to his long-term future. It is not surprising that my ill-timed query about his occupational aspirations met with only an impatient glare. ...

The definitions of aspirations and expectations given [earlier] suggest that an assessment of the opportunity structure and of one's capabilities impinge on one's preferences for the future. However, the portrait of the Hallway Hangers painted in these pages makes clear that "impinge" is not a strong enough word. But are the leveled aspirations and pessimistic expectations of the Hallway Hangers a result of strong negative assessments of their capabilities or of the opportunity structure?

This is not an easy question to answer. Doubtless, both factors come into play, but in the case of the Hallway Hangers, evaluation of the opportunity structure has the dominant role. Although in a discussion of why they do not succeed in school, the Hallway Hangers point to personal inadequacy ("We're all just fucking burnouts"; "We never did good anyways"), they look to outside forces as well. In general, they are confident of their own abilities.

(*In a group interview*)

JM: If you've got five kids up the high school with all A's, now are you gonna be able to say that any of them are smarter than any of you?

SLICK: (*immediately*) No.

JM: So how'd that happen?

SLICK: Because they're smarter in some areas just like we're smarter in some areas. You put them out here, right? And you put us up where they're living—they won't be able to survive out here.

SHORTY: But we'd be able to survive up there.

FRANKIE: See, what it is—they're smarter more academically because they're taught by teachers that teach academics.

JM: Not even streetwise, just academically, do you think you could be up where they are?

FRANKIE: Yeah.

CHRIS: Yeah.

SHORTY: Yeah.

JM: When it comes down to it, you're just as smart?

FRANKIE: Yeah.

SLICK: (*matter-of-factly*) We could be smarter.

FRANKIE: Definitely.

CHRIS: On the street, like.

FRANKIE: We're smart, we're smart, but we're just smart [inaudible]. It's fucking, y'know, we're just out to make money, man. I know if I ever went to fucking high school and college in a business course ...

SLICK: And concentrated on studying ...

FRANKIE: I know I could make it. I am a businessman.

JM: So all of you are sure that if you put out in school ...

FRANKIE: Yeah! If I went into business, I would, yeah. If I had the fucking money to start out with like some of these fucking rich kids, I'd be a millionaire. Fucking right I would be.

Although these comments were influenced by the dynamics of the group interview, they jibe with the general sense of self-confidence the Hallway Hangers radiate and indicate that they do not have low perceptions of their own abilities.

If their assessments of their own abilities do not account for the low aspirations of the Hallway Hangers, we are left, by way of explanation, with their perceptions of the job opportunity structure. The dominant view in the United States is that American society is an open one that values and differentially rewards individuals on the basis of their merits. The Hallway Hangers question this view, for it runs against the grain of their neighbors' experiences, their families' experiences, and their own encounters with the labor market.

The Clarendon Heights community, as a public housing development, is by definition made up of individuals who do not hold even modestly remunerative jobs. A large majority are on additional forms of public assistance; many are unemployed. Like most old housing projects, Clarendon Heights tends to be a cloistered, insular neighborhood, isolated from the surrounding community. Although younger residents certainly have external points of reference, their horizons are nevertheless very narrow. Their immediate world is composed almost entirely of people who have not "made it." To look around at a great variety of people—some lazy, some alcoholics, some energetic, some dedicated, some clever, some resourceful—and to realize all of them have been unsuccessful on the job market is powerful testimony against what is billed as an open society.

The second and much more intimate contact these boys have with the job market is through their families, whose occupational histories only can be viewed as sad and disillusioning by the Hallway Hangers. These are not people who are slothful or slow-witted; rather, they are generally industrious, intelligent, and very willing to work. With members of their families holding low-paying, unstable jobs or unable to find work at all, the Hallway Hangers are unlikely to view the job opportunity structure as an open one.

The third level of experience on which the Hallway Hangers draw is their own. These boys are not newcomers to the job market. As we have seen, all have held a variety of jobs. All except Steve are now on the job market year round, but only Stoney has a steady job. With the exceptions of Chris, who presently is satisfied with his success peddling drugs, and Steve, who is still in school, the Hallway Hangers are actively in search of decent work. Although they always seem to be following up on some promising lead, they are all unemployed. Furthermore, some who were counting on prospective employment have had their hopes dashed when it fell through. The work they have been able to secure typically has been in menial, dead-end jobs paying minimum wage.

Thus, their personal experience on the job market and the experiences of their family members and their neighbors have taught the Hallway Hangers that the job market does not necessarily reward talent or effort. Neither they nor their parents, older siblings, and friends have shared in the "spoils" of economic success. In short, the Hallway Hangers are under no illusions about the openness of the job opportunity structure. They are conscious, albeit vaguely, of a number of class-based obstacles to economic and social advancement. Slick, the most perceptive and articulate of the Hallway Hangers, points out particular barriers they must face.

SLICK: Out here, there's not the opportunity to make money. That's how you get into stealin' and all that shit.

(*in a separate interview*)

SLICK: That's why I went into the army—cuz there's no jobs out here right now for people that, y'know, live out here. You have to know somebody, right?

In discussing the problems of getting a job, both Slick and Shorty are vocal.

SLICK: All right, to get a job, first of all, this is a handicap, out here. If you say you're from the projects or anywhere in this area, that can hurt you. Right off the bat: reputation.

SHORTY: Is this dude gonna rip me off, is he ...

SLICK: Is he gonna stab me?

SHORTY: Will he rip me off? Is he gonna set up the place to do a score or somethin'? I tried to get a couple of my buddies jobs at a place where I was working construction, but the guy says, "I don't want 'em if they're from there. I know you; you ain't a thief or nothing."

Frankie also points out the reservations prospective employers have about hiring people who live in Clarendon Heights. "A rich kid would have a better chance of getting a job than me, yeah. Me, from where I live, y'know, a high crime area, I was prob'ly crime-breaking myself, which they think your nice honest rich kid from a very respected family would never do."

Frankie also feels that he is discriminated against because of the reputation that attaches to him because of his brothers' illegal exploits. "Especially me, like I've had a few opportunities for a job, y'know. I didn't get it cuz of my name, because of my brothers, y'know. So I was deprived right there, bang. Y'know they said, 'No, no, no, we ain't havin' no Dougherty work for us.'" In a separate discussion, Frankie again makes this point. Arguing that he would have almost no chance to be hired as a fireman, despite ostensibly meritocratic hiring procedures, even if he scored very highly on the test, Frankie concludes, "Just cuz fuckin' where I'm from and what my name is."

The Hallway Hangers' belief that the opportunity structure is not open also emerges when we consider their responses to the question of whether they have the same chance as a middle- or upper-class boy to get a good job. The Hallway Hangers generally respond in the negative. When pushed to explain why, Jinks and Steve made these responses, which are typical.

(*in separate interviews*)
JINKS: Their parents got pull and shit.
STEVE: Their fucking parents know people.

Considering the boys' employment experiences and those of their families, it is not surprising that the Hallway Hangers' view of the job market does not conform to the dominant belief in the openness of the opportunity structure. They see a job market where rewards are based not on meritocratic criteria, but on "who you know." If "con-nections" are the keys to success, the Hallway Hangers know that they are in trouble.

Aside from their assessment of the job opportunity structure, the Hallway Hangers are aware of other forces weighing on their futures. A general feeling of despondency pervades the group. As Slick puts it, "The younger kids have nothing to hope for." The Hallway Hangers often draw attention to specific incidents that support their general and vague feelings of hopelessness and of the futility of nurturing aspirations or high expectations. Tales of police brutality, of uncaring probation officers and callous judges, and of the "pull and hook-ups of the rich kids" all have a common theme, which Chris summarizes, "We don't get a fair shake and shit." Although they sometimes internalize the blame for their plight (Boo-Boo: "I just screwed up"; Chris: "I guess I just don't have what it takes"; Frankie: "We've just fucked up"), the Hallway Hangers also see, albeit in a vague and imprecise manner, a number of hurdles in their path to success with which others from higher social strata do not have to contend.

Insofar as contemporary conditions under capitalism can be conceptualized as a race by the many for relatively few positions of wealth and prestige, the low aspirations of the Hallway Hangers, more than anything else, seem to be a decision, conscious or unconscious, to withdraw from the running. The competition, they reason, is not a fair one when some people have an unobstructed lane. As Frankie maintains, the Hallway Hangers face numerous barriers: "It's a steeplechase, man. It's a motherfucking steeplechase." The Hallway Hangers respond in a way that suggests only a "sucker" would compete seriously under such conditions.

Chris's perspective seems a poignant, accurate description of the situation in which the Hallway Hangers find themselves.

CHRIS: I gotta get a job, any fucking job. Just a job. Make some decent money. If I could make a hundred bucks a week, I'd work. I just wanna get my mother out of the projects, that's all. But I'm fucking up in school. It ain't easy, Jay. I hang out there [in doorway #13] 'til about one o'clock every night. I never want to go to school. I'd much rather hang out and get high again. It's not that I'm dumb. You gimme thirty bucks today, and I'll give you one hundred tomorrow. I dunno. It's like I'm in a hole I can't get out of. I guess I could get out, but it's hard as hell. It's fucked up.

The Brothers: Ready at the Starting Line

Just as the pessimism and uncertainty with which the Hallway Hangers view their futures emerges when we consider what they perceive their lives will be like in twenty years, so do the Brothers' long-term visions serve as a valuable backdrop to our discussion of their aspirations. The ethos of the Brothers' peer group is a positive one; they are not resigned to a bleak future but are hoping for a bright one. Nowhere does this optimism surface more clearly than in the Brothers' responses to the question of what they will be doing in twenty years. Note the centrality of work in their views of the future.

(*all in separate interviews*)

SUPER: I'll have a house, a nice car, no one bothering me. Won't have to take no hard time from no one. Yeah, I'll have a good job, too.

JUAN: I'll have a regular house, y'know, with a yard and everything. I'll have a steady job, a good job. I'll be living the good life, the easy life.

MIKE: I might have a wife, some kids. I might be holding down a regular business job like an old guy. I hope I'll be able to do a lot of skiing and stuff like that when I'm old.

CRAIG: I'll probably be having a good job on my hands, I think. Working in an office as an architect, y'know, with my own drawing board, doing my own stuff, or at least close to there.

James takes a comic look into his future without being prompted to do so. "The ones who work hard in school, eventually it's gonna pay off for them and everything, and they're gonna have a good job and a family and all that. Not me though! I'm gonna have *myself*. I'm gonna have some money. And a different girl every day. And a different car. And be like this (*poses with one arm around an imaginary girl and the other on a steering wheel*)."

The Brothers do not hesitate to name their occupational goals. Although some of the Brothers are unsure of their occupational aspirations, none seems to feel that nurturing an aspiration is a futile exercise. The Brothers have not resigned themselves to taking whatever they can get. Rather, they articulate specific occupational aspirations (although these often are subject to change and revision).

Like all the Brothers, Super has not had extensive experience on the job market; he only has worked at summer jobs. For the past three summers, he has worked for the city doing maintenance work in parks and school buildings through a CETA-sponsored summer youth employment program. During the last year, Super's occupational aspirations have fluctuated widely. His initial desire to become a doctor was met with laughter from his friends. Deterred by their mocking and by a realization of the schooling required to be a doctor, Super immediately decided that he would rather go into business: "Maybe I can own my own shop and shit." This aspiration, however, also was ridiculed. "Yeah, right," commented Mokey, "Super'll be pimping the girls, that kinda business." In private, however, Super still clings to the hope of becoming a doctor, although he cites work in the computer field as a more realistic hope. "Really, I don't know what I should do now. I'm kinda confused. First I said I wanna go into computers, right? Take up that or a doctor." The vagueness of Super's aspirations is important; once again, we get a glimpse of how little is known about the world of middle-class work, even for somebody who clearly aspires to it. Of one thing Super is certain: "I just know I wanna get a good job."

Although Super does not distinguish between what constitutes a good job and what does not, he does allude to criteria by which the quality of a job can be judged. First, a good job must not demand that one "work on your feet," a distinction, apparently, between white and blue-collar work. Second, a good job implies at least some authority in one's workplace, a point Super makes clearly, if in a disjointed manner. "Bosses—if you don't come on time, they yell at you and stuff like that.

They want you to do work and not sit down and relax and stuff like that, y'know. I want to try and be a boss, y'know, tell people what to do. See, I don't always want people telling me what to do, y'know—the low rank. I wanna try to be with people in the high rank." Although Super does not know what occupation he would like to enter, he is certain that he wants a job that is relatively high up in a vaguely defined occupational hierarchy. ...

The Brothers display none of the cockiness about their own capabilities that the Hallway Hangers exhibit. Instead, they attribute lack of success on the job market exclusively to personal inadequacy. This is particularly true when the Brothers speculate about the future jobs the Hallway Hangers and their own friends will have. According to the Brothers, the Hallway Hangers (in Super's words) "ain't gonna get nowhere," not because of the harshness of the job market but because they are personally lacking. The rest of the Brothers share this view.

JM: Some of those guys who hang with Frankie, they're actually pretty smart. They just don't channel that intelligence into school, it seems to me.

CRAIG: I call that stupid, man. That's what they are.

JM: I dunno.

CRAIG: Lazy.

(*in a separate interview*)

SUPER: They think they're so tough they don't have to do work. That don't make sense, really. You ain't gonna get nowhere; all's you gonna do is be back in the projects like your mother. Depend on your mother to give you money every week. You ain't gonna get a good job. As you get older, you'll think about that, y'know. It'll come to your mind. "Wow, I can't believe, I should've just went to school and got my education."

(*in a separate interview*)

MOKEY: They all got attitude problems. They just don't got their shit together. Like Steve. They have to improve themselves.

In the eyes of the Brothers, the Hallway Hangers have attitude problems, are incapable of considering their long-term future, and are lazy or stupid.

Because this evidence is tainted (no love is lost between the two peer groups), it is significant that the Brothers apply the same criteria in judging each other's chances to gain meaningful employment. James thinks Mokey is headed for a dead-end job because he is immature and undisciplined. He also blames Juan for currently being out of work. "Juan's outta school, and Juan does *not* have a job (*said with contempt*). Now that's some kind of a senior. When I'm a senior, I'm gonna have a job already. I can see if you're gonna go to college right when you get out of school, but Juan's not doin' nothin'. He's just stayin' home." Juan, in turn, ththat Mokey and Super will have difficulty finding valuable work because of their attitudes. He predicts that Derek and Craig will be successful for the same reason.

These viewpoints are consistent with the dominant ideology in America; barriers to success are seen as personal rather than social. By attributing failure to personal inadequacy, the Brothers exonerate the opportunity structure. Indeed, it is amazing how often they affirm the openness of American society.

(*all in separate interviews*)

DEREK: If you put your mind to it, if you want to make a future for yourself, there's no reason why you can't. It's a question of attitude.

SUPER: It's easy to do anything, as long as you set your mind to it, if you wanna do it. If you really want to do it, if you really want to be something. If you don't want to do it ... you ain't gonna make it. I gotta get that through my mind: I wanna do it. I wanna be somethin'. I don't wanna be livin' in the projects the rest of my life.

MOKEY: It's not like if they're rich they get picked [for a job]; it's just mattered by the knowledge of their mind.

CRAIG: If you work hard, it'll pay off in the end.

MIKE: If you work hard, really put your mind to it, you can do it. You can make it.

This view of the opportunity structure as an essentially open one that rewards intelligence, effort, and ingenuity is shared by all the Brothers. Asked whether their chances of securing a remunerative job are as good as those of an upper-class boy from a wealthy district of the city, they all responded affirmatively. Not a single member of the Hallway Hangers, in contrast, affirms the openness of American society. ...

Reproduction Theory Reconsidered

This basic finding—that two substantially different paths are followed within the general framework of social reproduction—is a major challenge to economically determinist theories. Two groups of boys from the same social stratum who live in the same housing project and attend the same school nevertheless experience the process of social reproduction in fundamentally different ways. This simple fact alone calls into question many of the theoretical formulations of Bowles and Gintis.[6] If, as they argue, social class is the overriding determinant in social reproduction, what accounts for the variance in the process between the Brothers and Hallway Hangers? Bowles and Gintis, in considering a single school, maintain that social reproduction takes place primarily through educational tracking. Differential socialization through educational tracking prepares working-class students for working-class jobs and middle-class students for middle-class jobs. But the Hallway Hangers and the Brothers, who are from the same social class background and exposed to the curricular structure of the school in the same manner, undergo the process of social reproduction in substantially different manners. The theory of Bowles and Gintis cannot explain this difference.

Bourdieu's notion of habitus, however, can be used to differentiate the Hallway Hangers and the Brothers.[7] The habitus, as defined by Giroux, is "the subjective dispositions which reflect a class-based social grammar of taste, knowledge, and behavior inscribed in ... each developing person."[8] According to Bourdieu, the habitus is primarily a function of social class. Bourdieu does not give an adequate sense of the internal structure of the habitus, but there is some precedent in his work for incorporating other factors into constructions of the habitus; for example, he differentiates people not only by gender and class, but also by whether they come from Paris or not. Although Bourdieu sometimes gives the impression of a homogeneity of habitus within the boundaries of social class, I understand habitus to be constituted at the level of the family and thus can include, as constitutive of the habitus, factors such as ethnicity, educational histories, peer associations, and demographic characteristics (e.g., geographical mobility, duration of tenancy in public housing, sibling order, and family size) as these shape individual action. Although Bourdieu never really develops the notion along these lines, he does allude to the complexity and interplay of mediations within the habitus. "The habitus acquired in the family underlies the structuring of school experiences, and the habitus transformed by schooling, itself diversified, in turn underlies the structuring of all subsequent experiences (e.g. the reception and assimilation of the messages of the culture industry or work experiences), and so on, from restructuring to restructuring."[9] When understood along the lines I have indicated, the concept of habitus becomes flexible enough to accommodate the interactions among ethnicity, family, schooling, work experiences, and peer associations that have been documented [here].

Although we may accept the notion of habitus as a useful explanatory tool, we must reject the inevitability of its *function* in Bourdieu's theoretical scheme. According to Bourdieu, the habitus functions discreetly to integrate individuals into a social world geared to the interests of the ruling classes; habitus engenders attitudes and conduct that are compatible with the reproduction of class inequality. The outstanding example of this process is the development by working-class individuals of depressed aspirations that mirror their actual chances for social advancement.

The circular relationship Bourdieu posits between objective opportunities and subjective hopes is incompatible with the findings [presented here]. The Brothers, whose objective life chances probably were lower originally than those available to the Hallway Hangers because of racial barriers to success, nevertheless nurture higher aspirations than do the Hallway Hangers. By emphasizing structural determinants at the expense of mediating factors that influence subjective renderings of objective probabilities, Bourdieu presumes too mechanistic and simplistic a relationship between aspiration and opportunity. This component of his theory fails to fathom how a number of factors lie between and mediate the influence of social class on individuals; Bourdieu cannot explain, for instance, how ethnicity intervenes in the process of aspiration formation and social reproduction.

Thus, the theoretical formulations of Bowles and Gintis and the deterministic elements of Bourdieu's theory, although elegant and intuitively plausible, are incapable of accounting for the processes of social reproduction as they have been observed and documented in Clarendon Heights. These theories give an excellent account of the hidden structural and ideological determinants that constrain members of the working class and limit the options of Clarendon Heights teenagers. What the Hallway Hangers and the Brothers demonstrate quite clearly, however, is that the way in which individuals and groups respond to structures of domination is open-ended. Although there is no way to avoid class-based constraints, the outcomes are not predefined. Bowles and Gintis and Bourdieu pay too little attention to the active, creative role of individual and group praxis. As Giroux maintains, what is missing from such theories "is not only the issue of resistance, but also any attempt to delineate the complex ways in which working-class subjectivities are constituted."[10]

From Ethnography to Theory

Once we descend into the world of actual human lives, we must take our theoretical bearings to make some sense of the social landscape, but in doing so we invariably find that the theories are incapable of accounting for much of what we see. The lives of the Hallway Hangers and the Brothers cannot be reduced to structural influences or causes; although structural forces weigh upon the individuals involved, it is necessary, in the words of Willis, "to give the social agents involved some meaningful scope for viewing, inhabiting, and constructing their own world in a way which is recognizably human and not theoretically reductive."[11] We must appreciate both the importance and the relative autonomy of the cultural level at which individuals, alone or in concert with others, wrest meaning out of the flux of their lives.

The possibilities open to these boys as lower-class teenagers are limited structurally from the outset. That they internalize the objective probabilities for social advancement to some degree is beyond question. The process by which this takes place, however, is influenced by a whole series of intermediate factors. Because gender is constant in the study discussed in these pages, race is the principal variable affecting the way in which these youths view their situation. Ethnicity introduces new structurally determined constraints on social mobility, but it also serves as a mediation through which the limitations of class are refracted and thus apprehended and understood differently by different racial groups. The Brothers comprehend and react to their situation in a manner entirely different from the response the Hallway Hangers make to a similar situation; ethnicity introduces a new dynamic that makes the Brothers more receptive to the achievement ideology. Their acceptance of this ideology affects their aspirations but also influences, in tandem with parental encouragement, their approach to school and the character of their peer group, factors that in turn bear upon their aspirations.

If we modify the habitus by changing the ethnicity variable and altering a few details of family occupational and educational histories and duration of tenancy in public housing, we would have the Hallway Hangers. As white lower-class youths, the Hallway Hangers view and interpret their situation in a different light, one that induces them to reject the achievement ideology and to develop aspirations and expectations quite apart from those the ideology attempts to generate. The resultant perspective, which is eventually reinforced by the Hallway Hangers' contact with the job market, informs the boys' approach to school and helps us understand the distinctive attributes of this peer group. Thus, although social class is of primary importance, there are intermediate factors at work that, as constitutive of the habitus, shape the subjective responses of the two groups of boys and produce quite different expectations and actions.

Having grown up in an environment where success is not common, the Hallway Hangers see that the connection between effort and reward is not as clearcut as the achievement ideology would have them believe. Because it runs counter to the evidence in their lives and because it represents a forceful assault on their self-esteem, the Hallway Hangers repudiate the achievement ideology. Given that their parents are inclined to see the ideology in the same light, they do not counter their sons' rejection of the American Dream.

A number of important ramifications follow from the Hallway Hangers' denial of the dominant ideology: the establishment of a peer group that provides alternative means of generating self-esteem, the rejection of school and antagonism toward teachers, and, of course, the leveling of aspirations. In schematizing the role of the peer group, it is difficult not to appear tautological, for the group does wield a reciprocal influence on the boys: It attracts those who are apt to reject school and the achievement ideology and those with low aspirations and then deepens these individuals' initial proclivities and further shapes them to fit the group. But at the same time, the peer subculture itself, handed down from older to younger boys, is the product of the particular factors that structure the lives of white teenagers in Clarendon Heights.

In addition to the peer group, the curricular structure of the school solidifies the low aspirations of the Hallway Hangers by channeling them into programs that prepare students for manual labor jobs. Low aspirations, in turn, make the Hallway Hangers more likely to dismiss school as irrelevant. Once on the job market, the Hallway Hangers' inability to secure even mediocre jobs further dampens their occupational hopes. Thus, although each individual ultimately retains autonomy in the subjective interpretation of his situation, the leveled aspirations of the Hallway Hangers are to a large degree a response to the limitations of social class as they are manifest in the Hallway Hangers' social world.

The Brothers' social class origins are only marginally different from those of the Hallway Hangers. Being black, the Brothers also must cope with racially rooted barriers to success that, affirmative action measures notwithstanding, structurally inhibit the probabilities for social advancement, although to a lesser degree than do shared class limitations. What appears to be a comparable objective situation to that of the Hallway Hangers, however, is apprehended in a very different manner by the Brothers.

As black teenagers, the Brothers interpret their families' occupational and educational records in a much different light than do the Hallway Hangers. Judging by the Brothers' constant affirmation of equality of opportunity, the boys believe that racial injustice has been curbed in the United States in the last twenty years. Whereas in their parents' time the link between effort and reward was very tenuous for blacks, the Brothers, in keeping with the achievement ideology, see the connection today as very strong: "If you work hard, it'll pay off in the end" (Craig). Hence, the achievement ideology is more compatible with the Brothers' attitudes than with those of the Hallway Hangers, for whom it cannot succeed against overwhelming contrary evidence. The ideology is not as emotionally painful for the Brothers to accept because past racial discrimination can help account for their families' poverty, whereas the Hallway Hangers, if the ideology stands, are afforded no explanation outside of laziness and stupidity for their parents' failures. The optimism that acceptance of the achievement ideology brings for the Brothers is encouraged and reinforced by their parents. Thus, we see how in the modified habitus ethnicity affects the Brothers' interpretation of their social circumstances and leads to acceptance of the achievement ideology, with all the concomitant results.

Notes

1. All names of neighborhoods and individuals have been changed to protect the anonymity of the study's subjects.

2. Erik H. Erikson, *Gandhi's Truth* (New York: Norton, 1969), p. 154.

3. Ronald Reagan, "State of the Union Address to Congress," *New York Times,* 6 February 1985, p. 17.

4. Kenneth I. Spenner and David L. Featherman, "Achievement Ambitions," *Annual Review of Sociology* 4 (1978):376–378.

5. Howard B. London, *The Culture of a Community College* (New York: Praeger, 1978).

6. Samuel Bowles and Herbert Gintis, *Schooling in Capitalist America* (New York: Basic Books, 1976).

7. See Pierre Bourdieu, *Outline of a Theory of Practice* (Cambridge: Cambridge University Press, 1977).

8. Henry A. Giroux, *Theory & Resistance in Education* (London: Heinemann Educational Books, 1983), p. 89.

9. Bourdieu, *Outline of a Theory of Practice*, p. 87.

10. Giroux, *Theory & Resistance*, p. 85.

11. Paul E. Willis, *Learning to Labor* (Aldershot: Gower, 1977), p. 172.

The "New Structuralism"

MICHAEL J. PIORE

The Dual Labor Market: Theory and Implications

The central tenet of [my] analysis is that the role of employment and of the disposition of manpower in perpetuating poverty can be best understood in terms of a dual labor market. One sector of that market, which I have termed elsewhere the primary market,[1] offers jobs which possess several of the following traits: high wages, good working conditions, employment stability and job security, equity and due process in the administration of work rules, and chances for advancement. The secondary sector has jobs that are decidedly less attractive, compared with those in the primary sector. They tend to involve low wages, poor working conditions, considerable variability in employment, harsh and often arbitrary discipline, and little opportunity to advance. The poor are confined to the secondary labor market. Eliminating poverty requires that they gain access to primary employment.

The factors that generate the dual market structure and confine the poor to the secondary sector are complex. With some injustice to that complexity, they may be summarized: First, the most important characteristic distinguishing primary from secondary jobs appears to be the behavioral requirements they impose upon the work force, particularly that of employment stability. Insofar as secondary workers are barred from primary jobs by a real qualification, it is generally their inability to show up for work regularly and on time. Secondary employers are far more tolerant of lateness and absenteeism, and many secondary jobs are of such short duration that these do not matter. Work skills, which re-

ceive considerable emphasis in most discussions of poverty and employment, do not appear a major barrier to primary employment (although, because regularity and punctuality are important to successful learning in school and on the job, such behavioral traits tend to be highly correlated with skills).

Second, certain workers who possess the behavioral traits required to operate efficiently in primary jobs are trapped in the secondary market because their superficial characteristics resemble those of secondary workers. This identification occurs because employment decisions are generally made on the basis of a few readily (and hence inexpensively) assessed traits like race, demeanor, accent, educational attainment, test scores, and the like. Such traits tend to be statistically correlated with job performance but not necessarily (and probably not usually) causally related to it. Hence, a number of candidates who are rejected because they possess the "wrong" traits are actually qualified for the job. Exclusion on this basis may be termed *statistical discrimination*. In addition to statistical discrimination, workers are also excluded from primary employment by *discrimination pure and simple*.

Discrimination of any kind enlarges the labor force that is captive in the secondary sector, and thus lowers the wages that secondary employers must pay to fill their jobs. Such employers thus have an economic stake in perpetuating discrimination. Since it limits the supply of labor in the primary sector and raises the wages of workers who have access to jobs there, primary workers also have a stake in discrimination. Discrimination pure and simple is not generally of economic value to primary employers, since it forces them to pay higher wages without obtaining corresponding economic gains. In statistical discrimination, however, the higher wages are compensated by the reduced cost of screening job candidates, and here primary employers share the interest of secondary employers and primary workers in perpetuating such discrimination.

Third, the distinction between primary and secondary jobs is not, apparently, technologically determinate. A portion—perhaps a substantial proportion—of the work in the economy can be organized for either stable or unstable workers. Work normally performed in the primary sector is sometimes shifted to the secondary sector through subcontracting, temporary help services, recycling of new employees through probationary periods, and the like. Nor is the primary-secondary distinction necessarily associated with a given enterprise. Some enterprises, most of whose jobs constitute primary employment and are filled with stable, committed workers, have subsections or departments with inferior job opportunities accommodated to an unstable work force. Secondary employers generally have a few primary jobs, and some have a large number of them. Nonetheless, despite a certain degree of elasticity in the distribution of work between the primary and secondary sections, shifts in the distribution generally involve changes in the techniques of production and management and in the institutional structure and procedures of the enterprises in which the work is performed. The investment necessary to effect these changes acts to strengthen resistance to antipoverty efforts.

Fourth, the behavioral traits associated with the secondary sector are reinforced by the process of working in secondary jobs and living among others whose life-style is accommodated to that type of employment. Hence, even people initially forced into the secondary sector by discrimination tend, over a period of time, to develop the traits predominant among secondary workers. Thus, a man who works in a world where employment is intermittent and erratic tends to lose habits of regularity and punctuality. Similarly, when reward and punishment in the work place are continually based upon personal relationships between worker and supervisor, workers forget how to operate within the impersonal, institutional grievance procedures of the primary sector. When such workers do gain access to primary jobs, they are frustrated by the system's failure to respond on a personal basis and by their own inability to make it respond on an institutional basis.

Finally, among the poor, income sources other than employment, especially public assistance and illicit activity, tend to be more compatible with secondary than with primary employment. The public assistance system discourages full-time work and forces those on welfare either into jobs that are part-time or into jobs that pay cash income which will not be reported to the social worker or can be quickly dropped or delayed when the social worker discovers them or seems in danger of doing so. The relationship between social worker and client builds upon the personal relationship that operates in the secondary sector, not on the institutional mechanisms that tend to operate in the primary sector. Illegitimate activity also tends to follow the intermittent work pattern prevalent in secondary employment, and the attractions of such activity, as well as life patterns and role models it presents to those not themselves involved but associating with people who are, foster behavioral traits antagonistic to primary employment.

The dual market interpretation of poverty has some central implications: the poor do participate in the economy; the manner of their participation, not the question of participation as such, constitutes the manpower problem of the poor; and their current mode of participation is ultimately a response to a series of pressures—economic, social, and technical—playing upon individuals and labor market institutions. This suggests that a distinction can be drawn between policies that are designed to alleviate the pressures which generate the dual market structure and those that attempt to attack the problem directly by moving individuals from secondary to primary employment. The latter policies combat prevailing pressures but leave intact the forces that generate them. The thrust of [my] argument is that in concentrating upon training, counseling, and placement services for the poor, manpower policy has overemphasized direct approaches, and that more weight should be placed upon policies which affect the environment in which employment decisions are made and the pressures which the environment generates. Among such policies are antidiscrimination policy, occupational licensing reform, and the structure of public assistance.

Analysis of the dual labor market suggests a further implication: because the "poor" do participate in the economy, certain groups are interested in that participation and how it occurs. Policies aimed at moving the poor out of the secondary market work against the interests of these groups and therefore are in danger of being subverted by them. This danger is a major reason for concentrating on indirect approaches that are not susceptible to the same kind of subversion; in fact, because such approaches alleviate the pressures generating the dual market structure, they reduce the resistance to policies that move directly against that structure. The dangers to which existing institutions subject programs designed to move the poor directly out of the secondary market are twofold. The new institutions created by these programs can be rejected by the prevailing economic system and isolated off to one side; a program, for example, would then recruit workers for training in skills that are little utilized in either the secondary or the primary market. Alternatively, the new institutions may be captured by the prevailing economic system and used to facilitate its operation; for example, neighborhood employment offices may recruit secondary workers for secondary jobs, and training may be provided in primary employment to workers who would have gotten it anyway in establishments that would have financed it themselves. The central problem in the design of direct approaches to manpower programs is to organize them in such a way that they can resist this twofold threat of rejection on the one hand and capture on the other.

These conclusions follow directly from the dual market interpretation of the poverty problem but they are not uniquely dependent upon it. The dual labor market is one of a class of theoretical constructs which views poverty in the United States in terms of a dichotomy in the economic and social structures. Such a dichotomy is implicit in the concept of a "culture of poverty" and in the expression of public policy goals associated with poverty in terms of an income cutoff. Most such views of poverty entertain the idea that the dichotomy is a product of forces endogenous to the economy (or, more broadly, the society as a whole). It follows that attempts to eliminate poverty will tend to run counter to the natural operation of the economy, and that they will be resisted by existing institutions and are in danger of rejection. To say all this is perhaps to say simply that if poverty were easy to eliminate, it wouldn't be around in the first place. But it does at least identify as a certain problem in the program design the task of equipping the institution which works with the poor to withstand the rejection pressures.

What the dual labor market interpretation implies that is not implicit in other dichotomous interpretations is that the poor are separated from the nonpoor not only in the negative sense of exclusion from activities and institutions to which the nonpoor have access, but also in the positive sense that they have economic value where they are; that, in other words, *there are groups actively interested in the perpetuation of poverty.* It is this interest that makes new institutions created to work with the poor in the labor market subject to threats of capture as well as of rejection.

Notes

1. See Michael J. Piore, "On-The-Job Training in the Dual Labor Market," in Arnold Weber, *et al., Public-Private Manpower Policies* (Madison, Wisc.: Industrial Relations Research Association, 1969), pp. 101–132.

AAGE B. SØRENSEN AND ARNE L. KALLEBERG

An Outline of a Theory of the Matching of Persons to Jobs

Much recent research in sociology has focused on labor market processes. These concerns include analysis of the processes that produce variation in individual earnings by characteristics of people and their jobs; the analysis of career patterns and job mobility processes; and the analysis of employment and unemployment patterns of various population groups. Sociologists share many of these concerns with economists, and there is much overlap in research topics among sociologists and economists.

Despite similarities in methodology and research design, the research traditions in sociology and economics have quite different intellectual backgrounds. Most empirical research on labor market processes in economics is guided by the dominant school of labor economics—the neoclassical theory of wage determination and labor supply, with marginal productivity theory accounting for the demand side and human capital theory taking care of the supply side. In contrast, sociological research on labor market phenomena has its origin in research describing socioeconomic attainment and social mobility processes for various population groups. Sociological research on attainment and mobility has not employed an explicitly stated conceptual apparatus that informs the choice of variables and the interpretation of parameters. Although there is a growing body of findings about the magnitude of the influences of various variables on the outcomes of labor market processes, particularly income attainment, there are few efforts by sociologists to identify the mechanisms that create the influences of personal and job characteristics on

income and earnings or on the other labor market outcomes.

There is no need for sociologists to develop a unique theory of labor market processes if the neoclassical economic theory adequately accounts for the findings of empirical research. With respect to a favorite variable of both economists and sociologists—that is, education—human capital theory does provide an interpretation of results. However, the economic theory does not provide a rationale for the sociological concern for occupational attainment. Job characteristics, including those presumably captured by the Socioeconomic Index (SEI) or prestige scores of occupations, play little or no role in the orthodox economic theory. Still, occupational status accounts for a substantial fraction of the explained variance in sociological income attainment models.

The amount of variance added to income attainment models by occupation is not necessarily a strong argument for replacing or supplementing the economic theory. Sociologists have not been able to account for very much variance in income attainment. Research informed by human capital theory (e.g., Mincer, 1974) has in fact been able to do as well or better without including occupation. A measure of occupational status must necessarily show some relation to income, reflecting the between-occupation variance in income that it captures. An observed effect of job characteristics on income or earnings may be attributed to a misspecification of sociological models, both with respect to functional form and omitted variables, and need not be considered a challenge to the economic theory.

There are, however, other reasons for critically evaluating the neoclassical or orthodox economic theory. The economic theory is powerful, and numerous predictions can be derived from it regarding the earnings attainment process and other labor market processes, particularly labor supply. (A list of such predictions is presented by Becker, 1964.) Some of these predictions are borne out by empirical observations; some are not. Thurow (1975, pp. 56–70) presents a list of deviations from the theory, pertaining to such issues as the relationship between wages and unemployment, changes in the distribution of earnings, and the relationship between the distribution of education and the distribution of income. Numerous others have identified features of the earnings attainment process and of labor markets that deviate from the assumptions and predictions of the neoclassical theory. A review of these challenges to orthodox theory has been presented by Cain (1976). Particularly important are those critiques that argue that labor markets are segmented and that stress the differences between either so-called primary and secondary jobs (cf. Doeringer & Piore, 1971); or monopoly, competitive, and state economic sectors (cf. Averitt, 1968; Bluestone, 1970; O'Connor, 1973); or wage competition and job competition sectors (Thurow, 1975); or internal and external markets (Doeringer & Piore, 1971; Kerr, 1954). These critiques all observe that jobs and job structures differ, contrary to the assumption about the homogeneous nature of labor markets made by the economic theory. They stress qualitative differences among jobs relevant for employment and earnings processes and claim to be able to account for the observations that deviate from the orthodox economic theory, as well as to provide different explanations for labor market processes that also can be explained by the orthodox theory. An example of such an alternative explanation is Thurow's (1975) interpretation of the relationship between education and earnings.

Most of the criticism comes from within economics, though there are examples of research and conceptual elaboration by sociologists pertaining to the issues raised by the segmented labor market theory (Sørensen, 1977; Spilerman, 1977; Stolzenberg, 1975). The issues are clearly relevant for sociological research, and more so since the alternatives to the neoclassical theory provide a rationale for introducing job characteristics sociologists are likely to continue to emphasize.

The classical sociological theorists did not leave labor market analysis to economists. Marx and Weber spent lifetimes analyzing the relation between economy and society, and their concerns in many ways parallel the issues raised in recent controversies. Marx's analysis of capitalist society is an analysis of the implications of the fundamental condition of capitalist production: Labor is treated as a commodity bought and sold freely in a market. This conception of the labor market, we shall argue in the following pages, parallels the conception of the orthodox economic theory.

Marx treated labor in capitalist society as a homogeneous abstract category, and though there are occasional remarks concerning deviations from this model of labor as a commodity and their relevance for class conflict (e.g., Marx, 1961, Vol. 1, chap. 14), no systematic analysis of alternative labor market structures is presented. Weber's long analysis of the sociological categories of economic action (Weber, 1947, Pt. I, chap. 2) provides, in contrast, numerous concepts relevant for the analysis of labor market structures (including nonmarket relationships), particularly in the sections on the social division of labor. The concepts are highly relevant for the issues raised by the challenges to orthodox economic theory, and some of Weber's basic concepts will be used extensively in this chapter.

The following pages provide a conceptual framework for the analysis of labor markets. Labor markets are arenas for the matching of persons to jobs. The conditions that determine the earnings outcome of this matching process are of primary interest here, particularly the identification of what determines the influence of job and personal characteristics on earnings. The purpose of this chapter is not to show the neoclassical theory to be wrong, but rather to identify the conditions for the emergence of the matching process associated with the labor market structure assumed in the orthodox economic theory. It will be argued that the conditions for the emergence of this matching process are not present in some segments of the labor market. The absence of these conditions leads to alternative matching processes, and a model of one important alternative matching process will be presented. The two contrasting matching processes will be shown to have very different implications for the earnings determination process and for other labor market processes.

Basic Concepts

The theory proposed in this chapter will rely on Weber's notion of open and closed social relationships (Weber, 1947, p. 139) to identify different job structures characterized by different matching processes.[1] The degree of closure, in turn, is seen as determined by the bargaining power of employers and employees. We shall, therefore, refer to the employment relationship as the crucial determinant of the notion of the matching process and its earnings outcome.

Employment relationships are social relationships created in the production of goods and services between an employer (or his agent) and an employee. We concentrate on employment relationships typical of capitalist production in which the employer appropriates the output from the production process and has complete possession over the nonhuman means of production. Our analysis will focus on the consequences for the earnings determination process and other labor market processes of variation in control over the job by the employer versus the employee. Two aspects of control over the job may be distinguished. One is control over the activities of the job, resulting in more or less autonomy for the employee; the other is control over access to the job, resulting in a more or less closed employment relationship. These two dimensions may vary independently. Particularly, control over access to the job will be considered crucial, because it influences the nature of competition among employees.

The degree of control over access is a continuum. At one extreme, the employee "owns" the job and no one else can get access unless the current incumbent voluntarily leaves it and a vacancy is established. The length of the employ-

ment is then completely controlled by the employee, and the employment relationship is closed to outsiders. At the other extreme, the employer may replace the incumbent at any time. The employment contract is reestablished in every short interval of time, and the employment relationship is completely open to outsiders.

The employment relationship is established in a process assumed to involve purposive actors as employers and employees where both parties are attempting to maximize earnings. The earnings of the employer are determined by the value of the product of the job-person combination in relation to costs of production. The value of production is a question of prices of products and quantity produced. Quantity produced in turn reflects the performance of the employee and the technology used, including the technical division of labor adopted. For purposes of this analysis, the main variable of interest is the performance of the employee and the main costs of production of interest are the wages paid to the employee and the costs of supervision.

The performance of employees or the quantity of labor supplied will be taken as determined by such attributes of the employees as their skills, abilities, and effort. The employer's return from production evidently depends on his or her ability to obtain the highest output at the lowest costs. While numerous factors may influence the overall level of wages, the employer's ability to minimize costs of production depends not only on the overall level of wages but also on the ability to tie variations in wages paid to variations in the employee's productivity. The main argument of this chapter is that the mechanisms the employer can use to relate wages to performance depend on the employment relationship, particularly the employee's control over access to the job, and that these different mechanisms identify important differences in labor market structures relevant also for labor market processes other than earnings.

The orthodox economic theory identifies a particular set of mechanisms for relating the productivity of employees to their earnings. We shall first consider these mechanisms and the employment relationships needed for these mechanisms to be effective.

The Neoclassical Theory of Earnings Determination

In the economic theory, a wage rate is generated by a labor market as a result of the demand and supply schedules of labor. Demand for labor varies with the derived demand for products, as reflected in their value. The link between wages and the value of products is established through the concept of marginal productivity, since profit-maximizing firms will be in equilibrium when the value of the marginal product equals the marginal cost or price of labor as a factor of production. This should produce different wage rates for identical labor supply because of differences in demand. However, the neoclassical theory emphasizes supply differences as a source of differences in wage rates and earnings, in particular those supply differences resulting from different skills and other individual characteristics related to an employee's productive capacity.

Differences in skills, according to human capital theory, determine different levels of productive capacity resulting in different wage rates. If skills were acquired at no cost, those wage differentials would soon lead to equalizing skill acquisition. But skills are acquired at costs. These costs are partly direct in the form of tuition and living expenses and partly opportunity costs in the form of earnings foregone. No one should undertake training if the returns from this training, in the form of increased earnings accumulated over the working life, are not at least equal to the costs of training.

If only skills acquired through training are relevant, earnings differentials would be exactly offsetting the differences in training costs. However, it is usually recognized that earnings differentials also capture variations in ability, where ability is used to refer to such characteristics as IQ, motivation, and creativity. Ability may be incorporated in the theory by recognizing that persons with different abilities have different investment costs and hence need different earnings to induce the undertaking of training. In addition, some aptitudes may be innate and scarce; these will command a rent because of their fixed supply. Finally, some variation in earnings can be attributed to different opportunities for financing training, particularly as a result of the unequal distribution of parental wealth in combination with the unwillingness of lenders to take collateral in human capital.

The basic proposition derived from the neoclassical theory is then that differences in earnings reflect differences in the productive capacity of persons as a result of their training, abilities, and training opportunities. There may be transient variations in earnings as a result of differences in derived demand in combination with market imperfections, but the basic source of inequality in earnings is unequal endowments in productive capacities among persons. In other words, identical persons are assumed to obtain almost identical earnings, regardless of the characteristics of the jobs they are in.

This theory can be used to account for a number of features of observed earnings attainment processes. Most importantly, it provides an explanation for the relation between education and earnings that interprets education as a source of marketable skills. Also, the theory predicts growth patterns for earnings, where earnings increase rapidly in the younger years and then gradually reach a stable level, with growth after entry into the labor market explained by investment in on-the-job training. Empirically, the theory fares well in accounting for variations in earnings among persons, using schooling and time in the labor force (as a proxy for on-the-job training and experience) as the main independent variables (Mincer, 1974).

The economic theory also emphasizes supply in accounting for other market processes. Most importantly, unemployment is seen as mostly voluntary, except in certain population groups (youngsters, blacks) where minimum wage laws make it impossible for employers to pay the market wage.

The focus in human capital theory on the supply side—that is, on characteristics of persons—reflects the job structure assumed in the theory—that is, one of a competitive and perfectly functioning labor market. To distinguish the neoclassical theory of the earnings determination process from the alternative model of the matching process that will be formulated later in the chapter, we will refer to the neoclassical theory as the *wage competition* model (following Thurow, 1975) to emphasize the focus on competition among employees for wages. ...

A competitive labor market that determines wage rates is one where employers make wage offers and workers bid for employment on the basis of their productivity. The match is made when the value of the marginal product demanded equals the wage rate of the employee. This presupposes that employees paid more than their value can be replaced by others who are willing to work at the wage rate that equals marginal productivity, whereas employees who are paid less than their value can get access to jobs where the wage rate reflects their productivity. Only when the employment relationship is completely open will such a clearing of the market through wage rates be possible. Closed employment relationships, where new recruits can only get access if the incumbent leaves, insulate incumbents from competition. Employers cannot resolve discrepancies between productivity and wage rates by threatening to replace or actually replacing the current employee by someone who is more productive at the same wage rate or who is willing to work at a lower wage rate.

It could be argued that the existence of closed employment relationships does not prevent the employer from relating wages to performance, even in the absence of the ability to replace an employee. Most importantly, the employer can use promotion schemes to reward performance and in this way obtain efficient production. This is correct. Our argument is not that closed employment relationships necessarily prevent efficient production, but that promotion systems represent very different mechanisms for relating wages to performance than the use of competition among employees in open employment relationships where employers make wage offers and employees bid for employment on the basis of their productivity. Promotions can take place only when there is a vacancy in a higher level job and are meaningless as rewards for performance unless jobs at different levels provide different wages, so that wages become attributes of jobs rather than of people. Although a firm with closed employment relationships may operate ef-

ficiently because of the overall match between job assignments and performance of employees, the wages for individual employees will reflect the jobs they hold and therefore, not only their performance, but also the rate at which vacancies appear, the organization of jobs, and the seniority of employees. A very different labor market structure exists from the one assumed in the neoclassical theory when wages are tied to jobs and not to individual variations in performance. ...

Vacancy Competition

When employees have control over access to the job, others can only get access to the job when incumbents leave. Hence, a vacancy must exist for a person to get access to a job. We will refer to the resulting matching process as *vacancy competition*. We do not wish to argue that this is the only alternative matching process to the wage competition model described by neoclassical economics. At least one other alternative employment relationship can be identified: This is the often met arrangement when employees are directly involved in the disposition of goods to the market, and the "salesperson" is paid some fraction of total earnings. But such relationships presuppose that jobs are not highly interdependent and that the salesperson is primarily involved in the disposition, rather than in the production, of goods.[2] Vacancy competition in contrast is likely to emerge in closed employment relationships where jobs are interdependent in a technical and social division of labor around production.

In vacancy competition, as in wage competition, employers are assumed to be concerned about hiring the most productive employee at the least cost. But because of the indeterminate length of the employment relationship and the lack of competition among employees over wages, it will not be possible for the employer to link marginal productivity to the wage rate. This has important consequences for (*a*) the determination of who should be hired; (*b*) the determination of earnings; and (*c*) the organization of jobs in job ladders. These consequences all follow from the employer's attempt to secure the highest possible return from production when faced with employee control over the job.

In wage competition, the employer can rely on the wage rate as a measure of a person's productive capacity. The employer need only be concerned that the value of marginal productivity equals the wage rate and can be indifferent to the relationship between personal characteristics of employees and their performances. In contrast, in vacancy competition, the employer should be very much concerned about the relationship between personal characteristics and productive capacity, because once hired the employee cannot be easily dismissed. Furthermore, it is a person's potential performance that will be of concern, including the person's ability to fulfill the training requirements of jobs. Previous experience, education, and such ascriptive characteristics as race and sex will be used as indicators of potential performance; the main requirements are that the indicators chosen are visible and in the employer's experience show some relationship to performance. Based on the information provided by these indicators, the employer will hire the most promising candidate among those available for a job. In other words, access to a vacancy will be determined by a ranking of job candidates. As proposed by Thurow (1975), the situation may be conceived of as one where a queue of job candidates is established for vacant jobs. A person's position in the labor queue will be determined, not by his or her absolute level of productive capacity, but by the rank order in relation to other job candidates according to characteristics deemed relevant by employers.

As there is a queue of persons for jobs, there will be a rank order or a queue of vacant jobs, where the rank order is established by the earnings provided by vacant jobs, the career trajectories they imply, and such other characteristics as status, pleasantness, and convenience. The matching process, then, is a matching of the queue of persons to the queue of vacant jobs. The highest placed person in the labor queue will get the best job in the job queue. Changes in the supply of persons with certain characteristics (say a change in the distribution of education) and changes in the availability of jobs at different levels of rewards will change the rank orderings. As a result,

whenever there is a change in the labor and job queues, persons with similar characteristics will tend to be hired into different jobs and persons in similar jobs may have different personal characteristics. The organization of jobs into career trajectories (discussed later) will further reinforce these tendencies.

Wage rates in vacancy competition are characteristics of jobs, not of persons. Because employers have no effective way of enforcing a translation of productivity variations into wage rates other than by promotions, wages will tend to become heavily influenced by such institutional forces as collective bargaining and employee desire to preserve traditional relative wage differentials. Internally, wage differentials will reflect the organization of jobs into job ladders.

The creation of job ladders in internal labor markets is, as already mentioned, a way for the employer to create an incentive structure in the absence of open employment relationships. The organization of jobs into promotion schedules further acts as a screening device, inducing low-performance employees to leave on their own decision by denying or delaying promotion in relation to other employees. To be effective, jobs at the same level in a promotion schedule should provide identical earnings, whereas jobs at different levels should provide a differential large enough to induce employees to compete for promotion opportunities. This further reinforces the tendency in vacancy competition for earnings to become a characteristic of jobs so that similar jobs provide similar earnings regardless of characteristics of the incumbents.

Actual promotion opportunities are created when persons leave the firm or a new job is added, setting in motion chains of vacancies (White, 1970). The number of job levels, the distribution of jobs at various levels, the seniority distribution of employees, and the demand for products influencing the creation of new jobs (or the elimination of jobs), all interact to produce promotion schedules governing the careers of employees. These promotion schedules will under certain conditions result in career lives that are similar to those predicted by human capital theory, even though the mechanisms are quite different (Sørensen, 1977).

In wage competition, employees can change their earnings only by changing their performance. In vacancy competition, changes in earnings are generated by moves in mobility regimes that are chains of vacancies in internal labor markets. There is, in vacancy competition, no automatic correspondence between the creation of promotion opportunities and whatever changes take place in a person's productive capacity. Employees may be promoted without a preceding change in productivity, and a change in productive capacity need not result in a promotion. This means that the cross-sectional association between personal characteristics and earnings will be attenuated, even though personal characteristics are crucial for access to jobs. (A formal derivation of this conclusion and an empirical illustration is presented by Wise, 1975.)

In vacancy competition, variations in earnings reflect variations in job characteristics and the organization of jobs in internal labor markets. This is in contrast to the situation in the neoclassical model of wage competition, where the primary source of variation is the variation in personal characteristics that determine a person's productive capacity.

Vacancy competition structures are likely to be similar to the job structures identified as primary jobs (e.g., Doeringer & Piore, 1971). However, the dualist literature has a very descriptive character, and there is also some confusion as to whether the labor market segmentation is a segmentation of jobs or of persons (blacks, poor, and women in the secondary sector, white skilled workers in the primary sector). The main conclusion derived from this literature is that there are good jobs and bad jobs.

Constraints on Growth in Earnings

The two polar models of the matching process suggest different constraints on a person's ability to increase his or her earnings. In wage competition, earnings directly reflect performance and hence the skills and abilities of a person. Increases in earnings then are obtained by increasing the skill level of a person, and the major constraint on growth in earnings will be limitations on acquiring additional human capital. In wage competition markets, the amount of training that can be provided in jobs will be low, since on-the-job training is a major cause of the emergence of vacancy competition (Thurow, 1975). Hence, the major source of income inequality among persons lies outside the labor market—that is, in the educational and other training institutions that produce skill differentiation.

In vacancy competition sectors, the major constraint on the attainment of income is access to jobs. If no job is available, a person will not be able to obtain earnings. Growth in earnings is produced by the utilization of opportunities for mobility to better jobs, and this opportunity structure, not changes in skills, governs the earnings variations over time. The major source of variation in earnings is then the restriction of access to jobs and the level of derived demand that determines the availability of jobs.

The different constraints on growth in earnings in wage competition and vacancy competition jobs imply that quite different policies will have to be used in an attempt to increase pretransfer earnings of poverty groups. In wage competition sectors, policies aimed at increasing skill levels either through schooling or—for those already having entered the labor market—through various off-the-job training programs would presumably be effective. In vacancy competition sectors such policies would be quite ineffective since such training would not make jobs available.

The rather limited success of worker training programs suggests that job vacancy competition indeed is predominant in the U.S. economy. More correctly, the fate of such programs suggests that it is indeed difficult to prepare low-skilled workers for jobs that demand high skill levels, since such jobs tend to be vacancy competition jobs.

Notes

This research was supported in part by funds granted to the Institute for Research on Poverty at the University of Wisconsin by the Office of Economic Opportunity pursuant to the provisions of the Economic Opportunity Act of 1964. The conclusions expressed herein are those of the authors.

1. The definitions are given in paragraph 10 in the section on "Basic Concepts" in *Economy and Society,* Volume 1. "A social relationship ... will be known as 'open' to those on the outside, if ... participation ... is ... not denied to anyone who is inclined to participate and is actually in a position to do so. The relationship will be known as 'closed' [if] participation of certain persons is excluded, limited or subject to conditions [Weber, 1947, p. 139]." Weber argues that market relationships are open and gives as an example of a closed relationship the "establishment of rights to and possession of particular jobs on the part of the worker [Weber, 1947, p. 141]." This identification of open relationships with market relationships (for the exchange of labor for wages) and of closed relationships with control over the job by the worker (and the absence of market relationships) will be relied on heavily in this chapter.

2. A similar arrangement accounts for the apparent contradiction of the argument presented here exemplified by the existence of wage competition among faculty at elite universities despite tenure. Here the individual scholar, and not the employer (i.e., the university), disposes himself of the products (articles and other contributions) to a competitive market and obtains himself the returns from this activity (i.e., prestige in the profession).

References

Averitt, R. T. 1968. *The Dual Economy.* New York: Norton.

Becker, G. S. 1964. *Human Capital.* New York: National Bureau of Economic Research.

Bluestone, B. 1970. "The tripartite economy: Labor markets and the working poor." *Poverty and Human Resources Abstracts* (5 March–April):15–35.

Cain, G. G. 1976. "The challenge of segmented labor market theories to orthodox theory: A survey." *Journal of Economic Literature* 14:1215–1257.

Doeringer, P. B., and M. J. Piore. 1971. *Internal Labor Markets and Manpower Analysis.* Lexington, Massachusetts: Heath.

Kerr, C. 1954. "The Balkanization of labor markets." In E. W. Bakke, P. M. Hauser, G. L. Palmer, C. A. Myers, D. Yoder, and C. Kerr (eds.), *Labor Mobility and Economic Opportunity.* Cambridge, Massachusetts: Technology Press of MIT.

Marx, K. 1961. *Capital* (Vol. 1–3). Moscow: Foreign Language Press. (Originally published in English, 1887)

Mincer, J. 1974. *Schooling, Experience and Earnings.* New York: National Bureau of Economic Research.

O'Connor, J. 1973. *The Fiscal Crisis of the State.* New York: St. Martin's.

Sørensen, A. B. 1977. "The structure of inequality and the process of attainment." *American Sociological Review* 42:965–978.

Spilerman, S. 1977. "Careers, labor market structure, and socioeconomic achievement." *American Journal of Sociology* 83:551–593.

Stolzenberg, R. M. 1975. "Occupations, labor markets and the process of wage attainment." *American Sociological Review* 40:645–665.

Thurow, L. C. 1975. *Generating Inequality.* New York: Basic.

Weber, M. 1947. [*The Theory of Social and Economic Organization*] (A. M. Henderson and T. Parsons, Trans.). New York: Oxford Univ. Press.

White, H. C. 1970. *Chains of Opportunity: System Models of Mobility in Organizations.* Cambridge, Massachusetts: Harvard Univ. Press.

Wise, D. A. 1975. "Personal attributes, job performance and probability of promotion." *Econometrica* 43:913–931.

MARK GRANOVETTER

Toward a Sociological Theory of Income Differences

In recent years the prosaic but basic question of why different people have different incomes has increasingly occupied social scientists. Most such attention focuses on earned income, and this chapter similarly limits itself. I contend that the main need in this area is not for further empirical research but for deeper and broader theoretical development. There is no shortage of theories on income differences, but the existing traditions are narrowly focused and tightly encapsulated from one another.

Any attempt at theoretical progress must overcome the current fragmentation of ideas. Some of the fragmentation lies within disciplines; this is especially true for economics, despite some sociologists' image of that field as monolithic. This chapter will focus more on the barriers that separate economic from sociological ideas. While sociologists and economists have become increasingly aware of one anothers' ideas, this has not led to genuine integration. When sociologists claim to be making use of economic theory, it is usually either lip service or some superficial version; similarly, when economists refer to sociological ideas, these are typically simplistic and often out of date.

My aim here is to sketch what a broad sociological theory of income differences would look like, one that took economic arguments seriously but put them in a broader framework. I think of this broader framework as sociological, but this may be only a disciplinary conceit and thus inessential to the argument. My plan is as follows: I will first raise some broad sociological questions that will lead to a classification of those factors that are important determinants of income. I will then use this classification as a device for comparing existing theories of income determination. ...

Some Broad Sociological Questions

Being as simpleminded as possible leads, I believe, to the conclusion that three main factors contribute to earned income: (*a*) the characteristics of the job and employer; (*b*) the characteristics of the individual who occupies the job; and (*c*) how *a* and *b* get linked together—what I will call *matching processes*. For analytical purposes, I want to argue that it makes sense to think of each of these as exerting a separate and independent influence on earnings and that, furthermore, each is related to fundamental social structural characteristics of the society in which income is earned.

Begin with job characteristics. The idea that there exist "jobs" whose identities are independent of incumbents, and that such positions are the economic norm, is relatively recent. The ideal type of such positions is perhaps best defined in Max Weber's discussion of bureaucracy (1921/1968, 956–1005), where the independent existence of positions depends on and is defined by their place in a technically rational division of labor. It is that place which determines the rewards allocated to the position, rather than any special characteristics of incumbents. This idea is so familiar that some well-known analyses of stratification implicitly assume that all positions have rewards independent of their holders; functionalist arguments (that unequal rewards are necessary because some positions in society are more important than others) and most Marxist arguments (that positions must be unequally rewarded because of their different relationships to the ownership and control of capital) have in common the assumption that the characteristics of incumbents have no impact on the rewards of positions held (see Davis & Moore, 1945; Wright, 1979, chap. 2).

We may pose as an empirical question whether there actually are circumstances where the nature of a position alone determines rewards. It is plausible that this is the case to the extent that socioeconomic roles are closely defined—that is, that there is little leeway for different results based on who performs the given role. It would follow that the extent and location of such leeway ought to be an important focus of study in the comparison of reward structures across socioeconomic systems. The Weberian analysis would suggest that the more modernized the society, the more roles are so closely structured that rewards are preset. Whether or not this is correct, it is clear that *some* roles in our society have this characteristic: that while performance must not fall below some minimal level, beyond that level the role is so closely defined and interdependent with other roles that additional skill, charm, talent, or diligence not only cannot improve the outcome, but may even worsen it. Where diligence is at issue, such an event is called *rate-busting;* where skill is involved, we hear of *overqualification* for the position. Both are considered disruptive influences precisely because they involve an attempt to redefine the position of a role within a division of labor in a way that is not considered feasible.

Assemblyline jobs are perhaps the prototypes of such positions; attempts to speed up would only throw the entire productive system out of kilter. But many other jobs share similar features: most secretarial jobs, for example, and probably even some executive positions, especially in stable and predictable industrial environments.

At the other extreme, we may imagine systems where only personal characteristics, and not at all those of roles, determine economic outcomes. In such systems, the usual sociological conception of "role" would hardly seem applicable, since there would be so little of the stylized reciprocal expectations we associate with this idea (e.g., Berger & Luckmann, 1967). And so it is in those systems anthropologists call *prestige economies,* where economic rewards are determined mainly by personal prestige, gained by force of personality and skill at assembling a following—as for the Mela-

nesian Big Men so well described by Douglas Oliver (1955). Such tribal economies do not indeed have stable roles; when one Big Man is eclipsed or dies, there is no well-defined slot that others believe needs to be filled.

In modern economies such as ours, some individuals continue to be rewarded according to this older pattern (i.e., mainly as a result of their personal characteristics). As Weber might have predicted, this is most obvious for the self-employed, such as doctors, lawyers, and writers, who operate outside of bureaucratic structures. But it extends as well to people employed by firms insofar as their value to the firm depends on their building up a following (e.g., professional entertainers, athletes, and salespersons).

In a system where rewards were determined entirely by personal characteristics, income differences could naturally be understood by studying only those characteristics. But as soon as the features of jobs start to exert an influence on rewards, so that these are determined for most people by some mixture of individual and job characteristics, a third factor becomes central: matching—how do individuals with certain characteristics get matched up with jobs of certain types? To the extent that individual and job characteristics determine wages jointly, this matching question is theoretically urgent. Yet, in both sociology and economics, analyses of the matching between specific individuals and roles are rare. Both functionalist sociologists and Marxist economists believe, for example, that inequality is due to the variation in rewards attached to different roles, but neither pays much attention to how individuals get linked to such roles. Yet it is hardly informative to say that someone earns a high income as the result of holding a high-wage job; one needs an account of what determines who *comes* to hold jobs with high or low wages, that is, an account of matching processes.

I argue, then, that in modern economic systems, with few exceptions, one's earnings are determined by three factors: personal characteristics, characteristics of the job or role occupied, and processes that match these two. Existing theories of income differences can be categorized by how much attention they pay to each of these. Whereas an adequate theory would need to consider and integrate all three, most existing ones pay them unequal attention, and can, in fact, usually be seen as focusing almost exclusively on one.

A Review of Existing Theories of Earnings Differences

Status Attainment and Human Capital Theories

The two traditions that dominate current research in sociology and economics—status attainment research and human capital theory, respectively—are curiously similar in their nearly exclusive attention to characteristics and decisions of individuals and their neglect of the nature of jobs and matching processes.

In sociology, since Blau and Duncan's *The American Occupational Structure* (1967), empirical work has focused heavily on structural equation models, most of which have asserted that the "attainment" of status or income is caused mainly by background, personal characteristics, and levels of achievement. (Note the implicit individual-level bias of the word *attainment;* the use of such language both reflects and reinforces the underlying assumptions.) Sewell and Hauser's statement is representative; "We postulate that socioeconomic background affects mental ability, that background and ability affect educational attainment, that background, ability and education affect occupational achievement, and that all of the preceding variables affect earnings [1975, p. 50]." Furthermore, this model "is basic ... because it exhausts the influence of fundamental conditions of ascription and achievement. ... Consequently factors of luck or chance are implicated in the process of achievement to the extent of indeterminacy in the outcomes of our basic model [1975, p. 184]."

This tradition pays little attention to employers and jobs or to matching processes. The question of how individual characteristics actually generate income differences is addressed only by citing the path decomposition of particular effects. Having found, for example, that "a year of educational attainment is worth just over $200 in annual earnings," Sewell and Hauser add the explanation that "of this effect, just over half is explained by the higher status jobs open to better educated men; even for men with jobs of equal status, an additional year of schooling is worth $97 [1975, p. 84]."

Fägerlind attempts to provide a theoretical framework for such assertions, in explaining results for his large sample of Swedish students: "The resources the individual has access to in early childhood, mainly family resources and personality assets, are converted into 'marketable assets' mainly through the formal educational system [1975, p. 78]." But the central question of how such "resources" are "converted" to income is here merely begged, and we are left with the assertion that individual-level characteristics generate income.

Writers in this tradition, of course, probably do not believe that structures of employment and matching are infinitely malleable to the distribution of individual characteristics nor that the partial regression slopes on which the conclusions rest are timeless. But even those who are clearly aware of this (e.g., Jencks *et al.,* 1979) do not analyze what economic or labor market conditions have brought these slopes to their present values or which conditions might change them. Without a more explicit theory of how these individual-level variables have their effects, it is difficult to form any opinion about how long they can be expected to persist (cf. Granovetter, 1976).

Some revisionism has recently appeared within the status attainment tradition, edging it away from its highly individualistic assumptions. In most cases this trend has consisted of assertions that slopes of individual-level variables will differ according to context; depending on the writer, the context is said to be occupation, industry, firm, or social class (e.g., Beck, Horan, & Tolbert, 1978; Bibb & Form, 1977; Stolzenberg, 1975; Talbert & Bose, 1977; Wright & Perrone, 1977). While this new emphasis is salutary, it is not theoretically coherent; its mode of formulation continues to give explicit causal priority to individual-level variables, without attempting to integrate these in any theoretical detail with the characteristics of jobs or of matching processes.

Some such revisionists describe their problem as one of determining whether the "rates of return" to individual-level variables (as measured by regression slopes) vary importantly by context (e.g., Beck *et al.,* 1978). I argue, however, that to cast the question in this way accepts too easily the idea that there is an uncomplicated relationship between such variables as education and income—that the statistical correlation does not reflect complex processes of negotiation or structural influences, but rather a direct translation of a "resource" into money. This view, as well as the "rate of return" language, is taken over from human capital theory in economics.

Despite criticism (e.g., Blaug, 1976), human capital theory remains the dominant tradition in current labor economics. Its rise to this position can only be understood via a brief history of economic theories of wages in the twentieth century. At least since the turn of the century, the theory of wages has been treated by economics as simply a special case of the theory of commodity prices. Underlying ideas have changed little since Hicks's classic 1932 exposition:

The theory of the determination of wages in a free market is simply a special case of the general theory of value. Wages are the price of labor; and thus, in the absence of control, they are determined, like all prices, by supply and demand. ... The demand for labor is only peculiar to this extent: that labor is a factor of production, and is thus demanded ... not because the work to be done is desired for and by itself, but because it is to be used in the production of some other thing which is directly desired [1932/1964, p. 1].

First consider demand. For most productive processes, holding constant the amount of capital employed, the value of the product generated by each additional unit of labor eventually declines (i.e., diminishing marginal returns to labor). In competitive markets, firms are assumed to be *pricetakers*—they face a market wage for labor that they cannot affect. Given this fixed wage, therefore, a rational (i.e., profit-maximizing) firm would add workers only until the point where the value of the additional product produced as a result of having hired the last unit of labor equaled the wage of that unit; diminishing returns implies that hiring beyond that point would reduce net revenues. (Note that the wage of the last unit is the same as the wage of any other unit—the given market wage.) Thus, for any wage, there is a de-

terminate number of labor units that a rational firm would demand; graphing together all such points (wage, number of labor units) generates the demand curve for labor. But by hypothesis, the wage is the same as the value of product added by hiring the last unit of labor—that is, any market wage is the same as the *marginal product of labor*. Thus, the demand curve for labor is identical to the curve that would be gotten by graphing the marginal product of labor against the number of labor units in use. The point where this curve is then intersected by the supply curve of labor is, in the usual way, the equilibrium price of labor.

Each unit of labor is thus paid the marginal product of labor. The argument is hence sometimes thought of as the *marginal product theory of wages.* This shorthand is deceptive, however, as it seems to imply that workers are paid as a result of those personal characteristics that make them more or less productive. Three points need to be made here about the notion of the marginal product of labor.

1. For any given industry, the amount of product resulting from a given number of labor units results from the nature of the existing technology—in economic language, from the production function. It follows that workers in an industry with backward technology will have lower marginal products for this reason alone; characteristics of the job rather than workers' skill levels determine this.

2. Marginal product is also determined by product price, since the demand for labor is derived from the demand for the product it produces—the number of physical units of product added by bringing in one more labor unit must be multiplied by product price to get the marginal (value) product used in this theory. It follows that if consumers change their demand in such a way as to want less of a product at any given price (i.e., if the product demand curve shifts to the left), the marginal product of labor is again reduced, with no relation to workers' skill.

3. The marginal product is determined in part by the supply schedule of labor; if it

shifted to the right (i.e., more workers available at any given wage), more workers would be hired at a lower wage—that is, the marginal product would have declined, again for reasons unrelated to workers' skills.

It is important, therefore, to remember that to say workers are paid the marginal product of labor is to say much more than that they are paid according to ability and experience.

Though abstractly reasonable, this neoclassical argument about wages tells us only what a rational firm pays a "unit" of labor. In other words, the theory works because it makes the simplifying assumption that labor is infinitely divisible into homogeneous units, as well-behaved neoclassical commodities are supposed to be. Labor, of course, is not well behaved and comes instead in inconvenient lumps called workers. The artifice adopted to deal with this problem as far back as Marx and Ricardo, and carried through by Marshall and modern economists, has been to imagine that there exists some fundamental minimal unit of labor, sometimes thought of as an entirely unskilled worker, and that other more skilled workers can be considered to present some multiple of this basic unit (see, e.g., Rees & Schultz, 1970, p. 6). Since the marginal product of labor is a feature of the basic unit, wage differences among workers would then be explained by differences in the number of units presented. But this then throws the explanation of inequality back on the question of what explains such differences, an issue not addressed by the original theory. The recognition that neoclassical theory thus had little to say about workers' wage differences led to the dominance in the 1940s and 1950s of labor economics by "an institutionalist tradition ... whose intellectual roots lay in the law and a sociological rather than an economic theory [Rees, 1973, p. viii]."

Human capital theory has changed this situation. In this fully neoclassical account, workers are seen as rational individuals who attempt to maximize their lifetime income by investing in their productive capacities (Becker, 1964; Mincer, 1974). Education is the prototypical investment, but the theory applies also to any other invest-

ment, such as health or on-the-job training, that can yield a return in income. Income differences are seen, then, as differing returns to different initial and continuing investments.

The theory, however, pays little attention to the mechanisms by which investments generate a stream of income. (For further comments on this theme, see Granovetter, 1977.) Responding to a deficiency in neoclassical theory in the analysis of labor supply, human capital ideas overreact by imagining that the supply side is *all* that need be analyzed to understand income differences. The imbalance is quite similar to that of status attainment arguments, which also assume that worker characteristics are sufficient to explain inequality. But this is implausible; it implies, for example, that wages would increase indefinitely if only individuals kept investing more in their productivity. Sørensen comments that some "basic predictions from the theory do not square well with reality; ... one would predict that changes in the distribution of education would alter the distribution of incomes [1977, p. 966]"; but empirical evidence since World War II does not support such a prediction.

The difficulty is that whether one's "investment" pays off depends on whether there is demand for what one's acquired skills can produce (i.e., on the characteristics of available jobs) and on whether one will be in a position to help meet that demand (i.e., on matching processes). It is naive to see productivity as a matter of individual skills and is, in fact, less theoretically sophisticated than the older neoclassical arguments on marginal productivity, which, whatever their shortcomings, at least recognized that wages are generated not only by skills but by skills in conjunction with consumer demand, technology, and a work position.

Institutional Economics: Wage Structures, Segmented Labor Markets, and Labor Queues

The classical assumption of infinitely divisible commodities, when applied to labor, is unable to deal efficiently with the existence of workers, who come only in inconvenient lumps. This supply-side deficiency gave rise to human capital theory. The same assumption makes the existence of jobs, a demand-side lumpiness, equally difficult to analyze. Yet, the empirical observations of institutional economists in the 1940s and 1950s, of whom John Dunlop is the best known, made clear that the wages of a job often depended crucially on where it stood in a structure of jobs. The inability of the standard neoclassical analysis to cope with such observations led in this case to a tradition that, unlike human capital theory, has diverged markedly from neoclassical assumptions.

Dunlop and his students stressed the concept of "wage-structure": "the complex of rates within firms differentiated by occupation and employee and the complex interfirm rate structures [J. Dunlop, 1957, p. 128]." The problem of wage determination, for this group, was to determine how a particular *job* comes to have the wage it has. This is accompanied by seeing where the job fits in relation to other jobs and the firm in relation to other firms. Well-defined systems of jobs and firms comprise the wage-structure. Certain jobs, for example, are central—"key jobs"—in that if their wages change, this will set off a chain reaction of other changes in associated jobs that all together make up a "job cluster." Among firms, a "wage contour is defined as a stable group of wage-determining units ... which are so linked together by 1) similarity of product markets, 2) resort to similar sources for a labor force or 3) common labor-market organization (custom) that they have common wage-making characteristics [J. Dunlop, 1957, p. 131]."

The ideas of job clusters and key jobs led directly to Doeringer and Piore's concept of the *internal labor market:* "an administrative unit, such as a manufacturing plant, within which the pricing and allocation of labor is governed by a set of administrative rules and procedures," in contrast to the labor market of conventional theory, "where pricing, allocation and training decisions are controlled directly by economic variables [1971, pp. 1–2]." In such tightly closed systems of jobs, they argue, wages are based mainly on job characteristics, with careful attention to consistency within the hierarchy. For example, jobs "which involve wide contacts with other workers

acquire a strategic position in the internal wage structure which makes it impossible to change their wages without adjustments throughout the system [1971, p. 89]."[1]

This stream of literature, then, takes for granted that jobs have well-defined identities independent of incumbents and that this, plus how the overall structure of jobs fits together, is what determines wages. Like human capital theory, which responded to a supply-side deficiency in neoclassical wage theory and ended analyzing *only* supply, this line of argument responded to difficulties in the analysis of demand and ended up attributing wages only to demand-side factors. Unlike human capital theorists, however, these authors did not claim to explain inequality by recourse only to one set of factors. They recognized that to argue that a job's wage is determined by its characteristics and its position in a system of jobs does not explain how particular individuals get linked up with high- or low-wage jobs, which one needs to know to understand wage differences among actual workers.

Attempts to explain this better led to what was first called *dual* then *segmented* labor market theory. (See the useful though skeptical review in Cain, 1976; a more sympathetic account is Gordon, 1972.) This argument, propounded especially but not exclusively by radical economists, asserts that internal labor markets are only one kind of work setting and offer to those in them substantial advantages, such as built-in career ladders and mobility opportunities—hence the designation of such markets as *primary.* Other workers are said to be confined to *secondary* labor markets, which are "composed of workers, especially women, blacks, teenagers and the urban poor, who follow a much more random series of jobs and are generally denied opportunities for acquiring skills and advancement [Edwards, 1975, p. 16]."

Empirically, there is some argument about the actual extent of confinement. Here I need only to point out that if workers are not actually confined to one such market segment, then the theory does not explain wage inequality except in the very short run. On the other hand, to the extent such confinement operates, the real causes of inequality lie in the matching processes that lead to this immobility in low-wage jobs.

But in practice, segmented labor market theorists pay little attention to matching processes. Instead they argue that confinement occurs because workers lack stable work habits. This surprising reductionism to the causal level of individual attitudes by scholars, many of whom are Marxist and might thus be expected to lean toward more structural explanations, is justified by the claim that secondary employers "do not expect, may even discourage and therefore fail to elicit stability [Edwards, 1975, p. 16]." I believe that this superficial treatment of *confinement* is closely related to the general failure of Marxist analysis to take seriously the question of how individuals and socioeconomic roles are matched up.

Beyond this, the theory has a curiously static and atomistic flavor. The economy is imagined to be cut up into some small number of separate markets (three in Piore's 1975 analysis—hence the shift to the *segmented* designation; more in other analyses) that are semi-impermeable to one another and have little mutual influence. Even if we could accept the notion that two, three, or six segments were enough to explain income inequality (unlikely in light of the finding of Jencks *et al.* that, when we divide workers into 435 detailed occupational categories, nearly two-thirds of income variation is still *within* occupational groups (1972, pp. 226, n61)), we would want to understand much more about the possibility of personnel flows among segments and other ways they could influence one another.

The original emphasis of scholars such as Dunlop and Livernash on how wage-structures were interdependent in complex ways—related to networks of economic complementarity and social relations within and between firms—seems to have been lost track of here as "sectors" of the market have been given the bulk of the explanatory attention. It has been assumed that within sectors, uniformity of wage-setting practices exists, so that the task to be accomplished is to show that such practices are demonstrably different across some definition of sectors. In practice this is achieved by regressing earnings on various variables separately in each sector (as, e.g., in Osterman, 1975) and looking for differences in

slopes. Insight into interactions and mobility among sectors or into matching processes is precluded by such a procedure.

A different attempt to show how workers end up in jobs whose incomes are more or less predetermined is made by Thurow (1975). Like wage-structure and segmented labor market theorists, he argues that a wage is determined mainly by the job rather than by the incumbent; his justification for this assertion is different, however, resting on the claim that "marginal products are inherent in jobs and not in individuals [1975, p. 85]." His solution to the question of how workers are matched with jobs at any given salary level is the idea of a *labor queue;* workers are said to be arranged by employers on such a queue in order of their *trainability*—the cost of training them for such jobs. If there are more workers at a given level of trainability than jobs that demand that level, some workers will get worse jobs than they "deserve" by this criterion: "In effect, they will participate in a lottery [1975, p. 92]."

Two comments are apt. First, the idea of trainability depends so heavily on workers' background characteristics and educational achievement (Thurow, 1975, pp. 86–88) that the labor queue idea is empirically difficult to distinguish from human capital or status attainment ideas of income causation. More importantly, the idea of such a queue, while perhaps more flexible than that of fixed labor market segments, hardly takes the complexity of matching processes seriously; it is radically inconsistent with both theoretical and empirical accounts of the matching of workers to jobs (see Granovetter, 1974).

Information and the Matching Problem

Analysis of theories preoccupied with the demand side of the labor market—those arguing that jobs' or industries' characteristics mainly determine wages—led me to pinpoint neglect of the matching between workers and jobs as the main defect in such arguments. It has taken economists longer to address the matching problem than to address other shortcomings in the neoclassical theory of wages. This may be because the matching problem is more subtle: In neoclassical markets there is no such problem—supply and demand are brought into balance and the market cleared by the movement toward equilibrium prices. For this movement to occur, however, market participants must have full knowledge of the market situation.

Local labor market studies from the 1930s on showed repeatedly, however, that information was highly imperfect; formal and easily accessible means of job placement, such as employment agencies and newspaper advertising, accounted for only a small proportion of actual hires. Most placements were mediated instead by information gotten from friends and relatives or by "blind" applications—a privatization of information radically at variance with the assumption of widespread or perfect knowledge. (See Granovetter, 1974, pp. 5–6, for a summary of the empirical studies.) This situation was generally considered by economists as reflecting workers' irrational behavior; the solution repeatedly prescribed was expansion of state and federal employment services and the implementation of computerized matching of workers to jobs.

This situation changed in the 1960s when economists began to integrate information considerations into standard theory. Stigler's 1961 formulation is quite general, pointing out that information is a scarce commodity, whose acquisition requires expenditures of time, effort, and money. It is thus a proper subject of economic analysis: Producers or consumers seeking information will incur the required costs only up to the point where these are outweighed by benefits—the standard maximizing assumption of marginal analysis.

Though this point applies in principle to information in all commodity markets, the great bulk of literature on the economics of information has referred to labor markets. Stigler initiated the analysis from the supply side in his 1962 article; not until the 1970s did economists pay serious attention to the employer's information problem, in theories of *signaling* or *screening*. As of 1981, little has been done in the way of meshing these two sides of the information problem, though I will argue that this is the crux of the matching process. I shall briefly review the supply- and demand-side analyses in turn.

On the supply side, first Stigler (1962) and later McCall and others (e.g., Lippman & McCall, 1976;

McCall, 1970), though their models differ in certain important ways (Lippman & McCall, 1976, is a useful literature survey), all conceive of workers as engaged in a process called *job search,* which is conducted in a rational manner. My study of a random sample of job changers in a Boston suburb added a sociological dimension to this discussion and highlights certain inadequacies in the economic notion of job search (Granovetter, 1974). I pointed out that workers (as well as employers) prefer information derived from their personal contacts. This preference is neither accidental nor irrational: Such information is less costly and of better quality than that obtained from impersonal sources. "[A] friend gives more than a simple job-description—he may also indicate if prospective workmates are congenial, if the boss is neurotic, and if the company is moving forward or is stagnant. ... Similarly, ... evaluations of prospective employees will be trusted better when the employer knows the evaluator personally [Granovetter, 1974, p. 13]." Income is closely related to these considerations: Nearly half of those using contacts to find a new job reported 1969 incomes over $15,000, whereas the corresponding proportion for those using agencies and ads is under one-third and for direct application under one-fifth (1974, p. 14).

The problem for economic models of job search is not that workers act irrationally in their acquisition of job information but rather that, empirically, it is often difficult to accept the implicit assertion that information results from "search." Fully 29% of my respondents denied having carried out any active search before taking their present job (see similar figures in U.S. Department of Labor, 1975); more significantly, this figure was strongly related to income: Whereas 21.0% of those reporting an income of $15,000 or less said they had not searched, 40.2% of those with incomes over $15,000 made this assertion. For those with incomes of $25,000 or more, over 55% said that information about the job taken did not come from a search they had undertaken (Granovetter, 1974, pp. 32–36). There are two reasons for these findings. One is that some jobs are found as the result of employer searches, rarely represented in job-search models; I will comment further on this later. Another is that job information is deeply imbedded in other social structural processes, in a way that makes it difficult to assert even that workers act *as if* they were conducting a rational search (the usual response of economists to assertions that economic actors do not empirically *report* rational market behavior). By this I mean that information, unlike most other commodities, may often be acquired as the by-product of other activities. A prototype of such a situation is learning about a new job at a party or in a tavern. It strains credulity to assert that the costs of having attended such occasions ought to be called a cost of job search and that one could expect workers to equate, either consciously or unconsciously, the marginal costs and benefits of such "search." More generally, there are few business-related activities that cannot be the occasion for information about new job opportunities to be acquired, whether or not this is the intent of the actors involved. When people transacting business know one another, as is typical in any regularized transactions, the social amenities of such acquaintanceship include inquiries about one's general satisfaction with one's situation and gossip about corporate and personal events. The typical assertion of job-search models, that search takes place from a position of unemployment, excludes such circumstances; this is highly unrealistic for populations such as the professional, technical, and managerial personnel that I studied. (Some further comments of mine on models of job search are reported in Petersen, 1980.)

On the demand side of the labor market, the main work has come in the 1970s as theories of "signaling" or "screening," (e.g., Spence, 1974; Stiglitz, 1975a), which take as their main problem "the uncertainty of the employer, which stems from the fact that he does not know, prior to hiring, how productive a particular employee will turn out to be; this is because the employer cannot directly observe productivity prior to hiring [Spence, 1974, p. 6]." The emphasis has been on how workers might invest in various kinds of certification devices, especially education, which employers can then read as signaling some level of productivity. The models entail that workers investing in such signals will receive a higher income, net of investment costs, than if they had not, since there would otherwise be no economic

motive for investment. But the argument has become controversial in economics since, though posed in a way that is quite consistent with neoclassical assumptions, it opposes directly the human capital account of why education is related to income: not necessarily because it makes workers more productive, but only because it certifies them as such, without necessarily increasing productivity at all (cf. Berg, 1970; Blaug, 1976, pp. 845–849).

In my view, the signaling argument is more sophisticated than that offered by human capital theory, because it allows the relation between signals and productivity to be an empirical question, rather than one which is decreed a priori. Two aspects of this literature, however, seem unrealistic. One is the exclusive concentration on the demand side. Spence points out that when "the employer and potential employee confront each other in the market ... neither is certain about the qualities of characteristics of the service which the other is offering for sale [1974, p. 6]." But his models treat only the employer's, not the employee's, uncertainty. It seems highly likely that employers also invest in signals meant to show that they are progressive and provide a pleasant working environment. (In some locales, such investment seems a major support for the landscaping industry.) But these investments are not treated in the literature, perhaps because they are less easily quantified than is education. Yet, given my earlier comments on the complex nature of "marginal productivity," it does seem mistaken for signaling theorists to talk, as human capital theorists also do, as if productivity resides only in workers. It would make as much sense to spin theories about how employers try to show that their jobs are productive (consistent, for example, with Thurow's argument that marginal productivity resides in jobs). Neither seems adequate to me, as both neglect the matching of the two sides of the market; marginal productivity results only from a combination of a worker with a job.

Furthermore, my empirical work suggests that the signal chosen in the usual models—education—is not actually the main conveyer of information in labor markets. It is true that most jobs have clear-cut educational requirements, such that employers assume workers lacking them to be ipso facto unqualified. This is, however, a crude screen indeed, and if used alone, would leave the employer still with a large and unmanageable information problem. On paper, there are few jobs for which large numbers of people are not qualified; in practice, employers use a more refined and differentiated signal than educational qualification: They use the recommendations of people personally known to both them and prospective employees. Similarly, prospective employees know better than to rely on landscaping or other signals put out by employers and attempt, instead, to find out the inside story from their contacts. Such facts are massive in their familiarity. Readers are invited to recall how they found a doctor, dentist, plumber, or electrician when first moving to their present locale.[2] Yet they are absent from economic models of screening, perhaps because of the difficulty of imagining how to analyze "investment." One has some control over the amount of education acquired (provided, that is, perfect capital markets). One has less control over who will form good opinions of oneself and repeat them to others; there is even less control over which people these opinions will be repeated to. There is little way of knowing who is known personally to people one meets; the amount of information required to be accurate about this is stupendous.

Systematic study of social structure is required for such analysis and does suggest some leads. I found, for example, that workers' acquaintances were more likely than their close friends to be instrumental in linking them up to new jobs, and argued that this was not accidental but resulted from the social structural fact that one's close friends are more likely than acquaintances to know the same people one already knows, hence less likely to be sources of information not already available (Granovetter, 1974, chap. 3; see also Granovetter, 1973; these findings are amplified with a different sample in Lin, Ensel, & Vaughn, 1979).

Can economic models be constructed that take such facts into account? Respondents in my study seemed surprised when, after reviewing their careers, they recognized the central role played by acquaintances in job mobility. Poor investment "choices," showing ignorance of these principles,

were clear in some cases—such as for workers who remained for many years in firms where other co-workers also did so, with the result that, when the firms were bought out in conglomerate mergers, they knew no one personally in other firms and consequently had great difficulty moving (Granovetter, 1974, chap. 6). On the other hand, one does hear talk about "investing" in one's reputation and "cultivating" contacts, especially those who are "well placed." Thus, there may be some scope for rational models. Boorman (1975) has followed up the weak-tie, strong-tie distinction proposed previously, and constructed an interesting and complex economic model of investment in contacts; the purpose assumed is not signaling but simply acquisition of information about jobs, so that this belongs more properly with the discussion of job search: It could, however, be adapted to the purposes of signaling. Whether empirical work could mesh with such models remains an open question.

I have discussed theories of job search on the supply side of the labor market and those of signaling on the demand side; in both cases I have commented that such theories ought properly to apply to both sides of the market. Employers as well as employees search, and employees as well as employers try to read signals from the other side of the market. The one-sidedness of both sets of ideas precludes sophisticated approaches to the question of how employers and employees are matched. Furthermore, an adequate theory would have to incorporate both searching and signaling, whereas present theories consider these as sequential activities. Spence, for example, comments that when "the employer and potential employee confront each other in the market (the confrontation may be preceded by a considerable amount of search by either party or both) neither is certain about the qualities ... the other is offering for sale [1974, p. 6]." But such a version implies that employers and employees first conduct a search in which *only the identities* of the others are learned and no signals read until the next stage of the process. In practice this seems highly unlikely.

Beyond these points, theories of search and signaling, as presently constituted, implicitly assume that only an information problem requires solution. There exists a distribution of workers on the one side and vacant jobs on the other that need only to be matched up. Two facts contradict this simple version and lead to a need for more emphasis on matching processes. First, many workers who move to new jobs have no interim period of unemployment; in my random sample of professional, technical, and managerial job changers, 89% of respondents fell in this category (Granovetter, 1974, p. 44). This means that it may often not be obvious to employers who, exactly, is "in the market." Correspondingly, workers may take new jobs not previously held by anyone, so that no "vacancy" can be said to have existed. In my sample, about 45% of new jobs filled could be called well-defined vacancies; 20% were jobs where no vacancy existed but where the job was essentially similar to other jobs of its kind already existing in the firm; and 35% of jobs were created de novo, in the sense that either the work was not being done or the tasks had not previously been combined into one position. Those finding jobs via personal contacts were twice as likely to have taken this last category of job (Granovetter, 1974, pp. 14–15). Interviews showed that in many cases, the job was created only because employers had come across a person whose characteristics and skills they considered particularly appropriate for this work—even when they had not actively searched for such a person. Any firm has a variety of projects on the back burner that may or may not come to fruition; the information and personnel pool it is linked up to may determine which of these are pursued. A complex process of negotiation between firm and prospective employee, in which the exact details, work, and salary of such jobs are hammered out, constitutes the matching process here. Search, signaling, and job creation are all inextricably intertwined, in a way that cannot be well captured by models more appropriate to situations where consumers are surveying department stores for the range of refrigerator prices or used car lots for an appropriate vehicle.

Thus, informationally based theories, mostly in economics, sometimes address the characteristics and decisions of workers, sometimes those of employers, but not both; and, as with other theories surveyed thus far, the mechanisms by which these two sides are matched are neglected. Like status attainment and human capital theories, and arguments from institutional economics, these models founder on their failure to give balanced attention to the three factors outlined at the beginning of this chapter. ...

Limitations and Prospects

A chapter of this length cannot adequately treat all factors impinging on earnings. In this section I mean not to repair the various omissions, but only to identify them and suggest how they relate to what has been discussed. Perhaps most glaring is the absence of any discussion of discrimination. I have neglected this important aspect of matching processes in part because it is already widely recognized and discussed and in part because proper perspective would have required too extensive a discussion for the present format. Instead, I chose to highlight less commonly analyzed issues.

It is time also to say that, while the tripartite division of causal factors into those of personal and job characteristics and matching processes has been a useful initial probe into the literature and a serviceable sorting device, it has certain limitations. In particular, it has some of the atomistic flavor I have criticized in other contexts. To take this classification literally entails the implicit assumption that workers and employers enter the system that determines earnings as individuals, without significant interaction and organization beyond this individual level. This is a gross oversimplification. Workers interact extensively with one another in an attempt to influence earnings. They do so by means of organizations of various kinds, the most obvious of which are trade unions. A recent review article concludes that the "ability of unions to extract wage gains over and above what could have been achieved in their absence is generally an accepted fact in academic literature. ... Debate instead has focused on the magnitude and nature of such effects [Parsley, 1980, p. 1]." Correspondingly, employers, especially though not exclusively in oligopolistic industries, combine both informally and in formal trade associations whose operations may have effects on wages.

Furthermore, most individuals are employed not in a one-on-one situation with an employer, but rather in an organization whose structure has some impact on earnings (see, e.g., Baron & Bielby, 1980). One central organizational feature in most firms, for example, is the existence of clear-cut hierarchies with well-defined levels. One of the reasons that wage changes for one job frequently entail wage changes in others is the need to maintain consistency among such levels (Doeringer & Piore, 1971). Simon (1957) has even suggested that the number of such levels may be the main determinant of the wages of those at the top of the pyramid in industrial firms (see also Lydall, 1968, pp. 127–133). Yet, there is considerable dispute in the literature on the question of exactly why firms typically have such hierarchies. The Weberian notion that a clear chain of command is efficient has been amplified in various ways by economists who argue that a rational firm requires hierarchy in order to minimize various costs that would otherwise be faced, such as transaction costs (O. Williamson, 1975) or the costs of acquiring information on employee productivity (Stiglitz, 1975b). Marxists, on the other hand, have argued that hierarchies have no economic function but rather are required in order to prevent workers from developing autonomy or an integrated understanding of the productive process, either of which would generate threats to capitalist hegemony (Marglin, 1974; Stone, 1975). White (1978) suggests a third view, that hierarchies may be the more or less adventitious result of ordinary productive and marketing activities, required neither for efficiency nor for repression. This debate is one example of the complexity of collective processes that have important impacts on earnings but are currently poorly understood. As with other issues discussed in this chapter, a confrontation of organizational ideas from sociology with efficiency considerations from economics and political ones from Marxist thought may help generate more sophisticated analysis.

The extent to which wages are influenced by interactions that take place in a network of firms is also an issue that requires a less atomistic paradigm than the one I have employed here. Dunlop's notion that there exist *wage contours*—sets of firms whose wages influence one another—and that such influence may be highly asymmetrical (e.g., Eckstein & Wilson, 1961), would repay further analysis. Developments in interorganizational analysis (summarized by Aldrich, 1979) could help clarify this situation.

Finally, an important omission from the present chapter is any discussion of the impact of macroeconomic forces on earnings differences. This is a complex subject on which clear positions have not been staked out by economists; hence existing schools of thought on wage differences tend to revolve mostly around microeconomic analysis. This is the case despite the fact that levels of employment and the "stickiness" of prices, including wages, in the face of demand and supply changes have been central issues in macroeconomics. Recent ferment and revisionism in this area (e.g., Eichner, 1979; Leijonhufvud, 1968) lead, however, to the hope that more systematic consideration of how this larger framework relates to inequality will soon come to occupy considerable attention.

Summary

It will be clear by now to the reader that the exercise I have indulged in here is not a theory, but rather the statement of a puzzle and a display of many of the pieces. In an area where intellectual interchange has been extremely fragmentary, this seems to me a necessary first step. More generally, I believe that a number of difficult problems lie on the border of sociology and economics and consequently receive more narrow and less sophisticated treatment than they require. Ultimately, both sociological and economic theory need to be reconstructed and integrated in ways that will yield a far more powerful apparatus than either now offers. Such a task is unlikely to be achieved as the result of purely abstract considerations, but rather step by step in the course of attacking specific problems. One such problem is that of earnings differences, and my main purpose here is to encourage the integration described by focusing attention on an issue that is of compelling theoretical as well as practical significance.

Notes

An earlier version of this chapter was delivered at the 1979 meetings of the American Sociological Association. The paper was begun at the Center for Advanced Study in the Behavioral Sciences, Stanford, California, where my stay was supported in part by the National Science Foundation and the Andrew Mellon Foundation. Partial support was also received from the University Awards Council of the State University of New York.

I am indebted to Mitchel Abolafia for his comments and his valuable literature review. The following individuals make up an incomplete list of those who have been extremely generous with their comments: Howard Aldrich, Daniel Cornfield, William Form, Christopher Jencks, Arne Kalleberg, Susan Mueller, John Padgett, Charles Perrow, James Rule, and Robert Willis.

1. Notice that *strategic* is defined here not with reference to a rational position in the division of labor, but rather by an implicit social psychological argument that workers are more likely to compare their wages to those of positions they frequently interact with. This argument is made explicit in an imaginative empirical study by Gartrell (1979).

2. For application of these ideas to the difficulties experienced in placement by institutions that rehabilitate handicapped or disabled workers, see Granovetter, 1979.

References

Aldrich, H. 1979. *Organizations and Environments.* Englewood Cliffs, New Jersey: Prentice-Hall.

Baron, J., and W. Bielby. 1980. "Bringing the firms back in: Stratification, segmentation and the organization of work." *American Sociological Review* 45(October):737–765.

Beck, E. M., P. Horan, and C. Tolbert. 1978. "Stratification in a dual economy." *American Sociological Review* 43(October):704–720.

Becker, G. 1964. *Human Capital.* New York: Columbia Univ. Press.

Berg, I. 1970. *Education and Jobs: The Great Training Robbery.* New York: Praeger.

Berger, P., and T. Luckmann. 1967. *The Social Construction of Reality.* New York: Doubleday.

Bibb, R., and W. Form. 1977. "The effects of industrial, occupational and sex stratification on wages in blue-collar markets." *Social Forces* 55(June):974–996.

Blau, P., and O. D. Duncan. 1967. *The American Occupational Structure.* New York: Wiley.

Blaug, M. 1976. "The empirical status of human capital theory: A slightly jaundiced survey." *Journal of Economic Literature* 14(September):827–855.

Boorman, S. 1975. "A combinatorial optimization model for transmission of job information through contact networks." *Bell Journal of Economics* 6 (Spring):216–249.

Cain, G. 1976. "The challenge of segmented labor market theories to orthodox theory." *Journal of Economic Literature* 14(December):1215–1257.

Davis, K., and W. Moore. 1945. "Some principles of stratification." *American Sociological Review* 19 (April):242–249.

Doeringer, P., and M. Piore. 1971. *Internal Labor Markets and Manpower Analysis.* Lexington, Massachusetts: Heath.

Dunlop, J. 1957. "The task of contemporary wage theory." In G. Taylor and F. Pierson (eds.), *New Concepts in Wage Determination.* New York: McGraw-Hill.

Eckstein, O., and T. Wilson. 1961. "The determination of money wages in American industry." *Quarterly Journal of Economics* 76(August):379–414.

Edwards, R. 1975. "The social relations of production in the firm and labor market structure." In R. Edwards, M. Reich, and D. Gordon (eds.), *Labor Market Segmentation.* Lexington, Massachusetts: Heath.

Eichner, A., Ed. 1979. *A Guide to Post-Keynesian Economics.* White Plains, New York: M. E. Sharpe.

Fägerlind, I. 1975. *Formal Education and Adult Earnings.* Stockholm: Almqvist and Wiksell.

Gartrell, D. 1979. "The social evaluation of compensation: Public employees in Cambridge, Massachusetts." Unpublished doctoral dissertation, Harvard University.

Gordon, D. 1972. *Theories of Poverty and Underemployment.* Lexington, Massachusetts: Heath.

Granovetter, M. 1973. "The strength of weak ties." *American Journal of Sociology* 78(May):1360–1380.

———. 1974. *Getting a Job: A Study of Contacts and Careers.* Cambridge, Massachusetts: Harvard Univ. Press.

———. 1976. Review of Sewall and Hauser's *Education, Occupation and Earnings. Harvard Educational Review* 46(February):123–127.

———. 1977. Review of Mincer's *Schooling, Experience and Earnings. Sociological Quarterly* 18(Autumn):608–612.

———. 1979. "Placement as brokerage: Information problems in the labor market for rehabilitated workers." In D. Vandergoot, R. Jacobsen, and J. Worall (eds.), *Placement in Rehabilitation: A Career Development Perspective*. Baltimore: University Park Press.

Hicks, J. R. 1964. *The Theory of Wages*. New York: St. Martin's. (Reprint of 1932 edition, with 1964 supplement.)

Jencks, C., S. Bartlett, M. Corcoran, J. Crouse, D. Eaglesfield, G. Jackson, K. McClelland, P. Mueser, M. Olneck, J. Schwartz, S. Ward, and J. Williams. 1979. *Who Gets Ahead?* New York: Basic Books.

Jencks, C., M. Smith, H. Acland, M. Bane, D. Cohen, H. Gintis, B. Heyns, and S. Michelson. 1972. *Inequality*. New York: Basic Books.

Leijonhufvud, A. 1968. *On Keynesian Economics and the Economics of Keynes*. London and New York: Oxford Univ. Press.

Lin, N., W. Ensel, and J. Vaughn. 1979. "Social resources, strength of ties, and occupational status attainment." Department of Sociology, State University of New York at Albany. (Mimeo)

Lippman, S., and J. McCall. 1976. "The economics of job search: A survey." *Economic Inquiry* 14(June):155–189.

Lydall, H. 1968. *The Structure of Earnings*. London and New York: Oxford Univ. Press.

Marglin, S. 1974. "What do bosses do? The origins and functions of hierarchy in capitalist production." *Review of Radical Political Economics* 6(Spring):60–112.

McCall, J. 1970. "Economics of information and job search." *Quarterly Journal of Economics* 84(February):113–126.

Mincer, J. 1974. *Schooling, Experience and Earnings*. New York: Columbia Univ. Press.

Oliver, D. 1955. *A Solomon Island Society*. Cambridge, Massachusetts: Harvard Univ. Press.

Osterman, P. 1975. "An empirical study of labor market segmentation." *Industrial and Labor Relations Review* 28(July):508–523.

Parsley, C. J. 1980. "Labor union effects on wage gains: A survey of recent literature." *Journal of Economic Literature* 18(March):1–31.

Peterson, J. 1980. "An agenda for socioeconomic life-cycle research." *Journal of Economics and Business* 32(Winter):95–110.

Piore, M. 1975. "Notes for a theory of labor market stratification." In R. Edwards, M. Reich, and D. Gordon (eds.), *Labor Market Segmentation*. Lexington, Massachusetts: Heath.

Rees, A. 1973. *The Economics of Work and Pay*. New York: Harper.

Rees, A., and G. Shultz. 1970. *Workers and Wages in an Urban Labor Market*. Chicago: Univ. of Chicago Press.

Sewell, W., and R. Hauser. 1975. *Education, Occupation, and Earnings*. New York: Academic Press.

Simon, H. 1957. "The compensation of executives." *Sociometry* 20(March):32–35.

Sørensen, A. 1977. "The structure of inequality and the process of attainment." *American Sociological Review* 42(December):965–978.

Spence, M. 1974. *Market Signaling*. Cambridge, Massachusetts: Harvard Univ. Press.

Stigler, G. 1961. "The economics of information." *Journal of Political Economy* 69(June):213–225.

———. 1962. "Information in the labor market." *Journal of Political Economy* 70 (October, Pt. 2):94–105.

Stiglitz, J. 1975a. "The theory of 'screening', education and the distribution of income." *American Economic Review* 65(June):283–300.

———. 1975b. "Incentives, risk and information: Notes towards a theory of hierarchy." *Bell Journal of Economics* 6(Autumn):552–578.

Stolzenberg, R. 1975. "Occupations, labor markets and the process of wage attainment." *American Sociological Review* 40(October):645–665.

Stone, K. 1975. "The origins of job structures in the steel industry." In R. Edwards, M. Reich, and D. Gordon (eds.), *Labor Market Segmentation*. Lexington, Massachusetts: Heath.

Talbert, J., and C. Bose. 1977. "Wage-attainment processes: The retail clerk case." *American Journal of Sociology* 83(September):403–424.

Thurow, L. 1975. *Generating Inequality*. New York: Basic Books.

U. S. Department of Labor. 1975. *Jobseeking Methods Used by American Workers*. Bureau of Labor Statistics Bulletin 1886. Washington, D. C.: US Govt Printing Office.

Weber, M. 1968. [*Economy and Society*] (G. Roth and C. Wittich, Trans.). Totowa, New Jersey: Bedminister Press. (Originally published, 1921.)

White, H. 1978. "Markets and hierarchies revisited." Department of Sociology, Harvard University. (Mimeo)

Williamson, O. 1975. *Markets and Hierarchies*. New York: Free Press.

Wright, E. O. 1979. *Class, Crisis and the State*. New York: Schocken.

Wright, E. O., and L. Perrone. 1977. "Marxist class categories and income inequality." *American Sociological Review* 42(February):32–55.

JAMES N. BARON

Reflections on Recent Generations of Mobility Research

The readings in this section demonstrate why mobility and attainment research has so influenced contemporary sociology. As Featherman (1981) notes, it is hard to find another sociological subfield in which as much cumulative development of theory, models, methods, and data has occurred. The stellar examples selected for this section display numerous attractive features that are too rare in sociological research: tight linkages between theory and methods; a preoccupation with data and measurement, including standard methods, models, and metrics for quantifying mobility and attainment; and a concern with temporal and comparative issues long before they became generally fashionable. This literature operationalized broad questions about the structure, functioning, and evolution of modern societies—for instance, how industrialization and democratization affect the social order—in terms of individuals' movements through the occupational structure. This made it possible for data, methods, and measures to be brought to bear on these questions in powerful and productive ways, including comparative studies across time and space.

Scientific schools of thought are defined and maintained as much by what they omit as by what they study, and this has been true in the case of mobility and attainment studies. Because of the focus on the movement of individuals through the occupational structure, a number of facets of "generating stratification"—the topic of this section of readings—were deemphasized. The success of mobility and attainment research made it an attractive target for revisionist critiques, some examples of which are provided by the last three readings in this section. Mobility and attainment research, it was argued, focused on individuals and abstracted from the structural forces shaping the distribution of labor market opportunities and outcomes. In part because they were harder to measure, such causal forces as class relations, organizational and industrial structure, and the polity were given less attention than an individual's family background, education, and occupational role.

One might contrast the structuralist agenda with mainstream research on mobility and attainment by suggesting that the former is interested in differentiating among *contexts*—understanding how stratification processes and outcomes vary across organizations, industries, classes, and other social units—whereas the latter concentrates on differentiating among *individuals*. However, it is more difficult to distinguish between the two approaches in practice.

For one thing, the contrast has often been framed in terms of "structural" versus "individualistic" variables: Attainment researchers are said to focus on individual-level ascribed and achieved resources that people bring into the labor market, whereas structuralists focus on the social structures within which they are placed and through which they move. Yet there is a difference between an individual-level *characteristic* and an individual-level *interpretation*. Some accounts of educa-

This is an original article prepared for this book.

tion in Japan (Rosenbaum and Kariya 1989) and the United States (Bowles and Gintis 1976), for instance, suggest that schooling could just as plausibly be construed as a "structural" influence—a hierarchy of educational organizations designed to match young people to work organizations of varying prestige—as an individualistic characteristic measuring endowments, aptitudes, and abilities. Similarly, knowing that individuals have high or low tenure in a firm may tell us not only about their accumulated schooling and experience but also about the personnel policies of that organization. (Indeed, some organization-level research has used average firm tenure as a proxy for the presence of internal labor markets.) Occupational categories capture differences in job-related skills, the actions of socioeconomic institutions (e.g., unions and professional associations), and norms about the value and prestige of different work roles. In short, it quickly becomes difficult to know who should get credit for the explained variance associated with any effect, particularly because each camp often omits variables from its models that its rivals would regard as crucial for interpreting the results.

Ironically, perhaps the highly institutionalized nature of stratification research helped to obscure the distinction between mainstream and structuralist accounts. Wedded to the same data sets, variables, and methods as the mainstream attainment researchers were using, the structuralists had an avowed interest in the underlying structure of economic activity and social inequality that quickly became translated into a search for main effects of so-called structural variables and interactions with so-called individualistic variables (such as schooling). Rather than examine directly their theories' claims about the structure of economic activity and how it varies across contexts, the new structuralism has instead focused largely on who gets what, without providing very powerful tests of the underlying structural ideas: Many structural results could plausibly be embraced by mainstream researchers, while structuralists could plausibly claim that many nonfindings reflect data limitations, measurement imperfections, or omitted variables or are not central to the underlying theory.

For instance, would anyone jettison Marxists' notions about class structure in advanced societies if wage and status attainment did not vary across class categories (Wright and Perrone 1977)? To what extent does the claim of a monopolistic sector of ultrapowerful economic actors, put forward by such institutional economists as Averitt and Galbraith, really stand or fall on evidence disaggregating attainment by industry sectors (see Hodson and Kaufman 1982)? Numerous structuralist studies have disaggregated attainment and mobility models by economic sectors to try to document distinct segments of dominant and subordinate organizations, despite considerable theoretical and empirical work casting doubt on the very premise that the economy is so bifurcated (see Baron and Bielby 1984). Moreover, it remains unclear how or whether positive findings of labor market dualism or segmentation necessarily contradict conventional approaches.[1]

Yet there were not simply problems in executing the new structuralist agenda: The whole contrast between so-called structuralist and individualistic perspectives on stratification may have been either misunderstood or overdrawn. In the remainder of this essay, I suggest why and then propose ways that future studies of mobility and attainment might profitably attend to some issues emphasized by structuralist approaches.

Structural Concerns in Mobility and Attainment Research

As already noted, orthodox mobility and attainment studies were criticized as inattentive to the structural bases of inequality in modern societies.[2] Some of the readings in this section make it clear, however, that abiding concerns about social, economic, and political structure are central to the conventional mobility and attainment literatures, despite their empirical focus on the occupational movements of individuals. Admittedly, much of the early quantitative research on mobility and attainment diverged from these intellectual concerns and seemed concerned primarily with quantifying the extent of upward and downward mobility and making generic comparisons across demographic groups, time periods, and countries (cf. Sharlin 1979). More recently, however, mobility investigators have begun focusing explicitly on the macro forces influencing the layout and rules of the stratification game, such as economic development and political systems, which influence both the shape of the occupational distribution and individuals' relative mobility chances (e.g., Hout 1988; Grusky 1983; Grusky and Hauser 1984; Hauser and Grusky 1988; Ultee and Luijkx 1986; Gagliani 1985). This renewed interest in understanding what drives variations and commonalities in the occupational structure dovetails in some sense with the "new structuralism."

Moreover, it may also be dubious to brand classical mobility and status-attainment approaches as individualistic. If any theoretical framework underlies mobility and attainment studies, the main contender seems to be a Parsonsian view of the social order as progressively rationalizing and differentiating, fueling universalistic and achievement-based reward allocations (Blau and Duncan 1967, ch. 12). The functionalist flavor of this body of work is nicely conveyed in Turner's piece on sponsored and contest mobility (and in selections by Kingsley Davis and Wilbert E. Moore and by Donald Treiman elsewhere in this volume). Viewed in this way, the behavior of specific organizations and institutions becomes relatively nonproblematic, just as it was for human capital economists: If every firm is doing what is socially or economically adaptive, given competitive pressures and society's functional imperatives, its behavior essentially "washes out" and no longer represents a major constraint on individual mobility. This may explain the absence of such terms as *organization, company, firm, employment,* and *job* from the index of *The American Occupational Structure,* despite the fact that its first author is a premier organizational theorist.

Thus, critics who lambasted status-attainment and mobility research for being functionalist (e.g., Horan 1978) were right for the wrong reasons: That research is functionalist not because it employs occupational status scores or analyzes individual-level data but because of its assumptions about the macro forces shaping the allocation of personnel in postindustrial societies. The functional theory of stratification that underlies much of the mobility and status-attainment literature is, after all, a theory about the criteria used to reward and staff *positions* within an advanced division of labor. But it does not focus attention on variations among organizations, industries, industrial societies, and the like because the forces of universalism and rationalization are thought to be ubiquitous.[3]

Notice that these functionalist assumptions lead to straightforward predictions about stratification trends, which cannot be said for much of the "new structuralism." Recent studies of occupational mobility and status attainment have put those predictions to the test, examining, for instance, whether there is indeed a trend toward greater universalism in social mobility; whether economic development and social democratic policies influence propensities toward occupational inheritance and opportunities for upward mobility; and whether the rationalization of employment policies, prompted largely by government intervention, has made careers more meritocratic. In their reading in this section, Erikson and Goldthorpe (1992) argue against the "industrialism and expanding universalism" thesis, but there is compelling evidence that can be marshaled on both sides of the debate (e.g., Grusky 1983; Grusky and Hauser 1984; Hauser and Grusky 1988; Hout 1988; DiPrete and Grusky 1990).

One might thus apprehend in these recent cross-national and over-time analyses of mobility and status attainment a return to this literature's structural roots. (In referring to the "new structuralism," Bielby and I were being facetious, implying that much of this literature was simply rediscovering or relabeling earlier ideas and approaches [Baron and Bielby 1980]. Apparently, this was far from clear.) Critics of mobility and status-attainment orthodoxy may have underestimated that work's potential for illuminating structural concerns.

On the flip side, the new structuralists may have overpromised and underdelivered. Space does not permit here a comprehensive evaluation of the new structuralism (see Baron and Pfeffer 1993; Smith 1990). Instead, I merely offer three observations: First, despite increasing recognition that organizations play a critical role in generating stratification within capitalist economies, there has been relatively little explicit study of that role. To some extent, this may reflect how institutionalized certain kinds of data, variables, and methods have become in the stratification industry. Second, when students of stratification and mobility have considered organizational and institutional mechanisms generating stratification, they have tended not to study them directly but instead to infer them from wage and mobility patterns. Differences in attainment across industrial sectors, social classes, occupations, firms, and the like are treated as evidence of some imperative shaping stratification—such as the economic and political clout of core firms, the hegemony of owners and managers, or a systematic devaluation of occupations staffed by women or nonwhites—but researchers' stories about the mechanisms generating stratification are seldom put to explicit or meaningful tests (for a similar evaluation, see Aage Sørensen's comments in Swedberg [1990]).

Third, the stories told by the new structuralists are surprisingly economistic. This literature has focused almost exclusively on the scale, technology, unionization, and market power of firms and industries in explaining differential wages and promotion regimes. The new structuralist sociology has documented that wage and occupational attainment is not homogeneous across industries and organizations, often using better data than the economists have analyzed. To show that wages are higher in firms that are large, technically advanced, unionized, and dominant in product markets is certainly worthwhile but leaves unanswered the question of why this is so. Economists have known for some time about these wage differences and propounded explanations for them. There is seldom much that is distinctly *sociological* in the structuralists' explanations of those variations. Does the new structuralism amount to anything more than the old institutional labor economics?

The structuralists may have gone astray in divorcing their interest in institutions from any concern with the social-psychological and relational dimensions of stratification, which figured so prominently in the classical viewpoints and in

such pioneering empirical inquiries as the study of Sewell, Haller, and Portes (1969). The structuralists tend to castigate labor economists and status-attainment researchers because it is difficult to discern *structure* in their analyses. One could just as easily fault the structuralists on the grounds that it is difficult to discern *individuals* and *social interaction* in their accounts. Aside from academic posturing, is there any reason why individual (including social-psychological) and structural sources of social inequality need to be framed as mutually exclusive?

For instance, the new structuralism has put much more emphasis than earlier work on the role that organizational contexts play in generating stratification. Recent research has documented that organizations differ systematically in the ways they organize work, assign rewards to roles, and staff positions and that these variations have important implications for the distribution of economic and noneconomic rewards. However, the organizational context is important not simply because it influences the resources available to be distributed to workers, the amount of education required for job mobility, and the like but also because it influences what workers come to value, how they gauge their attainments relative to various comparison groups, and so on. MacLeod's (1987) description of the Hallway Hangers and the Brothers makes this point quite poignantly: These two groups of young men differ less in the objective circumstances of their existence than in the way those circumstances (especially race) influence the standards, benchmarks, and dimensions they use in assessing what is possible and thus what is desirable. Similarly, schools differ not only in the educational resources they make available to students (e.g., class size, teacher quality) but also in how they track students and thus influence who comes into contact with whom and how students form educational and occupational aspirations. The same is true within work organizations—the presence of a union, for instance, influences not only objective opportunities available to workers but also social relations among workers and thus the kinds of reactions workers are likely to have to those rewards and opportunities.

This point is especially important if one bears in mind how much attention the classical viewpoints devoted to the *consequences* of social mobility. The readings by Lipset, Bendix, and Zetterberg (1964)[4] and by Goldthorpe (1987) highlight the long-standing interest of sociologists in mobility because of its putative implications for politics, life-styles, social integration, and the like. Accordingly, researchers cannot ignore the factors that influence workers' relative standing within local hierarchies, as well as their comparison groups, aspiration levels, and other subjective dimensions of career achievement, for these are likely to be critical in determining the various outcomes that accompany, if not motivate, (im)mobility.

Where Do We Go from Here?

One might be tempted to contrast the mainstream and new structuralist approaches in terms of what statisticians call "reduced-form" versus "structural-form" modeling approaches.[5] Structuralists have chastised mainstream approaches for paying inadequate attention to the underlying structures responsible for individual-level relationships among such variables as social origins, schooling, and income. However, I have implied that this contrast may be overstated. I have argued that the conceptual framework underlying status-attainment research is "structural" in a sociological sense, whether or not the analyses have been "structural" in the statistical sense. In other words, the trends and relationships among variables observed in attainment studies are seen to reflect fundamental transformations in the linkages among the institutions of family, education, work, and the polity in advanced economies rather than, say, innate differences (Sorokin 1959; Blau and Duncan 1967). Moreover, I have noted how work on mobility and attainment has recently become more structural in the statistical sense, modeling explicitly the structural forces that generate variations in mobility and attainment. At the same time, my review of the new structuralism has implied that much of it reflects its own brand of reduced-form analysis, in which the institutions, mechanisms, and processes re-

sponsible for structural effects on labor market outcomes remain largely unexplored. Let me conclude with a few scattered thoughts about avenues the mobility and attainment literature—structuralist or otherwise—might profitably explore in the future.

Because survey respondents can rank the prestige or status of occupations with some consensus and stability over time, researchers have come to believe that this is the right way to conceptualize and measure labor market position. Yet Lipset, Bendix, and Zetterberg (1964), like many theorists before and after them, emphasized the importance of local status hierarchies and competing dimensions of social standing. They noted that much of the status mobility taking place within and between generations might appear "horizontal" in the typical occupation-based analyses of stratification and mobility. Consistent with their claim, Baron, Davis-Blake, and Bielby (1986) found that most organizational promotion ladders were circumscribed *within* detailed occupations. Moreover, they encountered firms having open bidding systems combined with a strict policy of internal promotion, where promotion ladders linked clerical and technical positions to production jobs in order to provide advancement opportunities for male clerks and technicians who otherwise would have reached dead ends. These promotions would be classified as downward moves in studies of intragenerational career mobility relying on occupational distinctions. The focus on global dimensions of stratification—income and occupational status—has advanced the study of mobility in recent decades but at the cost of ignoring local dimensions of status and the social and psychological benchmarks governing career aspirations, decisions, and satisfactions. (One would have thought this point would be self-evident to any academic who has fretted about getting tenure or agonized over the choice between job offers at different universities.)

Researchers' preoccupation with standard occupational classification schemes and status scales has also obscured the fact that structural and social-psychological forces influence the way work roles are defined in particular settings, which means that workers doing the same tasks in different settings may not even belong to the same standard occupational category because organizations define the same role differently. In a sample of California establishments that William Bielby and I studied, for instance, organizations having only one full-time personnel specialist tended to classify that person as a personnel *manager or administrator* if he was male and as a *clerk* if female (Baron 1992; also see Bridges and Nelson 1989). This evidence is reminiscent of Margo Conk's (1978) evidence about how race and other cultural stereotypes helped frame the original distinctions among skilled, semiskilled, and unskilled occupations created by Alba Edwards in designing the U.S. census classification scheme.

In other words, how work activities get classified into job categories (and, eventually, into occupations) depends considerably on who is doing the work and who is doing the classifying. Most workers do not move through "the occupational structure" but rather through structures and sequences of jobs, which are social labels attached to work activities done by specific actors in particular settings. Recent research has shown how the way positions are defined and labeled in a specific setting influences, in turn, the rewards and opportunities available to incumbents in ways that would be masked in studies employing conventional occupational taxonomies and data sets that do not illuminate the context of employment (see Baron 1992).

Of course, the theoretical justification for focusing on occupations can be traced back to Weber, who argued that classes should be delineated in terms of differential *market capacities,* particularly skills, which researchers subsequently came to equate with differences across occupations. Moreover, to the extent that members of different occupational groups characteristically exhibit distinct styles of life (e.g., similar wages, education levels, leisure activities), then occupational groups approximate Weber's concept of *status groups.*

However, social and economic developments might be weakening somewhat the link between occupations on the one hand and market capacities and styles of life on the other. First, the very notion and logic of an "occupation" has to some extent become institutionalized and diffused throughout the economy, blurring the boundaries among occupational categories. Many semiprofessional, lower-level white-collar, and even blue-collar lines of work now seek to organize themselves along lines similar to the traditional autonomous professionals—generating educational and training-based entry requirements, adopting distinctive languages and codes of conduct, and so on, with the objective of reducing their social and economic distance from the well-established professions. At the same time, work traditionally done by autonomous professionals increasingly is controlled by large bureaucracies and complex technological systems; the result is a blurring of some of the differences in status, autonomy, and training that occupations have been presumed to capture. (The growing prevalence of temporary personnel services specializing in the placement of high-status legal, medical, financial, and other professionals in organizations on a contract basis is testimony to this trend.) We might therefore expect to observe less conspicuous differences in working conditions, economic opportunities, and subjective experiences across nominally different occupations.

Second, organizational differentiation has increased dramatically since Weber (or even many of his disciples) wrote (see Stinchcombe 1965). There is not only a much wider range of organizational sizes and forms devoted to any given type of activity but no doubt a wider range of technologies and organizational "cultures" as well. To the extent this is true, we would expect correspondingly greater organization-based variations in work arrangements, career opportunities, and rewards among those employed within the same occupation (see Jencks et al. 1988).

Third, within the United States, regional variations in housing prices (which dwarf regional variations in wages) now mean that two practitioners of the same occupation making roughly the same wage but located in distinct parts of the country can be in dramatically different situations with respect to style of life. These variations in housing markets also mean that an important vehicle for intergenerational transmission of privilege may no longer coincide with occupation—namely, home equity, which can be used to fund education, housing, or business opportunities for one's offspring.

Fourth, a number of developments seem to be pushing organizations toward treating workers performing different occupations more similarly, in which case organizational affiliation is presumably becoming increasingly important relative to occupational affiliation. Standards of internal equity, the rise of strong affiliative organizational cultures, a preoccupation with cross-training and labor flexibility in order to deal with anticipated labor shortages, and legal restrictions mandating comparable treatment of all organizational members (e.g., in benefit and pension plans) are examples of forces that might blur differences in opportunity and treatment across occupations within a given organization. Recent economic research corroborates that high- (low-) wage firms and industries tend to pay high (low) wages in *all* occupations (see Thaler 1989), and that establishment differentials in wages dwarf occupational ones, at least within manufacturing (Groshen 1991, 1992).

These observations suggest that the role of occupations as the building blocks of stratification may itself vary across time and space (see Kalleberg and Lincoln 1988). This is a potentially troubling assertion, however, given its implications for comparative research: A number of the readings included in this section are testimony to the progress that has been made by imposing common and invariant metrics of mobility and attainment on different nation-states. (An equally vexing possibility is that national boundaries are themselves of diminishing relevance to stratification in a world of global competition, instantaneous communication, inexpensive transportation, international trade alliances, extraordinary international migration, multinational conglomerates, wildly fluctuating exchange rates, and extensive political intervention in the economy.)

In sum, mobility and attainment researchers have been very successful in refining their measurements of some of the "surface phenomena" concerning stratification—specifically, the movement of individuals through the occupational and wage structure—but less so in refining and developing their theories about the "deep structures" that generate those movements. We have many more coherent findings now about how specific variables affect mobility or attainment than we have coherent stories about why (and under what circumstances) those results obtain. Broad notions about industrialism, democratization, economic development, and expanding universalism, which undergirded most of the initial work on mobility and status-attainment processes, have received some—but hardly overwhelming—support from empirical studies. Other theoretical perspectives, such as neo-Marxism and economic segmentation, have been no more successful in their liaisons with data. None of them seems to provide a parsimonious and compelling account of the origins, patterning, trend, or consequences of inequality.

Attending to the organizational context of attainment is likely to change significantly our understandings about what generates stratification and what its consequences are. It may also change our estimates of the extent of mobility and inequality. Recent studies of trends in occupational and pay inequality by race and sex, for instance, demonstrate that attending to the organizational context of employment is likely to affect one's assessments of how much progress toward racial and gender equality has occurred, where, and why (e.g., Smith and Welch 1984; Bridges and Nelson 1989; Baron 1992). Predictions about the future of racial and gender equality are in large part predictions about how work organizations respond to changes in their environments. Moreover, perhaps researchers have been frustrated in searching for pervasive *consequences* of occupational standing and mobility (e.g., Davis 1982) because they have focused on global occupational position rather than on standing within more local organizational hierarchies.

What may therefore be called for is a reshaping not only of the phenomena analyzed and data and methods employed by students of mobility and attainment but also of our theories about what shapes stratification and economic activity in the first place. The conventional mobility and attainment approaches, which have served us well, may not be capable of addressing a number of the issues I have highlighted. Nevertheless, I realize the danger of throwing the baby out with the bath water. In the final analysis, as Thomas Kuhn

(1970, 157–158) writes: "The issue is which paradigm should in the future guide research on problems many of which neither competitor can yet claim to resolve completely. ... [That] decision must be based less on past achievement than future promise. ... A decision of that kind can only be made on faith."

Notes

David Featherman, Robert Hauser, and Christopher Jencks provided helpful comments on a draft of this essay. Conversations with Jeffrey Pfeffer have influenced my thinking on many issues discussed here. David Grusky made numerous insightful comments, provided stimulating conversation, and displayed extraordinary patience. I also gratefully acknowledge generous research support from the Stanford Graduate School of Business, including faculty fellowships from Robert M. and Anne T. Bass and the Business School Trust.

1. Many segmentation studies seem targeted at economists' notions of a perfectly competitive market more than at sociologists' assumptions regarding status-attainment processes. Different rates of return to individual and job characteristics have been interpreted as evidence that not all workers were governed by the same labor market regime. I doubt many labor economists would quarrel with the notion that corporate lawyers and housekeepers compete in different labor markets or with many other findings from dualist and segmentation studies (e.g., Lang and Dickens 1988; Farkas et al. 1988; Smith 1990). In my view, other structuralist studies speak more directly to assumptions underlying traditional attainment research, such as research showing how organizations differ in their reliance on social origins, schooling, and other factors in allocating people to jobs (e.g., Pfeffer 1977; Stolzenberg 1978; Collins 1979; Cohen and Pfeffer 1986). These studies underscore that any general trend toward increased universalism and rationalization masks tremendous diversity among organizations in technical, cultural, institutional, and other forces shaping job allocation regimes.

2. Some of this criticism may reflect the political climate of the 1960s and 1970s, in which studies focusing on the effects of schooling, IQ, aspirations, and the like were sometimes perceived by social critics as placing credit or blame for career success largely on individuals rather than on the "system." Some of the disapproval might also have reflected the novelty of the research methods and statistical techniques employed.

3. An alternative functionalist approach, based on neo-Marxism, has underpinned some studies of mobility and attainment (e.g., by Erik Wright and economists Bowles and Gintis). Here too the focus is on linking large-scale economic and political developments to patterns of labor market achievement. However, different predictions are made about the direction, relative importance, and distribution of effects throughout the population (see Baron and Bielby 1980).

4. This reading is listed in the references under the Lipset and Bendix (1964) book, one chapter of which was written by Lipset and Zetterberg.

5. In "reduced-form" analyses, the underlying influences or processes responsible for the association between two variables (such as social origins and income) are not directly modeled; by contrast, "structural-form" analyses explicitly represent those underlying forces. As Duncan (1975, 61) notes: "If one cared to know only the *total* effect of the exogenous variable on a dependent variable, the reduced-form coefficient tells the whole story. But if one is interested in how that effect comes about, the greater detail of the structural model is informative. After all, in the reduced form, a great deal of the 'structure' is buried."

References

Baron, James N. 1992. "Organizational Evidence of Ascription in Labor Markets." Pp. 113–143 in Richard Cornwall and Phanindra Wunnava, eds., *New Approaches to Economic and Social Analyses of Discrimination.* New York: Praeger.

Baron, James N., and William T. Bielby. 1980. "Bringing the Firms Back In: Stratification, Segmentation, and the Organization of Work." *American Sociological Review* 45 (October): 737–765.

———. 1984. "The Organization of Work in a Segmented Economy." *American Sociological Review* 49 (August): 454–473.

Baron, James N., Alison Davis-Blake, and William T. Bielby. 1986. "The Structure of Opportunity: How Promotion Ladders Vary Within and Among Organizations." *Administrative Science Quarterly* 31 (June): 248–273.

Baron, James N., and Jeffrey Pfeffer. 1993. "The Social Psychology of Organizations and Inequality." Unpublished manuscript, Graduate School of Business, Stanford University.

Blau, Peter M., and Otis D. Duncan. 1967. *The American Occupational Structure.* New York: Wiley.

Bowles, Samuel, and Herbert Gintis. 1976. *Schooling in Capitalist America.* New York: Basic.

Bridges, William P., and Robert L. Nelson. 1989. "Markets in Hierarchies: Organizational and Market Influences on Gender Inequality in a State Pay System." *American Journal of Sociology* 95 (November): 616–658.

Cohen, Yinon, and Jeffrey Pfeffer. 1986. "Organizational Hiring Standards." *Administrative Science Quarterly* 31:1–24.

Collins, Randall. 1979. *The Credential Society.* New York: Academic.

Conk, Margo A. 1978. "Occupational Classification in the United States Census: 1870–1940." *Journal of Interdisciplinary History* 9:111–130.

Davis, James A. 1982. "Achievement Variables and Class Cultures: Family, Schooling, Job, and Forty-nine Dependent Variables in the Cumulative GSS." *American Sociological Review* 47 (October): 569–586.

DiPrete, Thomas A., and David B. Grusky. 1990. "Structure and Trend in the Process of Stratification for American Men and Women." *American Journal of Sociology* 96 (July): 107–143.

Duncan, Otis D. 1975. *Introduction to Structural Equation Models.* New York: Academic.

Erikson, Robert, and John H. Goldthorpe. 1992. *The Constant Flux: A Study of Class Mobility in Industrial Societies.* Oxford: Clarendon Press.

Farkas, George, Paula England, and Margaret Barton. 1988. "Structural Effects upon Wages: Sociological and Economic Views." Pp. 93–112 in George Farkas and Paula England, eds., *Industries, Firms, and Jobs: Sociological and Economic Approaches.* New York: Plenum.

Featherman, David L. 1981. "Social Stratification and Mobility: Two Decades of Cumulative Social Science." *American Behavioral Scientist* 24 (January-February): 364–385.

Gagliani, Giorgio. 1985. "Long-term Changes in the Occupational Structure." *European Sociological Review* 1 (December): 183–210.

Goldthorpe, John H. 1987. *Social Mobility and Class Structure in Modern Britain.* 2d ed. Oxford: Clarendon Press.

Groshen, Erica L. 1991. "Five Reasons Why Wages Vary Among Employers: A Review of the Literature." *Industrial Relations* 30 (3): 350–381.

———. 1992. "The Structure of the Female/Male Wage Differential: Is It Who You Are, What You Do, or Where You Work?" *Journal of Human Resources* 27 (3): 457–472.

Grusky, David B. 1983. "Industrialization and the Status-Attainment Process: The Thesis of Industrialism Reconsidered." *American Sociological Review* 48 (August): 494–506.

Grusky, David B., and Robert M. Hauser. 1984. "Comparative Social Mobility Revisited: Models of Convergence and Divergence in Sixteen Countries." *American Sociological Review* 49 (February): 19–38.

Hauser, Robert M., and David B. Grusky. 1988. "Cross-National Variation in Occupational Distributions, Relative Mobility Chances, and Intergenerational Shifts in Occupational Distributions." *American Sociological Review* 53 (October): 723–741.

Hodson, Randy, and Robert L. Kaufman. 1982. "Economic Dualism: A Critical Review." *American Sociological Review* 47:727–739.

Horan, Patrick M. 1978. "Is Status-Attainment Research Atheoretical?" *American Sociological Review* 43 (August): 534–541.

Hout, Michael. 1988. "More Universalism, Less Structural Mobility: The American Occupational Structure in the 1980s." *American Journal of Sociology* 93 (May): 1358–1400.

Jencks, Christopher, Lauri Perman, and Lee Rainwater. 1988. "What Is a Good Job? A New Measure of Labor-Market Success." *American Journal of Sociology* 93 (May): 1322–1357.

Kalleberg, Arne L., and James R. Lincoln. 1988. "The Structure of Earnings Inequality in the United States and Japan." *American Journal of Sociology* 94 (Supplement): S121–S153.

Kuhn, Thomas S. 1970. *The Structure of Scientific Revolutions.* 2d ed. Chicago: University of Chicago Press.

Lang, Kevin, and William T. Dickens. 1988. "Neoclassical and Sociological Perspectives on Segmented Labor Markets." Pp. 65–88 in George Farkas and Paula England, eds., *Industries, Firms, and Jobs: Sociological and Economic Approaches.* New York: Plenum.

Lipset, Seymour Martin, and Reinhard Bendix. 1964. *Social Mobility in Industrial Society.* Berkeley and Los Angeles: University of California Press.

MacLeod, Jay. 1987. *Ain't No Makin' It: Leveled Aspirations in a Low-Income Neighborhood.* Boulder, Colo.: Westview.

Pfeffer, Jeffrey. 1977. "Toward an Examination of Stratification in Organizations." *Administrative Science Quarterly* 22:553–567.

Rosenbaum, James E., and Takehiro Kariya. 1989. "From High School to Work: Market and Institutional Mechanisms in Japan." *American Journal of Sociology* 94:1334–1365.

Sewell, William H., Archibald O. Haller, and Alejandro Portes. 1969. "The Educational and Early Occupational Attainment Process." *American Sociological Review* 34:82–92.

Sharlin, Allan. 1979. "From the Study of Social Mobility to the Study of Society." *American Journal of Sociology* 85:338–360.

Smith, James P., and Finis Welch. 1984. "Affirmative Action and Labor Markets." *Journal of Labor Economics* 2 (2): 269–301.

Smith, Michael R. 1990. "What Is New in 'New Structuralist' Analyses of Earnings?" *American Sociological Review* 55 (December): 827–841.

Sorokin, Pitirim A. 1959. *Social and Cultural Mobility.* New York: Free Press.

Stinchcombe, Arthur L. 1965. "Social Structure and Organizations." Pp. 142–193 in J. G. March, ed., *Handbook of Organizations.* Chicago: Rand McNally.

Stolzenberg, Ross M. 1978. "Bringing the Boss Back in: Employer Size, Employee Schooling, and Socioeconomic Achievement." *American Sociological Review* 43:813–828.

Swedberg, Richard. 1990. *Economics and Sociology.* Princeton, N.J.: Princeton University Press.

Thaler, Richard H. 1989. "Anomalies: Interindustry Wage Differentials." *Journal of Economic Perspectives* 3 (Spring): 181–193.

Ultee, Wout, and Ruud Luijkx. 1986. "Intergenerational Standard-of-Living Mobility in Nine EEC Countries: Country Characteristics, Competitive Balance, and Social Fluidity." *European Sociological Review* 2 (December): 191–207.

Wright, Erik O., and Luca Perrone. 1977. "Marxist Class Categories and Income Inequality." *American Sociological Review* 42:32–55.

Part V
The Consequences of Stratification

Life-Styles and Consumption Patterns

Attitudes and Personalities

THORSTEIN VEBLEN

The Theory of the Leisure Class

Pecuniary Emulation

The end of acquisition and accumulation is conventionally held to be the consumption of the goods accumulated—whether it is consumption directly by the owner of the goods or by the household attached to him and for this purpose identified with him in theory. This is at least felt to be the economically legitimate end of acquisition, which alone it is incumbent on the theory to take account of. Such consumption may of course be conceived to serve the consumer's physical wants—his physical comfort—or his so-called higher wants—spiritual, æsthetic, intellectual, or what not; the latter class of wants being served indirectly by an expenditure of goods, after the fashion familiar to all economic readers.

But it is only when taken in a sense far removed from its naïve meaning that consumption of goods can be said to afford the incentive from which accumulation invariably proceeds. The motive that lies at the root of ownership is emulation; and the same motive of emulation continues active in the further development of the institution to which it has given rise and in the development of all those features of the social structure which this institution of ownership touches. The possession of wealth confers honor; it is an invidious distinction. Nothing equally cogent can be said for the consumption of goods, nor for any other conceivable incentive to acquisition, and especially not for any incentive to the accumulation of wealth.

It is of course not to be overlooked that in a community where nearly all goods are private property the necessity of earning a livelihood is a powerful and ever-present incentive for the poorer members of the community. The need of subsistence and of an increase of physical comfort may for a time be the dominant motive of acquisition for those classes who are habitually employed at manual labor, whose subsistence is on a precarious footing, who possess little and ordinarily accumulate little; but it will appear in the course of the discussion that even in the case of these impecunious classes the predominance of the motive of physical want is not so decided as has sometimes been assumed. On the other hand, so far as regards those members and classes of the community who are chiefly concerned in the accumulation of wealth, the incentive of subsistence or of physical comfort never plays a considerable part. Ownership began and grew into a human institution on grounds unrelated to the subsistence minimum. The dominant incentive was from the outset the invidious distinction attaching to wealth, and, save temporarily and by exception, no other motive has usurped the primacy at any later stage of the development. ...

In any community where goods are held in severalty it is necessary, in order to ensure his own peace of mind, that an individual should possess as large a portion of goods as others with whom he is accustomed to class himself; and it is extremely gratifying to possess something more than others. But as fast as a person makes new acquisitions, and becomes accustomed to the resulting new standard of wealth, the new standard forthwith ceases to afford appreciably greater satisfaction than the earlier standard did. The tendency in any case is constantly to make the present pecuniary standard the point of departure for a fresh increase of wealth; and this in turn gives rise to a new standard of sufficiency and a new pecuniary classification of one's self as compared with one's neighbors. So far as concerns the present question, the end sought by accumulation is to rank high in comparison with the rest of the community in point of pecuniary strength. So long as the comparison is distinctly unfavorable to himself, the normal, average individual will live in chronic dissatisfaction with his present lot; and when he has reached what may be called the normal pecuniary standard of the community, or of his class in the community, this chronic dissatisfaction will give place to a restless straining to place a wider and ever-widening pecuniary interval between himself and this average standard. The invidious comparison can never become so favorable to the individual making it that he would not gladly rate himself still higher relatively to his competitors in the struggle for pecuniary reputability.

In the nature of the case, the desire for wealth can scarcely be satiated in any individual instance, and evidently a satiation of the average or general desire for wealth is out of the question. However widely, or equally, or "fairly," it may be distributed, no general increase of the community's wealth can make any approach to satiating this need, the ground of which is the desire of everyone to excel everyone else in the accumulation of goods. If, as is sometimes assumed, the incentive to accumulation were the want of subsistence or of physical comfort, then the aggregate economic wants of a community might conceivably be satisfied at some point in the advance of industrial efficiency; but since the struggle is substantially a race for reputability on the basis of an invidious comparison, no approach to a definitive attainment is possible.

What has just been said must not be taken to mean that there are no other incentives to acquisition and accumulation than this desire to excel in pecuniary standing and so gain the esteem and envy of one's fellowmen. The desire for added comfort and security from want is present as a motive at every stage of the process of accumulation in a modern industrial community; although the standard of sufficiency in these respects is in turn greatly affected by the habit of pecuniary emulation. To a great extent this emulation shapes the methods and selects the objects of expenditure for personal comfort and decent livelihood.

Besides this, the power conferred by wealth also affords a motive to accumulation. That propensity for purposeful activity and that repugnance to all futility of effort which belong to man by virtue of his character as an agent do not desert him when he emerges from the naïve communal culture where the dominant note of life is the unanalyzed and undifferentiated solidarity of the individual with the group with which his life is bound up. When he enters upon the predatory stage, where self-seeking in the narrower sense becomes the dominant note, this propensity goes with him still, as the pervasive trait that shapes his scheme of life. The propensity for achievement and the repugnance to futility remain the underlying economic motive. The propensity changes only in the form of its expression and in the proximate objects to which it directs the man's activity. Under the regime of individual ownership the most available means of visibly achieving a purpose is that afforded by the acquisition and accumulation of goods; and as the self-regarding antithesis between man and man reaches fuller consciousness, the propensity for achievement—the instinct of workmanship—tends more and more to shape itself into a straining to excel others in pecuniary achievement. Relative success, tested by an invidious pecuniary comparison with other men, becomes the conventional end of action. The currently accepted legitimate end of effort becomes the achievement of a favorable comparison with other men; and therefore the repugnance to futility to a good extent coalesces with the incentive of emulation. It acts to accentuate the struggle for pecuniary reputability by visiting with a sharper disapproval all shortcoming and all evidence of shortcoming in point of pecuniary success. Purposeful effort comes to mean, primarily, effort directed to or resulting in a more creditable showing of accumulated wealth.

Among the motives which lead men to accumulate wealth, the primacy, both in scope and intensity, therefore, continues to belong to this motive of pecuniary emulation.

In making use of the term "invidious," it may perhaps be unnecessary to remark, there is no intention to extol or depreciate, or to commend or deplore any of the phenomena which the word is used to characterize. The term is used in a technical sense as describing a comparison of persons with a view to rating and grading them in respect of relative worth or value—in an æsthetic or moral sense—and so awarding and defining the relative degrees of complacency with which they may legitimately be contemplated by themselves and by others. An invidious comparison is a process of valuation of persons in respect of worth.

Conspicuous Leisure

If its working were not disturbed by other economic forces or other features of the emulative process, the immediate effect of such a pecuniary struggle as has just been described in outline would be to make men industrious and frugal. This result actually follows, in some measure, so far as regards the lower classes, whose ordinary means of acquiring goods is productive labor. This is more especially true of the laboring classes in a sedentary community which is at an agricultural stage of industry, in which there is a considerable subdivision of property, and whose laws and customs secure to these classes a more or less definite share of the product of their industry. These lower classes can in any case not avoid labor, and the imputation of labor is therefore not greatly derogatory to them, at least not within their class. Rather, since labor is their recognized and accepted mode of life, they take some emulative pride in a reputation for efficiency in their work, this being often the only line of emulation that is open to them. For those for whom acquisition and emulation is possible only within the field of productive efficiency and thrift, the struggle for pecuniary reputability will in some measure work out in an increase of diligence and parsimony. But certain secondary features of the emulative process, yet to be spoken of, come in to

very materially circumscribe and modify emulation in these directions among the pecuniarily inferior classes as well as among the superior class.

But it is otherwise with the superior pecuniary class, with which we are here immediately concerned. For this class also the incentive to diligence and thrift is not absent; but its action is so greatly qualified by the secondary demands of pecuniary emulation, that any inclination in this direction is practically overborne and any incentive to diligence tends to be of no effect. The most imperative of these secondary demands of emulation, as well as the one of widest scope, is the requirement of abstention from productive work. … During the predatory culture labor comes to be associated in men's habits of thought with weakness and subjection to a master. It is therefore a mark of inferiority, and therefore comes to be accounted unworthy of man in his best estate. By virtue of this tradition labor is felt to be debasing, and this tradition has never died out. On the contrary, with the advance of social differentiation it has acquired the axiomatic force due to ancient and unquestioned prescription.

In order to gain and to hold the esteem of men it is not sufficient merely to possess wealth or power. The wealth or power must be put in evidence, for esteem is awarded only on evidence. And not only does the evidence of wealth serve to impress one's importance on others and to keep their sense of importance alive and alert, but it is of scarcely less use in building up and preserving one's self-complacency. In all but the lowest stages of culture the normally constituted man is comforted and upheld in his self-respect by "decent surroundings" and by exemption from "menial offices." Enforced departure from his habitual standard of decency, either in the paraphernalia of life or in the kind and amount of his everyday activity, is felt to be a slight upon his human dignity, even apart from all conscious consideration of the approval or disapproval of his fellows.

The archaic theoretical distinction between the base and the honorable in the manner of a man's life retains very much of its ancient force even today. So much so that there are few of the better class who are not possessed of an instinctive repugnance for the vulgar forms of labor. We have a realizing sense of ceremonial uncleanness attaching in an especial degree to the occupations which are associated in our habits of thought with menial service. It is felt by all persons of refined taste that a spiritual contamination is inseparable from certain offices that are conventionally required of servants. Vulgar surroundings, mean (that is to say, inexpensive) habitations, and vulgarly productive occupations are unhesitatingly condemned and avoided. They are incompatible with life on a satisfactory spiritual plane—with "high thinking." From the days of the Greek philosophers to the present, a degree of leisure and of exemption from contact with such industrial processes as serve the immediate everyday purposes of human life has ever been recognized by thoughtful men as a prerequisite to a worthy or beautiful, or even a blameless, human life. In itself and in its consequences the life of leisure is beautiful and ennobling in all civilized men's eyes.

This direct, subjective value of leisure and of other evidences of wealth is no doubt in great part secondary and derivative. It is in part a reflex of the utility of leisure as a means of gaining the respect of others, and in part it is the result of a mental substitution. The performance of labor has been accepted as a conventional evidence of inferior force; therefore it comes itself, by a mental shortcut, to be regarded as intrinsically base. ...

Conspicuous Consumption

In the earlier phases of the predatory culture the only economic differentiation is a broad distinction between an honorable superior class made up of the able-bodied men on the one side, and a base inferior class of laboring women on the other. According to the ideal scheme of life in force at that time it is the office of the men to consume what the women produce. Such consumption as falls to the women is merely incidental to their work; it is a means to their continued labor, and not a consumption directed to their own comfort and fullness of life. Unproductive consumption of goods is honorable, primarily as a mark of prowess and a perquisite of human dignity; secondarily it becomes substantially honorable in itself, especially the consumption of the

more desirable things. The consumption of choice articles of food, and frequently also of rare articles of adornment, becomes tabu to the women and children; and if there is a base (servile) class of men, the tabu holds also for them. With a further advance in culture this tabu may change into simple custom of a more or less rigorous character; but whatever be the theoretical basis of the distinction which is maintained, whether it be a tabu or a larger conventionality, the features of the conventional scheme of consumption do not change easily. When the quasi-peaceable stage of industry is reached, with its fundamental institution of chattel slavery, the general principle, more or less rigorously applied, is that the base, industrious class should consume only what may be necessary to their subsistence. In the nature of things, luxuries and the comforts of life belong to the leisure class. Under the tabu, certain victuals, and more particularly certain beverages, are strictly reserved for the use of the superior class. ...

As wealth accumulates, the leisure class develops further in function and structure, and there arises a differentiation within the class. There is a more or less elaborate system of rank and grades. This differentiation is furthered by the inheritance of wealth and the consequent inheritance of gentility. With the inheritance of gentility goes the inheritance of obligatory leisure; and gentility of a sufficient potency to entail a life of leisure may be inherited without the complement of wealth required to maintain a dignified leisure. Gentle blood may be transmitted without goods enough to afford a reputably free consumption at one's ease. Hence results a class of impecunious gentlemen of leisure. These half-caste gentlemen of leisure fall into a system of hierarchical gradations. Those who stand near the higher and the highest grades of the wealthy leisure class, in point of birth, or in point of wealth, or both, outrank the remoter-born and the pecuniarily weaker. These lower grades, especially the impecunious, or marginal, gentlemen of leisure, affiliate themselves by a system of dependence or fealty to the great ones; by so doing they gain an increment of repute, or of the means with which to lead a life of leisure, from their patron. They become his courtiers or retainers, servants; and being fed and countenanced by their patron they are indices of his rank and vicarious consumers of his superfluous wealth. Many of these affiliated gentlemen of leisure are at the same time lesser men of substance in their own right; so that some of them are scarcely at all, others only partially, to be rated as vicarious consumers. So many of them, however, as make up the retainers and hangers-on of the patron may be classed as vicarious consumers without qualification. Many of these again, and also many of the other aristocracy of less degree, have in turn attached to their persons a more or less comprehensive group of vicarious consumers in the persons of their wives and children, their servants, retainers, etc.

Throughout this graduated scheme of vicarious leisure and vicarious consumption the rule holds that these offices must be performed in some such manner, or under some such circumstance or insignia, as shall point plainly to the master to whom this leisure or consumption pertains, and to whom therefore the resulting increment of good repute of right inures. The consumption and leisure executed by these persons for their master or patron represents an investment on his part with a view to an increase of good fame. ...

With the disappearance of servitude, the number of vicarious consumers attached to any one gentleman tends, on the whole, to decrease. The like is of course true, and perhaps in a still higher degree, of the number of dependents who perform vicarious leisure for him. In a general way, though not wholly nor consistently, these two groups coincide. The dependent who was first delegated for these duties was the wife, or the chief wife; and, as would be expected, in the later development of the institution, when the number of persons by whom these duties are customarily performed gradually narrows, the wife remains the last. In the higher grades of society a large volume of both these kinds of service is required; and here the wife is of course still assisted in the work by a more or less numerous corps of menials. But as we descend the social scale, the point is presently reached where the duties of vicarious leisure and consumption devolve upon the wife alone. In the communities of the Western culture,

this point is at present found among the lower middle class.

And here occurs a curious inversion. It is a fact of common observance that in this lower middle class there is no pretense of leisure on the part of the head of the household. Through force of circumstances it has fallen into disuse. But the middle-class wife still carries on the business of vicarious leisure, for the good name of the household and its master. In descending the social scale in any modern industrial community, the primary fact—the conspicuous leisure of the master of the household—disappears at a relatively high point. The head of the middle-class household has been reduced by economic circumstances to turn his hand to gaining a livelihood by occupations which often partake largely of the character of industry, as in the case of the ordinary business man of today. But the derivative fact—the vicarious leisure and consumption rendered by the wife, and the auxiliary vicarious performance of leisure by menials—remains in vogue as a conventionality which the demands of reputability will not suffer to be slighted. It is by no means an uncommon spectacle to find a man applying himself to work with the utmost assiduity, in order that his wife may in due form render for him that degree of vicarious leisure which the common sense of the time demands.

The leisure rendered by the wife in such cases is, of course, not a simple manifestation of idleness or indolence. It almost invariably occurs disguised under some form of work or household duties or social amenities, which prove on analysis to serve little or no ulterior end beyond showing that she does not occupy herself with anything that is gainful or that is of substantial use. The greater part of the customary round of domestic cares to which the middle-class housewife gives her time and effort is of this character. Not that the results of her attention to household matters, of a decorative and mundificatory character, are not pleasing to the sense of men trained in middle-class proprieties; but the taste to which these effects of household adornment and tidiness appeal is a taste which has been formed under the selective guidance of a canon of propriety that demands just these evidences of wasted effort. The effects are pleasing to us chiefly because we have been taught to find them pleasing. There goes into these domestic duties much solicitude for a proper combination of form and color, and for other ends that are to be classed as æsthetic in the proper sense of the term; and it is not denied that effects having some substantial æsthetic value are sometimes attained. Pretty much all that is here insisted on is that, as regards these amenities of life, the housewife's efforts are under the guidance of traditions that have been shaped by the law of conspicuously wasteful expenditure of time and substance. If beauty or comfort is achieved—and it is a more or less fortuitous circumstance if they are—they must be achieved by means and methods that commend themselves to the great economic law of wasted effort. The more reputable, "presentable" portion of middle-class household paraphernalia are, on the one hand, items of conspicuous consumption, and on the other hand, apparatus for putting in evidence the vicarious leisure rendered by the housewife.

The requirement of vicarious consumption at the hands of the wife continues in force even at a lower point in the pecuniary scale than the requirement of vicarious leisure. At a point below which little if any pretense of wasted effort, in ceremonial cleanness and the like, is observable, and where there is assuredly no conscious attempt at ostensible leisure, decency still requires the wife to consume some goods conspicuously for the reputability of the household and its head. So that, as the latter-day outcome of this evolution of an archaic institution, the wife, who was at the outset the drudge and chattel of the man, both in fact and in theory—the producer of goods for him to consume—has become the ceremonial consumer of goods which he produces. But she still quite unmistakably remains his chattel in theory; for the habitual rendering of vicarious leisure and consumption is the abiding mark of the unfree servant.

This vicarious consumption practiced by the household of the middle and lower classes can not be counted as a direct expression of the leisure-class scheme of life, since the household of this pecuniary grade does not belong within the leisure class. It is rather that the leisure-class scheme of life here comes to an expression at the second remove. The leisure class stands at the head of the social structure in point of reputability; and its manner of life and its standards of worth therefore afford the norm of reputability for the community. The observance of these standards, in some degree of approximation, becomes incumbent upon all classes lower in the scale. In modern civilized communities the lines of demarcation between social classes have grown vague and transient, and wherever this happens the norm of reputability imposed by the upper class extends its coercive influence with but slight hindrance down through the social structure to the lowest strata. The result is that the members of each stratum accept as their ideal of decency the scheme of life in vogue in the next higher stratum, and bend their energies to live up to that ideal. On pain of forfeiting their good name and their self-respect in case of failure, they must conform to the accepted code, at least in appearance.

The basis on which good repute in any highly organized industrial community ultimately rests is pecuniary strength; and the means of showing pecuniary strength, and so of gaining or retaining a good name, are leisure and a conspicuous consumption of goods. Accordingly, both of these methods are in vogue as far down the scale as it remains possible; and in the lower strata in which the two methods are employed, both offices are in great part delegated to the wife and children of the household. Lower still, where any degree of leisure, even ostensible, has become impracticable for the wife, the conspicuous consumption of goods remains and is carried on by the wife and children. The man of the household also can do something in this direction, and indeed, he commonly does; but with a still lower descent into the levels of indigence—along the margin of the slums—the man, and presently also the children, virtually cease to consume valuable goods for appearances, and the woman remains virtually the sole exponent of the household's pecuniary decency. No class of society, not even the most abjectly poor, forgoes all customary conspicuous consumption. The last items of this category of consumption are not given up except under stress of the direst necessity. Very much of squalor and discomfort will be endured before the last trinket or the last pretense of pecuniary decency is put away. There is no class and no country that has yielded so abjectly before the pressure of physical want as to deny themselves all gratification of this higher or spiritual need.

From the foregoing survey of the growth of conspicuous leisure and consumption, it appears that the utility of both alike for the purposes of reputability lies in the element of waste that is common to both. In the one case it is a waste of time and effort, in the other it is a waste of goods. Both are methods of demonstrating the possession of wealth, and the two are conventionally accepted as equivalents. The choice between them is a question of advertising expediency simply, except so far as it may be affected by other standards of propriety, springing from a different source. On grounds of expediency the preference may be given to the one or the other at different stages of the economic development. The question is, which of the two methods will most effectively reach the persons whose convictions it is desired to affect. Usage has answered this question in different ways under different circumstances.

So long as the community or social group is small enough and compact enough to be effectually reached by common notoriety alone—that is to say, so long as the human environment to which the individual is required to adapt himself in respect of reputability is comprised within his sphere of personal acquaintance and neighborhood gossip—so long the one method is about as effective as the other. Each will therefore serve about equally well during the earlier stages of social growth. But when the differentiation has gone farther and it becomes necessary to reach a wider human environment, consumption begins to hold over leisure as an ordinary means of decency. This is especially true during the later, peaceable economic stage. The means of communication and the mobility of the population now expose the individual to the observation of many persons who have no other means of judging of his reputability than the display of goods (and perhaps of breeding) which he is able to make while he is under their direct observation.

The modern organization of industry works in the same direction also by another line. The exigencies of the modern industrial system frequently place individuals and households in juxtaposition between whom there is little contact in any other sense than that of juxtaposition. One's neighbors, mechanically speaking, often are socially not one's neighbors, or even acquaintances; and still their transient good opinion has a high degree of utility. The only practicable means of impressing one's pecuniary ability on these unsympathetic observers of one's everyday life is an unremitting demonstration of ability to pay. In the modern community there is also a more frequent attendance at large gatherings of people to whom one's everyday life is unknown; in such places as churches, theaters, ballrooms, hotels, parks, shops, and the like. In order to impress these transient observers, and to retain one's self-complacency under their observation, the signature of one's pecuniary strength should be written in characters which he who runs may read. It is evident, therefore, that the present trend of the development is in the direction of heightening the utility of conspicuous consumption as compared with leisure. ...

Pecuniary Canons of Taste

The requirements of pecuniary decency have, to a very appreciable extent, influenced the sense of beauty and of utility in articles of use or beauty. Articles are to an extent preferred for use on account of their being conspicuously wasteful; they are felt to be serviceable somewhat in proportion as they are wasteful and ill adapted to their ostensible use. ...

By habituation to an appreciative perception of the marks of expensiveness in goods, and by habitually identifying beauty with reputability, it comes about that a beautiful article which is not expensive is accounted not beautiful. In this way it has happened, for instance, that some beautiful flowers pass conventionally for offensive weeds; others that can be cultivated with relative ease are accepted and admired by the lower middle class, who can afford no more expensive luxuries of this kind; but these varieties are rejected as vulgar by those people who are better able to pay for expensive flowers and who are educated to a higher schedule of pecuniary beauty in the florist's products; while still other flowers, of no greater intrinsic beauty than these, are cultivated at great cost and call out much admiration from flower-lovers whose tastes have been matured under the critical guidance of a polite environment.

The same variation in matters of taste, from one class of society to another, is visible also as regards many other kinds of consumable goods, as, for example, is the case with furniture, houses, parks, and gardens. This diversity of views as to what is beautiful in these various classes of goods is not a diversity of the norm according to which the unsophisticated sense of the beautiful works. It is not a constitutional difference of endow-ments in the æsthetic respect, but rather a difference in the code of reputability which specifies what objects properly lie within the scope of honorific consumption for the class to which the critic belongs. It is a difference in the traditions of propriety with respect to the kinds of things which may, without derogation to the consumer, be consumed under the head of objects of taste and art. With a certain allowance for variations to be accounted for on other grounds, these traditions are determined, more or less rigidly, by the pecuniary plane of life of the class.

PIERRE BOURDIEU

Distinction: A Social Critique of the Judgement of Taste

The Social Space

The distribution of the different classes (and class fractions) runs from those who are best provided with both economic and cultural capital to those who are most deprived in both respects (see figures 1 and 2). The members of the professions, who have high incomes and high qualifications, who very often (52.9 percent) originate from the dominant class (professions or senior executives), who receive and consume a large quantity of both material and cultural goods, are opposed in almost all respects to the office workers, who have low qualifications, often originate from the working or middle classes, who receive little and consume little, devoting a high proportion of their time to care maintenance and home improvement; and they are even more opposed to the skilled or semi-skilled workers, and still more to unskilled workers or farm labourers, who have the lowest incomes, no qualifications, and origi-nate almost exclusively (90.5 percent of farm labourers, 84.5 percent of unskilled workers) from the working classes.[1]

The differences stemming from the total volume of capital almost always conceal, both from common awareness and also from 'scientific' knowledge, the secondary differences which, within each of the classes defined by overall volume of capital, separate class fractions, defined by different asset structures, i.e., different distributions of their total capital among the different kinds of capital [economic and cultural].

Once one takes account of the structure of total assets—and not only, as has always been done implicitly, of the dominant kind in a given structure, 'birth', 'fortune' or 'talents', as the nineteenth century put it—one has the means of making more precise divisions and also of observing the specific effects of the structure of distribution between the different kinds of capital. This may, for example, be symmetrical (as in the case of the professions, which combine very high income with very high cultural capital) or asymmetrical (in the case of higher-education and secondary teachers or employers, with cultural capital dominant in one case, economic capital in the other). One thus discovers two sets of homologous positions. The fractions whose reproduction depends on economic capital, usually inherited—industrial and commercial employers at the higher level, craftsmen and shopkeepers at the intermediate level—are opposed to the fractions which are least endowed (relatively, of course) with economic capital, and whose reproduction mainly depends on cultural capital—higher-education and secondary teachers at the higher level, primary teachers at the intermediate level. ...

The Habitus

The mere fact that the social space described here can be presented as a diagram indicates that it is an abstract representation, deliberately constructed, like a map, to give a bird's-eye view, a point of view on the whole set of points from which ordinary agents (including the sociologist and his reader, in their ordinary behaviour) see the social world. Bringing together in simultaneity, in the scope of a single glance—this is its heuristic value—positions which the agents can never apprehend in their totality and in their multiple relationships, social space is to the practical space of everyday life, with its distances which are kept or signalled, and neighbours who may be more remote than strangers, what geometrical space is to the 'travelling space' (*espace hodologique*) of ordinary experience, with its gaps and discontinuities.

But the most crucial thing to note is that the question of this space is raised within the space itself—that the agents have points of view on this objective space which depend on their position within it and in which their will to transform or conserve it is often expressed. Thus many of the words which sociology uses to designate the classes it constructs are borrowed from ordinary usage, where they serve to express the (generally polemical) view that one group has of another. As if carried away by their quest for greater objectivity,

sociologists almost always forget that the 'objects' they classify produce not only objectively classifiable practices but also classifying operations that are no less objective and are themselves classifiable. The division into classes performed by sociology leads to the common root of the classifiable practices which agents produce and of the classificatory judgements they make of other agents' practices and their own. The habitus is both the generative principle of objectively classifiable judgements and the system of classification (*principium divisionis*) of these practices. It is in the relationship between the two capacities which define the habitus, the capacity to produce classifiable practices and works, and the capacity to differentiate and appreciate these practices and products (taste), that the represented social world, i.e., the space of life-styles, is constituted.

The relationship that is actually established between the pertinent characteristics of economic and social condition (capital volume and composition, in both synchronic and diachronic aspects) and the distinctive features associated with the corresponding position in the universe of life-styles only becomes intelligible when the habitus is constructed as the generative formula which makes it possible to account both for the classifiable practices and products and for the judgements, themselves classified, which make these practices and works into a system of distinctive signs. When one speaks of the aristocratic asceticism of teachers or the pretension of the petite bourgeoisie, one is not only describing these groups by one, or even the most important, of their properties, but also endeavouring to name the principle which generates all their properties and all their judgements of their, or other people's, properties. The habitus is necessity internalized and converted into a disposition that generates meaningful practices and meaning-giving perceptions; it is a general, transposable disposition which carries out a systematic, universal application—beyond the limits of what has been directly learnt—of the necessity inherent in the learning conditions. That is why an agent's whole set of practices (or those of a whole set of agents produced by similar conditions) are both systematic, inasmuch as they are the product of the application of identical (or interchangeable)

FIGURE 1 The space of social positions (shown in black)
FIGURE 2 The space of life-styles (shown in grey)

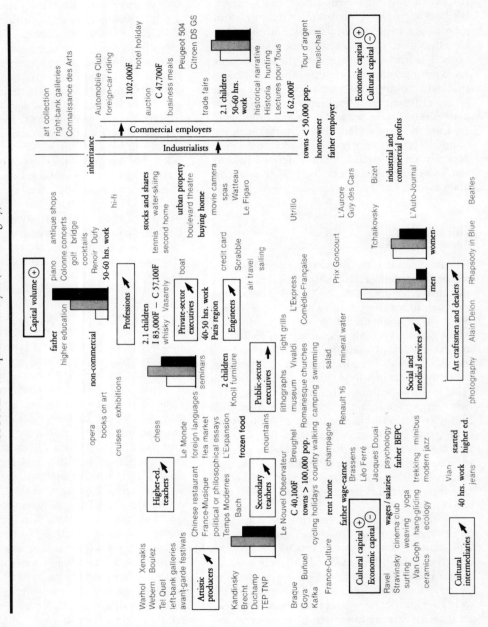

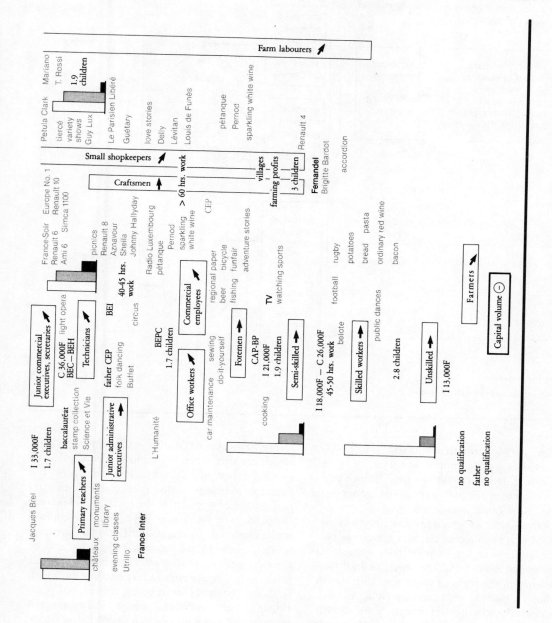

FIGURE 3
Conditions of existence, habitus, and life-style

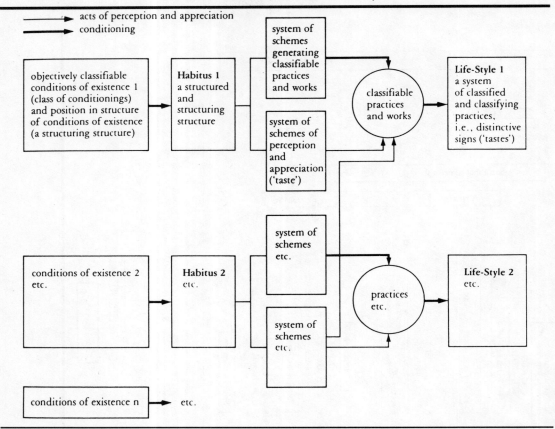

schemes, and systematically distinct from the practices constituting another life-style.

Because different conditions of existence produce different habitus—systems of generative schemes applicable, by simple transfer, to the most varied areas of practice—the practices engendered by the different habitus appear as systematic configurations of properties expressing the differences objectively inscribed in conditions of existence in the form of systems of differential deviations which, when perceived by agents endowed with the schemes of perception and appreciation necessary in order to identify, interpret and evaluate their pertinent features, function as life-styles (see figure 3).[2]

The habitus is not only a structuring structure, which organizes practices and the perception of practices, but also a structured structure: the principle of division into logical classes which organizes the perception of the social world is itself the product of internalization of the division into social classes. Each class condition is defined, simultaneously, by its intrinsic properties and by the relational properties which it derives from its position in the system of class conditions, which is also a system of differences, differential positions, i.e., by everything which distinguishes it from what it is not and especially from everything it is opposed to; social identity is defined and asserted through difference. This means that inevitably inscribed within the dispositions of the habitus is the whole structure of the system of conditions, as it presents itself in the experience of a life-condition occupying a particular position within that structure. The most fundamental oppositions in the structure (high/low, rich/poor etc.) tend to establish themselves as the fundamental structuring principles of practices and the perception of practices. As a system of practice-generating schemes which expresses systematically the necessity and freedom inherent in its class condition and the difference constituting that position, the habitus apprehends differences between conditions, which it grasps in the form of differences between classified, classifying practices (products of other habitus), in accordance with principles of differentiation which, being themselves the product of these differences, are objectively attuned to them and therefore tend to perceive them as natural.

While it must be reasserted, against all forms of mechanism, that ordinary experience of the social world is a cognition, it is equally important to realize—contrary to the illusion of the spontaneous generation of consciousness which so many theories of the 'awakening of class consciousness' (*prise de conscience*) amount to—that primary cognition is misrecognition, recognition of an order which is also established in the mind. Life-styles are thus the systematic products of habitus, which, perceived in their mutual relations through the schemes of the habitus, become sign systems that are socially qualified (as 'distinguished', 'vulgar' etc.). The dialectic of conditions and habitus is the basis of an alchemy which transforms the distribution of capital, the balance-sheet of a power relation, into a system of perceived differences, distinctive properties, that is, a distribution of symbolic capital, legitimate capital, whose objective truth is misrecognized.

As structured products (*opus operatum*) which a structuring structure (*modus operandi*) produces through retranslations according to the specific logic of the different *fields,* all the practices and products of a given agent are objectively harmonized among themselves, without any deliberate pursuit of coherence, and objectively orchestrated, without any conscious concertation, with those of all members of the same class. The

habitus continuously generates practical metaphors, that is to say, transfers (of which the transfer of motor habits is only one example) or, more precisely, systematic transpositions required by the particular conditions in which the habitus is 'put into practice' (so that, for example, the ascetic ethos which might be expected always to express itself in saving may, in a given context, express itself in a particular way of using credit). The practices of the same agent, and, more generally, the practices of all agents of the same class, owe the stylistic affinity which makes each of them a metaphor of any of the others to the fact that they are the product of transfers of the same schemes of action from one field to another. An obvious paradigm would be the disposition called 'handwriting', a singular way of tracing letters which always produces the same writing, i.e., graphic forms which, in spite of all the differences of size, material or colour due to the surface (paper or blackboard) or the instrument (pen or chalk)—in spite, therefore, of the different use of muscles—present an immediately perceptible family resemblance, like all the features of style or manner whereby a painter or writer can be recognized as infallibly as a man by his walk.

Systematicity is found in the opus operatum because it is in the modus operandi.[3] It is found in all the properties—and property—with which individuals and groups surround themselves, houses, furniture, paintings, books, cars, spirits, cigarettes, perfume, clothes, and in the practices in which they manifest their distinction, sports, games, entertainments, only because it is in the synthetic unity of the habitus, the unifying, generative principle of all practices. Taste, the propensity and capacity to appropriate (materially or symbolically) a given class of classified, classifying objects or practices, is the generative formula of life-style, a unitary set of distinctive preferences which express the same expressive intention in the specific logic of each of the symbolic sub-spaces, furniture, clothing, language or body hexis. Each dimension of life-style 'symbolizes with' the others, in Leibniz's phrase, and symbolizes them. An old cabinetmaker's world view, the way he manages his budget, his time or his body, his use of language and choice of clothing are fully present in his ethic of scrupulous, impeccable craftsmanship and in the aesthetic of work for work's sake which leads him to measure the beauty of his products by the care and patience that have gone into them.

The system of matching properties, which includes people—one speaks of a 'well-matched couple', and friends like to say they have the same tastes—is organized by taste, a system of classificatory schemes which may only very partially become conscious although, as one rises in the social hierarchy, life-style is increasingly a matter of what Weber calls the 'stylization of life'. Taste is the basis of the mutual adjustment of all the features associated with a person, which the old aesthetic recommended for the sake of the mutual reinforcement they give one another; the countless pieces of information a person consciously or unconsciously imparts endlessly underline and confirm one another, offering the alert observer the same pleasure an art-lover derives from the symmetries and correspondences produced by a harmonious distribution of redundancies. The over-determination that results from these redundancies is felt the more strongly because the different features which have to be isolated for observation or measurement strongly interpenetrate in ordinary perception; each item of information imparted in practice (e.g., a judgement of a painting) is contaminated—and, if it deviates from the probable feature, corrected—by the effect of the whole set of features previously or simultaneously perceived. That is why a survey which tends to isolate features—for example, by dissociating the things said from the way they are said—and detach them from the system of correlative features tends to minimize the deviation, on each point, between the classes, especially that between the petit bourgeois and the bourgeois. In the ordinary situations of bourgeois life, banalities about art, literature or cinema are inseparable from the steady tone, the slow, casual diction, the distant or self-assured smile, the measured gesture, the well-tailored suit and the bourgeois salon of the person who pronounces them.

Taste is the practical operator of the transmutation of things into distinct and distinctive signs, of continuous distributions into discontinuous oppositions; it raises the differences inscribed in the physical order of bodies to the symbolic order of significant distinctions. It transforms objectively classified practices, in which a class condition signifies itself (through taste), into classifying practices, that is, into a symbolic expression of class position, by perceiving them in their mutual relations and in terms of social classificatory schemes. Taste is thus the source of the system of distinctive features which cannot fail to be perceived as a systematic expression of a particular class of conditions of existence, i.e., as a distinctive life-style, by anyone who possesses practical knowledge of the relationships between distinctive signs and positions in the distributions—between the universe of objective properties, which is brought to light by scientific construction, and the no less objective universe of life-styles, which exists as such for and through ordinary experience.

This classificatory system, which is the product of the internalization of the structure of social space, in the form in which it impinges through the experience of a particular position in that space, is, within the limits of economic possibilities and impossibilities (which it tends to reproduce in its own logic), the generator of practices adjusted to the regularities inherent in a condition. It continuously transforms necessities into strategies, constraints into preferences, and, without any mechanical determination, it generates the set of 'choices' constituting life-styles, which derive their meaning, i.e., their value, from their position in a system of oppositions and correlations.[4] It is a virtue made of necessity which continuously transforms necessity into virtue by inducing 'choices' which correspond to the condition of which it is the product. As can be seen whenever a change in social position puts the habitus into new conditions, so that its specific efficacy can be isolated, it is taste—the taste of necessity or the taste of luxury—and not high or low income which commands the practices objectively adjusted to these resources. Through taste, an agent has what he likes because he likes what he has, that is, the properties actually given to him in the distributions and legitimately assigned to him in the classifications.[5]

The Homology Between the Spaces

Bearing in mind all that precedes, in particular the fact that the generative schemes of the habitus are applied, by simple transfer, to the most dissimilar areas of practice, one can immediately understand that the practices or goods associated with the different classes in the different areas of practice are organized in accordance with structures of opposition which are homologous to one another because they are all homologous to the structure of objective oppositions between class conditions. Without presuming to demonstrate here in a few pages what the whole of the rest of this work will endeavour to establish—but lest the reader fail to see the wood for the trees of detailed analysis—I shall merely indicate, very schematically, how the two major organizing principles of the social space govern the structure and modification of the space of cultural consumption, and, more generally, the whole universe of life-styles.

In cultural consumption, the main opposition, by overall capital value, is between the practices designated by their rarity as distinguished, those of the fractions richest in both economic and cultural capital, and the practices socially identified as vulgar because they are both easy and common, those of the fractions poorest in both these respects. In the intermediate position are the practices which are perceived as pretentious, because of the manifest discrepancy between ambition and possibilities. In opposition to the dominated condition, characterized, from the point of view of the dominant, by the combination of forced poverty and unjustified laxity, the dominant aesthetic—of which the work of art and the aesthetic disposition are the most complete embodiments—proposes the combination of ease and asceticism, i.e., self-imposed austerity, restraint, reserve, which are affirmed in that absolute manifestation of excellence, relaxation in tension.

This fundamental opposition is specified according to capital composition. Through the mediation of the means of appropriation available to them, exclusively or principally cultural on the one hand, mainly economic on the other, and the different forms of relation to works of art which result from them, the different fractions of the dominant class are oriented towards cultural practices so different in their style and object and sometimes so antagonistic (those of 'artists' and 'bourgeois')[6] that it is easy to forget that they are variants of the same fundamental relationship to necessity and to those who remain subject to it, and that each pursues the exclusive appropriation of legitimate cultural goods and the associated symbolic profits. Whereas the dominant fractions of the dominant class (the 'bourgeoisie') demand of art a high degree of denial of the social world and incline towards a hedonistic aesthetic of ease and facility, symbolized by boulevard theatre or Impressionist painting, the dominated fractions (the 'intellectuals' and 'artists') have affinities with the ascetic aspect of aesthetics and are inclined to support all artistic revolutions conducted in the name of purity and purification, refusal of ostentation and the bourgeois taste for ornament; and the dispositions towards the social world which they owe to their status as poor relations incline them to welcome a pessimistic representation of the social world.

While it is clear that art offers it the greatest scope, there is no area of practice in which the intention of purifying, refining and sublimating facile impulses and primary needs cannot assert itself, or in which the stylization of life, i.e., the primacy of form over function, which leads to the denial of function, does not produce the same effects. In language, it gives the opposition between popular outspokenness and the highly censored language of the bourgeois, between the expressionist pursuit of the picturesque or the rhetorical effect and the choice of restraint and false simplicity (litotes). The same economy of means is found in body language: here too, agitation and haste, grimaces and gesticulation are opposed to slowness—'the slow gestures, the slow glance' of nobility, according to Nietzsche[7]—to the restraint and impassivity which signify elevation. Even the field of primary tastes is organized according to the fundamental opposition, with the antithesis between quantity and quality, belly and palate, matter and manners, substance and form.

Form and Substance

The fact that in the realm of food the main opposition broadly corresponds to differences in income has masked the secondary opposition which exists, both within the middle classes and within the dominant class, between the fractions richer in cultural capital and less rich in economic capital and those whose assets are structured in the opposite way. Observers tend to see a simple effect of income in the fact that, as one rises in the social hierarchy, the proportion of income spent on food diminishes, or that, within the food budget, the proportion spent on heavy, fatty, fattening foods, which are also cheap—pasta, potatoes, beans, bacon, pork—declines (C.S. III), as does that spent on wine, whereas an increasing proportion is spent on leaner, lighter (more digestible), non-fattening foods (beef, veal, mutton, lamb, and especially fresh fruit and vegetables).[8] Because the real principle of preferences is taste, a virtue made of necessity, the theory which makes consumption a simple function of income has all the appearances to support it, since income plays an important part in determining distance from necessity. However, it cannot account for cases in which the same income is associated with totally different consumption patterns. Thus, foremen remain attached to 'popular' taste although they earn more than clerical and commercial employees, whose taste differs radically from that of manual workers and is closer to that of teachers.

For a real explanation of the variations which J. F. Engel's law merely records, one has to take account of all the characteristics of social condition which are (statistically) associated from earliest childhood with possession of high or low income and which tend to shape tastes adjusted to these conditions.[9] The true basis of the differences found in the area of consumption, and far beyond it, is the opposition between the tastes of luxury (or freedom) and the tastes of necessity. The former are the tastes of individuals who are the product of material conditions of existence defined by distance from necessity, by the freedoms or facilities stemming from possession of capital; the latter express, precisely in their adjustment, the necessities of which they are the product. Thus it is possible to deduce popular tastes for the foods that are simultaneously most 'filling' and

most economical[10] from the necessity of reproducing labour power at the lowest cost which is forced on the proletariat as its very definition. The idea of taste, typically bourgeois, since it presupposes absolute freedom of choice, is so closely associated with the idea of freedom that many people find it hard to grasp the paradoxes of the taste of necessity. Some simply sweep it aside, making practice a direct product of economic necessity (workers eat beans because they cannot afford anything else), failing to realize that necessity can only be fulfilled, most of the time, because the agents are inclined to fulfil it, because they have a taste for what they are anyway condemned to. Others turn it into a taste of freedom, forgetting the conditionings of which it is the product, and so reduce it to pathological or morbid preference for (basic) essentials, a sort of congenital coarseness, the pretext for a class racism which associates the populace with everything heavy, thick and fat.[11] Taste is *amor fati*, the choice of destiny, but a forced choice, produced by conditions of existence which rule out all alternatives as mere daydreams and leave no choice but the taste for the necessary.

The taste of necessity can only be the basis of a life-style 'in-itself', which is defined as such only negatively, by an absence, by the relationship of privation between itself and the other life-styles. For some, there are elective emblems, for others stigmata which they bear in their very bodies. 'As the chosen people bore in their features the sign that they were the property of Jehovah, so the division of labour brands the manufacturing worker as the property of capital.'[12] The brand which Marx speaks of is nothing other than life-style, through which the most deprived immediately betray themselves, even in their use of spare time; in so doing they inevitably serve as a foil to every distinction and contribute, purely negatively, to the dialectic of pretension and distinction which fuels the incessant changing of taste. Not content with lacking virtually all the knowledge or manners which are valued in the markets of academic examination or polite conversation nor with only possessing skills which have no value there, they are the people 'who don't know how to live', who sacrifice most to material foods, and to the heaviest, grossest and most fattening of them, bread, potatoes, fats, and the most vulgar, such as wine; who spend least on clothing and cosmetics, appearance and beauty; those who 'don't know how to relax', 'who always have to be doing something', who set off in their Renault 5 or Simca 1000 to join the great traffic jams of the holiday exodus, who picnic beside major roads, cram their tents into overcrowded campsites, fling themselves into the prefabricated leisure activities designed for them by the engineers of cultural mass production; those who by all these uninspired 'choices' confirm class racism, if it needed to be confirmed, in its conviction that they only get what they deserve.

The art of eating and drinking remains one of the few areas in which the working classes explicitly challenge the legitimate art of living. In the face of the new ethic of sobriety for the sake of slimness, which is most recognized at the highest levels of the social hierarchy, peasants and especially industrial workers maintain an ethic of convivial indulgence. A bon vivant is not just someone who enjoys eating and drinking; he is someone capable of entering into the generous and familiar—that is, both simple and free—relationship that is encouraged and symbolized by eating and drinking together, in a conviviality which sweeps away restraints and reticence.

The boundary marking the break with the popular relation to food runs, without any doubt, between the manual workers and the clerical and commercial employees (C.S. II). Clerical workers spend less on food than skilled manual workers, both in absolute terms (9,376 francs as against 10,347 francs) and in relative terms (34.2 percent as against 38.3 percent); they consume less bread, pork, pork products (*charcuterie*), milk, cheese, rabbit, poultry, dried vegetables and fats, and, within a smaller food budget, spend as much on meat—beef, veal, mutton and lamb—and slightly more on fish, fresh fruit and aperitifs. These changes in the structure of spending on food are accompanied by increased spending on health and beauty care and clothing, and a slight increase in spending on cultural and leisure activities. When it is noted that the reduced spending on food, especially on the most earthly, earthy, down-to-earth foods, is accompanied by a lower birth-rate, it is reasonable to suppose that it con-

stitutes one aspect of an overall transformation of the relationship to the world. The 'modest' taste which can defer its gratifications is opposed to the spontaneous materialism of the working classes, who refuse to participate in the Benthamite calculation of pleasures and pains, benefits and costs (e.g., for health and beauty). In other words, these two relations to the 'fruits of the earth' are grounded in two dispositions towards the future which are themselves related in circular causality to two objective futures. Against the imaginary anthropology of economics, which has never shrunk from formulating universal laws of 'temporal preference', it has to be pointed out that the propensity to subordinate present desires to future desires depends on the extent to which this sacrifice is 'reasonable', that is, on the likelihood, in any case, of obtaining future satisfactions superior to those sacrificed.[13]

Among the economic conditions of the propensity to sacrifice immediate satisfactions to expected satisfactions one must include the probability of these future satisfactions which is inscribed in the present condition. There is still a sort of economic calculation in the unwillingness to subject existence to economic calculation. The hedonism which seizes day by day the rare satisfactions ('good times') of the immediate present is the only philosophy conceivable to those who 'have no future' and, in any case, little to expect from the future.[14] It becomes clearer why the practical materialism which is particularly manifested in the relation to food is one of the most fundamental components of the popular ethos and even the popular ethic. The being-in-the-present which is affirmed in the readiness to take advantage of the good times and take time as it comes is, in itself, an affirmation of solidarity with others (who are often the only present guarantee against the threats of the future), inasmuch as this temporal immanentism is a recognition of the limits which define the condition. This is why the sobriety of the petit bourgeois is felt as a break: in abstaining from having a good time and from having it with others, the would-be petit bourgeois betrays his ambition of escaping from the common present, when, that is, he does not construct his whole self-image around the opposition between his home and the café, abstinence and intemperance, in other words, between individual salvation and collective solidarities.

The café is not a place a man goes to for a drink but a place he goes to in order to drink in company, where he can establish relationships of familiarity based on the suspension of the censorships, conventions and proprieties that prevail among strangers. In contrast to the bourgeois or petit-bourgeois café or restaurant, where each table is a separate, appropriated territory (one asks permission to borrow a chair or the salt), the working-class café is a site of companionship (each new arrival gives a collective greeting, 'Salut la compagnie!' etc.). Its focus is the counter, to be leaned on after shaking hands with the landlord—who is thus defined as the host (he often leads the conversation)—and sometimes shaking hands with the whole company; the tables, if there are any, are left to 'strangers', or women who have come in to get a drink for their child or make a phone call. In the café free rein is given to the typically popular art of the joke—the art of seeing everything as a joke (hence the reiterated 'Joking apart' or 'No joke', which mark a return to serious matters or prelude a second-degree joke), but also the art of making or playing jokes, often at the expense of the 'fat man'. He is always good for a laugh, because, in the popular code, his fatness is more a picturesque peculiarity than a defect, and because the good nature he is presumed to have predisposes him to take it in good heart and see the funny side. The joke, in other words, is the art of making fun without raising anger, by means of ritual mockery or insults which are neutralized by their very excess and which, presupposing a great familiarity, both in the knowledge they use and the freedom with which they use it, are in fact tokens of attention or affection, ways of building up while seeming to run down, of accepting while seeming to condemn—although they may also be used to test out those who show signs of stand-offishness.[15]

Three Styles of Distinction

The basic opposition between the tastes of luxury and the tastes of necessity is specified in as many oppositions as there are different ways of asserting one's distinction vis-à-vis the working class and its primary needs, or—which amounts to the same thing—different powers whereby necessity can be kept at a distance. Thus, within the dominant class, one can, for the sake of simplicity, distinguish three structures of the consumption distributed under three items: food, culture and presentation (clothing, beauty care, toiletries, domestic servants). These structures take strictly opposite forms—like the structures of their capital—among the teachers as against the industrial and commercial employers (see table 1). Whereas the latter have exceptionally high expenditure on food (37 percent of the budget), low cultural costs and medium spending on presentation and representation, the former, whose total spending is lower on average, have low expenditure on food (relatively less than manual workers), limited expenditure on presentation (though their expenditure on health is one of the highest) and relatively high expenditure on culture (books, papers, entertainments, sport, toys, music, radio and record-player). Opposed to both these groups are the members of the professions, who devote the same proportion of their budget to food as the teachers (24.4 percent), but out of much greater total expenditure (57,122 francs as against 40,884 francs), and who spend much more on presentation and representation than all other fractions, especially if the costs of domestic service are included, whereas their cultural expenditure is lower than that of the teachers (or even the engineers and senior executives, who are situated between the teachers and the professionals, though nearer the latter, for almost all items).

The system of differences becomes clearer when one looks more closely at the patterns of spending on food. In this respect the industrial and commercial employers differ markedly from the professionals, and a fortiori from the teachers, by virtue of the importance they give to cereal-based products (especially cakes and pastries), wine, meat preserves (foie gras, etc.) and game, and their relatively low spending on meat, fresh fruit and vegetables. The teachers, whose food

TABLE 1

Yearly Spending by Teachers, Professionals, and Industrial and Commercial Employers, 1972

Type of spending	Teachers (higher and secondary)		Professionals		Industrial and commercial employers	
	Francs	% of total	Francs	% of total	Francs	% of total
Food[a]	9,969	24.4	13,956	24.4	16,578	37.4
Presentation[b]	4,912	12.0	12,680	22.2	5,616	12.7
Culture[c]	1,753	4.3	1,298	2.3	574	1.3

Source: C.S. II (1972).

a. Includes restaurant or canteen meals.

b. Clothes, shoes, repairs and cleaning, toiletries, hairdressing, domestic servants.

c. Books, newspapers and magazines, stationery, records, sport, toys, music, entertainments.

purchases are almost identically structured to those of office workers, spend more than all other fractions on bread, milk products, sugar, fruit preserves and non-alcoholic drinks, less on wine and spirits and distinctly less than the professions on expensive products such as meat—especially the most expensive meats, such as mutton and lamb—and fresh fruit and vegetables. The members of the professions are mainly distinguished by the high proportion of their spending which goes on expensive products, particularly meat (18.3 percent of their food budget), and especially the most expensive meat (veal, lamb, mutton), fresh fruit and vegetables, fish and shellfish, cheese and aperitifs.[16]

Thus, when one moves from the manual workers to the industrial and commercial employers, through foremen, craftsmen and small shopkeepers, economic constraints tend to relax without any fundamental change in the pattern of spending (see figure 4). The opposition between the two extremes is here established between the poor and the rich (nouveau riche), between *la bouffe* and *la grande bouffe*;[17] the food consumed is increasingly rich (both in cost and in calories) and increasingly heavy (game, foie gras). By contrast, the taste of the professionals or senior executives defines the popular taste, by negation, as the taste for the heavy, the fat and the coarse, by tending towards the light, the refined and the delicate (see table 2). The disappearance of economic constraints is accompanied by a strengthening of the

social censorships which forbid coarseness and fatness, in favour of slimness and distinction. The taste for rare, aristocratic foods points to a traditional cuisine, rich in expensive or rare products (fresh vegetables, meat). Finally, the teachers, richer in cultural capital than in economic capital, and therefore inclined to ascetic consumption in all areas, pursue originality at the lowest economic cost and go in for exoticism (Italian, Chinese cooking etc.)[18] and culinary populism (peasant dishes). They are thus almost consciously opposed to the (new) rich with their rich food, the buyers and sellers of *grosse bouffe*, the 'fat cats',[19] gross in body and mind, who have the economic means to flaunt, with an arrogance perceived as 'vulgar', a life-style which remains very close to that of the working classes as regards economic and cultural consumption.

Eating habits, especially when represented solely by the produce consumed, cannot of course be considered independently of the whole life-style. The most obvious reason for this is that the taste for particular dishes (of which the statistical shopping-basket gives only the vaguest idea) is associated, through preparation and cooking, with a whole conception of the domestic economy and of the division of labour between the sexes. A taste for elaborate casserole dishes (pot-au-feu, *blanquette*, *daube*), which demand a big investment of time and interest, is linked to a traditional conception of woman's role. Thus there is a particularly strong opposition in this respect

FIGURE 4
The food space

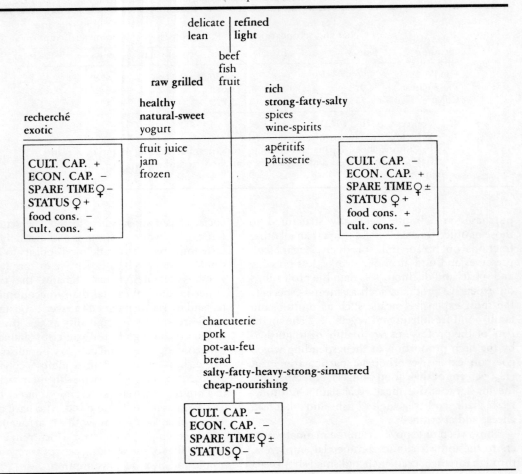

between the working classes and the dominated fractions of the dominant class, in which the women, whose labour has a high market value (and who, perhaps as a result, have a higher sense of their own value) tend to devote their spare time rather to child care and the transmission of cultural capital, and to contest the traditional division of domestic labour. The aim of saving time and labour in preparation combines with the search for light, low-calorie products, and points towards grilled meat and fish, raw vegetables ('*salades composées*'), frozen foods, yogurt and other milk products, all of which are diametrically opposed to popular dishes, the most typical of which is pot-au-feu, made with cheap meat that is boiled (as opposed to grilled or roasted), a method of cooking that chiefly demands time. It is no accident that this form of cooking symbolizes one state of female existence and of the sexual division of labour (a woman entirely devoted to housework is called 'pot-au-feu'), just as the slippers put on before dinner symbolize the complementary male rôle.

Small industrial and commercial employers, the incarnation of the 'grocer' traditionally execrated by artists, are the category who most often (60 percent) say they change into their carpet slippers every day before dinner, whereas the professions and the senior executives are most inclined to reject this petit-bourgeois symbol (35 percent say they never do it). The particularly high consumption of carpet slippers by working-class women (both urban and rural) no doubt reflects the relation to the body and to self-presentation entailed by confinement to the home and to domestic life. (The wives of craftsmen, shopkeepers and manual workers are those who most often say that their choice of clothes is mainly guided by a concern to please their husbands.)

It is among manual workers that most time and interest is devoted to cooking: 69 percent of those questioned say they like doing elaborate cooking (*la grande cuisine*), as against 59 percent of the junior executives, 52 percent of the small shopkeepers and 51 percent of the senior executives, professionals and industrialists (C.S. V). (Another indirect index of these differences as regards the sexual division of labour is that whereas the teachers and senior executives seem to give priority to a washing machine and a dishwasher, for the professionals and industrial or commercial employers priority seems to go rather to a TV set and a car—C.S. II.) Finally, when invited to choose their two favourite dishes from a list of seven, the farm workers and manual workers, who, like all other categories, give the highest rank to roast leg of lamb, are the most inclined (45 percent and 34 percent, as against 28 percent of the clerical workers, 20 percent of the senior executives and 19 percent of the small employers) to choose pot-au-feu (the farm workers are almost the only ones who choose andouillette—pork tripe sausage—14 percent of them, as against 4 percent of the manual workers, clerical workers and junior executives, 3 percent of the senior executives and 0 percent of the small employers). Manual workers and small employers

also favour coq au vin (50 percent and 48 percent), a dish typical of small restaurants aiming to be 'posh', and perhaps for this reason associated with the idea of 'eating out' (compared with 42 percent of the clerical workers, 39 percent of the senior executives and 37 percent of the farm workers). The executives, professionals and big employers clearly distinguish themselves solely by choosing—from a list which for them is particularly narrow—the dish which is both relatively 'light' and symbolically marked (in contrast to the ordinary routine of petit-bourgeois cooking), bouillabaisse (31 percent, as against 22 percent of the clerical workers, 17 percent of the small employers, 10 percent of the manual workers, 7 percent of the farm workers), in which the opposition between fish and meat (especially the pork in sauerkraut or *cassoulet*) is clearly strengthened by regionalist and touristic connotations (C.S. IV). It is obvious that the imprecise classifications used in this survey prevent one from seeing the effects of the secondary opposition between the fractions, and that the tendencies observed would have been more marked if, for example, it had been possible to isolate the teachers or if the list of dishes had been more diversified in the sociologically pertinent respects.

Tastes in food also depend on the idea each class has of the body and of the effects of food on the body, that is, on its strength, health and beauty; and on the categories it uses to evaluate these effects, some of which may be important for one class and ignored by another, and which the different classes may rank in very different ways. Thus, whereas the working classes are more attentive to the strength of the (male) body than its shape, and tend to go for products that are both cheap and nutritious, the professions prefer products that are tasty, health-giving, light and not fattening. Taste, a class culture turned into nature, that is, *embodied,* helps to shape the class body. It is an incorporated principle of classification which governs all forms of incorporation, choosing and modifying everything that the body ingests and digests and assimilates, physiologically

TABLE 2

Annual Household Expenditures on Food: Fractions of the Dominant Class, 1972

	Teachers (higher and secondary)		Senior executives		Professions		Engineers		Industrial and commercial employers	
Average number persons per household	3.11		3.6		3.5		3.6		3.6	
Average total household expenditure (francs)	40,844		52,156		57,122		49,822		44,339	
Average total household expenditure on food (francs)	9,969		13,158		13,956		12,666		16,578	
Expenditure on food as % of total expenditure	24.4		25.2		24.4		25.4		37.4	
	Average exp.		Average exp.		Average exp.		Average exp.		Average exp.	
Type of Food	Francs	As % of all food exp.	Francs	As % of all food exp.	Francs	As % of all food exp.	Francs	As % of all food exp.	Francs	As % of all food exp.
Cereals	865	8.7	993	7.5	1,011	7.2	951	7.5	1,535	9.2
bread	322	3.2	347	2.6	326	2.3	312	2.5	454	2.5
cakes, pastries	452	4.5	552	4.1	548	4.0	539	4.2	989	5.6
rusks	16	0.2	27	0.2	33	0.2	28	0.2	29	0.1
rice	35	0.3	32	0.2	62	0.4	41	0.3	33	0.1
flour	40	0.4	35	0.2	41	0.3	31	0.2	28	0.1
Vegetables	766	7.7	1,015	7.7	1,100	7.9	899	7.1	1,222	7.4
potatoes	81	0.8	94	0.7	95	0.7	98	0.7	152	0.8
fresh vegetables	555	5.6	729	5.5	811	5.8	647	5.1	915	5.1
dried or canned	131	1.3	191	1.4	216	1.5	154	1.2	153	0.8
Fruit	632	6.3	871	6.6	990	7.2	864	6.8	877	5.2
fresh fruit	295	2.9	405	3.1	586	4.2	424	3.3	547	3.1
citrus fruit, bananas	236	2.4	343	2.6	303	2.2	324	2.5	256	1.4
dried	102	1.0	122	0.9	98	0.7	116	0.9	72	0.4
Butcher's meat	1,556	15.6	2,358	18.0	2,552	18.3	2,073	16.4	2,323	14.0
beef	814	8.1	1,291	9.8	1,212	8.7	1,144	9.0	1,273	7.2
veal	335	3.4	452	3.4	630	4.5	402	3.1	377	2.3
mutton, lamb	156	1.6	315	2.3	438	3.2	242	1.9	390	2.2
horse	31	0.3	49	0.3	31	0.2	37	0.3	94	0.5
pork (fresh)	221	2.2	251	1.7	239	1.7	247	1.9	187	1.3

Pork products	634	6.3	741	5.6	774	5.5	705	5.6	812	4.9
Meat preserves	336	3.4	350	2.6	233	1.7	310	2.4	1,362	8.0
Fish, shellfish	336	3.4	503	3.8	719	5.1	396	3.1	588	3.5
Poultry	235	2.3	311	2.4	399	2.8	310	2.4	333	2.0
Rabbit, game	36	0.3	97	0.7	148	1.1	89	0.7	289	1.7
Eggs	149	1.4	172	1.3	190	1.4	178	1.4	185	1.1
Milk	299	3.0	271	2.0	249	1.8	287	2.3	309	1.9
Cheese, yogurt	692	6.9	776	5.9	843	6.0	785	6.1	1,090	6.5
Fats	399	4.0	564	4.3	525	3.8	504	4.0	551	3.3
butter	320	3.2	408	3.1	379	2.7	371	2.9	405	2.4
oil	66	0.6	136	1.0	132	1.0	103	0.8	112	0.6
margarine	12	0.1	17	0.1	12	0.1	29	0.2	19	0.1
lard	1	0	2	0	1	0	1	0	13	0.1
Sugar, confectionery, cocoa	304	3.0	395	3.0	265	1.9	327	2.6	407	2.4
Alcohol	711	7.1	1,365	10.3	1,329	9.5	937	7.4	2,218	13.4
wine	457	4.6	869	6.6	899	6.4	392	3.1	1,881	11.8
beer	82	0.8	91	0.7	40	0.3	184	1.4	93	0.5
cider	13	0.1	12	0	0	0	8	0	5	
apéritifs, liqueurs etc.	157	1.6	391	3.0	389	2.8	352	2.8	237	1.4
Non-alcoholic drinks	344	3.4	342	2.6	267	1.9	295	2.3	327	2.0
Coffee, tea	152	1.5	215	1.5	291	2.1	178	1.4	298	1.8
Restaurant meals	829	8.3	1,863	13.0	1,562	11.2	1,372	10.8	1,179	7.1
Canteen meals	745	7.5	562	4.0	221	1.6	773	6.1	299	1.8
Miscellaneous	264	2.6	379	2.7	258	1.8	432	3.4	324	1.9

Source: C.S. II (1972).

and psychologically. It follows that the body is the most indisputable materialization of class taste, which it manifests in several ways. It does this first in the seemingly most natural features of the body, the dimensions (volume, height, weight) and shapes (round or square, stiff or supple, straight or curved) of its visible forms, which express in countless ways a whole relation to the body, i.e., a way of treating it, caring for it, feeding it, maintaining it, which reveals the deepest dispositions of the habitus. It is in fact through preferences with regard to food which may be perpetuated beyond their social conditions of production (as, in other areas, an accent, a walk etc.),[20] and also, of course, through the uses of the body in work and leisure which are bound up with them, that the class distribution of bodily properties is determined.

The quasi-conscious representation of the approved form of the perceived body, and in particular its thinness or fatness, is not the only mediation through which the social definition of appropriate foods is established. At a deeper level, the whole body schema, in particular the physical approach to the act of eating, governs the selection of certain foods. For example, in the working classes, fish tends to be regarded as an unsuitable food for men, not only because it is a light food, insufficiently 'filling', which would only be cooked for health reasons, i.e., for invalids and children, but also because, like fruit (except bananas) it is one of the 'fiddly' things which a man's hands cannot cope with and which make him childlike (the woman, adopting a maternal role, as in all similar cases, will prepare the fish on the plate or peel the pear); but above all, it is because fish has to be eaten in a way which totally contradicts the masculine way of eating, that is, with restraint, in small mouthfuls, chewed gently, with the front of the mouth, on the tips of the teeth (because of the bones). The whole masculine identity—what is called virility—is involved in these two ways of eating, nibbling and picking, as befits a woman, or with whole-hearted male gulps and mouthfuls, just as it is involved in the two (perfectly homologous) ways of talking, with the front of the mouth or the whole mouth, especially the back of the mouth, the throat (in accordance with the opposition, noted in an earlier study, between the manners symbolized by *la bouche* and *la gueule*).[21]

This opposition can be found in each of the uses of the body, especially in the most insignificant-looking ones, which, as such, are predisposed to serve as 'memory joggers' charged with the group's deepest values, its most fundamental 'beliefs'. It would be easy to show, for example, that Kleenex tissues, which have to be used delicately, with a little sniff from the tip of the nose, are to the big cotton handkerchief, which is blown into sharply and loudly, with the eyes closed and the nose held tightly, as repressed laughter is to a belly laugh, with wrinkled nose, wide-open mouth and deep breathing ('doubled up with laughter'), as if to amplify to the utmost an experience which will not suffer containment, not least because it has to be shared, and therefore clearly manifested for the benefit of others.

And the practical philosophy of the male body as a sort of power, big and strong, with enormous, imperative, brutal needs, which is asserted in every male posture, especially when eating, is also the principle of the division of foods between the sexes, a division which both sexes recognize in their practices and their language. It behooves a man to drink and eat more, and to eat and drink stronger things. Thus, men will have two rounds of aperitifs (more on special occasions), big ones in big glasses (the success of Ricard or Pernod is no doubt partly due to its being a drink both strong and copious—not a dainty 'thimbleful'), and they leave the tit-bits (savoury biscuits, peanuts) to the children and the women, who have a small measure (not enough to 'get tipsy') of homemade aperitif (for which they swap recipes). Similarly, among the hors d'oeuvres, the *charcuterie* is more for the men, and later the cheese, especially if it is strong, whereas the *crudités* (raw vegetables) are more for the women, like the salad; and these affinities are marked by taking a second helping or sharing what is left over. Meat, the nourishing food par excellence, strong and strong-making, giving vigour, blood, and health, is the dish for the men, who take a second helping, whereas the women are satisfied with a small portion. It is not that they are stinting themselves; they really don't want what others might need, especially the men, the natural meat-eaters, and they derive a sort of authority from what they do not see as a privation. Besides, they don't have a taste for men's food, which is reputed to be harmful when eaten to excess (for example, a surfeit of meat can 'turn the blood', over-excite, bring you out in spots etc.) and may even arouse a sort of disgust.

Strictly biological differences are underlined and symbolically accentuated by differences in bearing, differences in gesture, posture and behaviour which express a whole relationship to the social world. To these are added all the deliberate modifications of appearance, especially by use of the set of marks—cosmetic (hairstyle, make-up, beard, moustache, whiskers etc.) or vestimentary—which, because they depend on the economic and cultural means that can be invested in them, function as social markers deriving their meaning and value from their position in the system of distinctive signs which they constitute and which is itself homologous with the system of social positions. The sign-bearing, sign-wearing body is also a producer of signs which are physically marked by the relationship to the body: thus the valorization of virility, expressed in a use of the mouth or a pitch of the voice, can determine the whole of working-class pronunciation. The body, a social product which is the only tangible manifestation of the 'person', is commonly perceived as the most natural expression of innermost nature. There are no merely 'physical' facial signs; the colour and thickness of lipstick, or expressions, as well as the shape of the face or the mouth, are immediately read as indices of a 'moral' physiognomy, socially characterized, i.e., of a 'vulgar' or 'distinguished' mind, naturally 'natural' or naturally 'cultivated'. The signs constituting the perceived body, cultural products which differentiate groups by their degree of culture, that is, their distance from nature, seem grounded in nature. The legitimate use of the body is spontaneously perceived as an index of moral uprightness, so that its opposite, a 'natural' body, is seen as an index of *laisser-aller* ('letting oneself go'), a culpable surrender to facility.

Thus one can begin to map out a universe of class bodies, which (biological accidents apart) tends to reproduce in its specific logic the universe of the social structure. It is no accident that bodily properties are perceived through social systems of classification which are not independent of the distribution of these properties among the social classes. The prevailing taxonomies tend to rank and contrast the properties most frequent among the dominant (i.e., the rarest ones) and those most frequent among the dominated.[22] The social representation of his own body which each agent has to reckon with,[23] from the very beginning, in order to build up his subjective image of his body and his bodily hexis, is thus obtained by applying a social system of classification based on the same principle as the social products to which it is applied. Thus, bodies would have every likelihood of receiving a value strictly corresponding to the positions of their owners in the distribution of the other fundamental properties—but for the fact that the logic of social heredity sometimes endows those least endowed in all other respects with the rarest bodily properties, such as beauty (sometimes 'fatally' attractive, because it threatens the other hierarchies), and, conversely, sometimes denies the 'high and mighty' the bodily attributes of their position, such as height or beauty.

Unpretentious or Uncouth?

It is clear that tastes in food cannot be considered in complete independence of the other dimensions of the relationship to the world, to others and to one's own body, through which the practical philosophy of each class is enacted. To demonstrate this, one would have to make a systematic comparison of the working-class and bourgeois ways of treating food, of serving, presenting and offering it, which are infinitely more revelatory than even the nature of the products involved (especially since most surveys of consumption ignore differences in quality). The analysis is a difficult one, because each life-style can only really be constructed in relation to the other, which is its objective and subjective negation, so that the meaning of behaviour is totally reversed depending on which point of view is adopted and on whether the common words which have to be used to name the conduct (e.g., 'manners') are invested with popular or bourgeois connotations.

Plain speaking, plain eating: the working-class meal is characterized by plenty (which does not exclude restrictions and limits) and above all by freedom. 'Elastic' and 'abundant' dishes are brought to the table—soups or sauces, pasta or potatoes (almost always included among the vegetables)—and served with a ladle or spoon, to avoid too much measuring and counting, in contrast to everything that has to be cut and divided, such as roasts.[24] This impression of abundance, which is the norm on special occasions, and always applies, so far as is possible, for the men, whose plates are filled twice (a privilege which marks a boy's accession to manhood), is often balanced, on ordinary occasions, by restrictions which generally apply to the women, who will share one portion between two, or eat the left-overs of the previous day; a girl's accession to womanhood is marked by doing without. It is part of men's status to eat and to eat well (and also to drink well); it is particularly insisted that they should eat, on the grounds that 'it won't keep', and there is something suspect about a refusal. On Sundays, while the women are on their feet, busily serving, clearing the table, washing up, the men remain seated, still eating and drinking. These strongly marked differences of social status (associated with sex and age) are accompanied by no practical differentiation (such as the bourgeois division between the dining room and the kitchen, where the servants eat and sometimes the children), and strict sequencing of the meal tends to be ignored. Everything may be put on the table at much the same time (which also saves walking), so that the women may have reached the dessert, and also the children, who will take their plates and watch television, while the men are still eating the main dish and the 'lad', who has arrived late, is swallowing his soup.

This freedom, which may be perceived as disorder or slovenliness, is adapted to its function. Firstly, it is labour-saving, which is seen as an advantage. Because men take no part in housework, not least because the women would not allow it—it would be a dishonour to see men step outside their rôle—every economy of effort is welcome. Thus, when the coffee is served, a single spoon may be passed around to stir it. But these short cuts are only permissible because one is and feels at home, among the family, where ceremony would be an affectation. For example, to save washing up, the dessert may be handed out on improvised plates torn from the cake-box (with a joke about 'taking the liberty', to mark the transgression), and the neighbour invited in for a meal will also receive his piece of cardboard (offering a plate would exclude him) as a sign of familiarity. Similarly, the plates are not changed between dishes. The soup plate, wiped with bread, can be used right through the meal. The hostess will certainly offer to 'change the plates', pushing back her chair with one hand and reaching with the other for the plate next to her, but everyone will protest ('It all gets mixed up inside you') and if she were to insist it would look as if she wanted to show off her crockery (which she is allowed to if it is a new present) or to treat her guests as strangers, as is sometimes deliberately done to intruders or 'scroungers' who never return the invitation. These unwanted guests may be frozen out by changing their plates despite their protests, not laughing at their jokes, or scolding the children for their behaviour ('No, no, *we* don't mind', say the guests; 'They ought to know better by now', the parents respond). The common root of all these 'liberties' is no doubt the sense that at least there will not be self-imposed controls, constraints and restrictions—especially not in eating, a primary need and a compensation—and especially not in the heart of domestic life, the one realm of freedom, when everywhere else, and at all other times, necessity prevails.

In opposition to the free-and-easy working-class meal, the bourgeoisie is concerned to eat with all due form. Form is first of all a matter of rhythm, which implies expectations, pauses, restraints; waiting until the last person served has started to eat, taking modest helpings, not appearing over-eager. A strict sequence is observed and all coexistence of dishes which the sequence separates, fish and meat, cheese and dessert, is excluded: for example, before the dessert is served, everything left on the table, even the salt-cellar, is removed, and the crumbs are swept up. This extension of rigorous rules into everyday life (the bourgeois male shaves and dresses first thing every morning, and not just to 'go out'), refusing the division between home and the exterior, the quotidian and the extra-quotidian, is not explained solely by the presence of strangers—servants and guests—in the familiar family world. It is the expression of a habitus of order, restraint and propriety which may not be abdicated. The relation to food—*the* primary need and pleasure—is only one dimension of the bourgeois relation to the social world. The opposition between the immediate and the deferred, the easy and the difficult, substance (or function) and form, which is exposed in a particularly striking fashion in bourgeois ways of eating, is the basis of all aestheticization of practice and every aesthetic. Through all the forms and formalisms imposed on the immediate appetite, what is demanded—and inculcated—is not only a disposition to discipline food consumption by a conventional structuring which is also a gentle, indirect, invisible censorship (quite different from enforced privations) and which is an element in an art of living (correct eating, for example, is a way of paying homage to one's hosts and to the mistress of the house, a tribute to her care and effort). It is also a whole relationship to animal nature, to primary needs and the populace who indulge them without restraint; it is a way of denying the meaning and primary function of consumption, which are essentially common, by making the meal a social ceremony, an affirmation of ethical tone and aesthetic refinement. The manner of presenting and consuming the food, the organization of the meal and setting of the places, strictly differentiated according to the sequence of dishes and arranged to please the eye, the presentation of the dishes, considered as much in terms of shape and colour (like works of art) as of their consumable substance, the etiquette governing posture and gesture, ways of serving oneself and others, of using the different utensils, the seating plan, strictly but discreetly hierarchical, the censorship of all bodily manifestations of the act or pleasure of eating (such as noise or haste), the very refinement of the things consumed, with quality more important than quantity—this whole commitment to stylization tends to shift the emphasis from substance and function to form and manner, and so to deny the crudely material reality of the act of eating and of the things consumed, or, which amounts to the same thing, the basely material

vulgarity of those who indulge in the immediate satisfactions of food and drink.[25]

Given the basic opposition between form and substance, one could re-generate each of the oppositions between the two antagonistic approaches to the treatment of food and the act of eating. In one case, food is claimed as a material reality, a nourishing substance which sustains the body and gives strength (hence the emphasis on heavy, fatty, strong foods, of which the paradigm is pork—fatty and salty—the antithesis of fish—light, lean and bland); in the other, the priority given to form (the shape of the body, for example) and social form, formality, puts the pursuit of strength and substance in the background and identifies true freedom with the elective asceticism of a self-imposed rule. And it could be shown that two antagonistic world views, two worlds, two representations of human excellence are contained in this matrix. Substance—or matter—is what is substantial, not only 'filling' but also real, as opposed to all appearances, all the fine words and empty gestures that 'butter no parsnips' and are, as the phrase goes, purely symbolic; reality, as against sham, imitation, window-dressing; the little eating-house with its marble-topped tables and paper napkins where you get an honest square meal and aren't 'paying for the wallpaper' as in fancy restaurants; being, as against seeming, nature and the natural, simplicity (pot-luck, 'take it as it comes', 'no standing on ceremony'), as against embarrassment, mincing and posturing, airs and graces, which are always suspected of being a substitute for substance, i.e., for sincerity, for feeling, for what is felt and proved in actions; it is the free-speech and language of the heart which make the true 'nice guy', blunt, straightforward, unbending, honest, genuine, 'straight down the line' and 'straight as a die', as opposed to everything that is pure form, done only for form's sake; it is freedom and the refusal of complications, as opposed to respect for all the forms and formalities spontaneously perceived as instruments of distinction and power. On these moralities, these world views, there is no neutral viewpoint; what for some is shameless and slovenly, for others is straightforward, unpretentious; familiarity is for some the most absolute form of recognition, the abdication of all distance, a trusting openness, a relation of equal to equal; for others, who shun familiarity, it is an unseemly liberty.

The popular realism which inclines working people to reduce practices to the reality of their function, to do what they do, and be what they are ('That's the way I am'), without 'kidding themselves' ('That's the way it is'), and the practical materialism which inclines them to censor the expression of feelings or to divert emotion into violence or oaths, are the near-perfect antithesis of the aesthetic disavowal which, by a sort of essential hypocrisy (seen, for example, in the opposition between pornography and eroticism) masks the interest in function by the primacy given to form, so that what people do, they do as if they were not doing it.

The Visible and the Invisible

But food—which the working classes place on the side of being and substance, whereas the bourgeoisie, refusing the distinction between inside and outside or 'at home' and 'for others', the quotidian and the extra-quotidian, introduces into it the categories of form and appearance—is itself related to clothing as inside to outside, the domestic to the public, being to seeming. And the inversion of the places of food and clothing in the contrast between the spending patterns of the working classes, who give priority to being, and the middle classes, where the concern for 'seeming' arises, is the sign of a reversal of the whole world view. The working classes make a realistic or, one might say, functionalist use of clothing. Looking for substance and function rather than form, they seek 'value for money' and choose what will 'last'. Ignoring the bourgeois concern to introduce formality and formal dress into the domestic world, the place for freedom—an apron and slippers (for women), bare chest or a vest (for men)—they scarcely mark the distinction between top clothes, visible, intended to be seen, and underclothes, invisible or hidden—unlike the middle classes, who have a degree of anxiety about external appearances, both sartorial and cosmetic, at least outside and at work (to which middle-class women more often have access).

Thus, despite the limits of the data available, one finds in men's clothing (which is much more socially marked, at the level of what can be grasped by statistics on purchases, than women's clothing) the equivalent of the major oppositions found in food consumption. In the first dimension of the space, the division again runs between the office workers and the manual workers and is marked particularly by the opposition between grey or white overalls and blue dungarees or boiler-suits, between town shoes and the more relaxed moccasins, kickers or sneakers (not to mention dressing-gowns, which clerical workers buy 3.5 times more often than manual workers). The increased quantity and quality of all purchases of men's clothing is summed up in the opposition between the suit, the prerogative of the senior executive, and the blue overall, the distinctive mark of the farmer and industrial worker (it is virtually unknown in other groups, except craftsmen); or between the overcoat, always much rarer among men than women, but much more frequent among senior executives than the other classes, and the fur-lined jacket or lumber jacket, mainly worn by agricultural and industrial workers. In between are the junior executives, who now scarcely ever wear working clothes but fairly often buy suits.

Among women, who, in all categories (except farmers and farm labourers), spend more than men (especially in the junior and senior executive, professional and other high-income categories), the number of purchases increases as one moves up the social hierarchy; the difference is greatest for suits and costumes—expensive garments—and smaller for dresses and especially skirts and jackets. The top-coat, which is increasingly frequent among women at higher social levels, is opposed to the 'all-purpose' raincoat, in the same way as overcoat and lumber jacket are opposed for men. The use of the smock and the apron, which in the working classes is virtually the housewife's uniform, increases as one moves down the hierarchy (in contrast to the dressing-gown, which is virtually unknown among peasants and industrial workers).

The interest the different classes have in self-presentation, the attention they devote to it, their awareness of the profits it gives and the investment of time, effort, sacrifice and care which they actually put into it are proportionate to the chances of material or symbolic profit they can reasonably expect from it. More precisely, they depend on the existence of a labour market in which physical appearance may be valorized in the performance of the job itself or in professional relations; and on the differential chances of access to this market and the sectors of this market in which beauty and deportment most strongly contribute to occupational value. A first indication of this correspondence between the propensity to cosmetic investments and the chances of profit may be seen in the gap, for all forms of beauty care, between those who work and those who do not (which must also vary according to the nature of the job and the work environment). It can be understood in terms of this logic why working-class women, who are less likely to have a job and much less likely to enter one of the occupations which most strictly demand conformity to the dominant norms of beauty, are less aware than all others of the 'market' value of beauty and much less inclined to invest time and effort, sacrifices and money in cultivating their bodies.

It is quite different with the women of the petite bourgeoisie, especially the new petite bourgeoisie, in the occupations involving presentation and representation, which often impose a uniform (*tenue*) intended, among other things, to abolish all traces of heterodox taste, and which always demand what is called *tenue,* in the sense of 'dignity of conduct and correctness of manners', implying, according to the dictionary, 'a refusal to give way to vulgarity or facility'. (In the specialized 'charm schools' which train hostesses, the working-class girls who select themselves on the basis of 'natural' beauty undergo a radical transformation in their way of walking, sitting, laughing, smiling, talking, dressing, making-up etc.) Women of the petite bourgeoisie who have sufficient interests in the market in which physical properties can function as capital to recognize the dominant image of the body unconditionally without possessing, at least in their own eyes (and no doubt objectively) enough body capital to obtain the highest profits, are, here too, at the site of greatest tension.

The self-assurance given by the certain knowledge of one's own value, especially that of one's body or speech, is in fact very closely linked to the position occupied in social space (and also, of course, to trajectory). Thus, the proportion of women who consider themselves below average in beauty, or who think they look older than they are, falls very rapidly as one moves up the social hierarchy. Similarly, the ratings women give themselves for the different parts of their bodies tend to rise with social position, and this despite the fact that the implicit demands rise too. It is not surprising that petit-bourgeois women—who are almost as dissatisfied with their bodies as working-class women (they are the ones who most often wish they looked different and who are most discontented with various parts of their bodies), while being more aware of the usefulness of beauty and more often recognizing the dominant ideal of physical excellence—devote such great investments, of self-denial and especially of time, to improving their appearance and are such unconditional believers in all forms of cosmetic voluntarism (e.g., plastic surgery).

As for the women of the dominant class, they derive a double assurance from their bodies. Believing, like petit-bourgeois women, in the value of beauty and the value of the effort to be beautiful, and so associating aesthetic value and moral value, they feel superior both in the intrinsic, natural beauty of their bodies and in the art of self-embellishment and everything they call *tenue,* a moral and aesthetic virtue which defines 'nature' negatively as sloppiness. Beauty can thus be simultaneously a gift of nature and a conquest of merit, as much opposed to the abdications of vulgarity as to ugliness.

Thus, the experience par excellence of the 'alienated body', embarrassment, and the opposite experience, ease, are clearly unequally probable for members of the petite bourgeoisie and the bourgeoisie, who grant the same recognition to the same representation of the legitimate body and legitimate deportment, but are unequally able to achieve it. The chances of experiencing one's own body as a vessel of grace, a continuous miracle, are that much greater when bodily capacity is commensurate with recognition; and, conversely, the probability of experiencing the body with unease, embarrassment, timidity grows with the disparity between the ideal body and the real body, the dream body and the 'looking-glass self' reflected in the reactions of others (the same laws are also true of speech).

Although it is not a petit-bourgeois monopoly, the petit-bourgeois experience of the world starts out from timidity, the embarrassment of someone who is uneasy in his body and his language and who, instead of being 'as one body with them', observes them from outside, through other people's eyes, watching, checking, correcting himself, and who, by his desperate attempts to reappropriate an alienated being-for-others, exposes himself to appropriation, giving himself away as much by hyper-correction as by clumsiness. The timidity which, despite itself, realizes the objectified body, which lets itself be trapped in the destiny proposed by collective perception and statement (nicknames etc.), is betrayed by a body that is subject to the representation of others even in its passive, unconscious reactions (one feels oneself blushing). By contrast, ease, a sort of indifference to the objectifying gaze of others which neutralizes its powers, presupposes the self-assurance which comes from the certainty of being able to objectify that objectification, appropriate that appropriation, of being capable of imposing the norms of apperception of one's own body, in short, of commanding all the powers which, even when they reside in the body and apparently borrow its most specific weapons, such as 'presence' or charm, are essentially irreducible to it. This is the real meaning of the findings of the experiment by W. D. Dannenmaier and F. J. Thumin, in which the subjects, when asked to assess the height of familiar persons from memory, tended to overestimate most of the height of those who had most authority or prestige in their eyes.[26] It would seem that the logic whereby the 'great' are perceived as physically greater than they are applies very generally, and that authority of whatever sort contains a power of seduction which it would be naive to reduce to the effect of self-interested servility. That is why political contestation has always made use of caricature, a distortion of the bodily image intended to break the charm and hold up to ridicule one of the principles of the effect of authority imposition.

Charm and charisma in fact designate the power, which certain people have, to impose their own self-image as the objective and collective image of their body and being; to persuade others, as in love or faith, to abdicate their generic power of objectification and delegate it to the person who should be its object, who thereby becomes an absolute subject, without an exterior (being his own Other), fully justified in existing, legitimated. The charismatic leader manages to be for the group what he is for himself, instead of being for himself, like those dominated in the symbolic struggle, what he is for others. He 'makes' the opinion which makes him; he constitutes himself as an absolute by a manipulation of symbolic power which is constitutive of his power since it enables him to produce and impose his own objectification.

The Universes of Stylistic Possibles

Thus, the spaces defined by preferences in food, clothing or cosmetics are organized according to the same fundamental structure, that of the social space determined by volume and composition of capital. Fully to construct the space of life-styles within which cultural practices are defined, one would first have to establish, for each class and class fraction, that is, for each of the configurations of capital, the generative formula of the habitus which retranslates the necessities and facilities characteristic of that class of (relatively) homogeneous conditions of existence into a particular life-style. One would then have to determine how the dispositions of the habitus are specified, for each of the major areas of practice, by implementing one of the stylistic possibles offered by each field (the field of sport, or music, or food, decoration, politics, language etc.). By superimposing these homologous spaces one would obtain a rigorous representation of the space of life-styles, making it possible to characterize each of the distinctive features (e.g., wearing a cap or playing the piano) in the two respects in which it is objectively defined, that is, on the one hand by reference to the set of features constituting the area in question (e.g., the system of hairstyles), and on the other hand by reference to the set of features constituting a particular life-style (e.g., the working-class life-style), within which its social significance is determined.

Sources

The survey on which the work was based was carried out in 1963, after a preliminary survey by extended interview and ethnographic observation, on a sample of 692 subjects (both sexes) in Paris, Lille and a small provincial town. To obtain a sample large enough to make it possible to analyse variations in practices and opinions in relation to sufficiently homogeneous social units, a complementary survey was carried out in 1967–68, bringing the total number of subjects to 1,217. Because the survey measured relatively stable dispositions, this time-lag does not seem to have affected the responses (except perhaps for the question on singers, an area of culture where fashions change more rapidly).

The following complementary sources (C.S.) were also used:

I. The 1966 survey on 'businessmen and senior executives' was carried out by SOFRES (Société française d'enquêtes par sondages) on behalf of the Centre d'études des supports de publicité (CESP). The sample consisted of 2,257 persons aged 15 and over, each living in a household the head of which was a large industrial or commercial employer, a member of the professions, a senior executive, an engineer or a secondary or higher-education teacher. The questionnaire included a set of questions on reading habits and the previous few days' reading of daily, weekly and monthly newspapers and magazines, use of radio and TV, standard of living, household equipment, life-style (holidays, sport, consumption), professional life (conferences, travel, business meals), cultural practices and the principal basic data (educational level, income, population of place of residence etc.). I had access to the whole set of distributions by the socio-occupational category of the head of household or individual.

II. The regular survey by INSEE (Institut national de la statistique et des études economiques) on household living conditions and expenditure was based in 1972 on a representative sample of 13,000 households. It consists of a survey by questionnaire dealing with the characteristics of the household (composition, ages, occupation of the head), accommodation and facilities, major expenditure (clothing, fuel etc.), periodic expenditure (rent, service charges etc.), combined with anal-

ysis of account books for current expenditure, left with each household for a week, collected and checked by the interviewer. This survey makes it possible to assess the whole range of expenditure (except certain major and infrequent items such as air travel, removal expenses etc.), as well as items of consumption not preceded by purchase (food in the case of farmers, items drawn from their stocks by craftsmen and shopkeepers), which are evaluated at their retail price to allow comparison with the other categories of households. This explains why consumption is considerably higher than income in the case of farmers and small businessmen (categories which are always particularly prone to under-declare their income). For the overall findings, see G. Bigata and B. Bouvier, 'Les conditions de vie des ménages en 1972', *Collections de l'INSEE*, ser. M, no. 32 (February 1972). The data presented here come from secondary analysis of tables by narrow categories produced at my request.

The other surveys consulted are simply listed below. These studies, almost always devoted to a particular area of cultural activity, are generally based on relatively limited samples. They mostly use a classification which groups the occupations into five categories: (1) *agriculteurs* (farmers and farm labourers); (2) *ouvriers* (industrial manual workers); (3) industrial and commercial employers; (4) clerical workers and junior executives; (5) senior executives and the 'liberal professions'.

III. INSEE, 'La consommation alimentaire des Français', *Collections de l'INSEE*. (The regular INSEE surveys on eating habits.)

IV. SOFRES, *Les habitudes de table des Français* (Paris, 1972).

V. SOFRES, *Les Français et la gastronomie*, July 1977. (Sample of 1,000.)

Notes

1. The gaps are more clear-cut and certainly more visible as regards education than income, because information on incomes (based on tax declarations) is much less reliable than information on qualifications. This is especially true of industrial and commercial employers (who, in the CESP survey—C.S. I—provided, along with doctors, the highest rate of non-response to the questions about income), craftsmen, shopkeepers and farmers.

2. It follows from this that the relationship between conditions of existence and practices or the meaning of practices is not to be understood in terms either of the logic of mechanism or of the logic of consciousness.

3. In contrast to the atomistic approach of social psychology, which breaks the unity of practice to establish partial 'laws' claiming to account for the products of practice, the *opus operatum*, the aim is to establish general laws reproducing the laws of production, the *modus operandi*.

4. Economic theory, which treats economic agents as interchangeable actors, paradoxically fails to take account of the economic dispositions, and is thereby prevented from really explaining the systems of preferences which define incommensurable and independent subjective use-values.

5. An ethic, which seeks to impose the principles of an ethos (i.e., the forced choices of a social condition) as a universal norm, is another, more subtle way of succumbing to *amor fati*, of being content with what one is and has. Such is the basis of the felt contradiction between ethics and revolutionary intent.

6. 'Bourgeois' is used here as shorthand for 'dominant fractions of the dominant class', and 'intellectual' or 'artist' functions in the same way for 'dominated fractions of the dominant class'.

7. F. Nietzsche, *Der Wille zur Macht* (Stuttgart, Alfred Kröner, 1964), no. 943, p. 630.

8. Bananas are the only fruit for which manual workers and farm workers have higher annual per capita spending (FF 23.26 and FF 25.20) than all other classes, especially the senior executives, who spend most on apples (FF 31.60 as against FF 21.00 for manual workers), whereas the rich, expensive fruits—grapes, peaches and nuts—are mainly eaten by professionals and industrial and commercial employers (FF 29.04 for grapes, 19.09 for peaches and 17.33 for nuts, as against FF 6.74, 11.78 and 4.90 respectively, for manual workers).

9. This whole paragraph is based on secondary analysis of the tables from the 1972 INSEE survey on household expenditure on 39 items by socio-occupational category (C.S. II).

10. A fuller translation of the original text would include: ' "les *nourritures* à la fois les plus *nourrissantes* et les plus *économiques*" (the double tautology showing the reduction to pure economic function).' (Translator's note.)

11. In the French: 'le gros et le gras, gros rouge, gros sabots, gros travaux, gros rire, grosses blagues, gros bon sens, plaisanteries grasses'—cheap red wine, clogs (i.e., obviousness), heavy work, belly laughs, crude common sense, crude jokes (translator).

12. K. Marx, *Capital*, I (Harmondsworth, Penguin, 1976), 482 (translator).

13. One fine example, taken from Böhm-Bawerk, will demonstrate this essentialism: 'We must now consider a *second* phenomenon of human experience—one that is heavily fraught with consequence. That is the fact that we feel less concerned about future sensations of joy and sorrow simply because they do lie in the future, and the lessening of our concern is in proportion to the remoteness of that future. Consequently we accord to goods which are intended to serve future ends a value which falls short of the true intensity of their future marginal utility. *We systematically undervalue our future wants and also the means which serve to satisfy them.*' E. Böhm-Bawerk, *Capital and Interest*, II (South Holland, Ill., 1959), 268, quoted by G. L. Stigler and G. S. Becker, 'De gustibus non est disputandum', *American Economic Review*, 67 (March 1977), 76–90.

14. We may assume that the deep-seated relation to the future (and also to one's own person—which is valued more at higher levels of the social hierarchy) is reflected in the small proportion of manual workers who say that 'there is a new life after death' (15 percent, compared with 18 percent of craftsmen and shopkeepers, office workers and middle managers, and 32 percent of senior executives).

15. It is not superfluous to point out that this art, which has its recognized virtuoso, the 'life and soul of the party', can sink into the caricature of jokes or remarks that are defined as stereotyped, stupid or coarse in terms of the criteria of popular taste.

16. The oppositions are much less clear-cut in the middle classes, although homologous differences are found between primary teachers and office workers on the one hand and shopkeepers on the other.

17. *La bouffe*: 'grub', 'nosh'; *grande bouffe*: 'blow-out' (translator).

18. The preference for foreign restaurants—Italian, Chinese, Japanese and, to a lesser extent, Russian—rises with level in the social hierarchy. The only exceptions are Spanish restaurants, which are associated with a more popular form of tourism, and North African restaurants, which are most favoured by junior executives (C.S. IV).

19. *Les gros*: the rich; *grosse bouffe*: bulk food (cf. *grossiste*: wholesaler, and English 'grocer'). See also note 17 above (translator).

20. That is why the body designates not only present position but also trajectory.

21. In 'The Economics of Linguistic Exchanges', *Social Science Information*, 26 (December 1977), 645–668, Bourdieu develops the opposition between two ways of speaking, rooted in two relations to the body and the world, which have a lexical reflection in the many idioms based on two words for 'mouth': *la bouche* and *la gueule*. *La bouche* is the 'standard' word for the mouth; but in opposition to *la gueule*—a slang or 'vulgar' word except when applied to animals—it tends to be restricted to the lips, whereas *la gueule* can include the

whole face or the throat. Most of the idioms using *la bouche* imply fastidiousness, effeminacy or disdain; those with *la gueule* connote vigour, strength or violence (translator's note).

22. This means that the taxonomies applied to the perceived body (fat/thin, strong/weak, big/small etc.) are, as always, at once arbitrary (e.g., the ideal female body may be fat or thin, in different economic and social contexts) and necessary, i.e., grounded in the specific reason of a given social order.

23. More than ever, the French possessive pronouns—which do not mark the owner's gender—ought to be translated 'his or her'. The 'sexism' of the text results from the male translator's reluctance to defy the dominant use of a sexist symbolic system (translator).

24. One could similarly contrast the bowl, which is generously filled and held two-handed for unpretentious drinking, and the cup, into which a little is poured, and more later ('Would you care for a little more coffee?'), and which is held between two fingers and sipped from.

25. Formality is a way of denying the truth of the social world and of social relations. Just as popular 'functionalism' is refused as regards food, so too there is a refusal of the realistic vision which leads the working classes to accept social exchanges for what they are (and, for example, to say, without cynicism, of someone who has done a favour or rendered a service, 'She knows I'll pay her back'). Suppressing avowal of the calculation which pervades social relations, there is a striving to see presents, received or given, as 'pure' testimonies of friendship, respect, affection, and equally 'pure' manifestations of generosity and moral worth.

26. W. D. Dannenmaier and F. J. Thumin, 'Authority Status as a Factor in Perceptual Distortion of Size', *Journal of Social Psychology*, 63 (1964), 361–365.

MELVIN L. KOHN

Job Complexity and Adult Personality

There have been several distinct approaches to the study of work, each of them emphasizing some aspect that bears on a particular theoretical concern of the investigator. Rarely, though, has that concern been the effect of work on personality. Sociologists have learned much about social stratification and mobility, for example, by focusing on the dimension of work most pertinent to the stratificational system, the status of the job (Blau and Duncan, 1967; Duncan, Featherman, and Duncan, 1972; Sewell, Hauser, and Featherman, 1976). But however important status may be for studies of mobility, it would be unwise to assume—as is often done—that the status of a job is equally pertinent for personality. In terms of impact on personality, job status serves mainly as a gross indicator of the job's location in the hierarchical organization of the economic and social system. The status of the job is closely linked to such structural conditions of work as how complex it is, how closely it is supervised, and what sorts of pressures it entails. It is these structural realities, not status as such, that affect personality (Kohn and Schooler, 1973).

It is also indisputable that economists have learned much about the functioning of the economic system by focusing on the extrinsic rewards the job confers—in particular, income. Just as with occupational status, though, it would be incorrect to assume that because income is important for an understanding of the economic system qua system, income is also the most significant aspect of the job in terms of the meaning of work to the worker or the impact of work on his sense of self and orientation to the rest of the world (Whyte, 1955; Kohn and Schooler, 1973).

Organizational theorists, both the Weberian sociologists and those more applied scholars who call themselves administrative scientists, have, by studying formal organizational structure, undoubtedly contributed much to our understanding of how organizations function (Blau and Schoenherr, 1971). But the very strength of their approach—its systematic attention to how formal organizations function as systems, regardless of the personalities of those who play the various organizational roles—means that they largely ignore the effect of organizational structure on the individual worker and his work. When they do pay attention to the individual worker, their interest rarely goes beyond his role as worker.

The human-relations-in-industry approach, in deliberate juxtaposition to the formal organizational approach, focuses on informal, interpersonal relationships and the symbolic systems that emerge out of such relationships (Whyte, 1961; 1969). Scholars using this approach supply a needed corrective to the formal organizational perspective. But they sometimes seem unaware that people not only relate to one another on the job; they also work. Moreover, this perspective has been concerned almost exclusively with the implications of work for on-the-job behavior, paying little attention to the effects of the job on other realms of life.

Occupational psychologists come close to understanding the relationship between work and personality, but there are two major limitations to their studies. First, many of them misinterpret Kurt Lewin (and, I would add, W. I. Thomas) by dealing exclusively with how people perceive their work while neglecting the actual conditions under which that work is performed. (This criticism applies as well to most sociological studies of alienation in work.) Thus, they measure boredom rather than routinization, interest in the work rather than its substantive complexity, and "alienation in work" rather than actual working conditions. Such an approach ignores the possibilities that there can be a gap between the conditions to which a person is subjected and his awareness of those conditions; that the existence or nonexistence of such a gap is itself problematic and may be structurally determined; and that conditions felt by the worker to be benign can have deleterious consequences, while conditions felt to be onerous can have beneficial consequences. The second limitation is the preoccupation of most occupational psychologists with job satisfaction, as if this were the only psychological consequence of work. I am less disturbed by the technical difficulties in measuring job satisfaction—a notoriously slippery concept—than I am by the assumption that work has no psychological ramifications beyond the time and place during and within which it occurs. Work affects people's values, self-conceptions, orientation to social reality, even their intellectual functioning. Job satisfaction is only one, and far from the most important, psychological consequence of work.

The research that comes closest of all to dealing straightforwardly with work and its consequences for personality employs an old tradition of sociological study—case studies of occupations. Practitioners of this art have sometimes done a magnificent job of depicting the reality of work as it impinges on the worker. Unfortunately, though, their studies cannot determine which aspects of work are most pertinent for which aspects of psychological functioning. W. Fred Cottrell's (1940) classic study of railroaders, for example, pointed out a multitude of ways that the job conditions of men who operate trains differ from those of men in many other occupations—including the unpredictability of working hours, geographical mobility, precision of timing, outsider status in the home community, and unusual recruitment and promotion practices. Since all these conditions are tied together in one occupational package, it is not possible to disentangle the psychological concomitants of each. More recent comparative studies face similar interpretative problems. For example, Robert Blauner's (1964) study of alienation among blue-collar workers in four industries, chosen to represent four technological levels, showed that differences in working conditions are systematically associated with the stage of technological development of the industry. But these differences, too, come in packages: Printing differs from automobile manufacture not only in technology and in the skill levels of workers but also in pace of the work, closeness of supervision, freedom of physical movement, and a multitude of other conditions. One cannot tell which, if any, of these interlocked occupational conditions are conducive to alienation.

Disentangling Occupational Conditions

Disentangling occupational conditions to assess their psychological impact requires a mode of research different from that employed in studies of particular occupations and particular industries. Carmi Schooler and I have dealt with the problem by shifting the focus from named occupations—carpenter, surgeon, or flight engineer—to dimensions of occupation (Kohn, 1969; Kohn and Schooler, 1969; 1973). Our strategy has been to secure a large and representative sample of employed men, who necessarily work in many occupations and many industries.[1] We have inventoried the men's job conditions and then differentiated the psychological concomitants of each facet of occupation by statistical analysis. In our most recent research, my colleagues and I have done comparable analyses for employed women (Miller et al., 1979).

Even though occupational conditions are intercorrelated, they are not perfectly intercorrelated. Thus, substantively complex jobs are likely also to be time-pressured; but there are enough jobs that are substantively complex yet not time-pressured, and enough that are substantively simple yet time-pressured, for us to examine the relationship between substantive complexity and, say, receptiveness or resistance to change, while statistically controlling time pressure. We can also look for statistical interaction between the two, asking whether the impact of substantive complexity on, let us say, stance toward change is different for men who are more time-pressured and for men who are less time-pressured. And, at the same time, we can statistically control many other occupational conditions, as well as important nonoccupational variables, for example, education, which usually precedes and is often a prerequisite for the job.

In all, we have indexed more than fifty separable dimensions of occupation, including such diverse aspects of work experience as the substantive complexity of work, the routinization or diversity of the flow of work, relationships with co-workers and with supervisors, pace of work and control thereof, physical and environmental conditions, job pressures and uncertainties, union membership and participation, bureaucratization, job protections, and fringe benefits. (For complete information, see Kohn, 1969, pp. 236, 244–253.) These indices provide the basis for a broad descriptive picture of the principal facets of occupations, as experienced by men in all types of industries and at all levels of the civilian economy.

I must admit that this approach—based as it is on a sample survey of all men employed in civilian occupations—is not optimum for securing some kinds of job information. Men may have only limited information about certain aspects of their jobs, such as the overall structure of the organization in which they work. Moreover, a sample of men scattered across many occupations and many work places does not contain enough people in any occupation or any workplace to trace out interpersonal networks and belief systems. Similarly, the method is not well adapted for studying the industrial and technological context in which the job is embedded. The method is most useful for studying the immediate conditions of a man's own job—what he does, who determines how he does it, in what physical and social circumstances he works, to what risks and rewards he is subject.

We found that nearly all of the more than fifty occupational conditions that we had inventoried are correlated with at least some of the several aspects of values, self-conception, social orientation, and intellectual functioning that we had measured (Kohn and Schooler, 1973).[2] But most of these statistical relationships reflect the interrelatedness of occupational conditions with one another and with education. Only twelve of the occupational conditions we studied appear to have any substantial relationship to men's psychological functioning when education and all other pertinent occupational conditions are statistically controlled. Few though they are, these twelve occupational conditions are sufficient to define the "structural imperatives of the job," in that they identify a man's position in the organizational structure, his opportunities for occupational self-direction, the principal job pressures to which he is subject, and the principal uncertainties built into his job.[3] These job conditions are "structural" in two senses: they are built into the structure of the job and they are largely determined by the job's location in the structures of the economy and the society.

Substantive Complexity

Because of its theoretical and empirical importance, I devote the remainder of this essay to one of the twelve structural imperatives of the job, the substantive complexity of work.[4] By the substantive complexity of work, I mean the degree to which the work, in its very substance, requires thought and independent judgment. Substantively complex work by its very nature requires making many decisions that must take into account ill-defined or apparently conflicting contingencies. Although, in general, work with data or with people is likely to be more complex than work with things, this is not always the case, and an index of the overall complexity of work should reflect its degree of complexity in each of these three types of activity. Work with things can vary in complexity from ditch digging to sculpting; similarly, work with people can vary in complexity from receiving simple directions or orders to giving legal advice; and work with data can vary from reading instructions to synthesizing abstract conceptual systems. Thus, the index of substantive complexity that we have generally employed is based on the degree of complexity of the person's work with things, with data, and with people; our appraisal of the overall complexity of his work, regardless of whether he works primarily with things, with data, or with people; and estimates of the amount of time he spends working at each type of activity (Kohn and Schooler, 1973; Kohn, 1976). The several components receive weightings based on a factor analysis.[5]

I focus on substantive complexity for two reasons. The first is that I conceive substantive complexity to be central to the experience of work. The other structural imperatives of the job—even closeness of supervision and routinization—set the conditions under which work is done but they do not characterize the work itself. The substantive complexity of work, by contrast, is at the heart of the experience of work. More than any other occupational condition, it gives meaning to this experience.

The second reason for my preoccupation with substantive complexity is empirical. Our analyses show that substantive complexity of work is strongly related to a wide range of psychological variables. The substantive complexity of work is of course correlated with job satisfaction and with occupational commitment. It also bears on many facets of off-the-job psychological functioning, ranging from valuation of self-direction to self-esteem to authoritarian conservatism to intellectual flexibility. It is even related to the intellectual demands of men's leisure-time pursuits. Moreover, these correlations remain statistically significant and large enough to be meaningful even when education and all other pertinent dimensions of occupation are statistically controlled. Thus, the substantive complexity of work has a strong, independent relationship to many facets of psychological functioning, a relationship stronger than that of any other dimension of occupation we have studied. This is true for men, and our most recent analyses show it to be equally true for employed women (Miller et al., 1979).

The Direction of Causal Effects

There is evidence that the substantive complexity of work is not only correlated with, but has a causal impact on, psychological functioning. The evidence of causal directionality is of two types. The more extensive but less definitive evidence comes from our analyses of cross-sectional data, derived from a large sample of men employed in civilian occupations. Social scientists have long recognized that one cannot make inferences about the direction of causal effects from cross-sectional data unless some of the described phenomena clearly preceded others in their time of occurrence. But where one can realistically assume reciprocity—that *a* affects *b* and *b* also affects *a*—it is possible to assess the magnitude of these reciprocal effects, using econometric techniques for solving simultaneous equations. The simplest of these, which we used, is called two-stage least squares.[6] With this technique, we have assessed the relationships between the substantive complexity of work and many facets of psychological functioning: occupational commitment, job satisfaction, valuation of self-direction or of conformity to external authority, anxiety, self-esteem, receptiveness or resistance to change, standards of morality, authoritarian conservatism, intellectual flexibility, the intellectuality of leisure-time activities, and three types of alienation—powerlessness, self-estrangement, and normlessness.

Our findings indicate that the substantive complexity of men's work affects all these facets of psychological functioning, independent of the selection processes that draw men into particular fields of work and independent of their efforts to mold their jobs to fit their needs, values, and capacities. Moreover, the substantive complexity of work in every instance affects psychological functioning more—often, much more—than the particular facet of psychological functioning affects the substantive complexity of work. This evidence is not definitive—only longitudinal studies can provide definitive evidence—but it does establish a strong prima facie case that the substantive complexity of work has a real and meaningful effect on a wide range of psychological phenomena.

More definitive, albeit less extensive, evidence comes from a follow-up study we conducted with a representative subsample of men in the original study ten years after the initial survey (Kohn and Schooler, 1978). Analyses of longitudinal data require the development of "measurement models" that separate unreliability of measurement from change in the phenomena studied. The essence of the method employed in constructing these models is the use of multiple indicators for each principal concept, inferring from the covariation of the indicators the degree to which each reflects the underlying concept that they are all hypothesized to reflect and the degree to which each reflects anything else, which for measurement purposes is considered to be error (see Jöreskog, 1969, and other papers cited in Kohn and Schooler, 1978). These models permit us to take into account that errors in the measurement of any indicator at the time of the initial survey may well be correlated with errors in the measurement of that same indicator at the time of the follow-up survey. Disregarding such correlated errors in the indicators might make the underlying concept seem more stable or less stable than it really is—thereby distorting any causal analysis in which that index is employed. ...

We chose intellectual flexibility as the first aspect of psychological functioning to be assessed because it offers us the greatest challenge—intellectual flexibility obviously affects recruitment into substantively complex jobs, and there is every reason to expect it to be resistant to change. Still, intellectual flexibility—though not much studied by sociologists—is so important a part of psychological functioning that we must not unthinkingly assume it to be entirely the product of genetics and early life experience. Rather, we should empirically test the possibility that intellectual flexibility may be responsive to adult occupational experience.

Our index of intellectual flexibility is meant to reflect men's actual intellectual performance in the interview situation. We used a variety of indicators—including the men's answers to seemingly simple but highly revealing cognitive problems, their handling of perceptual and projective tests, their propensity to agree when asked "agree-disagree" questions, and the impression they made on the interviewer during a long session that required a great deal of thought and reflection. None of these indicators is believed to be completely valid; but we do believe that all the indicators reflect, to some substantial degree, men's flexibility in coping with an intellectually demanding situation.

The stability of intellectual flexibility, thus measured, is remarkably high over time: The correlation between men's intellectual flexibility at the time of the original study and their intellectual flexibility ten years later, shorn of measurement error, is 0.93. It would be erroneous to assume, though, that the high over-time stability of intellectual flexibility means that it is unaffected by adult experience; it might even be that this stability reflects unchanging life circumstances. In fact, we find that the effect of the substantive complexity of work on intellectual flexibility is striking—on the order of one-fourth as great as that of the men's ten-year-earlier levels of intellectual flexibility. This effect is essentially contemporaneous: The path from the substantive complexity of the job held at the time of the initial survey to intellectual flexibility at the time of the follow-up survey ten years later is small and statistically nonsignificant, while the path from the substantive complexity of the current job to current intellectual flexibility is much more substantial and is statistically significant.[7]

The reciprocal effect of intellectual flexibility on substantive complexity is still more impressive than the effect of substantive complexity on intellectual flexibility. This effect is entirely lagged, that is, it is the men's intellectual flexibility at the time of the initial survey that significantly affects the substantive complexity of their current jobs, and not their current intellectual flexibility. The longitudinal analysis thus demonstrates something that no cross-sectional analysis could show—that, over time, the relationship between substantive complexity and intellectual flexibility is truly reciprocal. The effect of substantive complexity on intellectual flexibility is more immediate: current job demands affect current thinking processes. Intellectual flexibility, by contrast, has a time-lagged effect on substantive complexity: current intellectual flexibility has scant effect on current job demands, but considerable effect on the future course of one's career. Cross-sectional analyses portray only part of this process, making it seem that the relationship between the substantive complexity of work and intellectual functioning were mainly unidirectional, with work affecting intellectual functioning but not the reverse. Longitudinal analysis portrays a more intricate and more interesting, truly reciprocal process.

The data thus demonstrate, beyond reasonable doubt, what heretofore could be stated only as a plausible thesis buttressed by presumptive evidence—that the substantive complexity of work both considerably affects, and is considerably affected by, intellectual flexibility.

My colleagues and I have recently completed two further analyses that extend these conclusions. A much more extensive longitudinal analysis of job conditions and intellectual flexibility (Kohn and Schooler, 1981) confirms that the substantive complexity of work affects intellectual flexibility not only when prior levels of intellectual flexibility and pertinent aspects of social background are taken into account but also when all other structural imperatives of the job are taken into account as well. We further find that substantive complexity is not the only job condition that affects intellectual flexibility; several other job conditions that stimulate and challenge the individual are conducive to intellectual flexibility. But, clearly, substantive complexity plays a key role, not only because it has such a great effect on intellectual flexibility, but also because it provides the principal mechanism through which other job conditions affect intellectual functioning.

In another analysis (Miller et al., 1979), we found that the substantive complexity of work is as important for women's psychological functioning as it is for men's. In particular, a causal analysis using measurement models similar to those described above, but limited to cross-sectional data, shows the contemporaneous effect of substantive complexity on intellectual flexibility to be at least as great for employed women as for employed men.

These findings come down solidly in support of those who hold that occupational conditions affect personality and in opposition to those who believe that the relationship between occupational conditions and personality results solely from selective recruitment and job molding. Ad-

mittedly, personality has great importance in determining who go into what types of jobs and how they perform those jobs; in fact, our analyses underline the importance of these processes. But that has never been seriously at issue. What has been disputed is whether the reverse phenomenon—of job conditions molding personality—also occurs. The evidence of our longitudinal analysis supports the position that it does occur.

In particular, this analysis adds to and helps specify the growing evidence that the structure of the environment has an important effect on cognitive development (Rosenbaum, 1976) and that cognitive processes do not become impervious to environmental influence after adolescence or early adulthood but continue to show "plasticity" throughout the life span (Baltes, 1968; Horn and Donaldson, 1976; Baltes and Schaie, 1976). Our findings reinforce this conclusion by showing that intellectual flexibility continues to be responsive to experience well into midcareer. In fact, it appears that the remarkable stability of intellectual flexibility reflects, at least in part, stability in people's life circumstances. Intellectual flexibility is ever responsive to changes in the substantive complexity of people's work; for most people, though, the substantive complexity of work does not fluctuate markedly.

This analysis demonstrates as well the importance of intellectual flexibility for substantive complexity. I think it noteworthy that this effect appears to be lagged rather than contemporaneous. The implication is that the structure of most jobs does not permit any considerable variation in the substantive complexity of the work: job conditions are not readily modified to suit the needs or capacities of the individual worker. But over a long enough time—certainly over a period as long as ten years—many men either modify their jobs or move on to other jobs more consonant with their intellectual functioning. Thus, the long-term effects of intellectual flexibility on substantive complexity are considerable, even though the contemporaneous effects appear to be negligible.

Our models, of course, deal mainly with the events of midcareer or later. I think it reasonable to assume that men's intellectual flexibility in childhood, adolescence, and early adulthood have had a considerable effect on their educational attainments, and our data show that educational attainment is very important for the substantive complexity of the early jobs in men's careers. Since the substantive complexity of early jobs is a primary determinant of the substantive complexity of later jobs, it seems safe to infer that intellectual flexibility's long-term, indirect effects on the substantive complexity of later jobs has been even greater than our analysis depicts.

The reciprocal relationship between substantive complexity and intellectual flexibility implies an internal dynamic by which relatively small differences in substantive complexity at early stages of a career may become magnified into larger differences in both substantive complexity and intellectual flexibility later in the career. If two men of equivalent intellectual flexibility were to start their careers in jobs differing in substantive complexity, the man in the more complex job would be likely to outstrip the other in further intellectual growth. This, in time, might lead to his attaining jobs of greater complexity, further affecting his intellectual growth. Meantime, the man in the less complex job would develop intellectually at a slower pace, perhaps not at all, and in the extreme case might even decline in his intellectual functioning. As a result, small differences in the substantive complexity of early jobs might lead to increasing differences in intellectual development. ...

Processes of Learning and Generalization

Why does substantive complexity have such widespread ramifications for personality? This question is still largely unanswered. Our findings suggest that the simplest type of learning-generalization process is operating here: that there is a direct translation of the lessons of the job to outside-the-job realities, rather than some indirect process, such as reaction formation or compensation (Breer and Locke, 1965). Thus, men who do complex work come to exercise their intellectual prowess not only on the job but also in their nonoccupational lives. They become more open to new experience. They come to value

self-direction more highly. They even come to engage in more intellectually demanding leisure-time activities. In short, the lessons of work are directly carried over to nonoccupational realms.

Several alternative interpretations have been advanced, but none has been adequately tested. One such interpretation is that doing more (or less) substantively complex work leads to a stronger (or weaker) sense of control over the forces that affect one's life, and that this sense of controlling or not controlling those forces influences one's self-concept, in particular, one's self-esteem. But why is it necessary to accord so strategic a role in the causal chain to "locus of control"? Why not say, more directly, that people who do substantively complex work come to think of themselves as capable of doing difficult and challenging tasks—and thus deserve respect in everyone's eyes, including their own? Similarly, people who do substantively simple work come to think of themselves as capable of nothing more than this simple-minded stuff.

I think the most reasonable hypothesis is the most straightforward: that in an industrial society, where work is central to people's lives, what people do in their work directly affects their values, their conceptions of self, and their orientation to the world around them—"I do, therefore I am." Hence, doing substantively complex work tends to increase one's respect for one's own capacities, one's valuation of self-direction, one's intellectuality (even in leisure-time pursuits), and one's sense that the problems one encounters in the world are manageable. There is no need to posit that locus of control or any other aspect of values and orientation plays a necessary intermediary role in this process; the substantive complexity of work can directly affect all aspects of people's conceptions of reality. ...

Still another possible interpretation is that occupational conditions do not affect all people similarly, but differently, depending on the individual's own needs, values, and abilities—the so-called "fit" hypothesis. Our analyses do not support this interpretation. We repeatedly find, for example, that the substantive complexity of work has much the same effects regardless of whether men value intrinsic or extrinsic aspects of their work more highly (Kohn and Schooler, 1973;

Kohn, 1976). But these analyses have been broad-gauge, and more detailed analyses of pertinent subpopulations might require us to modify our views. Moreover, our analyses of this issue have thus far not been longitudinal. But since our data demonstrate that people's values and even their abilities are affected by their job conditions, it is clear that only longitudinal assessments can be conclusive.

Our studies have led me to conclude that the intrinsic meaning and psychological impact of a job result not just from the status or income or interpersonal relationships that the job provides but also—and especially—from the meaningful challenges the work itself poses (or fails to pose). The most important challenge is that of mastering complex tasks, that is, the substantive complexity of the work. Our data indicate that substantive complexity affects people's psychological functioning regardless of their needs, values, and personal capacities and regardless of their social class (but, of course, the type of work one does is intimately related to one's social class; so, too, are one's values). What matters most about work, in short, is not any of its attendant rewards or social experiences, but the work itself.

Moreover, the relationship between work and psychological functioning is quintessentially reciprocal. There is an ongoing process, throughout all of adult life, whereby the occupational conditions encountered by the individual both mold his psychological processes and in turn are molded by his personality and behavior. No theory of adult personality development that fails to take account of the ongoing effects of occupational (and, presumably, other social) conditions can be regarded as realistic. By the same token, no social psychology of occupations that fails to take account of the ongoing effects of individual psychological functioning can be regarded as realistic.

Notes

1. Our primary source of data is a sample survey of 3,101 men, representative of all men employed in civilian occupations in the United States. These men were interviewed for us by the National Opinion Research Center (NORC) in the spring and summer of 1964. For more detailed information on sample and research design, see Kohn, 1969, pp. 235–264. In 1974 NORC reinterviewed a representative subsample of these men for us; this time, the wives (and, where applicable, one of the children) were interviewed, too. For detailed information on the follow-up study, see Kohn and Schooler (1978) and Kohn (1977).

2. Our principal indices of psychological functioning measure subjective reactions to the job itself (that is, job satisfaction and occupational commitment), valuation of self-direction or of conformity to external authority (both for oneself and for one's children), self-conception (self-confidence, self-deprecation, fatalism, anxiety, and idea conformity), social orientation (authoritarian conservatism, criteria of morality, trustfulness, and receptiveness or resistance to change), alienation (powerlessness, self-estrangement, and normlessness), and intellectual functioning (intellectual flexibility, intellectuality of leisure-time activities). For detailed information about our definitions of these concepts and our methods of indexing them, see Kohn, 1969, pp. 47–58, 73–84, 265–269; Kohn and Schooler, 1973, pp. 99–101; Kohn, 1976, pp. 114–118.

3. Specifically, these twelve crucial occupational conditions are: (1) ownership/nonownership; (2) bureaucratization; (3) position in the supervisory hierarchy; (4) closeness of supervision; (5) routinization of the work; (6) substantive complexity of the work; (7) frequency of time-pressure; (8) heaviness of work; (9) dirtiness of work; (10) the likelihood, in this field, of there occurring a sudden and dramatic change in a person's income, reputation, or position; (11) the probability, in this line of work, of being held responsible for things outside one's control; and (12) the risk of loss of one's job or business.

4. The concept "substantive complexity" has been the subject of much research that goes considerably beyond the issues addressed in this essay. Many writers have adopted the concept and used it for such diverse purposes as reinterpreting the status-attainment model (Spaeth, 1976), proposing a new method of classifying the occupational structure of the U.S. economy (Temme, 1975), reassessing the psychological effects of complex role sets (Coser, 1975), interpreting the effects of fathers' occupational experiences on their sons' occupational choices (Mortimer, 1974; 1976), and searching out the sources of powerlessness (Tudor, 1972).

5. To validate this index, which is specifically tailored to each respondent's description of his own job, we have compared it to assessments of the average level of complexity of work with things, with data, and with people for the entire occupation, made by trained occupational analysts for the *Dictionary of Occupational Titles* (United States Department of Labor, 1965). The

multiple correlation between our index of substantive complexity and the independently coded *Dictionary* ratings is 0.78—sufficiently high to assure us that our appraisals of substantive complexity accurately reflect the reality of people's work.

6. The two-stage least squares technique is described in detail by Kohn and Schooler (1973) and the references cited therein. This method attempts to "purge" each variable of the effects of all others with which it is reciprocally related by estimating from other pertinent data what each individual's score on that variable would have been if the other variables had not had an opportunity to affect it. These estimated scores are then used as independent variables in the (second stage) multiple-regression equations.

7. Concretely, the time-lagged path (that is, from substantive complexity in 1964 to intellectual flexibility in 1974) is 0.05 and the contemporaneous path is 0.18. A path of 0.18 might not under ordinary circumstances be considered striking; but a continuing effect of this magnitude on so stable a phenomenon as intellectual flexibility is impressive, because the cumulative impact will be much greater than the immediate effect at any one time. Continuing effects, even small-to-moderate continuing effects, on highly stable phenomena become magnified in importance. The effect of the substantive complexity of work on intellectual flexibility is especially noteworthy when we take into account that we are dealing with men who are at least ten years into their occupational careers.

References

Baltes, Paul B. 1968. Longitudinal and cross-sectional sequences in the study of age and generation effects. *Human Development*, 11:145–171.

Baltes, Paul B., and K. Warner Schaie. 1976. On the plasticity of intelligence in adulthood and old age. *American Psychologist*, 31:720–725.

Blau, Peter M., and Otis Duncan. 1967. *The American occupational structure.* New York: Wiley.

Blau, Peter M., and Richard A. Schoenherr. 1971. *The structure of organizations.* New York: Basic Books.

Blauner, Robert. 1964. *Alienation and freedom: the factory worker and his industry.* Chicago: University of Chicago Press.

Breer, Paul E., and Edwin A. Locke. 1965. *Task experience as a source of attitudes.* Homewood, Ill.: Dorsey.

Coser, Rose Laub. 1975. The complexity of roles as a seedbed of individual autonomy. In *The idea of social structure: papers in honor of Robert K. Merton,* ed. L. A. Coser. New York: Harcourt Brace Jovanovich.

Cottrell, W. Fred. 1940. *The railroader.* Stanford: Stanford University Press.

Duncan, Otis D., David L. Featherman, and Beverly Duncan. 1972. *Socioeconomic background and achievement.* New York: Seminar Press.

Horn, John L., and Gary Donaldson. 1976. On the myth of intellectual decline in adulthood. *American Psychologist,* 31:701–719.

Jöreskog, Karl G. 1969. A general approach to confirmatory maximum likelihood factor analysis. *Psychometrika,* 34:183–202.

Kohn, Melvin L. 1977. Reassessment, 1977. In *Class and conformity: a study in values.* 2nd ed. Chicago: University of Chicago Press.

———. 1976. Occupational structure and alienation. *American Journal of Sociology* 82:111–130.

———. 1969. *Class and conformity: a study in values.* Homewood, Ill.: Dorsey. (2nd ed., Chicago: University of Chicago Press, 1977.)

Kohn, Melvin L., and Carmi Schooler. 1981. Job conditions and intellectual flexibility: a longitudinal assessment of their reciprocal effects. In *Factor analysis and measurement in sociological research: a multidimensional perspective,* ed. E. F. Borgatta and D. J. Jackson. Beverly Hills: Sage Publications.

———. 1978. The reciprocal effects of the substantive complexity of work and intellectual flexibility: a longitudinal assessment. *American Journal of Sociology,* 84:24–52.

———. 1973. Occupational experience and psychological functioning: an assessment of reciprocal effects. *American Sociological Review,* 38:97–118.

———. 1969. Class, occupation, and orientation. *American Sociological Review,* 34:659–678.

Miller, Joanne, Carmi Schooler, Melvin L. Kohn, and Karen A. Miller. 1979. Women and work: the psychological effects of occupational conditions. *American Journal of Sociology,* 85:66–94.

Mortimer, Jeylan T. 1976. Social class, work, and the family: some implications of the father's occupation for familial relationships and sons' career decisions. *Journal of Marriage and the Family,* 38:241–256.

———. 1974. Patterns of intergenerational occupational movements: a smallest-space analysis. *American Journal of Sociology,* 79:1278–1299.

Rosenbaum, James E. 1976. *Making inequality: the hidden curriculum of high school tracking.* New York: Wiley.

Sewell, William H., Robert M. Hauser, and David L. Featherman, eds. 1976. *Schooling and achievement in American society.* New York: Academic Press.

Spaeth, Joe L. 1976. Cognitive complexity: a dimension underlying the socioeconomic achievement process. In *Schooling and achievement in American society,* ed.

William H. Sewell, Robert M. Hauser, and David L. Featherman. New York: Academic Press.

Temme, Lloyd V. 1975. *Occupation: meanings and measures.* Washington, D.C.: Bureau of Social Science Research.

Tudor, Bill. 1972. A specification of relationships between job complexity and powerlessness. *American Sociological Review,* 37:596–604.

United States Department of Labor. 1965. *Dictionary of occupational titles.* Washington, D. C.: United States Government Printing Office. 3rd ed.

Whyte, William F. 1969. *Organizational behavior: theory and application.* Homewood, Ill.: Richard D. Irwin.

———. 1961. *Men at work.* Homewood, Ill.: Dorsey.

———. 1955. *Money and motivation: an analysis of incentives in industry.* New York: Harper.

JAMES A. DAVIS

Achievement Variables and Class Cultures: Family, Schooling, Job, and Forty-Nine Dependent Variables in the Cumulative GSS

Introduction

Blau and Duncan (1967) call their book *The American Occupational Structure* but its main effect has been to recast rank variables as stages in an achievement *process* whose core variables (Duncan et al., 1972:5) are:

$$family \rightarrow schooling \rightarrow job.$$

Since occupational levels remain fairly constant in the later adult years, this perspective has tended to view job (and earnings) as the end of the line, dependent variables to be explained by family background, intervening events, or residual random fate. Thus, for example, Coleman and Rainwater (1978:4–5) argue:

In the development of empirical sociological approaches to social stratification, a number of problems have aroused researchers' interests … the principal question must be (sic) that of the actual distribution of goods … Sociologists have been interested mainly in the distribution of occupations and secondarily in the distribution of education. Economists have concentrated on the size distribution of income.

Jencks, et al. (1979) summarize this focus crisply in the title of their book, *Who Gets Ahead?*

The attainment approach has tended to eclipse an older tradition which studies the effects of stratification, both objective (crime, family stability, mortality, morbidity, etc.) and subjective (morale, attitudes, values, political preferences, etc.). This paper is in this older tradition of treating scores on rank measures as independent variables. It follows a sequence of studies dating back many decades (Sorokin, 1927; Centers, 1949; Stouffer, 1955; Lipset, 1959; Hyman, 1966; Glenn and Alston, 1968; Kohn, 1969; Curtis and Jackson, 1977; Hyman and Wright, 1979).

Such novelty as this report may hold lies not in the problem—whether and how achievement variables influence subjective and behavioral variables—but in two recent technical advances, the NORC General Social Survey (Davis et al., 1980) and the "Goodman techniques" (1978) for analyzing tabular data.

TABLE 1
Dependent Items (GSS Mnemonic Topic, Wording, Contrasted Categories, and N)

Morale

1) ANOMIA5 — *Average man:* ". . . the lot of the average man is getting worse, not better." (Disagree, Don't Know) vs (Agree), 5689.

2) ANOMIA6 — *The Future:* "It's hardly fair to bring a child into the world with the way things look for the future." (Disagree, Don't Know) vs (Agree), 5688.

3) HAPPY — *Happiness:* "Taken all together, how would you say things are these days . . ." (Very Happy) vs (Pretty Happy, Not Too Happy), 9480.

4) HAPMAR — *Marriage Happiness:* "Taking all things together . . . would you say your marriage is . . ." (Very happy) vs (Pretty happy, not too happy), 5420.

5) LIFE — *Life exciting?:* "In general, do you find life exciting, pretty routine, or dull?" (Exciting) vs (Routine, dull, No opinion), 5608.

6) SATFAM — *Family Satisfaction:* "Tell me the number that shows how much satisfaction you get from . . . your family life." (A very great deal) vs (A great deal, Quite a bit, A fair amount, Some, A little, None), 7965.

7) SATFIN — *Financial Satisfaction:* "So far as you and your family are concerned, would you say you are . . . with your present financial situation?" (Pretty well satisfied) vs (More or less satisfied, Not satisfied at all), 9156.

8) SATFRIND — *Friendship Satisfaction:* "Tell me the number that shows how much satisfaction you get from . . . Your friendships" (A very great deal) vs (A great deal, Quite a bit, A fair amount, Some, A little, None), 5688.

9) SATJOB — *Job Satisfaction:* "On the whole, how satisfied are you with the work you do?" (note: includes housewives) (Very satisfied) vs (Moderately satisfied, A little dissatisfied, Very dissatisfied), 7377.

Attachment

10) ANOMIA7 — *Public Officials:* "Most public officials are not really interested in the problems of the average man." (Disagree, Don't know) vs (Agree), 5688.

11) ATTEND — *Church Attendance:* "How often do you attend religious services?" (Never, Less than once a year, About once or twice a year, Several times a year) vs (About once a month, 2–3 times a month, Nearly every week, Every week, Several times a week), 9142.

12) DIVORCE — *Divorced:* "Have you ever been divorced or legally separated?" (Yes or Marital Status = Divorced or Separated) vs (No) (Note: Never Married are excluded), 7950.

13) GETAHEAD — *Hard Work:* "Some people say that people get ahead by their own hard work; others say that lucky breaks or help from other people are more important. Which do you think is most important?" (Hard work most important) vs (Hard work and luck equally important, Luck most important), 5565.

14) HELPFUL — *People Helpful:* "Would you say that most of the time people try to be helpful, or that they are mostly just looking out for themselves?" (Try to be helpful) vs (Just look out for themselves, Depends), 6821.

15) MEMNUM — *Memberships:* "Here is a list of various kinds of organizations. Could you tell me whether or not you are a member of each type? (Total of 2 through 16) vs (zero or one), 5764.

16) PARTYID — *Neither Party:* "Generally speaking, do you usually think of yourself as a Republican, Democrat, Independent, or what?" (Independent close to neither party) vs (Republican, Democrat, or Independent close to Republican or Democrat), 9002.

17) RELIG — *No Religion:* "What is your religious preference? Is it Protestant, Catholic, Jewish, some other religion, or no religion?" (None) vs (Protestant, Catholic, Jewish, Other), 9165.

18) RELITEN — *Strong Religion:* "Would you call yourself a strong (religion)?" (Strong) vs (Somewhat strong, Not very strong) (Note: No religion excluded), 6305.

19) SOCOMMUN — *Neighboring:* "How often do you spend a social evening with someone who lives in your neighborhood?" (Almost every day, Once or twice a week, Several times a month, About once a month, Several times a year, About once a year, Never), 4652.

20) SOCFREND — *Social Friends:* "How often do you spend a social evening with friends who live outside the neighborhood?" (Almost every day, Once or twice a week, Several times a month) vs (About once a month, Several times a year, About once a year, Never), 4657.

21) TRUST — *People Trustworthy:* "Generally speaking, would you say that most people can be trusted or that you can't be too careful in dealing with people?" (Most people can be trusted) vs (Can't be too careful, Other, Depends), 6812.

TABLE 1
(continued)

Politics

22) COMMUN
Anti-Communism: "Thinking about all the different kinds of governments in the world today, which of these statements comes closest to how you feel about Communism as a form of government? (It's a good form of government, It's all right for some countries, It's bad, but no worse than some others) vs (It's the worst kind of all), 5551.

23) EQWLTH
Redistribution: "Some people think that the government in Washington ought to reduce the income differences between the rich and the poor, perhaps by raising the taxes of wealthy families or by giving income assistance to the poor. Others think the government should not concern itself with reducing this income difference between the rich and the poor. (On a scale from 1 = government should to 7 = government shouldn't) Which score between 1 and 7 comes closest to the way you feel?" (4–7) vs (1–3), 1673.

24) NATARMS
Military Spending: ". . . are we spending too much, too little, or about the right amount on the military, armaments, and defense?" (Too little) vs (About the right amount, Too much), 7540.

25) NATCITY
Urban Spending: ". . . are we spending too much, too little, or about the right amount on solving the problems of the big cities?" (Too little) vs (About the right amount, Too much), 6992.

26) NATCRIME
Anticrime Spending: ". . . are we spending too much, too little or about the right amount on halting the rising crime rate?" (Too Little) vs (About the right amount, Too Much), 7603.

27) NATFARE
Welfare Spending: ". . . are we spending too much, too little or about the right amount on welfare?" (Too little, About the right amount) vs (Too much), 7673.

28) PARTYID
Republican: "Generally speaking, do you think of yourself as a Republican, Democrat, Independent, or what?" (Republican) vs (Democrat), 7829. (Note: Independents are excluded).

29) POLVIEWS
Conservative: "Where would you place yourself on this scale (1 to 7) from Extremely Liberal to Extremely Conservative?" (1–2–3–4) vs (5–6–7), 3962.

30) SPKCOM
Free Speech: "Suppose this admitted Communist wanted to make a speech in your community. Should he be allowed to speak or not?" (Yes, allowed to speak) vs (Not allowed, Don't know), 6824.

Values and Tastes

31) CHLDIDEL
Fertility Norms: "What do you think is the ideal number of children for a family to have?" (0–1–2) vs (3–7), 6332.

32) JOBINC
Lucrative Job: "Would you please look at this card and tell which one thing on this list you would most prefer in a job? High income." (Most, Next) vs (3rd, 4th, 5th), 5565.

33) JOBMEANS
Meaningful Work: (Same as #32) "Work important and gives a feeling of accomplishment." (Most, Next) vs (3rd, 4th, 5th), 5565.

34) JOBPROMO
Chance to Advance: (Same as #32) "Chances for advancement." (3rd, 4th, 5th) vs (Most, Next), 5565.

35) JOBSEC
Job Security: (Same as #32) "No danger of being fired." (3rd, 4th, 5th) vs (Most, Next), 5565.

36) NEWS
Newspaper Reading: "How often do you read the newspaper?" (Every Day) vs (A few times a week, Once a week, Less than once a week, Never), 4696.

37) RICHWORK
Work Ethic: "If you were to get enough money to live as comfortably as you would like for the rest of your life, would you continue to work or would you stop working?" (Continue to work) vs (Stop working, Don't know), 3582.

38) TV HOURS
TV watching: "On the average day, about how many hours do you personally watch television?" (zero, 1) vs (2 through 24), 4626.

TABLE 1
(continued)

Social Issues

39) CAPPUN — *Death Penalty:* "Do you favor or oppose the death penalty for persons convicted of murder?" (Favor) vs (Oppose, Don't know), 6860.

40) COURTS — *Courts Tough:* "In general, do you think the courts in this area deal too harshly or not harshly enough with criminals?" (Too harshly, About right) vs (Not harshly enough), 8012.

41) DIVLAW: — *Ease Divorce:* "Should divorce in this country be easier or more difficult to obtain than it is now?" (Easier, Stay as it is) vs (More Difficult), 5499.

42) FEHOME — Women's Place: "Women should take care of running their homes and leave running the country up to men." (Disagree) vs (Agree), 4527.

43) FEWORK — *Wives Work:* "Do you approve or disapprove of a married woman earning money in business or industry if she has a husband capable of supporting her?" (Approve) vs (Disapprove), 5721.

44) GRASS — *Marijuana:* "Do you think the use of marijuana should be made legal or not?" (Should, Don't know) vs (Should not), 5665.

45) HOMOSEX — *Gay Sex:* "What about sexual relations between two *adults* of the *same* sex; do you think it is always wrong, almost always wrong, wrong only sometimes, or not wrong at all?" (Almost always wrong, Wrong only sometimes, Not wrong at all) vs (Always wrong), 5354.

46) PREMARSX — *Premarital:* "If a man and a woman have sex relations before marriage, do you think it is . . ." (Almost always wrong, Wrong only sometimes, Not wrong at all) vs (Always wrong), 5613.

47) RACMAR — *Intermarriage:* "Do you think there should be laws against marriages between (Negroes/Blacks) and whites?" (No) vs (Yes, Don't know) (Note: tabulation based on whites only), 7167.

48) RACOPEN — *Open Housing:* "Suppose there is a community-wide vote on the general housing issue . . . Which law would you vote for?" (The second law says that a homeowner cannot refuse to sell to someone because of their race or color) vs (One law says that a homeowner can decide for himself whom to sell his house to, even if he prefers not to sell to Negroes/Blacks) (Note: tabulation based on whites only), 5014.

49) XMARSEX — *Extramarital:* "What is your opinion about a *married* person having sexual relations with someone *other* than the marriage partner—is it . . ." (Almost always wrong, Wrong only sometimes, Not wrong at all) vs (Always wrong), 5606.

GSS

The cumulative General Social Survey (GSS) pools eight national NORC personal interview surveys between 1972 and 1980 totalling 12,120 respondents representing continental U.S., English-speaking persons, 18 years of age and older, living in noninstitutional quarters. Since most GSS items are repeated annually or in a rotation scheme, one may combine the individual surveys to increase the case total and dampen effects of current events near fieldwork times. The 49 tables analyzed here have Ns ranging from 1,673 to 9,480, with a median of 5,700.

Since the GSS was designed to be eclectic, it is possible to find items on most topics covered in previous research and in some cases exact replications. No standard grouping of "subjective and behavioral" variables exists, but the studies cited cover similar themes from Centers's "class sympathies and antipathies, racial and ethnic prejudices, religion, women, success and opportunity, satisfactions and frustrations, values and desires" (1949:214–16) to Jackson and Curtis's "formal social participation, informal social participation, political liberalism, satisfaction and symptoms of stress, intolerance, anomie, and aspirations for son" (1972:707). I chose 49 GSS items which seemed to tap issues raised in the literature, grouping them as (1) morale, (2) attachments, (3) politics, (4) values and tastes, and (5) social issues. Readers who prefer their own groupings may use Table 9 for that purpose.

I can hardly claim the 49 are a representative sampling of any universe of content, but I am prepared to argue (1) no major themes in prior research are missing, (2) because the GSS was designed with the advice of many sociologists, the topics cover areas of interest to professional sociology, and (3) these results are based on considerably more items and considerably larger or more representative sampling than any previous studies.

Table 1 gives the items, mnemonics, wordings, category groupings, and Ns.

For the achievement variables I chose Father's Occupational stratum (PAOCC16), "What kind of work did your father (father substitute) normally do while you were growing up?"; Respondent's Education (EDUC), "What is the highest grade in elementary school or high school that you finished and got credit for?"; and Respondent's Occupational stratum (OCC), "What kind of work do you (did you) normally do?" Occupations were coded into the standard fivefold Census groups (a=Professional, Technical and kindred, Managers and Administrators; b=Clerical and Sales; c=Craftsmen and kindred; d=Operatives, Laborers, Service workers; e=Farm), and education was trichotomized as 0–11, 12, and 13 or more years. Table 2 shows the marginals.

Because so few contemporary Americans are farmers, the "e" category was excluded from Respondent's Occupation (but not, of course, Father's) to avoid empty cells. Note that the sample includes both men and women, and furthermore retirees, housewives, and the unemployed are not currently holding the job they report as their normal occupation.

These three achievement variables were cross-tabulated against each of the 49 dependent variables to see whether and how family (father's occupation), schooling (years completed), and job (respondent's normal occupation) are related to various attitudes and behaviors.

Goodman Analysis

The Goodman approach (iterative proportional fitting of hierarchical models) enables us to make

TABLE 2
Marginals for Achievement Variables (N = 9,749)
(percent)

	Father	Respondent
Occupation		
a = Professional, Technical, and Kindred; Managers and Administrators	19.7%	24.2%
b = Clerical and Sales	6.9	26.3
c = Craftsmen and Kindred	22.8	12.7
d = Operatives, Laborers, Service	29.3	34.0
e = Farm	21.3	2.8
	100.0%	100.0%
Years of Education		
13+		32.5%
12		36.8
0–11		30.7
		100.0%

significance tests for seven possible associations involving a dependent variable, D. Calling Father's Occupation, "F," Educational Attainment, "E," and Respondent's Occupation, "R," the possible associations or "effects" involving D are FERD, FED, FRD, ERD, RD, ED, and FD. A table showing the seven effects for each of the 49 Ds, i.e., 343 tests, would constitute an answer to our research question.

RD, ED, and FD are the partial associations of Respondent's Occupational stratum, Respondent's Educational Attainment, and Father's Occupational stratum with the dependent variables. What each "really measures" is not easy to say. Education differences have been interpreted as consequences of curriculum, native intelligence, docile perseverance, and exposure to unconventional ideas. Occupational differences have been interpreted as consequences of economic or political interest, diffuse subcultures, specific skills (e.g., "head work" vs "hand work"), and simple gradations of job desirability. I reserve further discussion until we have seen the results.

F, E, and R are not only of considerable sociological interest as predictor variables, their combinations allow us to generate operational definitions of several theoretical ideas.

Note that an F × R table defines the classic "Father-Son/Daughter mobility matrix" and an

TABLE 3
Hypothetical Mobility Data

| | | (a) *Score Mobility* | | | Differences | |
| | | R's Score | | | Med. vs Low | High vs Medium |
		Low = 2	Medium = 5	High = 7		
F's Score	High = 7	−5	−2	0	+3	+2
	Medium = 5	−3	0	+2	+3	+2
	Low = 2	0	+3	+5	+3	+2
Differences	High vs Medium	−2	−2	−2		
	Medium vs Low	−3	−3	−3		

| | | (b) *Sheer Mobility* | | | Differences | |
| | | R's Score | | | Med. vs Low | High vs Medium |
		Low = 2	Medium = 5	High = 7		
F's Score	High = 7	5	2	0	−3	−2
	Medium = 5	3	0	2	−3	+2
	Low = 2	0	3	5	+3	+2
Differences	High vs Medium	+2	+2	−2		
	Medium vs Low	+3	−3	−3		

E × R table defines combinations of interest to theorists of status consistency or, alternatively, those who view occupation as a return on educational investment. Thus, a closer examination of the possible effects may enable us to build a bit more sociology into what otherwise would be a routine analysis.

I start with mobility. Mobility effects have been much studied and debated. I draw on the discussion by Curtis and Jackson (1977:110–15), but recast their ideas into the lingo of contingency tables, using a hypothetical example to make the points. Consider a fictitious numerical variable with pre- and post-measures (e.g., F and R) and for simplicity, just three scores, as shown in Table 3.

Each cell in Table 3a is the mobility score for respondents with a particular origin and destination, e.g., the upper left-hand corner cell is associated with people who started at 7, ended up at 2, and *hence* have a mobility score of −5. Call this "score mobility." Any measure of score mobility or any dependent variable which is a linear function of score mobility should track the cell values in Table 3a. Let us consider what to expect when

we analyze an F × R × D table for a D closely related to score mobility. The right hand columns and bottom rows in Table 3a give the answer. Consider first, the effect of R scores on D with a given value of F. The +2s in the far right column tell us that when we compare High and Medium Rs from the same origins we always get a difference of +2, and when we compare Medium and Low Rs we always get a difference of +3. That is, controlling for origin, the higher the destination the greater the mobility. Similarly, when we look at the effects of origin (F) on level of D we see the same difference values, but the signs *reverse*. Controlling for destination, the higher the origin, the *less* the mobility. Combining these two results:

1) In an origin by destination by dependent variable (F×R×D) table, score mobility effects will produce FD and RD effects with opposite signs.

2) If only one of these effects, FD or RD, is present, we doubt that score mobility is generating the effect although there will probably be a zero-order association between mobility scores and D. If FD and RD

have the same sign and similar magnitudes, the evidence is strongly against a mobility interpretation and the zero-order association between mobility scores and D will be very small.

The great theorists of the discipline, however, have often used their sociological imaginations to produce a different definition of mobility. Sorokin (1927:509), for example, wrote:

When a man throughout his life works at the same occupation and has the same economic and social status, his mind is decidedly marked ... he is doomed to think and to look at the world through the glasses of his "social box". ... Another picture is given by the mind of a man who passes from occupation to occupation, from poverty to riches, from subordination to domination and *vice versa*. (emphasis in original)

And Durkheim ([1897]1951:252) said:

In the case of economic disasters, indeed, something like declassification occurs which suddenly casts certain individuals into a lower state than their previous one ... their moral education has to be recommenced. ... It is the same if the source of the crisis is an abrupt growth of power and wealth ... the scale is upset and a new scale cannot be immediately improvised.

The notion here is that the sheer amount or fact of change is more important than its direction. I will call this second version "sheer mobility."

If sheer mobility were operating on D, we would remove the signs from the cell entries in Table 3a to get Table 3b. Necessarily the pattern of differences for FD and RD changes, producing an interaction effect: the sign of RD varies according to level of F (if you start at the bottom, the higher your R, the greater your sheer mobility, but if you start at the top, the higher your R, the less your sheer mobility). Of mathematical necessity FD will have a similar interaction. Thus:

In an origin by destination by dependent variable (F×R×D) table, sheer mobility effects will appear as an FRD interaction.

This is a necessary but not sufficient condition. If and when such interactions turn up (Curtis and

Jackson's results do not lead us to be optimistic), we must inspect the cell by cell results to see whether they follow the diagonal pattern suggested by Table 3b.

In summary, when looking at FD, RD, and FRD:

1) An FRD interaction suggests examining the data for *sheer* mobility effects.

2) FD and RD effects with opposite signs and no interaction suggest the operation of mobility *scores*.

3) All other patterns suggest "mobility" is a poor concept for interpreting the results.

Exactly the same reasoning may be applied to ED, RD, and ERD, giving us operational definitions of the concepts "return on investment" and "status consistency."

Achievement research is heavily influenced by economics in general and the "human capital" approach in particular. Many sociologists interpret Educational Attainment as an "investment" with adult occupation and income as "returns" on that investment. Whether the generality of Americans apply an "investment psychology" to their achievement, however, has not been studied. How would data behave if investment psychology were operating? Exactly like the pattern for score mobility, I argue. If occupation operates as a return, then at any level of education, the higher the occupation the *greater* the return, while at any level of occupation, the greater the education, the *less* the return.

Sociology itself has provided a second concept for interpreting ED and RD, "status consistency" (Jackson and Curtis, 1972). The notion is that particular combinations of, say, Education and Occupation, produce particularly high or low scores on D. Often consistency theorists argue that for highly correlated variables like E and R scores off the main diagonal in either direction generate inconsistency effects. In other words, we would expect an ERD interaction.

In summary, when looking at ED, RD, and FRD:

1) An ERD interaction suggests the operation of *status consistency.*

2) ED and RD effects with opposite signs and no interaction suggest the operation of a *return on investment* psychology.

The concepts score mobility, sheer mobility, status consistency, and return on investment give us a framework for interpreting any RD, ED, FRD, and ERD effects which turn up. The two remaining effects involving D, FERD and FED, seem to have no precursors in the theoretical literature. I will worry about them if and when we catch one.

Substantively, what should we expect? The literature leads us to expect: (1) Higher rank will be associated with higher morale, stronger attachments, conservative economic positions, distinctive tastes and values, and liberal positions on social issues. (2) Sheer mobility and status inconsistency should be associated with lower morale, lesser attachments, and more liberal politics and social attitudes. (This follows from the theoretical tradition. The empirical research tradition is to believe neither variable is related to anything.) (3) In the absence of a theoretical literature, common sense suggests the greater the occupational return on educational investment, the greater the morale and the more conservative the politics ("I made it, why don't those people just get jobs?"). (4) It is difficult to predict for score mobility since few theorists distinguish between sheer and score mobility, but my intuition suggests the greater the mobility the higher the morale and the more conservative the politics.

More generally, we also wish to consider the magnitude of the various associations to see whether achievement has strong and diverse effects or weak and scattered ones and also to see which of the achievement variables, occupation or education, seems the more powerful predictor—if they differ.

Collectively these questions test the hypothesis of "class cultures." To the extent the effects are large in magnitude, pervasive across content, and involve both achievement variables operating in the same direction, the notion that the United States is layered into class cultures seems fruitful. To the extent the effects are small in magnitude, concentrated in limited topics, and limited to one or the other achievement variable or opposite in sign, the notion of class cultures would seem forced or artificial.

To test these various hypotheses and concepts I tested the fit of eight hierarchical models for each of the 49 Ds in Table 1. The models are defined in Table 4 and their rationale will be explained as they turn up in the discussion of the results.

Results

Interactions

The findings for interaction are clear cut: there aren't any. Consider Table 4 and line 1 of Table 5. The model $H_1 = (FER)(FD)(ED)(RD)$ excludes all four interactions involving D (FERD, FED, FRD, ERD). H_1 fails to fit the data at the .05 level using textbook formulas in just 3 of 49 tables. Since one would expect 2.45 out of 49 failures when testing 49 independent sets of random data when using the .05 level, the three exceptions are not very persuasive.

But even these results are extravagant since they assume simple random sampling (SRS). Since the General Social Survey, like all modern national samples, is clustered, the raw Ns overestimate its power. The rule-of-thumb advice (Davis et al., 1980:187) is to treat N as .667N, that is, to consider a sample of 1,500 to have the power of an SRS sample of 1,000. When this is done (right-hand column of Table 5), none of the 49 tests produces a significant discrepancy for H_1.

H_1, of course, is a test of the shotgun null hypothesis that the four D interactions are collectively nil. It is possible (but not likely) that one is significant and the others very much not, so as a group the effects are weak. Lines 2–4 shoot down this notion. Since the models H2, H3, and H4 differ from H_1 only by the presence of FED (H2), FRD (H3), or ERD (H4), differences between each and H_1 test the null hypothesis that a particular three-variable interaction is nil. Rows 2–4 of Table 5 show the results: we are tempted to reject the null hypothesis only once for cluster-adjusted Ns and at most 6 out of 49 times (FRD) under SRS assumptions.

TABLE 4
Details of Test Models*

Effects Type	Variables	H1	H2	H3	H4	H5	H6	H7	H8
4 Variable Interactions	F E R D	−	−	−	−	−	−	−	−
3 Variable Interactions	F E R	M	M	M	M	M	M	M	M
	F E D	−	(M)	−	−	−	−	−	−
	F R D	−	−	(M)	−	−	−	−	−
	E R D	−	−	−	(M)	−	−	−	−
2 Variable Associations With dependent	F D	M	+	+	M	(−)	(−)	M	M
	E D	M	+	M	−	(−)	M	(−)	M
	R D	M	M	+	+	(−)	M	M	(−)
Among priors	F E	+	+	+	+	+	+	+	+
	F R	+	+	+	+	+	+	+	+
	E R	+	+	+	+	+	+	+	+
1 Variable Skews	F	+	+	+	+	+	+	+	+
	E	+	+	+	+	+	+	+	+
	R	+	+	+	+	+	+	+	+
	D	+	+	+	+	+	+	+	+
Degrees of Freedom		50	42	38	44	59	54	52	53

* Symbols

Variables: F = Father's Occupation, E = Respondent's Educational Attainment. R = Respondent's Occupation. D = Dependent Variable

Models: H1 = No interactions = (F E R) (F D) (E D) (R D)
H2 = FED interactions only = (F E R) (R E D) (R D)
H3 = FRD interactions only = (F E R) (F R D) (E D)
H4 = ERD interactions only = (F E R) (E R D) (F D)
H5 = No D effects = (F E R) (D)
H6 = No interactions, no FD association = (F E R) (E D) (R D)
H7 = No interactions, no ED association = (F E R) (F D) (R D)
H8 = No interactions, no RD association = (F E R) (F D) (E D)

Cell entries:
M = Fitted marginals
( ) = Differs from H1
+ = Implied by fitted marginals
− = Assumed absent (odds ratio = 1.000)

These results are so negative one is almost puzzled. Do we, perhaps, lack power to detect interactions? Since the median N over the 49 tables is 5,700 (3,800 cluster adjusted), sample size is hardly the problem. Therefore it is of some comfort to find that GSS data can actually produce a significant "mobility" effect, though not for our achievement variables. The aphorism, "converts are more Catholic than the Pope," suggests that if one looks at religious mobility against a dependent measure of religiosity, an interaction effect of the "sheer mobility" type might turn up. That is, we might find religious switchers either way score higher on religiosity than Catholics who remain Catholic and non-Catholics who remain non-Catholic. Table 6 shows the results, using Item #18 from Table 1 ("Would you call yourself a strong _____ ?") as the measure of religiosity.

Table 6 does show a "sheer mobility effect," albeit opposite to the aphorism's prediction. Converts are less "strong" (36.9 percent and 30.6 percent) than the religiously stable (42.2 percent and

TABLE 5
Significance Test Results (Likelihood Ratio Chi-Square, L^2)

		Significance over 49 dependent items*			
Null Hypothesis	Accept if . . .	Neither	SRS Only	Adjusted	Total
Interactions					
(1) All insignificant	H1 fits	46	3	0	49
(2) FED insignificant	H2 vs H1 insignificant	43	5	1	49
(3) FRD insignificant	H3 vs H1 insignificant	43	6	0	49
(4) ERD insignificant	H4 vs H1 insignificant	45	4	0	49
2 Variable Associations					
(5) All insignificant	H5 vs H1 insignificant	2	0	47	49
(6) FD insignificant	H6 vs H1 insignificant	14	5	30	49
(7) ED insignificant	H7 vs H1 insignificant	7	7	35	49
(8) RD insignificant	H8 vs H1 insignificant	7	5	37	49

* Adjusted = Significant at the .05 level after Chi-Square multiplied by .667 to adjust for clustering in sample design.
SRS only = Significant at the .05 level for raw Chi-Square, but not significant for adjusted.
Neither = Not significant at .05 level.

TABLE 6

Religious Mobility and Religious Intensity
(GSS 1974–1980)
(C = Proportion "Strong" on Religion Item)

A = In What Religion Were You Raised?	B = Current Religious Preference	
	Other	Catholic
Catholic	36.9%	42.4%
	(225)	(1,996)
Other*	41.4%	30.6%
	(5,789)	(242)

* = Protestant, Jewish, Other Religion
For the model (A B) (A C) (B C),
Chi-Square = 11.334

	N = 8,252
No Religion on A or B	646
No answer	105
	9,003

41.1 percent). This "ABC" interaction is statistically significant as the model (AB) (AC) (BC) generates a Likelihood Ratio Chi-Square (L^2) of 11.334, which exceeds the 1 d.f. criterion level of 3.84 even after correction for clustering (11.334 × .667 = 7.56). The mobility effect in Table 6 is not very strong (this will be justified later) but it is precious, as I suspect it is the only statistically and intuitively plausible support for the Sorokin-

Durkheim sheer mobility hypothesis in the history of social science. Movement to or from Catholicism appears to lower religiosity.

Back to the less exciting findings on achievement interactions; rows 1–4 in Table 5 suggest the following substantive conclusions:

- **Conclusion 1:** There is no evidence to support the hypothesis of sheer mobility effects for these 49 dependent items.

- **Conclusion 2:** There is no evidence to support the hypothesis of status consistency effects (Education and Occupation or Father's Occupation and Education) for these 49 dependent items.

Conclusions 1 and 2 unambiguously confirm, update, and extend the conclusions in Jackson and Curtis (1972).

Two-variable Effects: An Overview

The plethora of negative results (low L^2s) evaporate when we shift to the two-variable effects, FD, ED, and RD. Consider them first as a package. H5 (Table 4) differs from H1 by setting FD and ED and RD to nil. When the difference between the

L^2s for H5 and H1 is small, we tend to accept the null hypothesis that the two-variable effects involving D are collectively nil; when the difference in L^2s is large, we tend to infer that some of the achievement variables are associated with D. It has been noted that comparisons like H1 vs H5 are analogous to the multiple correlation in regression.

Line 5 in Table 5 gives the verdict. H5 almost never fits. In 47 out of 49 cases the cluster-adjusted chi-squares are statistically significant. With the exceptions of "Hard Work" (#13 in Table 1) and "Chance to Advance" (#34), the achievement triad shows significant relations across the board—morale, attachment, politics, values and tastes, and social issues.

But how strong are these statistical effects? With Ns averaging 5,700 statistical significance per se doesn't mean much. L^2 is the obvious candidate as a measure of magnitude, but it requires a bit of doctoring as chi-square is a notoriously ambiguous measure of association strength. First, chi-square is strictly proportional to sample size. If you double sample size, you will double chi-square. Because our Ns range from 1,673 to 9,480 (not all Ds appear in every GSS) it is necessary to correct for sample size. We begin by dividing L^2 by N, but this gives inconveniently small figures, e.g., $7.56/8,252 = .0009161$. Multiplying L^2/N by the arbitrary value 1,500 changes things to a more convenient order of magnitude ($.0009161 \times 1,500 = 1.37$). Although 1,500 is arbitrary, such results may be interpreted as the L^2 one would get if these data came from a single GSS. Second, the chi-square distribution also varies with the degrees of freedom, d.f. Researchers often divide chi-square by d.f., but this is an overcorrection as the relationship between d.f. and chi-square at a given probability level is virtually linear but not proportional. For example, at the .05 level the criterion value for 10 d.f., 18.307, is only 4.8 times the 1 d.f. value 3.841. Dividing by d.f. tends to bias magnitude measures against effects with more degrees of freedom. Taking our "data" from the standard chi-square table, we find the following results when regressing chi-square on d.f. values 1 through 20: The slope varies with the probability level, but not much, increasing from 1.00 to 1.41 to 1.75 as we shift from probability levels .50 to .05

TABLE 7

Linear Regression, Chi-Square and D.F. 1–20

Probability Level	Equation	r^2
.50	$-.5958 + 0.9929$ d.f.	.999
.05	$3.7421 + 1.4136$ d.f.	.997
.001	$11.3179 + 1.7521$ d.f.	.994

to .001 as shown in Table 7. Since we are generally more interested in magnitude when chi-square is significant and since we are looking for a plausible approximation rather than an exact function, I will use the rule of thumb that chi-square increases 1.5 per d.f. at any particular probability level. As with N, it is convenient to take an arbitrary yardstick value. I chose 2 d.f. Combining the two corrections:

$$L^2 \text{ adjusted } = \left(L^2 \times \frac{1500}{N}\right) - [(df - 2) \times 1.5]. \quad (1)$$

The adjusted L^2 may be interpreted as a rough estimate of what L^2 would have been if the data had come from a single GSS and the test used two degrees of freedom, as in testing the significance of a two-variable effect for a dichotomy and a trichotomy. One might tack on a .667 for multistage sampling but in this paper that would be a constant. It is easier to multiply the two d.f., .05 criterion value, 5.992, by 1.5 to get 8.9865, or for all practical purposes, 9.

The results in Table 6 illustrate the adjustment. The raw data give us an L^2 value of 11.334 for 1 d.f. and an N of 8,252. To adjust for N, we divide 1,500 by 8,252 getting .182 and multiply 11.334 by .182 to get 2.06, the L^2 "one would get" if these data had come from a single GSS. Then we add 1.5 as a rule-of-thumb guess of what the result would have been if the test had used two degrees of freedom rather than one. Thus our adjusted L^2 equals $(11.334 \times .182) + (1.5) = 3.6$. Since 3.6 is a lot less than 9.0, we conclude: while our L^2 is statistically significant when applying SRS assumptions to an N of 8,252, in a smaller (one GSS) sample with the critical value adjusted for clustering, the interaction would not be statistically significant.

TABLE 8
Summary of Effect Magnitudes (L^2 adjusted)

<table>
<tr><td colspan="6">(a) Median Net Effects of F, E, and R on 49
Dependent Items</td><td colspan="4">(b) Adjusted L^2s for FD, ED, and RD</td></tr>
<tr><td></td><td></td><td></td><td></td><td></td><td></td><td>Adjusted L^2</td><td>FD</td><td>ED</td><td>RD</td></tr>
<tr><td></td><td></td><td></td><td></td><td></td><td>(Median)</td><td>100+</td><td>0</td><td>0</td><td>0</td></tr>
<tr><td>FER on D</td><td>—</td><td>H5</td><td>vs</td><td>H1</td><td>27</td><td>67–99</td><td>0</td><td>2</td><td>0</td></tr>
<tr><td>F on D</td><td>E,R</td><td>H6</td><td>vs</td><td>H1</td><td>2</td><td>34–66</td><td>1</td><td>8</td><td>0</td></tr>
<tr><td>E on D</td><td>F,R</td><td>H7</td><td>vs</td><td>H1</td><td>8</td><td>9–33</td><td>10</td><td>14</td><td>18</td></tr>
<tr><td>R on D</td><td>E,F</td><td>H8</td><td>vs</td><td>H1</td><td>4</td><td>< 9</td><td>38</td><td>25</td><td>31</td></tr>
<tr><td></td><td></td><td></td><td></td><td></td><td></td><td>Total</td><td>49</td><td>49</td><td>49</td></tr>
</table>

We will use equation (1) to roughly equate chi-squares from various sample sizes and comparisons with various degrees of freedom, using the value of 9 or larger to sort out relationships that would presumably be significant in a single GSS. As insurance, however, we will also look at the findings in terms of the more familiar percentage difference.

As happens so often when one shifts from significance tests to magnitudes when analyzing large samples, the subjective and behavioral effects of the achievement triad appear less impressive in Table 8, where the adjusted L^2s are summarized.

Starting in the top panel of Table 8a we see median adjusted scores of 27, 2, 8, and 4 for FER, F, E, and R. In terms of the benchmark value of 9, the joint F-E-R effect is "usually significant" (in a single GSS) but the median values for F and R alone are well below 9 and the median of 8 for E is borderline. Only 53 out of 147 (36%) of the adjusted direct effects in Table 8b exceed 9. In other words, if one picks a single GSS and tabulates the FER triad against a variety of dependent variables one would routinely find *something* going on, but one would not routinely find that *each* item in the triad has a significant association with most dependent variables. The impressive significance levels in Table 5 are very much influenced by the extra large sample sizes of the cumulative GSS.
...

- **Conclusion 3:** The associations of achievement variables with the 49 subjective and behavioral variables are mostly weak and

not generally statistically significant except in extra large samples.

Percentage Differences

These conclusions on magnitude, of course, depend on the plausibility of the adjusted L^2 measure. Readers who are dubious about the measure may use the right-hand columns in Table 9 to explore the same questions using the traditional percentage difference. The entries are pooled ds (Davis, 1975:126–29) or variance weighted averages of ds over combinations of control categories. In each case one category is chosen as a reference—for FD and RD it is category "a," professional, technical, and managerial, and for ED it is 13 or more years. Consider the top line and the dependent item "the future." The blanks for the columns headed FD say the adjusted L^2 for FD was less than 9 (the left side of the table shows it to be 2.6). The −.09 for "12" under ED says that the percentage of optimistic respondents among high school graduates averages 9 points less than the percentage among those with a year or more of college, and −.24 says that respondents with 0–11 years of school are 24 points lower than the college group. The −.07, −.09, and −.17 under the columns headed RD say that in contrast to professionals and managers, clerical workers average 7 points lower on optimism, crafts workers average 9 points, and the operative-service-labor workers average 17 points lower. There are 143 ds in Table 9 and only 15 (10 percent) are 20 points or more, only 3 exceed 30 points. (Nothing is lost, believe me, by leaving out the percentages for L^2s

TABLE 9
Adjusted Chi-Square and ds for Individual Items

Item	All 3	FD	ED	RD	b	c	d	f	12	0–11	b	c	d
		Chi Square (L²)				FD			ED		RD		
Morale													
The future	145.3*	2.6*	45.9*	17.0*					−.09	−.24	−.07	−.09	−.17
Life exciting	82.4*	1.7*	37.4*	1.5					−.15	−.23			
Average man	65.2*	0.2	17.2*	11.8*					−.10	−.15	−.04	−.09	−.14
Job satisfaction	28.4*	4.9*	1.1	25.4							−.11	−.10	−.20
Financial satisfaction	13.7*	6.7*	0.5	10.1*									
Happiness	7.8*	4.7*	0.2	5.4*							−.04	−.08	−.13
Marriage happy	6.4*	1.2*	1.7	2.6*									
Family	1.6*	0.0	4.4*	1.3*									
Friendship satisfaction	0.0	2.3*	1.7	1.2*									
Attachments													
Memberships	110.3*	0.0	40.1*	19.0*					−.12	−.23	−.13	−.06	−.14
People trustworthy	94.6*	0.0	20.8*	22.8*					−.07	−.19	−.07	−.11	−.18
Public officials	45.5*	0.2	10.7*	9.2*					−.09	−.24	−.07	−.09	−.17
People helpful	39.0*	0.0	4.9*	18.0*							−.01	−.17	−.11
Social friends	35.5*	11.2*	16.1*	1.4	+.01	−.03	+.01	−.14	−.05	−.15			
Low church attendance	27.3*	21.3*	0.4	13.9*	−.05	−.04	−.04	−.19					
No religion	17.2*	2.5*	12.3*	0.6*					−.05	−.06	−.03	−.12	−.03
Strong religion	15.8*	12.0*	0.6	9.3*	−.02	−.03	−.03	+.09					
Divorced	3.5*	0.0	2.7	4.2*							+.00	−.12	−.05
Neighboring	0.0*	0.0	8.2*	0.0									
Neither party	0.0*	1.1*	1.1	0.1									
Hard work	0.0	0.1	0.4	0.0									
Politics													
Free speech	204.1*	33.5*	75.7*	1.2*	−.00	−.06	−.07	−.23	−.15	−.33			
Anti-Communism	63.6*	2.9*	36.1*	6.6*					−.16	−.23			
Republican	48.6*	11.0*	3.3*	12.2*	+.04	−.06	−.12	−.02			−.02	−.12	−.12
Redistribution (anti)	27.4*	2.3	29.3*	0.5					−.10	−.25			
Welfare spending	15.9*	0.0	8.2*	9.8*							−.06	−.01	−.12
Conservative	13.1*	10.3*	5.3*	3.3*	−.02	−.05	−.05	−.18					
Urban spending	8.3*	6.0*	1.8	4.0*									
Military spending	2.0*	0.0	3.0*	2.2*									
Anticrime spending	0.0*	0.0	1.3	0.0									
Values and Tastes													
Meaningful work	122.0*	3.1*	27.0*	23.2*					−.07	−.19	−.04	−.11	−.12
Job security	64.9*	1.7*	17.2*	11.4*					−.06	−.12	−.00	−.10	−.06
TV watching	47.6*	0.0	20.3*	6.0*					−.12	−.15			
Fertility norms	28.0*	5.9*	12.8*	0.0					−.04	−.12			
Newspaper reading	27.7*	0.0*	2.8	16.1*							−.08	−.10	−.15
Wore ethic	22.7*	0.0	10.2*	9.5*					−.08	−.11	−.11	−.05	−.04
Lucrative job	3.9*	0.0	0.8	6.1*									
Chance to advance	0.0	0.0	1.9	0.7									
Social Issues													
Intermarriage	229.9*	30.1*	91.7*	4.3*	−.02	−.06	−.05	−.21	−.11	−.34			
Women's place	165.2*	8.6*	63.8*	8.6*					−.12	−.28			
Gay sex	131.8*	21.9*	43.7*	3.8*	−.02	−.08	−.03	−.16	−.14	−.22			
Wives work	116.5*	6.8*	49.2*	2.5*					−.11	−.25			
Marijuana	89.5*	22.0*	34.9*	4.4*	+.01	−.05	−.06	−.16	−.13	−.19			
Premarital	80.5*	42.7*	19.9*	5.8*	−.05	−.07	−.05	−.28	−.08	−.16			
Extramarital	80.5*	15.7*	26.3*	0.6	−.02	−.07	−.04	−.15	−.11	−.19			
Open housing	25.4*	3.8*	17.1*	0.7					−.09	−.14			
Death penalty	15.9*	2.7*	5.5*	11.2*							+.01	−.08	+.06
Ease divorce	14.6*	3.0*	8.5*	0.0									
Courts tough	1.4*	0.0	5.2*	2.8*									

* = Significant at .05 level with N = .6667 of the raw N.

under 9. I have looked at them and there is nothing interesting in percentage terms there.)

Occupation

Respondent's Occupation has significant net associations (cluster adjusted controlling for Education and Father's Occupation) with 37 of 49 items (76 percent) but:

1) using the more conservative L²adj measure, it produces values of 9 or more for only 18 of 49 (37 percent), and

2) the highest L²adj, Job Satisfaction, is 25.4.

Glancing at the specific items in Table 9, the effects of Occupation appear pervasive and diffuse, but a closer inspection modifies the impression. With the exception of Death Penalty, where craftsmen are more harsh (perhaps partly because they are almost all males), there are no effects at all in the "social issues" cluster and the remaining items tend to bunch up in two areas:

Narrowly occupational and economic: Lower prestige workers are less satisfied with their jobs (25.4), give less priority to meaningful work (23.2), give more priority to secure jobs (11.4), report less financial satisfaction (10.1), are more favorable to welfare spending (9.8), and are less likely to espouse the work ethic (9.5).

Cynicism: Lower prestige workers are less likely to say others are trustworthy (22.8), to say others are helpful (18.0), to be optimistic about the future (17.0), to believe the lot of the average man is improving (11.8), or to think well of public officials (9.2).

The theme here seems to fit the dictionary definition of cynicism ("distrustful of human nature and motives") better than the original classification of "morale" or "attachments," since lower prestige strata do not differ on happiness, marital happiness, family satisfaction, sociability, neighboring, religiosity, etc.

Aside from these clusters, the net effects of oc-

cupation boil down to these: compared with a's (Professional, Technical, Managers, Administrators):

1) b-c-d workers have fewer voluntary association memberships and are less likely to read newspapers, and

2) c workers (heavily male) are lower on church attendance and religious intensity and more favorable to the Death Penalty, and

3) c workers and d workers (blue-collar workers) are less likely to be Republicans.

The three columns of differences at the right of Table 9 give us insight into classical "white-collar vs blue-collar" issues since we can use them to calculate the differences between adjacent strata. (Thus for "the future" in the top line, since the b−a difference is −.07 and the c−a difference is −.09, the c−d difference is −.02.) Table 10 summarizes the differences among adjacent strata.

If in each case the category differences in the D proportion were in the order a-b-c-d, the stratum comparisons would all have negative signs. If, on the other hand, the big gulf was between collar levels, we would find all negative d values for c vs b, but not for b vs a, or d vs c. I read Table 10 as follows:

TABLE 10

Occupational Stratum Differences
from Table 9

Difference	Stratum Comparisons*			
	b vs a	c vs b	d vs c	Total
+.05 or more		2	4	6
+.00 to +.094	3	2	3	8
−.00 to −.04	6	5	1	12
−.05 or more	8	8	9	25
Total	17	17	17	51
Number Negative	14	13	10	37
Median	−.04	−.04	−.05	−.04
Mean	−.05	−.04	−.02	−.04

*d = Operatives, Service, Labor.
c = Crafts.
b = Sales, Clerical.
a = Professional, Technical, Managerial.

1) Most of the differences (37 of 51 or 73 percent) are negative, with an average value of −.04.

2) For each comparison of adjacent strata, the mean and median are negative, as are 59 percent to 82 percent of the items. Of the adjacent comparisons, the d-c (operatives-service-labor vs crafts) gap seems least sharp. But of the seven positive d values, the three largest, Death Penalty, Church Attendance, and No Religion, are probably inflated by the concentration of males in crafts jobs and sex differences in these items.

All in all, these data seem to support Glenn and Alston (1968:365), who concluded, "Although there is not a sharp distinction ... between manual and nonmanual working, the distinction between the working class and the middle class still seems more useful than the concept of a 'middle mass.'"

Another way of viewing these findings is to say they cast considerable doubt on the "class culture" notion that occupational strata have vast and diffuse effects on the texture of our lives. Centers (1949:141), for example, claims:

The differences in basic politico-economic orientations found to exist between classes ... do not by any means exhaust the existing contrast in psychological characteristics between them. ... Differences exist, for example, in sympathies and antipathies, prejudices, beliefs, satisfactions and dissatisfactions, goals and desires.

To be sure, Centers does not define class strictly in terms of occupation, but the notion of broad cultural differences between the occupational strata permeates academic and pop social science through such concepts as "middle-class values," "the culture of poverty," "hard hat mentality," "bourgeois morality," "working class authoritarianism," etc.

The GSS data do show some occupational differences that suggest cultural patterns: newspaper reading, membership in voluntary associations, and party identification. But the same data do not show occupational differences (once Education is controlled) for attitudes toward free speech, Communism, military spending, race relations, sex roles, chastity, marital happiness, marijuana, etc., etc.

The rather small net effects of occupational stratum are perhaps the most surprising findings in this paper since they seem to disconfirm both popular and professional assumptions. Negative findings are among the hardest to explain, but the following considerations may be relevant.

First, these results are not actually dramatically different from others' findings. The percentage differences in Glenn and Alston (1968:370) are much like those in Table 10, and their conclusions (excerpted from their abstract, p. 365) are quite guarded: "The estimated differences are rather small both among the manual categories and among the nonmanual categories ... (and) there is not a sharp disjunction in reported attitudes and behavior between manual and nonmanual workers." Curtis and Jackson (1977:322) are similarly cautious, saying, "The effects of *occupation* in our analyses were fairly [*sic*] pervasive, although usually it did not exercise the strongest net effect. ... Certainly, significant portions of the zero-order correlations could be accounted for by the direct effects of education and income." Thus, in part, the surprise may be because no one has forcibly called our attention to the emperor's attire.

Second, Education and Father's Occupation are partialled out in these analyses. Bivariate tables will necessarily show stronger differences by occupational stratum, but they don't seem to be *due to* occupational stratum.

Third, let us consider some possible flaws in this study. Have we been misled by the unreliability of our items? I argued against that position in [Davis 1982:579] and note further that unreliability in the Ds can not account for the *differential* strength of their relations with Occupation and Education. Is Census group a poor measure of occupation? Perhaps a purer measure of prestige would improve things. Perhaps, but since a cross-tab of our GSS occupational levels against Hodge-Siegel-Rossi prestige scores in four categories gives an adjusted L^2 of 1,648, this line does not seem promising. Perhaps Census group does not tap the important qualitative dimensions of occupations. Perhaps, but not necessarily. Consider, for example, "authority." If one cross-tabulates our four R categories against the combination of GSS items on authority (WKSUB = "Do you have a supervisor on your job?"; WKSUP = "In your job do you supervise anyone who is directly responsible to you?") we get an adjusted L^2 of 124, which suggests the Census categories do get at sociologically interesting aspects of work. Are the data diluted by workers new at their jobs or long retired from them? Possibly, but extensive research on mobility routinely finds that workers tend to stay within strata for long periods. Furthermore, almost all of the respondents have been away from school for many years, but the Education effects, as we shall see, are stronger than the Occupational ones. ...

In sum, my conclusion is that occupational stratum simply does not have the diffuse and strong effects on our nonvocational attitudes and opinions that sociologists have generally assumed.

- **Conclusion 4:** Respondent's Occupational stratum has nontrivial net associations with about a third of the dependent items. The differences tend to follow the prestige order of the strata but the magnitudes are weak and the associations are concentrated in two clusters, cynicism and items directly related to jobs and economic security.

Father's Occupation

If the effects of respondent's occupation are disappointing, they are enormous compared with the associations for father's occupation (stratum of origin). Thus:

1) 30 of 49 (61 percent) of the associations are statistically significant (cluster adjusted) in the raw data.
2) The median adjusted L^2 is 2.
3) 11 of 49 (22 percent) have L^2adj values of 9 or more.
4) The largest adjusted L^2 is 42.7 for Premarital.

Scrutiny of Table 9 suggests that even these modest results are overstated. The big differences are concentrated in the column headed "f" (e.g., $-.28$ for Premarital, $-.23$ for Free Speech, $-.21$ for Intermarriage). That is, for the eleven "keepers" with magnitudes of 9 or more the big difference is between people who grew up on the farm and nonfarm people from whatever stratum. This hypothesis is easily tested by reanalyzing the eleven large effects after removing respondents from farm backgrounds. The result is clear: when the farm-reared are removed only six of the eleven are still statistically significant (cluster adjusted) and none of the adjusted L^2 values exceeds 4.8.

- **Conclusion 5:** Among Americans from nonfarm backgrounds, prestige stratum of Father's Occupation has no net association with any of the 49 items. Persons from farm backgrounds tend to be more conservative as adults.

Recalling that the signed mobility hypothesis implies opposite signs for RD and FD:

- **Conclusion 6:** The evidence is strongly against the hypothesis that sign mobility per se affects any of the 49 items.

I am not aware of any sociologists since the Warner school who have placed much stress on the net effects of origin stratum. Certainly such differences are a staple of Anglo-American literature (from the Yoknapatawpha novels of William Faulkner to *The Great Gatsby* to *My Fair Lady*) and again the language is rich with phrases such as "nouveau riche," "parvenu," "social climber," "arriviste," "come down in the world," "upstart," and "genteel poverty" which imply our behavior is shaped by where we came from as well as where we ended up. Nevertheless, Table 9 suggests 38 exceptions to the idea. The eleven nonexceptions—effects produced by farm origins—have the further consequence of suggesting that when parental social location has lasting effects, they stem from some qualitative or subcultural aspect of social structure, not from the ranked layers implicit in the word "stratification."

These conclusions do not imply that people who grew up in different occupational strata are totally homogeneous. The relationships among the FED variables are so strong they can produce zero-order associations when some net effects are nil. For example, Table 9 shows adjusted L^2s of 2.0, 36.1, and 6.6 for FD, ED, and RD when D is "Anti-Communism." ED has a healthy value, but when Education is controlled, Father's Occupation and Respondent's Occupation have virtually no effect on attitudes toward Communism. But if one runs the bivariate tables for FD and RD one gets respectable L^2s of 17.8 for FD and 20.6 for RD—both explained by Education. Americans of different occupational strata, past or present, differ in their attitudes to Communism, but their Educational differences account for both associations.

Education

Educational attainment has a more impressive box score. ED is significant (cluster adjusted) for 35 of 49 (71 percent) items, has adjusted L^2s of 9 or more for 24 of 49 (49 percent) items, and has adjusted L^2s of 25 or more for 13 items (26 percent).

Intermarriage	91.7	Life Exciting	37.4
Free Speech	75.7	Anti-Communism	36.1
Woman's Place	63.8	Marijuana	34.9
Wives work	49.2	Redistribution	29.3
Future	45.9	Meaningful work	27.0
Gay Sex	43.7	Extramarital	26.3
Memberships	40.1		

Thus, a hypothetical "typical GSS" would turn up significant net associations for about half of our items and nontrivial magnitudes for about a quarter.

Again the figures in Table 9 may be used to ask whether a relationship is ordinal. For the 24 cases with adjusted L^2s of 9 or more, each difference is negative and in each case the magnitude for 0–11 vs 13+ is larger than 12 vs 13+, i.e., all the differences are ordinal. For 12 years vs 13+ the mean is −.10, the median −.10; for 0–11 vs 12, the mean is −.20, the median −.08. When nontrivial net Education differences appear, the typical gap be-

tween college and high school graduates or between high school graduates and fewer years is about 10 percentage points.

As the literature persistently suggests, controlling for father's and respondent's occupations, better educated Americans tend to be more optimistic and less cynical (but not happier or more happily married), joiners, more sociable, less anti-Communist, give greater priority to intrinsic aspects of work, are less addicted to TV, less favorable to large families, more permissive on issues of sex behavior and women's roles, and (among whites) more liberal on race prejudice items.

These reports are solid, but short of colossal. After all, half the time "ED" "doesn't work" and other analyses (Davis, 1979) show that items associated with Education tend to be associated with Age (being young or perhaps being born more recently almost always operates in the same direction as having more schooling), so when Age is controlled the education association is usually reduced, though seldom eliminated. Nevertheless, Education is a much better predictor than Occupation. It has more "9s" (49 percent vs 37 percent) and more "25s" (26 percent vs 2 percent). If we simply take the difference between the adjusted L^2s for ED and RD, ED is stronger in 34 of 49 cases (69 percent) and surpasses RD by 25 points in 11 cases, while there is no item where RD exceeds ED by 25 points—the Job Satisfaction difference of 24.3 being the largest value of RD–ED.

The magnitudes of adjusted L^2 for ED and RD are uncorrelated ($r = -.003$), and when both happen to have an effect their "signs" never disagree. Hence there is zero support for the "investment psychology" hypothesis. Even for Job Satisfaction itself, within levels of occupation there is no association between Education and Satisfaction—although the investment hypothesis would predict a strong negative association.

- **Conclusion 7:** There is no evidence that Education acts as an investment and Occupation as a return in terms of attitudes and behaviors.

The zero correlation between the effect sizes for ED and RD casts doubt on yet another familiar sociological concept—the notion of an underlying "socioeconomic status dimension" with various stratification measures acting like items in a test.

To summarize:

- **Conclusion 8:** Of the three achievement variables, education is clearly the most powerful predictor. It explains any associations between Father's stratum and the dependent items and it has more and stronger associations with dependent items than does Respondent's Occupational stratum.

- **Conclusion 9:** All in all, given the weak magnitudes, disappointing effects of Occupation, and lack of agreement between occupational and education effects, the notion of class cultures receives little support from these data.

Again, these results are hardly unprecedented. Hyman and Wright's book (1979) is a virtual panegyric on the attitudinal effects of education and the less exuberant team of Curtis and Jackson are moved to say, "a major conclusion from this study is that the single most influential rank dimension is education" (1977:321). And again it is not obvious why the data come out this way. Neither this study nor its predecessors analyzes intervening variables that might explain how Educational Attainment "works." As for prior variables that might make part or all of the associations spurious, there are at least two obvious candidates, Age/Cohort and "social class." Younger/more recently born Americans are better educated (for GSS 1972–77 the adjusted L^2 for birth cohort by Education, with three categories each, is 137) and have attitudes characteristic of the better educated. The issue deserves systematic attention but enough published studies and informal GSS tabulations exist to justify the prediction that when Age/Cohort is controlled, Educational effects will be reduced a bit but definitely not eliminated. As for the social class hypothesis, this report lays it to rest. If the apparent effect of Education is spurious, it is definitely not because Education reinforces the values of the various occupational strata.

Conclusion

The carnage here has been considerable. Despite large and representative samples and a broad spectrum of dependent variable possibilities, we have failed to find a shred of support for the "obvious" propositions that Americans' attitudes and opinions are shaped by (1) intergenerational occupational mobility, "sheer" or "score," (2) occupational return on educational "investment," (3) status consistency, or (4) parental occupational stratum in a vertical sense. We did see some significant statistical effects for (1) farm vs nonfarm origins, (2) current occupational stratum, and (3) educational attainment. However, the significant associations are seldom of impressive magnitude and the occupational associations are centered on limited topics.

Negative findings seldom generate concise, trenchant conclusions. If there is a general implication here, it may be this: in the last twenty years sociology, empirical and theoretical, has shown an almost obsessive interest in the occupational structure of modern societies. Consequently, we have learned an enormous amount about these structures and their demographic metabolism. It is quite possible, however, that this knowledge is self-contained and if we are to understand other facets of contemporary societies, new theories, perhaps more cultural than structural, may be in order.

Notes

Direct all correspondence to: James A. Davis, Department of Sociology, Harvard University, Cambridge, MA 02138.

The research reported here was supported by the National Science Foundation grant SOC–7703279.

References

Blau, Peter M. and Otis Dudley Duncan. 1967. The American Occupational Structure. New York: Wiley.

Centers, Richard. 1949. The Psychology of Social Classes: A Study of Class Consciousness. Princeton: Princeton University Press.

Coleman, Richard P. and Lee Rainwater. 1978. Social Standing in America: New Dimensions of Class. New York: Basic Books.

Curtis, Richard F. and Elton F. Jackson. 1977. Inequality in American Communities. New York: Academic Press.

Davis, James A. 1975. "Analysing contingency tables with linear flow graphs: D systems." Pp. 111–45 in David Heise (ed.), Sociological Methodology 1976. San Francisco: Jossey-Bass.

———. 1979. Background Variables and Opinions in the 1972–1977 NORC General Social Surveys: Ten Generalizations about Age, Education, Occupational Prestige, Race, Region, Religion, and Sex and Forty-Nine Opinion Items. GSS Technical Report No. 18, Chicago: NORC.

Davis, James A., Tom W. Smith and C. Bruce Stephenson. 1980. General Social Surveys, 1972–1980: Cumulative Codebook. Chicago: NORC.

Durkheim, Emile. [1897]. Suicide. Glencoe, IL: Free Press. 1951.

Glenn, Norval D. and Jon P. Alston. 1968. "Cultural differences among occupational categories." American Sociological Review 33:365–82.

Goodman, Leo A. 1978. Analyzing Qualitative/Categorical Data. Cambridge, MA: Abt Books.

Hyman, Herbert H. 1966. "The value systems of different classes." Pp. 488–99 in Reinhard Bendix and Seymour M. Lipset (eds.), Class, Status, and Power. 2nd edition. Glencoe, IL: Free Press.

Hyman, Herbert H. and Charles R. Wright. 1979. Education's Lasting Influence on Values. Chicago: University of Chicago Press.

Jackson, Elton F. and Richard F. Curtis. 1972. "Effects of vertical mobility and status inconsistency: a body of negative evidence." American Sociological Review 37:701–13.

Jencks, Christopher et al. 1979. Who Gets Ahead? New York: Basic Books.

Kohn, Melvin L. 1969. Class and Conformity: A Study in Values. Homewood, IL: Dorsey Press.

Lipset, Seymour Martin. 1959. "Democracy and working class authoritarianism." American Sociological Review 24:482–501.

Sorokin, Pitirim. 1927. Social Mobility. New York: Harper & Brothers.

Stouffer, Samuel A. 1955. Communism, Conformity and Civil Liberties. New York: Doubleday.

PAUL DiMAGGIO

Social Stratification, Life-Style, and Social Cognition

Measures of class and related variables, as well as such other axes of stratification as gender and race, have long been the crack troops in sociologists' war on unexplained variance. Hardly an aspect of human experience—the clothes one wears, the number of siblings one has, the diseases one is likely to contract, the music to which one listens, the chances that one will serve in the armed forces or fall prey to violent crime—is uncorrelated with some dimension of social rank.

This section focuses on two especially interesting and well-developed literatures: one on the relationship among stratification, life-style, and consumption patterns and one addressing the interactions among class, personality, and attitudes. Such work considers the consequences of stratification for the cultural styles and personalities of individuals and groups. But it goes beyond this, as well, to explore the *effects* of cultural style and personality on people's life chances. And scholars in each tradition have explored the role of history and social structure in shaping the relationships observed in studies in which individuals are the units of analysis.

Culture, Life-Style, and Consumption

The starting point for any discussion of life-styles and consumption patterns must be the work of Thorstein Veblen and Pierre Bourdieu. Although

both authors believe that social stratification has profound effects on life-style, beyond this their approaches vary. First, they call attention to different aspects of stratification. Veblen uses the term "class" rhetorically, but his emphasis is on a continuous prestige hierarchy, "rated and graded" by similarity to a "leisure-class" cultural ideal. Bourdieu, by contrast, posits discrete "class fractions" sharing similar positions with respect to education, income, and occupation, each united by a *habitus* or worldview derived from similar life experiences and common images of the way of life appropriate for people "like us." Moreover, the social functions of taste are less complicated for Veblen than for Bourdieu. Veblen portrays pecuniary emulation and conspicuous consumption as strategies that individuals employ against their peers in struggling for status. By contrast, like Max Weber (on status groups, 1968; Collins 1979) and Mary Douglas (Douglas and Isherwood 1979), Bourdieu views tastes as signs of group affiliation—of horizontal connections as well as vertical distinctions (DiMaggio 1990).

Bourdieu's work has inspired a body of empirical research on the origins and effects of "cultural capital," usually operationalized by measures of survey respondents' knowledge of, interest in, or experience with the arts. Studies in Australia, Greece, Hungary, the Netherlands, Sweden, and the United States have all documented robust effects of parental education (and, to a lesser extent, occupation) on children's cultural capital (DiMaggio and Mohr 1985; DeGraff 1986; Ganzeboom 1982, 1986; Katsillas and Rubinson 1990; Lamb 1989; Mohr and DiMaggio 1990; Roe 1983).

This is an original article prepared for this book.

Similarly, researchers agree that adults' tastes (and related behaviors) are associated with educational attainment and, to a lesser extent, occupation (DiMaggio and Ostrower 1990; Hughes and Peterson 1983; Laumann and House 1970; Marsden and Reed 1983; Robinson 1985). Significant effects of students' cultural capital on such outcomes as school grades (DiMaggio 1982a; Roe 1983), educational aspirations (Lamb 1989) and attainment (DiMaggio and Mohr 1985; Ganzeboom 1986), and marital selection (DiMaggio and Mohr 1985) have been demonstrated by most but not all (e.g., DeGraff 1986; Katsillas and Rubinson 1990) studies of these topics.

The results are more consistent with Bourdieu's approach than with Veblen's formulation of the problem. Research on the predictors of cultural capital finds that schooling, which Bourdieu views as the key institution controlling access to cultural capital, is a far better predictor of taste than income, which Veblen regarded as central. Similarly, using direct measures of home cultural climate, Mohr and DiMaggio (1990) demonstrate that these affect strongly the cultural capital of adolescents, mediating most of the effects of parental education and occupation. At the same time, other results are consistent with *both* Veblen and Bourdieu's orientations. For example, research supports status-competitive over cognitive explanations of class differences: Tastes cluster more by the prestige of goods (e.g., liking fine art and classical music) than by their formal similarities (e.g., liking all kinds of music) (DiMaggio 1982a; Ganzeboom 1982). Attitudes toward high culture and arts attendance predict achievement better than what students actually know about the arts (DiMaggio 1982a), and early socialization in the arts has been found to be more strongly related to educational attainment than to subsequent arts attendance (Ganzeboom 1986).

Not all the evidence is consistent with Bourdieu's argument, however. Indeed, although taste is *differentiated* by social status, there is no sign of discrete taste classes with sharply *segmented* preferences. Educational attainment is strongly related to participation in prestigious art forms, but it is positively associated with consumption of most kinds of popular culture as well (DiMaggio and Ostrower 1990; Gans 1986;

Ganzeboom 1986; Hughes and Peterson 1983; Robinson 1985; Wilensky 1964). Moreover, although all researchers report positive associations between measures of socioeconomic status and taste, the proportion of variance that these measures explain is often low.

The definition of cultural capital has also suffered from considerable ambiguity (Lamont and Lareau 1988). On theoretical grounds, the use of the "capital" metaphor is potentially misleading insofar as it suggests an analogy with human capital. Whereas human capital comprises individual skills that are task-related, the components of cultural capital are socially constructed or, as Bourdieu has put it, "arbitrary." At the societal level, stocks of human capital contribute directly to the economic productivity of labor; indeed, human capital theory emerged as a way of explaining surprising positive residuals in gross national products during periods of educational expansion (Schultz 1961). By contrast, there is no intrinsic reason that "stocks" of cultural capital should boost aggregate productivity; any positive economic effect is likely to be incidental and to operate on economic institutions (primarily by increasing levels of trust) rather than in the realm of production. At the individual level, whereas human capital is a product of investment, cultural capital is more likely to be acquired effortlessly as a by-product of socialization. (To be sure, one can strive for "culture," but the product of such striving is by its very nature viewed as less "authentic" and is thus less valuable than an easy familiarity acquired without conscious intent.) To put it another way, whereas the acquisition of human capital expresses an individual logic of strategic competition, the acquisition and maintenance of cultural capital express a collective logic of monopolistic closure at the level of the status group. In this respect, then, the rationalistic imagery of the "capital" metaphor obscures the social-organizational basis from which the efficacy of cultural resources derives.

Ambiguity also reigns in the operationalization of cultural capital. Most studies have followed Bourdieu's early work (1973) in using measures of participation in the high-culture arts, although the concept is much broader. Why aesthetic measures have performed so well is not entirely clear.

The arts are arguably the most thoroughly institutionalized form of prestigious culture in modern industrial societies (DiMaggio 1982a), but the extent to which aesthetic orientations per se are important in their own right or are proxies for unmeasured forms of cultural capital—self-presentation, linguistic skills, orientations toward status-seeking, or, as Lamont (1992) suggests, moral stances—cannot be determined. Sophisticated studies of face-to-face interaction, which analyze particular cues that serve as bases of interpersonal trust and positive evaluations, are helpful in addressing the puzzle (Bernstein 1977; Erickson and Schultz 1982). Yet intensive local studies cannot resolve the matter because they cannot distinguish between cultural resources that help people get ahead in narrow social circles and well-institutionalized cultural capital of more general utility.

Indeed, insofar as the "capital" metaphor can be justified, it is in calling attention to the institutional apparatus that guarantees the wide validity of certain cultural signals. For example, local or ephemeral cultural resources (e.g., those related to cuisine or styles of dress) tend to lack such institutional backing, whereas other, more fully institutionalized cultural resources (e.g., the high-culture arts or, earlier, forms of religious expression) constitute a currency ("cultural capital" proper) of wide social, geographic, and temporal scope. Ultimately, combining fine-grained studies of social interaction and national surveys with a broader than customary range of cultural measures will be necessary to resolve these operational issues.

Finally, we need to understand why certain tastes or styles become valued more highly than others. The contemporary hierarchy of aesthetic taste, for example, was the product of early industrial class formation and political change, varying in detail but similar in result in Europe and the United States (DeNora 1991; DiMaggio 1982b, 1982c; Reddy 1984). It is clear that cultural hierarchies are maintained by economic investments (e.g., expenditures on humanities courses) and state power (e.g., government grants to high-cultural arts organizations or laws mandating the use of a single language in linguistically diverse communities). It is equally plain that they are eroded by other processes (e.g., increases in the proportion of cultural goods financed through market exchange as opposed to elite philanthropy). But we still lack a comprehensive theory of the manner in which such hierarchies change.

Personality and Attitudes

In the long history of research on the relationship between class and personality, there is no more creative and influential work than the research program of Melvin Kohn and his colleagues. Whereas the readings from Veblen and Bourdieu emphasize class differences in consumption, Kohn explores the relationship between one's place in the stratification order and the inner self of values and attitudes.

Actually, Kohn's work has more in common with Bourdieu's than this implies, for Bourdieu's *Distinction* treats class fractions as differing not only in tastes but also in both *ethos* (underlying evaluative dispositions) and *habitus* (experience-based schema that generate consistent behaviors across an infinite range of situations). Thus, these authors agree that both normative and cognitive orientations are linked to class and occupational positions because shared experiences associated with these positions are generalized by social learning and shaped into enduring dispositions.

Beyond this, though, the two differ markedly. Whereas Bourdieu emphasizes struggle among class fractions and strategic interaction in complex social "fields," Kohn and his colleagues rely on learning theory to the exclusion of strategic mechanisms and focus on the individual level of analysis. In addition, although each views human personalities or *habitus* as both stable and plastic, Bourdieu places relatively more weight on the role of the family and the broader social environment, whereas Kohn and his colleagues focus almost exclusively on the influence of work.

Both approaches have generated impressive long-term research programs. The work of Melvin Kohn, Carmi Schooler, and their colleagues spans more than three decades from the publication of Kohn's first paper on social class and parental values (1959) to research testing U.S. findings in comparative perspective (1990). The early studies (Kohn and Schooler 1969) documented moderate but robust associations between men's socioeconomic status (a weighted combination of education and occupational position) and numerous values and orientations: the extent to which the men interviewed valued self-directedness or conformity in their children; the characteristics they valued in themselves; the extent to which they judged their work according to intrinsic standards or extrinsic rewards; their attitudes toward morality and change; and their authoritarianism, self-confidence, and confidence in others. Social class was related to more self-directed, optimistic, and flexible responses in all these areas, with educational attainment and occupation (but not income) playing independent roles in predicting orientations and values. Most effects of occupation were captured by measures of opportunities for self-directedness inherent in the job.

Kohn and Schooler reinterviewed many of the same men ten years later and used the results to test the causal inferences in their earlier work (Kohn and Schooler 1978, 1982). After analyzing data from both time periods, they reported that although values and orientations were stable over time, men whose jobs were complex and who exercised considerable self-direction actually became more flexible, whereas men who did simple work and were highly supervised became less so. These findings have been sustained, extended, and elaborated in subsequent comparative work carried out on Polish men, Japanese men and women, and American women working in the paid labor force and at home (Miller et al. 1979; Schooler et al. 1984; Schooler and Naoi 1985; Kohn et al. 1990; Naoi and Schooler 1990). As in the case of research on cultural capital, students of work and personality have stepped back to explore social-structural as well as individual-level effects on values. For example, Schooler (1976, 1990) has argued that the strength and endurance of feudalism are associated with lower levels of individualism in both Europe and the Far East.

This work has yielded a substantial body of knowledge. Perhaps most notable, given the mass of research documenting statistical associations between measures of social rank and almost everything else, is the success with which Kohn, Schooler, and their colleagues have identified

what it is about class (and occupation) that makes the difference. Rarely has stratification been defined and operationalized with such theoretical precision. Equally important, as with research on cultural capital, the work demonstrates that the *effects* of desirable positions in the stratification order are themselves *resources* that help men and women get ahead.

A few questions remain open. The effects of self-direction and complexity on values are more notable for their ubiquity and robustness than for their strength. We know little about the factors that may account for the variance that work content does not explain. Moreover, the research has focused on men's and women's occupational lives; it has yet to explicate the role of schooling and early childhood socialization in setting men and women on trajectories that later occupational experience may either moderate or, more likely, reinforce.

In comparison to Kohn's explicit focus on the mechanisms by which class affects psychological functioning, James Davis (1982) assesses the gross association between several stratification measures and answers to forty-nine diverse attitude questions. The relatively weak associations that emerge suggest an important lesson: Simplistic notions about "class cultures" or expectations that people's attitudes arise mechanically from their locations in the social order are naive. So are some more sophisticated and widely held views (e.g., the status-inconsistency framework, which Davis also finds explanatorily impotent). Although one might regard this lesson as obvious, many sociologists do make broad claims about the connection between class and attitudes. The reading by Davis inoculates us against them. It would be wrong, however, to infer that class does not matter. Rather, as Davis concludes, his results point to the need for more sophisticated theories that explain why specific kinds of stratification influence the distribution of particular kinds of attitudes.

Davis also suggests that "new theories, perhaps more cultural than structural, may be in order." A partial example is the theory of the "new class" (Gouldner 1979), which holds that highly educated workers, especially those employed by public and nonprofit organizations, share a "culture of critical discourse" engendering oppositional and antiauthoritarian political beliefs. In his assessment of the theory, Brint (1984) reported that tolerance was associated not with upper-middle-class status per se but with particular locations within that class: Cultural and social-service professionals, for example, were more tolerant than technical professionals or business managers. Similarly, Macy (1988) found greater tolerance among professionals employed in the nonprofit and public sectors than among those employed by corporations. New class approaches edge toward the cultural in emphasizing independent effects of socialization and of humanistic and social-scientific education on cognitive and discursive styles, but they remain structural in that they view the political expression of such styles as shaped by interests associated with workers' positions in the division of labor.

Rather than suggesting that class does not matter, such results imply that class matters in complex ways. A synthesis of work on racial attitudes by Schuman, Steeh, and Bobo (1985) likewise supports this view. Schuman and colleagues found that educational stratification influenced some white attitudes but not others: For example, education had a strong liberalizing effect on abstract attitudes toward racial tolerance and equality but only weak effects on support for explicit government civil rights initiatives. There is no better guide to research on class and attitudes than the quotation from Alfred North Whitehead that Schuman, Steeh, and Bobo placed at the head of their concluding chapter: "Seek simplicity and distrust it." Understanding regularities in relationships between class, culture, and attitudes requires complex models, different models for different aspects of culture and different kinds of attitudes, and theories of how macrostructural variation among societies affects the relationship between individual-level measures of class, culture, and attitudes within them.

Conclusions

Each body of literature reviewed here demonstrates the effects of aspects of stratification on culture, life-style, values, or attitudes. Each reports reciprocal effects on life chances of styles or values with which hierarchically advantaged people are especially well endowed. And each has explored the role of institutional and social-structural change in accounting for relationships observed at the individual level.

The same is true of many other analyses that demonstrate stratification effects on noneconomic outcomes. Research on physical and mental health, for example, reveals that illness, mortality, and emotional distress are unequally allocated throughout the stratification system, with those at the bottom receiving far more than their share (Kessler 1982; Williams 1990). Studies of access to social networks similarly find that Euro-Americans, men, and people with more education have wider social networks and more resourceful connections than do African Americans, women, and the less educated (Marsden 1987). Still other research suggests that these findings are related: When poor people face misfortune, they have weaker social support on which to rely and therefore experience even more distress (Williams 1990). Like values and life-styles, health and networks are predictors as well as consequences of success. Emotional distress and illness keep people from getting ahead; robust social networks help them push forward (Granovetter 1974; Lin et al. 1983).

Taken together, the findings of research on noneconomic consequences of stratification (and the reciprocal effects of these consequences) demonstrate processes of cumulative advantage and disadvantage that are sometimes referred to as *social reproduction* (Bourdieu and Passeron 1977). We must distinguish between *micro-* and *macroreproduction* in order to pursue this point.

A social process is "reproductive" in the micro sense insofar as attitudes, values, and tastes linked to social origins are themselves causally related to hierarchical position at some later point in a manner that reinforces initial advantage or disadvantage. Microreproduction occurs both intra- and intergenerationally. Further, it entails both direct reciprocal relationships between pairs of variables (e.g., job complexity and intellectual flexibility) and more complex causal chains (e.g., having middle-class parents gives one a wide-ranging social network that makes it easier to get an attractive and complex job, thus increasing one's intellectual flexibility).

The strength of microreproduction is an open question. Although studies of the relationship between class and particular kinds of life-styles or attitudes often find significant but relatively small effects, we have been remiss in investigating the ways in which such myriad small effects cumulate and interact. Rarely, if ever, do researchers explore the relationship between position in the stratification order and a wide range of life-style variables (attitudes, values, cultural capital, linguistic capital, social networks, and health) in a single set of models featuring reciprocal effects and appropriate interaction terms. The extent to which such analyses would reveal stronger microreproductive processes than appear in more limited studies is an empirical question. To address it and thus take microreproduction seriously, we must relax otherwise productive barriers of specialization between different research subfields, each with its own set of dependent variables, in the interest of theoretical and empirical synthesis.

Whatever the results of such studies in particular national contexts, the effects of class on attitudes and life-style are likely to vary over time and cross-nationally as a result of macrostructural factors. By macroreproduction, I refer to large-scale structural change (e.g., the rise and fall of industries or communities), political decisions (e.g., those that alter the redistributive effects of the tax system), legal factors (e.g., definitions of property rights), or institutional developments (e.g., the emergence of formal organizations devoted to "high culture") that strengthen individual-level relationships between social origin and individual life chances.

There are many macrostructural processes that merit further study: How might the effect (or character) of pecuniary emulation vary between Western societies, where highly differentiated consumer goods are allocated on the basis of price, and socialist (or postsocialist) societies, where narrower selections of goods are allocated on the basis of queuing and rationing? What are the effects of macrostructural conditions (e.g., level of economic development or degree of religious and racial heterogeneity) on the extent to which individual political attitudes are stratified

by occupational and educational attainment? What are the processes and mechanisms by which classes develop new tastes or abandon old ones? If we are to answer such questions, historical and international comparative work must assume even more central places in the study of stratification.

Notes

I am grateful to David Grusky for superb and extensive substantive and editorial suggestions, which greatly strengthened the paper.

References

Bernstein, Basil. 1977. *Class, Codes, and Control*, vol. 3. London: Routledge & Kegan Paul.

Bourdieu, Pierre. 1973. "Cultural Reproduction and Social Reproduction." Pp. 71–112 in Richard Brown, ed., *Knowledge, Education, and Cultural Change*. London: Tavistock.

———. 1990a. *The Logic of Practice*. Stanford: Stanford University Press.

———. 1990b. *In Other Words*. Stanford: Stanford University Press.

Bourdieu, Pierre, and Jean-Claude Passeron. 1977. *Reproduction in Education, Society, and Culture*. Beverly Hills: Sage Publications.

Brint, Steven. 1984. "'New Class' and Cumulative Trend Explanations of Liberal Political Attitudes of Professionals." *American Journal of Sociology* 90:30–71.

Collins, Randall. 1979. *The Credential Society: An Historical Sociology of Education*. New York: Academic Press.

Davis, James A. 1982. "Achievement Variables and Class Cultures: Family, Schooling, Job, and Forty-nine Dependent Variables in the Cumulative GSS." *American Sociological Review* 47:569–586.

DeGraff, Paul M. 1986. "The Impact of Financial and Cultural Resources on Educational Attainment in the Netherlands." *Sociology of Education* 59:237–246.

DeNora, Tia. 1991. "Musical Patronage and Social Change at the Time of Beethoven's Arrival in Vienna." *American Journal of Sociology* 97:310–346.

DiMaggio, Paul. 1982a. "Cultural Capital and School Success: The Impact of Status Culture Participation on the Grades of U.S. High School Students." *American Sociological Review* 47:189–201.

_____. 1982b. "Cultural Entrepreneurship in Nineteenth-Century Boston, I: The Creation of an Organizational Base for High Culture in America." *Media, Culture, and Society* 4:33–50.

_____. 1982c. "Cultural Entrepreneurship in Nineteenth-Century Boston, II: The Classification and Framing of American Art." *Media, Culture, and Society* 4:303–322.

_____. 1990. "Cultural Aspects of Economic Action and Organization." Pp. 113–136 in Roger Friedland and A. F. Robertson, eds., *Beyond the Marketplace: Rethinking Economy and Society*. Chicago: Aldine.

DiMaggio, Paul, and John Mohr. 1985. "Cultural Capital, Educational Attainment, and Marital Selection." *American Journal of Sociology* 90:1231–1261.

DiMaggio, Paul, and Francie Ostrower. 1990. "Participation in the Arts by Black and White Americans." *Social Forces* 68:753–778.

Douglas, Mary, and Baron Isherwood. 1979. *The World of Goods: Toward an Anthropology of Consumption*. New York: W. W. Norton.

Erickson, Fred, and Jeffrey Schultz. 1982. *The Counselor as Gatekeeper: Social Interaction in Interviews*. New York: Academic Press.

Gans, Herbert J. 1986. "American Popular Culture and High Culture in a Changing Class Structure." Pp. 17–38 in *Prospects: An Annual of American Cultural Studies*, vol. 10. New York: Cambridge University Press.

Ganzeboom, Harry B.G. 1982. "Explaining Differential Participation in High-Cultural Activities: A Confrontation of Information-Processing and Status-Seeking Theories." Pp. 186–205 in Werner Raub, ed., *Theoretical Models and Empirical Analyses: Contributions to the Explanation of Individual Actions and Collective Phenomena*. Utrecht: E. S. Publications.

_____. 1986. "Cultural Socialization and Social Reproduction: A Cross-National Test of Bourdieu's Theory of Stratification." Paper presented at the International Sociological Association World Congress, New Delhi, India.

Gouldner, Alvin. 1979. *The Future of Intellectuals and the Rise of the New Class*. New York: Seabury Press.

Granovetter, Mark S. 1974. *Getting a Job: A Study of Contacts and Careers*. Cambridge: Harvard University Press.

Hughes, Michael, and Richard A. Peterson. 1983. "Isolating Cultural Choice Patterns in a U.S. Population." *American Behavioral Scientist* 26:459–478.

Katsillas, John, and Richard Rubinson. 1990. "Cultural Capital, Student Achievement, and Educational Reproduction in Greece." *American Sociological Review* 55:270–279.

Kessler, Ronald. 1982. "Socioeconomic Status and Psychological Distress." *American Sociological Review* 47:752–763.

Kohn, Melvin. 1959. "Social Class and Parental Values." *American Journal of Sociology* 64:337–351.

Kohn, Melvin L., Atsushi Naoi, Carrie Schoenbach, Carmi Schooler, and Kazimierz M. Slomczynski. 1990. "Position in the Class Structure and Psychological Functioning in the United States, Japan, and Poland." *American Journal of Sociology* 94:964–1008.

Kohn, Melvin L., and Carmi Schooler. 1969. "Class, Occupation, and Orientation." *American Sociological Review* 34:659–678.

_____. 1978. "The Reciprocal Effects of the Substantive Complexity of Work and Intellectual Flexibility: A Longitudinal Assessment." *American Journal of Sociology* 84:24–52.

_____. 1982. "Job Conditions and Personality: A Longitudinal Assessment of Their Reciprocal Effects." *American Journal of Sociology* 87:1257–1286.

Lamb, Stephen. 1989. "Cultural Consumption and the Educational Plans of Australian Secondary School Students." *Sociology of Education* 62:95–108.

Lamont, Michele. 1992. *Money, Morals, and Manners: Thee Culture of the French and American Upper-Middle Class*. Chicago: University of Chicago Press.

Lamont, Michele, and Annette Lareau. 1988. "Cultural Capital: Allusions, Gaps, and Glissandos in Recent Theoretical Developments." *Sociological Theory* 6:153–168.

Laumann, Edward O., and James S. House. 1970. "Living Room Styles and Social Attributes: The Patterning of Material Artifacts in a Modern Urban Commnity." *Sociology and Social Research* 54:321–342.

Lin, Nan, William M. Ensel, and John C. Vaughn. 1983. "Social Resources and Strength of Ties: Structural Factors in Occupational Status Attainment." *American Sociological Review* 46:393–405.

Macy, Michael. 1988. "New-Class Dissent Among Social-Cultural Specialists: The Effects of Occupational Self-Direction and Location in the Public Sector." *Sociological Forum* 3:325–356.

Marsden, Peter V. 1987. "Core Discussion Networks of Americans." *American Sociological Review* 52:122–131.

Marsden, Peter V., and John Shelton Reed. 1983. "Cultural Choice Among Southerners." *American Behavioral Scientist* 52:122–131.

Miller, Joanne, Carmi Schooler, Melvin Kohn, and K. A. Miller. 1979. "Women and Work: The Psychological Effects of Occupational Conditions." *American Journal of Sociology* 85:66–94.

Mohr, John, and Paul DiMaggio. 1990. "Patterns of Occupational Inheritance of Cultural Capital." Paper presented at the 1990 meetings of the American Sociological Association, Washington, D.C.

Naoi, Michiko, and Carmi Schooler. 1990. "Psychological Consequences of Occupational Conditions Among Japanese Wives." *Social Psychology Quarterly* 58:100–116.

Reddy, William M. 1984. *The Rise of Market Culture: The Textile Trade and French Society, 1750–1900.* Cambridge: Cambridge University Press.

Robinson, John. 1985. *Public Participation in the Arts: A Project Summary.* College Park: University of Maryland Survey Center.

Roe, Keith. 1983. *Mass Media and Adolescent Schooling: Conflict or Co-Existence?* Stockholm: Almqvist & Wiksell, 1983.

Schooler, Carmi. 1976. "Serfdom's Legacy: An Ethnic Continuum." *American Journal of Sociology* 81:1265–1286.

———. 1987. "Psychological Effects of Complex Environments During the Life Span: A Review and Theory." Pp. 24–49 in Carmi Schooler and K. Warner Schaie, eds., *Cognitive Functioning and Social Structure over the Life Course.* Norwood, N.J.: Ablex Publishing.

———. 1990. "The Individual in Japanese History: Parallels to and Divergences from the European Experience." *Sociological Forum* 5:569–594.

Schooler, Carmi, Joanne Miller, K. A. Miller, and C. N. Richtand. 1984. "Work for the Household: Its Nature and Consequences for Husbands and Wives." *American Journal of Sociology* 90:97–124.

Schooler, Carmi, and Atsushi Naoi. 1985. "Occupational Conditions and Psychological Functioning in Japan." *American Journal of Sociology* 90:729–752.

Schultz, T. W. 1961. "Investment in Human Capital." *American Economic Review* 51:1–17.

Schuman, Howard, Charlotte Steeh, and Lawrence Bobo. 1985. *Racial Attitudes in America: Trends and Interpretations.* Cambridge: Harvard University Press.

Weber, Max. 1968. *Economy and Society.* Berkeley: University of California Press.

Wilensky, Harold L. 1964. "Mass Society and Mass Culture: Interdependence or Independence." *American Sociological Review* 29:173–197.

Williams, David R. 1990. "Socioeconomic Differentials in Health: A Review and Redirection." *Social Psychology Quarterly* 53:81–99.

Part VI
Ascriptive Processes

Racial and Ethnic Stratification
Theories of Ethnic Stratification
The Evolution of Ethnic Stratification
The Underclass

Gender Stratification
Gender and Class
Occupational and Wage Discrimination

THEORIES OF ETHNIC STRATIFICATION

MICHAEL REICH

The Economics of Racism

This paper presents a radical analysis of racism and its historical persistence in America, focusing on the effects of racism on whites. The paper contrasts the conventional approach of neoclassical economic analysis—with its optimistic conclusions concerning the possibility of eliminating racism—with a radical approach—which argues that racism is deeply rooted in the current economic institutions of America, and is likely to survive as long as they do. A statistical model and empirical evidence are presented which support the radical approach and cast doubt on the conventional approach. The specific mechanisms by which racism operates among whites are also discussed briefly.

The Pervasiveness of Racism

When conventional economists attempt to analyze racism, they usually begin by trying to separate various forms of racial discrimination. For example, they define "pure wage discrimination" as the racial difference in wages paid to equivalent workers, i.e., those with similar years and quality of schooling, skill training, previous employment experience and seniority, age, health, job attitudes, and a host of other factors. They presume that they can analyze the sources of "pure wage

discrimination" without simultaneously analyzing the extent to which discrimination also affects the factors they hold constant.

But such a technique distorts reality. The various forms of discrimination are not separable in real life. Employers' hiring and promotion practices, resource allocation in city schools, the structure of transportation systems, residential segregation and housing quality, availability of decent health care, behavior of policemen and judges, foremen's prejudices, images of blacks presented in the media and the schools, price gouging in ghetto stores—these and the other forms of social and economic discrimination interact strongly with each other in determining the occupational status and annual income, and welfare, of black people. The processes are not simply additive, but are mutually reinforcing. Often, a decrease in one narrow form of discrimination is accompanied by an increase in another form. Since all aspects of racism interact, an analysis of racism should incorporate all of its aspects in a unified manner.

No single quantitative index could adequately measure racism in all its social, cultural, psychological, and economic dimensions. But, while racism is far more than a narrow economic phenomenon, it does have very definite economic consequences: blacks have far lower incomes than whites. The ratio of median black to median white incomes thus provides a rough, but useful, quantitative index of the economic consequences of racism for blacks as it reflects the operation of racism in the schools, in residential location, in health care—as well as in the labor market itself. We shall use this index statistically to analyze the causes of racism's persistence in the United States. While this approach overemphasizes the economic aspects of racism, it is nevertheless an improvement over the narrower approach taken by conventional economists.

Competing Explanations of Racism

How is the historical persistence of racism in the United States to be explained? The most prominent analysis of discrimination among economists was formulated in 1957 by Gary Becker in his book *The Economics of Discrimination*.[1] Racism, according to Becker, is fundamentally a problem of tastes and attitudes. Whites are defined to have a "taste for discrimination" if they are willing to forfeit income in order to be associated with other whites instead of blacks. Since white employers and employees prefer not to associate with blacks, they require a monetary compensation for the psychic cost of such association. In Becker's principal model white employers have a taste for discrimination; marginal productivity analysis is invoked to show that white employers hire fewer black workers than efficiency criteria would dictate—as a result, white employers lose (in monetary terms) while white workers gain from discrimination against blacks.

Becker does not try to explain the source of white tastes for discrimination. For him, these attitudes are determined outside of the economic system. (Racism could presumably be ended simply by changing these attitudes, perhaps by appeal to whites on moral grounds.) According to Becker's analysis, employers would find the ending of racism to be in their economic self-interest, but white workers would not. The persistence of racism is thus implicitly laid at the door of white workers. Becker suggests that long-run market forces will lead to the end of discrimination anyway—less discriminatory employers, with no "psychic costs" to enter in their accounts, will be

able to operate at lower costs by hiring equivalent black workers at lower wages, thus driving the more discriminatory employers out of business.[2]

The radical approach to racism argued in this paper is entirely different. Racism is viewed as rooted in the economic system and not in "exogenously determined" attitudes. Historically, the American Empire was founded on the racist extermination of American Indians, was financed in large part by profits from slavery, and was extended by a string of interventions, beginning with the Mexican War of the 1840s, which have been at least partially justified by white supremacist ideology.

Today, transferring the locus of whites' perceptions of the source of many of their problems from capitalism and toward blacks, racism continues to serve the needs of the capitalist system. Although an individual employer might gain by refusing to discriminate and agreeing to hire blacks at above the going black wage rate, it is not true that the capitalist class as a whole would profit if racism were eliminated and labor were more efficiently allocated without regard to skin color. I will show below that the divisiveness of racism weakens workers' strength when bargaining with employers; the economic consequences of racism are not only lower incomes for blacks, but also higher incomes for the capitalist class coupled with lower incomes for white workers. Although capitalists may not have conspired consciously to create racism, and although capitalists may not be its principal perpetuators, nevertheless racism does support the continued well-being of the American capitalist system.

Capitalist society in turn encourages the persistence of racism. Whatever the origins of racism, it is likely to take root firmly in a society which breeds an individualistic and competitive ethos, status fears among marginal groups, and the need for visible scapegoats on which to blame the alienating quality of life in America—such a society is unlikely magnanimously to eliminate racism even though historically racism may not have been created by capitalism.

Racism cannot be eliminated just by moral suasion; nor will it gradually disappear because of market forces. Racism has become institutionalized and will persist under capitalism. Its elimination will require more than a change of attitudes; a change in institutions is necessary.

We have, then, two alternative approaches to the analysis of racism. The first suggests that capitalists lose and white workers gain from racism. The second predicts the opposite—that capitalists gain while workers lose. The first says that racist "tastes for discrimination" are formed independently of the economic system; the second argues that racism is symbiotic with capitalistic economic institutions.

The two approaches reflect the theoretical paradigms of society from which each was developed. Becker follows the paradigm of neoclassical economics in taking "tastes" as exogenously determined and fixed, and then letting the market mechanism determine outcomes. The radical approach follows the Marxian paradigm in arguing that racial attitudes and racist institutions must be seen as part of a larger social system, in placing emphasis on conflict between classes and the use of power to determine the outcomes of such conflicts. The test as to which explanation of racism is superior is, in some ways, an illustrative test of the relative explanatory power of these competing social paradigms.

The very persistence of racism in the United States lends support to the radical approach. So do repeated instances of employers using blacks as strikebreakers, as in the massive steel strike of 1919, and employer-instigated exacerbation of racial antagonisms during that strike and many others.[3] However, the particular virulence of racism among many blue- and white-collar workers and their families seems to refute the radical approach and support Becker.

The Empirical Evidence

Which of the two models better explains reality? We have already mentioned that the radical approach predicts that capitalists gain and workers lose from racism, while the conventional Beckerian approach predicts precisely the opposite. In the latter approach racism has an equalizing effect on the white income distribution, while in the former racism has an unequalizing effect. The statistical relationship between the extent of racism and the degree of inequality among whites provides a simple, yet clear test of the two approaches. This section describes that test and its results.

First we shall need a measure of racism. The index we use, for reasons already mentioned, is the ratio of black median family income to white median family income (B/W). A low numerical value for this ratio indicates a high degree of racism. We have calculated values of this racism index, using data from the 1960 Census, for each of the largest forty-eight standard metropolitan statistical areas (SMSA's). It turns out there is a great deal of variation from SMSA to SMSA in the B/W index of racism, even within the North; Southern SMSA's generally demonstrated a greater degree of racism. The statistical technique we shall use exploits this variation.

We shall also need measures of inequality among whites. Two convenient measures are (1) S_1, the percentage share of all white income which is received by the top 1 percent of white families, and (2) G_W, the Gini coefficient of white incomes, a measure that captures inequality within as well as between social classes.[4]

Both of these inequality measures vary considerably among the SMSA's; there is also a substantial amount of variation in these variables within the subsample of Northern SMSA's. Therefore, it is interesting to examine whether the pattern of variation of the inequality and racism variables can be explained by causal hypotheses. This is our first statistical test.

A systematic relationship across SMSA's between racism and white inequality does exist and is highly significant: the correlation coefficient is $-.47$.[5] The negative sign of the correlation coefficient indicates that where racism is greater, income inequality *among whites* is also greater. This result is consistent with the radical model and is inconsistent with the predictions of Becker's model.

This evidence, however, should not be accepted too quickly. The correlations reported may not reflect actual causality, since other independent forces may be simultaneously influencing both variables in the same way. As is the case with many other statistical analyses, the model must be expanded to control for such other factors. We know from previous inter-SMSA income distribution studies that the most important additional factors that should be introduced into our model are (1) the industrial and occupational structure of the SMSA's; (2) the region in which the SMSA's are located; (3) the average income of the SMSA's; and (4) the proportion of the SMSA population that is black. These factors were introduced into the model by the technique of multiple regression analysis. Separate equations were estimated with G_W and S_1 as measures of white inequality.

In all the equations the statistical results were strikingly uniform: racism was a significantly unequalizing force on the white income distribution, even when other factors were held constant. A 1 percent increase in the ratio of black to white median incomes (i.e., a 1 percent decrease in racism) was associated with a .2 percent decrease in white inequality, as measured by the Gini coefficient. The corresponding effect on S_1 was two-and-a-half times as large, indicating that most of the inequality among whites generated by racism was associated with increased income for the richest 1 percent of white families. Further statistical investigation revealed that increases in racism had an insignificant effect on the share received by the poorest whites, and resulted in a small decrease in the income share of whites in the middle-income brackets.[6]

The Mechanisms of the Radical Model

Within the radical model, we can specify a number of mechanisms which further explain the statistical finding that racism increases inequality among whites. We shall consider two mechanisms here: (1) total wages of white labor are reduced by racial antagonisms, in part because union growth and labor militancy are inhibited; and (2) the supply of public services, especially in education, available to low- and middle-income whites is reduced as a result of racial antagonisms.

Wages of white labor are lessened by racism because the fear of a cheaper and underemployed black labor supply in the area is invoked by employers when labor presents its wage demands. Racial antagonisms on the shop floor deflect attention from labor grievances related to working conditions, permitting employers to cut costs. Racial divisions among labor prevent the development of united worker organizations both within the workplace and in the labor movement as a whole. As a result, union strength and union militancy will be less, the greater the extent of racism. A historical example of this process is the already mentioned use of racial and ethnic divisions to destroy the solidarity of the 1919 steel strikers. By contrast, during the 1890s, black-white class solidarity greatly aided mine-workers in building militant unions among workers in Alabama, West Virginia, Illinois, and other coalfield areas.[7]

The above argument and examples contradict the common belief that an exclusionary racial policy will strengthen rather than weaken the bargaining power of unions. But racial exclusion increases bargaining power only when entry into an occupation or industry can be effectively limited. Industrial-type unions are much less able to restrict entry than craft unions or organizations such as the American Medical Association. This is not to deny that much of organized labor is egregiously racist.[8] But it is important to distinguish actual discrimination practice from the objective economic self-interest of union members.

The second mechanism we shall consider concerns the allocation of expenditures for public services. The most important of these services is education. Racial antagonisms dilute both the desire and the ability of poor white parents to improve educational opportunities for their children. Antagonism between blacks and poor whites drives wedges between the two groups and reduces their ability to join in a united political movement pressing for improved and more equal education. Moreover, many poor whites recognize that however inferior their own schools, black schools are even worse. This provides some degree of satisfaction and identification with the status quo, reducing the desire of poor whites to press politically for better schools in their neighborhoods. Ghettos tend to be located near poor white neighborhoods more often than near rich white neighborhoods; racism thus reduces the potential tax base of school districts containing poor whites. Also, pressure by teachers' groups to improve all poor schools is reduced by racial antagonisms between predominantly white teaching staffs and black children and parents.[9]

The statistical validity of the above mechanisms can be tested in a causal model. The effect of racism on unionism is tested by estimating an equation in which the percentage of the SMSA labor force which is unionized is the dependent variable, with racism and the structural variables (such as the SMSA industrial structure) as the independent variables. The schooling mechanism is tested by estimating a similar equation in which the dependent variable is inequality in years of schooling completed among white males aged 25 to 29 years old.[10]

Once again, the results of this statistical test strongly confirm the hypotheses of the radical model. The racism variable is statistically significant in all the equations and has the predicted sign: a greater degree of racism results in lower unionization rates and greater amounts of schooling inequality among whites. This empirical evidence again suggests that racism is in the economic interests of capitalists and other rich whites and against the economic interests of poor whites and white workers.

However, a full assessment of the importance of racism for capitalism would probably conclude that the primary significance of racism is not strictly economic. The simple economics of racism does not explain why many workers seem to be so vehemently racist, when racism is not in their economic self-interest. In extra-economic ways, racism helps to legitimize inequality, alienation, and powerlessness—legitimization which is necessary for the stability of the capitalist system as a whole. For example, many whites believe that welfare payments to blacks are a far more important factor in their high taxes than is military spending. Through racism, poor whites come to believe that their poverty is caused by blacks who are willing to take away their jobs, and at lower wages, thus concealing the fact that a substantial amount of income inequality is inevitable in a capitalist society.

Racism also provides some psychological benefits to poor and working-class whites. For example, the opportunity to participate in another's oppression may compensate for one's own misery. The parallel here is to the subjugation of women

in the family: after a day of alienating labor, the tired husband can compensate by oppressing his wife. Furthermore, not being at the bottom of the heap is some solace for an unsatisfying life; this argument was successfully used by the Southern oligarchy against poor whites allied with blacks in the inter-racial Populist movement of the late nineteenth century.

In general, blacks as a group provide a convenient and visible scapegoat for problems that actually derive from the institutions of capitalism. As long as building a real alternative to capitalism does not seem feasible to most whites, we can expect that identifiable and vulnerable scapegoats will always prove functional to the status quo. These extra-economic factors thus neatly dovetail with the economic aspects of racism discussed in the main body of this paper in their mutual service to the perpetuation of capitalism.

Notes

1. University of Chicago Press.

2. Some economists writing on discrimination reject Becker's "tastes" approach, but accept the marginal productivity method of analysis. See, for example, L. Thurow, *Poverty and Discrimination* (Washington, D.C.: Brookings Institution, 1969). The main substantive difference in their conclusions is that for Thurow, the entire white "community" gains from racism; therefore, racism will be a little harder to uproot. See also A. Krueger, "The Economics of Discrimination," *Journal of Political Economy*, October 1963.

3. See, for example, David Brody, *Steelworkers in America: The Nonunion Era* (Cambridge: Harvard University Press, 1960); Herbert Gutman, "The Negro and the United Mineworkers," in J. Jacobson, ed., *The Negro and the American Labor Movement* (Garden City, N.Y.: Anchor, 1968); S. Spero and A. Harris, *The Black Worker* (New York: Atheneum, 1968), *passim*.

4. The Gini coefficient varies between 0 and 1, with 0 indicating perfect equality, and 1 indicating perfect inequality. For a more complete exposition, see H. Miller, *Income Distribution in the United States* (Washington, D.C.: Government Printing Office, 1966). Data for the computation of G_W and S_1 for 48 SMSA's were taken from the 1960 Census. A full description of the computational techniques used is available in my dissertation.

5. The correlation coefficient reported in the text is between G_W and B/W. The equivalent correlation be-

tween S_1 and B/W is r = −.55. A similar calculation by S. Bowles, across states instead of SMSA's, resulted in an r = −.58.

6. A more rigorous presentation of these variables and the statistical results is available in my dissertation.

7. See footnote 3.

8. See Herbert Hill, "The Racial Practices of Organized Labor," in J. Jacobson, ed., *The Negro and the American Labor Movement* (Garden City, N.Y.: Anchor paperback, 1968).

9. In a similar fashion, racial antagonisms reduce the political pressure on governmental agencies to provide other public services which would have a pro-poor distributional impact. The two principal items in this category are public health services and welfare payments in the Aid to Families with Dependent Children program.

10. These dependent variables do not perfectly represent the phenomena described, but serve as reasonable proxy variables for these purposes.

EDNA BONACICH

A Theory of Ethnic Antagonism: The Split Labor Market

Societies vary considerably in their degree of ethnic and racial antagonism. Such territories as Brazil, Mexico, and Hawaii are generally acknowledged to be relatively low on this dimension; while South Africa, Australia, and the United States are considered especially high. Literally hundreds of variables have been adduced to account for these differences, ranging from religions of dominant groups, to whether the groups who migrate are dominant or subordinate, to degrees of difference in skin color, to an irreducible "tradition" of ethnocentrism. While some writers have attempted to synthesize or systematize some subset of these (e.g., Lieberson, 1961; Mason, 1970; Noel, 1968; Schermerhorn, 1970; van den Berghe, 1966), one is generally struck by the absence of a developed theory accounting for variations in ethnic antagonism.

One approach to this problem is to consider an apparent anomaly, namely that ethnic antagonism has taken two major, seemingly antithetical forms: exclusion movements, and so-called caste systems.[1] An example of the former is the "white Australia" policy; while South Africa's color bar illustrates the latter. The United States has shown both forms, with a racial caste system in the South and exclusion of Asian and "new" immigrants[2] from the Pacific and eastern seaboards respectively. Apart from manifesting antagonism between ethnic elements, exclusion and caste seem to have little in common. In the one, an effort is made to prevent an ethnically different group from being part of the society. In the other, an ethnically different group is essential to the society: it is an exploited class supporting the entire edifice. The deep south felt it could not survive without its black people; the Pacific coast could not survive with its Japanese. This puzzle may be used as a touchstone for solving the general problem of ethnic antagonism, for to be adequate a theory must be able to explain it.

The theory presented here is, in part, a synthesis of some of the ideas used by Oliver Cox to explain the Japanese-white conflict on the U.S. Pacific coast (Cox, 1948:408–22), and by Marvin Harris to analyze the difference between Brazil and the deep south in rigidity of the "color line" (Harris, 1964:79–94). It stresses the role of a certain kind of economic competition in the development of ethnic antagonism. Economic factors have, of course, not gone unnoticed, though until recently sociological literature has tended to point them out briefly, then move on to more "irrational" factors (even such works as The Economics of Discrimination, Becker, 1957). A resurgence of Marxian analysis (e.g. Blauner, 1969; Reich, 1971) has thrust economic considerations to the fore, but I shall argue that even this approach cannot adequately deal with the problem posed by exclusion movements and caste systems. In addition, both Marxist and non-Marxist writers assume that racial and cultural differences in themselves prompt the development of ethnic antagonism. This theory challenges that assumption, suggesting that economic processes are more fundamental.

No effort is made to prove the accuracy of the following model. Such proof depends on a lengthier exposition. Historical illustrations are presented to support it.

Ethnic Antagonism

"Ethnic" rather than "racial" antagonism was selected as the dependent variable because the former is seen to subsume the latter. Both terms refer to groups defined socially as sharing a common ancestry in which membership is therefore inherited or ascribed, whether or not members are currently physically or culturally distinctive.[3] The difference between race and ethnicity lies in the size of the locale from which a group stems, races generally coming from continents, and ethnicities from national sub-sections of continents. In the past the term "race" has been used to refer to both levels, but general usage today has reversed this practice (e.g. Schermerhorn, 1970; Shibutani and Kwan, 1965). Ethnicity has become the generic term.

Another reason for choosing this term is that exclusion attempts and caste-like arrangements are found among national groupings within a racial category. For example, in 1924 whites (Europeans) attempted to exclude whites of different national backgrounds from the United States by setting up stringent immigration quotas.

The term "antagonism" is intended to encompass all levels of intergroup conflict, including ideologies and beliefs (such as racism and prejudice), behaviors (such as discrimination, lynchings, riots), and institutions (such as laws perpetuating segregation). Exclusion movements and caste systems may be seen as the culmination of many pronouncements, actions, and enactments, and are continuously supported by more of the same. "Antagonism" was chosen over terms like prejudice and discrimination because it carries fewer moralistic and theoretical assumptions (see Schermerhorn, 1970:6–9). For example, both of these terms see conflict as emanating primarily from one side: the dominant group. Antagonism allows for the possibility that conflict is mutual; i.e. a product of interaction.

The Split Labor Market

The central hypothesis is that ethnic antagonism first germinates in a labor market split along ethnic lines. To be split, a labor market must contain at least two groups of workers whose price of labor differs for the same work, or would differ if they did the same work. The concept "price of labor" refers to labor's total cost to the employer, including not only wages, but the cost of recruitment, transportation, room and board, education, health care (if the employer must bear these), and the costs of labor unrest. The degree of worker "freedom" does not interfere with this calculus; the cost of a slave can be estimated in the same monetary units as that of a wage earner, from his purchase price, living expenses, policing requirements, and so on.

The price of a group of workers can be roughly calculated in advance and comparisons made even though two groups are not engaged in the same activity at the same time. Thus in 1841 in the colony of New South Wales, the Legislative Council's Committee on Immigration estimated the relative costs of recruiting three groups of laborers to become shepherds. Table 1 shows their findings. The estimate of free white labor, for example, was based on what it would take to attract these men from competing activities.

TABLE 1
Estimated Cost of Three Types of Labor to Be
Shepherds in New South Wales, 1841*

	Free Man (White)			Prisoner (White)			Coolie (Indian)		
	£	s.	d.	£	s.	d.	£	s.	d.
Rations	16	18	0	13	14	4	9	6	4
Clothing	—	—	—	3	3	0	1	1	8
Wages	25	0	0	—	—	—	6	0	0
Passage from India	—	—	—	—	—	—	2	0	0
Total per An-num	41	18	0	16	17	4	18	8	0

*From Yarwood (1968:13).

Factors Affecting the Initial Price of Labor

Labor markets that are split by the entrance of a new group develop a dynamic which may in turn affect the price of labor. One must therefore distinguish initial from later price determinants. The initial factors can be divided into two broad categories: resources and motives.

1. Resources

Three types of resources are important price determinants. These are:

a. Level of Living, or Economic Resources—The ethnic groups forming the labor market in a contact situation derive from different economic systems, either abroad or within a conquered territory. For members of an ethnic group to be drawn into moving, they must at least raise their wage level. In general, the poorer the economy of the recruits, the less the inducement needed for them to enter the new labor market. Crushing poverty may drive them to sell their labor relatively cheaply. For example, Lind (1968:199) describes the effect of the living level on the wage scale received by immigrant workers to Hawaii:

In every case [of labor importations] the superior opportunities for gaining a livelihood have been broadcast in regions of surplus manpower, transportation facilities have been provided, and finally a monetary return larger than that already received has been of-fered to the prospective laborer. The monetary inducement has varied considerably, chiefly according to the plane of living of the population being recruited, and the cheapest available labor markets have, of course, been most extensively drawn upon.

Workers need not accept the original wage agreement for long after they have immigrated, since other opportunities may exist; for instance, there may be ample, cheap land available for individual farming. One capitalist device for keeping wages low at least for a time is to bind immigrants to contracts before they leave the old economy. The Indian indenture system, for example, rested on such an arrangement (Gillion, 1962:19–38).

b. Information—Immigrants may be pushed into signing contracts out of ignorance. They may agree to a specific wage in their homeland not knowing the prevailing wage in the new country, or having been beguiled by a false account of life and opportunity there. Williams (1944:11), for example, describes some of the false promises made to draw British and Germans as workers to West Indian sugar plantations before the advent of African slavery. Chinese labor to Australia was similarly "obtained under 'false and specious pretences'" (Willard, 1967:9).

The possibilities for defrauding a population lacking access to the truth are obvious. In general, the more people know about conditions obtaining in the labor market to which they are moving, the better can they protect themselves against disadvantageous wage agreements.

c. Political Resources—By political resources I mean the benefits to a group of organizing. Organization can exist at the level of labor, or it can occur at higher levels, for example, in a government that protects them. These levels are generally related in that a strong government can help organize its emigrants. There are exceptions, however: strong emigrant governments tend not to extend protection to their deported convicts or political exiles; and some highly organized groups, like the Jews in the United States, have not received protection from the old country.

Governments vary in the degree to which they protect their emigrants. Japan kept close watch over the fate of her nationals who migrated to Hawaii and the Pacific coast; and the British colonial government in India tried to guard against abuses of the indenture system (for example, by refusing to permit Natal to import Indian workers for their sugar plantations until satisfactory terms had been agreed to; cf. Ferguson-Davie, 1952:4–10). In contrast Mexican migrant workers to the United States have received little protection from their government, and African states were unable to intervene on behalf of slaves brought to America. Often the indigenous populations of colonized territories have been politically weak following conquest. Thus African nations in South Africa have been unable to protect their migrant workers in the cities.

In general, the weaker a group politically, the more vulnerable it is to the use of force, hence to an unfavorable wage bargain (or to no wage bargain at all, as with slavery). The price of a labor group varies inversely with the amount of force that can be used against it, which in turn depends on its political resources.

2. Motives

Two motives affect the price of labor, both related to the worker's intention of not remaining permanently in the labor force. Temporary workers tend to cost less than permanent workers for two reasons. First, they are more willing to put up with undesirable work conditions since these need not be endured forever. If they are migrants, this tolerance may extend to the general standard of living. Often migrant temporary workers are males who have left the comforts of home behind and whose employers need not bear the cost of housing and educating their families. Even when families accompany them, such workers tend to be willing to accept a lower standard of living since it is only short term.

Second, temporary workers avoid involvement in lengthy labor disputes. Since they will be in the labor market a short while, their main concern is immediate employment. They may be willing to undercut wage standards if need be to get a job, and are therefore ripe candidates for strike-breaking. Permanent workers also stand to lose from lengthy conflict, but they hope for benefits to

their progeny. If temporary workers are from elsewhere, they have no such interest in future business-labor relations. Altogether, temporary workers have little reason to join the organizations and unions of a permanent work force, and tend not to do so.

a. Fixed or Supplementary Income Goal—Some temporary workers enter the market either to supplement family income, or to work toward a specific purchase. The worker's standard of living does not, therefore, depend on his earnings on the job in question, since his central source of employment or income lies elsewhere. Examples of this phenomenon are to be found throughout Africa:

… the characteristic feature of the labor market in most of Africa has always been the massive circulation of Africans between their villages and paid employment outside. In some places villagers engage in wage-earning seasonally. More commonly today they work for continuous though short-term periods of roughly one to three years, after which they return to the villages. … the African villager, the potential migrant into paid employment, has a relatively low, clearly-defined and rigid income goal; he wants money to pay head and hut taxes, to make marriage payments required of prospective bridegrooms, or to purchase some specific consumer durable (a bicycle, a rifle, a sewing machine, a given quantity of clothing or textiles, etc.) (Berg, 1966:116–8).

Such a motive produces the "backward-sloping labor supply function" characteristic of many native peoples in colonized territories. In addition to the general depressing effects on wages of being temporary, this motive leads to a fairly rapid turnover in personnel, making organization more difficult and hindering the development of valuable skills which could be used for bargaining. If wages were to rise, workers would reach their desired income and withdraw more quickly from the market, thereby lessening their chances of developing the political resources necessary to raise their wages further.

b. Fortune Seeking—Many groups, commonly called sojourners (see Siu, 1952), migrate long distances to seek their fortune, with the ultimate intention of improving their position in their homeland. Such was the case with Japanese immigrants on the west coast and Italian immigrants in the east. Such workers stay longer in the labor market, and can develop political resources. However, since they are temporary they have little incentive to join the organizations of the settled population. Instead they tend to create competing organizations composed of people who will play a part in their future in the homeland, i.e. members of the same ethnic group.

Sojourner laborers have at least three features which affect the price of labor: lower wages, longer hours, and convenience to the employer. The Japanese show all three. Millis (1915:45) cites the U.S. Immigration Commission on the question of relative wages:

The Japanese have usually worked for a lower wage than the members of any other race save the Chinese and the Mexican. In the salmon canneries the Chinese have been paid higher wages than the Japanese engaged in the same occupations. In the lumber industry, all races, including the East Indian, have been paid higher wages than the Japanese doing the same kind of work. As section hands and laborers in railway shops they have been paid as much or more than the Mexicans, but as a rule less than the white men of many races.

And so on. The lower wage level of Japanese workers reflects both a lower standard of living, and a desire to get a foothold in the labor market. As Iwata (1962:27) puts it: "Their willingness to accept even lower wages than laborers of other races enabled the Japanese to secure employment readily."

Millis (1915:155) describes a basket factory in Florin, California, where Japanese workers had displaced white female workers because the latter were unwilling to work more than ten hours a day or on weekends. The Japanese, anxious to return to Japan as quickly as possible, were willing to work twelve to fourteen hours per day and on weekends, thereby saving their employers the costs of a special overtime work force.

The Japanese immigrants developed political resources through a high degree of community organization. This could be used for the convenience of the employer, by solving his recruitment problems, seeing that work got done, and providing workers with board and lodging. In the case of seasonal labor, the Japanese community could provide for members during the off-season by various boarding arrangements and clubs, and by transporting labor to areas of demand (Ichihashi, 1932:172–6; Millis, 1915:44–5). These conveniences saved the employer money.[4]

As the reader may have noted, I have omitted a factor usually considered vital in determining the price of labor, i.e. differences in skills. I would contend, however, that this does not in itself lead to that difference in price for the same work which distinguishes a split labor market. While a skilled worker may be able to get a higher paying job, an unskilled laborer of another ethnicity may be trained to fill that job for the same wage. Skills are only indirectly important in that they can be used to develop political resources, which in turn may lead to a difference in wage level for the same work.

Price of Labor and Ethnicity

Ethnic differences need not always produce a price differential. Thus, if several ethnic groups who are approximately equal in resources and/or goals enter the same economic system, a split labor market will not develop. Alternatively, in a two-group contact situation, if one ethnic group occupies the position of a business elite and has no members in the labor force (or in a class that could easily be pushed into the labor force, e.g. low-capital farmers) then regardless of the other group's price, the labor market will not be split. This statement is a generalization of the point made by Harris (1964) that the critical difference in race relations between the deep south and Brazil was that the former had a white yeomanry in direct competition with ex-slaves, while the Portuguese only occupied the role of a business elite (plantation owners).

Conversely, a split labor force does not only stem from ethnic differences. For example, prison and female labor have often been cheaper than free male labor in western societies. Prison labor has been cheap because prisoners lack political resources, while women often labor for supplementary incomes (cf. Hutchinson, 1968:59–61; Heneman and Yoder, 1965:543–4).

That initial price discrepancies in labor should ever fall along ethnic lines is a function of two forces. First, the original wage agreement arrived at between business and new labor often takes place in the labor group's point of origin. This is more obviously a feature of immigrant labor, but also occurs within a territory when conquered peoples enter their conquerors' economy. In other words, the wage agreement is often concluded within a national context, these nationalities coming to comprise the ethnic elements of the new labor market. One would thus expect the initial wages of co-nationals to be similar.

Second, nations or peoples that have lived relatively separately from one another are likely to have developed different employment motives and levels of resources (wealth, organization, communication channels.) In other words, the factors that affect the price of labor are likely to differ grossly between nations, even though there may be considerable variation within each nation, and overlap between nations. Color differences in the initial price of labor only seem to be a factor because resources have historically been roughly correlated with color around the world.[5] When color and resources are not correlated in the "expected" way, then I would predict that price follows resources and motives rather than color.

In sum, the prejudices of business do not determine the price of labor, darker skinned or culturally different persons being paid less because of them. Rather, business tries to pay as little as possible for labor, regardless of ethnicity, and is held in check by the resources and motives of labor groups. Since these often vary by ethnicity, it is common to find ethnically split labor markets.

The Dynamics of Split Labor Markets

In split labor markets, conflict develops between three key classes: business, higher paid labor, and cheaper labor. The chief interests of these classes are as follows:

1. Business or employers—This class aims at having as cheap and docile a labor force as possi-

ble to compete effectively with other businesses. If labor costs are too high (owing to such price determinants as unions), employers may turn to cheaper sources, importing overseas groups or using indigenous conquered populations. In the colony of Queensland in Australia, for example, it was believed that cotton farming would be the most suitable economic enterprise:

However, such plantations (being too large) could not be worked, much less cleared, by their owners; neither could the work be done by European laborers because sufficient numbers of these were not available—while even had there been an adequate supply, the high rates of wages would have been prohibitive. This was a consideration which assumed vast importance when it was realized that cotton would have to be cultivated in Queensland at a considerably lower cost than in the United States in order to compensate for the heavier freights from Queensland—the more distant country from England. It seemed then that there was no possibility of successful competition with America unless the importation of some form of cheap labor was permitted (Moles, 1968:41).

Cheaper labor may be used to create a new industry having substantially lower labor costs than the rest of the labor market, as in Queensland. Or they may be used as strikebreakers or replacements to undercut a labor force trying to improve its bargaining position with business. If cheap labor is unavailable, business may turn to mechanization, or try to relocate firms in areas of the world where the price of labor is lower.

2. Higher Paid Labor—This class is very threatened by the introduction of cheaper labor into the market, fearing that it will either force them to leave the territory or reduce them to its level. If the labor market is split ethnically, the class antagonism takes the form of ethnic antagonism. It is my contention (following Cox, 1948:411n) that, while much rhetoric of ethnic antagonism concentrates on ethnicity and race, it really in large measure (though probably not entirely) expresses this class conflict.

The group comprising higher paid labor may have two components. First, it may include current employees demanding a greater share of the profits or trying to maintain their position in the face of possible cuts. A second element is the small, independent, entrepreneur, like the subsistence farmer or individual miner. The introduction of cheaper labor into these peoples' line can undermine their position, since the employer of cheaper labor can produce at lower cost. The independent operator is then driven into the labor market. The following sequence occurs in many colonies: settlement by farmers who work their own land, the introduction of intensive farming using cheaper labor, a rise in land value and a consequent displacement of independent farmers. The displaced class may move on (as occurred in many of the West Indies when African slave labor was introduced to raise sugar), but if it remains, it comes to play the role of higher paid labor.

The presence of cheaper labor in areas of the economy where higher paid labor is not currently employed is also threatening to the latter, since the former attract older industries. The importance of potential competition cannot be overstressed. Oftentimes writers assert the irrationality of ethnic antagonism when direct economic competition is not yet in evidence owing to few competitors having entered the labor market, or to competitors having concentrated in a few industries. Thus Daniels (1966:29) belittles the role of trade unions in the Asiatic Exclusion League by describing one of the major contributors as "an organization whose members, like most trade unionists in California, were never faced with job competition from Japanese." It does not take direct competition for members of a higher priced labor group to see the possible threat to their well-being, and to try to prevent its materializing. If they have reason to believe many more low-priced workers are likely to follow an initial "insignificant trickle" (as Daniels, 1966:1, describes the Japanese immigration, failing to mention that it was insignificant precisely because a larger anticipated flow had been thwarted, and diverted to Brazil), or if they see a large concentration of cheaper labor in a few industries which could easily be used to undercut them in their own, they will attempt to forestall undercutting.

Lest you think this fear misguided, take note that, when business could override the interests of more expensive labor, the latter have indeed been

displaced or undercut. In British Guiana the local labor force, composed mainly of African ex-slaves, called a series of strikes in 1842 and 1847 against planters' attempts to reduce their wages. Plantation owners responded by using public funds to import over 50,000 cheaper East Indian indentured workers (Despres, 1969). A similar situation obtained in Mississippi, where Chinese were brought in to undercut freed blacks. Loewen (1971:23) describes the thinking of white land-owners: "the 'Chinaman' would not only himself supply a cheaper and less troublesome work force but in addition his presence as a threatening alternative would intimidate the Negro into resuming his former docile behavior." Such displacement has occurred not only to non-white more expensive labor, but, as the effects of slavery in the West Indies show, to whites by white capitalists.

3. Cheaper Labor—The employer uses this class partly to undermine the position of more expensive labor, through strikebreaking and undercutting. The forces that make the cheaper group cost less permit this to occur. In other words, either they lack the resources to resist an offer or use of force by business, or they seek a quick return to another economic and social base.

With the possible exception of sojourners, cheaper labor does not intentionally undermine more expensive labor; it is paradoxically its weakness that makes it so threatening, for business can more thoroughly control it. Cox makes this point (1948:417–8) in analyzing why Pacific coast white and Asian workers could not unite in a coalition against business:

... the first generation of Asiatic workers is ordinarily very much under the control of labor contractors and employers, hence it is easier for the employer to frustrate any plans for their organization. Clearly this cultural bar helped antagonize white workers against the Asiatics. The latter were conceived of as being in alliance with the employer. It would probably have taken two or three generations before, say, the East Indian low-caste worker on the Coast became sufficiently Americanized to adjust easily to the policies and aims of organized labor.

Ethnic antagonism is specifically produced by the competition that arises from a price differential. An oversupply of equal-priced labor does not produce such antagonism, though it too threatens people with the loss of their job. However, hiring practices will not necessarily fall along ethnic lines, there being no advantage to the employer in hiring workers of one or another ethnicity. All workingmen are on the same footing, competing for scarce jobs (cf. Blalock, 1967:84–92, who uses this model of labor competition). When one ethnic group is decidedly cheaper than another (i.e. when the labor market is split) the higher paid worker faces more than the loss of his job; he faces the possibility that the wage standard in all jobs will be undermined by cheaper labor.

Victory for More Expensive Labor

If an expensive labor group is strong enough (strength generally depending on the same factors that influence price), they may be able to resist being displaced. Both exclusion and caste systems represent such victories for higher paid labor.

1. Exclusion—Exclusion movements generally occur when the majority of a cheaper labor group resides outside a given territory but desires to enter it (often at the request of business groups). The exclusion movement tries to prevent the physical presence of cheaper labor in the employment area, thereby preserving a non-split, higher priced labor market.

There are many examples of exclusion attempts around the world. In Australia, for instance, a group of white workers was able to prevent capitalists from importing cheaper labor from India, China, Japan and the Pacific Islands. Attempts at importation were met with strikes, boycotts, petitions and deputations (Willard, 1967:51–7). Ultimately, organized white labor pressed for strong exclusion measures, and vigilantly ensured their enforcement. As Yarwood (1964:151–2) puts it: "A comparison of the records of various governments during our period [1896–1923] leaves no doubt as to the special role of the Labour Party as the guardian of the ports." In other words, a white Australia policy (i.e. the exclusion of Asian and Polynesian immigrants) appears to have sprung from a conflict of interests between employers

who wanted to import cheap labor, and a labor force sufficiently organized to ward off such a move.

California's treatment of Chinese and Japanese labor is another example of exclusion. A socialist, Cameron H. King, Jr., articulates the threatened labor group's position:

Unskilled labor has felt this competition [from the Japanese] for some time being compelled to relinquish job after job to the low standard of living it could not endure. The unskilled laborers are largely unorganized and voiceless. But as the tide rises it is reaching the skilled laborers and the small merchants. These are neither unorganized nor voiceless, and viewing the menace to their livelihood they loudly demand protection of their material interests. We of the Pacific Coast certainly know that exclusion is an effective solution. In the seventh decade of the nineteenth century the problem arose of the immigration of Chinese laborers. The Republican and Democratic parties failed to give heed to the necessities of the situation and the Workingman's party arose and swept the state with the campaign cry of "The Chinese must go." Then the two old parties woke up and have since realized that to hold the labor vote they must stand for Asiatic exclusion (King, 1908:665–6).

King wrote this around the time of the Gentlemen's Agreement, an arrangement of the U.S. and Japanese governments to prevent further immigration of Japanese labor to the Pacific Coast (Bailey, 1934). The Agreement was aimed specifically at labor and not other Japanese immigrants, suggesting that economic and not racial factors were at issue.

Exclusion movements clearly serve the interests of higher paid labor. Its standards are protected, while the capitalist class is deprived of cheaper labor.

2. Caste—If cheaper labor is present in the market, and cannot be excluded, then higher paid labor will resort to a caste arrangement, which depends on exclusiveness rather than exclusion. Caste is essentially an aristocracy of labor (a term borrowed from Lenin, e.g. 1964), in which higher paid labor deals with the undercutting potential of cheaper labor by excluding them from certain types of work. The higher paid group controls certain jobs exclusively and gets paid at one scale of wages, while the cheaper group is restricted to another set of jobs and is paid at a lower scale. The labor market split is submerged because the differentially priced workers ideally never occupy the same position.

Ethnically distinct cheaper groups (as opposed to women, for example, who face a caste arrangement in many Western societies) may reside in a territory for two reasons: either they were indigenous or they were imported early in capitalist-labor relations, when the higher paid group could not prevent the move. Two outstanding examples of labor aristocracies based on ethnicity are South Africa, where cheaper labor was primarily indigenous, and the U.S. south, where they were imported as slaves.

Unlike exclusion movements, caste systems retain the underlying reality of a price differential, for if a member of the subordinate group were to occupy the same position as a member of the stronger labor group he would be paid less. Hence, caste systems tend to become rigid and vigilant, developing an elaborate battery of laws, customs and beliefs aimed to prevent undercutting. The victory has three facets. First, the higher paid group tries to ensure its power in relation to business by monopolizing the acquisition of certain essential skills, thereby ensuring the effectiveness of strike action, or by controlling such important resources as purchasing power. Second, it tries to prevent the immediate use of cheaper labor as undercutters and strikebreakers by denying them access to general education thereby making their training as quick replacements more difficult, or by ensuring through such devices as "influx control" that the cheaper group will retain a base in their traditional economies. The latter move ensures a backward-sloping labor supply function (cf. Berg, 1966) undesirable to business. Third, it tries to weaken the cheaper group politically, to prevent their pushing for those resources that would make them useful as undercutters. In other words, the solution to the devastating potential of weak, cheap labor is, paradoxically, to weaken them further, until it is no longer in business' immediate interest to use them as replacements.

South Africa is perhaps the most extreme modern example of an ethnic caste system. A split labor market first appeared there in the mining industry. With the discovery of diamonds in 1869, a white working class emerged.[6] At first individual whites did the searching, but, as with the displacement of small farms by plantations, they were displaced by consolidated, high-capital operations, and became employees of the latter (Doxey, 1961:18). It was this class together with imported skilled miners from Cornwall (lured to Africa by high wages) which fought the capitalists over the use of African labor. Africans were cheaper because they came to the mines with a fixed income goal (e.g. the price of a rifle) and did not view the mines as their main source of livelihood. By contrast, European workers remained in the mines and developed organizations to further their interests.

Clearly, it would have been to the advantage of businessmen, once they knew the skills involved, to train Africans to replace the white miners at a fraction of the cost; but this did not happen. The mining companies accepted a labor aristocracy, not out of ethnic solidarity with the white workers but:

(as was to be the case throughout the later history of mining) they had little or no choice because of the collective strength of the white miners. ... The pattern which was to emerge was that of the Europeans showing every sign of preparedness to use their collective strength to ensure their exclusive supremacy in the labour market. Gradually the concept of trade unionism, and, for that matter, of socialism, became accepted in the minds of the European artisans as the means of maintaining their own position against non-white inroads (Doxey, 1961:23–4).

The final showdown between mine owners and white workers occurred in the 1920's when the owners tried to substitute cheaper non-white labor for white labor in certain semi-skilled occupations. This move precipitated the "Rand Revolt," a general strike of white workers on the Witwatersrand, countered by the calling in of troops and the declaration of martial law. The result was a coalition between Afrikaner nationalists (predominantly workers and small-scale farmers being pushed off the land by larger, British owned farms) and the English-speaking Labor Party (Van der Horst, 1965:117–8). The Revolt "showed the lengths to which white labour was prepared to go to defend its privileged position. From that time on, mine managements have never directly challenged the colour-bar in the mining industry" (Van der Horst, 1965:118).

The legislative history of much of South Africa (and of the post-bellum deep south) consists in attempts by higher priced white labor to ward off undercutting by cheaper groups, and to entrench its exclusive control of certain jobs.[7]

This interpretation of caste contrasts with the Marxist argument that the capitalist class purposefully plays off one segment of the working class against the other (e.g. Reich, 1971). Business, I would contend, rather than desiring to protect a segment of the working class supports a liberal or laissez faire ideology that would permit all workers to compete freely in an open market. Such open competition would displace higher paid labor. Only under duress does business yield to labor aristocracy, a point made in Deep South, a book written when the depression had caused the displacement of white tenant farmers and industrial workers by blacks:

The economic interests of these groups [employers] would also demand that cheaper colored labor should be employed in the "white collar" jobs in business offices, governmental offices, stores, and banks. In this field, however, the interests of the employer group conflict not only with those of the lower economic group of whites but also with those of the more literate and aggressive middle group of whites. A white store which employed colored clerks, for example, would be boycotted by both these groups. The taboo upon the employment of colored workers in such fields is the result of the political and purchasing power of the white middle and lower groups (Davis, *et. al.*, 1941:480).

In sum, exclusion and caste are similar reactions to a split labor market. They represent victories for higher paid labor. The victory of exclusion is more complete in that cheaper labor is less available to business. For this reason I would hypothesize that a higher paid group prefers exclusion to caste, even though exclusion means they have to do the dirty work. Evidence for this comes from Australia where, in early attempts to import Asian labor, business tried to buy off white labor's opposition by offering to form them into a class of "mechanics" and foremen over the "coolies"

(Yarwood, 1968:16, 42). The offer was heartily rejected in favor of exclusion. Apartheid in South Africa can be seen as an attempt to move from caste to the exclusion of the African work force.

Most of our examples have contained a white capitalist class, a higher paid white labor group, and a cheaper, non-white labor group. Conditions in Europe and around the world, and not skin color, yield such models. White capitalists would gladly dispense with and undercut their white working-class brethren if they could, and have done so whenever they had the opportunity. In the words of one agitator for excluding Chinese from the U.S. Pacific coast: "I have seen men … American born, who certainly would, if I may use a strong expression, employ devils from Hell if the devils would work for 25 cents less than a white man" (cited in Daniels and Kitano, 1970:43).

In addition, cases have occurred of white workers playing the role of cheap labor, and facing the same kind of ethnic antagonism as non-white workers. Consider the riots against Italian strikebreakers in the coal fields of Pennsylvania in 1874 (Higham, 1965:47–8). In the words of one writer: "Unions resented the apparently inexhaustible cheap and relatively docile labor supply which was streaming from Europe obviously for the benefit of their employers" (Wittke, 1953:10).

Even when no ethnic differences exist, split labor markets may produce ethnic-like antagonism. Carey McWilliams (1945:82–3) describes an instance:

During the depression years, "Old Stock"—that is, white, Protestant, Anglo-Saxon Americans, from Oklahoma, Arkansas, and Texas—were roundly denounced in California as "interlopers." The same charges were made against them that were made against the Japanese: they were "dirty"; they had "enormous families"; they engaged in unfair competition; they threatened to "invade" the state and to "undermine" its institutions. During these turgid years (1930–1938) California attempted *to exclude*, by various extra-legal devices, those yeoman farmers just as it had excluded the Chinese and Japanese. "Okies" were "inferior" and "immoral." There was much family discord when Okie girl met California boy, and vice versa. … The prejudice against the Okies was obviously not "race" prejudice; yet it functioned in much the same manner.

Conclusion

Obviously, this type of three-way conflict is not the only important factor in ethnic relations. But it does help explain some puzzles, including, of course, the exclusion-caste anomaly. For example, Philip Mason (1970:64) develops a typology of race relations and finds that it relates to numerical proportions without being able to explain the dynamic behind this correlation. Table 2 presents a modified version of his chart. My theory can explain these relationships. Paternalism arises in situations where the cleavage between business and labor corresponds to an ethnic difference. A small business elite rules a large group of workers who entered the labor market at approximately the same price or strength. No split labor market existed, hence no ethnic caste system arises. The higher proportion of the dominant ethnicity under "Domination" means that part of the dominant group must be working class. A labor element that shares ethnicity with people who have sufficient resources to become the business elite is generally likely to come from a fairly wealthy country and have resources of its own. Such systems are likely to develop split labor markets. Finally, competition has under it societies whose cheaper labor groups have not been a major threat because the indigenous population available as cheap labor has been small and/or exclusion has effectively kept business groups from importing cheap labor in large numbers.

This theory helps elucidate other observations. One is the underlying similarity in the situation of blacks and women. Another is the history of political sympathy between California and the South. And, a third is the conservatism of the American white working class, or what Daniels and Kitano (1970:45) consider to be an "essential paradox of American life: [that] movements for economic democracy have usually been violently opposed to a thorough-going ethnic democracy." Without having to resort to psychological constructs like "authoritarianism," this theory is able to explain the apparent paradox.

In sum, in comparing those countries with the most ethnic antagonism with those having the least, it is evident that the difference does not lie

TABLE 2
Numerical Proportion of Dominant to Subordinate Ethnic Groups*

Category		
Domination	Paternalism	Competition
Situations		
South Africa (1960) 1–4	Nigeria (1952) 1–2000	Britain (1968) 50–1
U.S. South (1960) 4–1	Nyasaland (1966) 1–570	U.S. North (1960) 15–1
Rhodesia (1960) 1–16	Tanganyika 1–450	New Zealand 13–1
	Uganda 1–650	

*Adapted from Mason (1970:64).

in the fact that the former are Protestant and the latter Catholic: Protestants are found in all three of Mason's types, and Hawaii is a Protestant dominated territory. It does not lie in whether the dominant or subordinate group moves: South African and the deep south show opposite patterns of movement. It is evident that some of the most antagonistic territories have been British colonies, but not all British colonies have had this attribute. The characteristic that those British colonies and other societies high on ethnic antagonism share is that they all have a powerful white, or more generally higher paid, working class.

Notes

1. I do not wish to enter the debate over the applicability of the term "caste" to race relations (cf. Cox, 1948; Davis, *et al.*, 1941). It is used here only for convenience and implies no particular theoretical bent.

2. The term "exclusion" has not usually been applied to immigrant quotas imposed on eastern and southern European immigrants; but such restrictions were, in effect, indistinguishable from the restrictions placed on Japanese immigration.

3. This usage contrasts with that of van den Berghe (1967a:9–10) who reserves the term "ethnic" for groups

socially defined by cultural differences. In his definition, ethnicity is not necessarily inherited. I would contend that, while persons of mixed ancestry may be problematic and are often assigned arbitrarily by the societies in which they reside, inheritance is implied in the common application of the word.

4. Sojourners often use their political resources and low price of labor to enter business for themselves (a process which will be fully analyzed in another paper). This does not remove the split in the labor market, though it makes the conflict more complex.

5. It is, of course, no accident that color and resources have been historically related. Poverty among non-white nations has in part resulted from European imperialism. Nevertheless, I would argue that the critical factor in the development of ethnic segmentation in a country is the meeting that occurs in the labor market of that country. The larger economic forces help determine the resources of entering parties, but it is not such forces to which workers respond. Rather they react to the immediate conflicts and threats in their daily lives.

6. Such a split was not found in the early Cape Colony, where business was one ethnicity—white, and labor another—non-white. Actually in neither case was the ethnic composition simple or homogeneous; but the important fact is that, among the laborers, who included so-called Hottentots, and slaves from Madagascar, Moçambique and the East Indies (cf. van den Berghe, 1967b:14), no element was significantly more expensive. The early Cape is thus structurally similar, in terms of the variables I consider important, to countries like Brazil and Mexico. And it is also noted for its "softened" tone of race relations as reflected in such practices as intermarriage.

7. Ethnically based labor aristocracies are much less sensitive about cheap labor in any form than are systems that do not arrive at this resolution because they are protected from it. Thus, Sutherland and Cressey (1970:561–2) report that both the deep south and South Africa continue to use various forms of prison contract labor, in contrast to the northern U.S. where the contract system was attacked by rising labor organizations as early as 1880.

References

Bailey, Thomas A. 1934. Theodore Roosevelt and the Japanese-American Crises. Stanford: Stanford University Press.

Becker, Gary. 1957. The Economics of Discrimination. Chicago: University of Chicago Press.

Berg, E. J. 1966. "Backward-sloping labor supply functions in dual economies—the Africa case." Pp. 114–36 in Immanuel Wallerstein (ed.), Social Change: The Colonial Situation. New York: Wiley.

Blalock, H. M., Jr. 1967. Toward a Theory of Minority-Group Relations. New York: Wiley.

Blauner, Robert. 1969. "Internal colonialism and ghetto revolt." Social Problems 16 (Spring):393–408.

Cox, Oliver C. 1948. Caste, Class and Race. New York: Modern Reader.

Daniels, Roger. 1966. The Politics of Prejudice. Gloucester, Massachusetts: Peter Smith.

Daniels, Roger, and Harry H. L. Kitano. 1970. American Racism. Englewood Cliffs: Prentice-Hall.

Davis, Allison W., B. B. Gardner and M. R. Gardner. 1941. Deep South. Chicago: University of Chicago Press.

Despres, Leo A. 1969. "Differential adaptations and micro-cultural evolution in Guyana." Southwestern Journal of Anthropology 25 (Spring):14–44.

Doxey, G. V. 1961. The Industrial Colour Bar in South Africa. Cape Town: Oxford University Press.

Ferguson-Davie, C. J. 1952. The Early History of Indians in Natal. Johannesburg: South African Institute of Race Relations.

Gillion, K. L. 1962. Fiji's Indian Migrants. Melbourne: Oxford University Press.

Harris, Marvin. 1964. Patterns of Race in the Americas. New York: Walker.

Heneman, H. G., and Dale Yoder. 1965. Labor Economics. Cincinnati: Southwestern.

Higham, John. 1965. Strangers in the Land. New York: Athenium.

Hutchison, Emilie J. 1968. Women's Wages. New York: Ams Press.

Ichihashi, Yamato. 1932. Japanese in the United States. Stanford: Stanford University Press.

Iwata, Masakazu. 1962. "The Japanese immigrants in California agriculture." Agricultural History 36 (January):25–37.

King, Cameron H., Jr. 1908. "Asiatic exclusion." International Socialist Review 8 (May):661–669.

Lenin, V. I. 1964. "Imperialism and the split in socialism." Pp. 105–120 in Collected Works, Volume 23, August 1916–March 1917. Moscow: Progress.

Lieberson, Stanley. 1961. "A societal theory of race and ethnic relations." American Sociological Review 26 (December):902–910.

Lind, Andrew W. 1968. An Island Community. New York: Greenwood.

Loewen, James W. 1971. The Mississippi Chinese. Cambridge: Harvard University Press.

Mason, Philip. 1970. Patterns of Dominance. London: Oxford University Press.

McWilliams, Carey. 1945. Prejudice: Japanese-Americans. Boston: Little, Brown.

Millis, H. A. 1915. The Japanese Problem in the United States. New York: Macmillan.

Moles, I. N. 1968. "The Indian coolie labour issue." Pp. 40–48 in A. T. Yarwood (ed.), Attitudes to Non-European Immigration. Melbourne: Cassell Australia.

Noel, Donald L. 1968. "A theory of the origin of ethnic stratification." Social Problems 16 (Fall):157–172.

Reich, Michael. 1971. "The economics of racism." Pp. 107–113 in David M. Gordon (ed.), Problems in Political Economy. Lexington, Massachusetts: Heath.

Schermerhorn, R. A. 1970. Comparative Ethnic Relations. New York: Random House.

Shibutani, Tamotsu, and Kian M. Kwan. 1965. Ethnic Stratification. New York: Macmillan.

Siu, Paul C. P. 1952. "The sojourner." American Journal of Sociology 58 (July):34–44.

Sutherland, Edwin H., and Donald R. Cressey. 1970. Criminology. Philadelphia: Lippincott.

van den Berghe, Pierre L. 1966. "Paternalistic versus competitive race relations: an ideal-type approach." Pp. 53–69 in Bernard E. Segal (ed.), Racial and Ethnic Relations. New York: Crowell.

_____. 1967a. Race and Racism. New York: Wiley.

_____. 1967b. South Africa: A Study in Conflict. Berkeley: University of California Press.

Van der Horst, Sheila T. 1965. "The effects of industrialization on race relations in South Africa." Pp. 97–140 in Guy Hunter (ed.), Industrialization and Race Relations. London: Oxford University Press.

Willard, Myra. 1967. History of the White Australia Policy to 1920. London: Melbourne University Press.

Williams, Eric. 1944. Capitalism and Slavery. Chapel Hill: University of North Carolina Press.

Wittke, Carl. 1953. "Immigration policy prior to World War I." Pp. 1–10 in Benjamin M. Ziegler (ed.), Immigration: An American Dilemma. Boston: Heath.

Yarwood, A. T. 1964. Asian Immigration to Australia. London: Cambridge University Press.

Yarwood, A. T. (ed.). 1968. Attitudes to Non-European Immigration. Melbourne: Cassell Australia.

MICHAEL HECHTER

Towards a Theory of Ethnic Change

I have seen, in my time, Frenchmen, Italians, and Russians; I even know, thanks to Montesquieu, that one may be a Persian; but as for man, *I declare that I have never met him in my life; if he exists, it is without my knowledge.*

—Joseph De Maistre

Every industrial and commercial center in England now possesses a working-class divided *into two* hostile *camps, English proletarians and Irish proletarians. The ordinary English worker hates the Irish worker as a competitor who lowers his standard of life. In relation to the Irish worker he feels himself a member of the ruling nation and so turns himself into a tool of the aristocrats and capitalists of his country* against Ireland, *thus strengthening their domination* over himself. *He cherishes religious, social and national prejudices against the Irish worker. His attitude towards him is much the same as that of the 'poor whites' to the 'niggers' of the former slave states of the USA. The Irishman pays him back with interest in his own money. He sees in the English worker at once the accomplice and the stupid tool of the* English domination in Ireland. ... *This antagonism is the* secret of the impotence of the English working-class, *despite their organization.*

—Karl Marx

The persistence of ethnic attachments in complex societies is in certain respects as vexing today as it was to these two very different nineteenth-century thinkers. The current flourish of national consciousness among cultural minorities in advanced industrial societies poses something of a sociological dilemma, for these frequently territorial conflicts involving language and religion have been assumed to be endemic to the early stages of national development.[1] Peripheral regions in developing countries have tended to resist the incursions of central authorities imposing their omnivorous bureaucracy and haughty culture.

However, the advent of sustained economic and social development presumably serves to undercut the traditional bases of solidarity among extant groups. A familiar list of processes catalogued under the heading of modernization systematically increases the individual's dependence upon and loyalty to the central government. The major foundation of political cleavage in industrial society is then thought to become functional rather than segmental, thereby producing 'alliances of similarly oriented subjects and households over wide ranges of localities.'[2] This provides the nucleus of a very generally held sociological theory of ethnic change. Such a theory predicts that the transformed conditions of industrial society alter the basis on which individuals form political associations. In consequence of modernization, the salience of cultural similarity as a social bond should give way to political alliances between individuals of similar market position, and thus, more generally, social class.

When the Western industrial working class was judged to have been granted the full rights of citizenship following militant trade-union and party organization, some observers relaxed enough to proclaim an end of ideology in the West. It now appears that the Flemings in Belgium, Celts in Britain and France, Slovaks in Czechoslovakia, French in Canada—to say nothing of various minorities in the United States—have not yet received the message.[3] There is a new fear that these phenomena are the rumblings of the eventual dissolution of the Western nation state. In ten years the pendulum has swung far indeed.[4] The specter of class warfare may have subsided only to be replaced by the hoarier aspect of 'racial' conflict. At any rate that state of social harmony sometimes referred to as national integration now seems to many an unexpectedly elusive goal.

In the context of the resurgence of ethnicity as a major political factor in industrial society it may be useful to examine the concept of national development and evaluate some of the alternative ways in which it has been used. Accordingly this chapter will have four related foci. First, it will introduce a simplified model for the empirical study of national development. Second, it will review the main currents of previous theory from the perspective of this model, and evaluate its adequacy, in the light of current research. Third, it will define the concept of ethnicity and discuss the social basis of ethnic identification. Finally, it will attempt to sketch some tentative hypotheses about the conditions governing the prospects for ethnic change.

Dimensions of National Development: An Exploratory Model

Among current concepts of social science, national development must rank high on a scale of ambiguity. One writer has detected five separate senses in which a related term has been used, varying not only in scope but in subject matter as well.[5] Others have denied the utility of this kind of concept outright, particularly in its evolutionary and deterministic form.[6] The general expansion of the size and scope of states since the late Middle Ages is justification enough for the utility of some concept of national development. Clearly

the social organization of the Athenian *polis* would be inadequate to maintain a society as large and diverse as the United States, the factor of communications technology aside. The specification of this evolutionary development was the major focus of nineteenth-century social theory. It is by now apparent that the classical social theorists overestimated the extent to which industrialization would lead to a fully national society.

A useful definition of national development would describe a process, the creation of a national society, rather than a particular state of affairs.[7] Here national development will refer to those processes by which a state characterized by sectional, or otherwise competing economies, polities, and cultures, within a given territory, is transformed into a society composed of a single, all-pervasive, and in this sense 'national' economy, polity, and culture. This definition, it should be noted, does not include the analytically distinct problem of the incorporation of excluded social classes into the national society.[8]

It should be understood at once that not much is known about national development in these terms. Since so little systematic empirical work has been done in this area many writers have assumed much about these processes on a purely *a priori* basis. For instance, the relationship between regional economic specialization and interregional political solidarity has never been carefully studied on a comparative basis. Nevertheless, writers will often take sides on this question largely on the basis of theoretical arguments. The difficulty is that a good theoretical case can be made for either side in the dispute.

In the following discussion I shall assume a simple model to illustrate processes of national development in industrial societies. In this model there are two collectivities or objectively distinct cultural groups: (1) the *core*, or dominant cultural group which occupies territory extending from the political center of the society (e.g. the locus of the central government) outward to those territories largely occupied by the subordinate, or (2) *peripheral* cultural group. The model therefore assumes that these respective cultural groups are to a large extent regionally concentrated.[9] For the moment I will assume that these two collectivities are perfectly solidary, and, loosely speaking, possess a group consciousness. Hence, when I conceive of a collectivity as an acting unit, this of course refers to the action of the bulk of its members. ...

Diffusion Models of National Development

Diffusion models of national development ultimately assert that core-periphery malintegration can be maintained only in the absence of sustained mutual contact.[10] Hence, the establishment of regular interaction between the core and the periphery is seen to be crucial for national development. Industrialization is usually conceived to be a necessary condition for intensifying contact between core and peripheral groups. Processes operating at various levels of social organization should reduce much of the diversity characteristic of pre-industrial societies. It may be useful to group diffusionist accounts of the integration of societies[11] into those which emphasize the dominant importance of cultural elements in the realization of national development and those which essentially seek to explain national development by reference to change in the social structure.

Cultural theories tend to presume a model in which the peripheral group is termed 'traditionally oriented' in contrast to the modernized core group. The most familiar elaboration of this dichotomy is Talcott Parsons's discussion of the pattern variables; they need not be discussed here. Once the peripheral group becomes exposed to the cultural modernity of the core, its values and normative orientations ought to undergo transformation. Frequently, however, this does not seem to occur. In the view of many of the cultural theorists, the maintenance of peripheral cultural forms and customs is an irrational reaction by groups which seek to preserve a backward lifestyle insulated from the rapid change of contemporary industrial society. The traditional life-style is a comfortable one. Groups tend to resist major change, in any case: there is a collective, if sometimes unstated, desire to optimize short-run interests while prospects for the long range are seriously compromised. The existence of a backward sloping labor supply curve, supposedly endemic to less developed societies, is commonly taken as evidence of a traditional normative orientation.[12]

The cultural theories thus seek to explain differences of values, norms, and life-styles among these collectivities as a function of the relative isolation of the peripheral group from the mainstream culture of the core. If only the choice between tradition and modernity could somehow be placed before individuals of the peripheral group, some have felt, modernity would easily win over. The solution to this problem of persisting cultural differences is, first, to stimulate a wide range of intercollectivity transactions, then, to let time work its inevitable course towards eventual cultural integration. Emile Durkheim presented an early statement of this theory when he discussed the effect of an increase in transactions between cultural groups as if it were analogous to the physical process of osmosis.[13] Cultural differences between collectivities would in effect be leveled, presumably according to the relative volumes (magnitudes?) of the respective groups.

This is one of the biological metaphors which Professor Parsons has so rightly disparaged in Durkheim's work. However, the anthropological version of this image, namely the process of *acculturation,* remains a rather current perspective in the study of intergroup relations. Acculturation is thought to occur when 'groups of individuals having different cultures come into continuous first-hand contact, with subsequent changes in the original culture patterns of either or both groups.'[14] Like osmosis, it is often conceived to proceed automatically and irreversibly. Once begun, the diffusion of symbols and institutions from the core to the periphery should lead to a gradual rapprochement, to a stable cultural equilibrium.[15] The proposition that the greater the frequency of interaction between collectivities, the greater the probability they will become more alike is sometimes held to follow from the experimental study of small groups.[16] Since it is not difficult to find evidence that intergroup contact often leads to hostility rather than mutual accommodation, less inviolable explanations must be sought.

Perhaps the most influential of these is the concept of social mobilization.[17] The social mobilization perspective, as well, assumes that the initiation of cultural contact between collectivities is generally beneficent. But interaction *per se* is seen to be an insufficient condition for the realization of national development. Much emphasis is placed on the power of the central government to coax or coerce the recalcitrant collectivity into acceptance of the core culture. This is best done by the manipulation of cultural symbols and values, especially through the use of communications media.[18] But the deployment of military force is also not ruled out. Social mobilization theorists such as Deutsch do not assume that any mere increase in the rate of intensity of interaction is sufficient to end culture maintenance in the periphery, since they recognize that it may be partially self-imposed. Hence, the active role of the central government is stressed, particularly in the establishment of what is often termed a national 'political culture.'[19] Control of the national information network enables a régime to set national goals, create a national identity, teach needed skills, centralize its power, extend the effective market, confer status on certain groups at the expense of others, and generally manipulate large numbers of individuals through well-developed techniques of mass persuasion.[20] However, with all these tools of behavioral management available, some well-established Western governments are facing ever stronger and more violent challenges to their authority along separatist lines.

Another of the technical means by which a central régime may gain adherents is through an inspiring brand of leadership. The Weberian category of charismatic legitimation has been often invoked to account for specific integration successes.[21] Recently, however, this explanation has come under criticism for certain theoretical inadequacies,[22] as well as the fact that a host of charismatic leaders in the Third World did not survive as long as their academic observers had anticipated.

Yet another factor which has been cited as having crucial importance for the process of national development is the encouragement of intercollectivity élite participation in shared, especially governmental, activities. It is thought that the experience gained in such activities encourages élite accommodation and mutual understanding, which then 'filters down' to the level of the masses. These so-called 'functional' theories of the political science literature[23] presume, however, a whole host of assumptions about the ability of each collectivity's élite to influence their respective rank-and-file members with the same effectiveness. In fact, there is good reason to believe the results of these filtering down activities to be highly differentiated by collectivity.

The theories of cultural diffusion have several obvious inadequacies. Since most of these hypotheses were derived from considering Third World failures of the integration process, they are not very applicable to the collectivities in developed societies. It is difficult to argue that peripheral groups in industrial societies are economically, politically, and culturally isolated from the core. This is evident from the most casual consideration of the history of Western European societies.

The development of national economies in Western Europe began in the sixteenth and seventeenth centuries with the ascendance of mercantilism.[24] Internal tariffs and other barriers to the free mobility of goods, labor, and capital were substantially eliminated. Weights, measures, and coinage were standardized throughout state territory. The central government succeeded in establishing control over foreign trade, especially in the realm of customs. Attempts to enforce central government control over techniques of production largely failed because of inadequate communications: the center was unable to carry out these policies because supervision was impossible in remote regions. National economies were basically realized after the Industrial Revolution made possible the proliferation of railway and canal systems throughout state borders.

Similarly, the evolution of strong central administration, begun in the fifteenth and sixteenth centuries,[25] was effectively completed in the nineteenth century, aided by means such as the standing army, which was capable of subduing internal threats to the central régime. Improved communications enabled the center to exert its control into the far reaches of the territory through its cultural influence and military might. Rural-urban migration and the creation of an urban proletariat forced an eventual extension of the suffrage to the working class, which resulted in the formation of mass national parties.[26]

Finally, the Industrial Revolution had direct and indirect effects on cultural isolation. In the late nineteenth century there were dramatic increases in mass literacy.[27] Newspapers reached into the dark corners of the land. Later, radio and television—often operated by the régime in power—penetrated all territorial space, trumpeting the culture of the core. The establishment of national school systems significantly narrowed socialization differences among the youth of separate collectivities. As a consequence of the penetration of the core's cultural institutions into the hinterlands, the maintenance of distinctive languages, and other cultural forms, was severely threatened. These trends indicate that the persistence of a distinctive culture in peripheral areas cannot be explained by the periphery's isolation from the core culture, at least in Western societies. Instead, the persistence of peripheral culture suggests a pattern of resistance to assimilation, a resistance so virile that powerful behavioral management techniques cannot overcome it.

Social structural diffusion theories claim that the malintegration of core and periphery arises from their essential differences of social organization. The 'modern' social organization of the core is characterized by a wide division of labor, high level of urbanization, capital-intensive production, small nuclear family, rationalistic bureaucratic structures, high *per capita* income, and those rational norms and values which naturally arise in such settings. On the contrary, the 'traditional' social organization of the periphery manifests a narrow division of labor, low level of urbanization, labor-intensive production, large extended family, personalistic and diffuse structures, lower *per capita* income, and traditional norms and values. These are the stereotypical differences between advanced industrial societies and relatively backward agricultural societies and are the stuff of the literature of modernization. What is slightly different in this situation is that this conflict of social systems occurs within the framework of the advanced industrial society. The structural diffusion theories suggest that eco-

nomic integration precedes, if it does not actually cause, cultural integration and subsequent national development.

How can this survival of traditionalism within a sea of modernity be accounted for? The simplest, and most frequent explanation is that the peripheral collectivity is not, in fact, economically integrated into the society.[28] How, then, can such integration be actively sought? One remedy is to incorporate the peripheral group into the modern industrial economy so that it becomes subject to the strains of structural differentiation. The widening of the division of labor loosens the hold of traditional authorities, creates new social needs and functions, and thus brings pressure for integration. 'Differentiation and upgrading processes may require the inclusion in a status of full membership in the relevant general community system of previously excluded groups which have developed legitimate capacities to "contribute" to the functioning of the system.[29] As the peripheral collectivity begins to participate in the national economic system, changes in its structural relations should lead to rational, performance-centered, and universalistic values.

A more equivocal response to this problem of integration leans on the tendency towards unbalanced growth in capitalist societies. It is well known that some regional sectors develop faster and more completely than others. Hence the solution to the problem of economic integration is to promote development in the relatively backward regions.[30] Neo-classical economic theory holds that the expansion of efficient capital, labor and commodity markets into regions dominated by traditionally oriented groups should decrease regional economic inequalities in the society as a whole.[31] Once the peripheral region is brought into the national network of commercial flows and transactions, inequality might temporarily increase; but in time an equilibrium will be reached and economic integration will be substantially achieved. This is another osmotic model, only in this case the causal factor is the exchange of material goods and services rather than the interaction of cultural elements *per se.*

Aside from the historical objections to the cultural diffusion theories discussed previously, there is a mounting body of evidence which seems to refute the thesis of peripheral isolation, particularly with respect to economic integration.[32] Thus there are two major difficulties with the structural and cultural diffusion theories. First, the persistence of relative economic backwardness in the periphery cannot satisfactorily be explained by reference to its isolation from the national economy. In effect, peripheral economic development has occurred more slowly than the theory would predict. This has led to analyses which tend to blame peripheral economic sluggishness on the oppressive traditional culture which is maintained.[33] But this points to the second problem: why is traditional culture so enduring in the periphery despite this substantial interaction with the core? Clearly the existence of a distinctive culture in the periphery cannot be taken as a given. The probability of successful acculturation, leading to the cultural homogenization of the two groups, should increase progressively with time. Here as well the diffusion theories present an overly optimistic assessment.

An Alternative Model: The Periphery as an Internal Colony

Common to both the structural and cultural diffusion theories is a unilateral conception of social and economic development. This type of development, as indicated by such measures as labor diversification indices and urbanization statistics, is assumed to spread from one locality to another though the mechanism of this diffusion is somewhat mysterious. However, an important distinction can be made between development which occurs as a result of factors endogenous to a specific society and that which is the result of basically exogenous forces. The second type of development—that usually associated with certain sectors of Third World societies—arose out of what Georges Balandier[34] has termed the 'colonial situation.' Typically this involves domination by a 'racially' and culturally different foreign conquering group, imposed in the name of a dogmatically asserted racial, ethnic, or cultural superiority, on a materially inferior indigenous people. There is contact between the different cultures. The domi-

nated society is condemned to an instrumental role by the metropolis. Finally, there is a recourse not only to force, to maintain political stability, but also to a complex of racial or cultural stereotypes, to legitimate metropolitan superordination.

The pattern of development characterising the colonial situation is markedly different in these respects from that which emerged from endogenous development in Western Europe and Japan. First, colonial development produces a cultural division of labor: a system of stratification where objective cultural distinctions are superimposed upon class lines. High status occupations tend to be reserved for those of metropolitan culture; while those of indigenous culture cluster at the bottom of the stratification system. The ecological pattern of development differs in the colonial situation, leading to what has been termed economic and social dualism. Since the colony's role is designed to be instrumental, development tends to be complementary to that of the metropolis. The colonial economy often specializes in the production of a narrow range of primary commodities or raw materials for export. Whereas cities arose to fulfill central place functions in societies having had endogenous development, the ecological distribution of cities looks very different in colonies, where they serve as way stations in the trade between colonial hinterlands and metropolitan ports. Hence cities tend to be located on coasts with direct access to the metropolis.[35] Similarly, transportation systems arise not to spur colonial development—they are seldom built to interconnect the various regions of the colony—but to facilitate the movement of commodities from the hinterland to the coastal cities.

Thus, the cultural contact engendered in the colonial situation did not lead to a type of social and economic development in the colony which was recognizably similar to that of the metropolis. Andre Gunder Frank has characterized the fruits of such contact as 'the development of underdevelopment.'[36] It must not, however, be assumed that this colonial type of development is to be found only in those areas subjected to nineteenth-century overseas imperialism.

Simultaneous to the overseas expansion of Western European states in the fifteenth and sixteenth centuries were similar thrusts into peripheral hinterlands:[37]

> The prime aim of the new rulers in their expansionist efforts was to bring under sway all territory not already theirs within the 'natural frontiers' dimly coming to be perceived ... small nationalities which had failed to develop as States were now swallowed up: Brittany (1491), Granada (1492), Navarre (1512), Ireland. Their languages and cultures persisted nevertheless and none of the governments succeeded fully in its program of unification. England strove in vain to absorb Scotland; Spain was only briefly able to absorb a reluctant Portugal. Frontiers thus surviving helped by mutual irritation to generate a corporate sentiment on both sides. By the seventeenth century an Englishman who did not look down on a Scotsman would have been only half an Englishman; a Scotsman who did not hate an Englishman would not have been a Scotsman at all.

These internal campaigns were not in any sense coincidental to overseas colonization. There is reason to believe that both movements were the result of the same social forces in these states, among which the search for new sources of foodstuffs may have been of primary importance. Fernand Braudel has referred to this territorial expansion of the Western European states as a quest for 'internal Americas.'[38]

This bears a striking resemblance to the description of internal colonialism which has emerged from consideration of the situation of Amerindian regions in several Latin American societies. This conception focuses on political conflict between core and peripheral groups as mediated by the central government. From this perspective the 'backwardness' of peripheral groups can only be aggravated by a systematic increase in transactions with the core. The peripheral collectivity is seen to be already suffused with exploitative connections to the core, such that it can be deemed to be an internal colony. The core collectivity practices discrimination against the culturally distinct peoples who have been forced onto less accessible inferior lands.

Some aspects of internal colonialism have been sketched, though not yet systematically demonstrated.[39] These bear many similarities to descriptions of the overseas colonial situation. Commerce and trade among members of the periphery tend to be monopolized by members of the core. Credit is similarly monopolized. When commercial prospects emerge, bankers, managers, and entrepreneurs tend to be recruited from the core. The peripheral economy is forced into complementary development to the core, and thus becomes dependent on external markets. Generally, this economy rests on a single primary export, either agricultural or mineral. The movement of peripheral labor is determined largely by forces exogenous to the periphery. Typically there is great migration and mobility of peripheral workers in response to price fluctuations of exported primary products. Economic dependence is reinforced through juridical, political, and military measures. There is a relative lack of services, lower standard of living and higher level of frustration, measured by such indicators as alcoholism, among members of the peripheral group. There is national discrimination on the basis of language, religion or other cultural forms.[40] Thus the aggregate economic differences between core and periphery are causally linked to their cultural differences.

In this description national development has less to do with automatic social structural or economic processes, and more with the exercise of control over government policies concerning the allocation of resources. Since increased contact between core and periphery does not tend to narrow the economic gap between the groups, national development will best be served by strengthening the political power of the peripheral group so that it may change the distribution of resources to its greater advantage. Ultimately this power must be based on political organization. One of the foundations upon which such organization might rest is, of course, cultural similarity, or the perception of a distinctive *ethnic identity* in the peripheral group. The obstacle to national development suggested by the internal colonial model analogy, therefore, relates not to a failure of peripheral integration with the core but to a malintegration established on terms increasingly regarded as unjust and illegitimate.

Thus the internal colonial model would appear to account for the persistence of backwardness in the midst of industrial society, as well as the apparent volatility of political integration. Further, by linking economic and occupational differences between groups to their cultural differences, this model has an additional advantage in that it suggests an explanation for the resiliency of peripheral culture. ...

On the Cause of Cultural Differences Between Collectivities

It is clear that culture maintenance in the periphery can be regarded as a weapon in that it provides the possibility of socialization, as well as political mobilization, contrary to state ends. Max Weber termed those collectivities having distinctive life-styles and cultures status groups (*Stände*), each of which is allocated a different ranking on a hierarchy of social honor, or prestige.[41] In effect, the difference between the type of social solidarity predominating in the core and that in the periphery is akin to the distinction Weber made between classes and status groups. Class solidarity is consonant with a high level of modernization and tends to be organized functionally in occupational groups. Trade unions, for instance, unite men in narrowly defined occupations at the primary, shop level, and confederations of unions tend to be much less solidary than constituent locals. Class solidarity assumes an individual orientation towards the marketplace, whereas status group solidarity involves a group, or collective orientation. The important question, of course, is to come to an understanding of the dynamics between class and status group solidarity. Why does status group solidarity appear to be stronger in the periphery than in the core?

The persistence of objective cultural distinctiveness in the periphery must itself be the function of the maintenance of an unequal distribution of resources between core and peripheral groups. Initially, individuals in the disadvantaged peripheral group are not permitted to become acculturated to the core. For Fredrik Barth,[42]

the persistence of ethnic groups in contact implies not only criteria and signals for identification, but also a

structuring of interaction which allows the persistence of cultural differences ... a set of prescriptions governing situations of contact, and allowing for articulation in some sectors or domains of activity, and a set of proscriptions on social situations preventing inter-ethnic interactions in other sectors, and thus insulating parts of the cultures from confrontation and modification.

Such boundaries are maintained by the differential allocation of social roles with the society:[43]

Common to all these systems is the principle that ethnic identity implies a series of constraints on the kinds of roles an individual is allowed to play, and the partners he may choose for different kinds of transaction. ... The persistence of stratified polyethnic systems thus entails the presence of factors that generate and maintain a categorically different distribution of assets: state controls, as in some modern plural and racist systems; marked differences in evaluation that canalize the efforts of actors in different directions, as in systems with polluting occupations; or differences in culture that generate marked differences in political organization, economic organization, or individual skills.

This system of stratification is, in effect, a *cultural division of labor.*

Ernest Gellner sees the initial advantage to one cultural group rather than another as an historical accident caused by the uneven spread of industrialization through territorial space. 'The wave creates acute cleavages of interest between sets of people hit by it at differing times—in other words the more and less advanced.'[44] This accounts for the ability of the superordinate group to impose the kinds of role restraints to which Barth makes reference. However, if the unequal distribution of resources is based on observable cultural differences there is always the possibility that the disadvantaged group in time will reactively assert its own culture as equal or superior to that of the advantaged group:[45]

This cleavage and hostility can express itself with particular sharpness if the more and the less advanced populations can easily distinguish each other, by genetic or rigid cultural traits. These aid discrimination and humiliation, and thus further exacerbate the conflict. If such differentiae are lacking, nothing happens: the 'backward' area becomes depopulated, or a depressed area within a larger unit, or an object of communal charity and assistance. If, however, the differentiating marks are available—whether through distance, 'race,' or cultural traits such as religion, they provide a strong incentive and a means for the backward region or population to start conceiving of itself as a separate 'nation' and to seek independence.

Hence, if at some initial point acculturation did not occur because the advantaged group would not permit it, at a later time acculturation may be inhibited by the desires of the disadvantaged group for independence from a situation increasingly regarded as oppressive. This accounts for the cultural 'rebirths' so characteristic of societies undergoing nationalistic ferment. It is not that these groups actually uncover evidence of their ancient cultural past as an independent people; most often such culture is created contemporaneously to legitimate demands for the present-day goal of independence, or the achievement of economic equality.[46]

Conclusion: The Politics of Ethnic Change

The internal colonial model would therefore seem to provide a more adequate explanation of the persistence of ethnic identity among peripheral groups in complex societies than do diffusion theories portraying the periphery as culturally and economically isolated from the core. In general, relations between core and peripheral groups may be schematized as follows:

The uneven wave of industrialization over territorial space creates relatively advanced and less advanced groups, and therefore acute cleavages of interest arise between these groups. As a consequence of this initial fortuitous advantage there is a crystallization of the unequal distribution of resources and power between the two groups.

The superordinate group, now ensconced as the core, seeks to stabilize and monopolize its advantages through policies aiming at the institutionalization and perpetuation of the existing stratification system. Ultimately, it seeks to regulate the allocation of social roles such that those roles commonly defined as having high status are generally reserved for its members. Conversely, individuals from the less advanced group tend to

be denied access to these roles. Let this stratification system be termed the cultural division of labor: it assigns individuals to specific roles in the social structure on the basis of objective cultural distinctions.

The cultural division of labor may be enforced *de jure*, when the individual from the disadvantaged collectivity is denied certain roles by the active intervention of the state. This is the racist solution to the maintenance of the *status quo*. The cultural division of labor may, alternatively, be preserved *de facto*, through policies providing differential access to institutions conferring status in the society at large, such as the educational, military, or ecclesiastical systems. This is the institutional racist solution to the maintenance of the *status quo*.[47] Both types of policies insure that the character of the cultural division of labor remains intact.

The existence of a cultural division of labor contributes to the development of distinctive ethnic identity in each of the two cultural groups. Actors come to categorize themselves and others according to the range of roles each may be expected to play. They are aided in this categorization by the presence of visible signs—distinctive life-styles, language, or religious practices—which are seen to characterize both groups. Such visible signals allow for intergroup interaction, necessarily involving a certain commonality of definitions on the part of interacting partners, in the face of objective cultural differences between groups. Acculturation need not occur because each individual can adjust his behavior in accordance with the other's status (which can be perceived visually) even before interaction takes place.[48]

Regarded as a status, ethnic identity is superordinate to most other statuses, and defines the permissible constellations of statuses or social personalities, which an individual with that identity may assume. In this respect ethnic identity is similar to sex and rank, in that it constrains the incumbent in all his activities, not only in some defined social situations.

The political position of the peripheral group within the society is likely to be feeble given this situation. This is so even in the most formally democratic polities since the peripheral collectivity is likely to be resource-poor relative to all other social groups. If the peripheral group is also a numerical minority its political situation is far worse. As a minority group it cannot independently force changes in central government policies, such as those which might provide a reallocation of income from the core group, on the strength of votes alone. This often results in politics of 'stable unrepresentation.'[49]

In most developed societies the above considerations hold only in a probabilistic sense. That is to say it is statistically possible for an individual of low ethnic status to achieve, for instance, high-status occupational roles, though of course it is very improbable. The realization of these conventionally forbidden roles makes it possible for statistically deviant individuals to reconsider their ethnic identity. They may have several types of options. By identifying with the advantaged group, these individuals may attempt to 'pass,' and thus undergo a subjective re-identification of their ethnic identity.[50] Alternatively, they may attempt to maximize their individual power by acting as brokers between the two groups. As 'ethnic leaders' they may seek to incrementally narrow the material differences between the groups by appealing to the universalistic norms which many industrial societies aspire to. Or they may reactively assert the equal or superior value of their culture, claim the separateness of their nation and seek independence.

The first option, basically one of selective co-optation, serves to remove potentially divisive leadership from the peripheral group and thereby ensures stabilization of the cultural division of labor. The ultimate consequences of the second choice are somewhat less clear, except for the probability that should any change occur it will be gradual. The slowness of actual economic integration in the face of larger expectations will most likely insure that a more militant group will form in the name of the ethnic nationalist position. In general, the probability of achieving economic integration within the society, as against other outcomes, such as actual secession or relative stasis, will be determined by factors such as the relative numbers of both groups, the indispensability of the periphery's role in the national economy, and

the kinds of policies adopted by the central government.

The existence of ethnic solidarity in a given group should therefore be regarded as a special instance of the general phenomenon of political mobilization. Hence, ethnic change facilitating political integration cannot be expected to result in the periphery until there is widespread satisfaction that the cultural division of labor has largely been eliminated. Once placed in this framework, it is easy to see the reason for the frequency of political demands along ethnic grounds in industrial society. The Marxian discussion of political mobilization points to two fundamental conditions for the emergence of group solidarity. Substantial economic inequalities must exist between individuals, such that these individuals may come to see this inequality as part of a pattern of collective oppression.

However, the aggregation of individual perceptions of economic inequality alone is insufficient for the development of collective solidarity. There must be an accompanying social awareness and definition of the situation as being unjust and illegitimate. Oppression by itself can, of course, if severe enough, precipitate random violence against the social system, as in the many instances of peasant *jacqueries* throughout history; but this is not the result of the attainment of group consciousness and hence lacks the organization and purposefulness to achieve effective ends.

Thus another vital condition for the advent of collective solidarity is adequate communication among members of the oppressed group.[51] Communication within collectivities generally occurs within the context of social institutions: neighborhoods, workplaces, schools, churches, social and recreational clubs, and the host of voluntary associations to which individuals may typically belong. To the extent that these contexts for social interaction are limited to members of a group sharing the social definition of an ethnic minority, the possibilities for intercommunication will be maximized. This is so because in the periphery there tends to be not only segregation in the workplace but also residential segregation as well. The concatenation of residential and occupational segregation gives a decisive advantage to the development of ethnic rather than class solidarity. Since the concept of social class seeks to deny the salience of cultural and residential differences among members of similar occupational groups, to the extent that such differences actually exist, class is ultimately more abstracted from the reality of everyday social life than is ethnicity.

Finally, the very economic backwardness of the periphery contributes to the inevitability of such residential and occupational segregation. As an impoverished and culturally alien region there is little incentive for members of the core group to migrate there in force. Typically the periphery has a declining population, an overabundance of the elderly, and a disproportionate number of females, all of which reflect the lack of adequate employment opportunity which is both a result of peripheral backwardness and a cause of further economic disadvantages.[52]

From these general observations it is possible to make three propositions concerning the prospects for the political integration of peripheral collectivities into the society as a whole:

1. The greater the economic inequalities between collectivities, the greater the probability that the less advantaged collectivity will be status solidary, and hence, will resist political integration.

2. The greater the frequency of intra-collectivity communication, the greater the status solidarity of the peripheral collectivity.

3. The greater the intergroup differences of culture, particularly in so far as identifiability is concerned, the greater the probability that the culturally distinct peripheral collectivity will be status solidary. Identifiable cultural differences include: language (accent), distinctive religious practices, and life-style.

It should be underlined that when objective cultural differences are superimposed[53] upon economic inequalities, forming a cultural division of labor, and when adequate communications exist as a facilitating factor, the chances for successful political integration of the peripheral collectivity into the national society are minimized. The internal colonial model predicts, and to some extent explains, the emergence of just such a cultural division in labor.

Notes

1. Clifford Geertz, 'The Integrative Revolution: Primordial Sentiments and Civic Politics in the New States' in C. Geertz, ed., *Old Societies and New States* (New York: 1963).

2. Seymour M. Lipset and Stein Rokkan, 'Introduction' in S. M. Lipset and S. Rokkan, eds, *Party Systems and Voter Alignments* (New York: 1967), p. 10.

3. E. Allardt and Y. Littunen, eds, *Cleavages, Ideologies, and Party Systems* (Helsinki: 1964); Robert A. Dahl, ed., *Political Oppositions in Western Democracies* (New Haven: 1966); and Stein Rokkan, *Citizens, Elections, and Parties* (New York and Oslo: 1970).

4. For a graphic demonstration compare two essays written at opposite poles of the past decade by Daniel Bell, 'The End of Ideology in the West' in *The End of Ideology* (New York: 1962), pp. 393–407, and 'Unstable America,' *Encounter*, 34 (1970), pp. 11–26.

5. Myron Weiner, 'Political integration and political development,' *Annals of the American Academy of Political Science*, 358 (1965), pp. 52–64.

6. Randall Collins, 'A Comparative Approach to Political Sociology' in Reinhard Bendix *et al.*, eds, *State and Society* (Boston: 1968), pp. 42–67.

7. Gunnar Myrdal, *An International Economy* (New York: 1956), pp. 9–11.

8. This problem has received substantially greater attention. See T. H. Marshall, 'Citizenship and Social Class' in *Class, Citizenship, and Social Development* (New York: 1964), pp. 71–134, and Reinhard Bendix, *Nation-Building and Citizenship* (New York: 1964).

9. This restriction limits the applicability of the model to a subset of the universe of settings for intergroup conflict. However, my central concern in this study is with industrialized societies where this model has wide relevance, except for those societies, like the United States, formed largely from voluntary migration. As R. A. Schermerhorn has argued, 'Studies of ethnic relations based chiefly on data from voluntary immigrations cannot serve as the model or foundation for ethnic relations as a whole.' *Comparative Ethnic Relations* (New York: 1970), p. 156.

10. A useful definition of diffusion is A. L. Kroeber, 'Diffusionism' in E.R.A. Seligman and A. Johnson, eds, *The Encyclopedia of the Social Sciences*, III (1930), reprinted in A. and E. Etzioni, eds, *Social Change: Sources, Patterns and Consequences* (New York: 1964).

11. This discussion does not pretend to offer a review of the literature bearing on these problems, but only on those *general* theoretical images of the mechanism of national development, i.e., a particular problem for the theory of social change. There is a vast anthropological literature on Third World societies which categorizes a variety of types of internal ethnic stratification as being more or less 'pluralistic,' without, however, attempting to theoretically account for changes in these situations.

12. Max Weber is among the many writers who have assumed this to be a defining characteristic of the traditional life-style, *The Protestant Ethic and the Spirit of Capitalism* (New York: 1958), p. 59. See also Wilbert E. Moore and Arnold Feldman, *Labor Commitment and Social Change in Developing Areas* (New York: 1960). For a somewhat skeptical view see Elliot J. Berg, 'Backward sloping labor supply functions in dual economies—the Africa case,' *Quarterly Journal of Economics*, 75, 3 (1961), pp. 468–92.

13. 'Some have seen [the increase in national homogeneity] to be a simple consequence of the law of imitation. But it is rather a leveling analogous to that which is produced between liquid masses put into communication. The partitions which separate the various cells of social life, being less thick, are more often broken through. ... Territorial divisions are thus less and less grounded in the nature of things, and, consequently, lose their significance. We can almost say that a people is as much more advanced as territorial divisions are more superficial.' *The Division of Labor in Society* (New York: 1964), p. 187.

14. This is the classical definition of acculturation from Robert Redfield *et al.,* 'Outline for the study of acculturation,' *American Anthropologist,* 38, 1 (1936). Since then there have been attempts to specify the types of situations in which contact lessens intergroup conflict. See Gordon W. Allport, *The Nature of Prejudice* (Cambridge, Mass.: 1954); Robin M. Williams, *Strangers Next Door* (New York: 1964); and Thomas F. Pettigrew, 'Racially separate or together?,' *Journal of Social Issues,* 25, 1 (1969).

15. This is not to deny that acculturative processes occur with some regularity as a result of interaction between collectivities. What is questioned is the simple assertion that acculturation *necessarily* leads to cultural integration under all circumstances. Acculturation studies have failed to describe the nature of the conditions under which assimilation can be expected to occur. 'Although Kroeber's characterization of acculturation as a passing fad was belied it was still true by 1960 that generally accepted propositions about the nature of change under contact conditions were lacking. ... [Subsequently] the main line of development of acculturation studies continued to be descriptive.' Edward H. Spicer, 'Acculturation,' *International Encyclopedia of the Social Sciences* (New York: 1968) vol. 1, p. 23. It might be added that the large literature on nationalist movements has similarly not yielded a theoretical perspective.

16. George C. Homans, *The Human Group* (New York: 1950), chapter 5.

17. Karl W. Deutsch, 'Social mobilization and political development,' *American Political Science Review,* 55, 3 (1961), pp. 493–514. Actually, Deutsch's precise position on this issue shifts from article to article and defies pinning down: see Walker Conner, 'Nation-building or nation-destroying?,' *World Politics,* 24, 3 (1972), pp. 319–55. I feel that, over all, his sympathies lie with the cultural diffusion model.

18. Lucian Pye, 'Introduction' in *Communications and Political Development* (Princeton: 1963), pp. 3–23.

19. Gabriel Almond and Sidney Verba, *The Civic Culture* (Princeton: 1963).

20. Wilbur Schramm, 'Communication Development and the Development Process' in Pye, *op. cit.,* pp. 30–57.

21. David Apter, *Ghana in Transition* (Princeton: 1963), and Seymour M. Lipset, *The First New Nation* (New York: 1963).

22. See Claude Ake, *A Theory of Political Integration* (Homewood, Ill.: 1967). It should be pointed out that these are less Weber's difficulties than those of many of his subsequent commentators.

23. Ernst Haas, *Beyond the Nation State* (Stanford: 1964) and Ernst Haas and Philippe Schmitter, 'Economies and differential pattern of political integration: projections about unity in Latin America,' *International Organization,* 18 (Autumn, 1964), pp. 705–37.

24. A very useful summary may be found in Eli Heckscher, *Mercantilism* (London: 1955), vol. I.

25. For England, the first state to undergo such political centralization, see G. R. Elton, *The Tudor Revolution in Government* (Cambridge: 1966).

26. Moisei Ostrogorski, *Democracy and the Organization of Political Parties* (New York: 1964).

27. Lawrence Stone, 'Literacy and education in England, 1640–1900,' *Past and Present,* 42 (1969), pp. 69–139.

28. Erik Allardt, 'A Theory of Solidarity and Legitimacy Conflicts,' in E. Allardt and Y. Littunen, eds, *op. cit.*

29. Talcott Parsons, *Societies: Evolutionary and Comparative Perspectives* (Englewood Cliffs: 1966), pp. 22–3. This general position has long been held, despite its evident empirical inadequacy. Thus, Max Weber goes to some length to discredit it with respect to the Indian caste system: 'One might believe, for instance, that the ritual caste antagonisms had made impossible the de-

velopment of 'large-scale enterprises' with a division of labor in the same workshop and might consider this to be decisive. But such is not the case. The law of caste has proved just as elastic in the face of the necessities of the concentration of labor in workshops as it did in the face of a need for concentration of labor and service in the noble household.' Hans Gerth and C. Wright Mills, eds, *From Max Weber: Essays in Sociology* (London: 1948), p. 412.

30. For a survey, see John Friedmann and William Alonso, eds, *Regional Development and Planning* (Cambridge, Mass.: 1964).

31. M. Tachi offers an example in 'Regional income disparity and internal migration of population in Japan,' *Economic Development and Cultural Change*, 12, 2 (1964), pp. 186–204.

32. For example, see Werner Baer, 'Regional inequality and economic growth in Brazil,' *Economic Development and Cultural Change*, 12, 3 (1964); J. R. Lasuén, 'Regional income inequalities and the problems of growth in Spain,' Regional Science Association: *Papers*, no. 8; and J. F. Riegelhaupt and Shepard Forman, 'Bodo was never Brazilian: economic integration and rural development among a contemporary peasantry,' *Journal of Economic History* 30, 1 (1970), pp. 100–16. If the economic isolation of peripheral groups cannot be demonstrated in these societies, then in industrial societies such groups are, *a fortiori*, fully incorporated into the national economy.

33. Edward C. Banfield, *The Moral Basis of a Backward Society* (New York: 1958).

34. Georges Balandier, *Sociologie actuelle de l'Afrique noire* (Paris: 1963).

35. Hence Christaller's theory predicting the location of cities in central places (cf. Edward Ullman, 'A theory of location for cities,' *American Journal of Sociology*, 46, 3 (1941), pp. 853–64), and devised from South German data, seems to apply best in Western Europe, or exactly that area which had endogenous development. After the sixteenth century, Eastern Europe experienced extensive refeudalization and came to serve as a major source of primary products for the Western maritime states. Hence these Eastern European societies exhibit many of the characteristics of an area of exogenous development. It has been claimed that this is a significant distinction in the development of feudalism as well. 'A rough general distinction may be drawn between feudalism (in an institutional sense) growing up "naturally" from below, or planted from above. West European feudalism seems to belong in the main to the former type. Peering with due caution into the mists of time and expert witness, one may associate this fact with the long Dark-Age struggle of its region of origin against the pressure of worse barbarism from outside.'

V. G. Kiernan, 'State and nation in Western Europe,' *Past and Present*, 31 (1965), pp. 21–2. The defensive nature of Western European feudalism, for Kiernan, led to conditions favoring social solidarity.

36. Andre Gunder Frank, *Capitalism and Underdevelopment in Latin America* (New York: 1969).

37. Kiernan, *op. cit.*, p. 33.

38. 'Mediterranean man has always had to fight against the swamps. Far more demanding than the problem of forest and scrubland, this colonization is the distinguishing feature of his rural history. In the same way that northern Europe established itself or at any rate expanded to the detriment of its forest marches so the Mediterranean found its New World, its own Americas in the plains.' *The Mediterranean and the Mediterranean World in the Age of Phillip II* (New York: 1972), p. 67.

39. Pablo Gonzáles-Casanova, 'Internal colonialism and national development,' *Studies in Comparative International Development*, 1, 4 (1965), pp. 27–37; Rodolpho Stavenhagen, 'Classes, colonialism, and acculturation,' *Studies in Comparative International Development*, 1, 6 (1965). Internal *colonialism*, or the political incorporation of culturally distinct groups by the core, must be distinguished from internal *colonization*, or the settlement of previously unoccupied territories within state borders. An example of the latter process may be cited from twelfth-century France: 'The wild unoccupied spaces belonged almost without exception to the highest nobility, and the attitude of the latter towards these open spaces underwent a change: they now decided to organize their colonization. This choice was frequently dictated by political considerations. It might be a question of securing the safety of a road by settling the forests through which it passed, or else of asserting control over the frontiers of a principality by establishing strong peasant communities obliged to perform armed service in wooded and deserted marches which had hitherto formed a protective ring round it.' Georges Duby, *Rural Economy and Country Life in the Medieval West* (London: 1968), p. 76.

40. There does not seem to be a general consensus on a small number of essential defining features of internal colonialism. Since the concept evolved from the study of ethnic conflict in Latin American societies, the above list is particularly applicable to societies with a similar history, especially with regard to Spanish and Portuguese patterns of colonialism. However, with certain modifications, the notion of internal colonialism may be much more general in scope. What if all but one or two conditions seem to be met? The danger, of course, is to so relax the meaning of internal colonialism that almost any instance of stratification may fall somewhere within its boundaries.

Let me give an example. A strict case study of internal colonialism should probably include *administrative differentiation,* such that there are both citizens and subjects, as dictated by the colonial analogy. This qualification is easily met by many Third World societies, but probably by only one developed society, the Republic of South Africa. Are we therefore to conclude that internal colonialism is an inappropriate concept in modern European history? Ireland is a perfect example of an internal colony under the old United Kingdom until 1829, when Catholics were nearly granted full civic and political rights. But it would be folly to consider that this legislation ended the essentially colonial status of the island. Are we then to refer to post-1829 Ireland as an instance of internal neo-colonialism?

Similarly, is *territoriality* a necessary condition, or can American Blacks be considered an internal colony as Robert Blauner ('Internal colonization and ghetto revolt,' *Social Problems,* 16, 4 (1969), pp. 393–408) and others have suggested? These are some of the problems that remain to be worked out if internal colonialism is indeed to become a useful concept.

41. Max Weber, *Economy and Society,* eds Guenther Roth and Claus Wittich (New York: 1968), vol. II, pp. 926–40.

42. Fredrik Barth, 'Introduction' in F. Barth, ed., *Ethnic Groups and Boundaries* (Boston: 1969), p. 16.

43. Barth, *op. cit.,* p. 17.

44. Ernest Gellner, 'Nationalism' in *Thought and Change* (London: 1969), p. 171.

45. *Ibid.,* pp. 171–2.

46. David C. Gordon, *History and Self-Determination in the Third World* (Princeton: 1971).

47. Stokely Carmichael and Charles V. Hamilton, *Black Power* (New York: 1967), pp. 3–4. The failure of national educational institutions to provide equal training for members of all status groups is now well recognized, and has generated an exhaustive literature.

48. Barth, *op. cit.,* p. 17.

49. This may be said to occur when the 'political system normally operates to prevent incipient competitors from achieving full entry into the political arena. Far from there being built-in mechanisms which keep the system responsive, such groups win entry only through the breakdown of the normal operation of the system or through demonstration on the part of challenging groups of a willingness to violate the "rules of the game" by resorting to illegitimate means for carrying on political conflict.' William A. Gamson, 'Stable unrepresentation in American society,' *American Behavioral Scientist,* 12, 2 (1968), p. 18.

50. It need hardly be added that to the extent that differential ethnicity is symbolized by phenotypical differences between groups such an option is correspondingly limited.

51. Karl Marx, *The Eighteenth Brumaire of Louis Bonaparte* (New York: 1926), p. 109.

52. This vicious circle of regional underdevelopment is lucidly discussed in Gunnar Myrdal, *Rich Lands and Poor* (New York: 1957), pp. 23–38.

53. For a parallel discussion of the effects of such superimposition on the intensity of class conflict, see Ralf Dahrendorf, *Class and Class Conflict in Industrial Society* (Stanford: 1959), pp. 213–18.

MICHAEL T. HANNAN

Dynamics of Ethnic Boundaries

Two seemingly contradictory facts characterize modern ethnicity and ethnic movements: (1) The spread of modern economic and political structures lowers ethnic diversity; and (2) high levels of economic and political modernization impart, under certain conditions, a renewed social and political importance to ethnic boundaries. The first observation is normally taken as evidence that ethnic distinctions are vestiges of former geographical and social isolation and that ethnicity becomes subordinate to modern national identities. The second observation, based on the study of ethnic separatist movements such as those in Quebec, Wales, Brittany, and the Basque provinces in Spain and France, is taken as evidence that ethnicity is primarily reactive and that modernization creates or invigorates ethnic distinctions.

This paper develops a theory that explains the seeming contradiction. It builds on Fredrik Barth's (1956, 1969) brilliant analysis of the cultural ecology of ethnic boundaries in premodern societies. The main outlines of the theory are as follows: Ethnic distinctions are often hierarchical in the sense that people have multiple identities (as members of family, clan, language group, and so forth) that relate to successively larger populations. Whether a particular ethnic identity endures and remains salient depends on which identities are activated in collective action and consequently which cultural boundaries are defended. When small-scale identities are salient, it is difficult to organize populations defined in terms of large-scale identities. Thus, when small-scale identities remain strong, effective and sustained action on the basis of broadly defined ethnic identities is unlikely. However, any process that lowers the salience of small-scale identities weakens this impediment to large-scale collective action. Economic and political modernization commonly has such effects.

When modern centers penetrate local communities, they undermine the salience of small-scale identities for a number of reasons. The theory advanced here places primary emphasis on disparities in power between the center and each locality in the periphery. Sustained mobilization in opposition to further penetration by the center must be on a scale commensurate with that of the center. Therefore, successful penetration by the social, economic, and political center of a social system alters the condition of competition among the various bases of collective action in favor of large-scale identities. Whether the basis of large-scale collective action is ethnic identity or some other identity, such as class, depends on the pattern of identities and on the manner in which the expansion of the center eliminates subsystem boundaries. This theory has the novel feature of relating the reemergence of ethnicity to the process that typically destroys ethnicity. It implies that the center can be so successful in breaking down subsystem boundaries that it creates the conditions for successful ethnic collective opposition.

Ethnic Organization

Discussions of ethnic organization and collective action are plagued by a lack of clarity in definitions. Thus, the initial problem is to provide a satisfactory definition of ethnicity and ethnic organization. Barth (1969) posits that ethnic identity is ascriptive (inherited on the basis of social origins), exclusive, and imperative (meaning that members do not have a choice of whether or not to invoke the ethnic identity in cross-ethnic interaction). Ethnicity is an organizing principle of populations: When interaction is organized around ascriptive, exclusive, and imperative distinctions, the population is fractionated into ethnic groups.

Barth's own research suggests that even this rather minimal definition may be too restrictive. Ethnicities are not necessarily rigidly ascribed; there is frequently considerable movement across certain stable ethnic boundaries (Horowitz 1975). These findings imply that ethnic identities are attributed to individuals on the basis of social origins and current behavior. When current behavior is weighted heavily, individuals have some choice over ethnic identity to the extent that they can make choices among alternative behaviors. But once a course of action is taken, attribution of ethnicity follows.

I follow Barth and use the following minimal definition: An ethnic identity is an attributed and imperative social identity that partitions a population; an ethnic group is a population organized with reference to an ethnic identity. The primordial-identity view typically stipulates that ethnic groups possess distinctive and integrated cultural content as well as a relatively closed field of social interaction. Including these elements as defining properties of ethnic organization assumes implicitly that ethnic boundaries are unproblematic. When ethnic boundaries are strong and persistent in time, cultural and social solidarity does ordinarily result. However, ethnic groups that are either emerging or declining need not exhibit such solidarity. Because the proposed theory attempts to account for both loss of ethnic diversity and the revival of ethnicity, it would be a mistake to add these additional stipulations to the definition of ethnicity. Instead, features of social and cultural solidarity are treated as consequences of particularly impenetrable ethnic organization and boundaries.

The Ecology of Ethnic Boundaries

The definition of ethnic identity implies the existence of a social boundary. Barth (1956, 1969) contends that the social functioning of ethnic organization can be best understood by examining the processes that maintain (and change) ethnic boundaries. He and his students have developed this perspective in the study of premodern systems in which ethnic boundaries remain fixed in space despite relatively high rates of movement across the ethnic boundaries. For instance, Haaland (1969) analyzed the relations between nomadic herders of Baggara ethnicity and settled horticulturalists of Fur ethnicity in Swat, North Pakistan. In this case, the ethnic boundary coincided with the form of production of the community (nomadic herding versus settled horticulture). Fur sometimes acquired cattle herds and contracted with Baggara to manage them in the uplands. Sometimes these herds grew large and became a substantial economic asset. In such cases, contracting for their care was thought to be too risky, and their Fur owners shifted to a nomadic life-style in order to better monitor and protect their assets. Haaland observed a strong tendency for the nomadic Fur to become Bagarra, thus preserving the equivalence of ethnic identity and basis of production.

Barth argues that two general processes determine ethnic boundaries in such systems. The first involves *competition and power relations* among ethnic groups. When two or more ethnically distinct populations attempt to exploit the same resources and occupy the same physical space, they stand in a relation of competition. Which of the competing groups can maintain themselves in the space depends on the military and social organizational capacities of the groups, according to Barth. In other words, the distribution of ethnic groups in social space depends on the result of competitive struggles among them.

The second process affecting the distributions of ethnic populations in social space is *ethnic identity change.* As already noted, Haaland (1969) observed that members of the Fur ethnic group became Baggara when they became full-time nomadic herders. The reason is that nomads cannot produce the life-styles necessary to be respectable according to the cultural standards of the Fur ethnicity. The constraints of the nomadic life rule out the requisite social organizational and cultural features. In this case, the population that moves to a nomadic life-style eventually comes to be viewed (by both sides) as members of the Baggara ethnic group.

Barth (1969) argues that the example of Fur becoming Baggara can be understood as an instance of a general process of ethnic boundary maintenance. According to this argument, systems of production constrain social organization, and value systems tend to develop in directions that are consistent with such constraints. In particular, actions that are feasible under the productive and organizational constraints facing a population tend to become valued. Ethnic identities, which tend to employ as cultural content those values that have widespread currency in the population, consequently crystallize around the distinctive properties of the productive niche (e.g., settled horticulture).

Action consistent with a particular ethnic identity is most feasible within the niche in which the ethnicity developed. Therefore, migrants (defined broadly) face the choice of engaging in action that is suboptimal or deviant from the perspective of their original ethnic identity or, when possible, they may undergo ethnic identity change. If migrants tend to choose the latter option, ethnic boundaries can remain stable in physical and social space even in the face of relatively high rates of migration across the boundaries.

Barth's argument can be summarized as positing that *ethnic boundaries tend to coincide with niche boundaries (in equilibrium).* Ethnic boundaries will be stable as long as the pattern of niches is stable and power relations are stable. But social changes that disrupt niche structures or power relations destabilize ethnic boundaries.

Niche Theory

Barth's argument and his detailed anthropological studies are consistent with general theories of niche structure. It is helpful to make these connections explicit. In order to do so, we must distinguish between fundamental and realized niches. The fundamental niche of an ethnic group is the set of environmental conditions in which the ethnic group can reproduce itself and maintain its defining social boundary. In general, ethnic identities that are specialized to a particular habitat and type of production have low survival values in regions in which the type of production is not feasible. In this sense, geophysical factors limit the fundamental niches of many types of ethnic organizations, particularly premodern varieties. The realized niche of an ethnic group is that part of the fundamental niche that can be exploited in the face of competition from other groups.

Barth's model can be adapted to apply to modern social structures. Doing so requires explicating the central process of ethnic competition. In particular, his ecological argument and especially his interpretation of ethnic interactions in Swat can be understood as positing that *the intensity of competition among ethnic groups is proportional to the degree to which their fundamental niches overlap.* The greater the similarity of resource exploitation of two resource-limited competitors, the lower the probability that a single environment or habitat can support both in equilibrium. The theory developed in this essay builds on this assumption.

When two or more ethnic groups with overlapping fundamental niches attempt to inhabit the same social space, intense competition among them routinely leads to ethnic conflict. Ethnic conflict usually results in exclusion of one or more ethnic groups from the resource ("competitive exclusion"). Thus, ethnic group boundaries are shaped by processes of competition and conflict among ethnic groups.

The distinction between fundamental and realized niches is crucial to the theory. The potential for competition and conflict among ethnic groups depends on the degree to which their fundamental niches (the resources that their social organizations can potentially exploit) overlap. But competition and conflict routinely lead to competitive exclusion, which means an absence of overlap in realized niches, as Barth's ethnographic work shows plainly.

Hannan (1979) argues that competitive processes of the sort previously described bear a strong resemblance to those analyzed by mathematical ecologists (especially to Lotka-Volterra models of ecological competition—see Hannan and Freeman 1977). Thinking of ethnic boundary dynamics as depending on resource-based competition and conflict allows one to use a rich body of formal ecological theory about competitive dynamics to explain how social, economic, and political change affects ethnic diversity and ethnic collective action.

Modernization and the Loss of Ethnic Diversity

The first stylized fact to be explained is that economic modernization and state building decrease ethnic diversity, measured in terms of numbers of distinct ethnic organizations. Such a result is consistent with the view that ethnic boundary dynamics are shaped by ecological competition, as suggested in the preceding section. Modern bioecological theories of the niche hold that species diversity is limited by the number of distinct resources and constraints. More precisely, no stable equilibrium can be attained by a community with m component groups and fewer than m distinct resources and other constraints on growth (for systems characterized by Lotka-Volterra forms of competitive interaction). In the long run, then, the diversity of resources and other constraints sets an upper bound to community diversity. Thus, environmental changes that add (eliminate) constraints from a system increase (decrease) the upper bound of diversity. If competition among ethnic groups takes the form of general ecological competition, then *any increase (decrease) in the number of constraints on the expansion of ethnic groups increases (decreases) the upper bound on ethnic diversity.*

The next step in the theory connects this ecological argument with large-scale economic change. Economic modernization involves at least three processes: (1) increasing application of non-human energy to production—that is, industrialization; (2) the freeing of labor and capital and the establishment of markets; and (3) increasing scale and complexity of production organization and the bureaucratization of production. Economic modernization is usually thought to increase social diversity. For instance, it is commonplace to point to the explosive growth of occupational titles over the past hundred years as evidence of the positive effect of modernization on social diversity. This evidence suggests that economic modernization increases the number of resources and other constraints.

I am persuaded that economic modernization has the opposite effect, at least in the long run. Expansion of a modern economic center has the consequence of breaking down local economic boundaries and incorporating labor and capital into larger exchange networks. As the process proceeds, individuals and organizations whose fates were weakly connected in the premodern economy come to stand in similar relations to events in the center and to events characterizing the entire economy. Disturbances created in one sector of a modern economy have much wider consequences than is the case in the economies they replaced. Consequently, modern economic units are adapted less to local conditions and more to national and global ones. In short, economic modernization simplifies the structure of constraints and reduces the number of distinct economic constraints within systems. That is, economic modernization tends to lower the upper bound for ethnic diversity within economic systems.

State building refers to the process by which potential centers of power eliminate rival forms of control over resources and events. This process usually proceeds in stages, with control estab-lished over successively smaller-scale organizations, resources, and actions in the society (Rokkan 1975). The emerging center must first eliminate other large-scale contenders to political control. Next, state building is oriented toward controlling specific resources and actions—for example, the state attempts land reform, control over markets, control over education, and so forth. Finally, the state attempts to incorporate individuals as agents of the state to conduct nation building (Bendix 1964). I think of state building as the construction of a hierarchical structure of political controls to successively lower levels of action, from control over the means to violence in a national territory to incorporation of the individual as an agent of the state.

State building obviously affects the structure of constraints: Effective state building eliminates local political boundaries and produces a unitary set of relations between the various peripheries and the center. In other words, effective state building tends to lower the upper bound for ethnic diversity within states.

These arguments relating economic modernization and state building to ethnic diversity also follow from consideration of *connectedness*. Economic modernization and effective state building increase the connectedness of social systems by joining the fates of previously unconnected populations. To pursue the implications of changes in connectedness, we make reference to an emerging theory on stability of multicomponent competitive systems. It seems intuitive that more complex systems ought to be more stable. However, it now appears that more connected systems are more vulnerable to environmental interference because a disturbance at any point propagates widely through the system. Simon (1973) has argued convincingly that nature (i.e., natural selection) "loves hierarchy" because hierarchies are less connected than other structures. Population biologists have advanced a number of mathematical and empirical arguments that less connected structures with the same number of components are more likely to attain a stable equilibrium (see May 1973).

Economic and political modernization increases both connectedness and strength of interaction. At some stage in the construction of the theory, it may be profitable to model each effect separately. For the present, I use the term *connectivity* to encompass both effects. Growing connectivity within society reduces ethnic diversity and changes the competitive balance in favor of collective action based on large-scale ethnic identities.

Modernization and the Rise of Ethnic Political Action

The second stylized fact to be explained is that ethnic collective action often increases in scale and intensity in advanced stages of modernization processes. Much of this activity appears oriented toward firming and defending ethnic boundaries. I use the term *ethnic political action* to refer to collective action, either institutional or noninstitutional, directed at maintaining, strengthening, or extending ethnic boundaries.

Historical evidence suggests that ethnic collective action occurs frequently and with considerable intensity in the early contacts of the ethnic groups that make up polyethnic nations—that is, primarily during the early conquest phase. Such action tends to decline once political and military control is established. In at least some cases, the rather extended period of ethnic quiescence is followed by a renewed intensity of creating and defending ethnic boundaries (Hechter 1974a, 1974b; Horowitz 1975; Nielsen 1980).

It seems safe to assume that threats to eliminate ethnic boundaries always lead to a certain amount of reactive political action. The problem is not to explain variations across situations in the likelihood that loss of an ethnic boundary generates a political reaction. Rather, the central question concerns conditions under which such a protopolitical tendency becomes activated in an organized fashion. After all, only when organized political action by those on the periphery encounters a response from the center does a boundary become reactively organized. The problem is to formulate a model that specifies the conditions under which the modernization processes eliminating ethnic boundaries encounter or produce *organized* resistance.

Consider a closed system containing m ethnic populations and $j < m$ expanding ethnically homogeneous centers. Suppose that each center controls a hinterland—that is, the larger system can be decomposed into j subsystems. Then arguments from the previous section imply that if modernization proceeds unhampered in each sector, ethnic diversity tends toward zero in each system. At some stage in this process, it is likely that the resulting j large-scale ethnic populations compete and engage in conflict. Because these ethnic populations are larger than those in the original set and because activities of the center are more widely noticed and more systematically recorded than those of the periphery, historians and other observers will likely conclude that the amount of ethnic activity has greatly increased. At least some of the increase might be spurious due to the inability of the observers to make ethnic distinctions among the initial periphery populations. There may also be a genuine increase in the importance of ethnic political activity to the system. Ethnic loyalties are likely to become activated in a greater proportion of political contests when the system is composed of a small number of relatively large ethnic groups because any outcome likely affects similarly many persons with the same ethnic identity.

The more usual—and more interesting—case involves the expansion of a single ethnically homogeneous center. To deal with this case, additional assumptions must be added to the general competition argument. I assume that sustained competition and conflict require some minimal power parity among the participants in the competition. The very fact of its expansion implies that the center surpasses the peripheries in resources, technology, and organization capacity. Organizations on the periphery must then have relatively large size if they are to sustain competition and conflict with the center. Under what conditions will organizations on the periphery acquire a scale sufficient to contest the expansion of the center?

Systems undergoing modernization are typically composed initially of many partially decomposable subsystems. The collection of subsystems contains many distinctive niches and associated ethnic identities and organizations. Most important, the average size and power of the ethnic populations are small relative to the emerging center. As long as the emerging center can contest with each ethnic organization singly, each contest will be brief and decisive in favor of the center.

If an ethnic stand is to be made against the center, it must be on the basis of some identity larger than that of the salient premodern ethnic identities. We need not assume that individuals have a single social identity. Quite to the contrary, individuals possess multiple social or cultural identities. For example, an individual may simultaneously be identified as a member of a clan, a local community, a religion, a linguistic community, and so forth. Each such cultural partition of a population forms the basis of potential ethnic organization. In some circumstances we notice organization around smaller-scale distinctions (e.g., clans) and in other circumstances around larger-scale distinctions (e.g., major language divisions). Because an individual's time and commitment are limited, increasing commitment to ethnic collective activity at one level implies a reduced commitment at other levels. In other words, ethnic identities at different levels compete for the time and intensity of commitment of their potential members. This is the same notion of competition previously described because the sum of time and commitment available is constant and some types of organizations grow only at the expense of other organizations.

Recall that Barth (1969) proposed that success in organizing an ethnic boundary around some set of cultural criteria depends on two factors: (1) the appropriateness of the cultural content to the behavioral contingencies of the local niche structure and (2) the power mobilized by the ethnic organization relative to the larger system. When the larger system exercises weak and infrequent constraints on the local systems, the first criterion dominates and small-scale and specialized ethnic organizations are more likely to attract members.

Modernization upsets the premodern equilibrium in the structure of niches. As the system becomes more connected, the size of the interacting population increases and the size of the largest competitor increases for all but the largest unit. This changes the conditions of organization (more precisely, of selection among forms of or-

ganization at different scale levels). Attempts at organizing around large-scale cultural identities, even if no less frequent or intense, ought to be more successful. Given the fixed time available for organization and participation, attempts at organizing or maintaining ethnic organizations premised on smaller-scale, more local identities ought to be correspondingly less successful.

The argument can be taken a step further. When boundaries around small-scale ethnic organizations are salient and successfully defended, any sort of large-scale collective action by sectors of the periphery is unlikely. As long as the lines of contest are drawn at the local level, populations that stand in the same relation to the center are unlikely to act collectively in opposition to the center. If the effect of modernization in reducing ethnic diversity results in the elimination of smaller-scale ethnic boundaries, the organizational potential of larger-scale ethnic organizations is increased.

All of these effects require that large-scale cultural identities be available. The situations of interest vary in the availability of such identities. One extreme is a segmental pattern in which identities are mutually exclusive and each identity includes the same-sized population. In a premodern equilibrium, each individual has presumably aligned himself or herself with the ethnic organization that maximizes the fit between cultural identities and current life circumstances. When modernization increases connectivity in the system, the gains of switching to an ethnic organization based on other available cultural identities are negative because all possible ethnic organizations have the same size and there are costs to ethnic change. Under these conditions, the center ought to be able to contest separately with each ethnic group and to eliminate each ethnic boundary in the system with little or no resistance.

On the other hand, when cultural identities form hierarchies (see Simon 1973) with respect to size of included populations, the processes I have described lead to selection in favor of organizations based on the largest-scale identities. Selection against boundaries at low levels in the hierarchy increases the size of the population that can be actively mobilized by organizing on the basis of larger-scale identities.

Discussion

In the preceding argument, I have indicated ways in which this ecological theory of ethnic boundary dynamics departs from sociological convention. These include use of a definition of ethnicity that focuses on boundaries rather than cultural content and on competition. To sharpen some distinctions, it is useful to contrast my argument with two recent and important sociological treatments of ethnic conflict: Hechter's analysis of the "cultural division of labor" and Bonacich's use of "split labor market theory."

Hechter (1974a, 1974b) contrasts two models of ethnic change. The functionalist theory argues that increasing social differentiation eliminates ethnic diversity. The so-called reactive theories argue that ethnicity is not threatened by contact with other populations; rather, ethnic boundaries are strengthened as a consequence of intense interaction with other populations. Hechter's specific reactive theory focuses on the role of ethnicity in the stratification system. He argues that ethnic solidarity arises from a cultural division of labor. Labor can be said to be culturally divided "when individuals are assigned to specific types of occupations and other social roles on the basis of observable cultural traits" (Hechter 1974b, 1154). In other words, ethnic solidarity is assumed to be most intense when culturally distinguishable populations occupy nonoverlapping segments of the occupational distribution.

Bonacich (1972, 1975) makes the opposite argument: Ethnic antagonism is most intense when two or more ethnic populations interact in a split labor market. According to Bonacich (1975, 603), "The central tenet of split labor market theory is that, when the price of labor for the same work differs by ethnic group, a three-way conflict develops among business, higher priced labor, and cheaper labor which may result in extreme ethnic antagonism." Note that the concept refers to differences in wage rates for the *same occupations*. So according to this theory, ethnic antagonism and ethnic solidarity are extreme when a cultural division of labor has been broken down. When the different ethnic populations enter the same occupations, the competition is most intense.

My theory agrees with a split labor market theory. It holds that competition is a function of niche overlap. The more similar the occupational distributions of two groups, the greater the competition between them. Bonacich's argument has a second desirable feature: It concerns a three-way competitive relationship. One cannot understand the dynamics of the competition between two ethnically distinct populations of laborers without considering the role of ownership. More important, the competition between any two elements in this system would be fundamentally altered by the elimination of the third from the system. The ecological theory of ethnic boundary dynamics suggests that processes of ethnic competition are complex. The formal theory (Hannan 1979) provides a convenient representation of the dynamics of N-party competitive processes. But there is a sense in which my argument demands a more comprehensive model of competition.

When this essay was first published, virtually all sociological treatments of ethnic competition treated ethnicity as primordial. Most dealt only with the case in which ethnic diversity arises due to immigration. In these cases, ethnic boundaries are unambiguous and the actors in the competitive play clearly defined. I have considered more complex situations, characterized by multiple levels of ethnic boundaries; in these situations, it is important to consider simultaneously two types of competition: (1) competition among ethnically organized populations and (2) competition among ethnic organizations for members. While ethnic populations compete for power and scarce resources, within each population there is competition among forms of organization for the time and commitment of potential members. In short, I argue that we should consider competition both among actual social organizations and among actual and potential forms of organization.[1]

Notes

Francois Nielsen, Jacques Delacroix, John W. Meyer, John Boli-Bennett, Richard Rubinson, and Susan Olzak made very helpful comments on drafts of the original essay. Susan Olzak also made helpful comments on a draft of the abridged version.

1. Since this paper first appeared, theories of ethnic competition have made much progress, especially in explicating the relationship between ethnic competition and ethnic conflict. Moreover, recent research has made clear that ethnic collective action and ethnic conflict are especially sensitive to changes in ethnic stratification systems (e.g., the breakdown of a cultural division of labor). See Nagel and Olzak (1982), Nielsen (1985), and Olzak (1992).

References

Barth, Fredrik. 1956. "Ecologic Relationships of Ethnic Groups in Swat, North Pakistan." *American Anthropologist* 58:1079–1089.

———. 1969. "Introduction." Pp. 9–38 in Fredrik Barth, ed., *Ethnic Groups and Boundaries*. Boston: Little, Brown.

Bendix, Reinhard. 1964. *Nation-Building and Citizenship*. New York: Wiley.

Bonacich, Edna. 1972. "A Theory of Ethnic Antagonism: The Split Labor Market." *American Sociological Review* 37:547–559.

———. 1975. "Abolition, the Extension of Slavery, and the Position of Free Blacks: A Study of Split Labor Markets in the United States, 1830–1863." *American Journal of Sociology* 81:601–628.

Haaland, Gunnar. 1969. "Economic Determinants in Ethnic Processes." Pp. 58–73 in Fredrik Barth, ed., *Ethnic Groups and Boundaries*. Boston: Little, Brown.

Hannan, Michael T. 1979. "The Dynamics of Ethnic Boundaries in Modern States." Pp. 253–275 in John W. Meyer and Michael T. Hannan, eds., *National Development and the World System*. Chicago: University of Chicago Press.

Hannan, Michael T., and John Freeman. 1977. "The Population Ecology of Organizations." *American Journal of Sociology* 82:929–964.

Hechter, Michael. 1974a. "The Political Economy of Ethnic Change." *American Journal of Sociology* 79:1151–1178.

———. 1974b. *Internal Colonialism: The Celtic Fringe in British National Development 1536–1966*. Berkeley: University of California Press.

Horowitz, Donald L. 1975. "Ethnic Identity." Pp. 111–140 in Nathan Glazer and Daniel P. Moynihan, eds., *Ethnicity: Theory and Experience*. Cambridge: Harvard University Press.

May, Robert M. 1973. *Stability and Complexity in Model Ecosystems*. Princeton: Princeton University Press.

Nagel, Joanne, and Susan Olzak. 1982. "Ethnic Mobilization in New and Old States: An Extension of the Competition Model." *Social Problems* 30:127–143.

Nielsen, François. 1980. "The Flemish Movement in Belgium After World War II: A Dynamic Analysis." *American Sociological Review* 45:76–94.

———. 1985. "Ethnic Solidarity in Modern Societies." *American Sociological Review* 50:133–145.

Olzak, Susan. 1992. *Dynamics of Ethnic Competition and Conflict*. Stanford: Stanford University Press.

Rokkan, Stein. 1975. "Dimensions of State Formation and Nation-building: A Possible Paradigm for Research on Variations Within Europe." Pp. 562–600 in Charles Tilly, ed., *The Formation of National States in Western Europe*. Princeton: Princeton University Press.

Simon, Herbert A. 1973. "The Organization of Complex Systems." Pp. 3–27 in Howard H. Patee, ed., *Hierarchy Theory*. New York: George Braziller.

ALEJANDRO PORTES AND ROBERT D. MANNING

The Immigrant Enclave: Theory and Empirical Examples

I. Introduction

The purpose of this chapter is to review existing theories about the process of immigrant adaptation to a new society and to recapitulate the empirical findings that have led to an emerging perspective on the topic. This emerging view revolves around the concepts of different modes of structural incorporation and of the immigrant enclave as one of them. These concepts are set in explicit opposition to two previous viewpoints on the adaptation process, generally identified as assimilation theory and the segmented labor markets approach.

The study of immigrant groups in the United States has produced a copious historical and sociological literature, written mostly from the assimilation perspective. Although the experiences of particular groups varied, the common theme of these writings is the unrelenting efforts of immigrant minorities to surmount obstacles impeding their entry into the "mainstream" of American society (Handlin, 1941, 1951; Wittke, 1952; Child, 1943; Vecoli, 1977). From this perspective, the adaptation process of particular immigrant groups followed a sequential path from initial economic hardship and discrimination to eventual socioeconomic mobility arising from increasing knowledge of American culture and acceptance by the host society (Warner and Srole, 1945; Gordon, 1964; Sowell, 1981). The focus on a "core" culture, the emphasis on consensus-building, and the assumption of a basic patterned sequence of adaptation represent central elements of assimilation theory.

From this perspective, the failure of individual immigrants or entire ethnic groups to move up through the social hierarchies is linked either to their reluctance to shed traditional values or to the resistance of the native majority to accept them because of racial, religious, or other shortcomings. Hence, successful adaptation depends, first of all, on the willingness of immigrants to relinquish a "backward" way of life and, second, on their acquisition of characteristics making them acceptable to the host society (Eisenstadt, 1970). Throughout, the emphasis is placed on the social psychological processes of motivation, learning, and interaction and on the cultural values and perceptions of the immigrants themselves and those who surround them.

The second general perspective takes issue with this psychosocial and culturalist orientation as well as with the assumption of a single basic assimilation path. This alternative view begins by noting that immigrants and their descendants do not necessarily "melt" into the mainstream and that many groups seem not to want to do so, preferring instead to preserve their distinct ethnic identities (Greeley, 1971; Glazer and Moynihan, 1970). A number of writers have focused on the resilience of these communities and described their functions as sources of mutual support and collective political power (Suttles, 1968; Alba and Chamlin, 1983; Parenti, 1967). Others have gone beyond descriptive accounts and attempted to establish the causes of the persistence of ethnicity.

Without exception, these writers have identified the roots of the phenomenon in the economic sphere and, more specifically, in the labor-market roles that immigrants have been called on to play.

Within this general perspective, several specific theoretical approaches exist. The first focuses on the situation of the so-called unmeltable ethnics—blacks, Chicanos, and American Indians—and finds the source of their plight in a history of internal colonialism during which these groups have been confined to specific areas and made to work under uniquely unfavorable conditions. In a sense, the role of colonized minorities has been to bypass the free labor market, yielding in the process distinct benefits both to direct employers of their labor and, indirectly, to other members of the dominant racial group (Blauner, 1972; Geschwender, 1978). The continuation of colonialist practices to our day explains, according to this view, the spatial isolation and occupational disadvantages of these minorities (Barrera, 1980).

A second approach attempts to explain the persistence of ethnic politics and ethnic mobilization on the basis of the organization of subordinate groups to combat a "cultural division of labor." The latter confined members of specific minorities to a quasi-permanent situation of exploitation and social inferiority. Unlike the first view, this second approach does not envision the persistence of ethnicity as a consequence of continuing exploitation, but rather as a "reactive formation" on the part of the minority to reaffirm its identity and its interests (Hechter, 1977; Despres, 1975). For this reason, ethnic mobilizations are often most common among groups who have already abandoned the bottom of the social ladder and started to compete for positions of advantage with members of the majority (Nagel and Olzak, 1982).

A final variant focuses on the situation of contemporary immigrants to the United States. Drawing on the dual labor market literature, this approach views recent immigrants as the latest entrants into the lower tier of a segmented labor market where women and other minorities already predominate. Relative to the latter, immigrants possess the advantages of their lack of experience in the new country, their legal vulnerability, and their greater initial motivation. All of these traits translate into higher productivity and lower labor costs for the firms that employ them (Sassen-Koob, 1980). Jobs in the secondary labor market are poorly paid, require few skills, and offer limited mobility opportunities. Hence, confinement of immigrants to this sector insures that those who do not return home are relegated to a quasi-permanent status as disadvantaged and discriminated minorities (Piore, 1975, 1979).

What these various structural theories have in common is the view of resilient ethnic communities formed as the result of a consistently disadvantageous economic position and the consequent absence of a smooth path of assimilation. These situations, ranging from slave labor to permanent confinement to the secondary labor market, are not altered easily. They have given rise, in time, either to hopeless communities of "unmeltable" ethnics or to militant minorities, conscious of a common identity and willing to support a collective strategy of self-defense rather than rely on individual assimilation.

These structural theories have provided an effective critique of the excessively benign image of the adaptation process presented by earlier writings. However, while undermining the former, the new structural perspective may have erred in the opposite direction. The basic hypothesis advanced in this chapter is that several identifiable modes of labor-market incorporation exist and that not all of them relegate newcomers to a permanent situation of exploitation and inferiority. Thus, while agreeing with the basic thrust of structural theories, we propose several modifications that are necessary for an adequate understanding of the different types of immigrant flows and their distinct processes of adaptation.

II. Modes of Incorporation

In the four decades since the end of World War II, immigration to the United States has experienced a vigorous surge reaching levels comparable only to those at the beginning of the century (National Research Council, 1985, chapter 2). Even if one restricts attention to this movement, disregarding multiple other migrations elsewhere in the world, it is not the case that the inflow has been of a homogeneous character. Low-wage labor immigration itself has taken different forms, including temporary contract flows, undocumented entries, and legal immigration. More importantly, it is not the case that all immigrants have been directed to the secondary labor market. For example, since the promulgation of the Immigration Act of 1965, thousands of professionals, technicians, and craftsmen have come to the United States, availing themselves of the occupational preference categories of the law. This type of inflow, dubbed "brain drain" in the sending nations, encompasses today sizable contingents of immigrants from such countries as India, South Korea, the Philippines, and Taiwan, each an important contributor to U.S. annual immigration.

The characteristics of this type of migration have been described in detail elsewhere (Portes, 1976, 1981). Two such traits deserve mention, however. First, occupationally skilled immigrants—including doctors, nurses, engineers, technicians, and craftsmen—generally enter the "primary" labor market; they contribute to alleviate domestic shortages in specific occupations and gain access, after a period of time, to the mobility ladders available to native workers. Second, immigration of this type does not generally give rise to spatially concentrated communities; instead, immigrants are dispersed throughout many cities and regions, following different career paths.

Another sizable contingent of entrants whose occupational future is not easily characterized *a priori* are political refugees. Large groups of refugees, primarily from Communist-controlled countries, have come to the United States, first after the occupation of Eastern Europe by the Soviet Army, then after the advent of Fidel Castro to power in Cuba, and finally in the aftermath of the Vietnam War. Unlike purely "economic" immigrants, refugees have often received resettlement assistance from various governmental agencies (Zolberg, 1983; Keely, 1981). All the available evidence runs contrary to the notion of a uniform entry of political refugees into low-wage secondary occupations; on the contrary, there are indications of their employment in many different lines of work.

A third mode of incorporation has gained the attention of a number of scholars in recent years. It consists of small groups of immigrants who are inserted or insert themselves as commercial intermediaries in a particular country or region. These "middleman minorities" are distinct in nationality, culture, and sometimes race from both the superordinate and subordinate groups to which they relate (Bonacich, 1973; Light, 1972). They can be used by dominant elites as a buffer to deflect mass frustration and also as an instrument to conduct commercial activities in impoverished areas. Middlemen accept these risks in exchange for the opportunity to share in the commercial and financial benefits gained through such instruments as taxation, higher retail prices, and usury. Jews in feudal and early modern Europe represent the classic instance of a middleman minority. Other examples include Indian merchants in East Africa, and Chinese entrepreneurs in Southeast Asia and throughout the Pacific Basin (Bonacich and Modell, 1980, chapter 1). Contemporary examples in the United States include Jewish, Korean, and other Oriental merchants in inner-city ghetto areas and Cubans in Puerto Rico (Kim, 1981; Cobas, 1984).

Primary labor immigration and middleman entrepreneurship represent two modes of incorporation that differ from the image of an homogeneous flow into low-wage employment. Political refugees, in turn, have followed a variety of paths, including both of the above as well as insertion into an ethnic enclave economy. The latter represents a fourth distinct mode. Although frequently confused with middleman minorities, the emergence and structure of an immigrant enclave possess distinct characteristics. The latter have significant theoretical and practical implications, for they set apart groups adopting this entry mode from those following alternative paths. We turn now to several examples of immigrant enclaves to clarify their internal dynamics and causes of their emergence.

III. Immigrant Enclaves

Immigration to the United States before World War I was, overwhelmingly, an unskilled labor movement. Impoverished peasants from southern Italy, Poland, and the eastern reaches of the Austro-Hungarian Empire settled in dilapidated and crowded areas, often immediately adjacent to their points of debarcation, and took any menial jobs available. From these harsh beginnings, immigrants commenced a slow and often painful process of acculturation and economic mobility. Theirs was the saga captured by innumerable subsequent volumes written from both the assimilation and the structural perspectives.

Two sizable immigrant groups did not follow this pattern, however. Their most apparent characteristic was the economic success of the first generation, even in the absence of extensive acculturation. On the contrary, both groups struggled fiercely to preserve their cultural identity and internal solidarity. Their approach to adaptation thus directly contradicted subsequent assimilation predictions concerning the causal priority of acculturation to economic mobility. Economic success and "clannishness" also earned for each minority the hostility of the surrounding population. These two immigrant groups did not have a language, religion, or even race in common and they never overlapped in significant numbers in any part of the United States. Yet, arriving at opposite ends of the continent, Jews and Japanese pursued patterns of economic adaptation that were quite similar both in content and in their eventual consequences.

A. Jews in Manhattan

The first major wave of Jewish immigration to the United States consisted of approximately 50,000 newcomers of German origin, arriving between 1840 and 1870. These immigrants went primarily into commerce and achieved, in the course of a few decades, remarkable success. By 1900, the average income of German-Jewish immigrants surpassed that of the American population (Rischin, 1962). Many individuals who started as street peddlers and small merchants had become, by that time, heads of major industrial, retail, and financial enterprises.

The second wave of Jewish immigration exhibited quite different characteristics. Between 1870 and 1914, over two million Jews left the Pale of Settlement and other Russian-dominated regions, escaping Czarist persecution. Major pogroms occurred before and during this exodus (Dinnerstein, 1977). Thus, unlike most immigrants of the period, the migration of Russian and Eastern Europe Jews was politically motivated and their move was much more permanent. In contrast to German Jews, who were relatively well educated, the Yiddish-speaking newcomers came, for the most part, from modest origins and had only a rudimentary education. Although they viewed the new Russian wave with great apprehension, German Jews promptly realized that their future as an ethnic minority depended on the successful integration of the newcomers (Rischin, 1962). Charitable societies were established to provide food, shelter, and other necessities, and private schools were set up to teach immigrants English, civics, and the customs of the new country (Howe and Libo, 1979).

Aside from its size and rapidity of arrival, turn-of-the-century Jewish immigration had two other distinct characteristics. First was its strong propensity toward commerce and self-employment in general in preference to wage labor; as German Jews before them, many Russian immigrants moved directly into street peddling and other commercial activities of the most modest sort. Second was its concentration into a single, densely populated urban area—the lower East Side of Manhattan. Within this area, those who did not become storekeepers and peddlers from the start found employment in factories owned by German Jews, learning the necessary rudiments for future self-employment (Sowell, 1981, chapter 4).

The economic activities of this population created, in the course of two decades, a dense network of industrial, commercial, and financial enterprises. Close physical proximity facilitated exchanges of information and access to credit and raw materials. Characteristic of this emerging Jewish enclave is that production and marketing of goods was not restricted to the ethnic community, but went well beyond it into the general economy. Jews entered the printing, metal, and building trades; they became increasingly prominent in jewelry and cigar-making; above all, the garment industry became the primary domain of Jewish entrepreneurship, with hundreds of firms of all sizes engaged in the trade (Rischin, 1962; Howe and Libo, 1979).

The economic success of many of these ventures did not require and did not entail rapid acculturation. Immigrants learned English and those instrumental aspects of the new culture required for economic advancement. For the rest, they preferred to remain with their own and maintained, for the most part, close adherence to their original religion, language, and values (Wirth, 1956; Howe, 1976). Jewish enclave capitalism depended, for its emergence and advancement, precisely on those resources made available by a solidaristic ethnic community: protected access to labor and markets, informal sources of credit, and business information. It was through these resources that upstart immigrant enterprises could survive and eventually compete effectively with better-established firms in the general economy.

The emergence of a Jewish enclave in East Manhattan helped this group bypass the conventional assimilation path and achieve significant economic mobility in the course of the first generation, well ahead of complete acculturation. Subsequent generations also pursued this path, but the resources accumulated through early immigrant entrepreneurship were dedicated primarily to further the education of children and their entry into the professions. It was at this point that outside hostility became most patent, as one university after another established quotas to prevent the onrush of Jewish students. The last of these quotas did not come to an end until after World War II (Dinnerstein, 1977).

Despite these and other obstacles, the movement of Jews into higher education continued. Building on the economic success of the first generation, subsequent ones achieved levels of education, occupation, and income that significantly exceed the national average (Featherman, 1971; Sowell, 1981, chapter 4). The original enclave is now only a memory, but it provided in its time the necessary platform for furthering the rapid social and economic mobility of the minority. Jews did enter the mainstream of American society, but they did not do so starting uniformly at the bottom, as most immigrant groups had done; instead, they translated resources made available by early ethnic entrepreneurship into rapid access to positions of social prestige and economic advantage.

B. Japanese on the West Coast

The specific features of Japanese immigration differ significantly from the movement of European Jews, but their subsequent adaptation and mobility patterns are similar. Beginning in 1890 and ending with the enactment of the Gentlemen's Agreement of 1908, approximately 150,000 Japanese men immigrated to the West Coast. They were followed primarily by their spouses until the Immigration Act of 1924 banned any further Asiatic immigration. Although nearly 300,000 Japanese immigrants are documented in this period (Daniels, 1977), less than half of this total remained in the United States (Petersen, 1971). This is due, in contrast to the case of the Jews, to the sojourner character of Japanese immigrants: the intention of many was to accumulate sufficient capital for purchasing farm land or settling debts in Japan. Hence this population movement included commercial and other members of the Japanese middle class who, not incidentally, were explicitly sponsored by their national government.

The residential patterns of Japanese immigrants were not as concentrated as those of Jews in Manhattan, but they were geographically clustered. Almost two-thirds of the 111,010 Japanese reported in the U.S. Census of 1920 lived in California. Further, one-third of California's Japanese residents lived in Los Angeles County in 1940, while another one-third lived in six nearby counties (Daniels, 1977). However, it was not the residential segregation of Japanese immigrants but rather their occupational patterns that eventually mobilized the hostility of the local population.

Japanese immigrants were initially welcomed and recruited as a form of cheap agricultural labor. Their reputation as thrifty and diligent workers made them preferable to other labor sources. Nativist hostilities crystallized, however, when Japanese immigrants shifted from wage labor to independent ownership and small-scale farming. This action not only reduced the supply of laborers but it also increased competition for domestic growers in the fresh-produce market. In 1900, only about 40 Japanese farmers in the entire United States leased or owned a total of 5000 acres of farmland. By 1909, the number of Japanese farmers had risen to 6000 and their collective holdings exceeded 210,000 acres (Petersen, 1971). Faced with such "unfair" competition, California growers turned to the political means at their disposal. In 1913, the state legislature passed the first Alien Land Law, which restricted land ownership by foreigners. This legislation did not prove sufficient, however, and, in subsequent years, the ever-accommodating legislature passed a series of acts closing other legal loopholes to Japanese farming (Petersen, 1971).

These proscriptions, which barred most of the Japanese from the lands, accelerated their entry into urban enterprise. In 1909, Japanese entrepreneurs owned almost 3000 small shops in several Western cities. Forty percent of Japanese men in Los Angeles were self-employed. They operated businesses such as dry-cleaning establishments, fisheries, lunch counters, and produce stands that marketed the production of Japanese farms (Light, 1972).

The ability of the first-generation *Issei* to escape the status of stoop labor in agriculture was based on the social cohesion of their community. Rotating credit associations offered scarce venture capital, while mutual-aid organizations provided assistance in operating farms and urban businesses. Light (1972) reports that capitalizations as high as $100,000 were financed through ethnic credit networks. Economic success was again accompanied by limited instrumental acculturation and by careful preservation of national identity and values. It was the availability of investment capital, cooperative business associations, and marketing practices (forward and backward economic linkages) within the ethnic enclave that enabled Japanese entrepreneurs to expand beyond its boundaries and compete effectively in the general economy. This is illustrated by the production and marketing of fresh produce. In 1920, the value of Japanese crops was about 10% of the total for California, when the Japanese comprised less than 1% of the state's population; many retail outlets traded exclusively with a non-Japanese clientele (Light, 1972; Petersen, 1971).

During the early 1940s, the Japanese ethnic economy was seriously disrupted but not eliminated by the property confiscations and camp internments accompanying World War II. After the war, economic prosperity and other factors combined to reduce local hostility toward the Japanese. Older *Issei* and many of their children returned to small business, while other second-generation *Nisei,* like their Jewish predecessors, pursued higher education and entered the white-collar occupations *en masse.* This mobility path was completed by the third or *Sansei* generation, with 88% of their members attending college. Other third-generation Japanese have continued, however, the entrepreneurial tradition of their parents (Bonacich and Modell, 1980). Like Jews before them, Japanese-Americans have made use of the resources made available by early immigrant entrepreneurship to enter the mainstream of society in positions of relative advantage. The mean educational and occupational attainment of the group's 600,000 members surpasses at present all other ethnic and native groups, while its average family income is exceeded among American ethnic groups only by the Jews (Sowell, 1981).[1] ...

IV. Conclusion: A Typology of the Process of Incorporation

We can now attempt a summary description of the characteristics of immigrant enclaves and how they differ from other paths. The emergence of an ethnic enclave economy has three prerequisites: first, the presence of a substantial number of immigrants, with business experience acquired in the sending country; second, the availability of sources of capital; and third, the availability of sources of labor. The latter two conditions are not too difficult to meet. The requisite labor can usually be drawn from family members and, more commonly, from recent arrivals. Surprisingly perhaps, capital is not a major impediment either since the sums initially required are usually small. When immigrants did not bring them from abroad, they could be accumulated through individual savings or pooled resources in the community. It is the first condition that appears critical. The presence of a number of immigrants skilled in what Franklin Frazier (1949) called the art of "buying and selling" is common [not only to the Jewish and Japanese cases reviewed above but also to contemporary enclave economies among Koreans and Cubans]. Such an entrepreneurial–commercial class among early immigrant cohorts can usually overcome other obstacles; conversely, its absence within an immigrant community will confine the community to wage employment even if sufficient resources of capital and labor are available.

Enclave businesses typically start small and cater exclusively to an ethnic clientele. Their expansion and entry into the broader market requires, as seen above, an effective mobilization of community resources. The social mechanism at work here seems to be a strong sense of reciprocity supported by collective solidarity that transcends the purely contractual character of business transactions. For example, receipt of a loan from a rotating credit association entails the duty of continuing to make contributions so that others can have access to the same source of capital. Although, in principle, it would make sense for the individual to withdraw once his loan is received, such action would cut him off from the very sources of community support on which his future business success depends (Light, 1972).

Similarly, relations between enclave employers and employees generally transcend a contractual wage bond. It is understood by both parties that the wage paid is inferior to the value of labor contributed. This is willingly accepted by many immigrant workers because the wage is only *one* form of compensation. Use of their labor represents often the key advantage making poorly capitalized enclave firms competitive. In reciprocity, employers are expected to respond to emergency needs of their workers and to promote their advancement through such means as on-the-job training, advancement to supervisory positions, and aid when they move into self-employment. These opportunities represent the other part of the "wage" received by enclave workers. The informal mobility ladders thus created are, of

course, absent in the secondary labor market where there is no primary bond between owners and workers or no common ethnic community to enforce the norm of reciprocity.

Paternalistic labor relations and strong community solidarity are also characteristic of middleman minorities. Although both modes of incorporation are similar and are thus frequently confused, there are three major structural differences between them. First, immigrant enclaves are not exclusively commercial. Unlike middleman minorities, whose economic role is to mediate commercial and financial transactions between elites and masses, enclave firms include in addition a sizable productive sector. The latter may comprise agriculture, light manufacturing, and construction enterprises; their production, marketed often by coethnic intermediaries, is directed toward the general economy and not exclusively to the immigrant community.

Second, relationships between enclave businesses and established native ones are problematic. Middleman groups tend to occupy positions complementary and subordinate to the local owning class; they fill economic niches either disdained or feared by the latter. Unlike them, enclave enterprises often enter in direct competition with existing domestic firms. There is no evidence, for example, that domestic elites deliberately established or supported the emergence of the Jewish, Japanese, Korean, or Cuban business communities as means to further their own economic interests. There is every indication, on the other hand, that this mode of incorporation was largely self-created by the immigrants, often in opposition to powerful domestic interests. Although it is true that enclave entrepreneurs have been frequently employed as subcontractors by outside firms in such activities as garment and construction (Bonacich, 1978), it is incorrect to characterize this role as the exclusive or dominant one among these enterprises.

Third, the enclave is concentrated and spatially identifiable. By the very nature of their activities, middleman minorities must often be dispersed among the mass of the population. Although the immigrants may live in certain limited areas, their businesses require proximity to their mass clientele and a measure of physical dispersion within it. It is true that middleman activities such as money-lending have been associated in several historical instances with certain streets and neighborhoods, but this is not a necessary or typical pattern. Street peddling and other forms of petty commerce require merchants to go into the areas where demand exists and avoid excessive concentration of the goods and services they offer. This is the typical pattern found today among middleman minorities in American cities (Cobas, 1984; Kim, 1981).

Enclave businesses, on the other hand, are spatially concentrated, especially in their early stages. This is so for three reasons: first, the need for proximity to the ethnic market which they initially serve; second, proximity to each other which facilitates exchange of information, access to credit, and other supportive activities; third, proximity to ethnic labor supplies on which they crucially depend. Unlike the Jewish, Korean, or Cuban cases, the Japanese enclave economy does partially depart from the pattern of high physical concentration. This can be attributed to the political persecution to which this group was subjected. Originally, Japanese concentration was a rural phenomenon based on small farms linked together by informal bonds and cooperative associations. Forced removal of this minority from the land compelled their entry into urban businesses and their partial dispersal into multiple activities.

Physical concentration of enclaves underlies their final characteristic. Once an enclave economy has fully developed, it is possible for a newcomer to live his life entirely within the confines of the community. Work, education, and access to health care, recreation, and a variety of other services can be found without leaving the bounds of the ethnic economy. This institutional completeness is what enables new immigrants to move ahead economically, despite very limited knowledge of the host culture and language. Supporting empirical evidence comes from studies showing low levels of English knowledge among enclave minorities and the absence of a net effect of knowledge of English on their average income levels (Light, 1980; Portes and Bach, 1985).

Table 1 summarizes this discussion by presenting the different modes of incorporation and their principal characteristics. Two caveats are necessary. First, this typology is not exhaustive, since other forms of adaptation have existed and will undoubtedly emerge in the future. Second, political refugees are not included, since this entry label does not necessarily entail a unique adaptation path. Instead, refugees can select or be channelled in many different directions, including self-employment, access to primary labor markets, or confinement to secondary sector occupations.

Having discussed the characteristics of enclaves and middleman minorities, a final word must be said about the third alternative to employment in the lower tier of a dual labor market. As a mode of incorporation, primary sector immigration also has distinct advantages, although they are of a different order from those pursued by "entrepreneurial" minorities. Dispersal throughout the receiving country and career mobility based on standard promotion criteria makes it imperative for immigrants in this mode to become fluent in the new language and culture (Stevens, Goodman, and Mick, 1978). Without a supporting ethnic community, the second generation also becomes thoroughly steeped in the ways of the host society. Primary sector immigration thus tends to lead to very rapid social and cultural integration. It represents the path that approximates most closely the predictions of assimilation theory with regard to (1) the necessity of acculturation for social and economic progress and (2) the subsequent rewards received by immigrants and their descendants for shedding their ethnic identities.

Clearly, however, this mode of incorporation is open only to a minority of immigrant groups. In addition, acculturation of professionals and other primary sector immigrants is qualitatively different from that undergone by others. Regardless of their differences, immigrants in other modes tend to learn the new language and culture with a heavy "local" content. Although acculturation may be slow, especially in the case of enclave groups, it carries with it elements unique to the surrounding community—its language inflections, particular traditions, and loyalties (Greeley, 1971; Suttles, 1968). On the contrary, acculturation of primary sector immigrants is of a more cosmopolitan sort. Because career requirements

TABLE 1

Typology of Modes of Incorporation

Variable	Primary sector immigration	Secondary sector immigration	Immigrant enclaves	Middleman minorities
Size of immigrant population	Small	Large	Large	Small
Spatial concentration, national	Dispersed	Dispersed	Concentrated	Concentrated
Spatial concentration, local	Dispersed	Concentrated	Concentrated	Dispersed
Original class composition	Homogeneous: skilled workers and professionals	Homogeneous: manual laborers	Heterogeneous: entrepreneurs, professionals, and workers	Homogeneous: merchants and some professionals
Present occupational status distribution	High mean status/low variance	Low mean status/low variance	Mean status/high variance	Mean status/low variance
Mobility opportunities	High: formal promotion ladders	Low	High: informal ethnic ladders	Average: informal ethnic ladders
Institutional diversification of ethnic community	None	Low: weak social institutions	High: institutional completeness	Medium: strong social and economic institutions
Participation in ethnic organizations	Little or none	Low	High	High
Resilience of ethnic culture	Low	Average	High	High
Knowledge of host country language	High	Low	Low	High
Knowledge of host country institutions	High	Low	Average	High
Modal reaction of host community	Acceptance	Discrimination	Hostility	Mixed: elite acceptance/mass hostility

often entail physical mobility, the new language and culture are learned more rapidly and more generally, without strong attachments to a particular community. Thus, while minorities entering menial labor, enclave, or middleman enterprise in the United States have eventually become identified with a certain city or region, the same is not true for immigrant professionals, who tend to "disappear," in a cultural sense, soon after their arrival (Stevens *et al.*, 1978; Cardona and Cruz, 1980).

Awareness of patterned differences among immigrant groups in their forms of entry and labor market incorporation represents a significant advance, in our view, from earlier undifferentiated descriptions of the adaptation process. This typology is, however, a provisional effort. Just as detailed research on the condition of particular minorities modified or replaced earlier broad generalizations, the propositions advanced here will require revision. New groups arriving in the United States at present and a revived interest in immigration should provide the required incentive for empirical studies and theoretical advances in the future.

Notes

[1]. The original article from which this excerpt was drawn includes a further discussion of contemporary Korean and Cuban enclaves.—ED.

References

Alba, Richard D., and Chamlin, Mitchell B. (1983). Ethnic identification among whites. *American Sociological Review* 48:240–47.

Barrera, Mario (1980). *Race and class in the Southwest: A theory of racial inequality.* Notre Dame, Indiana: Notre Dame University Press.

Blauner, Robert (1972). *Racial oppression in America.* New York: Harper and Row.

Bonacich, Edna (1973). A theory of middleman minorities. *American Sociological Review* 38(October):583–594.

Bonacich, Edna (1978). U.S. capitalism and Korean immigrant small business. Riverside, California: Department of Sociology, University of California—Riverside, mimeographed.

Bonacich, Edna, and Modell, John (1980). *The economic basis of ethnic solidarity: Small business in the Japanese-American community.* Berkeley, California: University of California Press.

Cardona, Ramiro C., and Cruz, Carmen I. (1980). *El exodo de Colombianos.* Bogota: Ediciones Tercer Mundo.

Child, Irving L. (1943). *Italian or American? The second generation in conflict.* New Haven, Connecticut: Yale University Press.

Cobas, Jose (1984). Participation in the ethnic economy, ethnic solidarity and ambivalence toward the host society: The case of Cuban emigres in Puerto Rico. Presented at the American Sociological Association Meeting, San Antonio, Texas (August).

Daniels, Roger (1977). The Japanese-American experience: 1890–1940. In *Uncertain Americans* (L. Dinnerstein and F. C. Jaher, eds.), pp. 250–267. New York: Oxford University Press.

Despres, Leo (1975). Toward a theory of ethnic phenomena. In *Ethnicity and resource competition* (Leo Despres, ed.), pp. 209–212. The Hague: Mouton.

Dinnerstein, Leonard (1977). The East European Jewish migration. In *Uncertain Americans* (L. Dinnerstein and F. C. Jaher, eds.), pp. 216–231. New York: Oxford University Press.

Eisenstadt, S. N. (1970). The process of absorbing new immigrants in Israel. In *Integration and development in Israel* (S. N. Eisenstadt, RivKah Bar Yosef, and Chaim Adler, eds.), pp. 341–367. Jerusalem: Israel University Press.

Featherman, David L. (1971). The socio-economic achievement of white religio-ethnic sub-groups: Social and psychological explanations. *American Sociological Review* 36(April):207–222.

Frazier, E. Franklin (1949). *The Negro in the United States.* New York: Macmillan.

Geschwender, James A. (1978). *Racial stratification in America.* Dubuque, Iowa: William C. Brown.

Glazer, Nathan, and Moynihan, Daniel P. (1970). *Beyond the melting pot: The Negroes, Puerto Ricans, Jews, Italians and Irish of New York City.* Cambridge, Massachusetts: M.I.T. Press.

Gordon, Milton M. (1964). *Assimilation in American life: The role of race, religion, and national origins.* New York: Oxford University Press.

Greeley, Andrew (1971). *Why can't they be like us? America's white ethnic groups.* New York: Dutton.

Handlin, Oscar (1941). *Boston's immigrants: A study of acculturation.* Cambridge: Harvard University Press.

Handlin, Oscar (1951). *The uprooted: The epic story of the great migrations that made the American people.* Boston: Little Brown.

Hechter, Michael (1977). *Internal colonialism, the Celtic fringe in British national development, 1536–1966.* Berkeley, California: University of California Press.

Howe, Irving (1976). *World of our fathers.* New York: Harcourt, Brace, Jovanovich.

Howe, Irving, and Libo, Kenneth (1979). *How we lived, a documentary history of immigrant Jews in America.* New York: Richard March.

Keely, Charles B. (1981). *Global refugee policy: The case for a development-oriented strategy.* New York: The Population Council.

Kim, Illsoo (1981). *New urban immigrants, the Korean community in New York.* Princeton, New Jersey: Princeton University Press.

Light, H. Ivan (1972). *Ethnic enterprise in America: Business and welfare among Chinese, Japanese, and Blacks.* Berkeley, California: University of California Press.

Light, H. Ivan (1980). Asian enterprise in America: Chinese, Japanese, and Koreans in small business. In *Self-help in urban America* (Scott Cummings, ed.) pp. 33–57. New York: Kennikat Press.

Nagel, Joane, and Olzak, Susan (1982). Ethnic mobilization in new and old states: An extension of the competition model. *Social Problems* 30:127–143.

National Research Council (1985). Immigration statistics: A story of neglect. Report of the Panel on Immigration Statistics. Washington, D.C.: National Academy of Sciences.

Parenti, Michael (1967). Ethnic politics and the persistence of ethnic identification. *American Political Science Review* 61:717–726.

Petersen, William (1971). *Japanese Americans, oppression and success.* New York: Random House.

Piore, Michael J. (1975). Notes for a theory of labor market stratification. In *Labor market segmentation* (Richard C. Edwards, Michael Reich, and David M. Gordon, eds.), pp. 125–171. Lexington, Massachusetts: Heath.

Piore, Michael J. (1979). *Birds of passage, migrant labor and industrial societies.* New York: Cambridge University Press.

Portes, Alejandro (1976). Determinants of the brain drain. *International Migration Review* 10(Winter):489–508.

Portes, Alejandro (1981). Modes of structural incorporation and theories of labor immigration. In *Global Trends in Migration, Theory and Research on International Population Movements* (Mary M. Kritz, Charles B. Keely, and Silvano M. Tomasi, eds.), pp. 279–297. New York: Center for Migration Studies.

Portes, Alejandro, and Bach, Robert L. (1985). *Latin journey, Cuban and Mexican immigrants in the United States.* Berkeley, California: University of California Press.

Rischin, Moses (1962). *The promised city, New York Jews 1870–1914.* Cambridge, Mass.: Harvard University Press.

Sassen-Koob, Saskia (1980). Immigrant and minority workers in the organization of the labor process. *Journal of Ethnic Studies* (1/Spring):1–34.

Sowell, Thomas (1981). *Ethnic America: A history.* New York: Basic Books.

Stevens, Rosemary, Goodman, Louis W., and Mick, Stephen (1978). *The alien doctors, foreign medical graduates in American hospitals.* New York: Wiley.

Suttles, Gerald D. (1968). *The social order of the slum, ethnicity and territory in the inner city.* Chicago: University of Chicago Press.

Vecoli, Rudolph (1977). The Italian Americans. In *Uncertain Americans* (L. Dinnerstein and F. C. Jaher, eds.), pp. 201–215. New York: Oxford University Press.

Warner, W. Lloyd, and Srole, Leo (1945). *The social systems of American ethnic groups.* New Haven: Yale University Press.

Wirth, Louis (1956). *The ghetto.* Chicago: University of Chicago Press.

Wittke, Carl (1952). *Refugees of revolution: The German Forty-eighters in America.* Philadelphia: University of Pennsylvania Press.

Zolberg, Aristide (1983). Contemporary transnational migrations in historical perspective: Patterns and dilemmas. In *U.S. immigration and refugee policy* (Mary M. Kritz, ed.), pp. 15–51. Lexington, Massachusetts: Heath.

WILLIAM JULIUS WILSON

The Declining Significance of Race: Blacks and Changing American Institutions

Race relations in America have undergone fundamental changes in recent years, so much so that now the life chances of individual blacks have more to do with their economic class position than with their day-to-day encounters with whites. In earlier years the systematic efforts of whites to suppress blacks were obvious to even the most insensitive observer. Blacks were denied access to valued and scarce resources through various ingenious schemes of racial exploitation, discrimination, and segregation, schemes that were reinforced by elaborate ideologies of racism. But the situation has changed. However determinative such practices were for the previous efforts of the black population to achieve racial equality, and however significant they were in the creation of poverty-stricken ghettoes and a vast underclass of black proletarians—that massive population at the very bottom of the social class ladder plagued by poor education and low-paying, unstable jobs—they do not provide a meaningful explanation of the life chances of black Americans today. The traditional patterns of interaction between blacks and whites, particularly in the labor market, have been fundamentally altered.

In the antebellum period, and in the latter half of the nineteenth century through the first half of the twentieth century, the continuous and explicit efforts of whites to construct racial barriers profoundly affected the lives of black Americans. Racial oppression was deliberate, overt, and is easily documented, ranging from slavery to segregation, from the endeavors of the white economic elite to exploit black labor to the actions of the white masses to eliminate or neutralize black competition, particularly economic competition.[1] As the nation has entered the latter half of the twentieth century, however, many of the traditional barriers have crumbled under the weight of the political, social, and economic changes of the civil rights era. A new set of obstacles has emerged from basic structural shifts in the economy. These obstacles are therefore impersonal but may prove to be even more formidable for certain segments of the black population. Specifically, whereas the previous barriers were usually designed to control and restrict the entire black population, the new barriers create hardships essentially for the black underclass; whereas the old barriers were based explicitly on racial motivations derived from intergroup contact, the new barriers have racial significance only in their consequences, not in their origins. In short, whereas the old barriers bore the pervasive features of racial oppression, the new barriers indicate an important and emerging form of class subordination.

It would be shortsighted to view the traditional forms of racial segregation and discrimination as having essentially disappeared in contemporary America; the presence of blacks is still firmly resisted in various institutions and social arrangements, for example, residential areas and private social clubs. However, in the economic sphere, class has become more important than race in determining black access to privilege and power. It is clearly evident in this connection that many talented and educated blacks are now entering positions of prestige and influence at a rate comparable to or, in some situations, exceeding that of whites with equivalent qualifications. It is equally clear that the black underclass is in a hopeless state of economic stagnation, falling further and further behind the rest of society. ...

Three Stages of American Race Relations

My basic thesis is that American society has experienced three major stages of black-white contact and that each stage embodies a different form of racial stratification structured by the particular arrangement of both the economy and the polity. Stage one coincides with antebellum slavery and the early post-bellum era and may be designated the period of *plantation economy and racial-caste oppression*. Stage two begins in the last quarter of the nineteenth century and ends at roughly the New Deal era and may be identified as the period of *industrial expansion, class conflict, and racial oppression*. Finally, stage three is associated with the modern, industrial, post–World War II era, which really began to crystallize during the 1960s and 1970s, and may be characterized as the period of *progressive transition from racial inequalities to class inequalities*. For the sake of brevity I shall identify the different periods respectively as the preindustrial, industrial, and modern industrial stages of American race relations.

Although this abbreviated designation of the periods of American race relations seems to relate racial change to fundamental economic changes rather directly, it bears repeating that the different stages of race relations are structured by the unique arrangements and interactions of the economy and the polity. Although I stress the economic basis of structured racial inequality in the preindustrial and industrial periods of race relations, I also attempt to show how the polity more or less interacted with the economy either to reinforce patterns of racial stratification or to mediate various forms of racial conflict. Moreover, for the modern industrial period, I try to show how race relations have been shaped as much by important economic changes as by important political changes. Indeed, it would not be possible to understand fully the subtle and manifest changes in race relations in the modern in-

dustrial period without recognizing the dual and often reciprocal influence of structural changes in the economy and political changes in the state. Thus, my central argument is that different systems of production and/or different arrangements of the polity have imposed different constraints on the way in which racial groups have interacted in the United States, constraints that have structured the relations between racial groups and that have produced dissimilar contexts not only for the manifestation of racial antagonisms but also for racial group access to rewards and privileges.

In contrast to the modern industrial period in which fundamental economic and political changes have made economic class affiliation more important than race in determining Negro prospects for occupational advancement, the preindustrial and industrial periods of black-white relations have one central feature in common, namely, overt efforts of whites to solidify economic racial domination (ranging from the manipulation of black labor to the neutralization or elimination of black economic competition) through various forms of juridical, political, and social discrimination. Since racial problems during these two periods were principally related to group struggles over economic resources, they readily lend themselves to the economic class theories of racial antagonisms that associate racial antipathy with class conflict. A brief consideration of these theories, followed by a discussion of their basic weaknesses, will help to raise a number of theoretical issues that will be useful for analyzing the dynamics of racial conflict in the preindustrial and industrial stages of American race relations. However, in a later section of this chapter I shall attempt to explain why these theories are not very relevant to the modern industrial stage of American race relations.

Economic Class Theories

Students of race relations have paid considerable attention to the economic basis of racial antagonism in recent years, particularly to the theme that racial problems in historical situations are related to the more general problems of economic class conflict. A common assumption of this theme is that racial conflict is merely a special manifestation of class conflict. Accordingly, ideologies of racism, racial prejudices, institutionalized discrimination, segregation, and other factors that reinforce or embody racial stratification are seen as simply part of a superstructure determined and shaped by the particular arrangement of the class structure.[2] However, given this basic assumption, which continues to be the most representative and widely used economic class argument,[3] proponents have advanced two major and somewhat divergent explanations of how class conflicts actually shape and determine racial relations—the orthodox Marxist theory of capitalist exploitation,[4] and the *split labor-market theory* of working class antagonisms.[5]

The orthodox Marxist theory, which is the most popular variant of the Marxists' explanations of race,[6] postulates that because the ultimate goal of the capitalist class is to maximize profits, efforts will be made to suppress workers' demands for increased wages and to weaken their bargaining power by promoting divisions within their ranks. The divisions occur along racial lines to the extent that the capitalist class is able to isolate the lower-priced black labor force by not only supporting job, housing, and educational discrimination against blacks, but also by developing or encouraging racial prejudices and ideologies of racial subjugation such as racism. The net effect of such a policy is to insure a marginal working class of blacks and to establish a relatively more privileged position for the established white labor force. Since discrimination guarantees a situation where the average wage rate of the black labor force is less than the average wage rate of the established white labor force, the probability of labor solidarity against the capitalist class is diminished.

At the same time, orthodox Marxists argue, the members of the capitalist class benefit not only because they have created a reserved army of labor that is not united against them and the appropriation of surplus from the black labor force is greater than the exploitation rate of the white labor force,[7] but also because they can counteract ambitious claims of the white labor force for higher wages either by threatening to increase the average wage rate of black workers or by replacing segments of the white labor force with segments of the black labor force in special situations such as strikes. The weaker the national labor force, the more likely it is that it will be replaced by lower-paid black labor especially during organized strikes demanding wage increases and improved working conditions. In short, orthodox Marxists argue that racial antagonism is designed to be a "mask for privilege" that effectively conceals the efforts of the ruling class to exploit subordinate minority groups and divide the working class.

In interesting contrast to the orthodox Marxist approach, the split labor-market theory posits the view that rather than attempting to protect a segment of the laboring class, business "supports a liberal or *laissez faire* ideology that would permit all workers to compete freely in an open market. Such open competition would displace higher paid labor. Only under duress does business yield to a labor aristocracy [i.e., a privileged position for white workers]."[8]

The central hypothesis of the split labor-market theory is that racial antagonism first develops in a labor market split along racial lines. The term "antagonism" includes all aspects of intergroup conflict, from beliefs and ideologies (e.g., racism), to overt behavior (e.g., discrimination), to institutions (e.g., segregationist laws). A split labor market occurs when the price of labor for the same work differs for at least two groups, or would differ if they performed the same work. The price of labor "refers to labor's total cost to the employer, including not only wages, but the cost of recruitment, transportation, room and board, education, health care (if the employer must bear these), and the cost of labor unrest."[9]

There are three distinct classes in a split labor market: (1) business or employers; (2) higher-paid labor; and (3) cheaper labor. Conflict develops between these three classes because of different interests. The main goal of business or employers is to maintain as cheap a labor force as possible in order to compete effectively with other businesses and to maximize economic returns. Employers will often import laborers from other areas if local labor costs are too high or if there is a labor shortage. Whenever a labor shortage exists, higher-paid labor is in a good bargaining position. Accordingly, if business is able to attract cheaper labor to the market place, the interests of higher-paid labor are threatened. They may lose some of the privileges they enjoy, they may lose their bargaining power, and they may even lose their jobs. Moreover, the presence of cheaper labor in a particular job market may not only represent actual competition but potential competition as well. An "insignificant trickle" could be seen as the beginning of a major immigration. If the labor market is split along ethnic lines, for example, if higher-paid labor is white and lower-paid labor is black, class antagonisms are transformed into racial antagonisms. Thus, "while much rhetoric of ethnic antagonism concentrates on ethnicity and race, it really in large measure (though probably not entirely) expresses this class conflict."[10]

In some cases members of the lower-paid laboring class, either from within the territorial boundaries of a given country or from another country, are drawn into or motivated to enter a labor market because they feel they can improve their standard of living. As Edna Bonacich points out, "the poorer the economy of the recruits, the less the inducement needed for them to enter the new labor market."[11] In other cases, individuals are forced into a new labor-market situation, such as the involuntary migration of blacks into a condition of slavery in the United States. In this connection, the greater the employer's control over lower-priced labor, the more threatening is lower-paid labor to higher-paid labor.

However, if more expensive labor is strong enough, that is, if it possesses the power resources to preserve its economic interests, it can prevent being replaced or undercut by cheaper labor. On the one hand it can exclude lower-paid labor from a given territory. "Exclusion movements clearly serve the interests of higher paid labor. Its standards are protected, while the capitalist class is deprived of cheaper labor."[12] On the other hand, if it is not possible for higher-paid labor to rely on exclusion (cheaper labor may be indigenous to the territory or may have been imported early in business-labor relations when higher-paid labor could not prevent the move) then it will institutionalize a system of ethnic stratification which could (1) monopolize skilled positions, thereby

ensuring the effectiveness of strike action; (2) prevent cheaper labor from developing the skills necessary to compete with higher-paid labor (for example, by imposing barriers to equal access to education); and (3) deny cheaper labor the political resources that would enable them to undercut higher-paid labor through, say, governmental regulations. "In other words, the solution to the devastating potential of weak, cheap labor is, paradoxically, to weaken them further, until it is no longer in business' immediate interest to use them as replacement."[13] Thus, whereas orthodox Marxist arguments associate the development and institutionalization of racial stratification with the motivations and activities of the capitalist class, the split labor-market theory traces racial stratification directly to the powerful, higher-paid working class.

Implicit in both of these economic class theories is a power-conflict thesis associating the regulation of labor or wages with properties (ownership of land or capital, monopolization of skilled positions) that determine the scope and degree of a group's ability to influence behavior in the labor market. Furthermore, both theories clearly demonstrate the need to focus on the different ways and situations in which various segments of the dominant racial group perceive and respond to the subordinate racial group. However, as I examine the historical stages of race relations in the United States, I find that the patterns of black/white interaction do not consistently and sometimes do not conveniently conform to the propositions outlined in these explanations of racial antagonism. In some cases, the orthodox Marxian explanation seems more appropriate; in other instances, the split labor-market theory seems more appropriate; and in still others, neither theory can, in isolation, adequately explain black-white conflict.

If we restrict our attention for the moment to the struggle over economic resources, then the general pattern that seems to have characterized race relations in the United States during the preindustrial and industrial stages was that the economic elite segments of the white population have been principally responsible for those forms of racial inequality that entail the exploitation of labor (as in slavery), whereas whites in the lower strata have been largely responsible for those forms of imposed racial stratification that are designed to eliminate economic competition (as in job segregation). Moreover, in some situations, the capitalist class and white workers form an alliance to keep blacks suppressed. Accordingly, restrictive arguments to the effect that racial stratification was the work of the capitalist class or was due to the "victory" of higher-paid white labor obscure the dynamics of complex and variable patterns of black-white interaction.

However, if we ignore the more categorical assertions that attribute responsibility for racial stratification to a particular class and focus seriously on the analyses of interracial contact in the labor market, then I will be able to demonstrate that, depending on the historical situation, each of the economic class theories provides arguments that help to illuminate race relations during the preindustrial and industrial periods of black-white contact. By the same token, I hope to explain why these theories have little application to the third, and present, stage of modern industrial race relations. My basic argument is that the meaningful application of the arguments in each theory for any given historical period depends considerably on knowledge of the constraints imposed by the particular systems of production and by the particular laws and policies of the state during that period, constraints that shape the structural relations between racial and class groups and which thereby produce different patterns of intergroup interaction. ...

The Influence of the System of Production

The term "system of production" not only refers to the technological basis of economic processes or, in Karl Marx's terms, the "forces of production," but it also implies the "social relations of production," that is, "the interaction (for example, through employment and property arrangement) into which men enter at a given level of the development of the forces of production."[14] As I previously indicated, different systems of production impose constraints on racial group interac-

tion. In the remainder of this section I should like to provide a firmer analytical basis for this distinction as it applies specifically to the three stages of American race relations, incorporating in my discussion relevant theoretical points raised in the foregoing sections of this chapter.

It has repeatedly been the case that a nonmanufacturing or plantation economy with a simple division of labor and a small aristocracy that dominates the economic and political life of a society has characteristically generated a paternalistic rather than a competitive form of race relations, and the antebellum South was no exception.[15] Paternalistic racial patterns reveal close symbiotic relationships marked by dominance and subservience, great social distance and little physical distance, and clearly symbolized rituals of racial etiquette. The southern white aristocracy created a split labor market along racial lines by enslaving blacks to perform tasks at a cheaper cost than free laborers of the dominant group. This preindustrial form of race relations was not based on the actions of dominant-group laborers, who, as we shall see, were relatively powerless to effect significant change in race relations during this period, but on the structure of the relations established by the aristocracy. Let me briefly amplify this point.

In the southern plantation economy, public power was overwhelmingly concentrated in the hands of the white aristocracy. This power was not only reflected in the control of economic resources and in the development of a juridical system that expressed the class interests of the aristocracy, but also in the way the aristocracy was able to impose its viewpoint on the larger society.[16] This is not to suggest that these aspects of public power have not been disproportionately controlled by the economic elite in modern industrialized Western societies; rather it indicates that the hegemony of the southern ruling elite was much greater in degree, not in kind, than in these societies. The southern elite's hegemony was embodied in an economy that required little horizontal or vertical mobility. Further, because of the absence of those gradations of labor power associated with complex divisions of labor, white workers in the antebellum and early postbellum South had little opportunity to challenge the control of the aristocracy. Because white laborers

lacked power resources in the southern plantation economy, their influence on the form and
quality of racial stratification was minimal
throughout the antebellum and early postbellum
periods. Racial stratification therefore primarily
reflected the relationships established between
blacks and the white aristocracy, relationships
which were not characterized by competition for
scarce resources but by the exploitation of black
labor.[17] Social distance tended to be clearly symbolized by rituals of racial etiquette: gestures and
behavior reflecting dominance and subservience.
Consequently, any effort to impose a system of
public segregation was superfluous. Furthermore,
since the social gap between the aristocracy and
black slaves was wide and stable, ideologies of
racism played less of a role in the subordination
of blacks than they subsequently did in the more
competitive systems of race relations following
the Civil War. In short, the relationship represented intergroup paternalism because it allowed
for "close symbiosis and even intimacy, without
any threat to status inequalities."[18] This was in
sharp contrast to the more competitive forms of
race relations that accompanied the development
of industrial capitalism in the late nineteenth century and first few decades of the twentieth century (the industrial period of American race relations), wherein the complex division of labor and
opportunities for greater mobility not only produced interaction, competition, and labor-market conflict between blacks and the white working
class, but also provided the latter with superior
resources (relative to those they possessed under
the plantation economy) to exert greater influence on the form and content of racial stratification.

The importance of the system of production in
understanding race relations is seen in a comparison of Brazil and the southern United States during the postslavery periods. In the United States,
the southern economy experienced a fairly rapid
rate of expansion during the late nineteenth century, thereby creating various middle level skilled
and unskilled positions that working-class whites
attempted to monopolize for themselves. The efforts of white workers to eliminate black competition in the south generated an elaborate system of
Jim Crow segregation that was reinforced by an

ideology of biological racism. The white working
class was aided not only by its numerical size, but
also by its increasing accumulation of political resources that accompanied changes in its relation
to the means of production.

As white workers gradually translated their increasing labor power into political power, blacks
experienced greater restrictions in their efforts to
achieve a satisfactory economic, political, and social life. In Brazil, on the other hand, the large Negro and mulatto population was not thrust into
competition with the much smaller white population over access to higher-status positions because, as Marvin Harris notes, "there was little
opportunity for any member of the lower class to
move upward in the social hierarchy."[19] No eco-
nomic-class group or racial group had much to
gain by instituting a rigid system of racial segregation or cultivating an ideology of racial inferiority. Racial distinctions were insignificant to the
landed aristocracy, who constituted a numerically
small upper class in what was basically a sharply
differentiated two-class society originally shaped
during slavery. The mulattoes, Negroes, and poor
whites were all in the same impoverished lower-
ranking position. "The general economic stagnation which has been characteristic of lowland
Latin America since the abolition of slavery," observes Marvin Harris, "tends to reinforce the pattern of pacific relationships among the various
racial groups in the lower ranking levels of the social hierarchy. Not only were the poor whites outnumbered by the mulattoes and Negroes, but
there was little of a significant material nature to
struggle over in view of the generally static condition of the economy."[20] Accordingly, in Brazil,
segregation, discrimination, and racist ideologies
failed to crystallize in the first several decades following the end of slavery. More recently, however,
industrialization has pushed Brazil toward a competitive type of race relations, particularly the
southern region (for example, São Paulo) which
has experienced rapid industrialization and has
blacks in economic competition with many
lower-status white immigrants.[21]

Whereas the racial antagonism in the United
States during the period of industrial race relations (such as the Jim Crow segregation movement in the South and the race riots in northern

cities) tended to be either directly or indirectly related to labor-market conflicts, racial antagonism in the period of modern industrial relations tends to originate outside the economic order and to have little connection with labor-market strife. Basic changes in the system of production have produced a segmented labor structure in which blacks are either isolated in the relatively non-unionized, low-paying, basically undesirable jobs of the noncorporate sector, or occupy the higher-paying corporate and government industry positions in which job competition is either controlled by powerful unions or is restricted to the highly trained and educated, regardless of race. If there is a basis for labor-market conflict in the modern industrial period, it is most probably related to the affirmative action programs originating from the civil rights legislation of the 1960s. However, since affirmative action programs are designed to improve job opportunities for the talented and educated, their major impact has been in the higher-paying jobs of the expanding government sector and the corporate sector. The sharp increase of the more privileged blacks in these industries has been facilitated by the combination of affirmative action and rapid industry growth. Indeed despite the effectiveness of affirmative action programs the very expansion of these sectors of the economy has kept racial friction over higher-paying corporate and government jobs to a minimum.

Unlike the occupational success achieved by the more talented and educated blacks, those in the black underclass find themselves locked in the low-paying and dead-end jobs of the noncorporate industries, jobs which are not in high demand and which therefore do not generate racial competition or strife among the national black and white labor force. Many of these jobs go unfilled, and employers often have to turn to cheap labor from Mexico and Puerto Rico. As Nathan Glazer has pointed out, "Expectations have changed, and fewer blacks and whites today will accept a life at menial labor with no hope for advancement, as their fathers and older brothers did and as European immigrants did."[22]

Thus in the modern industrial era neither the corporate or government sectors nor the noncorporate low-wage sector provide the basis for the kind of interracial competition and conflict that has traditionally plagued the labor market in the United States. This, then, is the basis for my earlier contention that the economic class theories which associate labor-market conflicts with racial antagonism have little application to the present period of modern industrial race relations.

The Polity and American Race Relations

If the patterned ways in which racial groups have interacted historically have been shaped in major measure by different systems of production, they have also been undeniably influenced by the changing policies and laws of the state. For analytical purposes, it would be a mistake to treat the influences of the polity and the economy as if they were separate and unrelated. The legal and political systems in the antebellum South were effectively used as instruments of the slaveholding elite to strengthen and legitimate the institution of slavery. But as industrialization altered the economic class structure in the postbellum South, the organizing power and political consciousness of the white lower class increased and its members were able to gain enough control of the political and juridical systems to legalize a new system of racial domination (Jim Crow segregation) that clearly reflected their class interests.

In effect, throughout the preindustrial period of race relations and the greater portion of the industrial period the role of the polity was to legitimate, reinforce, and regulate patterns of racial inequality. However, it would be unwarranted to assume that the relationship between the economic and political aspects of race necessarily implies that the latter is simply a derivative phenomenon based on the more fundamental processes of the former. The increasing intervention, since the mid-twentieth century, of state and federal government agencies in resolving or mediating racial conflicts has convincingly demonstrated the political system's autonomy in handling contemporary racial problems. Instead of merely formalizing existing racial alignments as in previous periods, the political system has, since the initial state and municipal legislation of the 1940s, increasingly created changes leading to the erosion of traditional racial alignments; in other words, instead of reinforcing racial barriers created during the preindustrial and industrial periods, the political system in recent years has tended to promote racial equality.

Thus, in the previous periods the polity was quite clearly an instrument of the white population in suppressing blacks. The government's racial practices varied, as I indicated above, depending on which segment of the white population was able to assert its class interests. However, in the past two decades the interests of the black population have been significantly reflected in the racial policies of the government, and this change is one of the clearest indications that the racial balance of power has been significantly altered. Since the early 1940s the black population has steadily gained political resources and, with the help of sympathetic white allies, has shown an increasing tendency to utilize these resources in promoting or protecting its group interests.

By the mid-twentieth century the black vote had proved to be a major vehicle for political pressure. The black vote not only influenced the outcome of national elections but many congressional, state, and municipal elections as well. Fear of the Negro vote produced enactment of public accommodation and fair employment practices laws in northern and western municipalities and states prior to the passage of federal civil rights legislation in 1964. This political resurgence for black Americans increased their sense of power, raised their expectations, and provided the foundation for the proliferation of demands which shaped the black revolt during the 1960s. But there were other factors that helped to buttress Negro demands and contributed to the developing sense of power and rising expectations, namely, a growing, politically active black middle class following World War II and the emergence of the newly independent African states.

The growth of the black middle class was concurrent with the growth of the black urban population. It was in the urban areas, with their expanding occupational opportunities, that a small but significant number of blacks were able to upgrade their occupations, increase their income, and improve their standard of living. The middle-class segment of an oppressed minority is most likely to participate in a drive for social justice that is disciplined and sustained. In the early phases of the civil rights movement, the black middle class channeled its energies through organizations such as the National Association for the Advancement of Colored People, which emphasized developing political resources and successful litigation through the courts. These developments were paralleled by the attack against traditional racial alignments in other parts of the world. The emerging newly independent African states led the assault. In America, the so-called "leader of the free world," the manifestation of racial tension and violence has been a constant source of embarrassment to national government officials. This sensitivity to world opinion made the national government more vulnerable to pressures of black protest at the very time when blacks had the greatest propensity to protest.

The development of black political resources that made the government more sensitive to Negro demands, the motivation and morale of the growing black middle class that resulted in the political drive for racial equality, and the emergence of the newly independent African states that increased the federal government's vulnerability to civil rights pressures all combined to create a new sense of power among black Americans and to raise their expectations as they prepared to enter the explosive decade of the 1960s. The national government was also aware of this developing sense of power and responded to the pressures of black protest in the 1960s with an unprecedented series of legislative enactments to protect black civil rights.

The problem for blacks today, in terms of government practices, is no longer one of legalized racial inequality. Rather the problem for blacks, especially the black underclass, is that the government is not organized to deal with the new barriers imposed by structural changes in the economy. With the passage of equal employment legislation and the authorization of affirmative action programs the government has helped clear the path for more privileged blacks, who have the requisite education and training, to enter the mainstream of American occupations. However, such government programs do not confront the impersonal economic barriers confronting members of the black underclass, who have been effectively screened out of the corporate and government industries. And the very attempts of the government to eliminate traditional racial barriers through such programs as affirmative action have had the unintentional effect of contributing to the growing economic class divisions within the black community.

Class Stratification and Changing Black Experiences

The problems of black Americans have always been compounded because of their low position in both the economic order (the average economic class position of blacks as a group) and the social order (the social prestige or honor accorded individual blacks because of their ascribed racial status). It is of course true that the low economic position of blacks has helped to shape the categorical social definitions attached to blacks as a racial group, but it is also true that the more blacks become segmented in terms of economic class position, the more their concerns about the social significance of race will vary.

In the preindustrial period of American race relations there was of course very little variation in the economic class position of blacks. The system of racial caste oppression relegated virtually all blacks to the bottom of the economic class hierarchy. Moreover, the social definitions of racial differences were heavily influenced by the ideology of racism and the doctrine of paternalism, both of which clearly assigned a subordinate status for blacks vis-à-vis whites. Occasionally, a few individual free blacks would emerge and accumulate some wealth or property, but they were the overwhelming exception. Thus the uniformly low economic class position of blacks reinforced and, in the eyes of most whites, substantiated the social definitions that asserted Negroes were culturally and biogenetically inferior to whites. The

uniformly low economic class position of blacks also removed the basis for any meaningful distinction between race issues and class issues within the black community.

The development of a black middle class accompanied the change from a preindustrial to an industrial system of production. Still, despite the fact that some blacks were able to upgrade their occupation and increase their education and income, there were severe limits on the areas in which blacks could in fact advance. Throughout most of the industrial period of race relations, the growth of the black middle class occurred because of the expansion of institutions created to serve the needs of a growing urbanized black population. The black doctor, lawyer, teacher, minister, businessman, mortician, excluded from the white community, was able to create a niche in the segregated black community. Although the income levels and life-styles of the black professionals were noticeably and sometimes conspicuously different from those of the black masses, the two groups had one basic thing in common, a racial status contemptuously regarded by most whites in society. If E. Franklin Frazier's analysis of the black bourgeosie is correct, the black professionals throughout the industrial period of American race relations tended to react to their low position in the social order by an ostentatious display of material possessions and a conspicuous effort to disassociate themselves from the black masses.[23]

Still, as long as the members of the black middle class were stigmatized by their racial status; as long as they were denied the social recognition accorded their white counterparts; more concretely, as long as they remained restricted in where they could live, work, socialize, and be educated, race would continue to be a far more salient and important issue in shaping their sense of group position than their economic class position. Indeed, it was the black middle class that provided the leadership and generated the momentum for the civil rights movement during the mid-twentieth century. The influence and interests of this class were clearly reflected in the way the race issues were defined and articulated. Thus, the concept of "freedom" quite clearly implied, in the early stages of the movement, the right to swim in certain swimming pools, to eat in certain restaurants, to attend certain movie theaters, and to have the same voting privileges as whites. These basic concerns were reflected in the 1964 Civil Rights Bill which helped to create the illusion that, when the needs of the black middle class were met, so were the needs of the entire black community.

However, although the civil rights movement initially failed to address the basic needs of the members of the black lower class, it did increase their awareness of racial oppression, heighten their expectations about improving race relations, and increase their impatience with existing racial arrangements. These feelings were dramatically manifested in a series of violent ghetto outbursts that rocked the nation throughout the late 1960s. These outbreaks constituted the most massive and sustained expression of lower-class black dissatisfaction in the nation's history. They also forced the political system to recognize the problems of human survival and de facto segregation in the nation's ghettoes—problems pertaining to unemployment and underemployment, inferior ghetto schools, and deteriorated housing.

However, in the period of modern industrial race relations, it would be difficult indeed to comprehend the plight of inner-city blacks by exclusively focusing on racial discrimination. For in a very real sense, the current problems of lower-class blacks are substantially related to fundamental structural changes in the economy. A history of discrimination and oppression created a huge black underclass, and the technological and economic revolutions have combined to insure it a permanent status.

As the black middle class rides on the wave of political and social changes, benefiting from the growth of employment opportunities in the growing corporate and government sectors of the economy, the black underclass falls behind the larger society in every conceivable respect. The economic and political systems in the United States have demonstrated remarkable flexibility in allowing talented blacks to fill positions of prestige and influence at the same time that these systems have shown persistent rigidity in handling the problems of lower-class blacks. As a result, for the first time in American history class issues can meaningfully compete with race issues in the way blacks develop or maintain a sense of group position.[24]

Conclusion

The foregoing sections of this chapter present an outline and a general analytical basis for the arguments that will be systematically explored [elsewhere].[25] I have tried to show that race relations in American society have been historically characterized by three major stages and that each stage is represented by a unique form of racial interaction which is shaped by the particular arrangement of the economy and the polity. My central argument is that different systems of production and/or different policies of the state have imposed different constraints on the way in which racial groups interact—constraints that have structured the relations between racial groups and produced dissimilar contexts not only for the manifestation of racial antagonisms but also for racial-group access to rewards and privileges. I emphasized in this connection that in the preindustrial and industrial periods of American race relations the systems of production primarily shaped the patterns of racial stratification and the role of the polity was to legitimate, reinforce, or regulate these patterns. In the modern industrial period, however, both the system of production and the polity assume major importance in creating new patterns of race relations and in altering the context of racial strife. Whereas the preindustrial and industrial stages were principally related to group struggles over economic resources as different segments of the white population overtly sought to create and solidify economic racial domination (ranging from the exploitation of black labor in the preindustrial period to the elimination of black competition for jobs in the industrial period) through various forms of political, juridical, and social discrimination; in the modern industrial period fundamental economic and political changes have made economic class position more important than race in determining black chances for occupational mobility. Finally, I have outlined the importance of racial norms or belief systems, especially as they relate to the general problem of race and class conflict in the preindustrial and industrial periods.

My argument that race relations in America have moved from economic racial oppression to a form of class subordination for the less privileged blacks is not meant to suggest that racial conflicts have disappeared or have even been substantially reduced. On the contrary, the basis of such conflicts have shifted from the economic sector to the sociopolitical order and therefore do not play as great a role in determining the life chances of individual black Americans as in the previous periods of overt economic racial oppression.

Notes

1. See, William J. Wilson, *Power, Racism and Privilege: Race Relations in Theoretical and Sociohistorical Perspectives* (New York: The Free Press, 1973).

2. In Marxist terminology, the "superstructure" refers to the arrangements of beliefs, norms, ideologies, and noneconomic institutions.

3. However, not all theorists who emphasize the importance of economic class in explanations of race relations simply relegate problems of race to the superstructure. The Marxist scholars Michael Burawoy and Eugene Genovese recognize the reciprocal influence between the economic class structure and aspects of the superstructure (belief systems, political systems, etc.), a position which I also share and which is developed more fully in subsequent sections of this chapter. See Eugene D. Genovese, *Roll, Jordan, Roll: The World the Slaves Made* (New York: Pantheon, 1974); idem, *In Red and Black: Marxian Explorations in Southern and Afro-American History* (New York: Vintage Press, 1971); and Michael Burawoy, "Race, Class, and Colonialism," *Social and Economic Studies* 23 (1974): 521–50.

4. Oliver C. Cox, *Caste, Class and Race: A Study in Social Dynamics* (Garden City, New York: Doubleday, 1948); Paul A. Baran and Paul M. Sweezy, *Monopoly Capital: An Essay on the American Economic and Social Order* (Harmondsworth: Penguin, 1966); Michael Reich, "The Economics of Racism," in *Problems in Political Economy,* ed. David M. Gordon (Lexington, Mass.: Heath, 1971); and M. Nikolinakos, "Notes on an Economic Theory of Racism," *Race: A Journal of Race and Group Relations* 14 (1973): 365–81.

5. Edna Bonacich, "A Theory of Ethnic Antagonism: The Split Labor Market," *American Sociological Review* 37 (October 1972): 547–59; idem, "Abolition, The Extension of Slavery and the Position of Free Blacks: A Study of Split Labor Markets in the United States," *American Journal of Sociology* 81 (1975): 601–28.

6. For examples of alternative and less orthodox Marxist explanations of race, see Eugene D. Genovese, *The Political Economy of Slavery: Studies in the Economy and Society of the Slave South* (New York: Pantheon, 1966); idem, *The World the Slaveholders Made: Two Essays in Interpretation* (New York: Pantheon, 1969); idem, *In Red and Black;* idem, *Roll, Jordan, Roll;* and Burawoy, "Race, Class, and Colonialism."

7. "Exploitation," in Marxian terminology, refers to the difference between the wages workers receive and the value of the goods they produce. The size of this difference, therefore, determines the degree of exploitation.

8. Bonacich, "A Theory of Ethnic Antagonism," p. 557.

9. Ibid., p. 549.

10. Ibid., p. 553.

11. Ibid., p. 549.

12. Ibid., p. 555.

13. Ibid., p. 556.

14. Neil J. Smelser, *Karl Marx on Society and Social Change* (Chicago: University of Chicago Press, 1974), p. xiv. According to Smelser, Marx used the notions "forces of production" and "social relations of production" as constituting the "mode of production." However, in Marx's writings the mode of production is often discussed as equivalent only to the "forces of production." To avoid confusion, I have chosen the term "system of production" which denotes the interrelation of the forces of production and the mode of production.

15. Pierre L. van den Berghe, *Race and Racism: A Comparative Perspective* (New York: John Wiley and Sons, 1967), p. 26.

16. See, for example, Genovese, *Roll, Jordan, Roll.*

17. An exception to this pattern occurred in the cities of the antebellum South, where nonslaveholding whites played a major role in the development of urban segregation. However, since an overwhelming majority of the population resided in rural areas, race relations in the antebellum southern cities were hardly representative of the region.

18. van den Berghe, *Race and Racism,* p. 27.

19. Marvin Harris, *Patterns of Race in the Americas* (New York: Walker, 1964), p. 96.

20. Ibid., p. 96.

21. van den Berghe, *Race and Racism,* p. 28.

22. Nathan Glazer, "Blacks and Ethnic Groups: The Difference, and the Political Difference It Makes," in *Key Issues in the Afro-American Experience,* ed. Nathan I. Huggins, Martin Kilson, and Daniel M. Fox (New York: Harcourt Brace Jovanovich, 1971), 2: 209.

23. E. Franklin Frazier, *Black Bourgeoisie* (New York: The Free Press, 1957). See also Nathan Hare, *Black Anglo-Saxons* (New York: Collier, 1965).

24. The theoretical implications of this development for ethnic groups in general are discussed by Milton Gordon under the concept "ethclass." See Milton M.

Gordon, *Assimilation in American Life* (New York: Oxford University Press, 1964).

[25]. See William Julius Wilson, *The Declining Significance of Race: Blacks and Changing American Institutions* (Chicago and London: University of Chicago Press, 1978).

MICHAEL HOUT

Occupational Mobility of Black Men: 1962 to 1973

Race relations in America have undergone fundamental changes in recent years, so much so that now the life chances of individual blacks have more to do with their economic class position than with their day-to-day encounters with whites.

—Wilson (1978:1)

Class and Race

In *The Declining Significance of Race,* William Julius Wilson (1978) argues that class has replaced race as the arbiter of economic opportunities for blacks in the United States. His thesis is that the occupational advance of some blacks (especially males) during the latter half of the 1960s introduced a dimension of class stratification that was not present in the black population before. One of the prime sources of evidence on class stratification of the type Wilson addresses is data on occupational mobility. The extent to which class can be said to be the arbiter of blacks' economic opportunities hinges on the strength of the association between the class positions of fathers' and sons' occupations and on the association between a man's occupational class at different points in his career.

Wilson's conclusion that class replaced race as the main determinant of blacks' occupational chances merits reexamination because it contradicts the empirical research on the occupational attainment and mobility of blacks published before Wilson's book. Most studies of both inter- and intragenerational mobility and achievement to that time replicated Duncan's (1969) finding that class effects are dwarfed by the evidence of racial discrimination in the early 1960s. Indeed, it was these studies that fostered the view that it was race and not class that affected blacks' chances.

As of 1962, blacks were poor not because they were born into poverty but because they were born black. Duncan and others could uncover no evidence of class effects on occupational or income achievements that could rival the effect of race on those outcomes of the stratification process. Race was such a powerful variable that even the more modest of the class effects that stratified whites were canceled by the skin color of blacks (Blau and Duncan, 1967:208–209). In short, up to the time of Wilson's writing, the best evidence was against him.

Wilson does not deny the results of prior research. His point is that the balance of class and race effects changed after 1962. He argues that the economic progress of blacks in the United States between the early 1960s and mid-1970s restructured opportunities for occupational advancement—not only the positions attained changed but also the process of attainment itself. He reasons that once blacks had greater access to the professional and managerial positions denied to all but a few for so long, class became at least as important for the economic opportunities of blacks as it is for the economic opportunities of whites. Wilson does not distinguish between inter- and intragenerational mobility in his discussion of the new balance of class and race effects, but it appears from the context of the discussion (Wilson, 1978:1–6, 21–26, 148–53) that he proposes that class is important for both forms of mobility.

Data on intragenerational mobility between 1962 and 1973 are important because if Wilson is right, the black men who could best take advantage of the new opportunities were those in the best positions in 1962. The empirical question is, "Who gained most from the improvements of the 1960s?" Wilson's answer is that those who gained most were those who were best off in 1962. That implies a strong association between occupational position in 1962 and occupational position in 1973.

Furthermore, Wilson's discussion of the emergence of a black middle class and the perpetuation of advantage implies that intergenerational mobility may also have been affected by the changes of the 1960s. The discussion suggests (there is nothing explicit enough to be called a prediction) a convergence of black and white patterns of intergenerational mobility. In the atmosphere of reduced exclusion of black men from middle-class occupations, the effect of father's occupation on son's occupation would likely be as strong among blacks as among whites (see especially pp. 148–53).

The problem with Wilson's argument is not in the logic. The problem is the data—more precisely, the lack of data. The data Wilson presents do not address the issue of mobility at all. There is certainly evidence of occupational upgrading among blacks in the labor force. But the crucial data on mobility between 1962 and 1973 and on changes in the pattern of intergenerational occu-

pational mobility over that period are lacking. In simple terms, Wilson's data only show evidence of change in the independent variable. That makes his argument plausible. What is needed to make the argument convincing is evidence that class affects intragenerational occupational mobility between the early 1960s and the 1970s, and intergenerational mobility up to a date in the 1970s more than intergenerational mobility up to a date in the 1960s.

The strongest evidence in support of Wilson comes from Featherman and Hauser's (1976, 1978: Ch. 6) analyses of changing conditions of racial stratification. They report a significant effect of father's status on son's status in 1973, a relationship that was markedly stronger than their replication of Duncan's finding of perverse openness in 1962 (Featherman and Hauser, 1978:334–40). Similar evidence is presented by Freeman (1981) and Hout (1984). Furthermore, the effect of occupational status in 1962 on status in 1973 (for men at work in both years) is strong and positive for blacks as well as for whites, and—for cohorts born since 1917—there is no black/white difference in the magnitude of the effect of status of first job on current status (Featherman and Hauser, 1978:361–64). Their summary statement could have come from Wilson himself (Featherman and Hauser, 1978:329):

At the same time that black skin has become a less restrictive impediment to occupational mobility than in prior decades, these greater opportunities for black achievement have been coupled to greater inequality of opportunity by socioeconomic background *within* the black population. (emphasis in the original)

This paper reanalyzes the Featherman and Hauser data. It advances their work by presenting the 1962–1973 occupational turnover tables not reported in *Opportunity and Change,* drawing attention to the relevance of the data for Wilson's thesis, developing log-linear models for the 1962–1973 tables, integrating findings on changing intergenerational mobility with occupational turnover during the 1962–1973 period, and showing important differences in mobility processes for the public and private sectors of the U.S. economy.[1]

Data and Methods

Source

Data for this report are drawn from the Occupational Changes in a Generation (OCG) surveys of March 1962 (Blau and Duncan, 1967) and March 1973 (Featherman and Hauser, 1978). Both surveys are representative samples of men in the experienced civilian labor force. In 1962 the age range is 20 to 64 years old at the time of the survey; the range is one year wider (20–65 years) in 1973. For the most part this analysis is limited to the subsample of black males. Blacks were oversampled in 1973 but not in 1962. Appropriate weights are used to assure representativeness and comparability (Featherman and Hauser, 1978:511–14). At one point data for white men are analyzed for comparison; they are differentially weighted to reflect the sampling probabilities of white men. The data are presented in the form of "effective counts." These are adjustments of the observed sample frequencies that compensate for the departures from simple random sampling in the OCG design (Featherman and Hauser, 1978:513–14).

The occupations analyzed in this paper are the father's (or other household head's) occupation at the time when the respondent was sixteen years old, the respondent's current occupation, and, for men in the 1973 sample, the respondent's occupation eleven years earlier. All occupations are coded according to the 1960 Census procedures and recoded to five categories: upper nonmanual; lower nonmanual; upper manual; lower manual; and farm.[2] More categories would be preferable, but many of the analyses below use three-way and four-way cross-classifications, and 1600 cases are spread too thin if too many categories are used. Also included in the analysis is a measure the Census Bureau calls "class of worker." It is an indicator of the *sector* of the economy in which the respondent is employed. The respondent's current sector and (for 1973 respondents) his retrospective report of 1962 sector are included. The Census categories are collapsed here into "public sector" and "other sector" because of limited sample size.

Models

The point of the data analysis is to test Wilson's hypothesis that since the early 1960s class has become a significant influence on the occupational mobility of black men—contrary to the known lack of class effects on mobility prior to 1962. In other words, the goal is to estimate for black men the effect of occupational class at one time on occupational class later. If Wilson is right, data for 1973 should show substantial class effects on intergenerational mobility and on intragenerational mobility since 1962.

Normally one would approach such an analysis much as Featherman and Hauser have—by regression methods. I use generalizations of the log-linear uniform association model proposed by Duncan (1979; see Goodman, 1979; Clogg, 1982) instead of regression because they make it possible to decompose the association between occupational origins and destinations into general and specific parts (Yamaguchi, 1983). General effects apply across the full range of occupational categories. They are interpreted much as regression coefficients—as differences in destination class that are attributable to differences in origin class.

Specific effects apply to particular combinations of origin and destination—typically cells along the diagonal of the mobility table, but other combinations may be modeled this way as well (Hout, 1983). This paper makes extensive use of specific effects for diagonal cells (so-called "Quasi-Uniform Association" models). Specific diagonal effects measure the amount of immobility intrinsic to or typical of the occupations in each category.

Wilson does not distinguish general from specific effects in his discussion, so strong effects of either type will constitute evidence in favor of Wilson's thesis. By cataloging the combination of general and specific effects present in the data, this analysis can advance beyond Featherman and Hauser's regression analysis and Wilson's original conceptualization of class effects.

The full range of modifications to uniform association proposed by Goodman (1979) and Clogg (1982) are employed here.[3] Note that uniform association imposes linear and additive constraints on the relationship between the odds on one destination relative to another and the class of origin. Row effects and diagonal effects allow departures from linearity. Column effects allow departures from additivity. Partial models impose constraints on effects across categories of third or fourth variables in multi-way classifications.[4]

Occupational Upgrading and Differentiation: 1962–1973

Before examining the mobility patterns, it is important to appreciate the extent of occupational upgrading and, more importantly for Wilson, occupational differentiation that took place between 1962 and 1973. Unpublished tabulations from the OCG data[5] show that unemployment and unpaid labor decreased while employment increased. Public-sector employment grew at a faster rate than employment in private businesses or self-employment. School enrollment was the fastest growing non–labor force activity, but withdrawals from the labor force also increased rapidly. The net increase in employment for black men between 1962 and 1973 was 749,000. This increase was accompanied by a redistribution of black labor into nonmanual (especially upper nonmanual) occupations, crafts, and semiskilled manufacturing jobs. Employment in service and unskilled jobs outside of manufacturing, the two largest occupations for black men in 1962, declined. So did employment in unskilled manufacturing jobs and farm labor.

From data of this type, Wilson reaches his conclusions about the ascendency of class and the decline of race in the stratification of blacks in the United States. While the data show substantial occupational differentiation and some occupational upgrading, they do not constitute evidence of a class effect on occupational attainment or mobility. A class effect of the type hypothesized by Wilson refers to the association between origins and destinations in a mobility table. The data in Wilson's book (e.g., Table 14, p. 131) are the marginals of such a table; they show nothing about association. The remainder of this paper presents mobility data and models of association in those data.

Mobility Between 1962 and 1973

Most of this analysis is limited to men who were employed in both 1962 and 1973. But not all of the occupational upgrading of blacks in general was due to individual upward mobility. Some of the greatest gains experienced by blacks are due to the improved first job placement of black men who entered the labor force between 1962 and 1973 (Featherman and Hauser, 1976). This section assesses the relative contributions of the influx of new workers into the work force between 1962 and 1973 and the net upward mobility of workers employed in both years. Table 1 presents the cross-tabulation of (retrospective report of) 1962 employment status and—for men at work in 1973—occupation in 1962 by 1973 occupation for black men in the experienced civilian labor force (ECLF) age 20 to 64 years in 1973.

The top panel of Table 1 shows the variation in recruitment patterns of the occupations in 1973. A substantial proportion of men in each occupation came from the ranks of new workers. The white-collar occupations recruited more from this source than did the blue-collar and farm occupations. Some of the occupational upgrading of the black population is due to the influx of new workers, but the difference between the proportional distribution of new workers and others is a trivial part of the total association in the table. Thus, while the new workers are an important mass, they need not be included in the search for class effects because nearly all of the association that could contain class effects lies in the 5 × 5 subtable of 1962 occupation by 1973 occupation for men employed in both years.[6]

The pattern of recruitment and supply found in the inflow and outflow percentages for men at work in both years shows evidence of a class effect

TABLE 1
Occupational Mobility Between 1962 and 1973: Black Men in the ECLF in 1973 by Employment Status in 1962

Employment Status and Occupation in 1962	Occupation in 1973						
	Upper Nonmanual	Lower Nonmanual	Upper Manual	Lower Manual	Farm	Total	(N)
	A. Inflow Percentages						
Employed							
Upper Nonmanual	30.6	2.0	1.2	1.2	.0	4.5	
Lower Nonmanual	7.7	22.6	5.0	2.8	.0	5.9	
Upper Manual	4.9	5.0	29.5	5.3	.0	8.7	
Lower Manual	12.2	24.2	31.1	47.3	9.7	36.9	
Farm	.2	.7	2.7	3.7	54.0	4.5	
Not Answered	.2	1.7	1.9	1.5	1.3	1.4	
Not Employed	41.0	40.1	24.9	32.6	26.7	33.0	
Unknown	3.0	3.7	3.8	5.7	8.3	4.9	
Total	100.0	100.0	100.0	100.0	100.0	100.0	
(N)	(309.5)	(318.9)	(422.9)	(1615.9)	(97.1)	(2764.3)	
	B. Outflow Percentages						
Employed							
Upper Nonmanual	75.5	5.2	4.1	15.2	.0	100.0	(125.1)
Lower Nonmanual	14.7	44.5	12.9	27.9	.0	100.0	(162.2)
Upper Manual	6.3	6.6	51.7	35.4	.0	100.0	(241.3)
Lower Manual	3.7	7.6	12.9	74.9	.9	100.0	(1020.9)
Farm	.6	1.7	9.1	46.9	41.7	100.0	(125.7)
Not Answered	1.7	14.0	20.3	60.6	3.4	100.0	(38.8)
Not Employed	13.9	14.0	11.5	57.7	2.8	100.0	(913.5)
Unknown	6.8	8.5	11.9	66.9	5.9	100.0	(136.8)
Total	11.2	11.5	15.3	58.5	3.5	100.0	(2764.3)

Source: 1973 OCG Survey.

of the type hypothesized by Wilson. The proportion of the outflow that arrives in the upper nonmanual stratum increases with class of origin, while the proportion that arrives in the lower manual stratum decreases with class of origin, except for a bulge on the diagonal. There is substantial regression toward the modal category (lower manual); in each row of the outflow table, lower manual is the most common destination for movers.

To test whether the apparent class effect in Table 1 is significant and to separate any significant effect into general and specific parts, a portion of the data in Table 1 was submitted to a log-linear analysis. Table 2 shows the preferred model for the 5 × 5 table obtained by deleting men who were not employed in 1962 or whose occupations

were unknown. Together the uniform and diagonal effects show a strong, positive association between class positions at the beginning and end of the period.[7]

The diagonal effects are significant in four of the five strata, indicating an important tendency for blacks in those positions to hold on to them. Significant immobility for black men, especially in nonmanual occupations, is a novel finding. Past studies of inter- and intragenerational mobility among blacks have pointed out the "perverse openness" of the mobility channels traveled by black men (Duncan, 1969) or "lack of articulation" in black men's careers (Featherman and Hauser, 1978:361–64). Openness of the type experienced by black men is perverse because it leads to substantial regression to a very low mean.

TABLE 2
Parameter Estimates and Standard Errors for
Quasi-Uniform Association Model of Mobility
Between 1962 and 1973: Black Men in the ECLF in 1973
Who Report Their 1962 Occupation[a]

Parameter	b	Standard Error
Uniform	.324*	.048
Diagonal		
Upper Nonmanual	1.830*	.324
Lower Nonmanual	1.330*	.206
Upper Manual	1.685*	.185
Lower Manual	.111	.186
Farm	3.957*	.385

[a] $N = 1675.3$; $L^2 = 10.11$; $df = 10$; $p = .43$; $\Delta = .013$.
The model also fits the marginal totals for 1962 and
1973 occupations.
    * $p < .05$.
Source: 1973 OCG Survey.

Without a substantial effect of origins on destinations even those few blacks who attain advantaged status cannot expect to hang on to that status very long. The evidence here contradicts that image in a way that provides support and elaboration for Wilson's hypothesis. Contrary to the perverse openness that returned most of those few blacks with high-class first occupations before 1962 to low-class 1962 occupations (Duncan, 1969), here is evidence of a pattern of immobility that kept advantaged blacks in their (relatively) privileged places over the 1962–73 period.

The uniform effect shows that, net of the tendency toward immobility in four of the five strata, the men who were in the nonmanual occupations in 1973 were disproportionately drawn from the middle class and upper working class of 1962. Conversely, the majority of black men who were "left behind" in the low-status occupations were drawn from the most disadvantaged portion of the black work force of 1962. If my reading of Wilson is correct, this is precisely what he meant when he said that class replaced race in deciding the economic opportunities of blacks.

Of course, data on black men alone cannot be used to assess the effect of race. The main effect of race is not in question. White men had much higher status than black men in both years (Featherman and Hauser, 1976). What is crucial

for Wilson's argument is the size of the general and specific class effects among whites relative to the size of comparable effects among blacks. Table 3 shows the preferred model for the 1962–73 mobility of white workers.[8] The uniform effect is significant, but as Hout (1983:60–65) shows, the interacting column effects modify the interpretation of this parameter. To facilitate interpretation, "implied slopes" are presented in Table 4. These calculations combine uniform and column effects to show the overall effect of class in 1962 on class in 1973. There are trivial differences between black and white men in the effect of 1962 class on mobility into nonfarm occupations in 1973. But while the same positive class effect applies to mobility into farm and nonfarm occupations among black men, the class effect on mobility into farming is negative for white men.[9]

Black and white men also differ in immobility in three of the four nonfarm categories. Immobility is greater for whites in the upper manual occupations; it is greater for blacks in both upper and lower nonmanual occupations. Bigger diagonal effects for blacks than whites are not necessarily evidence of black progress. If the big diagonal effects were in the lower manual category, the evidence would favor the "cycle of poverty" argument. But this study is not different from others in the finding that, for all the disadvantages affecting the mobility of black men in America, there is no cycle of poverty. In fact, for neither blacks nor whites is there a significant diagonal effect for lower manual occupations. There is no need for special theories to account for the observation that three-fourths of the black men who held lower manual occupations in 1962 did so in 1973 as well. The prevalence of lower manual occupations means that black men are more likely to find themselves in that category than in the upper manual category whether they start out above or below upper manual status.[10] What significant immobility in occupations other than the semiskilled and unskilled lower manual jobs means for the occupational upgrading of blacks in the 1962–73 period is that part of the group mobility was due to individual immobility—the fact that many of the blacks who held prestigious positions in 1962 held on to the prestige (if not the exact positions) through the decade.

TABLE 3

Parameter Estimates and Standard Errors for Preferred Association Model of Mobility Between 1962 and 1973: White Men in the ECLF in 1973 Who Report Their 1962 Occupation[a]

Parameter	Uniform & Diagonal Effects		Row Effects		Column Effects	
	b	Standard Error	b	Standard Error	b	Standard Error
Uniform	.065*	.033	—	—	—	—
Diagonal, Row, or Column						
Upper Nonmanual	.042	.257	—	—	—	—
Lower Nonmanual	.867*	.116	−.143*	.075	−.313*	.070
Upper Manual	2.023*	.064	−.322*	.050	−.563*	.057
Lower Manual	.053	.123	−.486*	.065	−.791*	.080
Farm	5.678*	.297	—	—	—	—

[a] N = 13,376.1; L^2 = 3.22; df = 3; p = .36; Δ = .002. The model also fits the marginal totals for 1962 and 1973 occupations and a special parameter for mobility between lower nonmanual and upper manual occupations. The special parameter has an absolute value of .305 with a standard error of .066. This parameter is positive for upward mobility and negative for downward mobility between the two categories.
* p < .05.
Source: 1973 OCG Survey.

TABLE 4

Implied Slopes[a] and Standard Errors for Log-Linear Regression of the Odds on a Higher-Status Occupation in 1973 on Occupation in 1962: Black and White Men in the ECLF in 1973 Who Report Their 1962 Occupation by Race

Odds	Black		White	
	b	Standard Error	b	Standard Error
Upper Nonmanual : Lower Nonmanual	.324*	.048	.378*	.043
Lower Nonmanual : Upper Manual	.324*	.048	.306*	.037
Upper Manual : Lower Manual	.324*	.048	.293*	.048
Lower Manual : Farm	.324*	.048	−.726*	.105

[a] The implied slope for category *j* relative to category *j'* is the uniform effect plus the column effect for category *j* (if there is one) minus the column effect for category *j'* (if there is one).
* p < .05.
Source: Tables 2 and 3.

This pattern of differential immobility tended to increase the effect of class on mobility among blacks more than among whites. Diagonal effects for nonmanual occupations are stronger among blacks, keeping advantaged blacks from regressing toward lower manual employment. The diagonal effects for upper manual and farm occupations are stronger for whites. These have little effect on the difference between class effects for blacks and whites because they have countervailing tendencies—decreasing downward mobility from upper manual occupations to about the same degree as they decrease upward mobility from farming.

Overall, the comparison between the class effects for blacks and whites reveals relatively small differences. The significant differences are evidence that class effects were greater among blacks than among whites during the 1962–73 period. The general (uniform and column) effects are virtually indistinguishable except for the small (and shrinking) farm category. The specific (diagonal) effects increased class distinctions for both blacks and whites, but their stratifying effects were somewhat greater among blacks. In sum, class effects on mobility during the 1960s were every bit as strong as Wilson supposed. Furthermore, the racial difference in class effects suggested by prior research on mobility from first to current occupations was certainly wiped out, and, to some extent, reversed.

Intergenerational Mobility

Wilson also describes the 1960s as a time of change in the intergenerational occupational mobility of black men. In 1962, the current occupations of black men were, for the most part, independent of their socioeconomic origins (Duncan, 1969; Featherman and Hauser, 1976; Hout, 1984). By 1973, a significant association between background and achievement (Featherman and Hauser, 1976) and between origin status and destination status (Hout, 1984) had emerged. Furthermore, the intergenerational mobility pattern of black men had become only trivially different from that of white men (Hout, 1984). The findings regarding 1973 were apparently unknown to Wilson, but, as pointed out above, they support his hypothesis of emerging stratification within the black population.

This section of the paper goes beyond the prior research by estimating the effects of father's (or other household head's) occupation on the son's occupation in 1962 and the net effects of those two occupations on the son's occupation in 1973. By inference these estimates can be used to assess the importance of background for 1962–73 mobility. It will be shown that class effects on the intergenerational mobility of black men emerged during the 1960s because the men who moved up the occupational ladder during the decade were the men from the most advantaged backgrounds.

The key to this section is the pattern of relationships in the causal chain from father's occupation to son's early occupation to son's later occupation. In general, the net effect of father's status on son's current status is less at each successive stage of the socioeconomic career. Blau and Duncan (1967:186–87) conclude from their synthetic cohort analysis that "factors salient at an early stage of a man's career may continue to play

a direct role as he grows older, but the direct effects of education and father's status are attenuated drastically with the passage of time." The significance of the direct effects of father's status on current occupation net of past achievements is open to question (Featherman, 1971, 1973; Kelley, 1973), especially after adjustment for response variability and measurement error (Hauser et al., 1983), but there is no question that background effects atrophy. However, the emergence of background effects in 1973 that were absent in 1962 as documented by Featherman and Hauser (1978) and Hout (1984) implies that, among black men, the usual pattern did not hold during the 1962–73 period.

The data for this section are in the cross-tabulation of father's occupation by son's 1962 occupation by son's 1973 occupation for black men employed in both years. A three-way quasi-uniform association model (Clogg, 1982; Hout, 1982) is preferred.[11] The parameter estimates are in Table 5.

The uniform effects support the proposition that the combined inter- and intragenerational mobility pattern of black men departs from the general pattern of diminishing background effects. The effect of father's occupation on son's 1962 occupation is of marginal statistical significance and slightly less than half the magnitude of the effect of father's occupation on 1973 occupation (.064/.139 = .460). The diagonal effects do not contradict this impression.[12]

These results support the thrust of Wilson's argument. They also go beyond Wilson by showing that the men most likely to move up the occupational ladder were the men from the relatively advantaged backgrounds. This is not a necessary consequence of the positive sign for the effect of father's occupation on son's 1973 occupation. A positive effect of background status on upward mobility depends on both the absolute size of the effect of father on son in each year and on the relative sizes of the two effects.[13] Figure 1 shows clearly how the odds on upward mobility between 1962 and 1973 varied with the status of father's occupation. The men most likely to move up from any 1962 status were those men from the highest status backgrounds. In other words, the opportunities that opened up were not evenly distributed, but disproportionately went to the men from rel-

TABLE 5

Parameter Estimates and Standard Errors for the Preferred Association Model of the Three-Way Cross-Tabulation of Father's Occupation, Son's 1962 Occupation, and Son's 1973 Occupation: Black Men in the ECLF in 1973 Who Report Their 1962 Occupation[a]

Parameter	Effect of Father's Occ. on 1962 Occ.		Effect of Father's Occ. on 1973 Occ.		Effect of 1962 Occ. on 1973 Occ.	
	b	Standard Error	b	Standard Error	b	Standard Error
Uniform	.064	.038	.139*	.036	.300*	.050
Diagonal						
Upper Nonmanual	.255	.514	.322	.477	1.819*	.338
Lower Nonmanual	−.156	.418	.778*	.354	1.332*	.218
Upper Manual	.568*	.254	−.451	.270	1.658*	.195
Lower Manual	−.153	.131	.011	.125	.188	.194
Farm	1.808*	.316	.765	.471	3.526*	.407

[a] N = 1,534.7; L^2 = 76.99; df = 94; p > .50; Δ = .049. The model also fits the marginal totals for all three variables.

* p < .05.

Source: 1973 OCG Survey.

FIGURE 1

Log-odds on upward mobility between 1962 and 1973 by father's occupation (lines for each occupational group in 1962 shown separately): Black men in the ECLF in 1973 who report their 1962 occupation

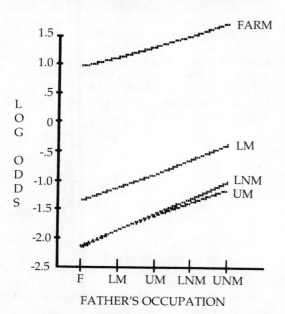

atively advantaged backgrounds. Note, however, that upward mobility was not the rule, even during this period of expanding opportunities; only among men in farming in 1962 are the odds on upward mobility better than even (log-odds greater than zero).

The positive sloping lines of Figure 1 suggest that the barriers that blocked the occupational advancement of black men most affected blacks from the upper strata. A pressure for advancement was built up by the blocked mobility of men who, if given the opportunity, would have advanced in a pattern similar to the pattern found among white men. When the barriers were cracked in the 1960s, the pattern emerged. The parameter estimates in Table 5 and the positive slopes of the lines in Figure 1 show that class effects on the intergenerational mobility of black men in 1973 were similar to those found among whites (see Hout, 1984) because *those blacks who moved up between 1962 and 1973 were those from the most advantaged backgrounds.* ...

Conclusions

William Julius Wilson argues that the occupational progress of blacks in the 1960s introduced an element of social stratification previously unknown in the black population. Although he has been criticized for this thesis by several writers, his contentions regarding occupational mobility were, until now, untested by critics or supporters. Relevant data are to be found in the literature, notably Featherman and Hauser (1978), but no direct tests have appeared.

The available evidence—both here and elsewhere—supports Wilson. By 1973 the occupational standing of black men depended on socioeconomic criteria to a greater extent than was true in 1962. The pattern of intragenerational occupational mobility between 1962 and 1973 departs substantially from the pattern of "perverse openness" found in the 1960s. Black men who held relatively high-status positions in 1962 did not experience the invidious regression toward the (very low) mean of black male achievement expected on the basis of past research (e.g., Featherman and Hauser, 1978:362) into the pattern of career mobility (first to current occupation). Men who beat the odds and attained a level of occupational success by 1962 were able to hold on to those positions to a greater extent than in the past (as judged by first-to-current occupational mobility studies for earlier cohorts), and the men who benefited most from the new opportunities were those men whose 1962 occupations were closest in status to the new occupations. Furthermore, outside of farming, the emergent stratification system affecting black men resembled that affecting whites, i.e., the effect of status on the mobility of blacks into nonfarm occupations in 1973 was not very different from the same effect for whites.

Also significant for Wilson's thesis is the evidence that the black men who moved up in status were drawn from relatively advantaged origins. Prior to 1962, discrimination blocked the occupational advancement of black men whose origins were comparable to those of whites who attained high-status occupations. Diminished discrimination between 1962 and 1973 was followed by upward mobility of blacks from relatively advantaged backgrounds, producing new class distinctions in life chances within the black population. In other words, the effect of socioeconomic origins on destinations among black men increased between 1962 and 1973 because the new opportunities that opened up for blacks during the 1962–73 period benefited men with relatively advantaged backgrounds more than it benefited other men. ...

Of course none of this implies equal occupational standing for blacks and whites. A huge socioeconomic gap still exists between majority and minority in the United States. At least as important is the growing gap between the households headed by women and those headed by men within the black population (Bianchi, 1981), a trend that Wilson notes. Wilson is also attentive to the divide between black men with jobs and the hypothesized underclass of men who are more or less permanently unemployed. These issues are beyond the scope of the research reported here. Evaluation of the theory of the underclass deserves a book in its own right. What this research has accomplished is a demonstration of how differential class effects no longer add to the gap that divides black and white male workers.

Appendix

The first step in deriving the effect of father's occupation on the odds on upward mobility between 1962 and 1973 is to write an equation for the frequencies expected under the model used to estimate the parameters in Table 5. Let R be the number of categories, i index son's 1973 occupation, j index son's 1962 occupation, and k index father's occupation. Then the expected frequency (F) in cell (i,j,k) is a multiplicative function of prevalence (α) effects, uniform association effects (β), and diagonal effects (δ):

$$F_{ijk} = \alpha_0 \alpha_{1i} \alpha_{2j} \alpha_{3k} \beta_1^{x_i x_j} \beta_2^{x_i x_k} \beta_3^{x_j x_k} \delta_{1i}^{z_{ij}}$$
$$\delta_{2i}^{z_{ik}} \delta_{3j}^{z_{jk}} \qquad (A.1)$$

where $\Pi_i \alpha_{1j} = \Pi_j \alpha_{2j} = \Pi_k \alpha_{3k} = 1$, $X_i = R - i$, $X_j = R - j$, $X_k = R - k$, $Z_{ij} = 1$ if $i = j$ and $= 0$ otherwise, $Z_{ik} = 1$ if $i = k$ and $= 0$ otherwise, and $Z_{jk} = 1$ if $j = k$ and $= 0$ otherwise.

The odds on upward mobility from 1962 occupation j for men with father's occupation k $(\Omega_{j.k})$ is the ratio of the number of men in 1973 occupations that are of higher status than j to the number of men in 1973 occupations that are of the same or lower status than j for each combination of j and k, i.e.,

$$\Omega_{j,k} = \frac{\sum_{i=1}^{j-1} F_{ijk}}{\sum_{i=j}^{R} F_{ijk}} \qquad (A.2)$$

Substituting equation (A.1) into equation (A.2) and cancelling redundant terms yields:

$$\Omega_{j,k} = \frac{\sum_{i=1}^{j-1} \alpha_{1i}(\beta_1^{x_j} \beta_2^{x_k})^{x_i} \delta_{2i}^{z_{ik}}}{\sum_{i=j}^{R} \alpha_{1i}(\beta_1^{x_j} \beta_2^{x_k})^{x_i} \delta_{1i}^{z_{ij}} \delta_{2i}^{z_{ik}}} \qquad (A.3)$$

Although equation (A.1) is log-linear in expected frequencies and logits, equation (A.3) is nonlinear even if both sides of the equation are logged. As Figure 1 shows, the combination of parameter values estimated for the mobility of black men between 1962 and 1973 yields a set of curves that is nearly log-linear when plotted against X_k, but that result is a property of the data, not the model. Specifically, it is due to the combination of strong β_2 and weak δ_{2i} for the mobility of black men over the 1962–73 period.

Notes

Direct all correspondence to: Michael Hout, Department of Sociology, University of Arizona, Tucson, AZ 85721.

I wish to thank Albert Bergesen, Beverly Duncan, Otis Dudley Duncan, Neil Fligstein, Doug McAdam, and Michael Sobel for their comments on earlier drafts of this paper. Penelope Hanke provided valuable research assistance. This research was paid for by the University of Arizona.

[1]. For reasons of space, the present reprint does not include Hout's analyses of cross-sector variability in mobility processes.—Ed.

2. Upper nonmanual occupations are professional, managerial, and nonretail sales jobs; lower nonmanual occupations are proprietorial, clerical, and retail sales jobs; upper manual occupations are supervisory and crafts jobs; lower manual occupations are service, semiskilled, and unskilled jobs; and farm occupations are farming and farm laboring.

3. Note, however, that the fitting methods described by Goodman (1979) and Clogg (1982) are not used in this paper. All estimates presented here are from Haberman's (1979) FREQ program that allows the researcher to constrain the diagonal parameters in ways that prove useful in this paper. The LOG-LINEAR subprogram in SPSSX uses the same algorithm. GLIM (Baker and Nelder, 1978) is also applicable (Breen, 1984).

4. Fit of the models is assessed using two measures. The first is the likelihood ratio chi-square: $L^2 = 2\Sigma f log (f/F)$, where the sum is over all cells in the table, f is the observed frequency, and F is the frequency expected under the model. L^2 is distributed as chi-square with degrees of freedom equal to the number of cells in the table minus the number of parameters in the model (see Goodman, 1979; Clogg, 1982 for details). The second statistic is the index of dissimilarity between the observed and expected frequencies: $\Delta = 1/2\Sigma |f–F|$. Δ tests no null hypothesis, but it is useful as a heuristic index of the proportion of cases misclassified by the model (see Hout, 1983:13–15).

5. These tabulations are available from the author on request.

6. The L^2 for the 2×5 table cross-classifying new workers and old workers by 1973 occupation is 31.42. With 4 degrees of freedom, that is significant at the .01 level. However, it is only 3.0 percent of the total L^2 of 1062.35 for the whole of Table 1. The L^2 for the 5×5 table cross-classifying 1962 occupation by 1973 occupation for men employed in both years is 963.37 (90.5 percent of the total). The remaining 6.5 percent of the total L^2 is to be found in the 3×5 cross-classification of employment status in 1962 by occupation in 1973.

7. The total association in the table is strong, as gauged by the L^2 for independence of 963.37. The insignificant L^2 of 10.11 for the preferred quasi-uniform association model shows that only a trivial portion of that total is not accounted for by the uniform and diagonal effects.

8. The standard models fail to fit the data for white men because of a departure from quasi-symmetry in the mobility upward and downward across the white-collar/blue-collar boundary. A special variable scored one for cell (3,2)—men who moved from upper manual to lower nonmanual occupations—and minus one for cell (2,3)—men who moved from lower nonmanual to upper manual occupations—captures the asymmetry. The addition of this special parameter to quasi-row and column effects I produces an acceptable fit. In part the greater complexity of the model for white men is due to the greater size of the white sample. The statistical power accruing to the greater effective size makes it possible to detect smaller effects for white men than can be detected using the smaller sample of black men.

9. A negative effect is perhaps a surprising result, but it is net of the very large intrinsic immobility of white farmers (d = 5.678 for whites).

10. The log-odds on an upper manual versus a lower manual occupation in 1973 are less than zero for all origins except upper manual.

11. The model fits the one-way marginals of the $5 \times 5 \times 5$ table, and it fits quasi-uniform association to each two-way interaction. No three-way interactions are included. The model fits the data very well ($L^2 = 76.99$; $df = 94$; $p > .50$; $\Delta = .049$).

12. There are three significant diagonal effects among the ten parameters estimated, but all of the father-to-son diagonal effects are small relative to the 1962-to-1973 diagonal effects.

13. Derivation of this result is appended.

References

Bianchi, Suzanne. 1981. Household Structure and Racial Inequality. New Brunswick, NJ: Rutgers University Press.

Baker, R. J. and J. A. Nelder. 1978. The GLIM System, Release 3: Generalized Linear Interactive Modelling. Oxford: Numerical Algorithms Group.

Blau, Peter M. and Otis Dudley Duncan. 1967. The American Occupational Structure. New York: Wiley.

Breen, Richard. 1984. "Fitting Nonhierarchical and Association Log-Linear Models Using GLIM." Sociological Methods and Research 13.

Clogg, Clifford C. 1982. "The analysis of association models for social data." Journal of the American Statistical Association 77:803–15.

Duncan, Otis Dudley. 1969. "Inheritance of poverty or inheritance of race?" Pp. 85–110 in Daniel P. Moynihan (ed.), On Understanding Poverty. New York: Basic Books.

_____. 1979. "How destination depends on origin in the occupational mobility table." American Journal of Sociology 84:793–804.

Featherman, David L. 1971. "A structural model for the socioeconomic career." American Journal of Sociology 77:293–304.

_____. 1973. "Comments on models for the socioeconomic career." American Sociological Review 38:785–90.

Featherman, David L. and Robert M. Hauser. 1976. "Changes in the socioeconomic stratification of the races, 1962–1973." American Journal of Sociology 82:621–51.

_____. 1978. Opportunity and Change. New York: Academic Press.

Freeman, Richard B. 1981. "Black economic progress since 1964: who has gained and why?" Pp. 247–94 in Sherwin Rosen (ed.), Studies in Labor Markets. Chicago: University of Chicago Press.

Goodman, Leo A. 1979. "Simple models for the analysis of association in cross-classifications having ordered rows and columns." Journal of the American Statistical Association 74:537–52.

Haberman, Shelby J. 1979. The Analysis of Qualitative Data. New York: Academic Press.

Hauser, Robert M., Shu-Ling Tsai and William H. Sewell. 1983. "A model of stratification with response error in social and psychological variables." Sociology of Education 56:20–46.

Hout, Michael. 1982. "Using uniform association models: examples from delinquency research." Pp. 115–28 in John Hagan (ed.), Methodological Advances in Delinquency Research. Beverly Hills: Sage.

_____. 1983. Mobility Tables. Beverly Hills: Sage.

_____. 1984. "Status, autonomy, and training in occupational mobility." American Journal of Sociology 89:1379–1409.

Kelley, Jonathan. 1973. "Causal chain models of the socioeconomic career." American Sociological Review 38:481–93.

Wilson, William Julius. 1978. The Declining Significance of Race. Chicago: University of Chicago Press.

Yamaguchi, Kazuo. 1983. "The structure of intergenerational occupational mobility: generality and specificity in occupational resources, channels, and barriers." American Journal of Sociology 88:718–45.

STANLEY LIEBERSON

A Piece of the Pie: Blacks and White Immigrants Since 1880

The source of European migrants to the United States shifted radically toward the end of the last century; Northwestern Europe declined in relative importance, thanks to the unheralded numbers arriving from the Southern, Central, and Eastern parts of Europe. These "new" sources, which had contributed less than one-tenth of all immigrants as late as 1880, were soon sending the vast majority of newcomers, until large-scale immigration was permanently cut off in the 1920s. For example, less than 1 percent of all immigrants in the 1860s had come from Italy, but in the first two decades of the twentieth century more migrants arrived from this one nation than from all of the Northwestern European countries combined (Lieberson, 1963, p. 550). These new European groups piled up in the slums of the great urban centers of the East and Midwest, as well as in the factory towns of those regions, and in the coal-mining districts of Pennsylvania and elsewhere. They were largely unskilled, minimally educated, poor, relegated to undesirable jobs and residences, and life was harsh.

The descendants of these South-Central-Eastern (SCE) European groups have done relatively well in the United States. By all accounts, their education, occupations, and incomes are presently close to—or even in excess of—white Americans from the earlier Northwestern European sources.[1] To be sure, there are still areas where they have not quite "made it." Americans of Italian and Slavic origin are underrepresented in *Who's Who in America*, although their numbers are growing (Lieberson and Carter, 1979, table 1). Every president of the United States has thus far been of old

European origin. Likewise, a study of the 106 largest Chicago-area corporations found Poles and Italians grossly underrepresented on the boards or as officers when compared with their proportion in the population in the metropolitan area (Institute of Urban Life, 1973).[2] There is also evidence of discrimination in the upper echelons of banking directed at Roman Catholics and Jews, to say nothing of nonwhites and women generally (United States Senate Committee on Banking, Housing and Urban Affairs, 1976, pp. 218–219, 223). For example, as of a few years ago there were only a handful of Jews employed as senior officers in all of New York City's eight giant banks and there were *no* Jews employed as senior officers in any of the nation's 50 largest non-New York banks (Mayer, 1974, p. 11).

Nevertheless, it is clear that the new Europeans have "made it" to a degree far in excess of that which would have been expected or predicted at the time of their arrival here. It is also equally apparent that blacks have not. Whether it be income, education, occupation, self-employment, power, position in major corporations, residential location, health, or living conditions, the average black status is distinctly below that held by the average white of SCE European origin. Numerous exceptions exist, of course, and progress has occurred: There are many blacks who have made it. But if these exceptions should not be overlooked, it is also the case that blacks and new Europeans occupy radically different average positions in society.

Since the end of slavery occurred about 20 years before the new Europeans started their massive move to the United States and because the latter groups seem to have done so well in this nation, there are numerous speculations as to why the groups have experienced such radically different outcomes. Most of these end up in one of two camps: either blacks were placed under greater disadvantages by the society and other forces outside of their control; or, by contrast, the new Europeans had more going for them in terms of their basic characteristics. Examples of the former explanation include: the race and skin color markers faced by blacks but not by SCE Europeans; greater discrimination against blacks in institutions ranging from courts to unions to schools; the preference that dominant whites had for other whites over blacks; and the decline in opportunities by the time blacks moved to the North in sizable numbers. Interpretations based on the assumption that the differences in success reflect superior new European attributes include speculations regarding family cohesion, work ethic, intelligence, acceptance of demeaning work, and a different outlook toward education as a means of mobility. Not only is it possible for both types of forces to be operating but their relative role could easily change over time, since a period of about 100 years is long enough to permit all sorts of feedback processes as well as broad societal changes which have consequences for the groups involved. Hence the problem is extremely complex. As one might expect, those sympathetic to the difficulties faced by blacks tend to emphasize the first factor; those emphasizing the second set of forces tend to be less sympathetic.

The answer to this issue is relevant to current social policies because an understanding of the causes would affect the ways proposed for dealing with the present black–white gap. In addition, there is the related issue of whether the SCE groups provide an analogy or a model for blacks. Finally, the historical causes of present-day circumstances are of grave concern to all those who are enmeshed in these events. Is the relatively favorable position enjoyed by the descendants of new European immigrants to be seen as purely a function of more blood, sweat, and tears such that easy access to the same goodies will in some sense desecrate all of these earlier struggles—let alone mean sharing future opportunities with blacks? If, on the other hand, the position held by blacks vis-à-vis the new Europeans is due to their skin color and the fact that blacks experience more severe forms of discrimination, then the present-day position of blacks is proof of the injustices that exist and the need to redress them. ...

A Theory of Intrinsic Differences

Ignoring blacks and new Europeans for a moment, consider the forces generating contact between racial and ethnic groups. These can be crudely divided into voluntary and involuntary forms of contact. Blacks were brought to the New World involuntarily as slaves; American Indians were already here but their contact with the white settlers was also involuntary insofar as they were overrun. By way of contrast, the movement of the new Europeans to the United States and the later migration of blacks from the South to the North are both examples of voluntary migration, international and internal, respectively. What do we know about voluntary migration? As a general rule, we can say that it is driven by economic forces, that is, people move from areas of low opportunity to areas of better opportunity. This is all relative, to be sure, but it means that the opportunity structure for a set of voluntary migrants is more favorable in the receiving area than in the sending area.[3] Because there is a lot of ignorance in these matters, as well as other satisfactions involved, a secondary counterflow to the sending area is sometimes rather substantial. Nevertheless, a net movement on the part of a group from one nation to another, or from one subarea within a nation to another subarea, is generally due to superior opportunities in the receiving area.

We also know that a set of potential sending areas differ from one another in their levels of living and opportunity structure. This means that the residents of countries (or subareas) A, B, C ... N will vary in their evaluation of the options available to them in the United States (or urban North for blacks in the South) because they will be affected by the different opportunity structures available in their respective homelands (or the South for potential black migrants to the North).

Migrants arriving in the United States from various sources will therefore differ in what is an acceptable job, depending on the options that exist for them in their homeland for the skills that they possess. A low-level menial job that might prove an attractive income alternative to someone with minimal skills from an extremely poor country would not be a migration "pull" for someone with more attractive alternatives in another homeland either because the level of living is higher or because the person possesses skills that can command a better job. Further, insofar as nations differ in their levels of development, it means that their labor forces will vary in the levels of skill for which they are capable as well as in their average educational levels.

Two important conclusions follow from these assumptions. First, there is an inherent reason for expecting differences between groups at the initial point of contact simply because the migrant groups differ in the alternatives available to them in the areas from which they are migrating. Ignoring special situations such as famine, social unrest, and oppression, emigrants from a nation with a relatively high level of living will tend to be both qualified for better jobs and have more attractive alternatives in their homeland than will those migrating from a nation with a lower level of living. Work acceptable to one group, in the sense of being a superior alternative to the opportunities available in the homeland, will not be attractive to members of another group (or to only a much smaller segment). Hence migrants from different sources will vary in their jobs and incomes not necessarily because of discrimination or work orientation but because of the alternatives available to them at home. Such groups at the initial point of contact in the United States differ not in their aspirations, but rather in the minimum they will settle for. And they differ in how little they will accept because of the alternatives at home that they must weigh them against. The second point is one well recognized in the work of Bonacich (1972, 1976), namely, workers in the receiving country will view migrants from nations with lower levels of living as potential competitors willing to work for less because of the alternatives at home.

However, of special interest here is the first issue, namely, whether earlier in this century and late in the last one the level of living in South-Central-Eastern Europe differed from the level of living for blacks in the South. If so, then the theory leads one to expect the group living in the poorer situation to have a lower minimum standard and so to accept working conditions and jobs that the other would reject. Deriving this conclusion is easier than testing it because to my knowledge there are no solid data on wages for the groups in comparable work which also take into account the cost of living encountered in each nation and the South at that time. Moreover, I cannot find data sets for per capita GNP during those periods for each of the countries. Consequently, I am obliged to rely on a reasonably good surrogate measure of the nature of life in these places, namely, life expectancy.

Table 1 compares life expectancy at birth ($\overset{\circ}{e}_0$) for blacks circa 1900, 1910, and 1920 with various nations in South, Central, and Eastern Europe. In addition, the average life table values in four southern cities in 1880 are compared with those for these same European nations. In 1880, when the sources of European migration first started to shift, $\overset{\circ}{e}_0$ in SCE Europe was generally superior to that experienced by blacks in the South. The expectation of life at birth for both black men and women in 1880, respectively, 22 and 26 years, is below that for any of the new European sources listed, the closest being Russia (males, 27; females, 29). Insofar as these life table values indicate general living conditions, one can infer that there would be jobs attractive to blacks that would not be attractive to the new Europeans.

Life expectancy was higher for Austrians, Bulgarians, Finns, Greeks, and Italians when compared with blacks in each of the four periods (Table 1). The only exception were the Russians who had lower levels in 1900–1902 and who had mixed results in the 1919–1920 comparison.[4] Incidentally, comparisons between Northwestern European nations and the South-Central-Eastern nations are consistent with this perspective; the former have generally more favorable mortality than do the new European sources.

In short, if the European and black life table values represent differences in levels of living,

TABLE 1
Life Expectancy at Birth in South, Central, and Eastern Europe and Among Blacks in the United States, 1880–1920

Nation	Sex	1880	1900–1902	1909–1911	1919–1920
Austria	Male	32.64	39.06	41.16	47.43
	Female	35.26	41.19	43.36	50.54
Bulgaria	Male	—	41.27	44.18	45.18
	Female	—	41.85	43.70	45.39
Finland	Male	—	44.13	46.53	49.08
	Female	—	46.52	49.68	53.03
Greece	Male	36.23	41.86	44.27	46.81
	Female	37.73	43.49	45.96	48.56
Italy	Male	34.33	43.60	45.66	48.64
	Female	34.84	44.11	46.50	50.01
Russia	Male	26.69	32.05	35.86	39.36
	Female	29.36	33.74	39.10	43.53
Black	Male	22.04	32.54	34.05	40.45
	Female	26.22	35.04	37.67	42.35

SOURCES: European nations from Dublin, Lotka, and Spiegelman, 1949, tables 87 and 88 (data interpolated to correspond to years above). Black data for original registration states in twentieth century are from Dublin, Lotka, and Spiegelman, 1949, tables 81 and 83. Data for blacks in 1880 are based on median figures for colored in four southern cities, Washington, D.C., Baltimore, Charleston, and New Orleans. Derived from data reported in Billings, 1886, pp. cxliv-cxlv.

then there is some reason to expect that the new Europeans might start off in a more favorable position than would blacks in the North even if there was no discrimination. Namely, if the average level of living for southern blacks was lower than that for whites residing in SCE Europe, then the relative attractiveness of certain job options in the North would differ for the groups. This does not mean that the upper end of their aspirations would differ, but it does mean that there is an intrinsic reason why blacks might start off lower. Of course, this situation is exacerbated by an additional force, the existence of even more discrimination against blacks than against SCE Europeans both in their initial jobs and later mobility. The "theory of intrinsic differences" developed here is sufficient to explain why groups will start off occupying different socioeconomic niches, but it

does not account for their continuation over time. Indeed, without discrimination or other factors one would expect such initial gaps to narrow progressively if there is intergenerational mobility (Lieberson and Fuguitt, 1967).[5] Accordingly, one must look elsewhere to understand why more discrimination was directed at blacks as well as why other forces have maintained these gaps.

Composition, the Latent Structure of Race Relations, and North-South Differences

Many have observed that the position of blacks started to deteriorate in this century as their numbers increased in the North. Basically two explanations for this have been offered: a shift in the "quality" of black migration and the response of whites to the radical increase in the numbers of blacks. In evaluating these explanations and offering an alternative, we should come closer to understanding the general forces that for so many decades have kept blacks from closing the initial gaps.

The quality interpretation is simply that migration northward became less selective over time, particularly after the decline in southern agriculture forced blacks to move in more or less helter-skelter fashion. There are two bodies of data that sharply challenge this thesis. Starting with the work of Bowles, Bacon, and Ritchey (1973) there is evidence to indicate that southern black migrants to the North in recent years have done relatively well when compared with northern-born blacks in terms of welfare, employment rates, earnings after background factors are taken into account, and so on. There is reason for this pattern to occur (Lieberson, 1978a), but the point here is that the results do not support the notion that the black position in the North was undermined by these migrants because of their qualities. A second data set, covering earlier decades as well, involves a comparison in each decade between the educational level of blacks living in the North in each decade with what would have occurred if there had been no migration into or out of the North during the preceding ten years. At most, the educational level of blacks in the North was only slightly different in each period from what it would have been without migration. This is due to the highly selective nature of black out-migration from the South (see Lieberson, 1978b).

As for the second explanation, namely, that changes in racial composition caused the black position to deteriorate, we know there was a massive increase in both the absolute number of blacks and their relative proportion of the population living in northern cities. The analysis of residential segregation in Lieberson (1980, chapter 9) fits in rather nicely with this perspective, with changes in the indexes accounted for by changes in population composition. But the segregation analysis involves a subtle difference from the assumption that the structure of race relations changed; it assumes that such dispositions were always present in a latent form and simply unfurl in accordance with shifts in population composition. To draw an analogy, if an automobile changes speed as we vary the pressure on the gas pedal, we do not assume that the engine changes in character with more or less gas. Rather we assume that the potential range of speeds was always there and is simply altered by the amount of gas received. In similar fashion, it is fruitful to assume that the reason for race relations changing with shifts in composition is not due to a radical alteration in the dispositions of whites, but rather that changes in composition affect the dispositions that existed all along. In other words, there is a latent structure to the race relations pattern in a given setting, with only certain parts of this structure observed at a given time. This fits in well with a long-standing ecological perspective on the influence of compositional changes on race and ethnic relations and competition (see, for example, Hawley, 1944). It also provides a rather novel perspective on North-South differences.

This way of thinking about the linkage between composition and race and ethnic relations has important consequences when approaching the deterioration in the position of blacks in the North and, indeed, the assumptions implicit to notions about the black position in various regions of the United States. How different was the situation for blacks in the South and non-South earlier in the century? Obviously there were very important historical differences between the regions. Even if there was far more to the Civil War than freeing the slaves, still the regions differed sharply in their history regarding slavery and their disposition toward the institution. Likewise, the customs were quite different in these regions with respect to such matters as poll taxes, Jim Crow laws, lynching, racial "etiquette," and the like. Some of these regional differences can probably be explained by the establishment of anti-black traditions that remain firm even after the causes have disappeared. Social events have a life of their own: once established, the customs persist long after causes vanish (see Lieberson, 1982).

But these important differences should not keep one from realizing that the North and South were still part of the same nation and shared certain qualities that were hidden only because the black composition in the regions was so radically different and because of historical forces. To be sure, if the small number of blacks living in a northern city had the vote, then they were unlikely to lose it when their proportion of the population increased to the point where it was of potential consequence to elections. But the latent structure of race relations in the North was not much different from the South on a variety of features. This has not been widely appreciated (a noteworthy exception being the analysis of the black position in the North before the end of slavery in the South by Litwack, 1961). It was not appreciated by those wanting to understand the changes in race relations as either due to the changing quality of blacks living in the North or some fundamental shifts in the United States. To be sure, there are a lot of complications affecting this comparison, witness the fact that the level of living was generally higher in the North and there were a number of institutional heritages in the South which blacks could avoid elsewhere. Hence there were strong incentives for migration from the South. But it is extremely helpful to recognize that the differences between regions with respect to bread-and-butter matters were not as radical as one would think by focusing exclusively on lynchings, poll taxes, race-baiting politicians, and legally sanctioned forms of segregation.

As noted [earlier], normally one does not ask why blacks in the South did not do as well as South-Central-Eastern Europeans. Until recently, circumstances were incredibly difficult for blacks in the South—witness, for example, the educational situation [described in Lieberson (1980, chapter 6)]. However, I believe there is reason to suspect that a substantial part of the North-South gap was really due to the much smaller proportion blacks were of the urban population in the North and their virtual absence from the rural North. As a consequence, certain similarities in disposition toward blacks and the conflict between lower and higher wage rates were concealed by these compositional factors. In other words, underlying the two regions were a large number of common dispositions. This, I might add, also helps us understand some of the shifts that have

occurred in the North when the black proportion of the population began to increase.

The Flow of Migrants

For more than a half century immigration from Europe has not been a significant factor in the SCE groups' growth, whereas the flow of blacks from South to North has been of importance in nearly all of this period. The significance of this widely cited difference is great. There are many more blacks who are recent migrants to the North whereas the immigrant component of the new Europeans drops off over time. Hence, at the very least it is important to make sure that generational factors are taken into account when comparing the ethnic groups. This is clearly an important consideration. For example, the median education of Japanese-American men increased massively between 1940 and 1960 in the United States—from 8.8 to 12.4 years of schooling. Almost all of this was due to changes in the generational composition of the group. With no immigration of any consequence for a number of decades, the foreign-born component dropped from 80 to 27 percent of the group. The actual shift in median education within the birthplace-specific components was rather small; from 8.3 to 8.8 years for the foreign-born and from 12.2 to 12.4 years for the American-born. In other words, almost all of the changes were simply due to shifts in generational composition (see Lieberson, 1973, pp. 562–563).

It is also argued that migration patterns are of significance because minimally skilled people no longer encounter the opportunities that once existed when the new Europeans were coming. This is not too convincing because there is every indication that occupational mobility is every bit as great now as it used to be. Second, black-white gaps in education are now narrowing rapidly. Finally, there is some reason to believe that intergenerational mobility in the North was never as good for blacks even in decades past (Thernstrom, 1973, pp. 183–194). I might add that the high unemployment rates among blacks in the

TABLE 2
Consequences of Black Population Increase for SCE European Jobs (queuing model)

Time	Percentage of population		Median percentile of jobs held		Increase in median percentile over previous time	
	Black	SCE European	Black	SCE European	Black	SCE European
1	5	10	2.5	10	—	—
2	10	10	5	15	2.5	5
3	20	10	10	25	5	10
4	30	10	15	35	5	10

NOTE: Median job percentile held is based on assumption that blacks received the lowest jobs in the community and that SCE European groups received the next lowest.

North are not as novel as some have suggested. This is because smaller black-white gaps in earlier periods were a reflection of the substantial concentration of blacks in the rural South and the hidden underemployment that represented (see Lieberson, 1980, chapter 8).

Notwithstanding the importance of drawing generational distinctions, there is another way of thinking about the end of European immigration and the continuous flow of blacks. Theoretically, such shifts have consequences of their own in a regular and orderly way. In terms of the occupational queuing notion [see Thurow, 1969, chapter 4], the increase in the black component means a rise in the median black occupational position in the community, but it will at the same time widen the gap between blacks and new Europeans. Assuming that there is an occupational queue in which blacks are at the bottom and the new Europeans are just above them, consider the hypothetical data shown in table 2. In the first period, 5 percent of the work force is black and 10 percent is new European. The median black job is at the 2.5 percentile because they hold the bottom 5 percent of the jobs; the median new European job is at the tenth percentile, because they hold the jobs that range from the fifth to the fifteenth percentiles. Suppose in each period the new European component of the work force remains at 10 percent whereas blacks go to 10, then 20, and finally 30 percent of the work force. In each period, the

average black percentile goes up but in each period the magnitude of the absolute gain in the average new European percentile goes up even faster. For example, from time 1 to time 2, the average black percentile goes up from 2.5 to 5, but the new European percentile goes up 5 points from 10 to 15. In similar fashion the new Europeans rise more rapidly when blacks go from 10 to 20 to 30 percent of the work force. This model ignores the fact that there will be some positive feedback as their component goes up because blacks will create a market for blacks pursuing such highly prestigious jobs as, for example, physicians, lawyers, dentists, merchants geared to blacks, and the like. Also, it assumes that the queuing is perfect such that the lowest SCE European enjoys a better job than the most highly placed black. Clearly this is false. But I believe the model does give one a clear understanding of how increases in the black component would upgrade the new Europeans at a more rapid rate as long as the queuing process remains intact. In effect, this queuing notion is compatible with the long-standing ladder model that holds that increases in a lower-ranked population would tend to upgrade the populations above them. In this sense, the growing presence of blacks did indeed benefit the new Europeans—not because they were more likely to discriminate against blacks than were other segments of the white population, but because blacks were lower on the hierarchy. This all operates insofar as there are strong enough barriers through unions, employers, and other discriminatory forces to stave off the potential undercutting of whites through the acceptance of lower wages by blacks.

The spectacular events since World War II should be seen in the context of these changes in the flow of migrants. The continuation of black migration to the North and the cessation of new European immigration helped upgrade the SCE groups in two additional ways besides the queuing process discussed above. These are the impact that newer segments of a group have on older segments and the overloading of special niches that each group tends to develop in the labor market. (None of this is to overlook the employment opportunities generated in the 1940s due to the massive demands of the war and in the post–World War II period. Bear in mind that there was a depression prior to the war and hence these demands not only meant new opportunities for blacks but also for the SCE European groups who were still higher on the queue.)

As for special niches, it is clear that most racial and ethnic groups tend to develop concentrations in certain jobs which either reflect some distinctive cultural characteristics, special skills initially held by some members, or the opportunity structure at the time of their arrival. In 1950 among the foreign-born men of different origins there were many such examples: 3.9 percent of Italians in the civilian labor force were barbers, eight times the level for all white men; 2.5 percent of the Irish were policemen or firemen, three times the rate for all white men; more than 2 percent of Scottish immigrants were accountants, about two and one-half times the level for whites; 9.4 percent of Swedish immigrants were carpenters, nearly four times the national level; 14.8 percent of Greek immigrant men ran eating and drinking establishments, 29 times the national level; and 3.3 percent of Russian immigrant men were tailors or furriers, 17 times the rate for all white men.[6] These concentrations are partially based on networks of ethnic contacts and experiences that in turn direct other compatriots in these directions. Each group does this and, because the job hierarchy is not a perfect system, such activities help give each group certain special niches that it might not otherwise have in a pure system of queues altered only by ethnic compatriot demands. In these cases, the group develops an "export" market in the sense of being able to supply needs and wants for other groups.

When the migration of a group accelerates, the ability to develop and exploit these special niches is badly handicapped. Such specialties can only absorb a small part of a group's total work force when its population grows rapidly or is a substantial proportion of the total population. After all, not everyone of Chinese origin could open a restaurant in a city where they are a sizable segment of the population, just as not all Jews could have opened stores in New York City. By contrast, when the numbers stabilize or increase at only a moderate clip, then the possibilities due to these ingroup concentrations are more sanguine. Thus, in communities where the group is a sizable segment of the population, it is more difficult for such niches to absorb much of the group.

The cessation of immigration, whether it involved the Japanese and Chinese or the South-Central-Eastern European groups, had long-run advantages to those members of the group already in the nation. (To be sure, there were certain negative costs such as the group's own natural market for compatriots' services or the expansion of demographically based power.) But these events help explain why blacks were unable to participate with the new Europeans in the massive socioeconomic shifts experienced in recent decades. In other words, it is more difficult to overcome the negative consequences of discrimination through special niches when the group is growing rapidly and/or is a large segment of the total population.

There is another way through which newcomers have a harmful effect on earlier arrivals and longer-standing residents from the same group. Sizable numbers of newcomers raise the level of ethnic and/or racial consciousness on the part of others in the city; moreover, if these newcomers are less able to compete for more desirable positions than are the longer-standing residents, they will tend to undercut the position of other members of the group. This is because the older residents and those of higher socioeconomic status cannot totally avoid the newcomers, although they work at it through subgroup residential isolation. Hence, there is some deterioration in the quality of residential areas, schools, and the like for those earlier residents who might otherwise enjoy more fully the rewards of their mobility. Beyond this, from the point of view of the dominant outsiders, the newcomers may reinforce stereotypes and negative dispositions that affect all members of the group.

Finally, I suspect that group boundaries shift and float in multiethnic or multiracial settings more than some recognize. Antagonisms and dispositions change in accordance with the group context. In this case, the movement of blacks to the North in sizable numbers reduced the negative disposition other whites had toward the new European groups. If the new Europeans rank higher in a queue, then the negative dispositions toward them would be muffled and modified in a setting where they would be viewed as relatively more desirable as neighbors, co-workers, political candidates, and so on than blacks. Ethnic ties and allegiances float and shift in accordance with the threats and alternatives that exist. The presence of blacks made it harder to discriminate against the new Europeans because the alternative was viewed even less favorably.

Under these circumstances, the rapid growth of the black population in the urban North during the last half century or so, accompanied by the opposite trend for the new Europeans, has significantly contributed to the differences in outcome experienced by these groups. These differences would be expected even if one ignores the latent structure of race relations tapped by these demographic changes in the North.

Further Analysis of Race

I believe there is further reason for speculating that race was not as crucial an issue as is commonly supposed for understanding the black outcome relative to the new Europeans. In order to avoid being misunderstood by the casual reader, let me reiterate that such a conclusion does not mean that other nonwhite groups or the new Europeans possessed certain favorable characteristics to a greater degree than did blacks. There is an alternative way of interpreting these events, namely, a substantial source of the disadvantage faced by blacks is due to their position with respect to certain structural conditions that affect race relations generally. Having been reviewed in this chapter, one should now make sense of black–new European gaps, but what about comparisons of blacks with other nonwhites? There are eight important factors to consider.

1. Although hard quantitative data are not available, there is every reason to believe that the response to Chinese and Japanese in the United States was every bit as severe and as violent initially as that toward blacks when the latter moved outside of their traditional niches.

2. There was a cessation of sizable immigration from Japan and China for a number of decades before these groups were able to advance in the society.

3. The cessation was due to the intense pressures within the United States against Asian migration, particularly by those whites who were threatened by these potential competitors.

4. This meant that the number of these groups in the nation is quite small relative to blacks. In the 1970 census there were 22,580,000 blacks recorded compared with 591,000 Japanese and 435,000 Chinese.

5. Because of factors 2 and 4 above, the opportunity for these Asian groups to occupy special niches was far greater than for blacks. Imagine more than 22 million Japanese Americans trying to carve out initial niches through truck farming!

6. Because of factor 2 there has been less negative effect on the general position of these groups due to recent immigrants (a situation that is now beginning to change somewhat for the Chinese).

7. Ignoring situations generated by direct competition between Asians and whites such as existed in the West earlier, there is some evidence that the white disposition toward blacks was otherwise even more unfavorable than that toward Asians. This is due to the ideologies that developed in connection with slavery as well as perhaps the images of Africa and its people stemming from exploration of the continent. Whatever the reason, one has the impression that whites have strikingly different attitudes toward the cultures

of China and Japan than toward those of blacks or of Africa.

8. The massive economic threat blacks posed for whites earlier in the century in both the South and North was not duplicated by the Asians except in certain parts of the West.

I am suggesting a general process that occurs when racial and ethnic groups have an inherent conflict—and certainly competition for jobs, power, position, maintenance of different subcultural systems, and the like are such conflicts. Under the circumstances, there is a tendency for the competitors to focus on differences between themselves. The observers (in this case the sociologists) may then assume that these differences are the sources of conflict. In point of fact, the rhetoric involving such differences may indeed inflame them, but we can be reasonably certain that the conflict would have occurred in their absence. To use a contemporary example, if Protestants in Northern Ireland had orange skin color and if the skin color of Roman Catholics in that country was green, then very likely these physical differences would be emphasized by observers seeking to explain the sharp conflict between these groups. Indeed, very likely such racial differences would be emphasized by the combatants themselves. No doubt such physical differences would enter into the situation as a secondary cause because the rhetoric would inflame that difference, but we can be reasonably certain that the conflict would occur in their absence. In the same fashion, differences between blacks and whites—real ones, imaginary ones, and those that are the product of earlier race relations—enter into the rhetoric of race and ethnic relations, but they are ultimately secondary to the conflict for society's goodies.

This certainly is the conclusion that can be generated from the classic experiment by Sherif and Sherif (1953) in which a homogeneous group of children at camp were randomly sorted into two groups and then competition and conflict between the groups was stimulated. The experiment resulted in each of the groups developing all sorts of images about themselves and the other group. Yet, unknown to them, the groups were identical in their initial distribution of characteristics.

In order to avoid a misunderstanding of a position that is radically different from that held by most observers, whether they be black or white, oriented toward one group or the other, let me restate this part of my thesis. There is powerful evidence that blacks were victims of more severe forms of discrimination than were the new Europeans—although the latter also suffered from intense discrimination. Much of the antagonism toward blacks was based on racial features, but one should not interpret this as the ultimate cause. Rather the racial emphasis resulted from the use of the most obvious feature(s) of the group to support the intergroup conflict generated by a fear of blacks based on their threat as economic competitors. If this analysis is correct, it also means that were the present-day conflict between blacks and dominant white groups to be resolved, then the race issue could rapidly disintegrate as a crucial barrier between the groups just as a very profound and deep distaste for Roman Catholics on the part of the dominant Protestants has diminished rather substantially (albeit not disappeared).

The Great Non Sequitur

The data comparing blacks and the new Europeans earlier in this century lead one to a rather clear conclusion about the initial question. The early living conditions of the new Europeans after their migration to the United States were extremely harsh and their point of entry into the socioeconomic system was quite low. However, it is a non sequitur to assume that new Europeans had it as bad as did blacks or that the failure of blacks to move upward as rapidly reflected some ethnic deficiencies. The situation for new Europeans in the United States, bad as it may have been, was not as bad as that experienced by blacks at the same time. Witness, for example, the differences in the disposition to ban openly blacks from unions at the turn of the century (Lieberson, 1980, chapter 11), the greater concentration of blacks in 1900 in service occupations and their smaller numbers in manufacturing and mechanical jobs (Lieberson, 1980, chapter 10), the higher black death rates in the North (Lieberson, 1980, chapter 2), and even the greater segregation of blacks with respect to the avenues of eminence open to them (Lieberson and Carter, 1979). It is a serious mistake to underestimate how far the new Europeans have come in the nation and how hard it all was, but it is equally erroneous to assume that the obstacles were as great as those faced by blacks or that the starting point was the same.

Notes

1. Compare the data on Italian, Polish, and Russian education in younger ages, occupation, and income with that for Americans of British origin in *Population Characteristics* (United States Bureau of the Census, 1973, tables 6–9). The traditional basis for allocating European sources into the old and new categories is somewhat arbitrary and, in some cases, does not correspond with the period of greatest immigration. For example, several Scandinavian sources were more important between 1880 and 1920 than they were in earlier decades. In keeping with traditional analysis, Germany is an old source and included with the Northwestern European nations even though it is a central European nation (Lieberson, 1963, p. 551).

2. This is a bit of an unfair comparison because these are national corporations and hence may tend to draw to some degree on the national market for executive recruitment and board members.

3. The distinction between "voluntary" and "involuntary" is sometimes not entirely clear, as in the case of starvation or political pressures in the sending country. Nevertheless, in those cases one can still argue that the motivation to move stems from more attractive conditions in the receiving country or subarea.

4. The original ten registration states used to provide data on black mortality in 1900, 1910, and 1920 were the six New England states and four elsewhere in the North. The reader may wonder if this is an appropriate measure for blacks because it is the living conditions of blacks in the South that are relevant here as an index for determining the jobs that they would accept in the North. Regional life tables, first available for 1930–1939, indicate that the three southern regions all have higher expectation of life at birth for nonwhite males than do either the North Atlantic or North-Central regions; this is also the case for two of the southern regions when compared to the Mountain and Pacific category. The gaps are not as great for nonwhite females (see Dublin, Lotka, and Spiegelman, 1949, tables 81, 83). The same sources also indicate that nonwhites in the rural South in 1939 had higher expectations of life than did nonwhites in either different regions or in different types of

communities. A special adjustment that takes into account this difficulty still supports the conclusion that life expectancy at birth for South-Central-Eastern European countries was generally more favorable. Because the West-South-Central states had the highest and the North-Central region the lowest $\mathring{e}_0$, the black data shown in table 1 were multiplied by the ratio of West-South-Central to North-Central regional black life table values in 1930–1939. This gave the most favorable increase to black values. In all periods the majority of SCE European nations still had higher life expectancy at birth even after this adjustment.

5. Another force probably operating in the same direction stems from the fact that the South was, of course, much closer to the North than was South-Central-Eastern Europe. If it is reasonable to assume that the minimum improvement necessary to stimulate migration will vary directly with distance, expressed in time-cost factors, then this force will also work toward generating an initial difference favoring the white groups.

6. Based on data reported in Hutchinson, 1956, table A-2a. See the table for detailed titles of the occupations described in the text.

References

Billings, John S. *Report on the Mortality and Vital Statistics of the United States, Part 2.* Washington, D.C.: Government Printing Office, 1886.

Bonacich, Edna. "A Theory of Ethnic Antagonism: The Split Labor Market." *American Sociological Review* 37 (1972): 547–559.

————. "Advanced Capitalism and Black/White Race Relations in the United States: A Split Labor Market Interpretation." *American Sociological Review* 41 (1976): 34–51.

Bowles, Gladys K., A. L. Bacon, and P. N. Ritchey. *Poverty Dimensions of Rural-to-Urban Migration: A Statistical Report.* Washington, D.C.: Economic Research Service, U.S. Department of Agriculture, 1973.

Dublin, Louis I., Alfred J. Lotka, and Mortimer Spiegelman. *Length of Life: A Study of the Life Table.* 2nd ed., rev. New York: Ronald Press, 1949.

Hawley, Amos H. "Dispersion Versus Segregation: Apropos of a Solution of Race Problems." Papers of the Michigan Academy of Science, Arts, and Letters 30 (1944): 667–674. Adopted in *Race: Individual and Collective Behavior,* edited by Edgar T. Thompson and Everett C. Hughes, pp. 199–204. Glencoe, Ill.: Free Press, 1958.

Hutchinson, E. P. *Immigrants and Their Children, 1850–1950.* New York: Wiley, 1956.

Institute of Urban Life. "Report on the Representation of Poles, Italians, Latins and Blacks in the Executive Suites of Chicago's Largest Corporations." Chicago: Institute of Urban Life, 1973.

Lieberson, Stanley. "The Old-New Distinction and Immigrants in Australia." *American Sociological Review* 28 (1963): 550–565.

———. "Generational Differences Among Blacks in the North." *American Journal of Sociology* 79 (1973): 550–565.

———. "A Reconsideration of the Income Differences Found Between Migrants and Northern-Born Blacks." *American Journal of Sociology* 83 (1978a): 940–966.

———. "Selective Black Migration from the South: A Historical View." In *Demography of Racial and Ethnic Groups,* edited by Frank D. Bean and W. Parker Frisbie, pp. 119–141. New York: Academic Press, 1978b.

———. *A Piece of the Pie: Blacks and White Immigrants Since 1880.* Berkeley: University of California Press, 1980.

———. "Forces Affecting Language Spread: Some Basic Propositions." In *Language Spread: Studies in Diffusion and Social Change,* edited by Robert L. Cooper, pp. 37–62. Bloomington: Indiana University Press, 1982.

Lieberson, Stanley, and Donna K. Carter. "Making It in America: Differences Between Eminent Blacks and White Ethnic Groups." *American Sociological Review* 44 (1979): 347–366.

Lieberson, Stanley, and Glenn V. Fuguitt. "Negro-White Occupational Differences in the Absence of Discrimination." *American Journal of Sociology* 73 (1967): 188–200.

Litwack, Leon F. *North of Slavery: The Negro in the Free States, 1790–1860.* Chicago: University of Chicago Press, 1961.

Mayer, Martin. *The Bankers.* New York: Weybright & Talley, 1974.

Sherif, Muzafer, and Carolyn W. Sherif. *Groups in Harmony and Tension: An Integration of Studies on Intergroup Relations.* New York: Harper & Brothers, 1953.

Thernstrom, Stephan. *The Other Bostonians: Poverty and Progress in the American Metropolis, 1880–1970.* Cambridge, Mass.: Harvard University Press, 1973.

Thurow, Lester C. *Poverty and Discrimination.* Washington, D.C.: Brookings Institution, 1969.

United States Bureau of the Census. *Population Characteristics.* "Characteristics of the Population by Ethnic Origin: March 1972 and 1971." Series P-20, No. 249. Washington, D.C.: Government Printing Office, 1973.

United States Senate Committee on Banking, Housing and Urban Affairs. *Treasury Department's Administration of the Contract Compliance Program for Financial Institutions.* Washington, D.C.: Government Printing Office, 1976.

DANIEL P. MOYNIHAN

The Tangle of Pathology

That the Negro American has survived at all is extraordinary—a lesser people might simply have died out, as indeed others have. That the Negro community has not only survived, but in this political generation has entered national affairs as a moderate, humane, and constructive national force is the highest testament to the healing powers of the democratic ideal and the creative vitality of the Negro people.

But it may not be supposed that the Negro American community has not paid a fearful price for the incredible mistreatment to which it has been subjected over the past three centuries.

In essence, the Negro community has been forced into a matriarchal structure which, because it is so out of line with the rest of the American society, seriously retards the progress of the group as a whole, and imposes a crushing burden on the Negro male and, in consequence, on a great many Negro women as well.

There is, presumably, no special reason why a society in which males are dominant in family relationships is to be preferred to a matriarchal arrangement. However, it is clearly a disadvantage for a minority group to be operating on one principle, while the great majority of the population, and the one with the most advantages to begin with, is operating on another. This is the present situation of the Negro. Ours is a society which presumes male leadership in private and public affairs. The arrangements of society facilitate such leadership and reward it. A subculture, such as that of the Negro American, in which this is not the pattern, is placed at a distinct disadvantage.

There is much evidence that a considerable number of Negro families have managed to break out of the tangle of pathology and to establish themselves as stable, effective units, living according to patterns of American society in general. E. Franklin Frazier has suggested that the middle-class Negro American family is, if anything, more patriarchal and protective of its children than the general run of such families.[1] Given equal opportunities, the children of these families will perform as well or better than their white peers. They need no help from anyone, and ask none.

While this phenomenon is not easily measured, one index is that middle-class Negroes have even fewer children than middle-class whites, indicating a desire to conserve the advances they have made and to insure that their children do as well or better. Negro women who marry early to uneducated laborers have more children than white women in the same situation; Negro women who marry at the common age for the middle class to educated men doing technical or professional work have only four-fifths as many children as their white counterparts.

It might be estimated that as much as half of the Negro community falls into the middle class. However, the remaining half is in desperate and deteriorating circumstances. Moreover, because of housing segregation it is immensely difficult for the stable half to escape from the cultural influences of the unstable one. The children of middle-class Negroes often as not must grow up in or next to the slums, an experience almost unknown to white middle-class children. They are therefore constantly exposed to the pathology of the disturbed group and constantly in danger of being drawn into it. It is for this reason that the propositions put forth in this study may be thought of as having a more or less general application.

In a word, most Negro youth are in *danger* of being caught up in the tangle of pathology that affects their world, and probably a majority are so entrapped. Many of those who escape do so for one generation only: as things now are, their children may have to run the gauntlet all over again. That is not the least vicious aspect of the world that white America has made for the Negro.

Obviously, not every instance of social pathology afflicting the Negro community can be traced to the weakness of family structure. If, for example, organized crime in the Negro community were not largely controlled by whites, there would be more capital accumulation among Negroes, and therefore probably more Negro business enterprises. If it were not for the hostility and fear many whites exhibit towards Negroes, they in turn would be less afflicted by hostility and fear and so on. There is no one Negro community. There is no one Negro problem. There is no one solution. Nonetheless, at the center of the tangle of pathology is the weakness of the family structure. Once or twice removed, it will be found to be the principal source of most of the aberrant, inadequate, or antisocial behavior that did not establish, but now serves to perpetuate the cycle of poverty and deprivation.

It was by destroying the Negro family under slavery that white America broke the will of the Negro People. Although that will has reasserted itself in our time, it is a resurgence doomed to frustration unless the viability of the Negro family is restored.

Matriarchy

A fundamental fact of Negro American family life is the often reversed roles of husband and wife.

Robert O. Blood, Jr., and Donald M. Wolfe, in a study of Detroit families, note that "Negro husbands have unusually low power,"[2] and while this is characteristic of all low income families, the pattern pervades the Negro social structure: "the cumulative result of discrimination in jobs … ,

the segregated housing, and the poor schooling of Negro men."[3] In 44 percent of the Negro families studied, the wife was dominant, as against 20 percent of white wives. "Whereas the majority of white families are equalitarian, the largest percentage of Negro families are dominated by the wife."[4]

The matriarchal pattern of so many Negro families reinforces itself over the generations. This process begins with education. Although the gap appears to be closing at the moment, for a long while, Negro females were better educated than Negro males, and this remains true today for the Negro population as a whole.

The difference in educational attainment between nonwhite men and women in the labor force is even greater; men lag 1.1 years behind women. …

Inevitably, these disparities have carried over to the area of employment and income.

In 1 out of 4 Negro families where the husband is present, is an earner, and someone else in the family works, the husband is not the principal earner. The comparable figure for whites is 18 percent.

More important, it is clear that Negro females have established a strong position for themselves in white collar and professional employment, precisely the areas of the economy which are growing most rapidly, and to which the highest prestige is accorded.

The President's Committee on Equal Employment Opportunity, making a preliminary report on employment in 1964 of over 16,000 companies with nearly 5 million employees, revealed this pattern with dramatic emphasis.

In this work force, Negro males outnumber Negro females by a ratio of 4 to 1. Yet Negro males represent only 1.2 percent of the males in white collar occupations, while Negro females represent 3.1 percent of the total female white collar work force. Negro males represent 1.1 percent of all male professionals, whereas Negro females represent roughly 6 percent of all female professionals. Again, in technician occupations, Negro males represent 2.1 percent of all male technicians while Negro females represent roughly 10 percent of all female technicians. It would appear therefore that there are proportionately 4 times as many Negro females in significant white collar jobs than Negro males.

Although it is evident that office and clerical jobs account for approximately 50 percent of all Negro female white collar workers, it is significant that 6 out of every 100 Negro females are in professional jobs. This is substantially similar to the rate of all females in such jobs. Approximately 7 out of every 100 Negro females are in technician jobs. This exceeds the proportion of all females in technician jobs—approximately 5 out of every 100.

Negro females in skilled jobs are almost the same as that of all females in such jobs. Nine out of every 100 Negro males are in skilled occupations while 21 out of 100 of all males are in such jobs.[5]

This pattern is to be seen in the Federal government, where special efforts have been made recently to insure equal employment opportunity for Negroes. These efforts have been notably successful in Departments such as Labor, where some 19 percent of employees are now Negro. (A not disproportionate percentage, given the composition of the work force in the areas where the main Department offices are located.) However, it may well be that these efforts have redounded mostly to the benefit of Negro women, and may even have accentuated the comparative disadvantage of Negro men. Seventy percent of the Negro employees of the Department of Labor are women, as contrasted with only 42 percent of the white employees.

Among nonprofessional Labor Department employees—where the most employment opportunities exist for all groups—Negro women outnumber Negro men 4 to 1, and average almost one grade higher in classification.

The testimony to the effects of these patterns in Negro family structure is widespread, and hardly to be doubted:

Duncan M. MacIntyre

The Negro illegitimacy rate always has been high—about eight times the white rate in 1940 and somewhat higher today even though the white illegitimacy rate also is climbing. The Negro statistics are symptomatic of some old socioeconomic problems, not the least of which are underemployment among Negro men and compensating higher labor force propensity among Negro women. Both operate to enlarge the mother's role, undercutting the status of the male and making many Negro families essentially matriarchal. The Negro man's uncertain employment prospects, matriarchy, and high cost of divorces combine to encourage desertion (the poor man's divorce), increase the number of couples not married, and thereby also increase the Negro illegitimacy rate. In the meantime, higher Negro birth rates are increasing the nonwhite population, while migration into cities like Detroit, New York, Philadelphia, and Washington, D.C., is making the public assistance rolls in such cities heavily, even predominantly, Negro.[6]

Robin M. Williams, Jr., in a Study of Elmira, New York

Only 57 percent of Negro adults reported themselves as married—spouse present, as compared with 78 percent of native white American gentiles, 91 percent of Italian-American, and 96 percent of Jewish informants. Of the 93 unmarried Negro youths interviewed, 22 percent did not have their mother living in the home with them, and 42 percent reported that their father was not living in their home. One-third of the youths did not know their father's present occupation, and two-thirds of a sample of 150 Negro adults did not know what the occupation of their father's father had been. Forty percent of the youths said that they had brothers and sisters living in other communities; another 40 percent reported relatives living in their home who were not parents, siblings, or grandparents.[7]

The Failure of Youth

Williams' account of Negro youth growing up with little knowledge of their fathers, less of their fathers' occupations, still less of family occupational traditions, is in sharp contrast to the experience of the white child. The white family, despite many variants, remains a powerful agency not only for transmitting property from one generation to the next, but also for transmitting no less valuable contacts with the world of education and work. In an earlier age, the Carpenters, Wainwrights, Weavers, Mercers, Farmers, Smiths acquired their names as well as their trades from their fathers and grandfathers. Children today still learn the patterns of work from their fathers even though they may no longer go into the same jobs.

White children without fathers at least perceive all about them the pattern of men working.

Negro children without fathers flounder—and fail.

Not always, to be sure. The Negro community produces its share, very possibly more than its share, of young people who have the something extra that carries them over the worst obstacles. But such persons are always a minority. The common run of young people in a group facing serious obstacles to success do not succeed.

A prime index of the disadvantage of Negro youth in the United States is their consistently poor performance on the mental tests that are a standard means of measuring ability and performance in the present generation.

There is absolutely no question of any genetic differential: Intelligence potential is distributed among Negro infants in the same proportion and pattern as among Icelanders or Chinese or any other group. American society, however, impairs the Negro potential. The statement of the HARYOU report that "there is no basic disagreement over the fact that central Harlem students are performing poorly in school"[8] may be taken as true of Negro slum children throughout the United States.

Eighth grade children in central Harlem have a median IQ of 87.7, which means that perhaps a third of the children are scoring at levels perilously near to those of retardation. IQ *declines* in the first decade of life, rising only slightly thereafter.

The effect of broken families on the performance of Negro youth has not been extensively measured, but studies that have been made show an unmistakable influence.

Martin Deutch and Bert Brown, investigating intelligence test differences between Negro and white 1st and 5th graders of different social classes, found that there is a direct relationship between social class and IQ. As the one rises so does the other: but more for whites than Negroes. This is surely a result of housing segregation, referred to earlier, which makes it difficult for middle-class Negro families to escape the slums.

The authors explain that "it is much more difficult for the Negro to attain identical middle- or upper-middle-class status with whites, and the social class gradations are less marked for Negroes because Negro life in a caste society is considerably more homogeneous than is life for the majority group."[9]

Therefore, the authors look for background variables other than social class which might explain the difference: "One of the most striking differences between the Negro and white groups is the consistently higher frequency of broken homes and resulting family disorganization in the Negro group."[10]

Further, they found that children from homes where fathers are present have significantly higher scores than children in homes without fathers.

The influence of the father's presence was then tested *within* the social classes and school grades for Negroes alone. They found that "a consistent trend within both grades at the lower SES [social class] level appears, and in no case is there a reversal of this trend: for males, females, and the combined group, the IQ's of children with fathers in the home are always higher than those who have no father in the home."[11]

The authors say that broken homes "may also account for some of the differences between Negro and white intelligence scores."[12]

The scores of fifth graders with fathers absent were lower than the scores of first graders with fathers absent, and while the authors point out that it is cross sectional data and does not reveal the duration of the fathers' absence, "What we might be tapping is the cumulative effect of fatherless years."[13]

This difference in ability to perform has its counterpart in statistics on actual school performance. Nonwhite boys from families with both parents present are more likely to be going to school than boys with only one parent present, and enrollment rates are even lower when neither parent is present.

When the boys from broken homes are in school, they do not do as well as the boys from whole families. Grade retardation is higher when only one parent is present, and highest when neither parent is present.

The loneliness of the Negro youth in making fundamental decisions about education is shown in a 1959 study of Negro and white dropouts in Connecticut high schools.

Only 29 percent of the Negro male dropouts discussed their decision to drop out of school with their fathers, compared with 65 percent of the white males (38 percent of the Negro males were from broken homes). In fact, 26 percent of the Negro males did not discuss this major decision in their lives with anyone at all, compared with only 8 percent of white males.

A study of Negro apprenticeship by the New York State Commission Against Discrimination[14] in 1960 concluded:

Negro youth are seldom exposed to influences which can lead to apprenticeship. Negroes are not apt to have relatives, friends, or neighbors in skilled occupations. Nor are they likely to be in secondary schools where they receive encouragement and direction from alternate role models. Within the minority community, skilled Negro "models" after whom the Negro youth might pattern himself are rare, while substitute sources which could provide the direction, encouragement, resources, and information needed to achieve skilled craft standing are nonexistent. ...

Alienation

The present generation of Negro youth growing up in the urban ghettos has probably less personal contact with the white world than any generation in the history of the Negro American.[15]

Until World War II it could be said that in general the Negro and white worlds lived, if not together, at least side by side. Certainly they did, and do, in the South.

Since World War II, however, the two worlds have drawn physically apart. The symbol of this development was the construction in the 1940's and 1950's of the vast white middle- and lower-middle class suburbs around all of the Nation's cities. Increasingly, the inner cities have been left to Negroes—who now share almost no community life with whites.

In turn, because of this new housing pattern—most of which has been financially assisted by the Federal government—it is probable that the American school system has become *more,* rather than less segregated in the past two decades.

School integration has not occurred in the South, where a decade after *Brown* v. *Board of Education* only 1 Negro in 9 is attending school with white children.

And in the North, despite strenuous official efforts, neighborhoods and therefore schools are becoming more and more of one class and one color.

In New York City, in the school year 1957–58 there were 64 schools that were 90 percent or more Negro or Puerto Rican. Six years later there were 134 such schools.

Along with the diminution of white middle-class contacts for a large percentage of Negroes, observers report that the Negro churches have all but lost contact with men in the Northern cities as well. This may be a normal condition of urban life, but it is probably a changed condition for the Negro American and cannot be a socially desirable development.

The only religious movement that appears to have enlisted a considerable number of lower-class Negro males in Northern cities of late is that of the Black Muslims: a movement based on total rejection of white society, even though it emulates white mores.

In a word: the tangle of pathology is tightening.

Notes

1. E. Franklin Frazier, *Black Bourgeoisie* (New York: Collier Books, 1962).
2. Robert O. Blood, Jr., and Donald M. Wolfe, *Husbands and Wives: The Dynamics of Married Living* (New York: The Free Press, 1960), p. 34.
3. *Ibid,* p. 35.
4. *Ibid.*
5. Based on preliminary draft of a report by the President's Committee on Equal Employment Opportunity.
6. Duncan M. MacIntyre, *Public Assistance: Too Much or Too Little?* (New York: New York State School of Industrial Relations, Cornell University, Bulletin 53-1, December 1964), pp. 73–74.
7. Robin M. Williams, Jr., *Strangers Next Door* (Englewood Cliffs, N.J.: Prentice-Hall, Inc., 1964), p. 240.
8. *Youth in the Ghetto* (New York: Harlem Youth Opportunities Unlimited), p. 195.
9. Martin Deutch and Bert Brown, "Social Influences in Negro–White Intelligence Differences," *Social Issues,* April 1964, p. 27.
10. *Ibid,* p. 29.
11. *Ibid.*
12. *Ibid,* p. 31.

13. *Ibid.*

14. "Negroes in Apprenticeship, New York State," *Monthly Labor Review,* September 1960, p. 955.

15. Nathan Glazer and Daniel Patrick Moynihan, *Beyond the Melting Pot* (Cambridge, Mass.: M.I.T. Press, 1965).

WILLIAM JULIUS WILSON

The Truly Disadvantaged: The Inner City, the Underclass, and Public Policy

In the mid-1960s, urban analysts began to speak of a new dimension to the urban crisis in the form of a large subpopulation of low-income families and individuals whose behavior contrasted sharply with the behavior of the general population.[1] Despite a high rate of poverty in ghetto neighborhoods throughout the first half of the twentieth century, rates of inner-city joblessness, teenage pregnancies, out-of-wedlock births, female-headed families, welfare dependency, and serious crime were significantly lower than in later years and did not reach catastrophic proportions until the mid-1970s.

These increasing rates of social dislocation signified changes in the social organization of inner-city areas. Blacks in Harlem and in other ghetto neighborhoods did not hesitate to sleep in parks, on fire escapes, and on rooftops during hot summer nights in the 1940s and 1950s, and whites frequently visited inner-city taverns and nightclubs.[2] There was crime, to be sure, but it had not reached the point where people were fearful of walking the streets at night, despite the overwhelming poverty in the area. There was joblessness, but it was nowhere near the proportions of unemployment and labor-force nonparticipation that have gripped ghetto communities since 1970. There were single-parent families, but they were a small minority of all black families and tended to be incorporated within extended family networks and to be headed not by unwed teenagers and young adult women but by middle-aged women who usually were widowed, separated, or divorced. There were welfare recipients, but only a very small percentage of the families could be said to be welfare-dependent. In short, unlike the present period, inner-city communities prior to 1960 exhibited the features of social organization—including a sense of community, positive neighborhood identification, and explicit norms and sanctions against aberrant behavior.[3]

Although liberal urban analysts in the mid-1960s hardly provided a definitive explanation of changes in the social organization of inner-city neighborhoods, they forcefully and candidly discussed the rise of social dislocations among the ghetto underclass. "The symptoms of lower-class society affect the dark ghettos of America—low aspirations, poor education, family instability, illegitimacy, unemployment, crime, drug addiction, and alcoholism, frequent illness and early death," stated Kenneth B. Clark, liberal author of a 1965 study of the black ghetto. "But because Negroes begin with the primary affliction of inferior racial status, the burdens of despair and hatred are more pervasive."[4] In raising important issues about the experiences of inequality, liberal scholars in the 1960s sensitively examined the cumulative effects of racial isolation and chronic subordination on life and behavior in the inner city. Whether the focus was on the social or the psychological dimensions of the ghetto, facts of inner-city life "that are usually forgotten or ignored in polite discussions" were vividly described and systematically analyzed.[5]

Indeed, what was both unique and important about these earlier studies was that discussions of the experiences of inequality were closely tied to discussions of the structure of inequality in an attempt to explain how the economic and social situations into which so many disadvantaged blacks are born produce modes of adaptation and create norms and patterns of behavior that take the form of a "self-perpetuating pathology."[6] Nonetheless, much of the evidence from which their conclusions were drawn was impressionistic—based mainly on data collected in ethnographic or urban field research that did not capture long-term trends.[7] Indeed, the only study that provided at least an abstract sense of how the problem had changed down through the years was the Moynihan report on the Negro family, which presented decennial census statistics on changing family structure by race.[8]

However, the controversy surrounding the Moynihan report had the effect of curtailing serious research on minority problems in the inner city for over a decade, as liberal scholars shied away from researching behavior construed as unflattering or stigmatizing to particular racial minorities. Thus, when liberal scholars returned to study these problems in the early 1980s, they were dumbfounded by the magnitude of the changes that had taken place and expressed little optimism about finding an adequate explanation. Indeed, it had become quite clear that there was little consensus on the description of the problem, the explanations advanced, or the policy recommendations proposed. There was even little agreement on a definition of the term *underclass*. From the perspective of liberal social scientists, policymakers, and others, the picture seemed more confused than ever.

However, if liberals lack a clear view of the recent social changes in the inner city, the perspective among informed conservatives has crystallized around a set of arguments that have received increasing public attention. Indeed, the debate over the problems of the ghetto underclass has been dominated in recent years by conservative spokespersons as the views of liberals have gradu-

ally become more diffused and ambiguous. Liberals have traditionally emphasized how the plight of disadvantaged groups can be related to the problems of the broader society, including problems of discrimination and social-class subordination. They have also emphasized the need for progressive social change, particularly through governmental programs, to open the opportunity structure. Conservatives, in contrast, have traditionally stressed the importance of different group values and competitive resources in accounting for the experiences of the disadvantaged; if reference is made to the larger society, it is in terms of the assumed adverse effects of various government programs on individual or group behavior and initiative.

In emphasizing this distinction, I do not want to convey the idea that serious research or discussion of the ghetto underclass is subordinated to ideological concerns. However, despite pious claims about objectivity in social research, it is true that values influence not only our selection of problems for investigation but also our interpretation of empirical data. And although there are no logical rules of discovery that would invalidate an explanation simply because if was influenced by a particular value premise or ideology, it is true that attempts to arrive at a satisfactory explanation may be impeded by ideological blinders or views restricted by value premises. The solution to this problem is not to try to divest social investigators of their values but to encourage a free and open discussion of the issues among people with different value premises in order that new questions can be raised, existing interpretations challenged, and new research stimulated. ...

The Ghetto Underclass and Social Dislocations

Why have the social conditions of the ghetto underclass deteriorated so rapidly in recent years? Racial discrimination is the most frequently invoked explanation, and it is undeniable that discrimination continues to aggravate the social and economic problems of poor blacks. But is discrimination really greater today than it was in

1948, when black unemployment was less than half of what it is now, and when the gap between black and white jobless rates was narrower?

As for the poor black family, it apparently began to fall apart not before but after the mid-twentieth century. Until publication in 1976 of Herbert Gutman's *The Black Family in Slavery and Freedom,* most scholars had believed otherwise. Stimulated by the acrimonious debate over the Moynihan report, Gutman produced data demonstrating that the black family was not significantly disrupted during slavery or even during the early years of the first migration to the urban North, beginning after the turn of the century. The problems of the modern black family, he implied, were associated with modern forces.

Those who cite discrimination as the root cause of poverty often fail to make a distinction between the effects of *historic* discrimination (i.e., discrimination prior to the mid-twentieth century) and the effects of *contemporary* discrimination. Thus they find it hard to explain why the economic position of the black underclass started to worsen soon after Congress enacted, and the White House began to enforce, the most sweeping civil rights legislation since Reconstruction.

The point to be emphasized is that historic discrimination is more important than contemporary discrimination in understanding the plight of the ghetto underclass—that in any event there is more to the story than discrimination (of whichever kind). Historic discrimination certainly helped create an impoverished urban black community in the first place. In his recent *A Piece of the Pie: Black and White Immigrants since 1880* (1980), Stanley Lieberson shows how, in many areas of life, including the labor market, black newcomers from the rural South were far more severely discriminated against in northern cities than were the new white immigrants from southern, central, and eastern Europe. Skin color was part of the problem but it was not all of it.

The disadvantage of skin color—the fact that the dominant whites preferred whites over non-whites—is one that blacks shared with the Japanese, Chinese, and others. Yet the experience of the Asians, who also experienced harsh discriminatory treatment in the communities where they were concentrated, but who went on to prosper in their adopted land, suggests that skin color per se was not an insuperable obstacle. Indeed Lieberson argues that the greater success enjoyed by Asians may well be explained largely by the different context of their contact with whites. Because changes in immigration policy cut off Asian migration to America in the late nineteenth century, the Japanese and Chinese population did not reach large numbers and therefore did not pose as great a threat as did blacks.

Furthermore, the discontinuation of large-scale immigration from Japan and China enabled those Chinese and Japanese already in the United States to solidify networks of ethnic contacts and to occupy particular occupational niches in small, relatively stable communities. For blacks, the situation was different. The 1970 census recorded 22,580,000 blacks in the United States but only 435,000 Chinese and 591,000 Japanese.

If different population sizes accounted for a good deal of the difference in the economic success of blacks and Asians, they also helped determine the dissimilar rates of progress of urban blacks and the new European arrivals. European immigration was curtailed during the 1920s, but black migration to the urban North continued through the 1960s. With each passing decade there were many more blacks who were recent migrants to the North, whereas the immigrant component of the new Europeans dropped off over time. Eventually, other whites muffled their dislike of the Poles and Italians and Jews and directed their antagonism against blacks.

In addition to the problem of historic discrimination, the black migration to New York, Philadelphia, Chicago, and other northern cities—the continued replenishment of black populations there by poor newcomers—predictably skewed the age profile of the urban black community and kept it relatively young. The number of central-city black youths aged sixteen to nineteen increased by almost 75 percent from 1960 to 1969. Young black adults (aged twenty to twenty-four) increased in number by two-thirds during the same period, three times the increase for young white adults. In the nation's inner cities in 1977, the median age for whites was 30.3, for blacks 23.9. The importance of this jump in the number of young minorities in the ghetto, many of them lacking one or more parents, cannot be overemphasized.

Age correlates with many things. For example, the higher the median age of a group, the higher its income; the lower the median age, the higher the unemployment rate and the higher the crime rate (more than half of those arrested in 1980 for violent and property crimes in American cities were under twenty-one). The younger a woman is, the more likely she is to bear a child out of wedlock, head up a new household, and depend on welfare. In short, part of what had gone awry in the ghetto was due to the sheer increase in the number of black youth.

The population explosion among minority youth occurred at a time when changes in the economy were beginning to pose serious problems for unskilled workers. Urban minorities have been particularly vulnerable to the structural economic changes of the past two decades: the shift from goods-producing to service-producing industries, the increasing polarization of the labor market into low-wage and high-wage sectors, innovations in technology, and the relocation of manufacturing industries out of the central cities.

Most unemployed blacks in the United States reside within the central cities. Their situation, already more difficult than that of any other major ethnic group in the country, continues to worsen. Not only are there more blacks without jobs every year; men, especially young males, are dropping out of the labor force in record proportions. Also, more and more black youth, including many who are no longer in school, are obtaining no job experience at all.

However, the growing problem of joblessness in the inner city both exacerbates and is in turn partly created by the changing social composition of inner-city neighborhoods. These areas have undergone a profound social transformation in the last several years, as reflected not only in their increasing rates of social dislocation but also in the changing class structure of ghetto neighborhoods. In the 1940s, 1950s, and even the 1960s, lower-class, working-class, and middle-class black urban families all resided more or less in the same ghetto areas, albeit on different streets. Although black middle-class professionals today tend to be employed in mainstream occupations outside the black community and neither live nor frequently interact with ghetto residents, the black middle-class professionals of the 1940s and 1950s (doctors, lawyers, teachers, social workers, etc.) resided in the higher-income areas of the inner city and serviced the ghetto community. The exodus of black middle-class professionals from the inner city has been increasingly accompanied by a movement of stable working-class blacks to higher-income neighborhoods in other parts of the city and to the suburbs. Confined by restrictive covenants to communities also inhabited by the urban black lower classes, the black working and middle classes in earlier years provided stability to inner-city neighborhoods and perpetuated and reinforced societal norms and values. In short, their very presence enhanced the social organization of ghetto communities. If strong norms and sanctions against aberrant behavior, a sense of community, and positive neighborhood identification are the essential features of social organization in urban areas, inner-city neighborhoods today suffer from a severe lack of social organization.

Unlike in previous years, today's ghetto residents represent almost exclusively the most disadvantaged segments of the urban black community—including those families that have experienced long-term spells of poverty and/or welfare dependency, individuals who lack training and skills and have either experienced periods of persistent unemployment or have dropped out of the labor force altogether, and individuals who are frequently involved in street criminal activity. The term *ghetto underclass* refers to this heterogeneous group of families and individuals who inhabit the cores of the nation's central cities. The term suggests that a fundamental social transformation has taken place in ghetto neighborhoods, and the groups represented by this term are collectively different from and much more socially isolated than those that lived in these communities in earlier years.

The significance of changes embodied in the social transformation of the inner city is perhaps best captured by the concepts *concentration effects* and *social buffer*. The former refers to the constraints and opportunities associated with living in a neighborhood in which the population is overwhelmingly socially disadvantaged—constraints and opportunities that include the kinds of ecological niches that the residents of these communities occupy in terms of access to jobs, availability of marriageable partners, and exposure to conventional role models. The latter refers to the presence of a sufficient number of working- and middle-class professional families to absorb the shock or cushion the effect of uneven economic growth and periodic recessions on inner-city neighborhoods. The basic thesis is not that ghetto culture went unchecked following the removal of higher-income families in the inner city, but that the removal of these families made it more difficult to sustain the basic institutions in the inner city (including churches, stores, schools, recreational facilities, etc.) in the face of prolonged joblessness. And as the basic institutions declined, the social organization of inner-city neighborhoods (defined here to include a sense of community, positive neighborhood identification, and explicit norms and sanctions against aberrant behavior) likewise declined. Indeed, the social organization of any neighborhood depends in large measure on the viability of social institutions in that neighborhood. It is true that the presence of stable working- and middle-class families in the ghetto provides mainstream role models that reinforce mainstream values pertaining to employment, education, and family structure. But, in the final analysis, a far more important effect is the institutional stability that these families are able to provide in their neighborhoods because of their greater economic and educational resources, especially during periods of an economic downturn—periods in which joblessness in poor urban areas tends to substantially increase.

In underlining joblessness as an important aspect of inner-city social transformations, we are reminded that in the 1960s scholars readily attributed poor black family deterioration to problems of employment. Nonetheless, in the last several years, in the face of the overwhelming attention given to welfare as the major source of black family breakup, concerns about the importance of joblessness have diminished, despite the existence of evidence strongly suggesting the need for renewed scholarly and public policy attention to the relationship between the disintegration of poor

black families and black male labor-market experiences.

Although changing social and cultural trends have often been said to explain some of the dynamic shifts in the structure of the family, they appear to have more relevance for changes in family structure among whites.[9] And contrary to popular opinion, there is little evidence to support the argument that welfare is the primary cause of family out-of-wedlock births, breakups, and female-headed households. Welfare does seem to have a modest effect on separation and divorce, particularly for white women, but recent evidence indicates that its total effect on the proportion of all female householders is small.[10]

By contrast, the evidence for the influence of joblessness on family structure is much more conclusive. Research has demonstrated, for example, a connection between an encouraging economic situation and the early marriage of young people. In this connection, black women are more likely to delay marriage and less likely to remarry. Although black and white teenagers expect to become parents at about the same ages, black teenagers expect to marry at later ages. The black delay in marriage and the lower rate of remarriage, each associated with high percentages of out-of-wedlock births and female-headed households, can be directly tied to the employment status of black males. Indeed, black women, especially young black women, are confronting a shrinking pool of "marriageable" (that is economically stable) men.[11]

White women are not experiencing this problem. Our "male marriageable pool index" shows that the number of employed white men per one hundred white women in different age categories has either remained roughly the same or has only slightly increased in the last two decades.[12] There is little reason, therefore, to assume a connection between the recent growth of female-headed white families and patterns of white male employment. That the pool of "marriageable" white men has not decreased over the years is perhaps reflected in the earlier age of first marriage and the higher rate of remarriage among white women. It is therefore reasonable to hypothesize that the rise in rates of separation and divorce among whites is due mainly to the increased economic independence of white women and related social and cultural factors embodied in the feminist movement.

The argument that the decline in the incidence of intact marriages among blacks is associated with the declining economic status of black men is further supported by an analysis of regional data on female headship and the "male marriageable pool."[13] Whereas changes in the ratios of employed men to women among whites have been minimal for all regions of the country regardless of age from 1960 to 1980, the ratios among blacks have declined significantly in all regions except the West, with the greatest declines in the northeastern and north-central regions of the country. On the basis of these trends, it would be expected that the growth in numbers of black female-headed households would occur most rapidly in the northern regions, followed by the South and the West. Regional data on the "male marriageable pool index" support this conclusion, except for the larger-than-expected increase in black female-headed families in the West—a function of patterns of selective black migration to the West.[14]

The sharp decline in the black "male marriageable pool" in the northeastern and north-central regions is related to recent changes in the basic economic organization in American society. In the two northern regions, the shift in economic activity from goods production to services has been associated with changes in the location of production, including an interregional movement of industry from the North to the South and West and, more important, a movement of certain industries out of the older central cities where blacks are concentrated. Moreover, the shrinkage of the male marriageable pool for ages sixteen to twenty-four in the South from 1960 to 1980 is related to the mechanization of agriculture, which lowered substantially the demand for low-skilled agricultural labor, especially during the 1960s. For all these reasons, it is often necessary to go beyond the specific issue of current racial discrimination to understand factors that contribute directly to poor black joblessness and indirectly to related social problems such as family instability in the inner city. But this point has not been readily grasped by policymakers and civil rights leaders.

The Limits of Race-specific Public Policy

In the early 1960s there was no comprehensive civil rights bill and Jim Crow segregation was still widespread in parts of the nation, particularly in the Deep South. With the passage of the 1964 Civil Rights Bill there was considerable optimism that racial progress would ensue and that the principle of equality of individual rights (namely, that candidates for positions stratified in terms of prestige, power, or other social criteria ought to be judged solely on individual merit and therefore should not be discriminated against on the basis of racial origin) would be upheld.

Programs based solely on this principle are inadequate, however, to deal with the complex problems of race in America because they are not designed to address the substantive inequality that exists at the time discrimination is eliminated. In other words, long periods of racial oppression can result in a system of inequality that may persist for indefinite periods of time even after racial barriers are removed. This is because the most disadvantaged members of racial minority groups, who suffer the cumulative effects of both race and class subjugation (including those effects passed on from generation to generation), are disproportionately represented among the segment of the general population that has been denied the resources to compete effectively in a free and open market.

On the other hand, the competitive resources developed by the *advantaged minority members*—resources that flow directly from the family stability, schooling, income, and peer groups that their parents have been able to provide—result in their benefiting disproportionately from policies that promote the rights of minority individuals by removing artificial barriers to valued positions.

Nevertheless, since 1970, government policy has tended to focus on formal programs designed and created both to prevent discrimination and to ensure that minorities are sufficiently represented in certain positions. This has resulted in a shift from the simple formal investigation and adjudication of complaints of racial discrimination to government-mandated affirmative action programs to increase minority representation in public programs, employment, and education.

However, if minority members from the most advantaged families profit disproportionately from policies based on the principle of equality of individual opportunity, they also reap disproportionate benefits from policies of affirmative action based solely on their group membership. This is because advantaged minority members are likely to be disproportionately represented among those of their racial group most qualified for valued positions, such as college admissions, higher paying jobs, and promotions. Thus, if policies of preferential treatment for such positions are developed in terms of racial group membership rather than the real disadvantages suffered by individuals, then these policies will further improve the opportunities of the advantaged without necessarily addressing the problems of the truly disadvantaged such as the ghetto underclass.[15] The problems of the truly disadvantaged may require *nonracial* solutions such as full employment, balanced economic growth, and manpower training and education (tied to—not isolated from—these two economic conditions).

By 1980 this argument was not widely recognized or truly appreciated. Therefore, because the government not only adopted and implemented antibias legislation to promote minority individual rights, but also mandated and enforced affirmative action and related programs to enhance minority group rights, many thoughtful American citizens, including supporters of civil rights, were puzzled by recent social developments in black communities. Despite the passage of civil rights legislation and the creation of affirmative action programs, they sensed that conditions were deteriorating instead of improving for a significant segment of the black American population. This perception had emerged because of the continuous flow of pessimistic reports concerning the sharp rise in black joblessness, the precipitous drop in the black-white family income ratio, the steady increase in the percentage of blacks on the welfare rolls, and the extraordinary growth in the number of female-headed families. This perception was strengthened by the almost uniform cry among black leaders that not only had conditions worsened, but that white Americans had forsaken the cause of blacks as well.

Meanwhile, the liberal architects of the War on Poverty became puzzled when Great Society programs failed to reduce poverty in America and when they could find few satisfactory explanations for the sharp rise in inner-city social dislocations during the 1970s. However, just as advocates for minority rights have been slow to comprehend that many of the current problems of race, particularly those that plague the minority poor, derived from the broader processes of societal organization and therefore may have no direct or indirect connection with race, so too have the architects of the War on Poverty failed to emphasize the relationship between poverty and the broader processes of American economic organization. Accordingly, given the most comprehensive civil rights and antipoverty programs in America's history, the liberals of the civil rights movement and the Great Society became demoralized when inner-city poverty proved to be more intractable than they realized and when they could not satisfactorily explain such events as the unprecedented rise in inner-city joblessness and the remarkable growth in the number of female-headed households. This demoralization cleared the path for conservative analysts to fundamentally shift the focus away from changing the environments of the minority poor to changing their values and behavior.

However, and to repeat, many of the problems of the ghetto underclass are related to the broader problems of societal organization, including economic organization. For example, as pointed out earlier, regional differences in changes in the "male marriageable pool index" signify the importance of industrial shifts in the Northeast and Midwest. Related research clearly demonstrated the declining labor-market opportunities in the older central cities. Indeed, blacks tend to be concentrated in areas where the number and characteristics of jobs have been most significantly altered by shifts in the location of production activity and from manufacturing to services. Since an overwhelming majority of inner-city blacks lacks the qualifications for the high-skilled segment of the service sector such as information processing, finance, and real estate, they tend to be concentrated in the low-skilled segment, which features unstable employment, restricted opportunities, and low wages.

Notes

1. Kenneth B. Clark, *Dark Ghetto: Dilemmas of Social Power* (New York: Harper and Row, 1965); Lee Rainwater, "Crucible of Identity: The Negro Lower-Class Family," *Daedalus* 95 (Winter 1966): 176–216; Daniel P. Moynihan, *The Negro Family: The Case for National Action* (Washington, D.C.: Office of Policy Planning and Research, U.S. Department of Labor, 1965); and idem, "Employment, Income and the Ordeal of the Negro Family," in *The Negro American,* ed. Talcott Parsons and Kenneth B. Clark (Boston: Beacon Press, 1965), pp. 134–59.

2. David L. Lewis, *When Harlem Was in Vogue* (New York: Alfred A. Knopf, 1981); Clark, *Dark Ghetto;* and Thomas Sowell, *Civil Rights: Rhetoric or Reality?* (New York: William Morrow, 1984).

3. See St. Clair Drake and Horace R. Cayton, *Black Metropolis: A Study of Negro Life in a Northern City,* vol. 2 (New York: Harper and Row, 1945).

4. Clark, *Dark Ghetto,* p. 27.

5. Rainwater, "Crucible of Identity," p. 173.

6. Clark, *Dark Ghetto,* p. 81.

7. See, e.g., Roger D. Abrahams, *Deep Down in the Jungle* (Hatboro, Pa.: Folklore Associates, 1964); Clark, *Dark Ghetto;* Rainwater, "Crucible of Identity"; and Elliot Liebow, *Tally's Corner: A Study of Negro Street-corner Men* (Boston: Little, Brown, 1967).

8. Moynihan, *Negro Family.*

[9]. For a relevant review of this literature, see William Julius Wilson, *The Truly Disadvantaged: The Inner City, the Underclass, and Public Policy* (Chicago: University of Chicago Press, 1987), ch. 3.—ED.

[10]. See Wilson, *The Truly Disadvantaged,* chs. 3, 4.—ED.

[11]. See Wilson, *The Truly Disadvantaged,* ch. 3.—ED.

[12]. See Wilson, *The Truly Disadvantaged,* ch. 3.—ED.

[13]. See Wilson, *The Truly Disadvantaged,* ch. 4.—ED.

[14]. See Wilson, *The Truly Disadvantaged,* ch. 4.—ED.

15. James Fishkin covers much of this ground very convincingly. See his *Justice, Equal Opportunity and the Family* (New Haven, Conn.: Yale University Press, 1983).

Gender Stratification

▶ GENDER AND CLASS

SHULAMITH FIRESTONE

The Dialectic of Sex

The immediate assumption of the layman that the unequal division of the sexes is "natural" may be well-founded. We need not immediately look beyond this. Unlike economic class, sex class sprang directly from a biological reality: men and women were created different, and not equally privileged. Although, as Simone de Beauvoir points out [in *The Second Sex*], this difference of itself did not necessitate the development of a class system—the domination of one group by another—the reproductive *functions* of these differences did. The biological family is an inherently unequal power distribution. The need for power leading to the development of classes arises from the psychosexual formation of each individual according to this basic imbalance, rather than, as Freud, Norman O. Brown, and others have, once again overshooting their mark, postulated, some irreducible conflict of Life against Death, Eros vs. Thanatos.

The *biological family*—the basic reproductive unit of male/female/infant, in whatever form of social organization—is characterized by these fundamental—if not immutable—facts:

1) That women throughout history before the advent of birth control were at the continual mercy of their biology—menstruation, menopause, and "female ills," constant painful childbirth, wetnursing and care of infants, all of which made them dependent on males (whether brother, father, husband, lover, or clan, government, community-at-large) for physical survival.

2) That human infants take an even longer time to grow up than animals, and thus are helpless and, for some short period at least, dependent on adults for physical survival.

3) That a basic mother/child interdependency has existed in some form in every society, past or present, and thus has shaped the psychology of every mature female and every infant.

4) That the natural reproductive difference between the sexes led directly to the first division of labor at the origins of class, as well as furnishing the paradigm of caste (discrimination based on biological characteristics).

These biological contingencies of the human family cannot be covered over with anthropological sophistries. Anyone observing animals mating, reproducing, and caring for their young will have a hard time accepting the "cultural relativity" line. For no matter how many tribes in Oceania you can find where the connection of the father to fertility is not known, no matter how many matrilineages, no matter how many cases of sex-role reversal, male housewifery, or even empathic labor pains, these facts prove only one thing: the amazing *flexibility* of human nature. But human nature is adaptable *to* something, it is, yes, determined by its environmental conditions. And the biological family that we have described has existed everywhere throughout time. Even in matriarchies where woman's fertility is worshipped, and the father's role is unknown or unimportant, if perhaps not on the genetic father, there is still some dependence of the female and the infant on the male. And though it is true that the nuclear family is only a recent development, one which only intensifies the psychological penalties of the biological family, though it is true that throughout history there have been many variations on this biological family, the contingencies I have described existed in all of them, causing specific psychosexual distortions in the human personality.

But to grant that the sexual imbalance of power is biologically based is not to lose our case. We are no longer just animals. And the Kingdom of Nature does not reign absolute. As Simone de Beauvoir herself admits:

The theory of historical materialism has brought to light some important truths. Humanity is not an animal species, it is a historical reality. Human society is an antiphysis—in a sense it is against nature; it does not passively submit to the presence of nature but rather takes over the control of nature on its own behalf. This arrogation is not an inward, subjective operation; it is accomplished objectively in practical action.

Thus, the "natural" is not necessarily a "human" value. Humanity has begun to outgrow nature: we can no longer justify the maintenance of a discriminatory sex class system on grounds of its origins in Nature. Indeed, for pragmatic reasons alone it is beginning to look as if we *must* get rid of it.

The problem becomes political, demanding more than a comprehensive historical analysis, when one realizes that, though man is increasingly capable of freeing himself from the biological conditions that created his tyranny over women and children, he has little reason to want to give this tyranny up. As Engels said, in the context of economic revolution:

It is the law of division of labor that lies at the basis of the division into classes [Note that this division itself grew out of a fundamental biological division]. But this does not prevent the ruling class, once having the upper hand, from consolidating its power at the expense of the working class, from turning its social leadership into an intensified exploitation of the masses.

Though the sex class system may have originated in fundamental biological conditions, this does not guarantee once the biological basis of their oppression has been swept away that women and children will be freed. On the contrary, the new technology, especially fertility control, may be used against them to reinforce the entrenched system of exploitation.

So that just as to assure elimination of economic classes requires the revolt of the underclass (the proletariat) and, in a temporary dictatorship, their seizure of the means of *production,* so to assure the elimination of sexual classes requires the revolt of the underclass (women) and the seizure of control of *reproduction:* not only the full restoration to women of ownership of their own bodies, but also their (temporary) seizure of control of human fertility—the new population biology as well as all the social institutions of childbearing and childrearing. And just as the end goal of socialist revolution was not only the elimination of the economic class *privilege* but of the economic class *distinction* itself, so the end goal of feminist revolution must be, unlike that of the first feminist movement, not just the elimination of male *privilege* but of the sex *distinction* itself: genital differences between human beings would no longer matter culturally. (A reversion to an unobstructed *pansexuality*—Freud's "polymorphous perversity"—would probably supersede hetero/homo/bi-sexuality.) The reproduction of the species by one sex for the benefit of both would be replaced by (at least the option of) artificial reproduction: children would be born to both sexes equally, or independently of either, however one chooses to look at it; the dependence of the child on the mother (and vice versa) would give way to a greatly shortened dependence on a small group of others in general, and any remaining inferiority to adults in physical strength would be compensated for culturally. The division of labor would be ended by the elimination of labor altogether (cybernation). The tyranny of the biological family would be broken.

And with it the psychology of power. As Engels claimed for strictly socialist revolution:

The existence of not simply this or that ruling class but of any ruling class at all [will have] become an obsolete anachronism.

That socialism has never come near achieving this predicated goal is not only the result of unfulfilled or misfired economic preconditions, but also because the Marxian analysis itself was insufficient:

it did not dig deep enough to the psychosexual roots of class. Marx was onto something more profound than he knew when he observed that the family contained within itself in embryo all the antagonisms that later develop on a wide scale within the society and the state. For unless revolution uproots the basic social organization, the biological family—the vinculum through which the psychology of power can always be smuggled—the tapeworm of exploitation will never be annihilated. We shall need a sexual revolution much larger than—inclusive of—a socialist one to truly eradicate all class systems.

HEIDI HARTMANN

The Unhappy Marriage of Marxism and Feminism: Towards a More Progressive Union

We can usefully define patriarchy as a set of social relations between men, which have a material base, and which, though hierarchical, establish or create interdependence and solidarity among men that enable them to dominate women. Though patriarchy is hierarchical and men of different classes, races, or ethnic groups have different places in the patriarchy, they also are united in their shared relationship of dominance over their women; they are dependent on each other to maintain that domination. Hierarchies "work" at least in part because they create vested interests in the status quo. Those at the higher levels can "buy off" those at the lower levels by offering them power over those still lower. In the hierarchy of patriarchy, all men, whatever their rank in the patriarchy, are bought off by being able to control at least some women. There is some evidence to suggest that when patriarchy was first institutionalized in state societies, the ascending rulers literally made men the heads of their families (enforcing their control over their wives and children) in exchange for the men's ceding some of their tribal resources to the new rulers.[1] Men are dependent on one another (despite their hierarchical ordering) to maintain their control over women.

The material base upon which patriarchy rests lies most fundamentally in men's control over women's labor power. Men maintain this control by excluding women from access to some essential productive resources (in capitalist societies, for example, jobs that pay living wages) and by restricting women's sexuality. Monogamous heterosexual marriage is one relatively recent and efficient form that seems to allow men to control both these areas. Controlling women's access to resources and their sexuality, in turn, allows men to control women's labor power, both for the purpose of serving men in many personal and sexual ways and for the purpose of rearing children. The services women render men, and which exonerate men from having to perform many unpleasant tasks (like cleaning toilets) occur outside as well as inside the family setting. Examples outside the family include the harassment of women workers and students by male bosses and professors as well as the common use of secretaries to run personal errands, make coffee, and provide "sexy" surroundings. Rearing children, whether or not the children's labor power is of immediate benefit to their fathers, is nevertheless a crucial task in perpetuating patriarchy as a system. Just as class society must be reproduced by schools, work places, consumption norms, etc., so must patriarchal social relations. In our society children are generally reared by women at home, women socially defined and recognized as inferior to men, while men appear in the domestic picture only rarely. Children raised in this way generally learn their places in the gender hierarchy well. Central to this process, however, are the areas outside the home where patriarchal behaviors are taught and the inferior position of women enforced and reinforced: churches, schools, sports, clubs, unions, armies, factories, offices, health centers, the media, etc.

The material base of patriarchy, then, does not rest solely on childrearing in the family, but on all the social structures that enable men to control women's labor. The aspects of social structures that perpetuate patriarchy are theoretically identifiable, hence separable from their other aspects. Gayle Rubin has increased our ability to identify the patriarchal element of these social structures enormously by identifying "sex/gender systems":

a "sex/gender system" is the set of arrangements by which a society transforms biological sexuality into products of human activity, and in which these transformed sexual needs are satisfied.[2]

We are born female and male, biological sexes, but we are created woman and man, socially recognized genders. *How* we are so created is that second aspect of the *mode* of production of which Engels spoke, "the production of human beings themselves, the propagation of the species."[3]

How people propagate the species is socially determined. If, biologically, people are sexually polymorphous, and society were organized in such a way that all forms of sexual expression were equally permissible, reproduction would result only from some sexual encounters, the heterosexual ones. The strict division of labor by sex, a social invention common to all known societies, creates two very separate genders and a need for men and women to get together for economic reasons. It thus helps to direct their sexual needs toward heterosexual fulfillment, and helps to ensure biological reproduction. In more imaginative societies, biological reproduction might be ensured by other techniques, but the division of labor by sex appears to be the universal solution to date. Although it is theoretically possible that a sexual division of labor not imply inequality between the sexes, in most known societies, the socially acceptable division of labor by sex is one which accords lower status to women's work. The sexual division of labor is also the underpinning of sexual subcultures in which men and women experience life differently; it is the material base of male power which is exercised (in our society) not just in not doing housework and in securing superior employment, but psychologically as well.

How people meet their sexual needs, how they reproduce, how they inculcate social norms in new generations, how they learn gender, how it feels to be a man or a woman—all occur in the realm Rubin labels the sex/gender system. Rubin emphasizes the influence of kinship (which tells you with whom you can satisfy sexual needs) and the development of gender specific personalities via childrearing and the "oedipal machine." In addition, however, we can use the concept of the sex/gender system to examine all other social institutions for the roles they play in defining and reinforcing gender hierarchies. Rubin notes that theoretically a sex/gender system could be female dominant, male dominant, or egalitarian, but declines to label various known sex/gender systems or to periodize history accordingly. We choose to label our present sex/gender system patriarchy, because it appropriately captures the notion of hierarchy and male dominance which we see as central to the present system.

Economic production (what marxists are used to referring to as *the* mode of production) and the production of people in the sex/gender sphere both determine "the social organization under which the people of a particular historical epoch and a particular country live," according to Engels. The whole of society, then, can be understood by looking at both these types of production and reproduction, people and things. There is no such thing as "pure capitalism," nor does "pure patriarchy" exist, for they must of necessity coexist. What exists is patriarchal capitalism, or patriarchal feudalism, or egalitarian hunting/gathering societies, or matriarchal horticultural societies, or patriarchal horticultural societies, and so on. There appears to be no necessary connection between *changes* in the one aspect of production and changes in the other. A society could undergo transition from capitalism to socialism, for example, and remain patriarchal. Common sense, history, and our experience tell us, however, that these two aspects of production are so closely intertwined, that change in one ordinarily creates movement, tension, or contradiction in the other.

Racial hierarchies can also be understood in this context. Further elaboration may be possible along the lines of defining color/race systems, arenas of social life that take biological color and turn it into a social category, race. Racial hierarchies, like gender hierarchies, are aspects of our social organization, of how people are produced and reproduced. They are not fundamentally ideological; they constitute that second aspect of our mode of production, the production and reproduction of people. It might be most accurate then to refer to our societies not as, for example, simply capitalist, but as patriarchal capitalist white supremacist.

Capitalist development creates the places for a hierarchy of workers, but traditional marxist categories cannot tell us who will fill which places. Gender and racial hierarchies determine who fills the empty places. *Patriarchy is not simply hierarchical organization,* but hierarchy in which *particular* people fill *particular* places. It is in studying patriarchy that we learn why it is women who are dominated and how. While we believe that most known societies have been patriarchal, we do not view patriarchy as a universal, unchanging phenomenon. Rather patriarchy, the set of interrelations among men that allow men to dominate women, has changed in form and intensity over time. It is crucial that the hierarchy among men, and their differential access to patriarchal bene-

fits, be examined. Surely, class, race, nationality, and even marital status and sexual orientation, as well as the obvious age, come into play here. And women of different class, race, national, marital status, or sexual orientation groups are subjected to different degrees of patriarchal power. Women may themselves exercise class, race, or national power, or even patriarchal power (through their family connections) over men lower in the patriarchal hierarchy than their own male kin.

To recapitulate, we define patriarchy as a set of social relations which has a material base and in which there are hierarchical relations between men and solidarity among them which enable them in turn to dominate women. The material base of patriarchy is men's control over women's labor power. That control is maintained by excluding women from access to necessary economically productive resources and by restricting women's sexuality. Men exercise their control in receiving personal service work from women, in not having to do housework or rear children, in having access to women's bodies for sex, and in feeling powerful and being powerful. The crucial elements of patriarchy as we *currently* experience them are: heterosexual marriage (and consequent homophobia), female childrearing and housework, women's economic dependence on men (enforced by arrangements in the labor market), the state, and numerous institutions based on social relations among men—clubs, sports, unions, professions, universities, churches, corporations, and armies. All of these elements need to be examined if we are to understand patriarchal capitalism. …

Industrialization and the Development of Family Wages

Marxists made quite logical inferences from a selection of the social phenomena they witnessed in the nineteenth century. But marxists ultimately underestimated the strength of the preexisting patriarchal social forces with which fledgling capital had to contend and the need for capital to adjust to these forces. The industrial revolution was drawing all people into the labor force, including women and children; in fact the first factories used child and female labor almost exclusively. That women and children could earn wages separately from men both undermined authority relations and kept wages low for everyone. Kautsky, writing in 1892, described the process this way:

[Then with] the wife and young children of the working-man ... able to take care of themselves, the wages of the male worker can safely be reduced to the level of his own personal needs without the risk of stopping the fresh supply of labor power.

The labor of women and children, moreover, affords the additional advantage that these are less capable of resistance than men [sic]; and their introduction into the ranks of the workers increases tremendously the quantity of labor that is offered for sale in the market.

Accordingly, the labor of women and children ... also diminishes [the] capacity [of the male worker] for resistance in that it overstocks the market; owing to both these circumstances it lowers the wages of the working-man.[4]

The terrible effects on working class family life of low wages and of forced participation of all family members in the labor force were recognized by marxists. Kautsky wrote:

The capitalist system of production does not in most cases destroy the single household of the workingman, but robs it of all but its unpleasant features. The activity of woman today in industrial pursuits ... means an increase of her former burden by a new one. *But one cannot serve two masters.* The household of the workingman suffers whenever his wife must help to earn the daily bread.[5]

Working men as well as Kautsky recognized the disadvantages of female wage labor. Not only were women "cheap competition" but working women were their very wives, who could not "serve two masters" well.

Male workers resisted the wholesale entrance of women and children into the labor force, and sought to exclude them from union membership and the labor force as well. In 1846 the *Ten-Hours' Advocate* stated:

It is needless for us to say, that all attempts to improve the morals and physical condition of female factory workers will be abortive, unless their hours are materially reduced. Indeed we may go so far as to say, that

married females would be much better occupied in performing the domestic duties of the household, than following the never-tiring motion of machinery. We therefore hope the day is not distant, when the husband will be able to provide for his wife and family, without sending the former to endure the drudgery of a cotton mill.[6]

In the United States in 1854 the National Typographical Union resolved not to "encourage by its act the employment of female compositors." Male unionists did not want to afford union protection to women workers; they tried to exclude them instead. In 1879 Adolph Strasser, president of the Cigarmakers International Union, said: "We cannot drive the females out of the trade, but we can restrict their daily quota of labor through factory laws."[7]

While the problem of cheap competition could have been solved by organizing the wage earning women and youths, the problem of disrupted family life could not be. Men reserved union protection for men and argued for protective labor laws for women and children. Protective labor laws, while they may have ameliorated some of the worst abuses of female and child labor, also limited the participation of adult women in many "male" jobs. Men sought to keep high wage jobs for themselves and to raise male wages generally. They argued for wages sufficient for their wage labor alone to support their families. This "family wage" system gradually came to be the norm for stable working class families at the end of the nineteenth century and the beginning of the twentieth. Several observers have declared the non wage-working wife to be part of the standard of living of male workers. Instead of fighting for equal wages for men and women, male workers sought the family wage, wanting to retain their wives' services at home. In the absence of patriarchy a unified working class might have confronted capitalism, but patriarchal social relations divided the working class, allowing one part (men) to be bought off at the expense of the other (women). Both the hierarchy between men and the solidarity among them were crucial in this process of resolution. Family wages may be understood as a resolution of the conflict over women's labor power which was occurring between patriarchal and capitalist interests at that time.

Family wages for most adult men imply men's acceptance, and collusion in, lower wages for others, young people, women and socially defined inferior men as well (Irish, blacks, etc., the lowest groups in the patriarchal hierarchy who are denied many of the patriarchal benefits). Lower wages for women and children and inferior men are enforced by job segregation in the labor market, in turn maintained by unions and management as well as by auxiliary institutions like schools, training programs, and even families. Job segregation by sex, by insuring that women have the lower paid jobs, both assures women's economic dependence on men and reinforces notions of appropriate spheres for women and men. For most men, then, the development of family wages secured the material base of male domination in two ways. First, men have the better jobs in the labor market and earn higher wages than women. The lower pay women receive in the labor market both perpetuates men's material advantage over women and encourages women to choose wifery as a career. Second, then, women do housework, childcare, and perform other services at home which benefit men directly. Women's home responsibilities in turn reinforce their inferior labor market position.

The resolution that developed in the early twentieth century can be seen to benefit capitalist interests as well as patriarchal interests. Capitalists, it is often argued, recognized that in the extreme conditions which prevailed in the early nineteenth century industrialization, working class families could not adequately reproduce themselves. They realized that housewives produced and maintained healthier workers than wage-working wives and that educated children became better workers than noneducated ones. The bargain, paying family wages to men and keeping women home, suited the capitalists at the time as well as the male workers. Although the terms of the bargain have altered over time, it is still true that the family and women's work in the family serve capital by providing a labor force and serve men as the space in which they exercise their privilege. Women, working to serve men and their families, also serve capital as consumers.[8] The family is also the place where dominance and submission are learned, as Firestone, the Frankfurt School, and many others have explained.[9]

Obedient children become obedient workers; girls and boys each learn their proper roles.

While the family wage shows that capitalism adjusts to patriarchy, the changing status of children shows that patriarchy adjusts to capital. Children, like women, came to be excluded from wage labor. As children's ability to earn money declined, their legal relationship to their parents changed. At the beginning of the industrial era in the United States, fulfilling children's need for their fathers was thought to be crucial, even primary, to their happy development; fathers had legal priority in cases of contested custody. As children's ability to contribute to the economic well-being of the family declined, mothers came increasingly to be viewed as crucial to the happy development of their children, and gained legal priority in cases of contested custody.[10] Here patriarchy adapted to the changing economic role of children: when children were productive, men claimed them; as children became unproductive, they were given to women. ...

The Family and the Family Wage Today

We argued above that, with respect to capitalism and patriarchy, the adaptation, or mutual accommodation, took the form of the development of the family wage in the early twentieth century. The family wage cemented the partnership between patriarchy and capital. Despite women's increased labor force participation, particularly rapid since World War II, the family wage is still, we argue, the cornerstone of the present sexual division of labor—in which women are primarily responsible for housework and men primarily for wage work. Women's lower wages in the labor market (combined with the need for children to be reared by someone) assure the continued existence of the family as a necessary income pooling unit. The family, supported by the family wage, thus allows the control of women's labor by men both within and without the family.

Though women's increased wage work may cause stress for the family (similar to the stress Kautsky and Engels noted in the nineteenth century), it would be wrong to think that as a consequence, the concepts and the realities of the family and of the sexual division of labor will soon disappear. The sexual division of labor reappears in the labor market, where women work at women's jobs, often the very jobs they used to do only at home—food preparation and service, cleaning of all kinds, caring for people, and so on. As these jobs are low-status and low-paying patriarchal relations remain intact, though their material base shifts somewhat from the family to the wage differential, from family-based to industrially-based patriarchy.[11]

Industrially based patriarchal relations are enforced in a variety of ways. Union contracts which specify lower wages, lesser benefits, and fewer advancement opportunities for women are not just atavistic hangovers—a case of sexist attitudes or male supremacist ideology—they maintain the material base of the patriarchal system. While some would go so far as to argue that patriarchy is already absent from the family (see, for example, Stewart Ewen, *Captains of Consciousness*),[12] we would not. Although the terms of the compromise between capital and patriarchy are changing as additional tasks formerly located in the family are capitalized, and the location of the deployment of women's labor power shifts, it is nevertheless true, as we have argued above, that the wage differential caused by extreme job segregation in the labor market reinforces the family, and, with it, the domestic division of labor, by encouraging women to marry. The "ideal" of the family wage—that a man can earn enough to support an entire family—may be giving way to a new ideal that both men and women contribute through wage earning to the cash income of the family. The wage differential, then, will become increasingly necessary in perpetuating patriarchy, the male control of women's labor power. The wage differential will aid in *defining* women's work as secondary to men's at the same time it necessitates women's actual continued economic dependence on men. The sexual division of labor in the labor market and elsewhere should be understood as a manifestation of patriarchy which serves to perpetuate it.

Many people have argued that though the partnership between capital and patriarchy exists now, it may *in the long run* prove intolerable to capitalism; capital may eventually destroy both familial relations and patriarchy. The argument

proceeds logically that capitalist social relations (of which the family is not an example) tend to become universalized, that women will become increasingly able to earn money and will increasingly refuse to submit to subordination in the family, and that since the family is oppressive particularly to women and children, it will collapse as soon as people can support themselves outside it.

We do not think that the patriarchal relations embodied in the family can be destroyed so easily by capital, and we see little evidence that the family system is presently disintegrating. Although the increasing labor force participation of women has made divorce more feasible, the incentives to divorce are not overwhelming for women. Women's wages allow very few women to support themselves and their children independently and adequately. The evidence for the decay of the traditional family is weak at best. The divorce rate has not so much increased, as it has evened out among classes; moreover, the remarriage rate is also very high. Up until the 1970 census, the first-marriage age was continuing its historic decline. Since 1970 people seem to have been delaying marriage and childbearing, but most recently, the birth rate has begun to increase again. It is true that larger proportions of the population are now living outside traditional families. Young people, especially, are leaving their parents' homes and establishing their own households before they marry and start traditional families. Older people, especially women, are finding themselves alone in their own households, after their children are grown and they experience separation or death of a spouse. Nevertheless, trends indicate that the new generations of young people will form nuclear families at some time in their adult lives in higher proportions than ever before. The cohorts, or groups of people, born since 1930 have much higher rates of eventual marriage and childrearing than previous cohorts. The duration of marriage and childrearing may be shortening, but its incidence is still spreading.[13]

The argument that capital destroys the family also overlooks the social forces which make family life appealing. Despite critiques of nuclear families as psychologically destructive, in a competitive society the family still meets real needs for many people. This is true not only of long-term monogamy, but even more so for raising children. Single parents bear both financial and psychic burdens. For working class women, in particular, these burdens make the "independence" of labor force participation illusory. Single parent families have recently been seen by policy analysts as transitional family formations which become two-parent families upon remarriage.[14]

It could be that the effects of women's increasing labor force participation are found in a declining sexual division of labor within the family, rather than in more frequent divorce, but evidence for this is also lacking. Statistics on who does housework, even in families with wage-earning wives, show little change in recent years; women still do most of it.[15] The double day is a reality for wage-working women. This is hardly surprising since the sexual division of labor outside the family, in the labor market, keeps women financially dependent on men—even when they earn a wage themselves. The future of patriarchy does not, however, rest solely on the future of familial relations. For patriarchy, like capital, can be surprisingly flexible and adaptable.

Notes

1. See Viana Muller, "The Formation of the State and the Oppression of Women: Some Theoretical Considerations and a Case Study in England and Wales," *Review of Radical Political Economics*, Vol. 9, no. 3 (Fall 1977), pp. 7–21.

2. Gayle Rubin, "The Traffic in Women," in *Toward an Anthropology of Women*, ed. Rayna Rapp Reiter (New York: Monthly Review Press, 1975), p. 159.

[3]. Frederick Engels, "Preface to the First Edition," *The Origin of the Family, Private Property and the State*, edited, with an introduction by Eleanor Burke Leacock (New York: International Publishers, 1972). The first aspect of the mode of production is, according to Engels, "the production of the means of existence, of food, clothing, and shelter and the tools necessary for that production."—ED.

4. Karl Kautsky, *The Class Struggle* (New York: Norton, 1971), pp. 25–26.

5. We might add, "outside the household." Kautsky, *Class Struggle*, p. 26, our emphasis.

6. Cited in Neil Smelser, *Social Change and the Industrial Revolution* (Chicago: University of Chicago Press, 1959), p. 301.

7. These examples are from Heidi I. Hartmann, "Capitalism, Patriarchy, and Job Segregation by Sex," *Signs: Journal of Women in Culture and Society*, Vol. 1, no. 3, pt. 2 (Spring 1976), pp. 162–163.

8. See Batya Weinbaum and Amy Bridges, "The Other Side of the Paycheck: Monopoly Capital and the Structure of Consumption," *Monthly Review*, Vol. 28, no. 3 (July-August 1976), pp. 88–103, for a discussion of women's consumption work.

9. Shulamith Firestone, *The Dialectic of Sex* (New York: Bantam Books, 1971). For the view of the Frankfurt School, see Max Horkheimer, "Authority and the Family," in *Critical Theory* (New York: Herder & Herder, 1972) and Frankfurt Institute of Social Research, "The Family," in *Aspects of Sociology* (Boston: Beacon, 1972).

10. Carol Brown, "Patriarchal Capitalism and the Female-Headed Family," *Social Scientist* (India); no. 40–41 (November-December 1975), pp. 28–39.

11. Carol Brown, in "Patriarchal Capitalism," argues, for example, that we are moving from "family based" to "industrially-based" patriarchy within capitalism.

12. Stewart Ewen, *Captains of Consciousness* (New York: Random House, 1976).

13. For the proportion of people in nuclear families, see Peter Uhlenberg, "Cohort Variations in Family Life Cycle Experiences of U.S. Females," *Journal of Marriage and the Family*, Vol. 36, no. 5 (May 1974), pp. 284–92. For remarriage rates see Paul C. Glick and Arthur J. Norton, "Perspectives on the Recent Upturn in Divorce and Remarriage," *Demography*, Vol. 10 (1974), pp. 301–14. For divorce and income levels see Arthur J. Norton and Paul C. Glick, "Marital Instability: Past, Present, and Future," *Journal of Social Issues*, Vol. 32, no. 1 (1976), pp. 5–20. Also see Mary Jo Bane, *Here to Stay: American Families in the Twentieth Century* (New York: Basic Books, 1976).

14. Heather L. Ross and Isabel B. Sawhill, *Time of Transition: The Growth of Families Headed by Women* (Washington, D.C.: The Urban Institute, 1975).

15. See Kathryn E. Walker and Margaret E. Woods, *Time Use: A Measure of Household Production of Family Goods and Services* (Washington, D.C.: American Home Economics Association, 1976); and Heidi I. Hartmann, "The Family as the Locus of Gender, Class, and Political Struggle: The Example of Housework," *Signs: Journal of Women in Culture and Society*, Vol. 6, no. 3 (Spring 1981).

SZONJA SZELÉNYI

Women and the Class Structure

There is a long history of debates addressing whether the primitive unit underlying stratification systems is the family or the individual. The purpose of this paper is to review, juxtapose, and critique the various class models that have emerged out of this debate. In the course of carrying out the review, I hope that several themes will emerge. The first such theme is that most of the theoretical contributions occur within very narrowly defined research traditions, and consequently the various participants do not feel obliged to pit their own preferred approach against the entire range of positions on record. I will further show that there is no one-to-one correspondence between the actual position taken and the larger theoretical or ideological stance of the protagonists. The same position often appeals to scholars coming from quite disparate theoretical orientations, and the resulting debate thus makes for strange ideological bedfellows. The final, and most disturbing, feature of these debates is that protagonists often fail to identify the theoretical underpinnings of their classification exercises, and the sociological consumer is therefore left without a "yardstick" against which to assess the contributions.

I shall review in straightforward fashion each of the conceptual stances that have so far been advanced. As the review unfolds, readers may find it useful to refer to Figure 1.

Conventional View

The position that dominated stratification theory and research from the 1950s to the early 1970s

rested on the assumption that (1) the family rather than the individual forms the basic unit of sociological analysis and (2) the social position of the family is properly indexed by the status of its (usually) male head. According to Parsons (1954), the occupational structure constitutes the main axis of social inequality, and as a result the status of families is defined by their ranking within the occupational hierarchy. However, because most wives do not have the opportunity to participate in the formal economy, the class position of their family is determined by their husband's occupation. The distinctive feature of Parsons (1954) is his resolutely functionalist interpretation of the sources of this gender-based division of labor. That is, he argues that segregating women in this fashion contributes to the stability of the family by eliminating competition for status between spouses and by allowing husbands to freely pursue labor market opportunities anywhere in the country without concern for their wives' careers.

Although the conventional viewpoint is routinely identified with a functionalist stance of this kind, it should be kept in mind that other theoretical orientations are also consistent with its propositions (Goldthorpe 1983). For example, Goldthorpe (1983) would agree with Parsons that the position of women in the class structure is merely derivative, but for Goldthorpe this arises from gender inequalities in power and advantage rather than from any functional need to reduce competition between husbands and wives. Whereas some feminists have argued that the

---

This is an original article prepared for this book.

FIGURE 1
A typology of approaches to locating women in the class structure

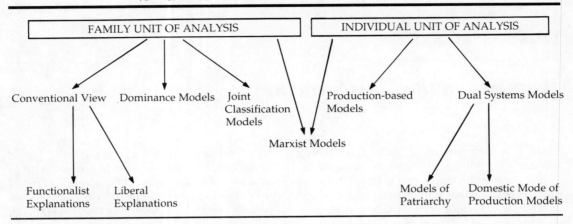

conventional view is a prime example of "intellectual sexism" (Acker 1973), Goldthorpe maintains that precisely the opposite is the case because his liberal rendition of the conventional view recognizes the derivative position of women and, therefore, underscores the importance of patriarchy.

The conventional view can nonetheless be criticized on other grounds. The most obvious difficulty is that it fails to appreciate the simple fact that women are entering the labor force in ever-increasing numbers. Although Goldthorpe would argue that the male head continues to maintain "the greatest commitment to, and continuity in, labor market participation" (1983, p. 470), this fallback position is unlikely to attract a large following given the (seemingly) revolutionary changes in the market position of women. The following facts are especially relevant here: (1) The proportion of all women who are unmarried has been on the increase since the 1970s, (2) women are marrying at older ages and are delaying the birth of their first child, (3) increasing numbers of women participate in the labor force on a continuous basis and with greater commitment to a career, and (4) full-time participation in the labor force is on the rise even among married women (see Szelényi 1992 for further details). Taken together, these trends indicate that women's life chances are increasingly defined by their own careers and not by their husbands' jobs.

Furthermore, if one follows Lockwood (1989) and Goldthorpe (1987) in defining classes as aggregates of occupations with similar market and work situations, the conventional viewpoint cannot be readily justified. To be sure, insofar as families pool income and function as unitary consumption classes, one might regard housewives as having the same market situation as their husbands. However, when the wife is employed, the pooled income for the family no longer reflects the income of the husband alone. The conceptual standing of the conventional model scarcely improves when the work conditions of spouses are compared. Although employed women may possibly have work conditions that are similar to those of their (employed) husbands, it is implausible in the extreme to assume that this equivalence will also hold for women working at home. It follows that the conventional view is tenable only if classes are defined solely in terms of market situation, and even here one must impose the further condition that wives are not employed and thus contribute no income to the family.

Dominance Model

Although many critics assume that the conventional view is the only family-based approach to defining the class position of women (e.g., Wright 1989), there are in fact several such approaches on offer, and not all of these treat the position of women as wholly derivative. In the so-called dominance model, Erikson (1984) identifies the class position of the family with that of the individual who is most highly ranked within a "dominance hierarchy," where this hierarchy is established by ordering family members in terms of their labor force participation and work situation. Under this formulation, the worker with the strongest attachment to the labor force always dominates, whereas in dual-career families the worker with the highest socioeconomic status dominates (see Erikson 1984 for elaboration and qualification).

In evaluating this approach, one again has to ask whether it captures the market and work situation of families adequately. Although the total income of the family (and thus its "market situation") will probably be better approximated by the income of the dominant family member than by that of the male head, it should be obvious that no single individual can possibly capture the total income of the family when both spouses are working. It is likewise the case that no single individual can adequately represent the work situations of all family members. In raising issues of this sort, we do not wish to prejudge which underlying model of class Erikson prefers, but regardless of what his preferences might be, the dominance model appears to be inadequate to the task. If, for example, the purpose of his "class" model is to capture patterns of deference and derogation between families, then one must ask whether the (seemingly) arbitrary rules that Erikson uses to establish dominance truly capture the social processes by which families are evaluated. Unfortunately, we know of no empirical work that addresses this issue directly, but classical theory (e.g., Shils 1970) does suggest that processes of status evaluation are somewhat more complex than the dominance model would imply.

Joint Classification Model

The second family-based approach that is often overlooked by critics of the conventional view is the joint classification model proposed by Britten

and Heath (1983). As the label suggests, Britten and Heath classify families in terms of the employment situation of both spouses, with the result thus being a "joint classification" that represents all possible combinations of their individual work statuses. If the intent of Britten and Heath is to capture the market and work situation of families, this approach is obviously superior to other family-based models because, by definition, the class position of the family is no longer reduced to that of any single family member.[1]

For our present purposes, the more important point is that Britten and Heath introduce, if only implicitly, a new definition of what constitutes a family-based approach. Whereas the conventional view seemingly implies that husbands and wives will have the same "scores" on class-related dependent variables such as voting behavior and subjective class identification, the joint classification approach no longer imposes this kind of equality constraint. In an analysis predicting such outcomes, we can reconceptualize the Britten-Heath model as allowing for (1) an individual-level effect for the respondent's occupation, (2) a contextual effect for the spouse's occupation, and (3) a possible interaction effect between the two. The viability of the Britten-Heath model therefore turns on the presence of contextual effects for both husbands and wives. By contrast, if the conventional view is recast in the same language of contextual effects, it implies a "mixed model" in which only individual effects are fitted for men and only contextual effects are fitted for women.

Marxist Models

Just as the family-based approach takes on many competing forms, so too there is no single individualistic model of class. The individualistic tradition nonetheless encompasses a somewhat less heterogeneous array of positions; at a minimum, all commentators within this tradition incorporate at least some women into their models of the class structure, even if they differ somewhat in their approaches to doing so. The common theme in all Marxist analyses, for example, is that both male and female wage workers are classified by the relationship of their individual jobs to the means of production. The variability within the Marxist camp arises only in their approaches to locating the class position of housewives. For classical Marxists (Engels 1968), housewives are seen as having no class position at all because they have no direct relationship to the means of production. To be sure, these theorists did not ignore altogether the subordination of women, but they viewed this as a mere remnant of past social relations and argued that it would disappear with the incorporation of women into the formal economy.

Among Marxists of the postwar era, housewives are no longer treated as peripheral to the class system but rather as explicitly involved in sustaining capitalist relations of production. This position takes on several forms. Whereas critical Marxists argue that housewives socialize children into a submissive role within capitalist relations of authority (Horkheimer 1982), other Marxists suggest that housewives provide male workers with an "emotional refuge in a cold and competitive society" (Lasch 1977, p. 6), and yet others claim that housewives constitute a reserve army of labor and thereby drive male wages down and undermine their strike potential (Beechey 1977). Under all of these viewpoints, women thus facilitate the exploitation of men but are not themselves exploited in a classical Marxian sense. By contrast, the domestic labor theorists argue that housewives are indirectly exploited by capital because their husbands are paid a "family wage" that reimburses them not only for their direct contribution to profit on the shopfloor but also for the daily reproduction of their labor power at home (Secombe 1974). This approach therefore converges with the conventional view because the position of housewives, albeit *not* employed women, again becomes derivative (Wright 1989). It is here, then, that we first see the debate over the class position of women producing strange bedfellows.

Production-based Models

The same sort of irony appears when attention is turned to "mainstream" stratification research and the production-based models that such re-

search typically deploys. Although feminist critics (Acker 1973) often assume that practitioners within this tradition adopt the conventional view, in fact their treatment of women bears a more striking similarity to the position taken by classical Marxists. In their studies of social mobility and status attainment, for example, mainstream researchers usually assign employed women to a class position that reflects their own job but treat housewives as outside the labor force and thus ignore them (Sewell, Hauser, and Wolf 1980; Hout 1988; Payne and Abbott 1990). This is not to suggest that exclusively male analyses are no longer carried out; however, the men in these studies are not typically regarded as proxies for their families but instead are seen as representing only themselves and therefore constituting only "half the story" (Grusky 1987, p. 7). It should finally be noted that mainstream stratification researchers have recently taken further steps to distance themselves from the conventional view by devising new occupational scales that reflect the socioeconomic standing of employed women as well as that of employed men (Stevens and Featherman 1981; Bose and Rossi 1983). In summary, although the "production-based" view elaborated here may not be explicitly theorized by its practitioners, it should be clear that contemporary research practices among most quantitative researchers are no longer consistent with the conventional view.

Dual Systems Models

The dual systems approach considers economic and sex-based inequality simultaneously and posits that "a healthy and strong partnership exists between patriarchy and capital" (Hartmann 1981, p. 19). Whereas Marxists see patriarchy as the handmaiden of capitalism (Horkheimer 1982), and radical feminists see capitalism as the handmaiden of patriarchy (Firestone 1971), dual system theorists emphasize the reciprocal relationship between these two structures of inequality. For example, Hartmann (1981) argues that women's domestic responsibilities make it difficult for them to compete for lucrative jobs, and this in turn generates a sex-segregated occupational structure. However, with the institutionalization of such segregation and the consequent emergence of a wage gap between genders, women have no choice but to be economically dependent on men. By emphasizing this reciprocal link between production and reproduction, the dual systems approach provides a fruitful conceptual framework.

The difficulty with this approach, at least for the present purposes, is that it is pitched at a highly abstract level and its classificatory implications are correspondingly unclear. It is possible, however, to identify two approaches to locating men and women in the stratification system that might be seen, albeit only indirectly, as having a dual systems heritage. The first such approach identifies the main line of patriarchal cleavage as being between men and women while the main lines of class cleavage are presumably captured by the conventional model of class (Firestone 1971). In most versions of this approach (e.g., models of patriarchy), the principal focus is on the structure of patriarchal relations, whereas little attention is paid to the nature of women's participation in the formal labor force (Millet 1970; Chodorow 1978; O'Brien 1981). The second such approach also adopts a dual systems framework, with the main line of patriarchal cleavage again occurring between men and women. But in describing the economic sphere, proponents of this view no longer see the conventional model of class as satisfactory, and they explicitly incorporate housewives within a *domestic mode of production* (e.g., Harrison 1973; Delphy 1984; Szelényi 1992). With this reformulation of the concept of class, these analysts theorize household labor as constituting a distinctive economic sphere and thereby recover a large segment of the working population that has been routinely ignored by previous class schemes.

I close by underlining just three points. First, the family-based models of class are especially difficult to evaluate, because their proponents sometimes fail to specify the dimensions of inequality that they ultimately seek to capture. The conceptual underpinnings of Marxist and other individualistic models are well specified by comparison; for example, when a Marxist asks whether housewives are properly conceived as members of the working class, this is clearly tantamount to asking whether they are exploited by

capital. Although one might quarrel with the claim that exploitation should be the criterion by which classes are defined, the conceptual "yardstick" against which the Marxist model can be evaluated is at least clear. Second, the joint classification model appears to take us in a useful direction, if only because it begins to recast the debate in the language of contextual effects. If this language is adopted and extended, one might reasonably ask whether the conjugal family is the only context of interest. As Parsons points out, it is perhaps high time to "divorce the concept of social class from its historic relation to both kinship and property" (1970, p. 24), given that individuals in modern society are embedded in a complex web of social communities (e.g., family of procreation, work organization, neighborhood, friendship networks), all of which may give rise to contextual effects. The third and final point is that the presence and strength of such contextual effects, including those pertaining to the family, are ultimately an empirical matter.

Notes

Support for this research was provided by grants from the Stanford Center for the Study of Families, Children, and Youth; the National Academy of Education Spencer Research Fellowship Program; and a McNamara Faculty Fellowship from the School of Humanities and Sciences at Stanford University. I thank Johannes Berger, Mariko Lin Chang, David Grusky, Paul Munroe, Jacqueline Olvera, and Winifred Poster for their helpful suggestions and advice. The opinions expressed herein are those of the author.

1. The irony here is that Goldthorpe (1983) in fact denies that the Britten-Heath approach is a viable *class* model. This conclusion could only be reached because Goldthorpe appears to abandon his earlier premise that classes should be defined in terms of market and work situations.

References

Acker, Joan. 1973. "Women and Social Stratification: A Case of Intellectual Sexism." *American Journal of Sociology* 78:936–945.

Beechey, Veronica. 1977. "Some Notes on Female Wage Labour in Capitalist Production." *Capital and Class* 3:45–66.

Bose, Christine E., and Peter H. Rossi. 1983. "Gender and Jobs: Prestige Standings of Occupations as Affected by Gender." *American Sociological Review* 48:316–330.

Britten, Nicky, and Anthony Heath. 1983. "Women, Men, and Social Class." Pp. 46–60 in Eva Gamarnikow, David Morgan, June Purvis, and Daphne Taylorson, eds., *Gender, Class, and Work*. London: Heinemann.

Chodorow, Christine. 1978. *The Reproduction of Mothering*. Berkeley: University of California Press.

Delphy, Christine. 1984. "The Main Enemy." Pp. 57–77 in Christine Delphy, *Close to Home*. Amherst: The University of Massachusetts Press.

Engels, Frederick. 1968. "The Origin of the Family, Private Property, and the State." Pp. 449–583 in Karl Marx and Frederick Engels, *Selected Works*. Moscow: Progress.

Erikson, Robert. 1984. "Social Class of Men, Women, and Families." *Sociology* 18:500–514.

Firestone, Shulamith. 1971. *The Dialectic of Sex*. New York: Bantam.

Goldthorpe, John H. 1983. "Women and Class Analysis: In Defense of the Conventional View." *Sociology* 17:465–88.

———. 1987. *Social Mobility and Class Structure in Modern Britain*, 2d ed. Oxford: Clarendon.

Grusky, David B. 1987. "American Social Mobility in the 19th and 20th Centuries." Working Paper 86-28. University of Wisconsin–Madison: Center for Demography and Ecology.

Harrison, John. 1973. "The Political Economy of Housework." *Bulletin of the Conference of Socialist Economists* 3 (Winter):35–51.

Hartmann, Heidi. 1981. "The Unhappy Marriage of Marxism and Feminism: Towards a More Progressive Union." Pp. 2–41 in Lydia Sargent, ed., *Women and Revolution*. Boston: South End.

Horkheimer, Max. 1982. *Critical Theory*. New York: Continuum.

Hout, Michael. 1988. "More Universalism, Less Structural Mobility: The American Occupational Structure in the 1980s." *Americal Journal of Sociology* 93:1358–1400.

Lasch, Christopher. 1977. *Haven in a Heartless World*. New York: Basic Books.

Lockwood, David. 1989. *The Blackcoated Worker*, 2d ed. Oxford: Clarendon.

Millett, Kate. 1970. *Sexual Politics*. New York: Ballantine Books.

O'Brien, Mary. 1981. *The Politics of Reproduction*. Boston: Routledge and Kegan Paul.

Parsons, Talcott. 1954. *Essays in Sociological Theory*. New York: The Free Press.

———. 1970. "Equality and Inequality in Modern Society, or Social Stratification Revisited." Pp. 13–72 in Edward O. Laumann, ed., *Social Stratification*. Indianapolis: Bobbs-Merrill.

Payne, Geoff, and Pamela Abbott. 1990. *The Social Mobility of Women: Beyond Male Mobility Models*. London: The Falmer Press.

Secombe, Wally. 1974. "The Housewife and Her Labour Under Capitalism." *New Left Review* 83:3–24.

Sewell, William H., Robert M. Hauser, and Wendy C. Wolf. 1980. "Sex, Schooling, and Occupational Status." *American Journal of Sociology* 86:551–583.

Shils, Edward A. 1970. "Deference." Pp. 420–448 in Edward O. Laumann, Paul M. Siegel, and Robert W. Hodge, eds., *The Logic of Social Hierarchies*. Chicago: Markham.

Stevens, Gillian, and David L. Featherman. 1981. "A Revised Socioeconomic Index of Occupational Status." *Social Science Research* 10:364–395.

Szelényi, Szonja. 1992. "Economic Subsystems and the Occupational Structure: A Comparison of Hungary and the United States." *Sociological Forum* 7:563–585.

Wright, Erik Olin, 1989. "Women in the Class Structure." *Politics and Society* 17:35–66.

▶ OCCUPATIONAL AND WAGE DISCRIMINATION

∼ Supply-Side Approaches

SOLOMON W. POLACHEK AND W. STANLEY SIEBERT

Gender in the Labour Market

Explaining why women seem relegated to an inferior economic position is important. If these patterns emerge because of unequal opportunities caused by unfair hiring practices, then the economy is failing to fully and appropriately utilise highly productive employees. Economic inefficiencies thereby come about, providing a justification for government intervention. On the other hand, if unequal economic outcomes result from differing individual choices despite equal opportunity, then government intervention to force 'equal pay' would lead to a distorted allocation of resources and inefficiencies within the economy. In this case, rather than helping disadvantaged groups, productive efficiency is hampered so that in the long run all end up suffering. Thus, the comprehension of the causes of gender differences in economic success is important.

In assessing the reasons for differences in pay between men and women it is useful to consider first the possibility of bias or discrimination *within* the labour market. 'Discrimination' can reasonably be defined as 'unlike treatment of likes'. In a labour market context, discrimination then occurs when men are paid more than women of the same productivity. Since the firm is the locus of such discrimination we can also call this 'demand-side' discrimination.

There is also the possibility of bias or discrimination *prior to* the labour market, in the education system, or in the family. Such bias affects the productivity characteristics (e.g., education, or motivation) which workers bring with them to the market. The family forms tastes and treats girl children differently from boy children. Many feel such different treatment to be a form of discrimination 'in the childhood formation of preferences' (Cain, 1976, 1236). Because tastes are difficult to measure economists have traditionally preferred to regard taste formation as a black box, and explain behaviour in terms of reactions to prices with tastes given (West and McKee, 1983, 1110). However, some studies exist of pre–labour market discrimination, and we will consider these. Since such discrimination affects the characteristics of the worker, and has nothing to do with the employer, we can call it 'supply-side' discrimination.

The supply and demand sides are inter-related, because expected demand discrimination will affect worker supply. For example, if women expect poor promotion prospects they will elect to have less education. However, the distinction is still useful for analytical purposes. ...

Differences in Tastes

We can generalise the definition of discrimination to mean 'unlike treatment of likes' in any field, including within the family. However to say that different treatment of boys and girls within the family—'playing doctor or playing nurse'—is discriminatory is then to imply that the sex of children does not or should not matter. There is no way of proving this. Psychological studies of parents indicate they have deeply held conceptions that their girls and boys are different: for example, parents rate girl babies as smaller than boy babies even when they are the same weight (Shepela and Viviano, 1984, 48). Parents, it seems, see what they want to see in this respect. This could be indicative of a deep biological and cultural necessity to have sexual differentiation—rather than some erroneous 'stereotyping' on the parents' part.

In any case, women's involvement in child rearing might be felt by the family to be good for the children. In Japan, where women have a more family-oriented role, they are strongly involved in pre-school education (Edwards, 1988, 245)—and Japanese children's educational performance is good by comparison with other countries. The mean mathematics score for thirteen year olds in Anderson's international study was 31.2 for Japan, 20.2 for Australia, 19.3 for England and 16.2 for the USA (Anderson, 1967, 191).

Whether the reasons be good or bad, men and women do appear to have different tastes and this affects occupational choice. Daymont and Andrisani (1984) analysed high school pupils' responses to questions about the importance of various job rewards when choosing a career. Women were found to be significantly more likely to be interested in a career with opportunities for helping others, and for working with people, and less likely to want a career with the emphasis on making money and being a leader. Proportions answering 'Yes' to questions about tastes were as follows (Daymont and Andrisani, 1984, 412):

	Male	Female
Very interested in a career with opportunities to help others	47%	72%
Very interested in working with people	40	68
Very interested in leading	22	11
Very interested in making money	22	13

Later, in college, the same sample of men and women were found to have different majors, with the men favouring business, engineering, and the professions, and the women health or biology, the humanities, and education (1984, 414). Tastes thus affect motivation and the type of education which an individual chooses, and these factors will then affect earnings.

Intermittent Participation and Reduced Human Capital

Women differ from men in their expectations of lifetime labourforce participation. Women, especially married women, tend to participate in the labourforce more intermittently than men. Using the 1967 National Longitudinal Survey, figures for years out of the workforce for married women at work in 1966 vary by age and education. For those aged thirty to thirty-four the figure is 9.9 years (4.2 years) for women with less than twelve (more than sixteen) years of education. Equivalent figures for the forty to forty-four age group are 15.7 (9.7) (see Mincer and Polachek, 1974; Mincer and Ofek, 1982). For those who had not worked since the birth of their first child (about 1/3 of the sample of 3,000) the period out of the workforce is about 50% higher. Those not at work in 1966, but who had ever worked, give an intermediate figure. Thus, to take a round figure, we might assume that ten years, on average, are spent out of the labourforce to bear and raise children. Still more time (about four years) is spent in intermittent participation as children are growing up. In the case of Britain, Joshi assumes eight years for 'Mrs. Typical' with two children (1987, 13).

Figure 1 depicts sex and marital status labourforce participation patterns for the United States. Married men have by far the highest labourforce participation. Married women have the lowest, peaking at about 43% at age twenty-three, and then again at forty-eight. The trough at around age thirty reflects labourforce intermittency related to child bearing. The gap between single men and single women is the narrowest. Single-never-married males and females have roughly similar lifetime work behaviour patterns. Over time, to be sure, the dip in participation for women in the twenty-five to thirty-seven age group has become much less marked. Neverthe-

FIGURE 1

Labourforce participation by marital status, US 1970. *Source:* Robert Fearn, *Labor Economics, The Emerging Synthesis,* Cambridge, MA: Winthrop Publishers, 1981.

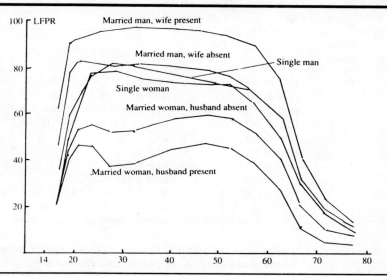

less women's labourforce participation remains much less than men's.

Human capital theory links occupations and wages to lifetime labourforce participation and the division of labour within the family. Because monetary gains from investment cannot be reaped when not at work, the average woman's returns from investment are reduced by the present value of the extra earnings from investment she would have earned had she continued to work instead of staying at home. Thus the effect of lower lifetime labourforce participation and intermittency is to lower gains from human capital investment.

Table 1 illustrates the position by contrasting two individuals, one of whom works continuously until age sixty-five, while the other leaves the workforce between ages twenty-six and thirty-five. The left-hand column shows that the present value of an arbitrary skill unit (i.e., an 'ed') assumed to raise wages by $1 a year falls smoothly with advancing age; the 'marginal gain' from investing in an 'ed' is almost $10 at age twenty, and falls to zero by age sixty-five. The right-hand column shows quite a different pattern. Due to the expected break in labourforce

participation (when nothing is earned), the present value of an 'ed' is much less at age twenty. The table shows the present value to be $5.81, falling to $3.28 at age twenty-five. Then for the next ten years the marginal gain to investment is increasing. But whether any investment is made is another matter. If post-school investment consists strictly of on-the-job training, then none can be made. The person's capital stock and capacity earnings will fall accordingly. Upon reentry at age thirty-six, marginal gain from investment follows the same path for both continuous and intermittent workers. ...

Intermittent Participation and Occupational Choice

Further, individuals expecting labourforce intermittency will choose occupations in which the penalty for intermittency—the 'atrophy' or depreciation of human capital—is lowest. Such occupations will have high starting wages and thus flat earnings (a job cannot have both a high starting wage and a high rate of increase of pay with

TABLE 1
Gains from Human Capital Investments for Continuous and Intermittent Workers

Age	Continuous worker: gain from 1 ed		Intermittent worker: gain from 1 ed	
	Partici- pation	MG_t	Partici- pation	FMG_t
20	1	10×0.986*	1	$10 \times (0.379 + 0.986 - 0.782) = 5.81$†
25	1	10×0.978	1	$10 \times (0 + 0.978 - 0.650) = 3.28$
30	1	10×0.964	0	$10 \times (0 + 0.964 - 0.436) = 5.25$
35	1	10×0.943	0	$10 \times (0 + 0.943 - 0.091) = 8.52$
40	1	10×0.908	1	10×0.908
45	1	10×0.851	1	10×0.851
50	1	10×0.761	1	10×0.761
55	1	10×0.614	1	10×0.614
60	1	10×0.379	1	10×0.379
65	1	0	1	0

Notes:

*Assume the value, w, of an ed is \$1 a year, i.e., buying 1 ed raises potential earnings, E, by \$1 a year for the rest of one's working life. Assume the discount rate is 10% (so buying 1 ed raises the value of the capital stock by $w/0.1 = \$10$), and people retire at age 65. If the ed is invested in at age 20, then the extra \$1 received for 45 years has a present value of

$$\frac{\$1}{0.1} \left[1 - \frac{1}{(1.1)^{45}} \right] = \$9.86.$$

†Assume the period out of the labour force lasts from age 26 to 35. Then the returns from an investment of 1 ed made at age 20 are gained for five years initially:

$$\frac{\$1}{0.1} \left[1 - \frac{1}{(1.1)^{5}} \right] = \$3.79$$

and then for 29 years in 16 years' time:

$$\frac{\$1}{0.1} \left[1 - \frac{1}{(1.1)^{45}} \right] - \frac{\$1}{0.1} \left[1 - \frac{1}{(1.1)^{16}} \right] = \$10 (0.986 - 0.782).$$

The total present value is therefore \$5.81.

experience, because everyone would go for that job). It would not make sense for someone who was expecting to leave the workforce to become a trainee manager, for example. Men who are not expecting to leave pull the starting wage of such jobs down. A worker who does leave will thus have incurred the penalty of a low trainee wage, and will not be around to enjoy the later higher wages.

One implication is that women will be less well represented in professional and managerial jobs for reasons of income-maximising choice (given competition from men)—quite apart from demand-side discrimination in hiring or promotion. Indeed we do find in practice that occupations with the highest depreciation during periods of hometime tend to have female workers with the fewest years out of the workforce. Professional and management jobs, for example, have high depreciation compared to the service job category, and the proportion of years spent as 'hometime' is about 30% for women in the former, compared to 60% in the latter.

Another implication of the hypothesis is that the jobs taken by single women will differ from those of married women, giving the latter's family care commitments, and be similar to those of single men. The empirical evidence here appears to support the proposition. Roos (1981) illustrates occupational patterns for employed women for twelve countries (mainly OECD). For each country except Israel and Sweden, a greater proportion of never married women are in professional, technical and administrative jobs. This contrasts with the large proportion of married women in more menial service and agricultural jobs. In addition there is a reasonably good correlation between occupations which have high percentage female, and those which employ women with high intermittency. England, however, does not find a correlation between per cent female and intermittency (per cent hometime) using detailed occupations (1982, table 4). But it is more appropriate to proxy intermittency with per cent home time than per cent female. Also, since the human capital model is designed to represent lifetime occupational choice, broad occupational categories are more appropriate than detailed (current) occupations.

Following up the point about expectations, a further implication of labourforce intermittency is that women who expect to remain in the workforce should choose jobs with lower starting salaries and steeper age-earnings profiles than those who did not. This has indeed been demonstrated empirically. A sample of young women (average age nineteen) were questioned as to whether they planned to be in the workforce at age thirty-five. Analysing their pay five years later, those who did have such plans were found to be earning 10% *less* than the others, but had much faster earnings growth (Sandell and Shapiro, 1980, 342). Individuals aiming to remain in the workforce thus appear to invest more in themselves, as we would expect.

Intermittent Participation and the Wage Gap

The effect of intermittency on the wage gap is illustrated in figure 2. $0''H$ represents an age-earnings profile for a typical individual with full lifetime labourforce participation, ignoring curvature for simplicity. It reflects earnings capacity at each level of experience, and thus rises with age.

Those labour market participants with intermittency have a different profile. First of all, initial labour market earnings (the vertical intercept) is smaller (point 0) because of the smaller investment in education. Second, the slope with respect to initial experience (e_1) is smaller (rising to level A). Third, earnings are essentially zero during the period (H) when one is out of the labourforce. And fourth, and perhaps most interesting, the reentry wage (B), after a period of intermittency, is lower in real terms than the wage at the point just prior to leaving the labour market (A).

The total loss in wages caused by intermittency can be expressed as segment (BK), the difference between reentry wage (B) and the wage the individual would have received had she been in the labourforce fully. This gap can be divided into three segments: (1) BC represents the direct depreciation of skills due to atrophy, (2) CD reflects the lost wages due to lost seniority, and (3) DK reflects the extra wage one would have obtained with initially high expectations of labourforce participation. This latter gap DK is composed of two parts, DG and GK. The gap DG reflects the additional earnings attributable to extra on-the-job training that would be obtained by those with expectations of complete labourforce continuity. Similarly, the gap GK reflects the additional earnings attributable to extra schooling (including the study of more market oriented fields) for those who plan to specialise more in a career than home activities. ...

FIGURE 2
The effect on earnings of labourforce intermittency

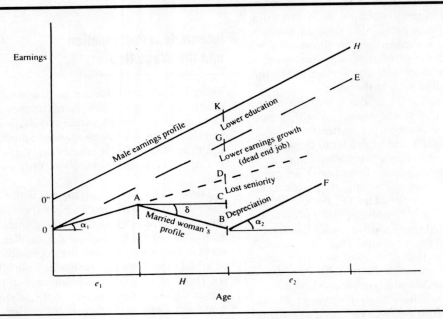

Current Policy

The wage gap has been a political issue at least since the early 1970s. Government policy promoting sexual equality in the market place has been oriented almost solely towards business. Firms are sued because they allegedly have unfair hiring practices and because they allegedly pay unequal wages for equal work. Britain has an Equal Pay Act, and a Sex Discrimination Act. The United States has Title VII of the Civil Rights Act of 1964, which prohibits discrimination on grounds of sex, religion, or national origin, and other legislation (for example, federal contractors must comply with affirmative action guidelines). In America, the government as well as individuals have brought class action suits at unprecedented levels.

Despite such legal activity, wage differentials have only narrowed slowly, and occupational distributions remain very different. This slow progress has most likely resulted because government legislation treats corporations as the primary culprit of most sex differences within the labour market.

As demonstrated above, such an approach is seriously limited in perspective because it neglects social factors. Whereas it may be true that some of the sex differences in labourforce participation are caused by women being discouraged from working continuously, we have argued that little of the differences are caused by firms. Rather it is the more subtle forms of social conditioning taking place directly within the family, and the power of gender specialisation within the household which are important. The specialisation factor is shown by the fact that single-never-been-married women have greater lifetime labourforce commitment than their married counterparts, as well as a higher level of earnings and better jobs. Specialisation within the household is also the reason that we observe that the gender wage gap is smaller for singles than marrieds, smaller at younger ages, and larger for those with children.

Despite the apparent failure of governmental equal employment opportunity type policies, greater sexual equality is coming about. It is not noticeable among all women, but is widely observed among the younger cohorts. Young women are entering the labour market in unprecedented numbers. They are doing so with expectations of greater labour market continuity brought about by postponing marriage, bearing fewer children, and having almost epidemic divorce rates. These expectations are causing the younger cohorts to increasingly invest in human capital skills. School attendance by women is becoming larger than that of men, and women are now entering what used to be occupations in the male domain. Law school, business school, and medical school enrolments which only a decade ago were at meagre levels for women are now approaching 40%. For these groups there is rough parity with men.

While the older cohorts are also increasing their role in the economy, they are at a great disadvantage. They are reentering the labour market after spending an average of about ten years out for child rearing responsibilities. Because of this time out, many of their skills have atrophied, resulting in an earnings power lower than it otherwise would have been. It is the inclusion of these reentrants that tend to bias downward the aggregate statistics measuring equality between the sexes.

Bibliography

Anderson, C. (1967), 'The International Comparative Study of Achievement in Mathematics', *Comparative Education Review*, June, 11: 182–96.

Cain, G. (1976), 'The Challenge of Segmented Labor Market Theories to Orthodox Theory: A Survey', *Journal of Economic Literature*, 14: 1215–57.

Daymont, T. and P. Andrisani (1984), 'Job Preferences, College Major, and the Gender Gap in Earnings', *Journal of Human Resources*, 19: 408–28.

Edwards, L. (1988), 'Equal Employment Opportunity in Japan: A View from the West', *Industrial and Labor Relations Review*, 41: 240–50.

England, P. (1982), 'The Failure of Human Capital Theory to Explain Occupational Sex Segregation', *Journal of Human Resources*, Spring, 17: 358–70.

Fearn, R. (1981), *Labor Economics, The Emerging Synthesis*, Cambridge, MA: Winthrop Publishers.

Joshi, H. (1987), 'The Cash Opportunity Costs of Child-Bearing', Economic Policy Research Unit Discussion Paper 208, London.

Mincer, J. and H. Ofek (1982), 'Interrupted Work Careers: Depreciation and Restoration of Human Capital', *Journal of Human Resources*, Winter, 17: 3–24.

Mincer, J. and S. Polachek (1974), 'Family Investments in Human Capital: Earnings of Women', *Journal of Political Economy*, Supplement, 82: S76–108.

Roos, P. (1981), 'Marital Differences in Occupational Distribution and Attainment', Paper presented at the Annual Population Association Meetings.

Sandell, S. and D. Shapiro (1980), 'Work Expectations, Human Capital Accumulation, and the Wages of Young Women', *Journal of Human Resources*, 15: 335–53.

Shepela, S. and A. Viviano (1984), 'Some Psychological Factors Affecting Job Segregation and Wages', in H. Remick (ed.), *Comparable Worth and Wage Discrimination: Technical Possibilities and Political Realities*, Philadelphia: Temple University Press.

West, E. and M. McKee (1983), 'De Gestibus Est Disputandum: The Phenomenon of "Merit Wants" Revisited', *American Economic Review*, 73: 1110–21.

PAULA ENGLAND

Wage Appreciation and Depreciation: A Test of Neoclassical Economic Explanations of Occupational Sex Segregation

Any theory of socioeconomic differences between women and men must have the sex segregation of jobs as its focus. Recent scholarship reflects this consensus on the importance of segregation (England, b), but our understanding of its causes has advanced little. The problem is not a lack of theoretically grounded propositions. On the contrary, virtually every perspective in the social sciences has spawned a theory about the causes of the sex segregation of jobs. Social psychologists focus on sex role socialization to explain sex-typical job choices (Marini and Brinton). Institutionalist economists and structuralist sociologists point to segmented labor markets and mobility ladders that perpetuate any segregation that occurs at firms' ports of entry (Blau and Jusenius; Roos and Reskin). Marxists argue that segregation by sex helps capitalists to "divide and conquer" workers (Edwards et al.). Theories of patriarchy see men operating as a class to keep women in roles with little power. Some neoclassical economists claim that segregation results from hiring discrimination motivated by employers' nonpecuniary "tastes." Other economists link segregation to employers' attempts to reduce information costs by engaging in statistical discrimination, that is, basing personnel decisions on sex group averages. Still other neoclassical economists have generated explanations of segregation from human capital theory. (For a critical review of the explanations above see England, c.)

With such a glut of explanations, it is more of an advance to weed out incorrect theories than to propose new ones. Segregation has more causes than any single theory can depict. But we should sharpen our focus to the most important factors generating and perpetuating segregation. In this spirit of parsimony, I present an analysis which pares down the literature by refuting two explanations of occupational sex segregation that have been generated from the neoclassical theory of human capital.

The two hypotheses I test explain segregation in terms of the occupational choices made by men and women. They are "labor-supply-side" explanations generated from human capital theory. (Both Becker and Mincer provide the seminal introductions to human capital theory.) Both hypotheses assume that men and women choose occupations that will maximize their lifetime earnings. Both theses take women's responsibility for childrearing as a given; they posit that the resulting sex differences in employment continuity make different occupational choices pecuniarily more rational for women than for men. Thus, optimizing choices made by male and female workers are seen by both theses to explain occupational sex segregation. Polachek's thesis (b, c, d, e) emphasizes the wage depreciation one suffers while out of the labor force; Zellner's hypothesis focuses on occupations' starting wages and returns to experience. The two theses are complementary rather than mutually exclusive.

Wage Depreciation: Polachek's Thesis

Polachek's (b, c, d, e) explanation of segregation focuses on the wage depreciation that occurs while women are engaged in full-time homemaking rather than employed for pay. Wage depreciation has occurred if a woman has lower real wages on returning to paid employment than she had when she quit her job to take up full-time homemaking. It is important to distinguish such depreciation from the wages or wage appreciation one foregoes by being out of the labor force. Two people with the same amount of employment experience may have different wages because the one whose employment has been broken by more or longer interruptions has suffered more wage depreciation. Polachek sees wage depreciation during home time as an atrophy of one's human capital—skills get rusty or obsolete. An interpretation less faithful to marginal productivity theory would acknowledge that such wage depreciation may result from institutional factors such as firms' or unions' rules dictating a loss of seniority rights upon resignation.

Polachek argues that some occupations entail a greater risk of depreciation than others. If this is true, women who anticipate intermittent employment may maximize lifetime earnings by choosing an occupation with low depreciation penalties. Since most men plan continuous employment, they have no such incentive to choose occupations with low depreciation rates. Thus sex differences in plans for employment continuity may lead to sex differences in the job choices that will maximize men's and women's lifetime earnings. Figure 1 depicts the proposition from Polachek's thesis that I test; it contrasts the rates of depreciation characterizing two types of occupations. To focus attention on Polachek's proposition regarding depreciation, I drew Figure 1 so that the jobs' wage profiles are identical except for their depreciation rates. Thus the occupations have identical starting wages and rates of return to experience. The two types of jobs differ only in the steepness of their depreciation penalties for time spent at home. (The drawings could include more than one period of home time.) According to Polachek, most occupations entail risks of depreciation, but some offer lower depreciation penalties than others. In his view, this is what leads some occupations to be chosen by women; hence I labeled the occupations with low depreciation rates "female occupations." The critical prediction from Polachek's thesis is that predominantly female occupations offer women lower depreciation rates than they experience in predominantly male occupations.

A number of published regression analyses estimate the effect of home time on subsequent wages, net of education, experience, and other variables (Corcoran; England, d; Mincer and Polachek, a, b; Polachek, a; Sandell and Shapiro). All analyses find a negative sign on the coefficient of home time. However, analyses differ in the size and significance of this coefficient indicating depreciation. But significant depreciation during home time is not all that Polachek's thesis predicts; it also specifies that depreciation is steeper in male than female occupations. The evidence that Polachek (b, c, d, e) presents in support of this latter prediction is of limited relevance because he does not classify occupations by their sex composition, and his estimates of penalties confound depreciation and appreciation. (For a more detailed critique of his specifications see England, d.) In an earlier analysis, I used data from the 1967 National Longitudinal Survey (NLS) to test whether the wage depreciation women suffer during time at home is lower if they are in predominantly female occupations (England, d). I found no evidence that women suffer less depreciation in female than male occupations. The present analysis serves as a replication on more recent data that is not restricted to women between the ages of 30 to 44 as the NLS is.

Starting Wages and Wage Appreciation: Zellner's Thesis

Zellner proposes an explanation of segregation that hinges on the fact that occupations differ in their starting wages and their rates of appreciation. Human capital theorists assume that jobs offering more wage appreciation will have lower starting wages; earnings foregone in early years are an investment in on-the-job training that leads to wage appreciation. Figure 2 contrasts occupations with high starting wages and flat appreciation to occupations with lower starting wages but steeper appreciation. Zellner reasons that many women are not employed enough years to allow an occupation's high appreciation rate to

FIGURE 1

A depiction of Polachek's explanation of occupational sex segregation in terms of different depreciation rates for female and male occupations. A broken line indicates hypothetical wage if one reentered the labor force at that point in time.

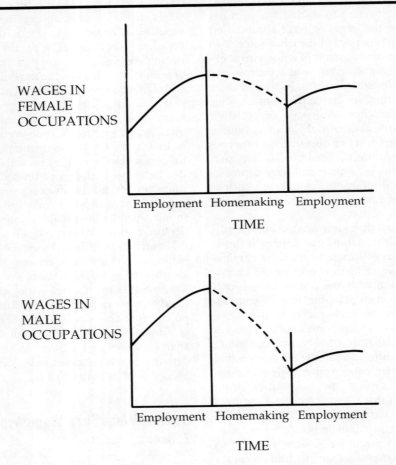

compensate for the lower starting wage. She hypothesizes that more women than men will maximize lifetime earnings by choosing occupations with high starting wages, despite the disadvantage of their flat appreciation. Thus, Figure 2 labels these "female occupations." The occupations labeled "male" will produce greater lifetime earnings for those who accumulate enough experience beyond the point where the two curves cross to make up for their lower starting wage. Thus sex differences in plans for employment continuity will lead men and women to different occupational choices if their aim is to optimize lifetime earnings. If women receive lower starting wages in male than female occupations, this is evidence that women have a pecuniary motivation to make occupational choices that perpetuate sex segregation.[1] If men experience steeper appreciation in male than female occupations such that lifetime earnings are greater in male occupations, this is evidence that males have a pecuniary incentive to make occupational choices that perpetuate sex

FIGURE 2

A depiction of Zellner's explanation of occupational sex segregation in terms of different starting wages and appreciation rates for female and male occupations

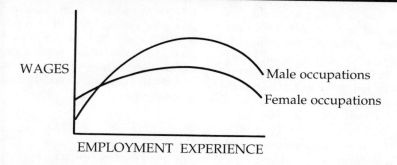

segregation. These are the two critical predictions of Zellner's thesis, but they have not received a direct test in past research. Rather, the thesis has been tested indirectly by ascertaining whether women with more continuous employment histories are more apt than other women to be in male occupations. Neither Zellner nor England (d) found such a relationship; but Wolf and Rosenfeld did find employment gaps to be more frequent among those in female occupations.

Methods

Data

This analysis uses the 1974 wave of the Panel Study of Income Dynamics (PSID) collected by the University of Michigan's Institute for Social Research (ISR).[2] This is a probability sample of households in the U.S. In the 1974 interviews, female household heads were asked about their occupations, earnings, and work histories. Male household heads were asked the same questions about themselves and their wives. (The PSID staff labeled the primary male in any household as its head. Women were considered heads of households only when no male mate was present.) Thus the 1974 information on wives comes from their husbands' reports. I assembled a male and a female subsample from the data. Records of all white

households with adult male heads provide information for the male subsample. A second pass through the data formed the female subsample out of all white households containing an adult woman. The female subsample includes both wives and heads (i.e., women who do not live with a husband). For each subsample I deleted records with missing values on any of the variables used in the analysis. This resulted in subsamples of 1,857 men and 1,209 women. These samples are a better basis for testing these theories about lifetime earnings and segregation than the commonly used National Longitudinal Survey because the male and female samples include adults of all ages. The mean age in my female subsample was 42; men averaged 43 years of age.

Variables

The dependent variable is the natural logarithm of average hourly earnings in 1973 (LNWAGE). Average hourly wages were computed by the PSID staff based on respondents' reports of total earnings and the number of weeks and hours worked in 1973.[3]

Independent variables in the regression analyses to follow include years of schooling completed (EDUC),[4] and years of employment experience (EXPER). The inclusion of EDUC and EXPER in the wage function follows from the neoclassical view of education and on-the-job learning as investments in human capital that enhance earnings. EXPER was computed the same way for males and females. Respondents were asked in how many years since age 18 they (or their wives) worked full-time all year, and in how many years they worked part-time or only part of the year. EXPER was computed as years of full-time employment experience plus one-half times the number of years of part-time or part-year experience.[5] The square of employment experience (EXPER^2) is also an independent variable in the analysis. Its coefficient captures the declining (and sometimes negative) rate of appreciation of human capital in the later years.

Home time (HT) is an independent variable that measures the number of post-school years spent out of paid employment. HT was computed as age minus employment experience since age 18, minus any years of schooling in excess of 12. By subtracting the years of schooling beyond high school, I avoid including years spent in college after age 18 in the measure of home time. Thus, for most women HT measures the amount of time they have spent out of the labor force in full-time homemaking since age 18. The coefficient on HT measures how much wages depreciate while one is out of the labor force.

The sex composition of individuals' occupations (OC%M) is a crucial independent variable in this analysis. I chose the 1974 wave of the PSID because it is the only one of the 11 waves (1968–78) with three-digit detail in the coding of occupations. The PSID tapes do not provide the sex composition of individuals' occupations. Therefore, OC%M was merged onto PSID records according to their three-digit Census occupational codes from a data file with these 1970 Census occupational categories as cases (U.S. Bureau of the Census).[6] OC%M measures the percent males were of all 1970 members of the experienced civilian labor force in the occupational category in which each PSID respondent was employed in 1974.

The independent variables also include three multiplicative interaction terms computed from the variables above:

$$\%MHT = OC\%M \times HT \qquad (1)$$
$$\%MEXP = OC\%M \times EXPER \qquad (2)$$
$$\%MEXP^2 = OC\%M \times EXPER^2 \qquad (3)$$

These three variables are necessary to operationalize the propositions advanced by Polachek and Zellner to explain segregation. A negative coefficient on %MHT would indicate that occupations with more males in them show steeper wage depreciation during home time. A positive effect of %MEXP would be evidence of steeper appreciation in male than female occupations. (For a lucid explanation of how to interpret nonlinear and nonadditive regression models such as these, see Stolzenberg.)

Analysis

The analysis uses ordinary least-squares regression to estimate how starting wages, appreciation, and depreciation vary by occupational sex composition for men and women. The dependent variable, hourly earnings in 1973, is converted to its natural logarithm. The semi-logarithmic specification of human capital functions was deductively derived by Mincer. Separate equations are estimated for men and women. Coefficients for models including different sets of independent variables are presented in the Appendix. The model including all the independent variables is:

$$\begin{aligned} LNWAGE = a &+ b_1 EDUC + b_2 EXPER + b_3 EXPER^2 \\ &+ b_4 HT + b_5 OC\%M + b_6 \%MEXP \\ &+ b_7 \%MEXP^2 + b_8 \%MHT \end{aligned} \qquad (4)$$

The operational hypotheses I test are listed below:

Hypothesis 1. Polachek argues that segregation arises because many women have a pecuniary motive to choose occupations with low depreciation penalties for time spent at home. This means that the negative effect of HT on women's wages is smaller in predominantly female than male occupations. If so, the interaction term, %MHT, should take on a significantly negative coefficient in the female regressions. (Since few men anticipate intermittent employment, the effect of %MHT in the male regressions is irrelevant to the validity of Polachek's thesis.)

Hypothesis 2. Zellner hypothesizes that women perpetuate segregation by choosing occupations with starting wages high enough to compensate for their lower appreciation rates, given the limited years of employment many women plan. If female occupations offer women higher starting wages than male occupations, computations from the female regression results should show a higher predicted wage at 0 years of experience for occupations with low values of OC%M. (Showing whether men receive higher starting wages in female or male occupations is not necessary to the validity of Zellner's thesis.)

Hypothesis 3. Zellner's thesis posits that segregation is perpetuated by men's optimizing choices of occupations with high appreciation rates. This implies that the male regression results show a significant positive coefficient on %MEXP, and this effect should be great enough to overshadow any negative effect of %MEXP^2. That is, the steeper appreciation in male occupations should outweigh any tendency of male occupations toward greater wage depreciation in the years before retirement. The effect of %MEXP should also be large enough to compensate for lower starting wages in male occupations if they occur. In short, Hypothesis 3 implies that men's lifetime earnings (prospectively evaluated) are higher in male than female occupations. From the regression results I will derive a function, F(x), relating experience to annual earnings. Given F(x), the prospective value of lifetime earnings is given by the standard formula for computing the present value of an annuity:

$$\sum_{x=1}^{x=n} \frac{\mathrm{F}(x)}{(1 + r)^x} \qquad (5)$$

where x = EXPER, r = a discount rate reflecting individuals' preference for present over future earnings, and n = number of years of experience at retirement. Evaluation of (5) with various assumed values of r and n will be used to test the prediction that men optimize lifetime earnings by choosing male occupations.

Assumptions of the Analysis

The theories of segregation being tested specify a dependent variable of lifetime earnings. Yet the operational specifications I use to test the hypotheses have hourly wages as the dependent variable. There are two assumptions embodied in this jump between theory and operationalization. The first assumption is needed to jump from findings about wages (hourly rates of pay) to conclusions about earnings (which reflect number of hours worked as well as wage rates). Since the analysis focuses on differences between the offerings of male and female occupations, the necessary assumption is that the availability of full-time employment to those who seek it is not correlated with the sex composition of occupations.[7]

A second assumption is needed to move from cross-sectional findings about how earnings vary with experience to conclusions about how lifetime earnings vary between occupations that differ in their appreciation rates. The assumption is that effects of employment experience observed in cross-sectional data are not a spurious reflection of some unspecified differences between the cohorts represented in each category of experience; that is, that every cohort will exhibit these effects of experience as they age. (See Palmore for a discussion of methodological issues in distinguishing age, cohort, and period effects.) This assumption is entailed in all conventional human capital analyses that use cross-sectional data to make inferences about the effects of experience accumulated over the life cycle.[8]

Findings

Tables 1 and 3 present regression results for women and men, respectively. The tables present only the preferred model for each sex—that is, the most saturated model in which all coefficients (except additive terms also involved in interactions) are significant. Appendices 1 and 2 present regression models with different sets of independent variables. The preferred models in Tables 1 and 3 were selected from these groups of models in Appendices 1 and 2.

Women's Wage Depreciation: Refutation of Hypothesis 1

Table 1 shows the effect of past home time on women's current earnings. The coefficient on HT

TABLE 1

Preferred[a] Regression Model Predicting Natural
Logarithm of White Females' 1973 Hourly Earnings
(LNWAGE)

Parameter	Coefficients[c]
Constant	4.4189*
	(.1065)
Unstandardized regression coefficient for[b]	
EDUC	.0819*
	(.0075)
EXPER	.0330*
	(.0050)
$EXPER^2$	−.0006*
	(.0001)
HT	−.0074*
	(.0018)
OC%M	.0019*
	(.0006)
%MEXP	—**
	—
$\%MEXP^2$	—**
	—
%MHT	—**
	—
R^2 (unadjusted)	.1895*

[a]This model is preferred over the others in Appendix 1 because it is the most saturated model for which all coefficients are significant.

[b]For key to variable names see text or Appendix 1.

[c]Standard errors in parentheses.

*Statistically significant at the .05 level, 2-tailed test.

**These variables did not have significant effects in any of the models in which they were included (see Appendix 1), so the variables were excluded in the estimation of coefficients for this preferred model.

shows that, net of earned or foregone appreciation (indexed by EXPER), women lose about .7 of 1 percent in current earnings for each past year they have been at home. But the critical test of Hypothesis 1 is not whether wages depreciate during time at home, but whether the depreciation women suffer during home time is greater in occupations containing more males. Thus, Hypothesis 1 is that %MHT has a significantly negative effect in the female regressions. The prediction is not upheld; Table 1 shows that this interaction term is not significant. I conclude that women do suffer wage depreciation during time at home, but that the rates of depreciation they suffer do not depend on whether they are in a typically male or female occupation. These PSID data indicate that Polachek is incorrect to assert that differences between the depreciation penalties in male and female occupations give women who work intermittently an incentive to choose female occupations. This finding replicates an earlier analysis on 1967 NLS data that also found no interactive effect of home time and occupational sex composition on earnings (England, d).

Women's Starting Wages: Refutation of Hypothesis 2

Hypothesis 2 states that women enjoy higher starting wages if they choose predominantly female occupations. The findings in Table 1 do not support this prediction from Zellner's thesis. Table 1 shows that women increase their wages about 3 percent for every year of employment experience. But women's returns to experience do not vary by the sex composition of their occupations; %MEXP does not have a significant effect.[9] Since the interaction effect (%MEXP) is not significant, estimates of how women's starting wages differ between male and female occupations depend on the additive effect of OC%M. The coefficient on OC%M shows that women earn significantly more in male than in female occupations at all levels of experience. An increment of 10 percent male in one's occupation leads to a 1.9 percent increase in wages, net of human capital. Women have higher starting wages and higher later wages if they are employed in occupations containing more men.

This is shown more concretely in the left two columns of Table 2. Table 2 displays predicted earnings at various levels of experience for occupations at the two extremes of sex composition—100 percent female and 100 percent male. The predicted earnings for females were computed from the equation in Table 1, the preferred model. Earnings were evaluated at the female mean level of education (12.6818) and years of home time (8.1045). The critical thing to notice about the

TABLE 2
Predicted Hourly Earnings of Women and Men in Female and Male Occupations at
Selected Levels of Employment Experience

Years of Employment Experience	Women[a]		Men[b]	
	Occupational Sex Composition			
	100% Female	100% Male[c]	100% Female[c]	100% Male
0	$2.21	$2.67	$3.31	$2.69
1	2.28	2.76	3.41	2.86
5	2.56	3.10	3.84	3.60
10	2.89	3.49	4.30	4.53
15	3.15	3.81	4.73	5.39
20	3.34	4.03	5.06	6.04
25	3.42	4.13	5.30	6.36
30	3.40	4.11	5.40	6.32
35	3.28	3.96	5.37	5.91
40	3.07	3.71	5.21	5.21
45	2.78	3.36	4.94	4.32
50	2.44	2.95	4.56	3.38
55	2.08	2.51	4.11	2.49

[a]Based on female equation in Table 1: LNWAGE = 4.4189 + .0819 (EDUC) + .0330 (EXPER) − .006 $(EXPER^2)$ − .0074 (HT) + .0019 (OC%M). Earnings were evaluated at the female mean level of EDUC (=12.6818) and HT (=8.1045).

[b]Based on male equation in Table 3: LNWAGE = 4.8739 + .0738 (EDUC) + .0312 (EXPER) − .0005 $(EXPER^2)$ − .0021 (OC%M) + .0003 (%MEXP) − .000007 $(\%MEXP^2)$. Earnings were evaluated at the male mean level of EDUC (=12.5671).

[c]There are no women in occupations that are 100% male or men in occupations that are 100% female, but these extremes of occupational sex composition were used for heuristic purposes (since, e.g., there are women in occupations that are 99.9% male).

predicted wages in the left two columns of Table 2 is that women's starting wages (experience = o) are higher in male than female occupations—the opposite of what Zellner predicted. Indeed, at every level of experience women make more in male than female occupations. Obviously, if women make more in male occupations at every level of experience, then their lifetime earnings are greater in male than female occupations. Thus, women have no pecuniary motive to choose predominantly female occupations.

Men's Lifetime Earnings: Equivocal Findings for Hypothesis 3

Zellner's thesis requires men to enjoy higher rates of appreciation in male than female occupations so their lifetime earnings will be higher in male occupations. This requires that %MEXP is significant and positive. Table 3 shows that %MEXP has a significant effect, but $\%MEXP^2$ is significant as well.

The negative sign on $\%MEXP^2$ means that men

experience a steeper decrease in their rate of appreciation in their later years if they are in occupations containing more males. This is made more concrete by the right two columns of Table 2. The male columns in Table 2 are computed from the regression equation in Table 3. At mean levels of education, men have higher wages in male than female occupations when they have between 10 and 40 years of experience. But before 10 years and after 40 years of experience female occupations offer men higher wages than male occupations do. This steeper decline in the rate of appreciation in male occupations may result because many male occupations are manual, and these skills decline more as men age than social or cognitive skills. Since the effect of occupational sex composition on men's wages varies across levels of experience, additional computations from the regression results are necessary to determine whether (controlling education) men have higher lifetime earnings in male or female occupations. If F(x) predicts annual earnings from experience, then the prospective value of men's lifetime earnings can be expressed as in (5) above. We need to define

TABLE 3

Preferred[a] Regression Model Predicting White Males'
1973 Hourly Earnings (LNWAGE)

Parameter	Coefficients[c]
Constant	4.8739*
	(.1412)
Unstandardized Regression Coefficient for[b]	
EDUC	.0738*
	(.0044)
EXPER	.0312*
	(.0137)
EXPER^2	−.0005
	(.0003)
HT	—**
OC%M	−.0021
	(.0015)
%MEXP	.0003*
	(.0002)
%MEXP^2	−.7E-5*
	(.3E-5)
%MHT	—**
R^2 (unadjusted)	.2423*

[a]This model is preferred over the others in Appendix 2 because it is the most saturated model for which all coefficients (except additive terms also involved in interactions) are significant.

[b]For key to variable names see text or Appendix 1.

[c]Standard errors in parentheses.

*Statistically significant at the .05 level, 2-tailed test.

**These variables did not have significant effects in any of the models in which they were included (see Appendix 2), so the variables were excluded in the estimation of coefficients for this preferred model.

F(x) to be consistent with the regression results from Equation VI in Appendix 2:

$$\text{LNWAGE} = 4.8739 + .0738(\text{EDUC})$$
$$+ .0312(\text{EXPER}) - .0005(\text{EXPER}^2)$$
$$- .0021(\text{OC\%M}) + .0003(\text{\%MEXP})$$
$$- .000007(\text{\%MEXP}^2) \qquad (6)$$

If we evaluate LNWAGE at the male mean level of education (12.5671), it can be expressed in terms of EXPER for occupations at the two extremes of

sex composition. To evaluate LNWAGE for occupations that are 100 percent male, (6) becomes:

$$\text{LNWAGE} = 4.8739 + (.0738)(12.5671)$$
$$+ .0312(\text{EXPER}) - .0005(\text{EXPER}^2)$$
$$- .0021(100) + .0003(100)(\text{EXPER})$$
$$- .000007(100)(\text{EXPER}^2) \qquad (7)$$
$$= 5.5914 + .0612(\text{EXPER})$$
$$- .0012(\text{EXPER}^2) \qquad (8)$$

Analogously, for female occupations that are 0 percent male, (6) becomes:

$$\text{LNWAGE} = 5.8014 + .0312(\text{EXPER})$$
$$- .0005(\text{EXPER}^2) \qquad (9)$$

To change (8) and (9) to functions predicting annual earnings we need to express F(x) in the metric of annual dollars rather than logged dollars. If we assume full-time employment (2,000 hours a year), (8) and (9) become:

$$F(x)_m = (20)_e^{(5.5914 + .0612x - .0012x^2)} \qquad (10)$$
$$F(x)_f = (20)_e^{(5.8014 + .0312x - .0005x^2)} \qquad (11)$$

where m denotes a male occupation and f denotes a female occupation. Substituting (10) and (11) into (5) allows estimation of lifetime earnings for males in male and female occupations under various assumptions about the length of men's work life and the discount rate they would use in prospectively comparing occupations' pecuniary value. Table 4 presents these results.

Economists' concepts of "discount rate" and "present value" need explanation to make Table 4 meaningful. One's discount rate is the rate of interest that would make one decide to save money rather than spend it. People with lower discount rates defer gratification farther into the future. Those with higher discount rates have a stronger preference for money in the present over money in the future. The theory being tested assumes that people choose an occupation at the beginning of their careers based on their present valuation of the earnings the occupation will yield over a lifetime. What that future stream of earnings is worth to a person evaluating it *prospectively* is called its "present value." To illustrate, consider two occupations that offer the same dollars of

TABLE 4

Prospective Value of Lifetime Earnings[a] for Men in Male and Female Occupations Under Selected Assumptions

Discount Rate (in percent)	Years of Experience at Retirement					
	35		45		55	
	Occupational Sex Composition					
	100% Female[b]	100% Male	100% Female[b]	100% Male	100% Female[b]	100% Male
5	$145,098	$147,848	$159,526	$160,473	$167,242	$165,359
10	80,642	79,739	82,903	81,737	83,666	82,226
15	52,994	50,935	53,365	51,283	53,450	51,338
20	38,756	36,424	38,830	36,490	38,841	36,497

[a]See text for computational procedures.

[b]There are no men in occupations that are 100% female. But this extreme value of occupational sex composition was used for heuristic purposes (since, e.g., there are men in occupations that are 99.9% female).

lifetime earnings but differ in the stages of the life cycle in which wages are the highest. Even though the two jobs offer the same dollars of lifetime earnings, their pecuniary value to those choosing an occupation differs according to their discount rates. Those with higher discount rates have a stronger preference for an extra dollar early in the career over an extra dollar later in the career. (For further discussion of these concepts see Alchian and Allen, 144–51.) By making the discount rate a variable in the calculation of the prospective value of occupations' lifetime earnings, as (5) does, Table 4 enumerates the pecuniary preferability of occupations in a way that is consistent with the theory being tested.

Table 4 shows that, for any discount rate of 10 percent or more, male earnings are slightly greater in female than male occupations. This is the opposite of what Zellner's thesis would predict. If we assume the discount rate to be only 5 percent, and experience at retirement to be 35 or 45 years, men have slightly higher lifetime earnings in male than female occupations, as Zellner's thesis predicts. Thus, the findings provide only equivocal support for Hypothesis 3 generated from human capital theory.

Conclusions

Regression analysis was used to test neoclassical economic explanations of occupational sex segre-

gation suggested by Polachek and Zellner. Both hypotheses assert that occupational sex segregation results from sex differences in men and women's employment continuity which give them incentives to choose occupations with different wage structures. Polachek and Zellner suggest that both men and women have a pecuniary motivation to choose occupations traditional for their sex. This analysis produced equivocal findings regarding whether males have higher lifetime earnings in male or female occupations—it depends on their discount rate and accumulated experience at retirement. But for females the findings are clear: at every level of experience—from starting wages to retirement—women have lower wages in female than male occupations. This is not the first research to find a net positive effect of occupations' percent male on earnings (see Blau; Bluestone; England, a; England and McLaughlin; England et al.; Hodge and Hodge; Jusenius; McLaughlin; Snyder and Hudis; Treiman and Terrell). But few previous analyses have been done on data containing a measure of experience so that additive effects of experience could be controlled and interaction effects tested. The evidence is now overwhelming that women pay a net wage penalty for being in sex-typical occupations. The evidence does not support the contention of human capital theorists that women maximize lifetime earnings by choosing female occupations. To the extent that women's segregation into traditional occupations can be explained from the labor-supply side, the relevant theory must specify nonpecuniary motivations, such as those created by sex role socialization. Future research should explore how such socialization dovetails with demand-side hiring discrimination and structured mobility ladders to perpetuate occupational sex segregation. The theory of human capital may explain many things, but occupational sex segregation is not among them.

APPENDIX 1
Regressions Predicting Natural Logarithm of White Females' 1973 Hourly Earnings[a]

Parameter	Equation							
	I	II[b]	III	IV	V	VI	VII	VIII
Constant	4.2086*	4.4189*	4.4207*	4.2391*	4.4363*	4.2306*	4.4264*	4.4276*
	(.0940)	(.1065)	(.1069)	(.0959)	(.1075)	(.0993)	(.1103)	(.1104)
Unstandardized Regression Coefficient for								
EDUC	.0963*	.0819*	.0820*	.0964*	.0825*	.0964*	.0825*	.0825*
	(.0067)	(.0075)	(.0075)	(.0067)	(.0075)	(.0067)	(.0075)	(.0076)
EXPER	.0271*	.0330*	.0331*	.0244*	.0307*	.0259*	.0325*	.0330*
	(.0049)	(.0050)	(.0051)	(.0052)	(.0054)	(.0068)	(.0070)	(.0071)
$EXPER^2$	−.0005*	−.0006*	−.0006*	−.0004*	−.0006*	−.0005*	−.0007*	−.0007*
	(.0001)	(.0001)	(.0001)	(.0001)	(.0001)	(.0002)	(.0002)	(.0002)
HT		−.0074*	−.0078*		−.0072*		−.0072*	−.0079*
		(.0018)	(.0025)		(.0018)		(.0018)	(.0026)
OC%M	.0018*	.0019*	.0018*	.0007	.0010	.0010	.0014	.0013
	(.0006)	(.0006)	(.0007)	(.0009)	(.0009)	(.0014)	(.0014)	(.0014)
%MEXP				.0001	.0001	.0000	−.0000	−.0000
				(.0001)	(.0001)	(.0002)	(.0002)	(.0002)
$\%MEXP^2$						.0000	.0000	.0000
						(.0000)	(.0000)	(.0000)
%MHT			.0000					.0000
			(.0001)					(.0001)
R^2 (unadjusted)	.1781*	.1895*	.1895*	.1798*	.1905*	.1799*	.1906*	.1907*

[a]N = 1209. Standard errors in parentheses.
[b]Preferred model. But see Note 9 regarding superiority of equation V in lon-logged specification.
*Statistically significant at the .05 level, 2-tailed test.

Key: WAGE = Average hourly wage in 1973; LNWAGE = Natural log of average hourly wage in 1973; EDUC = Years of schooling; EXPER = Years of employment experience; $EXPER^2$ = Square of EXPER; HT = Years of home time since schooling completed (i.e., time not employed); OC%M = Percent male of respondent's 3-digit Census occupational category; %MEXP = Interaction term: (OC%M) · (EXPER); $\%MEXP^2$ = Interaction term: (OC%M) · $(EXPER^2)$; %MHT = Interaction term: (OC%M) · (HT).

APPENDIX 2
Regressions Predicting Natural Logarithm of White Males' 1973 Hourly Earnings[a]

Parameter	Equation							
	I	II	III	IV	V	VI[b]	VII	VIII
Constant	4.6918*	4.6662*	4.6823*	4.6846*	4.6598*	4.8739*	4.8483*	4.8469*
	(.0875)	(.1016)	(.1051)	(.1115)	(.1223)	(.1412)	(.1495)	(.1496)
Unstandardized Regression Coefficient for								
EDUC	.0737*	.0755*	.0754*	.0737*	.0755*	.0738*	.0757*	.0756*
	(.0044)	(.0057)	(.0057)	(.0044)	(.0057)	(.0044)	(.0056)	(.0057)
EXPER	.0584*	.0582*	.0582*	.0588*	.0585*	.0312*	.0308*	.0318*
	(.0034)	(.0034)	(.0034)	(.0052)	(.0052)	(.0137)	(.0137)	(.0141)
$EXPER^2$	−.0011*	−.0011*	−.0011*	−.0011*	−.0011*	−.0005	−.0005	−.0005
	(.0001)	(.0001)	(.0001)	(.0001)	(.0007)	(.0003)	(.0003)	(.0003)
HT		.0031	0.0092		.0031		.0033	−.0033
		(.0063)	(.0213)		(.0063)		(.0063)	(.0002)
OC%M	.0002	.0002	.0000	.0003	.0002	−.0021	−.0021	−.0021
	(.0006)	(.0006)	(.0007)	(.0011)	(.0011)	(.0015)	(.0015)	(.0015)
%MEXP				.0000	−.0000	.0003*	.0003*	.0003
				(.0000)	(.0000)	(.0002)	(.0002)	(.0002)
$%MEXP^2$						−.7E-5*	−.7E-5*	−.7E-5*
						(.3E-5)	(.3E-5)	(.3E-5)
%MHT			.0001					.0001
			(.0002)					(.0003)
R^2 (unadjusted)	.2415*	.2416*	.2417*	.2415*	.2416*	.2423*	.2435*	.2436*

[a]N = 1857. For key to variable names see Appendix 1. Standard errors in parentheses.
[b]Preferred model.
*Statistically significant at the .05 level. 2-tailed test.

Notes

An earlier version of this paper was presented at the 1981 meetings of the American Sociological Association. I am indebted to E. M. Beck, Tabitha Doescher, Charles Tolbert, and Linda Waite for comments on an earlier draft; and to Margaret Barton, John Cardascia, Jay Cummings, Robert Nash Parker, Helen Reynolds, Wayne Ruhter, and John Wiorkowski for technical advice. Part of this research was funded by NSF Grant SES-8107345.

1. Polachek's metaphoric use of the term "atrophy" suggests that his theory of segregation is about differences in the *depreciation* rather than appreciation rates of male and female occupations. But his measures of atrophy tap both depreciation and foregone appreciation (England, d). He has confirmed in conversation that he accepts Zellner's thesis as implied in his own. However, I have attributed the explanation involving starting wages and appreciation to Zellner rather than Polachek. This is because Zellner's writing makes explicit the important point that it is a finding of higher starting wages (rather than low appreciation) in female occupations that is critical to the theory's ability to explain segregation in terms of the pecuniary incentives women face. Low appreciation, per se, is a disadvantage regardless of how few years of employment one plans.

2. The data utilized in this paper were made available by the Inter-University Consortium for Political and Social Research. The PSID data were originally collected under the supervision of James N. Morgan. Neither the original source or collectors of the data nor the Consortium bear any responsibility for the analyses or interpretations presented here.

3. The PSID data contain two women and two men reporting earnings of more than $40 per hour in 1973. I

deleted these four extreme outliers because of their large effects on the regression results and my suspicion that the high earnings reflect coding errors.

4. In the 1974 PSID data, years of schooling is bracketed into 8 ordinal categories. The 1975 PSID data records schooling in years. Since regression assumes an interval level of measurement a measure of schooling coded in years is preferable for this analysis. Thus, I assigned the 1975 number of schooling years to any man or woman for whom the number of years reported in 1975 fell within the bracket reported in 1974. If the number of years reported in 1975 did not fit into the 1974 bracket (perhaps because of continued schooling between 1974 and 1975), or if 1975 data were missing, I assigned the midpoint of the 1974 bracketed category. When assignments had to be made for those with more than a B.A., the highest 1974 ordinal category, I assigned 18.5 years.

5. PSID respondents were asked what percent of the time they worked during years in which they did not work full-time. This percent (rather than one-half) could have been used to weight the number of years worked less than full-time in the formula used to compute EXPER. I rejected this strategy because about half the records have missing codes on this question, probably indicating that respondents could not remember the answer. I used one-half as the weight since it was near the mean proportion of time worked in non-full-time years among respondents who did answer the question.

6. I am grateful to Steven McLaughlin for providing me with these 1970 occupational Census data in machine-readable form (U.S. Bureau of the Census).

7. Beck et al. have stressed the fact that discrimination can take the form of limiting women and minorities to jobs which offer less than full-time or year-round employment. My assumption that male and female occupations do not differ in the availability of full-time stable employment is probably unwarranted. The assumption gives a benefit of doubt to the theories I am testing. If the assumption is wrong and male occupations offer more stable employment, this buttresses my conclusion that women have no pecuniary incentive to choose female occupations.

8. In research currently in progress, I am testing these economic hypotheses using the longitudinal features of the NLS data.

9. I have run all regressions reported in Tables 1 and 3 and Appendices 1 and 2 in their non-logged as well as semi-logarithmic form. Results from the semi-logarithmic specifications are presented since this functional form is implied by the deductive logic of human capital theory (Mincer). For both men and women the same coefficients are significant in the logged as the

non-logged specifications, with one exception. Female regressions on wages (rather than on LNWAGE) show the interaction term, %MEXP, to be significant, as Zellner predicts. This means that absolute appreciation is greater for women in male occupations than in female occupations, though this is not true when appreciation is expressed in terms of percentage increases. Despite this interaction, computations of predicted wages from the non-logged regression equation shows that women do not earn higher wages at 0 years of experience in female than male occupations. Thus, neither the non-logged nor the semi-logarithmic specification shows female occupations to offer women the higher starting wages that are critical to the theory's prediction.

References

Alchian, Armen, and William Allen. 1964. *Exchange and Production.* Wadsworth, 1977.

Beck, E. M., Patrick M. Horan, and Charles Tolbert II. 1980. "Industrial Segmentation and Labor Market Discrimination." *Social Problems* 28:113–30.

Becker, Gary. 1964. *Human Capital.* Columbia University Press.

Blau, Francine D. 1977. *Equal Pay in the Office.* Heath.

Blau, F. D., and C. L. Jusenius. 1976. "Economists' Approaches to Sex Segregation in the Labor Market: An Appraisal." In Martha Blaxall and Barbara Reagan (eds.), *Women and the Workplace.* University of Chicago Press.

Bluestone, Barry. 1974. "The Personal Earnings Distribution: Individual and Institutional Determinants." Unpublished Ph.D. dissertation, University of Michigan.

Corcoran, M. 1979. "Work Experience, Labor Force Withdrawals, and Women's Wages: Empirical Results Using the 1976 Panel of Income Dynamics." In Cynthia B. Lloyd, Emily S. Andrews, and Curtis L. Gilroy (eds.), *Women in the Labor Market.* Columbia University Press.

Edwards, R. C., M. Reich, and D. M. Gordon. 1975. "Introduction." In Richard C. Edwards, Michael Reich, and David M. Gordon (eds.), *Labor Market Segmentation.* Heath.

England, P. a:1979. "Women and Occupational Prestige: A Case of Vacuous Sex Equality." *Signs: Journal of Women in Culture and Society* 5:252–65.

———. b:1981. "Assessing Trends in Occupational Sex Segregation, 1900–1976." In Ivar Berg (ed.), *Sociological Perspectives on Labor Markets.* Academic Press.

———. c:1981. "Explanations of Occupational Sex Segregation: An Interdisciplinary Review." Paper presented at the Southwest Social Science meetings.

———. d:1982. "The Failure of Human Capital Theory to Explain Occupational Sex Segregation." *Journal of Human Resources* 17:358–70.

England, P., and S. McLaughlin. 1979. "Sex Segregation of Jobs and Male-Female Income Differentials." In Rodolfo Alvarez, Kenneth Lutterman and Associates (eds.), *Discrimination in Organizations.* Jossey-Bass.

England, P., M. Chassie, and L. McCormack. 1982. "Skill Demands and Earnings in Female and Male Occupations." *Sociology and Social Research* 66:147–68.

Hodge, R. W., and P. Hodge. 1965. "Occupational Assimilation as a Competitive Process." *American Journal of Sociology* 71:249–64.

Institute for Social Research. 1974. *A Panel Study of Income Dynamics, Procedures and Tape Codes, 1974 Interviewing Year, Wave VII.* University of Michigan.

Jusenius, C. L. 1977. "The Influence of Work Experience, Skill Requirements, and Occupational Segregation on Women's Earnings." *Journal of Economics and Business* 29:107–15.

McLaughlin, Steven. 1978. "Occupational Sex Identification and the Assessment of Male and Female Earnings Inequality." *American Sociological Review* 43:909–21.

Marini, Margaret Mooney, and Mary Brinton. 1982. "Sex Stereotyping in Occupational Socialization." In Barbara F. Reskin (ed.), *Sex Segregation in the Workplace.* National Academy.

Mincer, Jacob. 1974. *Schooling, Experience and Earnings.* National Bureau for Economic Research.

Mincer, J., and S. Polachek. a:1974. "Family Investments in Human Capital: Earnings of Women." *Journal of Political Economy* 82:S76–S108.

———. b:1978. "Women's Earnings Reexamined." *Journal of Human Resources* 13:118–34.

Palmore, E. 1978. "When Can Age, Period, and Cohort be Separated?" *Social Forces* 57:282–95.

Polachek, S. a:1975. "Discontinuous Labor Force Participation and Its Effects on Women's Market Earnings." In Cynthia Lloyd (ed.), *Sex, Discrimination, and the Division of Labor.* Columbia University Press.

———. b:1976. "Occupational Segregation: An Alternative Hypothesis." *Journal of Contemporary Business* 5:1–12.

———. c:1978. "Sex Difference in College Major." *Industrial and Labor Relations Review* 31:498–508.

———. d:1979. "Occupational Segregation Among Women: Theory, Evidence and a Prognosis." In Cynthia Lloyd (ed.), *Women in the Labor Market.* Columbia University Press.

———. e:1981. "Occupational Self-Selection: A Human Capital Approach to Sex Differences in Occupational Structure." *Review of Economics and Statistics* 58:60–69.

Roos, Patricia, and Barbara Reskin. 1982. "Institutional Factors Affecting Job Access and Mobility for Women: A Review of Institutional Explanations for Occupational Sex Segregation." Paper presented at Workshop on Job Segregation by Sex, National Research Council, Washington, D.C.

Sandell, S., and D. Shapiro. 1978. "The Theory of Human Capital and the Earnings of Women: A Reexamination of the Evidence." *Journal of Human Resources* 13:103–17.

Snyder, D., and P. M. Hudis. 1976. "Occupational Income and the Effects of Minority Competition and Segregation." *American Sociological Review* 41:209–34.

Stolzenberg, R. M. 1979. "The Measurement and Decomposition of Causal Effects in Nonlinear and Nonadditive Models." In Karl F. Schuessler (ed.), *Sociological Methodology 1980.* Jossey-Bass.

Treiman, D. J., and K. Terrell. 1975. "Women, Work, and Wages—Trends in the Female Occupational Structure Since 1940." In Kenneth Land and Seymour Spilerman (eds.), *Social Indicator Models.* Russell Sage.

U.S. Bureau of the Census. 1973. "Occupational Characteristics." Subject Report, *1970 Census of the Population.* GPO.

Wolf, W. C., and R. Rosenfeld. 1978. "Sex Structure of Jobs and Job Mobility." *Social Forces* 56:823–44.

Zellner, H. 1975. "The Determinants of Occupational Segregation." In Cynthia Lloyd (ed.), *Sex, Discrimination, and the Division of Labor.* Columbia University Press.

~ **Demand-Side Approaches**

KENNETH J. ARROW

The Theory of Discrimination

The fact that different groups of workers, be they skilled or unskilled, black or white, male or female, receive different wages, invites the explanation that the different groups must differ according to some characteristic valued on the market. In standard economic theory, we think first of differences in productivity. The notion of discrimination involves the additional concept that personal characteristics of the worker unrelated to productivity are also valued on the market. Such personal characteristics as race, ethnic background, and sex have been frequently adduced in this context.

Assume that there are two groups of workers, to be denoted by B and W, which are perfect substitutes in production. For the simplest model, then, we have a large number of firms all producing the same product with the same production function. Discrimination means that some economic agent has some negative valuation for B or positive valuation for W, or both, a valuation for which the agent both is willing to pay and has the opportunity to pay.[1] The agents who could possibly discriminate are the employer, who might sacrifice profits to reduce or eliminate B employment in his plant, or the W workers who might accept a lower wage to work in a plant with more W and less B workers. (It is also possible that, for products sold on a face-to-face basis, customers might discriminate by being willing to pay higher prices to buy from W workers; this case could be studied along similar lines but will not be dealt with here.) Not all discriminatory feelings can find expression in the market; an entrepreneur who has a distaste for competing against firms

with B workers has no way, within the economic system at least, of expressing his tastes and therefore of influencing wage levels. ...

Employer discrimination also can be thought of as reflecting not tastes but perception of reality. That is, if employers have the preconceived idea that B workers have lower productivity than W workers, they may be expected to be willing to hire them only at lower wages. (Phelps has independently introduced a similar thesis.)[2] One must examine in detail the conditions under which this argument can be maintained, that is, the conditions under which the effects of these preconceptions are the same as those of discrimination in the strict sense of tastes.

First, the employer must be able to distinguish *W* workers from *B* workers. More precisely, the cost of making the distinction should be reasonably low. An employer might derive from his reading the opinion that an employee with an unresolved Oedipus complex will be disloyal to him as a father-substitute; but if the only way of determining the existence of an unresolved Oedipus complex is a psychoanalysis of several years at the usual rates, he may well decide that it is not worthwhile for him to use this as a basis for hiring. Skin color and sex are cheap sources of information. Therefore prejudices (in the literal sense of pre-judgments, judgments made in advance of the evidence) about such differentia can be easily implemented. School diplomas undoubtedly play an excessive role in employer decisions for much the same reason.

Second, the employer must incur some cost before he can determine the employee's true productivity. If the productivity could be determined costlessly, there would be no reason to use surrogate information, necessarily less valid even under the most favorable conditions. I suppose, therefore, that the employer must hire the employee first and then incur a personnel investment cost before he can determine the worker's productivity. This personnel investment might, for example, include a period of training, only after which is it possible to ascertain the worker's productivity; or indeed it may be only a period of observation long enough for reliable determination of productivity. In the absence of a personnel investment cost, after all, the employer could simply hire everyone who applied and fire those unqualified, or pay them according to productivity.

Third, it must be assumed that the employer has some idea or at any rate preconception of the distribution of productivity within each of the two categories of workers.

The simplest model to bring out the implication of these assumptions seems to be the following. Suppose there are two kinds of jobs, complementary to each other, say unskilled and skilled. All workers are qualified to perform unskilled jobs, and this is known to all employers. Only some workers, however, are *qualified* to hold skilled jobs. The employers need make no personnel investment in hiring unskilled workers but must make such an investment for skilled workers. The employer cannot know whether any given worker is qualified; however, he does believe that the probability that a random W worker is qualified is p_W and that a random B worker is qualified is p_B. An employer will eventually know whether or not a worker hired for a skilled position is in fact qualified, but this information is not available to other employers. He thus can count on keeping the qualified workers he hires.

Let r be the necessary return per worker on the personnel investment for skilled jobs. If a W worker is hired, then with probability p_W he is qualified; his productivity is MP_S, the marginal productivity of skilled workers, but the employer must pay a wage, w_W, so that the net gain to the employer is $MP_S - w_W$. On the other hand, if the worker hired turns out to be unqualified, the em-

ployer receives nothing. Hence, the expected return to a W worker hired is $(MP_S - w_W)\, p_W$. If the employer is risk-neutral, this must be equal to r. Similarly,

$$r = (MP_S - w_B)p_B, \qquad (1)$$

and therefore,

$$w_W = q\,w_B + (1 - q)MP_S, \qquad (2)$$

where $q = p_B/p_W$. Thus, if, for any reason, $p_B < p_W$, w_W is a weighted average of w_B and MP_S and therefore lies between them; since from (1) we must have $w_B < MP_S$ (in order that the employer recoup his personnel investment), it follows that $w_W > w_B$, i.e. the effect of the differential judgment as to the probability of being qualified is reflected in a wage differential.

If there are price rigidities which prevent w_B from falling much below w_W, the same forces may be reflected in a refusal to hire B workers at all for skilled jobs.

Once we shift the explanation of discriminatory behavior from unanalyzable (or at any rate unanalyzed) tastes to beliefs, we are led to seek to explain these beliefs. One possible explanation runs in terms of theories of psychological equilibrium, of which Festinger's theory of cognitive dissonance is one of the most developed.[3] The argument is that beliefs and actions should come into some sort of equilibrium; in particular, if individuals act in a discriminatory manner, they will tend to acquire or develop beliefs which justify such actions. Hence, discriminatory behavior and beliefs in differential abilities will tend to come into equilibrium. Indeed, the very fact that there are strong ethical beliefs which are in conflict with discriminatory behavior will, according to this theory, make the employer even more willing to accept subjective probabilities which will supply an appropriate justification for his conduct.

Notes

1. See Gary Becker, *The Economics of Discrimination* (Chicago: University of Chicago Press, 1959).

2. See Edwin S. Phelps, "The Statistical Theory of Racism and Sexism," *American Economic Review,* 62 (1972), 659–661.

3. For a more theoretical analysis see Leon Festinger, *A Theory of Cognitive Dissonance* (Evanston, Ill.: Row, Peterson, 1957).

WILLIAM T. BIELBY AND JAMES N. BARON

Men and Women at Work: Sex Segregation and Statistical Discrimination

The magnitude, determinants, and consequences of sex segregation are of concern to both researchers and policymakers. Whatever its causes, job segregation by sex is the principal source of gender differences in labor market outcomes, and policies to remedy gender inequality differ in their assumptions about the extent, sources, and effects of the sexual division of labor. For instance, comparable worth advocates regard segregation as pervasive and resistant to change (in the short run, at least) and thus seek to achieve pay equity by recalibrating the value of jobs women now perform. Policies emphasizing improved educational and training opportunities for women, in contrast, involve quite different assumptions about the sources of segregated work.

Though the sexual division of labor may not be inevitable, it is certainly persistent. Recent research has shown that the level of occupational sex segregation has changed very little since 1900, despite changes in the sex composition of specific occupations (England 1981). Roughly 60%–70% of male (or female) workers would require reclassification across detailed occupations to equalize the sexual division of labor, although this percentage has declined somewhat over the past 20 years (Blau and Hendricks 1979; Beller 1984). While this result implies that the occupational structure is divided substantially along gender

lines, it also shows that occupational specialization by sex is far from complete. During any given period, there are numerous occupations in which the sex composition is balanced.

However, a recent study at the organizational level (Bielby and Baron 1984) portrayed sex segregation as much more pervasive than did previous occupation-level research, showing that men and women rarely share job titles within establishments. Our present article seeks to reconcile those results with findings based on census occupational data. We show that men and women in the same census occupation are sorted into distinct organizations or are segregated by job titles within work settings. One set of explanations for this segregation stresses the optimal choices of employees and employers, sex differences in skills, and the technical requirements of work roles. These factors, it is argued, not only produce a sexual division of labor *across* occupations but also channel women into specific types of organizations or job classifications, even within occupational roles performed by both sexes. The first section of the article summarizes this explanation for sex segregation. The perspective is operationalized with a statistical model that predicts the sex composition of particular jobs within occupations employing both men and women. Hypotheses about the parameters of that model are tested with data from a diverse sample of work organizations in California.

Analyzing segregation within lines of work pursued by both men and women reduces the impact of socialization, occupational choice, and "supply-side" factors in general. That women are either pushed or pulled into a narrow range of occupations is well documented, although the causes of this "crowding" are still debated (Bergmann 1974; Polachek 1979; England 1982). We do not attempt here to explain differences in the occupational distributions of men and women. Instead, we examine areas of work in which both men and women are available to staff a role, so any differential allocation to jobs is probably attributable to deliberate actions by employees and employers. In particular, we are interested in the degree to which pervasive segregation by sex, even in mixed occupations, can be attributed to technical features of work and its organizational context. We conclude that the patterns of segregation we observe are difficult to reconcile with perspectives stressing employer rationality on the one hand or workers' vocational "investments" on the other hand. Accordingly, we suggest how sex segregation is built into the hierarchy of organizational positions and is sustained by sex stereotypes and workplace social relations. The final section summarizes several major implications of our findings, identifying some priorities for future research on gender segregation.

Is Organizational Sex Segregation "Efficient"? The Statistical Discrimination Perspective

No doubt sex differences in labor supply account for some of the segregation we observe, even within mixed occupations. That is, sex-based work role specialization could exist, even within narrowly defined lines of work. For example, women bus drivers may choose employment with school districts because of the attractiveness of part-time work. Metropolitan and intercity bus lines may offer more lucrative compensation, but such benefits may not outweigh the disadvantage

of longer hours to women burdened with child care and other household responsibilities. However, supply-side factors cannot fully account for the nearly complete segregation we document below. There is too much overlap between the sexes in the distribution of job-relevant skills and aptitudes for sex differences to account for near-complete segregation within and across organizations (Marini and Brinton 1984). Indeed, whatever sex differences in skills exist within representative samples of adults are likely to be much weaker among the select group of men and women in the same detailed occupation (Deaux 1985).

The model of statistical discrimination offers a compelling explanation for the existence of extreme segregation despite considerable overlap between the sexes in workers' attributes (Phelps 1972; Arrow 1973; Thurow 1975; Aigner and Cain 1977; Blau 1984). The model assumes employers perceive that *on average* the marginal productivity of men and of women differ for a given line of work. For example, within a specific occupation, women may be more likely to quit their jobs. If an employer incurs significant turnover costs due to the expense of finding and training new employees, the expected net contribution of the average female job applicant is less than that of an otherwise comparable male applicant. The model also assumes that it is unduly costly to ascertain these differences among individual male and female job applicants. For example, employers may be unable to devise any procedure for screening individual applicants with respect to quit propensity or work commitment.

Given these assumptions, profit-maximizing employers will reserve jobs with high replacement costs for the group with the greater expected productivity. Group differences may in fact be small relative to variation within groups; there may be many female applicants with lower quit propensities and greater work commitment than the average male applicant. But if employers are unable to obtain this information for individual applicants, expected profits are maximized by segregating workers by sex. Females will be allocated to jobs with low turnover costs. Consequently, economically efficient behavior by employers who face uncertain information about applicants can lead to extreme sex segregation across and within organizations, corresponding to differences in the average expected net productivity of male and female job applicants. Even when women fill the same occupational roles as men, they are likely to be concentrated in less demanding jobs or firms, where the turnover costs are lower. Moreover, statistical discrimination produces inequities between men and women in wages and other career outcomes. Qualified, highly committed women obtain work assignments with lower pay and few opportunities for on-the-job investments in productivity-enhancing skills, which limits future wages as well. Conversely, men with weak work commitment are posited to receive the same favorable work assignments as the average male.

The model of statistical discrimination avoids invoking bias, prejudice, or "tastes" for discrimination, so long as employers' perceptions of group differences are accurate. In fact, economists argue that segregation would not persist if employers' beliefs were incorrect, since employers not sharing those beliefs would gain a competitive advantage by hiring women to perform tasks from which they are excluded in rival firms (Arrow 1973; Aigner and Cain 1977). However, empirical evidence on sex differences in turnover behavior is mixed. Recent studies show that quit rates are indeed higher overall for women than for men but that these differences disappear when worker, labor market, and job characteristics are controlled (Viscusi 1980; Blau and Kahn 1981; Osterman 1982; Haber, Lamas, and Green 1983; Shorey 1983). In other words, turnover behavior differs little among women and men with comparable human capital and job responsibilities.

We have highlighted explanations of segregation based on skill differences and rational employer responses to uncertainty for several reasons. First, as noted above, we have already documented near-complete segregation at the level of job assignments within organizations (Bielby and Baron 1984), and the model of statistical discrimination purports to account for such findings. Second, that model is based largely on untested assumptions about the technical features of jobs and firms staffed by men versus women. Our data, based on detailed information about

jobs in diverse organizations, are well suited for testing these assumptions. Third, alternative explanations of segregation emphasize subjective attitudes and intentions of employers and workers on the one hand and power relations among men and women on the other hand. Comparative information across organizations on those dimensions is difficult to obtain, and our data in these areas are qualitative and suggestive at best. Finally, the idea that workplace inequality reflects individual choices, technical demands, and optimal decision making figures prominently in economics, as well as in public opinion and social policy. It implies a particular set of remedies for gender inequality, namely, encouraging female workers to invest in certain vocational skills and providing accurate information to employers about the labor market behavior of men and women. The validity of such policies depends on whether there is empirical evidence of the optimality of existing arrangements.

In other words, many sociological and economic theories take for granted either the truth or falsity of the view that sex segregation arises from employers' satisficing behavior. However, we know of few studies that examine how consistent employers' hiring practices and staffing patterns are with the predictions of the statistical discrimination framework. Consequently, we develop hypotheses from that approach, examining the extent to which sex segregation within mixed occupations reflects: (a) differences (perceived or real) in the traits and abilities of female versus male workers and (b) differences in turnover costs confronting employers. Our analyses clearly do not represent a definitive "test" of rational accounts of segregation. They do, however, allow us to assess the extent to which workers and employers act *as if* those accounts are correct, based on the allocation of men and women within mixed occupations to specific establishments and job titles.

The next section describes our data, hypotheses, and statistical model. We then present findings on the extent and determinants of sex segregation within and across organizations. First, we describe how occupation-level studies of segregation obscure the sexual division of labor by overlooking segregation within and across organizations, even within occupations that appear integrated. Then we report results from our statistical models that operationalize the efficiency accounts of segregation reviewed above. The concluding section considers alternatives to the efficiency-based account of sex segregation and suggests avenues for further research.

Data and Methods

Our data on the sex composition of mixed occupations were collected in 290 economic establishments in California between 1964 and 1979 by the California Occupational Analysis Field Center of the U.S. Employment Service.[1] This information is used primarily in preparing the *Dictionary of Occupational Titles* (hereafter, *DOT*). Over half the establishments are independent businesses; the rest are branches, regional divisions, subsidiaries, or production sites. Although the establishments do not constitute a probability sample from a distinct population, they reflect the diversity of California's work settings. Industries represented include agriculture, aircraft manufacturing, electronics manufacturing, banking, food processing, public utilities, eating and drinking places, hotels, and medical services (among many others). Manufacturing establishments are over-represented, and major California industries not represented include construction trades, trucking, department stores, insurance carriers, and miscellaneous business services (see Baron 1982, chaps. 2, 3; Bielby and Baron 1984).[2] About 40,000 males and 11,000 females are employed in over 10,000 official job titles in the 290 establishments in our sample.

Occupational Classification and Sex Segregation

Empirical assessments of sex segregation almost always measure differences in the occupational distributions of men and women. Occupations are collections of jobs involving similar activities across establishments, whereas a job consists of positions in an establishment in which workers perform the same activities (Reiss 1961, pp. 10–11; Miller et al. 1980, p. 216). Almost every job involves some tasks and skills that are not easily transferable across work settings, so occupational boundaries are never clear-cut. Most available data are coded to census three-digit occupational specifications, and that system has become the standard for segregation studies, largely by default.

However, the sex composition of an occupation conceals two patterns of segregation. First, a given line of work can be done exclusively by men in some organizational settings and by women in others. For example, most restaurants employ either male waiters or female waitresses, but it is unusual to find both in the same enterprise. Such patterns presumably reflect differences among organizations in employment and reward practices, work arrangements, and labor supply, and these differences often contribute to very different career prospects for men and women in the same occupation. Second, men and women can do equivalent work within an organization but hold distinct job titles. For example, male "operatives" and female "assemblers" in separate departments of a manufacturing establishment may do virtually identical work, although their similar duties may not be reflected in their paychecks or statuses. In short, empirical research must attend to two distinct phenomena: segregation *among* organizations, arising from gender-based differentiation of occupational labor markets across enterprises, and segregation *within* organizations, sustained by a differentiation of positions held by men and women in the same setting. It is important to know how much our understanding of sex segregation is obscured by studies at different levels of occupational detail.

Major occupational groups.—Government agencies that monitor compliance with EEO regulations do collect data on the sex composition of jobs in specific enterprises. However, government monitoring efforts are based almost exclusively on measures of sex composition across highly aggregated occupational groups. The EEOC requires private employers to report employment in nine categories: officials and managers, professionals, technicians, sales workers, office and clerical workers, skilled craft workers, semiskilled operatives, unskilled laborers, and service workers (U.S. EEOC 1982). It is therefore of interest to determine how much gender segregation is obscured by the highly aggregated scheme used to monitor trends. Five of the nine EEOC categories can be readily reconstructed from the *DOT*, but it is sometimes difficult to distinguish professionals from technicians and semiskilled from unskilled laborers. Consequently, we collapsed those categories to obtain seven major groups. Males tend to be overrepresented in each of the two major groups we combined (U.S. EEOC 1977) and therefore our measures of segregation across seven major groups should be comparable with those computed from the nine-group EEOC classification scheme.

Detailed occupational categories.—Because the three-digit *DOT* classification scheme used by the Employment Service differs considerably from that of the Census Bureau (Cain and Treiman 1981), we have taken two steps to improve comparability. First, unlike the Census Bureau, the *DOT* does not distinguish between skilled craft workers and operatives in manual occupations. Consequently, we divided each three-digit *DOT* production classification into skilled and unskilled categories on the basis of the *DOT* index of worker involvement with things.[3] Within a three-digit manual category, job titles having a rating of zero, one, or two (the three highest levels of technical complexity) constituted the skilled subcategory, and all others represented semiskilled or unskilled jobs.

Second, several three-digit *DOT* categories are based primarily on industrial distinctions. As a result, some *DOT* production classifications actually include both manual and nonmanual work; for instance, "miscellaneous transportation occupations, not elsewhere classified" includes both ticket agents and truck drivers. After examining six-digit production occupations in the third edition of the *DOT*, we discovered that titles having simple involvements with things (complexity ratings of three to seven) *and* moderate to high rat-

ings on complexity with data (zero to four) are almost always nonmanual occupations. Therefore, manual and nonmanual subcategories of three-digit titles were constructed accordingly.[4] These two modifications of the *DOT* three-digit classification increased the number of detailed categories in our sample from 455 to 645. Since our scheme is more detailed than the Census Bureau three-digit taxonomy (which included about 450 categories in 1970), segregation levels computed across the more detailed categories will be somewhat higher as well.

The first set of empirical analyses we report assesses aggregation biases in occupational measures of segregation. We compute indices of segregation across: (*a*) the seven major occupational groups, (*b*) our 645 detailed occupational categories, and (*c*) establishment job titles. Our measure of segregation is the index of dissimilarity—the percentage of female (or male) workers that would have to be reclassified to equalize the distributions of work roles by sex (Duncan and Duncan 1955).

Sex Composition of Jobs in Mixed Occupations

The second set of analyses attempts to account for variation in the sex composition of jobs in "mixed" occupations. For our purposes, a detailed occupational category is "mixed" if males account for no less than 20% of employment (in our sample) and no more than 80%.[5] Of 645 detailed occupational categories, only 84 were mixed according to this criterion, accounting for 24% of employment in our 290 establishments.[6]

Since we are interested in the determinants of segregation across and within organizations, we partition the sex composition of a job into two components. We denote the percentage female in the ith job in occupation j within establishment k as p_{ijk}. Averaging over jobs in one establishment yields $p_{.jk}$ and over jobs and establishments gives $p_{.j.}$. The sex composition of jobs within a given occupation can be partitioned into the sum of within- and between-establishment components:

TABLE 1
Hypothesized Relationships Between Job Characteristics, Organizational Context, and Percentage Female
in Jobs in Mixed Occupations

Independent Variable	Description	Hypothesized Effect on % Female
Organizational context:		
z_1	Organizational scale	−
z_2	Formal governance structures	−
z_3	Process technology	−
Job characteristics:		
x_1	Specialization	−
x_2	Training time	−
x_3	Technical complexity	−
x_4	Numerical skills	−
x_5	Verbal skills	+
x_6	Motor coordination	+
x_7	Manual dexterity	−
x_8	Finger dexterity	+
x_9	Clerical perception	+
x_{10}	Spatial skills	−
x_{11}	Eye/hand/foot coordination	−
x_{12}	Physical strength	−
x_{13}	Varied duties	+
x_{14}	Performance standards	+
x_{15}	Repetitiveness	+
x_{16}	Interpersonal skills	+
x_{17}	Direction or planning skills	−

$$(p_{ijk} - p_{.j.}) = (p_{ijk} - p_{.jk}) + (p_{.jk} - p_{.j.}).$$

Below we test hypotheses about characteristics of jobs and organizational context that explain why some establishments employ men while others employ women in the same mixed occupation. That is, we account for variation in the between-establishment component, $(p_{.jk} - p_{.j.})$. We also examine why a given establishment assigns men to some job classifications and women to others within the same detailed occupation. That is, we examine variation in the within-establishment component, $(p_{ijk} - p_{.jk})$.

For example, over 2,000 workers in our sample are employed in the classification "packaging occupations," and about 55% are women, giving the appearance of an integrated line of work. The workers are distributed across 106 establishments, and our analysis seeks to explain why some of those organizations employ mostly (or exclu-

sively) male packagers while others rely on women. Twenty-eight of those establishments employ both male and female packagers but assign them distinct job titles. Therefore, our analyses also attempt to explain why within those organizations, male and female packagers are usually assigned distinct job titles.

Determinants of Sex Composition of Jobs in Mixed Occupations: Hypotheses and Operationalization

Table 1 lists attributes of organizations and jobs that are hypothesized to affect the sex composition of jobs in mixed occupations, according to the efficiency-based accounts of sex segregation outlined above. Collectively, these measures index the turnover costs, training requirements, and technical features of work roles that are assumed

TABLE 2

Descriptive Statistics for Attributes of Establishments and Jobs in Mixed Occupations

Variable	Attribute	Metric	Mean	SD*
Attributes of 290 establishments:				
z_1	Organizational scale	Log_e employment	3.68	1.56
z_2	Union or bidding arrangements	0-1	.29	...
z_3	Process technology	0-1	.11	...
Organizational sex composition (% female) ..		...	33	27
Attributes of 2,997 jobs:				
x_1	Specialization†	Log_e workers	.60	1.0
x_2	Training time	1-9	4.4	2.1
x_3	Complexity of involvement with things (*DOT* rating)‡	0-7	5.8	1.9
x_4	Numerical aptitude§	1-5	3.3	.9
x_5	Verbal aptitude	1-5	3.2	.9
x_6	Motor coordination aptitude	1-5	3.5	.6
x_7	Manual dexterity aptitude	1-5	3.4	.6
x_8	Finger dexterity aptitude	1-5	3.5	.6
x_9	Clerical perception aptitude	1-5	3.4	1.0
x_{10}	Spatial skills aptitude	1-5	3.0	.5
x_{11}	Eye/hand/foot coordination aptitude	1-5	4.8	.4
x_{12}	Physical strength, lifting $\geq$ 25 lbs.	0-1	.27	...
x_{13}	Varied duties temperament	0-1	.23	...
x_{14}	Performance standards temperament	0-1	.39	...
x_{15}	Repetitiveness temperament	0-1	.56	...
x_{16}	Dealing with people temperament	0-1	.32	...
x_{17}	Direction, control, planning temperament	0-1	.21	...
Job sex composition (% female)		...	43	48

*Not reported for dichotomous variables.
†Low scores correspond to high specialization. Signs have been reversed on results computed below.
‡Low scores correspond to high complexity. Signs have been reversed on results reported below.
§Low scores correspond to high skills on the eight aptitude measures. Signs have been reversed on results reported below.

to influence staffing decisions by employers and employees. Although some are more direct measures of theoretically relevant dimensions than others, there is ample precedent in previous research for including each measure in table 1 in our statistical model. Descriptive statistics are reported in table 2.

Organizational context.—Large organizations typically have formal job ladders and other personnel procedures that facilitate on-the-job training and reduce turnover costs. Oi argues: "The initial fixed investments in recruiting and training employees are likely to be greater in large firms for two reasons. First, smaller firms with shorter, uncertain lives have less opportunity to capture the returns. Second, training yields higher returns when workers must be taught to conform with prescribed production methods. Large firms are thus provided with more incentives to design pay and personnel policies which can reduce labor turnover, thereby increasing the

returns to firm-specific human capital" (1983, p. 150). Empirical results on the relationship between establishment size, job tenure, and personnel practices support Oi's contention (Bielby and Baron 1983; Oi 1983; Barth, Cordes, and Haber 1984; Pfeffer and Cohen 1984; Wholey 1984). Consequently, the efficiency-based perspective suggests that within mixed occupations, women typically find employment in organizations operating on a smaller scale. We measure scale (z_1) as the natural logarithm of total establishment employment.

Williamson (1981) argues that formal governance structures regulating the employment relationship are implemented to economize on the cost of turnover and job-specific training. Accordingly, we expect women in mixed occupations to be underrepresented in organizations covered by a union contract or formal job posting and bidding procedures. A binary variable (z_2) denotes the presence of such arrangements.

When production technology creates interdependence among workers, they are less likely to be interchangeable and the costs of replacing workers who quit should be higher. Such interdependence is characteristic of automated production processes (Blauner 1964; Woodward 1965). Our specification includes a binary variable (z_3) denoting whether an establishment utilizes continuous process production techniques as its primary production technology. Within mixed occupations, we expect that women are underrepresented in establishments engaged in highly automated production.

Job characteristics.—We measure task specialization (x_1) at the job level by the natural logarithm of the number of workers allocated to an establishment job title. Workers who monopolize an organizational position are likely to have specialized duties and responsibilities. If many people are assigned to a position, however, workers are more likely to be interchangeable and turnover costs should be lower. Consequently, we hypothesize that job-level specialization has a negative effect on female representation in jobs within mixed occupations.

The remaining 16 measures are ratings of job attributes from the *DOT* (U.S. Department of Labor 1972). For about 30% of the jobs in our sample, these ratings were obtained from Employment Service analysts' on-site evaluations. Detailed job analyses were not performed for the remaining jobs, and ratings were obtained from the published *Dictionary* based on the nine-digit *DOT* classifications assigned to jobs.[7]

Our single direct measure of training time (x_2) is the *DOT* rating of specific vocational preparation (SVP). The scale ranges from one ("short demonstration only") to nine (over 10 years). The typical job in our sample from mixed occupations requires about six months' training, and we expect women to be overrepresented in jobs requiring little training.[8]

Technical complexity, like specialization, is assumed to be associated with higher training and turnover costs and therefore an underrepresentation of females. Our measure (x_3) is the *DOT* rating of the job's complexity of involvement with things.

The next eight measures, x_4 through x_{11}, are based on *DOT* ratings of job aptitudes, "the specific capacities or abilities required of an individual in order to facilitate the learning of some task or job duty" (U.S. Department of Labor 1972, p. 233). Each is measured on the following scale: (1) the top 10% of the working population, (2) the ninetieth to sixty-seventh percentile, (3) the middle third, (4) the thirty-third to tenth percentile, and (5) the bottom decile.

Previous research has documented small but significant differences between men and women on traits corresponding to these eight aptitude measures (Maccoby and Jacklin 1974; Marini and Brinton 1984), and hypothesized signs in table 1 correspond to the directions of those differences. That is, we expect men to dominate employment in jobs requiring numerical ability, manual dexterity, or spatial skills, but not verbal skills, motor coordination, finger dexterity, or clerical perception.[9] Since sex differences across individuals are modest on these dimensions, however, male-female aptitude differences alone cannot explain extreme sex segregation across jobs; an efficiency-based account must also assume that employers statistically discriminate based on these aptitudes. For example, within a mixed line of work, it is difficult to explain why only women would choose to apply for jobs requiring finger dexterity, when many men also have the requisite skills.[10] However, if there is no reliable, less expensive method of measuring whether applicants can accurately manipulate small objects, employers are likely to reserve jobs requiring such tasks for women.

On average, men have greater upper-body strength than women. Strength is one of the few physical traits related to work roles for which nontrivial sex differences exist (Maccoby and Jacklin 1974; Marini and Brinton 1984). Our binary indicator (x_{12}) is based on *DOT* ratings of the amount of lifting required on the job (U.S. Department of Labor 1972, pp. 325–27) and is coded one for jobs requiring lifting 25 pounds or more (zero otherwise).

Our last five measures of job characteristics are based on dichotomous *DOT* ratings of "temperaments," defined as "the adaptability requirements made on the worker by specific types of job-worker situations" (U.S. Department of Labor

1972, p. 297). The varied duties temperament (x_{13}) characterizes jobs requiring "adaptability to performing a variety of duties, often changing from one task to another of a different nature without loss of efficiency or composure" (U.S. Department of Labor 1972, pp. 309–10). Within mixed occupations, such jobs are likely to have lower turnover costs owing to lower firm- and job-specific skill content. Consequently, we expect women to be overrepresented in jobs coded one on this measure.

The performance standards temperament (x_{14}) denotes "adaptability to situations requiring the precise attainment of set limits, tolerances, or standards" (U.S. Department of Labor 1972, pp. 308–9). It should characterize work that is sufficiently routinized that control is embodied in technical standards of performance (Edwards 1979). Since training and turnover costs should be lower, women should be overrepresented in jobs characterized by this temperament. Similarly, within mixed occupations women should be concentrated in jobs requiring the repetitiveness temperament (x_{15}): "adaptability to performing repetitive work, or continuously performing the same work, according to set procedures, sequence or pace" (U.S. Department of Labor 1972, p. 305).

Finally, we expect women to be overrepresented in jobs characterized by the interpersonal or "dealing with people" temperament (x_{16}) and underrepresented in jobs requiring the direction, control, and planning of activities (x_{17}). The former is assigned to jobs requiring cooperativeness, the ability to work in teams, and ease in working relations (U.S. Department of Labor 1972, p. 304), interpersonal traits often thought to be more characteristic of women than men (Marini and Brinton 1984). Conversely, the latter temperament corresponds to interpersonal traits more often attributed to men (Deaux 1985).

Our model attempts to represent efficiency-based accounts of sex segregation as accurately as possible, given the available data. Some variables included in our model, however, also apply to other perspectives on segregation. In some cases, other accounts suggest hypotheses about variables that are the opposite of those in table 1. For example, various organizational theories argue that larger organizations are more visible to and

dependent on the state and are therefore more vulnerable to political pressures to provide employment opportunities for women and minorities (e.g., Salancik 1979). If so, women in mixed occupations should be overrepresented in large establishments, contrary to the hypothesis in table 1. In other instances, competing perspectives on segregation suggest effects similar to those hypothesized in table 1, but for different reasons. For example, male-dominated unions might make deliberate efforts on behalf of male workers to exclude women from more desirable jobs (Deaux and Ullman 1983);[11] we cannot distinguish that effect from the one hypothesized above for formal governance structures merely on the basis of our statistical model. We have opted to formulate a reasonably complete representation of one dominant approach to segregation, the efficiency-based account, rather than include weak measures from competing perspectives within a single statistical model. That is, we have taken the statistical discrimination perspective seriously and operationalized it as faithfully as possible. We rely on two kinds of evidence in evaluating how well that perspective explains sex segregation within mixed occupations: the estimates obtained from our statistical model and, in a later section of the article, qualitative information about employment practices in specific organizations.

Statistical Model

We represent the determinants of percentage female in the ith job in occupation j within establishment k as:

$$p_{ijk} = a + \mathbf{b}_1'\mathbf{x}_{ijk} + \mathbf{b}_2'\mathbf{z}_k + u_j + e_{ijk}, \quad (1)$$

where $\mathbf{x}_{ijk}$ is a vector of job attributes (x_1 through x_{17} in tables 1 and 2) and $\mathbf{z}_k$ includes establishment characteristics (z_1 through z_3 in tables 1 and 2). The term u_j represents all (unmeasured) occupational attributes that affect the sex composition of jobs in that line of work, and e_{ijk} is an orthogonal job-specific stochastic disturbance.

Averaging equation (1) across jobs in an establishment yields

$$p_{.jk} = a + \mathbf{b_1}'\mathbf{x}_{.jk} + \mathbf{b_2}'\mathbf{z}_k + u_j + e_{.jk}, \quad (2)$$

and averaging equation (2) across jobs in all establishments for the *j*th occupation gives

$$p_{.j.} = a + \mathbf{b_1}'\mathbf{x}_{.j.} + \mathbf{b_2}'\mathbf{z}_. + u_j + e_{.j.}. \quad (3)$$

Subtracting equation (2) from (1) provides the equation estimated for the within-establishment analysis:

$$(p_{ijk} - p_{.jk}) = \mathbf{b_1}'(\mathbf{x}_{ijk} - \mathbf{x}_{.jk}) + (e_{ijk} - e_{.jk}). \quad (4)$$

Subtracting equation (3) from (2) gives the equation estimated in the between-establishment analyses:

$$(p_{.jk} - p_{.j.}) = \mathbf{b_1}'(\mathbf{x}_{.jk} - \mathbf{x}_{.j.}) + \mathbf{b_2}'(\mathbf{z}_k - \mathbf{z}_.) + (e_{.jk} - e_{.j.}). \quad (5)$$

OLS regression provides unbiased estimates of both equations (4) and (5). Furthermore, all occupational characteristics that affect the propensity to employ females have been differenced out of both equations and can be ignored (see Judge et al. 1980, pp. 325–43). In addition, all attributes that characterize establishments have been differenced out of equation (4) and can be ignored in the within-establishment analyses.[12] Equation (4) is estimated for the 2,997 jobs employing 5,771 men and 6,311 women within 80 mixed occupational categories. To estimate equation (5), we aggregate across all specific jobs in an enterprise in a given mixed occupation. Doing that for every mixed occupation in each establishment yields the 1,385 observations (instances of mixed occupations in 266 establishments) used to estimate equation (5). Below, we report estimates of $\mathbf{b_1}$, the effects of job attributes, obtained from equation (4) and estimates of $\mathbf{b_2}$, the effects of establishment characteristics, from equation (5).[13]

Organizational scale and job specialization are entered in logarithmic form (base *e*) in equations (1)–(5), since we assume that *proportionate* differences have equal effects on sex composition.

Results

A Note on Segregation Across Occupations and Jobs

Table 3 shows how occupational measures of sex segregation overstate the extent to which men and women share comparable work assignments. It compares segregation indices computed across major occupational groups, detailed occupations, and job titles. To equalize the distribution of men and women across the seven major groups listed in table 3, only 36.5% of female (or male) workers would have to be reclassified.[14] In contrast, over three-fourths of the women (or men) would require reclassification across the 645 detailed occupations (bottom row, table 3). This is slightly higher than the index values reported for 1970 census three-digit categories (England 1981). The difference is not surprising, since our classification scheme is more detailed, particularly among highly segregated manufacturing occupations.

At the level of establishment job titles, sex segregation is nearly complete. In our sample, over 96% of the women would have to be transferred to different job titles to equalize sex ratios.[15] Indeed, only 8% of the workers in our sample shared job titles with members of the opposite sex, and only 4% of the titles were mixed.

Nor is there much difference in job segregation across major occupational groups, despite modest differences at the level of detailed occupations (compare the last two cols. of table 3). Administrative work (managers and officials) seems modestly desegregated, but job-level segregation is uniformly high (indeed, almost complete) in six of the seven groups and only slightly lower among managers and officials. Men and women may share occupational designations in a few lines of work; but even then they almost always work in different organizations or hold different job titles within an establishment.

Table 4 demonstrates how assessments of segregation within establishments are affected by aggregation. A classification scheme similar to the one used by EEOC portrays 28% of the establishments as having segregation indices less than 40, and the same fraction has indices of 90 or above.

TABLE 3

Sex Segregation Among Occupations and Job Titles by Major Occupational Groups

Major Occupational Group	No. of Workers	% Female	No. of Occupations	No. of Titles	Δ Segregation Across	
					3-Digit Occupations	Job Titles
1. Professional and technical workers	3,597	50	59	1,035	70.7	94.4
2. Managers and officials	2,879	19	20	1.602	48.4	86.0
3. Skilled production workers	14,744	4	190	1,860	89.4	98.9
4. Unskilled and semiskilled production workers	14,308	29	198	2,606	68.6	96.9
5. Clerical workers	10,115	42	97	2,644	67.7	95.1
6. Sales workers	1,805	18	33	169	85.1	93.3
7. Service workers	3,390	20	48	609	73.7	96.1
Total	50,838	21	645	10,525	75.1	96.3

Yet only a handful of enterprises were even modestly desegregated at the level of detailed occupations or establishment job titles.[16] Indeed, only 42% of the 290 establishments had *any* job titles to which both men and women were assigned. An overwhelming majority of the work settings were either completely sex segregated by job title or nearly so.

In sum, tables 3 and 4 demonstrate that occupational segregation in specific establishments is typically much higher than segregation computed from sex composition figures aggregated across establishments. Consequently, for many detailed occupations there appears to be disagreement across work settings about the sex label of specific occupational roles. Moreover, results reported in table 4 imply that even when an establishment employs both sexes in the same (detailed) line of work, men and women are usually assigned different official job titles. In the next section, we examine whether patterns of sex composition between and within establishments are consistent with accounts linking segregation to optimal employer decision making.

Segregation in Mixed Occupations: Statistical Models

All but 24 of the 290 establishments in our sample employed workers in at least one mixed occupation.[17] However, only 144 enterprises employed *both* men and women in mixed occupations. Roughly 12,000 workers in our sample (24%)

were employed in seemingly mixed occupations, and over 4,000 of those were in organizations that did not hire members of the opposite sex in their line of work. Working in the same job classification with members of the opposite sex is even rarer. Of nearly 3,000 job titles in mixed occupations, only 215 were filled by both men and women. Just five establishments account for 85 (40%) of these mixed job titles.

In short, the majority of workers in our sample did *not* work in mixed occupations, and those that did were typically engaged in routine administrative tasks (e.g., bookkeepers, production clerks), production work (e.g., assemblers, packagers), or service jobs (e.g., hotel clerks, waiters, and waitresses). Workers in mixed occupations occasionally labored in settings where members of the opposite sex had similar roles, but men and women were rarely assigned the same job titles in the same enterprise. Thus, even when men and women are not segregated occupationally, they are often segregated organizationally.

Table 5 reports the effects of organizational and job characteristics on the gender composition (percentage female) of jobs in mixed occupations. The results modestly support the hypotheses we derived from efficiency-based explanations of sex segregation. All but three of the hypothesized effects are statistically significant; the strongest effects are associated with physical demands, training time, specialization, and finger dexterity. For example, consider two otherwise comparable jobs that differ on the binary variable denoting heavy

TABLE 4

Distributions of Establishments by Levels of Segregation Computed Across Major Occupational Groups,
Detailed Occupations, and Job Titles

	Δ ACROSS MAJOR GROUPS		Δ ACROSS OCCUPATIONS		Δ ACROSS JOB TITLES	
SEGREGATION LEVEL	No of Establishments	%	No of Establishments	%	No. of Establishments	%
Δ < 20	23	8	3	1	1	0
20 ≤ Δ < 40	59	20	7	2	5	2
40 ≤ Δ < 60	61	21	23	8	7	2
60 ≤ Δ < 80	37	13	57	20	24	8
80 ≤ Δ < 90	29	10	33	11	22	8
90 ≤ Δ < 95	19	7	20	7	17	6
95 ≤ Δ < 100	15	5	33	11	45	16
Δ = 100 (mixed)	23	9	90	34	145	50
Δ = 100 (all male)	17	6	17	6	17	6
Δ = 100 (all female)	7	3	7	2	7	2
Total	290	100	290	100	290	100
Median		60.6		95.0		100
Interquartile range		57.6		23.0		5.9

lifting, that differ by one point on the finger dexterity aptitude, and that are a standard deviation apart on specialization and training time. The expected difference in percentage female is 68, with the job that is less specialized, requires less training, involves greater finger dexterity, and does not require heavy lifting likely to be allocated to women.

However, the statistical model specified in equation (1) is at odds with the empirical data in one important respect. The model assumes that job sex composition has a continuous distribution and varies in response to marginal changes in organizational and job characteristics. In effect, the model assumes that both the sex composition of the applicant pool and the propensity of employers to hire females in mixed occupations are distributed continuously. Given the distributions on the independent variables and the coefficient estimates reported in table 5, nearly two-thirds (63%) of the jobs in our sample are predicted to have between 20% and 80% females. However, only 6% actually did; 54% of the jobs in our sample from mixed occupations contained no women and 39% were 100% female.[18]

Thus men and women differ much more in their job assignments within mixed occupations than one would expect if segregation primarily reflects labor supply. That is, the women in our sample of mixed occupations have already eschewed "female" work roles; consequently, it seems unlikely that the vast majority of them would have *chosen* to be segregated from men, either by organizational setting or by virtue of their specific job classification. Nor does it seem very likely that their abilities and aptitudes would be sufficiently different from their male counterparts within the same work role to explain the pervasive sex segregation within mixed occupations. Instead, the sharp discontinuity in the distribution of sex composition among jobs suggests that statistical discrimination by employers on the demand side has a far greater impact on segregation within mixed occupations than do labor supply constraints. Suppose, for example, that employers rank jobs with respect to their appropriateness for female applicants based on their perceptions of requisite skills, training, and turnover costs. Then, using some type of mental discriminant function, they classify jobs into one cluster reserved for males and another reserved for females. Such behavior is consistent with the model of statistical discrimination and with the dichotomous distribution of gender composition observed in our job-level data.

To test this notion more adequately, we reformulated our statistical model to account for whether or not women were excluded from a given job. That is, we specify the gender mix of a job as a dichotomous (rather than continuous) outcome, affected by the same factors that we suggested above are weighed by employers. Ac-

TABLE 5

Determinants of Sex Composition (% Female) of Work in Mixed Occupations, Metric Coefficients for Regression
(N = 2,997)

Independent Variable	Description	Metric	Coefficient Estimate[a]
Organizational context:			
z_1	Organizational scale	Log employment	−2.7**
z_2	Union or bidding arrangements	0-1	−8.8**
z_3	Process technology	0-1	−5.9**
Job characteristics:			
x_1	Specialization	Log workers[b]	−6.5**
x_2	Training time	1-7	−6.6**
x_3	Complexity of involvement with things	0-7[c]	−3.8**
x_4	Numerical aptitude	1-5[d]	−3.9*
x_5	Verbal aptitude	1-5	7.3**
x_6	Motor coordination aptitude	1-5	1.2
x_7	Manual dexterity aptitude	1-5	−2.4
x_8	Finger dexterity aptitude	1-5	13.3**
x_9	Clerical perception aptitude	1-5	7.4**
x_{10}	Spatial skills aptitude	1-5	−6.5**
x_{11}	Eye/hand/foot coordination aptitude	1-5	−7.1**
x_{12}	Physical strength, lifting ≥ 25 lbs.	0-1	−34.2**
x_{13}	Varied duties temperament	0-1	10.2**
x_{14}	Performance standards temperament	0-1	5.7**
x_{15}	Repetitiveness temperament	0-1	6.2**
x_{16}	Dealing with people temperament	0-1	−14.3**
x_{17}	Direction, control, planning temperament	0-1	1.0

Variance explained:	Between Establishments $(p_{.jk} - p_{.j.})$	Within Establishments $(p_{ijk} - p_{.jk})$
Adjusted R^2	.142	.156
Standard error of estimate	34.5	25.0

[a] Estimated effects of organizational context are from the between-establishment equation, and estimated effects of job characteristics are from the within-establishment equation; see n. 13.

[b] Sign reversed so that high scores correspond to more specialized jobs.

[c] Sign reversed so that high scores correspond to more complex jobs.

[d] Sign reversed so that high scores correspond to greater aptitude.

* $P < .05$ (two-tailed test).

** $P < .001$ (two-tailed test).

cordingly, we respecified equation (1) as a logistic model:

$$O_{ijk} = \exp(a + \mathbf{b}_1'\mathbf{x}_{ijk} + \mathbf{b}_2'\mathbf{z}_k), \qquad (6)$$

where O_{ijk} represents the conditional odds that women are excluded from the ith job in occupation j in establishment k. Estimates of logistic coefficients are reported in table 6, along with the net effect of each variable on the probability of female exclusion (Hanushek and Jackson 1977, p. 189). (Effects are evaluated with all independent variables set to their mean values.)

The coefficients are comparable in relative size with those reported in table 5. Women in mixed occupations are most likely to be excluded from job classifications that are specialized; require heavy lifting; do not require finger dexterity, verbal aptitude, or clerical perception; or have longer training requirements. Women are also more likely to be absent from jobs that involve variable tasks, spatial skills, eye/hand/foot coordination; that are in larger establishments; or that are in enterprises with unions or formal bidding arrangements.

The differences between tables 5 and 6 are informative. The predictive power of the model in table 5 was quite weak, since it attempted to locate jobs along a continuum of percentage female, when in fact most jobs had values of zero or 100. The model explained just 14% of the variance in sex composition of mixed occupations across establishments and only 16% of the variance in the sex composition of jobs within establishments.[19] In contrast, the logistic regression model in table 6 is remarkably successful in predicting whether or not women are excluded from a job, correctly classifying 82% of the 3,000 jobs.

In short, the statistical results suggest that employers do reserve some jobs for men and others for women, based on their knowledge of technical and organizational features of work and their perceptions (however accurate) of sex differences in skills and work orientations. Technical features of jobs in the same mixed occupation are similar in many respects, but they are not identical. Our findings indicate that small differences in job requirements get amplified into large differences in gender composition. In the organizations we examined, the propensity to hire females in a mixed line of work appears to be an all-or-nothing proposition. With few exceptions, a job was either inappropriate for women or appropriate only for women, regardless of the amount of overlap in the attributes of prospective male and female employees.

As we noted above, economists often *assume* that such employment practices are economically optimal and not based on bias or prejudice, even if those policies are disadvantageous to individual women or men. Our statistical model, however, does not test that assumption, and we are not prepared to accept it as axiomatic. Indeed, case materials on employment practices in specific organizations, which we examine next, lead us to question that assumption.

Is Statistical Discrimination Efficient? Anecdotal Evidence Regarding Employers' Staffing Decisions

Employers' practices regarding the placement of women in jobs requiring strenuous physical effort are particularly difficult to reconcile with an efficiency perspective on sex segregation. According to table 6, whether or not a job required lifting 25 pounds or more was one of the strongest predictors of the likelihood of excluding women from that job. Since an individual's ability to lift heavy objects seems neither difficult nor costly to measure, it should be possible to devise more efficient screening mechanisms for physically demanding jobs than totally excluding women who are in that line of work.

Policies such as those summarized in Appendix A provide the context for our statistical results and suggest alternative explanations for our findings. Appendix A lists the observations of some Employment Service analysts about employer policies toward female employment. This information is compiled from narrative reports for 153 of the 290 establishments in our sample.[20] Physical demands of work are mentioned in 41% of those reports, and Appendix A lists examples in which physical requirements figured explicitly or implicitly in employers' policies for assigning women to specific jobs.

TABLE 6

Determinants of Likelihood That Women Are Excluded from Jobs in Mixed Occupations, Logistic Regression Coefficients (N = 2,997)

Independent Variable	Description	Coefficient Estimate[a]	Effect on Probability[b]
Organizational context:			
z_1	Organizational scale	.20**	.05
z_2	Union or bidding arrangements	.59**	.14
z_3	Process technology	...	...
Job characteristics:			
x_1	Specialization[c]	.60**	.14
x_2	Training time	.29**	.07
x_3	Complexity of involvement with things	...	...
x_4	Numerical aptitude[d]	.33**	.08
x_5	Verbal aptitude	− .70**	− .17
x_6	Motor coordination aptitude	...	...
x_7	Manual dexterity aptitude	...	...
x_8	Finger dexterity aptitude	− 1.13**	− .26
x_9	Clerical perception aptitude	− .58**	− .14
x_{10}	Spatial skill aptitude	.52**	.12
x_{11}	Eye/hand/foot coordination aptitude	.52**	.12
x_{12}	Physical strength, lifting ≥ 25 lbs.	1.45**	.32
x_{13}	Varied duties temperament	− .27	− .07
x_{14}	Performance standards temperament	...	...
x_{15}	Repetitiveness temperament	− .39*	− .10
x_{16}	Dealing with people temperament	...	...
x_{17}	Direction, control, planning temperament	...	...

NOTE.—Likelihood ratio χ^2 = 1001.4 with 22 df; 82% of cases correctly classified.

[a] Maximum likelihood estimate of linear net effect on log odds of exclusion. Three dots denote variables with insignificant effects in the full model and dropped from the final model.

[b] Net effect on probability of exclusion of a one-unit change in the independent variable, evaluated at the mean.

[c] Sign reversed so that high scores correspond to more specialized jobs.

[d] Signs reversed so that high scores correspond to greater aptitude.

* $P < .05$ (two-tailed test).

** $P < .001$ (two-tailed test).

The comments in Appendix A (and others we encountered like them) underscore the diversity of organizational and industrial contexts in which restrictions based on physical demands were invoked, such as finance, transportation, utilities, and recreation, as well as light and heavy manufacturing. Narratives for some establishments (e.g., the airline in App. A) mentioned state legal restrictions that, until struck down by the California Supreme Court in 1970, restricted women's lifting to 25 pounds. No doubt those restrictions provided the rationale for excluding women from heavy physical work in many other establishments as well. Nevertheless, our data contain numerous instances in which employer policy cited heavy lifting as the reason for excluding women from specific jobs, although detailed job analyses revealed that those jobs required *no strenuous physical exertion* (see also Deaux and Ullman 1983). Thus, our statistical model understates the impact of such policies on sex segregation, since it assesses only the extent to which women were excluded from jobs that actually required lifting in excess of the (pre-1971) legal limit.

Since legal restrictions on lifting for women became unconstitutional after 1970, we would expect rational, profit-maximizing employers to cease using sex as an inefficient screen for that job requirement, instead filling physically demanding jobs with workers of either sex who could demonstrate the capability to perform the work. Indeed, policies restricting women's employment based on physical demands were mentioned less frequently in narrative reports after 1970. Although 45% of the 124 reports prepared between 1965 and 1970 mentioned such restrictions, only 24% of the 29 reports prepared between 1971 and 1979 did so.

However, if employer policy—as articulated to Employment Service analysts—changed after 1970, employer practices apparently did not. We added two binary terms to our logistic regression model to test whether the tendency to exclude women from jobs requiring heavy lifting declined after 1970. The first was coded one if the establishment was studied after 1970, and the second was an interaction term coded one if the job required lifting 25 pounds or more and was studied after 1970. If anything, however, women were *more* likely to be excluded from jobs requiring heavy lifting in establishments studied after 1970. The logistic coefficient for the main effect of physical demands (the effect for establishments studied before 1971) was 1.1, but the sum of main and interaction effects for physical demands (the effect for establishments studied after 1970) was 2.6.[21]

In short, strenuous physical effort appears to have justified excluding women from specific jobs for some time after the legal rationale disappeared. On the one hand, these results suggest that employers persisted in a practice for which they could be held liable under both state and federal civil rights legislation. On the other hand, staffing patterns observed in the 1970s partially reflect both job assignments made before the era of effective EEO enforcement and inertia in women's work preferences. For all these reasons, organizational practices endure long after the circumstances that warranted them have disappeared (Stinchcombe 1965).

Although women are typically excluded from work perceived as physically demanding, they are often given exclusive access to tasks viewed as routine and requiring attention to detail. Unlike the practices summarized in Appendix A, policies regarding employment of women in "detail" work have not been sanctioned by protective legislation and regulations. Nevertheless, as the examples in Appendix B show, an employer's beliefs about the work habits and skills of women can become part of an organization's personnel policy. A job in assembly or packaging may be labeled "men's work" or "women's work" depending on whether it is identified as physically demanding—and therefore suitable only for men—or routine and requiring attention to detail—and thus suitable only for women. For example, women worked as bottlers and packers in several of the pharmaceutical enterprises in our sample, whereas men did remarkably similar tasks in a brewery (where a union refers job applicants to the plant).

The labeling of "men's work" and "women's work" for similar tasks occurs within organizations as well. Table 7 reports staffing patterns in packing jobs for a pharmaceutical establishment. An Employment Service analyst classified each job into the same nine-digit *DOT* category of "packager, machine." The establishment, however, recognized 10 distinct job classifications for the eight men and 85 women performing this occupational role, terming men "technicians" and women "operators." An establishment that processes sugar, studied in 1972, had a staffing pattern for the same *DOT* category that was the mirror image of the one in table 7. Over 120 male packagers were distributed across 15 job titles, and 19 women were employed in three different job classifications. For both establishments, our original statistical model in table 5, based on measures of job requirements and organizational context, predicts that each job would have between 30% and 50% female incumbents. However, these

TABLE 7

Staffing Patterns for Packaging Jobs in Same Nine-Digit *DOT* Classification: 1968, Pharmaceutical Manufacturing

Job Title	Men	Women
Senior aerosol technician	1	0
Aerosol technician	1	0
Floorlady	0	3
Senior aerosol operator	0	3
Aerosol operator (entry)	0	14
Senior packaging technician	2	0
Packaging technician	4	0
Floorlady	0	4
Senior packaging operator	0	20
Packaging operator (entry)	0	41

jobs were actually fully segregated by sex, as were many others like them in our sample. In other words, the role of machine packager has some characteristics of traditionally "male" jobs, such as heavy lifting requirements, and of traditionally "female" jobs, such as repetitive tasks, low training requirements, low spatial skills, and modest finger dexterity. Thus, there appears to be no compelling technical rationale for attaching a specific sex label to each particular job, yet employers did so. Accounting for these gender distinctions among work roles requires going beyond efficiency perspectives on organizations and inequality, and we suggest some alternatives in the concluding section.

Discussion and Conclusion

Overview

Historian Joan Wallach Scott offers this description of 19th-century textile factories: "The specific jobs done by men and women varied from mill to mill, but the separation of male and female work was almost universal; in most mills many rooms were staffed entirely by women. Thus the separate realms of work for men and women remained undisturbed" (1982, pp. 171–72). Sex segregation appears just as pervasive within and across organizations in almost every line of work represented in our diverse sample of California establishments, even within seemingly integrated occupations. Work done by both men and women is often done in distinct organizational settings, and when enterprises employ both sexes in the same occupation, they typically assign them different job titles. Once established, sex labels of job titles acquire tremendous inertia, even when similar work is done by the opposite sex elsewhere in the same establishment or in other settings.

To be sure, differences in the allocation of men and women across occupational roles, whether by choice or by constraint, *do* account for much of the segregation we observe. For example, as recently as 1980, men outnumbered women by more than two to one in managerial occupations, whereas the ratio was about one to three in clerical work. Women still make up less than 3% of workers in the construction trades, whereas less than 4% of all registered nurses are men (U.S. Department of Commerce 1983). But as we have shown, there is considerable sex segregation within and across organizations, even within detailed occupational categories. This article focused on occupational roles that are filled by both men and women, allowing us to reduce the impact of vocational choice on segregation.

Within the mixed occupations in our sample, men tended to be employed in larger organizations and in establishments with unions or formal bidding arrangements. They also tended to monopolize specialized jobs with more complex tasks and firm-specific training requirements.

Physically demanding work was typically not performed by women, whereas tasks requiring finger dexterity were rarely done by men. The organizations in our sample utilized diverse technologies, drew from many different labor pools, and ranged from small family businesses to massive bureaucracies. Yet men and women were found in distinct job classifications in almost every setting, even when their roles were so similar that they belonged to the same detailed (nine-digit) occupational classification.

Our research has several important implications for studying the sexual division of labor. First, the aggregation biases we illustrate clearly underscore the limits of occupation-level analyses. Second, our finding of almost complete job-level segregation by sex, even within seemingly integrated occupations, suggests a structural basis for sex differences in promotion opportunities, occupational status, and earnings trajectories. Third, our regression results are consistent with models of statistical discrimination, but they are difficult to reconcile with the view that such decision making is rational or optimal. Our findings suggest two important directions for future research: analyses of the role played by employers' beliefs and perceptions and studies of the institutionalization of gender-biased employment practices. Finally, our research demonstrates the importance of attending to changes in job- and organization-level structures and processes in studying labor force trends. We discuss each of these issues briefly.

Implications

Reevaluating the Results of Research on Occupations.—Our findings point to several limitations of research that ignores intraoccupational patterns of sex segregation. First, trends in the sex composition of occupational categories mask how segregation develops between and within firms. Although aggregate statistics on occupational composition show a very modest trend toward gender integration (Snyder, Hayward, and Hudis 1978; England 1981; Beller 1982), this may partly reflect increased sex-based differentiation of *jobs* as men and women have become more

similar occupationally. Our data from the late 1960s and early 1970s show that few work settings could have been more segregated at the job level. This suggests that as detailed occupations become mixed, intraoccupational segregation within and across work settings becomes more prevalent. Therefore, a more balanced sex mix in a given occupational category need not reflect increased equity of job opportunities in specific work settings. The appearance of increasing occupational integration between men and women may mask: (1) growth in female employment confined to specific work settings, such as when driving school buses becomes "women's work" while intercity bus driving remains "men's work"; (2) increased employment of women in segregated job titles in organizations already utilizing male workers, as appears to be the case in some areas of data processing; or (3) transitory employment patterns as an occupation's sex label changes from "men's" to "women's work" (e.g., telephone operator and bank teller early in the century).[22]

Second, using major occupational groups to monitor segregation, as EEOC does, seems virtually worthless. Biases in EEO-1 data have been documented by Smith and Welch (1984). They find that establishments that are covered by contract compliance regulations apparently have a broad view of what constitutes a managerial job when classifying women and minority workers. Moreover, these data are limited even when classification into major groups is done accurately. In our data, establishments that appeared integrated according to the major group classification were seldom desegregated by official job titles, which usually form the basis for workers' duties, pay, promotion opportunities, and responsibilities. In short, what gets reported on an EEO-1 form may have little to do with differences in work experiences and outcomes by sex.

Third, in addition to aggregation biases, contemporary research efforts are limited because they restrict our understanding of the social organization of work. For example, in an imaginative analysis of occupational and industrial data, Bridges (1982) found that highly unionized industries have lower levels of occupational sex segregation. Our finding that unionized enterprises are *more* segregated by job titles (Bielby and Baron

1984) is not necessarily inconsistent with Bridges's results. The proliferation of work rules, seniority systems, and detailed job hierarchies in unionized settings might facilitate the pattern we observe: employment of men and women in the same *occupation* but in distinct job titles (see Aronowitz 1973, p. 131; Deaux and Ullman 1983). In any event, reconciling the two sets of results demands attention to organizational arrangements. Work tasks, authority relations, personnel practices, and wage determination are largely designed and implemented at the organizational level. Nowhere is that more evident than in the way sex differences become incorporated into work arrangements.

Segregation and Job Hierarchies.—If jobs are almost perfectly segregated by sex, authority hierarchies and career ladders are likely to be segregated as well. Preliminary analyses of our data on job hierarchies show that women in positions of authority almost always supervised other women, though it is also common for women to be supervised by men. Women are much less likely to be in jobs with promotion opportunities, and career ladders are typically longer for men. The few jobs containing men and women are mostly in entry-level slots at the bottom of organizational hierarchies, and typically women's promotion opportunities diminish almost entirely after moving a step or two beyond entry level (Baron and Bielby 1984; Baron, Davis-Blake, and Bielby 1984).

Our data also provide numerous examples of men's apparent ability to circumvent formal promotion rules. In these cases, an entry-level position was monopolized by women, and that position was listed as requisite experience for promotion to the next level. However, all occupants of the next highest position were men. Employment Service analysts were sometimes quite explicit in conveying such inequalities:

"[MOLDING MECHANIC] workers [three males] are usually obtained from outside the plant. ... Promotion from OPERATOR, MOLDING MACHINE [to MOLDING MECHANIC] within the company is not normal since these workers are all female" (Job analysis schedule 2909975, pen and pencil company, 1965). This recurrent pattern underscores the political aspect of credentials, skills, and experience (Collins 1979).

Apparently, men can often substitute alternative qualifications for those required and obtained in the internal labor market, but women rarely enjoy this option.

Thus, job-level segregation affects the structure of organizational authority and promotion, with dramatic consequences for the careers of men and women. Indeed, our analyses are consistent with case study results that document "rank segregation" as the basis of gender inequalities in job rewards (Malkiel and Malkiel 1973; Grimm and Stern 1974; Halaby 1979; Cabral, Ferber, and Greene 1981; Rosenbaum 1983) and access to high-wage employers as an additional source of male advantage (Mennerick 1975; Blau 1977; Talbert and Bose 1977). Future research should examine how job structures were first implemented and subsequently institutionalized and whose interests are currently served.

Limitations of Efficiency-based Accounts of Segregation.—It is difficult to reconcile our findings with supply-side accounts of sex segregation within mixed occupations. It is of course possible that a given female "invests" in becoming an assistant professor, but not an associate or full professor; or in becoming a training representative, but only in firms where that job is done exclusively by women. However, such extensions of supply-side accounts of segregation require us to assume not only that women "disinvest" in certain general lines of work (occupations) but also that those who *do* pursue male or integrated work roles avoid certain specific titles and organizational settings.

Our findings are consistent with the model of statistical discrimination in one respect. Employers seem to reserve some jobs for men and others for women in a manner consistent with their perceptions of sex differences in skills, turnover costs, and work orientations. However, gender seems to be a very inefficient screen for attributes as easy to measure as physical strength and finger dexterity, and these job requirements had some of the strongest effects on the sex composition of jobs in our statistical models. In short, the end result—near-complete sex segregation across organizations and job titles in mixed occupations—may be consistent with the model of statistical discrimination, but there is considerable qualitative evidence that appears to undermine the notion that such decision making is optimal.

However, we do not mean to imply that employers are simply irrational, indulging their personal biases at the expense of profits. It is possible that employer actions are a rational response to the interests of male employees in excluding women from their job categories. For example, in Becker's (1957) model, given "tastes for discrimination" among male employees, an employer must pay a wage premium to men in order to induce them to work in an integrated setting. Under such circumstances, labor costs are minimized by employing either men or women exclusively.

We cannot completely dismiss this explanation. The interests and attitudes of male employees almost certainly play a role in generating sex segregation. Given the diversity of organizational and technical arrangements represented in our sample, there is almost certainly variation across jobs and establishments in the desire and ability of male workers to exclude women. For instance, where production is highly interdependent, male workers may perceive the entry of women as particularly disruptive to stable work group relationships. Similarly, employers in competitive markets are least able to absorb the additional costs required to induce male employees to work alongside women. However, even within mixed occupations, we found that women were almost invariably segregated from men by job title or organizational context. Thus, at least some of the intraoccupational segregation that we observed probably does not reflect the exclusionary interests and actions of male coworkers. We hope that future theory and research will devote more attention to specifying when male workers might have both interests in promoting segregation and the means to realize those interests.

Statistical Discrimination as a Self-fulfilling Prophecy.—Some economists maintain that statistical discrimination based on mistaken beliefs should not persist in a market economy. In contrast, social psychologists maintain that stereotypes are cognitive structures that are a normal part of one's perception of others, a shorthand invoked to conserve our limited information-pro-

cessing resources (Ashmore and Del Boca 1981, 1985). Even employers must cope with bounded rationality (Simon 1972). If workers' performances are not exogenous but influenced by the social context of work (Roethlisberger and Dickson 1939; Hackman and Oldham 1980), employer beliefs and perceptions might actually elicit the very behaviors employers expect. That is, given their initial beliefs, however accurate, employers might assign females to routine tasks and dead-end jobs, in which a particular woman's actual skills remain invisible to the employer (Milgrom and Oster 1984). In response to such work conditions, rational women may exhibit higher turnover and lower work involvement, just as employers predicted. While some organizational research has shown the substantial impact of expectations on worker performance (Berlew and Hall 1966), the effect on subsequent employment policies and practices has to date been documented only in case studies (e.g., Kanter 1977).

Another reason that statistical discrimination might not vanish in a market economy is that individuals are more likely to attend to and retain information that confirms their stereotypes and to ignore information that does not fit expectations (Hamilton 1981). Employers are probably no exception. Such "expectancy confirmation sequences" have been documented repeatedly in laboratory experiments (for reviews, see Berger, Rosenholtz, and Zelditch 1980; Darley and Fazio 1980).

The Institutionalization of Gender-based Job Assignments.—Beliefs and perceptions alone cannot account for the extent to which segregated arrangements are built into the structure of work. We need to understand how sex-based job assignments become standard organizational procedure. For example, as noted above, laws against assigning women to heavy manual work rationalized segregation by job title until the early 1970s. Case materials from our data repeatedly cited the California labor code to justify excluding women from some jobs, but we found no evidence of changes in job assignments after the laws were repealed. Thus, understanding current personnel practices and staffing patterns requires studying a legacy of interests that coalesced throughout this

TABLE 8
Gender Composition of Jobs in California Personnel System, Full-Time Workers, Jobs with Two or More
Incumbents: December 31, 1984

	% of Jobs		% of Full-Time Workers	
% female in job:				
100	29.5	(28.8)	6.9	(7.0)
90.0–99.9	2.6	(2.4)	11.9	(11.9)
80.0–89.9	3.2	(2.9)	6.0	(5.9)
70.0–79.9	2.6	(2.4)	5.3	(5.3)
60.0–69.9	3.3	(3.0)	10.1	(10.1)
50.0–59.9	6.6	(6.0)	5.2	(5.2)
40.0–49.9	1.9	(1.7)	3.0	(2.9)
30.0–39.9	3.6	(3.3)	4.3	(4.2)
20.0–29.9	4.5	(4.1)	8.0	(7.9)
10.0–19.9	3.4	(3.1)	12.4	(12.3)
.1– 9.9	2.2	(2.0)	17.1	(17.0)
0	36.5	(40.3)	9.9	(10.3)
N	8,159	(8,957)	121,962	(122,760)
Gender mix:				
No workers of opposite sex ..	66.0	(69.1)	16.8	(17.3)
< 10% workers of one sex ...	70.8	(73.5)	45.8	(46.2)
< 20% workers of one sex ...	77.4	(79.5)	64.2	(64.4)
< 30% workers of one sex ...	84.5	(86.0)	77.5	(77.6)
< 40% workers of one sex ...	91.4	(92.3)	91.9	(91.9)

NOTE.—When the same job class occurred in multiple agencies, each occurrence was treated as a separate job in the table. Figures in parentheses include the 798 job classifications having one incumbent each (632 men, 166 women).

century in support of protective legislation and learning how bureaucratic inertia, cultural stereotypes, and contemporary interests sustain practices that are now illegal.

Indeed, social histories of personnel practices in diverse lines of work, such as Tyack and Strober's (1981) study of the teaching profession, can reveal how sex labels are assigned to jobs and formalized through organizational procedures. A promising line of inquiry would be to study new occupational specialties in rapidly growing fields to learn how definitions and sex labels of job titles emerge and are translated into organizational arrangements for personnel practices.

Monitoring Labor Force Changes.—Our data do not capture very recent employment trends as employers have responded to EEO pressures and changing career aspirations. However, although gender segregation has certainly abated during the decade or so since our typical firm was studied, we should not overstate how much progress has occurred. Consider, for instance, the data summarized in table 8, describing the gender composition of jobs in the civil service personnel system of California at the end of 1984. These data are of particular interest because they almost certainly provide a lower boundary on the degree of job segregation in the private economy. The vigor with which EEO has been pursued in this state's public sector and the greater ability of agencies to pass along the costs of equality to customers (taxpayers) imply less job segregation than in the private sector as a whole.

According to table 8, job-level segregation is less extreme than in our sample but still pervasive. Even with the exclusion of the 798 jobs having one incumbent, 66% of the jobs (employing 17% of state workers) are perfectly segregated. Kanter (1977) and Pettigrew (1975) argue that the psychological and social effects of tokenism become manifested when a role or group has roughly 80% or more of its members in one category. According to that criterion, over 64% of the full-time employees in the state civil service system are in positions whose gender balance is severely skewed. Also, male workers employed by the state are about three times more likely than women to be in job classes with no members of the opposite sex, suggesting that there are considerably fewer women doing "men's work" than there are men doing "women's work."

Moreover, unpublished statistics supplied by the California State Personnel Board document numerous instances of the same forms of intra-occupational segregation encountered in our sample: sex-specific job titles within the same occupation and the segregation of women from men in mixed occupations across specific agencies or bureaus. In sum, notwithstanding recent changes in the sexual division of labor, the patterns documented in our research appear applicable to contemporary organizations.

In case after case, as EEO officials, corporate leaders, and reformers try to effect (or avoid) changes in traditional employment patterns, they encounter intransigent organizational structures and processes that sustain the patterns of sex segregation documented in this article. Our findings were consistent with the theory of statistical discrimination as applied to gender segregation, but they are difficult to reconcile with explanations emphasizing optimal employer decision making under uncertainty. Instead, we have suggested some features of organizations and their environments that foster and sustain the sexual division of labor. Researchers studying workplace inequalities should be examining these features directly. Ignoring them is likely to hinder both social science and social policy.

The employment of women is primarily confined to the home economics and clerical classifications because of the physical nature of other jobs (1964, natural gas utility).

Employment opportunities for women are limited in the production sections due to the physical requirements of many of the jobs (1971, felt goods manufacturing).

The nature of the work (medium to very heavy) does not lend itself to employment in production of either women or the handicapped, although these people are hired for office positions (1973, wire manufacturing).

Normally they [women] are excluded from jobs requiring heavy physical exertion such as *DRIVER, PUTPOST INSTRUCTOR*, and *SWIMMING INSTRUCTOR*. They are specified for the job of *ARTS AND CRAFTS INSTRUCTOR* (1965, coeducational summer camp).

Women are hired for office work classifications in all divisions. Women are also hired exclusively to fill *HOSTESS*, hostess supervisory, and training and cabin cleaning positions. They are preferred applicants for positions in reservations and counter sales. They are generally excluded from the passenger service counter, cargo service, and terminal operations because of the physical labor involved. Women are not hired as maintenance or flight crew personnel primarily because those jobs have been traditionally filled by men and because workers are often required to lift or carry objects in excess of the 25 pound limit set by state law for women (1964, commercial airline).

Males are hired as *FLOOR REPORTERS* and females as *CLERKS, GENERAL*. Both entry jobs are on the trading floor. *FLOOR REPORTERS* stand and walk constantly and *CLERKS, GENERAL* stand and walk about 50% of the time. … According to a stock exchange executive, the *FLOOR REPORTER* classification is a "training ground" for young men starting a career in the securities business (1968, securities exchange).

Women are hired in clerical occupations and in other plant areas where the physical requirements of the tasks involved do not preclude it (1968, pharmaceutical manufacturing).

SOURCE.—Narrative reports prepared by U.S. Employment Service Analysts for selected establishments.

Appendix A: Policies Regarding Employment of Women in Physically Demanding Jobs

The job of *UTILITY WORKER, FEMALE* could be considered a dead-end job. Women are restricted to that title due to physical demands and working conditions (1964, brick and tile manufacturing).

Appendix B: Policies Regarding Employment of Women in "Detail" Work

Female employees perform work of repetitive nature under exacting standards and must possess the temper-

628

ament for confining work at one station (1970, ordnance manufacturing).

Women are used almost exclusively in Packing and Carton Departments where the work is somewhat routine. The work requires considerable standing and walking, and demands a high degree of finger dexterity, close attention to details, and near acuity of color vision (1969, bottle manufacturing).

Women perform all of the assembly operations, since the work is light and merely requires good hand and finger dexterity and a willingness to perform monotonous work (1965, wooden box manufacturing).

The work force of this establishment is predominantly female, as the employer feels they are best suited to this type of work (1967, jewelry manufacturing).

When hiring new employees the company favors older women because of increased stability and favorable attitudes toward job responsibility. Women are employed for practically all production jobs (1970, electronics manufacturing).

Only women are hired for packing and inspection duties, because various aptitude tests indicate that women are more manually adept at this type of work. However, according to the employer, in company plants in other countries throughout the world, the reverse has been found (1966, chewing gum production).

Source.—Narrative reports prepared by U.S. Employment Service Analysts for selected establishments.

Notes

This research was supported in part by grants from the National Science Foundation to the authors (SES 79-24905) and to the Center for Advanced Study in the Behavioral Sciences (BNS 76-22943) and by research funds from the Stanford Graduate School of Business. We thank Clifford Clogg, Kay Deaux, Beverly Duncan, Henry Farber, Robert Flanagan, Neil Fligstein, Christopher Jencks, Brian Mittman, Marilyn Pearman, Barbara Reskin, Allyn Romanow, Pat Roos, Rachel Rosenfeld, Lynne Zucker, and the *AJS* reviewers for helpful comments and for assistance.

1. Procedures for collecting these data are described in U.S. Department of Labor (1972), Miller et al. (1980), and Spenner (1980).

2. The Employment Service changed its occupational classification system around 1964. Consequently, establishments studied before 1964, which were included in our earlier paper (Bielby and Baron 1984), are not analyzed here. Those establishments we have excluded are neither more nor less segregated than the ones analyzed in this article.

3. The second three digits of the *DOT* code are the ratings of complexity of involvement with data, people, and things, respectively. High scores correspond to low levels of complexity, but we have inverted the scales in our statistical analyses so that high scores denote complexity (see Cain and Treiman 1981).

4. Third-edition *DOT* ratings of data and things appear to undervalue the technical complexity of women's work. The "no significant relationship" classification (ratings of seven or eight on data and eight on things) was used more for jobs done by women than for comparable jobs done by men (Miller et al. 1980). This bias was eliminated in the fourth edition by dropping the "no significant relationship" classification. We have corrected the bias in third-edition ratings by truncating the data scale at six and the things scale at seven. The other *DOT* variables used in this study did not change appreciably between the third and fourth editions, and there is no evidence to suggest they are biased by sex (Miller et al. 1980, chap. 7).

5. By including occupations with sex ratios no greater than four to one, we capture a diverse range of occupational roles while excluding lines of work clearly dominated by one sex (see Kanter 1977, p. 209).

6. Four of the 84 occupations occurred in only one establishment and were excluded from our analysis. Of the 290 establishments, 24 employed no workers in mixed occupations. Over half (58%) of the women in our sample were in mixed occupations. However, many of these women were in a few job titles in several very large manufacturing establishments (17% of the women in mixed occupations were concentrated in just five job titles). Consequently, these figures differ considerably from labor force statistics. Apart from employment in these organizations, our data were consistent with statistics that show women disproportionately represented in a small number of occupations that occur in diverse industrial settings (e.g., clerical, service, and light assembly work).

7. Both on-site and published *DOT* ratings were available for about 500 jobs. Correlations between *DOT* and on-site ratings for these jobs generally ranged from .7 to .8. Correlations of about .9 were obtained for training time; complexity of involvement with things; verbal aptitude; dealing with people; and the direction, control, and planning temperament. The lowest correlations between *DOT* and on-site ratings were for motor and eye/hand/foot coordination (about .4).

8. This measure includes some training that is not firm specific and therefore may not perfectly index employers' incentives to reduce turnover. Among a sample of 1,750 jobs analyzed by the Employment Service for

which estimates of general versus firm-specific training were available, the SVP measure correlated about .6 with a similar variable based on specific skills. We would argue, however, that employers have an incentive to retain highly trained workers, even when some of that training is not firm specific, because of the costs of disrupting stable work relations and of replacing such a worker.

9. Clerical perception is the "ability to perceive pertinent detail in verbal or tabular material. To observe differences in copy, to proofread words and numbers, and to avoid perceptual errors in arithmetic computation" (U.S. Department of Labor 1972, p. 267).

10. Supply-side differences in aptitudes can explain extreme sex segregation *within* mixed occupations only if sex differences in aptitudes are greater within detailed occupations than in the general adult population. For example, if women with an aptitude for tasks requiring finger dexterity self-select into an occupation and men without such skills also choose that line of work, perhaps a supply-side account could explain differential job assignments by sex within that line of work. Of course, we would then need to explain why men with the relevant skills avoided specializing in an occupation that utilizes those skills and why men without skills were attracted to the occupation.

11. On the contrary, unions and formal job bidding procedures might constrain employers' ability to use ascriptive criteria in job assignment and thus facilitate integration of work roles (Bridges 1982; Freeman and Medoff 1984; Roos and Reskin 1984).

12. Estimation by OLS is unbiased but not efficient, since the variance of the composite disturbance is a function of the number of jobs within an occupation in a given establishment (N_{jk}). Consequently, the OLS estimates reproduced here are less precise than optimal GLS estimates, and significance levels should be interpreted with caution. However, since our analyses are based on thousands of observations, any effect that is substantively important should be statistically significant well beyond conventional levels. Both OLS and GLS estimates of eq. (5) are biased to the extent that relevant variables are omitted from $\mathbf{x}_{ijk}$ and $\mathbf{z}_k$ in eq. (1), but estimates for eq. (4) are unaffected by omissions from $\mathbf{z}_k$. The OLS estimates reported here were computed from pairwise present correlations, since *DOT* ratings of aptitudes, temperaments, physical demands, and training time were missing for about 8% of the jobs in our sample.

13. In fact, we have two estimates of the coefficients that make up $\mathbf{b}_1$, since $\mathbf{b}_1$ appears on the right side of both eqq. (4) and (5). We ignore estimates of $\mathbf{b}_1$ from eq. (5) for two reasons. First, those estimates can be biased because of omissions of relevant organizational variables in $\mathbf{z}_k$, whereas estimates from eq. (4) are immune from that specification error. Second, estimates of $\mathbf{b}_1$ from the two equations will differ if there are nontrivial "contextual" effects of job attributes. We have no substantive rationale for hypothesizing contextual effects, so we do not interpret differences in the effect of $\mathbf{x}_{ijk}$ as estimated from eqq. (4) and (5). Instead, we assume that any apparent contextual effects actually reflect omitted establishment characteristics in eq. (5).

14. In comparison, the index for the same seven groups among California establishments that filed reports with EEOC in 1975 was 42.6 across all industries and 44.6 in manufacturing (U.S. EEOC 1977). Our sample includes some small establishments not covered by the EEOC, which are likely to be more segregated (Bielby and Baron 1984). Among establishments in our sample with at least 100 employees, the segregation index across major groups equaled 38.4. Note that this figure is smaller than that computed from EEOC data, so it seems unlikely that our sample is biased toward establishments and industries that are more segregated than average.

15. Although segregation is complete *by definition* for jobs with one incumbent, eliminating those jobs hardly affects the level of segregation. The segregation index computed among jobs with two or more workers is 95.9.

16. In other analyses, we applied sampling weights to reproduce the size distribution of establishments within California industries and the distribution of establishments across industries. These reweightings had little effect on the statistics reported in table 4.

17. The 24 that do not employ workers in mixed occupations account for just 0.5% of total employment in our sample.

18. Of course, jobs with one employee cannot be mixed. Among 1,323 jobs with two or more incumbents, only 12% are between 20% and 80% female, whereas 48% are exclusively male and 36% are exclusively female. Reestimating the model for those jobs yields results almost identical to those reported in table 5.

19. The squared correlation between predicted and actual percentage female—an estimate of the proportion of variance explained by eq. (1)—is .34. Adjusted R^2 statistics reported in table 3 pertain to the differenced equations, not to the original substantive specification in eq. (1). Consequently, those statistics do not reflect variance attributable to unobserved differences among occupations.

20. Procedures for preparing narrative reports are summarized in U.S. Department of Labor (1972, pp. 59–68). In summarizing an establishment's "hiring requirements and its method of placement," analysts are

guided by the following questions regarding employment of women: "What openings for women are there in this establishment? What is the establishment's attitude toward their employment? Have jobs been restructured to facilitate their employment?" (p. 61).

21. Evaluated at the mean, the effect of physical demands on the probability of female exclusion is .24 for establishments studied between 1965 and 1970 and .40 for establishments studied since then.

22. An extreme contemporary example is the occupational category "hucksters and peddlers." It changed from being overwhelmingly male to predominantly female between 1950 and 1970 (Snyder et al. 1978; Blau and Hendricks 1979), but not necessarily because women took over the task of selling vacuum cleaners and encyclopedias door-to-door. A more likely explanation is that fewer salesmen are continuing their trade, becoming outnumbered by women selling cosmetics and kitchenware for such firms as Avon, Mary Kay, and Amway. Similarly, women are becoming pharmacists, but they are concentrated in organizational settings and job titles that provide lower wages than their male counterparts receive (Barbara F. Reskin, personal communication).

References

Aigner, Dennis J., and Glen C. Cain. 1977. "Statistical Theories of Discrimination in Labor Markets." *Industrial and Labor Relations Review* 30:175–87.

Aronowitz, Stanley. 1973. *False Promises.* New York: McGraw-Hill.

Arrow, Kenneth. 1973. "The Theory of Discrimination." Pp. 3–33 in *Discrimination in Labor Markets,* edited by O. Ashenfelter and A. Rees. Princeton, N.J.: Princeton University Press.

Ashmore, Richard D., and Frances K. Del Boca. 1981. "Conceptual Approaches to Stereotypes and Stereotyping." Pp. 1–35 in *Cognitive Processes in Stereotyping and Intergroup Behavior,* edited by David L. Hamilton. Hillsdale, N.J.: Erlbaum.

———. 1985. *The Social Psychology of Male-Female Relations.* New York: Academic Press.

Baron, James N. 1982. "Economic Segmentation and the Organization of Work." Ph.D. dissertation, University of California, Santa Barbara.

Baron, James N., and William T. Bielby. 1984. "Organizational Barriers to Gender Equality: Sex Segregation of Jobs and Opportunities." Pp. 233–51 in *Gender and the Life Course,* edited by Alice S. Rossi. New York: Aldine.

Baron, James N., Alison Davis-Blake, and William T. Bielby. 1984. "The Structure and Location of Internal Labor Markets." Paper presented at the annual meeting of the Academy of Management, Boston.

Barth, James R., Joseph J. Cordes, and Sheldon E. Haber. 1984. "Employee Characteristics and Firm Size: Are There Any Systematic Empirical Relationships?" Unpublished manuscript, Department of Economics, George Washington University.

Becker, Gary. 1957. *The Economics of Discrimination.* Chicago: University of Chicago Press.

Beller, Andrea H. 1982. "Occupational Segregation by Sex: Determinants and Changes." *Journal of Human Resources* 17:371–92.

———. 1984. "Trends in Occupational Segregation by Sex and Race, 1960–1981." Pp. 11–26 in *Sex Segregation in the Workplace,* edited by Barbara F. Reskin. Washington, D.C.: National Academy.

Berger, Joseph, Susan J. Rosenholtz, and Morris Zelditch. 1980. "Status Organizing Processes." *Annual Review of Sociology* 6:479–508.

Bergmann, Barbara R. 1974. "Occupational Segregation, Wages, and Profits When Employers Discriminate by Race or Sex." *Eastern Economic Journal* 1:103–10.

Berlew, David E., and Douglas T. Hall. 1966. "The Socialization of Managers: Effects of Expectations on Performance." *Administrative Science Quarterly* 11:207–23.

Bielby, William T., and James N. Baron. 1983. "Organizations, Technology, and Worker Attachment to the Firm." *Research in Social Stratification and Mobility* 2:77–113.

———. 1984. "A Woman's Place Is with Other Women: Sex Segregation within Organizations." Pp. 27–55 in *Sex Segregation in the Workplace,* edited by Barbara F. Reskin. Washington, D.C.: National Academy.

Blau, Francine D. 1977. *Equal Pay in the Office.* Lexington, Mass.: Heath.

———. 1984. "Discrimination against Women: Theory and Evidence." Pp. 53–89 in *Labor Economics: Modern Views,* edited by William Darity, Jr. Boston: Kluwer-Nijhoff.

Blau, Francine D., and Wallace E. Hendricks. 1979. "Occupational Segregation by Sex: Trends and Prospects." *Journal of Human Resources* 14:197–210.

Blau, Francine D., and Lawrence M. Kahn. 1981. "Race and Sex Differences in Quits by Young Workers." *Industrial and Labor Relations Review* 34:563–77.

Blauner, Robert. 1964. *Alienation and Freedom.* Chicago: University of Chicago Press.

Bridges, William P. 1982. "The Sexual Segregation of Occupations: Theories of Labor Stratification in Industry." *American Journal of Sociology* 88:270–95.

Cabral, Robert, Marianne A. Ferber, and Carole A. Greene. 1981. "Men and Women in Fiduciary Institutions: A Study of Sex Differences in Career Development." *Review of Economics and Statistics* 63:573–80.

Cain, Pamela S., and Donald J. Treiman. 1981. "The Dictionary of Occupational Titles as a Source of Occupational Data." *American Sociological Review* 46:253–78.

Collins, Randall. 1979. *The Credential Society.* New York: Academic Press.

Darley, J. M., and R. H. Fazio. 1980. "Expectancy Confirmation Sequences." *American Psychologist* 35:867–81.

Deaux, Kay. 1985. "Sex and Gender." *Annual Review of Psychology* 36:49–81.

Deaux, Kay, and J. C. Ullman. 1983. *Women of Steel: Female Blue Collar Workers in the Basic Steel Industry.* New York: Praeger.

Duncan, Otis D., and Beverly Duncan. 1955. "A Methodological Analysis of Segregation Indices." *American Sociological Review* 20:200–217.

Edwards, Richard C. 1979. *Contested Terrain.* New York: Basic.

England, Paula. 1981. "Assessing Trends in Occupational Sex Segregation, 1900–1976." Pp. 273–95 in *Sociological Perspectives on Labor Markets,* edited by Ivar Berg. New York: Academic Press.

———. 1982. "The Failure of Human Capital Theory to Explain Occupational Sex Segregation." *Journal of Human Resources* 17:358–70.

Freeman, Richard B., and James L. Medoff. 1984. *What Do Unions Do?* New York: Basic.

Grimm, James W., and Robert N. Stern. 1974. "Sex Roles and Internal Labor Market Structures: The 'Female' Semi-Professions." *Social Problems* 21:690–705.

Haber, Sheldon E., Enrique J. Lamas, and Gordon Green. 1983. "A New Method for Estimating Job Separations by Sex." *Monthly Labor Review* 106 (June): 20–27.

Hackman, J. Richard, and Greg R. Oldham. 1980. *Work Redesign.* Reading, Mass.: Addison-Wesley.

Halaby, Charles N. 1979. "Job-specific Sex Differences in Organizational Reward Attainment: Wage Discrimination vs. Rank Segregation." *Social Forces* 58:108–27.

Hamilton, David L., ed. 1981. *Cognitive Processes in Stereotyping and Intergroup Behavior.* Hillsdale, N.J.: Erlbaum.

Hanushek, Eric A., and John E. Jackson. 1977. *Statistical Methods for Social Scientists.* New York: Academic Press.

Judge, George F., William E. Griffiths, R. Carter Hill, and Tsoung-Chao Lee. 1980. *The Theory and Practice of Econometrics.* New York: Wiley.

Kanter, Rosabeth M. 1977. *Men and Women of the Corporation.* New York: Basic.

Maccoby, Eleanor G., and Carol N. Jacklin. 1974. *The Psychology of Sex Differences.* Stanford, Calif.: Stanford University Press.

Malkiel, Burton G., and Judith A. Malkiel. 1973. "Male-Female Wage Differentials in Professional Employment." *American Economic Review* 63:693–704.

Marini, Margaret Mooney, and Mary C. Brinton. 1984. "Sex Stereotyping in Occupational Socialization." Pp. 192–232 in *Sex Segregation in the Workplace,* edited by Barbara F. Reskin. Washington, D.C.: National Academy.

Mennerick, Lewis A. 1975. "Organizational Structuring of Sex Roles in a Nonstereotyped Industry." *Administrative Science Quarterly* 20:570–86.

Milgrom, Paul, and Sharon Oster. 1984. "Job Discrimination, Market Forces, and the Invisibility Hypothesis." Unpublished manuscript, Yale University, School of Organization and Management.

Miller, Ann, Donald J. Treiman, Pamela S. Cain, and Patricia A. Roos. 1980. *Work, Jobs, and Occupations: A Critical Review of the Dictionary of Occupational Titles.* Washington, D.C.: National Academy.

Oi, Walter Y. 1983. "Heterogeneous Firms and the Organization of Production." *Economic Inquiry* 21:147–71.

Osterman, Paul. 1982. "Affirmative Action and Opportunity: A Study of Female Quit Rates." *Review of Economics and Statistics* 64:604–12.

Pettigrew, Thomas F. 1975. "The Racial Integration of Schools." Pp. 224–39 in *Racial Discrimination in the United States,* edited by Thomas F. Pettigrew. New York: Harper & Row.

Pfeffer, Jeffrey, and Yinon Cohen. 1984. "Determinants of Internal Labor Market Arrangements in Organizations." *Administrative Science Quarterly* 29:550–72.

Phelps, E. S. 1972. "The Statistical Theory of Racism and Sexism." *American Economic Review* 62:659–61.

Polachek, S. 1979. "Occupational Segregation among Women: Theory, Evidence, and a Prognosis." Pp. 137–57 in *Women in the Labor Market,* edited by Cynthia B. Lloyd, Emily S. Andrews, and Curtis L. Gilroy. New York: Columbia University Press.

Reiss, Albert J., Jr. 1961. *Occupations and Social Status.* New York: Free Press.

Roethlisberger, F. J., and W. J. Dickson. 1939. *Management and the Worker.* Cambridge, Mass.: Harvard University Press.

Roos, Patricia A., and Barbara F. Reskin. 1984. "Institutional Factors Contributing to Sex Segregation in the

Workplace." Pp. 235–60 in *Sex Segregation in the Workplace,* edited by Barbara F. Reskin. Washington, D.C.: National Academy.

Rosenbaum, James E. 1983. "Why Do the Rear Wheels Fall Further Behind? The Impact of Jobs and Job Statuses on Women's Earnings Gains from Affirmative Action." Paper presented at the National Research Council's Seminar on Comparable Worth Research, Hilton Head, N.C., October 7–8.

Salancik, Gerald R. 1979. "Interorganizational Dependence and Responsiveness to Affirmative Action: The Case of Women and Defense Contractors." *Academy of Management Journal* 22:375–94.

Scott, Joan Wallach. 1982. "The Mechanization of Women's Work." *Scientific American* 247 (September): 166–87.

Shorey, John. 1983. "An Analysis of Sex Differences in Quits." *Oxford Economic Papers* 35:213–27.

Simon, Herbert A. 1972. "Theories of Bounded Rationality." In *Decision and Organization,* edited by C. B. McGuire and Roy Radner. Amsterdam: Elsevier–North-Holland.

Smith, James P., and Finis Welch. 1984. "Affirmative Action and Labor Markets." *Journal of Labor Economics* 2:269–301.

Snyder, David, Mark D. Hayward, and Paula M. Hudis. 1978. "The Location of Change in the Sexual Structure of Occupations, 1950–1970: Insights from Labor Market Segmentation Theory." *American Journal of Sociology* 84:706–17.

Spenner, Kenneth I. 1980. "Occupational Characteristics and Classification Systems: New Uses of the Dictionary of Occupational Titles in Social Research." *Sociological Methods and Research* 9:239–64.

Stinchcombe, Arthur L. 1965. "Social Structure and Organizations." Pp. 142–93 in *Handbook of Organizations,* edited by James G. March. Chicago: Rand McNally.

Talbert, Joan, and Christine E. Bose. 1977. "Wage-Attainment Processes: The Retail Clerk Case." *American Journal of Sociology* 78:962–74.

Thurow, Lester C. 1975. *Generating Inequality.* New York: Basic.

Tyack, David, and Myra Strober. 1981. "Jobs and Gender: A History of the Structuring of Educational Employment by Sex." Pp. 131–52 in *Educational Policy and Management: Sex Differentials,* edited by Patricia Schmuck and W. W. Charters. New York: Academic Press.

U.S. Department of Commerce. 1983. *Detailed Occupation and Years of School Completed by Age, for the Civilian Labor Force by Sex, Race, and Spanish Origin: 1980.* Report no. PC80-S1-8. Washington, D.C.: Government Printing Office.

U.S. Department of Labor. 1972. *Handbook for Analyzing Jobs.* Washington, D.C.: Government Printing Office.

U.S. Equal Employment Opportunity Commission. 1977. *Equal Employment Opportunity Report—1975.* Washington, D.C.: Government Printing Office.

———. 1982. *Equal Employment Opportunity Report—1980.* Washington, D.C.: Government Printing Office.

Viscusi, W. Kip. 1980. "Sex Differences in Worker Quitting." *Review of Economics and Statistics* 62:388–98.

Wholey, Douglas R. 1984. "Impacts of Firm Specific Skills and Organizational Demographics on Law Firm Internal Labor Markets." Paper presented at the annual meeting of the Academy of Management, Boston.

Williamson, Oliver E. 1981. "The Economics of Organization: The Transaction Cost Approach." *American Journal of Sociology* 87:548–77.

Woodward, Joan. 1965. *Industrial Organization: Theory and Practice.* London: Oxford University Press.

~ Gender and Status Hierarchies

WILLIAM H. SEWELL, ROBERT M. HAUSER, AND WENDY C. WOLF

Sex, Schooling, and Occupational Status

Within the past few years there has been increasing research interest in processes of sexual stratification in American labor markets. It is well known that between men and women there are large and persistent differentials in earnings and that there are pervasive patterns of occupational segregation by sex. At the same time structural-equation models of occupational attainment have shown surprisingly modest differences between the sexes in occupational prestige or socioeconomic status. In several national samples, there have been minimal differences between the sexes in levels of occupational status and in the effect of schooling on occupational status; occupational status is slightly less variable among women than among men (Treiman and Terrell 1975; McClendon 1976; Featherman and Hauser 1976; Spaeth 1977). Of the several arguments advanced to explain these anomalously small differences (Fligstein and Wolf 1978; Powers and Holmberg 1978), the most appealing is that prestige or socioeconomic status metrics do not adequately reflect important aspects of sexual inequality in labor market positions (Tyree and Treas 1974, p. 294; Wolf and Fligstein 1979a, 1979b; Hauser, Featherman, and Hogan 1977, pp. 192–93; McClendon 1976; Huber 1980). There is merit in the argument, but a closer look at the labor market careers of men and women reveals marked sex differences in occupational status and in the processes by which it is obtained. Paradoxically, differences in the occupational careers of men and women are consistent with and help explain the earlier findings of similarity between the sexes in current occupational status.

This study investigates the occupational attainment process from adolescence through mid-life in a cohort of male and female Wisconsin high school graduates who have been followed from 1957 to 1975. The analysis is based on a recursive social psychological model of achievement, which is displayed schematically in figure 1. It elaborates the well-known Blau-Duncan (1967) model of occupational achievement by introducing social-psychological variables related to school experience and aspirations, as well as a more extensive set of social background characteristics. Earlier versions of this model have been used in analyses of educational aspiration and attainment, of occupational status, and of earnings early in the career of the Wisconsin cohort (Sewell and Hauser 1980). To date, comparisons between the sexes have been reported only in summary form (Sewell 1971; Hauser, Sewell, and Alwin 1976).

Sources of Data

Previous analyses of occupational achievement in the Wisconsin sample focused on jobs held in 1964, seven years after high school graduation. Here, we analyze new data about occupational achievement through 1975, obtained from telephone interviews with the respondents. This was a particularly opportune time to study the achievements of the members of our sample, for schooling was virtually completed in the cohort, and many women who had borne children had returned to the work force.

FIGURE 1
Schematic diagram of a social psychological model of occupational achievement

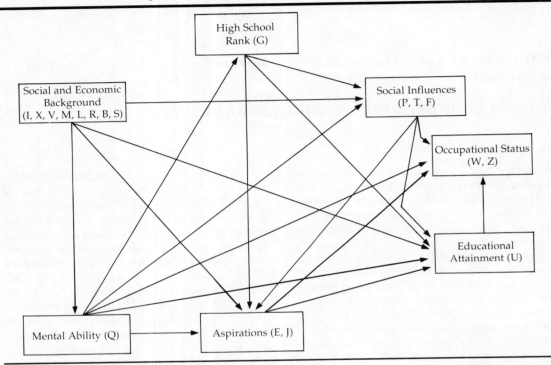

The Wisconsin longitudinal data come from several sources: (1) A survey of background, school experiences, and aspirations among all high school seniors in Wisconsin public, private, and parochial schools was conducted in 1957. From this survey a random sample consisting of 4,994 men and 5,323 women was drawn. (2) Information was taken from school and public records, with proper precautions to protect the privacy of individual information, on such matters as parental income, students' measured intelligence, and high school rank. (3) In 1964 the sample was followed up using questionnaires directed to parents. (4) In 1975 a second follow-up study was conducted in which approximately 90% of the original sample members were located and interviewed (Clarridge, Sheehy, and Hauser 1977).

Table 1 describes the source and coding of each of the variables in the model; the place of each

variable in the model is indicated by a symbol in figure 1. Most of this material is self-explanatory, but a few supplementary comments may be useful. In addition to parental education, occupation, and income, the set of social background characteristics includes maternal employment (L), rural origin (R), intact family (B), and number of siblings (S). It has often been suggested that maternal employment affects the socioeconomic life chances of children—especially of daughters—because it raises the family standard of living, because it competes with other familial activities, or because it provides a favorable role model (Hoffman and Nye 1974, chap. 6). The socioeconomic effects of rural upbringing, marital disruption, and large sibships are well known (Duncan, Featherman, and Duncan 1972; Featherman and Hauser 1978; Sewell 1964; Sewell and Orenstein 1965; Sewell, Haller, and Ohlendorf 1970; Yang

TABLE 1

Variables in Models of the Stratification Process

Symbol	Variable Name	Source*	Description
I.....	Parental income	Wisconsin tax records (1975 survey)	Average for all available years, 1957–60; scaled in $100 and truncated at $25,000
X.....	Occupational status of father (or other head of household)	1975 survey (Wis. tax records)	In 1957; Duncan SEI value of detailed census occupation
V.....	Education of father (or other head of household)	1975 survey (1957 survey)	Years of school completed
M....	Education of mother	1975 survey (1957 survey)	Years of school completed
L.....	Mother's employment	1975 survey	Scored 1 if R's† mother was employed in 1957; scored 0 otherwise
R....	Rural origin	1957 survey and school records	Scored 1 if R's father was a farmer or R's high school was in a place of fewer than 2,500 persons; scored 0 otherwise
B......	Intact family	1975 survey	Scored 1 if R lived with both parents most of the time up to high school graduation; scored 0 otherwise
S......	Number of siblings	1975 survey	Brothers and sisters (including step- and adoptive)
Q......	Mental ability	Wisconsin testing service	IQ based on Henman-Nelson test, given in grade 11
G.....	High school grades	School records	Based on average of grades in high school, ranked and normalized
P......	Parental encouragement	1957 survey	Scored 1 if R reported parental encouragement to attend college; scored 0 otherwise
T......	Teachers' encouragement	1957 survey	Scored 1 if R reported teachers' encouragement to attend college; scored 0 otherwise
F......	Friends' college plans	1957 survey	Scored 1 if R reported most friends were planning to attend college; scored 0 otherwise
E......	College plans	1957 survey	Scored 1 if R planned to attend a college or university; scored 0 otherwise
J......	Occupational status aspiration	1957 survey	Duncan SEI value of occupation R hoped eventually to enter
U.....	Educational attainment	1975 survey	Years of regular (not vocational or technical) schooling completed, e.g., 12 years for high school graduates, 16 years for college graduates
W.....	Occupational status of first job	1975 survey	Duncan SEI value of detailed census occupation, first full-time civilian job held after completing the highest grade of regular schooling
Z......	Occupational status of current (or last) job	1975 survey	Duncan SEI value of detailed census occupation held at survey date or of last occupation held within the preceding five years

* If data were missing, they were obtained from the secondary source given in parentheses.
† R = respondent.

1976). Before 1975, measures of sibship size and of intact family were not available in the Wisconsin data.

Following Featherman and Hauser (1978, pp. 23–24), the 1975 survey measured the status of the first full-time civilian job (*W*) held by the respondent after the completion of formal schooling, as well as the status of the current (or last) job (*Z*). Previously, first jobs had been excluded in comparisons of the occupational attainments of men and women. The importance of first job in explaining men's subsequent occupational attainment has been amply demonstrated (Blau and Duncan 1967; Duncan et al. 1972; Ornstein 1976; Featherman and Hauser 1978, chap. 5). Specifically, the inclusion of first job in our models allows us to ascertain (1) whether the ways in which education affects current occupational status are different for men and women (by decomposing the total effect of education on current status) and (2) whether the effect of status of first job on status of current job differs for men and women. Also, we are able to ascertain whether the effects of socioeconomic background and the social-psychological variables (mainly involving the school experience) diminish over time, as evidenced by their effects on status of first job and status of current job.

Sample Selection, Attrition, and Missing Data

Male and female respondents in the 1975 survey were included in this analysis if they were employed in civilian jobs in 1975 (or in the five years preceding the 1975 survey) and if information was available on all of the relevant variables. Sample attrition and selection are summarized in table 2. The final sample consisted of 3,411 men and 2,620 women. We believe that the sample restrictions and data losses do not substantially affect the generality of our findings about the achievement processes among men or women or about differences between the sexes in those processes.

Fligstein and Wolf (1978) have shown that the restriction of the National Longitudinal Survey (Parnes) sample to employed women does not

bias parameters of structural models of occupational achievement; the alternative hypothesis is that the differential selection of women into or out of the labor force does affect structural parameters of the process (Heckman 1974). While the analyses reported here are based on the restricted samples of men and women, we have carried out parallel analyses with more inclusive samples and have obtained similar results. Neither among men nor among women do there appear large or systematic differences between the analysis samples and the full samples. To take an extreme example, we carried out two regression analyses of the status of first jobs: one for women in the final sample and a second for women with complete data who ever held full-time civilian jobs after leaving school. The second analysis differs from the first by including almost 1,000 women who held full-time civilian jobs after leaving school but who were not employed between 1970 and 1975. There was a reassuring similarity between the parameter estimates in the two samples. Since we chose a contrast in sample definition that was extreme in its potential impact on our findings, we believe that our analyses are quite robust. We also estimated the equations in our model from pairwise present sample moments, and again the results did not vary in any important respect from those reported here.

Our findings in the Wisconsin cohort reflect the experiences of a broad segment of American youth, that of native, white high school graduates. Other important segments of the population are not well represented, especially high school dropouts and nonwhites. For example, Sewell and Hauser concluded that "in the late 1950s, school retention to grade 12 was markedly higher in Wisconsin than in the total United States and that from 75% to 80% of the Wisconsin men of high school age at about that time might have appeared in a sample of high school graduates" (1975, p. 215). Coverage of women is probably better than that of men in the Wisconsin sample. For example, in the 1960 census 74.7% of 20-year-old Wisconsin men and 79.5% of 20-year-old Wisconsin women had completed high school or were then enrolled in grade 12 (U.S. Bureau of the Census 1963, pt. 1, tables 168, 172, pt. 51, tables 101, 102). Furthermore, in 1960 only 2.4% of Wiscon-

TABLE 2

Sources of Nonresponse and Sample Selection in the Wisconsin Cohort

	Men (%) (N = 4,994)		Women (%) (N = 5,323)	
1. Nonrespondents in 1975.....................	13.3		9.7	
a) Deceased................................		2.4		1.1
b) Not found...............................		3.0		2.6
c) No telephone contact (disabled or institutionalized, no or unpublished phone, not in U.S.).		3.4		3.0
d) Refused.................................		4.5		3.0
2. Respondents in 1975........................	86.7		90.3	
a) Ineligible (in military or no civilian job in past 5 years)................................		0.8		25.0
b) Missing data............................		17.7		16.1
c) Analysis subsample......................		68.2		49.2
Total.............................	100.0	100.0	100.0	100.0

sin's population was nonwhite, and fewer than 1% of 1975 respondents were of African, Asian, or Native American descent.

In spite of these limitations of the sample, we have also obtained substantial agreement between our structural-equation models and those based on national samples of men for which comparable measurements were available (Sewell and Hauser 1975, chap. 3). Together with the fact that other researchers using our models have generally replicated our findings (Sewell and Hauser 1980), this agreement strengthens our confidence in findings based on the Wisconsin sample.

Achievements of Men and Women

The means and standard deviations of the social and psychological variables are reported in table 3. Sex differences in social background and academic performance in the Wisconsin sample have been discussed elsewhere (Sewell 1971; Hauser, Sewell, and Alwin 1976; Sewell, Hauser, and Wolf, in press). In spite of deficits of parental encouragement (P) and educational aspiration (E), women aspired to occupations (J) which were slightly higher in status than those to which men aspired. At the same time, the range of occupations to which women aspired was highly restricted in status relative to the range of men's occupational aspirations.

Up to a point, sex differences in educational attainment and occupational status parallel those in educational and occupational aspirations. First, the mean educational attainment (U) of men is almost a year greater than that of women, and the variance in educational attainment is restricted among women. This finding is contrary to past research comparing the educational achievements of employed men and women (or of husbands and wives), which has found similar distributions of schooling among men and women; the advantage, if any, has belonged to women (Treiman and Terrell 1975; McClendon 1976; Featherman and Hauser 1976). This discrepancy may be due to the fact that women were historically more likely than men to graduate from high school but less likely than men to attend or complete college (Folger and Nam 1967; Sewell and Shah 1967, 1968). Second, on the average the statuses of women's first jobs (W) are six points higher on the Duncan scale than those of men. This differential is larger than that separating the occupational aspirations of men and women. Also, just as in the case of occupational aspirations, the variability in the statuses of first jobs held by women is restricted relative to that among men.

Beyond this point the parallel between sex differences in aspirations and in achievements no longer holds. Despite the initial advantage of women in occupational status, by mid-life the average occupational standing of men is about five points higher on the Duncan scale than that of

TABLE 3

Means and Standard Deviations of Social and Psychological Variables by Sex in the Analysis Subsample

| | MEN (N = 3,411) | | WOMEN (N = 2,620) | |
VARIABLE	Mean	SD	Mean	SD
I.........	65.11	45.73	60.83	39.90
X.........	35.11	23.06	33.90	22.27
V.........	9.85	3.47	9.59	3.25
M.........	10.62	2.82	10.33	2.78
L.........	.346	.476	.397	.489
R.........	.369	.483	.369	.483
B.........	.916	.277	.913	.283
S.........	3.132	2.552	3.305	2.658
Q.........	101.64	14.74	101.48	13.94
G.........	97.75	13.92	104.64	13.76
P.........	.600	.400	.470	.499
T.........	.466	.499	.432	.495
F.........	.366	.482	.377	.485
E.........	.400	.490	.283	.451
J.........	48.72	27.51	50.34	16.34
U.........	13.81	2.44	12.99	1.77
W.........	40.97	26.74	47.07	18.34
Z.........	49.98	23.69	44.74	20.00

NOTE.—Variables are: I = parents' income, X = father's occupational status, V = father's education, M = mother's education, L = mother's employment, R = rural origin, B = intact family, S = number of siblings, Q = mental ability, G = high school grades, P = parental encouragement, T = teachers' encouragement, F = friends' college plans, E = college plans, J = occupational status aspiration, U = educational attainment, W = status of first occupation, Z = status of current occupation.

women. Indeed, not only is the initial sex difference reversed, as men gain about nine points in occupational standing, but also women lose an average of about two points in occupational standing between their first and current or last jobs.

These findings about occupational status square with other studies of life-cycle variation in occupational attainment among men and women. In a study of Rhode Island women (Wolf 1975) and in a national survey of middle-aged women (Rosenfeld 1976), women's average occupational standing was essentially constant over the life cycle. Obversely, several national surveys show that among men mean occupational status grows markedly over the course of working life (Ornstein and Rossi 1970; Sørensen 1975; Duncan et al. 1972; Featherman and Hauser 1978). At the same time, our findings seem inconsistent with national cross-section surveys in which the mean occupational standing of men and of women was virtually the same (Featherman and Hauser 1976; McClendon 1976; Treiman and Terrell 1975). The latter studies, however, were based on samples with broad age ranges over which the relationship between the mean occupational attainments of men and those of women might be expected to change. If in the life cycle the occupational standing of women is at first higher and then lower than that of men, a sex differential in occupational standing need not appear in a sample that is heterogeneous with respect to age.

As in the case of occupational aspirations and first jobs, the variability of occupational status is much less in current jobs among women than among men. Still, this differential appears to have declined as the cohort aged. We believe that sex differentials in the variability of occupational standing reflect restrictions in the occupational opportunities open to women. In comparative studies of occupational standing, sociologists are accustomed to summarizing differentials between populations by using a measure of central tendency like the mean (Duncan 1968; Hauser and Featherman 1974), but the differential occupational opportunities of men and of women cannot be so conveniently summarized. ...

The Process of Achievement

We have compared the coefficients for men and women in each equation [implied by figure 1]. The sex differences mentioned in the following discussion are statistically significant beyond the .05 probability level in a two-tailed *t*-test.[1]

The present analysis focuses on educational and occupational achievement, and we shall only summarize the equations for variables prior to educational attainment.[2] While the process of educational and occupational aspiration is broadly similar among men and women, there are also marked differences between the sexes. Where these differences occur, it is because men are more sensitive than women to the variables that influence aspiration in both sexes. Men's occupational aspirations are more influenced than women's by paternal occupation. Men's educational and occupational aspirations are also more influenced by ability, by high school grades, and by the support and example of significant others. We believe that all of these differentials reflect the limits imposed by traditional sex role definitions in the late 1950s.

Among men and women, educational attainment (U) is affected directly by parental income (I), father's education (V), ability (Q), grades (G), friends' plans (F), and aspirations (E and J). In addition, women's schooling is affected directly by mother's education (M), and men's schooling is affected directly by the encouragement of parents (P) and teachers (T). None of these effects (of M, P, or T) is significantly different for men and women, but there are other significant sex interactions. The direct effect of father's education (V) on son's education is three times larger than its effect on daughter's education; there is an opposite but nonsignificant interaction between sex and the influence of mother's education (M). The direct effect of ability (Q) on schooling is more than twice as large among men as among women, and the direct effect of grades (G) is nearly four times larger among men than women. Further, the direct influence of high-aspiring friends (F) on educational attainment is nearly three times larger among men than among women. At the same time, the effect of educational aspiration (E) on educational attainment is about 40% larger among women than among men. Thus, after controlling aspirations, the social and psychological variables responsible for variation in aspiration continue to have more influence on the educational attainments of men than women. Once educational aspirations have been formed among women, however, their effect on attainment is larger than among men. Neither maternal employment (L), rural origin (R), intact family (B), nor sibship size (S) affects educational attainment (U) directly among men or women; yet there is an interesting sex interaction in the effect of maternal employment (L). The effect of maternal employment is small and positive among men and small and negative among women; the difference between the two coefficients is statistically significant. While the evidence is insufficient to show that maternal employment helps men's and hurts women's educational attainment, it does show that maternal employment is less helpful to women than to men. It is sometimes suggested that the role model of the working mother leads daughters to higher aspirations and achievements. Our evidence does not support this interpretation. If maternal employment has any influence, it is probably economic and directed more to improving the life chances of sons than of daughters.

Of course, the final equation in educational attainment does not fully elucidate the process of educational attainment or sex differences in that process. Tables 4 and 5 give reduced-form equations for men and women (Alwin and Hauser 1975). Each of the social background variables in our model except maternal employment (L) and intact family (B) affects significantly the schooling of men or women or both (see lines 1 of tables 4 and 5). Rural origins (R) improve the educational chances of women but not of men. Each later social psychological variable affects significantly the educational attainment of men and of women; these effects are partly mediated through later variables. Hauser et al. (1976) have elaborated this aspect of the model, so we focus our discussion on sex interactions in the reduced-form coefficients. We have already noted the larger effects among men of father's education (V) and maternal employment (L) in the final schooling equation (line 5); these interactions ap-

TABLE 4

Coefficients of Reduced-Form Equations in the Model of Occupational Attainment: Men (N = 3,411)

a) Regression Coefficient (SE)

DEPENDENT VARIABLE	I[a]	X	V	M	L	R	B	S	Q	G	P	T	F	E	J	U	W	Constant
1) U	.730 (.099)	.0142 (.0021)	.1103 (.0142)	.0529 (.0160)	.138 (.082)	−.149 (.087)	.090 (.140)	−.067 (.016)										11.32
2) U	.550 (.090)	.0093 (.0020)	.0858 (.0130)	.0293 (.0146)	.077 (.075)	−.101 (.079)	.026 (.128)	−.043 (.014)	.0651 (.0025)									5.48
3) U	.553 (.083)	.0098 (.0018)	.0828 (.0120)	.0301 (.0135)	.148 (.070)	−.220 (.073)	−.056 (.118)	−.028 (.013)	.0262 (.0028)	.0696 (.0029)								2.68
4) U	.380 (.079)	.0048 (.0017)	.0675 (.0114)	.0124 (.0127)	.116 (.066)	−.118 (.070)	−.054 (.111)	−.004 (.013)	.0182 (.0028)	.0523 (.0029)	.671 (.077)	.366 (.072)	1.016 (.074)					4.76
5) U	.266 (.075)	.0024 (.0016)	.0602 (.0107)	.0086 (.0120)	.103 (.062)	−.086 (.066)	−.067 (.105)	.003 (.012)	.0137 (.0027)	.0399 (.0028)	.235 (.075)	.150 (.069)	.627 (.072)	1.535 (.098)	.0041 (.0017)			6.37
6) W	5.386 (1.081)	.200 (.023)	.869 (.156)	.411 (.175)	2.505 (.902)	−5.369 (.952)	.617 (1.534)	−.870 (.172)										20.8
7) W	3.731 (1.019)	.154 (.022)	.644 (.147)	.194 (.164)	1.945 (.848)	−4.932 (.895)	.026 (1.441)	−.646 (.162)	.599 (.028)									−33.0
8) W	3.753 (.974)	.159 (.021)	.618 (.140)	.200 (.157)	2.557 (.812)	−5.953 (.858)	−.673 (1.379)	−.515 (.155)	.265 (.033)	.598 (.034)								−57.1
9) W	2.187 (.942)	.110 (.020)	.478 (.135)	.028 (.151)	2.202 (.781)	−5.078 (.828)	−.611 (1.325)	−.285 (.150)	.185 (.032)	.421 (.034)	6.88 (.91)	4.83 (.86)	8.46 (.88)					−36.2
10) W	1.481 (.919)	.086 (.020)	.428 (.132)	−.003 (.147)	1.346 (.760)	−4.001 (.814)	−.358 (1.289)	−.224 (.146)	.133 (.031)	.313 (.034)	3.41 (.93)	3.20 (.89)	5.34 (.88)	5.08 (1.21)	.184 (.021)			−26.1
11) W	−.440 (.745)	.069 (.016)	−.006 (.107)	−.065 (.119)	.126 (.615)	−3.382 (.659)	.204 (1.044)	−.248 (.118)	.035 (.025)	.026 (.029)	1.71 (.75)	2.11 (.68)	.81 (.72)	−5.99 (1.01)	.154 (.017)	7.215 (.171)		−72.0
12) Z	4.663 (.968)	.180 (.021)	.582 (.140)	.323 (.156)	1.692 (.808)	−6.363 (.853)	.204 (1.373)	−.318 (.154)										34.0
13) Z	3.222 (.915)	.140 (.020)	.386 (.132)	.135 (.148)	1.204 (.762)	−5.983 (.804)	.312 (1.295)	−.123 (.146)	.521 (.025)									−12.8
14) Z	3.236 (.895)	.143 (.020)	.370 (.129)	.014 (.145)	1.596 (.746)	−6.637 (.788)	−.759 (1.267)	−.039 (.143)	.307 (.030)	.383 (.031)								−28.2
15) Z	2.116 (.895)	.108 (.019)	.269 (.126)	.014 (.141)	1.308 (.746)	−6.002 (.773)	−.709 (1.237)	.135 (.140)	.249 (.030)	.256 (.032)	5.59 (.85)	3.33 (.80)	5.66 (.82)					−13.3
16) Z	1.734 (.879)	.089 (.019)	.240 (.124)	−.008 (.139)	1.228 (.729)	−4.934 (.766)	−.387 (1.214)	.176 (.138)	.207 (.029)	.181 (.032)	3.28 (.87)	2.28 (.80)	3.58 (.83)	.31 (1.14)	.187 (.020)			−7.7
17) Z	.732 (.820)	.080 (.018)	.013 (.118)	.040 (.131)	.842 (.677)	−4.611 (.725)	−.135 (1.148)	.164 (.130)	.156 (.028)	.031 (.031)	2.39 (.87)	1.71 (.75)	1.22 (.80)	−5.47 (1.11)	.171 (.019)	3.764 (.188)		−31.7
18) Z	.884 (.778)	.056 (.017)	.015 (.112)	−.017 (.125)	.376 (.643)	−3.439 (.691)	−.178 (1.090)	.250 (.124)	.144 (.026)	.022 (.030)	1.80 (.78)	.98 (.72)	.93 (.76)	−3.39 (1.06)	.118 (.018)	1.264 (.220)	.347 (.018)	−6.7

b) Path Coefficient

DEPENDENT VARIABLE	I[a]	X	V	M	L	R	B	S	Q	G	P	T	F	E	J	U	W	R^2
1) U	.137*	.134*	.157*	.061*	.027	−.029	.010	−.070*										.169
2) U	.103*	.087*	.122*	.034*	.015	−.019	.003	−.045*	.393*									.308
3) U	.103*	.092*	.118*	.035*	.029*	−.044*	−.006	−.029*	.158*	.396*								.410
4) U	.071*	.045*	.096*	.014	.023	−.023	−.006	−.004	.110*	.298*	.135*	.075*	.200*					.477
5) U	.050*	.023	.086*	.043*	.020	−.017	−.008	−.003	.083*	.227*	.047*	.031*	.124*	.308*	.046*			.535
6) W	.092*	.172*	.113*	.021	.045*	−.097*	.006	−.083*										.168
7) W	.064*	.133*	.084*	.003	.035*	−.089*	.000	−.062*	.330*									.266
8) W	.064*	.137*	.080*	−.000	.045*	−.107*	−.007	−.049*	.146*	.311*								.329
9) W	.037*	.095*	.062*	−.007	.039*	−.092*	−.006	−.027	.102*	.219*	.126*	.090*	.152*					.381
10) W	.025	.074*	.056*	−.000	.024*	−.072*	−.004	−.021	.074*	.163*	.062*	.060*	.096*	.093*	.189*			.415
11) W	−.008	.059*	−.001	−.007	.002	−.061*	.001	−.024*	.019	.013	.031*	.039*	.015	−.110*	.159*	.659*		.617
12) Z	.090*	.137*	.085*	.038*	.034*	−.122*	.002	−.034*										.150
13) Z	.062*	.139*	.057*	.016	.032*	−.130*	−.004	−.013	.324*									.245
14) Z	.062*	.105*	.054*	.017	.026	−.135*	−.009	−.004	.191*	.225*								.278
15) Z	.041*	.087*	.039*	−.001	.025	−.122*	−.008	.015	.155*	.150*	.116*	.070*	.115*					.312
16) Z	.033*	.078*	.035	−.001	.017	−.101*	−.005	.019	.129*	.106*	.068*	.048*	.073*	.006	.217*			.339
17) Z	.014	.056	.002	−.005	.008	−.094*	−.002	.018	.097*	.018	.050*	.036*	.025	−.113*	.199*	.388*		.409
18) Z	.017	.055*	.002	−.002	.002	−.070*	−.002	.027*	.090*	.013	.037*	.021	.019	−.070*	.137*	.130*	.391*	.468

NOTE.—Variables are: I = parents' income, X = father's occupational status, V = father's education, M = mother's education, L = mother's employment, R = rural origin, B = intact family, S = number of siblings, Q = mental ability, G = high school grades, P = parental encouragement, T = teachers' encouragement, F = friends' college plans, E = college plans, J = status of first occupation, U = educational aspiration, W = status of current occupation, Z = status of current occupation.

Regression coefficients and their standard errors in this column have been multiplied by 100 for ease of presentation.

* Significant at .05 level.

TABLE 5
Coefficients of Reduced-Form Equations in the Model of Occupational Attainment: Women (N = 2,620)

a) Regression Coefficient (SE)

Dependent Variable	I[a]	X	V	M	L	R	B	S	Q	G	P	T	F	E	J	U	W	Constant
1) U	.585 (.094)	.0086 (.0018)	.0701 (.0122)	.1084 (.0131)	-.115 (.066)	.172 (.072)	-.090 (.115)	-.063 (.013)										10.82
2) U	.544 (.094)	.0074 (.0018)	.0566 (.0118)	.0839 (.0127)	-.109 (.063)	.149 (.070)	-.102 (.110)	-.050 (.012)	.0326 (.0023)									7.94
3) U	.603 (.090)	.0071 (.0017)	.0545 (.0118)	.0743 (.0124)	-.089 (.062)	.072 (.070)	-.110 (.108)	-.038 (.012)	.0124 (.0028)	.0332 (.0028)								6.64
4) U	.478 (.088)	.0035 (.0017)	.0351 (.0114)	.0430 (.0118)	-.109 (.058)	.038 (.068)	-.161 (.108)	-.015 (.012)	.0065 (.0026)	.0217 (.0028)	.702 (.069)	.367 (.067)	.540 (.068)					8.38
5) U	.230 (.083)	.0011 (.0016)	.0198 (.0108)	.0236 (.0098)	-.077 (.048)	.013 (.065)	-.051 (.101)	-.005 (.009)	.0062 (.0022)	.0101 (.0023)	.109 (.059)	.082 (.056)	.228 (.057)	2.180 (.073)	.0052 (.0019)			9.74
6) W	4.034 (1.021)	.030 (.020)	.539 (.133)	.717 (.143)	-1.101 (.718)	.325 (.789)	3.396 (1.250)	-.661 (.138)										30.4
7) W	3.626 (.990)	.018 (.019)	.405 (.129)	.472 (.140)	-1.045 (.696)	.092 (.765)	3.279 (1.212)	-.525 (.134)	.325 (.025)									1.6
8) W	4.267 (.966)	.015 (.019)	.382 (.126)	.367 (.137)	-.818 (.678)	-.750 (.749)	2.624 (1.182)	-.392 (.131)	.104 (.031)	.364 (.031)								-12.6
9) W	4.024 (.968)	.008 (.018)	.343 (.126)	.309 (.138)	-.886 (.678)	-.891 (.754)	2.651 (1.181)	-.348 (.131)	.092 (.031)	.338 (.032)	1.57 (.80)	1.10 (.78)	.58 (.79)					-8.9
10) W	2.364 (.919)	.001 (.018)	.307 (.119)	.190 (.130)	-.800 (.640)	-.687 (.712)	2.646 (1.116)	-.266 (.124)	.077 (.029)	.221 (.031)	-1.34 (.79)	-.57 (.75)	-1.09 (.76)	4.37 (.98)	.334 (.025)			-7.9
11) W	1.492 (.833)	-.003 (.017)	.232 (.114)	.101 (.125)	-.509 (.614)	-.736 (.683)	2.840 (1.070)	-.248 (.119)	.054 (.028)	.183 (.030)	-1.75 (.76)	-.88 (.72)	-1.95 (.73)	-3.88 (1.08)	.314 (.024)	3.783 (.250)		-44.8
12) Z	3.994 (1.118)	.047 (.021)	.453 (.145)	.735 (.157)	-.682 (.787)	-1.031 (.864)	2.718 (1.370)	-.610 (.151)										29.0
13) Z	3.494 (1.076)	.031 (.021)	.289 (.140)	.435 (.152)	-.614 (.756)	-1.316 (.831)	2.576 (1.317)	-.443 (.145)	.398 (.027)									-6.2
14) Z	4.019 (1.062)	.029 (.020)	.270 (.138)	.349 (.150)	-.428 (.746)	-2.006 (.823)	2.038 (1.300)	-.335 (.144)	.217 (.034)	.298 (.034)								-17.9
15) Z	3.441 (1.056)	.011 (.020)	.174 (.138)	.193 (.151)	-.516 (.740)	-2.150 (.823)	2.120 (1.288)	-.222 (.143)	.189 (.034)	.251 (.035)	4.05 (.87)	.80 (.85)	2.54 (.86)					-10.3
16) Z	2.362 (1.045)	.004 (.020)	.134 (.136)	.113 (.148)	-.428 (.728)	-2.106 (.810)	2.264 (1.269)	-.173 (.141)	.182 (.033)	.184 (.035)	1.91 (.90)	-.34 (.85)	1.35 (.86)	5.30 (1.11)	.145 (.028)			-7.7
17) Z	1.499 (1.015)	.000 (.019)	.060 (.132)	.025 (.144)	-.140 (.706)	-2.154 (.785)	2.456 (1.229)	-.155 (.137)	.159 (.032)	.147 (.034)	1.50 (.87)	-.65 (.82)	.50 (.84)	-2.87 (1.25)	.126 (.027)	3.747 (.287)		-44.2
18) Z	1.113 (.990)	.000 (.019)	.000 (.128)	-.001 (.140)	-.008 (.688)	-1.964 (.765)	1.723 (1.200)	-.091 (.134)	.146 (.031)	.099 (.034)	1.95 (.85)	.42 (.80)	1.00 (.82)	-1.87 (1.22)	.045 (.027)	2.771 (.292)	.258 (.022)	-32.6

b) Path Coefficient

Dependent Variable	I[a]	X	V	M	L	R	B	S	Q	G	P	T	F	E	J	U	W	R²
1) U	.132*	.108*	.129*	.170*	-.02	.047*	-.014	-.095*										.177
2) U	.122*	.092*	.104*	.132*	-.030	.040*	-.016	-.074*	.256*									.237
3) U	.136*	.089*	.100*	.117*	-.025	.020	-.026	-.056*	.097*	.258*								.276
4) U	.108*	.044*	.064*	.067*	-.030	.004	-.023	-.022	.051*	.169*	.198*	.102*	.148*					.360
5) U	.052*	.014	.036*	.037*	-.021	.002	-.008	-.007	.048*	.078*	.031	.023	.062*	.554*	.048*			.562
6) W	.079*	.037	.096*	.109*	-.029	.009	.052*	-.096*										.084
7) W	.093*	.022	.072*	.072*	-.028	.002	.051*	-.076*	.247*									.140
8) W	.088*	.018	.068*	.056*	-.022	-.020	.040*	-.057*	.079*	.273*								.184
9) W	.088*	.010	.061*	.047*	-.024	.002	.041*	-.050*	.070*	.254*	.043	.030	.015					.187
10) W	.051*	.001	.054*	.029	-.021	-.023	.041*	-.039*	.058*	.166*	-.037	-.015	-.029	.107*	.297*			.276
11) W	.032	-.004	.041*	.015	-.014	.018	.044*	-.036*	.041	.137*	-.048*	-.024	-.052*	-.095*	.280*	.366*		.335
12) Z	.080*	-.052*	.074*	.102*	-.017	.019	.038	-.081*										.076
13) Z	.080*	.035	.047*	.061*	-.015	-.025	.036	-.059*	.277*									.146
14) Z	.069*	.032	.044	.049*	-.010	-.032	.029	-.044*	.151*	.205*								.171
15) Z	.047*	.012	.028	.027	-.013	-.048*	.030	-.030	.132*	.173*	.101*	.020	.061*					.186
16) Z	.030	.004	.022	.016	-.010	-.052*	.032	-.023	.127*	.127*	.048*	-.008	.033	.119*	.118*			.213
17) Z	.047*	.000	.010	.003	-.003	-.051*	.035	-.021	.111*	.101*	.037	-.016	.012	-.065*	.103	.332*		.261
18) Z	.022	.001	.000	-.000	-.000	-.047*	.024	-.012	.101*	.068*	.049*	-.010	.024	-.042	.036	.246*	.237*	.299

NOTE.—Variables are: I = parents' income, X = father's education, V = father's occupational status, M = mother's education, L = mother's employment, R = rural origin, B = intact family, S = number of siblings, Q = mental ability, G = high school grades, P = parental encouragement, T = teachers' encouragement, F = friends' college plans, E = college plans, J = aspiration, U = educational attainment, W = status of first occupation, Z = status of current occupation.

[a] Regression coefficients and their standard errors in this column have been multiplied by 100 for ease of presentation.

* Significant at .05 level.

pear also in the reduced form (line 1). Further, the total effect of father's occupational status (X) is larger among men than women. At the same time, mother's education (M) has a larger total effect among women than among men; together with the opposite interaction of father's education (V), this suggests that a process of same-sex role modeling supplements the impact of both parents' educations on men and women. The total effect of ability (Q) on schooling is twice as large among men as among women; a 10-point difference in men's IQs leads to a 0.65-year increase in post–high school education, but the same difference in women's abilities leads only to a 0.33-year difference in schooling. Similarly, the total effect of a 10-point difference in grades (G) is twice as large among men (0.70 years) as among women (0.33 years). Last, the total effect of having high-aspiring friends (F) is also twice as great among men (1.02 years) as among women (0.54 years).

The occupational status of first job (W) is directly affected by several variables, but the most powerful effects are those of educational attainment (U) and occupational status aspirations (J) (see lines 11 in tables 4 and 5). The effects on first job of other variables in the model (background, ability, grades, significant others) are largely mediated by more proximate influences on occupational status.

Despite this general similarity in the estimates for men and women, there are marked sex interactions in the occupational status equations. In the final equation (line 11), father's occupational status (X) has a positive effect on men's first-job status, but not upon that of women. Similarly, rural origins (R) significantly reduce the status of the first job among men, but not among women. These effects parallel interactions in the final equations for occupational aspiration, but the sex differences in effects on status of first jobs persist even when occupational aspirations and educational attainment are controlled. Moreover, the effects of father's status and rural origins appear even in the initial equation for men (line 6), but these variables have no influence on initial occupational status among women. Maternal employment (L) has a small positive effect on men's initial occupational status; it leads to a 2.5-point increase in status in the initial equation (line 6)

and a 1.3-point increase in status in the final equation (line 11). No similar effect occurs among women. While the negative effects of maternal employment on women's first-job status are not statistically significant, the slopes for women are significantly less than those for men in every equation (lines 6–11). As in the determination of schooling, maternal employment is of greater benefit to sons than to daughters.

The total effect of ability (Q) on status of first occupation (W) is almost twice as large for men (0.60 points on the Duncan SEI) as for women (0.32 points; lines 7 of tables 4 and 5). This interaction is a result of the larger effect of ability on schooling among men than among women. It disappears when educational attainment is controlled, because ability has no substantial direct influence on status of first job for either sex (line 11). Similarly, in the first equation where grades (G) appear (line 8), the total effect of grades is 64% larger among men (0.60) than among women (0.36). Again, this interaction is explained by the larger effect of grades on educational attainment among men than among women; in the final equation for first-job status (line 11), the coefficient of grades becomes insignificant among men. Among women, on the other hand, there remains a significant positive direct effect of grades on initial occupational status that is half as large as the total effect of grades and that is significantly larger than the direct effect of grades among men. Thus, the total effect of high school grades on initial occupational status is larger among men than among women because high school grades are more likely to facilitate men's postsecondary schooling. Yet, when schooling is complete, high school grades substantially affect the occupational chances of women but not of men. We think this is because the skills acquired in school may be more relevant in the jobs women enter (e.g., clerical and sales work, nursing, and teaching) than in those men enter.

The total and direct effects of occupational aspirations (J) on initial occupational status (W) are about twice as large among women as men (lines 10 and 11 of tables 4 and 5); among women each unit difference in occupational aspiration results in a one-third–unit difference in initial occupational status when other variables in the model are controlled. This appears to parallel the special importance of educational aspirations in women's educational attainments. It is ironic that women's aspirations are less responsive than those of men to several of the causal factors in the attainment process but are also of greater significance in their later attainments than are men's aspirations. Traditional female role expectations seem to limit the range of women's aspirations; yet those goals are more likely to affect the socioeconomic life chances of women than of men.

The influence of a year of post–high school education on the status of first jobs is almost two times larger among men (7.22 points on the Duncan SEI) than among women (3.78 points). While educational attainment (U) has a larger effect on initial job status than does any other variable, women clearly obtain a lower payoff for their schooling than men at the time of initial labor force entry. We have ruled out two artifactual explanations of this finding—nonlinearity in the effect of schooling and differential timing of labor force entry—but space limitations preclude our presenting the details here. The effects of postsecondary schooling on initial occupational status are roughly linear. With less than a college education, women obtain higher-status first jobs than men; with a college degree or postgraduate education, men obtain higher-status first jobs than women. Further, the process of labor market entry is more protracted among men than among women.

Among men and women alike, the status of current (1975 or most recent) occupation (Z) is directly and strongly influenced by ability (Q), educational attainment (U), and status of first job (W). In addition, occupational aspiration (J) has a substantial direct effect on the current occupational status of men, but not of women (lines 18 of tables 4 and 5). The effects of other social and psychological variables are primarily indirect, through schooling or the status of first jobs. As in the determination of initial occupational status, the effects of father's occupational status (X) and rural origin (R) on current occupational status are larger among men than among women; in the case of father's occupation, the interaction effect remains significant even when status of first job is controlled. Sex interactions in the reduced-form

coefficients of ability (Q) and significant others (T, F) are mediated by later variables in the model; they do not appear in the final equation.

Ability (Q) has a small, positive direct effect on current occupational status (Z); among men and women status increases by 1.4 points for each 10-point difference in IQ when all other variables in the model are controlled. Ability is the only variable in the model whose direct effect on current occupational status is substantially larger than its direct effect on initial occupational status. Formal qualifications such as educational attainment and grades may be more important than ability for placement in first jobs, but the data suggest that ability increases in importance as it is expressed through labor market activity.

The most important sex interactions occur in the effects of educational attainment (U) and status of first job (W) on current occupational status (Z). In the final equation (line 18), the coefficient of schooling is more than twice as large among women (2.77 points on the SEI) as among men (1.26 points). Obversely, the effect of initial occupational status is one-third larger among men (0.35) than among women (0.26). These two interaction effects suggest that women, because they often have to find new jobs after interruptions in employment, continue to rely on educational attainment instead of work experience as the basis of occupational placement. Men rely heavily on education for initial job placement, but, because they tend to have continuous work histories, their later occupational status depends mainly on earlier occupational status.

This explanation is in accord with studies of occupational attainment among women with differing amounts of employment experiences or labor force interruptions. Both Wolf (1975) and Rosenfeld (1976) have found that (1) education has a larger net effect on current occupational status for women with less work experience than for women with more work experience, (2) the status of an earlier job has a larger net effect on the status of the current job for women with fewer interruptions in employment, and (3) employment experience is more important than education for the determination of current occupational status for women with fewer employment interruptions, but not for women with more interruptions.

TABLE 6

Regression of Occupational SEI on Schooling and Status of First Job by Sex and by Marital/Child Status of
Women: Persons Employed Within the Past Five Years

		WOMEN				
				Ever Married		
REGRESSION COEFFICIENT	MEN	All	Never Married	Childless	1–2 Children	3+ Children
1. First job on schooling...	7.22 (.17)	3.78 (.25)	3.98 (.59)	2.17 (.58)	4.28 (.43)	3.89 (.49)
2. 1975 (or last) job on schooling:						
a) Total...........	3.76 (.19)	3.75 (.29)	2.43 (.63)	3.00 (.72)	3.74 (.48)	3.74 (.56)
b) Direct..........	1.26 (.22)	2.77 (.29)	.27 (.62)	1.91 (.69)	2.50 (.49)	3.07 (.57)
3. 1975 (or last) job on first job.................	.347 (.018)	.258 (.022)	.543 (.070)	.503 (.085)	.291 (.037)	.171 (.032)

NOTE.—Parenthetic entries are standard errors. Each regression equation also includes 15 variables representing social background, high school experiences, and aspirations.

Unfortunately, our 1975 survey included only a partial work history for women, but we have further elaborated the influence of women's schooling on occupational status using our marital and child status classification as a proxy measure of work experience. Table 6 shows relevant coefficients in the equations for first and current occupational status by sex and marital and childbearing status. In the equations for status of first job (line 1), the effect of schooling is larger among men than among any of the groups of women. In the reduced-form equations for current occupational status (line 2a), the total effects of schooling are virtually the same among men as among the majority of women who had married and borne children. The total effects are lower among never-married women (2.43) and childless married women (3.00), but these differences are not statistically significant. The direct effects of schooling on status of current jobs (line 2b) vary in the expected fashion across marital/child status groups; the coefficient is least among never-married women, and it increases with the number of children born to ever-married women. Last, there is an opposite pattern of variation in the autoregression of occupational status across the marital/child status categories. Status persistence is greatest among the never-married women (.543)

and least among the married women with three or more children (.171). Persistence is more than half again as large among never-married women as among men, and it is half as large among married women with three or more children as among men. Even among childless and never-married women, the process of occupational attainment differs from that among men; yet married women with children account for most of the differences between men and women in occupational status attainment.

Our finding of sex differences in the effect of postsecondary schooling on occupational status attainment may appear to be inconsistent with earlier studies that showed unexpected similarity in the influence of schooling on occupational status among men and women (Treiman and Terrell 1975; McClendon 1976; Featherman and Hauser 1976). We find larger direct effects of schooling on the status of first jobs among men than among women, and we find larger direct effects of schooling on the status of current jobs among women than among men. In fact, there is no necessary inconsistency, for earlier studies have not included the status of the first occupation. In our reduced-form equations giving the total effects of educational attainment on current occupational status (lines 17 of tables 4 and 5), the schooling coefficients are almost identical for men and women (3.7 points on the SEI per year of schooling). According to our model, the equal effects of schooling are brought about by the larger initial effect and smaller delayed effect for men, combined with greater persistence of occupational status among men. Obversely, among women both the initial effect of schooling and the persistence of occupational status are less than among men, but schooling has a much larger delayed effect on current occupational status for women than for men. Despite sexual equality in the total effects of schooling on current occupational status, the mechanisms by which schooling affects occupational standing at mid-life appear to be quite different among men and women.

Discussion

Past research has suggested that the attainment of occupational status occurs in essentially the same ways for employed men and women. The means and standard deviations of current occupational status are similar among men and women, as are the effects of socioeconomic background and educational attainment on current occupational status. Of course, similarity between the sexes in the attainment of occupational status does not imply similarity in other aspects of the jobs held by men and women or in the processes by which those jobs are obtained. We have shown [elsewhere] that marked occupational segregation of men and women in the Wisconsin sample coexists with similarity in average levels of current occupational status; we have shown, also, that women tend to be excluded from the extremes of the occupational status distribution (see Sewell, Hauser, and Wolf 1980, pp. 559–561). We are well aware that occupational status is not the only important outcome of labor force activity, but we believe that it is a very important outcome.

Our analysis helps explain findings of similarity between the sexes in the effects of socioeconomic background and in the total effect of education on occupational status at mid-life. We have shown, however, that the similarity in the total effects of education is deceptive. By including status of first job in our models, we have revealed striking sex differences in the occupational attainment process. However, these sex differences do not unilaterally disadvantage women. In fact, the nature of the sex differences suggests a complex process, whereby women are advantaged at certain stages and men at others. Women obtain first jobs whose occupational status is, on the average, six points higher on the Duncan SEI than those of men, while at the same time women have a much narrower range of variation in first-job statuses than do men. At mid-life men's mean occupational status level is higher than women's because men have gained occupational status over the course of their work lives, whereas women have lost some ground. Thus, we find that women are advantaged with respect to at least some aspects of first job placement but seem clearly to be disadvantaged from that point onward.

An inspection of the process through which men and women are sorted into positions of occupational status at mid-life on the basis of their own prior achievements (education and status of first job) suggests a very complicated allocation process. Despite striking sex differences, the total returns that men and women obtain for their educational attainment are essentially the same. With regard to the status of their first jobs, women obtain much smaller returns on their education than men do. Later in the life cycle, women obtain higher occupational status returns on their educational qualifications than do men, whereas men obtain higher returns on their earlier occupational achievements. We believe that these latter differences are easily understood if the patterns of employment of men and women at different points in the life cycle are taken into account. Women are forced to rely at mid-life on formal qualifications such as educational attainment for occupational placement because they frequently reenter the labor market after interruptions, whereas men are better able to build on their earlier occupational experience because of their more continuous work histories.

Male-female differences in reliance on educational qualifications and on work experience are articulated with patterns of job segregation between the sexes. The fact that women have relatively high levels of status in first jobs can be explained in part by what we know about the kinds of occupations women enter. Women have higher-status first jobs than men because women with educational levels between 12 and 15 years usually take first jobs in lower-white-collar occupations (clerical and sales jobs), which have higher occupational statuses than the occupations that men with the same levels of education tend to enter (blue-collar jobs).

The fact that women fail to gain occupational status over the course of their work lives can also be explained by occupational segregation. First, it should be noted that the lack of mobility is not due entirely to the fact that women interrupt employment because of family obligations. While we have demonstrated a correlation between women's marital/childbearing histories and the resemblance between men's and women's occupational careers, even women without children have gained little occupational status over the course of their working lives (see Sewell, Hauser, and Wolf 1980, pp. 561–564). Similar findings are reported by Wolf (1975) and Rosenfeld (1976). Wolf and Rosenfeld (1978) have speculated that female-dominated occupations may be easier to reenter after interruptions in employment, yet do not offer much chance for upward mobility. Their empirical analysis offers some confirmation of this speculation. Grimm and Stern (1974) have shown that, although women are highly represented in certain professional occupations (nursing, social work, schoolteaching, library work), men are overrepresented in the higher-level positions within these same occupations. This implies that if "female-typed" occupations offer chances of advancement, it is men in these occupations who are more likely to be promoted. Research based on the Wisconsin data also indicates that women are much less likely than men to be in positions of authority—control over the work process of others—even when the effects of educational attainment, level of occupational status, and self-employment are held constant (Wolf and Fligstein 1979a, 1979b). These pieces of evidence suggest that women, in part because of their concentration in female-typed occupations, are less likely than men to be upwardly mobile over their working careers and tend not to be promoted to higher-level supervisory positions. On the other hand, even though men have lower-status first jobs, they are much more likely to obtain higher-status jobs later in the life cycle.

Our analysis has also pointed to other ways in which the attainments of women are limited or proscribed relative to those of men. Women's educational and occupational aspirations are more limited in range and less responsive to several of the factors that affect men's aspirations. At the same time, women's aspirations more strongly influence educational and early occupational attainments. Father's occupational standing affects the occupational aspirations and attainments of men, but not of women. In contrast, mother's employment does not contribute to the educational attainments of women; if anything, it is more helpful to men than to women to have had a working mother. While men's academic performance in high school is primarily important in facilitating higher education, among women high school grades have less effect on educational attainment but continue to have a direct and lasting effect on occupational status.

Given the complex allocation process that we have observed, the strategies for producing equality of opportunity for men and women are not obvious. Extending the chances for advancement of women in female-dominated occupations would clearly improve the situation. Also, women should have increased opportunities to obtain the graduate and professional education necessary for entry into the higher professions and higher levels of administration in both the private and public sectors. But this is not enough. We think it unlikely that much progress will be made in reducing occupational (or economic) inequalities between the sexes unless and until sex role socialization differences and occupational sex typing are substantially reduced.

Notes

This research was supported by a grant from the National Institute of Mental Health (MH-06275). Computation was supported by a grant to the Center for Demography and Ecology at the University of Wisconsin—Madison from the Center for Population Research of the National Institute of Child Health and Human Development (HD-05876). An earlier draft of this paper was presented at the American Sociological Association meetings in Chicago, September 1977. We acknowledge gratefully the helpful comments of William Bielby and Christopher Jencks and the computational assistance of Nancy Bode, Richard Williams, and Harold Varnis. The opinions expressed herein are our own.

[1]. See Sewell, Hauser, and Wolf (1980) for a full listing of the estimated structural coefficients.—Ed.

2. For detailed discussion of these equations of the model, see Sewell (1971); Hauser, Sewell, and Alwin (1976); and Sewell, Hauser, and Wolf (in press).

References

Alwin, Duane F., and Robert M. Hauser. 1975. "The Decomposition of Effects in Path Analysis." *American Sociological Review* 40 (February): 37–47.

Blau, Peter M., and Otis Dudley Duncan. 1967. *The American Occupational Structure.* New York: Wiley.

Clarridge, Brian R., Linda L. Sheehy, and Taissa S. Hauser. 1977. "Tracing Members of a Panel: A 17-Year Follow-Up." Pp. 185–203 in *Sociological Methodology 1978,* edited by Karl F. Schuessler. San Francisco: Jossey-Bass.

Duncan, Otis Dudley. 1961. "A Socioeconomic Index for All Occupations." Chap. 6 in *Occupations and Social Status,* by A. Reiss, Jr., et al. Glencoe, Ill.: Free Press.

———. 1968. "Inheritance of Poverty or Inheritance of Race?" Pp. 85–110 in *On Understanding Poverty: Perspectives from the Social Sciences,* edited by Daniel P. Moynihan. New York: Basic.

Duncan, Otis Dudley, David L. Featherman, and Beverly Duncan. 1972. *Socioeconomic Background and Achievement.* New York: Seminar.

Featherman, David L., and Robert M. Hauser. 1976. "Sexual Inequalities and Socioeconomic Achievement in the U.S., 1962–1973." *American Sociological Review* 41 (June): 462–83.

———. 1978. *Opportunity and Change.* New York: Academic Press.

Fligstein, Neil, and Wendy Wolf. 1978. "Sex Similarities in Occupational Status Attainment: Are the Results Due to the Restriction of the Sample to Employed Women?" *Social Science Research* 7 (June): 197–212.

Folger, John K., and Charles B. Nam. 1967. *Education of the American Population.* Washington, D.C.: Government Printing Office.

Grimm, James, and Robert Stern. 1974. "Sex Roles and Internal Labor Market Structures: The Female Semi-Professions." *Social Problems* 21 (June): 690–705.

Hauser, Robert M., and David L. Featherman. 1974. "Socioeconomic Achievements of U.S. Men, 1962–1972." *Science* 185 (July 26): 325–31.

Hauser, Robert M., David L. Featherman, and Dennis P. Hogan. 1977. "Sex in the Structure of Occupational Mobility in the United States, 1962." Pp. 191–215 in *The Process of Stratification: Trends and Analyses,* edited by Robert M. Hauser and David L. Featherman. New York: Academic Press.

Hauser, Robert M., William H. Sewell, and Duane F. Alwin. 1976. "High School Effects on Achievement." Pp. 309–41 in *Schooling and Achievement in American Society,* edited by William H. Sewell, Robert M. Hauser, and David L. Featherman. New York: Academic Press.

Heckman, James. 1974. "Shadow Prices, Market Wages, and Labor Supply." *Econometrica* 42 (July): 679–94.

Hoffman, Lois Wladis, and F. Ivan Nye. 1974. *Working Mothers.* San Francisco: Jossey-Bass.

Huber, Joan. 1980. "Ransacking Mobility Tables." *Contemporary Sociology* 9 (January): 5–8.

McClendon, McKee J. 1976. "The Occupational Status Attainment Processes of Males and Females." *American Sociological Review* 41 (February): 52–64.

Ornstein, Michael D. 1976. *Entry into the American Labor Force.* New York: Academic Press.

Ornstein, Michael D., and Peter H. Rossi. 1970. "Going to Work: An Analysis of the Determinants and Consequences of Entry into the Labor Force." Report no. 75. Baltimore: Center for the Study of the Social Organization of Schools, Johns Hopkins University.

Powers, Mary G., and Joan J. Holmberg. 1978. "Occupational Status Scores: Changes Introduced by the Inclusion of Women." *Demography* 15 (May): 183–92.

Rosenfeld, Rachel A. 1976. "Women's Employment Patterns and Occupational Achievements." Ph.D. dissertation, University of Wisconsin–Madison.

Sewell, William H. 1964. "Community of Residence and College Plans." *American Sociological Review* 29 (February): 24–38.

———. 1971. "Inequality of Opportunity for Higher Education." *American Sociological Review* 36 (October): 793–813.

Sewell, William H., Archibald O. Haller, and George W. Ohlendorf. 1970. "The Educational and Early Occupational Status Attainment Process: Replication and Revision." *American Sociological Review* 35 (December): 1014–27.

Sewell, William H., and Robert M. Hauser. 1975. *Education, Occupation, and Earnings: Achievement in the Early Career.* New York: Academic Press.

———. 1980. "The Wisconsin Longitudinal Study of Social and Psychological Factors in Aspirations and Achievements." Pp. 59–99 in *Research in Sociology of*

Education and Socialization: A Research Annual, edited by Alan C. Kerckhoff. Vol. 1. Greenwich, Conn.: JAI.

Sewell, William H., Robert M. Hauser, and Wendy C. Wolf. 1980. "Sex, Schooling, and Occupational Status." *American Journal of Sociology* 86 (November): 551–83.

——. In press. "A Comparative Analysis of the Occupational Achievements of a Cohort of Wisconsin Women and Men from High School Graduation to Mid-Life." In *Social Stratification in Japan and the United States,* edited by Donald Treiman and Ken'ichi Tominaga.

Sewell, William H., and Alan Orenstein. 1965. "Community of Residence and Occupational Choice." *American Journal of Sociology* 70 (March): 551–63.

Sewell, William H., and Vimal P. Shah. 1967. "Socioeconomic Status, Intelligence, and the Attainment of Higher Education." *Sociology of Education* 40 (Winter): 1–23.

——. 1968. "Parents' Education and Children's Educational Aspirations and Achievements." *American Sociological Review* 33 (April): 191–209.

Sørensen, Aage B. 1975. "The Structure of Intergenerational Mobility." *American Sociological Review* 40 (August): 456–71.

Spaeth, Joseph. 1977. "Differences in the Occupational Achievement Process between Male and Female College Graduates." *Sociology of Education* 50 (July): 206–17.

Treiman, Donald J., and Kermit Terrell. 1975. "Sex and the Process of Status Attainment: A Comparison of Working Women and Men." *American Sociological Review* 40 (April): 174–200.

Tyree, Andrea, and Judith Treas. 1974. "The Occupational and Marital Mobility of Women." *American Sociological Review* 39 (June): 293–302.

U.S. Bureau of the Census. 1963. *U.S. Census of Population, 1960.* Vol. 1. *Characteristics of the Population.* Pt. 1. *U.S. Summary.* Pt. 51. *Wisconsin.* Washington, D.C.: Government Printing Office.

Wolf, Wendy C. 1975. "Occupational Attainment of Married Women: Do Career Contingencies Matter?" Ph.D. dissertation, Johns Hopkins University.

Wolf, Wendy C., and Neil D. Fligstein. 1979*a*. "Sex and Authority in the Workplace: The Causes of Sexual Inequality." *American Sociological Review* 44 (April): 235–52.

——. 1979*b*. "Sexual Stratification: Differences in Power in the Work Setting." *Social Forces* 58 (September): 94–107.

Wolf, Wendy C., and Rachel A. Rosenfeld. 1978. "Sex Structure of Occupations and Job Mobility." *Social Forces* 56 (March): 823–44.

Yang, Charlotte W. 1976. "The Influence of Residence and Migration on Socioeconomic Achievement." Ph.D. dissertation, University of Wisconsin–Madison.

STANLEY LIEBERSON

Understanding Ascriptive Stratification: Some Issues and Principles

Ascriptive stratification based on gender and age is essentially universal, and ethnic-racial stratification is almost as widespread.[1] As a consequence, the specific issues in ascriptive stratification that capture public attention vary widely over time and place, often shifting in dramatic and sometimes unanticipated ways. For example, at different times prominent black-white issues in the United States have included slavery, lynching, discrimination in college fraternities, voting rights, membership in labor unions, de jure school segregation, affirmative action, the underclass, assimilation, Jim Crow segregation, and race riots.[2] The readings included here on ascriptive processes are largely directed at issues in the United States, particularly those of a contemporary nature. The discussions focus on the black family, capitalism and race relations, differences between blacks and white ethnic groups, contemporary issues of the underclass, the influence of race net of class, the occupational mobility of blacks and whites, comparisons of blacks with women, the contemporary class position of women, and the occupational attainment of women. By contrast, the readings by Hechter and by Hannan analyze problems of ethnic relations that go beyond contemporary or purely American affairs, while the readings by Firestone and by

Hartmann examine the broader contours of gender relations. This emphasis on current issues in gender or ethnicity is understandable, but there is a danger of thereby ignoring broad considerations that operate in a wide variety of specific situations. These general principles of ascriptive stratification remain relatively stable and are applicable to a range of settings; they will remain so even as the specific content changes in the years ahead. Specific contemporary events can be understood as reflecting these broader underlying issues.

As a supplement to the readings offered on these topics, I address three issues: (1) some important differences among types of ascribed stratification; (2) the macrosocietal issues that are common to all forms of ascriptive stratification; (3) the special difficulties in studying ascriptive stratification. Space limitations prevent an extensive treatment in this brief essay, but the lines of thought suggest further consideration for researchers, theorists, and students.

Differences

All forms of ascribed stratification have certain common features: By definition, they provide differential opportunities, rewards, privileges, and power to individuals based exclusively on criteria fixed at birth that the individual is normally un-

This is an original article prepared for this book.

able to alter. At issue here is whether there are any inherent differences among these types of stratification. This inquiry is different from asking if the disadvantages are of an equal magnitude in a given society—for example, whether the gender gap in income is of the same magnitude as the racial gap, or whether the stereotypes about older people are more unfavorable than those about some other ascribed population. Rather, there are two separate theoretical questions: First, how do age, gender, and ethnic subordination differ in their impact on individuals? Secondly, how do these forms of stratification differ in their impact on societal maintenance?

From the perspective of a given individual, each form of stratification has different consequences. For those experiencing a full life cycle, age stratification is "equitable" under conditions of societal stability—the ascribed disadvantages at one age compensate for the ascribed advantages of another. If seniority provides older persons certain advantages at work, for example, then younger workers will expect similar privileges as they age. Likewise, if young adults aid their aging parents, then they will in turn expect similar support from their own children. In periods of change or societal instability, or for those who cannot expect a full life cycle, the interchange of age-based advantages and disadvantages may disappear or is at least not assured. Under such circumstances, clashes may occur between the interests of different age cohorts. These problems are particularly likely in complex advanced societies where the obligations and duties with each age can change and thereby disrupt the system. Consider, for example, the situation facing young workers who may never benefit from a seniority system because the factory or the jobs may not be there for them in the years ahead. Nevertheless, in a stable system, the benefits and losses from age-based forms of ascriptive stratification are potentially neutral for a given individual. There are compensations at one age for disadvantages at another.[3]

The compensation system operates differently for gender-based forms of stratification; any compensation occurs for the family unit rather than the individual. In a stable family, with an equal number of males and females, gender discrimina-

tion creates no net loss for the unit per se, since what one member loses another member gains. There are two forces operating to undermine this pattern. First, the tolerance of unit-based compensation declines radically as the family system becomes unstable, and this then becomes an incentive for women to resist gender-based stratification: They are less assured of spending their life in a stable family with the compensations due them. Second, and probably more important, even without divorce and desertion, there are costs for those members of the disadvantaged sex because their *personal* opportunities, potential roles, restrictions, notions of self, and other imposed handicaps are *not* compensated on an individual basis. The movement toward individuation—that is, a sense of self-interest separate from the larger family entity—makes gender stratification more of an issue for women because they are, as individuals, disadvantaged even if the males in their family receive compensating privileges. The system provides no compensation for them as individuals.

In ethnic stratification, there is no compensation for members of the disadvantaged group per se, either within the life span of the individual or within the family unit. Only members of the society who belong to another ethnic-racial group benefit from the privileges denied through their subordination.[4] In the absence of extraordinarily high levels of intermarriage or some other exceptional situation such as an identification with the larger corporate entity that includes the groups who gain, there are *no* personal compensations.

Ethnic groups are also distinctive in their potential impact on the maintenance of the nation-state. To be sure, all three forms of ascribed stratification may generate reform movements seeking to reduce or eliminate disadvantages in the existing system. However, only ethnic-racial groups have the potential not only to seek reform or revolution but also to separate from the existing nation-state. This is more than hypothetical but is an actuality: Separatism is a threat in many societies (witness Russia, Canada, Cyprus, and Sri Lanka at present) and has occurred in many other settings throughout the decades. Not only can an ethnic-racial group maintain its own society indefinitely, but members often are spatially concentrated in a small number of regions—which makes a cleavage even more feasible. A disadvantaged sex or age group does not have the same potential for separatism, if only because members' spatial concentrations are insignificant (nil for gender and relatively minor for age). More critical, simple biological restrictions make it difficult for one age group or one sex to continue its own society indefinitely.[5]

As a consequence, the nation-state must deal with the potential threat of its disintegration or splintering along ethnic-racial lines. There is a certain tension when the nation-state seeks to maintain the political allegiance of subordinated ethnic-racial groups, since the same political system inevitably helps to maintain ethnic-racial forms of stratification (see the next section). The latter force sometimes leads to extreme oppression. At other times, there is a continuous interplay among groups seeking to alter the system that oppresses them and a nation that modifies its stratification no more than is necessary to maintain itself. (For a more detailed discussion of the distinctive quality of ethnic-racial stratification, see Lieberson [1970]; for an analysis of the types of ethnic-racial contact particularly likely to generate separatist movements, see Lieberson [1961].)

Common Features: Some Political Examples

In this brief essay, it is impossible to discuss all of the general principles influencing the conditions faced by ascribed groups. In most instances of ascriptive stratification, it is probably the case that efforts are made to socialize subordinate groups to their roles. Nevertheless, it is difficult to visualize ascriptive stratification without a coercive dimension that depends—directly or indirectly—on the operation of political institutions. Political processes are therefore a battleground, real or potential, as the advantaged strata maintain their favorable situation and the subordinates seek to alter it. The four political principles that follow illustrate ways of thinking that help us understand more than specific contemporary issues in gender and ethnic-racial relations.

1. The nature and forms of opposition to ascriptive stratification are affected by the way the dominant group responds to reform leaders.

2. All political events alter the relative positions of the dominant and subordinate groups. In the strict sense, there are no neutral political decisions. This accounts, at least in part, for the high degree of political mobilization among subordinate groups.

3. There is a two-way causal interaction between the political position of a group and its economic and social positions. Political power affects economic and social positions, and these positions affect political power.

4. Political power is a "real good" for a group, as suggested previously. But it is also a symbolic good, having a value to each group in and of itself.

Leadership

From the perspective of most contemporary societies, it is startling to realize that ascriptive subordination has not always been considered "illegitimate" by the subordinates themselves, let alone subject to challenge. Indeed, it would be a valuable exercise to consider the broad sweep of social events leading to the rejection of such belief systems. Under any circumstance, it is important to recognize certain principles that operate to affect the nature of leadership when subordination is under challenge. At any given time, many different ideas are circulating within a subordinate group about both the causes of its difficulties and the appropriate actions for correcting them. These ideas and their advocates are implicitly in competition for supporters. The efforts to introduce change typically start in a relatively conservative fashion with leaders who try to ameliorate their group's position by working within the existing system (witness the history of the black protest movement). The leaders—and the ideologies underlying their proposals for change—ultimately stand or fall on the response of the dominant group. Leaders successful in introducing changes will not only retain their following but will probably expand it, and their interpretation of both the group's problems and the appropriate solutions are reinforced. If the dominant group fails to respond positively to these movements, a new set of leaders will emerge who espouse a more aggressive ideology based on a different interpretation of the group's problems. Sometimes this trend is not immediately obvious because all leaders and ideologies are temporarily silenced through oppressive measures. However, in the present era, it is only a matter of time before more aggressive ideologies and leaders surface. Indeed, if extreme oppression has occurred, it is almost certain that the new ideologies and leaders will be extreme as well. The net effect, in either case, is that actions of the dominant group affect the competition of ideologies and leaders within the subordinate group.

No Political Decisions Are Neutral

All political decisions differentially affect social groups, whether the group is delineated by ascribed or achieved characteristics. Why is this? In essence, no matter what the basis of a group's formation, members will differ with respect to a wide range of other attributes that can be directly affected by political decisions. Consider how coin collectors, widowers, postal workers, tobacco farmers, joggers, residents of Idaho, gays, and the rural poor will—in the aggregate—each differ on a variety of other attributes such as income, occupation, political affiliation, values, health concerns, civil and social attitudes, and environmental concerns. As a result, political actions that affect the latter attributes will perforce affect these groups, albeit often in relatively minor ways. For example, one could analyze the differential effects of farm support policies, environmental policies, pay raises for employees of the U.S. Postal Service, and Supreme Court appointments on the well-being of the population of joggers. Since joggers are a nonrandom subset of the nation's population, they will differ on other attributes and therefore are differentially affected by these political events. This means that governmental policies and actions cannot be neutral in their impact on these groups, although the impact often is trivial

and sometimes is not obvious at the time it occurs.[6] However, no interest group—ascriptive or otherwise—would attempt to address every political event that in some conceivable way affects it; rather, the group will concentrate on those events of greatest real or symbolic consequence (see Lieberson 1971).

There are several factors that make the nonneutral nature of political decisions especially significant for ascriptive groups and motivate them to respond through political means. Let us ignore political issues that have obvious relevance—for example, suffrage for women, elimination of slavery, antidiscrimination legislation, or acts designed to protect or benefit children or the elderly. The direct significance of such issues for specific ascriptive groups are obvious and no different than would be tobacco price supports for tobacco farmers or the funding of AIDS research for gays. Beyond this, however, ascriptive groups are likely to share a broader range of common interests than are most other groupings in the society. Since ascriptive groups are relatively more homogeneous on a larger number of characteristics, a commonality of responses will occur for a far greater array of political events. The differential impact of a wider array of political actions will be more sharply delineated if a group is more distinctive (in quantitative terms) on a larger number of attributes.

Also, since ascriptive disadvantages are usually imposed or at least maintained by political institutions, a high degree of political mobilization occurs as these groups attempt to eliminate their subordination. Keep in mind the key feature of ascriptive group membership: It is involuntary, imposed from the outside, and one cannot escape from it. Not only do disadvantaged ascriptive groups often have stronger bonds for action, but there is a greater likelihood that these nonneutral acts of government will have symbolic overtones insofar as they represent the disposition of government toward the group. When government is the linchpin of ascriptive stratification, more diverse actions are considered of importance because they are taken to represent the disposition of government toward the group, a matter of relatively stronger general concern to them. The members of the National Rifle Association

(NRA), by contrast, probably have a less generalized and less intensive view of governmental actions beyond those that would impact on their concerns as members of the organization.[7]

Political Power: Its Interaction with the Economic and Social

A two-way interaction exists between political power and the economic and social position of a group. On the one hand, groups use political power to advance their positions in the economic and social spheres. On the other hand, economic and social power is often convertible into political power. It is, as it were, a situation in which the "rich get richer and the poor get poorer." However, there are social factors that alter a group's situation over time. Many exogenous variables can impact on the social order and thereby upset the existing ascriptive stratification system; examples include wars, new labor-force needs, alliances with other groups, demographic shifts, international politics, the clash of ascriptive stratification with other beliefs in the society, and economic changes. Also, as a group gains in one area (say, educational attainment, voting strength, or economic position), the gain changes the balance in other domains, and these changes in turn have additional feedback effects (for an incisive description of early changes in the black population, see Ogburn [1961]). We must recognize not only the feedback nature of these linkages but also that the groups are in competition in what is often a zero-sum situation. With a constant number of senators, for example, the electoral gain of one group is at the expense of other groups. Likewise, there is competition for social and economic positions. An analytical understanding of the ascriptive processes is incomplete if this inherent competition is not understood or is ignored.

This two-way interaction is especially important for ascriptive groups because economically successful members frequently retain considerable identification with their groups and use their economic power in the political realm to advance the position of other members. Usually this identification is retained in part because the larger society still imposes restrictions and subtle prejudices on economically successful members of ascribed groups. By contrast, individuals who are upwardly mobile within the class system are less likely to apply their newfound economic power against class-based advantages because the residue of prejudice and discrimination they experience by virtue of their *class* origins is relatively minor. This suggests that potential members of anticlass movements might be "bought off" more readily than potential members of antiascription movements.

Symbolism

Above and beyond the impact of governmental activities on a group's material well-being and institutional position, government also has a symbolic dimension for these subordinated populations. The election of ethnic or gender compatriots—as well as their participation in the judiciary or appointment to political office—matters not only because such people are believed to better understand ascriptive stratification, are thought to be more committed to reducing it, and may be better able to convey the group perspective to others, but also because holding these offices symbolizes the group position in the society. A group's political position is taken as a *representation* of its members' place in the nation—particularly when in the past such positions were difficult to attain through formal or informal prohibitions. The value is all the more enhanced when requiring the support (through appointments or election) of "others." One must never lose sight of the bread-and-butter importance of these positions, but an added value is in their symbolic meaning, pure and simple. This line of reasoning accounts for the tendency of subordinated populations to monitor their level of political representation so closely.

Caution: Special Difficulties

All forms of ascriptive stratification are emotionally tinged—and for good reason. Since one's gender, ethnicity, age, and other ascribed features are permanent (short of such procedures as passing as a member of another race or ethnic group, undergoing radical surgery, or alteration of appearance through face-lifts or hair transplants), disadvantages stemming from membership in subordinated strata are of great significance. One's own life is deeply affected by these stratification systems, as are other family members, friends, acquaintances, neighbors, and the like (depending on the particular type of stratification). As a consequence, comments about one's group, the interpretation of members' subordination, portrayals in the media, and actual or proposed policies are all significant issues. Particularly important are the perspectives held by the dominant ascriptive group because, by definition, its members hold power and advantage over the subordinate strata. Persons holding a subordinate status often wish to convey the disadvantages experienced, if only because the dominant group does not fully understand and appreciate these difficulties. Moreover, beliefs held among the dominant population affect the subordinate group.

Also, as part of the larger society, members learn many disparaging notions about their group, and it is unsettling to hear them repeated. Women, ethnic groups, and the elderly are intensely aware of the stereotypes held about them by others and of the potential influence of these notions on group position (Lieberson 1982). In addition, the impact of these stereotypes within the ascribed subordinate group itself is important insofar as it affects self-conceptions, patterns of behavior, and the development of strategies for improving the group's position. Conversely, members of the dominant group often interpret their favorable position as deserved rather than as the product of oppressive or discriminatory behavior.

Given these considerations, it is vital to distinguish between two potentially contradictory goals. One goal is the effort to demonstrate that a group is treated unjustly and therefore changes are needed or, obversely, that the group is treated fairly and no change is needed. The second goal is to determine the evidence about a given situation and evaluate stratification theories by the criterion of how closely they account for the data. In the first approach, one is an advocate or attorney for the group, presenting the group's case or argument in a particular light. In the latter approach, all possibilities are on the table, subject to scientific investigation, regardless of the empirical outcome. In a democratic society, it is acceptable and appropriate that groups with given interests attempt to present their case in a convincing manner to achieve a certain outcome. Conversely, it is acceptable and appropriate in a scientific endeavor that evidence and theories be evaluated without regard to their polemical utility or outcome. If these two distinct roles and goals are confused, the result can be ineffective political action (a scientist makes a poor advocate) or disastrous social science (an advocate makes a poor scientist).

When the advocate-scientist distinction is confused or glossed over, it is all too easy to judge scientific work by its impact on the group's position and image in the society rather than to use the same scientific criteria that would have been applied to problems and issues less deeply felt. Ironically, the very intense personal feelings that motivate and stimulate research and theorizing about a topic can undercut the goals of scientific analysis. As already noted, members of the favored group can have difficulties in approaching these topics too. One group is no more intrinsically objective than another. Critical for both social scientists and readers of social science is that theories of ascription and empirical data be evaluated in terms of their scientific validity—in the same way as one evaluates statements about, say, the factors affecting maple syrup production. Data and theories must not be evaluated in terms of either a subordinate group's effort to improve its situation or the dominant group's eagerness to justify maintenance of the existing advantages. These goals and criteria should not be confused. *The scientific goal should not be evaluated in terms of its impact on advocacy; in turn, the advocacy goal is ultimately a statement of values and norms—scientific evidence may be relevant, but it is not the critical issue.*

It is particularly important to be careful about the terms used to analyze ascriptive stratification. Obviously, special concepts help us understand the processes and provide easy ways to summarize complex matters. Nevertheless, there is a danger in using these terms in a polemical rather than an analytical way. In particular, we must keep in mind that the terms "racist" and "sexist" are increasingly used not only to describe a set of behaviors and attitudes that have been measured and evaluated in a rigorous and objective way but are also used as polemical terms. Social scientists have to consider whether a clear definition of racist or sexist exists such that criteria are applicable in a rigorous manner for a given setting. Otherwise, this is no different from the disposition of some conservatives to label every political proposal that they oppose as "communist." If a woman applies for a job and is not hired, for example, the reason could be sexist or it could not be. Rigorous research and sharply defined criteria are necessary before the assertion is appropriate.

Social-science analyses of ascriptive stratification are also distinctive from popular discussions because there is an effort to verify empirical assertions rather than assume they are true without any evidence. Assertions about the causes of group differences are empirical problems; they are not automatically viewed as true or false in accordance with one's polemical position. In addition, social science at its best does not take a simplistic good-bad approach to these forms of stratification (although the practitioners may personally feel that way as private citizens). Social science does not automatically view the disadvantaged group as largely "deserving" its subordination for reasons such as culture, physical features, or biological origins or in some other fashion such that it is a "fair" outcome. Likewise, all claims about a group's current characteristics are not automatically denied such that the only emphasis is on reform of either the larger social structure and/or on the dispositions of groups enjoying ascriptive advantages at the time.

This means, then, that caution is needed to avoid drawing premature conclusions without sufficient evidence simply because they fit into various polemical positions. The fact is that major macrosocietal questions about gender and ethnic-racial stratification are presently unresolved. This is itself not inherently worrisome;

uncertainty and incomplete knowledge are common to any scientific endeavor. What is important, however, is to recognize existing limitations, turning them into research problems rather than claiming more knowledge than is justifiable now.

Consider, by way of illustration, some of the current theorizing on the effects of capitalism on ethnic or gender oppression; these types of macrosocietal effects are often assumed to be present when, in fact, much more rigorous investigation is called for. Although Marxists and others often observe the presence of severe ascriptive stratification in many capitalist societies, this observation, which is unquestionably true, does not itself imply that capitalism is a simple explanation of oppressive ethnic or gender relations. To focus only on stratification in capitalist societies is to execute a logical error. In other words, in order to determine if X_1 causes Y more often (or increases the severity of Y) than does X_2, it is insufficient to look only at Y when X_1 is present. Rather, we must compare the levels of Y in the two conditions, X_1 and X_2. Similarly, to gauge the influence of one type of political economy on gender or ethnic-racial stratification, one must also compare stratification found in other economic settings. The logic of this is, I would hope, fairly obvious. The reader is well-advised, however, to keep it in mind when the influence of capitalism on ascriptive stratification is asserted without presentation of rigorous comparative data. It is one issue to decide if such ascription is present in capitalist countries; it is another to conclude that capitalism per se causes such forms of stratification. If the latter is true, then one should find lower levels in other types of societies. And this is an empirical question.

The cautions discussed in this last section are familiar to those espousing a rigorous social science that attempts to minimize the impact of personal values on the evaluation of theories and research. However, since one's personal feelings are sometimes at odds with one's intellectual perspective, with the latter overpowered by the former, it is important that the reader keep in mind the especially strong tension that can exist between the two spheres in the analysis of ascriptive stratification.

Notes

1. Henceforth in this essay the terms *ethnic* and *ethnic-racial* are used interchangeably in referring to both racial and ethnic forms.

2. Some of these issues may come and go as fashionable research topics. For example, race riots were a central concern during and immediately after each world war and again in the late 1960s.

3. This premise ignores inequities that can occur for someone who is exceptional and would fare quite favorably at a wide range of ages. Conversely, a highly incompetent person may gain more from the period when age protects him or her than is lost at the disadvantaged age. This is an individual problem—not trivial, to be sure—but not a problem intrinsic to one birth cohort versus another.

4. To be sure, there are some members of the subordinated group who occupy advantageous positions because of their group's situation, but they are inevitably a relatively small number.

5. However, it is now at least possible for women to maintain a society indefinitely through the use of sperm banks and the elimination of male babies.

6. Acts can have unintended consequences, and even social policies developed with a specific group in mind can have unforeseen side effects.

7. This would occur even if members of the organization tend to share other concerns and dispositions regarding events of no consequence to the issue of gun control.

References

Lieberson, Stanley. 1961. "A Societal Theory of Race and Ethnic Relations." *American Sociological Review* 26 (December): 902–910.

_____. 1970. "Stratification and Ethnic Groups." *Sociological Inquiry* 40 (Spring): 172–181.

_____. 1971. "An Empirical Study of Military-Industrial Linkages." *American Journal of Sociology* 76 (January): 562–584.

_____. 1982. "Stereotypes: Their Consequences for Race and Ethnic Interaction." Pp. 47–68 in Robert M. Hauser, David Mechanic, Archibald O. Haller, and Taissa S. Hauser, eds., *Social Structure and Behavior: Essays in Honor of William H. Sewell.* New York: Academic Press.

Ogburn, William Fielding. 1961. "Social Change and Race Relations." Pp. 200–207 in Jitsuichi Masuoka and Preston Valien, eds., *Race Relations: Problems and Theory.* Chapel Hill: University of North Carolina Press.

Part VII
The Evolution
of Modern Stratification

Theories of Industrialism and Modernity

Theories of Post-Industrialism and Post-Modernity

New Class Theories

CLARK KERR, JOHN T. DUNLOP, FREDERICK H. HARBISON, AND CHARLES A. MYERS

Industrialism and Industrial Man

The Logic of Industrialization

Although industrialization follows widely differing patterns in different countries, some characteristics of the industrialization process are common to all. These "universals" arise from the imperatives intrinsic to the process. They are the prerequisites and the concomitants of industrial evolution. Once under way, the logic of industrialization sets in motion many trends which do more or less violence to the traditional pre-industrial society.

In the actual course of history, the inherent tendencies of the industrial process are never likely to be fully realized. The pre-existing societies and conditions shape and constrain these inherent features. The leaders of economic development influence the directions and the rate of industrial growth; and the existing resources and the contemporaneous developments in other countries are also likely to affect actual events. These influences will be important in every case of industrialization. They do not, however, deny the validity of searching for some of the fundamental directions in which industrialization will haul and pull. Indeed, an understanding of these tendencies is requisite to a full appreciation of the influence of historical, cultural, and economic factors on the actual course of industrialization.

What, then, are some of the imperatives of the industrialization process? Given the character of science and technology and the requirements in-

herent in modern methods of production and distribution, what may be deduced as to the necessary or the likely characteristics of workers and managers and their interrelations? What are the inherent implications of industrialization for the work place and the larger community? What, in sum do the actual histories of those societies with either brief or more extensive industrializing experience suggest about the principal forces implicit in an "industrial revolution"?

The Industrial Work Force

[The workman] becomes an appendage of the machine, and it is only the most simple, most monotonous, and most easily acquired knack, that is required of him. (*Manifesto*, p. 65) ... Hence, in the place of the hierarchy of specialized workmen that characterizes manufacture, there steps, in the automatic factory, a tendency to equalise and reduce to one and the same level every kind of work that has to be done by the minders of the machines ... (*Capital*, p. 420). The more modern industry becomes developed, the more is the labour of men superseded by that of women (*Manifesto*, p. 66) ... The various interests and conditions of life within the ranks of the proletariat are more and more equalised, in proportion as machinery obliterates all distinctions of labour, and nearly everywhere reduces wages to the same low level (*Manifesto*, p. 69). ... The essential division is, into workmen who are actually employed on the machines (among whom are included a few who look after the engine), and into mere attendants (almost exclusively children) of these workmen. ... In addition to these two principal classes, there is a numerically unimportant class of persons, whose occupation is to look after the whole of the machinery and repair it from time to time such as engineers, mechanics, joiners, etc. (*Capital*, p. 420).[1]

These quotations from the *Manifesto* and *Capital* envisage as the consequence of capitalist production the destruction of the hierarchy of specialized workmen in pre-industrial society and the subsequent leveling of skill, a minor number of skilled labor, engineers, and managers, and the use of women and children for a growing number of unskilled tending and feeding jobs. The historical evidence of the past century, however, suggests a quite different pattern of evolution for the industrial work force.

Industrialization in fact develops and depends upon a concentrated, disciplined industrial work force—a work force with new skills and a wide variety of skills, with high skill levels and constantly changing skill requirements.

The industrialization process utilizes a level of technology far in advance of that of earlier societies. Moreover, the associated scientific revolution generates continual and rapid changes in technology which have decisive consequences for workers, managers, the state, and their interrelations.

The industrial system requires a wide range of skills and professional competency broadly distributed throughout the work force. These specialized human resources are indispensable to the science and technology of industrialism, and their development is one of the major problems of a society engaged in industrialization. The absence of a highly qualified labor force is as serious an impediment as a shortage of capital goods. The professional, technical, and managerial component of the labor force is particularly strategic since it largely carries the responsibility of developing and ordering the manual and clerical components.

Mobility and the Open Society. The dynamic science and technology of the industrial society creates frequent changes in the skills, responsibilities, and occupations of the work force. Some are made redundant and new ones are created. The work force is confronted with repeated object lessons of the general futility of fighting these changes, and comes to be reconciled, by and large, to repeated changes in ways of earning a living. But there may be continuing conflict over the timing of change and the division of the gains. The industrial society requires continual training and retraining of the work force; the content of an occupation or job classification is seldom set for life, as in the traditional society. Occupational mobility is associated with a high degree of geographical movement in a work force and with social mobility in the larger community both upwards and downwards.

One indication of the extent of occupational shifts which occur in the course of industrialization is reflected in Table 1 for the United States in the period 1900–1960.

Industrialization tends to produce an open society, inconsistent with the assignment of managers or workers to occupations or to jobs by traditional caste, by racial groups, by sex, or by family status. There is no place for the extended family; it is on balance an impediment to requisite mobility. The primary family provides a larger and more mobile labor force. The function of the family under industrialism is constricted: it engages in very little production; it provides little, if any, formal education and occupational training; the family business is substantially displaced by professional management. "... economic growth and a transference of women's work from the household to the market go closely hand in hand."[2] In the industrial society the primary family is largely a source of labor supply, a unit of decision-making for household expenditures and savings, and a unit of cultural activity.

This society is always in flux and in motion. As a result of its science and technology, it is continuously rearranging what people do for a living, where they work and where they live, and on what they spend their incomes. Their children come to expect to live different lives from their parents. But mobility in the industrial society is not random; it comes to be organized and governed by a complex of rules of the work community.

Education—The Handmaiden of Industrialism. Industrialization requires an educational system

TABLE 1

Occupational Distribution of Employment, United States, 1900–1960 (thousands of people, 14 years of age and older)

Occupational Group	1960	1900	Change 1900–1960	Per Cent Increase 1900–1960
Total	66,159	29,030	+37,129	128
Total Farm Employment	5,037	10,888	−5,851	−54
Total Non-Farm Employment	61,122	18,142	+42,980	237
White Collar Workers	28,507	5,115	+23,392	457
Professional, Technical, and Kindred Workers	7,418	1,234	+6,184	501
Managers, Officials, and Proprietors	7,032	1,697	+5,335	314
Clerical and Kindred Workers	9,710	877	+8,833	1,007
Sales Workers	4,347	1,306	+3,041	233
Blue Collar Workers	24,280	10,401	+13,879	133
Craftsmen, Foremen, and Kindred Workers	8,606	3,062	+5,544	181
Operatives and Kindred Workers	11,988	3,720	+8,268	222
Laborers	3,686	3,620	+66	2
Service Workers	8,335	2,626	+5,709	217
Service Workers Excluding Household Workers	6,134	1,047	+5,087	486
Private Household Workers	2,201	1,579	+622	39

Source: U.S. Department of Labor, Bureau of Labor Statistics, *Employment and Earnings, 1960;* and U.S. Department of Commerce, "Occupational Trends in the United States," Bureau of the Census Working Paper No. 5 (Washington, 1958), pp. 6–7.

functionally related to the skills and professions imperative to its technology. Such an educational system is not primarily concerned with conserving traditional values or perpetuating the classics; it does not adopt a static view of society, and it does not place great emphasis on training in the traditional law. The higher educational system of the industrial society stresses the natural sciences, engineering, medicine, managerial training—whether private or public—and administrative law. It must steadily adapt to new disciplines and fields of specialization. There is a relatively smaller place for the humanities and arts, while the social sciences are strongly related to the training of managerial groups and technicians for the enterprise and the government. The increased leisure time of industrialism, however, can afford a broader public appreciation of the humanities and the arts.

As in all societies, there is debate over what the youth is to be taught. The largest part of the higher educational system tends to be specialized and designed to produce the very large volume of professionals, technicians, and managers required

in the industrial society. There is a case for some degree of generality in the educational system because of the rapidity of change and growth of knowledge during the course of a career. A technically trained work force needs to be able to follow and to adapt to changes in its specialties and to learn to shift to new fields. Generality is also requisite for those coordinating and leading the specialists.

The industrial society tends to create an increasing level of general education for all citizens, not only because it facilitates training and flexibility in the work force, but also because, as incomes rise, natural curiosity increases the demand for formal education, and education becomes one of the principal means of vertical social mobility. It will be observed that the industrial society tends to transform drastically the educational system of the pre-industrial society. Further, the high level of technical and general education requisite to the industrial society cannot but have significant consequences for political life. The means of mass communication play a significant role both in raising standards of general education and in conditioning political activity and shaping political control.

The Structure of the Labor Force. The labor force of the industrial society is highly differentiated by occupations and job classifications, by rates of compensation, and by a variety of relative rights and duties in the work place community. It has form and structure vastly different from the more homogeneous labor force of the traditional society.

The variety of skills, responsibilities, and working conditions at the work place requires an ordering or a hierarchy. There are successive levels of authority of managers and the managed, as well as considerable specialization of function at each level of the hierarchy. Job evaluation and salary plans symbolize the ordering of the industrial work force by function and compensation.[3]

The work force in the industrial society is also structured in the sense that movement within the work community is subjected to a set of rules; hiring, temporary layoffs, permanent redundance, promotions, shift changes, transfers, and retirement are applied to individual workers and managers according to their position, station, seniority, technical competency, or some other measure of status in a group rather than in random fashion. Not all jobs are open at all times to all bidders. The ports of entry into an enterprise are limited, and priorities in selection are established. Movement tends to be relatively easier within than among job families in an enterprise. Delineation of job families may also vary and will often depend upon whether movement involves promotion, layoff, or transfer.

The industrial system changes the hours of work that prevail in predominantly agricultural societies. The silent night of pre-industrial society yields to the sometimes insistent requirements of continuous operations. The work force is geared to shift operations and the community to a changed attitude toward working at night. Even the holidays and religious days of the traditional society do not escape transformation.

Scale of Society

The technology and specialization of the industrial society are necessarily and distinctively associated with large-scale organizations. Great metropolitan areas arise in the course of industrialization. The national government machinery expands significantly. Economic activity is carried on by large-scale enterprises which require extensive coordination of managers and the managed. A wide variety of rules and norms are essential to secure this coordination.

Urban Dominance. The industrial society is an urban society, concentrated in metropolitan areas with their suburbs and satellite communities. While substantial cities have arisen in pre-industrial societies as commercial and religious centers,[4] urban ways come to permeate the whole of industrial society. Rapid means of transportation and mass communication reduce the variance of subcultures, particularly those based on geography and the contrast between farm and city.

In the industrial society agriculture is simply another industry; it is not a "way of life" to be preserved for its own value or because it constituted a traditional and antecedent form of society. Agricultural units of production (farms) tend to be specialized according to products, and the general farm, substantially self-sufficient, has little place. Indeed, the proportion of the work force engaged in agriculture is a rough index of the degree of industrialization of a society.[5] "To the economic eye a community which needs to have the majority of its people working on the land is merely demonstrating its inefficiency."[6]

Table 2 shows the relative role of agriculture in a number of countries; it reflects the low proportion of agriculture in the economically advanced countries and the high percentage of agricultural population in the less economically advanced societies.

Industrialization tends to promote the values, folkways, and heroes of the city and to weaken those of the farm. Even the art and music of the highly industrialized society can be expected to be substantially different from that of the pre-industrial society.

Large Role for Government. The industrial society is necessarily characterized by a substantial range and scale of activities by the government. In a society of advanced technology there are a larger number of activities for government; for

TABLE 2
Agricultural Population

Country	Per Cent of Active Population in Agriculture
United Kingdom (1951)	5
United States (1950)	12
Sweden (1950)	20
W. Germany (1950)	23
France (1957)	26
Italy (1957)	31
Japan (1957)	39
U.S.S.R. (1950)	50
Brazil (1950)	58
Egypt (1947)	65
India	71
Iran (ca. 1953)	80
Afghanistan (1954)	85
Nyasaland (1949)	90
Nepal (1952/54)	93

Source: Norton Ginsburg, *Atlas of Economic Development*, Research Paper No. 68, Department of Geography (Chicago: The University of Chicago Press, 1961), pp. 32–33.

instance, roads and highways, airports, the regulation of traffic, radio and television. Urban development has the same consequences. Technology also creates a more complex military establishment, extending in many directions the activities of government. The more integrated character of the world increases governmental activities in the area of international relations. The scale of some scientific applications and the capital needs of new technologies, such as atomic energy development or space exploration, increase the scope of public agencies. As income rises, the demand of consumers may be for services largely provided by governments, such as education, parks, roads, and health services.

The role of government in countries entering upon industrialization, regardless of political form, may therefore be expected to be greater than before. There is wisdom in the observation: "… it is extremely unlikely that the highly modernized systems of the world today could have developed indigenously on the basis of any system other than ones that relied very heavily indeed on private individual operations, and it is extremely unlikely that latecomers can carry out such devel-opment without relying very heavily on public operations."[7]

The industrial society and individual freedom, however, are not necessarily to be regarded as antagonists. A high degree of discipline in the work place and a large range of governmental activities is fully consistent with a larger freedom for the individual in greater leisure, a greater range of choice in occupations and place of residence, a greater range of alternatives in goods and services on which to use income, and a very wide range of subgroups or associations in which to choose participation. It is a mistake to regard the industrial society as antithetical to individual freedom by citing ways in which the scope of public and private governments has increased without also noting ways in which industrialization expands individual freedom.

The Web of Rules. The production of goods and services in the industrial society is largely in the hands of large-scale organizations. They consist of hierarchies composed of relatively few managers and staff advisers and a great many to be managed. The managers and the managed are necessarily connected by an elaborate web of rules that is made the more intricate and complex by technology, specialization, and the large scale of operations.

At any one time, the rights and duties of all those in the hierarchy must be established and understood by all.

The web of rules of the work place concerns compensation, discipline, layoffs, transfers and promotions, grievances, and a vast array of matters, some common to all work places and others specialized for the type of activity—factory, airline, railroad, mine, or office—and to the specific establishment. The rules also establish norms of output, pace, and performance. Moreover, the web of rules is never static, and procedures arise for the orderly change of these rules. The industrial system creates an elaborate "government" at the work place and in the work community. It is often observed that primitive societies have extensive rules, customs, and taboos, but a study of the industrial society reflects an even greater complex and a quite different set of detailed rules.

The web of rules depends partially on those technological features and market or budgetary constraints of the work place which are generally common to all types of industrializing countries, and partially on the particular resources and the political and economic forms of the country. The relative strength of these factors, and their mode of interaction, is important to an understanding of any particular industrial society. Cultural and national differences are less significant to the substantive web of rules, the more a country has industrialized. The impact of cultural and national heritage is more clearly discerned in the differences to be found in the process for formulating and promulgating the rules affecting men at work than in the content of the rules themselves.

The tug of industrialization—whatever these initial differences—is toward a greater role for the state in an eventual pluralistic rule-making system. The state does not evolve simply as a class apparatus and instrument for the oppression of another class, as Marx asserted.[8] Nor does it "wither away" in the ultimate "good society."[9] Governments have a significant role in determining the substantive rules of the work community or in establishing the procedures and responsibilities of those with this power. In the highly industrialized society, enterprise managers, workers, and the government tend to share in the establishment and administration of the rules. The industrial relations system of the industrial society is genuinely tripartite.

Consensus in Society

The industrial society, like any established society, develops a distinctive consensus which relates individuals and groups to each other and provides an integrated body of ideas, beliefs, and value judgments. Various forms of the industrial society may create some distinctive ideological features, but all industrialized societies have some common values.

In the industrial society science and technical knowledge have high values, and scientists and technologists enjoy high prestige and rewards.

Taboos against technical change are eliminated, and high values are placed on being "modern" and "up-to-date," and in "progress" for their own sake.

Education also has a high value because of the fundamental importance of science and the utility of education as a means of social mobility.

The industrial society is an open community encouraging occupational and geographic mobility and social mobility. Industrialization calls for flexibility and competition; it is against tradition and status based upon family, class, religion, race, or caste.

It is pluralistic, with a great variety of associations and groups and of large-scale operations; the individual is attached to a variety of such groups and organizations.

Goods and services have a high value in the industrial society, and the "demonstration effect" is very strong on the part of individuals and groups seeking to imitate the standards of those with higher income levels.

The work force is dedicated to hard work, a high pace of work, and a keen sense of individual responsibility for performance of assigned norms and tasks. Industrial countries may differ with respect to the ideals and drives which underlie devotion to duty and responsibility for performance, but industrialization requires an ideology and an ethic which motivate individual workers. Strict supervision imposed on a lethargic work force will not suffice; personal responsibility for performance must be implanted within workers, front-line supervisors, and top managers.[10]

It is not by accident that the leaders of industrializing countries today exhort their peoples to hard work. "This generation is sentenced to hard labor" (Nehru). "We shall march forward as one people who have vowed to work and to proceed on a holy march of industrializing ..." (Nasser). "The chief preoccupation of every Communist regime between the Elbe and the China Sea is how to make people work; how to induce them to sow, harvest, mine, build, manufacture and so forth. It is the most vital problem which confronts them day in, day out, and it shapes their domestic policies and to a considerable extent their attitude toward the outside world."[11] There are many counterparts for the Protestant ethic.

The Western tradition has been to harness the drive of individual self-interest; the communist method combines in varying proportions at varying times money incentives, devotion to a revolutionary creed, and the compulsion of terror. Regardless of means, industrialization entails a pace of work and an exercise of personal responsibility seldom known in economic activity in traditional societies.

The function of making explicit a consensus and of combining discrete beliefs and convictions into a reasonably consistent body of ideas is the task of intellectuals in every society. There are probably more intellectuals in the industrial society because of the higher levels of general education, income, and leisure. There are also new patrons to the intellectuals—the university, enterprise, labor organization, voluntary association and government—in place of the old aristocratic patrons. The function of formulating and restating the major values, premises, and consensus of a society from time to time, of reconciling the new industrial processes with the old order, plays a significant role in industrialization. The intellectuals accordingly are an influential group in the creation and molding of industrial society. ...

The Road Ahead: Pluralistic Industrialism

Men attempt to peer ahead, to understand the structure of history, to alter the process of history, if possible, in accord with their preferences. The history of industrialization to date has not been a smoothly unilinear one; it has been uneven and multilinear. It is likely that in the future it will continue to be both somewhat uneven and multilinear; and there will continue to be some latitude for choice and for chance. Chance may elude man, but choice need not; and the choice of men, within fairly broad limits, can shape history. To predict the future with any accuracy, men must choose their future. The future they appear to be choosing and pressing for is what might be called "pluralistic industrialism."

This term is used to refer to an industrial society which is governed neither by one all-powerful elite (the monistic model) nor by the impersonal interaction of innumerable small groups with relatively equal and fractionalized power (the atomistic model in economic theory). The complexity of the fully developed industrial society requires,

in the name of efficiency and initiative, a degree of decentralization of control, particularly in the consumer goods and service trades industries; but it also requires a large measure of central control by the state and conduct of many operations by large-scale organizations.

As the skill level rises and jobs become more responsible, any regime must be more interested in consent, in drawing forth relatively full cooperation. For the sake of real efficiency, this must be freely given. The discipline of the labor gang no longer suffices. With skill and responsibility goes the need for consent, and with consent goes influence and even authority. Occupational and professional groups, of necessity, achieve some prestige and authority as against both the central organs of society and the individual members of the occupation or profession.

Education brings in its wake a new economic equality and a new community of political outlook. This in turn, along with many other developments, helps bring consensus to society. The harsh use of power by the state is no longer so necessary to hold society together at the seams. Education also opens the mind to curiosity and to inquiry, and the individual seeks more freedom to think and to act. It brings a demand for liberty, and can help create conditions in which liberty can safely be assumed. It leads to comparisons among nations with respect to progress and participation.

Industrialism is so complex and subject to such contrary internal pressures that it never can assume a single uniform unchanging structure; but it *can* vary around a general central theme, and that theme is pluralism. While it will take generations before this theme will become universal in societies around the world, the direction of the movement already seems sufficiently clear:

The State that Does Not Wither Away. The state will be powerful. It will, at the minimum, have the responsibility for the economic growth rate; the over-all distribution of income among uses and among individuals; the basic security of individuals (the family formerly was the basic security unit); the stability of the system; providing the essential public services of education, transportation, recreational areas, cultural facilities, and the like; and the responsibility of providing a favorable physical environment for urban man.

In addition, any pluralistic society is subject to three great potential internal problems, and the state is responsible for handling each. One is the conflict among the various power elements in a pluralistic society. The state must set the rules of the game within which such conflict will occur, enforce these rules, and act as mediator; conflicts between managers and the managed are the most noticeable, but by no means the only ones. Another is the control of collusion by producers against consumers, by any profession against its clients, and by labor and management against the public. Undue aggrandizement of sectional interests is always endemic if not epidemic in a pluralistic society; in fact, one of the arguments for monism and atomism alike is the avoidance of sectionalism. Additionally, the state will come generally, under pluralistic industrialism, to set the rules relating members to their organizations—who may get in, who may stay in, what rights and obligations the members have, what the boundaries are for the activities of the organization, and so on. It will, almost of necessity, be against too much conflict among, or collusion between, or domination of the members by the subsidiary organizations in society.

All these responsibilities mean the state will never "wither away"; that Marx was more utopian than the despised utopians. The state will be the dominant organization in any industrial society. But it may itself be less than fully unitary. It may itself be subject to checks and balances, including the check of public acceptance of its current leadership and its policies.

The Crucial Role of the Enterprise—The Middle Class and the Middle Bureaucracy.
The productive enterprise, whether private or public, will be a dominant position under pluralistic industrialism. It will often be large and it must always have substantial authority in order to produce efficiently. This authority will not be complete, for it will be checked by the state, by the occupational association, by the individual employee; but it will be substantial.

The distinction between the private and the public manager will decrease just as the distinction between the private and the public enterprise will diminish; and the distinction among managers will be more according to the size, the product, and the nature of their enterprises. The controlled market and the controlled budget will bring more nearly the same pressures on them. The private enterprise, however, will usually have more freedom of action than the public enterprise; but the middle class and the middle bureaucracy will look much alike.

Associated Man.
The occupational or professional association will range alongside the state and the enterprise as a locus of power in pluralistic industrialism; and there will be more occupations and particularly more professions seeking association. Group organizations around skill and position in the productive mechanism will be well-nigh universal. These organizations will affect output norms, comparative incomes, access to employment, and codes of ethics in nearly every occupational walk of life. Their containment within reasonable limits will be a continuing problem; and some of the groups will always seek to invade and infiltrate the government mechanisms which are intended to supervise them.

The Web of Rules.
Uniting the state, the enterprise, and the association will be a great web of rules set by the efforts of all the elements, but particularly by the state. This web of rules will also relate the individual to each of these elements. In the contest over who should make the web of rules, the end solution will be that they will be made or influenced by more than one element; they will not be set by the state alone or by the enterprise alone or by the association alone. The web of rules will not equally cover all aspects of life.

From Class War to Bureaucratic Gamesmanship.
Conflict will take place in a system of pluralistic industrialism, but it will take less the form of the open strife or the revolt and more the form of the bureaucratic contest. Groups will jockey for position over the placement of individuals, the setting of jurisdictions, the location of authority to make decisions, the forming of alliances, the establishment of formulas, the half-evident with-

drawal of support and of effort, the use of precedents and arguments and statistics. Persuasion, pressure, and manipulation will take the place of the face-to-face combat of an earlier age. The battles will be in the corridors instead of the streets, and memos will flow instead of blood. The conflict also will be, by and large, over narrower issues than in earlier times when there was real disagreement over the nature of and the arrangements within industrial society. It will be less between the broad programs of capital and labor, and of agriculture and industry; and more over budgets, rates of compensation, work norms, job assignments. The great battles over conflicting manifestos will be replaced by a myriad of minor contests over comparative details.

From Class Movement to Special Interest Group. Labor-management relations will conform to this new context. Labor organizations will not be component parts of class movements urging programs of total reform, for the consensus of a pluralistic society will have settled over the scene. Nor may they be very heavily identified by industry, particularly with the increasing multiplication and fractionalization of industries. Rather, they may tend to take more the craft, or perhaps better, the occupational form. With skills more diverse, at a generally higher level, and obtained more through formal education, and with geographical mobility greatly increased, professional-type interests should mean more to workers than industry or class ties.

The purpose of these occupational and professional associations will be relatively narrow, mostly the improvement of the status of the occupation in terms of income, prestige, and specification of the rights and duties that accompany it. Generally these organizations will be a conservative force in society, opposed to new ways of doing things, resistant to increased efforts by members of the occupation. The enterprise managers will be the more progressive elements in the society, although they too may become heavily weighted down by checks and balances and rules.

The techniques of the professional associations for achieving their ends will be those of the bureaucratic organization everywhere; a far cry from the individual withdrawal, or the guerilla

warfare, or the strike or the political reform movement of earlier times. They will constitute the quarrels between the semi-managed and the semi-managers.

Individuals will identify themselves more closely with their occupation, particularly if it involves a formal training period for entry, and mobility will follow more the lines of the occupation than the lines of the industry or the job possibilities of the immediate geographical area. In terms of identification, the orientation will be more nearly that of the member of a guild than of a class or of a plant community. Mayo will turn out to be as wrong as Marx. Just as the class will lose its meaning, so also will the plant community fail to become the modern counterpart of the primitive tribe. The occupational interest group will represent the employee in his occupational concerns and the occupation will draw his allegiance. Status in the tribe will not give way to status in the plant; nor will status have given way to the individual contract through the march of civilization; rather interest identification will take the place of both status and individual contract in ordering the productive arrangements of men.

Education, occupation, occupational organization will all be drawn together to structure the life-line and the economic interests of many if not most employees.

The New Bohemianism. The individual will be in a mixed situation far removed either from that of the independent farmer organizing most aspects of his own life or from that of the Chinese peasant in the commune under total surveillance. In his working life he will be subject to great conformity imposed not only by the enterprise manager but also by the state and by his own occupational association. For most people, any complete scope for the independent spirit on the job will be missing. However, the skilled worker, while under rules, does get some control over his job, some chance to organize it as he sees fit, some possession of it. Within the narrow limits of this kind of "job control," the worker will have some freedom. But the productive process tends to regiment. People must perform as expected or it breaks down. This is now and will be increasingly accepted as an immutable fact. The state, the manager, the occupational association are all disciplinary agents. But discipline is often achieved by a measure of persuasion and incentive. The worker will be semi-independent with some choice among jobs, some control of the job, and some scope for the effects of morale; but he will also be confined by labor organizations, pensions, and seniority rules, and all sorts of rules governing the conduct of the job.

Outside his working life the individual may have more freedom under pluralistic industrialism than in most earlier forms of society. Politically he can have some influence. Society has achieved consensus and the state need not exercise rigid political control. Nor in this "Brave New World" need genetic and chemical means be employed to avoid revolt. There will not be any rebellion, anyway, except little bureaucratic revolts that can be settled piecemeal. An educated population will want political choice and can effectively use it. There will also be a reasonable amount of choice in the controlled labor market, subject to the confining limits of one's occupation, and in the controlled product market.

The great new freedom may come in the leisure-time life of individuals. Higher standards of living, more free time, and more education make this not only possible but almost inevitable. Leisure will be the happy hunting ground for the independent spirit. Along with the bureaucratic conservatism of economic and political life may well go a New Bohemianism in the other aspects of life—partly as a reaction to the confining nature of the productive side of society. There may well come a new search for individuality and a new meaning to liberty. The economic system may be highly ordered and the political system barren ideologically; but the social and recreational and cultural aspects of life should be quite diverse and quite changing.

The world will be for the first time a totally literate world. It will be an organization society, but it need not be peopled by "organization men" whose total lives are ruled by their occupational roles.

The areas closest to technology will be the most conformist; those farthest from the requirements of its service, the most free. The rule of technology need not, as Marx thought it would, reach into every corner of society. In fact, there may come a new emphasis on diversity, on the preservation of national and group traits that runs quite counter to the predictions of uniform mass consumption. The new slavery to technology may bring a new dedication to diversity and individuality. This is the two-sided face of pluralistic industrialism that makes it forever a split personality looking in two directions at the same time. The new slavery and the new freedom go hand in hand.

Utopia never arrives, but men may well settle for the benefits of a greater scope for freedom in their personal lives at the cost of considerable conformity in their working lives. If pluralistic industrialism can be said to have a split personality, then the individual in this society will lead a split life too; he will be a pluralistic individual with more than one pattern of behavior and one dominant allegiance.

Social systems will be reasonably uniform around the world as compared with today's situation; but there may be substantial diversity within geographical and cultural areas as men and groups seek to establish and maintain their identity. The differences will be between and among individuals and groups and subcultures rather than primarily between and among the major geographical areas of the world. Society at large may become more like the great metropolitan complexes of Paris or London or New York or Tokyo, urbanized and committed to the industrial way of life, but marked by infinite variety in its details.

Pluralistic industrialism will never reach a final equilibrium. The contest between the forces for uniformity and for diversity will give it life and movement and change. This is a contest which will never reach an ultimate solution. Manager and managed also will struggle all up and down the line of hierarchies all around the world; quiet but often desperate little battles will be fought all over the social landscape.

The uniformity that draws on technology, and the diversity that draws on individuality; the authority that stems from the managers, and the rebellion, however muted, that stems from the managed—these are destined to be the everlasting threads of the future. They will continue in force when class war, and the contest over private versus public initiative, and the battle between the monistic and atomistic ideologies all have been left far behind in the sedimentary layers of history.

Notes

1. The page citations in the *Manifesto* are to K. Marx and F. Engels, *Manifesto of the Communist Party* (Moscow: Foreign Languages Publishing House, 1955); page citations in *Capital* are to Karl Marx, *Capital,* First edition (Moscow: Foreign Languages Publishing House, 1954), English edition. Chapter XV in this first volume of *Capital* is entitled, "Machinery and Modern Industry," pp. 371–507.

2. W. Arthur Lewis, *The Theory of Economic Growth* (London: George Allen and Unwin Ltd., 1955), p. 116.

3. The 32 labor grades in the basic steel industry and the many thousands of jobs described and rated in the manual in use in the United States are eloquent testimony to the way in which an industrial work force is structured. While the details of the ordering vary among countries, the steel industry of all countries reflects a highly differentiated and ordered work force. See Jack Stieber, *The Steel Industry Wage Structure* (Cambridge, Massachusetts: Harvard University Press, 1959). Compare American Iron and Steel Institute, *Steel in the Soviet Union* (New York: 1959), pp. 287–376.

4. Bert F. Hoselitz, "The City, The Factory, and Economic Growth," *American Economic Review* (May 1955), pp. 166–184.

5. If industrializing countries are arrayed in groups according to product per capita, the proportion of the labor force in agriculture and related industries varies from 61.2 per cent in the least developed group to 14.4 per cent in the group with the highest product per capita. See Simon Kuznets, *Six Lectures on Economic Growth* (Glencoe, Illinois: The Free Press, 1959), pp. 44–45.

6. W. Arthur Lewis, *The Theory of Economic Growth,* p. 92.

7. Marion J. Levy, Jr., "Some Social Obstacles to 'Capital Formation' in 'Underdeveloped Areas,'" in *Capital Formation and Economic Growth,* A Conference of the Universities—National Bureau Committee for Economic Research (New Jersey: Princeton University Press, 1955), p. 461.

8. "Political power, properly so called, is merely the organized power of one class for oppressing another." K. Marx and F. Engels, *Manifesto of the Communist Party* (Moscow: Foreign Languages Publishing House, 1955), p. 95. The highest purpose of the state is the protection of private property; it is an instrument of class domination. See also F. Engels, *Origin of the Family, Private Property and the State,* translated by Ernest Untermann (Chicago: C. H. Kerr & Co., 1902), p. 130, and Paul H. Sweezy, *The Theory of Capitalist Development, Principles of Marxian Political Economy* (New York: Oxford University Press, 1942), pp. 243–244.

9. In the good society which Marx believed to be the final and inevitable result of the dialectical process, there would no longer be a division of society into economic classes. Since he held the state to be merely an instrument of class coercion, with the disappearance of classes, there would follow a concomitant "withering away" of the state. "The society that is to reorganize production on the basis of free and equal association of the producers, will transfer the machinery of state where it will then belong—into the Museum of Antiquities by the side of the spinning wheel and the bronze age." F. Engels, *Origin of the Family, Private Property and the State,* p. 211.

10. Daniel Bell, *Work and Its Discontents* (Boston: Beacon Press, 1956). "Although religion declined, the significance of work was that it could still mobilize emotional energies into creative challenges" (p. 56).

11. Eric Hoffer, "Readiness to Work" (unpublished manuscript).

TALCOTT PARSONS

Equality and Inequality in Modern Society, or Social Stratification Revisited

Sociological interest has tended to focus on inequality and its forms, causes, and justifications. There has been, however, for several centuries now, a trend to the institutionalization of continually extending bases of equality. This came to an important partial culmination in the eighteenth century, which happened to be the founding period of the politically independent American variant of Western society. Such cultural influences as the conceptions of natural rights or the rights of man had a profound effect on the normative definition of the nature of the new society and received a particularly important embodiment in the Bill of Rights, which was built into the United States Constitution as the first ten amendments. The egalitarian focus of this system of "rights" was unmistakable. It was also, however, closely associated with the nearly contemporary emphases of the French Revolution on the concept of citizenship. In the United States this could, to a degree impossible in the Europe of that time, be dissociated from religious and ethnic bases of the solidarity of societal communities, since the pattern of separation of church and state and denominational pluralism in the religious sphere was already well launched. This "liberalizing" tendency was reinforced by the beginnings of the attenuation of the assumption that the new American societal community was "essentially" Anglo-Saxon. Though English remained the common language for the whole society, the ethnic and religious diversity of the elements entering the society by immigration strongly reinforced the pluralistic potentials which were present in the cultural tradition. In-

deed, the Negro, recently the most difficult element to include, has, after a long and tragic history, begun to change status quite markedly in the direction of equality. Though there is a good deal of skepticism on this score, the indications of the trend point, in my judgment, to broadly successful inclusion after much further tension and struggle over a protracted period. Thus we can say that two of the most deep-seated ascriptive bases of inequality, religion and ethnicity, have lost much of their force in a society which in both respects has become notably pluralistic in composition. ...

Equality and Social Class

In spite of its "oversimplification," the Marxian conception remains a very useful point of reference. It was not fully accurate, even in 1848, and has certainly become progressively less so for the principal modern societies. But what have been the principal changes? On the kinship side, the most important one has been the attenuation of lineages with their intergeneration solidarity, leading to an increased "isolation" of the nuclear family. The most important single shift has been from total or virtual "arrangement" of marriages to a situation of relatively high degree of individual freedom of marriage choice, not without ascriptive "preferences," but still allowing much more mixing across ascriptive lines than before. This in turn has been associated with the loosening of the ties of the family to the other three ascriptive contexts, namely, religious affiliation—

indexed by the increase of "mixed" marriages—ethnicity, and local particularism. These more specific bases of class identification have tended to be replaced by more generalized "style of life" patterns related to income levels and access to consumers' goods.

On the "property" side, we can clearly no longer speak of a "capitalistic" propertied class which has replaced the earlier "feudal" landed class. The changes are principally of two types. One concerns the immense extent to which household income has come from occupational rather than property sources, extending upward in status terms from the proletarian wage worker to the very top of the occupational scale. This clearly leaves the problem of the relation of the income–receiver to the employing organization problematical, but it clearly cannot be simply dichotomized into the case of the classical "worker," who is simply paid by those who control the means of production, and the "owner," who, if he has a salary, essentially must be conceived to "pay himself." The second type of change is the relative dissociation of rights to property income from effective control of the means of production. Thus most of the recipients of corporate dividends have no more control of the enterprises in which they invest than do customers over those from which they buy.

The Marxian synthesis essentially asserted the *codetermination* of class status by economic *and* political factors—ownership of economic facilities giving *control*, in a political sense, of the firm as an organization. This in turn was conceived to be synthesized with the kinship system in its lineage aspect. The process of differentiation in modern society has, however, broken down this double synthesis, insofar as it existed at all, in classical nineteenth-century "capitalism." In consequence, not only has the mobility of economic and political resources been greatly enhanced but the door has been opened to the involvement of factors other than the classical three of kinship solidarity, proprietorship, and political power in private organizations. One effect is to make it possible for other ascriptive factors to have a continued or even revived existence, in the enhanced independence of "minority" religious and ethnic solidarities, and also relative to the "micro-

ascriptions" of which Mayhew [1968] speaks. But the main macrosocial structure has moved much farther away from ascriptive foci, even that of class, than the Marxian analysis would have it.

At the same time, the "property" complex has become much more highly differentiated. Not only have the ownership component as claim to income and the political power component as right to control become differentiated from each other, but the variegated occupational system has developed a wide range of qualitatively different types. The most important new element is probably the injection, on a scale not even vaguely envisioned by Marx, of many kinds of trained competence as factors in effective occupational performance. This has established a set of links between the occupational system and that of education, especially higher education, which did not exist before. The growth of a vast range of white-collar occupations for which secondary education is prerequisite is one major consequence, but perhaps the most important is the emergence into a new prominence of the professions, dependent as these are on university level training.

Occupation rather than property having become the primary focus of household status, both through the prestige value of occupational positions and functions themselves and through the income and style of life they ground, there is neither a simple dichotomy nor a single neat hierarchical continuum in the status system—and least of all is there such a continuum hinging on ownership as distinguished from employed status. There is, of course, an hierarchical dimension to the occupational system; but, especially in the upper ranges, it is only one of several dimensions of differentiation. It is particularly important that there is no clear-cut break between an upper and a lower "class;" even the famous line between manual and nonmanual work has ceased to be of primary significance.[1]

In the light of these developments, we may suggest the usefulness of divorcing the concept of social class from its historic relation to both kinship and property as such; to define *class status*, for the unit of social structure, as position on the hierarchical dimension of the differentiation of the societal system; and to consider *social class* as an aggregate of such units, individual and/or collective, that in their own estimation and those of others in the society occupy positions of approximately equal status in this respect.

As we will argue later in the paper, class status and the "division of society into classes"—to use a phrase of Malthus'—represent a more or less successful resultant of mechanisms dealing with integrative problems of the society, notably those having to do with the balance between factors of equality and of inequality.

Certainly for the male individual as unit, the two primary foci of class status are occupation and kinship. The former is articulated with a variety of the other predominantly universalistic and functionally specific structures of the society, particularly the market system, with special reference to the very complex phenomena of the labor market and the structure of power and authority especially in specific-function organizations, and the educational system and other foci of the institutionalization of differences of kind and level of competence.

Kinship, on the other hand, is for both the individual member and the social system, diffuse in function; it is the most important residual basis of diffuse solidarity and personal security. It, then, is articulated with the other principal bases of diffuse solidarity, which include the massive historic ones of ethnicity and religion and the relations between household and more extended kinship groupings, as well as those of residential neighborhood and, extending from this, a complex variety of solidarities associated with territorial localism, extending up to the societal community itself. Class status, for the unit, must include the whole complex of membership in diffusely solidary collectivities.

Diffuse solidarities, in this sense, constitute the structure of modern "communities." It is important to our general argument to be clear that there is no one community in a sociologically relevant sense but that a modern society is a very complex composite of differentiated and articulating—sometimes conflicting—units of community. This is one of the two primary respects in which such societies are "pluralistic." The typical individual participates not in one, but in several of them. He is, of course, a family member; but there are two typical family memberships for each indi-

vidual, not one. Both his ethnic and his religious identification may be in part independent of family membership—e.g., he may "intermarry" both ethnically and religiously. In even modestly high-status neighborhoods, he probably lives in one which is "mixed" from such points of view, as well as heterogeneous by occupational roles. Even at the level of the societal community as a whole there is major variation, e.g., as to the degrees to which people have transnational affiliations, on the basis of kinship, occupation or other grounds.

The other primary respect in which modern societies are pluralistic has to do with the functionally specific roles of which occupation is prototypical. Besides occupation itself, which is, like marriage, in the normal case a one-at-a-time involvement, this pluralism has above all to do with memberships in more or less formalized voluntary associations, which, for the participating individual, have immensely varying modes and levels of significance.

In order to throw more light on the nature of the integrative problems involved in the class hierarchy of a modern society, we must first turn to the aspects of their structure in which the egalitarian emphasis is strong and indeed newly prominent in the most recent phase of development. We have linked the emergence of this phase with the weakening of certain aspects of historic ascription of status. It should, however, be clear that equality versus inequality and ascription versus achievement should be treated as independently variable. We are suggesting here not their identity, but specific connections between them, namely, that the weakening of historic ascriptions "opens the door" to new modes and forms both of equality and of inequality. Hence a new situation comes into being for defining the relations between them.

Contexts of the Institutionalization of Equality

The case of Constitutional rights provides the most convenient point of reference for raising the question of the status of the relatively "unconditional" egalitarian component of the modern status system. The conception of equality of opportunity then forms, from the egalitarian side, the most important institutional link, not between equality and inequality generally, but between equality and that set of components of the latter which could be most fully integrated with the equality context, via achievement and functionally justified authority.

Especially since the work of T. H. Marshall (1965), the "rights" component of patterns of equality which he calls "civil" has come to be seen as part of a broader complex, which above all, following Marshall, may be said to include both "political" and "social" components. To these, should, I think, be added another which may in a rather vague and residual sense, be called "cultural." Each of the four categories is at the same time a focus of the institutionalization of components of equality of status and of the legitimation of components of stratification.

The rights that are institutionalized in the legal or civil context insure basic equalities with respect to freedom of the person, speech, assembly, association, and the like. At the same time, however, they institutionalize "equal freedoms" that permit those who enjoy them to engage in actions, the consequences of which are likely to produce differences of status. Thus the freedom of religion, as based in the first amendment to the United States Constitution, legitimizes the choice of a more prestigeful religious affiliation, given that denominations will in fact vary in terms of social prestige. Of course, the same applies to other aspects of the freedom of association. In this respect, however, probably the most important "legal" complex is that of the freedom of contract. The more commercial and financial aspects of contract have of course been highly important, but perhaps particularly important to stratification has been the inclusion here of the contract of employment. With the tendency of the occupational system to move its center of gravity from statuses of proprietorship—e.g., as peasant holder, craftsman or small business man—to that of functionally specific organizations, the immediate basis of the participation of the individual has tended to become increasingly contractual. The relation of freedom of contract to the pattern of equality of opportunity is clear.

The potentials of freedom of contract for facilitating inequality should not, however, be used to minimize the importance of the egalitarian trend of the "rights" complex. Recent legal trends in fields other than civil rights strongly emphasize this.

Similar dual involvements with the problems both of equality and of the legitimation of components of stratification should be seen in the second of Marshall's citizenship complexes, which he calls political. Historically, the central change came with an egalitarian thrust, namely, the enfranchisement of the mass of citizens through the democratic revolution. Rokkan (1960) in particular has shown how fundamental and universal, within at least the "liberal" world, has been the institutionalization of equalities in this aspect of government. That parallel developments have occurred with respect to a vast welter of private associations does not need to be stressed.

This phenomenon of course raises the question of the other side of the coin. In one respect the development of the democratic franchise, governmental or private, constituted a response to a crisis in the legitimacy of "arbitrary" authority, i.e., that based on grounds other than the explicit consent if not mandate of the governed. It has, however, also given rise to a new basis of the legitimation of inequality, namely in the authority and power of incumbents of elective office relative to that of the larger numbers on whose electoral decisions this grant of power rests.

As noted, this new legitimation of inequality of power extends to the sphere of private associations. At the same time, it is not unrelated to the legitimation of authority in the more bureaucratic aspects of modern formal organization. The most obvious case is that of governmental executive organization where the authority of elective office legitimizes appointive powers. In modern governments this, of course, becomes a very extensive phenomenon indeed.

One special type of case is the business corporation which, historically at least, has been a quasi-democratic association in its top authority, based on the votes of shares of capital rather than numbers of persons participating. Historically, of course, this is in turn a derivative of the rights of proprietorship, which in its earlier phases was neither strictly political nor strictly economic in its functional significance. In the case of the corporation, its economic functions have taken precedence over the political and thereby largely escaped the egalitarian pressures of modern political organization.

To sum up the political aspect of the citizenship complex in Marshall's sense, the focus of equality has been the democratic franchise on the principle of one member, one vote. Most large democratic associations, however, are governed on a representative basis, with elected officers acting on behalf of their constituents. The representative principle is also often combined with that of the separation of powers, as in the cases of the American federal and state constitutions.

Recently there has been a new wave of advocacy of so-called participatory democracy which, in its more extreme form, would go so far as to erase the distinction between basic membership status and elective office—"every member his own officer." A common slogan has been the importance of people coming to "control the decisions which affect their lives." Again the sheer fact of social interdependence makes this an absurdity if carried to the extreme, because if A controls all the decisions which affect his life, he *ipso facto* must control many decisions which affect the lives of others and thus deprive them of the order of control which he claims for himself. Nevertheless, the drive is clearly to extend participation well beyond the traditional limits of representative systems.

The largest scale American example has been the attempt to develop "maximum feasible participation" on the part of the "poor" concerning the administration of the programs associated with the "war on poverty" (cf. Moynihan, 1969a, 1969b). The principal targets in this case have been the welfare and secondarily educational "bureaucracies" which have had a primary responsibility to taxpayers as well as to clients and parents. In the more extreme cases there has been a direct bid of local groups to assume full control of the spending of such funds. Another major example, by no means confined to this country, has been of course the drive of student groups for more participation in academic decision-making, challenging not only the more bureaucratic component of university "administrations"—including their fiduciary boards—but also the professional prerogatives of faculties.

Again these movements are not altogether new. To take only the American case, "populist" movements were very prominent for a considerable time in our history and scored in such fields as the referendum, the recall and the popular election of judges.

It is indeed difficult to assess the limits of such movements; the history of populism would suggest that the limits for stable institutionalization are relatively narrow, though under popular pressure they may go quite far. It is, however, important to bear in mind that this participation movement concerns a complex balance among modes of what, in the analytical sense, is the political control of collective processes, and that there are at least three nonegalitarian modes which are being attacked, namely, the most obviously appropriate target, bureaucratic hierarchy, but also professional control of functions requiring special competence and, finally, the inequalities of power inherent in the institution of elective office, even though the procedures of election are thoroughly democratic. At one level the drive is to widen the scope of affairs organized in terms of the democratic association, but also beyond that, further to "democratize" the democratic association itself by reducing the powers of elected officers relative to those of the average member.

The third of Marshall's components of citizenship governed by egalitarian principles, he calls "social." It has often been said that this has proved necessary to give "substance" to the more "formal" legal and political equalities. It is of course notable that every "industrial" society has adopted more or less of the features of the so-called "welfare state." In terms of content, it comes close to the jurisdiction of the American federal department of "Health, Education and Welfare."

From our point of view there is here, as in the other contexts, a striking duality of reference. The one aspect, focussing on income level, concerns the state of economic welfare in which different sectors of the population find themselves. This includes access to health services and other conditions of welfare. The other aspect brings us to the opportunity complex, with the implication that there will be inevitable differentiation among those who have equivalent opportunities at the start.

It is perhaps correct to say that, in American society at least, there has been a notable shift of concern over the last two generations, from worry about the inequities of the advantages enjoyed by the rich—today, in this context, it is much more inequality of power than of wealth which is the focus—to concern about the other end of the scale, namely the problem of poverty. It is also notable that the weight of evidence indicates that, in a generation, there has been relatively little change in the main pattern of income distribution.[2] Since the general level has been rising, the "poor" are not in any absolute sense "worse off," so that a major problem is raised as to why there has been such a wave of new concern.

As Rainwater (1969) in particular has made clear, the essential answer to the nondisappearance of the problem in the face of increasing general productivity, lies in *relative deprivation,* a view which is of particular relevance in the present context. This is to say that those groups which, for whatever reason, have incomes sufficiently below the normal level of "average" families, are unable, in a variety of ways, to participate fully in normal activities and to utilize normal symbols of self-respect. The evidence indicates that the result tends to be a withdrawal, partly by self-isolation, partly by pressure of other groups, into a "subculture of poverty" which maintains a rather unstable partial integration in the larger society. There has been an increasingly vocal and impressive body of opinion arguing that by far the most effective single remedy for this situation is a massive redistribution of economic resources to the lowest sector of the income scale.

In this connection the emphasis is on the economic factor as such, but the development of the subculture of poverty seems to indicate that the main problem is societal integration and that we are here talking about one major condition of integrating a major sector of the population into the larger community. It seems reasonable, with respect to this integration, to distinguish two analytically separate components, although they overlap and interpenetrate empirically. One may

be said to be that of the "style of life," which focuses on what are usually called "consumption" standards, which are not necessarily essential elements of the conditions of developing capacities to exploit opportunities. Much of the area of dress, housing, and furnishings, of food habits and the like belongs in this category. The other concerns the factors of capacity and motivation to take advantage of opportunities for some kind of social mobility.

Economic underpinning is exceedingly important to both, but its provision may probably be relied on to operate more nearly automatically in the former sphere than in the latter. Probably the most important case in point here is education. Whatever may be said about the inferior quality of slum schools, in any drastic sense the "poor" cannot simply be said to have been denied access to educational opportunity. There is of course much argument on various aspects of the problem, but both the findings of the "Coleman report" (1966) and of much recent research in class-linkages in the cognitive aspect of child development seem to indicate that a genuine component of capacity is prominently involved, and that this in turn is a function of the culture of poverty (cf. Bowles, 1963; Coleman *et al.,* 1966; Kagan, 1967). Equal access to education is clearly one of the most important components of the equality of opportunity complex, helping enormously to lift those who can take advantage of it out of economic dependency and to open doors to higher levels of occupational and other success. At the same time it is more than that, not only in the negative sense that the capacities of the deprived are seriously impaired, but also in the sense that levels of education become exceedingly important conditions of the more general participations which symbolize full citizenship. Here what is meant is participation in a sense which includes shares in collective decision-making, but which is more broadly the sense of belonging and "being accepted" in many situations of social interaction. Thus, much as highbrows tend to look down on the mass media and the cultural levels of what they purvey, genuine participation in many aspects of mass media culture is essential to a sense of belonging in the society—a participation which includes politics and more specifically "cultural" concerns.

In several connections I have stressed the importance to modern society of the so-called educational revolution (cf. Parsons and Platt, 1972). If this emphasis is well placed, it should follow that the quality-inequality "variable" should have a cultural dimension as well as legal, political, and economic dimensions. In a society where cultural advancement is a process of fundamental importance, it is out of the question that there should be a "flat" equality of cultural level in a large population. Indeed much has been made, often with strongly aristocratic overtones, of the differences between elite and "mass" culture (cf. Ortega y Gasset, 1932; White, 1961). However justified such distinctions may be, it does not follow that there is not an equality problem in this area and that it is not structurally similar to those in the political and economic spheres.

One aspect of the problem concerns the extent to which "elite" culture must be ascriptively integrated with diffuse patterns of stratification, as has conspicuously been the case in societies characterized by the strong institutionalization of aristocracy. One major modern trend in this respect has been in the direction of increasing specificity of cultural bases of status, notable perhaps in the field of the intellectual disciplines and the professions. Cultural superiority as a component of the competence essential to an occupational role *is quite different* from the cultural "refinement" of the aristocrat.

If, as seems to be the case, modern society is strongly committed, on value grounds, to the minimization of institutionalized aristocracy, an acute question is raised about the nature and problems of what is sometimes called "general education" (cf. Parsons, 1966a). Here there is a problem not only of equality of "levels" but of "commonality" in the sense of transcending specializations. On the side of equality, the modern commitment to mass education clearly implies that there must be a "floor" below which only the "mentally retarded" should be allowed to fall. This floor was first set at simple literacy, but has been steadily rising. Whatever the crudity of the demographic measures of educational level, it is a cardinal fact of the society of our generation that

completion of secondary education has become normative for the *whole* of the age cohort. There is a "poverty" problem in the field of education as truly as in that of income, and it is the "dropouts" who cannot or will not complete secondary education who are becoming the core of the "educational poor."

If cultural standards are to constitute, "across the board," a criterion of position on a scale of stratification, the question of what constitutes a "level" of cultural attainment becomes a critical one. In the lower reaches the problem is relatively simple; virtually no one extols the cultural virtues of illiteracy or inability to understand simple arithmetic. The foundation clearly includes certain basic cognitive skills, and a fund of basic information. At more "advanced" levels problems clearly emerge having to do at the least with differences of competence among the ramified branches of the cognitive universe, and then with ideological and religious differences.

The broad answer is that the factor of "communality" as I have called it is above all a function of the level of generality of cultural orientation, and hence of the capacity to "subsume" differing varieties in the cultural sphere under more general categories. The ecumenical trend in religion is perhaps the most conspicuous example in a socio-cultural field, where points of view previously treated as nearly totally alien to each other have come more or less to be "included" in a single meaningful cultural system. The application of this principle to the sciences is relatively clear. Specialization has, to be sure, proceeded apace, but so has the integration of the corpus of scientific knowledge; indeed this process has begun to bridge the gap between the "natural" and the "behavioral" sciences, perhaps even of science in relation to the humanities.

Another way of putting the point is to say that we have been living in an increasingly pluralistic culture, which is intimately linked to the pluralization of the structure of modern society. In both cases, however, the differentiation which produces pluralization must be matched by corresponding integrative processes and patterns. In another idiom, the universalistic character of the more general cultural patterns has gained a certain ascendancy over the particularism of less generally significant "sectors" of the cultural universe. To me the only sensible way to define "general" education in a sense which permits progressive upgrading is in terms of participation in this process of universalistically defined generalization of the cultural tradition.

The System of Equality Dimensions

It has thus been possible to identify four principal contexts in which the equality-inequality problem arises, and to give at least reasonable indications why, in a highly differentiated and hence pluralistic modern society, they are to significant degrees independently variable. These are the "legal," political, economic, and social and cultural contexts. They all seem to open the door to opportunity for differential achievement which can be both legitimized and differentially rewarded in various ways. We have also reviewed some of the principal ways in which conditions have been or are being institutionalized, under which such differences are regarded as legitimate.

When the four are looked at as a system, however, an important element of asymmetry appears. This lies in the fact that, while economic, political, and cultural inequalities are legitimized under the general formula of equality of opportunity—and of course other conditions such as "fair competition" and the like—the same is not true in the same way for the legal category. The old constitutional formula about "inalienable" rights seems to be appropriate here. It is significant in particular that the principle of equality in the form of nondiscrimination has been institutionalized for two fundamental "boundary conditions" of human action, both in the formula common to the fifth and fourteenth amendments to the United States Constitution. The first of these concerns the ascriptive qualities of the organism as labelled by the terms "race" and "color." Presumptively other biological fundamentals are so closely related as to fall in the same broad category, namely age and sex. The second concerns the "ultimate" boundary at the cultural end of the cybernetic scale. Here the context is that of religion, and the constitutional word is "creed," but also the provisions about the "establishment" and

the "free exercise" of religion in the first amendment are central (cf. Parsons, 1966b: 9ff, Freund and Ulich, 1965).

Those considerations suggest, on theoretical grounds, that the "legal" complex has, relative to the other three, pattern-maintenance functions. It has evolved in most modern societies to the point of institutionalizing the principle that there shall be a "base" in the status of citizenship, with respect to which all individual citizens stand as equals, and that these patterns of equality apply in at least three spheres, namely, the citizen's rights of participation *in* government, e.g., through the franchise, his rights *vis-a-vis* government, and, within a considerable range, his rights in contexts of private association. Here the situation is somewhat less obvious, but recent court decisions have made it quite clear that, especially *vis-a-vis* race, but also religion, the freedom to discriminate within private associational contexts is substantially restricted. It seems a fairly safe prediction that these restrictions will tend to increase rather than the reverse.

In my two previous general papers on stratification theory (Parsons 1954), I have strongly stressed the importance of values as legitimizing differences of ranking. If the present interpretation that in the legal complex we are dealing with a pattern-maintenance function is correct, I should like to suggest that this valuational emphasis applies not only, as is obvious, to the factors of differential ranking, but also to equality—that the evaluative backing of constitutional law in this case constitutes the *specification* of the general value system of the society to the level of the *normative structure of the societal community*. It amounts to saying that the modern societal community shall be "basically" a "company of equals" and hence, so far as empirically possible, legitimate inequalities shall be "won" from a base of equal opportunity and that the rewards which go to differential statuses and achievements shall be justified in terms of functional contribution to the development and welfare of the society (cf. Davis and Moore, 1945). It should be noted that this formula can legitimize some differential opportunity, through the kinship system, for the children of the more favored groups, if they can be held to sufficiently high obligations to contribute. What in effect such a qualification does is to extend the equality of opportunity pattern beyond the span of one generation; indeed it connects with the old aristocratic formula of *noblesse oblige*.[3]

In this connection it is particularly important to be clear about system-references. When I speak of the legal or civil component of the citizenship complex as having pattern-maintenance functions, I do *not* refer to the total society but to the *societal community* as the system within and on behalf of which this component has pattern-maintenance functions. The societal community is here conceived as a primary, functionally differentiated *subsystem of a society* (cf. Parsons, 1969a: chap. 2). This is clearly to be distinguished from the pattern-maintenance subsystem of the society as a whole. The latter clearly centers in the system of institutionalized values at the general level and is in that sense especially closely related with the cultural system. The "value-premises" of the rights and obligations here regarded as both egalitarian and inalienable, should be conceived as residing in that more general value system, but the particular relevant "forms" they take, are specifications from these premises on the basis on which that aspect of value-commitments more generally have been analyzed (cf. Parsons, 1969b).

I have just argued that the equality component of the normative structure of modern society comes to focus in the legal or civil complex of citizenship with its presumption of basic equalities of rights—and correlatively of obligations. This complex is normatively grounded in the general societal value system. In a sense underlying the more specific contexts in which the equality-inequality problem arises, which have been reviewed on one level and will be discussed again presently, there are two particularly significant contexts of value-specification which go one step farther than the specification just discussed to the level of the societal community.

The first of these I shall call the *fiduciary* complex. It is grounded in the fact that one basis of inequality lies in the incapacity, for a very wide variety of reasons, of all members of a societal community to take effective responsibility for the protection and furtherance of their own rights and interests, hence there is a necessity for "en-trusting" these interests to persons or groups on which such responsibility is focussed.

This principle operates most obviously in those collectivities which have responsibility for the interests of dependent persons, an excellent example being the small child, whose interests are in the first instance entrusted to his parents, but also to various other agencies. In this sense there is a fiduciary component in virtually all differentiated responsibility for societal function. The connection with the legal system is, however, particularly prominent as in the case of the courts taking formal responsibility for the administration of such matters as wardships and guardianships, various kinds of trusts and the like. Indeed we shall note that the courts of law themselves are primarily fiduciary institutions in that small groups of persons are given responsibility for very widespread interests of others. There are, however, two particularly salient and more general cases, the "fiduciary board" as a governing body in organizations, and, in a more diffuse sense, the modern professions.

What I have called the fiduciary complex has an important though complex and often ambiguous relation to the legitimizing functions of government. Indeed, there is an important sense in which the private corporation, in the modern world, has been said to constitute a "delegation" of governmental authority to private groups, as does the institution of private property itself, if we go farther back. Such a line of argument, however, depends on the view that government is the primary matrix from which a main process of differentiation occurs. It seems to me that the appropriate matrix is more the societal community than government and that in the modern phase of societal development government itself has been in process of differentiating from this more diffuse matrix, with the democratic franchise marking one main phase of that differentiation. Thus it seems sounder to regard property and the corporation on the one hand, and government on the other, as two different "branch" developments from the same evolutionary trunk. Both of them involve the institutionalization of authority and power, and hence the elements of inequality inherent in such institutionalization. Both, however, rest on a common basis of legitimation through common values, rather than the former of being legitimized by the latter. Not to understand this fact of differentiatedness may perhaps be called the "Rousseauistic fallacy."

The other component of the "fiduciary" complex which is particularly important to the modern world, and which should be looked at in the present context, is the complex of the professions. Among their basic characteristics is a level of special technical competence that must be acquired through formal training and that necessitates special mechanisms of social control in relation to the recipients of services because of the "competence gap" which makes it unlikely that the "layman" can properly evaluate the quality of such services or the credentials of those who offer them. Professional competence, in this sense, is grounded in the mastery of knowledge of one or a combination of the intellectual disciplines, though of course other factors than knowledge as such are also involved.

What I have called the "competence gap" necessitates a component of inequality in the professional complex, e.g., between physician and patient, lawyer and client, or teacher and student. At the same time, *within* the context of professional organization, in spite of differences in competence, there is a strong tendency to an egalitarian type of associationalism on the principle that a person either is or is not a member of the profession in question, or one of its subdivisions, such as a university faculty or department, and that all such members have a certain equality of status, including the democratic franchise in collective decision-making. This is the most important case where a system of occupational roles is organized on such a basis, which may be called collegial.

It is clear that, though the factor of competence makes for a critical element of inequality—with fiduciary responsibility—it also puts a premium on capacity independent of ascriptively particularistic considerations and hence enhances the general societal stress on equality of opportunity. Indeed, this is particularly important because it operates in the higher levels of the modern occupational system. While classical bureaucratic organization is also in principle governed by equality of opportunity, it is at the same time bound up

with an hierarchical pattern of operating organization, much more than in the case of the professions. On the other hand the operation of large modern organizations has become so complex and technical that neither "direct democracy" nor elective office, crucial as the role especially of the latter is, can cover a very large proportion of its functioning, though the latter can form "top" control.

The "educational revolution" has brought the professional complex to an increasingly prominent place in the structure of the society, a prominence by no means confined to the academic world as such nor to the traditional "practicing" professions, but above all permeating both industry and government on a large scale and substantially modifying their patterns of organization, including stratification. It has above all created a new basis of solidarity, cross-cutting the traditional divisions between such spheres as those of "government" and "business." Hence the professional complex, as I am calling it, has the potential not only of a powerful instrumental influence in societal functioning but also as a focus of integrative mechanisms. These can operate above all through a process of balancing the necessary differentiations based on competence and authority, with patterns of equality.

Professions, like many other structurally differentiated groups, also pose problems of control. Since on some level only their members are competent to judge the competence of their fellow members, there is a built-in possibility of monopolistic practices in several contexts such as the restriction of access to membership. In the United States the medical profession, especially through the American Medical Association, has perhaps gone farthest in this direction. This would seem to be one of the inherent hazards to the "public interest" in a modern type of social organization.

Another major point concerns the relations between the "rights" complex of egalitarianism and the "political" complex. In a general institutional context clearly the former takes precedence in that such rights as the democratic franchise must be legally grounded, as we often put it, at constitutional levels. From this point of view the system of courts, and their equivalents in other systems, does not consist only in a "third branch," e.g., of the federal government, but is the fiduciary guardian of the more general legal order within which government itself operates—the institution of judicial review of acts both of the executive and the legislative branches clearly asserts this. This is a special case of the fiduciary principle, which is not, in the usual sense, democratic. Furthermore it is notable that, in most modern societies, these functions are performed by members of an institutionalized professional group which is structurally anchored in many nongovernmental ways in the society and has a long *cultural* tradition of its own which was not created by any act of government, nor of an electorate at any particular time.

The second field of specification referred to above is that of the generalized media of societal interchange, as I have called them. Earlier in the paper I have stressed the importance of the erosion of ascriptive structures and the consequent increase in the mobility of many kinds of resources and the related openness of opportunities. As first became clearly evident in the field of the economic market, the widespread openness of opportunities and extensiveness of markets, as well as high degrees of the division of labor, depended on the development of money as a medium of exchange, and beyond that, as an instrument of credit.

It has proved possible to extend the conception of a generalized medium of interchange beyond the case of money to include political power and what some of us have been calling influence and value-commitments (cf. Parsons, 1969a: chaps. 14–16).

The processes of interchange and the situations in which they occur open up greatly widened possibilities for units in the social system to pursue whatever goals and interests they may be committed to. The media themselves, however, cannot in the same sense be "managed" by unit-interests, but must in some sense become an object of fiduciary responsibility. This has become obvious in the case of money, where the monetary system is a fundamental responsibility of government and certain specialized organs of it. Similar things can be said of the constitutional aspect of the organization of political power, not only that of government, but also as institutionalized in private organizations. Such regulation seems to be necessary

because it is the very process of the development of such media, and especially the mobilization of the factors of production and of collective effectiveness, which has opened up new possibilities of inequality and of "exploitation." Thus Marxian doctrine was not fortuitously associated with the maturing of the industrial revolution and its complex relations to the democratic revolution.

It is possible to say comparable things about the relation of value-commitments as a generalized medium to the institutionalization of the culturally interpenetrating pattern-maintenance systems of modern societies. Indeed one source of modern "anti-intellectualism" seems to be a sense of inferiority, and hence of being, if not "exploited"—certainly not in the strictly economic sense—"put upon" by the superiorities of those who have enjoyed superior access to cultural resources. Indeed, the educational revolution has shifted the locus of felt conflict away from the older foci, especially of economic inequality, but also of political power, in the direction of cultural inequality.

If what has just been said about the importance of money, power, and value-commitments is correct, what of the fourth, namely influence as that especially institutionalized with reference to the societal community? My suggestion is that one principal function of influence as a medium, perhaps the most important, is as a mechanism for "handling" the tensions which continually arise in a dynamic society over the balances between the egalitarian and the elitist components of the normative structure of the society and the realistic implementations of this balance. In previous discussions of influence, it has been emphasized that one of the principal functions of the use of influence lay in the "justification" of actions which ego was trying to persuade alter ego to perform; here, justification has been specifically distinguished from legitimation (cf. Parsons, 1969a).

Here it becomes particularly significant that, in normative terms, the pattern-maintenance "base" of the modern societal community is essentially egalitarian. In this perspective, seen in the stratification context, a primary function of influence is to justify functionally necessary forms of *in*equality. At the "pure" social system level, we have argued, these can be reduced to three main types namely, (1) through control of monetary assets, access to generalized economic resources; (2) through political power, access to factors of collective effectiveness; and (3) through value-commitments, access to "cultural resources." The attempt, then is to "*persuade*" the otherwise given holders of such "resources" to make them available for societally justified functional use, *even though* this allocation stands in conflict with some previously established egalitarian "right." In this respect, for example, the equal rights of members of an electorate are "sacrificed" to the cause of effectiveness by the granting of power to elected representatives. Similarly, resources controlled through monetary mechanisms are differentially allocated among claimants. But the burden of proof is shifted to the side of justifying inequalities.

It is a very important feature of the theoretical scheme we have been using here that at each of the main boundaries of a given primary system or subsystem there is a "zone of interpenetration" between the system of reference and the adjacent system. This conception may be employed here by suggesting that certain crucially important equality patterns, all three of them cases of the more general principle of equality of opportunity, can be located in these zones of interpenetration between the societal community and the other primary functional subsystems of a society.

The first of these, at the boundary *vis-a-vis* the economy, is the "classical" economic conception of the purely competitive market. This has of course been conceived in contrast with monopoly and essentially means that all participants in the operation of such an ideal type of market should have equal opportunities of access, either to the effective demand of consumers of the relevant product, or to the factors of production, or both. When, however, the reference is to pure *competition,* it is made clear that equality of *outcome* of the process is not to be expected. If, however, the competition is "fair," it is expected that differential success will be accounted for mainly by differential efficiency of the competing units, "ultimately" in "satisfying the wants" of consumers or of producing "utility." This then falls under our conception of contribution to the welfare of the societal system. The justification, in the above

sense, of "free enterprise" competition thus rests in the assertion that a competitive element in economic production contributes to more efficiency than, for example, a centrally controlled socialist form of organization.[4]

This justification, however, is contingent on keeping monopolistic tendencies under control. Differential success in market operations inevitably produces, for the next stage, differential advantages in competition. If, as is the case for most economic analyses, the firm is taken as the unit entering into the competitive process, it is very unlikely that "pure" competitive equality will prevail realistically over a large share of the market system. If, on the other hand, the step is taken to the socialistic alternative, then the justification problem becomes a matter of the appropriateness of governmental machinery which, we would in general argue, cannot have the primacy of productive efficiency in the economic (but not technological) sense which a market-oriented firm can have.

Turning to the boundary *vis-a-vis* the polity, we conceive the democratic association to be a boundary structure here, which is part integrative, part political in function. The equality of membership rights, anchored especially in the "one member, one vote" principle, is primarily a constituent of the societal community, i.e., the integrative system. Other aspects of the equal rights complex are of course also involved, perhaps above all those associated with freedom of communication, so that the free play of influence can be protected.

Of course, the most conspicuous outcome of the democratic revolution has been the institutionalization of the democratic franchise in the citizenship complex. It should not be forgotten that major developments in this respect have been taking place very recently (viz, the recent U.S. Supreme Court decisions on legislative apportionment) and that the process is probably far from being complete even in democratically "advanced" societies. Second, however, is the exceedingly important development of the same basic set of principles in the organization of many types of private association.

In various discussions of the place of the polity in societal systems, we have argued that its principal value standard is *effectiveness* of collective goal-attainment. There is an obvious tension between the equality principle in the field of participation and the functional imperative of effectiveness (cf. Parsons, 1969a: chaps. 13, 14). Effectiveness in turn is a function of concentration of authority and power, not necessarily maximal, but still—where memberships are large and collective functions are both complex and urgent—an appreciable concentration. The most generally evolved institutional solution for reduction—never complete elimination—of this tension is the institution of elective office. Here of course citizens—or members of other associations—exercise their equal rights in contributing to the choice of their elected representatives, but in so doing they establish a special form of *inequality*, namely, as between office-holders and "ordinary" members. My suggestion is, in line with the above discussion, that the justification of this inequality must focus in the importance, to the collectivity of reference, of effectiveness in arriving at collective decisions—i.e., those *binding* on the collectivity—and implementing the decisions arrived at, above all through the mobilization of obligations to contribute to effective collective goal-attainment. ...

As in the other two cases, the culturally "common man" must sacrifice some of his egalitarian prerogative in recognizing the merits of cultural superiority. It is thus not surprising that there are new currents of what is sometimes called anti-intellectualism, and hence the idealization of a state of affairs where competence above the general level does not count—as well as derogation of the validity of claims to superior competence.

The line of justification of this category of inequalities clearly must rest first on assertions of the functional importance to the society of the institutionalization of the requisite aspects of culture, of its advancement, transmission, and application. The recognition of superiority then must be balanced by what I have referred to above as "fiduciary" responsibility. There must be institutionalized ways of assuring, with tolerable probability, that superior competence will be used in ways which are compatible with societal interests—as in the case of the medical assertion of concern for the "welfare of the patient."

If we are correct that the main center of gravity of the differentiation of that sector of the pattern-maintenance subsystem of modern society in which cultural interests have primacy is the system of higher education, it should not be surprising that the problem of the justification of inequality in matters of cultural competence should be particularly acute at the present time. Furthermore, among the classes of "laymen" in academic matters, students are particularly closely involved through their partial and somewhat equivocal membership in academic collectivities, in such ways that they are subject both to authority and to economic pressures in this relationship. This set of circumstances seems to be important in the background of the present wave of disturbances in the relations of students to universities and colleges. ...

Conclusion

A few crucial points can be made in conclusion which tie up the rather involved preceding analysis. The first is that though difficult balances must be held within complex social systems between the imperatives of equality and those of stratification, both sets of imperatives operate in such a wide variety of different respects and contexts that there is no guarantee that they will cohere in a form which is functionally viable for the larger system unless there are mechanisms which are functionally specialized in the relevant modes of integration.

There is no simple alternative as between an egalitarian and a stratified society, or even a question of acceptable "degrees" of stratification in general. Four patterns for the "maximization" of one mode of balance may be noted. The first, which was more popular a generation and more ago than now, is based on the strict application of the model of the competitive economic market. The combination of the ideal of equality of opportunity with the justification of the inequalities generated in the competitive process seems to provide one basis of reconciling these two opposed imperatives, with the implication that the successful in the competition of the market "deserve" not only such rewards as high income, but also the larger share in control over the processes of the economy that the resulting concentration brings about.

Interpenetrating with this there are two political models. The one with egalitarian emphasis is that all integration on the equality-inequality axis should occur through the pattern of the democratic association, so that the only inequalities permitted should be the superiorities accorded to incumbents of elective office who are held strictly accountable to a fully democratic constituency. This is often held to be the sole basis of a principled legitimation of inequality which would in turn make possible the justification of more particular forms of inequality.

Largely antithetical with this is the model of the centralization of inequalities by the self-conceived bearers of a higher order of value-commitments; this in turn allegedly justifies the assumption of central control and all the other primary spheres of inequality—as exemplified in our time by the fascist and communist dictatorships. There is an important sense in which this pattern is the obverse of radical democratic associationalism in that both tend to bring matters to focus on the problem of *control* of collective decisions and resources and thereby to "politicize" the integrative process. Dictatorship in this sense is generally legitimized in terms of a pattern I have often called "value-absolutism." The stance is that "the values to which *we* are committed clearly take precedence, at the value level, over any others operative in the relevant field, hence we have the legitimate right to take control and to suppress opposition." The content of the values may be economic, as in the communist case, nationalistic-political as in that of fascism, or religious, as in that of the early Calvinists; in our terms there is a basic similarity of pattern.

As against all three of these "models" of integration, the kind of pluralistic society which has become dominant in the modern world is dependent for its integration on complicated cross-relations among these different bases of claims to equality and justification of inequality respectively. This has certain important consequences, of which three may be noted. First, bases of prestige, in the sense in which we have used that term, must be functionally diffuse, i.e., a resultant of plural components rather than any one. Thus in a professional case, competence alone is a limiting case unless it is combined with a reputation for "integrity" in the sense of concern for the interests affected by the use of such competence. The access to influence which results from a position of prestige—higher than average—is thus a function of *plural* factors in this sense.

Secondly, since we have taken the position that there is a presumption in favor of equality of status and hence inequalities need to be specifically justified, the problem of *accountability* has acquired a new salience. This very old concept has had its most prominent uses in the fields first of "moral" accountability symbolized above all in terms of accountability to a deity or to a "moral community" legitimated at the highest level. The democratic version of accountability to a constituency involves many familiar complications. That of competitive success in the economic sense attempts to eliminate the problem by suggesting that an automatic mechanism insures that the successful are also the "deserving."

We suggest that the problem of accountability cannot, in a pluralistic society, be "solved" by any one of these three ways or by any combination of them. Hence, third, we suggest that a fourth focus, which has been discussed at some length above, is necessary, namely, what we have called the *fiduciary* focus. Here the term "responsibility" seems to have a rather special resonance. In this, as in so many contexts, system-references are crucial. For my present purposes, therefore, fiduciary responsibility is to be defined in terms of the social system of reference for most of this discussion, the society. In proportion as such a system is pluralistically differentiated, it becomes less meaningful to focus such responsibility in any one functional context—it is in this sense inherently "diffuse." Thus where government has come to be highly differentiated from the societal community, high governmental office has progressively less of a monopoly of fiduciary responsibility and with it, prestige.

There is here an important kind of relativity. If we take the perspective of any one primary functional context, the fiduciary component must arise from its articulations with others. Thus the socially responsible business man is one who has interests other than those in economic productivity in mind—similarly the socially responsible politician, interests other than those of effective government, to say nothing of his own power. In the academic world, assuming the primacy of cultural commitments, the socially responsible member of the profession is concerned with implementation of the relevant cultural commitments *plus* a concern for their impact on and conditioning by other factors in the society.

There was a sense in which, some centuries ago, a hereditary aristocracy could serve as the focus of fiduciary responsibility at the higher levels. This possibility has clearly been destroyed by the basic conflict of the modern egalitarian complex with the principle of heredity of status. In this structural reference it can perhaps be said that one of the greatest integrative needs of modern society is for a functional equivalent of aristocracy.

Notes

1. It is well known that, in Communist countries, the higher nonmanual occupations, including those of industrial managers and scientists, are classified as belonging to the "intelligentsia," which is explicitly said to be part of the "working class." Of course theoretically in such societies there is no longer a "bourgeois" class.

2. S. M. Miller points out that the economic aspect of welfare would take three components into account, namely, income, assets and services. On income distributions, a convenient source is Herman Miller (1964).

3. Earlier societies, notably in the Western orbit, however, positively institutionalized a pattern of *diffuse* inequality through the institution of aristocracy. This seems to link up with a conception of inherent "substance," i.e., quality in pattern-variable terms. In some respects the "class" division of the Christian church was similar, namely into the "religious" and the "lay" components. The process of "elimination" of this diffuse superiority-inferiority distinction has, significantly, typically taken the form of upgrading of the status of the "common" or "lay" component rather than the reverse. See Parsons, 1968. It is probably correct to regard the persisting stigmatization of groups on grounds of "race" and "poverty" or the combination of the two, as a residuum of this more general historic division.

4. It may of course be contended that it is not efficiency of production so much as the opportunity of the individual producer to "do his own thing" (in contemporary phrasing) which justifies competition. On this whole complex problem area, see the famous essay of Frank H. Knight (1935).

References

Bowles, F. 1963. Access to Higher Education. New York: Columbia University Press.

Coleman, J., *et al.* 1966. Equality of Educational Opportunity. Washington, D.C.: U.S. Office of Education.

Davis, K., and W. E. Moore. 1945. "Some principles of stratification." American Sociological Review 10, No. 2: 242–249.

Freund, F., and Ulich. 1965. Religion in the Public School. Cambridge, Mass.: Harvard University Press.

Kagan, J. (ed.). 1967. Creativity and Learning. Boston: Houghton Mifflin.

Knight, F. H. 1935. "The ethics of competition." in Ethics of Competition. New York: Harper.

Marshall, T. H. 1965. Class, Citizenship and Social Development. Garden City, New York: Anchor Books.

Mayhew, Leon. 1968. "Ascription in modern societies." Sociological Inquiry (Spring): 105–120.

Miller, Herman. 1964. Rich Man, Poor Man. New York: Signet Books.

Moynihan, Daniel P. 1969a. On Understanding Poverty. New York: Basic Books.

_____. 1969b. Maximum Feasible Misunderstanding. New York: The Free Press.

Ortega y Gassett, J. 1932. The Revolt of the Masses. New York: Norton.

Parsons, Talcott. 1954. Essays in Sociological Theory. New York: The Free Press.

_____. 1966a. Societies: Evolutionary and Comparative Perspectives. Englewood Cliffs, N.J.: Prentice-Hall.

_____. 1966b. "Youth behavior and values." in E. Landy and A. Kroll (eds.), Needs and Influencing Forces. Cambridge, Mass.: Harvard Graduate School of Education.

_____. 1968. "Professions." in David Sills (ed.), The International Encyclopedia of the Social Sciences. New York: Macmillan Company and The Free Press. 12:536–547.

_____. 1969a. Politics and Social Structure. New York: The Free Press.

_____. 1969b. "On the concept of influence"; "On the concept of political power"; "On the concept of value commitments." in Politics and Social Structure. New York: The Free Press.

Parsons, T., and G. M. Platt. 1972. "Higher education, changing socialization, and contemporary student dissent." in Matilda Riley, *et al.* (eds.), Aging and Society. New York: The Russell Sage Foundation.

Rainwater, Lee. 1969. "The problem of lower-class culture and poverty war strategy." in Moynihan (ed.), On Understanding Poverty. New York: Basic Books.

Rokkan, Stein. 1960. "Citizen participation in political life." International Social Science Journal 12.

White, Winston. 1961. Beyond Conformity. New York: The Free Press.

Theories of Post-Industrialism and Post-Modernity

DANIEL BELL

The Coming of Post-Industrial Society

The concept of the post-industrial society deals primarily with changes *in the social structure*, the way in which the economy is being transformed and the occupational system reworked, and with the new relations between theory and empiricism, particularly science and technology. These changes can be charted, as I seek to do in this [chapter]. But I do not claim that these changes in social structure *determine* corresponding changes in the polity or the culture. Rather, the changes in social structure pose *questions* for the rest of society in three ways. First, the social structure—especially the social structure—is a structure of roles, designed to coordinate the actions of individuals to achieve specific ends. Roles segment individuals by defining limited modes of behavior appropriate to a particular position, but individuals do not always willingly accept the requirements of a role. One aspect of the post-industrial society, for example, is the increasing bureaucratization of science and the increasing specialization of intellectual work into minute parts. Yet it is not clear that individuals entering science will accept this segmentation, as did the individuals who entered the factory system a hundred and fifty years ago.

Second, changes in social structure pose "management" problems for the political system. In a society which becomes increasingly conscious of its fate, and seeks to control its own fortunes, the political order necessarily becomes paramount.

Since the post-industrial society increases the importance of the technical component of knowledge, it forces the hierophants of the new society—the scientists, engineers, and technocrats—either to compete with politicians or become their allies. The relationship between the social structure and the political order thus becomes one of the chief problems of power in a post-industrial society. And, third, the new modes of life, which depend strongly on the primacy of cognitive and theoretical knowledge, inevitably challenge the tendencies of the culture, which strives for the enhancement of the self and turns increasingly antinomian and anti-institutional.

In this [chapter], I am concerned chiefly with the social structural and political consequences of the post-industrial society. In a later work I shall deal with its relation to culture. But the heart of the endeavor is to trace the societal changes primarily within the social structure.

"Too large a generalization," Alfred North Whitehead wrote, "leads to mere barrenness. It is the large generalization, limited by a happy particularity, which is the fruitful conception."[1] It is easy—and particularly so today—to set forth an extravagant theory which, in its historical sweep, makes a striking claim to originality. But when tested eventually by reality, it turns into a caricature—viz. James Burnham's theory of the managerial revolution thirty years ago, or C. Wright Mills's conception of the power elite, or W. W.

Rostow's stages of economic growth. I have tried to resist that impulse. Instead, I am dealing here with *tendencies,* and have sought to explore the meaning and consequences of those tendencies if the changes in social structure that I describe were to work themselves to their logical limits. But there is no guarantee that they will. Social tensions and social conflicts may modify a society considerably; wars and recriminations can destroy it; the tendencies may provoke a set of reactions that inhibit change. Thus I am writing what Hans Vahinger called an "as if," a fiction, a logical construction of what *could* be, against which the future social reality can be compared in order to see what intervened to change society in the direction it did take.

The concept of the post-industrial society is a large generalization. Its meaning can be more easily understood if one specifies [eleven] dimensions, or components, of the term:

1. *The centrality of theoretical knowledge.* Every society has always existed on the basis of knowledge, but only now has there been a change whereby the codification of theoretical knowledge and materials science becomes the basis of innovations in technology. One sees this primarily in the new science-based industries—computers, electronics, optics, polymers—that mark the last third of the century.

2. *The creation of a new intellectual technology.* Through new mathematical and economic techniques—based on the computer linear programming, Markov chains, stochastic processes and the like—we can utilize modeling, simulation and other tools of system analysis and decision theory in order to chart more efficient, "rational" solutions to economic and engineering, if not social, problems.

3. *The spread of a knowledge class.* The fastest growing group in society is the technical and professional class. In the United States this group, together with managers, made up 25 percent of a labor force of eight million persons in 1975. By the year 2000, the technical and professional class will be the largest single group in the society.

4. *The change from goods to services.* In the United States today more than 65 out of every 100 persons are engaged in services. By 1980, the figure will be about 70 in every 100. A large service sector exists in every society. In a pre-industrial society this is mainly a household and domestic class. (In England, it was the single largest class in the society until about 1870.) In an industrial society, the services are transportation, utilities, and finance, which are auxiliary to the production of goods, and personal service (beauticians, restaurant employees, and so forth). But in a post-industrial society, the new services are primarily human services (principally in health, education and social services) and professional and technical services (e.g., research, evaluation, computers, and systems analysis). The expansion of these services becomes a constraint on economic growth and a source of persistent inflation.

5. *A change in the character of work.* In a pre-industrial world, life is a game against nature in which men wrest their living from the soil, the waters, or the forests, working usually in small groups, subject to the vicissitudes of nature. In an industrial society, work is a game against fabricated nature, in which men become dwarfed by machines as they turn out goods and things. But in a post-industrial world, work is primarily a "game between persons" (between bureaucrat and client, doctor and patient, teacher and student, or within research groups, office groups, service groups). Thus in the experience of work and the daily routine, nature is excluded, artifacts are excluded, and persons have to learn how to live with one another. In the history of human society, this is a completely new and unparalleled state of affairs.

6. *The role of women.* Work in the industrial sector (e.g., the factory) has largely been men's work, from which women have been usually excluded. Work in the post-industrial sector (e.g., human services) provides expanded employment opportunities for women. For the first time, one can say that women have a secure base for economic independence. One sees this in the steadily rising curve of women's participation in the labor force, in the number of families (now 60 percent of the total) that have more than one regular wage earner, and in the rising incidence of divorce as women increasingly feel less dependent, economically, on men.

7. *Science as the imago.* The scientific community, going back to the seventeenth century, has

been a unique institution in human society. It has been charismatic, in that it has been revolutionary in its quest for truth and open in its methods and procedures; it derives its legitimacy from the credo that knowledge itself, not any specific instrumental ends, is the goal of science. Unlike other charismatic communities (principally religious groups and messianic political movements), it has not "routinized" its creeds and enforced official dogmas. Yet until recently, science did not have to deal with the bureaucratization of research, the subordination of its inquiries to state-directed goals, and the "test" of its results on the basis of some instrumental payoff. Now science has become inextricably intertwined not only with technology but with the military and with social technologies and societal needs. In all this—a central feature of the post-industrial society—the character of the new scientific institutions—will be crucial for the future of free inquiry and knowledge.

8. *Situses as political units.* Most of sociological analysis has focused its attention on classes or strata, horizontal units of society that exist in superior-subordinate relation to each other. Yet for the post-industrial sectors, it may well be that *situses* (from the Latin *situ*, location), a set of vertical orders, will be the more important loci of political attachment. On pp. 692–693 I sketch the possible situses of the post-industrial order. There are four *functional* situses—scientific, technological (i.e., applied skills: engineering, economics, medicine), administrative and cultural—and five *institutional* situses—economic enterprises, government bureaus, universities and research complexes, social complexes (e.g., hospitals, social-service centers), and the military. My argument is that the major interest conflicts will be between the situs groups, and that the attachments to these situses might be sufficiently strong to prevent the organization of the new professional groups into a coherent class in society.[2]

9. *Meritocracy.* A post-industrial society, being primarily a technical society, awards place less on the basis of inheritance or property (though these can command wealth or cultural advantage) than on education and skill. Inevitably the question of a meritocracy becomes a crucial normative question. In this [chapter] I attempt to define the character of meritocracy and defend the idea of a "just meritocracy," or of place based on achievement, through the respect of peers.

10. *The end of scarcity?* Most socialist and utopian theories of the nineteenth century ascribed almost all the ills of society to the scarcity of goods and the competition of men for these scarce goods. In fact, one of the most common definitions of economics characterized it as the art of efficient allocation of scarce goods among competing ends. Marx and other socialists argued that abundance was the precondition for socialism and claimed, in fact, that under socialism there would be no need to adopt normative rules of just distribution, since there would be enough for everyone's needs. In that sense, the definition of communism was the abolition of economics, or the "material embodiment" of philosophy. Yet it is quite clear that scarcity will always be with us. I mean not just the question of scarce resources (for this is still a moot point) but that a post-industrial society, by its nature, brings new scarcities which nineteenth- and early-twentieth-century writers had never thought of. The socialists and liberals had talked of the scarcities of goods; but in the post-industrial society there will be scarcities of information and of time. And the problems of allocation inevitably remain, in the crueler form, even, of man becoming *homo economicus* in the disposition of his leisure time.

11. *The economics of information.* Information is by its nature a collective, not a private, good (i.e., a property). In the marketing of individual goods, it is clear that a "competitive" strategy between producers is to be preferred lest enterprise become slothful or monopolistic. Yet for the optimal social investment in knowledge, we have to follow a "cooperative" strategy in order to increase the spread and use of knowledge in society. This new problem regarding information poses the most fascinating challenges to economists and decision makers in respect to both theory and policy in the post-industrial society. ...

Who Holds Power?

Decisions are a matter of power, and the crucial questions in any society are: *Who* holds power?

TABLE 1
Stratification and Power

	PRE-INDUSTRIAL	INDUSTRIAL	POST-INDUSTRIAL
Resource	Land	Machinery	Knowledge
Social locus	Farm Plantation	Business firm	University Research institute
Dominant figures	Landowner Military	Businessmen	Scientists Research men
Means of power	Direct control of force	Indirect influence on politics	Balance of technical-political forces Franchises and rights
Class base	Property Military force	Property Political organization Technical skill	Technical skill Political organization
Access	Inheritance Seizure by armies	Inheritance Patronage Education	Education Mobilization Co-optation

and *how* is power held? How power is held is a *system* concept; who holds power is a *group* concept. How one comes to power defines the base and route; who identifies the persons. Clearly, when there is a change in the nature of the system, new groups come to power. (In the tableau of pre-industrial, industrial, and post-industrial societies, the major differences can be shown schematically—see Table 1 on Stratification and Power.)

In the post-industrial society, technical skill becomes the base of and education the mode of access to power; those (or the elite of the group) who come to the fore in this fashion are the scientists. But this does not mean that the scientists are monolithic and act as a corporate group. In actual political situations scientists may divide ideologically (as they have in the recent ABM debate), and different groups of scientists will align themselves with different segments of other elites. In the nature of politics, few groups are monolithic ("the" military, "the" scientists, "the" business class), and any group contending for power will seek allies from different groups. (Thus, in the Soviet Union, for example, where the interest groups are more clear-cut in functional terms—factory managers, central planners, army officers, party officials—and the power struggle more naked, any faction in the Politburo *seeking* power will make alliances *across* group lines. Yet once in

power, the victors will have to make decisions *between* groups and affect the relative distribution of power of the functional units and shift the weights of the *system*.) In the change of the system in the post-industrial society, two propositions become evident:

1. As a *stratum*, scientists, or more widely the technical intelligentsia, now have to be taken into account in the political process, though they may not have been before.
2. Science itself is ruled by an ethos which is different from the ethos of other major social groups (e.g. business, the military), and this ethos will *predispose* scientists to act in a different fashion, politically, from other groups.

Forty-five years ago Thorstein Veblen, in his *Engineers and the Price System,* foresaw a new society based on technical organization and industrial management, a "soviet of technicians," as he put it in the striking language he loved to use in order to scare and mystify the academic world. In making this prediction, Veblen shared the illusion of that earlier technocrat, Henri de Saint-Simon, that the complexity of the industrial system and the indispensability of the technician made military and political revolutions a thing of the past. "Revolutions in the eighteenth century," Veblen wrote, "were military and political; and the Elder Statesmen who now believe themselves to be making history still believe that revolutions can be made and unmade by the same ways and means in the twentieth century. But any substantial or effectual overturn in the twentieth century will necessarily be an industrial overturn, and by the same token, any twentieth-century revolution can be combatted or neutralized only by industrial ways and means."

If a revolution were to come about in the United States—as a practiced skeptic Veblen was highly dubious of that prospect—it would not be led by a minority political party, as in Soviet Russia, which was a loose-knit and backward industrial region, nor would it come from the trade-union "votaries of the dinner pail," who, as a vested interest themselves, simply sought to keep prices up and labor supply down. It would occur, he said, along the lines "already laid down by the material conditions of its productive industry." And, turning this Marxist prism to his own perceptions, Veblen continued: "These main lines of revolutionary strategy are lines of technical organization and industrial management; essentially lines of industrial engineering; such as will fit the organization to take care of the highly technical industrial system that constitutes the indispensable material foundation of any modern civilized community."

The heart of Veblen's assessment of the revolutionary class is thus summed up in his identification of the "production engineers" as the indispensable "General Staff of the industrial system." "Without their immediate and unremitting guidance and correction the industrial system will not work. It is a mechanically organized structure of the technical processes designed, installed, and conducted by the production engineers. Without them and their constant attention to the industrial equipment, the mechanical appliances of industry will foot up to just so much junk."

This syndicalist idea that revolution in the twentieth century could only be an "industrial overturn" exemplifies the fallacy in so much of Veblen's thought. For as we have learned, no matter how technical social processes may be, the crucial turning points in a society occur in a political form. It is not the technocrat who ultimately holds power, but the politician.

The major changes that have reshaped American society over the past thirty years—the creation of a managed economy, a welfare society, and a mobilized polity—grew out of political responses: in the first instances to accommodate the demands of economically insecure and disadvantaged groups—the farmers, workers, blacks and the poor—for protection from the hazards of the market; and later because of the concentration of resources and political objectives following the mobilized postures of the cold war and the space race.

All of this opens up a broader and more theoretical perspective about the changing nature of class and social position in contemporary society. *Class, in the final sense, denotes not a specific group of persons but a system that has institutionalized the ground rules for acquiring, holding, and transferring differential power and its attendant privileges.* In Western society, the dominant system has been property, guaranteed and safeguarded by the legal order, and transmitted through a system of marriage and family. But over the past twenty-five to fifty years, the property system has been breaking up. In American society today, there are three modes of power and social mobility, and this baffles students of society who seek to tease out the contradictory sources of class positions. There is the historic mode of property as the basis of wealth and power, with inheritance as the major route of access. There is technical skill as the basis of power and position, with education as the necessary route of access to skill. And finally there is political office as a base of power, with organization of a machine as the route of access.

One can, in a simplified way, present these modes in Table 2.

The difficulty in the analysis of power in modern Western societies is that these three systems [in Table 2] co-exist, overlap, and interpenetrate. While the family loses its importance as an economic unit, particularly with the decline of family-firms and the break-up of family capitalism, family background is still advantageous in providing impetus (financial, cultural and personal connections) for the family member. Ethnic groups, often blocked in the economic access to

TABLE 2
Reduced Model

Base of Power:	Property	Political Position	Skill
Mode of Access:	Inheritance Entrepreneurial Ability	Machine Membership Co-optation	Education
Social Unit:	Family	Group Party	Individual

position, have resorted to the political route to gain privilege and wealth. And, increasingly, in the post-industrial society, technical skill becomes an overriding condition of competence for place and position. A son may succeed a father as head of a firm, but without the managerial skill to run the enterprise, the firm may lose out in competition with other, professionally managed corporations. To some extent, the owner of a firm and the politician may hire technicians and experts; yet, unless the owner or politician themselves know enough about the technical issues, their judgments may falter.

The rise of the new elites based on skill derives from the simple fact that knowledge and planning—military planning, economic planning, social planning—have become the basic requisites for all organized action in a modern society. The members of this new technocratic elite, with their new techniques of decision-making (systems analysis, linear programming, and program budgeting), have now become essential to the formulation and analysis of decisions on which political judgments have to be made, if not to the wielding of power. It is in this broad sense that the spread of education, research, and administration has created a new constituency—the technical and professional intelligentsia.

While these technologists are not bound by a sufficient common interest to make them a political class, they do have common characteristics. They are, first, the products of a new system in the recruitment for power (just as property and inheritance were the essence of the old system). The norms of the new intelligentsia—the norms of professionalism—are a departure from the hitherto prevailing norms of economic self-interest which have guided a business civilization. In the

upper reaches of this new elite—that is, in the scientific community—men hold significantly different values, which could become the foundation of the new ethos for such a class.

Actually, the institution of property itself is undergoing a fundamental revision, in a significant way. In Western society for the past several hundred years, property, as the protection of private rights to wealth, has been the economic basis of individualism. Traditionally the institution of property, as Charles Reich of the Yale Law School has put it, "guards the troubled boundary between individual man and the state." In modern life property has changed in two distinctive ways. One of these is elementary: Individual property has become corporate, and property is no longer controlled by owners but by managers. In a more subtle and diffuse way, however, a new kind of property has emerged, and with it a different kind of legal relationship. To put it more baldly, property today consists not only of visible things (land, possessions, titles) but also of claims, grants, and contracts. The property relationship is not only between persons but between the individual and the government. As Reich points out, "The valuables dispensed by government take many forms, but they all share one characteristic. They are steadily taking the place of the traditional forms of wealth—forms which are held as private property. Social insurance substitutes for savings, a government contract replaces a businessman's customers and goodwill. ... Increasingly, Americans live on government largess—allocated by government on its own terms, and held by recipients subject to conditions which express 'the public interest.'"[3]

While many forms of this "new property" represent direct grants (subsidies to farmers, corporations, and universities) or are contracts for services or goods (to industry and universities), the most pervasive form is claims held by individuals (social security, medical care, housing allowances) which derive from a new definition of social rights: claims on the community to ensure equality of treatment, claims legitimately due a person so that he will be able to share in the social heritage. And the most important claim of all is full access to education, within the limits of one's talent and potential.

The result of all this is to enlarge the arena of power, and at the same time to complicate the modes of decision-making. The domestic political process initiated by the New Deal was in effect a broadening of the "brokerage" system—the system of political deals between constituencies—although there are now many participants in the game. But there is also a new dimension in the political process, which has given the technocrats a new role. Matters of foreign policy have not been a reflex of internal political forces, but a judgment about the national interest, involving strategy decisions based on the calculation of an opponent's strength and intentions. Once the fundamental policy decision was made to oppose the communist power, many technical decisions, based on military technology and strategic assessments, took on the highest importance in the shaping of subsequent policy. Even a reworking of the economic map of the United States followed as well, with Texas and California gaining great importance because of the electronics and aerospace industries. In these instances technology and strategy laid down the requirements, and only then could business and local political groups seek to modify, or take advantage of, these decisions so as to protect their own economic interests.

In all this, the technical intelligentsia holds a double position. To the extent that it has interests in research, and positions in the universities, it becomes a new constituency—just as the military is a distinct new constituency, since this country has never before had a permanent military establishment seeking money and support for science, for research and development. Thus the intelligentsia becomes a claimant, like other groups, for public support (though its influence is felt in the bureaucratic and administrative labyrinth, rather than in the electoral system or mass pressure). At the same time, the technicians represent an indispensable administrative staff for the political office holder with his public following. ...

If one turns, then, to the societal structure of the post-industrial society considered along these two historical axes [of class and power], two conclusions are evident. First, the major class of the emerging new society is primarily a professional class, based on knowledge rather than property. But second, the control system of the society is lodged not in a successor-occupational class but in the political order, and the question of who manages the political order is an open one. (See "Schema: The Societal Structure of the Post-Industrial Society.")

In terms of status (esteem and recognition, and possibly income), the knowledge class may be the highest class in the new society, but in the nature of that structure there is no intrinsic reason for this class, on the basis of some coherent or corporate identity, to become a new economic interest class, or a new political class which would bid for power. The reasons for this are evident from an inspection of the Schema.

The professional class as I define it is made up of four estates: the scientific, the technological, the administrative, and the cultural.[4] While the estates, as a whole, are bound by a common ethos, there is no intrinsic interest that binds one to the other, except for a common defense of the idea of learning; in fact there are large disjunctions between them. The scientific estate is concerned with the pursuit of basic knowledge and seeks, legitimately, to defend the conditions of such pursuit, untrammeled by political or extraneous influence. The technologists, whether engineers, economists, or physicians, base their work on a codified body of knowledge, but in the application of that knowledge to social or economic purposes they are constrained by the policies of the different situses they are obedient to. The administrative estate is concerned with the management of organizations and is bound by the self-interest of the organization itself (its perpetuation and aggrandizement) as well as the implementation of social purposes, and may come into conflict with one or another of the estates. The cultural es-

Schema: The Societal Structure of the Post-Industrial Society (U.S. Model)

I. *Statuses: Axis of Stratification—Based on Knowledge*
   (Horizontal Structures)
   A. The professional class: the four estates
      1. Scientific
      2. Technological (applied skills: engineering, economics, medicine)
      3. Administrative
      4. Cultural (artistic and religious)
   B. Technicians and semi-professional
   C. Clerical and sales
   D. Craftsmen and semi-skilled (blue-collar)
II. *Situses: Locations of Occupational Activities*
    (Vertical Structures)
    A. Economic enterprises and business firms
    B. Government (bureaucratic: judicial and administrative)
    C. Universities and research institutions
    D. Social complexes (hospitals, social-service centers, etc.)
    E. The military
III. *Control System: The Political Order*
     A. The directorate
        1. Office of the President
        2. Legislative leaders
        3. Bureaucratic chiefs
        4. Military chiefs
     B. The polities: constituencies and claimants
        1. Parties
        2. Elites (scientific, academic, business, military)
        3. Mobilized groups
           a) Functional groups (business, professional, labor)
           b) Ethnic groups
           c) Special-focus groups
              (1) Functional (mayors of cities, poor, etc.)
              (2) Expressive (youth, women, homosexual, etc.)

tate—artistic and religious—is involved with the expressive symbolism (plastic or ideational) of forms and meanings, but to the extent that it is more intensively concerned with meanings, it may find itself increasingly hostile to the technological and administrative estates. As I noted in the introduction, the axial principle of modern culture, in its concern with the self, is antinomian and anti-institutional, and thus hostile to the functional rationality which tends to dominate the application of knowledge by the technological and administrative estates. Thus in the post-in-dustrial society one finds increasingly a disjunction between social structure and culture which inevitably affects the cohesiveness if not the corporate consciousness of the four estates.[5]

While the classes may be represented, horizontally, by *statuses* (headed by the four estates), the society is organized, vertically, by *situses,* which are the actual loci of occupational activities and interests. I use this unfamiliar sociological word *situses* to emphasize the fact that in day-to-day activities the actual play and conflict of interests exist between the organizations to which men belong, rather than between the more diffuse class or status identities. In a capitalist society, the property owner or businessman, as a class, is located exclusively in the business firm or corporation, so that status and situs are joined. In the post-industrial society, however, the four estates are distributed among many different situses. Scientists can work for economic enterprises, government, universities, social complexes, or the military (though the bulk of the "pure" scientists are to be found in the university). And the same distributions hold for the technologists and the managers. Because of this "cross-cutting," the likelihood of a pure "estate" consciousness for political purposes tends to diminish.

Finally, if the major historical turn in the last quarter-century has been the subordination of the economic function to societal goals, the political order necessarily becomes the control system of the society. But who runs it, and for whose (or what) ends? In one respect, what the change may mean is that traditional social conflicts have simply shifted from one arena to another, so that what the traditional classes fought out in the economic realm, where men sought comparative advantage in place, privilege and domination, is now transferred to the political realm, and as that arena widens, the special foci and ethnic groups (the poor and the blacks) now seek to gain through politics the privileges and advantages they could not obtain in the economic order. This is what has been taking place in recent years, and it will continue. The second, and structurally more pervasive, shift is that in the post-industrial society the *situses* rather than the *statuses* would be the major political-interest units in the society. To some extent this is evident in the familiar phenomenon of pressure groups. But in the post-industrial society it is more likely that the *situses* will achieve greater corporate cohesiveness vis-à-vis one another and become the major claimants for public support and the major constituencies in the determination of public policy.[6] And yet the very forces which have re-emphasized the primacy of the political order in a technical world make it imperative to define some coherent goals for the society as a whole and, in the process, to articulate a public philosophy which is more than the sum of what particular situses or social

groups may want. In the efforts to forge some such coherence one may find the seeds of the cohesiveness of the professional class in the post-industrial society.

A new social system, contrary to Marx, does not always arise necessarily within the shell of an old one but sometimes outside of it. The framework of feudal society was made up of noblemen, lords, soldiers, and priests whose wealth was based on land. The bourgeois society that took hold in the thirteenth century was made up of artisans, merchants, and free professionals whose property lay in their skills or their willingness to take risks, and whose mundane values were far removed from the fading theatrics of the chivalric style of life. It arose, however, outside the feudal landed structure, in the free communes, or towns, that were no longer seignorial dependencies. And these self-ruling small communes became the cornerstones of the future European mercantile and industrial society.[7]

So, too, the process today. The roots of post-industrial society lie in the inexorable influence of science on productive methods, particularly in the transformation of the electrical and chemical industries at the beginning of the twentieth century. But as Robert Heilbroner has observed: "Science, as we know it, began well before capitalism existed and did not experience its full growth until well after capitalism was solidly entrenched." And science, as a quasi-autonomous force, would extend beyond capitalism. By this token, one can say that the scientific estate—its ethos and its organization—is the monad that contains within itself the imago of the future society.[8] ...

Meritocracy and Equality

In 1958, the English sociologist Michael Young wrote a fable, *The Rise of the Meritocracy*.[9] It purports to be a "manuscript," written in the year 2033, which breaks off inconclusively for reasons the "narrator" failed to comprehend. The theme is the transformation of English society, by the turn of the twenty-first century, owing to the victory of the principle of achievement over that of ascription (i.e. the gaining of place by assignment or inheritance). For centuries, the elite positions in the society had been held by the children of the nobility on the hereditary principle of succession. But in the nature of modern society, "the rate of social progress depend[ed] on the degree to which power is matched with intelligence." Britain could no longer afford a ruling class without the necessary technical skills. Through the successive school-reform acts, the principle of merit slowly became established. Each man had his place in the society on the basis of "IQ and Effort." By 1990 or thereabouts, all adults with IQs over 125 belonged to the meritocracy.

But with that transformation came an unexpected reaction. Previously, talent had been distributed throughout the society, and each class or social group had its own natural leaders. Now all men of talent were raised into a common elite, and those below had no excuses for their failures; they bore the stigma of rejection, they were known inferiors.

By the year 2034 the Populists had revolted. Though the majority of the rebels were members of the lower classes, the leaders were high-status women, often the wives of leading scientists. Relegated during the early married years to the household because of the need to nurture high-IQ children, the activist women had demanded equality between the sexes, a movement that was then generalized into the demand for equality for all, and for a classless society. Life was not to be ruled by "a mathematical measure" but each person would develop his own diverse capacities for leading his own life.[10] The Populists won. After little more than half a century, the Meritocracy had come to an end.

Is this, too, the fate of the post-industrial society? The post-industrial society, in its initial logic, is a meritocracy. Differential status and differential income are based on technical skills and higher education. Without those achievements one cannot fulfill the requirements of the new social division of labor which is a feature of that society. And there are few high places open without those skills. To that extent, the post-industrial society differs from society at the turn of the twentieth century. The initial change, of course, came in the professions. Seventy years or so ago, one could still "read" law in a lawyer's office and take the bar examination without a college degree. Today, in medicine, law, accounting, and a dozen other professions, one needs a college degree and accrediting, through examination, by legally sanctioned committees of the profession, before one can practice one's art. For many years, until after World War II, business was the chief route open to an ambitious and aggressive person who wanted to strike out for himself. And the rags-to-riches ascent (or, more accurately, clerk-to-capitalist, if one follows the career of a Rockefeller, Harriman, or Carnegie) required drive and ruthlessness rather than education and skills. One can still start various kinds of small businesses (usually, now, by franchise from a larger corporation), but the expansion of such enterprises takes vastly different skills than in the past. Within the corporation, as managerial positions have become professionalized, individuals are rarely promoted from shop jobs below but are chosen from the outside, with a college degree as the passport of recognition. Only in politics, where position may be achieved through the ability to recruit a following, or through patronage, is there a relatively open ladder without formal credentials.

Technical skill, in the post-industrial society, is what the economists call "human capital." An "investment" in four years of college, according to initial estimates of Gary Becker, yields, over the average working life of the male graduate, an annual return of about 13 percent.[11] Graduation from an elite college (or elite law school or business school) gives one a further differential advantage over graduates from "mass" or state schools. Thus, the university, which once reflected the status system of the society, has now become the arbiter of class position. As the gatekeeper, it has gained a quasi-monopoly in determining the future stratification of the society.[12]

Any institution which gains a quasi-monopoly power over the fate of individuals is likely, in a free society, to be subject to quick attack. Thus, it is striking that the populist revolt, which Michael Young foresaw several decades hence, has already begun, at the very onset of the post-industrial society. One sees this in the derogation of the IQ and the denunciation of theories espousing a genetic basis of intelligence; the demand for "open admission" to universities on the part of minority groups in the large urban centers; the pressure for increased numbers of blacks, women, and specific minority groups such as Puerto Ricans and Chicanos in the faculties of universities, by quotas if necessary; and the attack on "credentials" and even schooling itself as the determinant of a man's position in the society. A post-industrial society reshapes the class structure of society by creating new technical elites. The populist reaction, which has begun in the 1970s, raises the demand for greater "equality" as a defense against being excluded from that society. Thus the issue of meritocracy versus equality. ...

The claim for group rights stands in formal contradiction to the principle of individualism, with its emphasis on achievement and universalism. But in reality it is no more than the extension, to hitherto excluded social units, of the group principle which has undergirded American politics from the start. The group process—which was the vaunted discovery of the "realists" of American political science—consisted largely of economic bargaining between functional or pressure groups operating outside the formal structure of the party system. What we now find are ethnic and ascriptive groups claiming formal representation both in the formal political structure and in all other institutions of the society as well.

These claims are legitimated, further, by the fact that America has been a pluralist society, or has come to accept a new definition of pluralism rather than the homogeneity of Americanism. Pluralism, in its classic conceptions,[13] made a claim for the continuing cultural identity of ethnic and religious groups and for the institutional autonomy of cultural institutions (e.g. universities) from politics. Pluralism was based on the separation of realms. But what we have today is a thoroughgoing politicizing of society in which not only the market is subordinated to political decision but all institutions have to bend to the demands of a political center and politicize themselves in group representational terms. Here, too, there has been another change. In functional group politics, membership was not fixed, and one could find cross-cutting allegiances or shifting coalitions. Today the groups that claim representation—in the political parties, in the universities, in the hospitals and the community—are

formed by primordial or biological ties, and one cannot erase the ascriptive nature of sex or color.

And yet, once one accepts the principle of redress and representation of the disadvantaged in the group terms that were initially formulated, it is difficult for the polity to deny those later claims. That is the logic of democracy which has always been present in the ambiguous legacy of the principle of equality.

Notes

1. Alfred North Whitehead, *Science and the Modern World* (New York, 1960; original edition, 1925), p. 46.

2. What is striking is that in the communist world, it is quite clear that *situses* play the major role in politics. One analyzes the play of power, not in class terms, but on the basis of the rivalries among the party, the military, the planning ministries, the industrial enterprises, the collective farms, the cultural institutions—all of which are *situses*.

3. Charles Reich, "The New Property," *The Public Interest,* no. 3 (Spring 1966), p. 57.

4. The suggestion of four estates is derived, of course, from Don K. Price's fruitful book *The Scientific Estate* (Cambridge, Mass., 1965). Price defines four functions in government—the scientific, professional, administrative, and political—and converts each function, as an ideal type, into an estate. My differences with Price are twofold: I think the estates can be represented more accurately as social groups, rather than functions; more importantly, I do not consider the *political* function coeval logically with the others, for I see the political as the control system of the entire societal structure. Terminologically, I have substituted the word "technological" (for the applied skills) where Price uses "professional," since I would reserve "professional" for the larger meaning of the entire class, and I have added a cultural estate, where Price has none. Nonetheless, my indebtedness to Price is great.

5. One might note that the more extreme forms of the "new consciousness" such as Theodore Rozsak's *The Making of a Counter-Culture* and Charles Reich's *The Greening of America* manifest a distinct hostility not only to scientism, but to science as well.

6. The limitation of this analysis is that while the post-industrial society, in its societal structure, increasingly becomes a *functional* society, the political order is not organized in functional terms. Thus the continuing existence of the traditional geographical districts and the dispersal of persons in this fashion means that the

political issues at any one time are much more diffuse than the interests of the particular statuses or situses. It would also indicate that the situses would, like the pressure groups, operate primarily through the lobbying of the legislative and executive branches, rather than work directly through the electoral process. Reality complicates immeasurably any ideal-type schemas.

7. Paradoxically, the growth of that society came about only after the self-contained economic life of the commune—its roots—was broken by the rise of larger-scale industry which, in branching out, could buy its raw materials in one town and sell in another, and which made its way, against both the older feudal society and the regulative restrictions of the commune, in alliance with the monarchical centralization of the newly emerging national state.

8. This is, indeed, Heilbroner's suggestion. See Robert Heilbroner, *The Limits of American Capitalism* (New York, 1966), p. 115.

9. Michael Young, *The Rise of the Meritocracy, 1870–2033* (London, 1958).

10. A theoretician of the Technicians party, Professor Eagle, had argued that marriage partners, in the na-

tional interest, should consult the intelligence register, for a high-IQ man who mates with a low-IQ woman is wasting his genes. The activist women, on the other hand, took romance as their banner and beauty as their flag, arguing that marriage should be based on attraction. Their favorite slogan was "Beauty is achievable by all."

11. Gary S. Becker, *Human Capital* (New York, 1964), p. 112. Later writers have suggested this figure may be too high; the point remains that a college degree does provide an investment "yield."

12. For a comprehensive discussion of this major social change, see Jencks and Riesman, *The Academic Revolution* (New York, 1968). For a survey of the reaction, see Stephen Graubard and Geno Ballotti, eds., *The Embattled University* (New York, 1970).

13. See, for example, the work of R. M. MacIver, *The More Perfect Union: A Program for the Control of Intergroup Discrimination* (New York, 1948), and on the religious side, John Courtney Murray, *We Hold These Truths: Reflections on the American Proposition* (New York, 1960).

GØSTA ESPING-ANDERSEN

Postindustrial Cleavage Structures: A Comparison of Evolving Patterns of Social Stratification in Germany, Sweden, and the United States

Introduction

Over the last few decades, most labor movements in the Western capitalist democracies have experienced crisis and decline. Trade unions have been weakened in terms of their capacity for cohesive collective action and, in some cases, have suffered fragmentation and eroded membership. Except in the Mediterranean basin, the social democratic or labor parties have been facing (sometimes devas-

tating) electoral decline, increased incapacity to forge governing coalitions, ideological flux and programmatic impasse, and frequently even decomposition.[1] We can attribute these problems to a host of factors, but the ongoing transformation in the class structure must surely count as decisive. Virtually all labor movements emerged as a response to the rise of industrialism, and logically built their organizations, programs, ideology, and mobilization strategies on the image of the industrial mass-worker. However, what is distinctive of our epoch is the rapid, and even revolutionary, decline of the "Fordist" model of industrial mass production. Within the shrunken manufacturing economy, the organization and division of work is being recast; service employment is burgeoning and/or we find growing joblessness and mass unemployment.[2]

These changes are producing a new occupational structure. Everywhere, industrial mass production workers are in decline and professionals are on the rise. However, within this broad trend, nations diverge; in some, like the United States, we see the birth of a new low-paid service proletariat in the consumer industries; in others, like Sweden, there is also a burgeoning new service proletariat, but concentrated in relatively well-paid and secure welfare state jobs. In Germany, postindustrialism is producing joblessness rather than services.

We can therefore identify two broad trends. The first is a *common* structural transformation: the decline of industry, the expansion of services, an overall skill upgrading and professionalization. The "Fordist" stratification system is in eclipse. The second is a *contingent* structural transformation whose shape depends ultimately on the institutional and political framework within which postindustrialization occurs. Because of institutional differences, nations embark upon distinct postindustrial trajectories.

The labor movements are likely to be seriously affected by both the common and contingent types of transformation, not only because they alter patterns of social stratification, but also because they are certain to spur the emergence of new social divisions, new forms of collectivity, new identities and, in the end, new axes of conflict.

The main purpose of this chapter is to examine, comparatively, the emerging patterns of stratification in the era of "postindustrialization," and to suggest how these result in new cleavage structures. This, in my view, is a precondition for addressing the larger question of emerging political alliances. Our focus is on three countries that follow decisively different trajectories: Germany, Sweden, and the United States.

Models of Stratification in Postindustrial Society

The literature on postindustrial societies and the new service economy is often preoccupied with the problem of class, precisely because its goal is to understand the prospects for equality and democracy. Postindustrial theory has its pessimistic and optimistic class scenarios. These scenarios are either implicitly or explicitly the basis for political extrapolations.

In Daniel Bell's generally optimistic model, the rise of science and information technologies creates a postindustrial society which is dominated by service employment and professional–technical cadres. Power and privilege derive from the control of scientific knowledge and hence meritocracy will become pre-eminent and the salience of class will decline. In his vision, the control over information will emerge as a principal axis of society. His model does not envisage the emergence of a new postindustrial proletariat. Much of the literature on "post-Fordism" and flexibility shares Bell's positive view, although its emphasis is on skill upgrading and the declining hierarchy within industry.[3]

There are essentially two pessimistic versions. One predicts that modern automation and technology cause the emergence of a workless society. Gershuny argues that the service economy will grow only marginally since households will engage in "self-servicing" via purchased material commodities. Thus emerges the possibility that the "service society" may engender mass joblessness rather than service employment.[4]

The jobless growth model is also envisaged in the Baumol theory of unbalanced growth, which argues that high wage costs in the less productive services will produce a cost-disease problem.[5] Following the Baumol model, mass unemployment can be averted if government "subsidizes" service jobs (i.e. welfare state jobs), or if service workers are willing to accept low wages.

If a large share of the service economy expands on the basis of low wages, we might anticipate the emergence of a new service proletarian class divide. Alternatively, as van Parijs argues, a postindustrial economy without job growth might result in an insider–outsider cleavage: a closed labor market of (upgraded) insiders enjoying high wages and job security (efficiency wages), and a swelling army of outsiders including youth, long-term unemployed, early retirees, and discouraged workers. Jobs, themselves, may become the key asset over which distributional struggles will center.[6]

The second pessimistic version emerges from the literature on deindustrialization. The argument here is that industrial decline generates redundancies mainly among the erstwhile well-paid unionized labor force; this is accompanied by a downward pressure on wages. The result is the "declining middle" and heightened labor market polarization between the top and the new proletarianized bottom. A rather similar model is found in the pessimistic variant of the flexibility literature which suggests the possibility of a "Napoli model" of flexibilization, where firms combine an internal upgraded labor force with a pool of peripheral, "numerically" flexible, labor.[7]

The nature of the welfare state is clearly important in shaping the patterns of postindustrial stratification. As the Baumol logic suggests, welfare state employment is an alternative to mass unemployment or to a low-wage job trajectory. As we shall see, the welfare state "option" has mainly been followed in the Scandinavian countries, accounting for almost all net job growth in the past decades. The Swedish welfare state labor market today accounts for 30 percent of total employment, and it has allowed female participation to increase phenomenally. This contrasts sharply with the transfer-biased Continental European countries where, because of fiscal overload or Christian Democratic preference, social service employment has grown only marginally.

Welfare state institutions also influence the structure of labor supply and the conditions for employment.[8] Opportunities for paid leave from work (ranging from sick pay and maternity to paid leave for education or trade union participation) decide women's capacity to work and pursue careers, and are thus instrumental in narrowing gender-based employment differentials. Yet, the high costs and risks that absenteeism impose on employers may have the adverse effect of inducing "statistical discrimination" in employer hiring strategies. There is little doubt that the extraordinarily high Swedish female participation rates *and* gender segregation are attributable to Sweden's liberal absenteeism policies.

While paid leave enhances female employment, education and retirement schemes can drastically reshape and reduce the supply of labor. Education delays employment entry, and early retirement schemes have in some cases drastically curtailed the normal age of exit. In countries like Germany, early retirement was used to lure the older unskilled labor force to retire as a means to accelerate industrial rationalization. In other words, retirement schemes have been the midwives of manual worker decline and, in countries like Germany, have been instrumental in nurturing a latent insider–outsider axis.

Welfare states differ sharply in their labor market bias and, as we shall see, this affects emerging stratification patterns. Hence, the nature of the welfare state will dictate the ways in which our traditional manufacturing economy is reorganized, the growth and shape of the service sector, the distribution of employment, and also how households organize social reproduction and their use of leisure time.

The Problem of "Classes"

Virtually all varieties of class theory were formulated with the industrial capitalist order in mind. Their target was to provide an understanding of the division of labor and the social hierarchies associated with the industrial divide. Since our task is to understand an emerging "postindustrial" order, I shall shun classical theory and, instead, construct "classes" in a purely heuristic way.

The following analyses of employment change are based on census and survey data for the period from 1960 to the 1980s, a period which is long enough to permit us to identify decisive structural shifts.[9] The analyses focus on three nations that are equally advanced economically and technologically, but which represent three distinct kinds of welfare state and industrial relations system: Germany, Sweden, and the United States.

The weakness of virtually all existing research is that it has focused on either sectoral employment shifts (the rise of jobs in services) or, less commonly, occupational change. In order to identify the outlines of a new stratificational order, we need to combine the two. This we shall undertake in the form of occupation–industry matrices.

The Classification of Industries

It is possible to divide the economy into two broad logics. In one we find the traditional activities associated with the Fordist system of mass production and mass consumption of standardized commodities. Leaving aside the primary sector completely, the principal sectors engaged in the Fordist industrial economy include manufacturing and distribution (wholesale and retail, transportation, utilities, infrastructure, and administration). One can speak of an internal organic interdependence between these sectors in the sense that the logic of mass industrial production necessitates mass distribution linkages, and vice versa.

In the other, we find the "postindustrial" service sectors whose vitality derives from fundamental changes in societal reproduction. We distinguish three service sectors, each identified by its unique role in reproduction. Firstly, *business services* mainly provide intermediate, nonphysical, inputs into industrial production and distribution (management consultancy, architectural/engineering services, software programming and systems design, legal and accounting services, financial services, and the like). Their growth is mainly fueled by growing demand for nonphysical, often tailormade, professionalized-scientific inputs into the production process. Business services emerge because industries are less willing to self-service.

Secondly, the growth of *social services* (health, education, and welfare services) reflects household export of the tasks associated with social reproduction, i.e. a decline in "social" self-servicing. The rise of social services is directly tied to

the emerging "postindustrial" life cycle: the participation of women in the economy, the equalization of career profiles, the reallocation of household time-use, the shrinking size of households, the phenomenal rise of one-person units, and also the changing demographic profile of modern societies.[10] Social services release time for paid employment and for leisure. They can be exported into the market or into the welfare state.

Thirdly, *consumer services*, like the two previous services, are an alternative to self-servicing, in this case associated with leisure reproduction. On one hand, their growth is connected to the work–social reproduction nexus: when women also work, households are more likely to visit restaurants and send their laundry out. On the other hand, their growth is also connected to the extension of leisure time and the income capacity to purchase entertainment and fun. It is in the consumer services that the Baumol logic, or self-servicing, is most likely to arrest employment growth, since it is in these activities that the commodity option is most available (microwave ovens, dishwashers, video machines, and so on).

The Classification of Occupations

Detailed occupational titles provide us with a reasonable description of the human capital, responsibilities, and work tasks of a person. Parallel to our sectoral classification, we distinguish a set of occupational classes. In one set, we group those that represent the traditional industrial division of labor; in the second set, we group those that are representative of the "postindustrial" division of labor. For each set, we can then classify occupations according to their place within the Fordist and postindustrial hierarchy, respectively. Our study once again will omit the primary sector occupations (farmers, etc.) entirely and also the military. We thus arrive at the following "classes."

1.　The Fordist hierarchy:
　(a)　managers and proprietors (includes executive personnel and the "petite bourgeoisie");
　(b)　clerical, administrative and sales workers (engaged in the more routine tasks

TABLE 1

The Distribution of Employment by Industry in the 1980s, and the Annual Average Percentage Rate of Change, 1960–1980s (in parentheses)

	Germany	Sweden	United States
Primary sector	4.9 (−2.6)	5.8 (−2.9)	3.1 (−2.0)
Industry	39.7 (−0.7)	31.5 (−1.3)	25.4 (−1.0)
Distribution	20.7 (+0.4)	20.4 (0.0)	22.7 (−0.1)
Total "Fordist" economy	65.3 (−0.8)	57.7 (−1.2)	51.2 (−0.8)
Government administration	7.8 (+2.7)	4.3 (+2.4)	4.8 (−0.2)
Consumer services	6.4 (+0.4)	5.5 (−1.6)	11.9 (+0.2)
Social services	12.0 (+6.2)	25.5 (+8.7)	20.9 (+3.2)
Business services	7.8 (+5.0)	7.1 (+7.2)	11.2 (+2.3)
Total service economy	26.2 (+3.5)	38.1 (+4.3)	44.0 (+1.8)

of control, distribution, and administration);

(c) manual production workers, subdivided between skilled/craft and the unskilled (these, of course, include also transport workers and other manual occupations engaged in manufacture and distribution, such as packers, truck drivers, haulers, and the like).

2. The postindustrial hierarchy:
   (a) professionals and scientists;
   (b) technicians and semi-professionals (school teachers, nurses, social workers, laboratory workers, technical designers, etc.);
   (c) service workers, subdivided between skilled (cooks, hairdressers, etc.) and unskilled (cleaners, waitresses, bartenders, baggage porters, etc.).[11]

It will be noticed that in each group the hierarchy reflects both a human capital structure and a kind of command/authority structure (managers command, clericals administer commands, and

workers execute), although the command structure is less clear-cut within the postindustrial hierarchy. In traditional industrial capitalism, the unskilled manual laborer constituted the archetypal proletarian position; we shall especially focus on the unskilled service worker in our assessment of the proletarianizing and polarizing potential of postindustrial economies.

Three Postindustrial Trajectories

To examine the trends in our three countries, we use 1960 as a benchmark since it marks generally the high point of the "Fordist" industrial epoch. In 1960, there were significant national differences (the United States being somewhat more managerial and service biased), but overall the countries were rather similar; all were basically dominated by the traditional industrial economy. The sectoral trends displayed in table 1, however, show that the nations have followed divergent employment paths.

The countries have all experienced a marked

TABLE 2

Occupational Distribution of Employment in the 1980s, and Average Annual Percentage Rate of Change, 1960–1980s (in parentheses)

	Germany	*Sweden*	*United States*
Managers	4.5 (+1.4)	4.8 (−0.6)	9.1 (+0.6)
Clerical/sale	29.6 (+1.1)	20.4 (+1.1)	28.3 (+0.8)
Manual	33.3 (−0.7)	29.2 (−1.3)	23.1 (−1.2)
All "Fordist" occupations	68.7 (+0.1)	54.4 (−0.6)	60.5 (−0.3)
Professional	5.9 (+4.3)	5.8 (+3.1)	8.8 (+2.3)
Semi-professional	11.4 (+4.9)	20.6 (+5.2)	9.3 (+1.8)
Skilled service	5.5 (+5.8)	3.1 (−0.4)	6.6 (+2.0)
Unskilled service	4.5 (−1.9)	10.5 (+1.7)	11.7 (−0.1)
All "postindustrial" occupations	26.1 (+1.5)	40.0 (+3.0)	36.4 (+1.1)

shift towards services, but the pace and direction of change differs importantly. In Germany, industry remains much more prominent than elsewhere while the social services are comparatively very underdeveloped. In fact, industry and, generally, the Fordist economy has declined very modestly in Germany.[12] In Sweden, virtually the entire change has been driven by the social services—consumer services have, indeed, declined sharply. And, in the United States, the service sector is very large, but with a comparatively heavy bias towards consumer services; still, it comes as a surprise that this welfare state laggard nation's social services are almost twice the size of their German counterpart.[13]

These shifts must be understood on the backdrop of labor market conditions which have been radically different in the three countries. In Germany, total employment has been stagnant, and women's participation has grown relatively little (it remains at about 55 percent). Sweden has experienced considerable overall employment growth, almost all of which is accounted for by the increase in women's employment (from about 60 percent in 1960 to about 82 percent today). Moreover, virtually the entire increase in Swedish

women's participation (75 percent) occurred in welfare state jobs (health, education, and welfare services). The United States has experienced a virtual job explosion over the two decades (almost a doubling of the labor force) with a rate of female increase that follows closely behind Sweden's.

In Germany, low female participation coincides with stagnant social services. But one should not jump to the conclusion that the social services are the only possible inroad for women workers. Women's employment growth in America has *not* been sectorally biased.[14] The stagnation and even decline in consumer services in *both* Germany and Sweden is best ascribed to Baumol's cost-disease problem.[15] While average hourly earnings in American eating and drinking establishments are only 44 percent of manufacturing wages, they are 65 percent in Germany and 80 percent in Sweden.

In table 2, the occupational data suggest even greater differentiation between the countries. Germany remains a very "workerist" society; its share of manual workers in the 1980s is equal to the American share in the 1960s! Within its overall jobless growth context, the German trajectory is unique in the degree of pervasive occupational upgrading and the very marginal importance of the service proletariat. Combining the share of manual and administrative occupations, we see that the German occupational structure remains heavily "Fordist."

In the 1960s, Sweden's occupational mix was not very different from Germany's; today, the two are almost opposites. Sweden has experienced a significant decline in manual workers (mainly among the unskilled), while the strongest growth has occurred among the semi-professionals and the new service proletariat (two groups, incidentally, heavily female biased). Sweden has comparatively very few administrative jobs. The single most surprising fact is the substantial growth of the new service proletariat—as we shall see, heavily concentrated in the welfare state.

Contrary to what the de-industrialization literature tells us, the momentum of the United States is clearly towards occupational upgrading. While the United States has become even more overmanaged/administrative than earlier, its proletarian component has declined, and the United States is a leader in professionalization.[16]

So far, our data on employment change suggest a number of important hypotheses. First, the Baumol cost-disease effect seems to apply principally to the lower-skilled jobs in the consumer services. The low wages among these groups in the United States are probably the best explanation for their much larger size. And, vice versa, high labor costs in Sweden and Germany make employment growth here prohibitive. The Baumol effect reflects institutional differences in industrial relations systems; strong and comprehensive trade unionism in Sweden and Germany has imposed greater wage equality and higher indirect labor costs (social contributions) across all employment categories.

Second, the data suggest that the marginal effect of an expansion in the service sectors is to increase the relative share of service proletarian jobs. Sweden has a huge service proletariat because social services have expanded so much; the United States, because the consumer services are so large. As we move towards the postindustrial economy, we may very well face a trade-off between strong job growth with a concomitantly large service proletariat, or employment stagnation with a better occupational mix (but probably also joblessness). Our subsequent analyses bring this "size effect" out much more clearly.

The Occupational Structure in the New Service Economy

As we now turn to the distribution of occupations within the new service sectors, we can begin to confront some of the main propositions in the literature. Is the postindustrial structure benign or malign? Is it following the professionalism scenario of Bell or the proletarianization model of Harrison and Bluestone? Can we expect the new social order to reproduce the kind of class divide and polarization that characterized the old industrial order? In table 3, we examine occupational polarization in traditional manufacturing and in our three postindustrial service sectors combined. The table shows, first, that manufacturing is deproletarianizing and professionalizing, indicating that traditional Fordist hierarchies are fading. While management has more or less stagnated, professionals have doubled over the period. The share of unskilled workers has declined significantly. This is the trend in all three countries.[17] The consequence is a sharp reduction in our "polarization ratio" of proletarians per managers/professionals. Being more heavily industrial, it was to be expected that the German ratio is more "workerist."

National variations are more accentuated within the service economy. In Germany and Sweden, the share of managers is very small (and in decline); in the United States, large (and growing). The services are heavily professional and, in all cases, increasingly so. The differences, however, are dramatic, especially between the 50 percent share in Sweden and the 29 percent in the United States. And, third, the size of the unskilled service proletariat is similar in the United States and Sweden, but only half as large in Germany. We can see that the polarization ratio has declined markedly in all three countries and that, anyhow, the new service economy is much less

TABLE 3

Hierarchy and Polarization in Manufacturing and the New Service Economy:
The Share of Select Occupations, 1980s

	Germany	Sweden	United States
Manufacturing			
Managers	2.7	2.3	9.3
Professional/			
semi-professional	11.5	15.8	10.7
Unskilled workers	31.7	34.1	37.3
Unskilled per			
manager + prof. 1960	4.0	3.3	3.4
1980	2.2	1.9	1.9
Service economy			
Managers	5.2	2.7	11.1
Professional/			
semi-professional	36.0	49.6	29.0
Unskilled service	12.8	24.5	24.0
Unskilled per			
manager + prof. 1960	0.8	0.8	1.0
1980	0.3	0.5	0.6

Unskilled workers combine unskilled manual and unskilled service
workers; the professional group also includes technicians. The 1980 data
refer to 1985 for Germany, 1980 for Sweden, and 1988 for the United States.

proletarian (and decreasingly so) than the traditional "Fordist" economy.

The occupational mix of the service economy
differs sharply by sector. In Sweden, where the
service economy is so heavily slanted toward the
social services, it has produced a paradoxical
combination of, on the one hand, an unusually
high professional (mainly semi-professional,
though) content and, on the other hand, a huge
social service proletariat. Vice versa, the low
American professional share has to do with the
relative dominance of consumer services.

Hence, there are two sources of proletarianization. In the United States, it is the consumer service industry (twice as large as in Sweden) which
furnishes heavy proletarianization; in Sweden, the
same occurs in the social service sector. In Germany, where neither of these service sectors has
grown significantly, proletarianization is substantially less. Consumer services constitute a core in
a possible proletarianized postindustrial society,
but this depends essentially on how large they are

permitted to grow. The powerful proletarian element in the Swedish social services is clearly not
the consequence of low wages. Rather, our "size
effect", in the case of social services, means that
each marginal increase in social services favors
additions of low-skilled manpower. Or, put differently, the welfare state is liberating women
from the traditionally self-serviced social activities (care of the elderly, for example) that involve
a heavy dose of unqualified labor.

The services can nurture a sizable growth in
traditionally "Fordist" jobs. In Germany and especially the United States, the social services include a very large managerial–administrative labor force. In the former case, this is primarily due
to the decentralized, "Lander-based" system of
service delivery; in the latter case, private sector
dominance in social protection, with its proliferation of private plans, compels a multiplicity of administration. In contrast, Sweden saves on administrative and control personnel because of its
consolidated and centralized welfare state, and

because means testing (requiring control) plays such a marginal role.

While the business services are quite professionalized, they are also occupationally speaking much closer to the Fordist model, and show less cross-national variation. If the Cohen and Zysman thesis is correct, the convergence found here is not very surprising.[18] Business services largely cater to externalized manufacturing functions which show much less variation across countries than do the services.

The data suggest that there is very little empirical support for the pessimistic postindustrial theories. The trend is almost universally towards deproletarianization and depolarization, most dramatically (and surprisingly) so in the United States where the total proletarian share declined by 24 percent (14 percent in Germany and 18 percent in Sweden). The consumer services are certainly a basis of proletarianization but, still, the American experience suggests that the proletarian element can decline (by 23 percent from 1960 to 1988). The only real case of increased proletarianization is found in Swedish social services (a full 33 percent increase).

A proletarian decline should produce less labor market polarization, and this is brought out quite clearly in our data. Our findings therefore sharply contradict the de-skilling and polarization theses. The postindustrialization of labor markets is generally producing job upgrading and less job polarization, especially within the new service industries.

Germany by and large exhibits the most favorable job structure in the new service economy, but this is basically because it is so small. Its favorable occupational mix is, so to speak, bought at the expense of a large "outsider" population, unable to enter into the labor market.

It is much more surprising that upgrading is so powerful in the United States, where employment growth has been both explosive and unregulated by either the welfare state or comprehensive trade unions. However, accumulated empirical evidence shows that the American upgrading process has been accompanied by growing earnings inequalities and a large base of low-paid jobs. As the data of Harrison and Bluestone and of Levy show,[19] there are sharp differences in the profile of job growth over the decades we study: the well-paid jobs exploded in the 1960s and 1970s, while the low-paid jobs dominated the growth profile of the 1980s. But the earnings data and the job data nonetheless show opposite trends, even for the 1980s. Thus, what we can surmise for the United States is a strong decoupling process at work between occupation and earnings. This is almost certainly attributable to the weak and dualistic system of trade unionism.

Finally, what the American labor force data do not show is the concomitant evolution of a new "outsider" population, akin to the situation in Germany. In the American case, however, the outsiders are especially weighted with highly vulnerable groups such as single mothers and black youth. Since, for reasons of education or social position, these groups are structurally barred from full labor market participation, and since the American welfare state fails to assure a comprehensive social safety net, the result is a harsher and more targeted dualism. Whereas poverty is a marginal phenomenon in the German "outsider" population, it is unusually concentrated in the American.[20]

Paradoxically, the social services in Sweden have contributed to a trend towards proletarianization and polarization. Relying on the welfare state to produce a socially benevolent postindustrial order may have secured maximum female labor force participation and certainly also a more favorable earnings structure, but at the cost of a large service proletariat and female ghettoization within the welfare state labor market. Today, almost 70 percent of total public employment is female.[21] ...

Conclusions

It is difficult to reach anything approximating firm conclusions from a study deliberately focused on societies in flux. What we can offer, instead, are some hypotheses.

First, developments *so far* suggest that we should not expect a fundamentally convergent pattern of postindustrialization. Certainly, there are trends that go in the same direction, but there are many more important ones that diverge.

This leads us to the second hypothesis. The welfare state and the system of industrial relations are decisive in terms of explaining postindustrial variation. In these two institutions lie both barriers and catalysts in realizing postindustrial employment potentialities.

Differences in welfare states have been important in blocking or spurring overall employment expansion. The transfer-biased German welfare state, hostile to collective service provision, has helped block job growth and has encouraged labor force exit; the service-biased Swedish, the opposite. When we take into account the enormous degree of tax subsidization of private social services in America, we have also identified an important source of their growth (and its heavy burden of administrative personnel).

From our comparisons emerge the outlines of a terrible dilemma. Our size effect hypothesis suggests that a marginal extra growth within the new services produces more service proletarians. In contrast, a no-growth labor market appears to hinder their emergence. If this is truly the case, the choice appears to be between a German-style insider–outsider scenario or a Swedish American-style expansionary but proletarianizing scenario (in the former, in terms of jobs; in the latter, in terms of earnings).

Notes

1. For an examination of the labor movements in Scandinavia, see G. Esping-Andersen, *Politics against Markets* (Princeton, NJ: Princeton University Press, 1985).

2. For a discussion of the concept of Fordism and post-Fordist alternatives, see R. Boyer (ed.), *The Search for Labor Market Flexibility* (Oxford: Oxford University Press, 1988).

3. D. Bell, *The Coming of Post-Industrial Society* (New York: Basic Books, 1976). Representative examples of the optimistic post-Fordist view are M. Piore and C. Sabel, *The Second Industrial Divide* (New York: Basic Books, 1984); H. Kern and R. Schumann, *Das Ende der Arbeitsteilung? Rationalisierung in der Industrielle Produktion* (Munich: C. H. Beck, 1984); see also Boyer, *The Search for Labor Market Flexibility*.

4. See, for example, J. Gershuny, *After Industrial Society* (London: Macmillan, 1978), and J. Gershuny, *Social Innovation and the Division of Labour* (Oxford: Oxford University Press, 1983).

5. W. Baumol, "The macro-economics of unbalanced growth," *American Economic Review,* 57 (1967), pp. 415–26.

6. P. van Parijs, "A revolution in class theory," *Politics and Society,* 15 (1987), pp. 453–82. Incidentally, a parallel insider–outsider model was developed by Max Adler in his analyses of mass unemployment during the 1930s Depression. See M. Adler, "Wandlung der Arbeiterklasse," *Der Kampf,* 26 (1933), pp. 367–82.

7. On the impact of de-industrialization, see B. Harrison and B. Bluestone, *The Great U-Turn* (New York: Basic Books, 1988). The pessimistic post-Fordist scenario is presented in Boyer, *The Search for Labor Market Flexibility,* and Piore and Sabel, *The Second Industrial Divide.*

8. See, for example, G. Esping-Andersen, *The Three Worlds of Welfare Capitalism* (Cambridge: Polity Press; Princeton, NJ: Princeton University Press, 1990).

9. For the United States, many would argue that the degree of employment change has been much more powerful in the 1980s than throughout the whole 1960–80 period. Since we have data for 1960, 1980 *and* 1988, we are able to identify whether this is indeed the case. In essentially *all* cases, both the industry and occupational structures are quite stable between 1980 and 1988. The two years are therefore substitutable.

The data in the following tables derive from the 1961 Census and the 1985 Mikrocenzus (Germany), the 1960 and 1980 Census (Sweden), and the 1960 and 1980 Census and the 1988 (March) *Current Population Survey* (United States).

10. See F. Block, *Postindustrial Possibilities* (Berkeley, CA: University of California Press, 1990), for a discussion of the new life cycle.

11. Our operational definition of the unskilled service proletariat is that it involves a job that anyone of us could do with no prior qualifications.

12. The high growth rates for services in Germany are mainly a function of their extremely low initial stage. Similarly, the American growth rates for all three service sectors appear modest, but we must remember that their initial stage was very high.

13. The point is that the United States is a welfare *state* laggard, but has produced an enormous (tax-financed) private welfare and education sector. When this is added to the public share, the total American welfare package absorbs almost the same amount of gross domestic product as does the typical European.

14. For a more detailed analysis of women's employment in the services, see Esping-Andersen, *The Three Worlds of Welfare Capitalism.*

15. For an econometric test of the cost-disease problem in our three countries, see G. Giannelli and G. Esping-Andersen, "Labor costs and service employment," European University Institute Working Papers, 1989.

16. Note, however, that the data supporting the declining middle thesis for the United States are based on earnings, not occupations. Our contradictory results suggest the real possibility that the traditionally stable relationship between jobs and earnings is being undone.

17. Because of space limitations we have not provided detailed occupational breakdowns for both 1960 and the 1980s. The discussion is thus based on data not shown here.

18. See S. Cohen and J. Zysman, *Manufacturing Matters* (New York: Basic Books, 1987).

19. Harrison and Bluestone, *The Great U-Turn;* F. Levy, *Dollars and Dreams* (New York: Norton, 1988).

20. For comparable data on poverty, see D. Mitchell, "Income transfer systems: a comparative study using microdata," Doctoral Dissertation, Australian National University, Canberra, 1990; J. Palmer, T. Smeeding, and B. Torrey, *The Vulnerable* (Washington, DC: The Urban Institute, 1988).

21. This compares with about 46 percent in the United States and less than 40 percent in Germany.

RON EYERMAN

Modernity and Social Movements

It is common today to distinguish "old" social movements from "new" ones (Melucci 1980, 1981). Such a distinction rests on two sets of criteria. The first, associated with Alain Touraine, builds on the theory of the historical transition from an old industrial society to a new postindustrial society (Touraine 1981). From this point of view the labor movement is an old social movement because it expresses the conflicts of industrial society and industrialization, that is, the conflicts between labor and capital. New social movements, such as the women's movement, express conflicts representative of the new postindustrial society. A second set of criteria differentiating between new and old social movements stems from the issues they raise and the locus of the changes they wish to bring about. In this case the labor movement not only reflects the old struggle between labor and capital but also is rooted in and concerned with the labor process itself in its demands for change and its vision of the future. New social movements, however, express concerns that according to established ways of thinking are outside the labor process. These concerns are primarily noneconomic issues, such as gender relations and the meaning of war and peace. The new social movements express concerns that are more cultural than economic. They aim at changing norms and values rather than productive and distributive relations.

These distinctions between old and new social movements provide a convenient way of categorizing various contemporary political conflicts and social movements. For one thing, classes and related class interests, which provided the prime source of collective identity and motivation for collective action in the past (at least in Europe), seem less a factor today, at least for explaining social movements. Contemporary social movements seem motivated by concerns other than those directly associated with income and economic security. In addition, rather than focusing on the labor process the realm of concern has shifted to what has been called the "life-world," which involves issues of personal identity, personal life, neighborhood, sexuality, and life-style.[1]

Finally, the types of demands put forward by the new social movements lie, to some extent, outside the realm of traditional compromise politics, whether that be labor-market politics or representative democracy as it currently exists. Unlike working-class movements, which can offer and withdraw their labor power in exchange for concessions from capital, the new social movements have little to offer in exchange. Their demands tend to be made in nonnegotiable terms and are usually expressed negatively: antiwar, antinuclear, and so on. Whether this approach represents tactics or is an early stage of movement development remains to be seen. The literature on social movements includes a long-standing discussion concerning the strategies and tactics of social movements (see Jenkins 1981). In any case the distinction between old and new social movements seems worthwhile to make from an analytical point of view. From the actor's point of view its validity seems beyond question.[2] ...

My task here is to connect this discussion [of old and new social movements] with the changes in economic and social structure that may be referred to as "postmodern." I argue that what I call "new" social movements are the expression of postmodernity.

Three societal dynamics underlie the development of postmodernity: the expansion of the state, the explosion of the knowledge industry, and the development of the new mass media. These three dynamics of social change have both influenced social movements and been influenced by them. The old social movements were at once the product of modernity and an essential element in its dynamism. The working class movement, for example, was the product of industrialization and urbanization, but modern democracy was a force in its development in specific directions. Similarly, new social movements are both the product of modernity and a reaction to it. It is important, however, to distinguish the postmodern critique of modernity from the premodern critique. The premodern, or Romantic, critique of modernity focused on modernization as such and based itself on an idyllic past, usually with right-wing political overtones. In contrast, the postmodern critique of modernity, although sharing some of the features of Romanticism—which

are especially evident in the environmental movement—represents a "progressive" transcendence of modernity rather than its outright rejection.

At this point I would like to discuss three of the changes underlying the postmodern condition. First, since the end of World War II Western societies have undergone an exceptional transformation in economic and social structure. To a great extent the root of this transformation lies in the expansion and intervention of the state into areas that previously were the domain of civil society, including private economic activity regulated by a market and social activity, such as child-care, regulated by tradition. This shifting ground between state and civil society, between public and private areas of action and responsibility, is part of the field of ambiguity and potential conflict from which new social movements emerge. State expansion and intervention have politicized private domains and provoked a reaction from both the political left and the political right.

Second, in the postwar period Western societies have also experienced a shift toward knowledge-based, capital-intensive production, which requires more highly educated workers. The state-supported transformation of the employment structure has been underpinned by a revolution in education in which the links between education and production have become more pronounced and rationalized through various forms of manpower planning. What I call the new social movements are to a great extent peopled by the highly educated and the content of their critique of modern society builds on both their educational experience and their occupational expectations.[3]

A related development important to the understanding of the new social movements is the expanded employment opportunities for women—especially married women—made possible by the knowledge industry and the general expansion of the public sector. The expansion of service, administrative, and care-giving occupations, which coincided with the growth of the state and its intervention into what previously were private services has opened up many new paid employment opportunities for women. New opportunities for work and education helped establish the condition in which the social values and norms that defined a proper "woman's place" could be challenged. Here the interplay between the beliefs of a sociopolitical movement (the women's movement) and a shifting economic and social structure of opportunity becomes clear. Structural possibilities and social conflicts grew together, opening fields of contention from which sociopolitical movements would emerge.

Third, the changes in representative democracy that occurred as part of modernity have laid the grounds for postmodernity. During the course of their development the old social movements became participatory movements. Whatever their original intentions or ideologies, they came more and more to be concerned with getting a piece of the modern pie and participating in modern politics as equal partners with capital and other powerful political and economic actors.[4] These movements—and here I think primarily of the labor movements of Western Europe—developed into organizations that became part of the institutionalized power and decision-making structures of modern society. Such movements developed into centralized organizations and associated with political parties, slowly gaining power and influence but losing the dynamism and the mass engagement with which they began. Perhaps this development was both necessary and successful, for no one can deny the actual power labor movements enjoy today in Western Europe. Except for ceremonial occasions, however, hardly anyone would deny that the "movement" aspect has disappeared.[5] Political power and participation were bought at the price of accepting a certain definition of modern politics, that of administration and redistribution through the centralized state, and of the loss of a social movement. In the dialectic between movement and organization, the movement got lost. This development is also important in understanding new social movements and their rejection of modernity. For the new movements modernity is associated with a particular type of politics. The new social movements are expressions of the rejection of the politics of administration and its representatives in both labor and capital. In this sense they are postmodern because they reject the identities of class and the ideology of political modernism. ...

Like the state and the knowledge industry, the new mass media have helped "create" the new social movements. Coverage in the mass media and the instant attention gained through modern communication technologies have helped build these movements into significant social and political forces and have influenced their internal strategies, organization, and leadership. As Todd Gitlin has documented in his brilliant account of the influence of the mass media on the development of the student movement in the United States, the media in many senses became the movement (Gitlin 1980). New social movements are shaped by the mass media in several ways. Activists are conscious of media attention. They are also aware of their own importance in making and shaping "events" and in catching the public eye. To be noticed by the media is to gain legitimacy and significance and the ability to influence policy as well as the public at large. Modern movements must learn to use the media; otherwise the media will use and abuse them.

Modern politics is played out before the public. The mass media are the producers as well as important interpreters of this drama. The mass media, either because of their form or because of the values they embody, are attracted to the spectacular and the flamboyant. This has the effect of making the media event and the colorful movement leader a significant factor in the development of modern social movements. Would such an organization as Greenpeace, one of the fastest-growing organizations in the environmentalist movement, be possible without the mass media and modern techniques of communication and administration? I think not.

Other movement organizations are also influenced by the modern media. Gitlin demonstrates that the American student organization Students for a Democratic Society (SDS), a rather small group of well-brought-up students, was given celebrity status through media attention, which transformed not only the organization and its leadership, giving precedence to the colorful and the violent, but also its aims and its ideology, giving precedence to "radical" ideas and positions even though such views had previously only had marginal status within the movement. Philip Lowe and David Morrison show how the media and media attention have significantly affected the tactics and the aims of British environmentalist organizations (Lowe and Morrison 1984). Unlike the SDS, environmentalist groups have for the most part received favorable coverage in the media, especially as long as environmental issues remain free from partisan politics. This explains why environmental activists have been at pains to steer free of political parties. Lowe and Morrison go so far as to suggest that modern environmentalism, as opposed to the earlier conservation movement, would never have achieved its influence without its creative use of the media.

No modern movement can hope to gain influence without taking into account the centralized state and its forms of discourse and organization, and no modern movement can afford to ignore the mass media. And just as taking the state into account entails paying the price of becoming organized and centralized, media attention has its own price. In this way modern social movements are shaped by various key aspects of modernity at the same time that they play a significant role in the development of modernity.

Notes

1. On the use of the phenomenological concept of life-world see Habermas 1981 and Peterson 1984.

2. Witness the "new" left and the conflicts within the Greens in Germany and elsewhere between the new and the old politics and forms of political identity.

3. Some, primarily Marxists, have interpreted these new social movements as the protests of the privileged, that is, as expressions of a new class or at least the new strata of an educated elite seeking to protect or to better its social standing against opponents in the old society, including both capital and labor. Alvin Gouldner's new class theory is a variation on this theme, as are the more traditional Marxist accounts of "proletarianization," "new working class theory," and the various attempts at

structuralist class analysis, from Poulantzas to E. Wright.

4. Let me be clear that this does not mean, except of course from a particular theoretical and political point of view, that they thus lost their mission or suffered *embourgeoisment* and the like. How one interprets this alteration, if it really was that, is a matter of preference, which I have discussed elsewhere (Eyerman 1981).

5. Again, interpreting this development is a matter of preference and there are differences of opinion. Walter Korpi (1979), for example, sees this development as an expression of increased power and maturity. From a more radical Marxist point of view the opposite would be the case.

References

Eyerman, R. 1981. *False consciousness and ideology in Marxist theory.* Stockholm: Almqvist and Wiksell and Humanities Press.

Gitlin, T. 1980. *The whole world is watching: Mass media in the making and the unmaking of the new left.* Berkeley: University of California Press.

Habermas, J. 1981. *Theorie des Kommunikativen Handelns.* Vol. 2. Frankfurt: Suhrkamp.

Jenkins, J. Craig. 1981. Sociopolitical movements. In *Handbook of political behavior,* 4:81–153. New York and London: Plenum Press.

Korpi, Walter. 1979. *The working class in welfare capitalism.* London: Routledge and Kegan Paul.

Lowe, P., and D. Morrison. 1984. Bad news or good news: Environmental politics and the media. *The Sociological Review* 32:75–90.

Melucci, A. 1980. The new social movements: A theoretical approach. Part 2. *Social Science Information* 19:199–226.

————. 1981. Ten hypotheses for the analysis of new movements. In *Contemporary Italian sociology,* ed. D. Pinto, 173–94. Cambridge: Cambridge University Press.

Peterson, A. 1984. The sex-gender dimension in Swedish politics. *Acta Sociologica* 27:3–18.

Touraine, A. 1981. *The voice and the eye: An analysis of social movements.* Cambridge: Cambridge University Press.

ALVIN W. GOULDNER

The Future of Intellectuals and the Rise of the New Class

In all countries that have in the twentieth century become part of the emerging world socio-economic order, a New Class composed of intellectuals and technical intelligentsia—not the same—enter into contention with the groups already in control of the society's economy, whether these are businessmen or party leaders. A new contest of classes and a new class system is slowly arising in the third world of developing nations, in the second world of the USSR and its client states, and in the first world of late capitalism of North America, Western Europe, and Japan.

The early historical evolution of the New Class in Western Europe, its emergence into the public sphere as a structurally differentiated and (relatively) autonomous social stratum, may be defined in terms of certain critical episodes. What follows is only a synoptic inventory of *some* episodes decisive in the formation of the New Class.

1. A process of secularization in which most intelligentsia are no longer trained by, living within, and subject to close supervision by a churchly organization, and thus separated from the everyday life of society.[1]

Secularization is important because it desacralizes authority-claims and facilitates challenges to definitions of social reality made by traditional authorities linked to the church. Secularization is important also because it is an infrastructure on which there develops the modern grammar of rationality, or culture of critical discourse, with its characteristic stress on self-groundedness—in Martin Heidegger's sense of the "mathematical project."[2]

2. A second episode in the emergence of the New Class is the rise of diverse vernacular languages, the corresponding decline of Latin as the language of intellectuals, and especially of their scholarly production. Latin becomes a ritual, rather than a technical language. This development further dissolves the membrane between everyday life and the intellectuals—whether clerical or secular.

3. There is a breakdown of the feudal and old regime system of personalized *patronage* relations between the old hegemonic elite and individual members of the New Class as cultural producers, and

4. A corresponding growth of an anonymous *market* for the products and services of the New Class, thus allowing them to make an independent living apart from close supervision and *personalized controls by patrons*. Along with secularization, this means that the residence and work of intellectuals are both now less closely supervised by others.

They may now more readily take personal initiatives in the public, political sphere, while also having a "private" life.

5. The character and development of the emerging New Class also depended importantly on the multi-national structure of European polities. That Europe was not a single empire with a central authority able to impose a single set of norms throughout its territory, but a system of competing and autonomous states with diverse cultures and religions, meant that dissenting intellectuals, scientists, and divines could and did protect their

own intellectual innovations by migrating from their home country when conditions there grew insupportable and sojourning in foreign lands. Even the enforced travel of exiled intellectuals also enabled them to enter into a European-wide communication network. In an article (as yet unpublished), Robert Wuthnow has suggested that their often extensive travel led many intellectuals to share a cosmopolitan identity transcending national limits and enhancing their autonomy from local elites.

6. A sixth episode in the formation of the New Class is the waning of the extended, patriarchical family system and its replacement by the smaller, nuclear family. As middle class women become educated and emancipated, they may increasingly challenge paternal authority and side with their children in resisting it. With declining paternal authority and growing maternal influence, the autonomy strivings of children are now more difficult to repress; hostility and rebellion against paternal authority can become more overt. There is, correspondingly, increasing difficulty experienced by paternal authority in imposing and reproducing its social values and political ideologies in their children.

7. Following the French Revolution, there is in many parts of Europe, especially France and Germany, a profound reformation and extension of *public, non*-church controlled, (relatively more) *multi-class* education, at the lower levels as well as at the college, polytechnical, and university levels. On the one hand, higher education in the public school becomes the institutional basis for the *mass* production of the New Class of intelligentsia and intellectuals. On the other hand, the expansion of primary and secondary public school teachers greatly increases the jobs available to the New Class.

As teachers, intellectuals come to be defined, and to define themselves, as responsible for and "representative" of society as a *whole*,[3] rather than as having allegiance to the class interests of their students or their parents. As teachers, they are not defined as having an *obligation* to reproduce parental values in their children. Public teachers supersede private tutors.

8. The new structurally differentiated educational system is increasingly insulated from the family system, becoming an important source of values among students divergent from those of their families. The socialization of the young by their families is now mediated by a *semi*-autonomous group of teachers.

9. While growing public education limits family influence on education, it also increases the influence of the state on education. The public educational system thus becomes a major *cosmopolitanizing* influence on its students, with a corresponding distancing from *localistic* interests and values.

10. Again, the new school system becomes a major setting for the intensive linguistic conversion of students from casual to reflexive speech, or (in Basil Bernstein's terms) from "restricted" linguistic codes to "elaborated" linguistic codes,[4] to a culture of discourse in which claims and assertions may *not* be justified by reference to the speaker's social status. This has the profound consequence of making all *authority-referring* claims potentially problematic.

11. This new culture of discourse often diverges from assumptions fundamental to everyday life, tending to put them into question even when they are linked to the upper classes. These school-inculcated modes of speech are, also, (relatively) situation-free language variants. Their situation-freeness is further heightened by the "communications revolution" in general, and by the development of printing technology, in particular. With the spread of printed materials, definitions of social reality available to intellectuals may now derive increasingly from *distant* persons, from groups geographically, culturally, and historically distant and even from dead persons, and may therefore diverge greatly from any local environment in which they are received. Definitions of social reality made by local elites may now be invidiously contrasted (by intellectuals) with definitions made in other places and times.

12. With the spread of public schools, literacy spreads; humanistic intellectuals lose their exclusiveness and privileged market position, and now experience a status disparity between their "high" culture, as they see it, and their lower deference, repute, income and social power. The social position of humanistic intellectuals, *particularly in a technocratic and industrial society*, becomes more

marginal and alienated than that of the technical intelligentsia. The New Class becomes internally differentiated.

13. Finally, a major episode in the emergence of the modern intelligentsia is the changing form of the revolutionary *organization*. Revolution itself becomes a technology to be pursued with "instrumental rationality." The revolutionary organization evolves from a ritualistic, oath-bound secret society into the modern "vanguard" party. When the *Communist Manifesto* remarks that Communists have nothing to hide,[5] it is exactly a proposed emergence into *public* life which is implied. The *Communist Manifesto* was written by Marx and Engels for the "League of Communists," which was born of the "League of the Just" which, in turn, was descended from the "League of Outlaws." This latter group of German emigrants in Paris had a pyramidal structure, made a sharp distinction between upper and lower members, blindfolded members during initiation ceremonies, used recognition signs and passwords, and bound members by an oath.[6] The vanguard organization, however, de-ritualizes participation and entails elements of both the "secret society" and of the public political party. In the vanguard organization, public refers to the public availability of the *doctrine* rather than the availability of the organization or its membership to public scrutiny. Here, to be "public" entails the organization's rejection of "secret doctrines" known only to an elite in the organization—as, for instance, Bakunin's doctrine of an elite dictatorship of anarchists.[7] The *modern* vanguard structure is first clearly encoded in Lenin's *What Is to Be Done?* Here it is plainly held that the proletariat cannot develop a *socialist* consciousness by itself, but must secure this from a scientific theory developed by the intelligentsia.[8] The "vanguard" party expresses the *modernizing* and elite ambitions of the New Class as well as an effort to overcome its political limitations. Lenin's call for the development of "professional" revolutionaries, as the core of the vanguard, is a rhetoric carrying the tacit promise of a *career*-like life which invites young members of the New Class to "normalize" the revolutionary existence.

I shall return to and enlarge upon *some* of the critical episodes inventoried above. Above all, the attempt is to formulate a frame of reference within which the New Class can be situated, giving some indication of the intellectual work— theoretical and empirical—that needs to be done to understand the New Class as a world historical phenomenon. Rather than viewing the New Class as if it were composed just of technicians or engineers, the effort that follows moves toward a *general* theory of the New Class as encompassing *both* technical intelligentsia *and* intellectuals. Rather than focusing in a parochial way on the United States alone, my interest is in the New Class in *both* late capitalism and in the authoritarian state socialism of the USSR, without arguing or implying any more general "convergence" thesis. I shall suggest that the two most important theoretical foundations needed for a general theory of the New Class will be, first, a theory of its distinctive language behavior, its distinctive culture of discourse and, secondly, a general theory of capital within which the New Class's "human capital" or the old class's moneyed capital will be special cases.

The analysis to follow is grounded in what I can only call my own version of a "neo-Hegelian" sociology, a neo-Hegelianism which is a "left" but certainly not a "young" Hegelianism. It is *left* Hegelianism in that it holds that knowledge and knowledge systems are important in shaping social outcomes, but, far from seeing these as disembodied eternal essences, views them as the ideology of special social classes; and while ready to believe that knowledge is one of the best hopes we have for a humane social reconstruction, also sees our knowledge systems as historically shaped forces that embody limits and, indeed, pathologies.

Like any social object, the New Class can be defined in terms of both its imputed value or goodness and its imputed power.[9] In most cultural grammars, a "normal" social world is supposed to be one in which the powerful are good and the bad, weak. The temptation to see the world in this manner, to *normalize* it, is difficult to resist and one sees it at work in conceptions of the New Class. Thus Noam Chomsky sees the New Class as cynically corrupt *and* as weak, pliable tools of others. Conversely, John Galbraith views the technical intelligentsia as productively benign *and* as already dominant. Such judgments bear the impress (albeit in different directions) of normalizing tendencies and ought to be routinely suspect.

In contrast to such normalizing tendencies, a left Hegelian sociology accepts dissonance as part of reality. It does not assume that the strong are good or the bad, weak. It accepts the possibility that those who are becoming stronger—such as the New Class—and to whom the future *may* belong, are not always the better and may, indeed, be morally ambiguous.

There are, then, several distinguishable conceptions of the New Class:

1. *New Class as Benign Technocrats:* Here the New Class is viewed as a new historical elite already entrenched in institutional influence which it uses in benign ways for society; it is more or less inevitable and trustworthy: e.g., Galbraith,[10] Bell,[11] Berle and Means.[12]

(*Sed contra:* This obscures the manner in which the New Class egoistically pursues its own special vested interests. Moreover, the power of the New Class today is scarcely entrenched. This view also ignores the limits on the rationality of the New Class.)

2. *New Class as Master Class:* Here the New Class is seen as another moment in a long-continuing circulation of historical elites, as a socialist intelligentsia that brings little new to the world and continues to exploit the rest of society as the old class had, but now uses education rather than money to exploit others: Bakunin,[13] Machajski.[14]

(*Sed contra:* The New Class is more historically unique and discontinuous than this sees; while protecting its own special interests, it is not bound by the same *limits* as the old class and, at least transiently, contributes to collective needs.)

3. *New Class as Old Class Ally:* The New Class is here seen as a benign group of dedicated "professionals" who will uplift the old (moneyed) class from a venal group to a collectivity-oriented elite and who, fusing with it, will forge a new, genteel elite continuous with but better than the past: Talcott Parsons.[15]

(*Sed contra:* Neither group is an especially morally bound agent; the old class is constrained to protect its profits, the New Class is cashing in on its education. Immersed in the present, this view misses the fact that each is ready to exploit the other, if need be, and shows little understanding of the profound (if different) limits imposed on the rationality and morality of each of these groups, and of the important tensions between them.)

4. *New Class as Servants of Power:* Here the New Class is viewed as subservient to the old (moneyed) class which is held to retain power much as it always did, and is simply using the New Class to maintain its domination of society: Noam Chomsky[16] and Maurice Zeitlin.[17]

(*Sed contra:* This ignores the revolutionary history of the twentieth century in which radicalized elements of the New Class played a major leadership role in the key revolutions of our time. It greatly overemphasizes the common interests binding the New and old class, systematically missing the tensions between them; it ignores the fact that elimination of the old class is an historical option open to the New Class. This static conception underestimates the growth in the numbers and influence of the New Class. The view is also unexpectedly Marcusean in overstressing the prospects of old class continuity; it really sees the old class as having no effective opponents, either in the New Class or in the old adversary class, the proletariat. It thus ends as seeing even less social change in prospect than the Parsonian view [#3 above].)

5. *New Class as Flawed Universal Class (my own view):* The New Class is elitist and self-seeking and uses its special knowledge to advance its own interests and power, and to control its own work situation. Yet the New Class may also be the best card that history has presently given us to play. The power of the New Class is growing. It is substantially more powerful and independent than Chomsky suggests, while still much less powerful than is suggested by Galbraith who seems to conflate present reality with future possibility. The power of this morally ambiguous New Class is on the ascendent and it holds a mortgage on at least *one* historical future.

In my own left Hegelian sociology, the New Class bearers of knowledge are seen as an embryonic new "universal class"—as the prefigured embodiment of such future as the working class still has. It is that part of the working class which will survive cybernation. At the same time, a left Hegelian sociology also insists that the New Class is profoundly flawed as a universal class. Moreover, the New Class is not some unified subject or a seamless whole; it, too, has its own internal contradictions. It is a class internally divided with tensions between (technical) intelligentsia and (humanistic) intellectuals. No celebration, mine is a critique of the New Class which does not view its growing power as inevitable, which sees it as morally ambivalent, embodying the collective interest but partially and transiently, while simultaneously cultivating its own guild advantage. ...

The New Class as a Cultural Bourgeoisie

1. The New Class and the old class are at first undifferentiated; the New Class commonly originates in classes with property advantages, that is, in the old class, or is sponsored by them. The New Class of intellectuals and intelligentsia are the relatively more *educated* counterpart—often the brothers, sisters, or children—of the old moneyed class. Thus the New Class contest sometimes has the character of *a civil war within the upper classes.* It is the differentiation of the old class into contentious factions. To understand the New Class contest it is vital to understand how the *privileged* and advantaged, not simply the suffering, come to be alienated from the very system that privileges them.

2. The "non-negotiable" objectives of the old moneyed class are to reproduce their capital, at a minimum, but, preferably, to make it accumulate and to appropriate profit: M-C-M', as Marx said. This is done within a structure in which all of them must compete with one another. This unrelenting competition exerts pressure to rationalize their productive and administrative efforts and unceasingly to heighten efficiency. (Marx called it, "revolutionizing" production.) But this rationalization is dependent increasingly on the efforts of the New Class intelligentsia and its expert skills. It is inherent in its structural situation,

then, that the old class must bring the New Class into existence.

3. Much of the New Class is at first trained under the direct control of the old class' firms or enterprises. Soon, however, the old class is separated from the reproduction of the New Class by the emergence and development of a public system of education whose costs are "socialized."[18]

4. The more that the New Class's reproduction derives from specialized systems of public education, the more the New Class develops an ideology that stresses its *autonomy,* its separation from and presumable independence of "business" or political interests. This autonomy is said to be grounded in the specialized knowledge or cultural capital transmitted by the educational system, along with an emphasis on the obligation of educated persons to attend to the welfare of the collectivity. In other words, the *ideology* of "professionalism" emerges.

5. Professionalism is one of the public *ideologies* of the New Class, and is the genteel subversion of the old class by the new. Professionalism is a phase in the historical development of the "collective consciousness" of the New Class. While not overtly a critique of the old class, professionalism is a tacit claim by the New Class to *technical and moral superiority* over the old class, implying that the latter lack technical credentials and are guided by motives of commercial venality. Professionalism silently installs the New Class as the paradigm of virtuous and legitimate authority, performing with technical skill and with dedicated concern for the society-at-large. Professionalism makes a focal claim for the legitimacy of the New Class which tacitly de-authorizes the old class.

On the one side, this is a bid for prestige *within* the established society; on the other, it tacitly presents the New Class as an *alternative* to the old. In asserting its own claims to authority, professionalism in effect *devalues the authority of the old class.*

6. The special privileges and powers of the New Class are grounded in their *individual* control of special cultures, languages, techniques, and of the skills resulting from these. The New Class is a cultural bourgeoisie who appropriates privately the advantages of an historically and collectively produced cultural capital. Let us be clear, then: the

New Class is not just *like* the old class; its special culture is not just *like* capital. No metaphor is intended. The special culture of the New Class *is* a stock of capital that generates a stream of income (some of) which it appropriates privately.

7. The fundamental objectives of the New Class are: to increase its own share of the national product; to produce and reproduce the special social conditions enabling them to appropriate privately larger shares of the incomes produced by the special cultures they possess; to control their work and their work settings; and to increase their political power partly in order to achieve the foregoing. The struggle of the New Class is, therefore, to *institutionalize a wage system*, i.e., a social system with a distinct principle of distributive justice: "from each according to his ability, to each according to his work," which is also the norm of "socialism." Correspondingly, the New Class may oppose other social systems and their different systems of privilege, for example, systems that allocate privileges and incomes on the basis of controlling stocks of money (i.e., old capital). The New Class, then, is prepared to be egalitarian so far as the privileges of the *old* class are concerned. That is, under certain conditions it is prepared to remove or restrict the special incomes of the old class: profits, rents, interest. The New Class is anti-egalitarian, however, in that it seeks special guild advantages—political powers and incomes—on the basis of its possession of cultural capital. ...

The New Class as a Speech Community

1. The culture of critical discourse (CCD)[19] is an historically evolved set of rules, a grammar of discourse, which (1) is concerned to *justify* its assertions, but (2) whose *mode* of justification does not proceed by invoking authorities, and (3) prefers to elicit the *voluntary* consent of those addressed solely on the basis of arguments adduced. CCD is centered on a specific speech act: justification. It is a culture of discourse in which there is nothing that speakers will on principle permanently refuse to discuss or make problematic; indeed, they are even willing to talk about the value of talk itself and its possible inferiority to silence or to practice. This grammar is the deep structure of the common ideology shared by the New Class. *The shared ideology of the intellectuals and intelligentsia is thus an ideology about discourse.* Apart from and underlying the various technical languages (or sociolects) spoken by specialized professions, intellectuals and intelligentsia are commonly committed to a culture of critical discourse (CCD). CCD is the latent but mobilizable infrastructure of modern "technical" languages.

2. The culture of critical discourse is characterized by speech that is *relatively* more *situation-free*, more context or field "independent." This speech culture thus values expressly legislated meanings and devalues tacit, context-limited meanings. Its ideal is: "one word, one meaning," for everyone and forever.

The New Class's special speech variant also stresses the importance of particular modes of *justification*, using especially explicit and articulate rules, rather than diffuse precedents or tacit features of the speech context. The culture of critical speech requires that the validity of claims be justified without reference to the speaker's *societal position or authority*. Here, good speech is speech that can make its own principles *explicit* and is oriented to conforming with them, rather than stressing context-sensitivity and context-variability. Good speech here thus has *theoreticity*.[20]

Being pattern-and-principle-oriented, CCD implies that that which is said may *not* be correct, and may be *wrong*. It recognizes that "What Is" may be mistaken or inadequate and is therefore open to alternatives. CCD is also relatively more *reflexive*, self-monitoring, capable of more meta-communication, that is, of talk about talk; it is able to make its own speech problematic, and to edit it with respect to its lexical and grammatical features, as well as making problematic the validity of its assertions. CCD thus requires considerable "expressive discipline," not to speak of "instinctual renunciation."

3. Most importantly, the culture of critical speech forbids reliance upon the speaker's person, authority, or status in society to justify his claims. As a result, CCD de-authorizes all speech grounded in traditional societal authority, while it authorizes itself, the elaborated speech variant of the culture of critical discourse, as the standard

of *all* "serious" speech. From now on, persons and their social positions must not be visible in their speech. Speech becomes impersonal. Speakers hide behind their speech. Speech seems to be dis-embodied, de-contextualized and self-grounded. (This is especially so for the speech of intellectuals and somewhat less so for technical intelligentsia who may not invoke CCD except when their paradigms break down.) The New Class becomes the guild masters of an invisible pedagogy.

4. The culture of critical discourse is the common ideology shared by the New Class, although technical intelligentsia sometimes keep it in latency. The skills and the social conditions required to reproduce it are among the common *interests* of the New Class. Correspondingly, it is in the common interest of the New Class to prevent or oppose all censorship of its speech variety and to install it as the standard of good speech. *The New Class thus has both a common ideology in CCD and common interests in its cultural capital.* ...

Intelligentsia and Intellectuals

1. There are at least two elites within the New Class: (1) *intelligentsia* whose intellectual interests are fundamentally "technical" and (2) *intellectuals* whose interests are primarily critical, emancipatory, hermeneutic and hence often political. Both elites utilize an elaborated linguistic variant and both are committed to the CCD. Both therefore resist the old class, although doing so in different ways in different settings and to different degrees.

While intellectuals often contribute to revolutionary leadership, they also serve to accommodate the future to the past and to reproduce the past in the future. That's what comes of the love of books. While the technical intelligentsia often wish nothing more than to be allowed to enjoy their opiate obsessions with technical puzzles, it is their social mission to revolutionize technology continually and hence disrupt established social solidarities and cultural values by never contenting themselves with the *status quo*. Revolutionary intellectuals are the medium of an ancient moral-

ity; accommodative intelligentsia are the medium of a new amorality. Which is more revolutionary?

2. The sociology and the social psychology of the occupational life of intellectuals and technical intelligentsia differ considerably, as do their cognitive procedures. Thomas Kuhn's notion of "normal science"[21] is a key to the cognitive life of technical intelligentsia and of their differences from intellectuals. A "normal science" is one whose members concentrate their efforts on solving the "puzzles" of "paradigms" on which normal science centers. Technical intelligentsia concentrate on operations within the paradigm(s) of their discipline, exploring its inner symbolic space, extending its principles to new fields, fine-tuning it. Intellectuals, in contrast, are those whose fields of activity more commonly lack consensually validated paradigms, may have several competing paradigms, and they therefore do not take normal science with its single dominating paradigm as the usual case. Intellectuals often transgress the boundaries of the conventional division of labor in intellectual life; they do not reject scholarship, however, but only the *normalization* of scholarship.

3. It would be tempting but far too simple to say, intellectuals produce the "lions" of the New Class, while the intelligentsia produce its "foxes." Who is a lion and who a fox depends on whose way upward is being blocked. Where recruitment of college teachers is under the close control of the national ministry, as for example in Israel, members of the Israeli Communist Party and any who seem well disposed toward it have little chance of being hired.[22] In parts of the Mid-East, then, it is often the case that teachers and other intellectuals are relatively prudent politically, while doctors, engineers, and lawyers—being "independent"—may be more openly radical. Ché Guevara, it will be remembered, was a doctor, as is George Habash; Yasir Arafat was trained as an engineer.

Old Line Bureaucrats, New Staff Intelligentsia

1. With the growth of the technical intelligentsia, the functional autonomy of the old class wanes. The intelligentsia of the New Class manage the

new means of production and administration; they also acquire at-hand control over the new means of communication and of *violence*. If we think of the state's repressive apparatus within the framework of Marxism there is no way to explain the recent revolutions in Ethiopia and Portugal, where the military played a singular role. In less developed countries, military intelligentsia are often the vanguard of the New Class.

Marxism misses the paradox that the old class can influence the state, or any other administrative system for that matter, only with the mediation of the New Class. It is not simply a matter of the split between "management and ownership" within capitalism, first, because that split is no less true of "socialism," and secondly, because the split is not confined to the production of commodities, but also includes the production of *violence*. As the organizational units of the economy and state become larger and more bureaucratic, the survival and control of the old class becomes more attenuated, more indirect, ever more dependent on the intelligentsia of the New Class.

2. The fundamental organizational instrument of our time, the bureaucratic organization, becomes increasingly scientized. The old bureaucratic officials at first provide a protective cover for the growth of the New Class. But as the number and importance of technical experts operating with CCD increases, there is a growing split between the old line bureaucrats and the technical intelligentsia. It becomes ever more difficult even for those *managing* the organization simply to understand the skills of the New Class, let alone to exert an ongoing, close control over them. The bureaucratic organization, as the dominant organizational type of the modern era, is controlled by an uneasy coalition of three elements: (i) top managing directors appointed from outside the bureaucracy and who do not usually control the technical expertise of the New Class or the complex details known to bureaucratic officials, (ii) New Class experts, and (iii) bureaucratic "line" officials whose modes of rationality differ.[23]

3. The cadre of the *old* bureaucratic structure are an officialdom, "bureaucrats," who ground their orders in terms of their legal *authority*: "do this because *I* say so, and I am authorized to say so." They are the *older* elite of the bureaucracy, the "bureaucrats" of legendary stigma, the "line" of-

ficials whose position depends simply on their rigorous conformity with organizational rules, obedience to their superiors' orders, the legality of their appointment, and sheer seniority. Their principal function is *control* over the behavior of those beneath them and those outside the organization. They are rooted in the elemental impulse of domination. In short, they are the organization's old "snake brain."

Having no reasons he can speak, the bureaucratic official does not justify his actions by arguing that they contribute to some desirable goal. He simply says he is conforming with the rules which, as Max Weber noted, he treats as "a basis of action for their own sake"; in the sinister phrase, he is "following orders." Either way, he serves as a transmission belt. He is passing on orders or policies that he is expected to obey whatever his personal feeling and whether or not he agrees with them.

These orders or policies are, then, placed beyond the domain of the culture of critical discourse. The old bureaucratic official was designed to be an "agent," uncritically obedient to the organization's top *managers* who, in turn, transmit the ideological and economic interests of social groups outside of the bureaucracy, and who are appointed because they can be relied upon to do just that. Bureaucratic officials are the agents of an internal colonialism, the instruments of an Indirect Rule. The bureaucratic officialdom are the brute part of bureaucracy, the barriers by which the technical intelligentsia are caged, and at the same time they are the protective covering for the New Class's first growth within the bureaucracy.

4. Unlike the older bureaucrats, the new intelligentsia have extensive cultural capital which increases their mobility. The old bureaucrat's skills are often little more than being able to read, write, file, and are limited to their employing bureaucracy. The new intelligentsia's greater cultural capital is, indeed, *more productive of goods and services* and they are, therefore, less concerned to vaunt their personal superiority or to extract deference from those below them. As a result, the old bureaucrats and the new intelligentsia develop and reproduce different systems of social control. Bureaucrats employ a control apparatus based on "ordering and forbidding," threatening and punishing the disobedient or resistant. The intelligen-

tsia of the New Class, capable of increasing services and production, typically seek to control by *rewarding* persons for conformity to their expectations, by providing more material incentives and, also, by educational indoctrination. The intelligentsia of the New Class is a task-centered and work-centered elite having considerable confidence in its own worth and its future and, correspondingly, has less status anxiety that they irrationally impose on others. They are less overbearing and less punishment-prone. They need not, moreover, seek status solely within their own organization and from its staff or clients. Rather, they also seek status in professional associations; they wish the good regard of the knowledgeable.

5. The technical intelligentsia of the New Class is controlled by those incompetent to judge its performances and whose control, therefore, is experienced as irrational.[24] The New Class intelligentsia, then, feel a certain contempt for their superiors; for they are not competent participants in the careful discourse concerning which technical decisions are made. The New Class's intelligentsia are controlled by two echelons above them: one, the *bureaucratic officialdom,* the "line officials," *directly* above them; two, the *political* appointees managing the bureaucracy at its pinnacle, who are not appointed on the basis of their technical competence, but because they represent money capital or politically reliable "commissars." The fundamental structure within which most technical intelligentsia work, then, systematically generates tensions between them, on the one side, and the bureaucratic officials and managers, on the other. It is within the bureaucratic structure that much of the technical intelligentsia of the New Class begins its struggle to rise. It has one of its first muffled confrontations with the old class within the precincts of a specific organizational structure, the bureaucracy.

6. By comparison with line bureaucrats, the technical intelligentsia of the New Class are veritable philosophers. By comparison with the intellectuals, the intelligentsia may seem *idiots savants.* In contrast to the bureaucrats, however, the intelligentsia seeks nothing for its own sake, gives reasons without invoking authority, and regards nothing as settled once for all. To them, nothing is exempt from re-examination. Unlike the bureau-

crats, intelligentsia are not "ritualists" pursuing something without regard to its effectiveness.

7. At the same time, however, nothing is sacred to them; their primary concern is with the technical effectiveness of their means rather than its moral propriety. They are pragmatic nihilists. They are capable of emancipating men from old shibboleths, but they are emancipators who know no limits. Their emancipation has a side effect: cultural destructiveness, *anomie.* The cultural dissolution they bring is precisely that always entailed by the culture of critical discourse, which commonly alienates persons from tradition.[25] In short, *like intellectuals, the intelligentsia, too, are a revolutionary force.* But the revolutionary power of the technical intelligentsia of the New Class is dammed-up by the bureaucratic barrier and the old form of property.

8. If the technical sub-elite of the New Class have the makings of a "benign" elite, they nonetheless remain an *elite.* They have no intention of instituting a social order in which all are *equal* regardless of their cultural capital. They do not think of themselves as an "intellectual proletariat," let alone as an ordinary proletariat. Contributing to the increase of the social surplus by the increased productivity of their cultural capital, they will benignly increase the funds available for welfare, may even accept worker participation in setting incentives, increase consumerism, even increasing job security. Although seeking it for themselves, they do not tolerate "workers' control" and they do not believe in equality.[26] Talk of "workers' control" is for the most part produced by a different sector of the New Class, by radicalized *intellectuals,* and not the technical intelligentsia.

9. Maoism was essentially an effort to avoid the resurgence of the old line bureaucratic officials *and* of the technical intelligentsia of the New Class. But the intelligentsia is the more rational elite, increasing both social productivity and social understanding, and now China is liquidating the "cultural revolution" and opting for the New Class.[27] Distilled to essentials, Maoism was an effort to strengthen the bargaining position of the working class (including the peasantry) in its inescapable, forthcoming negotiations with the New Class. For its part, and unlike Maoism, Stalinism was a profoundly regressive force because

it sought to subordinate the technical intelligentsia to the most archaic sector, the old bureaucratic officialdom.[28]

As the old class deteriorates and loses control, especially with the rise of state socialism, the real choices are between the new technical intelligentsia and the old line bureaucrats. And it *is* a real choice. The rule of the bureaucratic officialdom is callous and authoritarian, while the rule of the new cultural elite, able to increase the level of productivity, can rely more on rewards than punishment and on the demystified performance of tasks without the mystique of authority or the extortion of personal deference. ...

The Flawed Universal Class

1. The New Class is the most progressive force in modern society and is a center of whatever human emancipation is possible in the foreseeable future. It has no motives to curtail the forces of production and no wish to develop them solely in terms of their profitability. The New Class possesses the scientific knowledge and technical skills on which the future of modern forces of production depend. At the same time, members of the New Class also manifest increasing sensitivity to the ecological "side effects" or distant diseconomies of continuing technical development. The New Class, further, is a center of opposition to almost all forms of censorship, thus embodying a universal societal interest in a kind of rationality broader than that invested in technology. Although the New Class is at the center of nationalist movements throughout the world, after that phase is secured, the New Class is also the most internationalist and most universalist of all social strata; it is the most cosmopolitan of all elites. Its control over ordinary "foreign" languages, as well as of technical sociolects, enable it to communicate with other nationalities and it is often a member of a technical guild of international scope.

2. For all that, however, the New Class is hardly the end of domination. While its ultimate significance is the end of the old moneyed class's domination, the New Class is also the nucleus of a *new*

hierarchy and the elite of a new form of cultural capital.

The historical limits of the New Class are inherent in both the nature of its own characteristic rationality, and in its ambitions as a cultural bourgeoisie. Its culture of critical discourse fosters a purely "theoretical" attitude toward the world. Speakers are held competent to the degree that they know and can *say* the rules, rather than just happening to follow them. The culture of critical discourse thus values the very theoreticity that the "common sense" long suspected was characteristic of intellectuals.

Intellectuals have long believed that those who know the rule, who know the theory by which they act, are superior because they lead an "examined" life. They thus exalt theory over practice, and are concerned less with the success of a practice than that the practice should have submitted itself to a reasonable rule. Since intellectuals and intelligentsia are concerned with doing things in the right way and for the right reason—in other words, since they value doctrinal conformity for its own sake—they (we) have a native tendency toward ritualism and *sectarianism*.

3. The culture of the New Class exacts still other costs: since its discourse emphasizes the importance of carefully edited speech, this has the vices of its virtues: in its *virtuous* aspect, self-editing implies a commendable circumspection, carefulness, self-discipline and "seriousness." In its negative modality, however, self-editing also disposes toward an unhealthy self-consciousness, toward stilted convoluted speech, an inhibition of play, imagination and passion, and continual pressure for expressive discipline. The new rationality thus becomes the source of a new alienation.

Calling for watchfulness and self-discipline, CCD is productive of intellectual reflexivity *and* the loss of warmth and spontaneity. Moreover, that very reflexivity stresses the importance of adjusting action to some pattern of propriety. There is, therefore, a structured inflexibility when facing changing situations; there is a certain disregard of the differences in situations, and an insistence on hewing to the required rule.

This inflexibility and insensitivity to the force of differing contexts, this inclination to impose one set of rules on different cases also goes by the ancient name of "dogmatism." Set in the context of human relationships, the vulnerability of the New Class to dogmatism along with its very *task-centeredness,* imply a certain insensitivity to *persons,* to their feelings and reactions, and open the way to the disruption of human solidarity. Political brutality, then, finds a grounding in the culture of critical discourse; the new rationality may paradoxically allow a new darkness at noon.

4. The paradox of the New Class is that it is both emancipatory *and* elitist. It subverts all establishments, social limits, and privileges, including its own. The New Class bears a culture of critical and careful discourse which is an historically emancipatory rationality. The new discourse (CCD) is the grounding for a critique of established forms of domination and provides an escape from tradition, but it also bears the seeds of a new domination. Its discourse is a lumbering machinery of argumentation that can wither imagination, discourage play, and curb expressivity. The culture of discourse of the New Class seeks to *control* everything, its topic and itself, believing that such domination is the only road to truth. The New Class begins by monopolizing truth and by making itself its guardian. It thereby makes even the claims of the old class dependent on it. The New Class sets itself above others, holding that its speech is better than theirs; that the examined life (*their* examination) is better than the unexamined life which, it says, is sleep and no better than death. Even as it subverts old inequities, the New Class silently inaugurates a new hierarchy of the knowing, the knowledgeable, the reflexive and insightful. Those who talk well, it is held, excel those who talk poorly or not at all. It is now no longer enough simply to be good. Now, one has to explain it. The New Class is the universal class in embryo, but badly flawed.

Notes

1. It is not my intention to suggest that modern intellectuals are merely the secular counterpart of clericals. Indeed, my own stress (as distinct, say, from Edward Shils who does appear to view intellectuals as priests *manqués*) is on the discontinuity of the two.

2. For full development of this, see chapter 2, especially p. 42, of my *Dialectic of Ideology and Technology* (New York, 1976).

3. Doubtless some will insist this is a "false consciousness." But this misses the point. My concern here is with their own definitions of their social role, precisely because these influence the manner in which they perform their roles. As W. I. Thomas and Florian Znaniecki long ago (and correctly) insisted, a thing defined as real is real in its consequences. Moreover, the state who employs most of these teachers is itself interested in having teachers consolidate the tie between students and it itself, rather than with the students' parents.

4. See Basil Bernstein, *Class, Codes and Control,* vol. 1, *Theoretical Studies Towards a Sociology of Language* (London, 1971), vol. 2, *Applied Studies Towards a Sociology of Language* (London, 1973), vol. 3, *Towards a Theory of Educational Transmission* (London, 1975). Bernstein's theory is used here in a critical appropriation facilitated by the work of Dell Hymes and William Labov. My own critique of Bernstein emerges, at least tacitly, in the discussion of [the "Flawed Universal Class"] in the text. It is developed explicitly in my *Dialectic of Ideology and Technology,* pp. 58–66. While Labov has sharply criticized Bernstein, he himself also stresses the general importance of self-monitored speech and of speech *reflexivity* in general (i.e., not only of careful pronunciation) thus converging with Bernstein's focus on reflexivity as characterizing the elaborated linguistic variant and distinguishing it from the restricted variant. See William Labov, *Sociolinguistic Patterns* (Philadelphia, 1972), p. 208.

5. For example: "The Communists disdain to conceal their views and aims. They openly declare ..." (*Communist Manifesto* [Chicago, 1888], authorized English edition edited by Engels, p. 58).

6. See E. Hobsbawm, *Primitive Rebels* (Manchester, 1959), p. 167 ff.

7. A secret doctrine is one which, because it is reserved only for the organization elite, can be made known only after persons join organizations and reach a certain membership position in it. A secret doctrine thus is never one which can have been a *motive* for joining the organization in the first instance.

8. Lenin's *What Is to Be Done?* was originally published in 1902.

9. I am grounding myself here in the analysis of dimensions of meaning common to social objects in the pioneering work of Charles Osgood and his collaborators. Their researches have recurrently found three dimensions: goodness/badness, weakness/strength, and activity/passivity. In the *Coming Crisis* I proposed an *equilibrium* condition for the first two dimensions,

speaking there of social worlds that were culturally permitted and those unpermitted, defining the latter in terms of a dissonance between imputed goodness/badness and weakness/strength. To "normalize" is to contrive to see an unpermitted world as if it were a permitted one, i.e., to remove the dissonance. See A. W. Gouldner, *The Coming Crisis of Western Sociology* (New York, 1970), especially pp. 484–88. For Osgood's first researches see Charles E. Osgood, George Suci, and Percy Tannenbaum, *The Measurement of Meaning* (Urbana, 1957).

10. *The New Industrial State* (Boston, 1967).

11. *The Coming of Post-Industrial Society* (New York, 1973).

12. *The Modern Corporation and Private Property* (New York, 1932).

13. "It stands to reason that the one who knows more will dominate the one who knows less," M. Bakouinine, *Oeuvres*, Vol. 5 (Paris, 1911), p. 106.

14. See V. F. Calverton, *The Making of Society* (New York, 1937).

15. Talcott Parsons, *The Social System* (Glencoe, 1951), chapter 10; *Essays in Sociological Theory* (Glencoe, 1954), chapter 18; "The Professions," *International Encyclopedia of Social Sciences* (New York, 1968).

16. While Chomsky's position is exhibited in various of his writings, I shall rely here on his most recent statement in his Huizinga lecture, "Intellectuals and the State," delivered at Leiden, 9 October 1977. Citations will be from the manuscript copy. Cf. N. Chomsky, *American Power and the New Mandarins* (New York, 1969).

17. Maurice Zeitlin, "Corporate Ownership and Control: The Large Corporations and the Capitalist Class," *American Journal of Sociology* (March 1974), pp. 1073–1119.

18. Cf. James O'Connor, *Corporations and the State* (New York, 1974), pp. 126–28 for the argument that government financing of R & D and advanced education constitute a socialization of part of the costs of production whose net surplus is privately appropriated.

19. This section is indebted to Basil Bernstein and is based on a critical appropriation of his "elaborated and restricted linguistic codes," which have gone through various re-workings. That controversial classic was published in J. J. Gumperz and D. Hymes, *Directions in Sociolinguistics* (New York, 1972). A recent re-working is to be found in Bernstein's, "Social Class, Language, and Socialization," in T. A. Sebeok, ed., *Current Trends in Linguistics* (The Hague, 1974). For full bibliographic and other details see note 4 above.

20. Cf. Peter McHugh, "A Common-Sense Perception of Deviance," in H. P. Dreitzel, ed., *Recent Sociology, Number 2* (London, 1970), p. 165 ff. For good speech as "serious" speech see David Silverman, "Speaking Seriously," *Theory and Society* (Spring, 1974).

21. Thomas S. Kuhn, *The Structure of Scientific Revolutions* (Chicago, 1970) second edition, enlarged.

22. See Khalil Nakhleh, "Palestinian Dilemma: Nationalist Consciousness and University Education" (ms., 1976).

23. For fuller discussion of the differences and contradictions between bureaucrats and technical intelligentsia, see my *Dialectic of Ideology and Technology*, p. 266 ff.

24. As a consequence, when technical intelligentsia are monitored by organizational superiors, "it is results that count" for it is often only these that *can* be judged.

25. The testimony on this is venerable: in Plato's *Republic*, Socrates proposes to defer training in the dialectic until students are in their thirties and have passed other tests. And then, he warns, great caution is needed: "Why great caution?" "Do you not remark," I said, "how great is the evil which dialectic has introduced?" "What evil?" he said. "The students of the art are filled with lawlessness" (*Republic*, 437 DE). For fuller discussion see my *Enter Plato* (New York, 1965), p. 279. In short, the dialectic, like CCD, has certain inherent costs which Nietzsche was among the first to notice. Thus CCD cannot simply be equated with "good" speech.

26. This is no less true for the Marxist contingent of the New Class than of others. Equality has never been a high priority value for Marxism.

27. While editing this, a recent people's congress in Peking eliminated the cultural revolution's "revolutionary committees" in factories and schools, began to refurbish wage differentials, and recharged higher education, the essential reproductive mechanism of the New Class.

28. Louis Althusser's argument, that Stalinism was a fumbled attack on the New Class, has many difficulties. Not least is the fact that among the delegates to the 18th Congress of the CPSU in 1939, two years after the purges, about 26% had higher education, compared to the 10% with higher education among delegates of the 17th Congress in 1934, who were a central target of Stalin's terror. For further discussion, see A. W. Gouldner, "Stalinism," *Telos* (Winter 1977–78).

IVÁN SZELÉNYI

Post-Industrialism, Post-Communism, and the New Class

The term "new class" was coined by M. Bakunin around 1870 in his book *The Knoto-Germanic Empire and the Social Revolution*. In analyzing the possible social consequences of the Marxist scenario of socialism, he wrote:

There will be … an extremely complex government, which will not content itself with governing and administering the masses politically, as all governments do today, but which will also administer them economically. … All that will demand an immense knowledge. … It will be the reign of scientific intelligence, the most aristocratic, despotic, arrogant and contemptuous of all regimes. There will be a new class, a new hierarchy of real and pretended scientists and scholars, and the world will be divided into a minority ruling in the name of knowledge and the immense ignorant majority.[1]

The idea of a postcapitalist class society in which domination is based not on ownership of wealth but on monopoly of knowledge has haunted the social sciences ever since.

The term "new class theory" describes a variety of approaches. In my search to provide an all-encompassing definition of new class theory, I found only two points upon which new class theorists tend to agree. First, they typically concur that Marx was correct in predicting that the class rule of the bourgeoisie under capitalism would not last forever; second, they further agree that Marx was incorrect in suggesting that the formation following capitalism would be either "classless" or the "dictatorship of the proletariat." All new class theorists claim that the postcapitalist formation will be a class society in which a new class, other than the proletarian, will rule, but beyond these two points they may have no common ground. The history of new class theories is a history of political and theoretical controversies.

After a century of debate, new class theorists have left the following questions unresolved: Who are the likely candidates for the new dominant class position? Will they be bureaucrats, technocrats, engineers, managers, or the critical, countercultural, adversary-culture intellectuals? On what grounds will the new class rule? Will it be on the basis of its bureaucratic position within the state or through its monopoly of knowledge? What type of knowledge will those agents who are most likely to form the new class need: technocratic or teleocratic, technical or theoretical? In what kind of society will the new class become dominant: state capitalist, socialist, or bureaucratic collectivist? Where is the new class more likely to emerge: in the former Soviet-type societies, in the West, or in both systems simultaneously? Will this new class be progressive, "our best card in history,"[2] or will it be the most despotic of all dominant classes? Is the new class a

---

This article, as prepared for this book, relies on two earlier publications. See Iván Szelényi and Bill Martin, "Three Waves of New Class Theories," *Theory and Society*, September 1988, 645–667; George Konrad and Iván Szelényi, "Intellectuals and Domination in Post-Communist Transition," in Pierre Bourdieu and James Coleman, eds., *Social Theory and Contemporary Society* (Boulder, Colo.: Westview, 1991).

"class" at all, or rather is it an "estate," a dominant "group,"[3] an "officialdom,"[4] or a "new priest-hood"?[5]

Different theorists have come forward with diametrically opposed answers to these questions. In this essay, I briefly review the history of the idea of the new class. I distinguish three versions of new class theories: the intellectual class theories elaborated by the anarchists, the techno-bureaucratic class theories of the 1930s through 1950s, and the knowledge class theories of the 1970s. Finally, I explore the relevance of new class theory for the analysis of modern postindustrial or postcommunist societies.

The Anarchist Theories of the Intellectual Class

The anarchists were quick to spot the latent scientism and elitism of the Marxian project of socialism. Bakunin's attack against Marx during their collaboration in the First International focused on the statist features of the Marxist conception of socialism. According to Bakunin, the complexity of the knowledge that a government-run economy and society requires will inevitably lead to rule by scholars and intellectuals.

Following this line of argument, W. Machajski, the Polish-Ukrainian anarchist, suggested that workers and intellectuals have different visions of socialism: The former expect socialism to be egalitarian, whereas the latter see the essence of socialism in state power.[6] Machajski believed that the statist vision of socialism is self-serving, since it allows intellectuals to use the working-class movement to promote their own rise to power through the state bureaucracies. The society that emerges would be as inegalitarian as capitalism is, except that privilege based on private capital is replaced by privilege based on the monopoly of knowledge.

Thus, both Bakunin and Machajski were skeptical about the role intellectuals would play in the socialist movement. According to their formulation, intellectuals not only construct ideologies that give primacy to the political over the economic in mass struggles, but they also underem-

phasize equality as a goal by focusing on the nature of state power. These ideologies serve the power aspirations of intellectuals but do not contribute to the emancipation of manual workers. In this view, then, we first see a cynical streak that reasserts itself throughout the history of new class theorizing.

The Technocratic-Bureaucratic Class Theories

Since the late 1930s, several theories have emerged claiming that a bureaucratic, a technocratic, or a managerial new dominant class is in the making or already in power in the former Soviet republics (in particular, Russia), in Western capitalism, or in both systems. These theories are rather heterogeneous: Indeed, the agents of the new class differ from theory to theory (ranging from Stalinist bureaucrats to American managers), and the scope of the theories differ as well, with some insisting that the new class formation is limited to the former Soviet states and others describing the evolution of a new dominant class under both capitalism and socialism. Still, the common feature of all these theories is the claim that class power based on individual ownership of capital has been superseded and a new structural position has been created from which economic command can be exercised.

Although such an analysis began to develop independently for Western societies in the work of Veblen and of Berle and Means,[7] most of the bureaucratic class theories can be traced to the work of Leon Trotsky[8] and to the empirical analysis of the early Stalinist Soviet Union. While Trotsky himself was not a new class theorist—he emphatically denied the class character of the bureaucracy—the first comprehensive theories describing the Soviet Union as a society dominated by a bureaucratic class were developed by former Trotskyites. Trotsky's former disciples moved beyond their teacher by pointing out the class nature of the ruling Soviet bureaucracy, and thus they offered a more radical analysis of the character of the Soviet Union. Two versions of such post-Trotskyist bureaucratic class theories can be distinguished: (1) According to some scholars (for instance, Tony Cliff), the Stalinist bureaucracy effectively turned the Soviet Union into a "state capitalist" society;[9] (2) other scholars, under the influence of Bruno Rizzi,[10] claimed that the Soviet Union represented a fundamentally new social system that was different from both capitalism and socialism and that rightfully should be called bureaucratic collectivism,[11] which referred to societies ruled by the state bureaucracy constituted as the new dominant class. However, despite these disagreements over the extent to which the Soviet Union might be seen as "state capitalist," both the early state capitalism and the bureaucratic collectivism theories assumed that the class power of the bureaucracy was based in a new form of ownership: The bureaucrats collectively own the means of production.

These early theories of the former Soviet Union as a new class society dominated by a collective ownership class—the bureaucracy—remained influential for some time. Their impact can be seen, at least in trace form, in theories emerging as late as the early 1970s. There have been, however, three notable reformulations of early bureaucratic class theories in the post-Stalinist epoch:

1. Djilas and, in the late 1960s Kuron and Modzelewski, accepted the idea of a new dominant bureaucratic class whose power is based on collective ownership, but they regarded the Soviet-type societies as "communist" or "state monopoly socialist."[12]

2. Maoists, led principally by Charles Bettelheim,[13] developed a new version of the state capitalism theory, according to which the Soviet Union restored capitalism and became a new class society. But unlike the post-Trotskyist theorists, they also believed that the agents who carried out this restoration were not Stalinist bureaucrats but enterprise managers. However, in a crucial respect, Bettelheim and the post-Trotskyist bureaucratic class theorists are in agreement: They both identify the base of the class power of the managerial technocracy in its collective ownership of the means of production.

3. During the 1970s, a new version of bureaucratic collectivism emerged in the works of Carlo (which contain traces of the Maoist influence) and, to some extent, in the writings of Castor-iadis.[14] Both Carlo and Castoriadis believed that the Soviet Union was obsessed with economic growth[15] and consequently it produced an economic system based on the premise of "production for production's sake."[16] Since production is an end in itself rather than a means of satisfying genuine social needs, the Soviet bureaucratic collectivism (Carlo) or total bureaucratic capitalism (Castoriadis) serves, in the last analysis, bureaucratic class interests.

The idea that in Soviet-type societies the class power of the old bourgeoisie was replaced by the power of those who control the means of production influenced the analysis of Western societies as well. Some of these Western new class theories are spin-offs from the Trotskyist analysis of the Soviet Union. James Burnham, a former Trotskyist, developed in the early 1940s the theory of "managerial society,"[17] wherein he claimed that the Russian Revolution replaced the bourgeoisie with managers as a dominant class. He also stated that the managerial revolution is a worldwide phenomenon. At the time, fascist Japan and Germany appeared to be moving toward managerialism, as did the United States with the New Deal. Thus, Burnham developed an East-West theory of the new class that forecasts the evolution of a new dominant class on a truly worldwide basis.

During the 1930s, the idea of a technocratic-managerial transformation of modern capitalism was advanced with either apologetic or critical overtones. Within the former camp, Berle and Means[18] stand out as important scholars: They reported with approval on the advance of managerial power in the United States. They claimed that capitalism is undergoing a major transformation in which private property is being dissolved and private owners are being replaced by managers in positions of economic power.[19]

The Knowledge Class Theories of the 1970s

During the 1970s, the political Right (neoconservatives) began to develop for the first time their own new class theories. (Earlier theories were, with few exceptions, left-wing critiques of

Marxist theory or Marxist-Leninist political practices.) Their argument was that the Left intelligentsia developed an "adversary culture"[20] that seeks to undermine the value system of modern democratic society and establish the power of a modern "priesthood" comprising moralizing leftist intelligentsia.[21] This intelligentsia, they contend, exercises undemocratic pressures through the media and creates its own class domination by controlling the welfare state, academia, or a combination of these institutions.[22]

Daniel Bell, in *The Coming of Post-Industrial Society*,[23] develops a politically less charged but in certain respects similar argument.[24] In the works of Bell, scientists are believed to play a fundamentally new role in postindustrial society. Scientific-theoretical knowledge, accordingly, becomes a major force of economic growth and social progress in the postindustrial epoch. Under such circumstances, there is room for a new, socially progressive knowledge class.[25]

Bell and the neoconservatives might be termed "knowledge class theorists," since both describe the development of new forms of knowledge that provide the basis for class domination by the intelligentsia. While for Bell the distinctive feature of this new knowledge is its abstractness and "theoreticity," for the neoconservatives this knowledge is simply destructive and subversive—it is adversarial knowledge that is antidemocratic and anticapitalist in orientation.

Alvin Gouldner offered the most comprehensive knowledge class theory. Gouldner's research project on the new class begins as a standard "sociology of knowledge" critique of Marxism and the role of leftist revolutionary intellectuals.[26] Gouldner identifies certain features of Marxism, in particular its "metaphoricality,"[27] that make it possible for Marxist intellectuals to pursue self-interested goals while pretending to represent universalistic interests. Armed with this knowledge, the revolutionary intelligentsia can substitute itself for the proletariat and emerge from the revolution as a new dominant class. In his two major works on the subject, *The Dialectic of Ideology and Technology*[28] and *The Future of Intellectuals and the Rise of the New Class*,[29] Gouldner develops a new class theory that not only encompasses the power aspirations of the Marxist

revolutionary vanguards but also speaks to the increasing power of the technocrats and scientists. The key concept Gouldner identifies is that of a "culture of critical discourse"—this constitutes the common feature and quality of knowledge shared by Marxist radicals, professionals, the technical intelligentsia, and adversary or countercultural intellectuals. The cultural capital thus acquired enables these social groupings to usurp from a position of power both old-line bureaucrats of state socialism and private capitalists.

Typically, knowledge class theories were devised in reaction to changing social relations in the West. My book, coauthored with George Konrad and titled *The Intellectuals on the Road to Class Power*,[30] offers an analysis quite similar to that of Gouldner, but the focus shifts to the socialist case. We argued that the intelligentsia in Eastern Europe, by virtue of its monopoly over "teleological knowledge" (i.e., its control over the definition of socially desirable ends), formulates claims for class power. In the post-Stalinist epoch, the bureaucracy has indeed opened up and joined forces with the intelligentsia as a new dominant class in incipient form.

Thus, the most recent new class theories explore the changing nature of knowledge. They typically argue that a new type of knowledge (be it adversary culture, teleological knowledge, or cultural capital) is gaining ground and the possessors of this knowledge are in a radically new relationship to domination. It is assumed that the possessors of this new type of knowledge can now make an autonomous bid for power.

Relevance of New Class Theories for the Analysis of Western Postindustrial Societies

In light of the evidence of the last century, new class theories might be seen as false prophecies, since neither intellectuals, technocrats, nor managers have yet succeeded in establishing their collective power. When bureaucrats seized power in Soviet-type societies, they proved to be too archaistic in their character; thus they ruled more as an estate than a class. The question that remains, however, is whether any of the agents the new class theorists have regarded so far as candidates for the new dominant class position will eventually acquire class power.

As far as Western postindustrial societies are concerned, I am highly skeptical about the possibility of such a transition. New class theories too readily assume that the agents who can become the new class will in fact want the class power emanating from that position. Gouldner did consider the possibility that these candidates will indeed seek power, and so did we in *The Intellectuals on the Road to Class Power*. However, even if a structural position is open to intellectuals and they have the opportunity to become "new masters," it is not certain that they would seize it. Our review of new class theories suggests that the highly educated would have to pay a very high price for class power: This price is bureaucratization. Bourgeois society at least offers the freedom of the *professions libres* and of academia, with economic security and privileges for the highly educated. Statist bureaucratization, without which a new class is hardly imaginable, would endanger such privileges. Would the intellectuals and the highly educated forgo these privileges, knowingly and willingly, just to exercise power? Paradoxically, the highly educated group may resist the temptation of its own class power not out of any altruistic dedication to social causes but out of self-interest. Furthermore, by resisting the temptation of class power, intellectuals may actually gain a different type of power, namely, "symbolic domination." It always has been an attraction to ideologues, both on the political Left and Right, to exercise influence through the possession of knowledge or information and thus remain behind the curtains in the theater of power. In summary, a genuine form of new class domination is possible in postcapitalist and postindustrial society, but it is not very probable.

Intellectuals and Domination in Postcommunist Transition

George Konrad and I completed *The Intellectuals on the Road to Class Power* in September 1974. In the last paragraph of the manuscript, we concluded that its publication by an official publishing house in an East European country would be the empirical proof that socialism had reached its "third period" in which intellectuals, rather than the bureaucratic elite, exercise class power.

Exactly fifteen years later, in October 1989, our book appeared in Hungary in print by a respectable publishing house. We owe answers to at least three important questions that our readers may pose: (1) Are current events indeed proof of the decline of bureaucratic domination and the growth of power of the intelligentsia? (2) Is the undoubtedly increased political activism and influence of the intellectuals a lasting phenomenon or merely a brief interval between communist bureaucratism and a new, possibly bourgeois class domination? In other words, is what we observe now a true third epoch in the making or just a brief period of transition? (3) And, last but not least, if the current stage is a third epoch rather than a brief transition period, can we characterize it as socialist in any meaningful sense of the term? I will address each of these questions in turn.

Currently, intellectuals play a fundamental role in the transformation of state socialist societies. This is particularly true for Hungary, the Czech Republic, and Poland; at least to some extent, it is also true for Russia. As the foundations of bureaucratic domination eroded and the old elite declined, intellectuals emerged as the only viable candidates for membership in the new elite. Never before in East European history have intellectuals exercised more collective power than they do today in Hungary, Poland, or the Czech Republic.

However, the power of intellectuals may be only a transitory phenomenon, just as it was for their predecessors during the French Revolution. As before, they may only be laying the foundations of a new type of domination for a class other than their own: The ultimate victors may well be a neobourgeoisie. However, one should not exclude the possibility that the new intellectual class, which is just appearing on the historical scene, may be able to reproduce itself in a uniquely East European configuration of economic and political institutions and social agents. Intellectuals are in a socially dominant position today, and it is far from obvious that they will give up their power voluntarily and without a fight. Whereas intellectuals in the Western world may never abandon the freedom of academia, intellectuals in Eastern Europe have already done so and may well act to preserve and extend their power.

I am less certain about the answer to the third and final question. I prefer to label the social and economic order we see emerging in Eastern Europe today as "postcommunist." With this label, I want to express my belief that I know better what we are leaving behind than what lies ahead of us. At this writing (winter 1992), the societies of Eastern Europe are socialist mixed economies with a still dominant but rapidly disintegrating statist economy. It is possible that postcommunism will not prove to be an epochal phenomenon but will instead be a brief interval between state socialism and some sort of capitalism. If this is the case, then the most likely near-term future of Eastern Europe is dependent capitalism. As Jadwiga Staniszkis has noted,[31] the transition from state socialism into dependent capitalism may take the form of political capitalism in which former cadres and the current intellectual ruling elite attempt to use their office to transform themselves into a propertied bourgeoisie.

I do not want to exaggerate the prescience of *The Intellectuals on the Road to Class Power*. It is true that intellectuals indeed came to power in Eastern Europe, but Konrad and I were right for the wrong reason: They did not achieve power by rationalizing redistributive power as we presupposed, but instead they defeated the bureaucracy in a "discursive revolution" of the kind Gouldner forecasted. And this may have been a Pyrrhic victory: If intellectuals eliminate the redistributive institutions along with the state socialist bureaucracy, they undermine in the long run the economic and social base of their own collective power as well.

Notes

1. M. Bakunin, "Marx, the Bismarck of Socialism," in Leonhard I. Krimmerman and Lewis Perry, eds., *Patterns of Anarchy* (New York: Anchor, 1966), 80–97.

2. Alvin Gouldner, *The Future of Intellectuals and the Rise of the New Class* (New York: Seabury, 1979).

3. F. Feher, A. Heller, and G. Markus, *Dictatorship over Needs* (New York: Basil Blackwell, 1983).

4. Zygmunt Bauman, "Officialdom and Class: Bases of Inequality in Socialist Society," in Frank Parkin, ed., *The Social Analysis of Class Structure* (London: Tavistock, 1974), 129–148.

5. H. Schelsky, *Die Arbeit Tun die Anderen* (Opladen: Westdeutscher Verlag, 1975).

6. See W. Machajski, "Selections from His Writings," in V. F. Calverton, ed., *The Making of Society* (New York: Modern Library, 1937). See also Max Nomad, "Masters, Old and New," in Calverton, *The Making of Society*; and Max Nomad, *Aspects of Revolt* (New York: Bookman, 1959).

7. Thorstein Veblen, *Engineers and the Price System* (New York: Harcourt Brace, 1963); A. A. Berle and G. C. Means, *The Modern Corporation and Private Property* (New York: Macmillan, 1932).

8. Leon Trotsky, *The Revolution Betrayed* (New York: Pathfinder, 1974).

9. Tony Cliff, *State Capitalism in Russia* (London: Pluto, 1979).

10. Bruno Rizzi, *The Bureaucratization of the World* (London: Tavistock, 1985).

11. Max Shachtman, *The Bureaucratic Revolution: The Rise of the Stalinist State* (New York: Donald, 1962).

12. See Milovan Djilas, *The New Class* (New York: Holt, Rinehart, and Winston, 1957); and J. Kuron and K. Modzelewski, *Il Marxismo Polacco all'Opposizione* (Rome, 1968), quoted in A. Carlo, "The Socio-economic Nature of the USSR," *Telos*, 21, Fall 1974, 55.

13. Charles Bettelheim, *Economic Calculations and Forms of Property* (London: Routledge and Kegan Paul, 1976).

14. A. Carlo, "The Socio-economic Nature of the USSR," *Telos*, 21, Fall 1974, 2–86.

15. C. Castoriadis, "The Social Regime in Russia," *Telos*, 38, Winter 1978-79, 212–248.

16. See Carlo, "The Socio-economic Nature of the USSR," 55.

17. James Burnham, *The Managerial Revolution* (Bloomington: Indiana University Press, 1962).

18. Berle and Means, *The Modern Corporation and Private Property*.

19. For a critique of this view, see Maurice Zeitlin, "Corporate Ownership and Control," *American Journal of Sociology* 79, March 1974, 1073–1119.

20. The term "adversary culture" was initially proposed by Lionel Trilling. See Lionel Trilling, *Beyond Culture* (New York: Harcourt Brace Jovanovich, 1965).

21. Schelsky, *Die Arbeit Tun die Anderen*.

22. See D. P. Moynihan, "Equalizing Education: In Whose Benefit?" *The Public Interest* 29, Fall 1972, 68–89.

23. Daniel Bell, *The Coming of Post-Industrial Society* (New York: Basic Books, 1976).

24. Bell is certainly less critical and more sympathetic to the emergent new class thesis than the neoconservative theorists are.

25. Veblen had similar ideas about the future role of engineers, and Galbraith, following Veblen, developed a parallel analysis about "technostructure." See Veblen, *Engineers and the Price System*; J. K. Galbraith, *The New Industrial State* (Boston: Houghton Mifflin, 1967), 71–82, 97–108, 291–303.

26. Alvin Gouldner, "Prologue to the Theory of Revolutionary Intellectuals," *Telos*, 30, Winter 1975-76, 3–36.

27. Alvin Gouldner, "The Metaphoricality of Marx-

ism and the Context-free Grammar of Socialism," *Theory and Society*, 4, Winter 1974, 387–414.

28. Alvin Gouldner, *The Dialectic of Ideology and Technology* (New York: Seabury, 1976), 9–13, 23–63, 195–294.

29. Gouldner, *The Future of Intellectuals and the Rise of the New Class.*

30. G. Konrad and Ivan Szelényi, *The Intellectuals on the Road to Class Power* (New York: Harcourt Brace Jovanovich, 1979).

31. Jadwiga Staniszkis, *The Dynamics of the Breakthrough in Eastern Europe* (Berkeley: University of California Press, 1991). See also Elemer Hankiss, *East European Alternatives: Are There Any?* (Oxford: Oxford University Press, 1990); and Hankiss, *Erzsebet Szalai: Gazdasag es Hatalom* (Budapest: Aula Kiado, 1990), 169–176, 181–186.

JOHN W. MEYER

The Evolution of Modern Stratification Systems

The sociological tendency, well represented in the readings for this section, has been to see modern stratification systems in a realist vein. Real component individuals and groups, competing and cooperating in real interdependencies, create and change a system of inequalities. Real systems—and thus some sort of functionalism, broadly defined—are involved: To be sure, some theories may place particular stress on competitive interdependence (as in class-conflict models), and others may emphasize economic over other interdependencies, but nearly all share a vision of society as a system made up of interdependent parts.

For example, Kerr and his colleagues see the modern economy as evolving toward greater complexity and thus as functionally requiring changing forms of inequality (including emphases on education and merit). Parsons takes much the same approach but with a broader and more social view of the functional requirements involved, so that requirements for social as well as economic integration are seen—the implication being that excess inequality is potentially destabilizing. Marxists often use exactly the same lines of argument, but for them the functional requirements are those of some economic elites or forces rather than society as a whole. Narrower Marxian ideas harmonize with Kerr's thinking of the technical requirements of modern capital; broader ones parallel Parsons's more general list of functional requirements, including social integration

(which can be called "hegemony"). Bell follows especially Kerr but also Parsons and sees both economic and social complexity as creating more and more functional requirements for new levels of knowledge and competence, and this leads to emergence of a new set of strata. Gouldner sees the same consequence arising from social tension and conflict; his is a darker but still recognizable version of Parsons's conception.

Despite their disagreements and conflicts, the authors of these lines of thought all share a general description and analysis of the evolution of modern stratification, a view rooted in a realist vision of modern society as a functioning system. Expansion produces differentiation and complexity—these require more reliance on education and ultimately new professional strata. As the system expands around the world, modern forms of stratification are found everywhere. The story is a standard sociological one, told with varying emphases on conflict and consensus; it is also very similar to the stories modern societies tell about themselves. We emphasize the latter point as of substantive importance in understanding modern societies, not so much as a criticism of stratification theories.

The story has some pronounced weaknesses: If expansion is the driving force, why does so much differentiation occur (e.g., in the modern Third World) even without expansion? If education and the new class are relied upon for technically efficient solutions, why can we not find better evidence of their efficiency (e.g., Berg 1971)? And above all, if stratification reflects real social requirements, why are the forms of stratification

---

This is an original article prepared for this book.

and mobility so strikingly similar across all the extreme variations of modern society?

There is a strong sociological tendency to leave cultural matters out of the equation—aside from some notions that individuals in society may have some socialized tastes in common or less accepted ideas of societies as built up from some general values (a notion illustrated in the Parsons reading). The idea that modern societies may with some collective self-consciousness be, through direct collective action, creating and changing their stratification system is not given much emphasis. "Class consciousness" is of interest as a dependent variable or as an intervening variable helping to account for various outcomes such as political mobilization. But this is class consciousness in the sense of Marx or Mannheim, who assume an underlying sociological reality and see some form of consciousness as its product. In research terms, it is class consciousness as a property of individuals and groups within society, not a property of the collective itself. More respect than imitation is given to Ossowski (1963), for whom the cultural aspects of stratification can be (1) independent variables and (2) collective or institutional properties.

Inattention to collective and cultural aspects of stratification has been a substantial limitation in the field. It has led to extraordinarily mistaken theoretical analyses and predictions (as with the whole families of theories that have overemphasized the causal and descriptive role of economic dimensions in stratification). And it has led to inattention to some obviously cultural aspects of stratification. In this essay, corrective reflections are suggested. We offer cultural interpretations of modern differentiation, the rise of education and the service sector, and the overall homogeneity of modern stratification systems.

The cultural perspective we emphasize is an alternative to what we are calling sociological realism on several dimensions that in a broader discussion could be distinguished. We may note two of them here. First, modern sociological realists see society as made up of individuals and groups that have prior and natural properties (e.g., motives and interests). Their strivings for equality and their inequality result from these properties and their interaction in social life. A more cul-

tural view treats the existence and standing (and motives and interests) of these entities as highly constructed—as the product of meaning and interpretation in modern schemes and scripts. The construction of modern citizens as formally equal, for instance, is seen as an evolution in culture and theory rather than as either natural equalities or a result of interests in interaction (e.g., mystifying tactics or compromises of dominant elites or functionally necessary responses to social complexity).

Second, sociological realism tends to emphasize social systems as affected by high levels of interactive interdependence among their components—as really social systems of interdependent parts. A more cultural view calls attention to the impact of cultural theories and ideologies about this putative interdependence: The high status and importance of many groups, such as the professions, in modern stratification systems arise from cultural ideologies (which in the modern world commonly take the form of functional theories) as much as from "real" interactive dominance and dependence.

Conceptions of Culture

Part of the problem lies with a very limited conception of culture as individual attitudes or vague collective sentiments. In fact, much sociology deeply shares the contemporary bias that modern systems (unlike the traditional ones that anthropologists study) are so overwhelmingly articulated and real that they do not have very much culture: In other words, the rationalism and functionalism of the cultures of modern society are taken as true by the analysts.

Another way to put this is to note that social-scientific stratification theories are themselves core cultural elements of modern society. They are institutionalized as constitutional principles, but they also may provide cultural bases for criticism and opposition. Although this is obvious with Marxist theories, it is also the case with most others, which provide normative bases with which to defend, attack, or ignore inequalities of various sorts. Stratification theorists may understate the importance of the cultures of modern systems *because stratification theories (though not necessarily only narrowly academic ones) are the central cultural elements involved*. Recognizing the cultural character of stratification would weaken the realist vision of society as a real system. It would also undercut some of the scientific claims of stratification theorists: If stratification is cultural theory, the theorists (as classic phenomenological critics have had it) are studying themselves.

Our point here is not to support the often-noted special importance of some intellectuals and scientific professions in modern society. It is to note that explicit theories and ideologies about licit and illicit inequalities are deeply ingrained in the public discussions of the modern system. Most great political conflicts in this system are explicitly and articulately about equality and inequality: Contemporary opinion surveys suggest that even ordinary persons are able to go on at length about inequalities and the conditions under which they are legitimate. Indeed, it is for this reason that the system tends to pick out for great attention some of the ideas of intellectuals (e.g., Smith or Marx) who might be quite obscure in other traditions. The culture of the system tends to make stratification theories important (rather than the theorists simply having some sort of mysterious dominance over the culture); carriers include everyone from ordinary members to political and economic elites as well as to specialized intellectuals.

Our emphasis on a cultural reinterpretation of stratification can be pursued in either a strong or weak form—the difference between the two is immaterial here, for the most part. The strong form (Meyer 1989; Mann 1986; Hall 1986) treats the modern (Western and now worldwide) stratification system as having distinctive cultural roots in such themes as equality and progress. A weak form might argue that more narrowly "real" social forces produced such Western structures as high capitalism or political democracy—after which institutionalization turned such arrangements into cultural recipes to be repeated throughout the world. Either form is good enough for present arguments.

We briefly review the cultural postures built into the stratification theories of modern soci-

eties. That is, in discussing what seem to be the most prominent substantive themes in stratification theories, we recognize that modern systems are much affected by their cultures and conceive of stratification theories as prominent parts of these cultures. One important theme is that persons are formally and ultimately equal; another is that inequalities can be justified only by contributions to collective progress. Many lines of sociological thought incorporate such matters as aspects of social reality—we treat them as the cultural rules of modern collective actors. We go on to consider the consequences these cultural postures may have—the things that can be better explained when we recognize the cultural character of stratification theory in the modern system.

Sociological thinking routinely recognizes that stratification systems in the premodern past were cultural constructions. Further, there is a tendency to imagine that in some future utopia (or dystopia) where inequalities are put right (or wrong), cultural principles could again hold sway. This is, obviously, a dramatic counterpoint to the aggressive realism about the present that is characteristic of Marxian theory. We apply the same perspective to contemporary modern society, seeing its stratification system as in part the realization of its cultural visions.

Stratification Principles

Clearly a first cultural principle built into the stratification models of modern theories and societies is the functional one. Society is a system—a rationally analyzable set of components organized as a purposive project—and inequalities among its parts are justified by inequalities in their contributions to collective goods and goals. For instance, one can defend enhanced inequalities by functional arguments: A greater return to private capital is required to promote more investment, or more pay and status are needed for teachers if we wish to select better ones and improve the performance of all. The idea of social progress is obviously involved in the principle.

The idea that inequality is justified only or mainly by functional considerations is so firmly established (e.g., Rawls 1971) that sociological critics of particular inequalities must argue that they are not really functional (but are rather products of tradition or power). In such analyses, socially useful achievement is set in opposition to two defective sources of inequality—discussing the issues involved is a modern (and a sociological) obsession. One opposition is mainly with the past and with tradition; achievement is set against ascription in a drama that combines issues of social efficiency with those of social justice. Thus there is great attention to whether favorable evaluations or opportunities are provided students or workers on merit or whether there is a direct effect of status background. Even if the analyses suggest merit is mainly involved, analysts go further—perhaps the standards of merit are status-biased, or perhaps the resources of those higher in status permit easier or more achievement. A second opposition is to set socially useful and legitimate achievement against power that may pervert goals or means (as when hegemonic capitalism is thought to substitute the requirements of capital for the good of society).

The issues involved here infuse the stratification literature as well as modern social discussion with much normative excitement. Minor details of the distribution of income or education become salient, and analyses of mobility give great attention to causal pathways distinguishable according to their justice and efficiency. On the one hand, there are many conflicts about what is really functional: Radical differences in the interpretation of the functions of private capital or of education can produce very different assessments. On the other hand, broad bands of agreement can be found: There are few defenders of extreme inequalities, of high levels of status consistency, or of high levels of status inheritance.

All this takes on more momentum given the second crucial principle of modern stratification (and theory): moral individualism. Individuals are to be ultimately morally equal, and justice is to be assessed in terms of inequality among individuals. There is considerable tension, naturally, between this principle and the legitimation of inequality on functional grounds—we later suggest that this tension is a source of a good deal of modern social change.

The individualism of modern stratification theory and research is striking. The important inequality is, for instance, individual income inequality. We do not much care if the genders (or races or families or ethnic groups or groups of differing class origins) have equal incomes. In fact, calculations of the income of a gender, race, ethnic group, or family as a group are very rare, in contrast to stratificational thinking in societies in which corporate groups (e.g., clans or villages) are more real than individuals. We care only, on a per capita basis, if individuals of each gender (or class background or race or ethnicity) have equal incomes. When we attend to cross-national comparisons, we calculate not income differences among countries but income differences per capita. On some questions, other units have moral standing (as when each country has certain rights in international relations, or as when each family or town may be represented in certain activities), but the utterly dominant unit is the individual: Justice is assessed in terms of the equality or inequality of individuals.

The Impact of Stratification Ideology on the Development of the Modern System

Imagine, thus, that the social changes of the modern period are going on under the continuing scrutiny of collective actors (including prominently the intellectual advisers and social theoreticians of these collective actors) concerned about the principles of functionality for the collective good and the ultimate equality of individuals. This is not so unrealistic an image: Most modern stratification theorists work with just these standards, and most aspire to affect public policy; more to the point, decisionmaking elites in modern systems operate in about the same way.

We can consider separately the impact of the first cultural principle, then the second principle, and finally the joint interaction of the two.

Theory of Progress

Some effects of the legitimation of inequality in terms of the rational pursuit of progress are noteworthy: First, it seems obvious that rationalistic and progressive ideas have played a role in supporting a great deal of modern social differentiation. Activities can be pulled out of social life and bundled into rationalized elements or roles; their inequalities thus are legitimated. The modern system has been profligate in its creation of new occupations, tasks, organizational forms, and so on. Not all of this is easy to explain in terms of standard arguments about the real functional requirements of modern development—it is still utterly unclear what actual (as opposed to culturally defined) functional requirements call for such occupations as sociologist or such organizations as therapeutic ones. Rationalistic models not only helped justify the evolution of these minor institutions but also played a role in the historically crucial early Western institutionalization of the capitalist class (in contrast to most other social systems).

Second, strong and highly culturally theorized notions of progress and the collective good help explain the homogeneity of modern stratification regimes (across country and time) despite much heterogeneity in immediate circumstances. The finding that occupational prestige systems and mobility regimes are relatively homogeneous has been an overpowering surprise in the research literature. One explanation has been a very broad functional image. A more realistic explanation is to see the cultural (functional) theories of modernity as widespread and as generating a good deal of stratificational isomorphism. This would also help explain why stratificational change (e.g., in the status of women or ethnic minorities, in the welfare correctives for the class structure, or in educational opportunity) tends to be global in character (Thomas et al. 1987).

Third, the institutionalization of ideas of rationality and progress can help explain the surprising worldwide rise of education as the critical dimension in all modern stratification systems. Education provides a clear legitimating account of sources of improved capacity and also locates this capacity in specific persons and groups (Meyer 1977). Thus, ascriptive and income/power considerations and even some of the functional ones of occupation tend to be replaced by education as the main dimension of status: Education

tends to correlate more highly with more outcomes than the other dimensions do, and intergenerational educational correlations are usually higher than the others. Empirical researchers routinely build education into their measures, but both researchers and theorists are slow to let go of their nineteenth-century (cultureless) models of society and continue to use terms like "class" or "socioeconomic status" when education is the main phenomenon at issue in their measures. This peculiarity of labeling variables in modern stratification research is quite revealing of its ideological base in modern culture.

The worldwide rise in educational certification for all sorts of social positions has been discussed as resulting from functional requirements. However, critics have noted the utter absence of evidence of such requirements and have seen the expansion as resulting instead from conflict processes (Collins 1979). The latter explanation is incomplete. Why would so many forces make education, as opposed to other institutional settings, the new arena of competition and conflict? Education becomes the competitive arena in part because myths of rational progress have made educational institutions culturally central.

Finally, we may note the extraordinary—and in the main, unpredicted—rise of the service sector and its new classes. Some social theories attribute great feats of power and manipulation to the professions and the state but give no real explanation about where the power and capacity come from. The cultural commitments to rational progress previously noted may provide some explanation for why societies supposedly dominated by their economies (Marx) or their state bureaucracies (Weber) in fact turn out to have the professions (analogous to, of all things, a priesthood) as their leading groups.

Effects of Individualism

There have been several effects of the institutionalization of individualism and equality on stratification: A first consequence is the expansion of social citizenship and of the dimensions of social life it comprehends. Stratification theorists have been so engrossed in the normative search for illicit inequality as to have avoided noticing the rise and expansion of a most important social status in terms of which all are formally equal. For example, Parsons, until his last discussion of stratification (see the reading in this section), essentially omitted citizenship as an element. Clearly, citizenship is now one of the more important dimensions of status throughout the world—and on such dependent variables as income perhaps the most important one. Obviously, claims for its expansion (in more welfare arenas) have been continuous throughout the modern period (and have tended to increase inequality among citizens of different countries and thus to redefine world stratification).

Second, the importance of individual equality has tended to expand education. Not only is education the crucial certifier of inequality, but mass education is a most important constructor of equality as well.

Third, the importance of individual equality has produced considerable expansion of protection of young and old persons (including extensions of personhood to prenatal periods). In this area, as in others, the rise of professional protectors and the growth of organizations with some type of protective agenda have been the most prominent developments.

Equal Persons, Unequal Roles

We next consider the impact of simultaneous emphases on equal individuals and unequal contributions to rational progress: Many observers have noted that the dualistic Western (and now worldwide) emphasis on both individual and collective good has been a mobilizing dynamic in modern history. We can consider a few ways this works out for stratification.

First, the simultaneous stress on the inequality of activities (i.e., societywide coordination) and the equality of persons generates a great deal of role differentiation. As already noted, theorists have tended to understate the cultural bases of such differentiation. But differentiation clearly has served to protect central myths in the modern system in two ways: (1) Elaborate role differentiation and the tight organization of activity systems (e.g., in such arrangements as modern formal organizations) help to sustain functional myths and

to define activity as primarily linked to social tasks rather than personal status. (2) More important, the modern system notoriously differentiates activities and roles from persons.

The second point is critical because all sorts of functional roots of this in efficiency pressures (for the most part, unproven) are alleged by the theorists. It is more important to note how much such individual/activity differentiations help sustain the principle of individual equality. In a modern system, we can have a societywide coordination of activity (e.g., public tax policy or other political and economic decisionmaking) implying the utter domination of the activities of millions or billions of people by the activities of a few without any serious violation of the normative stratificational principle of equality. In a system of this kind, the activities control each other but not the persons: Differentiation is crucial to sustaining the principle of individual equality.

Consider how this works out in terms of measures of income inequality. As Lenski (1966) noted, agrarian societies (e.g., medieval states) had very high levels of income inequality; the disparity is greatly lowered by the modern system. But in the medieval world, all the income of the state was attributed to the king personally, so that the king appeared to be very rich. In the modern world, a differentiation is established: A president gets only a modestly high salary (higher than the best sociologists but lower than the best economists) personally but may control a monumental budget as a property of the presidential role. If this budget were attributed to the president personally, as in medieval accounting, the modern system would show enormously high levels of inequality (a typical head of a modern state would be recorded has having up to half the national income). Neither the medieval accounting (with state income attributed to the king) nor the modern differentiated one is wrong: The point is that because a great change in organizational accounting has occurred, enormous societywide political control can result with only modest levels of accounted interpersonal inequality.

As a result of the modern differentiation between person and role, decreasing proportions of monetary flows are recorded as individual income, and the well-known growth in all sorts of corporate actors occurs. Our point is that one pressure in this direction arises from the modern demand for individual equality, combined with the modern pressures for rationalization and progress. Differentiation permits increasingly equal individuals in a system of increasingly unequal and ordered activities: It involves, of course, an elaborate modern differentiation between the tastes and motives attributed to persons and those attributed to organizations (Meyer 1986).

Consider how both forms of differentiation—between persons and roles and between different roles—help sustain equality in a modern organization like a university. Some equalities in status and salary among professors are maintained. But some professors may control huge research grants, hiring many servants and much equipment; in both social custom and in tax law, this is not attributed to their persons but to their roles. Further, if the inequalities among professorial roles become too great, a further differentiation occurs, such that the wealth of one professor is located in a specialized institute and controlled by the professor as director of the institute. This control can produce social accountings reflecting great equality of income and power among the professors as persons but great inequality among their roles or activities.

The overall point is that much of the role differentiation of the modern system (between roles and between roles and persons) solves cultural problems related to stratification theory and can be seen as having cultural or legitimating significance. A sociologically realist perspective treats all this differentiation as arising step-by-step out of the pressures of organizational life: Such a perspective has great difficulty explaining why such similar differentiation occurs in many different places (regardless of variation in local problems or needs), is hard pressed to explain the fact that much of the differentiation seems only symbolic in character, and must resort to unsubstantiated arguments about the presumed efficiencies involved in much differentiation. The idea employed here—that the functional theory involved is acting as a cultural principle—simplifies the problem.

What are the mechanisms by which cultural commitments produce this sort of differentiation? In our argument, they occur through the relatively articulate and explicit activity of collective actors—public political elites, intellectual and professional theorists, and the like. Modern systems are constantly under scrutiny by cultural theorists looking for precisely such illicit inequalities. Both tax laws and common opinion may penalize the insufficient differentiation of personal and organizational resources and reward instances of clear and "rational" differentiation.

Second, the tension between equal individuals and unequal roles can be seen as one of the sources of ever-expanding educational credentialism and its related institutions: More and more social boundaries and mechanisms are installed to keep the structural inconsistency involved maintained. There are the educational credentials themselves, which can be used to legitimate the allocation of formally equal individuals to unequal roles. The legitimation problem then reduces to accounting for interindividual variations in the "investment" in education. There is no shortage of ancillary social theories with this orientation. Moreover, there are also theories of variations in abilities as well as in tastes that treat role differentiation as a matter of individual choice. Such effects work through the mechanism of relatively articulate collective consciousness and action. Clearly, many groups advocate and states often require the replacement of less legitimated and more ascriptive criteria of role entry by educational credentials: This is argued to indicate merit, to deserve public respect and trust, and thus to enhance legitimate status.

Third, all of these characteristics are institutionalized in an expanding modern personnel bureaucracy. A surprising feature of modern organizational development, from the point of view of most theories, has been the elaboration of the citizenship of persons within organizations. Many individual rights have expanded to provide organizational protection of individuals from potentially threatening inequalities. Such bureaucracy is seen as both more progressive and more just.

Conclusions

Two closely related themes arise from our discussion. One conclusion is about modern societies:

Many aspects of their stratification systems reflect cultural properties of the modern system, as with the expansion of education, the service sector, the personnel bureaucracy, and so on. This was mostly unexpected by theorists emphasizing the economic or political realism of the modern system; from their point of view, much of the modern social structure reflects distortion, false consciousness, or mystification. The theories tend to be mistaken, precisely in their inattention to the modern system's sensitivity to and cultural analysis of its own stratification system.

A second conclusion is that the underlying culture of the modern stratification system is closely tied to the social-scientific analyses we call stratification theory: The obsessions of theory (e.g., with individual inequality and with the distinction between just and functional inequalities and unjust or power and ascription-ridden ones) are the main cultural themes of modern stratification.

These cultural commitments in fact drive much social change. This can help explain many of the puzzling aspects of modern stratification regimes: their homogeneity across time and space; their constant shifts toward education and the service sector; their high levels of differentiation among roles (and especially between roles and persons); and the worldwide expansion in citizenship statuses.

We can illustrate these points by noting that in recent decades, the world itself has come to be conceptualized as a unitary social system or society. The shift to such conceptions is rapidly changing public and scientific stratification analyses: Distinctions among individuals in different countries now require rectification (from the point of view of both dependency and human rights ideologies), and a differentiated set of world institutions is rapidly developing. The ultimate goal of stratification theories—both lay and scientific—is no longer the articulation of equal individual personhood combined with social progress at the nation-state level: A bigger arena will

presumably undercut some of the structures of the older one. For instance, it may delegitimate some efforts to produce equality within developed nation-states at the cost of enhanced international inequality.

Notes

This paper benefited from useful comments on earlier drafts by David Grusky, Ron Jepperson, David Strang, Marc Ventresca, and members of the Stanford Stratification Seminar.

References

Berg, Ivar. 1971. *Education and Jobs: The Great Training Robbery*. Boston: Beacon.

Collins, Randall. 1979. *The Credential Society: A Historical Sociology of Education and Stratification*. New York: Academic Press.

Hall, John. 1986. *Powers and Liberties*. New York: Penguin.

Lenski, Gerhard. 1966. *Power and Privilege*. New York: McGraw-Hill.

Mann, Michael. 1986. *The Sources of Social Power*. Cambridge: Cambridge University Press.

Meyer, John. 1977. "The Effects of Education as an Institution." *American Journal of Sociology* 83 (July): 55–77.

———. 1986. "The Self and the Life Course." Pp. 199–216 in A. B. Sorensen, F. E. Weinert, and L. R. Sherrod, eds., *Human Development and the Life Course*. Hillsdale, N.J.: Erlbaum.

———. 1989. "Conceptions of Christendom." Pp. 395–413 in M. Kohn, ed., *Cross-National Research in Sociology*. Newbury Park: Sage.

Ossowski, Stanislaw. 1963. *Class Structure in the Social Consciousness*. New York: Free Press.

Rawls, John. 1971. *A Theory of Justice*. Cambridge: Belknap.

Thomas, George, John Meyer, Francisco Ramirez, and John Boli. 1987. *Institutional Structure*. Newbury Park: Sage.

About the Book and Editor

The field of stratification is being transformed and reshaped by advances in theory and quantitative modeling as well as by new approaches to the analysis of economic, racial, and gender inequality. Although these developments are revolutionary in their implications, until now there has been no comprehensive effort to bring together the classic articles that have defined and redefined the contours of the field.

In this up-to-date anthology, the history of stratification research unfolds in systematic fashion, with the introductory articles in each section providing examples of the major research traditions in the field and the concluding essays (commissioned from leading scholars) providing broader programmatic statements that identify current controversies and unresolved issues. The resulting collection of articles both celebrates the diversity of theoretical approaches and reveals the cumulative nature of ongoing research.

This comprehensive reader is designed as a primary text for introductory courses on social stratification and as a supplementary text for advanced courses on social classes, occupations, labor markets, or social mobility. The following types of questions and debates are addressed in the six sections of the reader:

1. Is stratification inevitable? Do the recent "experiments with destratification" in Eastern Europe and elsewhere provide new insights into the functionalist theory of inequality?

2. Can we identify a set of organized and cohesive "social classes" in advanced industrial societies? Does it make sense to refer to a ruling class, a "political class," or a "power elite" in these societies?

3. Are the basic contours of occupational mobility the same within all advanced industrial societies? Have the "new structuralists" led us astray in our attempts to understand the sources and causes of occupational attainment?

4. Are there fundamental differences across social classes in styles of life, patterns of consumption, and attitudes toward work? Are these "class-specific cultures" attenuating as we move into advanced industrialism?

5. Is there an emerging underclass in America? What are the principal sources of racial, ethnic, and gender inequality?

6. Can we identify a "teleological dynamic" driving the development of stratification systems? Are new forms of stratification and inequality emerging as Eastern Europe enters its postsocialist stage?

The volume offers essential reading for undergraduates who require an introduction to the field, for graduate students who wish to broaden their understanding of stratification research, and for advanced scholars who seek a basic reference guide. Although most of the selections are middle-range theoretical pieces suitable for introductory courses, the anthology also includes advanced contributions on the cutting edge of research. The editor outlines a modified study plan for undergraduate students requiring a basic introduction to the field.

David B. Grusky is associate professor of sociology at Stanford University and coeditor (with Marta Tienda) of the Westview Press Social Inequality Series.

Index

(continued from page vi)

Max Weber, "The Rationalization of Education and Training": Reprinted by permission from *Max Weber: Essays in Sociology* (New York: Oxford University Press, 1946), translated by H. H. Gerth and C. Wright Mills, pp. 240–243.

Anthony Giddens, "The Class Structure of the Advanced Societies": Approximately 25 pages from *The Class Structure of the Advanced Societies* by Anthony Giddens. Copyright © 1973 by Anthony Giddens. Reprinted by permission of HarperCollins Publishers, Inc., and by permission of Routledge Chapman & Hall.

Frank Parkin, "Marxism and Class Theory: A Bourgeois Critique": Reprinted from Frank Parkin, *Marxism and Class Theory: A Bourgeois Critique* (New York: Columbia University Press, 1979), pp. 11–13, 23–25, 27–28, 44–50, 53–58, 62–64, 67–73, 112–113.

Gaetano Mosca, "The Ruling Class": Reprinted from Arthur Livingston, ed., *The Ruling Class,* translated by Hannah D. Kahn (New York: McGraw-Hill, 1939), pp. 50–54, 56–62, 65–66, by permission of McGraw-Hill.

C. Wright Mills, "The Power Elite": Reprinted by permission from C. Wright Mills, *The Power Elite* (London: Oxford University Press, 1956), pp. 3–18, 20–23, 365–367.

Anthony Giddens, "Elites and Power": Approximately 25 pages from *The Class Structure of the Advanced Societies* by Anthony Giddens. Copyright © 1973 by Anthony Giddens. Reprinted by permission of HarperCollins Publishers, Inc., and by permission of Century Hutchinson, a division of Random House UK Ltd.

Michael Useem, "The Inner Circle": Reprinted by permission from Michael Useem, *The Inner Circle* (New York: Oxford University Press, 1984), pp. 3–6, 9–16, 59–61, 74–75, 201–202, 206–207. The excerpts included here are not presented in the same order as they appear in *The Inner Circle.*

Edward A. Shils, "The Political Class in the Age of Mass Society: Collectivistic Liberalism and Social Democracy": Reprinted from pp. 16–18, 20–22, 27–32 of *Does Who Governs Matter? Elite Circulation in Contemporary Societies,* edited by Moshe M. Czudnowski. © 1982 by Northern Illinois University Press. Reprinted with permission of the publisher.

W. Lloyd Warner, with Marchia Meeker and Kenneth Eells, "Social Class in America": Approximately 14 pages from *Social Class in America* by W. Lloyd Warner. Copyright © 1960 by Harper & Row, Publishers, Inc. Reprinted by permission of HarperCollins Publishers, Inc. Chart I, from Allison Davis, Burleigh B. Gardner, and Mary B. Gardner, *Deep South* (Chicago: University of Chicago Press, 1941) (copyright © 1941 University of Chicago Press), is reprinted by permission of the University of Chicago Press.

Edward Shils, "Deference": Reprinted from J. A. Jackson, ed., *Social Stratification* (Cambridge: Cambridge University Press, 1968), pp. 104–108, 115–117, 119–122, 126–129, with the permission of Cambridge University Press.

Peter M. Blau and Otis Dudley Duncan (with the collaboration of Andrea Tyree), "Measuring the Status of Occupations": Edited and reprinted with the permission of The Free Press from pp. 118–124 of *The American Occupational Structure* by Peter M. Blau and Otis Dudley Duncan. Copyright © 1967 by Peter M. Blau and Otis Dudley Duncan.

Donald R. Treiman, "Occupational Prestige in Comparative Perspective": Reprinted from *The Journal of Interdisciplinary History,* VII (1976), 285–290, with the permission of the editors of *The Journal of Interdisciplinary History* and the MIT Press, Cambridge, Massachusetts. © 1976 by The Massachusetts Institute of Technology and the editors of *The Journal of Interdisciplinary History.*

John H. Goldthorpe and Keith Hope, "Occupational Grading and Occupational Prestige": © Nuffield College, Oxford 1972. Reprinted from pp. 23–24, 26–27, 30–37, 78–79 of *The Analysis of Social Mobility: Methods and Approaches,* edited by

Jay MacLeod, "Ain't No Makin' It: Leveled Aspirations in a Low-Income Neighborhood": Reprinted from Jay MacLeod, *Ain't No Makin' It: Leveled Aspirations in a Low-Income Neighborhood* (Boulder: Westview Press, 1987), pp. 1–2, 4–5, 8, 60–63, 69–75, 78–79, 81, 137–141, 162.

Michael J. Piore, "The Dual Labor Market: Theory and Implications": Reprinted from Samuel H. Beer and Richard E. Barringer, eds., *The State and the Poor* (Cambridge MA: Winthrop Publishers, 1970), pp. 55–59.

Aage B. Sørensen and Arne L. Kalleberg, "An Outline of a Theory of the Matching of Persons to Jobs": Reprinted by permission from Ivar Berg, ed., *Sociological Perspectives on Labor Markets* (New York: Academic Press, 1981), pp. 49–57, 65–69, 72–74. The excerpts included here are not presented in the order in which they appear in the original article.

Mark Granovetter, "Toward a Sociological Theory of Income Differences": Reprinted by permission from Ivar Berg, ed., *Sociological Perspectives on Labor Markets* (New York: Academic Press, 1981), pp. 11–27, 40–47.

Thorstein Veblen, "The Theory of the Leisure Class": Reprinted from Thorstein Veblen, *The Theory of the Leisure Class* (Boston: Houghton Mifflin Company, 1973), pp. 35–36, 38–43, 61, 65–72, 94, 98.

Pierre Bourdieu, "Distinction: A Social Critique of the Judgement of Taste": Reprinted by permission of the publishers and of Routledge and Kegan Paul Ltd from pp. 114–115, 128–129, 169–180, 183–197, 199–202, 206–209, 503, 519–521, 523, 572–576 of *Distinction: A Social Critique of the Judgement of Taste* by Pierre Bourdieu, Cambridge, Mass.: Harvard University Press, Copyright © 1984 by the President and Fellows of Harvard College and Routledge and Kegan Paul Ltd. This chapter is based on survey data collected by Bourdieu and on additional complementary sources (denoted by C.S. I–C.S. V) described at the end of the chapter. The passages reproduced in sans serif type, set off by rules, contain "illus-trative examples or discussion of ancillary issues" (Bourdieu, *Distinction*, p. xiii). For the purpose of conserving space, some of these passages had to be excised. It was also necessary to excise some of the more detailed tables.

Melvin L. Kohn, "Job Complexity and Adult Personality": Reprinted by permission of the publishers from pp. 193–210 of *Themes of Work and Love in Adulthood* edited by Neil J. Smelser and Erik H. Erikson, Cambridge, Mass.: Harvard University Press, Copyright © 1980 by the President and Fellows of Harvard College.

James A. Davis, "Achievement Variables and Class Cultures: Family, Schooling, Job, and Forty-Nine Dependent Variables in the Cumulative GSS": Reprinted from *American Sociological Review* 47 (October 1982), pp. 569–586, by permission of the American Sociological Association and the author.

Michael Reich, "The Economics of Racism": Reprinted by permission of Michael Reich from David M. Gordon, ed., *Problems in Political Economy: An Urban Perspective* (Lexington MA: D. C. Heath and Company, 1977), pp. 184–188.

Edna Bonacich, "A Theory of Ethnic Antagonism: The Split Labor Market": Reprinted from *American Sociological Review* 37 (October 1972), pp. 547–559, by permission of the American Sociological Association and the author.

Michael Hechter, "Towards a Theory of Ethnic Change": Reprinted from *Internal Colonialism: The Celtic Fringe in British National Development, 1536–1966* by Michael Hechter (Berkeley: University of California Press, 1975), pp. 15–18, 22–34, 37–43. Copyright © 1975 Michael Hechter. Reprinted by permission of the University of California Press and the author.

Michael T. Hannan, "Dynamics of Ethnic Boundaries": This essay is adapted by the author from "The Dynamics of Ethnic Boundaries in Modern States," John W. Meyer and Michael T. Hannan, eds., *National Development and the World System*

Social Inequality Series
Marta Tienda and David B. Grusky, *Series Editors*

The field of stratification is being transformed and reshaped by advances in theory and quantitative modeling as well as by new approaches to the analysis of economic, racial, and gender inequality. Although these developments are revolutionary in their implications, until now there has been no comprehensive effort to bring together the classic articles that have defined and redefined the contours of the field.

In this up-to-date anthology, the history of stratification research unfolds in systematic fashion, with the introductory articles in each section providing examples of the major research traditions in the field and the concluding essays (commissioned from leading scholars) providing broader programmatic statements that identify current controversies and unresolved issues. This comprehensive reader is designed as a primary text for introductory courses on social stratification and as a supplementary text for advanced courses on social classes, occupations, labor markets, or social mobility.

This volume offers essential reading for undergraduates who require an introduction to the field, for graduate students who wish to broaden their understanding of stratification research, and for advanced scholars who seek a basic reference guide. Although most of the selections are middle-range theoretical pieces suitable for introductory courses, the anthology also includes advanced contributions on the cutting edge of research. The editor outlines a modified study plan for undergraduate students requiring a basic introduction to the field.

David B. Grusky is associate professor of sociology at Stanford University and a National Science Foundation Presidential Young Investigator.

Praise for SOCIAL STRATIFICATION

"A very important collection of the most significant contributions to this core area of sociology, including excellent coverage of the most recent work in the field. The anthology surely will become the standard classroom text and an invaluable reference."

—*Aage B. Sørensen*
Harvard University

"Sociologists have not had an up-to-date reader on social stratification for twenty years. This novel collection does the job. Its coverage is both broad and deep, running the theoretical gamut from functionalism through class analysis to post-industrialism, yet also challenging the reader to work through the key quantitative studies on the cutting edge of research."

—*Robert M. Hauser*
University of Wisconsin

For order and other information, please write to:

Westview Press
5500 Central Avenue • Boulder, Colorado 80301-2877
36 Lonsdale Road • Summertown • Oxford OX2 7EW
or use the enclosed inquiry card.

ISBN 0-8133-1065-2

90000

9 780813 310657